THE OXFORD HANDBOOK OF MEMORY

THE OXFORD HANDBOOK OF MEMORY

EDITED BY

Endel Tulving
Fergus I. M. Craik

OXFORD
UNIVERSITY PRESS

2000

OXFORD
UNIVERSITY PRESS

Oxford   New York

Athens Auckland Bangkok Bogotá Buenos Aires Calcutta
Cape Town Chennai Dar es Salaam Delhi Florence Hong Kong Istanbul
Karachi Kuala Lumpur Madrid Melbourne Mexico City Mumbai
Nairobi Paris São Paulo Singapore Taipei Tokyo Toronto Warsaw

and associated companies in
Berlin   Ibadan

Copyright © 2000 by Endel Tulving and Fergus I. M. Craik

Published by Oxford University Press, Inc.
198 Madison Avenue, New York, New York 10016

Oxford is a registered trademark of Oxford University Press

Library of Congress Cataloging-in-Publication Data
The Oxford handbook of memory / edited by
  Endel Tulving, Fergus I. M. Craik.
      p. cm.
   Includes bibliographical references and index.
   ISBN 0-19-512265-8
   1. Memory.   I. Tulving, Endel.
  II. Craik, Fergus I. M.
  BF371.O84   2000
  153.1′2—dc21   99-27533

9 8 7 6 5 4 3 2 1

Printed in the United States of America
on acid-free paper

Preface

Memory is usually thought of as the ability to recollect past events and to bring learned facts and ideas back to mind. Memory and learning have these functions indeed, but an adequate definition must necessarily bring in further aspects. For example, whereas past happenings may be re-experienced consciously, they can also affect behavior in the absence of such conscious awareness. In addition, the mental activities of learning and memory clearly have their neural counterparts in brain activities, and a full understanding of memory and related functions must therefore involve an understanding of the brain mechanisms of acquisition, storage, and retrieval. Recent scientific studies thus deal with memory and learning at the levels of experience, behavior, and neural mechanisms; each level can be understood in its own terms, but any final theory must also show how the different levels of description map onto each other. Because memory and learning are such all-pervasive shapers of human existence, their scientific study has never been far from center stage in experimental psychology and related brain sciences.

Memory reaches its evolutionary culmination in human beings. Human memory has been systematically studied for over a hundred years, and a great deal has been found out about its nature, functions, and manifestations. This has become possible through the invention and adoption of clever methods suitable for the objective analysis of something as ineffable as memory. Much of the success of these methods has consisted in meticulous delineation and elaboration of facts about memory that would not surprise anyone, but a good deal has involved the discovery of aspects that for long had remained hidden not only from the "expert users of memory," that is, ordinary people in everyday life—but also from the more interested and focused professional investigators.

The result of these activities is a massive, rich, and rapidly expanding accumulation of knowledge about memory in its many forms, together with continually increasing ability and sophistication in the development and adoption of tools required to add to this knowledge, and to make theoretical sense of it. An important characteristic of the factual data base of memory is its remarkable reliability. In a world as complex as that of memory it would be natural to think that observations about it sometimes take the form of "now you see it, now you do not." But as in a number of other established branches of psychology, accepted facts about memory are remarkably firm. When an expert claims that under such and such conditions such and such occurs, because this is what objective study has shown, there are seldom reasons to question the claim. The uncertain parts of our science— and there are always some such in every living and growing enterprise—have to do with theory, with the question of how best to interpret and integrate the massive amounts of data that experimental and clinical studies of memory have yielded. This is where the present challenge lies, and will continue to lie for some time to come.

The Oxford Handbook of Memory was put together to summarize the current state of the science of memory. It was meant to inform the reader what this science is all about, how memory has been and is being studied, where the action has been, what the study of memory has achieved in the past, and where we are likely to go from here. Strictly speaking, the *Handbook* is not concerned as much with memory as it is with its scientific study. A more accurate title for it therefore might have been something like "The Oxford Handbook of the Scientific Study of Memory." But in addition to being awkward, this title probably would have frightened away many a potential reader who might find something interesting or even useful in the volume. Hence the short version of the title.

The *Handbook* deals largely with memory as seen from the perspectives of experimental psychology and its contemporary offshoots— cognitive psychology, neuropsychology, developmental psychology, and cognitive neuroscience. These perspectives deal primarily with human memory and treat it from the behavioral and cognitive points of view. For practical reasons alone—the amount of the material, the breadth of the expected readership, the expertise of the editors—it was not possible to embrace the equally successful and voluminous memory research conducted with other animals and at other biological levels of analysis. Even in the narrower field of "systems-level analysis" of human memory, work in several lively subareas had to be omitted from the present volume for what might be called technical reasons.

Given the exciting, rich, and vast field of memory, it may sound odd that this is the first handbook of memory ever published. There are thousands of books on memory, and thousands of handbooks on all other subjects, but, until now, there has never been a *handbook* of memory. Why not?

Like any other question of this sort, this one allows many possible answers. The one we like is that much of the early work now classified under "memory" was originally called something else. Until the 1960s memory in its current sense was researched, and written about, but mostly apologetically and unobtrusively. Until then the fashionable word, at least in North American psychology, was "learning"; and, indeed, various handbooks of learning were published. After about 1970, more and more psychologists began studying "memory" rather than "learning." They also began making new discoveries about memory, and having new ideas of a kind that would not fit into the learning framework. In no time at all memory became a tremendously successful growth industry. Because of the feverish pace at which research on memory was conducted, and new things about memory discovered, its practitioners were simply too busy to find time to write about old "solid" achievements, the typical fare one expects to find in volumes labeled "Handbook."

This, at least, is one possible explanation of why the present volume is the first handbook of memory ever published. The research area of human memory and learning is a vast one, and the *Handbook* does not attempt to deal with all possible aspects. We did, however, try to cover the major theories, findings, and methods that are current in the more restricted field of memory, especially those associated with the perspectives of cognitive psychology and cognitive neuroscience.

The scope of the *Handbook* is reflected in the organization of its sections. Part I sets the scene for the rest of the book by laying out some basic presuppositions, concepts, and methods in a historical context. Part II is concerned with memory in the laboratory—how memory has been studied from the "verbal learning" and "cognitive" standpoints. This section provides a survey of the major hypotheses, methods, results, and conclusions that form the central core of work on memory at the present time. The level of analysis in such laboratory studies has traditionally been that of behavior, but more recent work has emphasized the roles of conscious awareness and reflection, so these perspectives are also given due prominence.

Part III deals with memory in the real world as opposed to in the laboratory. It covers the development of memory in infancy and childhood, and also the decline of memory seen in normal aging and in some pathological conditions. This section also contains chapters on personal memories for events and knowledge, on spatial memory, and on the role of emotion. The final section contains two sets of chapters. Those in the first set describe the fascinating current work that links the behavioral and experiential aspects of memory to brain mechanisms; it is not an exaggeration to say that the new technologies of neuroimaging have revolutionized this approach to the study of memory, and that the area is one of the most exciting and dynamic in present-day science. The chapters in the second set bring many of the previously described findings and ideas together under the heading of current theories, which again reflect the experiential, behavioral, and neural levels of analysis. Finally— the culmination of our "39 steps to wisdom"! —Larry Weiskrantz provides some reflections on the whole enterprise.

A word about responsibility, or accountability. The editors are responsible for the general contents and the organization of the volume, as well as the selection of the authors of individual chapters. It is worth noting that every author who was invited accepted the challenge of the task presented to him or her. This means that as far as the editors were concerned they were working with the "first team." The authors were given general guidelines as to the nature of the whole enterprise (intended audience, level of writing) and the quantitative scope of their chapters, but otherwise were left free to "do their own thing." By and large, however, the editors did not meddle with what the writers wanted to say.

All this means that the editors do not take, cannot take, any responsibility for the actual substantive contents of individual chapters. In a field as much in flux as is memory, a field that is still struggling to find its first Kuhnian paradigm, a field in which theories vie with facts for the observers' attention, it is impossible for any collection of writers to put together a menu that pleases every reader, be the reader the editor of the collection, a happy owner of the *Handbook*, or an equally happy borrower of it in the library. There are things said by writers of chapters that the editors do not believe or do not approve of, in addition to the majority of things that they do. These matters will be discussed in the ordinary course of scientific "business"—interchanges at scientific meetings, on the pages of specialty journals,

and by personal correspondence. Readers of the Handbook are invited to initiate and partake in such discussions. The current snail-mail and e-mail addresses of all the authors are given at the beginning of the volume.

As is always the case in the creation of serious books we too are happy to acknowledge the gracious help of many people "without whom this book could not have happened," as the saying goes. Our most heartfelt thanks go, of course, to our colleagues and friends who accepted our invitation to contribute to the *Handbook*. We are very pleased that we were able to rely on the expertise, knowledge, and skills of such an outstanding collection of individuals. We expect the *Handbook* to become a major reference source for people who want to get started in the field, or who wish to check things outside their own regional area. Such an ambition can become reality only if the source of the information lies in the expertise of the most qualified writers on every topic.

Among others "without whom," we especially wish to express our gratitude to Alison Mudditt who, out of the blue, provided the initial spark for the whole venture. We are also most grateful to Joan Bossert, the Executive Editor at the Oxford University Press who was most enthusiastic, encouraging, and helpful with a number of details from the very beginning, and whose continued support has been essential throughout the venture. Our very special gratitude goes to Sharyn Kreuger, who provided invaluable help in the closing stages of editing and checking manuscripts. Finally, we acknowledge the less visible but equally important contributions of the many parents, teachers, spouses, colleagues, and students of the people who have written chapters for the *Handbook*. We regret that it is not possible to mention them all by name, but we do sincerely thank them all, not only on our behalf and that of the authors of the chapters, but also on behalf of the many prospective readers and users of *The Oxford Handbook of Memory*.

Endel Tulving

Fergus Craik

Contents

Contributors   xi

Part I Study of Memory

1. A Brief History of Memory Research   3
   Gordon H. Bower
2. Concepts of Memory   33
   Endel Tulving
3. Methods of Memory Research   45
   Robert S. Lockhart
4. Contingency Analyses of Memory   59
   Michael J. Kahana

Part II Memory in the Laboratory

ACTS OF MEMORY

5. Short-Term and Working Memory   77
   Alan Baddeley
6. Encoding and Retrieval of
   Information   93
   Scott C. Brown & Fergus I. M. Craik
7. Transfer and Expertise   109
   Daniel R. Kimball & Keith J. Holyoak

CONTENTS OF MEMORY

8. Serial Learning: Cognition and
   Behavior   125
   Robert G. Crowder & Robert L. Greene
9. Remembering Actions and Words   137
   Lars-Göran Nilsson
10. Distortions of Memory   149
    Henry L. Roediger &
    Kathleen B. McDermott

REFLECTIONS IN MEMORY

11. Memory Judgments   165
    Douglas L. Hintzman
12. Source Monitoring: Attributing Mental
    Experiences   179
    Karen J. Mitchell & Marcia K. Johnson
13. Metamemory: Theory and Data   197
    Janet Metcalfe

AWARENESS IN MEMORY

14. Recollection and Familiarity:
    Process-Dissociation   215
    Colleen M. Kelley & Larry L. Jacoby

15. Remembering and Knowing 229
   John M. Gardiner &
      Alan Richardson-Klavehn
16. Nonconscious Forms of Human
   Memory 245
   Jeffrey P. Toth

Part III Memory in Life

MEMORY IN DEVELOPMENT

17. Memory in Infancy and Early
   Childhood 267
   Carolyn Rovee-Collier &
      Harlene Hayne
18. Socialization of Memory 283
   Katherine Nelson & Robyn Fivush
19. Memory and Theory of Mind 297
   Josef Perner

MEMORY IN USE

20. Remembering Life Experiences 315
   Ulric Neisser & Lisa K. Libby
21. Control Processes in
   Remembering 333
   Asher Koriat
22. Long-Term Maintenance of
   Knowledge 347
   Harry P. Bahrick
23. Remembering Spaces 363
   Barbara Tversky
24. Memory for Emotional Events 379
   Jonathan W. Schooler & Eric Eich

MEMORY IN DECLINE

25. Memory Changes in Healthy Older
   Adults 395
   David A. Balota, Patrick O. Dolan,
      & Janet M. Duchek
26. Memory in the Aging Brain 411
   Nicole D. Anderson &
      Fergus I. M. Craik
27. Selective Memory Disorders 427
   Andrew R. Mayes
28. Memory in the Dementias 441
   John R. Hodges

Part IV Organization of Memory

NEURAL SUBSTRATES OF MEMORY

29. Neuroanatomy of Memory 465
   Hans J. Markowitsch
30. The Medial Temporal Lobe and
   the Hippocampus 485
   Stuart M. Zola & Larry R. Squire
31. Brain Imaging of Memory 501
   Lars Nyberg & Roberto Cabeza
32. Event-Related Potential Studies of
   Memory 521
   Michael D. Rugg & Kevin Allan
33. Psychopharmacological Perspectives
   on Memory 539
   H. Valerie Curran

THEORIES OF MEMORY

34. The Adaptive Nature of Memory 557
   John R. Anderson & Lael J. Schooler
35. Memory Models 571
   Roger Ratcliff & Gail McKoon
36. Connectionist Models of Memory 583
   James L. McClelland
37. Episodic Memory and Autonoetic
   Awareness 597
   Mark A. Wheeler
38. Theories of Memory and
   Consciousness 609
   Morris Moscovitch
39. Memory Systems of 1999 627
   Daniel L. Schacter,
      Anthony D. Wagner,
      & Randy L. Buckner

EPILOGUE

   The Story of Memory, and Memory of
   the Story 645
   L. Weiskrantz

Subject Index 649

Name Index 675

Contributors

Kevin Allan
Wellcome Brain Research Group
School of Psychology
University of St. Andrews
St. Andrews KY169JU U.K.
Email: ka@st-andrews.ac.uk

Nicole D. Anderson
The Gerry & Nancy Pencer Brain Tumor
    Centre
Department of Psychiatry, Faculty of
    Medicine
University of Toronto
610 University Ave. 18-728
Toronto, ON M5G 3G3 Canada
Email: NicoleAnderson@pmh.toronto.on.ca

John R. Anderson
Department of Psychology
Carnegie-Mellon University
Pittsburgh, PA 15213
Email: JA+@CMU.EDU

Alan D. Baddeley
Department of Psychology
University of Bristol
8 Woodland Road
Bristol BS8 1TN England
Email: Alan.Baddeley@bristol.ac.uk

Harry P. Bahrick
Department of Psychology
Ohio Wesleyan University
127 Elmwood Drive
Delaware, OH 43015–2398
Email: hpbahric@cc.owu.edu

David A. Balota
Department of Psychology
Washington University
St. Louis, MO 63130
Email: dbalota@artsci.wustl.edu

Gordon H. Bower
Department of Psychology
Stanford University
Stanford, CA 94305
Email: gordon@psych.stanford.edu

Scott C. Brown
University of Michigan
ISR/RCGD
426 Thompson St.
Ann Arbor, MI 48106-1248
Email: scbrown@umich.edu

Randy L. Buckner
Department of Psychology
Washington University
St. Louis, MO 63130–4899
Email: rbuckner@artsci.wustl.edu

Roberto Cabeza
Department of Psychology
University of Alberta
Edmonton, AB T6G 2E9 Canada
Email: roberto.cabeza@ualberta.ca

Fergus I.M. Craik
Department of Psychology
University of Toronto
Toronto, ON M5S 3G3 Canada
Email: craik@psych.toronto.edu

Robert G. Crowder
Department of Psychology
PO Box 208205
Yale University
New Haven, CT 06520–8205
Email: robert.crowder@yale.edu

Valerie Curran
Department of Psychology
University College London
Gower Street
London, WC1E 6BT U.K.
Email: v.curran@ucl.ac.uk

Patrick O. Dolan
Department of Psychology
Washington University
St. Louis, MO 63130–4899
Email: pdolan@artsci.wustl.edu

Janet M. Duchek
Department of Psychology
Washington University
St. Louis, MO 63130–4899
Email: jand@ot-link.wustl.edu

Eric Eich
Department of Psychology
University of British Columbia
Vancouver, BC V6T 1Z4 Canada
Email: ee@cortex.psych.ubc.ca

Robyn Fivush
Department of Psychology
Emory University
Atlanta, GA 30322–1100
Email: psyrf@emory.edu

John M. Gardiner
Psychology Department
City University
Northampton Square
London EC1V 4P8, U.K
Email: J.M.Gardiner@city.ac.uk

Robert Greene
Department of Psychology
Case Western Reserve University
Cleveland, OH 44106
Email: rlg2@po.cwru.edu

Harlene Hayne
Department of Psychology
University of Otago
Dunedin, New Zealand
Email: hayne@psy.otago.ac.nz.

Douglas L. Hintzman
Department of Psychology
University of Oregon
Eugene, OR 97403–1205
Email: hintzman@OREGON.UOREGON.EDU

John R. Hodges
MRC Cognition and Brain Sciences Unit
15 Chaucer Rd.
Cambridge, CB2 2EF U.K.
Email: jrh24@mrc-cbu.cam.ac.uk

Keith J. Holyoak
Department of Psychology
6613 Franz Hall
UCLA
Los Angeles, CA 90024–1301
Email: holyoak@lifesci.ucla.edu

Larry Jacoby
Department of Psychology
McMaster University
Hamilton, ON L8S 4K1 Canada
Email: jacoby@mcmaster.ca

Marcia K. Johnson
Department of Psychology
Princeton University, Green Hall
Princeton, NJ 08544–101
Email: mkj@clarity.princeton.edu

Michael J. Kahana
Center for Complex Systems
Brandeis University
Waltham, MA 02254–9110
E-mail: kahana@cs.brandeis.edu

Colleen M. Kelley
Department of Psychology
The Florida State University
Tallahassee, FL 32306–1270
Email: kelley@darwin.psy.fsu.edu

Daniel R. Kimball
Department of Psychology
UCLA
Los Angeles, CA 90024–1301
Email: kimball@psych.ucla.edu

Asher Koriat
Department of Psychology
University of Haifa
Haifa, 31905 Israel
Email: akoriat@psy.haifa.ac.il

Lisa K. Libby
Department of Psychology
Cornell University
Uris Hall
Ithaca, NY 14853
Email: lkl3@cornell.edu

Robert S. Lockhart
Department of Psychology
University of Toronto
Toronto, ON M5S 1A1 Canada
Email: lockhart@psych.utoronto.ca

Hans J. Markowitsch
Physiological Psychology
University of Bielefeld
P.O. Box 10 01 31
D-33501 Bielefeld, Germany
Email: hjmarkowitch@post.Uni-Bielefeld.DE

Andrew R. Mayes
Department of Clinical Neurology
Royal Hallamshire Hospital,
Glossop Road
Sheffield S10 2JF U.K.
Email: A.Mayes@sheffield.ac.uk

James L. McClelland
Center for the Neural Basis of Cognition
115 Mellon Institute
4400 Fifth Avenue
Pittsburgh, PA 15213
Email: jlm@cnbc.cmu.edu

Kathleen B. McDermott
Washington University School of Medicine
Division of Radiological Sciences
4525 Scott Avenue, Campus Box 8225
St. Louis, MO 63110
Email: kmcd@npg.wustl.edu

Gail McKoon
Department of Psychology
Northwestern University
Evanston, IL 60208
Email: g-mckoon@nwu.edu

Janet Metcalfe
Department of Psychology
Columbia University
New York, NY 10027
Email: metcalfe@psych.columbia.edu

Karen J. Mitchell
Department of Psychology
Princeton University, Green Hall
Princeton, NJ 08544–1010
Email: kmitchel@Princeton.edu

Morris Moscovitch
Rotman Research Institute
Baycrest Centre for Geriatric Care
3560 Bathurst Street
North York, ON M6A 2E1 Canada
Email: momos@credit.erin.utoronto.ca

Ulric Neisser
Department of Psychology
Cornell University
Uris Hall
Ithaca, NY 14853
Email: un13@cornell.edu

Katherine Nelson
Department of Developmental Psychology
CUNY Graduate School & University Center
33 W 42nd Street
New York, NY 10036
Email: knelson@Email.gc.cuny.edu

Lars-Göran Nilsson
Department of Psychology
Stockholm University
S-10691 Stockholm, Sweden
Email: lgn@psychology.su.se

Lars Nyberg
Department of Psychology
Umea University
S-901 87 Umea, Sweden
Email: lars.nyberg@psy.umu.se

Josef Perner
Department of Psychologie
University of Salzburg
Hellbrunnerstrasse 34
A-5020 Salzburg, Austria
Email: josef.perner@mh.sbg.ac.at

Roger Ratcliff
Department of Psychology
Northwestern University
2029 Sheridan Road
Swift Hall 102
Evanston, IL 60208–0001
Email: roger@eccles.psych.nwu.ed

Alan Richardson-Klavehn
Division of Psychology
University of Westminster
309 Regent Street
London W1R 8AL U.K.
Email: a.r.klavehn@wmin.ac.uk

Henry L. Roediger, III
Department of Psychology
Washington University
St. Louis, MO 63130–4899
Email: roediger@artsci.wustl.edu

Carolyn Rovee-Collier
Department of Psychology
Rutgers University
Busch Campus
New Brunswick, NJ 08903
Email: rovee@rci.rutgers.edu

Michael D. Rugg
Institute of Cognitive Neuroscience
University College London
17, Queen Square
London WC1N 3AR England
Email: m.rugg@ucl.ac.uk

Daniel L. Schacter
Department of Psychology
William James Hall
Harvard University
Cambridge, MA 02138
Email: dls@wjh.harvard.edu

Jonathan W. Schooler
635 Learning Research and Development
    Center
University of Pittsburgh
3939 O'Hara St
Pittsburgh PA 15260
Email: schooler+@pitt.edu

Lael J. Schooler
Department of Psychology
Pennsylvania State University
University Park, PA 16802–1009
Email: ljs24@psu.edu

Larry R. Squire
Vet. Admin. Medical Center, V116A
University of California, San Diego
3350 La Jolla Village Drive
San Diego, CA 92161
Email: lsquire@ucsd.edu

Jeffrey Toth
School of Psychology
Georgia Institute of Technology
Atlanta, GA 30332–0170
Email: jt104@prism.gatech.edu

Endel Tulving
Rotman Research Institute
Baycrest Centre for Geriatric Care
3560 Bathurst Street
North York, ON M6A 2E1 Canada
Email: tulving@psych.utoronto.ca

Barbara Tversky
Department of Psychology
Stanford University
Stanford, CA 94305–2130
Email: bt@psych.stanford.edu

Anthony D. Wagner
Massachusetts General Hospital NMR Center
Harvard Medical School
Boston, MA 02129
Email: adwagner@NMR.MGH.Harvard.EDU

Lawrence Weiskrantz
Department of Experimental Psychology
South Parks Road
Oxford OX1 3UD, England
Email: larry.weiskrantz@psy.ox.ac.uk

Mark A. Wheeler
Department of Psychology
Temple University
Philadelphia PA 19122
Email: mwheeler@nimbus.ocis.temple.edu

Stuart M. Zola
Department of Psychiatry 0603
University of California, San Diego
9500 Gilman Drive
San Diego, CA 92093–0603
Email: szola@ucsd.edu

Part I: Study of Memory

A Brief History of Memory Research

GORDON H. BOWER

Background: Associationism

Psychology as a discipline developed out of philosophical discussions regarding the nature of the mind and mental life. The study of memory and learning arose from philosophical questions regarding how people come to know things about their world. Learning is assuredly the primary way we acquire knowledge, and remembering is a primary means by which people support knowledge claims, as when a witness in court asserts "I remember seeing Jones with a revolver in his hand."

Philosophical speculations about learning were prominent among advocates of *empiricism*, which is the view that sensory experiences are the only ultimate source of knowledge and truths about the world (contra innate ideas or religious authorities). People's ideas about the world are alleged to derive from sense impressions either as simple copies or as combinations of simple ideas. Objects such as oranges, dogs, and houses are allegedly constellations of many sensory qualities (e.g., the color, shape, taste, and texture of an orange).

The empiricist program required some means for learning these constellations. Thus was introduced the fundamental theory of *association by contiguity* (Warren, 1921). Complex ideas are allegedly formed in the mind by connecting together in memory simple ideas based on sensations that are experienced contiguously in time and/or space. The memory that sensory quality or event A was experienced together with, or immediately preceding, sensory quality or event B is recorded in the memory bank as an *association* from idea *a* to idea *b*. Reviving these associative sequences from memory (when recurrence of event A makes us think of event B) is the presumed method by which people's past experiences cause their later thoughts to progress from one idea to the next. This basic notion can be elaborated to account for the way humans develop coordinated expectations about properties of objects, expectations about causal sequences of events, predictions about future events, explanations of how or why something came about, and plans of action designed to bring about particular outcomes. These are basic abilities of the mind.

Throughout the seventeenth to nineteenth centuries, empiricist philosophers such as John Locke, John Stuart Mill, and Thomas Brown speculated about various factors that might affect the degree or strength of particular associations (Warren, 1921). They recognized that associations would vary in their strength according to the *vividness* or distinctiveness of the original experience, its *duration* (study time), its *frequency* (repetitions), and its *interest* for the observer. Revival of associations from memory was hypothesized to vary with the *resemblance* of the stimulating cue to the memory, the *recency* of the experience, the coexistence of *fewer alternative associates* to the cue (called "interference"), and "*temporary diversities of state*" (intoxication, delirium, depression). Such conjectures have generated much experimental research on learning and memory, and every learning theory deals with these factors in some way (Bower & Hilgard, 1981).

The scientific investigation of association formation began with the work of a German scientist, Hermann Ebbinghaus, whose pioneering research (with himself as sole subject) was published in his treatise *On Memory* in 1885. Discussion of his work will be postponed in order to examine briefly another major influence on studies of learning—namely, the doctrine of *behaviorism*, which became wedded for many years to the doctrine of associationism.

Behaviorism and S-R Psychology

The Behaviorist Philosophy

Behaviorism is a positivist philosophy which argues that all that observers can ever know about other persons or animals is provided by close observations of their overt actions or behaviors in specific situations (and human behavior includes speech). Behaviorism grew out of a desire for scientific objectivity in observations and for parsimony in explanations; it was especially critical of the undisciplined, introspective "mentalism" that at the turn of the century was being passed off as an explanation for behavior. On the behaviorist view, to predict someone's behavior, all one needs is a catalog of specific facts and generalizations about his or her past responses to situations resembling the present one. These generalizations about a person's past situation-to-action regularities are presumably carried in his or her nervous system as a set of stimulus-response (S-R) *habits*.

Antecedents of Behaviorism

While antecedents to behaviorism were many, an assured one was Charles Darwin's theory of biological evolution, which suggested the continuity of all species, including *Homo sapiens*

(Darwin, 1859). Human learning was seen as an adaptive mechanism that evolved over millions of years throughout the animal kingdom by small variations and minor accretions in the neural hardware that carries out the various learning tasks with which organisms are confronted. This "biological continuity" view justifies the many comparative studies by psychologists of behavioral adaptation and learning in lower animals. Since animals do not talk, those studies led in turn to a strong behaviorist orientation toward learning. Thus, learning came to be viewed as a change in an organism's behavioral dispositions in particular situations (S-R habits) as a result of its experiences. It was recognized, of course, that the responses may be complex skills and the stimuli may be those stemming from a complex environment, including intricate and subtle social situations.

Behaviorist approaches to learning were greatly encouraged around the turn of the twentieth century by the pioneering studies of conditioned reflexes by the Russian physiologist Ivan Pavlov (1927) and by early studies of "trial-and-error" (instrumental) learning by Edward Thorndike (1898, 1903), an influential educational psychologist in America. This behaviorist orientation was promulgated by many influential psychologists throughout the first half of the twentieth century—from John Watson (1919, 1924), to Clark Hull (1943), to B. F. Skinner (1953, 1957). This orientation strongly affected the way in which human learning was studied and explained. That orientation began to fade with the coming of the "cognitive revolution" that began in the late 1950s and early 1960s. However, before discussing those events, we return to the earlier work of Hermann Ebbinghaus and the rote learning tradition that followed his pioneering studies. The rote learning tradition was characterized by a fusion of associationism and behaviorism.

Ebbinghaus and the Rote Learning Tradition

Ebbinghaus (1885) set out to investigate the formation of novel associations using controlled systematic experiments with careful measurements of his own learning. He introduced strict controls regarding the timing and number of study trials, recall time permitted, and retention interval (to study forgetting). He invented the notion of the nonsense syllable (like DAX, QEH) to provide himself with learning materials of homogeneous difficulty, thus avoiding the variability of familiar words or prose. He taught himself by studying serial lists of 6 to 20 syllables, reading them aloud in sequence in pace with a metronome and then trying to recite the series from memory. The serial list was his analog of the associative chain of ideas about which philosophers had speculated.

Ebbinghaus introduced many important ideas and methods (see the Ebbinghaus symposium published in the July 1985 issue (volume 11) of the *Journal of Experimental Psychology: Learning, Memory, and Cognition*). He measured the difficulty of learning a list by the number of study trials required for him to attain one errorless recitation of it. He noted how difficulty increased disproportionately with the length of the list being learned. He introduced the idea of measurable "degrees of learning" (or forgetting) by noting the savings in relearning a list he had learned earlier. The percent savings was the difference in trials for original learning (say, 9 trials) minus those needed for later relearning (say, 3) divided by the original learning trials (so, $(9 - 3)/9 = 67\%$). Using this measure, he was able to plot his famous forgetting curve relating percent savings to retention interval. This curve (figure 1.1) showed very rapid losses over the first few hours or days, with more gradual but steady decline over subsequent days, weeks, and months. Ebbinghaus also found that forgetting of a list decreased with multiple relearnings of it, that overlearning increased retention, and that widely distributed study trials (say, 1 per hour) were more effective than closely packed trials (say, 1 per minute) for long-term retention.

Ebbinghaus's new paradigm (adults learning lists of nonsense materials) defined a task in which a multitude of variables can be defined and their influences on "remembering" behaviors observed. The phenomena that he discovered, his ideas, and his methods cast a long shadow throughout the twentieth century of research on human memory. Subsequent research has invented several other paradigms and teased out many variables that determine memory performance in these settings. The memories established can be tested by either recall, recognition, and reconstruction, or by a variety of indirect measures. The nature of the materials can be varied, as can their mode of presentation, strategies subjects use in studying them, expectations regarding the memory test, and relationships among several sets of materials being learned. As variables have been isolated and studied, a huge backlog of empirical information has accumulated about how humans learn in these situations. And many theoretical hypotheses have been proposed and tested to integrate and account for the evidence surrounding specific topics.

Analysis of Laboratory Rote Learning Tasks

The rote learning tradition was established around the intensive study of three different kinds of learning paradigms—serial learning, paired-associate learning, and perceptual–motor skill learning. We will briefly characterize each of these learning tasks and a few of their findings.

Serial Learning

The task Ebbinghaus used is called *serial learning*, an analog of learning the alphabet or learning to put letters in sequence to spell a word: the subject learns to output in a specified order a small set of temporally ordered, discrete items (letters, nonsense syllables, written or spoken words, pictured objects, sentences). Subjects are asked to remember both the items and their serial order. Retrieval may be tested by asking subjects either to reproduce (recall) all items in the order presented, or to recall what item followed a specific cued item, or to reconstruct the presented order when given the items (on flashcards) in scrambled order. In some experiments, a number of series are presented only once for recall (e.g., for measuring the immediate memory span). In other experiments, the same items may be presented many times in the same order for repeated study and test trials to examine accumulative learning.

Studies of serial learning have uncovered many facts. Increasing the study trials and time per item increases learning; increasing the time subjects are given to anticipate the next successor in the series improves their performance. While making the items very similar to one another (e.g., XON, NEH, XEH, NOH) improves their recallability, this similarity creates many confusion errors about their ordering. A robust finding is that items at the beginning and end of the list are easier to learn than items in the middle (see figure 1.2), a fact that has provoked many explanatory attempts (Johnson, 1991).

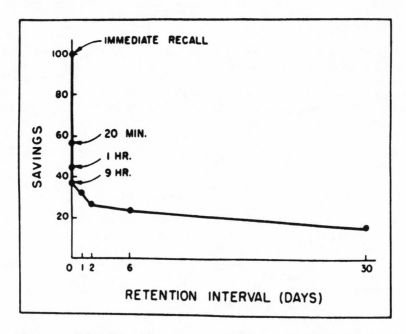

Figure 1.1 Ebbinghaus's forgetting curve. The savings percentages are plotted as a function of retention interval. After Ebbinghaus (1885).

Figure 1.2 Predicted and observed relative serial position error curves for 8-, 11-, and 14-item lists. Data from Hovland (1940). The fit to the data is provided by Johnson's theory of relative distinctiveness of different serial positions. (From figure 1 of "A distinctiveness model of serial learning" by G. J. Johnson (1991). *Psychological Review, 98*, pp. 204–217. Reprinted by permission.)

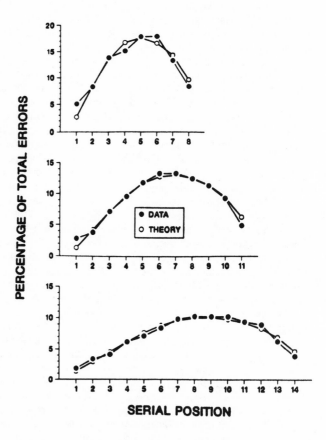

Conjectures regarding the effective stimulus for the next response in the series have also provoked much research. The natural hypothesis is that the series is learned by chaining together a set of pairwise associations, so that the series A-B-C-D is stored as the unordered pairs C-D, A-B, B-C. Thus, item C is both a response to its preceding cue, B, and in turn a cue for its successor, D. However, predictions from this pairwise chaining hypothesis frequently fail, suggesting that some more abstract "mental slots" for relative position ("first—A, second—B, . . . last—D") may be the effective cues for the ordered associations.

Paired-Associates Learning

Soon after Ebbinghaus's studies, an American investigator, Mary Calkins (1894), introduced the method of *paired-associates* learning. In this task, subjects study a set of pairs of discrete units (syllables, words, pictured objects) and are asked to learn to recall a specific member of a pair (the "response") when tested by presenting the other member of the pair (the "stimulus"). The retrieval test might also request discrimination ("recognition") of studied pairs compared to rearranged pairs. Examples of paired associates include learning French to English vocabulary with flashcards, names to faces, names of wife-husband pairs, countries with their major exports, and so on. In many respects, paired-associate learning closely mimics the S-R associationist analysis of all learning; for that reason it came to be favored for many rote learning studies.

Paired associate learning involves three distinct but overlapping phases: (1) learning the nominal response terms as integrated units (e.g., French words, nonsense syllables, etc.); (2) discriminating and reducing confusions among the stimulus terms of the many pairs being learned; and (3) associating the correct response term to its appropriate stimulus. Increasing the prior familiarity and meaningfulness of the response terms (e.g., English versus Turkish words) lowers the difficulty of the first phase. Increasing the similarity among the nominal stimuli in the list of pairs increases the difficulty of the second, discrimination phase; confusions between two similar stimuli persist until the subject selects a differentiating cue that distinguishes between them (e.g., noting that the stimuli QEH and HEQ differ in order). The difficulty of the third, associative phase is reduced by using words that are already weakly associated or

ones for which subjects can easily discover meaningful relationships. This issue will be revisited later.

Skills

Many categories of human skills have been studied systematically since the turn of the century (for reviews, see Rosenbaum, 1991; Schmidt, 1988). They vary greatly and include (1) *perceptual motor skills* such as typing and telegraphy, athletic skills such as diving and shooting basketball, musical skills such as violin and piano playing, and laboratory tasks such as pursuit rotor tracking and reverse-mirror tracing; and (2) *cognitive skills* such as computer text editing, computer programming, chess playing, and geometry theorem proving (see Anderson, 1995). The skills differ in the degree to which they can be imparted by verbal instruction and by the learner imitating the performance of a coach or model. The development of skills in everyday life typically requires a huge amount of practice—hundreds and perhaps thousands of hours of patient, deliberate practice. Laboratory tasks are selected for study so that significant improvement can be tracked over a few minutes or hours of practice. Skills are almost always tested by subjects' ability to perform (rather than verbally describe) the requisite activity at some level of competence.

An early hypothesis was that skills could be well represented in memory as a linear chain of associations in which proprioceptive (and external) feedback following a given response component provided the stimulus for the next response component in the chain. That hypothesis has been replaced, however, by more complex modern hypotheses involving hierarchical control of integrated motor programs (see Rosenbaum, 1991).

A major finding is that the curve plotting performance (e.g., time to do the task) against practice trials almost always approximates a power function of the form $P = aN^b$, where P is performance, N is number of practice trials, and b (negative when P is time) determines the rate of improvement per practice trial. This function (called the "No pain, no gain" principle) says that performance speed improves rapidly at first, but then increasingly slowly as practice proceeds. But improvements can always be eked out by further practice—captured in the slogan "The difference between ordinary and extraordinary is that little bit extra."

Second, as practice proceeds, the skill can be carried out with progressively less attention and cognitive effort (on "automatic pilot"), enabling the person to attend to other matters. This aspect of automatization is often conveyed in the slogan "When the going gets tough, the tough get going"—meaning that high-level performance can be maintained in the face of stress and distractions.

Third, the basis for most perceptual motor skills is largely nonconscious, not available to conscious introspection, beyond the skilled person's ability to describe in useful detail how he or she does the skilled action. Highly skilled baseball hitters cannot adequately describe how they know where the pitched ball is going to be and how to adjust their swing to hit an inside versus outside pitch (the same inarticulateness characterizes golf putters or tennis pros hitting a graceful backhand). Despite this unverbalizable character of high-level skills, some of the very best, most effective instruction is conducted by athletic coaches and music instructors who provide daily demonstrations and subtle feedback to bring out the very best in their pupils. (Even tennis pros continue to have coaches.) Curiously, no such intense coaching occurs in academic subjects such as mathematics or psychology.

The Nature of S-R Theory for Rote Learning

The several tasks mentioned have been studied in many variations along with attendant theories of how humans master the tasks. For reviews, see McGeoch and Irion (1952), Hall (1971), Kausler (1974), and later chapters in this *handbook*. An important development was that the investigation of human learning was expropriated in the 1930s and 1940s by strong proponents of S-R behaviorism—a marriage that was to lead to a stormy separation later during the "cognitive revolution." To illustrate the nature of an S-R theory of human learning, its analysis of paired-associate learning in which subjects learn a collection of S-R pairs will be reviewed.

Considering each paired associate alone, the general idea is that reinforced repetitions of the pair gradually build up its associative strength (S-R habit) toward a maximum, as illustrated in figure 1.3. Associative strength of the pairing is presumed to be reflected in the probability and latency (retrieval time) for the correct response to the stimulus as well as its resistance to later forgetting. In figure 1.3, two different thresholds are postulated: the S-R strength must be above the lower, "recognition" threshold in order to support the sub-

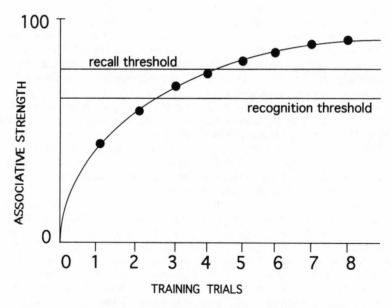

Figure 1.3 Hypothetical curve of increase in associative strength of an S-R habit as it receives rewarded practice. A lower "recognition threshold" and higher "recall threshold" are indicated.

ject's accuracy on a pair *recognition* test; and the strength must be above the upper, "recall" threshold in order to support accurate response *recall* to the stimulus member of the pair. Strengths below these thresholds lead to errors or omissions. If the momentary strength fluctuates somewhat from trial to trial around the mean plotted in figure 1.3, then correct response proportions will gradually increase from zero to one rather than abruptly shifting from zero to one when the mean crosses the threshold.

These two thresholds reflect the general belief that recognition tests are easier than recall tests, and are more sensitive for detecting small differences among weak associations. Three implications follow: first, that any S-R pair that is recalled can also be recognized; second, that initial study trials can build up associative strength to the S-R connection in a "subthreshold" manner, even before these effects are revealed in accurate recognition or recall (this will also produce savings in relearning of "forgotten" pairs); and third, repetitions beyond the point of recall ("overlearning") continue to strengthen the habit, and this would be revealed in its retrieval speed and its resistance to later forgetting.

These remarks about single S-R connections need to be elaborated somewhat to deal with subjects' learning of a list of many pairs. First, suppose that subjects are learning a list of 12 pairs that include the pairs *king–table, prince–throne,* and *dog–car.* The associationist would first note that the stimulus words have preexisting associations from past learning, such as *king* having associates of *queen, royalty, throne, Arthur, Henry,* and so on. Thus, the new, to-be-learned association *king–table* must be strengthened sufficiently to overcome these preexisting ones.

Second, the theory imagines that each stimulus word will show initial generalization or confusions (based on the similarities of their appearance or meanings) to other stimuli in the list. These generalization tendencies are illustrated by dashed lines in figure 1.4. These generalization tendencies can produce errors by evoking the wrong response to a similar stimulus. However, the correct response to each stimulus will be rewarded each trial (by knowledge of results), and thus strengthened, whereas generalized responses (e.g., saying *throne* to *king,* or *table* to *prince*) will be non-reinforced (punished) and hence extinguished or inhibited. Thus, over repeated study trials, the correct association is expected to be

STIMULI   RESPONSES

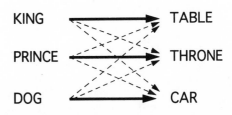

Figure 1.4 Hypothetical stimulus (left) to response (right) associations involved in learning three noun-noun pairs. The direct, correct associations (solid lines) must overcome competition from the generalized error associations (dashed lines) to produce correct recall. Adapted from Gibson (1940).

strengthened sufficiently to win out in competition with both the preexisting and the generalized associates.

This generalization analysis explains the fact that pairs with similar stimuli and/or responses will lead to many confusion errors (e.g., saying *throne* to *king* more often than to *car*) and thus take longer to learn. The analysis also recognizes that preexisting associations that conflict with the correct response (such as *king–throne*) and that are strongly primed by other pairs in the list can create many errors of commission ("intrusions") before the correct, novel association wins out. (Obviously, if the preexisting associate were the correct one for this list, this would be a positive influence.)

Two other aspects of this analysis may be noted. First, subjects are often observed to learn such novel pairs (*king–table*) by finding and utilizing preexisting associations, such as *king–[Arthur–roundtable]–table.* These are called *mediators* and they chain together internal (covert) associates that successively cue one another and lead to the correct response. Note that these mediating associates are assumed to act like internal "responses" that provide stimulating aftereffects, so in some sense they preserve the stimulus-response character of the theory despite being (for the moment) unobservable. Moreover, an "editing monitor" needs to be postulated to enable the model (subject) to withhold the mediators (not to say *Arthur* to *king*) but to give overtly only the correct response. It has often been noted that such mediators serve as only a temporary crutch during early learning; as practice proceeds and the direct *king–table* association is repeatedly reinforced, it is retrieved more quickly, thus short-circuiting (and beating out) the mediating associative chain that then drops away.

A second aspect of this generalization-discrimination analysis is that after learning—which, remember, occurred by inhibiting the preexisting and generalized responses—the passage of a retention interval allows the inhibition of errors to decay, thus leading to the partial recovery of errors over time. Therefore, although once inhibited, error responses such as *throne–king* may recover in strength over a delay interval, creating forgetting via errors of commission. While this hypothesis (due to Gibson, 1940) explains forgetting in terms of the familiar conditioning concept of spontaneous recovery, it must be admitted that it fares poorly against the evidence (see Underwood, 1961). For example, contrary to implication, once learned, high-similarity paired-associate lists are not forgotten at a higher rate than low-similarity lists.

Materials Variations

The foregoing illustrates that even in Ebbinghaus's earliest experiments, it was clear that learning depended greatly on the nature of the materials—whether numbers, nonsense syllables, words, meaningful sentences, coherent prose, or poetry. These vary greatly in their familiarity and meaningfulness for subjects—for example, in how much prior experience subjects have had with such materials and how rich the network is of associations subjects have surrounding the units to be learned.

Researchers in the Ebbinghaus tradition soon noticed that even their favored nonsense syllables differed greatly in how many words and other associations they evoked among learners, and that syllables evoking more associations were learned more easily. To deal with this variability, researchers tested many subjects to tabulate "association norms" or "meaningfulness norms" for collections of nonsense syllables (Glaze, 1928), other nonsense materials (consonant trigrams such as XMQ; Witmer, 1935), and words (Noble, 1952; Noble & Parker, 1969). These norms were used to compose lists of materials that were of specified associative difficulty.

Implicit in this emphasis on the association value of to-be-learned material was an important underlying idea—namely, that people learn most easily by relating the new material to things they already know. They look for the "mediators" mentioned previously. They try to transform (recode) the to-be-learned material into something familiar or close to something that is meaningful to them. Thus, the nonsense syllable MIK is recoded as "MIKE with the E missing" and JQA as "the initials of John Quincy Adams" (see Montague, 1972). Learners then remember their recoding, and convert it back into the to-be-remembered series when they are asked to recall.

This observation led different investigators in three different directions. One direction was to account for the kind of mediators subjects came up with; for example, Montague and Kiess (1968) showed that learning of a paired associate was highly predictable from the ease with which adults came up with a mediator for it; and Prytulak (1971) predicted the memorability of different nonsense trigrams by how complicated were the "mental steps" subjects required to convert them into familiar words. A second and predominant direction for researchers was to abandon use of nonsense materials (as too variable) for studying elementary learning and move on to studies of learning of already meaningful materials such as words, sentences, texts, pictures of common objects, and video events; this predominant trend accounts for the fact that nonsense-syllable learning studies practically disappeared in the memory literature after the late 1960s. The third direction for researchers was to examine carefully how past learning was brought to bear upon a person's current learning. These were called studies of "transfer" of past knowledge—a topic to be discussed briefly now.

Transfer of Knowledge

By assumption adult learners always come into a given learning situation with considerable knowledge, learning strategies, and specific associations that they use as best they can to optimize performance on the given task. These transfer effects include both general methods of attack for solving particular learning problems and more specific associations among units employed in the new task.

Nonspecific Transfer

General (nonspecific) transfer includes strategies for studying particular kinds of materials, selecting discriminating cues from the nominal stimuli, composing mediators for particular materials, optimizing use of immediate memory, and adjusting to the temporal pacing of the study and test trials in the laboratory task. An example of such general transfer effects is demonstrated in an experiment by Thune (1951). His college-student subjects learned three new unrelated lists of 10 paired adjectives on each of 5 successive days, each list practiced for 10 trials. The average correct responses over the first 5 trials on each list (in figure 1.5) reveals a swift rise in performance across the three new lists within each day (reflecting "warm up" adjustments) along with a slower improvement across days (reflecting "learning to learn" lists of this kind). Many studies of this general kind have examined the benefits of explicitly teaching subjects various mnemonic devices (Bower, 1970a), as well as useful techniques for learning educational materials (e.g., history or science textbooks), including how to analyze texts for important ideas and their relationships, memorize, organize one's study time, and recite and review the material (see, e.g., Dansereau, 1978; Mayer, 1987; O'Neil, 1978).

Specific Transfer

The second class of transfer studies examine the influence of specific prior associations, and these are of two types. One type of study examines subjects' preexisting associations learned over a lifetime, and investigators then notice how these operate in transfer to new learning situations—understanding, of course, that these past learnings may vary widely across subjects owing to their differing experiences. An example here is the use of familiar words rather than unfamiliar letter strings as learning materials. The perceptual system divides or segregates stimuli into discrete groups or "chunks," and looks for a match in

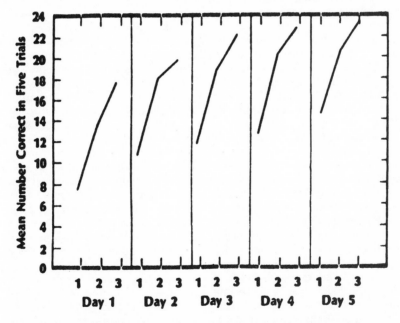

Figure 1.5 Trends in nonspecific transfer with practice. Three paired associate lists were learned for 10 trials on each of 5 days; average number of correct responses over first 5 trials on each list is plotted. Contrast the large gains within sessions with the smaller ones between sessions. (From L. E. Thune (1951), "Warm-up effect as a function of level of practice in verbal learning." *Journal of Experimental Psychology, 42*, pp. 250–256. Reproduced by permission.)

memory to these perceptual chunks. A *chunk* is defined as a familiar collection of more elementary units that have been interassociated and stored in memory repeatedly and that act as a coherent, integrated group when retrieved (Miller, 1956; Simon, 1974). The brain's mechanism for learning begins its operation (of association formation) by linking together elementary units into larger chunks. The difference can be seen in comparing, for example, letter strings such as IBF versus FBI versus FIB: the first is three chunks, the second a meaningful but unpronounceable chunk, and the third a pronounceable and meaningful word. A simple rule is that novel material will be remembered more easily the fewer chunks contained in it. This, of course, requires a suitably educated person who has the requisite familiarity with the verbal units.

Beyond examining these preexisting language chunks, however, investigators may aim to study the composition of transferable habits and their mode of operation by explicitly teaching subjects prior associations and then noticing how these affect later learning of related material. Different arrangements can produce either positive, negative, or zero transfer on a second learning task.

Classic cases of negative transfer arise when subjects must learn a new arbitrary response to an old stimulus. For example, having already learned who is married to whom (e.g., *Bill–Sally* and *Dan–Ruth*), subjects then learn new pairings as couples divorce and remarry, requiring new associations such as *Bill–Jane* and *Dan–Sally*. This situation produces large negative transfer relative to a control condition, because the prior specific associations compete with and interfere with the subject's quickly learning the new associations. The old associations keep coming to mind and blocking retrieval of the new associations. The effect here is similar to that in the earlier illustration of *king–throne* interfering with remembering *king–table*. The amount of negative transfer is greater the more the first-learned associations are aroused by the second stimuli. Thus, if the word-stimuli in list 2 were close in meaning to the stimuli in list 2, then the earlier associations will generalize to the second-list stimuli, creating more negative transfer the greater their similarity. In contrast, transfer is rather different when the relationship of the nominal response terms in the successive pairs is varied. When words are used as paired associates, positive transfer is observed when the successive responses to a

stimulus are closely related in meaning. Having learned *prince–throne*, for example, subjects would be quick to learn *prince–chair*, presumably because the first associate is used as a mediator to aid learning of the second pair.

The topic of transfer is far richer and more complex than this brief discussion can indicate. For example, psychologists have examined the generally positive transfer that occurs when adults learn two computer programming languages or two computer text editors (see Singley & Anderson, 1989). In those situations positive transfer appears to arise owing to similar problem-solving steps that are utilized in the two domains, despite differences in details. For example, the general plan for how to "cut and paste" text must logically be nearly the same for every text editor (so that that plan transfers), whereas the specific key strokes required may differ somewhat in the two editors, causing minor negative transfer at that level.

Forgetting

The stimulus-response approach easily accommodates three basic reasons for forgetting associations after they have been learned. The first reason is simply autonomous decay in the strength of the S-R association due to physiological and metabolic processes that cause progressive erosion of the synaptic changes in the brain that had encoded the original association. The second reason for forgetting is performance loss due to a type of stimulus generalization: the training cue (or total stimulus complex) is allegedly progressively altered between training and testing owing to natural forces, so that the full stimulus complex is not reinstated at testing, resulting in progressively poorer retrieval of the original association. As a hypothetical example, suppose that the full training complex were composed of the simultaneous cues A, B, C, D, all associated with response R. If only cue A were present later (because B, C, D are altered, missing, or forgotten), then A is unlikely to retrieve the whole associative complex, so response R will not be recalled. The B, C, D cues in this example might refer to any of a diverse set of what are called "contextual stimuli"—internal postural, sensory stimuli plus emotional and associative responses of the subject, as well as environmental cues besides those experimenters explicitly recognize in their description of the stimulus situation.

A third reason in S-R theory for forgetting is that other associations learned before or after the target association in question may come over time to compete with, displace, or block out and *interfere* with retrieval of the target material. This happens, for example, when people have trouble remembering the name of a woman's second husband because her first husband's name is quite familiar and it keeps coming to mind and getting in the way. Another example is that people often misremember attributes of a person they met earlier by intruding those appropriate to the ethnic stereotype that they had assigned to that person.

The evidence for each of these three causes of forgetting is simply overwhelming. Throughout the history of research on forgetting, attempts have been made to eliminate theoretically one or another factor, or to explain one factor as really due to another (e.g., decay eliminated in favor of interference—see McGeoch & Irion, 1952; or decay eliminated in favor of progressive drift over time in the retrieval context—see Estes, 1955). Because all three factors are usually highly correlated, these attempts at colonization are typically insufficient, often requiring assumptions that are equivalent to the other factors to account for the full range of data.

The interference factor has been most often studied in the laboratory. In the paradigm most easily studied, subjects learn two or more lists of associations bearing particular relationships to one another. To illustrate with paired associates, let A-B denote a generic list of many pairs, where A and B denote the generic stimulus and response terms, respectively. In *retroactive interference* studies, recall of a first learned list of homogeneous A-B pairs is substantially impaired after subjects learn a second list with the same stimuli but different responses (denoted generically as A-C). The amount of retroactive interference is assessed by comparison to a control condition in which subjects learn the A-B list but then rest or engage in a distracting task for an equivalent time before receiving a recall test with their A-B list. This A-B, A-C arrangement is the same as that noted earlier that produces negative transfer in learning the second association. Indeed, across conditions, negative transfer in second-list learning correlates highly with the amount of later forgetting produced by interference. *Proactive interference* conditions are the converse, examining the decrement in second-list (A-C) recall caused

by prior learning of a first list (A-B). The control subjects in this case learn only the A-C list.

Many facts are known about forgetting caused by such interference (see Postman, 1971). First, the stronger the training of the target response compared to the competing associates, the better it will withstand interference from other associates. Second, the stronger or more numerous are the interfering associates (e.g., multiple lists such as A-C, A-D, A-E learned before or after the A-B target list), the greater the decrement in recall of the target associates. Examples of these relationships are shown in figure 1.6 (from Briggs, 1957): in this study, after 2, 5, 10, or 20 trials of second-list training, subjects were asked to give the first response that each "A" stimulus brought to mind. The panels of the figure show the data for subjects who received 2, 5, 10, or 20 trials of original learning (OL) in figure 1.6 on A-B. The more A-C trials that accumulated, the more A-C came to the fore; but the more original learning (A-B) trials, the longer A-B predominated before losing out.

Another fact about interference is that a longer interval or gap between learning of the two lists reduces the extent to which they interfere with one another. Furthermore, as the interval from the second-learned list to testing is lengthened, proactive interference increases whereas retroactive interference decreases. Such results are explicable by the ideas that all associative strengths decay, and that competing associates suppressed during learning recover somewhat as time passes and their suppression dissipates.

Interference effects are not solely a function of overt intrusion errors of the explicit competing responses. The subject may think of the competing response but recognize it as not the requested target-response, so withhold it (a process called "list discrimination"). On other occasions, interference arises as a total blocking or inability of the subject to think of any relevant response (an "omission" error). Thus, for example, if after learning two lists in an A-B, A-C relationship subjects are asked to recall both responses to the stimulus terms, they can recall both responses to some extent, but progressively more C's and fewer B's, the greater the amount of training they have just received on the second (A-C) list (Barnes & Underwood, 1959).

Although interference effects have been illustrated with paired-associate learning, the basic ideas apply to analyses of forgetting in

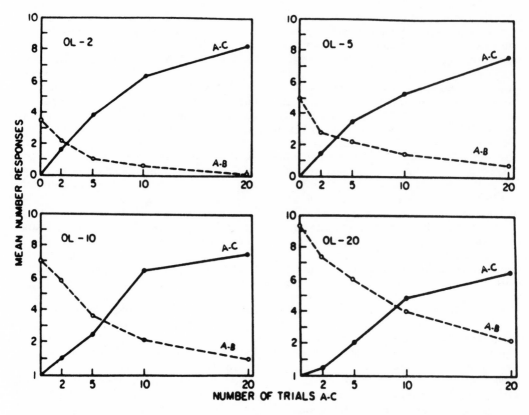

Figure 1.6 Relative frequencies of the originally learned response (A-B) and the newly learned response (A-C) during learning of the new response. The four graphs are from four different groups of subjects given 2, 5, 10, or 20 trials of original learning (OL). (From G. E. Briggs (1957), "Retroactive inhibition as a function of original and interpolated learning." *Journal of Experimental Psychology, 53*, p. 64. Reprinted with permission.)

all learning situations such as serial learning, free recall, memorizing addition and multiplication tables, and remembering in which of multiple lists (or contexts) particular items occurred. It also applies to forgetting sentences, paragraphs, and stories when similar concepts are involved (see Anderson, 1995).

Cognitive Psychology

The Information Processing Perspective

While interest in cognitive (thought) processes had been a continuing minor sideline throughout the first half of the twentieth century, major momentum to cognitivism was imparted by developments in the 1950s and 1960s. One of the antecedents was information (communi-

cation) theory, with its concepts of encoding and decoding messages, and the concept of "limited capacity," which applied to any communication channel (for a review, see Garner, 1962). The metaphor was that the human perceptual system analyzed the stimulus array, extracted information from it in the form of neural codes (e.g., in visual or auditory modalities), and that these codes entered into mental programs designed either to store them in memory, or to reason, make decisions, and guide actions. Donald Broadbent (1958) adapted several ideas from this approach in his studies of selective attention, especially using the dichotic ("two ears") task in which adults with earphones immediately followed in mimicry ("shadowed") speech heard in one ear while trying to ignore a message piped into the other ear. Broadbent's studies led him to postulate selective sensory filters along with a brief short-term memory that could hold unattended speech sounds for several seconds before attention could be switched over to deal with them.

Computer Models of Cognition

A second impetus to cognitive psychology was the work of Allen Newell and Herbert Simon (1961, 1972), who constructed computer programs designed to simulate details of the thought processes that people go through as they solve various kinds of problems (e.g., logic proofs, analogies, chess playing, intelligent search). Such simulation programs clearly had to have very large memories of structured knowledge about a given domain (such as rules and moves of chess), have a means for putting new information into the system (e.g., an opponent's chess moves), have a means for reasoning about the current situation by manipulating symbolic expressions in a central processor (or "short-term memory"), and have some means for reporting out the "actions" (moves) the program had decided to take. These activities are easily viewed as analogous to activities of the human mind. Simon and Newell noted that the stimulus-response analyses of problem solving were of no help whatsoever in deciding how to structure the knowledge base of the programs in order to carry out efficient retrieval, or how to reason effectively to achieve specific goals. Along with other researchers in artificial intelligence, they proceeded to create a number of computer programs that, by manipulating symbols, displayed an impressive amount of simulated "intelligent behavior" of a sort formerly carried out only by humans (see an early account by Feigenbaum & Feldman, 1963). This included not only reasoning programs but also learning programs (the EPAM program of Feigenbaum, 1959; Simon & Feigenbaum, 1964; Richmond & Simon, 1989) and many others. For reviews, see the handbooks by Barr and Feigenbaum (1981a, 1981b) and Cohen and Feigenbaum (1981).

Memory theorists were inspired by such developments to step outside the strictures of S-R theory and to begin to theorize about perceptual and attentional processes, as well as strategies and knowledge structures that were learned and used to acquire new knowledge. The "call to revolution" was urged in two important books: *Plans and the Structure of Behavior* by George Miller, Eugene Galanter, and Karl Pribram (1960), and *Cognitive Psychology* by Ulric Neisser (1967). These inspirational books provided arguments and exciting new agendas for an "information processing" view of humans. People were seen as taking information into a perceptual system, selectively attending to parts of it, encoding or transforming it for use by their cognitive abilities, storing it in memory, and later retrieving it from memory when an appropriate plan and retrieval cue were activated. The analysis of perception, attention, immediate sensory memories, short-term memory, and the structure of long-term memory became prominent topics. Since S-R theory had very little to contribute to these topics, the major developments in memory theory began breaking away from the S-R perspective.

Critiques of S-R Theory

Concurrent with these developments from communication engineering and artificial intelligence were a series of effective critiques of S-R theory as a means for dealing with complex varieties of human cognition. The critiques attacked the S-R accounts of motor skills (Lashley, 1951), thinking (Bruner, Goodnow, & Austin, 1956; Newell, Shaw, & Simon, 1958; Newell & Simon, 1961), pattern recognition (Neisser, 1967; Selfridge & Neisser, 1960), memory (Anderson & Bower, 1973; Asch, 1969; Bartlett, 1932; Bower, 1970c; Tulving & Madigan, 1970), and language (Fodor, Bever, & Garrett, 1974; Chomsky, 1959, 1972). Even in the traditional S-R domain of conditioning, new investigations of higher cognitive processes in nonhuman animals, especially higher primates and dolphins, were introducing major revisions in conceptualizations of cognitive processes (and learning) in lower organisms (e.g., Roitblat, Bever, & Terrace, 1984).

One of the most well-known critiques was that by the linguist Noam Chomsky (1959, 1972) in his review of B. F. Skinner's book *Verbal Behavior* (1957). In his book, Skinner, the radical arch-behaviorist, attempted an S-R account of language acquisition and use. Chomsky argued that Skinner's account (and by implication, all S-R accounts) was doomed to superficiality since it ignored the obvious cognitive processes that intervene between a situation and language utterances. He argued further that extrapolations of terms such as "stimulus," "response," "reinforcement," and "discrimination" from their animal-laboratory setting (the "Skinner box") to interpret language behavior were vague, metaphorical, and no better than common sense. Moreover, Chomsky argued strongly that the simple ideas of S-R associationism were inadequate in principle to account for the way children learn their language from experience. Children learn nonconscious linguistic rules that are far more abstract and complex than warranted by the language samples they hear, especially the realistic samples containing their many errors, back-ups, false starts, and ungrammatical utterances (see Chomsky, 1968, 1972). Chomsky similarly argued that S-R concepts were not rich enough to adequately explain the complexities of humans' abilities to comprehend and generate sentences in context.

Chomsky's critique and those of his associates established a new direction for the study of language; the new field of *psycholinguistics* drew its ideas and inspiration from new linguistic theories rather than S-R psychology (Fodor, Bever, & Garrett, 1974; Miller & McNeill, 1969). In turn, psycholinguistics had a very strong influence on ideas of memory researchers who recognized that some day they would have to understand in detail how and what people learn from language inputs—which, after all, is the medium through which most education proceeds.

Popularity of Different Memory Tasks

As noted, experiments within the S-R paradigm intensively investigated serial learning and paired-associate learning. With the advent of the cognitive approach to memory, somewhat different questions about memory were asked, leading to different memory paradigms that became popular because they provided a means for studying different kinds of memory processes. These experimental arrangements were free recall, context judgments about memorized events, and indirect memory tests, along with a renewed emphasis on short-term memory. We shall discuss these newly popular memory tasks.

Free Recall

In a free recall task, following presentation of a set of discrete experiences (words, pictures of common objects, actions), subjects are asked to recall them in *any* order that they choose for convenience. The set of items may be repeatedly presented, often in new scrambled orders, and repeatedly recalled. A frequent finding is that items presented at the beginning ("primacy") and end ("recency") of the list are typically recalled earlier and more often than items presented in the middle of the list (see figure 1.7). Longer lists and shorter study times per item cause poorer overall recall, except for the final ("recency") items of the list. These effects are obvious in the recall curves of figure 1.7.

Free recall was difficult for S-R theories to explain, since no specific stimulus appeared to be involved and subjects were not obviously making overt responses as they were exposed to the study list. Moreover, subjects' performance seemed to reveal a variety of "organizational processes" at work—a fact emphasized by Tulving (1968, 1962). For example, when multiple study and recall trials are given with the same list of supposedly unrelated words, subjects' improving recall is usually accompanied by increasing stereotypy or consistency in what items they recall together as clusters (Tulving, 1962). The clusters are often idiosyncratic groups of 3 to 7 list words among which a subject finds some kind of meaningful relationship. With training, these subjective clusters grow longer (include more items) and become more stable. Recall can be substantially increased by using words in the list that have strong prior connections (e.g., instances of a taxonomic category), since subjects are likely to discover these inter-item relationships and use them for organizing their recall (see also Bower, 1970c; Mandler, 1967). Such results suggest that learners are not the passive *tabula rasa* (blank slate) assumed in traditional associationism; rather, they are very active in using what they already know to search for meaningful relationships among the learning materials that they can utilize to ease their memorization task.

Another impressive fact about free recall is that subjects know far more of the list words than they are able to recall when given the general request to "recall the words of that list you studied." When provided with more specific associative cues (e.g., a category name), subjects now recall many list items they formerly failed to retrieve (Tulving & Pearlstone, 1966; Tulving & Psotka, 1971). In an impressive *tour de force* regarding the power of retrieval cues, Mäntylä (1986) had subjects write 3 meaningful associates to each of 600 target words, with no instructions for remembering. Seven days later they received a recall test. When given none of their associates as cues,

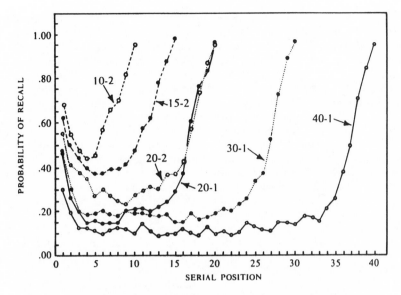

Figure 1.7 Serial position curves for free recall of lists of 10, 15, 20, 30, or 40 words each presented for 1 or 2 seconds of study (e.g., 15-2 denotes 15 words presented at a 2-second rate). (From B. B. Murdock, Jr. (1962), "The serial position effect of free recall." *Journal of Experimental Psychology, 64*, pp. 482–488. Reprinted by permission.)

they recalled only 6% of the target words; when given their 3 associates as cues, they recalled 65% of the 600 target words. Mäntylä and Nilsson (1988) produced even more dramatic recall (94% at 3 weeks), even without instructions for memorizing, by asking subjects to produce unique and/or distinctive associates during original exposure to the target words. The results illustrate the differing power of different retrieval cues (viz., one's associates versus "the list studied"). It suggests that when a memory is claimed to have been forgotten, the claim should be limited to the particular kind of retrieval test that failed. If one retrieval cue fails, perhaps a more potent set of cues could be found that would revive the temporarily inaccessible memory.

Context Judgments from Memory

In this paradigm, having been presented with one or more sets of discrete items, subjects are presented with a copy of the old items (and perhaps similar new ones) and asked to retrieve and judge something about that item's context of earlier presentation. The judgment may be whether or not the item was presented in the earlier, specified list (called a "recognition memory" test). If items were presented in several different lists, subjects may be asked to indicate in which list, if any, the test item was presented. Items may be presented several times in each of two or more distinguishable lists, and subjects later may be asked to indicate how often a test item was presented in each list. Subjects may also be asked to recall aspects of the "source"—who said the word, where or when it was presented, in what manner of voice (male or female speaker), or characteristics of its visual presentation (type font of word, size, colored vs. black-and-white slides). Some experimenters refer to all these judgments as "source memory," whereas others distinguish "recognition memory" judgments (which could be based on an undifferentiated feeling of recent familiarity of an item) from the other explicit source judgments.

Source Memory. Source memories are laboratory analogs of people remembering where and from whom they learned certain information. The difficulty these performances raise for an S-R theory is that in no case are subjects overtly responding to these aspects of the experience as they are studying the items. Rather, it seems that the perceptual system is almost automatically recording something like sensory images that are retrieved later to support such judgments.

A basic finding of source memory is that remembering which source provided particular information grows worse the more similar are the salient properties of the several sources. For example, people are more likely to confuse in memory which of two unfamiliar speakers said a particular message if the speakers look and sound alike. Source confusions also increase the less associated are the contents of the messages with their respective sources. For example, readers are more likely to ascribe their memory of an alien abduction story to having read it in the *National Enquirer* than in the more credible *New York Times*.

A second fact is that material people imagine or produce themselves (e.g., as associates to something they saw) can be confused later in memory with something they actually saw or heard. This discrimination of "my internal vs. his external" event improves the more thinking or cognitive effort subjects engage in while generating the imagined scene originally. This is likely due to the fact that the imagined scene was stored along with a record of the cognitive operations needed to create the scene. Later retrieval of these traces helps people judge the memory as an imagined one (see Johnson & Raye, 1981; Johnson, Hashtroudi & Lindsay, 1993).

Frequency Judgments.   Frequency judgments ask subjects how often a given word or picture was presented in a list. Hintzman (1976; Hintzman & Block, 1971) has brought these frequency-in-context judgments to bear upon a fundamental issue in memory theory—namely, how multiple repetitions of the nominally same item are treated by the memory system. The traditional theory is that different presentations of, say, the word *table* simply strengthen the one association of that memory unit to the list context, and that later judgments of its presentation frequency could be derived from the strength of this one association.

The alternative view favored by Hintzman is that each presentation of the same nominal stimulus establishes a new memory trace, each associated with its accompanying spe-

cific time, place, and mode of presentation (its "context," as he says). As evidence, Hintzman found that subjects were often able to retrieve some contextual details about each presentation of an item, almost in the manner of a videotape recording. For example, subjects might experience presentation of a long list in which 30 unrelated words are presented once mixed in among 15 presented twice and 10 presented four times, all scattered randomly throughout a 100-presentation list. Upon later testing with the test word *table*, a hypothetical subject might be able to report correctly that "the word *table* was presented twice: its first presentation was in the first quarter of the list and was spoken in a male voice; its second presentation was in the third quarter of the list and it was presented visually in red Gothic letters." While such contextual details are generally poorly recalled (as would be expected by the similarity-based interference they suffer), their moderate accuracy indicates that subjects are often successfully storing detailed records of several different experienced presentations of the same word. This in turn supports the multiple-trace over the strengthened single-trace account of how repetition works in memory. With higher frequencies (10 or more), individual memories of a given item's presentations greatly interfere with one another, and subjects appear to shift to a "frequency estimation" rather than "memory counting" strategy for making judgments of these higher frequencies.

Another interesting type of contextual judgment is the relative recency of an event. For example, the subject might be asked to estimate how many items back in a series (or how long ago) the word *table* (vs. *prince*) had been presented. In general, accuracy of judgments declines as a power function of intervening items or time elapsed; and discrimination of which of two items was more recent follows a logarithmic function—that is, discrimination varies with the ratio of their recency difference divided by the recency of the more recent one (Yntema & Trask, 1963). A multiple-trace theory also provides a better account of how repetitions of an item affects its apparent recency judgment (Flexser & Bower, 1974).

Recognition Memory.   In recognition memory experiments, subjects judge whether or not a test item was explicitly presented on a list studied earlier. A basic fact is that access to an item's memory requires that subjects interpret (or "encode") the item at test in roughly the same manner as they did when it was originally studied. This basic fact has been demonstrated for a variety of stimuli that have ambiguous (multiple) interpretations, including simple drawings (the *duck–rabbit* picture; the *young wife–old crone* picture), naturalistic sounds (*trotting horses* vs. *tap dancers*), and polysemous words (kitchen *TABLE* vs. math *TABLE*). The point is that the nominal stimulus during the test must arouse the same percept or meaningful interpretation it did during study in order for it to make contact with the memory trace of the original event. This is the sense of the "encoding specificity principle" proposed by Tulving (1983; Tulving & Thomson, 1973).

Tulving believes the principle applies far more widely than with just ambiguous words or pictures, since the context of presentation can activate somewhat different properties and associations to thousands of words or pictures that are otherwise unambiguous. For example, people think of different aspects of a *piano* if they speak about tuning it versus lifting it. The aspect aroused by the word during its original context of presentation can then serve later as the more potent retrieval cue for re-arousing that memory.

Indirect Memory Tests

The tasks above are called "direct" tests since subjects are asked explicitly to try to remember an earlier episode, perhaps to recall several features of the context surrounding the presented event. These tests may be contrasted with indirect tests of memory in which subjects answer general knowledge questions that presumably do not refer to recent, specific experiences (Richardson-Klavehn & Bjork, 1988; Schacter, 1987). Yet it can be shown that recent experiences affect the speed and content of what is retrieved from one's general knowledge.

The prototypic example is *repetition priming* wherein a word (or picture of a common object) is accessed more readily if it is a repetition of one recently presented. Such priming (say, of *robin*) shows up in facilitated perceptual identification (seeing it more accurately in a degraded or quick flash), in lexical decisions (that *robin* is a word, but *ribon* is not), and in fragment completion ("Give the first word you can think of to complete *r_bi_*,")

The primed word is also more likely to be generated as a member of a category (list some *birds*) or as an associate to a related cue ("Perched in a tree is a red-breasted _____ _____."). In such indirect tests, the subject may produce the primed item with a frequency far above an unprimed baseline, and yet have no subjective awareness of remembering any specific episode from his or her past. The nature of indirect memory tests and their relation to direct tests are topics of great interest in current research (see, e.g., Bower, 1996; Tulving & Schacter, 1990), and several chapters of this handbook will touch on these issues.

Short-Term Memory Models

In the early 1960s, considerable interest arose in the study of immediate (or "short-term") memory. While the limits of immediate memory and the "memory span" had been known since Ebbinghaus (and described by William James, 1890), the novel, startling fact observed by Lloyd and Margaret Peterson (1959) was that people very rapidly forget a few unrelated letters or words (such as *T G K* or *glass, pen, wood*) that they have just read if they are distracted and occupied with another task for just a few seconds. Figure 1.8 illustrates this rapid loss as subjects were engaged for 1 to 18 seconds in a simple subtraction task (subtracting successive 3's from a starting number) before being asked to recall the three items they had just read. Early investigators had apparently overlooked this rapid fall-off in memory for trivially small amounts of material because they typically had used serial lists well beyond subjects' capability for perfect immediate recall. Such results suggest a *short-term memory* of extreme fragility, lasting only a few seconds after the subject's attention is drawn elsewhere. This rapid loss may be contrasted to the *long-term* memories for information people have stored in their knowledge base.

The next decade in memory research was filled with many studies of such short-term memories: many different paradigms were investigated, and many variables that controlled short-term retention were investigated. As evidence accumulated, several formal theories were proposed to explain the interaction between short-term and long-term memory. These built on the earlier proposals of Broadbent (1958), Bower (1964), and Waugh and Norman (1965) (reviewed in Murdock, 1974).

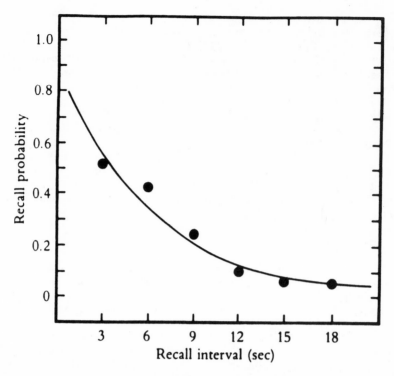

Figure 1.8 Correct recall of 3 letters as a function of a retention interval filled with a "counting backwards" distraction task. (From L. R. Peterson and M. J. Peterson (1959), "Short-term retention of individual verbal items," *Journal of Experimental Psychology, 58*, pp. 193–198. Copyright 1959 by the American Psychological Association. Reprinted by permission.)

The most popular model of this period was that proposed by Atkinson and Shiffrin (1968, 1971) because it was the most explicit and was applied to the widest range of results.

A Popular Model of Short-Term Memory

Figure 1.9 shows the general structure of the three memory stores postulated: a sensory store that held briefly glimpsed (or heard) messages for a couple of seconds before their traces decayed. Stimulus traces in the sensory store that are attended to, identified, and re-coded are thereby entered into a short-term memory (STM). The STM is of limited capacity, holding at most only a few items (e.g., 4 words or 2 paired associates). If the items are to be learned, the central-control processes initiate a plan for memorizing, such as covert rehearsal (silently going over the words). The model assumes that each rehearsal cycle also

transfers into the more durable long-term memory information about the associations being studied. Information transferred to long-term memory can also be forgotten, but at a much slower rate than the information in STM. A to-be-remembered item will be eventually displaced or lost from STM since newly arriving information enters STM and bumps out the earlier items. The greater the demands or difficulty of the interpolated task, the more rehearsal suffers and so the poorer the retention of the target items.

Benefits of the Short-Term Memory Model

Several features of such models should be emphasized. First, they permit flexibility in the initial encoding of the input coding. For normal speakers, many to-be-remembered stimuli will be encoded by their names or descriptors. Thus, later confusions in recall of letter or

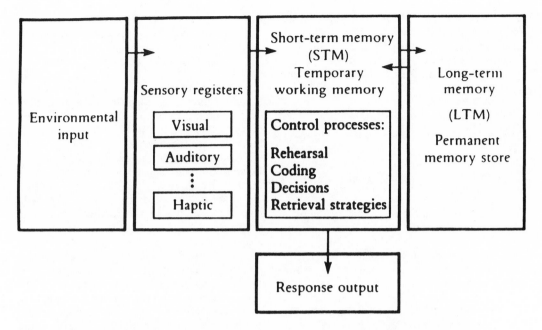

Figure 1.9 The flow of information through the three memory stores postulated in Atkinson-Shiffrin's model. (From R. C. Atkinson and R. M. Shiffrin (1971), "The control of short-term memory," *Scientific American, 225*, pp. 82–90. Copyright by *Scientific American*. Reprinted by permission.)

word strings will often be greater for items with similar pronunciations (e.g., recalling the similar letters B, T, V, C versus the dissimilar B, X, W, Q—see Conrad, 1962, 1964). Second, multiple study trials aid later recall by accumulating strength of the association recorded in LTM. Third, the model distinguishes memory structures from the momentary plans ("control structures") that utilize these mental structures to help memorization or recall. One such memorizing plan is verbal rehearsal and Atkinson and Shiffrin developed their model's main predictions by assuming that motivated subjects in a learning situation engage in steady verbal rehearsal when they have the opportunity. One implication of the verbal rehearsal strategy is that the number of items that can be held in the rehearsal STM increases with their covert speech rate. Thus, immediate memory span would be lower for longer words, for people who speak slowly (e.g., younger children), and for languages whose digit names take longer to pronounce (see Baddeley, 1986, 1990).

The model's distinction between memory structures and control processes (strategies) permits an understanding of the differing results that arise if subjects use other learning strategies—such as concentrating rehearsal on some high-valued (or surprising) items at the expense of low-valued items, or searching in LTM for mediators (of the type mentioned earlier) as a way to aid association learning. This approach allows a role for motivational and individual-ability differences in partly determining memory.

The STM models were partly inspired by neurological patients (the famous H.M.) with organic amnesia caused by bilateral damage to the medial temporal lobe and hippocampus. Such patients have an intact short-term memory and long-term memory, but are greatly impaired in transferring new verbal information to long-term memory. This is exactly the pattern to be expected if the STM-LTM transfer process were impaired.

Such STM-LTM models had a ready explanation for the serial position curves seen in free recall (see the earlier figure 1.7). The better recall of the beginning words ("primacy" effect) was due to their entering an empty STM and thus receiving greater amounts of rehearsal compared to later words before being displaced; the better recall of the end-final items ("recency") was due supposedly to subjects reading them out of STM at list's ending before they return to LTM to retrieve earlier list items (see the curves in figure 1.7). Items presented for more study (2 vs. 1 sec in figure 1.7) transfer more information into LTM, thus raising recall levels of early and middle items.

Shortcomings of the Short-Term Memory Models

Although STM models explained many facts, they suffered from several shortcomings that caused the basic ideas to be altered and elaborated. Included among these shortcomings are the following:

1. In order for a familiar word or chunk to be identified, the stimulus must first access its matching code in LTM. Thus, it seems as though the diagram in figure 1.8 should have LTM accessed by the stimulus *before* its code is entered into STM. Alternatively, it may be more logical to consider STM as only an activated portion of LTM (see, e.g., Anderson, 1995).
2. Several secondary tasks (e.g., repeating 4 digits) were found to have little or no effect on free recall memory for visually presented word lists. This suggested to Baddeley and Hitch (1974) that adults could place small amounts of irrelevant verbal material (the digits) into a repetitive articulatory loop whose operation did not interfere with subjects encoding and learning the visual words. The implication is that adults have multiple regions for short-term storage of stimuli received from different sensory modalities (see Baddeley, 1990).
3. Fast, repetitive, going over of verbal items results in very little memory later—that is, "mindless" rehearsal per se is not sufficient to create durable memories. Rather, some kind of meaningful associations and elaborations (some "deeper processing" to use the term of Craik & Lockhart, 1972; Craik & Tulving, 1975), connecting the new material with old chunks of knowledge already in memory, are needed to create more durable memories.
4. The model assumes that STM is the "entrance" to transferring materials into LTM; but several neurological patients were soon reported (Shallice & Warrington, 1970, 1974) who could learn visual paired associates quite normally despite having severely impaired auditory immediate memory. Such patients suggest

that structures that produce durable long-term traces may be somewhat independent from those responsible for short-term maintenance of information.

In reaction to such criticisms, more recent theorists have revised and recast important aspects of the Atkinson-Shiffrin model. Baddeley (1986, 1990) has hypothesized several modality-specific short-term stores that he calls *working memories*—a phonological store for speech-based material, a visuo-spatial store for visual images, and an "executive controller" that holds plans that program and coordinate the activities of the separate short-term stores. Anderson (1983, 1995) has argued that rather than a separate "storage place," short-term memory should be conceived as the temporary activation of information chunks in a single memory. According to this view, items can be in various states of momentary activation. Items that are highly activated are readily available for recall or for entering into other cognitive activities. To deal with long-term recall, Anderson supposes that different memory traces also differ in their strength or ability to be reactivated later by relevant cues. We will return later to discuss the representation of memories in the long-term store.

The Episodic/Semantic Memory Distinction

Following observations by philosophers writing about memory (e.g., Bergson, 1911; Russell, 1921), Endel Tulving (1972) introduced to psychologists the distinction between *episodic* memory and *semantic* memory. An episodic memory is about a specific event that occurred at a particular time and place, such as your memory of getting a traffic ticket or observing a car accident. In contrast, semantic memory is the "mental thesaurus, organized knowledge a person possesses about words and other verbal symbols, their meaning and referents, about relations among them, and about rules, formulas, and algorithms" for manipulating them (Tulving, 1972, p. 386). In these terms, the memories typically being acquired and tested in verbal learning experiments are episodic (e.g., "I just studied the pair *king–table*"). Semantic memories are the abstracted words, concepts, and rules stored in our long-term memory whose context of acquisition was long ago forgotten (e.g., most people cannot say when they first learned the meaning of the word *king*).

Tulving noted several properties of these two classes of memories. First, episodic memories are more susceptible to forgetting. Second, retrieval of an episodic memory is usually accompanied by an explicit or implicit reference to, and image of, the time and/or place of the episode (e.g., "In the list you just learned, what was *king* paired with?"). Third, retrieval of any information is itself another episode that creates its own episodic memory (e.g., people can remember a test trial and how they performed). Fourth, autobiographic memories are typically dated episodic memories, although people also have many abstract generalizations about long stretches of their life that are not themselves distinct episodes (e.g., people can recall that they went to college for four years, although they may not now be recalling any specific incident).

Tulving (1983) believed the differences between episodic and semantic memories were sufficiently striking and hard-wired that he hypothesized the existence of two different memory systems—episodic and semantic. (Later he added a procedural memory system in recognition of perceptual motor skills.) These memory systems were contrasted in terms of their conditions and consequences of retrieval, nature of the stored information, vulnerability to interference, and interdependence. This hypothesis has led to much discussion in the literature (see, e.g., the discussion around the article by Tulving, 1986, in *Brain and Behavioral Sciences*). Critics contend that semantic knowledge consists of abstractions in LTM derived from many episodic memories (e.g., occasions when a word was used or spelled correctly for the person); they argue that although the two classes of memories clearly differ in their contents, strengths, and specific time-place contextual references, the two classes are otherwise similar in their properties. This productive discussion has continued over the years; a recent development has proposed use of brain neuroimaging data gathered during episodic versus semantic retrieval tasks in hopes of obtaining discriminating evidence for the brain-basis for the distinction (see Buckner, 1996).

Knowledge Structures in Long-Term Memory

Propositions

We noted above the development of computer models to simulate reasoning, problem solving, and learning. Appreciable developments also arose in computer models for natural language understanding and learning from language input. A computer model that attempts to understand language (typed into it) obviously needs several components: a word lexicon that calls up a network of interrelated concepts in long-term memory; a syntactic component that will take in a sentence, parse it, and assign a grammatical structure to its constituents (e.g., word classes, noun phase, verb phrase, logical roles of agent, action, object), and an interpreter that splices together the grammatical structure with the indicated concepts to compose a full interpretation of the sentence in the context (see Harris, 1985; Schank & Riesbeck, 1981; Winograd, 1972, 1983). A final necessity is a sentence-production module that is called upon to paraphrase what it has been told, draw inferences, and answer questions based on what it has been told or can retrieve from memory (see references cited).

In such systems a primary concern is in how knowledge units are to be represented in the memory of the model. Many proposals have been advanced on this topic. An early proposal is that the unit of knowledge should be elementary propositions such as subject-predicate structures (e.g., Anderson & Bower, 1973; Kintsch, 1974). Propositional structures may be either one-place predicates ("Roses are red" rendered as Red(roses)); two-place predicates (Mother-of (Mary, Jesus)); or three-place predicates (loaned (library, book, John)). The "arguments" in such propositions are concepts that exist in long-term memory; the proposition asserts (and records) a new kind of property or relation among the concepts. When someone comprehends a proposition, the theories conceive of that act as establishing in his or her memory new associations corresponding to the asserted relationships among the concepts. Thus, in comprehending "A man gave a book to a woman," people are setting up in memory a *giving* predicate that interrelates instances of their preexisting concepts of *man* as the donor, *woman* as the recipient, and a new instance of a *book* as the object transferred. Note that in such cases the verb (*give*) comes with a collection of expected roles—donor, recipient, object, implicitly a time and place of the event, and a set of inferences (e.g., the woman now has the book). These roles act like empty slots to be filled by the other concepts (arguments) in the proposition. This is an elementary example of a "schema," a notion elaborated below.

Concepts and Schemas

As noted, language understanders require a huge network of concepts and their interrelations. Psychologists have speculated extensively about the nature of concepts and how they might be structured in human memory. Concepts are obviously represented in terms of their associated properties, perceptual features, intended uses or functions, and their relations to other concepts. While an early view was that concepts should be represented in memory as a set of defining features that are all necessary and jointly sufficient to recognize instances (e.g., the concept of a *triangle*), the more comprehensive view that has emerged proposes that naturalistic concepts are better represented in memory as probabilistic prototypes (like a summary). Different features of the prototype are more or less diagnostic, and features that are not at all diagnostic may nonetheless be so characteristic of the class that they are used for rapid identification of instances (see Smith & Medin, 1981; Rosch & Mervis, 1975). If concepts are probabilistic prototypes, different examples will vary in how closely they match the prototype, and hence vary in how "good" (or typical) an example they are of the concept. For example, a *robin* is a very typical *bird*, a *stork* somewhat less, and an *ostrich* or *chicken* a very poor example of a *bird*.

In addition to such object concepts, semantic memory includes many concepts about relations such as spatial prepositions (*on, in, around, left of*) and actions. Actions are typically represented as verbs in English, and have associated *frames* or *schemas* that stipulate roles for participants in the action scenario. Verbs like *buy, rent,* or *steal* denote schemas that put together concepts in a certain scenario. So, "John bought Bill's car" means that Bill transferred ownership of a car to John, and John transferred ownership of something valuable (probably money) to Bill in exchange for his car.

Schemas (or *frames*) are good candidates for how long-term memory might be structured (Rumelhart & Ortony, 1977). Schemas capture clusters of organized expectations and represent abstract knowledge about some domain. Schemas can be of any "size" or "grain," and some schemas (e.g., eyes and mouth) can be embedded within other schemas (human face). Common examples of schemas come from common objects (e.g., birds, horses, cars, faces, rooms), ethnic and personality stereo-

types, and routine, stereotyped actions (e.g., making a telephone call, visiting the dentist, buying cinema tickets, buying groceries at a check-out counter, attending a classroom lecture). Each stereotyped activity is composed of an ordered sequence of actions to achieve some goal, and it "runs off" in behavior (and in recall chunks) more or less automatically. People use their schema knowledge not only to guide their actions but also to understand those of others (as viewed or described in narratives). Through experience people acquire schemas regarding novel activities (e.g., rollerblading, talking on cellular phones). They also acquire schemas for familiar narrative forms, their coherence (e.g., the hero acts in order to resolve some problem), and the genre of different narratives (e.g., cowboy Westerns, science fiction, parodies). It is often claimed that people understand events (or their narration) by being able to explain them by fitting them into familiar schemas—familiar abstract patterns of relationships. Thus, movie viewers understand immediately why a sheriff in a Western movie jumps on his horse to chase bank robbers: his motivations flow from his role and his plans along with constraints imposed by his limited resources.

A final point is that these structured schemas can be viewed as simply large clusters of elementary associations (or expectations) such as those studied in the laboratory. When a subject hears a sentence asserting new relationships (e.g., "President Clinton is now visiting South Africa"), memory theorists can think of this as the person recording into memory a novel set of associations that the subject did not have before—associations which can be used to answer questions ("Where's Clinton now?") and to draw inferences using other knowledge (e.g., "He's probably not speaking at the U.N. today").

The new wrinkle that is added to traditional associationism is that the associations are *labeled* according to their logical type or schematic role (see Anderson & Bower, 1973: Norman & Rumelhart, 1975). To illustrate, *canary* is associated with the concepts of *bird, yellow, legs*, and *Tweety*, yet people appreciate the different relationships—namely, that a canary *is a kind* of bird, *yellow* is a *property of* its appearance, *legs* are a *part of* canaries, and *Tweety* is an *example* of a canary. These kinds of relations are appreciated as rapidly as the items themselves. Moreover, relations are useful for carrying out directed search and retrieval operations, as when people are asked to "List some *parts of* canaries." So, in more recent models of memory, the associations are assumed to be recorded into memory along with an attached relational label specifying its type (see, e.g., Anderson & Bower, 1973; Norman & Rumelhart, 1975).

Visual Imagery

Before the 1960s, most memory research examined *verbal* memory for language units, and the verbal associations to these language units were emphasized. Starting in the 1960s and thereafter, a contingent of memory researchers began investigations of visual imagery and its properties, including image associations and memories for words. This movement was led by Allan Paivio (1969, 1971) with support by Roger Shepard (1978; Shepard & Metzler, 1971), Stephen Kosslyn (1975, 1981), Lee Brooks (1968), and others (Bower, 1970a, 1970b, 1972; Finke, 1984). Paivio conceived of nonverbal imagery as a form of coding and symbolic representation of information that was alternative to the verbal coding system. He brought forth a number of compelling facts in support of his emphasis on the role of mental imagery in learning. Let us consider a few of these.

First, words differ greatly in the extent to which they evoke imagery. While this is usually correlated with whether they refer to concrete objects (*apple*) or abstract ideas (*fidelity*), many nonconcrete but image-arousing words exist (e.g., *unicorn, ghost, angel*). Paivio found that the imagery-arousing value of a word was the most potent determinant of its rate of learning—whether in paired associates or free recall. Second, subjects learning paired associates with high-imagery words were more likely to report spontaneous imagery mediators ("mental pictures") to learn the associations; and pairs for which imagery mediators were reported were learned more rapidly. Third, subjects instructed to use visual imagery to relate word pairs together learned far more rapidly than uninstructed subjects or other subjects instructed to use verbal repetition (Bower, 1970a, 1972). Fourth, Paivio found that pictures of common concrete objects (or presentation of the objects themselves) were even more effective items for learning than were their names.

From such facts Paivio (1971) argued that verbal and nonverbal codes provide the inputs to two separate memory stores. Imagery provides a coding system; items coded in this manner are stored in an "imagery" memory store that is more durable than the verbal memory store. Although the two coding systems are closely interconnected (so people can translate between them), memory traces established in the two systems are functionally independent. A picture of a common object is remembered better than its name because pictures typically have more distinctive codes that suffer less interference. A word that evokes a corresponding image (either spontaneous or by instruction) will be better remembered because its presentation lays down two redundant memory traces at least one of which is more likely to survive over a retention interval.

While Paivio emphasized the role of imagery in verbal learning, Kosslyn (1981), Shepard (1978) and Finke (1984) concentrated on how memory images could be manipulated in reasoning and used to extract information. The image manipulations studied included scanning across or around a two-dimensional image, enlarging or shrinking it, rotating it in either the picture plane or in depth, and so on. Measurements taken as subjects perform such tasks suggest that operations on the mental image are closely isomorphic to their corresponding perceptual operations. Moreover, evidence was obtained for modality-specific interference (Brooks, 1968; Farah, 1985; Segal & Fusella, 1970): that is, requiring people to process external sounds or spatial arrays caused selective degradation in auditory or visuo-spatial images, respectively.

While acknowledging these strong effects of imagery on memory, the critics of the imagery approach have raised questions regarding the interpreted categorical, and "proposition-like," features of many images (Anderson, 1978; Pylyshyn, 1973). Anderson has suggested that most imagery effects can be modeled with an associative network using propositions referring to points in space connected with spatial predicates, and that computational processes can be provided that will operate over these networks to simulate manipulations of images (e.g., magnifying, rotating them). Clearly, this is what is being done in the visual graphic design and graphic display programs (such as Adobe Photoshop) for modern computers.

Multiple Memory Systems

With the proliferation of theories about different kinds of memories—short-term/long-term, visual/auditory sensory stores, precategorical/postcategorical stores, episodic/semantic, verbal/imagery, cognitive/motor—it was perhaps inevitable that attempts would be made to coordinate these different types of memories to different parts of the mammalian brain. This research has proceeded on several fronts—examining behavioral effects of specified brain lesions created in animals and of brain damage that humans accidently suffer due to head injuries, strokes, tumors, and cerebral disorders. Additionally, the activity of the human brain may be recorded indirectly (via blood-flow patterns) using functional magnetic resonance imaging as people work on a variety of cognitive or memory tasks.

These researchers have found that parts of the medial temporal and hippocampus region seem to be needed for humans to store new episodic memories, but not for learning procedural or motor skills or for showing repetition priming (Squire, 1987). Parts of the posterior parietal cortex are strongly implicated in mental imagery and visual memory. The left temporal and right parietal cerebral cortices are especially implicated in verbal and visual memory, respectively (Kolb & Whishaw, 1991; Kosslyn, 1991). The amygdala and limbic systems of the brain seem closely related to storage of highly emotional memories. The cerebellum, motor, premotor cortex and basal ganglia are closely linked to learning and performance of motor skills. The primary sensory cortices (striate and occipital for vision, temporal for audition, somatosensory for touch) are intimately involved in the modality-specific memories displayed in repetition priming. The frontal and prefrontal cortex appear to serve working (short-term) memory, with different parts specialized for briefly maintaining either verbal, object pattern, or spatial location information. The prefrontal cortex also is strongly implicated in strategic aspects of performance and memory; it supports people's ability to follow lengthy recall plans, keep things in order, search for obscure memories, and update working memory in rapidly changing scenarios (e.g., air traffic controllers keeping track of many airplanes entering and leaving their air space).

One of the fascinating mysteries is to relate the person's sense of conscious recollection to selective activation of different parts of the brain. It is clear that many indirect tests that utilize primed semantic knowledge are performed without people being aware that their facilitated performance stems from an earlier experience. On the other hand, requests to retrieve specific episodic memories typically bring forth the subject's feeling of being in mental contact and conscious of a specific moment experienced in the past. Tulving, Kapur, Craik, Moscovitch, & Houle (1994; also Nyberg, Cabeza, & Tulving, 1996) conjectured that retrieval of these two types of memories—the conscious, explicit episodic ones versus the primed semantic ones—utilizes two different parts of the frontal cortex. This speculation has already generated considerable research that has led to advances in the understanding of the brain basis of memory. The successes of the past decade in relating cognitive and memory functions to different parts of the brain have been quite remarkable and may be expected to accelerate into the future.

The Everyday Memory Theme

The research reviewed above has all been based on laboratory work, either that of normal subjects learning tasks involving artificial materials or brain-injured patients being tested in the neurological clinic. In reaction to this dominant laboratory tradition, a group of researchers have argued that attention should be turned to the ways in which people use memory in their everyday tasks (Neisser, 1978, 1982). This movement toward "ecological validity" stemmed from concerns that the principles learned from laboratory studies of memory may not help elucidate many everyday memory phenomena and may not aid in such practical tasks as rehabilitation of stroke or Alzheimer's patients who suffer from particular disorders.

As a consequence, a plethora of research has been published on the extent and frequencies of common types of memory errors and mental slips in everyday life, on how people commonly remember appointments, medicine-taking schedules, names, faces, dogs, cars, license plates, shopping lists, errands, parts of machinery, and so on. (An infinity of domains could be studied.) Detailed studies have also been made of memory experts, how they perform their feats, and what memory mechanisms are involved. Examples are studies of people who were trained to achieve a digit span of 80 (Ericsson, Chase & Falloon, 1980; Chase & Ericsson, 1981), novice taxi drivers learning city routes (Chase & Ericsson, 1981), musicians who memorize complex and lengthy musical scores (Ericsson, Krampe, &

Tesch-Romer, 1993; Rubin, 1995), restaurant waiters who remember large number of meal orders (Ericsson et al., 1993), and repertory actors who memorize and must rapidly retrieve lengthy roles in several plays (Noice, 1991, 1992). These studies often provide valuable insights into the means by which people use limited resources very efficiently in order to surmount limitations of memory. However, Banaji and Crowder (1989) have argued that the "everyday memory" movement has turned up very few novel phenomena or principles that had not already been known for many years based on laboratory research. (For opposing arguments, see articles in the *American Psychologist*, January 1991 [volume 46, Issue #1], pp. 16–48.)

One especially fascinating aspect of the everyday-memory movement is its investigation of autobiographical memory (e.g., Rubin, 1986; Conway, 1992; Conway & Bekerian, 1987; Conway & Rubin, 1993). By collecting and classifying phenomenological reports, psychologists have constructed theories of how people structure in memory large segments of their life, how they use salient "marking events" (e.g., graduations, marriage, birth of a child, beginning a job, moving) as signposts for ordering and reconstructing the temporal and logical sequence of events. Although people clearly have conceptual knowledge corresponding to long stretches of their past, different event memories are also multiply cross-indexed in memory according to life themes, what happened, where it happened, who was involved, and what the significance was of the event for one's life. Some of the knowledge is in the form of personal episodic memories that are experienced in recall with imagery and often some emotion; and it has been noted that these specific memories can often be a mistaken blend of fact and fiction (Loftus & Ketcham, 1994). In addition to these episodic memories, large portions of people's autobiography are in narrative generalizations with no more sense of "personally being there" than they have for the knowledge that they were born on a specific date.

An interesting aspect of autobiographic memory is that it is intimately tied to conceptions of *self*—of who and what we are. Many studies have found that memories are reconstructed to satisfy self-serving motives, and that people remember themselves in a more favorable light than is warranted (see Greenwald, 1980; Loftus & Ketcham, 1994). People also tend to distort their memory of how they used to behave (or their former opinions) to be more consistent with their opinion of today (Ross, 1989). These and other tendencies suggest that social, motivational, and personality factors play a significant role in the way memories are altered over time. More studies of this kind can be expected as the field advances and makes better contact with other branches of psychology.

References

Anderson, J. R. (1978). Arguments concerning representations for mental imagery. *Psychological Review, 85*, 249–277.

Anderson, J. R. (1983). *The architecture of cognition.* Cambridge, MA: Harvard University Press.

Anderson, J. R. (1995). *Learning and memory: An integrated approach.* New York: John Wiley.

Anderson, J. R., & Bower, G. H. (1973). *Human associative memory.* Washington, D.C.: D. H. Winston.

Asch, S. E. (1969). Reformulation of the problem of association. *American Psychologist, 24*, 92–102.

Atkinson, R. C., & Shiffrin, R. M. (1968). Human memory: A proposed system and its control processes. In K. W. Spence & J. T. Spence (Eds.), *The psychology of learning and motivation: Advances in research and theory* (Vol. 2; pp. 90–197). New York: Academic Press.

Atkinson, R. C., & Shiffrin, R. M. (1971). The control of short-term memory. *Scientific American, 225*, 82–90.

Baddeley, A. D. (1986). *Working memory.* Oxford: Oxford University Press.

Baddeley, A. D. (1990). *Human memory: Theory and practice.* Boston: Allyn & Bacon.

Baddeley, A. D., & Hitch, G. (1974). Working memory. In G. H. Bower (Ed.), *The Psychology of Learning and Motivation: Advances in research and theory* (Vol. 8; pp. 47–90). New York: Academic Press.

Banaji, M. R., & Crowder, R. G. (1989). The bankruptcy of everyday memory. *American Psychologist, 44*, 1185–1193.

Barnes, J. M., & Underwood, B. J. (1959). Fate of first-list associations and transfer theory. *Journal of Experimental Psychology, 58*, 97–105.

Barr, A., & Feigenbaum, E. A. (Eds.). (1981a). *The handbook of artificial intelligence.* Volume 1. Los Altos, CA: Kaufman.

Barr, A., & Feigenbaum, E. A. (Eds.). (1981b). *The handbook of artificial intelligence.* Volume 2. Los Altos, CA: Kaufman.

Bartlett, F. C. (1932). *Remembering: A study in experimental and social psychology.* Cambridge: Cambridge University Press.

Bergson, H. (1911). *Matter and memory.* London: Allen & Unwin.

Bower, G. H. (1964). A descriptive theory of memory. Speech presented at the Second International Inter-Disciplinary Conference on Learning, Remembering, and Forgetting. Princeton, New Jersey. (Published in D. T. Kimble (Ed.) (1967), *The Organization of Recall* (pp. 112–185). New York: New York Academy of Sciences.

Bower, G. H. (1970a). Analysis of a mnemonic device. *American Scientist, 58,* 496–510.

Bower, G. H. (1970b). Imagery as a relational organizer in associative learning. *Journal of Verbal Learning and Verbal Behavior, 9,* 529–533.

Bower, G. H. (1970c). Organizational factors in memory. *Cognitive Psychology, 1,* 18–46.

Bower, G. H. (1972). Mental imagery and associative learning. In L. Gregg (Ed.), *Cognition in learning and memory* (pp. 51–88). New York: John Wiley.

Bower, G. H. (1996). Reactivating a reactivation theory of implicit memory. *Consciousness & Cognition, 5,* 27–72.

Bower, G. H., & Hilgard, E. R. (1981). *Theories of learning* (5th ed.). Englewood Cliffs, NJ: Prentice-Hall.

Briggs, G. E. (1957). Retroactive inhibition as a function of original and interpolated learning. *Journal of Experimental Psychology, 53,* 64.

Broadbent, D. E. (1958). *Perception and communication.* London: Pergamon Press.

Brooks, L. (1968). Spatial and verbal components of the act of recall. *Canadian Journal of Psychology, 22,* 349–368.

Bruner, J. F., Goodnow, J., & Austin, G. (1956). *The study of thinking.* New York: John Wiley.

Buckner, R. (1996). Beyond HERA: Contributions of specific prefrontal brain areas to long-term memory retrieval. *Psychonomic Bulletin Review, 3,* 149–158.

Calkins, M. W. (1894). Association. *Psychological Review, 1,* 476–483.

Chase, W. G., & Ericsson, K. A. (1981). Skilled memory. In J. R. Anderson (Ed.), *Cognitive skills and their acquisition* (pp. 141–189). Hillsdale, NJ: Erlbaum.

Chomsky, N. (1959). Review of Skinner's *"Verbal Behavior." Language, 35,* 26–58.

Chomsky, N. (1968). *Language and mind.* New York: Harcourt, Brace, Jovanovich.

Chomsky, N. (1972). Psychology and ideology: The case against B. F. Skinner. *Cognition, 1,* 11–46.

Cohen, P. R., & Feigenbaum. E. A. (Eds.). (1981). *The handbook of artificial intelligence.* Volume 3. Los Altos, CA: Kaufman.

Conrad, R. (1962). An association between memory errors and acoustic confusions of speech. *Nature, 93,* 1314–1315.

Conrad, R. (1964). Acoustic confusion in immediate memory. *British Journal of Psychology, 55,* 75–84.

Conway, M. A. (1992). A structural model of autobiographical memory. In M. A. Conway, D. C. Rubin, H. Spinnler, & W. A. Wagenaar (Eds.), *Theoretical perspectives on autobiographical memory* (pp. 167–193). Dordrect, The Netherlands: Kluwer.

Conway, M. A., & Bekerian, D. A. (1987). Organization in autobiographical memory. *Memory and Cognition, 15,* 119–132.

Conway, M. A., & Rubin, D. C. (1993). The structure of autobiographical memory. In A. E. Collins, F. E. Gathercole, M. A. Conway, & T. E. Morris (Eds.), *Theories of memory* (pp. 103–137). Hillsdale, NJ: Erlbaum.

Craik, F. I. M., & Lockhart, R. S. (1972). Levels of processing: A framework for memory research. *Journal of Verbal Learning and Verbal Behavior, 11,* 671–684.

Craik, F. I. M., & Tulving, E. (1975). Depth of processing and the retention of words in episodic memory. *Journal of Experimental Psychology: General, 104,* 268–294.

Dansereau, D. F. (1978). The development of a learning strategies curriculum. In H. F. O'Neil Jr. (Ed.), *Learning strategies* (pp. 1–29). New York: Academic Press.

Darwin, C. (1859). *Origin of species by means of natural selection.* London: John Murry.

Ebbinghaus, H. (1885). *On memory* (H. A. Ruger & C. E. Bussenius, Trans.). New York: Teachers' College, 1913. Paperback edition, New York: Dover, 1964.

Ericsson, K. A., Chase, W. G., & Falloon, F. (1980). Acquisition of a memory skill. *Science, 208,* 1181–1182.

Ericsson, K. A., Krampe, R. E., & Tesch-Romer, C. (1993). The role of deliberate practice in the acquisition of expert performance. *Psychological Review, 100,* 363–406.

Estes, W. K. (1955). Statistical theory of spontaneous recovery and regression. *Psychological Review, 62,* 369–377.

Farah, M. (1985). Psychophysical evidence for a shared representational medium for mental images and percepts. *Journal of Ex-*

perimental Psychology: General, 114, 91–103.

Feigenbaum, E. A. (1959). *An information processing theory of verbal learning.* RAND Corporation paper, P-1817, October.

Feigenbaum, E. A., & Feldman, J. (1963). *Computers and thought.* New York: McGraw-Hill.

Finke, R. A. (1984). Mental imagery and the visual system. *Scientific American, 254*, no. 3, 88–95.

Flexser, A. J., & Bower, G. H. (1974). How frequency affects recency judgments: A model for recency discrimination. *Journal of Experimental Psychology, 103*, 706–716.

Fodor, J. A., Bever, T. G., & Garrett, M. F. (1974). *The Psychology of language: An introduction to psycholinguistics and generative grammar.* New York: McGraw-Hill.

Garner, W. R. (1962). *Uncertainty and structure as psychological concepts.* New York: John Wiley.

Gibson, E. J. (1940). A systematic application of the concepts of generalization and differentiation to verbal learning. *Psychological Review, 47*, 196–229.

Glaze, J. A. (1928). The association value of nonsense syllables. *Genetic Psychology, 35*, 255–267.

Greenwald, A. G. (1980). The totalitarian ego: Fabrication and revision of personal history. *American Psychologist, 35*, 603–618.

Hall, J. F. (1971). *Verbal learning and retention.* Philadelphia: J. B. Lippincott.

Harris, M. D. (1985). *Introduction to natural language processing.* Resten, VA: Resten Publishing.

Hintzman, D. L. (1976). Repetition and memory. In G. H. Bower (Ed.), *The psychology of learning and motivation* (Vol. 10; pp. 47–91). New York: Academic Press.

Hintzman, D. L., & Block, R. A. (1971). Repetition and memory: Evidence for a multiple trace hypothesis. *Journal of Experimental Psychology, 88*, 297–306.

Hovland, C. I. (1940). Experimental studies in rote-learning theory: Number 7. Distribution of practice with varying lengths of list. *Journal of Experimental Psychology, 27*, 271–284.

Hull, C. L. (1943). *Principles of behavior: An introduction to behavior theory.* New York: Appleton-Century-Crofts.

James, W. (1890). *The principles of psychology.* New York: Henry Holt.

Johnson, G. J. (1991). A distinctiveness model of serial learning. *Psychological Review, 98*, 204–217

Johnson, M. K., Hashtroudi, S., & Lindsay, D. S. (1993). Source monitoring. *Psychological Bulletin, 114*, 3–28.

Johnson, M. K., & Raye, C. L. (1981). Reality monitoring. *Psychological Review, 88*, 67–85.

Kausler, D. H. (1974). *Psychology of verbal learning and memory.* New York: Academic Press.

Kintsch, W. (1974). *The representation of meaning in memory.* Hillsdale, NJ: Erlbaum.

Kolb, B., & Whishaw, I. Q. (1991). *Fundamentals of human neuropsychology* (3rd. ed.). New York: W. H. Freeman.

Kosslyn, S. (1975). Information representation in visual images. *Cognitive Psychology, 7*, 341–370.

Kosslyn, S. (1981). *Image and mind.* Cambridge, MA: Harvard University Press.

Kosslyn, S. M. (1991). A cognitive neuroscience of visual cognition: Further developments. In R. Logie & M. Denis (Eds.), *Mental images in human cognition: Advances in psychology series* (Vol. 80; pp. 351–381). Amsterdam: North Holland.

Lashley, K. S. (1951). The problem of serial order in behavior. In L. A. Jefress (Ed.), *Cerebral mechanisms in behavior* (pp. 112–131). New York: John Wiley.

Loftus, E. F., & Ketcham, K. (1994). *The myth of repressed memory: False memories and allegations of abuse.* New York: St. Martin's.

Mandler, G. (1967). Organization and memory. In K. Spence & J. T. Spence (Eds.), *The psychology of learning and motivation* (Vol. 1; pp. 327–372). New York: Academic Press.

Mäntylä, T. (1986). Optimizing cue effectiveness: Recall of 500 and 600 incidentally learned words. *Journal of Experimental Psychology: Learning, Memory and Cognition, 12*, 66–71.

Mäntylä, T. & Nilsson, L-G. (1988). Cue distinctiveness and forgetting: Effectiveness of self-generated retrieval cues in delayed recall. *Journal of Experimental Psychology: Learning, Memory and Cognition, 14*, 502–509.

Mayer, R. E. (1987). *Educational psychology: A cognitive approach.* Boston: Little, Brown.

McGeoch, J. A., & Irion, A. L. (1952). *The psychology of human learning.* New York: Longmans & Green.

Miller, G. A. (1956). The magical number 7, plus or minus 2: Some limits on our capacity for processing information. *Psychological Review, 63*, 81–97.

Miller, G. A., Galanter, E., & Pribram, K. H. (1960). *Plans and the structure of behavior*. New York: Holt, Rinehart & Winston.

Miller, G. A., & McNeill, D. (1969). Psycholinguistics. In G. Lindzey & E. Aronson (Eds.), *The Handbook of social psychology* (pp. 666–794) 2nd ed., vol. 3; Reading, MA: Addison-Wesley.

Montague, W. E. (1972). Elaborative strategies in verbal learning and memory. In G. H. Bower (Ed.), *The psychology of learning and motivation: Advances in research and theory* (pp. 225–302). New York: Academic Press.

Montague, W. E., & Kiess, H. O. (1968). The associability of CVC pairs. *Journal of Experimental Psychology Monograph, Supplement 78*, no. 2, part 2, 1–23.

Murdock, B. B., Jr. (1962). The serial position effect of free recall. *Journal of Experimental Psychology, 64*, 482–488.

Murdock, B. B., Jr. (1974). *Human memory: Theory and data*. Potomac, MD: Erlbaum.

Neisser, U. (1967). *Cognitive psychology*. New York: Appleton-Century-Crofts.

Neisser, U. (1978). Memory: What are the important questions? In M. M. Gruneberg, P. E. Morris, & R. N. Sykes (Eds.), *Practical aspects of memory* (pp. 1–24). London: Academic Press.

Neisser, U. (Ed.). (1982). *Memory observed: Remembering in natural contexts*. San Francisco: Freeman.

Newell, A., Shaw, J. C., & Simon, H. A. (1958). Elements of a theory of human problem-solving. *Psychological Review, 65*, 151–166.

Newell, A., & Simon, H. A. (1961). Computer simulation of human thinking. *Science, 134*, 2011–2017.

Newell, A., & Simon, H. A. (1972). *Human problem-solving*. Englewood Cliffs, NJ: Prentice-Hall.

Noble, C. E. (1952). An analysis of meaning. *Psychological Review, 59*, 421–430.

Noble, C. E., & Parker, G. V. C. (1969). The Montana scale of meaningfulness (m). *Psychological Reports, 7*, 325–331.

Noice, H. (1991). The role of explanations and plan recognition in the learning of theatrical scripts. *Cognitive Psychology, 15*, 425–460.

Noice, H. (1992). Elaborative memory strategies of professional actors. *Applied Cognitive Psychology, 6*, 417–427.

Norman, D. A., & Rumelhart, D. E. (Eds.). (1975). *Explorations in cognition*. San Francisco: Freeman.

Nyberg, L., Cabeza, R., & Tulving, E. (1996). PET studies of encoding and retrieval: The HERA model. *Psychonomic Bulletin & Review, 3*, 135–148.

O'Neil, H. F., Jr. (Ed.). (1978). *Learning strategies*. New York: Academic Press.

Paivio, A. (1969). Mental imagery in associative learning and memory. *Psychological Review, 76*, 241–263.

Paivio, A. (1971). *Imagery and verbal processes*. New York: Holt, Rinehart & Winston.

Pavlov, I. P. (1927). *Conditioned reflexes*. London: Clarendon Press.

Peterson, L. R., & Peterson, M. J. (1959). Short-term retention of individual verbal items. *Journal of Experimental Psychology, 58*, 193–198.

Postman, L. (1971). Transfer, interference and forgetting. In J. W. Kling & L. A. Riggs (Eds.), *Woodworth and Schlosberg's Experimental Psychology* (3rd ed., pp. 1019–1132). New York: Holt, Reinhardt, & Winston.

Prytulak, L. S. (1971). Natural language mediation. *Cognitive Psychology, 2*, 1–56.

Pylyshyn, Z. W. (1973). What the mind's eye tells the mind's brain: A critique of mental imagery. *Psychological Bulletin, 80*, 1–24.

Richardson-Klavehn, A., & Bjork, R. A. (1988). Measures of memory. *Annual Review of Psychology, 36*, 475–543.

Richman, H. B., & Simon, H. A. (1989). Context defects in letter perception: Comparison of two theories. *Psychological Review, 96*, 417–432.

Roitblat, H. L., Bever, T. G., & Terrace, H. S. (Eds.). (1984). *Animal cognition*. Hillsdale, NJ: Erlbaum.

Rosch, E., & Mervis, C. B. (1975). Family resemblances: Studies in the internal structure of categories. *Cognitive Psychology, 7*, 573–605.

Rosenbaum, D. A. (1991). *Human motor control*. San Diego: Academic Press.

Ross, M. (1989). Relation of implicit theory to the construction of personal histories. *Psychological Review, 96*, 341–357.

Rubin, D. C. (Ed.). (1986). *Autobiographical memory*. Cambridge, UK: Cambridge University Press.

Rubin, D. C. (1995). *Memory in oral traditions*. New York: Oxford University Press.

Russell, B. (1921). *The analysis of mind*. London: Allen & Unwin.

Rumelhart, D. E., & Ortony, A. (1977). The representation of knowledge in memory. In R. C. Anderson, R. J. Spiro, & W. E. Montague (Eds.), *Schooling and the acquisition of knowledge* (pp. 99–135). Hillsdale, NJ: Erlbaum.

Schacter, D. L. (1987). Implicit memory: History and current status. *Journal of Experimental Psychology: Learning, Memory, and Cognition, 13*, 501–518.

Schank, R. C., & Riesbeck, C. K. (1981). *Inside computer understanding.* Hillsdale, NJ: Erlbaum.

Schmidt, R. A. (1988). *Motor control and learning: A behavioral emphasis.* Champaign, IL: Human Kinetics.

Segal, S. J., & Fusella, V. (1970). Influence of imaged pictures and sounds on detection of visual and auditory signals. *Journal of Experimental Psychology, 83*, 458–464.

Selfridge, O. G., & Neisser, U. (1960). Pattern recognition by machine. *Scientific American, 203*, 60–80.

Shallice, T., & Warrington, E. K. (1970). Independent functioning of verbal memory stores: A neuropsychological study. *Quarterly Journal of Experimental Psychology, 22*, 261–273.

Shallice, T., & Warrington, E. K. (1974). The dissociation between short-term retention of meaningful sounds and verbal material. *Neuropsychologia, 12*, 553–555.

Shepard, R. N. (1978). The mental image. *American Psychologist, 33*, 125–137.

Shepard, R. N., & Metzler, J. (1971). Mental rotation of three-dimensional objects. *Science, 191*, 952–954.

Simon, H. A. (1974). How big is a chunk? *Science, 183*, 482–488.

Simon, H. A., & Feigenbaum, E. A. (1964). An information processing theory of some effects of similarity, familiarization, and meaningfulness in verbal learning. *Journal of Verbal Learning and Verbal Behavior, 3*, 385–396.

Singley, M. K., & Anderson, J. R. (1989). *The transfer of cognitive skill.* Harvard University Press: Cambridge, MA.

Skinner, B. F. (1953). *Science and human behavior.* New York: Macmillan.

Skinner, B. F. (1957). *Verbal behavior.* Englewood Cliffs, NJ: Prentice-Hall.

Smith, E. E., & Medin, D. L. (1981). *Categories and concepts.* MA: Harvard University Press.

Squire, L. R. (1987). *Memory and brain.* Oxford: Oxford University Press.

Thorndike, E. L. (1898). Animal intelligence: An experimental study of the associative processes in animals. *Psychological Review,* Monograph Suppl., Vol. 2, no. 8.

Thorndike, E. L. (1903). *Educational psychology.* New York: Lemcke & Buchner.

Thune, L. E. (1951). Warm-up effect as a function of level of practice in verbal learning. *Journal of Experimental Psychology, 42*, 250–256.

Tulving, E. (1962). Subjective organization in free recall of "unrelated" words. *Psychological Review, 69*, 344–354.

Tulving, E. (1968). Theoretical issues in free recall. In T. R. Dixon & D. L. Horton (Eds.), *Verbal behavior and general behavior theory* (pp. 2–36). Englewood Cliffs, NJ: Prentice-Hall.

Tulving, E. (1972). Episodic and semantic memory. In E. Tulving & W. Donaldson (Eds.), *Organization of memory* (pp. 381–403). New York: Academic Press.

Tulving, E. (1983). *Elements of episodic memory.* New York: Oxford University Press.

Tulving, E. (1986). Episodic and semantic memory: Where should we go from here? *Behavioral Brain Sciences, 9*, 573–577.

Tulving, E., Kapur, S., Craik, F. I. M., Moscovitch, M., & Houle, S. (1994). Hemispheric encoding/retrieval asymmetry in episodic memory: Positron emission tomography findings. In *Proceedings of the National Academy of Science, 91*, 2016–2020.

Tulving, E., & Madigan, S. A. (1970). Memory and verbal learning. *Annual Review of Psychology, 21*, 437–484.

Tulving, E., & Pearlstone, Z. (1966). Availability versus accessibility of information in memory for words. *Journal of Verbal Learning and Verbal Behavior, 5*, 381–391.

Tulving, E., & Psotka, J. (1971). Retroactive inhibition in free recall: Inaccessibility of information available in the memory store. *Journal of Experimental Psychology, 87*, 1–8.

Tulving, E., & Schacter, D. L. (1990). Priming and human memory systems. *Science, 247*, 301–306.

Tulving, E., & Thomson, D. M. (1973). Encoding specificity and retrieval processes in episodic memory. *Psychological Review, 80*, 352–373.

Underwood B. J. (1961). An evaluation of the Gibson theory of verbal learning. In C. N. Cofer (Ed.), *Verbal learning and verbal behavior* (pp. 197–217). New York: McGraw-Hill.

Warren, H. C. (1921). *A history of the association philosophy.* New York: Charles Scribner's Sons.

Watson, J. B. (1919). *Psychology from the standpoint of a behaviorist.* Philadelphia: J. B. Lippincott.

Watson, J. B. (1924). *Behaviorism.* New York: Norton.

Waugh, N. C., & Norman, D. A. (1965). Primary memory. *Psychological Review, 72*, 89–104.

Winograd, T. (1972). *Understanding natural language.* New York: Academic Press.

Winograd, T. (1983). *Language as a cognitive process.* Reading, MA: Addison-Wesley.

Witmer, L. R. (1935). The association value of 3-place consonant syllables. *Journal of Genetic Psychology, 47*, 337–360.

Yntema, D. B., & Trask, F. P. (1963). Recall as a search process. *Journal of verbal learning and verbal behavior, 2*, 65–74.

2

Concepts of Memory

ENDEL TULVING

Scientific research can be thought of as a game of communication involving two parties: scientists and nature. In some fields scientists do experiments that put questions to nature. If the questions are posed intelligibly, nature yields bits and pieces of clues and hints of answers. It is then up to the scientists to make sense of these bits and pieces, to have fruitful ideas about them, and ideally to come up with coherent descriptions of their subject-matter domain. In other situations, nature has voluntarily strewn bits and pieces of various answers around for the scientists to notice and to make up questions about them. The whole enterprise depends crucially on the cooperation of the two parties: nature's job is to provide the raw materials (data, facts, findings, observations) and the scientists' job is to make it meaningful by inventing and applying the mortar that binds the nature-given materials and man-made ideas (hypotheses, models, theories, conceptualizations) into complete scientific edifices.

The purely human side of science making ('theorizing') can be divided into two separate but intertwined branches. One consists of making up and answering 'what' questions about the domain of interest. The most basic form of this kind of question is 'What is X?' where X stands for any one of a very large number of words or expressions. In the science of memory, X could represent things

such as accessibility, association, encoding, implicit memory, item, retrieval, source amnesia, working memory, and a long string of others. Other forms of 'what' questions arise in more closely circumscribed contexts. In the context of discussing, say, encoding, the question could be posed: 'Encoding of *what*?' In the context of remembering: 'Remembering *what*?' One can extend this series practically endlessly. These are not idle questions. Answers to them, or ideas about possible answers, shape the thinking of memory experimenters and theorists alike, and determine how the end products of research are recorded.

The other branch of theorizing consists of the construction of theories and models. In contemporary studies of memory these theories and models are typically descriptions and explanations of observed regularities in a chosen domain. The many chapters of this handbook are full of more or less complete theories and models of this kind.

This chapter is about concepts of memory. Concepts can be thought of as answers to 'what' questions. When we answer a question such as, 'What is implicit memory?' or 'What is it that people remember?' we have specified a concept, the concept of "implicit memory" in one case and the concept of, say, "previous experience" in the other. Both the premise and the thesis of the chapter is that conceptual analysis of memory is as important to progress in the field as is gathering facts and constructing models and theories. Because little systematic work on concepts of memory has been done, and because there is almost no literature on the subject, the discussion herein is uncertain and tentative. Everything is subject to revision. Some previous musings, even more rudimentary than those here, can be found elsewhere (Tulving, 1979, 1985, 1991).

The chapter consists of six parts: 1. Why should we care about concepts? 2. Terms, concepts, and reality. 3. The concept of "memory." 4. Idioms of memory: behavior and cognition. 5. Priming and implicit memory: a case study. 6. Centrality of concepts. The six parts are followed by a conclusion.

Why Should We Care about Concepts?

With rare exceptions students of memory do not explicitly discuss the concepts they use in their work (Mitchell & Hunt, 1989; Gardiner & Java, 1993; also see Chapter 1 by Bower, and Chapter 3 by Lockhart). Given the premise of this chapter—that concepts play a vital role in any science, including ours—such a lack may seem surprising.

There are at least three reasons for the benign oversight of concepts in our field. First, we have managed to do pretty well so far without any formal analyses of the terms we use, and without fretting about the exact meanings of the concepts that the terms designate. The progress that we can call our own may have depended on the development and elaboration of concepts, but all this has occurred rather naturally, in the course of normal gathering of facts and making up theories about the observed phenomena. There is no evidence that the absence of any focused emphasis on concepts has been an impediment of any kind.

The second reason for the neglect of concepts lies in the fact that our research community as a whole does not perceive much value in conceptual analysis; there is no promise of social reinforcement for any single individual who might be attracted to the enterprise. Under the circumstances, clever people, especially if they are young, resist any temptation to get involved.

The third reason, mushiest of them all yet possibly most pertinent, is that conceptual analysis is far too easily judged, or instinc-

tively felt to be scientifically irrelevant. Sure, one can wring one's hands over definitions and meanings of terms and usefulness of concepts, but real practicing scientists steer clear of such questionable intellectual neighborhoods. It is a game best left to philosophers, or linguists, or even semioticians who have much more time on their hands.

Note that psychologists' avoidance of concepts is highly specific to scientific or theoretical concepts as tools they use in their own day-to-day activity. Concepts formed and used by those that psychologists observe, in real life or in the laboratory, are embraced without embarrassment. Thus, concepts constitute basic components of network models of memory (Anderson & Bower, 1973; Balota & Lorch, 1986; Nelson, Bajo, & Canas, 1987), and topics such as concept learning (Smith & Medin, 1981), concepts and categories (Rosch & Mervis, 1975), conceptual processes (Roediger, 1989), and conceptual priming (Moscovitch, chapter 38 of this handbook) figure prominently in explorations of learning and memory.

Now, if it is true that students of memory have tacitly agreed to avoid conceptual analysis of their field, why should anyone wish to bother with it? Why a whole chapter on concepts in this handbook?

At least three reasons can be given. They are briefly mentioned here, and elaborated throughout the rest of the chapter. First, formal and focused attention paid to concepts is highly likely to result in greater terminological and conceptual clarity of thought and communication in the discipline. Right now there is altogether too much confusion in this respect. Given that we have trouble enough to coax nature to do its part in the joint venture, why should we compound the difficulties by deliberate carelessness on our own part? Second, concepts are crucial components of theories of memory, and therefore the goodness of our theories depends on the goodness of concepts. No sound concepts, no sound theory. The third reason has to do with our self-respect as students of memory. Surely one thing we should strive for are as clear and useful terms and concepts as we possibly can have at any given stage of the development of our science. Surely one thing we should avoid as much as possible is sloppiness and vagueness in our thinking about what the terms we use stand for. How can we respect ourselves, and how can we expect other scientists to respect us for what we have achieved, if the language we speak frequently sounds like babel?

It is widely accepted that the maturity of any scientific discipline is reflected in the maturity and sharpness of its terms and concepts (Holton & Brush, 1973; Mayr, 1982). Although our terms and concepts cannot be better than what the current stage of the development of our field allows, it also need not be worse than that. If we wish to see our discipline grow and blossom, we have to start paying attention to 'what?'

Terms, Concepts, and Reality

Concepts, like most other good things in life, come in many different forms and varieties, and they can be thought about in many ways. In order to optimize communication, some comments about the concepts of "term" and "concept" are necessary. These comments are based on Mario Bunge's lucid (1998, chap. 2 & 3) presentation and discussion of scientific concepts from the point of view of philosophy of science. His thorough conceptual analysis of terms and concepts, their place in scientific language, classification and taxonomy, systematics of concepts, vagueness and sharpening of concepts, definition and interpretation, and elucidation of concepts—a main mission of science—cannot help but enlighten every thoughtful scientist and is therefore highly recommended. Here only the barest outline of the central ideas can be given.

Bunge (1998) distinguishes among linguistic, conceptual, and physical levels of analysis, and uses the word *designation* to describe the relation between the linguistic and conceptual levels, the word *reference* to describe the relation between the linguistic and conceptual levels on the one hand and the physical level on the other hand, and the word *denotation* to represent the union of *designation* and *reference*. He further suggests using the convention of enclosing linguistic entities ('terms') in single quotes and conceptual entities ("concepts") in double quotes. Bunge's three-dimensional concept-space and terminological conventions are observed in this chapter wherever possible because they greatly contribute to the clarity of communication. Thus, a reader familiar with these distinctions who compares one sentence (such as, 'X' designates "Y") with another (such as, "X" refers to Y), will know something that a person unaware of the subtle but important distinction possibly cannot. Such purity, of course, is not always possible: we live in an imperfect world and are coping with pesky problems in an unfinished science.

At any rate, Bunge's (1998) analysis means that it is necessary to distinguish, as clearly as possible, among three kinds of interrelated existences: (1) *things*, entities existing in the *real world*; (2) *concepts*, entities existing in the form of pure abstract *thoughts* about real-world entities; and (3) *terms*, linguistic or other symbolic *signs*, entities that also exist in the real world but whose sole function is to denote concepts and their associated real-world correspondences. One interesting implication inherent in this conceptualization of the term 'concept' is that it would be most unusual for two individuals to completely share—that is, agree on the meaning of—any complex concept. Once we realize this fact and keep it in mind at all times, we can take appropriate precautionary measures and thereby simplify our lives.

It is important to emphasize at this point that real-world existences include purely mental, phenomenal *experiences*, of the kind that have been usually labeled as 'subjective.' Thus, the feeling of warmth or pain by a sentient organism, and seeing red or hearing the sound of the waves crashing on to the shore, are kinds of real-world entities that one can have thoughts about (make up concepts about) and can designate by signs. They are nonphysical in the standard sense of the term, and they differ in basic ways from physical objects and events, yet they are part of the real world because they exist, as products of neural activity, in the four-dimensional space-time continuum, and they do so independently of concepts referring to them or signs designating them. For scientific purposes it is immaterial whether their existence is observed directly or is inferred from indirect evidence.

In brief, in this chapter, the 'concepts of memory' under scrutiny are *pure abstractions*, in the sense that they have no other existence than that in the minds of individuals. Concepts do not exist in any form in the real nonabstract world. To render them amenable to rational analysis, however, they are connected to the real world in two ways: they can be designated by signs (words or other symbols) and they refer to (are associated with) objects, situations, and events in the real world.

The Concept of "Memory"

Given the three-dimensional concept-space in the science of memory—term, concept, and brain/behavior operations—difficulties arise not within a single dimension but between them. The one that occurs most frequently is the one-many relation between terms and concepts: one and the same term is used to designate many different concepts.

The problem has been discussed by Gardiner and Java (1993), who pointed out that a common source of confusion in theoretical discussions lies in the failure to make necessary terminological distinctions. Frequently, they argue, the same term—for example 'implicit memory'—is applied to (1) both memory tasks and memory systems, (2) both memory systems and memory processes, (3) both memory processes and the state of the rememberer's awareness, and (4) both states of awareness and memory tasks. Such indiscriminate use of a single sign to denote rather different concepts does not just breed confusion, it also is directly responsible for needless and frequently counterproductive arguments.

Gardiner and Java (1993) propose a rule of *incontrovertibility of terms*: any given term should be allowed to denote only a single concept or entity. Thus, if 'implicit memory' refers to a memory task in which the subject has no need to remember any particular past event, then terms such as 'implicit memory system' or 'implicit memory processes' should not be used. If, on the other hand, 'implicit memory' designates a particular process of retrieving stored information, then it should not be used in any other sense.

The idea of a rule such as *incontrovertibility of terms* is admirable, and beneficial, in more ways than one. In a perfect world its merits would not be even debated (although its label might be shortened). However, in the real world, it would be difficult to effect the general acceptance of the rule. There are powerful forces of history and tradition that militate against such rational behavior. As an illustration, consider the term 'memory' that designates the central concept of all the chapters in this handbook. What does it mean— that is, how is it used by students of memory?

The term 'memory,' in addition to denoting a field of study, can designate a number of different concepts. Among the more frequently occurring meanings of 'memory' are (1) memory as neurocognitive capacity to encode, store, and retrieve information; (2) memory as a hypothetical store in which information is held; (3) memory as the information in that store; (4) memory as some property of that information; (5) memory as a componential

process of retrieval of that information; and (6) memory as an individual's phenomenal awareness of remembering something. In addition there are other senses in which writers use 'memory,' although such uses tend to be idiosyncratic.

Let us consider more concrete illustrations of these various concepts of "memory." Thus, when one speaks about 'testing a patient's memory' or about 'profound losses of memory,' one usually has in mind 'memory' in the broad sense of *"neurocognitive capability"* of a particular kind, one that is related to but separable from other neurocognitive capabilities such as perception and thought.

When one speaks about things such as 'encoding information into memory' or 'retrieving information into memory,' one usually has in mind, not the overall memory capability as such, but rather something more properly referred to as *"memory store."* (People who worry that the word *store* implies the acceptance of spatial (Roediger, 1980) or warehouse (Tulving, 1983) metaphors of memory can relax: it is perfectly possible to define "memory store" as a stage of information processing between encoding and retrieval.)

The term 'memory' in expressions such as 'amnesia is like normal memory weakened by reduced study time,' or 'memory changes after initial learning,' or 'memory decays rapidly,' or 'medial temporal damage affects recently acquired memories more than memories acquired long ago,' designates neither the overall capacity nor the memory store. Instead, the term 'memory' in these expressions corresponds to something like *"the information stored about an item or an event."*

Propositions such as 'time in the short-term store is not a major determinant of memory,' or 'memory is a function of depth and elaboration,' are not claims made about memory as a capability, or the memory store, or the nature and kind of information in the store. Instead these sorts of claims refer to a certain hypothetical property of the stored information, something that more specifically could be thought of as the *"strength"* or *"accessibility"* of *"the memory trace"* of an item or event.

When 'memory' occurs in an expression such as 'signal-detection theory enables us to separate the subjects' performance into two components, memory and decision,' it designates a hypothesized component of the *process* of retrieval.

Finally, 'memory' in an expression such as 'memory without awareness' designates the *experiential* (phenomenological) flavor of the act of retrieval. As discussed by Roediger and McDermott in chapter 10 of this handbook, this kind of memory can be experienced even when the remembered events did not happen.

In most cases, the context within which a proposition is made is sufficient to specify the particular sense in which 'memory' is used: general capability, memory store, memory trace in the store, property of the memory trace, a process of retrieval, and phenomenal experience at retrieval, or what not. In the absence of adequate supporting context, the meaning of memory may, of course, remain unclear. Thus, for example, just reading that 'memory is largely a function of depth and elaboration' does not in itself provide information as to whether reference is made to the contents of an engram, the strength of the memory trace, the probability of recall or recognition, or something else.

Ideally, of course, we would curtail the abandon with which the central term of our discipline is used, and instead of the general term 'memory' would use terms such as memory store, stored information, memory trace, trace strength, mnemonic information (as one of the determinants of measured recognition performance), and recollection. It would aid communication and free time for more fruitful pursuits. It would also help outsiders who may now wonder how it is possible to have memories that contain memories that contain memories, a state of affairs logically embedded in the nexus of concepts of "memory" as discussed.

Idioms of Memory: Behavior and Cognition

We consider now another vital conceptual distinction that must be made in the study of memory. The distinction—yet another dichotomy, which we know that scientists love even if nature does not—pits pure action against pure thought, or behavior against cognition. People and other animals can acquire, through learning and memory, a wide variety of *behaviors* that are useful for their survival. They can also acquire a great deal of *knowledge* about the world in which they live and survive, and in which they practice their learned behaviors along with innately determined ones.

Reflection, as well as the results of a good deal of objective study, reveal that it is perfectly possible for people to engage in highly complicated forms of learned behavior without anything resembling the corresponding knowledge. Young children's ability to speak grammatically is one of the most obvious examples. An outfielder catching the near-home-run ball near the top of the high back fence of the field is another. The outfielder can talk about his feat in a way that a young child cannot, but such a verbal description is secondary (epiphenomenal) and plays no role in the execution of the highly skillful behavior. On the other hand, two masters can play chess without the board and pieces, entirely within their own minds. They need to rely on overt behavior only to communicate the results of their thoughts to each other, and for the loser to congratulate the winner at the end! In this situation behavior is an incidental by-product (epiphenomenon) of the exercise of thought.

A basic conceptual issue has to do with whether 'memory' whose operations are expressed purely in behavior, in the absence of corresponding (conscious) thought, can be regarded as the same kind of 'memory' whose operations are expressed in pure thought, in the absence of any *necessity* to convert the thought into behavior. That is, the issue concerns the extent to which the two *idioms* of memory, behavioral versus cognitive, mark the boundaries of rather different domains within which the search for unifying principles may turn out to be difficult if not futile. The concept of "idiom" of memory is introduced here to facilitate communication. 'Idioms of memory designate the particular ways in which memory manifests itself, or the mode in which the products of memory are expressed. The three main "idioms of memory" are related to behavior, knowledge, and remembering. Here the focus is on the contrast between behavior and knowledge. Analytical and empirical comparisons between knowledge and remembering can be found elsewhere (Tulving & Markowitsch, 1998; Wheeler, Stuss, & Tulving, 1997).

The basic distinction between behavior and cognition, or action and thought, is reflected in the distinction between procedural and declarative (cognitive) forms of memory, which is universally accepted today. Hodges (chapter 28), as well as Mayes (chapter 27) and Markowitsch (chapter 29) discuss neuropsychological evidence pertaining to the distinction. Schacter and his colleagues (chapter 39) describe neuronal correlates of procedural and declarative memory as revealed by functional brain imaging methods.

Why is the distinction between the two idioms of memory important?

Apart from the fact that it contributes to terminological clarity and hence enhances the quality of communication, the distinction has a number of practical implications. Its main advantage lies in the needed constraints it places on facts and theories. Behavioral and cognitive memory have features in common (otherwise we would not classify both as memory), but they also differ in many ways. One consequence of these differences is that not every question that can be posed for one idiom makes sense in the other, and not every fact that is true of one idiom is true of the other. Keeping behavior apart from cognition frees us from the necessity of going through unnatural contortions if we tried to speak the same kind of language about both of these forms of memory. In the cognitive idiom, it is natural to speak about encoding and storing of information that represents what there is or could be in the world, as it is to speak about retrieving bits and pieces and various aspects of such information. The study of encoding, retrieval, and their interaction has occupied center stage of the cognitive idiom of memory for a long time, as many chapters in this handbook demonstrate (see especially chapter 6 by Brown & Craik). Trying to bring these concepts into play in the study of, say, behavioral skills such as reading or writing is awkward at best and silly at worst.

Consider another example. A great deal of experimental and theoretical effort has been devoted to the study of recall and recognition tests and processes assumed to underlie the performance on these tests. But the whole problem complex can arise only in the cognitive idiom, in situations where subjects' *thoughts* about the products of retrieval can be expressed in the production (recall) of appropriate responses or in the proper identification (recognition) of test items. The distinction between recall and recognition is devoid of meaning in the behavioral idiom. There is no way of telling whether a monkey in a delayed-matching-to-nonsample test (see chapter 30 by Zola and Squire) is engaged in recall or in recognition. The same argument applies to studies with human infants, described by Rovee-Collier and Hayne in chapter 17. Infants are capable of learning to make responses that activate the mobile, and they respond differentially to familiar and novel mobiles. But there is no way of classifying their task as that of recalling or recognizing.

The point is that fundamental distinctions that have occupied the focus of experimental and theoretical attention in the cognitive idiom of memory for a long time are meaningless in the behavioral idiom. We are well advised, therefore, to explicitly conceptualize behavioral memory different from cognitive memory. Unless we do so, we run the risk of tacitly assuming that behavior and knowledge are highly correlated ("the doctrine of concordance"; Tulving, 1989), and end up playing Procrustes in modern times: our ideas will end up mutilated.

Priming and Implicit Memory: A Case Study

A persistent theme of this chapter is that one can take any one of a very large number of terms that one finds in the memory literature and subject it to a thorough analysis. In many situations such action, of course, would border on madness; in some situations the payoff would not be worth the cost, but in many other situations the exercise might be worthwhile. As a case study let us consider the topic of priming and implicit memory.

An exceedingly important ability that organisms must possess in order to survive is that of responding discriminatively to different environmental stimuli. The first requirement for taking appropriate action about objects encountered in one's surroundings is telling them apart. In humans, whose environments have been largely shaped by civilization and culture, this ability has reached a very high level of development at which an adult has learned to identify, and discriminate among, tens upon tens of thousands of different objects.

'Identification,' like any other term, can be defined in many different ways. Here it means the assignment of a given object to a specific conceptual category. The category itself has to be socially shared rather than idiosyncratic, to distinguish object identification from, say, episodic-memory recognition where the categories "old" and "new" are specific to the individual in a given situation. But within such socially shared categories, many classifications are possible. A two-dimensional visual object may be categorized, and thus identified, as an indistinct blob, a roundish shape, a face, a human face, the face of a woman, a familiar face, the face of a well-known movie star of the past, the face of Marlene Dietrich, the face of my great-aunt. This ordering illustrates two points. One, a general term such as 'familiarity' (one of the most frequently used terms in the memory literature) designates a large number of different concepts. The face of a complete stranger is a familiar object in one sense, the face of my great-aunt is familiar in another sense. Two, and more directly relevant in this context, in any discussion of object identification it is mandatory to specify the concept to which the term applies.

In the laboratory, the subject is typically informed of the general nature of the relevant supra-category and the question put about each stimulus, 'What is this object?' The subject responds by naming or in some other way describing the appropriate subcategory. Various derivatives of the basic question are also used: 'Is this object X?' (e.g., 'Is this string of letters a word? Does this word represent a living thing?), or 'Tell me about objects in category X' (e.g., 'Name words beginning with letter "L", or 'List all the Presidents of U.S.', or even 'Draw a house'). The study of variables affecting identification of objects has been a favorite pastime of psychologists for ages. Many different kinds of objects and many different tasks of object identification have been used. In perceptual identification tasks, the examiner shows the subject a Mooney figure and asks whether it represents a face or not, or flashes a word on the screen and asks the subject to name the word. In clinical tests, patients suspected of suffering from agnosia are shown pictures of common objects and the patient asked to name them. In intelligence (knowledge, language, vocabulary) tests, subjects are asked questions: What does 'tranquil' mean? What is another name for interstellar space? What is the capital of France? Do you know two European capitals whose names have the same two initial letters and the same three final letters? In studies of semantic memory, the participant may be asked: Name colors, or writers, or famous singers. Do canaries have wings? Is X famous for any reason?

In all of these cases the respondent's success on the identification task depends on relevant skills and knowledge, and on the nature of the information provided. For an adult to answer the question about the capital of France comes effortlessly, whereas the question about the two other capitals with similar names is difficult, despite the fact that everyone knows the two names. (This last example illustrates the problems involved in the concept of "identification" but also those in the concept of "knowing."

Memory—more precisely, cognitive memory—is relevant to the issue of object identification in two ways. First, the knowledge base whose use makes the answering of identification questions possible is clearly a product of (cognitive) memory. (Note that there is no generally accepted term that designates this knowledge base. What should it be called, other than the ungraceful and vague 'knowledge base'?) Second, changes in this knowledge base (expansion, enrichment, elaboration, refinement, as well as reduction, impoverishment, degradation) occur continuously throughout life, and some of these changes can be observed, analyzed, and measured in the laboratory and in the clinic, in studies of memory. One such change is known as priming.

Priming and Object Identification

Priming is the name of the hypothetical process that underlies an observed improvement in identification performance that is attributable to previous experience. It is also used as a term to denote such improvement. There are three general categories of situations in which priming has been studied. One kind of priming is studied in a paradigm introduced by Meyer and Schvaneveldt (1971). It is described and discussed by Balota and colleagues in chapter 25, under the label of 'semantic priming.'

The second kind of priming occurs in connection with the use of successive tests. The idea is that the first test, say yes/no recognition, may affect the subject's performance on the second test, say cued recall, resulting in the second-test performance that reflects both the initial study and priming by the first test (Humphreys & Bowyer, 1980). This kind of successive-test priming is discussed by Kahana in chapter 4.

The third type of priming, currently the most intensely studied one, has to do with *identification* of objects in the sense of answering the question 'what?' about a presented stimulus. The spirit of the question put to the subject in a test for priming is *always* this: 'I am thinking of an object. Indeed, it is recorded here on my answer sheet. I want you to tell me what it is. Here is a clue about the object. What is the object?' The subject also usually knows the *general* category to which the *target* object is to be assigned: it is the name of a place or a person, or an English word, or a line drawing of a concrete thing, or the photograph of a celebrity, or whatever. (See table 16.1 in Toth's chapter 16 for an extensive listing.)

Initially the type of priming that is observed in these kinds of situations was referred to as 'repetition' priming, because the clue at test was seen as a kind of a repetition (even if partial or fragmentary) of the target item (see Bower, chapter 1, and Lockhart, chapter 3). Actual repeated presentation of the to-be-identified objects, however, occurs only in some priming tasks. For example, picture naming (Mitchell & Brown, 1988) and lexical decisions about pairs of words (Goshen-Gottstein & Moscovitch, 1995) are faster when the picture or pair is presented for the second time in a particular context. Similarly, after reading a word in a list, the subject is more likely to produce that word when a conceptually related clue is given and the subject instructed to say the first word, or the first *n* words, that 'comes to mind.' In many other priming situations, however, no such direct repetition of stimuli between study and test occurs, and 'repetition' priming is a misnomer. More appropriate are labels that identify the nature of the clue used in the identification task. The two major categories are 'perceptual' and 'conceptual' clues, and accordingly a distinction is drawn between 'perceptual' priming and 'conceptual' priming (Roediger & Blaxton, 1987; Tulving & Schacter, 1990; also see Toth, chapter 16).

Priming and
Implicit Memory

As mentioned earlier, the knowledge base that makes identification of objects possible is *acquired*. It is a *result of* learning: perceptual learning for identification of an object on the basis of its appearance; conceptual learning for the identification of an object on the basis of its meaning. This is as true of experimentally nonprimed as it is of experimentally primed identification.

Many experiments have demonstrated that the use of previously acquired knowledge for the purpose of object identification can be totally independent of remembering the past (Toth, chapter 16). Normally, indeed, people are oblivious to the fact that any memory of any kind is involved in perceiving an object, regardless of whether such perceiving has been experimentally primed or not. They are retrieving (using) stored information, but are not aware that they are doing so. Therefore, object

identification, whether specifically primed or not, could be said to represent an instance of 'implicit retrieval' (Schacter, 1987).

Although this proposal should be generally acceptable to all students of memory, it is not. Whereas there is little disagreement in the literature concerning the implicit nature of priming, there is considerable disagreement as to whether (unprimed) retrieval of information from the general knowledge store is to be thought of as implicit or explicit. Many writers take the stance that, for example, identifying Paris as the capital of France represents an instance of explicit retrieval because the subject is fully aware that she is relying on her (semantic) memory when she answers the question or thinks of the fact on her own. These writers believe that only *changes* in this knowledge occur implicitly. Thus, nonprimed retrieval is explicit, priming is implicit.

On the other hand, there are others who believe that both unprimed and primed retrieval of semantic information, such as that concerning Paris, should be thought of as implicit, in keeping with the definition of 'implicit' in terms of the individual's lack of awareness of the nature of the relation between a current identification task and any previous happening (Graf & Schacter, 1985). This definition is satisfied in typical situations in which the individual retrieves information from the general knowledge store, regardless of whether the information is used for object identification or for answering questions about the world, and regardless of the priming status of the information.

The disagreement here—is retrieval of "unprimed" semantic information explicit or implicit?—clearly has its roots in different concepts of "implicit memory." If 'implicit' is conceptualized in terms of the individual's lack of awareness of the relation between current performance and any previous event (Graf & Schacter, 1985), then answering the Paris question clearly is an instance of implicit retrieval. If, on the other hand, 'implicit' designates the individual's lack of awareness that he is now retrieving previously acquired knowledge, then answering the Paris question is not an instance of implicit retrieval. Both views may be held, of course, but not by the same person at the same time.

Centrality of Concepts

In the last section of the chapter we return to the issue of the central role that concepts play in living science, and consider yet another example that involves the concept of "memory."

As is well known, there exist today two large classes of students of memory—those who believe in a unitary memory and those who believe in multiple memories. They can be differentiated in terms of their answers to the question: 'What is memory?' (Tulving, 1999). They can also be distinguished by analyzing the terms they use. Thus, for example, unitarians use terms such as 'direct' (or 'explicit') versus 'indirect' (or 'implicit') *measures of memory* (Richardson-Klavehn & Bjork, 1988), on the assumption that memory is one, but the ways in which it can be measured vary. Believers of multiple-memory systems, on the other hand, would claim that an expression such as 'direct versus indirect measures of memory' makes no sense, because there is no such single thing as memory. They would argue that different aspects or operations of different kinds of memory can be measured in different ways, and that it can be done with respect to changes in stored information originating in a given event.

The issue of unitary versus multiple memory systems is hotly debated at the present time (Foster & Jelicic, 1999), and it revolves around the concept of memory, around the answer to the question of 'what is memory?' The kind of answer one gives, or calls his own, regardless of the manner of its articulation, has fundamental implications for how one proceeds in one's study of memory.

For a unitarian, an interesting finding might be that even when an event cannot be retrieved consciously, as in a recall or recognition test, it may nevertheless be retrieved nonconsciously or implicitly. The important word in the immediately preceding sentence is *it*. The task now necessarily becomes that of explaining the dissociation. Hundreds of experiments can be conducted to find out how different conditions affect the presence, absence, or the magnitude of the dissociation. The task dissociation, say one between 'aware' and 'unaware' memory, has become a *phenomenon to be explained*.

A multiple-systems person, who begins with the idea that there are many different memory systems and subsystems, has a different research program. As a unitary-system person seeks to describe and understand all of memory, so the multiple-systems person seeks to describe and understand each different system, and to ascertain their similarities and differences. Multiple-systems people would not

spend much time trying to explain (answering 'how' and 'why' questions) about dissociations between aware and unaware memory tasks for the same reason that they would not wonder about the meaning of dissociations between, say, vision and audition. Vision and audition are different evolved adaptations by which organisms receive and internalize information about their environment, and there exist no a priori reasons to expect that they operate according to the same principles, although there may be some similarities. Different forms of memory, or different memory systems, are different evolved adaptations by which organisms can benefit from past experiences in meeting the exigencies of the present situation, and there exist no a priori reasons to expect they operate similarly in every respect. Therefore, the dissociation between aware and unaware memory is not a phenomenon to be explained; rather, it is an *item of relevant information* by which properties of different systems can be identified.

The point is that the debate concerning unitary and multiple memories is not something that would clearly or directly benefit from doing experiments and constructing process theories or models. The debate is to a large extent a conceptual one. Because there exist no practical criteria that could be used to assess the truth or goodness of concepts and terms, and no useful rules for judging the correctness of answers to the 'what' questions, it is not possible for anyone to adjudicate the various disagreements and conflicts that openly enliven the happenings on the conceptual scene or that lie hidden behind theoretical debates in memory research today. As always in science, the merits of different ways of classifying and thinking about things in the broad domain of memory will become clear only in the future.

Concepts of memory are continually molded and shaped by empirical findings in the field, and by people's thoughts about the findings. However, experience suggests that conceptual changes in memory research occur with the speed of the movement of tectonic plates. Although it is not entirely unknown for an individual scientist to radically alter his or her ideas about 'what X is,' the usual mechanism for conceptual change lies in the gradual flow, and passing, of generations of practitioners.

Under the circumstances, where the world in which we live and work cannot be changed, and where we cannot change our basic convictions as to *what* the entities are that we study and work on, we must be alert to two things that are perfectly possible: (1) making sure that we understand the similarities and differences between each others' terms and concepts; and (2) making sure we understand the nature of debates and disagreements: Are we arguing about 'how' and 'why,' or are we disagreeing about 'what?'

Conclusion

In science, 'what' questions are at least as important as 'how' and 'why' questions. 'What' questions are about concepts. In the science of memory, as in any other field, terms and concepts play a central role in shaping the inquiry and articulating its fruits.

In the past, relatively little explicit attention has been paid to terms and concepts. As a result, problems have arisen. A frequent source of confusion lies in the use of one and the same term to designate rather different concepts. The term 'memory,' for example, has at least six, and probably many more, clearly different meanings. Sometimes important concepts cannot be discussed because of the lack of appropriate terminology. Thus, although behavioral and cognitive memory clearly represent rather disparate entities, and although differences between them are generally accepted, the language for comparing them is not clearly available. In this chapter the two are thought of as two of the main three *idioms* of memory, remembering representing the third.

The conceptual issues that face today's memory researchers are illustrated with the analysis of a paradigmatic case study of object identification, priming, and implicit memory—terms that are among the most popular ones in the contemporary science of memory.

A final illustration of the centrality of concepts involved the distinction between unitary and multiple memory systems. This distinction has led to a heated debate that to many appears to be revolving around interpretations of facts and explanations of phenomena, but which in fact is rooted in a conceptual disagreement. The different concepts of the parties have led to radically different research programs.

The terms and concepts of memory that have been useful in the pursuit of the understanding of nature's secrets have evolved as natural by-products of the normal data-gathering and hypothesis-making activities of students of memory. The time may be ripe now to switch from the hunting and gathering mode to one of planned cultivation.

Acknowledgment The author's research is supported by NSERC (Grant A8632) and a foundation by Anne and Max Tanenbaum in support of research in cognitive neuroscience.

References

Anderson, J. R., & Bower, G. H. (1973). *Human associative memory*. Washington, DC: D. H. Winston.

Balota, D. A., & Lorch, R. F., Jr. (1986). Depth of automatic spreading of activation: Mediated priming effects in pronunciation but not in lexical decision. *Journal of Experimental Psychology: Learning, Memory, and Cognition, 12*, 336–345.

Bunge, M. (1998). *Philosophy of science, Vol. 1.* New Brunswick, NJ: Transaction Publishers.

Foster, J. K., & Jelicic, M. (Eds.). (1999). *Memory: Structure, function, or process?* Oxford: Oxford University Press.

Gardiner, J. M., & Java, R. I. (1993). Recognising and remembering. In A. Collins, S. Gathercole, M. Conway, & P. Morris (Eds.), *Theories of memory* (pp. 163–188). Hillsdale, NJ: Erlbaum.

Goshen-Gottstein, Y., & Moscovitch, M. (1995). Repetition priming for newly formed and preexisting associations: Perceptual and conceptual influences. *Journal of Experimental Psychology: Learning, Memory, & Cognition, 21*, 1229–1248.

Graf, P., & Schacter, D. L. (1985). Implicit and explicit memory for new associations in normal subjects and amnesic patients. *Journal of Experimental Psychology: Learning, Memory, and Cognition, 11*, 501–518.

Holton, G., & Brush, S. G. (1973). *Introduction to concepts and theories of physical science*. Reading, MA: Addison-Wesley.

Humphreys, M. S., & Bowyer, P. A. (1980). Sequential testing effects and the relationship between recognition and recognition failure. *Memory and Cognition, 8*, 271–277.

Mayr, E. (1982). *The growth of biological thought*. Cambridge, MA: Harvard University Press.

Meyer, D. E., & Schvaneveldt, R. W. (1971). Facilitation in recognizing pairs of words: Evidence of a dependence between retrieval operations. *Journal of Experimental Psychology, 90*, 227–234.

Mitchell, D. B., & Brown, A. S. (1988). Persistent repetition priming in picture naming and its dissociation from recognition memory. *Journal of Experimental Psychology: Learning, Memory, and Cognition, 14*, 213–222.

Mitchell, D. B., & Hunt, R. R. (1989). How much "effort" should be devoted to memory? *Memory and Cognition, 17*, 337–348.

Nelson, D. L., Bajo, T. M., & Canas, J. (1987). Prior knowledge and memory: The episodic encoding of implicitly activated associates and rhymes. *Journal of Experimental Psychology: Learning, Memory, and Cognition, 13*, 54–63.

Richardson-Klavehn, A., & Bjork, R. A. (1988). Measures of memory. *Annual Review of Psychology, 39*, 475–543.

Roediger, H. L. (1980). Memory metaphors in cognitive psychology. *Memory & Cognition, 8*, 231–246.

Roediger, H. L., & Blaxton, T. A. (1987). Retrieval modes produce dissociations in memory for surface information. In D. Gorfein & R. R. Hoffman (Eds.), *Memory and cognitive processes: The Ebbinghaus Centennial Conference* (pp. 349–379). Hillsdale, NJ: Erlbaum.

Roediger, H. L., Weldon, M. S., & Challis, B. H. (1989). Explaining dissociations between implicit and explicit measures of retention; a processing account. In H. L. Roediger & F. I. M. Craik (Eds.), *Varieties of memory and consciousness: Essays in honour of Endel Tulving* (pp. 3–41). Hillsdale, NJ: Erlbaum.

Rosch, E., & Mervis, C. B. (1975). Family resemblance studies in the internal structure of categories. *Cognitive Psychology, 7*, 573–605.

Schacter, D. L. (1987). Implicit memory: History and current status. *Journal of Experimental Psychology: Learning, Memory, and Cognition, 13*, 501–518.

Smith, E. E., & Medin, D. L. (1981). *Categories and concepts.* Cambridge, MA: Harvard University Press.

Tulving, E. (1979). Memory research: What kind of progress? In L-G. Nilsson (Ed.), *Perspectives in memory research* (pp. 19–34). Hillsdale, NJ: Erlbaum.

Tulving, E. (1983). *Elements of episodic memory.* Oxford: Clarendon Press.

Tulving, E. (1985). On the classification problem in learning and memory. In L-G. Nilsson and T. Archer (Eds.), *Perspectives in learning and memory* (pp. 67–94). Hillsdale, NJ: Erlbaum.

Tulving, E. (1989). Memory: Performance, knowledge, and experience. *European Journal of Cognitive Psychology, 1*, 3–26.

Tulving, E. (1991). Concepts of human memory. In L. R. Squire, G. Lynch, N. M. Weinberger, & J. L. McGaugh (Eds.), *Memory: Organization and locus of change* (pp. 3–32). New York: Oxford University Press.

Tulving, E. (1999). Study of memory: Processes and systems. In J. K. Foster & M. Jelicic (Eds.), *Memory: Systems, process, or function?* (pp. 11–30). Oxford: Oxford University Press.

Tulving, E., & Markowitsch, H. J. (1998). Episodic and declarative memory: Role of the hippocampus. *Hippocampus, 8*, 198–204.

Tulving, E., & Schacter, D. L. (1990). Priming and human memory systems. *Science, 247*, 301–306.

Wheeler, M., Stuss, D. T., & Tulving, E. (1997). Toward a theory of episodic memory: The frontal lobes and autonoetic consciousness. *Psychological Bulletin, 121*, 331–354.

3

Methods of Memory Research

ROBERT S. LOCKHART

Progress in memory research owes much to the richness of its methodology. The field's many experimental paradigms and various techniques for measuring memory have provided the empirical foundation on which contemporary theory has been built. This is no minor achievement; the task of developing a behavioral methodology that will support inferences about memory systems and processes that are themselves not directly observable is a formidable challenge. This chapter describes some of the key methodological strategies that memory research has used in confronting this challenge. Space does not permit a complete catalogue of the various measurement techniques and experimental paradigms that have been used, and even if space were available, such a descriptive list would make tedious reading. As other chapters in this handbook demonstrate, methodology becomes exciting in the context of its achievements.

A reasonable first question is whether behavioral methods are of more than historical interest. Recent advances in brain imaging technology might suggest that a solution based on direct observation is now at hand, rendering prior behavioral methodology as obsolete as the methods used to diagnose broken bones before the availability of X-rays. Such a view is badly mistaken. The misleading nature of the metaphor becomes apparent as soon as

one asks a few simple questions: What task should the brain be performing while being scanned? How does one know that the brain activity being observed has anything to do with memory? Are there different kinds of remembering, and if so, are they associated with different patterns of brain activity? The fact is that successful imaging studies depend crucially on the judicious selection of tasks for the subject to perform, and those tasks are the fruit of decades of behavioral research. This research has yielded a large range of procedures that are not only thoroughly documented, but have a well-developed theoretical rationale. Only in this context of continuing behavioral research can image data be related to measures of memory performance in a way that is theoretically meaningful. It is for this reason that one of the most salient features of current brain imaging technology applied to the study of memory is its heavy reliance on behavioral methodology and the theoretical concepts derived from it.

The Three Phases of a Memory Experiment

The beginning of experimental methodology in the study of memory is generally attributed to the 1885 publication of Hermann Ebbinghaus's *Über das Gedächtnis*. Ebbinghaus displayed a zeal for experimental control and sound experimental method that remains exemplary more than a century later. The reward for such methodological obsessiveness was data that were so orderly as to completely undermine any claim that memory was not amenable to scientific study. However, as impressive as it is, this experimental rigor was not the most revolutionary aspect of Ebbinghaus's methodology. That distinction belongs to a feature of his work that is so fundamental to contemporary methodology that we are inclined to take it for granted.

Prior to Ebbinghaus, the subject matter of memory research was deemed to be the investigation of existing memories laid down over the natural course of everyday experience. The truly revolutionary concept in *Über das Gedächtnis* was the idea that memories should be created in the laboratory as an integral part of the experimental procedure. It is interesting to note that Bartlett (1932), while harshly criticizing many features of Ebbinghaus's methods (such as his use of nonsense syllables), did not question this particular aspect. Indeed, creating and modifying memories within a laboratory context is a basic feature of Bartlett's own research.

Ebbinghaus's methodological revolution notwithstanding, the study of memories laid down in the course of everyday experience remains an important and legitimate part of memory research, as several chapters in this handbook demonstrate. Such studies are also of great practical significance, especially in domains such as legal testimony and psychotherapy. Autobiographical memory is a term used to describe much of this work to which Conway (1990) provides a comprehensive introduction. The need for careful methodology in this area has been underlined by the large body of evidence demonstrating the inaccuracies and distortions of everyday memory. Schacter (1995, 1996) provides an extensive review of this research.

While acknowledging the importance of investigating natural memories, it is Ebbinghaus's experimental framework that remains the prototype for memory research. Despite innumerable variations and elaborations, the contemporary memory experiment consists of three phases: a study or encoding phase in which material is presented to the subject, a retention interval, and finally a retrieval or test phase in which the subject attempts to respond to a question, the answer to which involves the use of the initially studied information. Memory methods, from Ebbinghaus to the present day, can thus be characterized in terms of the conditions they establish for each of these three phases. The fundamental research strategy has been to vary the conditions obtaining at each of these three phases, and the paradigms of memory research have consisted largely of an ever-increasing number of variations in the conditions for each phase.

Prior to the cognitive revolution of the 1960s, each of the three components could be given a simple characterization: The acquisition phase established a trace strength, the retention interval saw the weakening (through decay and/or interference) of that strength, and the retrieval (test) phase served to provide a measure of residual trace strength. Research methods were aimed at establishing functional relations that documented the influence of various acquisition and retention-interval conditions on test-phase performance.

The cognitive revolution did not bring about radical changes in this basic methodology, but it did give old methods new purpose, leading to a shift of emphasis and the spawning of many novel procedures. Each of the three phases was no longer simply a matter of changes in trace strength, but was now seen as a set of complex operations to be understood in terms of an active information processor. Moreover, the focus of these methods shifted increasingly from documenting the independent additive effects occurring at each phase, to attempts to understand their *interactive* relationship. For example, rather than ask how different encoding processes influenced performance levels, the question of greater interest became how remembering was determined by the interaction of particular encoding processes with different conditions at the time of retrieval.

Closely related to this shift of focus was a growing debate as to the number and form of memory systems. For example, did long-term and short-term memory constitute different memory subsystems? Was memory performance influenced by processes outside a subject's conscious control? What were the implications of a nonunitary view of memory for the measurement of memory? Do traditional measures such as recognition and recall each tap a distinct memory system? Do these measures reflect the joint influence of more than one memory system?

Retrieval Conditions and the Measurement of Memory

Although the retrieval phase is the final stage of the typical memory experiment, it is the logical starting point for an account of methods because it is this phase that defines the response measure and thus establishes the phenomenon under investigation. This point of view reflects something of the shift in emphasis that followed the cognitive revolution. For most researchers prior to 1970, the various methods of evaluating memory (recognition or recall, for example) were seen as alternative methods for measuring a common underlying construct. Differences among measures were regarded as a matter of methodological detail rather than an issue of theoretical importance. The fact that recognition typically yielded higher performance levels than did recall was seen simply to reflect the fact that recognition was a more sensitive measure of trace strength, or of whether an item was still "in memory." So entrenched was this view that the reaction to Tulving's demonstration that under certain conditions items could be recalled but not recognized was met with a mixture of disbelief and incomprehension (see Tulving, 1983, chap. 13).

An important conclusion that emerged as part of the cognitive revolution was that memory performance was not the manifestation of an underlying unitary construct. Measuring memory was no longer seen to be like measuring length or weight; rather, memory was now regarded as an umbrella term used to cover a complex phenomenon. Different memory tasks, such as those described in the next section, were now viewed as possibly involving different processes that potentially tapped different memory subsystems. Equally important was the acknowledgment that a single memory task such as a recognition test might not be a pure measure of any one memory system, but be jointly determined by two or more subsystems.

At the retrieval phase of a memory experiment, subjects are given clear instructions that they should try to remember some designated experience. Such methods can be termed *explicit memory tests* in order to distinguish them from *implicit tests* (described below) in which the subject is led to believe that the task is for some purpose other than the evaluation of memory. One way of characterizing differences among various explicit memory tests is in terms of the type and amount of information (the retrieval cues) available at the time when retrieval is attempted.

Recognition Tests

In these tests, subjects are presented with a replica of the previously presented material so that the experimenter-provided retrieval information can be thought of as a "copy cue" (Tulving, 1983). In a *free-choice* ("yes-no") recognition test, items are presented singly as a randomly ordered sequence of old and new items (usually, but not necessarily, an equal number of each) and subjects are required to judge each item as either old ("yes") or new ("no"). In a *forced-choice* recognition test, each previously studied ("old") item is presented, grouped with a small number of not previously presented items called distractors, or "new" items, and the subject is asked to choose which of these items is old. Thus in a three-alternative forced-choice test, subjects are shown sets of three items, one of which is old, the other two new.

Recognition tests, especially free-choice recognition, pose a difficulty that is commonly construed as a problem of guessing or of chance success. Although the difficulty is a genuine one, concepts such as guessing are misleading and do not provide the basis of an adequate solution, at least in the case of free-choice recognition. For example, in a yes-no recognition test in which half the test items are old and half new, it is tempting to consider the chance success rate to be 50%. After all, this would be the expected success rate of a subject who had no memory and simply guessed at random. To see why this is a dangerous oversimplification, consider the four possible outcomes involved in the yes-no test as set out below.

	Test Item Type	
Decision	Item Old	Item New
"Yes"	hit	false alarm
"No"	miss	correct rejection

When a yes-no decision must be made about each individual item, the subject's confidence in the correctness of the decision will typically be less than 100%, and so a response criterion must be set. How confident must a subject be that an item is in fact old before answering "yes"? As with any such binary decision under uncertainty, the decision maker must set some subjective criterion that will strike a balance between correct recognition of old items (hits) and the incorrect identification of new items as old (false alarms). Thus the hit rate reflects not only the degree of familiarity of old items but also the strictness of the subjective decision criterion that a subject sets for responding "old." A very lax criterion for calling an item old could yield a high hit rate even if recognition memory is poor, a situation that would be reflected in a correspondingly high false alarm rate. How does one compare a hit rate of .8 with one of .6 if the former is associated with a false alarm rate of .5 and the latter with one of .25? This confounding of familiarity with a decision criterion makes the use of hit rates alone a dubious measure of recognition memory, especially if there is any possibility that different conditions within an experiment might encourage different criteria and thus different false alarm rates.

A number of solutions have been proposed to solve this problem posed by the confounding of memory and decision processes. The simplest of these is to use as a measure of recognition performance the difference between the hit and false alarm rates. Notice that with this measure, the hit rate of .8 in the preceding paragraph reflects poorer recognition than the hit rate of .6. Insofar as the concept of chance success has any legitimacy in this situation, it is reflected in the false alarm rate, which in general will not be 50%. A hit rate of .4 with an associated false alarm rate of .2 reflects recognition performance well above chance, whereas a hit rate of .6 associated with a false alarm rate of .6 reflects chance-level performance—a complete failure to discriminate between old and new test items.

Some experimental manipulations produce systematic changes in the relation between hits and false alarms, and in these cases it may be appropriate to report these two measures separately. For example, a number of variables (such as word frequency) have opposite effects on hit and false alarm rates: low frequency words produce higher hit rates and lower false alarm rates than do high frequency words, a phenomenon known as the "mirror effect" (see Glanzer & Adams, 1985, 1990).

The most sophisticated of the various proposals for measuring recognition memory involves the application of the theory of signal detection. Banks (1970) describes the basic rationale for this application. The task of correctly recognizing an old item is construed as formally equivalent to identifying an auditory signal presented in a noisy background. Each new item is assumed to elicit a degree of familiarity that is "noise" only, whereas each old item is assumed to elicit a degree of familiarity that is noise plus an increment in familiarity attributable to the item's prior presentation. Familiarity is considered a random variable and the familiarity associated with signal and noise items is treated as two overlapping distributions on a familiarity continuum. It is then possible to derive an estimate of the degree of separation of these signal and noise distributions as a measure of recognition performance. This measure, usually written as d' ("d-prime"), is an index of the discriminability of old and new items that is independent of changes in the balance between hits and false alarms caused by shifts in the response criterion.

The application of signal detection theory is based on a number of assumptions, some of which may be questionable (Lockhart and Murdock, 1970). Such assumptions are usually evaluated by plotting receiver-operating characteristics (ROCs). ROCs are plots that show hits (y-axis value) as a function of false alarms (x-axis value) for different decision criteria. There are several methods for obtaining such plots, but the most economical way is to have subjects rate the confidence of their yes-no decision and treat this confidence level as a decision criterion. For example, a point on the plot corresponding to a very strict criterion can be obtained by considering as hits and false alarms only those "yes" responses receiving the highest confidence rating. Other ROC points corresponding to more lax criteria can be obtained using lower confidence levels to define hits and false alarms. The shape of the resulting ROC can then be used to evaluate assumptions such as whether the signal and noise distributions have equal variances.

The application of signal detection theory has been presented at some length for two reasons. One is that it provides an example of how simple theoretical concepts have been used to provide a solution to a problem of measurement. The second reason is less obvious. The assumptions underlying signal detection theory are usually thought to have only nuisance value, and are often given as arguments against its use. However, there are circumstances under which evaluation of these assumptions can be turned to the researcher's advantage, such as when competing theories make different predictions for the shape of the ROCs. Under these circumstances the form of the ROC can become a valuable diagnostic tool in evaluating theoretical claims such as the hypothesis that more than a single process underlies recognition memory. Yonelinas (1994, 1997), for example, has used ROCs to argue for a two-process theory of recognition. The two processes are simple familiarity not consciously attached to any specific prior event, and the conscious recollection of the prior event. The theory is described elsewhere (Kelley & Jacoby, chapter 14) but is mentioned here as an example of the close interrelationship between memory measurement and memory theory.

The decision process does not pose a serious problem in the case of forced-choice recognition tests because, when presented with two or more alternatives (one of which is a previously presented item), it is reasonable to assume that the subject makes an unbiased judgment from among the alternatives. Insofar as any bias exists, its most likely source is the order of presentation of the alternatives, a bias that randomization of the order will effectively eliminate. Although simple assumptions make it possible to apply a correction for chance success, such corrections are usually unnecessary because in the typical memory experiment there is no interest in the absolute level of performance, but only in differences among conditions. Any correction for chance success will not influence the ordering of differences among conditions.

Performance on either a free- or forced-choice recognition test will depend on the nature of the distractors and, in particular, on their relation to the old items with respect to some dimension such as semantic similarity, or to the overlap of perceptual features. For example, old items that are paired with synonyms as distractors pose a more difficult memory test than if paired with distractors that are semantically unrelated. In planning experiments, care must therefore be taken to ensure that, across conditions, distractors do not differ in their similarity to old items, a requirement that can be difficult to enforce if the comparison is between different stimulus types such as words versus pictures or faces.

A measurement difficulty that can arise with accuracy-based measures of recognition is the occurrence of performance levels that are too high to allow the potential effects of an experimental manipulation to show themselves. To overcome these ceiling effects, response times might replace accuracy as the primary response measure. Routine use of response times requires very high accuracy levels in that typically only response times for correct responses are used. However, even with very high accuracy levels, performance is usually not entirely error free. Under these circumstances speed-accuracy tradeoffs can pose a problem, if error rates differ among conditions. A speed-accuracy tradeoff exists if faster responding is associated with higher error rates. For this reason, as well as because response times are typically based on correct responses only, it is important that research using response times should also report the error rates for each condition.

The direct use of confidence ratings provides another alternative to accuracy judgments. In one version of this method, subjects make an old/new judgment and then supplement this decision with a rating of how confident they are about the accuracy of their judgment. An alternative version is to dispense with the old/new decision, and have subjects rate all items (both old and new) in terms of their confidence that the item was old. Both these methods are based on the assumption that such confidence judgments are positively correlated with accuracy. Although this assumption is often justified (Murdock, 1974), it is not difficult to arrange conditions so that high confidence becomes associated with low accuracy (e.g., Chandler, 1994) and there is ample evidence that real-world memories can display such a negative relation (e.g., Loftus, 1979; Neisser & Harsch, 1992).

In review, the measurement of recognition memory is not a simple matter. For straightforward applications requiring a single index of performance level, a measure such as hits minus false alarms for the yes-no procedure, or proportion correct for the forced-choice procedure, will usually be satisfactory. There is little to recommend the routine use of signal detection theory outside the context of a model within which the assumptions underlying the calculation of d' can be evaluated. However, in the context of theories that explicitly model memory and decision processes, more sophisticated measures such as d' and ROCs may not only be justified, but essential to the appropriate evaluation of the model. Finally, for cases in which experimental manipulations produce systematic changes in the relation between hits and false alarms, it may be appropriate to report these two measures separately.

Cued Recall

Memory researchers have devised a large number of tasks in which subjects are presented with a cue and required to recall an item associated with that cue. The cues are described as intra-list cues if they appear along with the target item during the presentation phase of the experiment and extra-list cues if they do not. Paired-associate paradigms provide the classic example of intra-list cues. In these paradigms, subjects study pairs of items and are instructed that they will be given one member of the pair and asked to recall the other. An example of extra-list cues would be labels of categories to which the to-be-recalled items belong, the labels not having been previously presented. This method was introduced by Tulving and Pearlstone (1966).

Intra-list cues can serve a dual role. In addition to providing information that potentially aids retrieval, such cues can serve to specify a designated target item. One methodological purpose of designating an item in this way is to eliminate or reduce the potential interfering effect of recalling an item on other items yet to be recalled ("output interference") by requiring the subject to recall only the cued item. In this case the cue is typically termed a probe. Classic examples are the partial report method used by Sperling (1960) to study very short-term visual memory and the procedure used by Waugh and Norman (1965) to study short-term verbal memory.

Serial and Free Recall

In serial recall, subjects are instructed to recall items in the order in which they were presented, whereas in free recall subjects are instructed to recall items in any order they choose. In both cases the only experimenter-provided cue is the general instruction designating the set of to-be-recalled items.

A much-used example of serial recall is the digit-span test found in many standard test batteries. Subjects are read a sequence of digits and immediately asked to recall the sequence in the same order. Digit span is the maximum list length that can be correctly recalled. Although less common, the same procedure can be used to measure span for other materials, such as letters of the alphabet or words.

In free recall, the performance measure commonly used is the number (or proportion) of items recalled. If the subject's recall attempt is allowed to begin immediately after the material has been presented, then recall levels will vary according to the serial position of the item in the list. In particular, the last few items to have been presented will be recalled at a much higher level than items in the middle of the list, a phenomenon known as the recency effect. As a performance measure, therefore, the number (or proportion) of items recalled is an aggregation (or averaging) over recall levels that vary systematically with serial position of an item's presentation. The usual interpretation of the recency effect is that the higher recall level of end-of-list items reflects the output of the contents of working or short-term memory, so that one method of removing the recency effect from the response measure is to delay recall. Another is to treat the last five or so items as nonlist or "buffer" items and ignore their presence in the recall protocol. A more sophisticated method is described by Craik (1968). In this procedure the recall protocol is partitioned into two components, one consisting of items recalled from working memory, the other items recalled from a longer term memory. Tulving and Colotla (1970) used this partitioning method to clarify the processes underlying the free recall of multilingual lists, providing a further example of the close relationship between theory and measurement.

Prospective Remembering

Prospective memory tasks require subjects to recall and perform some action at a designated future time. An everyday example is the instruction to buy bread on the way home from work. With such tasks, even the instruction to remember is absent, at least at the point in time when remembering is required, making it the least cue-supported form of recall of those we have considered. Various methods have been used to designate the point at which the act of remembering is to be performed, but a helpful distinction is between time-based and event-based tasks (see Einstein and McDaniel, 1996). In time-based prospective remembering, an action must be performed at a specified time in the future, such as remembering to turn off the burner in ten minutes. In event-based prospective remembering, an action must be performed contingent on the occurrence of some other event, such as remembering to follow an instruction to lock the door on the way out.

Implicit Remembering

All the methods considered thus far have used explicit instructions as to the nature of the memory task and in this sense they all entail what has been termed explicit remembering: a conscious effort to fulfill the instructional demand to remember. Implicit tasks are those in which memory is revealed in the absence of any instructions to remember, possibly without the subject being aware that a form of remembering has occurred.

An example of a task used to investigate implicit memory is word-fragment completion. Subjects are shown a word fragment such as _ r _ c o _ _ l _ and asked to state the word of which it is a fragment (crocodile). As a method of studying implicit remembering, the procedure follows the usual three phases of memory experiments: study, retention interval, and test. However, subjects are typically not informed that the experiment has anything to do with remembering. A list of words is shown and subjects are instructed to perform some implicit task, such as judging the word on some attribute. Following the retention interval, subjects are given a series of word fragments; some are fragments of words previously shown, others of words not previously shown. The measure of implicit remembering is the degree of superiority of fragment completion for previously presented words over words not previously presented.

The facilitation of a task such as word-fragment completion through implicit memory is termed *priming*. In the example just given, the response is primed by the prior presentation of the word itself. The presentation of "crocodile" facilitates the response crocodile to the fragment _ r _ c o _ _ l _. Such priming is termed *repetition priming* to distinguish it from other forms of priming, such as *associative priming* (prior presentation of "doctor" facilitates the response "nurse") or *conceptual priming* (prior presentation of "dog" facilitates the response "beagle").

Other tasks can be substituted for word-fragment completion and Toth (chapter 16) provides a comprehensive list. In some of these tasks (such as word-fragment completion) there may be more than one correct completion. In such cases, care must be taken to ensure that subjects respond with the first word that comes to mind. If subjects attempt to complete a word fragment by consciously trying to recall an item from the previously presented list, then the procedure has changed from one of implicit recall to a form of explicit cued recall.

No matter how careful the instructions, any implicit task is likely to involve both conscious recollection and implicit memory. Jacoby (1991) introduced a method called process dissociation aimed at separating these components. This separation cannot be achieved using the normal priming procedure because with this procedure both conscious recollection and implicit memory exert an influence in the same direction: the completion of the stem with a word previously seen. The novel aspect of Jacoby's method is to include a condition (called an *exclusion test*) in which subjects are instructed to complete a fragment or stem with a word that was *not* previously shown. The two processes now exert opposite influences, with conscious recollection leading to the suppression of previously shown words, and automatic responding leading to the unwitting use of previously shown words. Under this exclusion condition any remaining priming effect can be attributed to implicit memory alone. The process dissociation method compares performance on this exclusion test with performance in an *inclusion test*, which is assumed to involve both explicit and implicit processes. Typical instructions for the inclusion test are for subjects to use words from the study list to complete the stem or fragment or, if no words are recalled, to use the first word to come to mind. For a fuller discussion of this method and its critics, see Jacoby (1998) and Kelley and Jacoby (chapter 14).

Encoding Conditions

A vast body of memory research has involved the manipulation of the processing that occurs in the study or encoding phase of an experienced event. Various methods exploit the fact that such encoding will be jointly determined by three broad factors: induced cognitive state, task demands, and the nature of the stimulus material.

Induced Cognitive or Mental State

The classic example of a manipulation of this kind is the study of proactive interference (PI), which examines the influence of prior experience on the encoding of the to-be-remembered material. A general paradigm to study proactive interference compares memory for some target event across conditions that vary in the nature and/or the number of events that preceded the presentation of the target event. A good example of this kind of manipulation is the phenomenon known as "release from PI" (Wickens, Born, & Allen, 1963). If subjects are given a sequence of trials, each requiring the recall of a set of consonants, then recall level drops off from one trial to the next, a decline attributed to the buildup of proactive interference. If the task suddenly switches to digits, then the recall level returns to its initial level, only to decline again as the digit trials continue.

Events immediately prior to the study phase can also induce a mental state that will influence encoding in a way that facilitates subsequent remembering. Bransford and Johnson (1972), for example, showed that prior information that aids the comprehension of a subsequently studied passage improved later memory for that passage.

Another class of methods aimed at influencing the encoding process involves the manipulation of the current mental state of the subject. Mood at the time of encoding has been manipulated through various means, including reading passages, seeing film clips, or listening to music, aimed at depressing or elating the subject's mood (See Eich, 1995, for a review). Other experiments have manipulated arousal level, alcohol and marijuana intoxication, and so forth. Perhaps the most exotic manipulation is that of Godden and Baddeley (1975), who had divers learn material either while underwater or while sitting on land. Many of these "mental state" experiments have simultaneously manipulated the same mental state at the time of retrieval in order to evaluate the state dependency of memory. With state dependency the question of interest is not whether a given mental state improves or lowers memory performance, but whether memory performance is better if the mental state at retrieval matches that at encoding.

Task Demands

In a typical memory experiment, subjects are instructed to "study" or "attend to" the events they are about to experience for the purpose of a subsequent test of their memory of those events. The nature of this memory test may or may not be explained to the subject. In this regard it should be noted that the available evidence (for example, Tversky, 1973) indicates that encoding processes are influenced by the form of the memory test (recognition versus recall) that subjects expect.

Instructions that warn subjects of a future memory test are often referred to as "intentional" and distinguished from "incidental" instructions under which subjects perform some orienting or cover task and remain uninformed about any subsequent memory test. Craik and Tulving (1975), for example, used a set of orienting tasks that is prototypical of what has come to be known as the "levels of processing manipulation." In their procedure subjects saw a series of items, each preceded by a question asking about either the word's appearance ("Is the word typed in capital letters?"), its sound (Does the word rhyme with "blame"?), or its meaning (Is the word something hot?). It is worth noting that if the orienting task is fully demanding of attention, then whether or not the subject is also forewarned of a subsequent memory test has little or no effect on recognition or recall.

Many other processing instructions have been investigated. The effect of instructions to form visual images has been much studied, as have various other traditional mnemonic devices. Various orienting tasks have been used. For example, Bower and Karlin (1974) showed subjects photographs of men and women and asked them to judge the person's sex (male or female) or honesty (above or below average). Judgments of honesty led to better recognition than judgments of sex. Slamecka and Graf (1978) showed that if subjects generated a word to a cue (for example, a synonym to the word *rapid* that begins with the letter *f*) memory was better than if they simply read the right hand word in the pair *rapid–fast*. This difference is called the *generation effect*. From a methodological perspective, the major purpose of comparing the effects of different instructions and orienting tasks is to use such differences as clues as to why certain forms of processing lead to better remembering than others. Why should semantic-level processing, imagery formation, or word generation yield better remembering than that obtained with other orienting tasks?

Another method that manipulates task demands requires the subject to engage in an independent secondary task while studying the to-be-remembered material. This dual or concurrent task methodology has a long history dating back to early research in divided attention (Cherry, 1953). As a method for understanding memory, its usual purpose is to examine the effects on remembering of restricting the subject's processing capacity. In the dichotic listening version of this methodology, subjects might be instructed to attend to a message being delivered to one ear and then be tested for memory of the independent message delivered to the other (unattended) ear. As a further example of a method of reducing processing capacity Craik (1982) used a concurrent task that required subjects to monitor a sequence of digits and report whenever they heard a sequence of three odd numbers. Baddeley (1986) and Baddeley and Hitch (1974) provide examples of the systematic use of dual-task methodology in the development of a model for working memory. The concurrent task can be chosen so as to interfere selectively with the processing of stimuli. For example, having subjects engage in concurrent articulation reduces the capacity of the articulatory rehearsal loop of Baddeley's working memory model.

Materials

In their effort to understand how encoding processes influence remembering, memory research has exploited the fact that the form of processing will be constrained by the nature of the materials. A broad distinction has been made between verbal and nonverbal materials, but much finer distinctions have been drawn within each of these domains. Within the broad class of verbal materials, memory experiments have used digits, letters, words, sentences, paragraphs, and longer prose passages. Various attributes of words have been studied: frequency, length, form class, and concrete versus abstract, to name only the most common. The modality of presentation of verbal materials (visual versus auditory) has been much studied. In the domain of nonverbal materials the major areas of research have been memory for pictures, faces, geometric forms, motor skills, odors, and performed actions.

From the viewpoint of methodology, the purpose of this vast body of research is not merely to catalogue the properties of the memory system as they apply to each of these materials. Rather, it is to illuminate a general theory of memory by exploiting the pattern of similarities and differences that are observed as materials are varied. Engelkamp and Zim-

mer (1994) provide an extensive review of this research strategy.

Conditions in the Retention Interval

For this phase of a memory experiment the two major conditions of interest have been the duration of the retention interval and the nature of events that occur during this interval. As a method of studying memory, the former is straightforward and needs little exposition except to note that formal studies of memory have used retention intervals ranging from zero seconds to at least 50 years. Less obvious are methods concerned with the impact of events that occur during this interval. Such methods fall into two classes: one class includes methods aimed at rehearsal prevention, the other is the systematic manipulation of the type of event occurring within the interval.

Rehearsal Prevention

A classic example of rehearsal-prevention methodology is the Brown-Peterson paradigm, so-called because of its independent introduction by Brown (1958) and Peterson and Peterson (1959). In this procedure the presentation of a study item (3 letters or 3 words, for example) is followed by a signal, at which point the subject begins performing some independent distractor task, such as rapidly counting backwards by 3's from a given number, until a second signal indicates that counting should end and recall of the study items attempted. Many distractor tasks other than backward counting have been used; the important point is that, whatever task is used, it should fully occupy processing capacity during the retention interval so that any rehearsal of the to-be-remembered items is impossible, a point demonstrated by Posner and Rossman (1965). Sequentially dependent tasks, such as backward counting, that demand keeping track of a series are particularly effective in this regard in that shifts of attention from the task to rehearsing an item will often lead to errors in the sequential task that can be detected by the experimenter.

Recoding Paradigms

The purpose of retention interval tasks such as backward counting is simply one of rehearsal prevention, and the task content bears no specific relation to the content of the to-be-remembered material. There are, however, methods in which the content of the retention interval is chosen to produce selective effects on the remembered event. Tulving (1983) refers to such methods as the recoding paradigm. The paradigm compares the memory performance in a group that has witnessed a selected interpolated event with performance in a group that has not. In some circumstances, it is appropriate to add a third control group that experiences only the interpolated event.

Traditional studies of retroactive interference (RI) fall within this domain. In the standard RI paradigm, subjects study pairs of items (designated A-B) with the aim of recalling B when given A as the cue. The experimental condition presents for study (as a potential source of retroactive interference) an A-C pair, interpolated between the original study of the A-B pair and the subsequent cued-recall test of B. There are several variations of this test procedure. One variation, misleadingly called modified free recall (MFR), allows subjects to recall either B or C to the A cue, a procedure that was itself modified (and labeled MMFR) by Barnes and Underwood (1959) to allow the recall of both B and C responses.

Not all methods involving the manipulation of events within the retention interval have been interested in simple forgetting. An interpolated representation of the to-be-remembered stimulus, or an interpolated recall opportunity, can be thought of as retention-interval manipulations, and there are many studies that have examined these factors, especially the number and temporal spacing of repetitions and of test trials. Other studies have focused on the influence that retention interval events can have on the accuracy of remembering rather than on the amount of forgetting. A much-cited example of such research is the work of Loftus on the accuracy of eyewitness testimony (Loftus 1975, 1979; Loftus, Miller, & Burns, 1978). The basic methodology is to insert misleading information into the retention interval and then evaluate the impact of this information on subsequent memory of the original event. For example, in one experiment subjects were shown a car ignoring a stop sign and then asked about its speed when it ignored the *yield* sign. In a subsequent forced-choice recognition test of the original scene, subjects were presented with a choice among a stop sign, a yield sign, or a one-way sign. Most mistakenly chose the yield sign over the other two; moreover when told they were wrong and given a second choice, as many subjects chose the (never-seen) one-way sign as chose the originally seen stop sign.

Another retention-interval condition is known as directed forgetting (Bjork, 1970). In such tasks, some of the presented items are designated as items to be remembered and others as items to be forgotten. Note that the designation follows the item's presentation, so that at the time of study, subjects do not know the item's status. Thus any differences in subsequent remembering cannot be attributed to differences in encoding but only to events within the retention interval. The directed forgetting paradigm has been used to study inhibitory processes in memory (see Bjork, 1989; Zacks, Radvansky, & Hasher, 1996 as examples).

Interactions among the Three Phases

The manipulation of conditions at encoding, during the retention interval, and for retrieval has been used to assemble a vast body of data. However, as previously mentioned, research methods have increasingly focused on what can be learned from studying the interactions associated with particular combinations of conditions at the three phases of a memory experiment. For example, the chapter by Brown and Craik (chapter 6) describes various encoding-retrieval interactions. The study of such interactions can advance theoretical understanding and illustrates why the experimental manipulation of each phase in isolation will at best lead to an incomplete picture of underlying processes, and at worst one that is seriously distorted.

A particular form of interaction known as functional dissociation is of special methodological interest in the identification of memory systems. The general logic of functional dissociation is that if two memory systems are functionally distinct, then there should exist variables that influence one system and exert either no influence on the other (called a single dissociation), or exert an influence in the opposite direction (called a double dissociation). Dissociation has been used to support distinction between implicit and explicit memory systems, between long-term and

short-term memory (e.g., Shallice, 1988), between semantic versus episodic memory (Tulving 1983), and for distinctions between cognitive functions in other areas such as
language comprehension.

As several critics have pointed out (e.g.,
Dunn & Kirsner, 1988), single or even double
dissociation does not logically exclude single-
system accounts. However, evidence of dissociations does greatly strengthen the case for
distinct systems, especially when it is obtained across many different manipulations.
Moreover, functional dissociations can be subject to further scrutiny through the use of imaging techniques such as PET and fMRI that
can monitor brain activity and establish
whether functional dissociations are validated
by corresponding differences in patterns of
neural activity.

The Use of Natural Variables

As part of its methodological armory, memory
research has exploited a class of variables having to do with individual, group, and species
differences. Rather than being manipulated by
the experimenter, variables such as age or
neurological state reflect existing attributes of
the subject. Memory research has been greatly
enhanced by the investigation of differences
in memory performance between individuals
or groups who differ in various ways. Among
the most frequently studied natural variables
have been expertise, age, and memory deficits
attributable to various neurological states. Although each of these variables is of considerable scientific interest and practical significance in its own right, methodologically such
natural variables are important because of
what they can contribute to a general theory
of memory. Three examples will illustrate this
point.

Expertise

Perhaps the most-studied area of expertise and
memory has been chess. Chess experts show
superior memory for chess positions compared to weak players, but only if the board
positions correspond to plausible game positions. If the chess pieces are assigned randomly to the board, then the superiority of the
experts disappears (de Groot 1965, 1966). As
well as documenting the memory abilities of
chess experts, this pattern of results tells us
something about the general relation of exper-

tise and memory. It indicates that memory superiority is limited to the area of expertise and
that the impact of expertise on memory lies in
the expert's ability to extract meaningful patterns from stimuli that to the novice are effectively random.

Age

Age changes in memory, especially over early
childhood and in old age, have been investigated extensively. The study of preverbal infant memory demands specialized methodology using indirect or implicit measures based
on habituation, novelty preference, and conditioning. Moscovitch (1984) provides a convenient source of examples of this methodology.
Moscovitch (1985) has argued that such studies validate the distinction between episodic
and other memory systems, episodic memory
being a late system that begins to emerge only
after 8–9 months. By showing differential
rates of decline across different memory tests,
studies of memory in the elderly have also
demonstrated the validity of distinctions between different memory systems.

Brain Damage

Warrington and Weiskrantz (1968, 1970) compared amnesic patients with normal subjects
using the word-fragment completion task.
They found that whereas amnesic patients recognized few words under standard explicit instructions, priming in the fragment completion task did not differ from that of the normal
subjects. The significance of this result goes
beyond the documentation of an interesting
feature of amnesia. It suggests (although in itself does not establish) that explicit and implicit tests of recognition involve (at least in
part) distinguishable memory systems.

Concluding Comments

The beginning of this chapter described the
challenge of developing a behavioral methodology that would support inferences about the
unobservable elements of memory systems
and processes. There has been notable progress, but only future research will reveal the
extent to which this challenge has been successfully met. Although neuropsychology and
brain imaging technology will play an increasingly important role in this ongoing evalua-

tion, these areas themselves will continue to depend on the development and refinement of behavioral methodology.

Acknowledgment I thank Joan Grusec for her comments on an earlier version of the manuscript.

References

Baddeley, A. D. (1986). *Working memory*. Oxford: Clarendon Press.

Baddeley, A. D., and Hitch, G. (1974). Working memory. In G. H. Bower (Ed.), *The psychology of learning and motivation*. New York: Academic Press.

Banks, W. P. (1970). Signal detection theory and human memory. *Psychological Bulletin, 74*, 81–99.

Barnes, J. M., & Underwood, B. J. (1959). "Fate" of first-list associations in transfer memory. *Journal of Experimental Psychology, 58*, 97–105.

Bartlett, F. C. (1932). *Remembering*. Cambridge: Cambridge University Press.

Bjork, R. A. (1970). Positive forgetting: The noninterference of items intentionally forgotten. *Journal of Verbal Learning and Verbal Behavior, 9*, 225–268.

Bjork, R. A. (1989). Retrieval inhibition as an adaptive mechanism in human memory. In H. L. Roediger, III & F. I. M. Craik (Eds.), *Varieties of memory and consciousness: Essays in honour of Endel Tulving* (pp. 309–330). Hillsdale, NJ: Erlbaum.

Bower, G. H., & Karlin, M. B. (1974). Depth of processing pictures of faces and recognition memory. *Journal of Experimental Psychology, 103*, 751–757.

Bransford, J. D., & Johnson, M. K. (1972). Contextual prerequisites for understanding: Some investigations of comprehension and recall. *Journal of Verbal Learning and Verbal Behavior, 11*, 717–726.

Brown, J. (1958). Some tests of the decay theory of immediate memory. *Quarterly Journal of Experimental Psychology, 10*, 12–21.

Chandler, C. (1994). Studying related pictures can reduce accuracy, but increase confidence, in a modified recognition test. *Memory & Cognition, 22*,145–174.

Cherry, E. C. (1953). Some experiments on the recognition of speech with one and two ears. *Journal of the Acoustical Society of America, 25*, 975–979.

Conway, M. A. (1990). *Autobiographical memory: An introduction*. Philadelphia: Open University Press.

Craik, F. I. M. (1968). Two components in free recall. *Journal of Verbal Learning and Verbal Behavior, 7*, 997–1004.

Craik, F. I. M. (1982). Selective changes in encoding as a function of reduced processing capacity. In F. Klix, J. Hoffman, & E. van der Meer (Eds.), *Cognitive research in psychology* (pp. 152–161). Berlin, Germany: Deutscher Verlag der Wissenschaffen.

Craik, F. I. M., & Tulving, E. (1975). Depth of processing and the retention of words in episodic memory. *Journal of Experimental Psychology: General, 104*, 269–294.

De Groot, A. (1965). *Thought and choice in chess*. The Hague: Mouton.

De Groot, A. (1966). Perception and memory versus thought: Some old ideas and recent findings. In B. Kleinmuntz (Ed.), *Problem solving* (pp. 19–50). New York: John Wiley.

Dunn, J. C., & Kirsner, K. (1988). Discovering functionally independent mental processes: The principle of reversed association. *Psychological Review, 95*, 91–101.

Ebbinghaus, H. (1885). *Über das Gedächtnis*. Leipzig: Duncker und Humblot.

Eich, E. (1995). Mood as a mediator of place dependent memory. *Journal of Experimental Psychology: General, 124*, 293–308.

Einstein, G. O., & McDaniel, M. A. (1996). Remembering to do things: Remembering a forgotten topic. In D. Herrmann et al. (Eds.), *Basic and applied memory research* (Vol. 2, pp. 123–138). Mahwah, NJ: Erlbaum.

Engelkamp, J., & Zimmer, H. D. (1994). *Human memory: A multimodal approach*. Toronto: Hogrefe & Huber.

Glanzer, M., & Adams, J. K. (1985). The mirror effect in recognition memory. *Memory and Cognition, 13*, 8–20.

Glanzer, M., & Adams, J. K. (1990). The mirror effect in recognition memory: Data and theory. *Journal of Experimental Psychology: Learning, Memory, and Cognition, 16*, 5–16.

Godden, D. R., & Baddeley, A. D. (1975). Context dependent memory in two natural environments: On land and under water. *British Journal of Psychology, 66*, 325–332.

Jacoby, L. L. (1991). A process dissociation framework: Separating automatic from intentional uses of memory. *Journal of Memory and Language, 30*, 513–541.

Jacoby, L. L. (1998). Invariance in automatic influences of memory: Toward a user's guide for the process-dissociation procedure. *Journal of Experimental Psychology: Human Learning and Memory, 24*, 3–26.

Lockhart, R. S., & Murdock B. B., Jr. (1970). Memory and the theory of signal detection. *Psychological Bulletin, 74*, 100–109.

Loftus, E. F. (1975). Leading questions and the eyewitness report. *Cognitive Psychology, 7*, 560–572.

Loftus, E. F. (1979). *Eyewitness testimony.* Cambridge, MA: Harvard University Press.

Loftus, E. F., Miller, D. G., & Burns, H. J. (1978). Semantic integration of verbal information into visual memory. *Journal of Experimental Psychology: Human Learning and Memory, 4*, 19–31.

Moscovitch, M. (Ed.). (1984). *Infant memory: Its relation to normal and pathological memory in human and other animals.* New York: Plenum.

Moscovitch, M. (1985). Memory from infancy to old age: Implications for theories of normal and pathological memory. *Annals of the New York Academy of Science, 444*, 78–96.

Murdock, B. B., Jr. (1974). *Human memory: Theory and data.* Hillsdale, NJ: Erlbaum.

Neisser, U., & Harsch, N. (1992). Phantom flashbulbs: False recollections of hearing the news about Challenger. In E. Winograd & U. Neisser (Eds.), *Affect and accuracy in recall: Studies in "flashbulb" memories* (pp. 9–31). Cambridge: Cambridge University Press.

Peterson, L. R., & Peterson, M. J. (1959). Short-term retention of individual items. *Journal of Experimental Psychology, 58*, 193–198.

Posner, M. I., & Rossman, E. (1965). Effect of size and location of informational transforms on short-term memory. *Journal of Experimental Psychology, 70*, 496–505.

Schacter, D. L. (Ed.). (1995). *Memory distortion: How minds, brains, and societies reconstruct the past.* Cambridge, MA: Harvard University Press.

Schacter, D. L. (1996). *Searching for memory: The brain, the mind, and the past.* New York: Basic Books.

Shallice, T. (1988). *From neuropsychology to mental structure.* Cambridge: Cambridge University Press.

Slamecka, N. J., & Graf, P. (1978). The generation effect: Delineation of a phenomenon. *Journal of Experimental Psychology: Human Learning and Memory, 4*, 592–604.

Sperling, G. (1960). The information available in brief visual presentations. *Psychological Monographs, 74*, (Whole No. 498).

Tulving, E. (1983). *Elements of episodic memory.* Oxford: Oxford University Press.

Tulving, E., & Colotla, V. A. (1970). Free recall of trilingual lists. *Cognitive Psychology, 1*, 86–98.

Tulving, E., & Pearlstone, Z. (1966). Availability versus accessibility of information in memory for words. *Journal of Verbal Learning and Verbal Behavior, 5*, 381–391.

Tversky, B. (1973). Encoding processes in recognition and recall. *Cognitive Psychology, 5*, 275–287.

Warrington, E., & Weiskrantz, L. (1968). A study of learning and retention in amnesic patients. *Neuropsychologia, 6*, 283–291.

Warrington, E., & Weiskrantz, L. (1970). Amnesia: Consolidation or retrieval? *Nature, 228*, 628–630.

Waugh, N. C., & Norman, D. A. (1965). Primary memory. *Psychological Review, 72*, 89–104.

Wickens, D. D., Born, D. G., & Allen, K. C. (1963). Proactive inhibition and item similarity in short-term memory. *Journal of Verbal Learning and Verbal Behavior, 2*, 440–445.

Yonelinas, A. P. (1994). Receiver operating characteristics in recognition memory: Evidence for a dual-process model. *Journal of Experimental Psychology: Learning, Memory, and Cognition, 20*, 1341–1354.

Yonelinas, A. P. (1997). Recognition memory ROCs for item and associative information: The contribution of recollection and familiarity. *Memory & Cognition, 25*, 747–763.

Zacks, R. T., Radvansky, G., & Hasher, L. (1996). Studies of directed forgetting in older adults. *Journal of Experimental Psychology: Learning, Memory, and Cognition, 22*, 143–156.

4

Contingency Analyses of Memory

MICHAEL J. KAHANA

Human memory subsumes a multitude of processes that undoubtedly rely on many different types of information, operations, and systems. Recognition of the complexity of human memory has driven scholars to broaden the scope of memory tasks that are studied, and to consider not only how a given memory task is performed but also how different kinds of memory tasks are interrelated. It is the study of the similarities and differences among memory tasks that may help us develop predictive models of the underlying information, operations, and systems that support this vital human capacity. The study of human memory thus requires techniques both for dissecting the information-processing components of a single task and for examining the relations between information-processing components of different tasks.

One standard method for separating components both within and between memory tasks is to look for experimental factors that have different effects on different memory tasks, or on different aspects of subjects' performance in a given task. This kind of task analysis has yielded numerous examples of parallel effects and dissociations among tasks (see Richardson-Klavehn & Bjork, 1988, for a review). Converging evidence for dissociations between memory tasks is taken by some researchers as evidence for the operation of

multiple memory systems (e.g., Nyberg & Tulving, 1996; Schacter & Tulving, 1994; Tulving, 1985).

Dissociations can also be observed within a single task. For example, dissociations between different portions of the serial position curve (e.g., Glanzer & Cunitz, 1966; Murdock, 1962) have been taken as evidence for the distinction between short-term and long-term memory systems. Techniques for performing task analysis with response time data (Sternberg, 1969) have enabled researchers to distinguish between stages of processing that are relatively independent of one another (see Sternberg, 1998, for a review).

This chapter is concerned with another method of task analysis: contingency analyses applied to the outcomes of successive memory tests. This method has been used to examine the correlation between the outcomes of successive memory tests at the level of an individual subject-item (e.g., DaPolito, 1967; Estes, 1960; Tulving & Wiseman, 1975). The correlation between the observed responses reflects, at least in part, the degree to which their memory processes tap common information, operations, and/or systems. Because the responses are usually dichotomous variables (recall of an item on test 1 and on test 2) these correlations are measured using a 2×2 contingency table. Correlations derived from contingency tables are susceptible to all of the potential con-foundings that face correlations between continuous measures. Fears of these potential confoundings have caused many investigators to shy away from using correlational measures to study memory. The position taken in this review is that such avoidance behavior is not well founded, and that these measures can provide information not present in simple measures of memory performance under different conditions.

The chapter is organized into six short sections. The first two sections briefly discuss functional and correlational approaches to provide a context for the discussion of contingency analyses. The fourth presents three applications of the use of contingency analyses in memory research. The next section reviews the controversy over the use of contingency analyses. Finally, the last section offers a summary and some concluding thoughts.

Functional Approaches

In laboratory memory experiments, the basic unit of information is a subject item in a given experimental condition. Under particular retrieval conditions one can ask whether the item is remembered (usually a binary outcome) and how long it takes for the response to be made (response time or RT). In general, RT and accuracy provide complementary but correlated pictures of human behavior (for a discussion of the relation between RT and accuracy in human memory, see Kahana & Loftus, 1999).

Whether or not a target item is remembered depends on (1) the subject, (2) the item, and (3) the experimental condition. In the functional approach, the latter effect is of sole interest. Mean values, computed over many subjects and many items, are compared among conditions and taken as estimates of the "effect" of the manipulated variable. Subject and item differences are typically controlled, either physically or statistically, so that the comparison of performance in one condition with that in another can be made with respect to the independent variable(s) of interest in the experiment. This functional approach teaches us how memory depends on the variables we have manipulated in our experiments.

Comparisons across tasks often reveal interactions. For example, the degree to which a delay between study and test affects retention of a given item is mediated by the kind of memory test employed (e.g., item recognition, fragment completion, free recall). This does not necessarily mean that these different kinds of memory tasks tap different kinds of information. Consider a simple model in which $S(t) = at^{-b}$ defines the strength of each item in memory as a function of time (in this equation, a and b are positive constants). Recognition succeeds when the strength is above a recognition threshold (K_1); recall succeeds when the strength is above a recall threshold (K_2). If $K_1 < K_2$, then there will be a statistical interaction between the retention interval and the kind of test (recognition vs. recall). In this simple model, the interaction results because of the nonlinearity in the forgetting function and not because recognition and recall tap different underlying sources of information.

Correlational Approaches

The correlational approach need not involve manipulating any variables. Rather, one can study the relations between different measures obtained from different tasks, a single task, or even a single response. Consider a single response in a recognition task that asks subjects to make confidence judgments. Murdock and Anderson (1975; see also Koppell, 1977) carefully documented the well-known finding that RT and confidence judgments covary—high-confidence judgments are made faster than low-confidence judgments. This positive correlation is consistent with the view that RT and confidence are both affected by the "strength" of the underlying memory (or, in contemporary terms, the strength of the context-item association).

Within the free-recall task, different aspects of performance are correlated. For example, Tulving (1962, 1966) showed that as subjects learn a list, their recall order becomes increasingly stereotyped (the phenomenon of *subjective organization*). Although plotted as a functional relationship, the experimenter does not directly manipulate either recall probability or subjective organization. Rather, the independent variable, number of study trials, produces correlated effects on both dependent variables.

Examining the correlation between different memory tasks, Kahana and Rizzuto (1999) measured subjects' performance on item-recognition, associative-recognition, and cued-recall tasks. The correlation between item recognition and cued recall was moderate ($r^2 = 0.33$) whereas the correlation between associative recognition and cued recall was high ($r^2 = 0.80$). These subject correlations involve computing an average for each subject across many items. Another correlational technique asks whether the ordering of performance across items in one task or situation is correlated with the ordering of performance across items in another task or situation. If recognition and recall tap common information, we would expect that the correlation across items is positive. For instance, if recognition and recall both tap "strength" but recall requires a higher threshold, we would expect a strong positive correlation across items. Because these techniques involve averaging (across either subjects *or* items), they allow the investigator to compute a Pearson product-moment correlation. Mandler (1959) demonstrated that correlations across subjects and items can often yield very different results. In some cases, correlations across subjects can be positive while correlations across items can be negative. The use of subject and item based correlations is fairly uncommon in memory research (for exceptions, see Rubin, 1981; Underwood, Boruch, & Malmi, 1978).

Contingency Analyses of Successive Tests

Taking this analysis of the recognition-recall relation one step further, we can examine the relation between recognition and recall at the level of individual subject items. To do this, we employ the method of successive tests. In the canonical procedure, subjects study pairs of items (A-B) and are then given two successive tests: item-recognition followed by cued recall. In the item recognition test, the experimenter presents B items from the studied pairs intermixed with nonstudied items (lures). Subjects judge each item as a target or a lure. In the second, cued-recall test, subjects attempt to recall the B items given the A items as cues. The same B items are tested twice—first using a recognition test and then, later, using a recall test. Because we cannot average over subjects or items we compute a *contingency table* from the pairs of outcomes on test 1 and test 2 for each subject item. Table 4.1 gives hypothetical data for successive item-recognition and cued-recall tests. These hypothetical data show the usual advantage for recognition over recall. However, examining the

Table 4.1 Hypothetical data comparing recognition and recall performance for the same subject-items tested successively.

Subject-Item	Test 1 (recognition)	Test 2 (recall)
1	1	0
2	0	0
3	1	1
4	1	0
5	0	0
6	1	0
7	1	1
8	0	1
9	1	1
10	1	0
11	0	0
12	1	0
13	1	1
14	1	0
15	1	1
16	1	0
17	1	0
18	1	1
19	0	0
20	1	0
21	0	1
22	1	1
23	0	0
24	1	1
25	0	0
26	1	1
Mean	0.69	0.42

contingency table allows us to say something stronger. For example, according to a simple strength theory of memory, recognition and recall tap exactly the same information, but recall requires a higher threshold. Strictly speaking, this means that an item that is recalled will always be recognized, making the correlation between recognition and recall, at the level of subject items, exactly one. The hypothetical data in table 4.1, and the real data of Tulving and Thomson (1973), indicate that there is recognition failure of recallable items —contradicting the predictions of strength theory.

Because the test outcomes are binary variables, we compute the subject-item correlation between recognition and recall by tabulating the data in a contingency table. This correlation is often referred to as contingency or dependency, as it is calculated from the cells in a 2 × 2 contingency table. Yule's Q is a popular measure of correlation for 2 × 2 contingency tables (Bishop, Feinberg, & Holland, 1975). Like a standard Pearson correlation, Yule's Q varies from −1.0 (perfect negative correlation) to +1.0 (perfect positive correlation). For a discussion of other correlational measures that are applicable to contingency tables, see Poldrack (1996).

Table 4.2 shows the results of a contingency analysis applied to the hypothetical data in table 4.1. For each subject item, the combination of outcomes on test 1 and test 2 determine the values of the four cells in the contingency table (A, B, C, & D). Yule's Q is given by the equation:

$$Q = \frac{A \times D - B \times C}{A \times D + B \times C}.$$

For the hypothetical data shown in table 4.1, the dependency between the item recognition and cued recall, as measured by Yule's Q, is 0.5. This dependency of 0.5, measured at the level of subject items, does not mean that the correlation across subjects is 0.5 or that the correlation across items is 0.5. As pointed out by Tulving (1985), correlations at the level of subjects, items, and subject items can yield very different values.

This example was chosen because there is a vast literature examining the relation between recognition and recall using the method of successive tests. This literature, first surveyed by Tulving and Wiseman (1975) and more recently reviewed by Nilsson and Gardiner (1993), reveals an invariance: successive-item recognition and cued-recall tasks almost always yield moderate correlations, with Yule's Q rarely deviating from the range 0.3 to 0.75. This makes the successive-testing data inconsistent with a simple strength-threshold theory (Tulving, 1983), and also with certain dis-

tributed memory models (Kahana & Rizzuto, 1999).

Together with Yule's Q, the percent correct for tests 1 and 2 fully characterize the data in our 2 × 2 contingency table. Without the correlational information, the accuracy data would do little to constrain theory. Because theories of memory make claims about the processes acting on a given subject item, it is important to consider not just accuracy data but also the correlation between tests.

The foregoing example illustrates the comparison of tasks using contingencies of outcomes on successive tests. In comparing performance across the two tests, it is important to recognize that the successive tests do not necessarily measure the "same thing." The first measure is of the consequences of study—subject to all the input/output interference effects that may operate on retrieval of individual list items (e.g., Tulving & Arbuckle, 1966). The second measure is affected not only by study and the interpolated conditions but also by the earlier test and its outcome.

One can also analyze contingencies across successive trials of the same task. This approach was fruitfully employed by Estes (1960) in his studies of one-trial learning and by Tulving (1964) in his analysis of inter- vs. intra-trial forgetting in multitrial free recall.

Empirical Regularities in Successive Testing Experiments

There are many interesting examples of the use of contingency analyses, but the most well-studied problems include comparisons of successive episodic memory tasks (Nilsson & Gardiner, 1993; Tulving & Wiseman, 1975), successive explicit and implicit memory tasks (Hayman & Tulving, 1989a, 1989b; Tulving, Schacter, & Stark, 1982), and successive implicit memory tasks (e.g., Hayman & Tulving, 1989b; Tulving & Hayman, 1995; Witherspoon & Moscovitch, 1989). Other important applications of successive tests include demonstrations of one-trial learning (e.g., Estes, 1960) and demonstrations of the independence of A-B and A-C associations in the retroaction (e.g., Greeno, James, & Dapolito, 1971). In this section, three applications are discussed: independence of A-B and A-C associations, the recognition failure paradigm, and some recent results pertaining to the classic

Table 4.2 Contingency table for the hypothetical data shown in table 1.

		Test 1	
		1	0
Test 2	1	a = 9	b = 2
	0	c = 9	d = 6

question of associative symmetry versus independent associations. These three examples were chosen because they yield correlations of approximately 0.1, 0.5, and 0.9, respectively.

Analysis of Competing A-B and A-C Associations

The classic associative interference theory of verbal learning played a prominent role in guiding a generation of research in verbal learning (see Postman & Underwood, 1973, for a review). A major technique used to study associative interference is the A-B/A-C paradigm. Subjects first master a list of A-B pairs. Next, subjects study a second list of A-C pairs to some degree of mastery. Briggs (1954) showed that with increasing trials of A-C learning comes a decrease in subjects' ability to recall the original A-B associations. To examine this retroactive interference effect under conditions designed to minimize response competition, Barnes and Underwood (1959) proposed the now-classic MMFR procedure (MMFR stands for modified-modified free recall). In this procedure, subjects study the A-B list, then study the A-C list, and then are given each of the A items and asked to recall *both* the B and C responses *in any order*. With increasing trials of A-C learning, subjects recall fewer B items and more C items, demonstrating the classic retroactive interference phenomenon. According to the Melton-Underwood unlearning-recovery hypothesis—a central tenet of associative interference theory—the decrease in A-B recall following A-C learning results from *specific* unlearning of the individual A-B associations. This contrasts with the earlier view (McGeoch, 1942) that associations are independent, but that the stronger response dominates. Here we have two very different theories that both explain the basic data on retroactive interference.

Applying a contingency analysis to the MMFR data, Dapolito (1967) examined the dependence between B and C recall. According to the unlearning-recovery hypothesis, learning A_i-C_i causes specific weakening of the A_i-B_i association. As a consequence, recall of B_i and C_i should be negatively correlated. In contrast to these predictions, Dapolito found near independence between recall of B_i and C_i. Numerous additional studies supported the independence position (Abra, 1969; Greeno et al., 1971; Martin, 1971; Wichawut & Martin, 1971). Because these studies did not report their results in terms of Yule's Q, it is hard to

compare their observations with other studies of correlations among successive tests. Appendix A presents a database of 32 experimental conditions obtained using the MMFR technique. Across these conditions, the mean value of Yule's Q is 0.08, with a standard deviation of 0.31. Again, contingency analyses reveal a regularity of human memory that distinguishes among theories of associative interference. Several major mathematical models of human memory (e.g., Murdock, 1982, 1997; Chappell & Humphreys, 1994; Mensink & Raaijmakers, 1988) have been framed in a way that captures the basic phenomenon of A-B, A-C independence.

The Recognition Failure Paradigm (Tulving & Thomson, 1973)

Perhaps the most common application of contingency analyses to the study of memory is the influential, if somewhat controversial, recognition-failure paradigm (Flexser & Tulving, 1978; Tulving & Thomson, 1973; Tulving & Wiseman, 1975). In this approach, discussed briefly in the previous section, subjects study a list of word pairs and are then tested successively, first by item recognition and then by cued recall. Tulving and Wiseman (1975) observed that the dependency relation between item recognition and cued recall, across a wide range of experimental conditions, was well fit by a quadratic formula relating the conditional probability of recognition given recall to the probability of recognition itself. This function, known as the Tulving-Wiseman function, describes a moderate degree of dependency between item recognition and cued recall.

Analyses based on the conditional probability of recognition given recall, $P(Rn|Rc)$, are subject to a number of problems: First, $P(Rn|Rc)$ is constrained to be less than $P(Rn)/P(Rc)$ in experiments where the probability of recall exceeds that of recognition (Hintzman & Hartry, 1990; Hintzman, 1992). Second, the predicted values of Yule's Q, derived from the Tulving-Wiseman function, can be less than -1 or greater than $+1$ for some combinations of $P(Rn)$ and $P(Rc)$. These potential constraints can be avoided by examining results in terms of both Yule's Q and the probability of success on test 1 and on test 2. The cells in a 2×2 contingency table are completely determined by either (1) knowing the probabilities of successful outcomes on tests one and two as well as the correlation (Yule's Q) between these outcomes, or (2) knowing the probability of success on test 1, the probability of success on test 2 conditional upon test 1 success, and the probability of success on test 2 conditional upon test 1 failure. (A proof of this assertion is available from the author upon request.) This later approach is used by Humphreys and Bowyer (1980) as well as Batchelder and Riefer (1995).

Using a measure of dependency such as Yule's Q, one typically obtains a value of approximately 0.55 in these experiments. Not all experiments using the successive testing methodology yield the moderate dependencies described by the Tulving-Wiseman function (Nilsson, Law, & Tulving, 1988; Nilsson & Gardiner, 1993). Higher recognition-recall dependencies can result from shallow encoding or from semantic redundancy of study pairs. Nilsson and Gardiner (1991) refer to these cases as boundary conditions on the Tulving-Wiseman function. A great many studies have looked at the dependency between item recognition and cued recall under varying conditions (see Nilsson & Gardiner, 1993, for a partial review). Examining the correlations summarized by Nilsson and Gardiner (1993) reveals significant variation around the mean value of 0.55. The reason for this variation is that many of these studies were especially constructed to push the correlation up or down. Appendix B presents a database of Yule's Q values from studies that gathered significant amounts of data using standard methods (i.e., subjects study a list of common word pairs and are then given a yes/no recognition test followed by a cued-recall test). Across these studies, the mean value of Yule's Q is 0.55 and the standard deviation is 0.12. The consistently obtained moderate correlation between item recognition and cued recall represents a basic fact of human memory.

Kahana and Rizzuto (1999) have shown that the moderate dependency obtained in successive item recognition and cued recall tasks is also found in successive item and associative recognition tasks ($Q = 0.59$). This suggests that the reason for the moderate dependency is that the one test taps item and the other test taps associative information. In contrast, when both tasks tap associative information (e.g., successive *associative* recognition and cued recall), the correlation rises substantially ($Q = 0.81$). Finally, for identical associative recognition tasks correlations approach unity ($Q = 0.94$).

Though the data are clear, there is still much debate over the interpretation of these findings. Metcalfe (1991) shows that under certain conditions, CHARM (a mathematical memory model that assumes composite and distributed storage of auto- and hetero-associative information) can account for both the Tulving-Wiseman function and conditions that result in deviations from the function. Kahana and Rizzuto (1999) found that several classes of memory models including Metcalfe's (1982, 1985) CHARM model, Murdock's (1982) TODAM model and the matrix model of Humphreys, Bain, and Pike (1989) can all produce the moderate dependencies required, but only if you allow for variability in the goodness of encoding (see also Hintzman, 1987). Each of the preceding models assumes that item and associative information have distinct representations. Models that assume identical representations for individual items and associations produce correlations that are too high, deviating from the experimental data for all reasonable parameter values. These results show that if models make explicit predictions about subject performance in the successive testing paradigm, contingency analyses place constraints on the models and, in doing so, provide insight into the function of human memory.

Associative Symmetry vs. Independent Associations

Another basic question in the study of human memory is the nature of associations. Two models of association are present in the classical literature: The independent associations model considers associations to be unidirectional links between stored items (e.g., Ebbinghaus, 1885/1913; Robinson, 1932). The holistic model considers associations to be newly formed patterns combining elements of each stored item (Kohler, 1940). In this model, forward and backward associations between items are symmetrical (Asch & Ebenholtz, 1962). Early studies addressing the differences between these two positions focused on whether forward recall is easier than backward recall (see Ekstrand, 1966, and Kahana, 1999, for a review). The evidence, from numerous studies, suggests that order of study has a minimal effect on associative strength. Findings of equivalent forward and backward retrieval have been taken as evidence for the position of associative symmetry; findings of asymmetric retrieval have been taken as evidence for the position of independent associations (e.g., Wollen, 1970a,b; Wolford, 1971).

A much stronger test of associative symmetry requires that for a given studied pair (A-B), the strength of the forward and backward associations, and hence the recall probabilities, must be identical. Evidence relevant to this question may be gleaned from contingency analyses applied to the outcomes of successive cued-recall tests. First, one association is tested (say, A is presented as a cue to recall B) and then the other association is tested (B is presented as a cue to recall A).

Kahana (1999) had subjects study lists of word pairs and then gave successive cued-recall tests of all pairs in the list. Across the two successive tests, word pairs were tested in all combinations of forward and backward orders: T1-forward/T2-forward, T1-forward/T2-backward, T1-backward/T2-forward, T1-backward/T2-backward. To test the symmetry principle, Yule's Q was computed for identical and reverse successive tests (separate Yule's Q values were calculated for each subject). For identical successive tests (i.e., forward-forward or backward-backward), the average Yule's Q value was 0.88 (SE = 0.012). For reverse successive tests (i.e., forward-backward or backward-forward), the average Yule's Q value was 0.91 (SE = 0.017). These effects did not differ statistically. The independent associations model of paired-associate learning (Wolford, 1971; Wollen, 1970a,b) can account for asymmetries that pose a resolvable challenge to symmetrical associative models (see Kahana, 1999), but they cannot explain the finding that correlations between forward and backward recall are near unity.

Other Applications

The previous three applications illustrated how intertask contingencies can vary quite dramatically and how they can be used to constrain theories of memory. There are a number of other important applications of contingency analyses that are not reviewed here. In particular, contingency analyses have been extensively applied to the study of implicit memory (Hayman & Tulving, 1989a, 1989b; Tulving et al., 1982; Tulving, Hayman, & Macdonald, 1991; Tulving & Hayman, 1995; Witherspoon & Moscovitch, 1989). These studies have shown that successive implicit tasks can yield dependencies ranging from near zero (with nonoverlapping cues) to around 0.5 (with identical cues). In contrast, successive explicit tasks yield dependencies ranging from around 0.5 (with different cues) to 1.0 (with identical cues). An important aspect of these results is that the dependency between fragment completion tasks can be dramatically affected by subjects' intentionality (i.e., whether or not subjects are instructed to focus retrieval on their memory for the study list). Tulving and colleagues have used this evidence, together with findings of functional independence, to support a multiple memory systems view (e.g., Schacter & Tulving, 1994).

The Controversy

Despite the fruitful application of contingency analyses to a broad range of memory paradigms, there has been considerable controversy surrounding their use as an analytic tool. Hintzman, a vocal critic, has argued that correlations between tasks, as measured by Yule's Q, are at best difficult to interpret and at worst uninterpretable. His arguments are based on Simpson's paradox (Hintzman, 1980). This refers to the fact that collapsing data across subjects or items *can* give rise to relations that were not present in the pre-collapsed data. In practice, what does this mean? Here we examine two cases, both using our familiar example of successive item-recognition and cued-recall tests (e.g., Tulving & Thomson, 1973). Recall that in these experiments, Yule's Q is almost always between 0.30 and 0.75.

Case 1. The experimenter presents a long list of A_i-B_i word pairs for study. As the list is being presented, subjects adopt the following strategy: they attend to the first few pairs and then close their eyes and keep rehearsing those pairs throughout the duration of the list presentation. Upon tabulating our results, we discover that all responses are segregated into cells A (+/+) and D (−/−) of the contingency table, with D (−/−) having the majority of responses. The few items that subjects rehearsed were both recognized on test 1 and recalled on test 2 (accounting for the responses in cell A). The remaining, unseen items, were neither recognized nor recalled (accounting for the responses in cell D). The resulting correlation is exactly +1.0. This result does not reflect common operations underlying recognition and recall; rather it is a spurious correlation induced by a third actor—variability in encoding.

Case 2. Here again, the experimenter presents a list of A_i-B_i pairs, and then gives successive item recognition and cued recall tests for B_i. Suppose we now divide our pairs into two groups: in group 1, we make the B-items easy to recognize but hard to recall, and in group 2, we make the B-items hard to recognize and easy to recall. We can manipulate recognition of B_i by varying its word frequency or its similarity to the lures. We can manipulate recall of B_i by varying the associative relations between A_i-B_i and between A_i-B_j. After tabulating our contingency table, most of the pairs in group 1 would be in cell C (+/−) and most of the pairs in group 2 would be in cell B (−/+). In this case, the correlation between item recognition and cued recall would be close to −1.0. This illustrates another spurious correlation: we identified factors that have different effects on recognition and recall and then specially selected pairs to induce a negative correlation.

In an attempt to show Simpson's paradox at work in successive recognition and fragment completion tests, Hintzman and Hartry (1990) found that selecting different subsets of items could produce large changes in the observed correlation between tasks. Such demonstrations do not teach us very much. They do point out, as all practitioners who use correlations ought to know, that spurious correlations can occur. In particular, variability that affects the two outcome variables in a correlated manner can induce an increase or decrease in the observed correlation.

Suppose that variability in subject ability and item difficulty both have positive effects on memory performance. In this case, the observed value of Yule's Q would be somewhat higher when collapsing across subjects or items. Flexser (1981) provided a useful technique for adjusting Yule's Q to account for these sources of variability. Another approach requires the collection of sufficient data across subjects and items to permit separate Yule's Q analyses for contingency tables that are collapsed across only subjects, or only items. When these techniques have been used, the correlation between successive tasks has *not* changed dramatically.

One problem with these approaches is that they do not adjust for potential variability at the level of subject items *that is caused by factors not intrinsic to the tasks being studied* (e.g., trial by trial fluctuations in attention). If this external source of variability, affecting the encoding of information important for both test 1 and test 2, is *much* larger than the mea-surable variability across subjects and items, then it is possible that the "true" correlation is smaller than what is observed experimentally.

One way to address this potential problem is to create lists in which the variability is artificially increased by mixing strong and weak items (where strength is manipulated by varying number of repetitions or presentation rate). One can assess the effect of variability on the dependency relations among tasks by comparing these mixed lists with pure lists (in which presentation rate, or number of repetitions, is uniform across all study pairs). Kahana and Rizzuto (1999) conducted two experiments of this kind and found significant increases in Yule's Q for the specially constructed, high-variability lists. However, the effects were extremely small (the largest changes in variability only increased Yule's Q by about 0.10). In contrast, informational manipulations produced dramatic changes in the correlations between successive tests. These findings strongly suggest that variability in goodness-of-encoding only plays a minor role in determining the correlations between successive memory tasks.

A final class of criticisms relate to the "priming" of second test performance by the first test (e.g., Humphreys & Bowyer, 1980). As stated previously, it is well known that the first test may affect performance on the second test, and therefore the second test is no longer a direct measure of the study event. Rather, the second test reflects both the study event and the effect of the first test on memory. Humphreys and Bowyer argue that the dependency between recognition and recall is increased by differential facilitation of later recall by prior recognition. In essence, recognized items may be strengthened during the recognition test more than nonrecognized items. This transfer effect enhances cued-recall performance for the recognized items more than for the nonrecognized items, thereby increasing the dependency between item recognition and cued recall. In several experiments, Humphreys and Bowyer found higher cued-recall performance for those items that were tested in the recognition phase (as compared with items only tested in the cued-recall phase).

If one assumes that only recognized items prime subsequent recall, Humphreys and Bowyer show that the observed moderate correlation between recognition and recall could be largely due to this priming effect. The problem with this account is that nonrecognized items can also facilitate subsequent recall (Begg, 1979; Donnelley, 1988). In addition, even experiments that fail to show significant "priming" yield moderate dependency between item recognition and cued recall (Wiseman & Tulving, 1976). These results suggest that although the outcome of the first recognition test does influence subsequent recall, this effect accounts only for some part of the observed dependency between these tasks.

Where, then, do we stand in the face of these potential confounds? Rather than running away from the complexities of contingency analyses we need to proceed with caution. Researchers have managed to obtain highly reliable and replicable results using the method of successive tests, and the variation in dependencies among tasks have been consistent and theoretically interpretable (Martin, 1981; Gardiner, 1991).

Conclusions

This chapter reviewed the use of contingency analyses applied to successive memory tasks. As shown in the applications section, the correlation between successive tests varies in reliable ways across different task comparisons. Successive item-recognition and cued-recall tasks yield moderate levels of dependency (Yule's Q ≈ 0.55) whereas successive tests of episodic memory with identical cues or cues containing identical information yield very high dependencies (Yule's Q ≈ 0.90).With implicit memory tasks, a very different pattern is observed: Yule's Q ranges from 0.1 to 0.5 as a function of cue overlap. This difference between implicit and explicit memory tasks has provided evidence supporting the multiple memory systems view (e.g., Tulving, 1985;

Schacter & Tulving, 1994). Although other explanations may well exist, contingency analyses have played an important role in this debate.

Applying contingency analyses to the relation between recognition and recall, researchers have shown that experimental variables that have a significant effect on overall levels of performance do not seem to affect the task-task contingencies (see Flexser & Tulving, 1978; Kahana & Rizzuto, 1999; Nilsson & Gardiner, 1993; Wiseman & Tulving, 1976). This finding highlights an important feature of intertask contingencies: they represent an added dependent variable that is independent of overall performance levels on the two successive tasks.

These and other examples of contingency analyses, reviewed in this chapter and elsewhere (e.g., Tulving, 1985; Tulving & Hayman, 1995) illustrate a striking feature of the correlations between successive tests: the dependency varies systematically with the nature of the two tests. Even in a situation in which the first test remains the same, the study conditions are the same, and the target items are the same, the exact form of the second test can dramatically alter the observed correlation (see Hayman & Tulving, 1989a; Tulving et al., 1991).

Repeated testing of the knowledge that subjects acquire in the laboratory has been of immense value in enriching our understanding of how human memory works—this despite the fear that many students of memory have exhibited, and problems of interpretation that require a different approach than that adopted for the study of the effects of independent variables. In this respect, these experiments resemble life in which, too, the results of an experience are frequently tested repeatedly.

Appendix A

A selected database of studies that examined the correlation between B and C responses in the MMFR paradigm. The mean Yule's Q value for the included conditions was 0.08 ± .11 (95% confidence interval).

Study	Condition	Yule's Q
Abra (1969)	48 hr.–0 hr.	−0.22
Abra (1969)	48 hr.–24 hr.	−0.13
Abra (1969)	48 hr.–48 hr.	0.47
Abra (1969)	24 hr.–24 hr.	−0.10
Delprato (1972)	AC(4,2)	−0.05
Delprato (1972)	AC(4)	0.29
Delprato (1972)	AC(8,4)	−0.32
Delprato (1972)	AC(8,8)	−0.16
Delprato (1972)	AC(16,8)	−0.38
Delprato (1972)	AC(16,16)	0.14
Koppenaal (1978)	Retention Interval = 1 min.	−0.32
Koppenaal (1978)	Retention Interval = 20 min.	0.00
Koppenaal (1978)	Retention Interval = 90 min.	0.37
Koppenaal (1978)	Retention Interval = 6 hours	−0.62
Koppenaal (1978)	Retention Interval = 24 hours	0.00
Koppenaal (1978)	Retention Interval = 72 hours	0.06
Koppenaal (1978)	Retention Interval = 1 week	0.23
Postman (1964)	set 1	−0.32
Postman (1964)	set 2	0.31
Postman (1964)	set 3	0.35
Postman and Gray (1977)	Substitution	−0.13
Tulving and Watkins (1974)	BC	0.16
Tulving and Watkins (1974)	$B'C'$	0.44
Tulving and Watkins (1974)	$B'C$	0.51
Tulving and Watkins (1974)	BC'	0.53
Tulving and Watkins (1974)	BC	0.39
Tulving and Watkins (1974)	$B'C'$	0.48
Tulving and Watkins (1974)	$B'C$	0.07
Tulving and Watkins (1974)	BC'	0.62
Wichawut and Martin (1971)	AC(4)	−0.24
Wichawut and Martin (1971)	AC(8)	0.13
Wichawut and Martin (1971)	AC(12)	0.00

Appendix B

A selected database of successive item recognition—cued-recall experimental conditions. Studies that used pairs of common English nouns, or weak associates, were included; studies that used strong associates or non-English materials were excluded. Studies that used categorization or free association before the successive tests were excluded. Finally, experiments where the standard error on Yule's Q was greater than 0.2 were also omitted. The mean Yule's Q value for included conditions was 0.55 ± 0.05 (95% confidence interval).

Study	Condition	Yule's Q
Bartling and Thompson (1977)	Noun-noun condition	0.50
Wallace (1978)	Weak cue target pairs, Rn, cued Rc	0.43
Wallace (1978)	Weak cue target pairs, Rn, cued Rc	0.76
Wallace (1978)	Weak cue target pairs, Rn, cued Rc, no lures	0.64
Begg (1979)	Meaningful instructions	0.19
Begg (1979)	Rote instructions	0.63
Bowyer & Humphreys (1979)	Weak cue-target pairs, between subject priming	0.41
Bowyer & Humphreys (1979)	Weak cue target pairs, within subject priming	0.53
Fisher (1979)	Repetition rehearsal, high-low cue target assoc.	0.75
Vining and Nelson (1979)	Weak cue target pairs	0.59
Vining and Nelson (1979)	Unrelated cue target pairs	0.51
Gardiner (1988)	Cued recall overall	0.66
Gardiner (1988)	Cued recall (ctrl), strict	0.65
Gardiner (1988)	Cued recall overall, strict	0.54
Gardiner (1988)	Cued recall (ctrl), lenient	0.73
Gardiner (1988)	Cued recall overall, lenient	0.49
Sandberg (1988)	Weak cue target pairs, cued recall instruction	0.55
Kahana and Rizzuto (1999)	Experiment 1 (Pure Strong)	0.54
Kahana and Rizzuto (1999)	Experiment 1 (Pure Weak)	0.49
Kahana and Rizzuto (1999)	Experiment 2 (Pure Strong)	0.49
Kahana and Rizzuto (1999)	Experiment 2 (Pure Weak)	0.52
Kahana and Rizzuto (1999)	Experiment 3 (item recognition)	0.57

Acknowledgments This research was funded by N.I.H. grant MH55687 to Brandeis University. I am grateful to Ben Murdock for his comments on a previous version of this chapter. Thanks are also due to Dan Rizutto and Marc Howard for very helpful comments and discussion. Correspondence should be addressed to M. J. Kahana, Center for Complex Systems, Brandeis University, Waltham, MA, 02454-9110. E-mail may be sent to: kahana@cs.brandeis.edu.

References

Abra, J. C. (1969). List-1 unlearning and recovery as a function of the point of interpolated learning. *Journal of Verbal Learning and Verbal Behavior, 8*, 494–500.

Asch, S. E., & Ebenholtz, S. M. (1962). The principle of associative symmetry. *Proceedings of the American Philosophical Society, 106*, 135–163.

Barnes, J. M., & Underwood, B. J. (1959). Fate of first-list associations in transfer theory. *Journal of Experimental Psychology, 58*, 97–105.

Bartling, C. A., & Thompson, P. (1977). Encoding specificity: Retrieval asymmetry in the recognition failure paradigm. *Journal of Experimental Psychology: Human Learning and Memory, 3(6)*, 690–700.

Batchelder, W. H., & Riefer, D. M. (1995). A multinomial modeling analysis of the recognition-failure paradigm. *Memory & Cognition, 23*, 611–630.

Begg, I. (1979). Trace loss and the recognition failure of unrecalled words. *Memory & Cognition, 7*, 113–123.

Bishop, Y. M. M., Fienberg, S. E., & Holland, P. W. (1975). *Discrete multivariate analysis: theory and practice*. Cambridge, Mass: MIT Press.

Bowyer, P. A., & Humphreys, M. S. (1979). Effect of a recognition test on a subsequent cued-recall test. *Journal of Experimental Psychology: Human Learning & Memory, 5*, 348–359.

Briggs, G. E. (1954). Acquisition, extinction, and recovery functions in retroactive inhibition. *Journal of Experimental Psychology, 47*, 285–293.

Chappell, M., & Humphreys, M. (1994). An autoassociative neural network for sparse representations: Analysis and application to models of recognition and cued recall. *Psychological Review, 101*, 103–128.

Dapolito, F. J. (1967). Proactive effects with independent retrieval of competing responses. *Dissertation Abstracts International, 27*, 2522–2523.

Delprato, D. (1972). Pair specific effects in retroactive inhibition. *Journal of Verbal Learning and Verbal Behavior, 11*, 566–572.

Donnelly, R. E. (1988). Priming effects in successive episodic tasks. *Journal of Experimental Psychology: Learning, Memory, & Cognition, 14*, 256–265.

Ebbinghaus, H. (1885/1913). *Memory: A contribution to experimental psychology*. New York: Teachers College, Columbia University.

Ekstrand, B. R. (1966). Backward associations. *Psychological Bulletin, 65*, 50–64.

Estes, W. K. (1960). Learning theory and the new "mental chemistry." *Psychological Review, 67*, 207–223.

Fisher, R. P. (1979). Retrieval operations in cued recall and recognition. *Memory & Cognition, 7*, 224–231.

Flexser, A. (1981). Homogenizing the 2×2 contingency table: A method for removing dependencies due to subject and item differences. *Psychological Review, 88*, 327–339.

Flexser, A. J., & Tulving, E. (1978). Retrieval independence in recognition and recall. *Psychological Review, 85*, 153–171.

Gardiner, J. M. (1988). Functional aspects of recollective experience. *Memory & Cognition, 16*, 309–313.

Gardiner, J. M. (1991). Contingency relations in successive tests: Accidents do not happen. *Journal of Experimental Psychology: Learning, Memory, & Cognition, 17*, 334–337.

Glanzer, M., & Cunitz, A. R. (1966). Two storage mechanisms in free recall. *Journal of Verbal Learning and Verbal Behavior, 5*, 351–360.

Greeno, J. G., James, C. T., & Dapolito, F. J. (1971). A cognitive interpretation of negative transfer and forgetting of paired associates. *Journal of Verbal Learning and Verbal Behavior, 10*, 331–345.

Hayman, G. A. C., & Tulving, E. (1989a). Contingent dissociation between recognition and fragment completion: The method of triangulation. *Journal of Experimental Psychology: Learning, Memory, & Cognition, 15*, 228–240.

Hayman, G. A. C., & Tulving, E. (1989b). Is priming in fragment completion based on a "traceless" memory system? *Journal of Experimental Psychology: Learning, Memory, & Cognition, 15*, 941–956.

Hintzman, D. L. (1980). Simpson's paradox and the analysis of memory retrieval. *Psychological Review, 87*, 398–410.

Hintzman, D. L. (1987). Recognition and recall in minerva 2: Analysis of the 'recognition-failure' paradigm. In P. Morris (Ed.), *Modelling cognition* (pp. 215–229). New York: Wiley.

Hintzman, D. L. (1992). Mathematical constraints on the Tulving-Wiseman function. *Psychological Review, 99*, 536–542.

Hintzman, D. L., & Hartry, A. L. (1990). Item effects in recognition and fragment completion: Contingency relations vary for different subsets of words. *Journal of Experimental Psychology: Learning: Memory, & Cognition, 16*, 965–969.

Humphreys, M. S., Bain, J. D., & Pike, R. (1989). Different ways to cue a coherent memory system: A theory for episodic, semantic, and procedural tasks. *Psychological Review, 96*, 208–233.

Humphreys, M. S., & Bowyer, P. A. (1980). Sequential testing effects and the relation between recognition and recognition failure. *Memory & Cognition, 8*, 271–277.

Kahana, M. J. (1999). Associative symmetry and memory theory. Submitted for publication.

Kahana, M. J., & Loftus, G. (1999). Response time versus accuracy in human memory. In R. J. Sternberg (Ed.), *The Nature of Cognition* (pp. 323–384). Cambridge, CA: MIT Press.

Kahana, M. J., & Rizzuto, D. S. (1999). An analysis of the recognition-recall relation in four distributed memory models. *Manuscript submitted for publication.*

Köhler, W. (1940). *Dynamics in Psychology.* New York: Liveright.

Koppell, S. (1977). Decision latencies in recognition memory: A signal detection theory analysis. *Journal of Experimental Psychology: Human Learning & Memory, 3*, 445–457.

Koppenaal, R. J. (1963). Time changes in the strengths of a-b, a-c lists; spontaneous recovery? *Journal of Verbal Learning and Verbal Behavior, 2*, 310–319.

Mandler, G. (1959). Stimulus variables and subject variables: A caution. *Psychological Review, 66*, 145–149.

Martin, E. (1971). Verbal learning theory and independent retrieval phenomena. *Psychological Review, 78*, 314–332.

Martin, E. (1981). Simpson's paradox resolved: A reply to Hintzman. *Psychological Review, 88*, 372–374.

McGeoch, J. A. (1942). *The psychology of human learning: An introduction.* New York: Longmans.

Mensink, G. J. M., & Raaijmakers, J. G. W. (1988). A model for interference and forgetting. *Psychological Review, 95*, 434–455.

Metcalfe, J. (1985). Levels of processing, encoding specificity, elaboration, and CHARM. *Psychological Review, 92*, 1–38.

Metcalfe, J. (1991). Recognition failure and the composite memory trace in CHARM. *Psychological Review, 98*, 529–553.

Metcalfe-Eich, J. (1982). A composite holographic associative recall model. *Psychological Review, 89*, 627–661.

Murdock, B. B. (1962). The serial position curve in free recall. *Journal of Experimental Psychology, 64*, 482–488.

Murdock, B. B. (1982). A theory for the storage and retrieval of item and associative information. *Psychological Review, 89*, 609–626.

Murdock, B. B. (1997). Context and mediators in a theory of distributed associative memory (TODAM2). *Psychological Review, 104*, 839–862.

Murdock, B. B., & Anderson, R. E. (1975). Encoding, storage and retrieval of item information. In R. L. Solso (Ed.), *Information Processing and Cognition: The Loyola Symposium* (pp. 145–194). Hillsdale, New Jersey: Lawrence Erlbaum Associates.

Nilsson, L. G., & Gardiner, J. M. (1991). Memory theory and the boundary conditions of the Tulving-Wiseman law. In W. E. Hockley & S. Lewandowsky (Eds.), *Relating theory and data: Essays on human memory in honor of Bennet B. Murdock* (pp. 57–74). Hillsdale, NJ: Lawrence Erlbaum Associates.

Nilsson, L. G., & Gardiner, J. M. (1993). Identifying exceptions in a database of recognition failure studies from 1973 to 1992. *Memory & Cognition, 21*, 397–410.

Nilsson, L. G., Law, J., & Tulving, E. (1988). Recognition failure of recallable unique names: Evidence for an empirical law of memory and learning. *Journal of Experimental Psychology: Learning, Memory, and Cognition, 14*, 266–277.

Nyberg, L., & Tulving, E. (1996). Classifying human long-term memory: Evidence from converging dissociations. *European Journal of Cognitive Psychology, 8*, 163–183.

Poldrack, R. A. (1996). On testing for stochastic dissociations. *Psychonomic Bulletin and Review, 3*, 434–448.

Postman, L. (1964). Studies of learning to learn ii. changes in transfer as a function of practice. *Journal of Verbal Learning and Verbal Behavior, 3*, 437–447.

Postman, L., & Gray, W. (1977). Maintenance of prior associations and proactive inhibition. *Journal of Experimental Psychology: Human Learning and Memory, 3*, 255–263.

Postman, L., & Underwood, B. (1973). Critical issues in interference theory. *Memory & Cognition, 1*, 19–40.

Richardson-Klavehn, A., & Bjork, R. A. (1988). Measures of memory. *Annual Review of Psychology, 39*, 475–543.

Robinson, E. S. (1932). *Association theory today; an essay in systematic psychology.* New York: The Century Co.

Rubin, D. C. (1981). First-order approximation to english, second-order approximation to english, and orthographic neighbor ratio norms for 925 nouns. *Behavior Research Methods, Instruments and Computers, 13*, 713–721.

Schacter, D., & Tulving, E. (1994). *Memory Systems 1994.* Cambridge, MA: MIT Press.

Sternberg, S. (1969). The discovery of processing stages: Extensions of Donders' method. *Acta Psychologica, 30*, 276–315.

Sternberg, S. (1998). Discovering mental processing stages: The method of additive factors. In D. Scarborough & S. Sternberg (Eds.), *Invitation to Cognitive Science: Vol. 4.: Methods, Models, and Conceptual Issues 2nd ed.* (pp. 703–861).

Tulving, E. (1962). Subjective organization in free recall of "unrelated" words. *Psychological Review, 69*, 344–354.

Tulving, E. (1964). Intra-trial and inter-trial retention: Notes towards a theory of free recall verbal learning. *Psychological Review, 71*, 219–237.

Tulving, E. (1966). Subjective organization and effects of repetition in multi-trial free-recall learning. *Journal of Experimental Psychology, 72*, 145–150.

Tulving, E. (1983). *Elements of Episodic Memory.* New York: Oxford.

Tulving, E. (1985). How many memory systems are there? *American Psychologist, 40*, 385–398.

Tulving, E., & Arbuckle, T. Y. (1966). Input and output interference in short-term associative memory. *Journal of Experimental Psychology, 72*, 145–150.

Tulving, E., Hayman, C. A. G., & Macdonald, C. A. (1991). Retroactive inhibition in free recall: Inaccessibility of information available in the memory store. *Journal of Verbal Learning and Verbal Behavior, 17*, 595–617.

Tulving, E., & Hayman, C. A. G. (1995). On measurement of priming: What is the correct baseline? *European Journal of Cognitive Psychology, 7*, 13–18.

Tulving, E., Schacter, D. L., & Stark, H. A. (1982). Priming effects in word-fragment completion are independent of recognition memory. *Journal of Experimental Psychology: Learning, Memory, and Cognition, 8*, 336–342.

Tulving, E., & Thomson, D. M. (1973). Encoding specificity and retrieval processes in episodic memory. *Psychological Review, 80*, 352–373.

Tulving, E., & Watkins, M. J. (1974). On negative transfer: Effects of testing one list on the recall of another. *Journal of Verbal Learning and Verbal Behavior, 13*, 181–193.

Tulving, E., & Wiseman, S. (1975). Relation between recognition and recognition failure of recallable words. *Bulletin of the Psychonomic Society, 6*, 79–82.

Underwood, B. J., Boruch, R. F., & Malmi, R. A. (1978). Composition of episodic memory. *Journal of Experimental Psychology: General, 107*, 393–419.

Vining, S. K., & Nelson, T. O. (1979). Some constraints on the generality and interpretation of the recognition failure of recallable words. *American Journal of Psychology, 92*, 257–276.

Wallace, W. P. (1978). Recognition failure of recallable words and recognizable words. *Journal of Experimental Psychology: Human Learning & Memory, 4*, 441–452.

Wichawut, C., & Martin, E. (1971). Independence of a–b and a–c associations in retroaction. *Journal of Verbal Learning and Verbal Behavior, 10*, 316–321.

Wiseman, S., & Tulving, E. (1976). Encoding specificity: Relation between recall superiority and recognition failure. *Journal of Experimental Psychology: Human Learning and Memory, 2*, 349–361.

Witherspoon, D., & Moscovitch, M. (1989). Stochastic independence between two implicit memory tasks. *Journal of Experimental Psychology: Learning, Memory, and Cognition, 15*, 22–30.

Wolford, G. (1971). Function of distinct associations for paired-associate performance. *Psychological Review, 78*, 303–313.

Wollen, K. (1970a). Effects of instructional set and materials upon forward and backward learning. *Journal of Experimental Psychology, 85*, 275–277.

Wollen, K. (1970b). Effects of set to learn A-B or B-A upon A-B and B-A tests. *Journal of Experimental Psychology, 86*, 186–189.

Part II: Memory in the Laboratory

ACTS OF MEMORY

5

Short-Term and Working Memory

ALAN BADDELEY

The study of short-term memory, the retention of small amounts of information over brief time intervals, formed a major component of the development of cognitive psychology during the 1960s. It had a strong theoretical component, derived from the increasingly influential computer metaphor, combined in Britain at least with a concern for application to problems such as those of air traffic communication (Broadbent, 1958) and of coding in telephony and postal systems (Conrad, 1964). The attempt to develop information-processing models of short-term memory (STM) led to some major controversies (see below). Unfortunately, resolving these issues unequivocally proved beyond the capability of the methods available at the time, resulting in a decline of interest in STM during the 1970s, and subsequently even to a declaration of its demise (Crowder, 1982).

However, as the old concept of STM was losing favor, it became incorporated within a more complex framework, *working memory* (WM), which proposed that the older concept of a unitary store be replaced by a multicomponent system that utilized storage as part of its function of facilitating complex cognitive activities such as learning, comprehending, and reasoning (Baddeley & Hitch, 1974). Interest in WM continued to develop through the 1980s, though with somewhat different emphases on different sides of the Atlantic. During the 1990s, the whole area has received a further boost from the development of functional imaging techniques, with the components of working memory offering an appropriate level of complexity for the developing techniques of brain scanning. This development was facilitated by the very fruitful relationship between cognitive psychology and the neuropsychology of working memory, which provided hypotheses as to which areas of the brain might be most likely to be involved in particular tasks, together with concepts that facilitate the linking of the neuroanatomy to a coherent cognitive framework. Finally, and coincidentally, some of the old applied problems are now beginning to resurface. In both the United States and Britain, for example, there is currently considerable concern about the best way to extend the ever-expanding series of telephone codes so as to optimize capacity without unduly increasing length, while new areas such as pharmaceutical prescribing errors are beginning to highlight the need for an understanding of the processes involved, and to draw upon the empirical work of the 1960s (Lambert, 1997).

As a result of these various developments, there is a growing interest in the field of STM and WM from scientists whose principal training has been in other areas, but who wish to incorporate measures of short-term and working memory into their work. Finally, the area continues to attract good young researchers who see the study of working memory as an important interface between research on memory, perception, and attention.

While there are many overviews of the area, ranging from the relatively brief (Baddeley, 1992) to the chapter length (Baddeley, 1996) and the book length (Gathercole, 1996; Miyake & Shah, in press), neither these nor journal articles tend to include the sort of practical detail that is so important if one wishes to carry out or evaluate experiments. The present chapter aims to go some way toward filling this gap, while bearing in mind that the only way to fully understand a technique is to use it. Here STM and WM are treated separately, since the relevant techniques, driven by the specific theoretical issues of the time, tend to be somewhat different. However, it is important to bear in mind that they do form part of the same tradition, and that it is increasingly common for 1960s techniques and methods to find new uses in the 1990s. It may be useful, however, to begin with some terminology.

Terminology

The division of memory into two or more systems was proposed by William James (1890), who distinguished between *primary memory*, which he regarded as closely associated with conscious awareness, and *secondary memory*, which referred to more durable memories. When the interest in fractionating memory revived in the late 1950s, the term STM was used to refer to tasks in which small amounts of material were retained over brief intervals, in contrast to LTM, which involved retention over more than a few seconds. It subsequently became clear that performance on STM tasks was not a pure reflection of the hypothetical underlying system, but was also influenced by LTM. To avoid confusion, some investigators used different terms to refer to the hypothetical underlying theoretical memory systems, such as *short-term* and *long-term store* (STS and LTS: Atkinson & Shiffrin, 1968), or reverting to *primary* and *secondary memory* (Waugh & Norman, 1965).

In recent years, the term *working memory* proposed by Miller, Galanter, and Pribram (1960) has been developed to emphasize the functional role of STM as part of an integrated system for holding and manipulating information during the performance of complex cognitive tasks (Baddeley & Hitch, 1974). Unfortunately, the same term has been used independently within the animal learning literature, where it refers to situations in which the animal needs to retain information across several trials during the same day (Olton, Walker, & Gage, 1978), almost certainly involving different mechanisms from those involved in the typical human WM task. Finally, the production system approach to computational modeling proposed by Newell and Simon (1972) postulates a working memory of unlimited capacity, although this is not assumed to be related to the limited capacity STM system proposed by experimentalists such as Baddeley and Hitch (1974). Fortunately, the context is usually sufficient to avoid too much confusion between the various users of the term.

Short-Term Memory

Methods and Techniques

Before going on to discuss recent theoretical developments in the area, it may be useful to describe some of the rich armament of methods and techniques that have been developed to study verbal and visual STM.

Verbal STM

Memory Span

Subjects are presented with a sequence of items, which they attempt to reproduce in the presented order. Typically, digits, consonants, or words are used. Presentation may be visual or auditory, with auditory presentation tending to give a slight advantage, particularly over the last one or two items, the so-called *modality effect*. Rates of presentation typically range from 0.5s to 2s per item, with 1s probably being the commonest. Presentation rate is not a major variable within this range, but faster rates run the risk of errors owing to failure to perceive, while slower rates give sufficient time for subjects to engage in complex and often highly variable rehearsal strategies.

Recall may be spoken or written. It is usual to require the subject to recall in the order of presentation, and to monitor that this is the case. Performance is typically measured in terms of the maximum level achieved, with span formally being the point at which the subject recalls the ordered sequence of items on 50% of occasions. This is not easy to determine directly, and hence a number of approximations are used. One simple method is to take the mean of the length of the three longest sequences correctly recalled, so a subject being correct on three out of four 7-item sequences, and one at length eight, would have a score of 7.33.

Memory span has the disadvantage that many of the data collected come from sequence lengths at which performance is perfect, hence providing little information. More information may be gained from using a procedure in which all sequences are presented at the same length, which should be at or slightly beyond span. Performance can then be scored either in terms of number of *sequences* completely correct or of number of *items* recalled in the correct serial position.

In his classic paper *The magic number seven*, George Miller (1956) speculated that in the area of absolute perceptual judgments, subjects could typically distinguish about 7 separate categories, while a typical digit span was about 7 items. He went on to emphasise that this latter conclusion was a gross oversimplification since it was possible to increase this substantially by *chunking*, a process whereby several items are aggregated into a larger super item. Perhaps the clearest demonstration of this is in immediate memory for prose material; memory span for unrelated words is about 5 or 6, whereas with meaningful sentences, spans of 16 words or more are not unusual (Baddeley, Vallar, & Wilson, 1987). Syntax and meaning make prose highly redundant, and an early paper by Miller and Selfridge (1950) showed that the more closely a string of words approximates to English prose, the longer the memory span. However, although absolute number of words increases with approximation to English, Tulving and Patkau (1962) showed that the number of chunks remains constant.

Free Recall

This simple task involves presenting the subject with a list, typically of words, that subjects attempt to recall in any order they wish. The classic serial position curve shows excellent recall of the last few items (the *recency effect*), somewhat better recall of the first one or two items (the *primacy effect*), and a relatively flat function between.

A brief filled delay will wipe out the recency effect while having little effect on ear-lier items. Virtually any variable that will influence long-term learning (e.g., rate of presentation, familiarity of material, the presence of a secondary task, or the age of the subject) will influence earlier items but have little or no impact on the recency effect (Glanzer, 1972). The recency effect reflects a strategy of first recalling the earlier items, and is abolished if subjects are dissuaded from this. It appears to be a very basic and robust strategy that is found in young children, amnesic patients, and even patients suffering from Alzheimer's disease (Glanzer, 1972; Baddeley & Hitch, 1993).

The primacy effect is less marked and less robust. It may reflect a number of variables, but in particular the tendency to give more attention and possibly more rehearsal to the initial item (Hockey, 1973).

While the typical serial position function operates across a wide range of lengths and presentation rates, most experimenters avoid sequences of less than 10 items, since there is a tendency for subjects to attempt to recall short sequences in serial order. Presentation rate is typically slower than in memory span, since this increases the amount of recall from the earlier long-term part of the curve, with 2s per item being the most common presentation rate. It is also not uncommon to use semantically categorized material, since this again increases performance and also gives some indication as to whether the subject is able to take advantage of meaning (Tulving & Pearlstone, 1966).

Short-Term Forgetting

The classic paradigm here was developed by Peterson and Peterson (1959); their subjects were presented with three consonants and required to retain them over a delay ranging from 0–18s, during which they counted backwards in threes. Performance reflects an STM component that declines over about 5 seconds (Baddeley & Scott, 1971), and an LTM component reflecting the extent to which items can be discriminated from prior items, the result of *proactive interference* (PI; Keppel & Underwood, 1962). PI can be prevented by changing the type of material to be remembered—for example, switching from animals to flowers (Wickens, 1970) or by inserting a delay between successive trials (Loess & Waugh, 1967), resulting in a recovery of performance (*release from PI*), followed by a further buildup of PI.

Memory Probe Techniques

The act of recalling an item can itself produce forgetting, either because the time taken to recall allows further trace decay or because the recall process disrupts the memory trace. One way of avoiding both of these is through probe techniques, whereby only part of the remembered material is sampled. For example, Sperling (1963) presented subjects with 3 rows of 4 letters. At recall, one of the 3 rows is cued by a tone. Since the subject does not know in advance which row, one can legitimately multiply that score by the number of rows to estimate the capacity of the memory system, which is typically greater than that obtained using more standard total recall methods. In a variant of this, Waugh and Norman (1965) presented their subjects with a series of digit strings varying in length. The experimenter then provided one item from the string and required the subject to produce the next in sequence. Recall performance showed a very clear recency effect, which was minimally affected by rate of presentation, suggesting that forgetting was principally due to the limited capacity of the short-term store rather than to temporal trace decay.

A variant of the memory probe technique was developed by Sternberg (1966), who used speed of response as a means of investigating the storage of items within the memory span. A digit list ranging in length from 1 to 6 was presented, followed by a probe digit. The task was to decide whether the probe digit had been part of the previously presented sequence. Reaction time increased linearly with the length of the presented sequence. This occurred not only for positive probes but also for negative probes, where the item had not been in the list. Sternberg proposed a model based on the analogy of a computer serially scanning its memory store, with the slope of the function relating RT to number items in store providing a measure of hypothetical scanning rate, typically about 40 ms per item. The fact that slopes for "yes" and "no" responses were the same prompted Sternberg to suggest that the search was exhaustive. If subjects could respond as soon as they detected a match with the probe, then the "yes" response slope should be shallower than the "no." This led to intensive experimental work that uncovered phenomena inconsistent with the scanning model, such as effects of recency (Corballis, Kirby, & Miller, 1972) and repetition effects (Baddeley & Ecob, 1973), leading to the proposal of alternative models (Anderson, 1973; Theios, 1973). With the growth in number of models and a lack of crucial experimental evidence, the technique became unfashionable, although it is still quite extensively used as a measure of cognitive deficit following drugs or stressors, for which it provides a neat and reasonably sensitive measure. In the absence of any broadly accepted theoretical interpretation, it continues to offer a theoretical challenge.

Nonverbal STM

Research on STM was dominated by verbal tasks, probably because the material is so easy to manipulate and record. However, analogous effects have been shown for visual memory. Dale (1973) required subjects to remember the location of a single point on an open field over a delay filled by verbal counting, finding that accuracy declined steadily over time. Phillips (1974) presented subjects with a matrix of which half the cells were filled, presenting a second matrix for recognition after a filled delay varying in length. Performance remained high over the delay for simple 2 × 2 matrices, with forgetting becoming steeper as the complexity of the matrix increased. In a subsequent study, Phillips and Christie (1977) presented subjects with a sequence of matrix patterns, observing that only the last pattern showed evidence of excellent initial performance followed by rapid decay, while earlier matrices showed a low level of performance. This pattern of results, therefore, suggests a short-term visual memory store that is limited to one pattern, with performance on that pattern being a function of its complexity. This has been used to develop a measure of pattern span in which the subject is shown a pattern and attempts to reproduce it on a matrix. The test begins with a 2 × 2 matrix with half the cells filled, increasing to a point at which the subject is no longer able to accurately reproduce the pattern, which for a normal adult is typically around 16 cells (Della Sala, Gray, Baddeley, & Wilson, 1997).

An alternative measure of visuo-spatial span is the Corsi block tapping task (Milner, 1968), in which the subject is faced with an array of 9 quasi-randomly arranged blocks. The experimenter taps a particular sequence of blocks and asks the subject to imitate, starting with just 2 and building up to a point at which performance breaks down, typically around 5 taps. This task has a sequential and motor component missing from the pattern span, and appears to measure a different aspect of visuo-spatial memory, since patients can be impaired on one but not the other; furthermore, spatial activity interferes with Corsi span, while intervening abstract pictures differentially interferes with pattern span (Della Sala, Gray, Baddeley, Allamano, & Wilson, in press).

Memory for location using a technique somewhat similar to that developed by Dale suggests that visual and verbal STM involve different brain regions (Smith & Jonides, 1995) and also that the maintenance of even a single item involves an active process involving the frontal lobes (Goldman-Rakic, 1996; Haxby, Ungerleider, Horwitz, Rapoport, & Grady, 1995).

Research on other nonverbal retention is less well developed, but studies of memory for kinaesthetic stimuli (Adams & Dijkstra, 1966) and tactile stimuli (Gilson & Baddeley, 1969) show rapid forgetting over a short delay, whereas memory for odors (Engen, Kuisma, & Eimas, 1973) does not.

Theoretical Issues

Despite earlier suggestions that there might be more than one kind of memory (Hebb, 1949; James, 1890), the issue was largely ignored until the discovery of the short-term forgetting of small amounts of information over filled intervals by Brown (1958) and Peterson and Peterson (1959), which led the investigators to propose separate LTM and STM memory systems, with short-term forgetting reflecting the spontaneous decay of the memory trace. This view was resisted, notably by Melton (1963), who argued strongly for a unitary memory system in which forgetting reflected associative interference between the items retained, rather than trace decay. The importance of PI in the STM paradigm (Keppel & Underwood, 1962) suggested that interference effects certainly occur in STM, although these in turn could be interpreted as reflecting limited capacity, rather than classic associative interference (Waugh & Norman, 1965). The issue of whether short-term forgetting reflects decay or interference remains unresolved.

During the mid-1960s proponents of a dichotomy between STM and LTM generated evidence from a range of sources, including:

Two Component Tasks: Tasks such as free recall appear to have separate components,

with the recency effect reflecting STM, while earlier items appear to depend upon LTM (Glanzer, 1972).

Acoustic and Semantic Coding: Conrad (1962) showed that errors in recalling visually presented consonants tended to be similar in sound to the correct items (e.g., *B* is remembered as *V*), suggesting that recall is based on an acoustic code. Baddeley (1966a, 1966b) showed that immediate recall sequences of 5 unrelated words was highly susceptible to acoustic similarity but insensitive to semantic similarity, while delayed recall of 10-word lists showed exactly the opposite pattern. Using a probe technique, Kintsch and Buschke (1969) showed that the recency part of the function reflected acoustic similarity effects, while performance on earlier items reflected semantic coding. These studies, therefore, appeared to suggest a predilection for acoustic coding in STM and semantic coding in LTM.

Neuropsychological Evidence: Amnesic patients such as the classic case HM (Milner, 1966) showed grossly impaired LTM, together with preserved span. Such patients also showed preserved recency, and if intellectually otherwise intact, normal performance on the Peterson Short-Term Forgetting Task (Baddeley & Warrington, 1970). In contrast, a second class of patient appeared to show the opposite pattern with digit spans of 1 or 2 items, very poor Peterson performance, and little or no recency, coupled with apparently normal LTM (Shallice & Warrington, 1970). This double dissociation strongly supported a separation of LTM and STM.

By the late 1960s, a range of models began to appear in which STM and LTM were conceptualized as separate systems. The most influential of these was the Atkinson and Shiffrin (1968) model, which became known as the *modal model*. As shown in figure 5.1, it assumes that information comes in from the environment through a parallel series of sensory memory systems into a limited-capacity short-term store, which forms a crucial bottleneck between perception and LTM. The STS was also assumed to be necessary for recall, and to act as a limited-capacity working memory.

In the early 1970s, the modal model encountered two major problems. The first concerned its assumptions regarding long-term learning, while the second involved its capac-

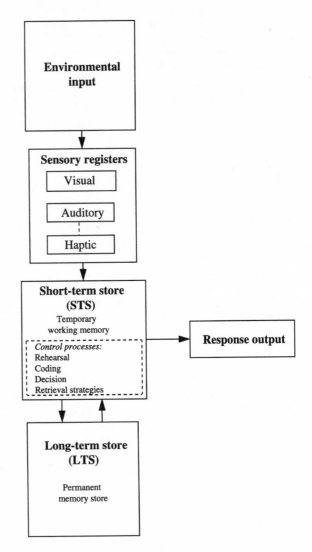

Figure 5.1 Atkinson & Shiffrin's (1968)
influential model of STM.

ity to explain the neuropsychological evidence.

The modal model assumed that the longer an item was held in STS, the greater the chance of its being transferred to the LTS. This assumption was challenged (e.g., Craik & Watkins, 1973), leading Craik and Lockhart (1972) to propose their levels of processing hypothesis. This proposes that the durability of memory increases with depth of processing, hence processing a word in terms of its visual appearance leads to little learning. Phonological processing in terms of sound is somewhat better, whereas deeper semantic processing leads

to the best retention. While the detailed application of this model can be criticized (Baddeley, 1978), there is no doubt that it represents a good account of a considerable amount of data, and that the underdevelopment of its treatment of coding represents a limitation of the modal model.

The second problem with the modal model stems from its apparent prediction that patients with a grossly impaired STS should encounter associated problems in long-term learning. Furthermore, since the STS was assumed to act as working memory, allowing complex information processing to proceed, then such patients should also have major general information-processing deficits. However, the few relatively pure cases studied appeared to have normal long-term memory and to lead largely normal lives (Shallice & Warrington, 1970; Vallar & Shallice, 1990).

Working Memory

In order to tackle this problem, Baddeley and Hitch (1974) proposed that the concept of a single unitary STM be replaced by a multi-component system, focusing on three subsystems. These comprised two slave systems; one, the *phonological loop* was concerned with storing acoustic and verbal information, while the second, the *visuo-spatial sketchpad*, was its visual equivalent (see figure 5.2). The overall system was assumed to be controlled by a limited-capacity attentional system, the *central executive*. While the details of this model and its terminology are by no means universally accepted, the last 20 years have seen an increasing tendency for the term *working memory* to be used, together with a broad general acceptance of the usefulness of postulating a system that combines executive control with more specialized storage systems that show important differences between visual and verbal material (Miyake & Shah, 1999). For that reason, the tripartite structure will be used as a basis for the review, while accepting that there may be a subsequent need to postulate other components.

Verbal Working Memory

This system, labeled by Baddeley and Hitch the *articulatory* or *phonological loop*, is closest in character to the original concept of a short-term store. It is assumed to be defective in the type of patient studied by Shallice and Warrington (1970). The general cognitive disruption implied by the modal model does not occur because the central executive is intact in such patients. The phonological loop is assumed to comprise two components, a store in which an acoustic or phonological memory trace is held. The trace is assumed to decay within about two seconds unless performance is maintained by the second component, the process of subvocal articulatory rehearsal. This process is not only able to refresh the memory trace but can also register visually presented but nameable material in the phonological store by means of articulation. The principal evidence for phonological coding is the previously described acoustic similarity effect, while the role of the articulatory process is supported by the *word length effect*, whereby the immediate memory span for words is a direct function of the length of the constituent items. A simple rule of thumb is that subjects can remember as many items as they can say in two seconds (Baddeley, Thompson, & Buchanan, 1975). Baddeley and Hitch explained this phenomenon in terms of trace decay, proposing that subvocal maintenance rehearsal occurs in real time, hence long words take longer to rehearse, allowing

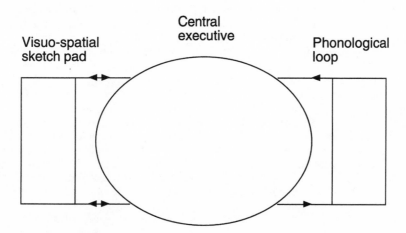

Figure 5.2 The Working Memory model proposed by Baddeley & Hitch (1974).

more forgetting through trace decay. Cowan et al. (1992) suggest that the word length effect principally is a function of forgetting during the process of recall, with longer words taking longer to produce, hence allowing more decay. As the effect can also be found, though to a lesser extent, with probed recall, it seems likely that both rehearsal rate and output time contribute to the word-length effect (Avons, Wright, & Pammer, 1994).

Articulatory suppression is a procedure whereby the subject is required to utter some repeated redundant sound such as the word "the" while performing another task such as memory span. Murray (1968) showed that suppression reduces performance and also eliminates the phonological similarity effect, with visual, though not with auditory, presentation. This is assumed to occur because suppression prevents the subject from converting the visual stimulus into a verbal code that is suitable for registering in the phonological store. With auditory presentation, access to the store is assumed to be automatic (Baddeley, 1986). The effect of suppression on the word-length effect is assumed to be somewhat different. Since the word-length effect is a direct function of rehearsal, suppression will remove the effect, regardless of whether presentation is auditory or visual, as indeed is the case (Baddeley, Lewis, & Vallar, 1984).

Another area of considerable activity and controversy in connection with the word-length effect relates to individual differences. If trace decay is responsible for the word-length effect, then subjects who rehearse more slowly should show poorer performance. This was indeed found by Baddeley et al. (1975). Nicolson (1981) observed that developmental changes in children's memory span were associated with changes in speed of articulation, suggesting that faster rehearsal might be responsible for the increase in span with age. The effect was replicated by subsequent studies (e.g., Hitch, Halliday, Dodd, & Littler, 1989), while research on serial recall of pictured objects suggested that verbal coding was a strategy that children begin to adopt between the ages of 7 and 10, as reflected by the influence on performance of the acoustic similarity of the names in the set and of their spoken length (Hitch, Halliday, Schaafstad, & Hefferman, 1991). Younger children appear to use some form of visual code, and hence perform more poorly when the items depicted are similar in shape—for example, a spoon, a pen, and a twig.

When material is presented auditorily, phonological similarity and word-length effects appear at a much earlier age, a result which was initially taken to suggest that rehearsal begins at this early stage. However, opinion is now shifting toward the assumption that this very early rehearsal reflects a different and relatively automatic process—more like a spontaneous internal echoing of the stimulus than a coherent cumulative rehearsal strategy such as is found in older children and adults (Gathercole & Hitch, 1993).

Finally, there has been considerable interest in recent years in the possible evolutionary function of the phonological loop; if patients can show gross impairment in memory span with little impact on everyday functioning, can the loop be of much biological significance? Initial work focused on the possible role of the loop in language comprehension (Vallar & Baddeley, 1984). Although there are some differences among patients, the general consensus is that most have difficulty only when syntactic structures require the literal maintenance of the first part of the sentence until it is disambiguated at the end, as for example in the case of self-embedded sentences (see Vallar & Shallice, 1990, for a review).

A much stronger case for the importance of the phonological loop can be made in the case of new phonological learning. For example, PV, a patient with a very pure STM deficit, showed no difficulty in learning to associate pairs of words in her own language, but was grossly impaired in capacity to learn the vocabulary of an unfamiliar language, Russian (Baddeley, Papagno, & Vallar, 1988). In a subsequent study, Gathercole and Baddeley (1990) found that children with a specific language disability were particularly impaired in their capacity to hear and repeat back unfamiliar sound sequences. This deficit was more pronounced than their language impairment and did not appear to be attributable to either perceptual or speech production problems. This work led to the development of a nonword repetition test in which the subject attempts to repeat spoken nonwords ranging in length from 2 syllables (e.g., *ballop*) to 5 (e.g., *voltularity*). Nonword repetition performance proved to correlate with level of vocabulary development across a wide range of ages; over the 4- to 5-year range, cross-lagged correlation suggested that nonword repetition was causally related to the subsequent development of vocabulary, rather than the reverse (see Baddeley, Gathercole, & Papagno, 1998, for a review). Finally, the phonological short-term store appears to be related to the capacity for second-language acquisition in both children (Service, 1992) and adults (Papagno, Valentine, & Baddeley, 1991), with variables such as articulatory suppression, phonological similarity, and word length all influencing the acquisition of novel word forms but not affecting the capacity to associate pairs of already familiar words, a process that is assumed to depend principally on semantic coding (Papagno & Vallar, 1992).

Neurobiological Evidence

Neuropsychological studies of STM patients suggested an impaired phonological store (Vallar & Baddeley, 1984; Vallar & Shallice, 1990). The capacity to articulate overtly is not necessary for rehearsal since dysarthric patients with a peripheral disruption to speech production appear to have normal rehearsal capacities (Baddeley & Wilson, 1985). However, dyspraxia, a disruption of the basic capacity to program speech output, does interfere with memory performance (Waters, Rochon, & Caplan, 1992).

More recently, functional imagery studies using PET and fMRI have produced clear evidence for a phonological short-term store located in the perisylvian region of the left hemisphere, together with a separate rehearsal component associated with Broca's area (Paulesu, Frith, & Frackowiak, 1993; Awh et al., 1996).

Visuo-Spatial Working Memory

As described earlier, evidence for the storage of visual information has been available for many years. The use of visuo-spatial coding for verbal material was demonstrated particularly neatly by Brooks (1967), using a technique in which subjects were induced to store a sequence of sentences by recoding them in terms of a path through a visually presented matrix. Using this paradigm, Baddeley, Grant, Wight, and Thomson (1973) showed that visuo-spatial tracking, but not verbal coding, interfered with visual-imagery-based performance, in contrast to a broadly equivalent verbally coded task. Further work suggested that the coding was specifically *spatial* (Baddeley & Lieberman, 1980). However, using a somewhat different memory paradigm involving the use of visual imagery in paired-associ-

ate learning, Logie (1986) showed that performance could be disrupted by the simple requirement to observe patterns or patches of color, a *visual* rather than a spatial task.

Most disrupting tasks tend to involve both visual and spatial processing, and may also tend to have an executive component (see Logie, 1995, for a review). The technique recently developed by Quinn and McConnell (1996) appears to minimize disruption to anything other than the visual component of the working memory system. Their disrupting task simply requires the subject to fixate on a screen on which a large matrix of cells is continuously flickering on and off. They find that this influences performance when subjects are learning paired associates using an imagery mnemonic, while having no effect on rote learning performance, in contrast to the effects of irrelevant speech, which produces the opposite pattern.

Further evidence for separating visual and spatial aspects of STM come from the observation that pattern span, in which subjects have to reproduce a pattern of filled and unfilled cells in a matrix, is disrupted by the subsequent requirement to look at a series of abstract pictures, but not by a spatial tapping task, in contrast to the more spatial and serial Corsi Block Tapping Task, which shows exactly the opposite pattern (Della Sala et al., in press).

Neurobiological Evidence

Evidence for separate visual and spatial components of the STM system come from neuropsychological studies, with separate patients capable of performing the Corsi Block but not the pattern span task and vice versa (Della Sala et al., in press). Finally, neuroradiological evidence indicates the separability of visual and verbal memory (Smith, Jonides, & Koeppe, 1996), and within that, a distinction between spatial and object-based components (Smith et al., 1995). This area continues to develop, and further fractionation seems probable (Baddeley, 1998b).

Executive Processes

Individual Difference in Working Memory Span

While work utilizing the Baddeley and Hitch model has tended to concentrate on the slave systems, postponing a more detailed analysis of the central executive, North American research on working memory has tended to follow the opposite pattern, though with notable exceptions. Furthermore, while neuropsychological evidence has played a particularly important role in European research on working memory, North American research has been more strongly influenced by the psychometric tradition with its concern for individual differences within the normal population. The two approaches are complementary and will be considered in turn.

In a classic paper, Daneman and Carpenter (1980) operationally defined working memory as the system responsible for the simultaneous storage and manipulation of information. They developed a measure, *working memory span*, in which subjects were required to read out a series of sentences and then recall the final word of each. The maximum number of sentences for which all the final words can be correctly recalled is the working memory span, which for normal subjects ranges between 2 and 5. Daneman and Carpenter then demonstrated that span correlated highly with reading comprehension in a sample of student subjects. This finding has been replicated many times (see Daneman & Merikle, 1996, for a review). A series of follow-up studies contrasted subjects who were high and low in span, demonstrating, for example, that there were qualitative differences in the way in which prose is processed by the two groups; for example, high-span subjects are more able to resolve textual ambiguities and to carry information across from one sentence to another in order to do so (Daneman & Carpenter, 1983).

Views differ as to whether the measure was concerned with a language-specific system as proposed, for example, by Daneman and Tardif (1987) or reflects a more general executive processing capacity, as suggested by Turner and Engle (1989), who showed that a measure they call *operation span*, based on arithmetic, predicts reading comprehension virtually as well as the original sentence span.

Further support for the working memory span measure comes from Kyllonen and Christal (1990), who demonstrate that performance on a cluster of working memory span tasks correlates highly with more traditional measures of fluid intelligence while being less subject to the influence of prior knowledge and providing better prediction of success in

acquiring practical skills such as programming than more traditional measures.

However, despite the apparent success of the working memory span measures, they have recently come under criticism, notably from Waters and Caplan (1996a, 1996b), who question the interpretation of earlier results and also report data from neuropsychological patients of various types that they claim are inconsistent with the theoretical interpretation offered by Carpenter and Just (1992). The criticism is relatively recent and the issue still unresolved (see Just, Carpenter, & Keller, 1996). It seems likely that working memory span probably involves the interaction of several cognitive subsystems. This highlights the importance of understanding the task if this approach is to continue to be fruitful.

Analysis of the WM span task has been one of the major problems tackled by Engle and his group. Engle (1996) showed that high-span subjects are better at generating items from semantic categories but, paradoxically, are more impaired than low-span subjects by the requirement to perform a concurrent task. This is interpreted as reflecting the successful use of attentional resources by the high-span subjects to minimize disruption from already generated items, a strategy that is disrupted by the concurrent load. Low-span subjects are unaffected by load because they are incapable or perhaps unwilling to use the inhibitory strategy, and are unaffected by a concurrent attentional demand. A similar intriguing pattern of results is obtained in studying performance on the Sternberg scanning task, for which there is again evidence for a qualitative difference in performance between high- and low-span subjects that is attributed to the capacity to maintain a memory representation against the disruption of potentially interfering items (Conway & Engle, 1994).

While Engle's work is highly creative in linking individual difference measures and more traditional memory measures such as category fluency and the Sternberg task, it appears to demonstrate qualitative differences in performance between high- and low-span subjects. These would seem to be at least as likely to result from differences in strategy as from a qualitative difference in the way in which the memory system works. In either case, the discontinuity casts doubt on using working memory span as a continuous measure. Even more seriously, these results suggest that many of the findings in this area, which are typically based on young students who are presumably of above-average intelligence for the population, may not generalize to samples of older subjects from a wider intellectual range. The success of Kyllonen in using the measures suggests that there is an important core to the work, but the measures are not yet well understood. At the very least, it would be useful to have work that separates out the role of the slave systems from that of executive processes. The necessity for such a separation is supported both by further psychometric research in the working memory span tradition (Shah & Miyake, 1996) and by the growing amount of evidence from functional imagery studies (Smith & Jonides, 1995).

Analysing the Central Executive

Work from a multicomponent approach to working memory has tended to use secondary task techniques, contrasting low processing load tasks such as articulatory suppression and spatial tapping that are targeted at the slave systems, with more demanding tasks, such as random generation of digits or key presses. Baddeley (1986) suggested that the capacity to produce a random stream of items such as digits or letters was constrained by the capacity of the central executive to break away from well-learned stereotypes such as the alphabet by continuously switching to new retrieval plans. Random generation does indeed dramatically impair complex tasks such as choosing the appropriate move in chess, in contrast to the simple suppression effect of reciting the alphabet (Robbins et al., 1996). Similarly, a concurrent digit span task can be shown to interfere with manual generation, with randomness decreasing linearly with digit load (Baddeley, Emslie, Kolodny, & Duncan, 1998).

The initial model of the central executive (Baddeley, 1986) was strongly influenced by Norman and Shallice's (1986) Supervisory Attentional System (SAS), and like the SAS was assumed to depend on the operation of the frontal lobes. However, a clear distinction was made between the question of anatomical localization and that of the functional analysis of the system assumed to reflect the operation of the central executive. It was suggested that the use of the term frontal syndrome should be avoided; the term *dysexecutive syndrome*

was proposed as an alternative (Baddeley & Wilson, 1988).

One danger with the concept of a central executive is that of postulating a homunculus that is simply assumed to have whatever capacities are necessary to account for the data (Parkin, 1998). One response to this charge (Baddeley, 1998a) is to argue for the value of homunculi as a means of allowing the investigator to set aside some of the more intractable problems. The danger occurs when the theorist treats the homunculus as a solution rather than as a problem to be solved.

The question of how to analyze the central executive remains a difficult one. One approach is, of course, that based on individual differences described above. A second is to attempt to understand the breakdown of executive processes following brain damage in frontal lobe patients (e.g., Shallice & Burgess, 1996) or in patients suffering from Alzheimer's disease (Baddeley, Bressi, Della Sala, Logie, & Spinnler, 1991). Both these approaches have proposed a number of separable executive subprocesses, such as the capacity to focus and switch attention and to divide it among a number of sources. Division of attention appears to be particularly impaired in Alzheimer's disease, for example, while being relatively preserved in normal elderly subjects (Baddeley et al., 1991). Given the richness and complexity of executive processes, fractionation is likely to be a long and complex task. There is evidence to suggest, however, that it will benefit substantially from the development of functional imagery studies, which are already giving a very clear indication that different areas of the frontal lobes may be specialized for different executive functions (for an overview, see the papers included in Roberts, Robbins, & Weiskrantz, 1998).

Suppose that we are successful in identifying a finite array of executive processes, will we then have solved the central executive problem? Clearly not, since a crucial issue is the way in which the constituent processes interact. At present we have little evidence to constrain the possibilities, which range from a hierarchical structure with one dominant function, to an array of executive processes of approximately equal status, with a set of rules of interaction from which consensus emerges. If the former, then what is the process that dominates and, if the latter, what are the mechanisms that allow consensus to be reached? The same question arises within the more specialized subsidiary systems accessed. We know that verbal memory span is strongly influenced by phonological factors, but is in addition somewhat sensitive to visual similarity and can, of course, be strongly influenced by semantic and linguistic factors when sentences are retained. As a recent survey of current models of working memory illustrates (Miyake & Shah, 1999), the question of how information from different sources is integrated lies at the heart of many approaches to working memory and is likely to offer one of the most important and challenging problems facing the study of working memory in the years to come.

Acknowledgment The support provided by grant G9423916 from the Medical Research Council is gratefully acknowledged.

References

Adams, J. A., & Dijkstra, S. (1966). Short-term memory for motor responses. *Journal of Experimental Psychology, 71*, 314–318.

Anderson, J. A. (1973). A theory for the recognition of items from short memorized lists. *Psychological Review, 80*, 417–438.

Atkinson, R. C., & Shiffrin, R. M. (1968). Human memory: A proposed system and its control processes. In K. W. Spence (Ed.), *The psychology of learning and motivation: Advances in research and theory* (pp. 89–195). New York: Academic Press.

Avons, S. E., Wright, K. L., & Pammer, K. (1994). The word-length effect in probed and serial recall. *Quarterly Journal of Experimental Psychology, 47a*, 207–231.

Awh, E., Jonides, J., Smith, E. E., Schumacher, E. H., Koeppe, R. A., & Katz, S. (1996). Dissociation of storage and retrieval in verbal working memory: Evidence from positron emission tomography. *Psychological Science, 7*, 25–31.

Baddeley, A. D. (1966a). Short-term memory for word sequences as a function of acoustic, semantic and formal similarity. *Quarterly Journal of Experimental Psychology, 18*, 362–365.

Baddeley, A. D. (1966b). The influence of acoustic and semantic similarity on long-term memory for word sequences. *Quarterly Journal of Experimental Psychology, 18*, 302–309.

Baddeley, A. D. (1978). The trouble with levels: A re-examination of Craik and Lockhart framework for memory research. *Psychological Review, 85*, 139–152.

Baddeley, A. D. (1986). *Working memory.* Oxford: Oxford University Press.

Baddeley, A. D. (1992). Working memory. *Science, 255*, 556–559.

Baddeley, A. D. (1996). The concept of working memory. In S. E. Gathercole (Ed.), *Models of short-term memory* (pp. 1–27). Hove, England: Psychology Press.

Baddeley, A. D. (1998a). The central executive: A concept and some misconceptions. *Journal of the International Neuropsychology Society, 4*, 523–526.

Baddeley, A. D. (1998b). Recent developments in working memory. *Current Opinion in Neurobiology, 8*, 234–238.

Baddeley, A. D., Bressi, S., Della Sala, S., Logie, R., & Spinnler, H. (1991). The decline of working memory in Alzheimer's disease: A longitudinal study. *Brain, 114*, 2521–2542.

Baddeley, A. D., & Ecob, J. R. (1973). Reaction time and short-term memory. Implications of repetition effects for the high-speed exhaustive scan hypothesis. *Quarterly Journal of Experimental Psychology, 25*, 229–240.

Baddeley, A. D., Emslie, H., Kolodny, J., & Duncan, J. (1998). Random generation and the executive control of working memory. *Quarterly Journal of Experimental Psychology, 51A*, 819–852.

Baddeley, A., Gathercole, S., & Papagno, C. (1998). The phonological loop as a language learning device. *Psychological Review, 105*, 158–173.

Baddeley, A. D., Grant, S., Wight, E., & Thomson, N. (1973). Imagery and visual working memory. In P. M. A. Rabbitt & S. Dornic (Eds.), *Attention and performance V* (pp. 205–217). London: Academic Press.

Baddeley, A. D., & Hitch, G. J. (1974). Working memory. In G. A. Bower (Ed.), *The psychology of learning and motivation* (pp. 47–89). New York: Academic Press.

Baddeley, A. D., & Hitch, G. J. (1993). The recency effect: Implicit learning with explicit retrieval? *Memory and Cognition, 21*, 146–155.

Baddeley, A. D., Lewis, V. J., & Vallar, G. (1984). Exploring the articulatory loop. *Quarterly Journal of Experimental Psychology, 36*, 233–252.

Baddeley, A. D., & Lieberman, K. (1980). Spatial working memory. In R. S. Nickerson (Ed.), *Attention and performance VIII* (pp. 521–539). Hillsdale: NJ: Erlbaum.

Baddeley, A. D., Papagno, C., & Vallar, G. (1988). When long-term learning depends on short-term storage. *Journal of Memory and Language, 27,* 586–595.

Baddeley, A. D., & Scott, D. (1971). Short-term forgetting in the absence of proactive interference. *Quarterly Journal of Experimental Psychology, 23,* 275–283.

Baddeley, A. D., Thomson, N., & Buchanan, M. (1975). Word length and the structure of short-term memory. *Journal of Verbal Learning and Verbal Behaviour, 14,* 575–589.

Baddeley, A. D., Vallar, G., & Wilson, B. A. (1987). Sentence comprehension and phonological memory: Some neuropsychological evidence. In M. Coltheart (Ed.), *Attention and performance XII: The psychology of reading* (pp. 509–529). London: Erlbaum.

Baddeley, A. D., & Warrington, E. K. (1970). Amnesia and the distinction between long- and short-term memory. *Journal of Verbal Learning and Verbal Behavior, 9,* 176–189.

Baddeley, A. D., & Wilson, B. (1985). Phonological coding and short-term memory in patients without speech. *Journal of Memory and Language, 24,* 490–502.

Baddeley, A. D., & Wilson, B. (1988). Frontal amnesia and the dysexecutive syndrome. *Brain & Cognition, 7*(2), 212–230.

Broadbent, D. E. (1958). *Perception and communication.* London: Pergamon Press.

Brooks, L. R. (1967). The suppression of visualization by reading. *Quarterly Journal of Experimental Psychology, 19,* 289–299.

Brown, J. (1958). Some tests of the decay theory of immediate memory. *Quarterly Journal of Experimental Psychology, 10,* 12–21.

Conrad, R. (1962). An association between memory errors and errors due to acoustic masking of speech. *Nature, 193,* 1314–1315.

Conrad, R. (1964). Acoustic confusion in immediate memory. *British Journal of Psychology, 55,* 75–84.

Conway, A. R. A., & Engle, R. W. (1994). Working memory and retrieval: A resource-dependent inhibition model. *Journal of Experimental Psychology: General, 123,* 354–373.

Corballis, M. C., Kirby, J., & Miller, A. (1972). Access to elements of a memorised list. *Journal of Experimental Psychology, 94,* 185–190.

Cowan, N., Day, L., Saults, J. S., Keller, T. A., Johnson, T., & Flores, L. (1992). The role of verbal output time and the effects of word length on immediate memory. *Journal of Memory and Language, 31,* 1–17.

Craik, F. I. M., & Lockhart, R. S. (1972). Levels of processing: A framework for memory research. *Journal of Verbal Learning and Verbal Behavior, 11,* 671–684.

Craik, F. I. M., & Watkins, M. J. (1973). The role of rehearsal in short-term memory. *Journal of Verbal Learning and Verbal Behavior, 11,* 671–684.

Crowder, R. G. (1982). The demise of short-term memory. *Acta Psychologica, 50,* 291–323.

Dale, H. C. A. (1973). Short-term memory for visual information. *British Journal of Psychology, 64,* 1–8.

Daneman, M., & Carpenter, P. A. (1980). Individual differences in working memory and reading. *Journal of Verbal Learning and Verbal Behaviour, 19,* 450–466.

Daneman, M., & Carpenter, P. A. (1983). Individual difference in integrating information between and within sentences. *Journal of Experimental Psychology: Learning, Memory and Cognition, 9,* 561–584.

Daneman, M., & Merikle, P. M. (1996). Working memory and language comprehension: A meta-analysis. *Psychonomic Bulletin & Review, 3,* 422–433.

Daneman, M., & Tardif, T. (1987). Working memory and reading skill re-examined. In M. Coltheart (Ed.), *Attention and performance* (pp. 491–508). Hove, England: Erlbaum.

Della Sala, S., Gray, C., Baddeley, A. D., Allamano, N., & Wilson, L. (in press). Pattern span: A means of unwelding visuo-spatial memory. *Neuropsychologia.*

Della Sala, S., Gray, C., Baddeley, A. D., & Wilson, L. (1997). *The visual patterns test: A test of short-term visual recall.* Flempton Bury & Edomonds, England: Thames Valley Test Company.

Engen, T., Kuisma, J. E., & Eimas, P. D. (1973). Short-term memory of odors. *Journal of Experimental Psychology, 99,* 222–225.

Engle, R. W. (1996). Working memory and retrieval: An inhibition-resource approach. In J. T. E. Richardson, R. W. Engle, L. Hasher, R. H. Logie, E. R. Stoltfus, & R. T. Zacks (Eds.), *Working memory and human cognition* (pp. 89–119). New York: Oxford University Press.

Gathercole, S. E. (1996). *Models of short-term memory.* Hove, England: Psychology Press.

Gathercole, S. E., & Baddeley, A. D. (1990). Phonological memory deficits in language-disordered children: Is there a causal connection? *Journal of Memory and Language, 29*, 336–360.

Gathercole, S. E., & Hitch, G. J. (1993). Developmental changes in short-term memory: A revised working memory perspective. In A. Collins, S. E. Gathercole, M. A. Conway, & P. E. Morris (Eds.), *Theories of memory*. Hove, England: Erlbaum.

Gilson, A. D., & Baddeley, A. D. (1969). Tactile short-term memory. *Quarterly Journal of Experimental Psychology, 21*, 180–184.

Glanzer, M. (1972). Storage mechanisms in recall. In G. H. Bower (Ed.), *The psychology of learning and motivation: Advances in research and theory*. New York: Academic Press.

Goldman-Rakic, P. S. (1996). The prefrontal landscape: Implications of functional architecture for understanding human mentation and the central executive. *Philosophical Transactions of the Royal Society (Biological Sciences), 351*, 1445–1453.

Haxby, J. V., Ungerleider, L. G., Horwitz, B., Rapoport, S. I., & Grady, C. L. (1995). Hemispheric differences in neural systems for face working memory: a PET-rCBF study. *Human Brain Mapping, 3*, 68–82.

Hebb, D. O. (1949). *Organization of behavior.* New York: John Wiley.

Hitch, G. J., Halliday, M. S., Dodd, A., & Littler, J. E. (1989). Development of rehearsal in short-term memory: Differences between pictorial and spoken stimuli. *British Journal of Developmental Psychology, 7*, 347–362.

Hitch, G. J., Halliday, M. S., Schaafstal, A. M., & Heffernan, T. M. (1991). Speech, "inner speech" and the development of short-term memory: Effects of picture labelling on recall. *Journal of Experimental Child Psychology, 51*, 220–234.

Hockey, G. R. J. (1973). Rate of presentation in running memory and direct manipulation of input processing strategies. *Quarterly Journal of Experimental Psychology, 25*, 104–111.

James, W. (1890). *The principles of psychology.* New York: Holt, Rinehart & Winston.

Just, M. A., Carpenter, P. A., & Keller, T. A. (1996). The capacity theory of comprehension: New frontiers of evidence and arguments. *Psychological Review, 103*, 773–780.

Keppel, G., & Underwood, B. J. (1962). Proactive inhibition in short-term retention of single items. *Journal of Verbal Learning and Verbal Behavior, 1*, 153–161.

Kintsch, W., & Buschke, H. (1969). Homophones and synonyms in short-term mem-

ory. *Journal of Experimental Psychology, 80*, 403–407.

Kyllonen, P. C., & Christal, R. E. (1990). Reasoning ability is (little more than) working memory capacity. *Intelligence, 14*, 389–433.

Lambert, B. L. (1997). Predicting look-alike and sound-alike medication errors. *American Journal of Health-system Pharmacy, 54*, 1161–1171.

Loess, H., & Waugh, N. C. (1967). Short-term memory and inter-trial interval. *Journal of Verbal Learning and Verbal Behaviour, 6*, 445–460.

Logie, R. H. (1986). Visuo-spatial processing in working memory. *Quarterly Journal of Experimental Psychology, 38A*, 229–247.

Logie, R. H. (1995). *Visuo-spatial working memory.* Hove, England: Erlbaum.

Melton, A. W. (1963). Implications of short-term memory for a general theory of memory. *Journal of Verbal Learning and Verbal Behavior, 2*, 1–21.

Miller, G. A. (1956). The magical number seven, plus or minus two: Some limits on our capacity for processing information. *Psychological Review, 63*, 81–97.

Miller, G. A., Galanter, E., & Pribram, K. H. (1960). *Plans and the structure of behavior.* New York: Holt, Reinhart & Winston.

Miller, G. A., & Selfridge, J. A. (1950). Verbal context and the recall of meaningful material. *American Journal of Psychology, 63*, 176–185.

Milner, B. (1966). Amnesia following operation on the temporal lobes. In C. W. M. Whitty & O. L. Zangwill (Eds.), *Amnesia* (pp. 109–133). London: Butterworths.

Milner, B. (1968). Visual recognition and recall after right temporal-lobe excision in man. *Neuropsychologia, 6*, 191–209.

Miyake, A., & Shah, P. (Eds.). (1999). *Models of working memory: Mechanisms of active maintenance and executive control.* New York: Cambridge University Press.

Murray, D. J. (1968). Articulation and acoustic confusability in short-term memory. *Journal of Experimental Psychology, 78*, 679–684.

Newell, A., & Simon, H. A. (1972). *Human problem solving.* Englewood Cliffs, NJ: Prentice-Hall.

Nicolson, R. (1981). The relationship between memory span and processing speed. In M. Friedman, J. P. Das, & N. O'Connor (Eds.), *Intelligence and learning* (pp. 179–184). New York: Plenum Press.

Norman, D. A., & Shallice, T. (1986). Attention to action: Willed and automatic control of behaviour. In R. J. Davidson, G. E. Schwarts, & D. Shapiro (Eds.), *Consciousness and self-regulation. Advances in research and theory* (pp. 1–18). New York: Plenum Press.

Olton, D. S., Walker, J. A., & Gage, F. H. (1978). Hippocampal connections and spatial discrimination. *Brain Research, 139*, 295–308.

Papagno, C., Valentine, T., & Baddeley, A. D. (1991). Phonological short-term memory and foreign language vocabulary learning. *Journal of Memory and Language, 30*, 331–347.

Papagno, C., & Vallar, G. (1992). Phonological short-term memory and the learning of novel words: The effect of phonological similarity and item length. *Quarterly Journal of Experimental Psychology, 44A*, 47–67.

Parkin, A. J. (1998). The central executive does not exist. *Journal of the International Neuropsychology Society, 4*, 518–522.

Paulesu, E., Frith, C. D., & Frackowiak, R. S. J. (1993). The neural correlates of the verbal component of working memory. *Nature, 362*, 342–345.

Peterson, L. R., & Peterson, M. J. (1959). Short-term retention of individual verbal items. *Journal of Experimental Psychology, 58*, 193–198.

Phillips, W. A. (1974). On the distinction between sensory storage and short-term visual memory. *Perception and Psychophysics, 16*, 283–290.

Phillips, W. A., & Christie, D. F. M. (1977). Components of visual memory. *Quarterly Journal of Experimental Psychology, 29*, 117–133.

Quinn, G., & McConnell, J. (1996). Irrelevant pictures in visual working memory. *Quarterly Journal of Experimental Psychology, 49A*, 200–215.

Robbins, T., Anderson, E., Barker, D., Bradley, A., Fearneyhough, C., Henson, R., Hudson, S., & Baddeley, A. D. (1996). Working memory in chess. *Memory and Cognition, 24*(1), 83–93.

Roberts, A. C., Robbins, T. W., & Weiskrantz, L. (1998). *The pre-frontal cortex: Executive and cognitive functions*. Oxford: Oxford University Press.

Service, E. (1992). Phonology, working memory and foreign-language learning. *Quarterly Journal of Experimental Psychology, 45A*, 21–50.

Shah, P., & Miyake, A. (1996). The separability of working memory resources for spatial thinking and language processing. *Journal of Experimental Psychology: General, 125*, 4–27.

Shallice, T., & Burgess, P. (1996). The domain of supervisory processes and temporal organization of behaviour. *Philosophical Transactions of the Royal Society of London Series B—Biological Sciences, 351*(1346), 1405–1411.

Shallice, T., & Warrington, E. K. (1970). Independent functioning of verbal memory stores: A neuropsychological study. *Quarterly Journal of Experimental Psychology, 22*, 261–273.

Smith, E. E., & Jonides, J. (1995). Working memory in humans: Neuropsychological Evidence. In M. Gazzaniga (Ed.), *The cognitive neurosciences* (pp. 109–1020). Cambridge, MA: MIT Press.

Smith, E., Jonides, J., & Koeppe, R. A. (1996). Dissociating verbal and spatial working memory using PET. *Cerebral Cortex, 6*, 11–20.

Smith, E. E., Jonides, J., Koeppe, R. A., Awh, E., Schumacher, E., & Minoshima, S. (1995). Spatial versus object working memory: PET investigations. *Journal of Cognitive Neuroscience, 7*, 337–358.

Sperling, G. (1963). A model for visual memory tasks. *Human Factors, 5*, 19–31.

Sternberg, S. (1966). High-speed scanning in human memory. *Science, 153*, 652–654.

Theios, J. (1973). Reaction time measurements in the study of memory process: Theory and data. In G. H. Bower (Ed.), *The Psychology of Learning & Motivation.* Vol. 7. (pp. 43–85). New York: Academic Press.

Tulving, E., & Patkau, J. E. (1962). Concurrent effects of contextual constraint and word frequency on immediate recall and learning of verbal material. *Canadian Journal of Psychology, 16*, 83–95.

Tulving, E., & Pearlstone, Z. (1966). Availability versus accessibility of information in memory for words. *Journal of Verbal Learning and Verbal Behavior, 5*, 381–391.

Turner, M. L., & Engel, R. W. (1989). Is working memory capacity task-dependent? *Journal of Memory and Language, 28*, 127–154.

Vallar, G., & Baddeley, A. D. (1984). Fractionation of working memory. Neuropsychological evidence for a phonological short-term store. *Journal of Verbal Learning and Verbal Behaviour, 23*, 151–161.

Vallar, G., & Shallice, T. (Eds.). (1990). *Neuropsychological impairments of short-term memory*. Cambridge: Cambridge University Press.

Waters, G. S., & Caplan, D. (1996a). The measurement of verbal working memory capacity and its relation to reading comprehension. *Quarterly Journal of Experimental Psychology, 49a*, 51–79.

Waters, G. S., & Caplan, D. (1996b). The capacity theory of sentence comprehension: Critique of Just & Carpenter (1992). *Psychological Review, 103*, 761–772.

Waters, G. S., Rochon, E., & Caplan, D.

(1992). The role of high-level speech planning in rehearsal: Evidence from patients with apraxia of speech. *Journal of Memory and Language, 31*, 54–73.

Waugh, N. C., & Norman, D. A. (1965). Primary memory. *Psychological Review, 72*, 89–104.

Wickens, D. D. (1970). Encoding categories of words: an empirical approach to meaning. *Psychological Review, 77*, 1–15.

6

Encoding and Retrieval of Information

SCOTT C. BROWN & FERGUS I. M. CRAIK

The purpose of this chapter is to outline some recent developments in our understanding of human memory processes—specifically, encoding and retrieval processes in long-term episodic memory. A brief history of work in this area is provided, followed by a discussion of memory codes. The nature of encoding and retrieval operations is then explored, with a discussion of how these two types of processes interact. The chapter concludes with a description of some factors that lead to enhancement and impairment of memory performance.

The Information Processing Framework

The terms *encoding* and *retrieval* have their origins in the information-processing framework of the 1960s, which characterized the human mind/brain as an information-processing device (see also Bower, chapter 1, for a more detailed history of memory research). In this model, the mind—like the computer—receives informational input that it retains for a variable duration and subsequently outputs in some meaningful form. *Encoding*, therefore, refers to the process of acquiring information or placing it into memory, whereas *retrieval* refers to the process of recovering previously encoded information. However, this early work focused less on encoding and retrieval than it did on storage or retention of information. In one of the more prominent variants of information-processing theory, sometimes called the multistore or modal model, information is presumed to flow through a series of mental stores (Atkinson & Shiffrin, 1971; and see also Bower, chapter 1). In this model, information enters the processing system through modality-specific sensory stores and then proceeds to a limited short-term or primary memory before entering a permanent and extensive long-term or secondary memory. The key to successful encoding in this model is attention—that is, in order for information to proceed to progressively more capacious and durable stores, the learner has to pay conscious attention to the information. The more rehearsal that the individual engages in, the greater the likelihood that the information will be transferred from short-term to permanent storage (Atkinson & Shiffrin, 1968). So, for example, when processing language, the "literal" sensory input decays rapidly unless selected by attentional mechanisms that transform it into short-term auditory or visual representations. Further processing usually transforms the short-term information into long-term semantic representations that can be recovered minutes or even years later. This information-processing model of memory has been very influential and is still in use some 30 years later.

However, the three-store model is not without its problems: For example, subsequent research showed that the capacity, coding, and forgetting characteristics of short-term memory varied as a function of people, materials, and tasks (e.g., Naveh-Benjamin & Ayres, 1986; Shulman, 1972). Moreover, models appealing to both passive stores and active processes were considered less parsimonious than one appealing solely to active processes. That is, if the experiential and behavioral aspects of memory can be accounted for by considering the characteristics of various encoding and retrieval processes themselves, the concept of a "memory store" loses theoretical meaning and thus becomes superfluous. As an alternative framework, Craik and Lockhart (1972) proposed that incoming stimuli were processed to different levels, or depths, within the cognitive system, from "shallow" or sensory levels to "deep" or meaningful levels of analysis. Memory is considered to be the by-product of such active perceptual and cognitive processes; the more deeply or meaningfully the information is processed, the more well retained the information will be. This levels-of-processing (LOP) view thus emphasizes the role of mental operations in memory, particularly encoding processes. Clearly, retrieval processes are also important and, as discussed later, a more complete model incorporates the LOP view of encoding with views emphasizing the compatibility of encoding and retrieval operations (e.g., Morris, Bransford, & Franks, 1977).

The Nature of Memory Codes

It seems likely that our memory for personally experienced events, along with accrued knowledge and skilled procedures, must ultimately be represented in the brain by complex networks of neurons. In this sense, specific neural networks represent various life experiences in a coded form, and the assumption is that when a particular network is active, we reexperience the event or recollect the fact. However, it is also possible to talk about memory codes at a cognitive level. That is, different aspects of an experienced event are encoded—for example, an object's shape, texture, location, and function—and part of the cognitive researcher's task is therefore to clas-

sify these qualitatively different dimensions of encoding, to work out their interrelations, and to specify their implications for later memory of the original event (Bower, 1967). If these different aspects of an encoded object or event are stored in somewhat different regions of the brain, an important problem concerns how the aspects are bound together during the encoding and retrieval processes to yield the experience of a single coherent object or event. This "binding problem" is ubiquitous in cognitive theorizing (see, e.g., Chalfonte & Johnson, 1996; and Johnson & Chalfonte, 1994).

One possibility is that all sensory modalities first represent and store rather literal copies of the surface aspects of objects (e.g., color, size, shape), and that subsequent interactions with the same objects reveal the relations among the sensory elements, as well as "deeper" aspects such as function, significance, and value. By this view, the cognitive system is organized hierarchically, with lower levels representing sensory aspects and higher levels representing derived aspects ("significance" or "meaning") of objects and events. The lower, shallow levels of processing may be driven predominantly by perceptual inputs (bottom-up or data-driven processing) and the higher (deeper) levels driven either by the same perceptual inputs, or activated "top down" by expectations and intentions (Norman, 1968). If shallow levels of representation are *not* well accessed by top-down processes, this may be one reason sensory codes are difficult to maintain and rehearse (e.g., Posner & Keele, 1967). A further difference between sensory and conceptual codes is that sensory codes are likely to be reused in many different combinations, just as the 26 letters of the alphabet are recombined to form many different unique words; conceptual codes, on the other hand, are more usually specific and differentiable (Moscovitch & Craik, 1976).

It is natural enough to regard these various coded representations as the *product* or residue of processing operations; that is, as *structures* of the mind and of the brain. Some theorists have taken a more radical position, however, and argued that the coded representations of experiences are the *processes* themselves (e.g., Kolers & Roediger, 1984). By this account, the activity of remembering is similar to the activity of perceiving; the mental experiences of perceiving and remembering occur only when the relevant processing operations are themselves occurring. It is even possible to think that the similarity between perceiving and remembering is more than an analogy; that memory encoding processes are identical to those processes carried out primarily for the purposes of perception and comprehension, and that memory retrieval processes represent the cognitive system's best efforts to reinstate the same pattern of mental activity that occurred during the original experience (Craik, 1983; Craik & Lockhart, 1972).

Of course, there must be *some* physical change in the brain that corresponds to the formation and storage of each new memory, but this material basis of memory may again be different from the pattern of neural activity that is the correlate of the mental experience of remembering. A videotape recording may provide an analogy here. The tape itself contains a static coded representation of the filmed events; the tape has the potential to give rise to a specific pattern of electromagnetic activity when run through the VCR, and this activity in turn causes the dynamic images (the "phenomenal experience") to appear on the video screen. When analyzing and researching memory codes we may, therefore, have to consider three very different levels of representation: a structural level of neurochemical changes in the brain, a pattern of neural activity that is triggered and guided by the first level, and the mental experience that is a correlate of activity at the second level. Each level of representation will have its own rules and characteristics, and there will also be "mapping rules" by which adjacent levels communicate. A comprehensive science of memory will, therefore, have to provide an account of memory codes at these various levels, as well as an account of how one set of codes maps on to the other sets (see Konorski, 1967; Velichkovsky, 1994, for similar ideas).

Types of Memory Code

This chapter is concerned with codes at the psychological level only; other chapters of the handbook deal with the neural correlates of these codes. Most memory research by cognitive psychologists has dealt with language or alphanumeric materials—numbers, letters, syllables, words, sentences, and texts—so the study of encoding processes has concentrated substantially on verbal codes. Pictures have been studied to a lesser extent, and some important contrasts have been drawn between pictorial and verbal codes. For example, Paivio (1971) proposed an influential dual-code

hypothesis in which he suggests that many events are represented in two very different ways: an analogue code that preserves the physical features of the object or scene (e.g., an image of a cat under a table), and a symbolic code that provides a verbal description of the event (e.g., "the cat is under the table"). In support of this hypothesis, researchers have shown that visual perception interferes with visual imagery (both sets of processes presumably utilizing the pictorial coding system), but that visual perception of scenes or objects interferes only negligibly with the mental manipulation of verbal material (Baddeley, 1983; Brooks, 1968). Paivio (1971) has also demonstrated that memory is enhanced when an event can be encoded by both systems; thus concrete nouns like TABLE and HORSE are readily encoded imaginally as well as verbally, whereas abstract nouns (e.g., TRUTH, JUSTICE) do not easily yield a pictorial image. The finding is that concrete nouns are better recalled than are abstract nouns; two codes are better than one.

The dual-coding hypothesis seems very much on the right track, but probably does not go far enough. There must also be codes for voices, melodies, textures, tastes, smells, and many other aspects of our perceptual experiences. But there is no reason to think that their memory codes obey different laws; it seems likely, in fact, that such stimuli encoded only in terms of their surface features will not be remembered well, and that those encoded "deeply" in terms of domain-relevant meaning will be well retained. It is important to note that "meaning" does not refer to linguistic meaning only; a familiar face, a well-known voice, an evocative picture, a spectacular chess move or football play—are all examples of stimuli that are meaningful and thus likely to be encoded deeply and well remembered. From this point of view, expertise in the domain of encoding under investigation is a prerequisite for attaining deeper levels of processing (Bransford, Franks, Morris, & Stein, 1979).

Some examples of investigations of these less usual encoding dimensions include studies of face recognition (Moscovitch, Winocur, & Behrmann, 1997) and voice recognition (Read & Craik, 1995). Pictures are extremely well recognized (e.g., Standing, 1973), presumably because we are all "experts" in visual perception. There is relatively little work on memory for touch, taste, or smell; Herz and Engen (1996) provide a useful review of studies of memory for odors. On the other hand,

Wilson and Emmorey (1997) have recently examined the nature of representation in sign language: it appears that deaf signers employ memory codes similar to hearing subjects (i.e., articulatory and phonological representations), albeit within the visuo-spatial domain. Finally, studies of musical memory (see Levitin, in press, for a review) suggest that melodies are encoded abstractly; that is, we tend to recall the relative frequencies and durations of musical notes rather than their absolute frequencies or durations. However, some absolute information is retained, as when nonmusicians sing their favorite song from memory and approximate the tones used in the original recording (Levitin, 1994). In summary, it appears that memories may be coded along a multitude of dimensions and that several codes may be retained from a single experienced event.

Another class of code is memory for contextual detail, as opposed to memory for the focal event itself. One example of context memory is memory for the source from which information was learned. Memory for the event itself and its source are often dissociable (Schacter, Harbluk, & McLachlan, 1984). Thus a person may remember some newly acquired fact but forget where he or she learned it. Older people are particularly vulnerable to this type of forgetting (McIntyre & Craik, 1987; Spencer & Raz, 1995), resulting in their "telling the same story twice" (Koriat, Ben-Zur, & Sheffer, 1988). Another common experience is what George Mandler (1980) referred to as "the butcher on the bus" phenomenon: when a person's face encountered in an atypical context seems very familiar, yet the perceiver cannot recollect where or when he has met the person. But does contextual information utilize a different type of memory code? It seems most likely that it does *not*; contextual or source information is qualitatively similar to focal event information and is classified as "context" merely because it is of lesser interest to the perceiver. The greater vulnerability of contextual information to forgetting is most likely attributable to its receiving less attention and less comprehensive and elaborate processing.

Encoding Operations

From the preceding discussion it should be clear that several factors are important ingredients of good encoding. Some factors are internal—for example, motivation, strategies, and relevant prior knowledge—and others are external, such as to-be-learned materials and experimental instructions. Some highlights are discussed in the present section.

First, it is important to bear in mind the goals and purposes of the learner. If a person wishes to hold a verbal sequence only briefly—retaining a string of numbers to make a telephone call, for example—then it may be more efficient to encode the string as a speech-motor sequence. This type of short-term articulatory code (the "articulatory loop" in the terminology of Baddeley, 1986) is excellent for short-term retention but poor for longer term memory, as most people know in connection with remembering the names of new acquaintances at a party! Clearly "paying attention" to new information is crucial. However, more than simply attending to something, we must also process it at an abstract, schematic, and conceptual level. For example, Craik and Tulving (1975) showed that when participants were asked questions about a series of words, semantic questions (e.g., "Is the word a type of fish?"—SHARK) led to higher levels of memory in a subsequent surprise test than did questions relating to phonemic ("Does the word rhyme with *park*?") or orthographic features ("Does the word start with *S*?"). Figure 6.1 shows subjects' mean recognition levels for these three conditions (Craik & Tulving, 1975, experiment 1). This result suggests that "paying attention" is not an end in itself; rather, what is crucial is the qualitative nature of the processing operations fueled by attentional resources.

Put another way, the type of rehearsal that the individual engages in determines the success of his or her encoding efforts. There are two main types of rehearsal that are pertinent to the LOP framework: maintenance rehearsal, in which information is kept passively in mind—for example, through rote repetition—and elaborative rehearsal, in which information is meaningfully related to other information, presented either previously or currently. The general finding is that the greater the elaboration—or extensiveness—of one's encodings, the better the subsequent memory (Craik & Tulving, 1975). For example, Craik and Tulving (1975) asked participants to decide whether a word would fit meaningfully in either a simple, medium, or complex sentence. Although all three types of sentences involved conceptual processing, the most complex sentences were remembered best,

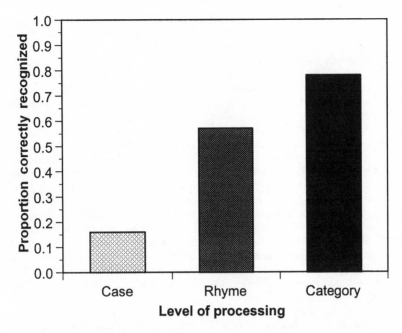

Figure 6.1 Mean proportions of words recognized as a function of processing condition (data from Craik & Tulving, 1975, experiment 1).

presumably because the complex sentences activated larger, richer cognitive structures than did the simpler sentences.

A related issue with rehearsal concerns the timing of the rehearsals: retention after a delay is best when rehearsals are distributed or spaced out over time, rather than massed together in a short period of time. The spacing of rehearsals may be mimicked by actually presenting items to be learned twice, either at short or long intervals. The finding here is that longer spaced repetitions are associated with higher levels of subsequent retention (e.g., Madigan, 1969). Why should this be? One suggestion is that items re-presented after longer intervals are more likely to be encoded somewhat differently from how they were on their first presentation. This encoding variability may be associated with a richer, more elaborate encoding of the item, which in turn supports better retention (Martin, 1968).

In addition to elaborative and distributed rehearsal, organization has been shown to be helpful when learning new information. Organization refers to the grouping together of items into larger units, usually based on meaningful relationships between items. One type of organization is called chunking, which involves grouping items into larger units on the basis of previous experience. Thus, a se-

ries of numbers may be recoded into chunks of adjacent numbers from dates, repetitions, or simple arithmetic sequences; as an example, the series 771968246333 can be broken into 4 chunks, namely 77-1968-246-333. This strategy of chunking may be quite useful during the initial stages of encoding, given claims about the limited capacity of short-term memory (e.g., Miller, 1956). Tulving (1962, 1968) extended the notion of grouping on the basis of previous learning to that of "subjective organization," measured by the consistency of a subject's responses in a series of recall trials from the same list. Tulving's argument was that "similar" items (however defined by the subject) will tend to be recalled together, and the growth of learning over a series of trials will be correlated to the strengthening of inter-item associations and thus to subjective organization. In fact, the results showed a correlation between subjective organization and learning (Tulving, 1962, 1968).

Finally, the distinctiveness of encodings, or the processing of stimulus-specific characteristics, has been shown to improve memory. Moscovitch and Craik (1976) had subjects encode words either shallowly or deeply, and either each word was given its own unique encoding question or groups of 10 words shared the same encoding question. These encoding questions were later presented as retrieval cues, and the finding was that the benefit of unique cues relative to shared cues was greater for deeper levels of encoding. Moscovitch and Craik concluded that deeper encoding establishes a higher ceiling on *potential* memory performance, and that the extent to which this potential is realized depends on the specificity of the cue-target relation. It therefore seems that, ideally, information should be encoded in terms of both item-specific features (characteristics that are unique to a particular stimulus) and associative features (characteristics shared with other information presented either concurrently or previously). In fact, several researchers (e.g., Ausubel, 1962; Einstein & Hunt, 1980) have suggested that both distinctive processing, or the encoding of differences among stimuli, and organization, or the encoding of similarities, are important for successful remembering.

There is also ample evidence that encoding may be guided by an individual's prior knowledge, values, and expectations (e.g., Bartlett, 1932; Bransford & Johnson, 1972). In particular, individuals call upon semantic memory or general world knowledge when encoding and retrieving new information (Neisser, 1998). The implication of these factors for memory is that subjects typically encode more than is presented to them in the stimulus, especially if the stimulus is rich in meaning—a sentence or a picture, for example. Barclay (1973) demonstrated that subjects encode inferences from meaningful sentences, and Barclay, Bransford, Franks, McCarrell, and Nitsch (1974) further showed that different contexts biased a word's encoding in different ways. In a related demonstration, Anderson et al. (1976) showed that people tend to encode particulars rather than generalities; after encoding the phrase, "Fish attacked swimmer," for example, SHARK was a better retrieval cue than FISH for later recall of the phrase.

Similarly, expertise may provide an important mental framework to which incoming information may be attached. For example, in a study of expert versus novice chess players, experts were better than novices at remembering the positions of chess pieces on a "legal" chessboard, but were no better than novices when recalling a "random" chess layout, where pieces' positions did not conform to the rules of chess (e.g., Chase & Simon, 1973; see also Bransford et al., 1979; and Kimball and Holyoak, chapter 7).

With regard to the role of external variables in encoding, much research has supported the notion that the type of material employed also determines the effectiveness of an encoding. In particular, there is the finding that pictures are typically remembered much better than words, known as the *picture superiority effect.* As described previously, Paivio (1971) has argued that this is the case because pictures are more likely to be encoded and stored in two independent codes (e.g., both verbal and imaginal codes) than are words (but see, e.g., Pylyshyn, 1973, for an alternative view). Instructions also play an important role, as most people are not fully knowledgeable about optimal learning strategies. Therefore, instructions to process items coherently and meaningfully (transforming word lists into stories or interacting images, for example) are typically beneficial (Bower, 1970; Paivio, 1971). On the other hand, the *intention* to learn something does not seem to be a factor in its own right, but simply a means of ensuring that some efficient encoding strategy will be used. This conclusion follows from studies showing that incidental (nonintentional) learning can be as effective as, or even more effective than, intentional learning provided that the incidental orienting task induces the learner to process the information in a meaningful, elaborate, and distinctive fashion (Craik & Tulving, 1975; Postman, 1964).

Retrieval Operations

Modern psychological research on memory developed from work on learning, and this shift resulted in an emphasis on the processes of encoding or acquisition; very little thought was given to the equally important problems of memory retrieval. This state of affairs was rectified by a series of studies from Endel Tulving's laboratory in the 1960s (see Tulving, 1983, for a summary account). First, Tulving distinguished two major reasons for forgetting—either the relevant memory trace was no longer *available* (i.e., it had been lost from the system) or it was still present but not *accessible* by means of the present cues (Tulving & Pearlstone, 1966). It is difficult to prove with certainty that a given trace is truly unavailable—it may be that the appropriate cues have not yet been provided—so Tulving's further work focused on the effectiveness of various types of cues. He proposed the notion that successful remembering is a joint function of trace information (reflecting encoding variables) and cue information (reflecting retrieval variables). That is, it is not possible to understand memory by considering either encoding or retrieval in isolation; remembering reflects the interaction between encoding and retrieval processes.

These ideas then led to the encoding specificity principle, which states in essence that a retrieval cue will be effective to the extent that information in the cue was incorporated in the trace of the target event at the time of its original encoding (Tulving, 1983; Tulving & Thomson, 1973). Thus, if the word BRIDGE is encoded as an engineering structure, the subsequent cue "a card game" will be ineffective, but the cue words "girder" or "span" would probably be quite effective. More subtly, if a certain characteristic of an object or event is stressed at encoding, then other salient aspects of the object will not function as effective cues. Barclay et al. (1974) demonstrated this by showing that if the word PIANO was encoded as "something heavy," then the later cue "a musical instrument" was not associated with high levels of recall.

Tulving and Thomson (1973) illustrated the encoding specificity principle in a 4-stage paradigm. First, target words were presented for subjects to learn in the context of a second word; for example, the target word BLACK was presented with the context word "train." In a second (ostensibly unrelated) phase, subjects were asked to generate 6 associations to a series of words; thus the word "white" might be provided and the subject might generate "sheet, snow, color, black, grey, crayon"). In a third (recognition) phase the subject was asked to circle any of his generated words that were on the initial list of target words to be learned. Finally, in phase 4, the original context words (e.g., "train") were re-presented as cues for a cued-recall test. The spectacular result of the study was that subjects recognized few (24%) of the target words from the words that they had previously generated, but were reasonably successful (63%) at recalling the target words when the context words were re-provided in phase 4. The conclusion is that BLACK in the context of "train" is encoded in a specific fashion, and this specific encoding is not "contacted" by BLACK in the context of "white." The result also casts doubt on the "generate-recognize" theory of recall (e.g., Bahrick, 1970; Kintsch, 1970), which states that recall reflects two processes: covert generation of plausible candidates based on the available cues, followed by selection of items for overt

responses by means of a subjective recognition test. The generate-recognize theory predicts that memory performance should be worse when two processes are required of the subject (e.g., recall) than when only one process is required (e.g., recognition). However, Tulving and Thomson found the opposite result, suggesting that the degree of overlap between study and test conditions is more predictive of memory performance than is the requirement to generate a response. Nonetheless, as discussed later, it seems certain that constructive, reconstructive, and generative processes do play an important part in retrieval under certain circumstances (see, e.g., Jacoby & Hollingshead, 1990).

A further dramatic example of encoding specificity is provided by Nilsson, Law, and Tulving (1988). They had subjects learn lists of famous names (e.g., George Washington, Charles Darwin) and well-known cities (e.g., Toronto, Stockholm). At the time of study these names were encoded in the context of compatible phrases (e.g., "A well known building for music in VIENNA"). In a subsequent test of names in the absence of context, subjects failed to recognize many of the names, although they were able to *recall* the names later when reprovided with the study contexts. Thus the phenomenon of recognition failure of recallable words extends even to salient and well-known proper nouns.

Perhaps the main message of the encoding specificity principle is that successful retrieval depends on the similarity of encoding and retrieval operations. This point is generally accepted, and is embodied in other current views of retrieval. For instance, Kolers (1973, 1979) suggested that recognition memory performance improves to the extent that the processing operations carried out during retrieval replicate those carried out at the time of encoding. In a similar vein, the concept of transfer-appropriate processing postulates that good memory performance is a positive function of the degree of overlap between encoding and retrieval processes (Morris et al., 1977; Roediger, Weldon, & Challis, 1989). But it does not appear to be the case that compatibility between encoding and retrieval operations is all that matters; the depth (or type) of initial encoding also plays a major role. For instance, Morris et al. (1977) demonstrated that when words were tested for recognition in terms of their rhyming characteristics, rhyme encoding cues were more effective than semantic encoding cues, but on the other hand, the combination of semantic encoding and semantic retrieval (standard item recognition) was superior to that of rhyme encoding and rhyme retrieval. The data from their Experiment 1 are shown in table 6.1. For target words associated with positive responses at encoding, the semantic-semantic and rhyme-rhyme encoding-test combinations yielded recognition scores of 0.84 and 0.49, respectively. Morris et al. argue that semantic processing is not necessarily superior to other types of encoding—memory performance will depend both on the compatibility between encoding and test, and on the purposes and expertise of the learner. Interestingly, table 6.1 also shows that the superiority of rhyme-rhyme over semantic-rhyme does not hold for targets associated with negative responses at encoding, perhaps because in this case the target words are not so richly encoded in terms of their rhyming characteristics. One way of summing up the situation is to say that the type of initial encoding sets limits on the probability of later retrieval; the degree to which this potential is realized then depends on the compatibility between encoding and retrieval information (Moscovitch & Craik, 1976).

One further salient characteristic of retrieval is its constructive or reconstructive nature. The cognitive approach to perception, learning, and the higher mental processes stresses the notion that the whole cognitive system is active and constructive, as opposed to the more passive and reactive view engendered by behaviorist approaches. Thus, even perception depends substantially on past experience and what we expect to perceive, and such "top-down" influences are particularly

evident in memory (Bartlett, 1932). By and large these constructive influences are positive and helpful, but they can also lead to errors, some of which may occur during the initial encoding of an event (or in storage; see, for example, the work of Loftus, 1998), but most of which probably occur at retrieval. The best evidence for these false memories comes from the recent work of Roediger, McDermott, and their associates, and the reader is referred to that work for further details (Roediger, McDermott, & Robinson, 1998; Roediger & McDermott, chapter 10).

Encoding/Retrieval Interactions

State dependency is a special example of encoding specificity or transfer-appropriate processing. The notion is that, just as retrieval depends on the effectiveness of retrieval cues, it also depends on the person's "state" or mental condition when he or she was encoding information. Moreover, the person's state at retrieval should ideally match that at encoding in order to ensure retrieval of the encoded information. For instance, if a person has learned certain facts or experienced particular events while "high" on drugs or alcohol, or while in a certain mood, then he or she may be better able to recall the facts or events when in a similar state of mind. Interestingly, state-dependent effects appear to be strongest when retrieval cues are weakest—for example, with free recall as opposed to recognition memory (Eich, 1980). One possible interpretation of this finding is that the person's mental state

Table 6.1 Proportions of words recognized (hits minus false alarms) as a function of encoding and test conditions (Morris, Bransford, & Franks, 1977, experiment 1).

		Positive responses			*Negative responses*		
		Test				*Test*	
		Standard	*Rhyme*			*Standard*	*Rhyme*
Encoding	Semantic	.84	.33	Semantic		.86	.33
	Rhyme	.63	.49	Rhyme		.52	.18

Note. At encoding, subjects answered semantic or rhyme questions about target words. These questions led either to a positive response (e.g., "Rhymes with legal?"—EAGLE) or a negative response (e.g., "Rhymes with sound?"—EAGLE). Subsequent recognition scores for targets associated with positive and negative responses are shown on the left and right respectively. The recognition test was either for the target word itself (e.g., EAGLE ?) or for a word rhyming with any target word (e.g., REGAL ?).

influences and guides the constructive aspects of retrieval, and that top-down constructive operations play a bigger part in recall than they do in recognition, which is relatively more data driven.

Just as a person's mental state can apparently modulate the encoding and retrieval of information, so too can the external context, provided that it is sufficiently rich and distinctive. An interesting example of this phenomenon is Godden and Baddeley's (1975) finding that when scuba divers learned lists of words either underwater or on dry land, they subsequently recalled more words when they were tested in the study location, as opposed to the alternative location not used at study. Figure 6.2 shows subjects' mean recall performance as a function of encoding and retrieval condition (Godden & Baddeley, 1975, experiment 1). Reinstatement of the encoding context at the time of retrieval can thus be very beneficial to remembering—an effect encountered in daily life under the term "revisiting the scene of the crime" or less dramatically by returning to room A after failing to remember what it was you went to room B to fetch! This notion was developed by Craik (1983, 1986) into the concept of "environmental support"

with the idea that older people are particularly dependent on help from compatible contexts when attempting to remember. Obviously people can remember facts and events when they are not in the original encoding context, and such remembering is therefore more reliant on "self-initiated mental activities." In fact, commonly used retrieval paradigms may be classified with respect to how much environmental support they provide and (in a complementary sense) how much self-initiated activity they require. Craik (1983) suggested that paradigms such as free recall and prospective remembering typically require a lot of self-initiated activity, whereas recognition memory and many procedural memory paradigms embody more environmental support and thus require less self-initiated activity. There is reasonable evidence to support the conclusion that adult age-related memory decrements are greatest in situations where environmental support is least available (see Anderson & Craik, chapter 26).

Earlier in this chapter, the importance of elaborate semantic processing operations was emphasized. Typically, the involvement of meaning at encoding, combined with the provision of compatible retrieval cues at the time

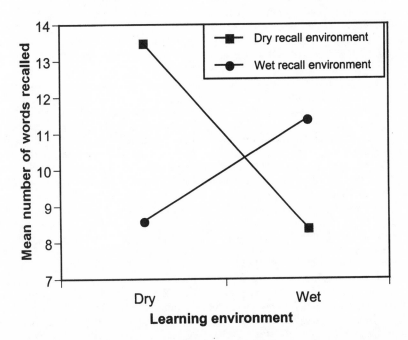

Figure 6.2 Mean number of words recalled as a function of learning and recall environment (data from Godden & Baddeley, 1975, experiment 1; adapted from Anderson, 1980, p. 210).

of testing, yields the highest levels of memory performance. However, a refinement to this general principle is suggested by investigations of paradigms that tap implicit memory (see Roediger & McDermott, 1993; Schacter, 1987; and Toth, chapter 16, for reviews). In these paradigms, subjects are not asked explicitly to recollect some earlier event; rather, the initial experience affects current performance, often in the absence of any conscious recollection of the original situation. In one such experiment, Jacoby and Dallas (1981) found that a levels-of-processing manipulation had no effect on later perceptual identification of re-presented words, although re-presented words were better identified than were new words, and the LOP manipulation did have the standard effect on explicit recognition memory. In a later study, Jacoby (1983) demonstrated that (visual) perceptual identification was sensitive to the amount of *visual* processing that had been done at the time of encoding. In general it seems that several implicit memory paradigms (e.g., word identification, word-fragment completion, word-stem completion) are positively affected by the compatibility of surface characteristics between study and test, whereas they are unaffected by semantic variables (Craik, Moscovitch, & McDowd, 1994). Other implicit memory tasks do deal with semantic or conceptual processing, however, and they are sensitive to the type and amount of conceptual processing carried out at encoding (e.g., Blaxton, 1989). Transfer-appropriate processing again appears to be the key in understanding variations in performance in these paradigms (Roediger et al., 1989).

A further interesting characteristic of at least some implicit memory tasks is that the compatibility effects between study and test are extremely long lasting. As one example, Tulving, Schacter, and Stark (1982) found very little "forgetting" in a word-fragment completion task between 1 hour and 7 days after initial presentation of the studied words. These long-lasting priming effects may be regarded as examples of perceptual learning rather than as episodic memory in the usual sense (Jacoby & Dallas, 1981), and they may be relevant to a puzzle in the literature on levels of processing. Craik and Lockhart (1972) postulated that shallow sensory codes were quite short-lasting, in line with current evidence from studies of sensory memory. However, Baddeley (1978) pointed out that some surface codes can be extremely *long* lasting; one dramatic example is Kolers' (1976) dem-

onstration of savings in reading speed one *year* later in subjects reading texts in transformed typography. It now seems that the resolution of the puzzle may involve differences between implicit and explicit tests of memory. In the latter cases, when subjects are asked to recollect an earlier event, sensory or surface information appears to play little part after a few seconds—in line with Craik and Lockhart's suggestion. For implicit tests, on the other hand, surface information is often of primary importance (Craik et al., 1994; Jacoby, 1983) and is very long lasting.

Memory Enhancement and Impairment

This final section deals briefly with some selected situations in which memory performance is either increased or reduced. The more general question of what factors lead to memory improvement or memory failure is better answered after a consideration of all of the chapters in this handbook!

Slamecka and Graf (1978) showed that memory for words was enhanced by requiring subjects to complete fragments of the words at the time of learning. In most cases the completions were extremely easy, and might be helped by an associated context word. For example, the word SLOW might be presented in its entirety (the "read" condition) or with some letters missing (the "generate" condition); that is, fast-SLOW or fast-S___ W. Surprisingly, the generate condition is consistently associated with higher levels of recall and recognition (see, e.g., Hirshman & Bjork, 1988, for a review). What underlies the effect? One possibility is that the necessity to complete the word forces the subject to process its meaning to a slightly greater degree, and that the generation effect is therefore another manifestation of "deeper" processing. This account is speculative, however.

A somewhat similar phenomenon is found in a paradigm requiring subjects to perform simple actions with common objects. These "subject-performed tasks," or SPTs, are contrasted with a list of verbal commands, with the former condition yielding better later memory for the items. Thus commands such as "pick up the toy car," "point to the book," or "stamp your foot" are either given in a list to be learned or are acted out by the subject. Both recall and recognition are enhanced by the SPT condition (Cohen, 1983; Engelkamp,

1998). As with the generation effect, there is no final agreement on the mechanism underlying the SPT effect. It seems likely that some item-specific encoding enhancement is involved (Engelkamp & Zimmer, 1994), possibly either greater elaboration of the phrase when it has to be enacted or possibly the verbal information is enriched by the addition of further visual and motor information in the case of SPTs (see Nilsson, chapter 9, for further discussion).

Although it seems paradoxical at first, an act of retrieval can either benefit or impair subsequent memory performance. The positive effects of retrieval are easier to understand. Tulving (1967) showed that test trials were as effective as further study trials in boosting learning; similarly, the simple procedure of retrieving some newly learned fact repeatedly (a new name, for instance), preferably at progressively longer spaced intervals, boosts subsequent recall performance (Landauer & Bjork, 1978). This effect of retrieval practice may have two major underlying causes. First, repeated successful retrievals may somehow reinforce the appropriate sequence of retrieval operations. Second, it is arguably the case that any conscious mental operation acts as an encoding operation whatever its primary purpose; so by this principle, retrieval processes (like perceptual processes) will provide further encoding opportunities (Bjork, 1975). Further, an act of retrieval is likely to be more effective as a second encoding to the extent that the retrieval processes involve deeper, semantic processing operations.

On the other hand, retrieval processes can act to inhibit the subsequent recall of information *associated with* successfully retrieved target information. In one such demonstration, Brown (1968) had subjects study 25 of the 50 U.S. states, followed by a recall attempt of all 50 states. Relative to a control group that had no preliminary study session, the first group recalled more of the studied 25, but fewer of the unstudied 25. Apparently study had inhibited recall from the complementary subset. A similar phenomenon was observed by Slamecka (1968) and has been studied exhaustively under the heading of "part-list cueing inhibition" (e.g., Roediger, 1973). In more recent work, Anderson, Bjork and Bjork (1994) had subjects practice retrieving half of the items from each of several categories. The finding is that in a subsequent recall attempt in which all items must be recalled, the non-practiced items' recall is inhibited relative to appropriate controls. According to Anderson and his colleagues, this is because nontarget items are inhibited or suppressed during the initial retrieval practice session, and this retrieval-induced inhibition persists to the second retrieval session. Apparently retrieval acts to facilitate the recall of wanted items by suppressing the recallability of associated but unwanted items.

Finally, several studies have now shown asymmetrical effects of divided attention on encoding and retrieval. Subjects in these studies carry out a secondary task while encoding or retrieving lists of words, say, and the finding is that division of attention has a strongly negative effect on later recall and recognition when the secondary task is performed during encoding, but relatively little effect when performed during retrieval (Baddeley, Lewis, Eldridge, & Thomson, 1984; Craik, Govoni, Naveh-Benjamin, & Anderson, 1996; Kellogg, Cocklin, & Bourne, 1982). This finding is of interest first because it may shed further light on the similarities and differences between encoding and retrieval processes (Craik, Naveh-Benjamin, & Anderson, 1998), and second because divided attention appears to have very similar effects to those caused by aging, intoxication, and sleep deprivation (Nilsson, Bäckman, & Karlsson, 1989). The common factor in these various conditions may be the temporary or permanent loss of processing resources (e.g., Craik & Byrd, 1982), but an alternative possibility is a breakdown of control of cognitive operations (Jacoby, 1991).

Conclusion

It seems likely that the next 10 years will see a clarification of several issues regarding encoding and retrieval processes. Specifically, investigators will continue to identify the similarities and differences between these two types of processes. In addition, recent developments in neuroscience (see, e.g., Nyberg & Cabeza, chapter 31; and Rugg & Allan, chapter 32) will likely provide us with a clearer account of the neural correlates of control or processing resources, and a fuller understanding of how they affect the processes of encoding and retrieval.

Acknowledgments The authors wish to thank Nicole Anderson and Aaron Benjamin for helpful comments on an earlier draft of this chapter. We are also grateful to the Natural Sciences and Engineering Research Council of Canada for a grant to FIMC that facilitated preparation of the chapter.

References

Anderson, J. R. (1980). *Cognitive psychology and its implications*. Freeman: San Francisco.

Anderson, M. C., Bjork, R. A., & Bjork, E. L. (1994). Remembering can cause forgetting: Retrieval dynamics in long-term memory. *Journal of Experimental Psychology: Learning, Memory, and Cognition, 20,* 1063–1087.

Anderson, R. C., Pichert, J. W., Goetz, E. T., Schallert, D. L., Stevens, K. V., & Trollip, S. R. (1976). Instantiation of general terms. *Journal of Verbal Learning and Verbal Behavior, 15,* 667–679.

Atkinson, R. C., & Shiffrin, R. M. (1968). Human memory: A proposed system and its control processes. In K. W. Spence & J. T. Spence (Eds.), *The psychology of learning and motivation: Advances in research and theory* (Vol. 2, pp. 89–195). New York: Academic Press.

Atkinson, R. C., & Shiffrin, R. M. (1971, August). The control of short-term memory. *Scientific American,* 82–90.

Ausubel, D. P. (1962). A subsumption theory of meaningful verbal learning and retention. *Journal of General Psychology, 66,* 213–244.

Baddeley, A. D. (1978). The trouble with levels: A reexamination of Craik & Lockhart's framework for memory research. *Psychological Review, 85,* 139–152.

Baddeley, A. D. (1983). Working memory. *Philosophical Transactions of the Royal Society of London, B 302,* 311–324.

Baddeley, A. D. (1986). *Working memory*. Oxford: Oxford University Press.

Baddeley, A. D., Lewis, V., Eldridge, M., & Thomson, N. (1984). Attention and retrieval from long-term memory. *Journal of Experimental Psychology: General, 113,* 518–540.

Bahrick, H. P. (1970). Two-phase model for prompted recall. *Psychological Review, 77,* 215–222.

Barclay, J. R. (1973). The role of comprehension in remembering sentences. *Cognitive Psychology, 4,* 229–254.

Barclay, J. R., Bransford, J. D., Franks, J. J., McCarrell, N. S., & Nitsch, K. (1974). Comprehension and semantic flexibility. *Journal of Verbal Learning and Verbal Behavior, 13,* 471–481.

Bartlett, F. C. (1932). *Remembering: A study in experimental and social psychology*. Cambridge, UK: Cambridge University Press.

Bjork, R. A. (1975). Retrieval as a memory modifier: An integration of negative recency and related phenomena. In R. Solso (Ed.), *Information processing and cognition: The Loyola symposium* (pp. 123–144). Hillsdale, NJ: Erlbaum.

Blaxton, T. A. (1989). Investigating dissociations among memory measures: Support for a transfer-appropriate processing framework. *Journal of Experimental Psychology: Learning, Memory, and Cognition, 10,* 3–9.

Bower, G. H. (1967). A multicomponent theory of the memory trace. In K. W. Spence & J. T. Spence (Eds.), *The psychology of learning and motivation: Advances in research and theory* (Vol. 1, pp. 229–325). New York: Academic Press.

Bower, G. H. (1970). Imagery as a relational organizer in associational learning. *Journal of Verbal Learning and Verbal Behavior, 9,* 529–533.

Bransford, J. D., Franks, J. J., Morris, C. D., & Stein, B. S. (1979). Some general constraints on learning and memory research. In L. S. Cermak & F. I. M. Craik (Eds.), *Levels of processing in human memory* (pp. 331–354). Hillsdale, NJ: Erlbaum.

Bransford, J. D., & Johnson, M. K. (1972). Contextual prerequisites for understanding: Some investigations of comprehension and recall. *Journal of Verbal Learning and Verbal Behavior, 11,* 717–726.

Brooks, L. R. (1968). Spatial and verbal components of the act of recall. *Canadian Journal of Psychology, 22,* 349–368.

Brown, J. (1968). Reciprocal facilitation and impairment of free recall. *Psychonomic Science, 10,* 41–42.

Chalfonte, B. L., & Johnson, M. K. (1996). Feature memory and binding in young and older adults. *Memory and Cognition, 24,* 403–416.

Chase, W. G., & Simon, H. A. (1973). The mind's eye in chess. In W. G. Chase (Ed.), *Visual information processing* (pp. 215–281). New York: Academic Press.

Cohen, R. L. (1983). The effect of encoding variables on the free recall of words and action events. *Memory and Cognition, 11,* 575–582.

Craik, F. I. M. (1983). On the transfer of information from temporary to permanent memory. *Philosophical Transactions of the*

Royal Society of London, Series B 302, 341–359.

Craik, F. I. M. (1986). A functional account of age differences in memory. In F. Klix & H. Hagendorf (Eds.), *Human memory and cognitive capabilities. Mechanisms and performances* (pp. 409–422). North-Holland: Elsevier.

Craik, F. I. M., & Byrd, M. (1982). Aging and cognitive deficits: The role of attentional resources. In F. I. M. Craik & S. Trehub (Eds.), *Aging and cognitive processes* (pp. 191–211). New York: Plenum.

Craik, F. I. M., Govoni, R., Naveh-Benjamin, M., & Anderson, N. D. (1996). The effects of divided attention on encoding and retrieval processes in human memory. *Journal of Experimental Psychology: General, 125*, 159–180.

Craik, F. I. M., & Lockhart, R. S. (1972). Levels of processing: A framework for memory research. *Journal of Verbal Learning and Verbal Behavior, 11*, 671–684.

Craik, F. I. M., Moscovitch, M., & McDowd, J. M. (1994). Contributions of surface and conceptual information to performance on implicit and explicit memory tasks. *Journal of Experimental Psychology: Learning, Memory, and Cognition, 20*, 864–875.

Craik, F. I. M., Naveh-Benjamin, M., & Anderson, N. D. (1998). Encoding and retrieval processes: Similarities and differences. In M. Conway, S. Gathercole, & C. Cornoldi (Eds.), *Theories of Memory II* (pp. 61–86). Hove, England: Psychology Press.

Craik, F. I. M., & Tulving, E. (1975). Depth of processing and the retention of words in episodic memory. *Journal of Experimental Psychology: General, 104*, 268–294.

Eich, J. E. (1980). The cue-dependent nature of state-dependent retention. *Memory and Cognition, 8*, 157–173.

Einstein, G. O., & Hunt, R. R. (1980). Levels of processing and organization: Additive effects of individual item and relational processing. *Journal of Experimental Psychology: Human Learning and Memory, 6*, 588–598.

Engelkamp, J. (1998). *Memory for actions*. Hove, England: Psychology Press.

Engelkamp, J., & Zimmer, H. D. (1994). Motor similarity in subject-performed tasks. *Psychological Research, 57*, 47–53.

Godden, D. R., & Baddeley, A. D. (1975). Context-dependent memory in two natural environments: On land and underwater. *British Journal of Psychology, 66*, 325–331.

Herz, R. S., & Engen, T. (1996). Odor memory: Review and analysis. *Psychonomic Bulletin and Review, 3*, 300–313.

Hirshman, E., & Bjork, R. A. (1988). The generation effect: Support for a two-factor theory. *Journal of Experimental Psychology: Learning, Memory, and Cognition, 14*, 484–494.

Jacoby, L. L. (1983). Remembering the data: Analyzing interactive processes in reading. *Journal of Verbal Learning and Verbal Behavior, 22*, 485–508.

Jacoby, L. L. (1991). A process dissociation framework: Separating automatic from intentional uses of memory. *Journal of Memory and Language, 30*, 513–541.

Jacoby, L. L., & Dallas, M. (1981). On the relationship between autobiographical memory and perceptual learning. *Journal of Experimental Psychology: General, 110*, 306–340.

Jacoby, L. L., & Hollingshead, A. (1990). Toward a generate/recognize model of performance on direct and indirect tests of memory. *Journal of Memory and Language, 29*, 433–454.

Johnson, M. K., & Chalfonte, B. L. (1994). Binding complex memories: The role of reactivation and the hippocampus. In D. L. Schacter & E. Tulving (Eds.), *Memory Systems 1994* (pp. 311–350). Cambridge, MA: MIT Press.

Kellogg, R. T., Cocklin, T., & Bourne, L. E. (1982). Conscious attentional demands of encoding and retrieval from long-term memory. *American Journal of Psychology, 95*, 183–198.

Kintsch, W. (1970). Models for free recall and recognition. In D. A. Norman (Ed.), *Models of human memory*. New York: Academic Press.

Kolers, P. A. (1973). Remembering operations. *Memory and Cognition, 1*, 347–355.

Kolers, P. A. (1976). Reading a year later. *Journal of Experimental Psychology: Human Learning and Memory, 2*, 554–565.

Kolers, P. A. (1979). Reading and knowing. *Canadian Journal of Psychology, 33*, 106–117.

Kolers, P. A., & Roediger, H. L. (1984). Procedures of mind. *Journal of Verbal Learning and Verbal Behavior, 23*, 425–449.

Konorski, J. (1967). *Integrative activity of the brain*. Chicago: University of Chicago Press.

Koriat, A., Ben-zur, H., & Sheffer, D. (1988). Telling the same story twice: Output monitoring and age. *Journal of Memory and Language, 27*, 23–39.

Landauer, T. K., & Bjork, R. A. (1978). Optimum rehearsal patterns and name learning. In M. M. Gruneberg, P. E. Morris, &

R. N. Sykes (Eds.), *Practical aspects of memory* (pp. 625–632). New York: Academic Press.

Levitin, D. J. (1994). Absolute memory for musical pitch: Evidence from the production of learned melodies. *Perception and Psychophysics, 56*, 414–423.

Levitin, D. J. (in press). Memory for musical attributes. In P. R. Cook (Ed.), *Music, cognition, and computerized sound: An introduction to psychoacoustics.* Cambridge, MA: MIT Press.

Loftus, E. F. (1998). Imaginary memories. In M. A. Conway, S. E. Gathercole, & C. Cornoldi (Eds.), *Theories of Memory II* (pp. 135–145). Hove, England: Psychology Press.

Madigan, S. A. (1969). Intraserial repetition and coding processes in free recall. *Journal of Verbal Learning and Verbal Behavior, 8*, 828–835.

Mandler, G. (1980). Recognizing: The judgment of previous occurrence. *Psychological Review, 87*, 252–271.

Martin, E. (1968). Stimulus meaningfulness and paired-associate transfer: An encoding variability hypothesis. *Psychological Review, 75*, 421–441.

McIntyre, J. S., & Craik, F. I. M. (1987). Age differences in memory for item and source information. *Canadian Journal of Psychology, 41*, 175–192.

Miller, G. A. (1956). The magical number seven, plus or minus two: Some limits on our capacity for processing information. *Psychological Review, 63*, 81–97.

Morris, C. D., Bransford, J. D., & Franks, J. J. (1977). Levels of processing versus test-appropriate strategies. *Journal of Verbal Learning and Verbal Behavior, 16*, 519–533.

Moscovitch, M., & Craik, F. I. M. (1976). Depth of processing, retrieval cues, and uniqueness of encoding as factors in recall. *Journal of Verbal Learning and Verbal Behavior, 15*, 447–458.

Moscovitch, M., Winocur, G., & Behrmann, M. (1997). What is special about face recognition? Nineteen experiments on a person with visual object agnosia and dyslexia but normal face recognition. *Journal of Cognitive Neuroscience, 9*, 555–604.

Naveh-Benjamin, M., & Ayres, T. J. (1986). Digit span, reading rate, and linguistic relativity. *Quarterly Journal of Experimental Psychology, 38*, 739–751.

Neisser, U. (1998). Stories, selves, and schemata: A review of ecological findings. In M. A. Conway, S. E. Gathercole, & C. Cornoldi (Eds.), *Theories of Memory II* (pp. 171–186). Hove, England: Psychology Press.

Nilsson, L. G., Bäckman, L., & Karlsson, T. (1989). Priming and cued recall in elderly, alcohol intoxicated and sleep deprived subjects: A case of functionally similar deficits. *Psychological Medicine, 19*, 423–433.

Nilsson, L. G., Law, J., & Tulving, E. (1988). Recognition failure of recallable unique names: Evidence for an empirical law of memory and learning. *Journal of Experimental Psychology: Learning, Memory, and Cognition, 14*, 266–277.

Norman, D. A. (1968). Toward a theory of memory and attention. *Psychological Review, 75*, 522–536.

Paivio, A. (1971). *Imagery and verbal processes.* New York: Holt, Rinehart, and Winston.

Posner, M. I., & Keele, S. W. (1967). Decay of visual information from a single letter. *Science, 158*, 137–139.

Postman, L. (1964). Short-term memory and incidental learning. In A. W. Melton (Ed.), *Categories of human learning* (pp. 145–201). New York: Academic Press.

Pylyshyn, Z. W. (1973). What the mind's eye tells the mind's brain: A critique of mental imagery. *Psychological Bulletin, 80*, 1–24.

Read, D., & Craik, F. I. M. (1995). Earwitness identification: Some influences on voice recognition. *Journal of Experimental Psychology: Applied, 1*, 6–18.

Roediger, H. L. (1973). Inhibition in recall from cueing with recall targets. *Journal of Verbal Learning and Verbal Behavior, 12*, 644–657.

Roediger, H. L., & McDermott, K. B. (1993). Implicit memory in normal human subjects. In H. Spinnler & F. Boller (Eds.), *Handbook of neuropsychology* (pp. 63–131). Amsterdam: Elsevier.

Roediger, H. L. McDermott, K. B., & Robinson, K. J. (1998). The role of associative processes in producing false remembering. In M. Conway, S. Gathercole, & C. Cornoldi (Eds.), *Theories of Memory II* (pp. 187–246). Hove, England: Psychology Press.

Roediger, H. L., Weldon, M. S., & Challis, B. H. (1989). Explaining dissociations between implicit and explicit measures of retention: A processing account. In H. L. Roediger, & F. I. M. Craik (Eds.), *Varieties of memory and consciousness: Essays in honour of Endel Tulving* (pp. 3–41). Hillsdale, NJ: Erlbaum.

Schacter, D. L. (1987). Implicit memory: History and current status. *Journal of Experimental Psychology: Learning, Memory, and Cognition, 13*, 501–518.

Schacter, D. L., Harbluk, J. L., & McLachlan, D. R. (1984). Retrieval without recollection: An experimental analysis of source amnesia. *Journal of Verbal Learning and Verbal Behavior, 23*, 593–611.

Shulman, H. G. (1972). Semantic confusion errors in short-term memory. *Journal of Verbal Learning and Verbal Behavior, 11*, 221–227.

Slamecka, N. J. (1968). An examination of trace storage in free recall. *Journal of Experimental Psychology, 76*, 504–513.

Slamecka, N. J., & Graf, P. (1978). The generation effect: Delineation of a phenomenon. *Journal of Experimental Psychology: Human Learning and Memory, 4*, 592–604.

Spencer, W. D., & Raz, N. (1995). Differential effects of aging on memory for content and context: A meta-analysis. *Psychology and Aging, 10*, 527–539.

Standing, L. (1973). Learning 10,000 pictures. *Quarterly Journal of Experimental Psychology, 25*, 207–222.

Tulving, E. (1962). Subjective organization in free recall of "unrelated" words. *Psychological Review, 69*, 344–354.

Tulving, E. (1967). The effects of presentation and recall of material in free-recall learning. *Journal of Verbal Learning and Verbal Behavior, 6*, 175–184.

Tulving, E. (1968). Theoretical issues in free recall. In T. R. Dixon & D. L. Horton (Eds.), *Verbal behavior and general behavior theory* (pp. 2–36). Englewood Cliffs, NJ: Prentice-Hall.

Tulving, E. (1983). *Elements of episodic memory.* New York: Oxford University Press.

Tulving, E., & Pearlstone, Z. (1966). Availability versus accessibility of information in memory for words. *Journal of Verbal Learning and Verbal Behavior, 5*, 381–391.

Tulving, E., Schacter, D. L., & Stark, H. A. (1982). Priming effects in word-fragment completion are independent of recognition memory. *Journal of Experimental Psychology: Learning, Memory, and Cognition, 8*, 336–342.

Tulving, E., & Thomson, D. M. (1973). Encoding specificity and retrieval processes in episodic memory. *Psychological Review, 80*, 352–373.

Velichkovsky, B. M. (1994). The levels endeavour in psychology and cognitive science. In P. Bertelson, P. Eelen, & G. d'Ydewalle (Eds.), *International perspectives in psychological science, Volume 1: Leading themes* (pp. 143–158). Hove, England: Erlbaum.

Wilson, M., & Emmorey, K. (1997). A visual-spatial 'phonological-loop' in working memory: Evidence from American Sign Language. *Memory and Cognition, 25*, 313–320.

7

Transfer and Expertise

DANIEL R. KIMBALL & KEITH J. HOLYOAK

Readers having a passing familiarity with research on transfer and expertise might think it somewhat odd to find these two topics covered in a single chapter. After all, one of the most common generalizations from research on expertise is that expertise is domain and task specific: experts in a domain are exceptional at performing familiar tasks within that domain, but often poor at transferring that expertise to other domains or even, in many cases, to novel tasks within the same domain (see, e.g., Ericsson & Charness, 1994). However, there are at least three ways in which transfer and expertise are related. First, transfer is a basic process in learning (perhaps synonymous with it; Gick & Holyoak, 1987), and therefore experts must use transfer in acquiring their expertise. Second, as we will see, level of expertise affects the degree and quality of subsequent transfer (Chi, Feltovich, & Glaser, 1981). Third, there appear to be types of expertise that *do* involve transfer of learning to novel tasks and domains; Hatano and Inagaki (1986) have termed such types "adaptive" expertise, which they contrast with the "routine" expertise associated with performance of familiar, domain-specific tasks. Most research to date has focused on routine expertise, perhaps because it is more conducive to exploration in the laboratory.

In this chapter, we touch on these related aspects of transfer and expertise in the context of a broader discussion of both fields. We first discuss transfer, providing a theoretical framework and outlining major research findings in the field. We then take up expertise, discussing the theories and empirical research regarding routine and adaptive expertise as they affect basic memory processes, knowledge representation, and transfer.

Transfer

Definitions and Taxonomy

Transfer is theoretically indistinguishable from learning, as can be seen by its definition: transfer is the degree to which prior performance of a task (the *training task*) affects performance on a second task (the *transfer task*) that varies in similarity to the training task (Gick & Holyoak, 1987). The two tasks may be identical (*self-transfer*), highly similar (*near transfer*), or very different (*far transfer*). While self-transfer may be regarded as the prototypical example of learning, it is also arguably rare to nonexistent, for at a minimum, the temporal, spatial, and other contextual conditions surrounding the two tasks always vary in some respect (Estes, 1955).

Closely related to the proximity of transfer is its generality. Transfer may be either *specific*, selectively influencing performance on a particular transfer task, or *general*, influencing a broader range of transfer tasks. Variations in generality of transfer are related to the distinction between the two types of expertise mentioned earlier: routine expertise, with its emphasis on domain- and task-specific knowledge, and adaptive expertise, with its emphasis on the development of general reasoning skills. We will return to this aspect of transfer in our discussion of expertise.

Transfer may be either positive or negative, depending on whether performance of the training task benefits or hinders performance of the transfer task. For example, learning to classify a small animal with a tail as a dog may result in positive transfer upon encountering a spaniel, but in negative transfer (overgeneralization) upon encountering a cat. Of course, often there will be no transfer at all, especially if the learning and transfer stimuli are very unrelated (e.g., learning to classify a small animal as a dog is unlikely to have any impact on classifying vehicles).

Factors Influencing the Magnitude and Direction of Transfer

In the preceding example, the existence and direction of transfer depend both on the characteristics of the two situations that are salient to the classifying person—the animal's size and shape of tail, perhaps, rather than the sound it may utter—as well as on the nature of the person's task—classifying animals into subclasses, rather than on some other basis (e.g., classifying them all as animals). These considerations exemplify the two main principles that determine magnitude and direction of transfer. First, the greater the overall *perceived* similarity between the training and transfer tasks, the greater will be the *magnitude* of transfer—that is, the more likely it is that transfer will be attempted. The theoretical basis for similarity is controversial, but the concept generally refers to the sharing of features and relations between the training and transfer tasks (see Tversky, 1977; Medin, Goldstone, & Gentner, 1993). However, perceived similarity may not correspond to objective similarity, because psychological factors such as context, knowledge, and expertise influence perceptions of similarity. For example, novice problem solvers in physics are often unaware of structural (functional, goal-relevant) similarities and dissimilarities between problems and therefore judge problems

as similar on the basis of surface (nonfunctional, goal-irrelevant) similarities, resulting in inappropriate attempts to transfer solution methods from the training to the transfer problems (Chi et al., 1981).

Once transfer is attempted, the direction of transfer is determined by the degree of objective structural similarity between the training and transfer tasks—the extent to which the two tasks share features or relations that are causally relevant to the goal or required response. Thus, in the physics example, negative transfer will result to the extent two problems differ in objective structural characteristics yet surface similarities lead the physics novices to attempt to transfer the solution. On the other hand, physics experts accurately perceive the objective structural dissimilarities between the two problems and do not attempt transfer. By contrast, experts exhibit positive transfer on problems that do share structural components, as do novices when the surface and objective structural characteristics of the two problems are both similar.

Empirical Evidence Regarding Transfer

Because transfer depends on the application of previously acquired knowledge, it is inherently dependent on memory. Accordingly, the following discussion of transfer is organized into two major sections, each representing an aspect of memory: episodic encoding effects and episodic retrieval effects.

Encoding of the Training Task

Degree of Learning. In some cases, subjects fail to induce the operative rule during training. For example, in a problem-solving paradigm, the training task may be underconstrained, in that subjects are able to solve a category of problems by using a strategy such as trial and error that is simpler than the complex rule that the experimenter intends to define the category (Sweller, 1980). In such cases, positive transfer to a problem requiring use of the complex rule is extremely unlikely.

Barring failure of learning, so long as the training and transfer tasks require structurally similar responses, positive transfer increases with the degree of original learning (Ellis, 1965). However, when the tasks differ structurally, the relationship between degree of learning and transfer is more complex: transfer initially becomes more and more negative as the degree of learning increases, but as learning continues to grow stronger, transfer begins to become less negative and eventually even becomes positive (Mandler, 1962). This reversal in the direction of transfer with increasingly strong learning may seem to contradict the principle that negative transfer results when training and transfer tasks are structurally inconsistent. However, what seems to happen in some cases is that additional training boosts learning of very general components of the training task that in fact are structurally similar to those of the transfer task, such as general problem-solving strategies common to both tasks (e.g., "win-stay, lose-shift" in discrimination learning) and higher order similarities between training and transfer responses (e.g., the relevance of color rather than other stimulus dimensions, even though the specific colors differ in the two tasks). Thus learning of the training task occurs at different levels of abstraction, and the content at some of the levels may be structurally consistent with the transfer task.

Learning Strategies. The optimal learning strategy for maximizing transfer depends upon characteristics of the training task. For example, when a category of problems is defined by a group of interdependent rules, none of which alone is sufficient for solving the problem, some form of implicit learning (e.g., observing or memorizing instances in the absence of instructions to learn rules) may sometimes be superior to an explicit hypothesis-testing strategy (for reviews, see Reber, 1993; Seger, 1994). Another example of the influence of learning strategy on transfer involves the use of means-ends versus forward-search problem-solving strategies. A means-ends strategy involves working backwards from the goal, whereas a forward-search strategy involves working forward from the givens. Sweller, Mawer, and Ward (1983) manipulated the specificity of the goal stated in a problem and found that more specific goal statements encouraged use of a means-ends strategy, and less specific goal statements encouraged forward search. Subjects who used forward search showed better transfer to new problems, apparently having induced rules connecting givens to problem-solving operations (also see Vollmeyer, Burns, & Holyoak, 1996). As we will see later, in many problem domains forward search is one of the hallmarks of expertise.

Number and Variability of Examples. Positive transfer increases with the number of examples provided during training (e.g., Homa & Cultice, 1984), but optimizing transfer also depends on the representativeness and variability of the training examples. Varying the surface features of the examples during training, thereby more completely representing a category, permits abstraction of increasingly accurate rules for determining category membership on the basis of shared structural components (e.g., Anderson, Kline, & Beasley, 1979). For example, Bassok and Holyoak (1989) found that students who learned arithmetic progression problems in algebra exhibited more positive transfer to an isomorphic problem category—constant acceleration problems in physics—than did students who learned the physics problems and were tested for transfer with the algebra problems. Bassok and Holyoak attributed this asymmetry in transfer in part to the exposure of the algebra-trained students to a wider range of examples during training, in contrast to the physics-trained students, whose training problems all involved objects in motion. However, Bassok (1990) found evidence that a more basic cause of the failure of transfer from physics to algebra was that subjects represented the acceleration problems as rate problems rather than more generally as constant-increase problems. This view is consistent with the principle discussed earlier, according to which transfer will fail if the perceived similarity of the training and transfer tasks is low.

As another example, Gick and Holyoak (1983) manipulated the number of problems used as training examples. They used analogous "convergence" problems as training and transfer tasks. Convergence problems are based on Duncker's (1945) "radiation problem," in which the reasoner must find a way to destroy a stomach tumor without destroying surrounding healthy tissue, by using a type of ray that at sufficiently high intensity will destroy the tumor, but at that same intensity would also destroy the surrounding tissue through which the ray must pass to reach the tumor. The convergence solution requires directing multiple, converging rays toward the tumor at different angles, with the intensity of each ray being sufficiently low to avoid destruction of the surrounding tissue, but the combined intensity of the rays being sufficiently high to destroy the tumor.

Gick and Holyoak (1983) trained subjects on either one or two convergence problem analogs and tested for transfer with a second analog. An example of an analog for the radiation problem involves a general who wants to amass his forces to attack a fortress, but all the roads leading to the fortress contain mines that will detonate if a sufficiently large group traverses the road. Subjects provided with two source analogs exhibited substantially more transfer than did subjects seeing only one source analog. Gick and Holyoak argued that providing multiple-source analogs permitted abstraction of a generalized schema for the problem category, improving the likelihood that subjects will spontaneously recognize the structural similarities among the problems, thereby facilitating transfer (see also Ross & Kennedy, 1990).

Order of Examples. Positive transfer may also depend on the ordering of low-variability and high-variability examples, as well as the use of an implicit or explicit mode of learning. Elio and Anderson (1984) found that when people use an explicit strategy, actively seeking a single, deterministic rule, they benefit from presentation of high-variability examples first. Presentation of high-variability examples early makes it less likely that learners will unduly restrict the rule they induce to a limited set of features. However, when people adopt an implicit mode of learning, they seem to benefit more from early presentation of low-variability examples, which may serve to establish a strong memory representation for the examples most central to the category.

Roles of Abstract Training and Examples. Presentation of examples and abstract rules or schemata during training both appear necessary to optimize transfer. Even when abstract rules or schemata are presented, providing examples appears to facilitate transfer by showing how an abstract concept can be instantiated, especially if the concept is not part of the intuitive repertoire of the learner. Conversely, presenting an abstract rule or schema along with training examples appears to facilitate transfer to novel examples, especially when the rule is difficult to induce from examples alone (see Nisbett, Fong, Lehman, & Cheng, 1987), or when the training and transfer examples are superficially dissimilar (Gick & Holyoak, 1983). Surface and structural similarity also appear to jointly affect the efficacy of presenting abstract rules, but in a complex way. Ross and Kilbane (1997) found that when

an abstract principle is presented separately from a training problem, transfer is worse for a transfer problem that reverses the structural roles of objects in the problem than for a transfer problem that uses dissimilar objects. However, when the abstract principle is instead embedded in the training problem, transfer is worse for the dissimilar-object problem than for the role-reversed problem. Thus, presenting an abstract principle separately from the training problem benefits transfer to a problem that has different surface features altogether, but impairs transfer to a problem using the same surface components in different structural roles.

Summary. In general, the conditions at encoding influence whether or not the training task is encoded in terms of structural components that are shared with the transfer task. Manipulations that foster the acquisition of generalized rules, sufficiently abstract to characterize both the training task and the subsequent transfer task, will increase positive transfer. The rules acquired must be well learned, and based on an overall set of examples diverse enough to allow generalization mechanisms to abstract the common structural components from surface differences. Direct abstract training in rules embodying appropriate solution procedures is likely to be useful, but rules for classifying novel instances into the category must also be acquired to ensure successful transfer. Unless such rules have been acquired earlier, it will be necessary to augment training in abstract rules with exposure to concrete examples.

Retrieval of Training Task at Transfer

Similarity of Surface and Structural Components. As might be expected from the principles discussed earlier, transfer is affected by manipulating similarity of training and transfer tasks. Varying the similarity of surface and structural components has different effects. For example, using the convergence-problem paradigm described earlier, Holyoak and Koh (1987) increased surface similarity to the radiation problem by using another analog involving the same type of critical object (rays), in which converging lasers were used to repair the filament of a light bulb. They found that increased surface similarity significantly improved spontaneous transfer (i.e., retrieval of the relevant analog), but did not affect use of the analogy after a hint to access the source analog was given (see also Keane, 1986; Ross & Bradshaw, 1994).

Holyoak and Koh also manipulated structural similarity by using two different versions of the light bulb analog, one in which the rationale for convergence was to avoid damaging the glass surrounding the filament—structurally analogous to avoiding destruction of healthy tissue in the radiation problem—and the other in which the convergence rationale was the unavailability of a sufficiently strong single laser source. Transfer was greater for the structurally analogous problem both before and after a hint was provided (see discussion below of uninformed versus informed transfer). The positive effect of structural similarity on spontaneous transfer suggests that similarity of relations as well as similarity of objects guides retrieval and hence transfer (also see Wharton, Holyoak, & Lange, 1996).

Procedural learning can also be influenced by the degree to which the training and transfer tasks can be characterized by structurally similar production rules. For example, Kieras and Bovair (1986) trained subjects to perform a series of procedures on a control panel device, manipulating the order of training to vary the degree to which previously learned production rules were included in new procedures either in original or modified form. Multiple regression analysis revealed that a new rule added approximately 70% more time to total training time on average than a previously encountered rule, and that the number of new production rules required by the new procedure was the best predictor of total training time for it. Thus, learning is faster and presumably easier to the extent that the training and transfer tasks are based on shared production rules.

Structural similarity between training and transfer tasks can in turn be influenced by pre-experimental knowledge, thereby affecting transfer. Bassok, Wu, and Olseth (1995) found that transfer in problem solving depends on how subjects use pre-experimental knowledge to interpret the structure of the training and transfer problems. Using isomorphic problems involving random assignment of elements from one set to another, Bassok et al. found that subjects induced a symmetric structure ("pair") if the two sets were similar types of people (e.g., doctors and doctors), but they induced an asymmetric structure ("get") if one set was objects and the other people (e.g.,

prizes and students). Transfer was facilitated if the interpreted structures matched, but was impaired if they mismatched (see also Bassok & Olseth, 1995).

Similarity of Processing. Positive transfer is more likely when the training and transfer tasks require use of similar processing, a phenomenon that has been termed "transfer-appropriate processing" (Morris, Bransford, & Franks, 1977). For example, McDaniel and Schlager (1990) trained subjects either by having them both generate a problem-solving strategy and implement it with specific operations (discovery condition), or by providing them with the strategy and simply having them implement it (implementation-only condition). Subjects were then tested on transfer problems that required either applying the learned strategy in a new context or generating a new strategy. Discovery subjects outperformed implementation-only subjects on the transfer problem requiring generation of a new strategy, but the two groups did not differ in performance of the transfer problem requiring only application of the learned strategy. Thus, transfer is improved when the training and transfer problems both require the same type of processing.

In another problem-solving study, Weisberg, Di Camillo, and Phillips (1978) had subjects attempt to solve Duncker's (1945) candle problem, which requires finding a way to attach a candle to a wall using given materials. On an earlier paired-associate task, some subjects had studied the word pair *box-candle*, which paired elements of the correct solution (emptying a box of tacks, tacking it to the wall, and putting the candle on the box). However, these subjects were no better at solving the problem than were subjects who had not seen the word pair. Weisberg et al. suggested that subjects use the goal, and not the separate problem elements, as the primary cue when searching memory. The processing required for the two tasks in this case, memorization and problem solving, were dissimilar, so transfer was poor.

Informed vs. Uninformed Transfer. Using the convergence problem paradigm, Gick and Holyoak (1980, 1983) established the general finding that informed transfer—transfer after subjects are given a hint as to the structural similarity of the tasks—is markedly more frequent than uninformed, spontaneous transfer, demonstrating that people can transfer learning if they are made aware of the structural similarities between training and transfer tasks. However, the hint may not be as effective after the subject has failed to transfer learning from the training task during an unsuccessful attempt to perform the transfer task. In such a case, the representation of the transfer task may become sufficiently dissimilar from that of the training task that retrieval of information about the training task after the hint will not increase the perception of structural similarity (Perfetto, Bransford, & Franks, 1983).

Expertise also affects transfer. For example, as mentioned earlier, experts generally tend to classify tasks on the basis of structural similarity more often than do novices, who use surface similarity more often (Chi et al., 1981). We now turn to expertise, examining it in a broader context before returning at the end of the discussion to consider the mutual effects of transfer and expertise in more detail.

Expertise

Focusing on the role of memory in expertise, we first examine research on routine expertise, involving memory for information related to typical tasks within the expert domain, and then the more limited body of research on adaptive expertise, involving the transfer of expert knowledge to novel tasks and domains.

Routine Expertise: Memory for Expert Domain Information

Routine experts differ from novices both in the structure of domain-related knowledge and in the ability to retrieve episodic domain-related information. Evidence indicates that experts represent domain information in long-term memory (LTM) in the form of schemas, knowledge structures that are hierarchically organized and highly interconnected semantically. With certain exceptions, experts exhibit superior episodic memory for domain-typical information largely because they can directly access LTM to rapidly and reliably encode and retrieve the information, rather than maintaining it in short-term memory (STM) alone. We first discuss the evidence regarding schematic organization of knowledge within the expert domain, and then the evidence and theories regarding the respective roles of STM and LTM in experts' domain-specific episodic memory performance.

Schematic Representation of Expert Domain Knowledge

Evidence supporting the schematic representation of knowledge in experts' LTM is largely indirect, arising from studies using episodic memory tasks, and is based on instances of both superior and inferior memory performance. Experts generally exhibit better recall and recognition than do novices for episodic information related to the expert domain, but this superiority is even more exaggerated for information that is related to the central goals within the domain. For example, Spilich, Vesonder, Chiesi, and Voss (1979) found that baseball experts recalling a baseball passage included more propositions and a higher proportion of both goal-related propositions and relations among the propositions than did novices. Spilich et al. interpreted these data as indicative of the experts' superior situation model, an instantiation of a well-developed schema. There is also evidence that experts use retrieval structures—instantiations of schemas—in episodic processing, as assumed in the theories of Ericsson and Kintsch (1995) and Gobet and Simon (1996c), discussed further below.

Even in cases in which expertise does not yield uniformly superior memory performance, performance may depend on the use of schemas in LTM. For example, Adelson (1984) found that, following a programming task, expert computer programmers had worse incidental recall than novices for details of code. This performance decrement resulted from the experts' paying greater attention to the goal structure of the programming task than to code details. Similarly, Schmidt and Boshuizen (1993) found that recall of patient information following a medical diagnosis task varied nonmonotonically with the level of expertise, exhibiting an inverted U function: subjects with an intermediate level of expertise recalled more than did those with either more or less expertise. Schmidt and Boshuizen attributed the poorer recall of the most expert subjects to an increase in selectivity and abstraction, consistent with the hierarchical, goal-driven nature of schemas (also see Patel & Groen, 1991). Studies such as these show that experts tend to pay more attention to goal-relevant information, consistent with processes of schema abstraction and instantiation, which often results in poorer memory for goal-irrelevant details.

Roles of LTM and STM in Expert Episodic Memory Performance

Theories seeking to explain the mechanisms underlying experts' generally superior episodic memory within the expert domain have differed in the degree to which they assume experts store and retrieve episodic information in STM versus LTM. We discuss three of these theories—the chunking theory of Chase and Simon (1973), the mutiple template hypothesis of Gobet and Simon (1996c), and the long-term working memory theory of Ericsson and Kintsch (1995)—and the evidence regarding STM and LTM involvement in experts' episodic memory.

Chunking Theory. A frequently cited example of superior domain-related memory is the finding by Chase and Simon (1973) that chess masters recall more piece locations from briefly presented boards reflecting actual middle-game and end-game positions than do novices, but that when the pieces are arranged randomly, this advantage disappears (or at least is extremely small; Gobet & Simon, 1996a). The masters' superior memory solely for game positions appears to be largely attributable to recognition of patterns previously encountered by the masters and stored in LTM (Gobet & Simon, 1996b). The finding of superior memory of experts for domain-typical but not domain-atypical stimuli holds in many domains other than chess, including bridge, music, medicine, computer programming, and open motor skills (see Ericsson & Lehmann, 1996, for a review).

Chase and Simon (1973) proposed a chunking theory of expertise to explain their findings. As elaborated by Gobet and Simon (1996c), this theory assumes that a chunk consists of a recurring pattern reflecting a characteristic relation (e.g., attack, defense) among a set of a few pieces. When a chunk is recognized in a newly encountered board position, a pointer is placed in STM referencing the LTM representation of the chunk, thereby reducing the effects of STM capacity limitations. The theory assumes, however, that there is no direct storage of the memory trace in LTM. Because chess masters have stored more and larger chunks in LTM, they can use the pointers in STM to access more information than novices about piece locations from a given board—at least when the board contains chunks corresponding to representations stored in LTM. However, when the pieces are randomly arranged, eliminating all but the occasional random chunk, masters cannot use their storehouse of chunks effectively, and their recall advantage over novices virtually disappears. Thus, the chunking theory accounts for the Chase and Simon results, and similar findings.

Evidence Challenging the Chunking Theory. Evidence has accumulated contesting the chunking theory's assumption that experts store episodic traces solely in STM (see Ericsson & Kintsch, 1995, for a review). For example, Charness (1976) found that chess masters' memory for briefly presented chess positions was not adversely affected by a delay, regardless of whether subjects rehearsed during the interval or performed a distractor task, even a visual chess task. Mnemonists capable of extraordinary digit spans also exhibit negligible decrements in recall after interference tasks (see Ericsson & Staszewski, 1989). As STM is presumably emptied of studied material during such delays, these findings call into question the assumption that STM alone is used to store the episodic trace.

Other evidence against exclusive STM storage includes the finding by Gobet and Simon (1996c) that chess masters who briefly viewed multiple boards recalled more chunks than STM is usually assumed to hold, and exhibited not only recency effects, indicative of STM storage, but also primacy effects, typically viewed as reflecting LTM storage. In addition, the largest chunks were larger than assumed by chunking theory and differed in size depending on the number of boards presented, contrary to the chunking theory's assumption that chunk size should not vary. Other studies indicate that experts also appear to store episodic information in LTM during incidental memory tasks, indicating that episodic storage in LTM takes place in the normal course of their activities. For example, Lane and Robertson (1979) found that incidental memory of chess positions is related to level of expertise, and so long as the study-phase task involves domain-relevant goals, incidental memory is as good as intentional memory.

The evidence indicating a direct role for LTM in experts' episodic storage and retrieval has given rise to two recent, similar theories, to which we now turn.

Multiple Template Hypothesis. Gobet and Simon (1996c) have proposed a theory of chess expertise that assumes that chess masters accumulate multiple "templates" in LTM during an episode involving presentation of multiple boards. The templates are essentially instantiations of LTM schemas and each comprises a substantial number of core piece locations and a number of variable slots. The slots can be filled by different configurations of less central pieces, as well as other information such as possible future moves and antecedent opening strategies, and may have revisable defaults. The authors note the similarity between their templates and other schematic memory structures such as frames (Minsky, 1977) and scripts (Schank & Abelson, 1977).

Gobet and Simon (1996c) view their hypothesis as a modification of the chunking theory, with the templates being more complex chunks in that they include variable slots. The hypothesis retains the chunking theory's assumption that pointers to LTM chunks and templates are placed in STM at encoding. Gobet and Simon note that filling the variable slots requires the use of some STM capacity, which they offer as an explanation for the decrease they observed in maximum chunk size as the number of studied boards increases. The hypothesis thus assumes that STM capacity limits the number of templates that can be reliably stored and retrieved in a given episode, barring the use of a deliberately acquired mnemonic retrieval structure that subsumes several templates. Gobet and Simon describe an example of a retrieval structure, comprising the list of world chess champions, that was used by a master in deliberate training to expand his memory for multiple boards.

Richman, Staszewski, and Simon (1995) applied a theory similar to the multiple template hypothesis to simulate extraordinary digit span using a revised version of the Elementary Perceiver and Memorizer computer program, EPAM IV. The program included retrieval structures in LTM similar to those reported by mnemonists in verbal protocols, as well as a discrimination net for recognition processes and an associative semantic memory. During encoding, the program associated the presented digits with aspects of both the retrieval structure and semantic memory. The program was able to simulate a mnemonist subject's learning curve in extending the digit span, as well as his free and cued recall performance, including overall accuracy, proactive inhibition with multiple lists, and the timing pattern for various operations. Especially critical to the simulation performance was the redundant storage of information in both the retrieval structure and semantic memory during encoding and rehearsal.

Long-Term Working Memory. Ericsson and Kintsch (1995) have proposed a theory, the long-term working memory theory, that is similar to the multiple template hypothesis in several respects, but is intended to apply more generally to a broader range of routine expertise. The theory assumes that experts develop skill in the rapid storage and retrieval of domain-specific information in and from LTM, using what Ericsson and Kintsch have described as long-term working memory (LT-WM). The experts' extensive domain knowledge facilitates the identification of the studied items that are most likely to require retrieval and the association of those items with the most effective retrieval cues. Experts are assumed to develop retrieval structures to aid in this process, either in the natural course of performing domain-related tasks or as a consequence of deliberate mnemonic effort. For example, one mnemonist with an extraordinary digit span associated the presented digits with long-distance running times (e.g., 3596 became 3 minutes 59.6 seconds or just under 4 minutes for running a mile; Chase & Ericsson, 1981). The association in LT-WM of the cues in these retrieval structures with the studied items during encoding facilitates the reinstatement of the cues in STM at retrieval, which in turn facilitates retrieval of the studied items from LTM. Because this association of cues and items takes place in LTM, interference tasks that are effective in preventing retrieval from STM have little or no effect on experts' memory.

Ericsson and Kintsch (1995) propose that two mechanisms, recency and elaboration, help experts overcome the proactive and retroactive interference that one might expect from association of multiple items with the same retrieval structures and cues. If the intertrial spacing at encoding is long enough, experts can take advantage of temporal distinctiveness by using recency in encoding and retrieving the information. Elaboration involves interassociation of items processed during a single trial or task, sometimes through use of higher order relations among chunks, thus providing redundant retrieval pathways. For example, Chase and Ericsson (1982) reported that a digit-span mnemonist elaborated higher order relations among sets of digits within a list to avoid interference effects from processing multiple lists of digits.

Ericsson and Kintsch (1995) surveyed research in five expert domains—mental abacus calculation, mental multiplication, dinner-order memory, medical expertise, and chess. All domains except one (mental abacus calculation) yielded evidence of substantial incidental recall and/or postsession recall by experts, indicating the encoding of new structures in LTM. For example, as noted above, Lane and Robertson (1979) found that incidental recall of chess positions is substantially equivalent to intentional recall. The exception to this pattern, mental abacus calculation, is a task requiring continuous updating of digits, resulting in severe retroactive inhibition (Hatano & Osawa, 1983). Experts in all five domains used retrieval structures. For example, medical experts reorganized randomly presented medical diagnosis information into a standard format for recall (e.g., Groen & Patel, 1988), and similarly a waiter with extraordinary memory for multiple dinner orders recalled the orders in a clockwise fashion regardless of input order (Ericsson & Polson, 1988).

Ericsson and Kintsch (1995) argue that LT-WM is a hallmark of expertise generally. To underscore that point, they offer text comprehension as an example of a domain in which expertise is common and in which they assert use of LT-WM is instrumental. They discuss the importance of LT-WM in Kintsch's (1988) computational construction-integration model, which assumes that both a propositional text base and an elaborated situation model are constructed during text processing through an alternating sequence of unconstrained semantic association and inference generation (construction) followed by constraint satisfaction (integration). Retrieval structures in LT-WM are used to store and continuously update the text base and situation models during text processing. Experienced readers become adept at building efficient retrieval structures based on accumulated domain knowledge that allows accurate anticipation of future retrieval re-

quirements. Such retrieval efficiency is particularly evident in text processing within an expert domain, as revealed, for example, in the study of baseball expertise by Spilich et al. (1979).

Comparison of Template Hypothesis and LT-WM Theory. Both the LT-WM theory and the multiple template theory assume experts encode episodic information directly into LTM, using retrieval structures to increase effective memory capacity and processing efficiency. However, the two theories differ in some respects. The multiple template hypothesis contemplates two varieties of retrieval structures, operating at different levels: templates that serve as chunks with variable slots; and deliberately acquired, mnemonic retrieval structures that subsume several templates and that experts use to overcome interference effects. Use of the latter is the only mechanism Gobet and Simon (1996c) offer for circumventing STM capacity limits when storing multiple templates. The LT-WM theory does not explicitly distinguish between these types of retrieval structures, but is more explicit in suggesting that retrieval structures may develop naturally in the course of acquiring domain experience, as well as through deliberate mnemonic acquisition. Ericsson and Kintsch (1995) also offer temporal and elaborative encoding as two additional mechanisms that allow experts to overcome proactive and retroactive interference when using the same retrieval structure repeatedly, and therefore they apparently assume that use of an overarching retrieval structure subsuming several retrieval structures is not necessary, although its use is possible. While the template hypothesis also contemplates elaborative associations based on semantic memory, Gobet and Simon have not explicitly suggested that such elaborations would be sufficient to overcome interference effects.

Summary

The research reviewed here indicates that experts use schemas to represent expert domain information in LTM. The evidence is also consistent with the direct encoding into LTM by experts of episodic information within the expert domain, and the association of that information with elements of retrieval structures. These structures, which amount to instantiated schemas, are acquired by experts naturally through domain-related experience or deliberately through mnemonic effort, and assist in the maintenance of rapid, flexible, and reliable access to the episodic information.

Adaptive Expertise: Transfer to Novel Tasks and Domains

Relative to the substantial amount of empirical and theoretical work that has been done on routine expertise within a task domain, considerably less research has focused on adaptive transfer of expertise. Nonetheless, some general themes have emerged. The key difference between routine and adaptive experts is the greater capacity of the latter to transfer learning to novel tasks within and beyond the initial domain (Hatano & Inagaki, 1986). Adaptive experts have a deeper conceptual understanding of the domain, possessing not just "know-how" and "know-what" but also "know-why." One might expect adaptive expertise to develop to a greater degree for tasks that are variable rather than stereotyped in nature, and to emerge from free exploration more than from direct focus on achieving highly specific goals (Sweller et al., 1983). Such conditions would be conducive to the development of more abstract, structural representations of domain knowledge, which would in turn better enable application of domain knowledge to novel situations that vary in surface characteristics from previously encountered situations.

It is readily apparent that experts in one domain do not necessarily exhibit comparable performance levels in other domains (see, e.g., Chiesi, Spilich, & Voss, 1979). There is even evidence that experts in a domain can be impaired relative to novices when both attempt a task outside the domain. For example, Wiley (1998) found that people with a high degree of baseball knowledge were impaired, relative to people with less baseball knowledge, at solving a "remote associates" task that required accessing non-baseball-related associates of baseball terms. For example, people with high knowledge of baseball were less likely than those with low knowledge to find a common associate linking the words *plate, broken, shot* (where the intended answer is *glass*), apparently because the competing baseball associations to the first word, *plate*, interfered with finding non-baseball associations.

Nonetheless, other studies have found positive transfer effects. For example, Gott, Hall,

Pokorny, Dibble, and Glaser (1993) found that avionics technicians who represented the functions of testing devices more abstractly showed greater flexibility in transferring their knowledge to new testing devices. Barnett and Koslowski (1997) presented unusual restaurant management problems to novice undergraduates, restaurant managers, and general business consultants. The authors coded the verbal protocols of these three groups for evidence of "deep reasoning," which was construed as an indicator of adaptive expertise. Deep reasoning involved the use of theoretical business concepts, the use of justifications and explanations to support recommendations, and discussion of complementary alternative solutions. Barnett and Koslowski found evidence of more deep reasoning among the general business consultants, compared to the restaurant managers and undergraduates, who did not differ in their use of deep reasoning. The authors suggested that the variation in business scenarios previously encountered by the consultants was crucial to the development of their adaptive expertise. The business consultants would have had more opportunity to abstract a schema applicable to general business problems, rather than those applicable only to restaurants.

Adaptive expertise may also involve shifts in problem-solving strategies. Experts often use forward search of the problem space, reasoning forward from the givens, whereas novices use backward search, reasoning backwards from the goal (Chi et al., 1981). However, some studies have found that experts adapt their search strategies to the constraints of the task. For example, expert computer programmers use backward search because the initial state places few constraints on the task (Anderson, Farrell, & Sauers, 1984; Jeffries, Turner, Polson, & Atwood, 1981). Nevertheless, the experts do still use a breadth-first search strategy in search of the goal structure, unlike novices, who use a depth-first strategy. More generally, expertise in complex tasks often is distinguished not by some single canonical search strategy but by flexible switching among alternative strategies (Dorner & Scholkopf, 1991). The determinant of strategy selection appears to be the goal structure of the task, which is consistent with schematic representation of expert knowledge and with adaptive transfer of that knowledge to novel situations.

These types of studies show that adaptive transfer can occur, given the appropriate training conditions. It also appears likely that certain abstract skills are candidates as widespread mediators of adaptive transfer. Metacognitive skills are perhaps the most important of these, as they facilitate reasoning from first principles and play a key role in assessing when understanding is lacking, when the strategy currently in use is unlikely to succeed, and when the task requires restructuring (Dorner & Scholkopf, 1991). Abstract mathematics skills may also have broad applicability in facilitating transfer (Novick, 1988; Novick & Holyoak, 1991). Abstract training in statistics and everyday deductive reasoning has been shown to facilitate transfer to novel problems (see Nisbett et al., 1987). Causal reasoning is another potential candidate as a mediator of adaptive transfer (e.g., Cheng, 1997).

In summary, there is evidence that expertise can sometimes be transferred to novel tasks within and beyond the initial domain. Broad-based experience with a variety of related situations allows the development of abstract knowledge representations and skills, which in turn facilitate transfer of the knowledge to novel situations.

Conclusions

Transfer generally, and transfer of expertise in particular, is influenced by a number of factors. The likelihood that transfer will be attempted at all is determined by the overall perceived similarity between the training and transfer tasks. Given that transfer is attempted, the degree of positive transfer is determined by the objective structural similarity of the tasks. The degree of transfer is determined jointly by whether encoding conditions permit abstraction of rules that are sufficiently general to cover both tasks (e.g., as a result of experiencing a variety of examples); whether the two tasks share surface and/or structural components; whether similar processing is used in the tasks; and whether prior experience affects the perception of the tasks.

An important way in which prior experience affects transfer is by the development of expertise. Existing theories provide a better account for routine expertise—the performance of familiar, domain-related tasks—than for adaptive expertise—characterized by a deeper conceptual understanding of the domain and transferability of knowledge and skills to novel tasks within and beyond the initial domain. Routine expertise appears to involve the organization of domain knowledge into relatively specific schemas and the use of schema instantiations and domain-specific retrieval structures to expand working memory by facilitating the rapid and reliable encoding and retrieval of episodic domain information into and from LTM. By contrast, adaptive expertise seems to require the development of more flexible and abstract learning mechanisms and schemas to promote a deeper conceptual understanding of the expert domain and the transfer of knowledge to novel tasks and domains.

Acknowledgment   Preparation of this paper was supported by NSF Grant SBR-9729023.

References

Adelson, B. (1984). When novices surpass experts: The difficulty of a task may increase with expertise. *Journal of Experimental Psychology: Learning, Memory and Cognition, 10*, 483–495.

Anderson, J. R., Farrell, R., & Sauers, R. (1984). Learning to program in LISP. *Cognitive Science, 8*, 87–129.

Anderson, J. R., Kline, P. J., & Beasley, C. M. (1979). A general learning theory and its application to schema abstraction. In G. H. Bower (Ed.), *The psychology of learning and motivation* (Vol. 13) (pp. 277–318). New York: Academic Press.

Barnett, S. M., & Koslowski, B. (1997). Deep processing and expertise: Etiology and applicability. In M. G. Shafto & P. Langley (Eds.), *Proceedings of the Nineteenth Annual Conference of the Cognitive Science Society* (p. 858). Mahwah, NJ: Erlbaum.

Bassok, M. (1990). Transfer of domain-specific problem solving procedures. *Journal of Experimental Psychology: Learning, Memory and Cognition, 16*, 522–533.

Bassok, M., & Holyoak, K. J. (1989). Interdomain transfer between isomorphic topics in algebra and physics. *Journal of Experimental Psychology: Learning, Memory and Cognition, 15*, 153–166.

Bassok, M., & Olseth, K. L. (1995). Object-based representations: Transfer between cases of continuous and discrete models of change. *Journal of Experimental Psychology: Learning, Memory and Cognition, 21*, 1522–1538.

Bassok, M., Wu, L., & Olseth, K. L. (1995). Judging a book by its cover: Interpretative effects of content on problem-solving transfer. *Memory & Cognition, 23*, 354–367.

Charness, N. (1976). Memory for chess positions: Resistance to interference. *Journal of Experimental Psychology: Human Learning and Memory, 2*, 641–653.

Chase, W. G., & Ericsson, K. A. (1981). Skilled memory. In J. R. Anderson (Ed.), *Cognitive skills and their acquisition* (pp. 141–190). Hillsdale, NJ: Erlbaum.

Chase, W. G., & Ericsson, K. A. (1982). Skill and working memory. In G. H. Bower (Ed.), *The psychology of learning and motivation* (Vol. 16, pp. 1–58). Hillsdale, NJ: Erlbaum.

Chase, W. G., & Simon, H. A. (1973). Perception in chess. *Cognitive Psychology, 4*, 55–81.

Cheng, P. W. (1997). From covariation to causation: A causal power theory. *Psychological Review, 104*, 367–405.

Chi, M. T. H., Feltovich, P. J., & Glaser, R. (1981). Categorization and representation of physics problems by experts and novices. *Cognitive Science, 5*, 121–152.

Chiesi, H. L., Spilich, G. J., & Voss, J. F. (1979). Acquisition of domain-related information in relation to high and low domain knowledge. *Journal of Verbal Learning and Verbal Behavior, 18*, 257–274.

Dorner, D., & Scholkopf, J. (1991). Controlling complex systems; or, expertise as "grandmother's know-how." In K. A. Ericsson & J. Smith (Eds.), *Toward a general theory of expertise: Prospects and limits* (pp. 218–239). New York: Cambridge University Press.

Duncker, K. (1945). On problem solving. *Psychological Monographs, 58* (Whole No. 270).

Elio, R., & Anderson, J. R. (1984). The effects of information order and learning mode on schema abstraction. *Memory & Cognition, 12*, 20–30.

Ellis, H. C. (1965). *The transfer of learning.* New York: Macmillan.

Ericsson, K. A., & Charness, N. (1994). Expert performance: Its structure and acquisition. *American Psychologist, 49*, 725–747.

Ericsson, K. A., & Kintsch, W. (1995). Long-term working memory. *Psychological Review, 102*, 211–245.

Ericsson, K. A., & Lehmann, A. C. (1996). Expert and exceptional performance: Evidence of maximal adaptation to task constraints. *Annual Review of Psychology, 47*, 273–305.

Ericsson, K. A., & Polson, P. G. (1988). An experimental analysis of a memory skill for dinner-orders. *Journal of Experimental Psychology: Learning, Memory and Cognition, 14*, 305–316.

Ericsson, K. A., & Staszewski, J. J. (1989). Skilled memory and expertise: Mechanisms of exceptional performance. In D. Klahr & K. Kotovsky (Eds.), *Complex information processing: the impact of Herbert A. Simon* (pp. 235–267). Hillsdale, NJ: Erlbaum.

Estes, W. K. (1955). Statistical theory of distributional phenomena in learning. *Psychological Review, 62*, 369–377.

Gick, M. L., & Holyoak, K. J. (1980). Analogical problem solving. *Cognitive Psychology, 12*, 306–355.

Gick, M. L., & Holyoak, K. J. (1983). Schema induction and analogical transfer. *Cognitive Psychology, 15*, 1–38.

Gick, M. L., & Holyoak, K. J. (1987). The cognitive basis of knowledge transfer. In S. M. Cormier & J. D. Hagman (Eds.), *Transfer of training: Contemporary research and applications* (pp. 9–46). New York: Academic Press.

Gobet, F., & Simon, H. A. (1996a). Recall of rapidly presented random chess positions is a function of skill. *Psychonomic Bulletin & Review, 3*, 159–163.

Gobet, F., & Simon, H. A. (1996b). The roles of recognition processes and look-ahead search in time-constrained expert problem-solving: Evidence from grand-master-level chess. *Psychological Science, 7*, 52–55.

Gobet, F., & Simon, H. A. (1996c). Templates in chess memory: A mechanism for recalling several boards. *Cognitive Psychology, 31*, 1–40.

Gott, S. P., Hall, E. P., Pokorny, R. A., Dibble, E., & Glaser, R. (1993). A naturalistic study of transfer: Adaptive expertise in technical domains. In D. K. Detterman & R. J. Sternberg (Eds.), *Transfer on trial: Intelligence, cognition, and instruction* (pp. 258–288). Norwood, NJ: Ablex.

Groen, G. J., & Patel, V. (1988). The relationship between comprehension and reasoning in medical expertise. In M. Chi, R. Glaser, & M. J. Farr (Eds.), *The nature of expertise* (pp. 287–310). Hillsdale, NJ: Erlbaum.

Hatano, G., & Inagaki, K. (1986). Two courses of expertise. In H. Stevenson, H. Azuma, & K. Hakuta (Eds.), *Child development and education in Japan* (pp. 262–272). San Francisco: Freeman.

Hatano, G., & Osawa, K. (1983). Digit memory of grand masters in abacus-derived mental calculation. *Cognition, 15*, 95–110.

Holyoak, K. J., & Koh, K. (1987). Surface and structural similarity in analogical transfer. *Memory & Cognition, 15*, 332–340.

Homa, D., & Cultice, J. (1984). Role of feedback, category size, and stimulus distortion on the acquisition and utilization of ill-defined categories. *Journal of Experimental Psychology: Learning, Memory and Cognition, 10*, 83–94.

Jeffries, R., Turner, A. T., Polson, P. G., & Atwood, M. E. (1981). The processes involved in designing software. In J. R. Anderson (Ed.), *Cognitive skills and their acquisition* (pp. 255–283). Hillsdale, NJ: Erlbaum.

Keane, M. T. (1986). On retrieving analogues when solving problems. *Quarterly Journal of Experimental Psychology, 39A*, 29–41.

Kieras, D. E., & Bovair, S. (1986). The acquisition of procedures from text: A production-system analysis of transfer of training. *Journal of Memory and Language, 25*, 507–524.

Kintsch, W. (1988). The use of knowledge in discourse processing: A construction-integration model. *Psychological Review, 95*, 163–182.

Lane, D. M., & Robertson, L. (1979). The generality of the levels of processing hypothesis: An application to memory for chess positions. *Memory and Cognition, 7*, 253–256.

Mandler, G. (1962). From association to structure. *Psychological Review, 69*, 415–427.

McDaniel, M. A., & Schlager, M. S. (1990). Discovery learning and transfer of problem-solving skills. *Cognition and Instruction, 7*, 129–159.

Medin, D., Goldstone, R., & Gentner, D. (1993). Respects for similarity. *Psychological Review, 100*, 254–278.

Minsky, M. (1977). Frame-system theory. In P. N. Johnson-Laird & P. C. Wason (Eds.), *Thinking: Readings in cognitive science* (pp. 355–376). Cambridge: Cambridge University Press.

Morris, C. D., Bransford, J. D., & Franks, J. J. (1977). Levels of processing versus transfer appropriate processing. *Journal of Verbal Learning and Verbal Behavior, 16*, 519–533.

Nisbett, R. E., Fong, G. T., Lehman, D. R., & Cheng, P. W. (1987). Teaching reasoning. *Science, 238*, 625–631.

Novick, L. R. (1988). Analogical transfer, problem similarity, and expertise. *Journal of Experimental Psychology: Learning, Memory and Cognition, 14*, 510–520.

Novick, L. R., & Holyoak, K. J. (1991). Mathematical problem solving by analogy. *Journal of Experimental Psychology: Learning, Memory and Cognition, 17*, 398–415.

Patel, V. L., & Groen, G. J. (1991). The general and specific nature of medical expertise: A critical look. In K. A. Ericsson & J. Smith (Eds.), *Toward a general theory of expertise: Prospects and limits* (pp. 93–125). New York: Cambridge University Press.

Perfetto, G., Bransford, J., & Franks, J. (1983). Constraints on access in a problem solving context. *Memory & Cognition, 11*, 24–31.

Reber, A. S. (1993). *Implicit learning and tacit knowledge: An essay on the cognitive unconscious.* New York: Oxford University Press.

Richman, H. B., Staszewski, J. J., & Simon, H. A. (1995). Simulation of expert memory using EPAM IV. *Psychological Review, 102*, 305–330.

Ross, B. H., & Bradshaw, G. L. (1994). Encoding effects of remindings. *Memory & Cognition, 22*, 591–605.

Ross, B. H., & Kennedy, P. T. (1990). Generalizing from the use of earlier examples in problem solving. *Journal of Experimental Psychology: Learning, Memory, and Cognition, 16*, 42–55.

Ross, B. H., & Kilbane, M. C. (1997). Effects of principle explanation and superficial similarity on analogical mapping in problem solving. *Journal of Experimental Psychology: Learning, Memory and Cognition, 23*, 427–440.

Schank, R. C., & Abelson, R. P. (1977). *Scripts, plans, goals, and understanding.* Hillsdale, NJ: Erlbaum.

Schmidt, H. G., & Boshuizen, H. P. A. (1993). On the origin of intermediate effects in clinical case recall. *Memory & Cognition, 21*, 338–351.

Seger, C. A. (1994). Implicit learning. *Psychological Bulletin, 115*, 163–196.

Spilich, G. J., Vesonder, G. T., Chiesi, H. L., & Voss, J. F. (1979). Text processing of domain-related information for individuals with high and low domain knowledge. *Journal of Verbal Learning and Verbal Behavior, 18*, 275–290.

Sweller, J. (1980). Hypothesis salience, task difficulty and sequential effects on problem solving. *American Journal of Psychology, 95*, 455–483.

Sweller, J., Mawer, R. F., & Ward M. R. (1983). Development of expertise in mathematical problem solving. *Journal of Experimental Psychology: General, 112*, 639–661.

Tversky, A. (1977). Features of similarity. *Psychological Review, 84*, 327–352.

Vollmeyer, R., Burns, B. D., & Holyoak, K. J. (1996). The impact of goal specificity on strategy use and the acquisition of problem structure. *Cognitive Science, 20*, 75–100.

Weisberg, R., Di Camillo, M., & Phillips, D. (1978). Transferring old associations to new situations: A non-automatic process. *Journal of Verbal Learning and Verbal Behavior, 17*, 219–228.

Wharton, C. M., Holyoak, K. J., & Lange, T. E. (1996). Remote analogical reminding. *Memory & Cognition, 24*, 629–643.

Wiley, J. (1998). Expertise as mental set: The effects of domain knowledge in creative problem solving. *Memory & Cognition, 26*, 716–730.

CONTENTS OF MEMORY

8

Serial Learning

Cognition and Behavior

ROBERT G. CROWDER & ROBERT L. GREENE

Probably no concept has been studied as long in the experimental study of memory as that of serial learning—that is, learning a series of items in order. Clearly, recalling things in the proper order is crucial in limited situations, such as remembering telephone numbers or word spellings. More generally, however, any skilled behavior critically depends on the mastery of order. Consider the most distinctively human skill—that of language. At least among adults, information is generally carried not by the use of novel stimuli but by the ordering of long-familiar words and phrases.

Ebbinghaus (1885/1964), who developed so much of the tradition followed by researchers in verbal learning, initiated this interest in memory for serial ordering. Indeed, with respect both to his methodology and his theoretical formulation, Ebbinghaus's work completely dominated research on serial learning for 80 years and continues to be influential today. One of his most striking methodological contributions was his choice of stimuli. He constructed sets of nonsense syllables (that is, sets of a consonant, vowel, and consonant). These stimuli were chosen to minimize the effects of meaning or prior familiarity on the experiments. Ebbinghaus himself was aware that these nonsense syllables were only an imperfect solution and noted that there were great differences among syllables in the ease with which they could be learned. Subsequent research has suggested that the ease of acquisi-

tion of a nonsense syllable is greatly influenced by the extent to which it follows the phonetic and orthographic rules of the subject's native language (Jenkins, 1985).

Ebbinghaus used himself as his sole subject in these pioneering experiments. He would create a series of nonsense syllables and then read the series to the beat of a metronome until it seemed that the series was on the verge of being mastered. He would then look away from the sheet on which the list was printed and try to recite it from memory. If he hesitated during a recitation, he would turn back to the sheet and resume reading from the spot of his hesitation. He kept track of the time or trials required for mastery of the list. When he wanted to measure delayed retention, he would attempt to relearn the list and then compare the time or trials required for relearning with those required for the original learning of the list. Retention could then be expressed as a savings score—that is, some indication of the percentage of time saved in relearning the series. Ebbinghaus's choice of savings as a measure of memory was characteristically wise, as this has proved to be a particularly sensitive measure, one that can detect memory even when recall and recognition are around zero (MacLeod, 1988; Nelson, 1985).

Measuring memory by the time required to master a list to a particular criterion is not an ideal approach for all situations. Research on serial learning in the last two decades has increasingly used a study-test procedure. With this procedure, a subject studies a list once and is then tested for retention of the order of the items. In most of these studies, the study-test procedure is repeated many times until the subject has gone through a number of lists. The test used is often serial (ordered) recall or list reconsideration (in which the subject is given all the items and has to arrange them in the correct order). However, these changes in procedure have had seemingly little impact either on the major phenomena found or on the theories developed to explain memory for serial order.

This chapter will have two major sections. In the first, we will discuss the major theoretical approaches that have been taken for the explanation of serial retention. Then, we will turn to some of the major empirical findings in the area.

Theoretical Accounts of Serial Learning

Interitem-Association Accounts

The Chaining Hypothesis

In addition to his other contributions to this area, Ebbinghaus (1885/1964) also created one of the classic theoretical approaches to serial learning. It took many decades for researchers to consider systematically any alternative to Ebbinghaus's account, now known as the chaining hypothesis. Ebbinghaus assumed that serial learning consists largely of the formation of associations between adjacent items. Reciting a well-learned list would then just involve traveling down this chain of associations from one item to the next. Ebbinghaus did not believe that these associations from one item to the next were the only mechanism through which serial order was learned. Indeed, he believed that every item on a list became associated with every other item and that remote associations (that is, associations between nonadjacent items) played an important (albeit secondary) role in serial learning. Because Ebbinghaus believed in the importance of remote associations, Slamecka (1985) suggested that "bundle hypothesis" is actually a more appropriate term than "chaining hypothesis" for Ebbinghaus's account.

Ebbinghaus (1885/1964) reported an experiment on transfer of training to derived lists as evidence for the reality of remote associations. If learning a list (e.g., SAF-POR-BUJ-SUV-WEL-KAG-LEV-VIT . . .) leads to the formation of associations between adjacent items, then a second list (e.g., of the form SAF-BUJ-WEL-LEV . . .) containing the same items but systematically skipping a fixed number of items (in this case, 1) should be relatively easy to learn. Ebbinghaus made a number of comparisons of this sort and concluded that remote associations are indeed formed during serial learning, with the strength of these associations being determined by the distance between the two items. There has been occasional debate about the evidence for the notion of remote associations (e.g., Slamecka, 1964; Shebilske & Ebenholtz, 1971), but little attention has been paid to this topic in recent decades.

The central mechanism in Ebbinghaus's (1885/1964) theory—namely, chaining composed of associations between adjacent items—itself came under fire as a result of a line of research initiated by Young (1959; for a review of the early experiments, see Young, 1968). According to the chaining hypothesis, a subject who has mastered the serial list FUG-MIS-PED-LUH-ZIF-MOQ-SIW-JUB . . . has done so by learning associations between FUG and MIS, MIS and PED, LUH and ZIF, and so on. What if this subject is then asked to learn a list of paired associates containing pairs such as LUH-ZIF, FUG-MIS, and MOQ-SIW? If the chaining hypothesis is true, such a list should be very easy to learn because the required associations had already been learned while mastering the serial list. However, Young repeatedly found that there was little or no positive transfer from the serial list to the paired-associate list, and concluded that the chaining hypothesis had to be wrong. Later experiments established boundary conditions on Young's conclusions by finding clear transfer between serial lists and paired-associate lists under some circumstances. For example, Jensen (1962) added a number of methodological changes, including informing subjects regarding the experimental design. Crowder (1968a) abandoned the potentially insensitive dependent variable of trials to criterion and used correct responses to individual pairs in a continuous paired-associate learning task to measure transfer. Both studies found evidence for chaining, but transfer was still far from complete in these studies. This has to be viewed as evidence against the chaining hypothesis as a complete account of serial learning.

Slamecka (1977) shed light on why the magnitude of transfer to paired-associate learning has been so disappointing. He noted that most studies in this vein had subjects learn the serial list through the anticipation method, where they would try to pronounce each item aloud before it is presented. In this methodology, it is possible that the physical processes involved in producing each item become associated with the identity of the succeeding item. That is, each item becomes associated not only with the preceding item but also with the physical actions required to pronounce the previous item. Slamecka found evidence in two experiments to support this notion.

It would be a mistake to view the chaining hypothesis as purely a museum piece. Indeed, Lewandowsky and Murdock (1989) developed a theory of serial learning that is based exclusively on chaining. These authors assumed that serial learning is based entirely on pairwise associations between adjacent items. At the time of recall, retrieval follows the chain of associations, beginning either at the beginning of the list or the end. Ironically, this model is even purer than Ebbinghaus's (1885/1964) original account given that Lewandowsky and Murdock chose to exclude the use of remote associations in serial order. Although the model has not been able to explain all aspects of the data on serial learning (Li & Lewandowsky, 1993), its success in accounting for much of the literature suggests that chaining remains a viable theory and likely makes some contribution to the retention of serial information.

Study-Phase Retrieval and Reminding

Anyone who sits through an experiment requiring study of a long list will experience the sensation that one item will bring to mind earlier items. Sometimes the reason for this reminding is obvious, as there may be a strong similarity between the current item and the one that was brought to mind. At other times the basis for this reminding is idiosyncratic and unclear. The term *reminding* is used to refer to an act of involuntary retrieval—that is, a person is not trying effortfully to bring to mind a particular memory, but it arrives unbidden, presumably as a result of its similarity to the person's current thoughts and percep-

tions. For our purposes this reminding process is interesting because it could convey information about serial order. For example, say that the presentation of one word on a list (e.g., *winter*) reminds a subject of an earlier word (e.g., *party*) on the list, perhaps because the subject's birthday is during winter. If the subject is able to remember that this reminding process took place, then there would be no question as to which of those words had been presented earlier because *winter* had brought the already-presented *party* to mind. A reminding process taking place during the presentation of a list is called study-phase retrieval.

Tzeng and Cotton (1980) helped to popularize this concept. They had their subjects study a 50-word list for an unspecified memory test. The list consisted either of 5 exemplars from 10 semantic categories or of semantically unrelated words. After presentation of the list was complete, subjects were given a recency-discrimination test—that is, they were given pairs of words from the study list one at a time and were asked to pick the word in each pair that had occurred later (i.e., more recently) on the study list. Subjects were correct on .65 of the trials when they had studied a list of unrelated words. Their performance was essentially identical (.66) when they had studied the list of 5 exemplars from 10 categories and were tested on pairs containing words from 2 different categories. However, their performance (.80) was greatly enhanced when they were tested on pairs containing 2 words from a single category. Tzeng and Cotton argued that study-phase retrieval had taken place. That is, when subjects encounter a word, it could easily bring to mind related words that had been shown. This reminding would later help subjects to remember the relative positions of those words. Nairne and Neumann (1993) showed that the same sort of similarity advantage could be found when memory was tested by reconstruction of order.

It should be noted that Tzeng and Cotton's (1980) reasoning was somewhat indirect. That is, they found that similarity enhanced recency discrimination and assumed that study-phase retrieval had taken place and mediated this effect. However, there was no direct evidence that any sort of reminding process took place. Winograd and Soloway (1985) addressed this by asking subjects to write down a free association to each word on a list that was being presented to them. These free-association responses could then be used to determine when study-phase retrieval had taken place. On a later recency-discrimination test, subjects were far more accurate on pairs of related words (where relatedness was determined by the occurrence of a study-phase retrieval) than on pairs of unrelated words. Thus, the existence of study-phase retrieval and its usefulness in remembering serial order appears to be on solid empirical ground.

Ironically, one can see this study-phase retrieval process as being one explanation for how remote associations (to use Ebbinghaus's terms) get formed. We have discussed how Ebbinghaus's (1885/1964) claim that associations are formed between nonadjacent items became controversial (Slamecka, 1964; Shebilske & Ebenholtz, 1971) and has largely been neglected. However, this study-phase retrieval process, in which two items that may have occurred at widely separated positions become connected in the mind, is exactly the sort of cognitive process that can be used to explain how remote associations come about. Although Tzeng and Cotton may have described this process in very different terms, the essential goal is still to explain how mental connections are formed in the absence of temporal contiguity.

Positional-Association Accounts

Historically, the chief alternative to accounts emphasizing inter-item associations have been those emphasizing associations between each item and some representation of the position that it occupied in the list. The notion that serial learning depends upon item-position associations seemingly dates back at least to a discussion in Ladd and Woodworth (1911, pp. 578–579) and to a mimeographed text by Woodworth and Poffenberger (1920, pp. 71–72). Scattered evidence supporting this notion was reported over the years. Melton and Irwin (1940) had subjects learn two unrelated serial lists; they reported that, when an intrusion from the first list was made on the second list, it was placed at the position it had occupied on the first list more often than would be expected by chance. Schultz (1955) reported that subjects were able to recall the position that an item occupied on a serial list. Still, it was not until Young (1959) raised doubts about the chaining hypothesis that this positional alternative attracted a lot of attention. Research has generally confirmed the propositions that subjects form associations between items and po-

sitions and that these associations may play some role in serial learning (see Ebenholtz, 1972, for a review).

There are actually several different versions of this account. For example, one could believe that subjects actually form associations between each item and the number representing its position on the list (Young, Hakes, & Hicks, 1967). Alternatively, associations could be formed between items and some representation of relative position (e.g., "third from last"; see Glanzer & Peters, 1962). Another version attributes serial learning to the formation of associations between items and points on a very abstract scale that represents time of occurrence. For example, Johnson (1991; see also Bower, 1971; Murdock, 1960) argued that subjects associate each item with an abstract representation of that item's distance from the center of the list.

This positional approach is usually seen as an alternative to accounts emphasizing inter-item associations. However, it is possible to combine these approaches. For example, Young, Patterson, and Benson (1963) suggested that positional associations are used to remember items occurring in the middle of a list while chaining is used for items at the beginning and end. Ebenholtz (1963) took exactly the opposite approach, saying that positional associations are used to recall terminal positions while chaining is used for interior positions. More generally, accounts emphasizing inter-item associations and those emphasizing positional associations are similar because they see serial learning as a process in which pairwise associations are built up and strengthened gradually and passively. Essentially, these approaches see serial learning as a form of paired-associate learning. However, in the last few decades, researchers have increasingly felt that serial learning involves the active constructions of a complex, hierarchical organization of the list.

Hierarchical Accounts of Serial Learning

Lashley (1951) is generally seen as the pivotal figure in the development of hierarchical accounts of serial order. Lashley based many of his arguments, not on serial learning per se, but on examples involving other skills. For instance, an account of language that relies on pairwise associations seems doomed to failure because there are so many different combinations and reorderings of words, letters, and phrases. Similarly, it is difficult to believe that the performance of a piece by a skilled pianist reflects the execution of pairwise associations of each note with the next or with its position in the piece. Lashley argued that a structure involving several levels of organization seems required for such serial behavior. Of course, one could argue (as have Lewandowsky & Murdock, 1989) that these arguments do not necessarily extend to traditional serial-learning experiments, where subjects usually have only limited experience with any particular list. Still, the force of Lashley's arguments has generally been accepted (Bruce, 1994).

Studies in which the experimenter has (indirectly) encouraged the use of organization during memorization have popularized the claim that memorized lists are structured hierarchically. Miller's (1956) classic paper brought concepts such as "recoding" and "chunking" to the mainstream of memory research. Wickelgren (1967) used pauses to induce a temporal-rhythmic structure to serial lists. Similarly, Bower and Winzenz (1969) used rhythmic stress to show how grouping can facilitate recall of digit strings. Of particular note is the development of the seriogram (Martin & Noreen, 1974), which traces the history of a single subject with a single list through many trials of serial learning to a fixed criterion. The logic here is that, if a set of items had been grouped together, then it is likely that either all of those items will be recalled or that none of them will be. Martin and Noreen kept track of which items were successfully recalled on each trial by a particular subject and then constructed a depiction of the development of the organizational structure used by that subject on a single list.

Another way of summarizing this approach is that theoretical accounts of serial learning have increasingly rejected the terminal meta-postulate (Bever, Fodor, & Garrett, 1968). Essentially, the terminal meta-postulate would say here that accounts of learning must include only potentially observable events (i.e., stimuli and responses) and the associations between events; such associations would presumably be built up gradually through repetition of co-occurrences. This meta-postulate would have been included as an unspoken assumption by most discussions of serial learning before Lashley (1951). In recent decades, the rejection of the terminal meta-postulate has been equally widespread. Mandler (1985) has noted that theories of serial organization have moved from a reliance on association to a reliance on structure as an explanatory mechanism.

Selected Empirical Phenomena in Serial Learning

Serial-Position Effects

In just about any task in which memory for order is required, performance is better on the first few and last few items than on the ones in the middle. The advantage at the beginning of the list is called the primacy effect, and the advantage at the end is called the recency effect. Priority for this finding belongs to an American physicist, Francis Nipher, who reported his findings in an 1878 paper that fell into obscurity before being rediscovered and republished by Stigler (1978). Nipher read lists composed of 6 digits to his subjects, who were required to write them down in order. Pronounced primacy and recency effects were present in Nipher's data. Unfortunately, Nipher's work attracted little attention, so it was left to Kirkpatrick (1894) and Ebbinghaus (1902) to rediscover serial-position effects for experimental psychology.

Up until the 1960s, research on serial-position effects was strongly linked to the serial-learning methodology. Therefore, it is not surprising that most of the early accounts of these effects grew out of theoretical approaches to serial learning. For example, Ribback and Underwood (1950) developed a chaining account of serial-position effects. They assumed that learning is a chaining process that starts at the two outside positions and works inward. The beginning and end of the list, where the chaining process starts, would be learned first and be least dependent on a long chain of associations. A slight complication with this approach is that typically the primacy effect in serial recall is larger than the recency effect. However, Ribback and Underwood noted that the chain starting at the beginning of the list would be based on forward associations from one item to the next, whereas the chain working inward from the end of the list would be based upon backward associations, which theorists from Ebbinghaus on have assumed to be weaker than forward associations. Therefore, an asymmetry in serial-position functions could be predicted. This account never generated much attention. A related but more complex formulation by Hull et al. (1940) generated somewhat more interest, but neither of these approaches survived the general rejection of associationist accounts beginning in the 1960s.

On the other hand, accounts of serial learning that emphasize the association of items with serial positions have long led to reasonably successful accounts of serial-position effects. The critical assumption here is that the first few and last few serial positions are more distinctive than the others and that the association between an item and its position will be enhanced if that position is a distinctive one. Johnson (1991) presents a typical account (see also Bower, 1971; Ebenholtz, 1972; Murdock, 1960, for similar approaches). Johnson assumed that serial learning consists of the formation of associations between items and serial positions, that items can become associated not only with their own positions but with other serial positions as well, and that the strength of the incorrect item-position associations depends upon the distinctiveness of the true position that the item occupied. The end result would be that there would be less ambiguity regarding the position of an item from the beginning or end of a list than of one from the middle.

One complication regarding any discussion of serial-position effects in serial learning is that it is uncertain whether an adequate theory should extend easily to serial-position effects in all of the other memory tasks in which they are found. Particularly critical is the recency effect found in free recall, which has often been explained in terms of a limited-capacity short-term memory store (Atkinson & Shiffrin, 1968; Glanzer, 1972; Waugh & Norman, 1965). This short-term store account, which usually assumes the existence of brief and fragile buffer, could not easily be extended to serial learning, where serial-position effects are found in a task that may require the subject to spend many trials mastering a long list using the anticipation method. However, there is some evidence that the short-term store account is not even satisfactory as a complete account of recency effects in free recall (Greene, 1986). On the other hand, the positional-distinctiveness account that Johnson (1991) and others suggested for serial recall can be extended quite naturally to free recall, as well as other tasks. The only added assumption required is that the distinctiveness of a serial position can influence the probability of retrieval (Bjork & Whitten, 1974). If one wants to create a single theory of serial-posi-

tion effects (and not all researchers do), this approach currently seems to be the most promising.

Modality Effects

In the typical experiment on modality differences in memory for order, subjects are given a list, often composed of randomly arranged digits, and are asked to recall them in order. Memory performance is generally enhanced if the items are presented auditorily, rather than visually. This auditory advantage is usually restricted to the end of the list; for earlier items, there is typically little difference as a function of presentation modality. Corballis (1966) brought this finding to the notice of modern researchers, although similar findings had been reported long ago (e.g., Washburn, 1916). This auditory advantage at the end of a list is known as the *modality effect*; another way of describing this effect is to say that the recency effect is far greater for auditory lists than for visual lists. A similar pattern is found when memory for order is tested using a list-reconstruction task (Neath, 1997).

For many years, the modality effect was often explained in terms of a precategorical acoustic store (Crowder & Morton, 1969), some sort of auditory sensory storage that would maintain information about the last few sounds that had been heard. By this account, the modality effect is not informative about the general processes used in serial recall but rather reflects the existence of a supplementary source of information that is briefly available for auditory items but not for visual items. However, one encounters the same problems with the modality effect as have been seen in our discussion with serial-position effects—namely, that it is not clear if one must evaluate theories in terms of how they deal with results from very different memory tasks. Long-term modality effects can be found under some circumstances when subjects are tested for delayed free recall (Gardiner & Gregg, 1979; Glenberg, 1984; Greene, 1985). Clearly, no attempt to explain modality and suffix effects in terms of short-lived precategorical acoustic stores is likely to be extended successfully here.

Glenberg and Swanson (1986) took a daring approach to this issue. Unlike Crowder and Morton (1969), Glenberg and Swanson argued that modality effects do not represent a supplementary source of information that is added to the processes generally used in serial learning, but rather that the modality effect truly represents an advantage in serial coding for auditory information. In other words, they assumed that serial (or temporal) memory truly is better for auditory information than for visual information. Glenberg and Swanson argued that time of occurrence is more accurately encoded for auditory information than for visual information and that such information is used not only in serial-recall tasks (where order information is explicitly required) but also to assist retrieval in free recall. Glenberg and Swanson's proposal inspired a burst of research comparing temporal coding for visual and auditory information. Some results have been supportive of this approach. For example, when subjects see a list of items and then have to make judgments about the position of particular items, an advantage for auditory presentation over visual presentation has been reported both for items at the beginning of the list and for items at the end (Glenberg & Fernandez, 1988; Greene & Crowder, 1988), though no difference was found for items that had occupied middle positions on the study list. Also, Glenberg, Mann, Altman, Forman, and Procise (1989) reported an advantage for auditory, as opposed to visual, presentation in the perception and reproduction of temporal rhythms, although it is possible that this auditory advantage is found only under very limited conditions (Watkins, LeCompte, Elliott, & Fish, 1992).

However, there have been other situations where an expected auditory advantage failed to appear. For example, Crowder and Greene (1987; see also Schab & Crowder, 1989) required subjects to remember the amount of time between the presentations of items that would occur at irregular rates. There would be different amounts of time between the occurrence of adjacent items. Performance on this task was generally unaffected by the modality of presentation of the items. More generally, Neath and Crowder (1990) found that aurally presented words seemed less sensitive than visually presented words to manipulations of temporal distinctiveness. Marks and Crowder (1997) have resolved some of the empirical conflicts regarding modality and temporal memory, but the status of Glenberg and Swanson's (1986) original claim, that time of occurrence is registered more accurately for auditory stimuli than for visual items, must be viewed as having at best limited generality.

Similarity

One is tempted to say that, while serial-position effects were considered the most important phenomenon to explain in older theories of serial learning, the effects of similarity were seen as being the critical data to explain starting in the 1960s. This is largely because similarity became an essential variable in differentiating between item and order information. Horowitz (1961) performed one of the most influential studies here. He had subjects learn lists of 12 trigrams that were either high in similarity (e.g., VXF, XVS, FSV, FXS, XSF, SVF, and so on) or lower (e.g., QSZ, KWX, SJM, WQJ, JZR, MRV, and so on). Free recall was higher for lists of high-similarity trigrams than for lists of low-similarity trigrams, implying that item information is enhanced by high similarity. However, order reconstruction (measured by putting the items on cards and asking the subject to arrange them in the right order) was more accurate when low-similarity trigrams were used. A similar sort of dissociation is found in recall, where free recall is enhanced but ordered serial recall is impaired by phonological similarity (Watkins, Watkins, & Crowder, 1974).

This sort of interaction between type of information and similarity has been critical for the argument that there is a fundamental distinction between item information and order information. Different theorists have approached this distinction in quite different ways. For example, Conrad (1965) argued that item information is primary and that order information is derivative; Conrad maintained that an order transposition is actually the result of two item errors. On the other hand, theories such as those of Estes (1972) and Wickelgren (1977) assume that item information is secondary to order information. In these theories, items (say, letters or words) depend upon the proper ordering of constituent elements (phonemes). A mistake that appears to be a loss of item information (e.g., recalling an item that was not included on the list) may actually represent a loss of order information, a misordering of the phonemes that made up one or more of the items.

However, one must be careful before accepting the conclusion that intra-list similarity enhances item information and impairs order information. Crowder (1979) questioned the first half of this pattern. By manipulating semantic similarity, he was able to replicate the standard pattern of free recall being higher, and serial recall being impaired, when lists of high similarity are used. However, when subjects were tested on recognition, which is normally viewed as a pure measure of item information, no effect of similarity was observed. Crowder suggested that the apparent similarity advantage in previous studies was actually due to a sophisticated guessing strategy, where subjects use the structure of the list to generate possible stimuli to recall.

The claim that high similarity inevitably impairs order information is also no longer tenable. One should recall the literature on study-phase retrieval, where similarity could lead to a reminding process that actually improved memory for order. Nairne and Neumann (1993) reported several examples of phonological or semantic similarity improving long-term memory for order. The simple generalization that similarity dissociates item from order information no longer seems valid.

In retrospect, the failure of this dissociation is reasonable. Item and order information are unlikely to differ in any fundamental way. In standard memory experiments, subjects are tested on familiar stimuli, and a test of item information, such as free recall or recognition, is really seeing whether the subjects know that these stimuli occurred at a particular time and place. However, that is what is meant by order information as well—that is, having the subject remember the time of occurrence of a particular event. As has been argued elsewhere (Crowder, 1979), order and item information differ only in terms of their frame of reference (either locating a time of occurrence on a list, as opposed to in other situations, or at a particular place on the list).

Intra-List Repetition of Items

Taking intra-item similarity to its maximum point would mean including items that are repetitions of earlier items. A moment's reflection would suggest that any stimulus-response account of serial learning would predict that the repetition of items on a list should be disastrous. A complete reliance on inter-item chaining would leave a subject unable to master a sequence like 736439285, where an item (in this case, the digit 3) occurs in two distinct locations. Remote associations may be used to assist learning, but one should still expect such a sequence to be far more challenging than one without a repetition. Similarly, an account emphasizing item-position associa-

tions would imply tremendous interference between the two positions associated with a repeated stimulus.

Considerable research (primarily using a study-test method in serial recall) has been carried out on intra-list repetition effects. A decrement in serial recall of repeated items is generally found; this finding is called the *Ranschburg effect*, after its German discoverer. Crowder and Melton (1965) introduced this effect to contemporary researchers. Still, perhaps the most striking aspect of the Ranschburg effect is not that it occurs because it would be predicted by seemingly any associationist account of serial order; rather, the most striking thing is that the Ranschburg effect is small in magnitude and limited in generality. Typically, the effect is found only when the two occurrences of the repeated item are spread apart, and the detrimental effect is found only on recall of the second occurrence, with recall of the first item unaffected. Even when these conditions are met, the Ranschburg effect is typically modest in size (for evidence for all of these claims, see Crowder, 1968b). Moreover, the Ranschburg effect probably does not predominantly reflect associative interference at all but rather response strategies, in which subjects hesitate to emit a response that they had already given while recalling a list (Greene, 1991; Hinrichs, Mewaldt, & Redding, 1973).

Given sufficiently sophisticated assumptions regarding coding processes and response strategies in serial recall, the literature on the Ranschburg effect can be satisfactorily explained (e.g., see Nairne's [1990] feature model of immediate serial recall). However, such a richness of assumptions is indeed required. No simple attempts to reduce serial learning to the mechanistic strengthening of pairwise associations will be able to explain the data in this area.

Conclusion

Research has been almost nonexistent for several decades on serial learning as earlier generations defined it—that is, the gradual mastery of a list of nonsense syllables. However, the issues raised by this task continue to be central in studies of human memory. Research on serial learning (broadly defined) has shed light on such contemporary issues as the nature of memory organization, the distinction between item and order information, the role of distinctiveness in retrieval, and the place of response strategies in accounts of behavior. As the methods used to study serial learning have become more varied, the theories on this topic have necessarily become more complex. However, this should be welcomed as a sign of the maturation of the research area after so many decades of study.

References

Atkinson, R. C., & Shiffrin, R. M. (1968). Human memory: A proposed system and its control processes. In K. W. Spence & J. T. Spence (Eds.), *The psychology of learning and motivation* (Vol. 2, pp. 89–105). New York: Academic Press.

Bever, T. G., Fodor, J. A., & Garrett, M. A. (1968). A formal limit of associationism. In T. R. Dixon & D. L. Horton (Eds.), *Verbal behavior and general behavior theory* (pp. 582–585). Englewood Cliffs, NJ: Prentice-Hall.

Bjork, R. A., & Whitten, W. B. (1974). Recency-sensitive retrieval processes in long-term free recall. *Cognitive Psychology, 6,* 173–189.

Bower, G. H. (1971). Adaptation-level coding of stimuli and serial position effects. In M. H. Appley (Ed.), *Adaptation-level theory* (pp. 175–201). New York: Academic Press.

Bower, G. H., & Winzenz, D. (1969). Group structure, coding, and memory for digit series. *Journal of Experimental Psychology Monograph Supplement, 80*(2), 1–17.

Bruce, D. (1994). Lashley and the problem of serial order. *American Psychologist, 49,* 93–103.

Conrad, R. (1965). Order errors in immediate recall of sequences. *Journal of Verbal Learning and Verbal Behavior, 4,* 161–169.

Corballis, M. C. (1966). Rehearsal and decay in immediate recall of visually and aurally presented items. *Canadian Journal of Psychology, 20,* 43–51.

Crowder, R. G. (1968a). Evidence for the chaining hypothesis of serial verbal learning. *Journal of Experimental Psychology, 76,* 497–500.

Crowder, R. G. (1968b). Intraserial repetition effects in immediate memory. *Journal of Verbal Learning and Verbal Behavior, 7,* 446–451.

Crowder, R. G. (1979). Similarity and order in memory. In G. Bower (Ed.), *The psychology of learning and motivation* (Vol. 13, pp. 319–353). San Diego, CA: Academic Press.

Crowder, R. G., & Greene, R. L. (1987). On the remembrance of times past: The irregular list technique. *Journal of Experimental Psychology: General, 116,* 265–278.

Crowder, R. G., & Melton, A. W. (1965). The Ranschburg phenomenon: Failures of immediate recall correlated with repetition of elements within a stimulus. *Psychonomic Science, 2,* 295–296.

Crowder, R. G., & Morton, J. (1969). Precategorical acoustic storage (PAS). *Perception & Psychophysics, 5,* 365–373.

Ebbinghaus, H. (1885/1964). *Memory: A contribution to experimental psychology.* New York: Dover.

Ebbinghaus, H. (1902). *Grundzüge der Psychologie.* Leipzig: Von Veit.

Ebenholtz, S. M. (1963). Position mediated transfer between serial learning and a spatial discrimination task. *Journal of Experimental Psychology, 65,* 603–608.

Ebenholtz, S. M. (1972). Serial learning and dimensional organization. In G. H. Bower (Ed.), *The psychology of learning and motivation* (Vol. 5, pp. 267–314). New York: Academic Press.

Estes, W. K. (1972). An associative basis for coding and organization in memory. In A. W. Melton & E. Martin (Eds.), *Coding processes in human memory* (pp. 161–190). Washington, DC: Winston.

Gardiner, J. M., & Gregg, V. H. (1979). When auditory memory is not overwritten. *Journal of Verbal Learning and Verbal Behavior, 18,* 705–719.

Glanzer, M. (1972). Storage mechanisms in recall. In G. H. Bower & J. T. Spence (Eds.), *The psychology of learning and motivation* (Vol. 5, pp. 129–193). New York: Academic Press.

Glanzer, M., & Peters, S. C. (1962). A re-examination of the serial position effect. *Journal of Experimental Psychology, 64,* 258–266.

Glenberg, A. M. (1984). A retrieval account of the long-term modality effect. *Journal of Experimental Psychology: Learning, Memory, and Cognition, 10,* 16–31.

Glenberg, A. M., & Fernandez, A. (1988). Evidence for auditory temporal distinctiveness: Modality effects in order and frequency judgments. *Journal of Experimental Psychology: Learning, Memory, and Cognition, 14,* 728–739.

Glenberg, A. M., Mann, S., Altman, L., Forman, T., & Procise, S. (1989). Modality effects in the coding and reproduction of rhythms. *Memory & Cognition, 17,* 373–383.

Glenberg, A. M., & Swanson, N. C. (1986). A temporal distinctiveness theory of recency and modality effects. *Journal of Experimental Psychology: Learning, Memory, and Cognition, 12*, 3–24.

Green, R. L. (1985). Constraints on the long-term modality effect. *Journal of Memory and Language, 24*, 526–541.

Greene, R. L. (1986). Sources of recency effects in free recall. *Psychological Bulletin, 99*, 221–228.

Greene, R. L. (1991). The Ranschburg effect: The role of guessing strategies. *Memory & Cognition, 19*, 313–317.

Greene, R. L., & Crowder, R. G. (1988). Memory for serial position: Effects of spacing, vocalization, and stimulus suffixes. *Journal of Experimental Psychology: Learning, Memory, and Cognition, 14*, 740–748.

Hinrichs, J. V., Mewaldt, S. P., & Redding, J. (1973). The Ranschburg effect: Repetition and guessing factors in short-term memory. *Journal of Verbal Learning and Verbal Behavior, 12*, 64–75.

Horowitz, L. M. (1961). Free recall and ordering of trigrams. *Journal of Experimental Psychology, 62*, 51–57.

Hull, C. L., Hovland, C. I., Ross, R. T., Hall, M., Perkins, D. T., & Fitch, F. B. (1940). *Mathematico-deductive theory of rote learning.* New Haven, CT: Yale University Press.

Jenkins, J. J. (1985). Nonsense syllables: Comprehending the "almost incomprehensible variation." *Journal of Experimental Psychology: Learning, Memory, and Cognition, 11*, 455–460.

Jensen, A. R. (1962). Temporal and spatial effects of serial position. *American Journal of Psychology, 75*, 390–400.

Johnson, G. J. (1991). A distinctiveness model of serial learning. *Psychological Review, 98*, 204–217.

Kirkpatrick, E. A. (1894). An experimental study of memory. *Psychological Review, 1*, 602–609.

Ladd, G. L., & Woodworth, R. S. (1911). *Elements of physiological psychology.* New York: Charles Scribner's Sons.

Lashley, K. S. (1951). The problem of serial order in behavior. In L. A. Jeffress (Ed.), *Cerebral mechanisms in behavior* (pp. 112–136). New York: John Wiley.

Lewandowsky, S., & Murdock, B. B., Jr. (1989). Memory for serial order. *Psychological Review, 96*, 25–57.

Li, S.-C., & Lewandowsky, S. (1993). Intralist distractors and recall direction: Constraints on models of memory for serial order. *Journal of Experimental Psychology: Learning, Memory, and Cognition, 19*, 895–908.

MacLeod, C. M. (1988). Forgotten but not gone: Savings for pictures and words in long-term memory. *Journal of Experimental Psychology: Learning, Memory, and Cognition, 14*, 195–212.

Mandler, G. (1985). From association to structure. *Journal of Experimental Psychology: Learning, Memory, and Cognition, 11*, 464–468.

Marks, A. R., & Crowder, R. G. (1997). Temporal distinctiveness and modality. *Journal of Experimental Psychology: Learning, Memory, and Cognition, 23*, 164–480.

Martin, E., & Noreen, D. L. (1974). Serial learning: Identification of subjective subsequences. *Cognitive Psychology, 6*, 421–435.

Melton, A. W., & Irwin, J. M. (1940). The influence of degree of interpolated learning on retroactive inhibition and the overt transfer of specific responses. *American Journal of Psychology, 53*, 173–203.

Miller, G. A. (1956). The magical number seven plus or minus two: Some limits on our capacity for processing information. *Psychological Review, 63*, 81–97.

Murdock, B. B., Jr. (1960). The distinctiveness of stimuli. *Psychological Review, 67*, 16–31.

Nairne, J. S. (1990). A feature model of immediate memory. *Memory & Cognition, 18*, 251–269.

Nairne, J. S., & Neumann, C. (1993). Enhancing effects of similarity on long-term memory for order. *Journal of Experimental Psychology: Learning, Memory, and Cognition, 19*, 329–337.

Neath, I. (1997). Modality, concreteness, and set-size effects in a free reconstruction of order task. *Memory & Cognition, 25*, 256–263.

Neath, I., & Crowder, R. G. (1990). Schedules of presentation and temporal distinctiveness in human memory. *Journal of Experimental Psychology: Learning, Memory, and Cognition, 16*, 316–327.

Nelson, T. O. (1985). Ebbinghaus' contribution to the measurement of retention: Savings during relearning. *Journal of Experimental Psychology: Learning, Memory, and Cognition, 11*, 472–479.

Ribback, A., & Underwood, B. J. (1950). An empirical explanation of the bowness of the serial position curve. *Journal of Experimental Psychology, 40*, 329–335.

Schab, F. R., & Crowder, R. G. (1989). Accuracy of temporal coding: Auditory-visual comparisons. *Memory & Cognition, 17,* 384–397.

Schultz, R. W. (1955). Generalization of serial position in rote serial learning. *Journal of Experimental Psychology, 49,* 267–272.

Shebilske, W., & Ebenholtz, S. M. (1971). Ebbinghaus' derived-list experiments reconsidered. *Psychological Review, 78,* 553–555.

Slamecka, N. J. (1964). An inquiry into the doctrine of remote associations. *Psychological Review, 71,* 61–76.

Slamecka, N. J. (1977). A case for response-produced cues in serial learning. *Journal of Experimental Psychology: Human Learning and Memory, 3,* 222–232.

Slamecka, N. J. (1985). Ebbinghaus: Some associations. *Journal of Experimental Psychology: Learning, Memory, and Cognition, 11,* 414–435.

Stigler, S. M. (1978). Some forgotten work on memory. *Journal of Experimental Psychology: Human Learning and Memory, 4,* 1–4.

Tzeng, O. J. L., & Cotton, B. (1980). A study-phase retrieval model of temporal coding. *Journal of Experimental Psychology: Human Learning and Memory, 6,* 705–716.

Washburn, M. F. (1916). *Movement and mental imagery.* Boston: Houghton Mifflin.

Watkins, M. J., LeCompte, D. C., Elliott, M. N., & Fish, S. B. (1992). Short-term memory for the timing of auditory and visual signals. *Journal of Experimental Psychology: Learning, Memory, and Cognition, 18,* 931–937.

Watkins, M. J., Watkins, O. C., & Crowder, R. G. (1974). The modality effect in free and serial recall as a function of phonological similarity. *Journal of Verbal Learning and Verbal Behavior, 13,* 430–447.

Waugh, N. C., & Norman, D. A. (1965). Primary memory. *Psychological Review, 72,* 89–104.

Wickelgren, W. A. (1967). Rehearsal grouping and hierarchical organization of serial position cues in short-term memory. *Quarterly Journal of Experimental Psychology, 19,* 97–102.

Wickelgren, W. A. (1977). *Learning and memory.* Englewood Cliffs, NJ: Prentice-Hall.

Winograd, E., & Soloway, R. M. (1985). Remindings as a basis for temporal judgments. *Journal of Experimental Psychology: Learning, Memory, and Cognition, 11,* 262–271.

Woodworth, R. S., & Poffenberger (1920). *Textbook of experimental psychology* (Mimeographed ed.). New York: Columbia University.

Young, R. K. (1959). A comparison of two methods of learning serial associations. *American Journal of Psychology, 72,* 554–559.

Young, R. K. (1968). Serial learning. In T. R. Dixon & D. L. Horton (Eds.), *Verbal behavior and general behavior theory* (pp. 122–148). Englewood Cliffs, NJ: Prentice-Hall.

Young, R. K., Hakes, D. T., & Hicks, R. Y. (1967). Ordinal position number as a cue in serial learning. *Journal of Experimental Psychology, 73,* 427–438.

Young, R. K., Patterson, J., & Benson, W. M. (1963). Backward serial learning. *Journal of Verbal Learning and Verbal Behavior, 1,* 335–338.

9

Remembering Actions and Words

LARS-GÖRAN NILSSON

In the beginning of the 1980s, a new experimental paradigm for studying remembering and memory was developed. This paradigm seemed to produce results that were not only different with respect to levels of performance in comparison to that obtained in verbal memory experiments but also revealed data suggesting that other laws, principles, or rules might be at work. Empirical phenomena that are reliably obtained in verbal learning experiments were not obtained when using this new paradigm.

Independently of each other, Cohen (1981), Engelkamp and Krumnacker (1980), and Saltz and Donnenwerth-Nolan (1981) invented this new paradigm. The paradigm is usually referred to as the enactment paradigm or the subject performed task (SPT) paradigm. It requires the subject to perform minitasks according to verbal instructions given by the experimenter (e.g., roll the ball, fold the paper, lift the pen). During a subsequent memory test the subject is asked to remember as many of these instructions as possible. The control condition consists of the same type of verbal commands presented to the subject without any instructions to perform the actions. The typical result obtained in such experiments is that memory for enacted action phrases is superior to that for events encoded without enactment (e.g., Cohen, 1981; Engelkamp & Zim-

mer, 1985). As will be seen below, many of the replicable classical phenomena demonstrated in memory experiments using words as the to-be-remembered (TBR) information have not been duplicated in action memory experiments.

The motivation for developing this paradigm was somewhat different for Cohen, Engelkamp, and Saltz, respectively. Cohen's (1981) aim with this paradigm was specifically to use it as a way to test the generality of memory phenomena that had been obtained on the basis of memory for lists of unrelated words. For Engelkamp and Krumnacker (1980) and for Saltz and Donnenwerth-Nolan (1981), the enactment condition was a means to study under which conditions memory can generally be improved.

Theory

The enactment paradigm invited a large number of experimental studies with the purpose of explaining the enactment effect. Four different theoretical approaches eventually emerged.

The first theoretical position was proposed by Cohen (1981, 1983). He argued that memory for action events is nonstrategic in the sense that it does not depend on acquisition strategies. The encoding of nonenacted events, in contrast, requires deliberate strategies for remembering. Memory events may be ordered on a continuum of sensitivity to encoding variables with words at the high sensitivity end of the continuum, and SPTs at the low sensitivity end (Cohen, 1983). The essence of Cohen's argument is that action memory constitutes an optimal form of encoding, which is not improved by the use of strategies. In these earlier versions of his theory, Cohen did not specify any mechanism as to why enactment encoding produces a superior memory performance other than an optimal encoding. Expressed otherwise, the difference in performance level occurs because subjects fail to find the most optimal encoding strategies in the case of verbal encoding. In later writings, Cohen (1989) proposed that enactment at study also facilitates retrieval by adding a motor dimension to the memory trace.

A second theory was suggested by Bäckman and Nilsson (1984, 1985). They argued that enactment during encoding automatically leads to multimodal processing, which in turn produces a rich encoding of information. The processing was stated as being multimodal simply because, in an SPT condition, subjects hear the verbal command by the experimenter, see the object which is referred to in the command, and feel the object haptically when carrying out the action. The multimodal nature of SPTs is sometimes even more emphasized when items like "eat the raisin" and "smell the perfume" are included among the commands to be enacted, thereby involving all five sensory modalities. This multimodal notion was later extended to state a dual code hypothesis (Bäckman, Nilsson, & Chalom, 1986)—namely, that physical properties of SPTs are encoded nonstrategically, whereas verbal components are encoded strategically. Thus, SPTs contain both verbal and physical properties, whereas verbal tasks (VTs) contain the verbal component only.

Nilsson and Bäckman (1989) have later argued that the physical component of the dual code is encoded incidentally and retrieved implicitly, whereas the verbal component normally is encoded intentionally and retrieved explicitly. Nilsson and Bäckman (1989) also argued that the implicitly accessed physical component of an SPT helps trigger the explicit retrieval of the verbal component of the SPT, thereby improving memory performance for SPTs in comparison to that of VTs. For VTs there is normally no physical component of the TBR item to help trigger the conscious re-

trieval of the verbal component. As a result there is a superior recall for SPTs.

The third theory to be discussed here was proposed by Engelkamp and Zimmer (1983, 1984, 1985; Zimmer & Engelkamp, 1985). These authors argued that encoding of SPTs is governed by programs, which are motoric, visual, and verbal in nature. In this way the Engelkamp and Zimmer conceptualization is an extension of the dual-code theory proposed by Paivio (1971). Whereas Paivio proposed a verbal code and a visual code, Engelkamp and Zimmer proposed separate codes for the verbal, visual, and motor modalities. Engelkamp and Zimmer further assumed that these programs are independent of each other in the sense that they have different representations, codes, and modality-specific properties. Moreover, motor encoding is more efficient than verbal and visual encoding, which is the reason, they claim, for the enactment effect. Motor encoding is also special because it improves item-specific encoding, whereas visual and verbal processing improves the relational encoding between items. Item-specific and relational encoding are regarded as central constructs in interpreting data from verbal memory experiments (Hunt & Einstein, 1981; Marschark, Richman, Yuille, & Hunt, 1987; McDaniel, Einstein, & Lollis, 1988). When Engelkamp (1990) applied this terminology to the enactment effect, he proposed that enactment improves item-specific processing and that there are two types of relational processing affecting performance in an SPT experiment. One form is the integration of actions in a list based on semantic category whereas the other form is about integration of the verb and the noun in a command (Engelkamp & Cohen, 1991). According to Engelkamp (1990), the first type of integration is independent of enactment, whereas the second form is hindered by enactment.

Saltz and Donnenwerth-Nolan (1981) took a rather similar theoretical position to Engelkamp and Zimmer (1983, 1984, 1985) in that they assumed enactment encoding to be modality specific. Moreover, Saltz and Donnenwerth-Nolan (1981) postulated that motor encoding produced a more distinctive image of the event to be remembered than did visual and verbal encoding. The more distinctive an encoding is, the more precisely the event will be registered in a multidimensional representational space.

A fourth theory differs quite radically from the three positions discussed so far. According to this view, proposed by Kormi-Nouri (1995), the encoding of action events is entirely strategic. Kormi-Nouri clearly opposes both the automatic, nonstrategic view of Cohen (1981, 1983) and the partially automatic, multimodal dual-conception view of Bäckman and Nilsson (1984, 1985). Kormi-Nouri (1995) noted that previous research has found that some encoding strategies may not affect SPTs (e.g., Cohen, 1981; Helstrup, 1987; Nilsson, Nyberg, Kormi-Nouri, & Rönnlund, 1995), whereas others do (e.g., Cohen, 1989; Helstrup, 1986; Nilsson & Craik, 1990). The reason for the enactment effect, according to Kormi-Nouri, is that enactment increases the degree of self-involvement at the time of encoding. Thus, there is no postulation of motor programs, motor images, and so on. A better self-awareness and a more obvious experiential registration in the case of SPTs make enactment encoding a more optimal case for episodic remembering than encoding without enactment as for VTs.

Integration is a central concept in Kormi-Nouri's terminology. The integration can be both semantic and episodic. Semantic integration concerns previously acquired general knowledge about the relation between the verb and the noun in the type of commands used in SPT experiments. Episodic integration concerns special knowledge of the relation between the verb and the noun in such commands; this integration is acquired by enactment at the time of study. According to Kormi-Nouri (1995; Kormi-Nouri & Nilsson, 1998, in press a, in press b), semantic integration increases the effect of enactment and the enactment increases the episodic integration between verb and noun, thus implying an interaction between semantic and episodic integration. Enactment integrates the encoding of an action verb and an object into a single memory unit, rendering more specificity to enacted than to nonenacted events.

Data

Support for Cohen's theoretical position comes from experimental manipulations known to affect memory performance in classical verbal learning experiments and from studies on individual differences. With respect to experimental manipulations, several empirical phenomena known from the verbal learning domain have been examined using the SPT paradigm. These data usually take the form of dissociations. The use of dissociations is a well-established way to demonstrate basic differences between hypothetical constructs or possible underlying mechanisms. Converging evidence from several cases or situations is required for arguing that differences are real (see e.g., Schacter & Tulving, 1994, regarding evidence on dissociations for supporting the notion of basic differences between episodic memory and semantic memory).

First, it has been repeatedly demonstrated (Cohen, 1981; Cohen & Bryant, 1991; Nilsson & Cohen, 1988; Nilsson & Craik, 1990) that the levels-of-processing effect (Craik & Lockhart, 1972), so frequently demonstrated in verbal learning experiments (e.g., Craik & Tulving, 1975), was not obtained when subjects were instructed to encode the to-be-remembered information by means of enactment. Second, the primacy effect always obtained in verbal learning experiments was not demonstrated in SPT experiments (Cohen, 1981; Bäckman & Nilsson, 1984). Third, the effect first demonstrated by Slamecka and Graf (1978), that subjects remember much better those items that they have generated on their own than items that have merely been presented, was not obtained in experiments where subjects were encoding the items by means of enactment (Nilsson & Cohen, 1988).

Still another effect demonstrated in experiments of verbal memory but not in experiments on action memory is the effect of rate of presentation (Cohen, 1985). Since action memory experiments have consistently used a minimal time interval between items, Cohen (1985) reasoned that the nonstrategic properties of the action memory experiments may have been due to the fast presentation rate and not to the nature of the items per se. Lengthening the inter-item interval might provide the subjects with a greater opportunity to use strategies, thereby improving the memory performance for SPTs even more. Although Cohen (1985) used inter-item intervals as long as 10 seconds, recall of commands encoded by means of enactment did not improve. For the nonenacted control condition there was an improvement in performance as a function of the length of the interitem interval.

One further difference pursued by Cohen concerns meta-memory. It is well established that subjects in verbal memory experiments can predict, during study, which verbal items they will subsequently recall successfully in a free-recall test (e.g., Arbuckle & Cuddy, 1969; Cohen, 1988; Lovelace, 1984; Underwood, 1966). In action memory experiments, Cohen

(1983, 1988, 1989; Cohen & Bryant, 1991) has repeatedly demonstrated that subjects fail in predicting their performance in a subsequent recall test. This suggests that subjects have more knowledge about the functioning of their verbal memory system than about their action memory system (Engelkamp & Cohen, 1991).

With respect to individual differences, Cohen and Stewart (1982) found no differences in memory performance between children of different ages, when the TBR information had been encoded by means of enactment, whereas such differences were found for nonenacted verbal events. Campione and Brown (1978) and many others have shown that intelligence is positively correlated with memory performance when the TBR information is composed of verbal materials. In contrast, Cohen and Bean (1983) found essentially no difference in memory performance for mentally retarded and normal controls, when the TBR information had been encoded by means of enactment. Some data from studies of aging and memory (Bäckman, 1985; Bäckman & Nilsson, 1984, 1985) are also regarded as a support for this view. In these studies the typical age deficit in episodic memory tasks was demonstrated for the nonenacted encoding task, whereas for enacted encoding condition no age deficit was found. Provided the optimal encoding conditions in SPTs are present, elderly subjects do not suffer. It is the necessary use of deliberate encoding strategies in nonenacted tasks that produces the age deficits, according to this theory.

Support for the multimodal dual-code theory proposed by Bäckman (Bäckman, 1985; Bäckman & Nilsson, 1984, 1985; Bäckman et al., 1986) comes largely from experiments in which subjects have encoded the TBR information at the same time as they carry out a secondary task. It has been consistently demonstrated that the verbal component of SPTs was more affected under conditions of divided attention than the physical components were (e.g., Bäckman et al., 1986; Bäckman, Nilsson, Herlitz, Nyberg, & Stigsdotter, 1991; Bäckman, Nilsson, & Kormi-Nouri, 1993), rendering support for the multimodal dual-code view of a strategic verbal component and a nonstrategic physical component.

It is well known in traditional verbal learning studies that subtle differences in features of verbal items may trigger an increased level of recall for some items. For example, using the classical release from proactive interference (PI) paradigm (Wickens, 1970), Gardiner, Craik, and Birtwistle (1972) demonstrated a dramatic PI release, although the shift in items from the first three trials to the fourth trial was as subtle as garden flowers to wild flowers. Nilsson and Bäckman (1991) applied the PI-release paradigm to studies of SPTs and found, first, stronger levels of PI release for SPTs than for VTs. Second, they argued that these levels of PI release due to physical features like weight, color, size, and texture of objects was more pronounced than could be expected on the basis of slight semantic differences of the items used by Gardiner et al. (1972).

A final set of data that has been used as support for the multimodal dual-code theory is the age by encoding task interaction reported by Bäckman (1985; Bäckman & Nilsson, 1984, 1985), who claimed that SPTs provide differential encoding support for old subjects by means of multimodal processing.

Support for the motor program theory by Engelkamp and Zimmer emanates primarily from experiments in which the importance of the actual motor activity is demonstrated. For example, Engelkamp and Zimmer (1985) have consistently demonstrated that recall is higher when subjects actually perform the verbal instructions, not only as compared to the regular verbal control but also as compared to a condition in which the subject watches the experimenter carrying out the action. Such a condition is usually referred to as experimenter performed task (EPT). Thus, the physical activity is important and enhances the encoding of simply seeing someone else enacting the verbal command.

Engelkamp, Zimmer, Mohr, and Sellen (1994) also argued that the data by Engelkamp and Zimmer (1983), showing essentially the same recall performance when enactment is carried out with real objects as compared to using imaginary objects, supports the notion of the specific importance for physical activity. Such data are regarded as evidence for the motor component view and against the theory of multimodality and richness of encoding proposed by Bäckman and Nilsson (1984, 1985). According to this latter view, it is the sensory input of seeing and touching the actual object that contributes to the enriched encoding of SPTs. In the same vein, data from Engelkamp, Zimmer, and Biegelmann (1993) are seen as support for the motor component theory. These authors demonstrated that enactment of the denoted actions is the critical factor because the SPT effect is present even if the subjects close their eyes while performing the action. That is, seeing the task performed by oneself is not necessary for obtaining the SPT effect. One further piece of support for the motor theory by Engelkamp and Zimmer is the finding by Mohr, Engelkamp, and Zimmer (1989) showing that the SPT effect is more pronounced in recognition than in recall. This finding supports the motor theory because enactment, according to Engelkamp and Zimmer, influences item-specific information rather than relational information, which is more related to verbal encoding.

The assumption by Engelkamp (1990) that enactment improves item-specific encoding and that enactment is neutral to the categorical-integration form of relational encoding has been confirmed in several studies (e.g., Engelkamp, 1988; Engelkamp, Zimmer, & Mohr, 1990; Mohr et al., 1989; Zimmer & Engelkamp, 1989). In contrast to Bäckman et al. (1986), several experiments by Engelkamp and his colleagues (Engelkamp & Zimmer, 1990; Engelkamp et al., 1990; Zimmer, 1991; Zimmer & Engelkamp, 1989) have demonstrated that organizational scores did not differ between conditions of enacted and nonenacted encoding.

The third assumption by Engelkamp (1990) in relation to the distinction between item-specific and relational encoding—that is, that the verb-noun integration is hindered by enactment—has also gained some support from experiments in his own laboratory (Engelkamp, 1986). However, others (e.g., Helstrup, 1989) have failed to replicate this result.

Engelkamp et al. (1993), Knopf (1991), and Mohr et al. (1989) used two types of commands at study followed by recognition tests to provide further support for the motor program theory. One type of command was that of a congruous relationship between verb and noun—for example, "open the book." Another type of command was that of an incongruous relationship between verb and noun—for example, "comb the toothbrush," "shave the kiwi." These latter commands were referred to as "bizarre" commands by Engelkamp and his colleagues. The studies showed an interaction between type of encoding and type of testing such that bizarre phrases were better recognized than ordinary phrases after verbal encoding, whereas after enacted encoding there was no such difference. The interpretation proposed by Engelkamp and his group was that bizarreness is a feature of a verbal episode but not of an action episode. According to

these authors, it is no doubt unusual to use a comb on a toothbrush, but the action pattern itself is not bizarre. This interpretation of bizarreness being part of the verbal episode but not the action episode may or may not be the correct one, but this does not matter in this context as a case supporting Cohen's notion of basic differences between enacted and nonenacted encoding. Perhaps the underlying mechanism is not related to bizarreness per se, but to frequency of occurrence. Combing a toothbrush or shaving a kiwi should reasonably be considered as low-frequency items, whereas items like opening a book should be considered as high-frequency items. A reliable phenomenon in memory research with words is the word frequency effect, showing that low-frequency words are better recognized than high-frequency words (e.g., Balota & Neely, 1980; Glanzer & Bowles, 1976; Gregg, 1976).

Support for Kormi-Nouri's theory comes from experiments demonstrating, first, that there are no additional enactment effects when subjects are asked to perform the actions at the time of test rather than simply recalling the commands verbally. Based on the encoding specificity principle (Tulving & Thomson, 1973), Kormi-Nouri, Nyberg, and Nilsson (1994) argued that motor retrieval cues should increase the enactment effect when subjects enact at retrieval. Since there was no increase in the enactment effect as compared to conditions where subjects enacted only at encoding, Kormi-Nouri concluded that the stored information for SPTs is in a verbal/conceptual rather than a motor code. The second source of support for Kormi-Nouri's interpretation of the enactment effect comes from experiments comparing the role of verbal and visual secondary tasks on motor memory. Engelkamp and Zimmer (1983, 1984, 1985) have argued that the processing of motor information is largely independent from the processing of a verbal or visual secondary task. Kormi-Nouri (1995) refers to experiments by Bäckman et al. (1993) and Kormi-Nouri, Nilsson, and Bäckman (1994) showing that the processing of motor information is also affected by secondary tasks that are of a verbal or visual nature.

Moreover, in the Kormi-Nouri (1995) study, SPT encoding, like VT encoding, was affected by a high semantic integration between verb and noun. A stronger integration effect was found for SPTs on free-recall tests, whereas the effect of integration was more striking for VTs than for SPTs on cued-recall tests. Moreover, Kormi-Nouri and Nilsson (1998), using the recognition failure paradigm (Tulving & Thomson, 1973), found that the combination of high semantic and episodic integration produced the highest degree of independence between recognition and recall. A low semantic and episodic integration resulted in a higher degree of dependence between recognition and recall.

Unresolved Issues

The theoretical accounts of the enactment effect, in particular those by Cohen (1981, 1983) and by Bäckman and Nilsson (1984, 1985), have been changed owing to new data and as a result, they have become more similar. First, the notion of a nonstrategic property for SPTs is now part of each of these theories (Engelkamp & Cohen, 1991). Second, Cohen's (1989) position is now also similar to that of Engelkamp and Zimmer (1983, 1984, 1985) in that it includes the specification that the physical movement is a crucial component of SPT encoding, although Cohen does not specifically postulate a motor program to accompany the visual and verbal programs in enacted encoding. The multimodality position proposed by Bäckman and Nilsson (1984, 1985) has also specified a specific role for the motor component in later versions Nilsson and Bäckman (1989, 1991).

Thus, a composite version of these three theories includes the notions of nonstrategic processing and motor activity as central components. Such a composite theory, as well as each of the three individual theories, stands in sharp contrast to the fourth theory of the enactment effect discussed in this chapter— that is, the integration theory proposed by Kormi-Nouri (1995). Whereas the motor component is an essential feature of Kormi-Nouri's theory as well, this theory is very explicit in stating that enacted encoding is deliberate and strategic; it is not automatic and nonstrategic. Thus, the theoretical controversy at the present time in this field of research is whether enacted encoding is strategic or nonstrategic, and whether a physical movement is a necessary component in accounting for the enactment effect. However, before coming to a close on this topic, it is necessary to point out and to evaluate the empirical inconsistencies that exist in relation to these two issues. Evaluation of these inconsistencies might help to clarify the theoretical positions still further.

Several empirical inconsistencies for particular phenomena have been reported. The most obvious inconsistencies have been observed for the potential differential roles of relational processing in SPTs and VTs, the role of integration of verbs and nouns in the commands used in these experiments, the role of real or imaginary objects, the role of the actual physical movement, and the role of age.

Relational Processing

Several studies (e.g., Engelkamp, 1988; Engelkamp et al., 1990; Mohr et al., 1989; Zimmer & Engelkamp, 1989) have lent support to Engelkamp's (1990) assumption that enactment not only improves item-specific encoding but is also neutral to the categorical-integration form of relational encoding. The assumption regarding item-specific encoding is noncontroversial, whereas the assumption of the organizational structure of the TBR information as mediated by categorical integration is not. Engelkamp and his colleagues (Engelkamp & Zimmer, 1990; Engelkamp et al., 1990; Zimmer, 1991; Zimmer & Engelkamp, 1989) have repeatedly demonstrated that organizational scores do not differ between conditions of enacted and nonenacted encoding. On the other hand, Bäckman and his colleagues (Bäckman & Nilsson, 1984, 1985; Bäckman et al., 1986; Kormi-Nouri & Nilsson, 1999) have shown repeatedly that such organizational scores were higher for enacted than for nonenacted encoding, suggesting that subjects benefit more from the the relational list structure when items have been encoded by means of enactment. The only difference in procedure between the Engelkamp and Bäckman experiments that might be of importance in this context is that Engelkamp and his colleagues have used imaginary objects in the enactment conditions, whereas Bäckman and his colleagues have used real objects. The difference between SPT items and VT items is thus larger in the Bäckman experiments, since no objects are used in the VT conditions in any of the two groups. It is likely, then, that the larger difference between SPT and VT items in the case of Bäckman has helped boost the organizational scores, without having any substantive importance for enactment per se. This inconsistency might then be ruled out as being artificial in that it cannot be used to clarify any theoretical position.

Integration

The other assumption regarding relational processing by Engelkamp (1990), that the integration of the verb and the noun in a command is hindered by enactment, is more controversial. As stated before, this assumption has gained some support from experiments in Engelkamp's own laboratory (Engelkamp, 1986), but others (e.g., Helstrup, 1989; Kormi-Nouri, 1995; Kormi-Nouri & Nilsson, 1998) have demonstrated repeatedly that this type of integration is actually essential for enactment. In fact, Kormi-Nouri (1995) states that the enactment effect depends explicitly on the interaction between semantic integration and episodic integration. This empirical inconsistency has been subject to considerable discussion. On the basis that Helstrup (1989) explicitly required his subjects to integrate verb and noun at the enactment encoding, Engelkamp (1989) argued that this instruction caused the SPT effect in Helstrup's cued-recall condition. Helstrup (1991) and Engelkamp, Mohr, and Zimmer (1991) tested this hypothesis by Engelkamp by varying encoding instructions systematically. In both these studies it was demonstrated that the instruction to interact is indeed a prerequisite for the SPT effect to occur. This interpretation is also in line with the results obtained by Kormi-Nouri (1995; Kormi-Nouri & Nilsson, 1999) in that the semantically well-integrated verb-noun pairs should foster integration, perhaps just as well as explicit instructions to integrate. Thus, this might not be a real inconsistency either and may therefore not be of any help in evaluating the different theoretical positions.

Real vs. Imaginary Objects

It has become a tradition in some laboratories to use real objects in the SPT conditions, whereas in other laboratories the use of imaginary objects is the rule. In some cases it has been proposed that this difference in the experimental setup has caused empirical inconsistencies. In a series of experiments Cohen (1981, 1983; Cohen & Bean, 1983) compared performance levels in SPT and EPT conditions with real objects in both conditions, and found consistently that recall levels were the same. When Engelkamp and his coworkers (e.g., Engelkamp & Krumnacker, 1980; Engelkamp & Zimmer, 1983) did the same comparisons, using imaginary objects, they con-

sistently found a superior recall for SPT conditions. As noted by Engelkamp and Cohen (1991), these discrepancies could easily be accounted for if an interaction between object and test condition was assumed. However, when testing this explicitly Engelkamp and Zimmer (1983) did not find any such interaction. Moreover, in contrast to Engelkamp and Zimmer (1983), Ratner and Hill (1991) found no difference between performance levels in SPT and EPT conditions, when using imaginary objects. There is no apparent explanation for these discrepancies and it is fair to state that this issue will need some further scrutiny in future research.

Physical Movement vs. Imaginary Movement

Engelkamp and Zimmer (1984, 1985; Engelkamp, in press) regard the movement component of SPTs as crucial for obtaining the enactment effect. In support of this claim they often refer to the experiments reported above showing a superiority in recall performance for SPTs as compared to EPTs. This is the way it should be if physical movement is crucial, since SPTs involve movement by the subject, whereas EPTs do not. As was reported above, Cohen (1981, 1983; Cohen & Bean, 1983) and Ratner and Hill (1991) found no differences between performance levels in the SPT condition and the EPT condition, apparently independently of whether real objects or imaginary objects were used. There is no straightforward explanation of this empirical inconsistency available.

Kormi-Nouri (1998b) recently addressed the issue of physical versus imaginary movement and object. He compared systematically control VTs (involving no enactment and no objects) with four different conditions of SPT encoding: real movement with real object, real movement with imaginary object, imaginary movement with real object, and imaginary movement with imaginary object. Three groups of subjects participated in the study: sighted subjects, sighted but blindfolded subjects, and blind subjects. Free recall data showed SPTs to be better recalled than VTs for all three groups of subjects. Moreover, there was no difference between the SPT conditions, but blind subjects performed at a lower level after imaginary instructions. Kormi-Nouri (1998) concluded that the integration of the movement and the object is the crucial cause of the enactment effect, rather than any of these two factors taken separately.

It might be concluded on the basis of the empirical inconsistencies reported in this section that the role of actual movement is indirect rather than direct. Physical movement does not seem to add any specific motoric dimension to the memory trace. Rather, movement improves memory if it leads to a better integration of the verb and the noun of the TBR command.

Age Differences in Memory

Bäckman and Nilsson (1984, 1985) were the first to contrast memory performance in SPTs and VTs as a function of age. In free recall of VTs there was a significant decline of performance as a function of age; for SPTs this decline was nonsignificant. Thus, the age deficit so consistently demonstrated in episodic memory tasks was found for nonenacted encoding, but not for enacted encoding. This finding of smaller age-related memory impairments after enacted encoding than after nonenacted encoding has later been replicated in several studies (Brooks & Gardiner, 1994; Cohen & Faulkner, 1990; Dick, Kean, & Sands, 1989; Nyberg, Nilsson, & Bäckman, 1992). However, a number of studies have also found rather similar age effects after enacted and nonenacted encoding (Cohen, Sandler, & Schroeder, 1987; Earles, 1996; Guttentag & Hunt, 1988; Knopf & Niedhardt, 1989; Nilsson & Craik, 1990; Nilsson et al., 1997). Several attempts have been made to explain this inconsistency in data in the results obtained across studies. So far, no explanation has been suggested for which there is general agreement. Task difficulty seems to be the most likely candidate explanation at present. That is, for difficult tasks the age deficits are parallel in SPTs and VTs, and for easy tasks (e.g., short lists, recognition test), there is an interaction between encoding task (enactment vs. no enactment), such that the age difference is smaller after enactment than after nonenactment. For example, Knopf and Niedhart (1989) found similar age effects for SPTs and VTs in a free-recall task, but in a subsequent recognition task with the same set of commands, the age deficit was essentially eliminated for SPTs. The theoretical interpretation of this pattern of data is that for easy tasks, subjects manage without a specific strategy, whereas for difficult tasks they have to employ a deliberate strategy. In doing this, it is reasonable to expect that old subjects suffer more than young subjects. However, this interpretation might be called into question on the basis that for easy tasks (e.g., recognition), the performance for young subjects tends to approach the ceiling. At any rate, inconsistencies in data with respect to aging effects might not be used for supporting or refuting any of the theories proposed.

A Solution

As stated earlier, the nonstrategic theory proposed by Cohen (1981, 1983) and the multimodal dual code theory by Bäckman and Nilsson (1984, 1985) have been subjected to changes and modifications because empirical findings have indicated problems with the original versions of the theories. Cohen (1989) proposed that physical movement should be considered as a crucial factor in explaining the enactment effect. This modification makes this theory rather similar to that of Engelkamp and Zimmer (1983, 1984, 1985), especially so when the latter theory also considers the nonstrategic notion a factor underlying the enactment effect (cf. Engelkamp & Cohen, 1991). A specific role for the motor component was also proposed by Nilsson and Bäckman (1989, 1991) to modify the original position by Bäckman and Nilsson (1984, 1985). Thus, these three theories now form a rather homogeneous category of theoretical positions with respect to the role of nonstrategic encoding and physical movement for the enactment effect.

In this sense, they stand in sharp contrast to the theory by Kormi-Nouri (1995; Kormi-Nouri & Nilsson, in press; Kormi-Nouri et al., 1994; Nilsson & Kormi-Nouri, in press), which holds that enactment encoding is strategic and that the motor component is not crucial. For Kormi-Nouri (1995; Kormi-Nouri & Nilsson, in press; Kormi-Nouri et al., 1994; Nilsson & Kormi-Nouri, in press), the critical role of enactment is to conceptually integrate the verb and the noun of the TBR command. This might indicate that the critical role of enactment is to increase the distinctiveness of the memory traces by adding item-specific and relational information. Kormi-Nouri's (1995) position is similar to Helstrup (1986, 1987), who argued that the use of deliberate strategies depends on the difficulty of the task. More difficult tasks require the use of explicit strategies and conceptual involvement. Viewed in this way encoding and retrieval become problem-solving tasks (Helstrup, 1986, 1987).

Given the fact that the empirical inconsistencies found with respect to the role of actual movement in accounting for the enactment effect seem to favor an indirect rather than a direct role, one might argue that the issue of strategic versus nonstrategic processing is the essence of the theoretical controversy in the field. The continuum of sensitivity to encoding variables envisaged by Cohen (1983) might be a useful starting point in trying to solve this controversy. Cohen (1983) argued that memory events may be ordered on a continuum of sensitivity to encoding variables with words at the high-sensitivity end of the continuum, and actions at the low-sensitivity end. Cohen's position was that action memory is an optimal form of encoding leaving nothing left to be influenced by deliberate encoding strategies. Maintaining this notion of a continuum, one need not take the standpoint that action memory is at the extreme end. An appealing thought might be to argue for a more quantitative difference between words and actions, instead of the qualitative difference proposed by Cohen (1983). Thus, rather than claiming a complete goal directedness for SPTs, one might argue that subjects can initiate deliberate encoding strategies under certain conditions. The determining factors for this subject initiated processing may involve variables like demands of the task. It seems reasonable to assume that strategies would be initiated, for example, in conditions of high semantic integration of the verb-noun pair in Kormi-Nouri's terminology (Kormi-Nouri, 1995; Kormi-Nouri & Nilsson, 1999). Similarly, it would seem reasonable to assume that self-initiation of strategies is employed when the task is too difficult or of too little guidance in directing the subjects how to manage encoding of the action command. Still maintaining the notion of a potential continuum of sensitivity to encoding variables, this conceptualization would then suggest that SPTs can be located in the middle range of this continuum. It is for this range that enactment constitutes an optimal encoding that requires little or no additional support in terms of deliberate strategies. For the end points of the continuum, deliberate strategies are initiated by the subjects in order to accomplish enough of a deep processing to manage to remember the TBR information.

This conceptualization, which is based on Craik's (1986; Craik & Jennings, 1992) notion of self-initiated processing for explaining age differences in memory, suggests that differences between memory for actions and words are quantitative rather than qualitative in nature. Despite those dissociations reported primarily by Cohen (1981, 1983, 1985) in support for a qualitative difference, it is argued here that a quantitative conceptualization is more tenable when including task demands as a determining factor for the relationship between strategic and nonstrategic processing. It was mentioned initially that claims have been made (e.g., Cohen, 1981, 1985) that action memory obeys other laws than those affecting verbal memory. However, on the basis of the literature reviewed here, it is concluded that the need for different laws for action memory is hardly warranted.

Acknowledgment   Comments from Reza Kormi-Nouri and Julie Yonker on an earlier version of this manuscript are gratefully acknowledged.

References

Arbuckle, T. Y., & Cuddy, L. L. (1969). Discrimination of item strength at time of presentation. *Journal of Experimental Psychology, 81*, 126–131.

Bäckman, L. (1985). Further evidence for the lack of adult age differences on free recall of subject-performed tasks: The importance of motor action. *Human Learning, 4*, 79–87.

Bäckman, L., & Nilsson, L.-G. (1984). Aging effects in free recall: An exception to the rule. *Human Learning, 3*, 53–69.

Bäckman, L., & Nilsson, L.-G. (1985). Prerequisites for lack of age differences in memory performance. *Experimental Aging Research, 11*, 67–73.

Bäckman, L., Nilsson, L.-G., & Chalom, D. (1986). New evidence on the nature of the encoding of action events. *Memory & Cognition, 14*, 339–346.

Bäckman, L., Nilsson, L.-G., Herlitz, A., Nyberg, L., & Stigsdotter, A. (1991). A dual conception of the encoding of action events. *Scandinavian Journal of Psychology, 32*, 289–299.

Bäckman, L., Nilsson, L.-G., & Kormi-Nouri, R. (1993). Attentional demands and recall of verbal and color information in action events. *Scandinavian Journal of Psychology, 34*, 246–254.

Balota, D. A., & Neely, J. H. (1980). Test-expectancy and word frequency effects in recall and recognition. *Journal of Experimental*

Psychology: Human Learning & Memory, 6, 576–587.

Brooks, B. M., & Gardiner, J. M. (1994). Age differences in memory for prospective compared with retrospective subject-performed tasks. *Memory & Cognition, 22,* 27–33.

Campione, J. C., & Brown, A. L. (1978). Toward a theory of intelligence: Contributions from research with retarded children. *Intelligence, 2,* 279–304.

Cohen, R. L. (1981). On the generality of some memory laws. *Scandinavian Journal of Psychology, 22,* 267–281.

Cohen, R. L. (1983). The effect of encoding variables on the free recall of words and action events. *Memory & Cognition, 11,* 575–582.

Cohen, R. L. (1984). Individual differences in event memory: A case for nonstrategic factors. *Memory & Cognition, 12,* 633–641.

Cohen, R. L. (1985). On the generality of the laws of memory. In L.-G. Nilsson & T. Archer (Eds.), *Perspectives on learning and memory* (pp. 247–277). Hillsdale, NJ: Erlbaum.

Cohen, R. L. (1988). Metamemory for words and enacted instructions: Predicting which items will be recalled. *Memory & Cognition, 16,* 452–460.

Cohen, R. L. (1989). Memory for action events: The power of enactment. *Educational Psychology Review, 1,* 57–80.

Cohen, R. L., & Bean, G. (1983). Memory in educable mentally retarded adults: Deficit in subject or experimenter. *Intelligence, 7,* 287–298.

Cohen, R. L., & Bryant, S. (1991). The role of duration in memory and metamemory of enacted instructions (SPTs). *Psychological Research, 53,* 183–187.

Cohen, R. L., & Faulkner, D. (1990). The effects of aging on perceived and generated memories. In L. W. Poon, D. C. Rubin, & B. A. Wilson (Eds.), *Everyday cognition in adulthood and late life* (pp. 222–243). New York: Cambridge University Press.

Cohen, R. L., Sandler, S. P., & Schroeder, K. (1987). Aging and memory for words and action events: Effects of item repetition and list length. *Psychology and Aging, 2,* 280–285.

Cohen, R. L., & Stewart, M. (1982). How to avoid developmental effects in free recall. *Scandinavian Journal of Psychology, 23,* 9–16.

Craik, F. I. M. (1986). A functional account of age differences in memory. In F. Klix & H. Hagendorf (Eds.), *Human memory and cognitive capabilities, mechanisms and perfor-*

mances (pp. 409–422). North-Holland: Elsevier.

Craik, F. I. M., & Jennings, J. M. (1992). Human memory. In F. I. M. Craik & T. A. Salthouse (Eds.), *Handbook of aging and cognition* (pp. 51–110). Hillsdale, NJ: Erlbaum.

Craik, F. I. M., & Lockhart, R. S. (1972). Levels of processing: A framework for memory research. *Journal of Verbal Learning and Verbal Behavior, 11,* 671–684.

Craik, F. I. M., & Tulving, E. (1975). Depth of processing and the retention of words in episodic memory. *Journal of Experimental Psychology: General, 104,* 268–294.

Dick, M. B., Kean, M.-L., & Sands, D. (1989). Memory for action events in Alzheimer type dementia: Further evidence for an encoding failure. *Brain and Cognition, 9,* 71–87.

Earles, J. L. (1996). Adult age differences in recall of performed and nonperformed items. *Psychology and Aging, 11,* 638–648.

Engelkamp, J. (1986). Nouns and verbs in paired-associate learning: Instruction effects. *Psychological Research, 48,* 153–159.

Engelkamp, J. (1988). Modality specific encoding and word class in verbal learning. In M. M. Gruneberg, P. E. Morris, & R. N. Sykes (Eds.), *Practical Aspects of Memory: Current Research and Issues* (Vol 1; pp. 415–420). Chichester: John Wiley.

Engelkamp, J. (1989). Memory for performed and imaged noun pairs and verb pairs: A comment on Tore Helstrup. *Psychological Research, 50,* 241–242.

Engelkamp, J. (1990). *Das menschliche Gedächtnis.* Göttingen: Hogrefe.

Engelkamp, J. (in press). Action memory: A system-oriented approach. In H. D. Zimmer (Ed.), *Action memory: A specific type of episodic memory?* Oxford: Oxford University Press.

Engelkamp, J., & Cohen, R. L. (1991). Current issues in memory of action events. *Psychological Research, 53,* 175–182.

Engelkamp, J., & Krumnacker, H. (1980). Imaginale und motorische Prozesse beim Behalten verbalen Materials. *Zeitschrift für experimentelle und angewandte Psychologie, 27,* 511–533.

Engelkamp, J., Mohr, G., & Zimmer, H. D. (1991). Pair-relational encoding of performed nouns and verbs. *Psychological Research, 53,* 232–239.

Engelkamp, J., & Zimmer, H. D. (1983). Zum Einfluss von Wahrnehmen und Tun auf das Behalten von Verb-Objekt-Phrasen. *Sprache und Kognition, 2,* 117–127.

Engelkamp, J., & Zimmer, H. D. (1984). Motor program information as a separable memory unit. *Psychological Research, 46*, 283–299.

Engelkamp, J., & Zimmer, H. D. (1985). Motor programs and their relation to semantic memory. *German Journal of Psychology, 9*, 239–254.

Engelkamp, J., & Zimmer, H. D. (1990). Imagery and action: Differential encoding of verbs and nouns. In P. J. Hampson, D. F. Marks, & J. T. E. Richardson (Eds.), *Imagery: Current developments* (pp. 150–168). London: Routledge & Kegan Paul.

Engelkamp, J., Zimmer, H. D., & Biegelmann, U. E. (1993). Bizarreness effects in verbal tasks and subject-performed tasks. *European Journal of Cognitive Psychology, 5*, 393–415.

Engelkamp, J., Zimmer, H. D., & Mohr, G. (1990). Differential memory effects of concrete nouns and action verbs. *Zeitschrift für Psychologie, 198*, 189–216.

Engelkamp, J., Zimmer, H. D., Mohr, G., & Sellen, O. (1994). Memory of self-performed tasks: Self-performing during recognition. *Memory & Cognition, 22*, 34–39.

Gardiner, J. M., Craik, F. I., & Birtwistle, J. (1972). Retrieval cues and release from proactive inhibition. *Journal of Verbal Learning and Verbal Behavior, 11*, 778–783.

Glanzer, M., & Bowles, N. (1976). Analysis of the word frequency effect in recognition memory. *Journal of Experimental Psychology: Human Learning and Memory, 2*, 21–31.

Gregg, V. (1976). Word frequency, recognition and recall. In J. Brown (Ed.), *Recall and Recognition* (pp. 183–216). London: John Wiley.

Guttentag, R. E., & Hunt, R. R. (1988). Adult age differences in memory for imagined and performed actions. *Journal of Gerontology: Psychological Sciences, 43*, 107–108.

Helstrup, T. (1986). Separate memory laws for recall of performed acts? *Scandinavian Journal of Psychology, 27*, 1–29.

Helstrup, T. (1987). One, two, or three memories? A problem solving approach to memory for performed acts. *Acta Psychologica, 66*, 37–68.

Helstrup, T. (1989). Memory for performed and imaged noun pairs and verb pairs. *Psychological Research, 50*, 237–240.

Helstrup, T. (1991). Integration versus nonintegration of noun pairs and verb pairs under enactment and nonenactment conditions. *Psychological Research, 53*, 240–245.

Hunt, R. R., & Einstein, G. O. (1981). Relational and item-specific information in memory. *Journal of Verbal Learning and Verbal Behavior, 20*, 497–514.

Knopf, M. (1991). Having shaved a kiwi fruit: Memory for unfamiliar subject-performed actions. *Psychological Research, 53*, 203–211.

Knopf, M., & Niedhart, E. (1989). Aging and memory for action events: The role of familiarity. *Developmental Psychology, 25*, 780–786.

Kormi-Nouri, R. (1995). The nature of memory for action events: An episodic integration view. *European Journal of Cognitive Psychology, 7*, 337–363.

Kormi-Nouri, R. (1998). The role of movement and object in action memory: A comparative study between blind, blindfolded, and sighted subjects. Manuscript submitted for publication.

Kormi-Nouri, R., & Nilsson, L.-G. (1998). The role of integration in recognition failure and action memory. *Memory & Cognition, 26*, 681–691.

Kormi-Nouri, R., & Nilsson, L.-G. (1999). Negative cueing effects with weak and strong intralist cues. *European Journal of Cognitive Psychology, 11(2)*, 199–218.

Kormi-Nouri, R., & Nilsson, L.-G. (in press). The motor component is not crucial! In H. D. Zimmer (Ed.), *Action memory: A specific type of episodic memory?* Oxford: Oxford University Press.

Kormi-Nouri, R., Nilsson, L.-G., & Bäckman, L. (1994). The dual conception view reexamined: Attentional demands and the encoding of verbal and physical information in action events. *Psychological Research, 51*, 181–187.

Kormi-Nouri, R., Nyberg, L., & Nilsson, L.-G. (1994). The effect of retrieval enactment on recall of subject-performed tasks and verbal tasks. *Memory & Cognition, 22*, 723–728.

Lovelace, F. A. (1984). Meta-memory: Monitoring future recallability during study. *Journal of Experimental Psychology: Learning, Memory & Cognition, 10*, 756–766.

Marschark, M., Richman, C. L., Yuille, J. C., & Hunt, R. R. (1987). The role of imagery in memory: On shared and distinctive information. *Psychological Bulletin, 102*, 28–41.

McDaniel, M. A., Einstein, G. O., & Lollis, T. (1988). Qualitative and quantitative considerations in encoding difficulty effect. *Memory & Cognition, 16*, 8–14.

Mohr, G., Engelkamp, J., & Zimmer, H. D. (1989). Recall and recognition of self-performed acts. *Psychological Research, 51*, 181–187.

Nilsson, L.-G., & Bäckman, L. (1989). Implicit memory and the enactment of verbal instructions. In S. Lewandowsky, J. Dunn, & K. Kirsner (Eds.), *Implicit memory: Theoretical issues* (pp. 173–183). Hillsdale, NJ: Erlbaum.

Nilsson, L.-G., & Bäckman, L. (1991). Encoding dimensions of subject-performed tasks. *Psychological Research, 53*, 212–218.

Nilsson, L.-G., Bäckman, L., Erngrund, K., Nyberg, L., Adolfsson, R., Bucht, G., Karlsson, S., Widing, M, & Winblad, B. (1997). The Betula prospective cohort study: Memory, health, and aging. *Aging, Neuropsychology, and Cognition, 4*, 1–32.

Nilsson, L.-G., & Cohen, R. L. (1988). Enrichment and generation in the recall of enacted and non-enacted instructions. In M. M. Gruneberg, P. E. Morris, & R. N. Sykes (Eds.), *Practical aspects of memory: Current research and issues* (Vol 1; pp. 427–432). Chichester: John Wiley.

Nilsson, L.-G., & Craik, F. I. M. (1990). Additive and interactive effects in memory for subject-performed tasks. *European Journal of Cognitive Psychology, 2*, 305–324.

Nilsson, L.-G., & Kormi-Nouri, R. (in press). What is the meaning of a memory-systems approach? In H. D. Zimmer (Ed.), *Action memory: A specific type of episodic memory?* Oxford: Oxford University Press.

Nilsson, L.-G., Nyberg, L., Kormi-Nouri, R., Rönnlund, M. (1995). Dissociative effects of elaboration on memory of enacted and non-enacted events: A case of a negative effect. *Scandinavian Journal of Psychology, 36*, 225–231.

Nyberg, L., Nilsson, L.-G., & Bäckman, L. (1991). A component analysis of action events. *Psychological Research, 53*, 219–225.

Nyberg, L., Nilsson, L.-G., & Bäckman, L. (1992). Recall of actions, sentences and nouns: Influence of adult age and passage of time. *Acta Psychologica, 79*, 1–10.

Paivio, A. (1971). *Imagery and verbal processes*. New York: Holt, Rinehart & Winston.

Ratner, H. H., & Hill, L. (1991). The development of children's action memory: When do actions speak louder than words? *Psychological Research, 53*, 195–202.

Saltz, E., & Donnenwerth-Nolan, S. (1981). Does motoric imagery facilitate memory for sentences: A selective interference test. *Journal of Verbal Learning and Verbal Behavior, 20*, 322–332.

Schacter, D. L., & Tulving, E. (1994). What are the memory systems of 1994? In D. L. Schacter & E. Tulving (Eds.), *Memory systems 1994* (pp. 1–38). Cambridge: MIT Press.

Slamecka, N. J., & Graf, P. (1978). The generation effect: Delineation of a phenomenon. *Journal of Experimental Psychology: Human Learning and Memory, 4*, 592–604.

Tulving, E., & Thomson, D. M. (1973). Encoding specificity and retrieval processes in episodic memory. *Psychological Review, 80*, 353–373.

Underwood, B. J. (1966). Individual and group predictions of item difficulty for free learning. *Journal of Experimental Psychology, 71*, 673–679.

Wickens, D. D. (1970). Encoding categories of words: An empirical approach to meaning. *Psychological Review, 77*, 1–15.

Zimmer, H. D. (1991). Memory after motoric encoding in a generation-recognition model. *Psychological Research, 53*, 226–231.

Zimmer, H. D., & Engelkamp, J. (1985). An attempt to distinguish between kinematic and motor memory components. *Acta Psychologica, 58*, 81–106.

Zimmer, H. D., & Engelkamp, J. (1989). Does motor encoding enhance relational information? *Psychological Research, 51*, 158–167.

10

Distortions of Memory

HENRY L. ROEDIGER & KATHLEEN B. MCDERMOTT

There are two general classes of errors in re-membering: omission and commission. In the former, people fail to recollect a prior event when they try to retrieve it. In the latter, people remember events quite differently from the way they happened, or they remember an event that never happened at all. No one doubts the reality of the first error; forgetting of needed information happens to everyone dozens of times each week. Psychologists have studied forgetting experimentally for 115 years, since Ebbinghaus's (1885/1964) meticulous studies showed the general nature of the forgetting function. However, errors of commission—memory distortions—are much more controversial and, over the years, have received much less attention. People would like to believe that their memories are more or less accurate renditions of the experiences that occurred to them in the past. How could a memory for an event be "false"? Where would the recollection come from, if not from stored traces of actual events? Demonstrations that such distortions can occur have thrust the issue of memory illusions and false memories onto center stage in contemporary cognitive psychology.

The aim of this chapter is to provide an overview of factors known to create memory distortions. We first provide a brief history of this field of study. Then, in the body of the chapter, we review the literature on distortions by considering six factors that seem to be responsible for their occurrence. We conclude with a discussion of some of the implications of memory distortion for wider problems in society, particularly the issues of accuracy of eyewitness testimony and the recovery of memories of childhood abuse.

History

The systematic experimental study of perception and memory began at roughly the same point in time—in the latter part of the nineteenth century. However, the study of errors and distortions received quite different treatment in the two domains of study. Researchers interested in perception quickly seized upon the phenomena of perceptual illusions and studied them assiduously. Coren and Girgus (1978) estimated that 200 scientific papers on perceptual illusions appeared before 1900.

The case was quite different in the study of memory. Most researchers examined correct performance, either directly (e.g., the number or proportion of events correctly recalled or recognized) or indirectly (e.g., through Ebbinghaus's ingenious relearning and savings technique). Not many researchers were interested in errors (also referred to as distortions of memory or memory illusions; Roediger, 1996). However, just as perceptual illusions may aid in our knowledge of perceiving, so should memory illusions offer a vantage point to aid our understanding of remembering. Although they were few, some studies of memory errors did appear in the early memory literature (see Schacter, 1995, for a fuller historical treatment).

Early in this century, Binet (1900) in France, Varendonck (1911) in Belgium, and Stern (1910) in Germany all conducted studies of the fallibility of children's recollections (see Ceci & Bruck, 1995, chap. 5). Typically, these studies examined how children's recollections could be altered by suggestions from an adult. For example, Binet (1900) showed children 5 objects (e.g., a button glued onto a board) for 10 seconds and then tested their memories of the objects with various types of questions. When given free recall instructions ("Write down everything you saw"), the children made few errors. However, when asked suggestive questions about the objects ("Wasn't the object attached to the board by a string?"), many errors occurred, as the children complied with the researcher's suggestion. Neutral questions elicited fewer errors than did the suggestive questions. The research by Binet and others was relatively well known even to readers of English at the time, owing to reviews in *Psychological Bulletin* by Whipple (1909, 1913). In addition, Munsterberg's (1908) *On the Witness Stand* emphasized the erratic nature of eyewitness testimony through examples. However, this early research did not thoroughly permeate experimentalists' attempts to understand human memory, which mostly continued in the tradition begun by Ebbinghaus.

In 1932, Bartlett published his great book *Remembering*, in which he described recollection as being a reconstructive process driven by schemas, or general organizational schemes. Bartlett's idea was that specific experiences may not be remembered, but that overall themes would be. When people tried to recover distant memories, they would be guided by general themes or schemas and fill in details that were consistent with the schemas (but which might be quite wrong). He conducted rather informal experiments with English college students in which they were given a Native American story, "The War of the Ghosts," and asked on several occasions to recollect it. He interpreted the systematic errors the students made as evidence for his schema theory. Although Bartlett's book is a milestone, it seems to have had curiously little impact on the field for many years. It was not until the 1970s that several lines of research began that were inspired in a general way by Bartlett's work, but which used much more rigorous techniques for eliciting errors of memory.

Another important contribution, published at the same time as Bartlett's book, was made by Carmichael, Hogan, and Walters (1932). They showed people ambiguous figures and labeled the figures with a single word. For example, one figure was labeled as either a rifle (for one group of subjects) or a broom (for a different group of subjects). Carmichael et al. later tested their subjects' abilities to accurately remember and draw the ambiguous objects they had seen. The form subjects drew was heavily influenced by the label given to the object: the ambiguous figure previously labeled a broom no longer looked ambiguous when recalled—it looked like a broom. In modern parlance, Carmichael et al. studied the effects of verbal recoding on remembrance of visual form: people do not remember objects as they exist in the world, but as their minds recode the objects (Miller, 1956; Schooler & Engstler-Schooler, 1990).

Analyses of errors in remembering were conducted from time to time in the next decades, but usually for some theoretical purpose rather than to study the fallibility of memory per se. For example, Melton and Irwin (1940) used intrusion analyses to identify what they called factor X (later identified as unlearning) in interference theory. Similarly, Deese (1959) examined errors in recall as a means of studying associative processes. Subsequently, other researchers used error patterns in attempts to identify the types of coding in short- and long-term memory. Conrad (1964) noted that errors in short-term memory represented acoustic confusions, even when the material was presented to subjects visually. Out of this observation grew the hypothesis that phonological codes underlie short-term retention (e.g., Baddeley, 1966). Errors in long-term retention seemed to be based more on meaning. Thus, error analyses were used to make theoretical points in two-store theories, but the study of errors in their own right and for showing the basic fallibility of human memory was not the purpose of these studies. In fact, errors were generally considered a nuisance by memory researchers, a factor that might indicate "guessing" on the part of the subjects and that therefore needed to be eliminated, controlled, or factored out of performance to get a "true" memory score. The corrections could either be simple (subtracting errors from correct responding) or more complex, as in the theory of signal detectability, but the errors themselves were considered to be of little interest in most experimental studies of memory.

The situation changed in the late 1960s and early 1970s. Neisser's (1967) *Cognitive Psychology*, which helped to launch and to name the cognitive revolution, revived Bartlett's approach to remembering. At about the same time, other researchers (e.g., Bransford & Franks, 1971; Cofer, 1973) began to study errors in retention using prose materials. This work was inspired by Bartlett and provided more secure evidence than did his own work for many of his key points. Loftus and Palmer (1974) introduced a paradigm for studying eyewitness recollection that also markedly changed the course of the field. In the past 25 to 30 years the study of memory distortion has been a central topic in the field. The remainder of the chapter surveys what we have learned.

Factors Creating Distortions of Memory

This part of the chapter is organized around six sets of factors that have been shown to cause distortions of memory. We categorize our review of the literature under the rubrics of relatedness effects in memory; interference effects; retrieval and guessing effects; effects of imagining; effects of social context; and individual differences in these processes—are some people more susceptible than others to memory distortion?

Relatedness Effects

This term is intended to cover a variety of phenomena that all follow the same general rule: if people experience a series of items that are strongly related, they will tend to remember other (nonpresented) items as having occurred if these nonpresented items are strongly related to those that did occur. The relation among items in the series can be of a categorical nature, can involve associative relations among similar elements in lists of words or pictures or in videotapes, or can be among themes and schemas in prose. The general idea is that when a person tries to retrieve

a prior episode, his or her general knowledge (semantic memory) may strongly influence this recollection; thus, episodic memory and semantic memory interact (Tulving, 1972). General knowledge of the world can help people fill out their episodic recollections.

As mentioned previously, Bartlett (1932) was one of the first researchers to demonstrate the role of schemas on memory. In his classic demonstration using the "War of the Ghosts," he noted that when people were asked to recall this story, which to them seemed rather disjointed and confusing, they seemed to engage in "effort after meaning." That is, people reinterpreted the story in light of their world knowledge; they imposed order where none had been present to make a more logical story. Bartlett referred to this process as *rationalization*.

One type of relatedness effect is remembering things implied but not specifically stated. Implications received substantial attention during the 1970s. For example, Sulin and Dooling (1974) presented subjects with short paragraphs about a troubled girl and tested for false recognition of nonpresented ideas. The paragraphs studied by two groups of subjects were identical, with the exception of the name of the protagonist: Helen Keller or Carol Harris. Subjects who read about Helen Keller often later erroneously recognized "She was deaf, dumb, and blind" as having been present in the paragraph, whereas those reading about Carol Harris rarely made this error. In addition, the probability of making such an error increased with the retention interval, consistent with Bartlett's informal observations.

Bransford and Franks (1971) and Johnson, Bransford, and Solomon (1973) made similar observations, showing that people often extract implications and remember them as having been explicitly stated. For example, Bransford and Franks (1971) presented subjects with short sentences such as "The rock rolled down the mountain" or "The rock crushed the hut." There were four ideas altogether that would make up the sentence "The rock rolled down the mountain and crushed the tiny hut." Bransford and Franks had people listen to sentences containing the ideas and then gave them a later test; they were asked to identify which sentences they had actually heard and which were new. The test sentences could themselves have 1, 2, 3, or 4 ideas and could either have been studied or not studied. However, even when the sentences per se had not been studied, other sentences representing the larger idea had been studied. Subjects rated their belief that the sentences had been presented earlier on a 10-point scale, from −5 (sure the sentence was new or nonstudied) to +5 (sure the sentence was old or studied). The results are shown in figure 10.1, where it can be seen that the more ideas the test sentence contained, the higher the recognition rating for the sentences. This relationship held whether the sentences were ones that had actually been studied or were new. In addition, except for the sentences expressing only one idea, there was little difference in recognition confidence between sentences that had actually been studied and those that had not been studied (but which were consistent with knowledge built up from other sentences). Subjects seemed to retain the meaning of the simple ideas quite accurately, but not to know whether the particular sentence on the test had been previously presented.

Brewer (1977) added an interesting twist to this research in studying pragmatic implications of sentences. Pragmatic implications are made when the person hearing a sentence infers something that is neither stated explicitly nor logically necessitated by the sentence. For example, "The karate champion hit the cinder block" implies that the cinder block was broken. However, it is perfectly possible that the block was struck but not broken. Thus, "breaking" is pragmatically (but not logically) implied. Brewer found that when people were given the first part of the sentence (e.g., *The karate champion*) as a cue to recall the rest of the sentence, people were more likely to recall the implied verb (in this example, *broke*) than the presented verb (*hit*).

Complex prose materials, leading to implications, are not necessary to obtain influences of semantic memory on episodic memory. In a classic study, Underwood (1965) demonstrated that recognition for lists of words can show similar effects. When presented with a continuous recognition task, in which words are presented one at a time and subjects must determine for each word whether it had been seen previously in the experiment, people sometimes erroneously recognized associates of previously presented words. For example, when *hard* was given in the list, subjects subsequently recognized *soft* as having occurred with probabilities greater than the background false alarm rate to unrelated words. Underwood proposed that implicit associative responses (IARs) were responsible for this effect. He believed that when a person encounters a word, he or she also thinks about a word (or words) related to it. That is, reading *hard* may elicit *soft*, either consciously or unconsciously. False recognition occurs as a result of a failure in what would, in current terminology, be called reality monitoring (Johnson & Raye, 1981); that is, false recognition arises when people confuse what they previously thought with what actually occurred.

Although Underwood (1965) is usually credited with discovering that associative processes can induce false memories in list-learning paradigms, there was an earlier demonstration that made a similar point. Deese (1959) showed that people sometimes erroneously recall a nonpresented word (e.g., *sleep*) when presented with 12 words associated to that nonpresented word (e.g., *bed, rest, awake*, etc). Deese's contribution was largely overlooked, however. This neglect was probably due to the fact that the paper was not structured as a demonstration of false recall. Instead, Deese was interested in showing how associative processes contribute to memory; in addition, many of the lists he used did not produce false recall.

Roediger and McDermott (1995) adapted Deese's (1959) paradigm for the study of false recall and extended it to the study of false recognition and to meta-memory judgments. They showed that when presented with 15 words strongly associated to a critical, nonpresented word, people often recalled, recognized, and claimed to remember the specific instance of

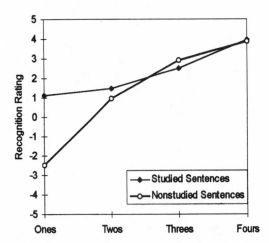

Figure 10.1 Mean recognition ratings for studied and nonstudied sentences as a function of number of propositions per sentence. Data from Bransford and Franks (1971).

presentation of the critical nonpresented associate (e.g., *sleep*). The recognition results from one experiment are shown in figure 10.2. The false alarm rate for the critical nonstudied words such as *sleep*, from the which the lists were derived, approximated the hit rate for words actually studied. In addition, the false alarm rate to the critical items was much higher than that for unrelated distracters. Considerable research on false recall and recognition has been developed through use of this paradigm (see Roediger, McDermott, & Robinson, 1998, for a review).

Although the relatedness effects discussed thus far are meaning based, preexisting semantic associations are not necessary to obtain these types of effects. Using a modified version of a pattern classification paradigm introduced by Posner and Keele (1968, 1970), Franks and Bransford (1971) showed that people will often erroneously recognize shape configurations that are the nonstudied prototypes of presented shape stimuli. Sommers and Lewis (1999) presented lists of words that were all from the same phonological neighborhood and found errors similar to those observed by Roediger and McDermott (1995). Therefore, relatedness effects need not arise from preexisting semantic representations.

In summary, relatedness is a powerful means by which false memories can arise. The relations can arise in the form of schemas, inferences, and associative bonds (both preexisting semantic or phonological links, as well as more abstract, figural prototypes). The presentation of related sets of information probably serves as a general means of producing false recollections for an event not in the original sets but strongly related to them.

Interference Effects

Müller and Pilzecker (1900) showed very early that interference could be a potent source of forgetting. Indeed, theorizing about forgetting in the middle part of this century was dominated by the interference theory of forgetting, which stressed how events happening before and after some critical event could create forgetting of that event (proactive and retroactive interference, respectively). One mechanism for the forgetting was postulated to be response competition—the interfering event competes with the original event, and sometimes people remember the interfering event as the original event. Thus, interference can also be a potent source of false memories. The general principle is that an event that occurs

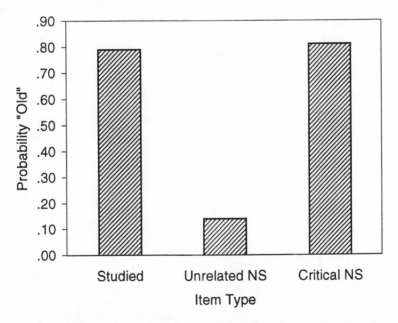

Figure 10.2 Mean proportion of studied, unrelated nonstudied, and critical nonstudied items classified as having been previously studied. Data from selected conditions of Roediger and McDermott (1995, experiment 2).

after (or before) some event of interest may later be retrieved as if it were the event of interest. Similarly, interference may influence the details retrieved regarding the original event. In general, the more similar the events (in content or in time of occurrence), the more likely these confusions will arise (see Crowder, 1976, chap. 10, for a review of interference theory).

Loftus and Palmer (1974) developed a tractable laboratory paradigm simulating an eyewitness viewing a traffic accident; the goal was to study how information could interfere with memory for an earlier event. People viewed a film in which a traffic accident was depicted. They were subsequently asked a question regarding how fast the cars had been traveling when the accident occurred. The critical aspect of the question was the verb used in the question. People who were asked "About how fast were the cars going when they smashed each other?" estimated a speed of 41 mph. When the critical verb was "hit" (instead of "smashed"), the estimates dropped to 34 mph. Not only did the leading question influence the quantitative estimation of speed, but it also tended to lead to the creation of distorted memories. When people were asked a week later whether they had seen any broken glass in the film, those who received the leading question containing "smashed" mistakenly reported having seen broken glass 32% of the time, whereas people receiving the "hit" question made this error only 14% of the time. Thus, a single word occurring in a single question in a series of questions was sufficient to interfere with peoples' memory for the witnessed event, both immediately and one week later.

In subsequent studies on the role of interference in producing false memories, Loftus and her colleagues have demonstrated the ease with which leading questions or misleading statements can alter subsequent recollections. Loftus, Miller, and Burns (1978) presented subjects with a series of slides; one of the slides depicted a car approaching an intersection with a stop sign. In a second phase of the experiment, subjects answered questions about the events, such as "Did another car pass the red Datsun while it was stopped at the intersection?" The subjects who received this question were given no information about the sign. For another group of subjects, the question was asked using the phrase "stop sign" in the question in place of "intersection" (the consistent information condition). A third group of subjects were given the same question but with "yield sign" substituted (the inconsistent or misleading information condition). In a third phase of the experiment, subjects were given a two-alternative forced-choice recognition test in which they were asked which type of sign had appeared at the intersection: a yield sign or a stop sign. The results are shown in figure 10.3, where it can be seen that, relative to the neutral condition provided with no information about the sign, subjects who had been given the misleading information performed worse, whereas those given the consistent information performed better. The misleading information seemed to undermine subjects' recollections of the information they had seen, and they actually scored below chance on the test; they reported a yield sign had been in the slides rather than a stop sign. Repetitions of the misinformation create even greater distortions (Zaragoza & Mitchell, 1996). More recent experiments demonstrate the ubiquity of the phenomenon of misleading information causing errors in recollections of the original events (see Ayers & Reder, 1998, for a recent review). Many (but not all) of these interference studies can be interpreted under the source memory framework (e.g., Johnson & Raye, 1981; Johnson, Hashtroudi, & Lindsay, 1993). That is, people sometimes remember events as having occurred in one situation when they actually occurred in another context; in the previous example, people would remember the yield sign from the questionnaire as having been the sign in the original slide sequence.

Another powerful demonstration of the role of interference in producing false memories lies in the false fame experiments developed by Jacoby and his colleagues (Jacoby, Kelley, Brown, & Jasechko, 1989; Jacoby, Woloshyn, & Kelley, 1989). In this paradigm, people read a series of ordinary, nonfamous names (e.g., Lester Dillard) in a first phase and are informed that all names they read are nonfamous. In a second phase of the experiment, which is ostensibly unrelated to the previous phase, the subjects are given another set of names and asked to determine whether or not each name refers to a famous person. Some of the names in this series overlap with the nonfamous names encountered earlier (Lester Dillard, in this example, mixed in with Winston Churchill and other names that are either famous or nonfamous). The assumption is that people perform this fame judgment task partly by examining feelings of familiarity that

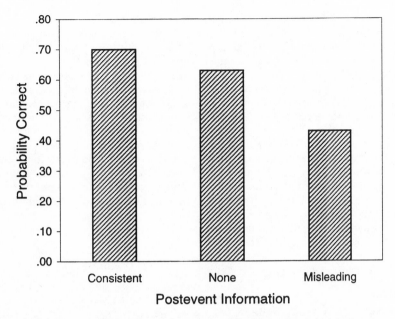

Figure 10.3 Probability correct (on a 2-alternative forced choice recognition test) as a function of whether subjects had received information consistent with what they had previously seen, information inconsistent with what had been seen, or no specific post-event information. Data from Loftus, Miller, and Burns (1978, experiment 2).

the names evoke. Therefore, if the recently encountered but nonfamous names seem familiar to subjects but are not recollected as having occurred earlier in the experimental setting, subjects may misattribute this strong feeling of familiarity as arising from fame. Consistent with these predictions, when people had read nonfamous names in a first phase, they sometimes incorrectly judged these nonfamous names to be those of famous people. The outcome in this paradigm is in some ways opposite that of the relatedness studies described in the previous section: In the false fame paradigm, researchers examine the interference exerted by a recent episode on semantic memory (fame) judgments, whereas in the relatedness studies, one observes the influence of semantic memory on memory for specific episodes.

In this section, we have reviewed some of the ways in which it has been shown that interference can induce false memories. In these cases, the interference has been external (e.g., leading questions or prior presentation of interfering information). Below we consider a related case, in which the interference is produced internally, by the rememberer. Specifi-

cally, we examine how imagination can induce false memories.

Imagination

Psychologists have generally extolled the power of imagery in aiding memory. Indeed, telling people to form images in remembering verbal materials typically enhances performance, and some mnemonic devices reveal spectacular powers of imagery in promoting accurate memories. However, in these cases people form images of events that happened or that they want to remember. What if people imagine events that did not happen? Will they come to remember them as actually having happened?

Raye, Johnson, and Taylor (1980) presented words visually to subjects varying numbers of times; subjects were also induced to internally generate the words from conceptual clues (without seeing them), again for varying numbers of times. Later subjects were asked to judge the frequency of the actual occurrence (seeing, but not imagining, the words). Raye et al. (1980) found that internal generation of words inflated the frequency with which the word was judged to have occurred. The more frequently a person had privately generated or imagined the word, the greater the inflation in estimating its frequency of actual occurrence.

Garry, Manning, Loftus, and Sherman (1996) asked subjects if they had experienced rather implausible childhood events. Garry et al. selected events that subjects believed had not occurred to them as children and later asked the subjects to vividly imagine these events. On a test given two weeks later, they once again asked subjects to rate the probability that the events had occurred in their childhood. The results showed what they termed *imagination inflation*: having imagined the occurrence of the event made subjects somewhat more likely to judge that it had previously occurred. Similar results have been reported by others (Heaps & Nash, 1999; Hyman & Pentland, 1996).

Because the studies just described used childhood events that were not under experimental control, the possibility exists that the imagining of the events reminded subjects of real events that had occurred in their childhood. If so, then the second estimate of whether the event happened might not reflect a memory illusion, but a more accurate recollection. Goff and Roediger (1998) developed a 3-phase laboratory paradigm to seek imagination inflation under controlled conditions, where this criticism is not possible. In an encoding phase subjects heard commands for action events, such as *push the toy car* or *break the toothpick*, a task widely used to study memory for actions (e.g., Engelkamp & Zimmer, 1984). Sometimes subjects performed the events as instructed, sometimes they only imagined doing so, and sometimes they just listened to the statements. In a second, imagination, phase, subjects imagined performing actions 0, 1, 3, or 5 times. Some imagined items had occurred in the encoding phase and others had not. Finally, in a test given two weeks after the first (encoding) session, subjects were asked to recognize action statements that had occurred in the first session and were also asked to judge whether they had actually performed the action, had imagined performing it, or had only listened to the statement.

The central issue in Goff and Roediger's (1998) experiments was whether repeatedly imagining an action during the second phase would lead to an inflation in recollections of having performed it in the first phase. In general, the answer was yes: the more frequently subjects had imagined performing the action,

the more likely they were both to falsely recognize the statement as having occurred in the original phase and to judge that they had actually completed an action that, in fact, they had only imagined completing. Imagination inflation was confirmed in a laboratory paradigm in which the problem of establishing what events actually had and had not occurred does not exist.

In brief, imagining events that never happened can lead people to remember them as having occurred. Just as imagining can enhance recollection of events that did happen, so can the process create memories of events that did not happen.

Retrieval Processes and Effects of Guessing

Retrieval processes contribute to the development of false recollections in at least two different ways. First, the nature of the retrieval query or the retrieval cue can determine the remembrance that a person reports. As noted above, Binet's (1900) early research indicated that children tested with free recall made fewer errors than those asked suggestive questions. A clear example of the power of the type of test question is shown in a previously cited study by Loftus and Palmer (1974) on eyewitness memory. Subjects' recollections depended upon the precise wording of the question: in one condition subjects were asked "About how fast were the two cars going when they contacted each other?" Other groups of subjects saw the same videotape and were given the question, but with the verb changed to *hit, bumped, collided*, and *smashed*. The mean speed estimates for the five verbs are reported in table 10.1. The form of the retrieval query determined in part the subjects' recollection of the speed of the cars. The range from 32 to 40 miles per hour may greatly mat-

Table 10.1 The effect of leading questions on memory. Data from Loftus and Palmer (1974).

Verb	Mean Speed Estimates
Smashed	40.8
Collided	39.3
Bumped	38.1
Hit	34.0
Contacted	31.8

ter in testimony if the speed limit were, say, 30 mph.

A second way retrieval processes can lead to false recollections is through repeated retrieval attempts. Most attention in the literature has been given to how testing can facilitate retrieval of studied events (e.g., Thompson, Wenger, & Bartling, 1978), but if other (nonexperienced) events are recalled as having been experienced, their probability of later retrieval is enhanced and so is the probability that the events will be confidently remembered. The general rule seems to be that if an event is retrieved from memory (whether accurately or inaccurately), it will tend to be retrieved again more readily at a later time. Retrieval not only indexes remembered events but can also modify them (Bjork, 1975). For example, McDermott (1996) presented subjects with related lists of words, using the Deese/Roediger-McDermott paradigm discussed previously. Some subjects took an immediate free-recall test (in which both veridical and false recall were measured), whereas others did not. Two days later both groups took a free-recall test for material presented in the initial study session. Having taken the prior recall test boosted recall of list items (.17 for subjects who received the prior test relative to .04 for those who had not—the standard testing effect), and the same effect occurred for critical nonstudied items (.24 versus .12). Note that the probability of false recall in the delayed test exceeded that of veridical recall. In addition, other experiments have shown that the act of prior recall increases the probability that subjects claim they can remember the moment of occurrence of events, even when the events did not occur (Roediger & McDermott, 1995; Roediger, Jacoby & McDermott, 1996).

These same processes seem partly responsible for the findings that pseudomemories can arise during hypnosis. Although hypnosis is sometimes used by therapists and law enforcement officials attempting to aid the recall of their clients or of witnesses, research generally shows that hypnotic procedures do not produce any benefit in retrieval (Smith, 1983; Erdelyi, 1994) and may in fact induce false memories (Branier & McConkey, 1992; see also Lynn, Lock, Myers, & Payne, 1997). While under hypnosis people are typically given instructions to let their minds roam freely and to report whatever comes to mind. When people produce information under these instructions, the act of recall may make the information seem more real, and when it is retrieved again

later the person may accept the retrieved information as fact, even though it may have been produced earlier under the demands of hypnosis. Unwarranted confidence in the remembered events can also result from hypnosis (Sheehan, 1988).

Recent research shows that instructing people to guess on tests can produce results similar to those seen under hypnosis. Ackil and Zaragoza (1998) used a paradigm in which subjects watched a videotape and then were forced to answer questions about events that had never happened in the video. Subjects knowingly fabricated the details, following the experimenter's request. A week later subjects returned to have their memories tested. At this time, subjects recalled details they had generated a week previously as if the events had occurred in the videotape. Further, children were more likely to make this error than were young adults. The act of guessing about possible events causes subjects to provide their own misinformation, which they later come to retrieve as memories. Ackil and Zaragoza's (1998) study shows that this outcome can occur even without hypnosis.

Social Factors

One area of inquiry that has received little investigation thus far is the influence that social factors can impose upon the memory of an individual. In a recent study of social factors on memory, which was modeled after Asch's (1956) studies on conformity in perception, Schneider and Watkins (1996) presented a list of words to pairs of subjects. One subject in each pair was a confederate. The subject's recognition response (yes/no) and confidence rating (on a 3-point scale) were influenced by the confederate's prior response. Interestingly, this bias was found to be greater for lures than for studied words, which leads to the conclusion that subjects might show greater social influence on false than on true memories.

Betz, Skowronski, and Ostrom (1996) provided converging evidence that social factors can influence veridical and false memories; further, they show that the degree of consensus among multiple confederates determines the extent to which memory distortion occurs. This outcome is similar to that in Asch's (1956) conformity paradigm in which the greater the number of confederates whose erroneous responses preceded that of the actual subject, the more likely the actual subject was to conform to the erroneous group judgment.

In some sense the experiments in the misinformation paradigm, in which people are given transcripts said to have been given by other witnesses of a stimulus event, can be thought of as demonstrations of social influences on memory, as well. This is especially true of such studies that have examined the credibility of the source providing the misleading information (Underwood & Pezdek, 1998). However, systematic studies manipulating social pressure and group consensus on false memories are just beginning to emerge.

Individual Differences

The role of individual differences in susceptibility to false memories has been the topic of much recent research. Although we cannot take the space to review the evidence for the various populations here, we note some general trends that appear to be emerging from the literature.

The effects of age have been of great interest to memory researchers. In general, both young children (e.g., Ackil & Zaragoza, 1998; Poole & White, 1993) and older adults (Norman & Schacter, 1997; Balota et al., 1999) are more susceptible to memory illusions than are young adults. Within the population of younger adults, those who score high on the Dissociative Experiences Scale (a self-report measure of one's tendency to "space out") tend to be more likely to experience false memories than those scoring low on the measure (Hyman & Billings, 1998; Winograd, Peluso, & Glover, 1998).

Schacter, Verfaellie, and Pradere (1996) have found evidence that some amnesic patients seem to have "impaired" false memories. That is, when presented with associated words in the Deese/Roediger-McDermott paradigm, amnesics manifested impaired accurate recognition, accompanied by lower levels of false recognition, relative to matched controls. Schacter and his colleagues have interpreted these findings as evidence that the processes underlying false recognition overlap to a great degree with those underlying accurate recognition. Interestingly, neuroimaging studies of false memories have tended to support this conclusion (Schacter et al. 1996; Schacter, Buckner, Koutstaal, Dale, & Rosen, 1998). However, this pattern of reduced false memories does not occur in all memory-impaired populations. Norman and Schacter (1997), using the same paradigm, found that false recall

was greater in a sample of older adults than in young adults, despite the fact that memory for studied words was impaired for older adults. These results are shown in figure 10.4. Balota et al. (1999) also found a greater tendency of false memories in patients with diseases of the Alzheimer's type, as well as in older adults, relative to younger adults. Assuming similar results are obtained in other false memory paradigms, aging would seem to pull a particularly pernicious double whammy on memory: older adults are more likely to forget events that actually occurred, but more likely to remember events that did not occur.

The study of individual differences in memory distortions is relatively new, and much work remains to be done. However, from the early studies, it seems clear that some groups are more susceptible than others, and we suspect that the patterns seen across populations will inform us with respect to memory processes (both intact and as they break down).

False Memories Outside the Laboratory

There are three primary arenas in which research on distorted memories has implications for issues arising outside the laboratory: eyewitness testimony for crimes, situations of possible child abuse in which children's testimony plays a critical role, and the possible delayed recovery of memories of abuse by adults. We discuss each issue in turn, albeit briefly, while providing references for fuller treatments for those interested in these applied issues.

Eyewitness testimony to crimes exerts powerful influence on a jury. If a witness can identify a person and say "That is the man who did it. I will never forget his face," most reasonable people will be persuaded that the defendant in a trial is the guilty party. However, eyewitnesses have no less fallible memories than subjects in memory experiments, and often their testimony comes under conditions known to lead to memory distortions: long delays since the event, many suggestions occurring during the interval, repeated recounting of the event (often with tacit demands to go beyond what the person remembers and to guess), and so on. The interfering effects of information introduced to the witness after an

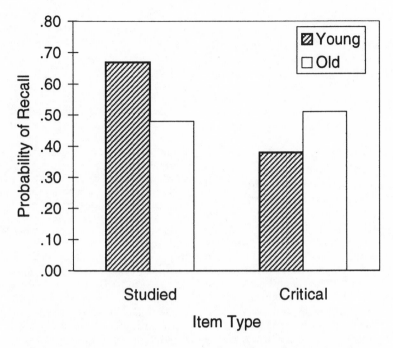

Figure 10.4 Probability of accurate recall (of studied items) and false recall (of critical nonstudied items) as a function of subject population. Data from Norman and Schacter (1997).

event can have a distorting effect, as in the misinformation experiments reported by Loftus and her associates, as well as many others. Indeed, these experiments were intended to model difficulties eyewitnesses may have in reporting on crimes. Loftus (1979) and Loftus and Ketcham (1991) air these issues more fully.

The child witness provides the judicial system with a difficult case. How well can children understand the questions presented to them? How well can they remember the events in question? Are children more suggestible than adults in response to leading questions and other forms of persuasion? These are difficult issues with which psychologists, social workers, lawyers, and judges must contend. Ceci and Bruck (1995) have reviewed the evidence at hand and, although the evidence is complex, the bottom line is that children do seem more susceptible to some forms of memory distortion (as mentioned above in the section on individual differences). In many experiments children's accurate memories for events have been shown to be less detailed than those of adults, and children also seem to be more easily misled.

A third type of case in which memory distortions must be considered is that of delayed or recovered memories of childhood abuse. Some adults, often women undergoing certain forms of psychotherapy, claim to recover horrific events of childhood sexual abuse, ones of which they had no inkling prior to the recovery of the memory. Often they remember a father, or uncle, or teacher having committed rape or other crimes; sometimes the people recovering the memories take the alleged perpetrators to court. These cases are very difficult because usually the alleged crimes were committed many years previously, and after this long delay, no physical evidence of abuse can reasonably be expected. Therefore, the entire case often hangs on the veracity of the recovered memories. However, the conditions in these cases seem particularly prone to memory errors. The retention interval is long and often the person recovering the memory has therapists and support groups recounting their own similar stories of recovered memories. Therefore, social influence processes may be at work, and often the therapeutic techniques used for memory recovery include imagination and the encouragement of guessing as to what might have happened—factors that can lead to false memories. Loftus (1993) and Lindsay and Read (1994), among many others, have discussed the many psychological factors that can lead to the "recovery" of false memories.

Conclusion

This chapter has provided a summary of what is known about memory distortions. At least six factors, and probably more, provide potent means of leading people to recollect events that never happened to them. False memories arise from inferences from series of related pieces of information, from interference from events surrounding the event of interest, from imagination of possible events that did not occur, from retrieval processes, and from social factors. Finally, there are individual differences in susceptibility to these memory illusions. The hope from studying memory illusions is that we can elucidate both the nature of these curious and interesting phenomena, but also shed light on processes occurring in "normal" remembering of events. In addition, the research on memory distortions has considerable implications for societal issues, particularly those of eyewitness testimony, children's testimony, and the delayed recovery of memories of sexual abuse.

References

Ackil, J. K., & Zaragoza, M. S. (1998). The memorial consequences of forced confabulation: Age differences in susceptibility to false memories. *Developmental Psychology, 34,* 1358–1372.

Asch, S. E. (1956). Studies in independence and conformity: A minority of one against a unanimous majority. *Psychological Monographs, 70,* (9, Whole No. 416).

Ayers, M. S., & Reder, L. M. (1998). A theoretical review of the misinformation effect: Predictions from an activation-based memory model. *Psychonomic Bulletin & Review, 5,* 1–21.

Baddeley, A. D. (1966). Short-term memory for word sequences as a function of acoustic, semantic, and formal similarity. *Quarterly Journal of Experimental Psychology, 18,* 362–365.

Balota, D. A., Cortese, M. J., Duchek, J. M., Adams, D., Roediger, H. L., McDermott, K. B., & Yerys, B. E. (1999). Veridical and false memories in healthy older adults and

in Dementia of the Alzheimer's type. *Cognitive Neuropsychology, 16,* 361–384.

Bartlett, F. C. (1932). *Remembering: A study in experimental and social psychology.* Cambridge, England: Cambridge University Press.

Betz, A. L., Skowronski, J. J., & Ostrom, T. M. (1996). Shared realities: Social influence and stimulus memory. *Social Cognition, 14,* 113–140.

Binet, A. (1900). *La suggestibilité.* Paris: Schleicher Freres.

Bjork, R. A. (1975). Retrieval as a memory modifier: An interpretation of negative recency and related phenomena. In R. L. Solso (Ed.), *Information processing and cognition* (pp. 123–144). New York: John Wiley.

Branier, A. J., & McConkey, K. M. (1992). Reports of real and false memories: The relevance of hypnosis, hypnotizability, and the context of memory test. *Journal of Abnormal Psychology, 101,* 521–527.

Bransford, J. D., & Franks, J. J. (1971). The abstraction of linguistic ideas. *Cognitive Psychology, 2,* 331–350.

Brewer, W. F. (1977). Memory for the pragmatic implications of sentences. *Memory & Cognition, 5,* 673–678.

Carmichael, L., Hogan, H. P., & Walters, A. A. (1932). An experimental study of the effect of language on the reproduction of visually perceived form. *Journal of Experimental Psychology, 15,* 73–86.

Ceci, S. J., & Bruck, M. (1995). *Jeopardy in the courtroom: A scientific analysis of children's testimony.* American Psychological Association Press: Washington, D.C.

Cofer, C. N. (1973). Constructive processes in memory. *American Scientist, 61,* 537–543.

Conrad, R. (1964). Acoustic confusions in immediate memory. *British Journal of Psychology, 55,* 75–84.

Coren, S., & Girgus, J. S. (1978). *Seeing is deceiving: The psychology of visual illusions.* Hillsdale, NJ: Erlbaum.

Crowder, R. G. (1976). *Principles of learning and memory.* Hillsdale, NJ: Erlbaum.

Deese, J. (1959). On the prediction of occurrence of particular verbal intrusions in immediate recall. *Journal of Experimental Psychology, 58,* 17–22.

Ebbinghaus, H. (1885/1964). *Memory: A contribution to experimental psychology.* New York: Dover.

Engelkamp, J., & Zimmer, H. D. (1984). Motor programme information as a separable memory unit. *Psychological Research, 46,* 283–299.

Erdelyi, M. (1994). Hypnotic hypermnesia: The empty set of hypermnesia. *International Journal of Clinical and Experimental Hypnosis, 42*, 379–390.

Franks, J. J., & Bransford, J. D. (1971). Abstraction of visual patterns. *Journal of Experimental psychology, 90*, 65–74.

Garry, M., Manning, C. G., Loftus, E. F., & Sherman, S. J. (1996). Imagination inflation: Imagining a childhood event inflates confidence that it occurred. *Psychonomic Bulletin & Review, 3*, 208–214.

Goff, L. M., & Roediger, H. L. (1998). Imagination inflation for action events: Repeated imaginings lead to illusory recollections. *Memory & Cognition, 26*, 20–33.

Heaps, C., & Nash, M. (1999). Individual differences in imagination inflation. *Psychonomic Bulletin & Review, 6*, 313–318.

Hyman, I. E., & Billings, F. J. (1998). Individual differences and the creation of false childhood memories. *Memory, 6*, 1–20.

Hyman, I. E., & Pentland, J. (1996). The role of mental imagery in the creation of false childhood memories. *Journal of Memory and Language, 35*, 101–117.

Jacoby, L. L., Kelley, C. M., Brown, J., & Jasechko, J. (1989). Becoming famous overnight: Limits on the ability to avoid unconscious influences of the past. *Journal of Personality and Social Psychology, 56*, 326–338.

Jacoby, L. L., Woloshyn, V., & Kelley, C. (1989). Becoming famous without being recognized: Unconscious influences of memory produced by dividing attention. *Journal of Experimental Psychology: General, 118*, 115–125.

Johnson, M. K., Bransford, J. D., & Solomon, S. K. (1973). Memory for tacit implications of sentences. *Journal of Experimental Psychology, 98*, 203–205.

Johnson, M. K., Hashtroudi, S., & Lindsay, D. S. (1993). Source monitoring. *Psychological Bulletin, 114*, 3–28.

Johnson, M. K., & Raye, C. L. (1981). Reality monitoring. *Psychological Review, 88*, 67–85.

Lindsay, D. S., & Read, J. D. (1994). Psychotherapy and memories of childhood sexual abuse: A cognitive perspective. *Applied Cognitive Psychology, 8*, 281–338.

Loftus, E. F. (1979). *Eyewitness Testimony.* Cambridge, MA: Harvard University Press.

Loftus, E. F. (1993). The reality of repressed memories. *American Psychologist, 48*, 518–537.

Loftus, E. F., & Ketcham, K. (1991). *Witness for the Defense: The accused, the eyewit-ness, and the expert who puts memory on trial.* New York: St. Martin's.

Loftus, E. F., Miller, D. G., & Burns, H. J. (1978). Semantic integration of verbal information into a visual memory. *Journal of Experimental Psychology: Human Learning and Memory, 4*, 19–31.

Loftus, E. F., & Palmer, J. C. (1974). Reconstruction of automobile destruction: An example of the interaction between language and memory. *Journal of Verbal Learning and Verbal Behavior, 13*, 585–589.

Lynn, S. J., Lock, T. G., Myers, B., & Payne, D. G. (1997). Recalling the unrecallable: Should hypnosis be used to recover memories in psychotherapy? *Current Directions in Psychological Science, 6*, 79–83.

McDermott, K. B. (1996). The persistence of false memories in list recall. *Journal of Memory and Language, 35*, 212–230.

Melton, A. W., & Irwin, J. M. (1940). The influence of degree of interpolated learning on retroactive inhibition and the overt transfer of specific responses. *American Journal of Psychology, 53*, 173–203.

Miller, G. A. (1956). The magical number seven plus or minus two: Some limits on our capacity for processing information. *Psychological Review, 63*, 81–97.

Müller, G. E., & Pilzecker, A. (1900). Experimentalle Beiträge zur Lehre vom Gedachtnis. *Zeitschrift fur Psychologie, 1*, 1–300.

Münsterberg, H. (1908). *On the witness stand: Essays on psychology and crime.* New York: Clark, Boardman, Doubleday.

Neisser, U. (1967). *Cognitive psychology.* New York: Appleton-Century-Crofts.

Norman, K. A., & Schacter, D. L. (1997). False recognition in younger and older adults: Exploring the characteristics of illusory memories. *Memory & Cognition, 25*, 838–848.

Poole, D. A., & White, L. T. (1993). Two years later: Effects of question repetition and retention interval on the eyewitness testimony of children and adults. *Developmental Psychology, 29*, 844–853.

Posner, M. I., & Keele, S. W. (1968). On the genesis of abstract ideas. *Journal of Experimental Psychology, 77*, 353–363.

Posner, M. I., & Keele, S. W. (1970). Retention of abstract ideas. *Journal of Experimental Psychology, 83*, 304–308.

Raye, C. L., Johnson, M. K., & Taylor, T. H. (1980). Is there something special about memory for internally generated information? *Memory & Cognition, 8*, 141–148.

Roediger, H. L. (1996). Memory illusions. *Journal of Memory and Language, 35*, 76–100.

Roediger, H. L., & McDermott, K. B. (1995). Creating false memories: Remembering words not presented in lists. *Journal of Experimental Psychology: Learning, Memory, and Cognition, 21,* 803–814.

Roediger, H. L., Jacoby, J. D., & McDermott, K. B. (1996). Misinformation effects in recall: Creating false memories through repeated retrieval. *Journal of Memory and Language, 35,* 300–318.

Roediger, H. L., McDermott, K. B., & Robinson, K. J. (1998). The role of associative processes in creating false memories. In M. A. Conway, S. E. Gathercole, & C. Cornoldi (Eds.), *Theories of memory II* (pp. 187–245). Hove, Sussex: Psychology Press.

Schacter, D. L. (1995). Memory distortion: History and current status. In D. L. Schacter, J. T. Coyle, G. D. Fischbach, M. M. Mesulam, & L. E. Sullivan (Eds.), *Memory distortion* (pp. 1–43). Cambridge, MA: Harvard University Press.

Schacter, D. L., Buckner, R. L., Koutstaal, W., Dale, A. M., & Rosen, B. R. (1998). Late onset of anterior prefrontal activity during true and false recognition: An event-related fMRI study. *Neuroimage, 6,* 259–269.

Schacter, D. L., Reiman, E., Curran, T., Yun, L. S., Bandy, D., McDermott, K. B., & Roediger, H. L. (1996). Neuroanatomical correlates of veridical and illusory recognition memory: Evidence from positron emission tomography. *Neuron, 17,* 267–274.

Schacter, D. L., Verfaellie, M., & Pradere, D. (1996). The neuropsychology of memory illusions: False recall and recognition in amnesic patients. *Journal of Memory and Language, 35,* 319–334.

Schneider, D. M., & Watkins, M. J. (1996). Response conformity in recognition testing. *Psychonomic Bulletin & Review, 3,* 481–485.

Schooler, J. W., & Engstler-Schooler, T. (1990). Verbal overshadowing of visual memories: Some things are better left unsaid. *Cognitive Psychology, 22,* 36–71.

Sheehan, P. W. (1988). Memory distortion in hypnosis. *International Journal of Experimental and Clinical Hypnosis, 36,* 296–311.

Smith, M. C. (1983). Hypnotic memory enhancement of witnesses: Does it work? *Psychological Bulletin, 94,* 387–407.

Sommers, M. S., & Lewis, B. R. (1999). Who really lives next door? Creating false memories with phonological neighbors. *Journal of Memory and Language, 40,* 83–108.

Spiro, R. J. (1980). Accommodative reconstruction in prose recall. *Journal of Verbal Learning and Verbal Behavior, 19,* 84–95.

Stern, W. (1910). Abstracts of lectures on the psychology of testimony and on the study of individuality. *American Journal of Psychology, 21,* 270–282.

Sulin, R. A., & Dooling, D. J. (1974). Intrusion of a thematic idea in the retention of prose. *Journal of Experimental Psychology, 103,* 255–262.

Thompson, C. P., Wenger, S. K., & Bartling, C. A. (1978). How recall facilitates subsequent recall: A reappraisal. *Journal of Experimental Psychology: Human Learning and Memory, 4,* 210–221.

Tulving, E. (1972). Episodic and semantic memory. In E. Tulving & W. Donaldson (Eds.), *Organization of memory* (pp. 381–403). New York: Academic Press.

Underwood, J. (1965). False recognition produced by implicit verbal responses. *Journal of Experimental Psychology, 70,* 122–129.

Underwood, B. J., & Pezdek, K. (1998). Memory suggestibility as an example of the sleeper effect. *Psychonomic Bulletin & Review, 5,* 449–453.

Varendonck, J. (1911). Les témoignages d' enfants dans un procès retentissant. *Archives de Psychologie, 11,* 129–171.

Whipple, G. M. (1909). The observer as reporter: A survey of the "psychology of testimony." *Psychological Bulletin, 6,* 153–170.

Whipple, G. M. (1913). Psychology of testimony and report. *Psychological Bulletin, 10,* 264–268.

Winograd, E., Peluso, J. P., & Glover, T. A. (1998). Individual differences in susceptibility to memory illusions. *Applied Cognitive Psychology, 12,* S5–S28.

Zaragoza, M. S., & Mitchell, K. J. (1996). Repeated exposure to suggestion and the creation of false memories. *Psychological Science, 7,* 294–300.

REFLECTIONS IN MEMORY

11

Memory Judgments

DOUGLAS L. HINTZMAN

There are two basic ways to query human memory. In *recall* tasks, the experimental subject must generate a representation of a past stimulus such as a word from memory. In *memory-judgment* tasks, a copy or representation of the stimulus is supplied by the experimenter at test, and the subject answers a specific question about it from memory. The question may be answered by rating or categorizing the test item, or by comparing it with one or more others on relevant dimensions. However, the subject does not have to generate the item itself.

Thus characterized, the number of possible memory-judgment tasks is essentially unlimited. The retrieval cue can be of any kind, ranging from simple (odors and colors) to complex (musical scores and the themes of books or movies). Some judgment tasks relate to specific experiences in one's past. These include recognition judgments (old vs. new in the experimental setting), judgments of membership in experimentally learned categories, judgments of presentation frequency, judgments of list membership, judgments of temporal order or recency, judgments of spatial order or location, and judgments of source such as input modality (auditory vs. visual) and reality monitoring (actually presented vs. imagined). Other judgment tasks concern generic knowledge. These include lexical deci-

sions (word vs. nonword), various kinds of semantic and conceptual ratings (e.g., concreteness, familiarity, and typicality), and judgments based on retrieved or generated imagery (e.g., judgments of relative loudness or size). They also include true-false and multiple-choice test formats, which are familiar from educational settings.

The ground covered by this chapter will necessarily be more limited. First, it will focus on laboratory investigations, in which learning occurs under controlled conditions. Thus, studies of everyday memory and of memory for semantic or generic information will not be included. Second, the chapter will concentrate on retention intervals longer than a few seconds, and will thus exclude immediate judgments of order and duration, as well as various psychophysical tasks, which usually rely to some extent on immediate memory. Third, it will ignore research on the learning of artificial concepts. Finally, to avoid redundancy with other chapters, this one will say less about recognition memory and about source and reality monitoring than would otherwise be warranted. This leaves us with a range of laboratory judgment tasks relating to episodic memory. It is the essence of specific personal experiences that they have spatio-temporal structure, so judgments of recency, frequency, modality, and spatial and temporal order have obvious relevance to the nature of episodic memory.

Historically, a contrast can be drawn between theorists who have emphasized the poverty, as opposed to the richness, of memory. Some theorists have stressed the poverty of memory for surface form, by proposing either that sensory details are discarded during initial processing (Sachs, 1967) or that they are quickly forgotten (Craik & Lockhart, 1972). In the extreme view, even abstract meaning has to be reconstructed from highly fragmented information (Bartlett, 1932; Neisser, 1967). Other theorists have assumed that a memory is a copy or "trace" of an earlier experience, which more or less faithfully retains its perceptual characteristics (Köhler, 1929; Wallach & Averbach, 1955).

Theories differ as well in the richness with which memory is thought to record the temporal aspects of experience. Variables such as repetition, exposure duration, and time since learning are often assumed to produce their effects via a single underlying quantity—the strength or familiarity of an association or representation (e.g., Hull et al., 1940; Kintsch, 1970). An obvious consequence of this simple strength hypothesis is that people should tend to confuse the effects of recency and frequency. In contrast is the view held by the Gestalt psychologists and others that temporal variables are directly encoded in memory. Koffka (1935), for example, hypothesized that memories are recorded in a "trace column" that spatially preserves their temporal order. The most extreme proponent of memory's richness may have been Penfield (1955), whose claim that the brain contains "a permanent record of the stream of consciousness" suggests a videotape recording (albeit one that is not limited to the auditory and visual aspects of experience). Such a memory would be rich in surface form and spatial relations, and also in temporal information.

Where does human episodic memory fall on this scale from extremely impoverished to extremely rich? Memory judgments, which focus on a subject's ability to answer specific questions about previous experience, offer a fairly direct way to answer this question. The following two sections contain a review of some of the basic experimental findings on memory for surface details and memory for temporal aspects of experience. Subsequent sections will discuss memory-judgement tasks in relation to retrieval dynamics, brain mechanisms, and conscious awareness.

Memory for Surface Form and Location

Two studies appearing in 1972 challenged the view that memory discards sensory information, by showing that people can remember the input modalities of words. Bray and Batchelder (1972) presented a mixed list of 32 auditory and visual words, had subjects free-recall the list, and then gave a 3-choice (auditory vs. visual vs. new) recognition and modality-judgment test. Conditionalized on recognition of the test word as old, modality judgments were correct about 80% of the time, regardless of whether the subjects had been forewarned of a modality-judgment test. Hintzman, Block and Inskeep (1972) had subjects free-recall eight 18-word mixed-modality lists, and followed this with an unexpected end-of-session recognition and modality-judgment test. Modality judgments, conditionalized on recognition, were about 74% correct. In two follow-up experiments, subjects showed poorer—but above-chance—memory for block vs. script type font (58%) and male vs. female voice (59%). These results suggested that memory for surface form is organized primarily by sensory modality and only secondarily by such within-modality distinctions as font and voice.

Some within-modality distinctions can be remembered quite accurately, however. Light, Stansbury, and Rubin (1973) had subjects study 48 slides, half showing pictures of objects and the other half showing names of objects. Subjects were warned of a memory test, but the type of test was not disclosed. At test, the subjects heard pairs of old and new object names, chose the member of each pair that they thought was old, and then indicated whether it had been studied as a name or as a picture. On both old-new judgments and word-picture judgments, accuracy was over 90%. A comparison across these studies suggests that the verbal-pictorial distinction may be more salient in memory than is the input modality of words.

Modality, voice, and type font are sometimes referred to as context, although they are intrinsic properties of the stimulus that must be processed for the stimulus to be correctly perceived. Extrinsic context is also often remembered. Rothkopf (1971) had subjects read a 12-page passage and then answer questions about it. For each question, they were also asked to indicate which quarter of the passage contained the answer and the eighth of the page (from top to bottom) where it had been located. Accuracy of both judgments was well above chance. In a less naturalistic study, Nairne and Dutta (1992) presented 35 words individually in a 5-location array, and had subjects rate them for pleasantness. Although subjects were not warned to memorize location, they were later able to reconstruct the words' spatial locations with an accuracy of about 70%.

Memory for
Temporal Variables

In the 1950's, the study of memory was dominated by interest in retroactive and proactive sources of forgetting, and the dominant explanation of forgetting was interference theory. This was essentially a strength theory, which assumed that strong associations compete with weaker ones at the time of retrieval (Postman, 1961). It gradually became evident, however, that competition according to strength could not account for all the relevant data, and that an additional process of "list differentiation" might be required. The list-discrimination task was invented as a more direct way to investigate this process (Winograd, 1968).

In the simplest list discrimination experiment, a subject studies two lists, perhaps separated by a filler task. At test, the subject must indicate whether each test item came from list 1 or list 2. Of course, list discrimination should benefit if the lists differ in semantic content or input modality. However, Winograd (1968) showed that list discrimination was harder when both lists were presented for the same frequency or number of trials than when the frequencies were different, and Hintzman and Waters (1969) showed that list discrimination was harder the closer together the two lists were in time. These findings suggest that more basic processes of frequency and recency discrimination contribute to the ability to discriminate between lists.

Single Study Presentations

Much of the early interest in memory judgments derived from a study of memory for recency, by Yntema and Trask (1963). Subjects inspected a series of 220 cards, most of which contained single words. An occasional card showed a word pair, and this indicated that the subject was to choose the word that was more recent. The data showed that recency discrimination increased both with the recency of the more recent word and with the lag or spacing between the words (see figure 11.1). In a version of the task introduced by Peterson (1967), subjects were tested with single items instead of with pairs, judging the number of items that intervened since each test item was last seen.

Upon what kind of information are recency judgments based? Yntema and Trask (1963) simply referred to this information as "time tags." Hinrichs (1970) proposed a quantitative theory in which apparent recency is determined by decaying memory strength. Consistent with this hypothesis, several studies have shown that repeated items seem more recent than nonrepeated ones (although the difference is small). Counting against the hypothesis, better remembered categories of items do not generally seem more recent than more poorly remembered items. Rather, the apparent recencies of the better-remembered items are more accurate (for pictures vs. words, see Fozard & Weinert, 1972; for words vs. consonant strings, see Greene, 1996).

Another problem for a strength theory is found in memory for serial position. In Hintzman and Block (1971, exp. 1) subjects saw a serial list of 50 words, which was followed by a recognition and position-judgment test in which they had to assign each word they judged "old" to a 10th or decile of the study list. Although judged decile increased monotonically with position throughout the list, the increase was most rapid over the first 10 positions—that is, primacies were better discriminated than recencies. This is the opposite of what a decaying-strength construct predicts. Hintzman, Block and Summers (1973a, exp. 2) had subjects study four different 20-word lists, each followed by a recognition test that included the 10 middle items from the list. Subjects were then unexpectedly asked to assign each of the 40 remaining words to one of the four lists, and to indicate whether it had appeared nearer the beginning or the end of its list. List-discrimination judgments were most accurate in list 1 and list 4, and errors showed generalization over time. Inconsistent with strict temporal generalization, however, judgments of position tended to be correct even when a test word was placed in the wrong list (see also Nairne, 1991).

In their experiment 3, Hintzman et al. (1973) presented three study lists, and compared performance on a list-and-position judg-

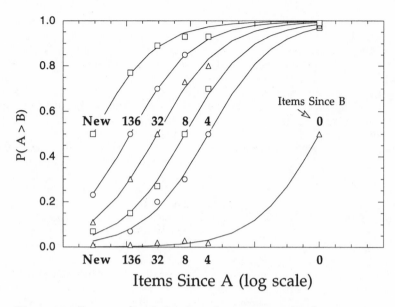

Figure 11.1 Recency discrimination of concrete nouns, from Yntema and Trask (1963). The probability of choosing word A as more recent than word B is plotted as a function of the recency of A (the abscissa) and the recovery of B (the parameter of the curves). New items were not seen before during the experiment. By assumption, P (A > B) is 0.5 when the recencies are equal. The fitted psychophysical functions assume a logarithmic scale.

ment test that either came immediately after list 3 or was delayed. A new analysis of those data shows an effect of delay on the ability to correctly assign words to lists 1, 2, and 3 (.62, .43, .62 immediate vs. .64, .35, .50 delayed), but no effect on the ability to assign words to within-list position (.60 immediate vs. .60 delayed). This suggests that decaying strength contributes to crude discriminations such as list 2 vs. list 3, but that more precise judgments of within-list position are based on contextual information of some kind. It may "feel" different to be studying list 1 than to be studying a later list, and it may feel different near the beginning of a list than approaching the end. If such contextual information is encoded into memory, it could become available at later retrieval for fortuitous use in a memory-judgment task.

Multiple Study Presentations

Some of the more surprising memory-judgment results relate to the ability to remember presentation frequency. As an example, consider experiment 2 of Hintzman and Rogers (1973). Subjects saw a sequence of 190 vaca-

tion slides, in which different scenes appeared 1, 2, or 3 times. Pictures with frequencies of 2 and 3 had repetition spacings of 0, 1, or 5 intervening items. Subjects were told to study the pictures for a later test, the nature of which was not disclosed. On the test, the old pictures were intermixed with new ones, and subjects were asked to indicate how many times each test picture had appeared in the study list. Mean frequency judgments are shown in figure 11.2. The judgments tracked actual study frequency closely when repetitions were widely spaced. Like judgments of recency and position, judgments of frequency are more accurate for better remembered items such as pictures than for more poorly remembered items such as words (Hintzman, Curran & Caulton, 1995). Figure 11.2 also shows the powerful effect of the spacing of repetitions. As is also seen in recall and recognition, the effect of a repetition is greatly diminished if it is massed. Frequency judgments are relatively unaffected by recency, however. Differences in recency ranging from a few seconds to several minutes have little effect on an item's apparent frequency (Galbraith & Underwood, 1973), although frequency information

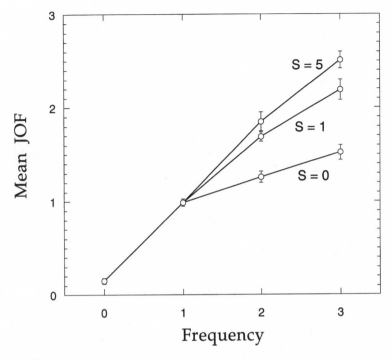

Figure 11.2 Mean judgments of picture frequency, from Hintzman and Rogers (1973). JOF = judgment of frequency, S = spacing of repetitions. Error bars represent the standard error of the mean.

is lost over retention intervals of hours to days (Hintzman & Stern, 1984; Leicht, 1968).

Memory for presentation frequency seems to accrue as an inevitable consequence of encoding repetitions into memory. Surprisingly, the ability to judge presentation frequencies of words shows little change with age, from grade 2 through college (Hasher & Chromiak, 1977). When subjects receive frequency-judgment test instructions they often complain of not being warned in advance, but in numerous experiments comparing the incidental and intentional learning of frequency, such warning has had little effect (see Hasher & Zacks, 1979).

Incidentally learned frequencies can also be apportioned accurately to different contexts. In Hintzman and Block (1971, exp. 3), subjects studied two lists; individual words occurred 0, 2, or 5 times in list 1, crossed with 0, 2, or 5 times in list 2. Afterward, the subjects were able to make separate list 1 and list 2 frequency judgments for a given word with considerable accuracy: about 87% of the variance among judgment means was related to frequency in the target list (list 1 or list 2),

and only about 8% to generalization from frequency in the nontarget list. Hockley and Cristi (1996) found a similar ability to apportion overall frequency to trials in which words had been seen individually, as opposed to as members of pairs. Subjects judged single-word frequency with little effect of pair frequency, and judged pair frequency with little effect of single-word frequency. They could also judge a word's overall frequency, combining singletons and pairs. Sometimes the ability to apportion frequency to different contexts breaks down in an asymmetrical fashion. In an early reality-monitoring experiment by Raye, Johnson, and Taylor (1980), subjects read words 2, 5, or 8 times, and generated the same words 2, 5, or 8 times. Judgments of reading frequency were affected by read and generate trials to about the same degree, but judgments of generate frequency were much less affected by read trials than by generate trials. This outcome suggests that generating an item produces more source-related contextual information than reading the item does.

Unlike memory for surface form, frequency information must be aggregated over multiple trials. Is the aggregate one in which individual events retain their identity? Hintzman, Block, and Summers (1973b) presented a list in which words occurred either once auditorily or visually (A or V), or twice in the same or both modalities (AA, AV, VA, or VV). Subjects were then asked to judge frequency and modality for each word, giving two ordered modality judgments if they thought the test word had occurred twice. Subjects' accuracy—particularly their ability to distinguish AV from VA—suggested that memories of individual event are preserved. Similarly, Hintzman, and Block (1971, exp. 2) had subjects make two serial-position judgments for any word they thought had occurred twice. Judgments of the first position were reliably affected by the word's first position but not by the second, and judgments of the second position showed the opposite pattern—an outcome that supports a multiple-trace account of memory for repetitions.

Flexser and Bower (1974) assumed such a multiple-trace account. They showed that if the first and second presentations of an item have independent but overlapping apparent-position distributions, then the first presentation will sometimes be remembered as occurring later than the second presentation. A repeated item will therefore seem more recent, on average, than an item that occurred only once. In accordance with this overlapping-distributions model, when subjects were asked which of two items occurred more recently in the study list, there was a bias to pick a repeated over a nonrepeated item. But there was a bias to pick a repeated item also when subjects were asked to make a distance judgment—that is, to choose the item that had occurred earlier in the study list. The bias in recency judgments is predicted by both the strength hypothesis and the overlapping-distributions hypothesis, but only the latter predicts the distance-judgment bias.

Despite this success, different presentations of a repeated item may not be represented independently, as the Flexser and Bower (1974) model assumes. If subjects study a list and then are asked to judge the spacings of pairs of events, those judgments are much more accurate for repetitions of the same word (e.g., war-war) than for pairs of unrelated words (e.g., spider-table). Hintzman, Summers, and Block (1975) proposed that a word's repetition reminds the subject of its earlier occurrence—including its recency—and that an implicit judgment of recency therefore becomes integrated into the trace of the second occurrence of the word. To test this hypothesis, they presented a list that included associatively related words (e.g., queen-king), which should also trigger reminding. As predicted, spacing judgments for the related words resembled those for repetitions. Tzeng and Cotton (1980) took this idea further, proposing that information encoded as a result of a reminding would also include word order. They showed that people are better able to discriminate the recencies of two words when they are related than when they are unrelated (see also Winograd & Solway, 1985). These findings suggest that events such as word presentations are encoded in memory not just in terms of what, how, when, and where, but also in terms of potentially meaningful relationships with surrounding events.

Theoretical Discussion

Theories that assume that surface information is discarded, and that effects of temporal variables are simply mediated by strength, receive little support from memory-judgment experiments. Given the centrality of the strength construct to interference theory, it was a noteworthy defection when one of the theory's strongest proponents dismissed strength as the mere "by-product" of a memory's "temporal, spatial, frequency, modality, orthographic, associative nonverbal, and associative verbal" attributes (Underwood, 1969). Impressed with the ability of children and adults to unintentionally absorb such information as frequency and spatial location, Hasher and Zacks (1979) proposed that certain attributes of memory are encoded "automatically"—that is, without demanding attentional capacity. As empirical criteria for this automaticity, Hasher and Zacks proposed that automatic encoding should not be affected by intentionality, instructions, practice, development, or reductions of attentional capacity.

Thus staking their case on the null hypothesis, Hasher and Zacks provoked a flurry of studies showing that the null hypothesis is not always true. Many of these demonstrations were not surprising. Consider just the case of memory for frequency: Conditions that impair learning in general, including "shallow" encoding (Fisk & Schneider, 1984) and massed repetition (see figure 11.2), lead to underestimation of presentation frequency. It is also obvious that frequency can be represented in more than one way (Brown, 1995), and that this is somewhat open to strategic manipulation. Thus, given the motivation and opportunity, subjects can sometimes be induced to count repetitions during study, or even to sequentially retrieve and count instances (e.g., category members) at test.

Such attentional and strategic influences notwithstanding, a robust knowledge of frequency seems inevitably to result when repetitions are encoded effectively into memory. One way to explain this phenomenon is to assume that each attended-to event leaves a separate trace in memory (the multiple-trace hypothesis), and that the number of traces is inferred at test from the total amount of trace activation produced by the retrieval cue. Hintzman (1988) showed that such a multiple-trace model can explain a variety of empirical findings surrounding recognition memory and judgments of frequency. Another possibility is that frequency-relevant information accumulates during study, as a consequence of remindings. That is, later encounters with an item might automatically remind the subject of earlier ones, so that the associated context comes to represent the item's increasing aggregate frequency. It remains to be seen whether a theory based on remindings can explain how subjects correctly apportion frequencies to different contexts, as in research that was described earlier.

Is memory so rich that theorists should take the videotape metaphor more seriously? There are several reasons to believe it is not. First, memory for surface information is far from perfect. Incidental retention of input modality for words that are recognized as old has typically run around 75%, where 50% is chance. Memory for font and for voice tend to be considerably lower under similar conditions, but memory for whether a concept was represented by a picture or a word appears to be much better. Memory for location is poor in the middle of a page or line, but good near edges and boundaries. Probably the best current approach to understanding such performance is the source-monitoring framework (Johnson, Hashtroudi, & Lindsay, 1993; also chapter 13), which holds that people judge the source of a memory by flexibly weighting various retrieved attributes, including perceptual details, semantic information, emotional reactions, and cognitive operations that were involved at the time of encoding. From this perspective, source judgments are attributions, based on whatever remembered pieces of in-

formation seem relevant to the judgment task. Memories may be rich in content even if they are reconstructed from fragments.

Studies of the temporal aspects of experience lead to a similar conclusion. In a broad-based review of the literature on memory for time, Friedman (1993) identified three basic ways in which memory might code the time of an earlier event: distance from the present (as might be represented by decreasing strength), location in time (time tags), and relative time (event X happened before event Y). Distance information is accurate for making crude temporal distinctions. For example, one would not think something had happened yesterday occurred only a minute ago, or as long as three years ago. Location per se seems to be coded in memory only rarely, as when a clock time or memorized date is retrieved by association. Subjects appear to infer that an item occurred near the beginning or end of a list based on contextual information—thus they can get the list wrong even when they know something about the item's within-list position. The fact that order and spacing judgments are better for related than for unrelated words suggests also that temporal location is often reconstructed from order information that was encoded into memory during remindings. Thus the personal experience most people have of a temporally ordered set of memories is, in Friedman's words, a "chronological illusion." "The sense of an absolute chronology in our lives is an illusion, a thin veneer on the more basic substance of coincidence, locations in recurrent patterns, and independent sequences of meaningfully related events" (Friedman, 1993, pp. 61–62).

This does not imply that the strength hypothesis should be completely abandoned, however. Anderson and Bower (1972) argued that recognition memory is just a variant of the list-discrimination task, except that instead of deciding whether a test item occurred in list 1 or list 2, the subject decides whether it occurred in the experimental or nonexperimental context. Thus described, the similarity of recognition and list discrimination seems obvious. On the other hand, "global matching" models have proved able to account for many recognition-memory phenomena based on a unidimensional strength or familiarity construct (see Clark & Gronlund, 1996). Even the multiple-trace model of Hintzman (1988), which was designed specifically to account for memory for frequency, assumes that recognition and frequency judgments are inferred from a strength-like sum of activation over traces. Although Johnson et al. (1993) accept recognition memory as a kind of source-monitoring task, they nevertheless allow that recognition judgments may be based primarily on less differentiated information, which requires less careful and systematic evaluation. Such undifferentiated information could also be called strength or familiarity. The idea that strength and context constitute different kinds of retrieved information is supported by data on the retrieval dynamics of memory judgments, as we see in the following section.

Retrieval Dynamics

Most memory-judgment tasks involve—or can be turned into—a choice between two simple responses. This makes memory judgments ideally suited for studying retrieval and decision dynamics. Traditionally, such questions have been addressed using reaction time (RT); but speed-accuracy tradeoff, and an unwillingness of subjects to respond based on a bare minimum of information, limits the usefulness of the RT measure. In the response-signal method, the experimenter takes primary control of response time away from the subject, and interest is focused on the speed-accuracy tradeoff itself. As the method typically is used, the subject makes a binary decision (e.g., old vs. new or auditory vs. visual) about each test item. The test item is displayed on the computer screen for a variable and unpredictable lag, which terminates with a signal such as a tone, whereupon the subject must respond immediately even if it is necessary to guess. Performance is at chance if the lag is as short as 50 ms, but grows to an asymptotic level, typically at lags of 1000 to 2000 ms. When judgment accuracy is plotted as a function of processing time, the curves for different tasks display different quantitative characteristics. Particularly interesting from a theoretical perspective is the point at which performance suddenly begins to rise above chance—the minimal retrieval time, or "intercept."

To illustrate, consider an experiment comparing retrieval dynamics in the recognition-memory and list-discrimination tasks (Hintzman, Caulton, & Levitin, 1998, exp. 2). In each block of the experiment, subjects studied two lists of 21 words, separated by a filler task. Some words occurred twice and others once in their respective lists. Following list 2, subjects were told whether the following test trials would require judgments of "old" vs. "new," or of "list 1" vs. "list 2." Test trials followed the response-signal procedure, with signals to respond coming at seven lags ranging from 100 to 2000 ms. Figure 11.3 shows accuracy (hit rate–false alarm rate) for both tasks and both presentation frequencies, as a function of processing time (lag plus response latency). Each retrieval function has been fitted with an exponential growth curve having a starting point or intercept that is shifted away from time = 0. What is most striking about these curves is that the intercept for recognition memory is about 100 ms earlier than that for list discrimination. (Sensory and motor times should be equal in all conditions.) Apparently, information is available during this 100 ms that is useful for discriminating old items from new items, but not for deciding whether a test word occurred in list 1 or list 2. It is also interesting that repetition seems to have had no effect on the intercept for recognition memory. The graph shows a slight reduction in the list-discrimination intercept with repetition, although it is not statistically reliable.

Gronlund, Edwards, and Ohrt (1997) compared the retrieval dynamics of recognition memory and location judgments, with similar results. When subjects judged whether a word was old or new, the intercept was 60 to 120 ms earlier than when they judged whether its spatial location was the same at study and test. And Hintzman and Caulton (1997) compared the retrieval dynamics of recognition memory with those of modality judgments. When each item was studied once, the recognition-memory intercept was about 100 ms earlier than the modality-judgment intercept. When words were studied in the same modality three times, the recognition-memory intercept did not appear to change, but the modality-judgment intercept became shorter (in keeping with the nonsignificant trend for list discrimination, in figure 11.3).

Frequency judgments, in contrast to list discrimination, location judgments, and modality judgments, appear to have retrieval dynamics like those of recognition memory. Subjects in experiment 1 of Hintzman and Curran (1994) were given response-signal tests on words that had occurred either 0, 1, or 2 times in the preceding study list. Prior to some test lists subjects were instructed to discriminate old items from new items (0 → "no"; 1 or 2 → "yes"), and prior to the other test lists they

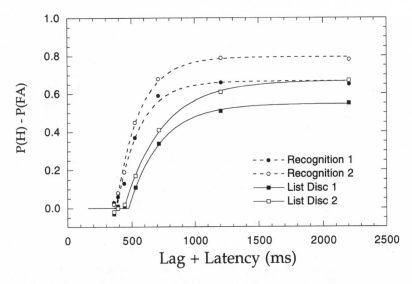

Figure 11.3 Speed-accuracy tradeoff curves for recognition-memory and list-discrimination judgments, from Hintzman, Caulton, and Levitin (1998). The dependent variable is the hit rate minus the false alarm rate (in the original figure it was logistic d'). Lag is the delay of signal, from onset of the test word, and latency is response time. The words were studied either one or two times.

were instructed to discriminate items that had occurred twice from those of lesser frequency (0 or 1 → "no"; 2 → "yes"). The ability to discriminate frequencies of 1 vs 2 rose above chance just as early as that to discriminate old vs new.

At present there are no well-developed theories of retrieval dynamics in memory judgments. As a first attempt to understand these results, however, we can relate them to theoretical notions discussed earlier. Suppose that studying an item has two distinct effects: it increases the item's strength or familiarity, which then decays over time; and it establishes a variety of associations to context (e.g., remindings, cognitive operations, sensory and spatial information). Familiarity is the simpler of the two kinds of information and is available earlier in retrieval. Because recognition testing usually takes place shortly after study, a test item's strength or familiarity is highly relevant to the question of whether it occurred in the experimental setting. This may help explain why global-matching models based on a strengthlike construct can account for many recognition-memory phenomena. Contextual information is complex and takes longer to retrieve and evaluate. Such information is needed for judging input modality, list mem-

bership, source, spacing, spatial location, and serial order. Judgments of overall experimental frequency often can be based on strength; but when frequencies must be apportioned separately to sources, such as different temporally defined lists, contextual information must be retrieved.

Brain Mechanisms

It is tempting to relate memory-judgment phenomena to the rapidly accumulating knowledge about brain mechanisms underlying memory (chapters 28–34, this volume). Recalling the modality in which a word was presented—its location, serial position, or list membership—requires the retrieval of various incidental attributes that were associated with or "bound to" the word's meaning at the time of encoding. The incoming, internal, and outgoing neural connections of the hippocampus appear ideally suited to carry out such a binding function. To oversimplify somewhat, it has been hypothesized that signals from cortical areas involved in an experience converge on the hippocampus, which serves to interconnect the attributes of the experience, and that a subset of those attributes, reinstated later, allows the hippocampus to reconstruct an approximation of the original experience (e.g., Treves & Rolls, 1993). Research with animals and humans suggests that there is, in addition, a medial temporal-lobe region that can function independently of the hippocampus, and that flags as familiar (but does not bind) the individual attributes of experience (Aggleton & Brown, 1999; Eichenbaum, Otto, & Cohen, 1994). Patients with focal lesions in hippocampus, fornix, and mammillary bodies, that spare this region, show large deficits in recall but only small deficits in recognition (Aggleton & Shaw, 1996). If the hippocampus is necessary for the recall of associated information but not for retrieval of strength or familiarity, this could help explain evidence reviewed in the previous section that list, location, and modality judgments rise above chance about 100 ms later in retrieval than recognition and frequency judgments. Brain imaging studies using memory-judgment tasks could throw further light on this proposed separation of function.

Several memory-judgment studies on neuropsychology patients have been interpreted as implicating the frontal lobes in these tasks. A classic investigation by Huppert and Piercy (1978) examined the independence of recency and frequency judgments in Korsakoff amnesics and alcoholic controls. Pictures were shown either 1 time or 3 times, either 24 hours or 10 minutes before testing. On successive tests, subjects judged whether test items had occurred today vs. yesterday, and then whether test items had occurred 1 time vs. 3 times. The Korsakoff patients were much more likely than controls to think that pictures seen 3 times yesterday had been seen today, and that pictures seen 1 time today had been seen 3 times. In both tasks, the Korsakoff patients seemed to be responding primarily on the basis of strength, while the controls, in keeping with the literature reviewed earlier, were able to make largely independent recency and frequency judgments. Because Korsakoff patients tend to have both frontal and diencephalic damage and are impaired on item (recognition) memory, the interpretation of this outcome is unclear. Squire (1982) compared the list-discrimination performance of Korsakoff patients, normal controls, and nonalcoholic amnesics, most of whom were patients undergoing electroshock treatment for depression. Subjects read two lists of sentences, separated by a filler task. They then were tested on old-new recognition and asked to identify the list

membership of sentences they judged to be "old." The Korsakoff patients were impaired about as much as the other amnesics on recognition, but performed much worse on list discrimination (they were essentially at chance).

Evidence that non-Korsakoff patients with frontal lesions are specifically impaired on memory for recency was presented by Milner, Corsi, and Leonard (1991). Surgery patients with various cortical areas excised were compared with controls on forced-choice recognition and recency discrimination, for words, drawings, and abstract paintings. Averaged across materials and transformed into d', performance of frontal patients was 78% that of the controls in recognition memory, but only 53% that of controls in recency judgments. Performance of unilateral temporal-lobe patients was 81% that of controls in recognition, and 89% in recency judgments. It has also been reported that patients with frontal-lobe excisions are differentially impaired on memory for frequency (Smith & Milner, 1988). In those data, however, differences appear confined to frequencies greater than 3, so there could be an impairment in the use of larger numbers, rather than in frequency judgment per se. It is important to note that frontal damage generally produces a recognition-memory deficit (Aggleton & Shaw, 1996; Wheeler, Stuss, & Tulving, 1995). To the extent that other memory-judgment tasks are more affected than recognition, it may be because the tasks require more difficult discriminations or more strategic evaluation of retrieved evidence (Moscovitch, 1992), not because they play a dedicated role in particular memory-judgment tasks.

Memory Judgments and Conscious Awareness

The study of memory has been marked recently by interest in retrieval and conscious awareness. A little explored aspect of this problem is the relationship between memory judgments and implicit memory (see chapter 18). Implicit memory measures such as priming in perceptual identification are affected by repetition of sensory details, and judgments of source such as modality, font, and voice also involve memory for sensory information. One might therefore expect variables that affect perceptual priming to have similar effects on appropriately chosen source judgments. However, if priming occurs in the initial processing areas of the cortex while memory judgments depend crucially on binding by the hippocampus, such a correspondence may not exist. A report that aging has a substantial effect on modality judgments but essentially no effect on modality effects in priming (Light, LaVoie, Valencia-Laver, Owens, & Mead, 1992) lends support to the latter view.

Another approach to memory and consciousness has subjects make old-new recognition decisions and then report whether each "old" decision was accompanied by awareness of details of the item's prior occurrence (a "remember" judgment) or not accompanied by such awareness (a "know" judgment—see chapter 17). It is reasonable to suppose that there must be a close connection between the willingness to report "remembering" a test item and the ability to accurately report its modality, serial position, and so on. The remember-know task, however, does not fit into the category of memory judgments as they have been defined in this chapter. The most important distinction lies in what the judgment is about: a memory judgment is about a study event that occurred earlier. A remember-know judgment, in contrast, is about one's state of consciousness during the recognition decision. In this sense, a remember-know judgment is like a confidence rating. Indeed, it has been noted that remember-know judgments can be analyzed using signal-detection theory, in just the way that is routine with confidence ratings (Donaldson, 1996; Hirshman & Master, 1997).

One consequence of the fact that memory judgments and remember-know judgments are about different things is that memory judgments can be scored for accuracy, but remember-know judgments cannot be. To doubt subjects' reports on their own awareness would appear problematic, but one can investigate the relation between remember-know judgments and memory-judgment accuracy. In a series of experiments, Perfect, Mayes, Downes, and Van Eijk (1996) asked subjects to indicate "remember" or "know" for words that they recognized as old, and then to give judgments of serial order, list membership, or spatial location. Memory judgments were considerably more accurate for "remembered" words than for words subjects said they just "knew." Even for items in the latter category, however, memory judgments were better than chance—significantly so in one out of four experiments. Moreover, in the one experiment which used both remember-know and confidence ratings,

these measures showed the same relationship to memory-judgment accuracy. Several interrelated questions are raised by these findings. One is whether remembering and knowing are best understood as discrete states of awareness or as regions on a continuum of retrieved information. Another is how remembering and knowing relate to the processes that underlie the distinct retrieval-dynamics curves discussed earlier. Still another question concerns the extent to which subjects can make accurate judgments of source, recency, frequency, and so on, in the absence of mediation by conscious awareness. Memory-judgment experiments should help to answer such questions.

Acknowledgments   Preparation of this chapter was supported in part by the National Science Foundation under Grant Nos. BNS-90-08909 and SBR-93-19265. Correspondence should be addressed to Douglas L. Hintzman, Department of Psychology, University of Oregon, 97403.

References

Aggleton, J. P., & Brown, M. W. (1999). Episodic memory, amnesia and the hippocampal-anterior thalamic axis. *Behavioral and Brain Sciences, 22*, 425–489.

Aggleton, J. P., & Shaw, C. (1996). Amnesia and recognition memory: a reanalysis of psychometric data. *Neuropsychologia, 34*, 51–62.

Anderson, J. R., & Bower, G. H. (1972). Recognition and retrieval processes in free recall. *Psychological Review, 79*, 97–123.

Bartlett, F. C. (1932). *Remembering.* Cambridge, England: Cambridge University Press.

Bray, N. W., & Batchelder, W. H. (1972). Effects of instructions and retention interval on memory of presentation mode. *Journal of Verbal Learning and Verbal Behavior, 11*, 367–374.

Brown, N. R. (1995). Estimation strategies and the judgment of event frequency. *Journal of Experimental Psychology: Learning, Memory, and Cognition, 21*, 1539–1553.

Clark, S. E., & Gronlund, S. D. (1996). Global matching models of recognition memory: How the models match the data. *Psychonomic Bulletin & Review, 3*, 37–60.

Craik, F. I. M., & Lockhart, R. S. (1972). Levels of processing: A framework for memory research. *Journal of Verbal Learning and Verbal Behavior, 11*, 671–684.

Donaldson, W. (1996). The role of decision processes in remembering and knowing. *Memory & Cognition, 24*, 523–533.

Eichenbaum, H., Otto, T., & Cohen, N. J. (1994). Two functional components of the hippocampal memory system. *Behavioral and Brain Sciences, 17*, 449–518.

Fisk, A. D., & Schneider, W. (1984). Memory as a function of attention, level of processing, and automatization. *Journal of Experimental Psychology: Learning, Memory, and Cognition, 10*, 181–197.

Flexser, A. J., & Bower, G. H. (1974). How frequency affects recency judgments: A model for recency discrimination. *Journal of Experimental Psychology, 103*, 706–716.

Fozard, J. L., & Weinert, J. R. (1972). Absolute judgments of recency for pictures and nouns after various numbers of intervening items. *Journal of Experimental Psychology, 95*, 472–474.

Friedman, W. J. (1993). Memory for the time of past events. *Psychological Bulletin, 113*, 44–66.

Galbraith, R. C., & Underwood, B. J. (1973). Perceived frequency of concrete and abstract words. *Memory & Cognition, 1*, 56–60.

Greene, R. L. (1996). Mirror effect in order and associative information: Role of response strategies. *Journal of Experimental Psychology: Learning, Memory, and Cognition, 22*, 687–695.

Gronlund, S. D., Edwards, M. B., & Ohrt, D. D. (1997). Comparison of the retrieval of item versus spatial position information. *Journal of Experimental Psychology: Learning, Memory, and Cognition, 23*, 1261–1274.

Hasher, L., & Chromiak, W. (1977). The processing of frequency information: An automatic mechanism? *Journal of Verbal Learning and Verbal Behavior, 16*, 173–184.

Hasher, L., & Zacks, R. T. (1979). Automatic and effortful processes in memory. *Journal of Experimental Psychology: General, 108*, 356–388.

Hinrichs, J. V. (1970). A two-process memory-strength theory for judgment of recency. *Psychological Review, 77*, 223–233.

Hintzman, D. L. (1988). Judgments of frequency and recognition memory in a multiple-trace memory model. *Psychological Review, 95*, 528–551.

Hintzman, D. L., & Block, R. A. (1971). Repetition and memory: Evidence for a multiple-trace hypothesis. *Journal of Experimental Psychology, 88*, 297–306.

Hintzman, D. L., Block, R. A., & Inskeep, N. R. (1972). Memory for mode of input. *Journal of Verbal Learning and Verbal Behavior, 11*, 741–749.

Hintzman, D. L., Block, R. A., & Summers, J. J. (1973a). Contextual associations and memory for serial position. *Journal of Experimental Psychology, 97*, 220–229.

Hintzman, D. L., Block, R. A., & Summers, J. J. (1973b). Modality tags and memory for repetitions: Locus of the spacing effect. *Journal of Verbal Learning and Verbal Behavior, 12*, 229–238.

Hintzman, D. L., & Caulton, D. A. (1997). Recognition memory and modality judgments: A comparison of retrieval dynamics. *Journal of Memory and Language, 37*, 1–23.

Hintzman, D. L., Caulton, D. A., & Levitin, D. J. (1998). Retrieval dynamics in recognition and list discrimination: Further evidence of separate processes of familiarity and recall. *Memory & Cognition, 26*, 449–462.

Hintzman, D. L., & Curran, T. (1994). Retrieval dynamics of recognition and frequency judgments: Evidence for separate processes of familiarity and recall. *Journal of Memory and Language, 33*, 1–18.

Hintzman, D. L., Curran, T., & Caulton, D. A. (1995). Scaling the episodic familiarities of pictures and words. *Psychological Science, 6*, 308–313.

Hintzman, D. L., & Rogers, M. K. (1973). Spacing effects in picture memory. *Memory & Cognition, 1*, 430–434.

Hintzman, D. L., & Stern, L. D. (1984). A comparison of forgetting rates in frequency discrimination and recognition. *Bulletin of the Psychonomic Society, 22*, 409–412.

Hintzman, D. L., Summers, J. J., & Block, R. A. (1975). Spacing judgments as an index of study-phase retrieval. *Journal of Experimental Psychology: Human Leaning and Memory, 1*, 31–40.

Hintzman, D. L., & Waters, R. M. (1969). Interlist and retention intervals in list discrimination. *Psychonomic Science, 17*, 357–358.

Hirshman, E., & Master, S. (1997). Modeling the conscious correlates of recognition memory: Reflections on the remember-know paradigm. *Memory & Cognition, 25*, 345–351.

Hockley, W. E., & Cristi, C. (1996). Tests of the separate retrieval of item and associative information using a frequency-judgment task. *Memory & Cognition, 24*, 796–811.

Hull, C. L., Hovland, C. I., Ross, R. T., Hall, M., Perkins, D. T., & Fitch, F. B. (1940). *Mathematico-deductive theory of rote learning.* New Haven: Yale University Press.

Huppert, F. A., & Piercy, M. (1978). The role of trace strength in recency and frequency judgements by amnesic and control subjects. *Quarterly Journal of Experimental Psychology, 30,* 347–354.

Johnson, M. K., Hastroudi, S., & Lindsay, D. S. (1993). Source monitoring. *Psychological Bulletin, 114,* 3–28.

Kintsch, W. (1970). Models for free recall and recognition. In D. A. Norman (Ed.), *Models of human memory* (pp. 331–373). New York: Academic Press.

Koffka, K. (1935). *Principles of gestalt psychology.* New York: Harcourt, Brace & World.

Köhler, W. (1929). *Gestalt psychology.* New York: Liveright.

Leicht, K. L. (1968). Recall and judged frequency of implicitly occurring words. *Journal of Verbal Learning and Verbal Behavior, 7,* 918–923.

Light, L. L., Stansbury, C., & Rubin, C. (1973). Memory for modality of presentation: Within-modality discrimination. *Memory & Cognition, 1,* 395–400.

Light, L. L., LaVoie, D., Valencia-Laver, D., Owens, S. A. A., & Mead, G. (1992). Direct and indirect measures of memory for modality in young and older adults. *Journal of Experimental Psychology: Learning, Memory, and Cognition, 18,* 1284–1297.

Milner, B., Corsi, P., & Leonard, G. (1991). Frontal-lobe contribution to recency judgments. *Neuropsychologia, 29,* 601–618.

Moscovitch, M. (1992). Memory and working-with-memory: A component process model based on modules and central systems. *Journal of Cognitive Neuroscience, 4,* 257–267.

Nairne, J. S. (1991). Positional uncertainty in long-term memory. *Memory & Cognition, 19,* 332–340.

Nairne, J. S., & Dutta, A. (1992). Spatial and temporal uncertainty in long-term memory. *Journal of Memory and Language, 31,* 396–407.

Neisser, U. (1967). *Cognitive psychology.* New York: Appleton-Century Crofts.

Penfield, W. (1955). The permanent record of the stream of consciousness. *Acta Psychologica, 11,* 47–69.

Perfect, T. J., Mayes, A. R., Downes, J. J., & Van Eijk, R. (1996). Does context discriminate recollection from familiarity in recog-

nition memory? *Quarterly Journal of Experimental Psychology, 49A,* 797–813.

Peterson, L. R. (1967). Search and judgment in memory. In B. Kleinmuntz (Ed.), *Concepts and the structure of memory.* (pp. 153–180). New York: John Wiley.

Postman, L. (1961). The present status of interference theory. In C. N. Cofer (Ed.), *Verbal learning and verbal behavior.* (pp. 152–179). New York: McGraw-Hill.

Raye, C. L., Johnson, M. K., & Taylor, T. H. (1980). Is there something special about memory for internally generated information? *Memory & Cognition, 8,* 141–148.

Rothkopf, E. Z. (1971). Incidental memory for location of information in text. *Journal of Verbal Learning and Verbal Behavior, 10,* 608–613.

Sachs, J. S. (1967). Recognition memory for syntactic and semantic aspects of connected discourse. *Perception & Psychophysics, 2,* 437–442.

Smith, M. L., & Milner, B. (1988). Estimation of frequency of occurrence of abstract designs after frontal or temporal lobectomy. *Neuropsychologica, 26,* 297–306.

Squire, L. R. (1982). Comparison between forms of amnesia: Some deficits are unique to Korsakoff's syndrome. *Journal of Experimental Psychology: Learning, Memory, and Cognition, 8,* 560–571.

Treves, A., & Rolls, E. T. (1993). Computational analysis of the role of the hippocampus in memory. *Hippocampus, 4,* 374–391.

Tzeng, O. J. L., & Cotton, B. (1980). A study-phase retrieval model of temporal coding. *Journal of Experimental Psychology: Human Learning and Memory, 6,* 705–716.

Underwood, B. J. (1969). Attributes of memory. *Psychological Review, 76,* 519–531.

Wallach, H., & Averbach, E. (1955). On memory modalities. *American Journal of Psychology, 68,* 249–257.

Wheeler, M. A., Stuss, D. T., & Tulving, E. (1995). Frontal lobe damage produces episodic memory impairment. *Journal of the International Neuropsychological Society, 1,* 525–536.

Winograd, E. (1968). List differentiation as a function of frequency and retention interval. *Journal of Experimental Psychology Monograph Supplement, 76,* 2 (Part 2).

Winograd, E., & Soloway, R. M. (1985). Reminding as a basis for temporal judgments. *Journal of Experimental Psychology: Learning, Memory, and Cognition, 11,* 262–271.

Yntema, D. B., & Trask, F. P. (1963). Recall as a search process. *Journal of Verbal Learning and Verbal Behavior, 2,* 65–74.

12

Source Monitoring

Attributing Mental Experiences

KAREN J. MITCHELL & MARCIA K. JOHNSON

To understand the problems that source monitoring research and theory address, consider the implications of a cognitive system that is capable of construction and reconstruction—that is, capable of generating information on its own and integrating information from multiple sources. Constructive and reconstructive processes that interpret, embellish, transform, and synthesize experiences are powerful engines for comprehension and creativity, but the potential cost is distorted memories and beliefs (e.g., Bartlett, 1932/1995; Bransford & Johnson, 1973; Neisser, 1967).

The constructive view of cognition was fueled by many observations. Among the most important were the consequences of schema-driven (e.g., Bartlett, 1932/1995), associative (e.g., Deese, 1959), and organizational (e.g., Tulving, 1962) processes. For example, while inter-item associations contribute to accurate recall (e.g., Jenkins & Russell, 1952), associations with an item not on the list can produce intrusions (Deese, 1959). Thus, it has long been clear that similar mechanisms produce both *accurate* and *inaccurate* memory.

The impact of constructive and reconstructive processes was strikingly apparent in studies carried out in the late 1960s and early 70s that were concerned with the comprehension of, and memory for, prose. For example, shortly after reading a passage, changes in wording that alter meaning are typically rejected, but changes in wording that preserve meaning (i.e., paraphrases) are likely to be recognized as old (e.g., Sachs, 1967). People told that *there is a box to the right of a tree* and that *there is a chair on the box*, often remember that they heard that *the tree is to the left of the chair* (Bransford, Barclay, & Franks, 1972). A key message of such studies was that encoding is not simply associative; it also produces complex representations of entire situations that reflect real-world knowledge (e.g., of spatial relationships). Furthermore, constructive processes are not a luxury. They allow us to use activated relevant knowledge to interpret, integrate, and retrieve an otherwise incomprehensible event and, consequently, remember much more than we could otherwise (e.g., Bransford & Johnson, 1973).

At the same time, the information, knowledge, and beliefs that help us encode and remember events can also produce errors. For example, participants told that the main character of a story was Helen Keller were more likely to remember reading the nonpresented sentence *She was deaf, dumb, and blind* than a control group told the main character's name was Carol Harris (Sulin & Dooling, 1974). What is remembered may even distort the meaning behind the message. For example, people hearing a story that included the sentence *The spy threw the secret document into the fireplace just in time since 30 seconds longer would have been too late* were later likely to falsely recognize a sentence that indicated that the spy burned the secret document (Johnson, Bransford, & Solomon, 1973). Thus, people were likely to make assumptions about the situation that might be incorrect (e.g., that a fire was lit in the fireplace and the spy wanted to destroy the document, whereas the fire might not have been lit and the spy might have wanted to hide the document) and these assumptions were taken by the rememberer to be part of the memory for the situation. Such memory distortions that go beyond logical paraphrase raise serious questions about the relation of a constructive memory system to reality. How does such a constructive memory system remain functional and not deteriorate into a pathological quagmire of real and imagined experience or recombinations of features of real experience?

The Johnson-Raye (1981) model of reality monitoring, and the more general source monitoring framework (SMF; Johnson, Hashtroudi, & Lindsay, 1993), are attempts to address this question. The proposed solution centers on the idea that construction and reconstruction alone do not create memory distortion. From both everyday experience and laboratory studies, it is clear that people sometimes succeed and sometimes fail at discriminating the origin of mental experiences. It follows that there must be mechanisms that allow us to discriminate correctly the origin of some mental experiences but not others. Johnson and colleagues proposed that these mechanisms are attributional judgment processes— that is, evaluative or monitoring processes by which mental experiences are attributed to different sources. Accordingly, constructions and reconstructions only constitute memory distortions when they are taken to be accurate memories.

The Source Monitoring Framework (SMF)

Memory representations reflect the processing activities occurring at acquisition (e.g., Johnson, 1983; Kolers & Roediger, 1984). According to the SMF, later activation of these representations (along with activation of other information at test) results in mental experiences that can range from general feelings of familiarity or strength to memory for specific features such as perceptual detail (e.g., color, shape), spatial and temporal information, semantic information, affective detail (e.g., emotional reactions), and the cognitive processes engaged (e.g., elaboration, retrieval of supporting information). Different types of acquisition processes (e.g., reading, thinking, inferring) and different types of events (e.g., movie, newspaper, dream) tend to produce memorial representations that are characteristically different from each other. For example, memories of imagined events typically have less vivid perceptual, temporal, and spatial information than perceived events and often include information about intentional cognitive operations (e.g., active generation and manipulation of visual images during problem solving). Memories of dreams are often perceptually vivid, typically do not include information about the cognitive operations that created them, and are often inconsistent with knowledge or other memories (Johnson, Kahan, & Raye, 1984). However, because of variability within these source types, the distributions of features of memories from different processes and events overlap. For example, representations of some perceived events are less detailed and perceptually vivid than representations of some imagined events. Some dreams are more plausible than some waking events. Thus, the characteristics of a mental experience cannot serve as a precise signature, or "tag," that specifies its origin. Rather, remembering always involves judgments about how the quantity and quality of these characteristics compare to expectations about characteristics of memories from various sources. So, for example, if a mental experience had substantial perceptual detail (e.g., visual), one would tend to attribute it to a perceived event (e.g., something one saw) since, on average, memories from perceived events contain quite a bit of perceptual detail.

Many source attributions are thus made rapidly and relatively nondeliberatively following the match-to-average-characteristics heuristic just described. However, the SMF posits that source monitoring sometimes also entails more systematic processes that are typically slower and more deliberate, involving, for example, retrieving additional information, discovering and noting relations, extended reasoning, and so on (see also Ross, 1997). Hence, even if you had a very vivid, perceptually rich memory of finding a money tree in the backyard, you might nonetheless accurately attribute that memory to a dream since you know that money does not grow on trees and you could therefore reason that this would, unfortunately, be impossible (Johnson, 1985).

Both heuristic and systematic source attributions are affected by a rememberer's biases, goals, agendas, and meta-memory skills. For example, you would probably engage in more stringent evaluative processing if you were trying to remember who proposed an interesting new theoretical argument that you want to cite than if you were trying to determine who told a particularly funny joke that you want to retell.

In sum, the ability to identify accurately the source of a memory depends on the type, amount, and quality of activated memory characteristics, whether the characteristics uniquely specify the source, the efficacy of the judgment processes engaged, the weights assigned to different features of the mental experience, and the criteria used when making the source attribution. Of course, as imperfect judgment processes are applied to mental representations that are themselves imperfect (in the sense that they are not exact copies of events) some errors are bound to occur. A basic tenet of the SMF is that illusory memories and veridical memories normally arise via exactly the same mechanisms (Johnson et al., 1993; Johnson & Raye, 1998). Nevertheless, we can specify factors likely to promote source monitoring errors, and hence, memory distortion.

For example, factors that disrupt normal encoding processes that bind features into a complex memory have been shown to increase source errors leading to memory distortions. Study conditions such as divided attention (e.g., Jacoby, Woloshyn, & Kelley, 1989) and focusing on one's own emotions rather than event details (Hashtroudi, Johnson, Vnek, & Ferguson, 1994; Johnson, Nolde, & De Leonardis, 1996) increase source errors, presumably because useful source-specifying information fails to be, or is weakly, bound into the memory (for other evidence that disruptions in binding can lead to illusory memories see, for example, Kroll, Knight, Metcalfe, Wolf, & Tulving, 1996; Reinitz, Lammers, & Cochran, 1992). Likewise, factors that decrease the specificity, or diagnosticity, of available source information can lead to increased source memory errors—for example, increased semantic similarity of statements (e.g., Lindsay, Johnson, & Kwon, 1991), decreased temporal separation of word lists (e.g., Winograd, 1968), decreased salience of cognitive

operations (e.g., Finke, Johnson, & Shyi, 1988; Rabinowitz, 1989), or a high degree of perceptual similarity between sources (Hashtroudi, Johnson, & Chrosniak, 1990; Johnson, Foley, & Leach, 1988; Lindsay et al., 1991). Similarly, factors at test that lead people to focus on less diagnostic memory characteristics also increase source misattributions (Marsh & Hicks, 1998). Factors that decrease the efficacy of the judgment process lead to increased errors—for example, inducing lax criteria, inappropriate feature weights, or less thorough evaluative processes (Dodson & Johnson, 1993; Lindsay & Johnson, 1989; Multhaup, 1995) or dividing attention at test (e.g., Dodson, Holland, & Shimamura, 1998; Dodson & Johnson, 1996; Gruppuso, Lindsay, & Kelley, 1997). Likewise, limiting the time available to make a source judgment is likely to negatively affect accuracy (e.g., Zaragoza & Lane, 1998). This last point is supported by studies using a response-signal method that shows that recognizing that an item is old typically precedes more specific source identification (Gronlund, Edwards, & Ohrt, 1997; Johnson, Kounios, & Reeder, 1994; see also Hintzman, chapter 11).

It should be noted that although explicit source identification tasks are often used to investigate memory distortion (see Johnson, 1997; Lindsay, 1994, for reviews), the SMF can be applied to a number of other attributional phenomena that result in illusory memories (e.g., *cryptomnesia*—that is, unconscious plagiarism; Marsh, Landau, & Hicks, 1997; misattributions in exclusion paradigms, such as the *false fame effect*; see Kelley & Jacoby, chapter 14; the *illusory truth effect*, in which participants' ratings of the truth [i.e., referential validity] of plausible statements about real-world situations increase with prior exposure, regardless of the actual truth of the statement; Bacon, 1979; Hasher, Goldstein, & Toppino, 1977). All of these phenomena reflect, in essence, source monitoring errors. Although not all of these paradigms are described as explicit source identification tasks, in some participants are told to avoid using information from a particular source in their answers (e.g., in cryptomnesia paradigms they are told to not give answers that have been previously provided), and all do, in fact, involve making attributions about the source of mental experiences.

We turn next to a specific class of source misattribution errors that has been especially well investigated—eyewitness suggestibility, or people's tendency to remember as part of a witnessed event information that was only suggested to them afterward. Systematic application of the principles of the SMF in recent years has advanced our understanding of the mechanisms underlying this phenomenon.

Eyewitness Suggestibility as Source Monitoring Error

The memorial task for eyewitnesses is to a large extent a source monitoring one. They must differentiate details of a witnessed event from related details such as relevant prior memories, general knowledge about events such as crimes, and, of particular interest here, memories of crime-specific information they are exposed to after the witnessed event (e.g., via police questioning, media exposure, casual conversations). Misattributing information from any of these sources to the witnessed event could have serious consequences, especially in cases where false information has been introduced (e.g., via misleading questioning by police, lawyers).

Many studies demonstrate that eyewitnesses can be led to report postevent suggestions as part of their memory for a witnessed event (see Belli & Loftus, 1994; Lindsay, 1994; Loftus, 1993; Zaragoza, Lane, Ackil, & Chambers, 1997, for reviews). Although there has been substantial controversy over the status of the original memory of the witnessed event after exposure to suggestion (see Lindsay, 1994; Loftus, 1993; Zaragoza et al., 1997, for reviews), it has become widely accepted among researchers in the eyewitness memory domain that the misinformation effect reflects, in great part, source confusion. That is to say, participants misattribute a memory from one source (postevent questions) to another source (the witnessed event). Thus, recent work has centered on more clearly delineating the circumstances under which source misattribution errors might be expected to obtain, and the factors that serve to increase/decrease these errors, in an eyewitness situation.

To maximize accuracy, most suggestibility studies carried out from the source monitoring perspective employ an adaptation of the three-phase suggestibility procedure in which the source identification requirements are made as clear as possible. Participants first "witness" an event (e.g., video of a crime). Later, in the context of a postevent narrative or questions about what they saw, participants are ex-

posed to some misleading suggestions (e.g., that the thief had a gun when, in fact, the thief had no weapon of any sort). During the test phase, participants are often explicitly informed that some of the information supplied in the postevent questions/narrative did not really appear in the original event (e.g., the video). They are then asked directly about their memory for the source of the suggestions (together with some filler items from the other source categories—that is, video only, both the video and questions, and new). Suggestibility is usually measured as participants' tendency to misattribute the misleading postevent information to the originally witnessed event (whether or not they also attribute it correctly to the postevent questions/narrative).[1]

Although the two events that need to be differentiated in an eyewitness situation (the originally witnessed event and the postevent questioning) should be clearly distinguishable in some respects (e.g., the first has richer visual detail), they share similar semantic information—including a common referent—and an abundance of contextual information (e.g., Lindsay, 1994). In fact, compared to actual eyewitness interrogations, objective overlap is maximized in the usual laboratory study because the postevent suggestions are typically embedded in a richly detailed account that essentially reinstates for the witness the event's contents and context (e.g., chronology). The fact that environmental context, such as the room and the experimenter, are typically also shared across the two events adds to the objective overlap. Given what we know about the effects of similarity in other source monitoring situations, perhaps it is not surprising that participants in suggestibility experiments become confused about the source of the suggested information. As mentioned earlier, evidence from other paradigms shows that increasing perceptual or semantic similarity between two sources increases the rate of source errors. For example, although people remembered the source of words quite well when they heard an experimenter read some of the words and imagined themselves saying some others, source errors increased when they were asked to distinguish between words the experimenter read aloud and words they imagined hearing *in the experimenter's voice* (Johnson et al., 1988). Likewise, increasing either the perceptual similarity of two speakers or the semantic similarity of the contents of their messages increases source errors (jointly increasing both forms of similarity makes the discrimination especially difficult; Lindsay et al., 1991).

Mitchell and Zaragoza (1999) shed some light on the relative importance of various dimensions of similarity for source monitoring in an eyewitness situation. They showed that reducing objective overlap between the originally witnessed event (a video) and the misleading postevent questioning episode (i.e., amount of true content information, chronology, environmental context) did not significantly improve participants' ability to discriminate between the two events as the source of the suggestions. In explaining this counterintuitive finding, Mitchell and Zaragoza proposed that as people attempt to answer postevent questions about the video they must reflect back on and reactivate their memory of the witnessed event (and perhaps image the suggested information as well). They argued that this process of reactivating and reflecting back on the witnessed event during postevent questioning may increase the functional similarity of the two events because it affords an opportunity for the postevent suggestions to acquire specific characteristics typical of the originally witnessed event (such as a high degree of sensory/perceptual detail). Alternatively, or in addition, as witnesses answer questions, they may create a representation (semantic product or mental model; Bransford & Johnson, 1973; Johnson-Laird, 1983) that includes elements from both the witnessed event and the suggestion, effectively binding them together. Then, when they are tested with the misinformation, it may activate elements from the original event that in turn might be taken as evidence that the misinformation was part of the event. In effect, people may base their judgment on a representation of their constructed understanding of an event rather than a representation of the event itself (e.g., Johnson, 1983; Reyna & Titcomb, 1997).

Consistent with the idea that the cognitive processes invoked during the postevent will determine the magnitude of the source misattribution effect, Zaragoza and Lane (1994) found that a postevent task, such as answering questions about the video, which required participants to retrieve the originally witnessed event while processing the misleading information, resulted in significantly more source misattributions than a task that did not require that they necessarily reflect back on the witnessed event (i.e., reading the misleading postevent information as a narrative). Re-

peatedly engaging in such reflective processing (e.g., responding to multiple questions about a scene in the video) increases errors (Zaragoza & Mitchell, 1996). Thus, it may be that the functional (as opposed to objective) similarity in cases where multiple events have the same referent is largely determined by the nature of the reflective operations that take place as the events are processed.

The hypothesis that suggestibility errors in this paradigm sometimes arise from the misattribution of specific qualitative characteristics (e.g., imagined perceptual detail) rather than (or more likely in addition to) general attributes such as a strong sense of familiarity is supported by the fact that participants in eyewitness suggestibility studies sometimes rate their false memories with high confidence (e.g., Zaragoza & Lane, 1994; Zaragoza & Mitchell, 1996) and claim to specifically "recollect" seeing the suggested information in the video (e.g., Zaragoza & Mitchell, 1996). Similarly, in other source memory paradigms, confidence in source judgments tends to be associated with higher levels of rated detail (e.g, Hashtroudi et al., 1990).

This is not to say that familiarity is never the basis of eyewitnesses' source decisions. Consistent with the idea that familiarity may be used when people set lax criteria, source errors decrease when the test format leads participants to consider more detailed information (e.g., Lindsay & Johnson, 1989; Multhaup, De Leonardis, & Johnson, 1999; Zaragoza & Koshmider, 1989; see also Dodson & Johnson, 1993). Likewise, Chambers and Zaragoza (1993) showed that eyewitnesses' identification of the source of postevent suggestion improves when the source of the suggestion is explicitly discredited (see also, for example, Dodd & Bradshaw, 1980; Underwood & Pezdek, 1998), although the beneficial effects of this discrediting decay quickly, as in the *sleeper effect* (a social persuasion phenomenon reflecting source monitoring failure, in which the impact of a persuasive message from a discredited source increases over time because people remember the message but forget they had a reason to discount it; e.g., Pratkanis, Greenwald, Leippe, & Baumgardner, 1988). The SMF predicts that eyewitness suggestibility would increase in situations in which the remember has but does not, or cannot, use available information and knowledge to prevent a source error—for example, by retrieving and reasoning from additional information (Johnson, Foley, Suengas, & Raye,

1988; Lindsay, 1994; Zaragoza & Lane, 1994; see also Ross, 1997). And, in fact, suggestibility has been shown to increase under conditions of speeded responding (Zaragoza & Lane, 1998).

It is interesting to note that although participants in suggestibility studies may confidently say they remember the suggested information from the witnessed event, they often also indicate that they remember, at quite high levels, that the suggested information was read in the postevent questions/narrative (e.g., Belli, Lindsay, Gales, & McCarthy, 1994; Fiedler, Walther, Armbruster, Fay, & Naumann, 1996; Zaragoza & Mitchell, 1996). Thus, even if a witness to an actual crime knows full well that some piece of information occurred in the context of postevent questioning (or other postevent exposure such as media coverage), they may still come to remember it as part of the originally witnessed event. In fact, even when people knowingly confabulate about a witnessed event (i.e., they are forced to generate false information in response to forced-recall questions), they sometimes later come to misremember their own confabulations as part of the witnessed event (Ackil & Zaragoza, 1998). This is consistent with the general source monitoring literature, which shows that individuals' awareness of their own cognitive operations at time 1 will not necessarily protect them from memory distortions at time 2. For example, individuals can know at time 1 that they are imagining an event and later, at time 2, believe they saw it, perhaps because the information regarding cognitive operations decays or other information becomes more salient (e.g., Durso & Johnson, 1980; Garry, Manning, Loftus, & Sherman, 1996; Goff & Roediger, 1998; Johnson, Raye, Wang, & Taylor, 1979; for evidence regarding the deleterious effects of explicit imagery instructions on eyewitness memory, see Zaragoza, Mitchell, & Drivdahl, 1997). The likelihood of such errors should increase with the ease of imagining (Dobson & Markham, 1993; Finke et al., 1988; see also Johnson et al., 1979). Findings such as these support the SMF assertion that memories are made up of collections of features (semantic and perceptual detail, cognitive operations, etc.) and that the accessibility, availability, and diagnosticity of these features change over time.

An increasingly active area of research in the eyewitness memory domain investigates developmental changes in source monitoring accuracy. For example, consistent with other findings in the source monitoring literature (e.g., Foley, Johnson, & Raye, 1983), Ackil and Zaragoza (1995) found that although no age group is completely resistant to source misattribution errors, young children (first- and fifth-graders) have an especially difficult time with source monitoring in eyewitness situations (see Qin, Quas, Redlich, & Goodman, 1997, for a general review of suggestibility in children). Although, relative to young adults, older adults often exhibit source memory deficits in other source monitoring situations (e.g., Glisky, Polster, & Routhieaux, 1995; Henkel, Johnson, & De Leonardis, 1998; Johnson, De Leonardis, Hashtroudi, & Ferguson, 1995; Schacter, Koutstaal, Johnson, Gross, & Angell, 1997), the picture from eyewitness paradigms is not clear. There is evidence to suggest both that older adults may be more suggestible than younger adults (e.g., Cohen & Faulkner, 1989) and that they may be no more suggestible than younger adults (e.g., Coxon & Valentine, 1997). The effects of aging on suggestibility thus remains an important issue in need of empirical attention.

Finally, we might note that the SMF is also useful for understanding other eyewitness suggestibility phenomena. As one example consider the case of *unconscious transference*, an eyewitness misidentification effect in which people identify in a lineup a previously viewed, but innocent, person (e.g., a bystander or someone seen in a mugshot; see Ross, Ceci, Dunning, & Toglia, 1994, for a review). From the SMF perspective, these errors are also likely source errors; the memory of the innocent person, acquired from the previous viewing, is misattributed to the criminal event (see, for example, Read, Tollestrup, Hammersley, McFadzen, & Christensen, 1990, for discussion of this and other possible factors).

As the empirical work discussed thus far illustrates, the SMF is a fruitful approach for systematically investigating both accurate and inaccurate memory. At the same time, several new lines of research have focused on refining some aspects of the source monitoring approach and on expanding its scope.

New Directions

Measuring Source Accuracy

Several groups of researchers have been working on better ways to measure source memory and on developing mathematical models of recognition and source monitoring processes.

Batchelder, Riefer, and colleagues have advanced a multinomial processing tree (MPT) approach that attempts to disentangle indices of old/new recognition (item detection) and source identification (discrimination) from various response biases likely to be operating in source identification tasks (e.g., Batchelder & Riefer, 1990). Additional efforts have been directed at improving the MPT approach to resolve ambiguities between memory and bias parameters and to extend the approach to multiple sources (e.g., Batchelder, Riefer, & Hu, 1994; Riefer, Hu, & Batchelder, 1994). The MPT approach has been criticized for simplifying high-threshold assumptions (e.g., Kinchla, 1994), and Batchelder et al. (1994) have proposed a low-threshold alternative and Bayen, Murnane, and Erdfelder (1996) have proposed a two-high-threshold alternative.

Jacoby and colleagues' process dissociation procedure also provides an approach to examining source memory. It employs two tasks that require source discriminations—an old/new recognition task (inclusion) and a source identification task (exclusion; see Kelley & Jacoby, chapter 14). The procedure is designed to generate estimates of "familiarity" and "recollection." Recollection allows one to discriminate familiar but nontarget items (e.g., list 1) from familiar, target items (e.g., list 2) in an "exclusion" recognition test that requires *yes* responses to list 2 old items and *no* to list 1 and new items. Process dissociation parameters for familiarity and recollection are similar to MPT parameters for item detection and source discrimination, and Buchner and colleagues have developed an MPT extension of the process dissociation procedure (Buchner, Erdfelder, & Vaterrodt-Plunnecke, 1995; see also the commentaries on this topic in *Consciousness & Cognition, 5(4)*).

Some researchers have proposed that signal-detection theory (SDT) models of the sort often used for recognition memory can account for source identification as well (e.g., Hoffman, 1997). Yonelinas (1994) combined an SDT approach with Jacoby's process dissociation procedure, proposing that familiarity is a signal-detection process (corresponding to d') whereas, as in Jacoby's procedure, recollection reflects a discrete retrieval process (i.e., with a threshold below which there is no recollection). Such a hybrid model is similar to earlier recognition models (e.g., Atkinson & Juola, 1974).

All of these techniques can help us extract systematic patterns from data, and each might be appropriate under some particular circumstances. However, as general theoretical models the process dissociation procedure and MPT approaches present an overly simplified way of thinking about memory because both imply that memories fall into discrete categories (e.g., familiar, recollected; detected, discriminated). In contrast, according to the SMF, the phenomenal experience of remembering can have intermediate qualities; neither familiarity nor recollection are discrete states. In addition, Dodson and Johnson (1996) have questioned the theoretical interpretation of the process dissociation procedure for not conceptually distinguishing between decisions based on phenomenal qualities (familiarity or specific detail) and processes by which those qualities arise (automatic vs controlled). For example, although familiarity may typically arise more quickly and automatically than specific detail, under some circumstances specific detail might arise quickly and automatically and under some familiarity might be used in a controlled way. Finally, SDT models have the advantage that they allow variations in amount of information relevant to judgments, but are limited in that they treat all information as falling on a single dimension. In contrast, the SMF emphasizes the multiple facets or features of memory, that features are not all equally diagnostic for any particular source attribution, that features are given flexible weights, and that decision thresholds vary depending on motives and circumstances.

Two recent developments are particularly interesting with respect to these issues. Consider variations in source information. For example, a participant might not remember which of four speakers said a word, but remember that it was one of the male speakers. Dodson et al. (1998) have proposed an extension of the MPT approach to estimate partial source information. A means for simplifying analyses involving multiple feature dimensions opens up the possibility of systematically studying the joint impact of memory characteristics in more complex situations (e.g., Bayen & Murnane, 1996; Johnson et al., 1995; Lindsay et al., 1991). The other development is an extension of signal detection methods to a multidimensional representation (Banks, Chen, & Prull, in press). This model is most consistent with the original descriptive theoretical framework proposed by Johnson and Raye (1981). It may provide an approach for systematically studying the effects of assigning differential feature weights.

In general, the increased attention to problems in measurement and to developing tractable formal models that address both more general (old/new recognition) and more specific source memory should further sharpen theoretical issues and help clarify our understanding of source attributions—both accurate and inaccurate.

Subjective Measures of Qualitative Characteristics of Memories

Understanding the qualitative characteristics that go into the phenomenal experience of remembering is of central interest in the SMF (e.g., Johnson et al., 1988; Suengas & Johnson, 1988). One way to measure the qualitative characteristics of people's memory is to ask them to discriminate between stimuli. Under the appropriate conditions (e.g., if asked which of two previously presented stimuli was red), accurate performance requires that the target characteristic is represented in memory. Such discrimination tasks have been used regularly to assess qualitative characteristics of memory (e.g., color, location, voice), and most of the studies discussed in previous sections are variations on this theme. Another way to assess memory characteristics is to score recall protocols not just for whether an event is remembered but for qualitative characteristics pertaining to how it is remembered (e.g., Brewer, 1988; Hashtroudi et al., 1990; Johnson, O'Connor, & Cantor, 1997).

Yet another way to assess people's memory for specific qualitative characteristics is to ask them for subjective reports. There has been a recent renewal of interest in such subjective measures (e.g., Brewer, 1988; Gardiner, chapter 15; Johnson et al., 1988; Tulving, 1985). For example, the remember/know paradigm asks people whether they are "recollecting" an event (i.e., they can remember specific memorial information such as color or temporal information) or only "know" that an event occurred in the past (i.e., they cannot remember specific information) (see Gardiner, chapter 15; Rajaram & Roediger, 1997, for reviews). Though useful, this procedure does not capture the nuances of subjective experience, and Gardiner and colleagues have begun asking participants about the basis for their memory decisions (e.g., Gardiner, Ramponi, & Richardson-Klavehn, 1998). These protocols can then be scored for specific characteristics (see also

Johnson et al., 1988; Johnson, Bush, & Mitchell, 1998).

More specific information is also obtained by using a Memory Characteristics Questionnaire (e.g., Johnson et al., 1988). Such questionnaires ask people to rate their phenomenal experience of both general memorial characteristics (e.g., "My memory for this event is: 1 = dim to 7 = sharp/clear") and/or more specific attributes in several categories such as perceptual detail (e.g., "My memory for this event involves smell: 1 = little or none to 7 = a lot"), temporal information (e.g., "My memory for the time when the event takes place is: 1 = vague to 7 = clear/distinct"), associated or supporting information (e.g., "I remember events relating to this memory that took place in advance of the event: 1 = not at all to 7 = yes, clearly"), and so on.

There is a fairly substantial body of research showing that people's subjective reports about their memory are sensitive to various manipulations and that memories from various sources differ in their qualitative characteristics (see, for example, Gardiner, chapter 15; Johnson et al., 1993; Rajaram & Roediger, 1997, for reviews). For example, sensory-perceptual and temporal information play a central role in autobiographical memory (e.g., Conway, 1992), and confidence in autobiographical memories increases with the amount of visual information recalled (Brewer, 1988). Consistent with this, Memory Characteristics Questionnaire ratings are typically higher for perceived than for imagined events (e.g., Suengas & Johnson, 1988; McGinnis & Roberts, 1996) and higher for memories of recent autobiographical events than for memories of older autobiographical events (i.e., those from childhood; e.g., Johnson et al., 1988). Other studies confirm that memory errors are associated with misattributing specific qualitative characteristics (e.g., voice) to a particular (in this case erroneous) source (e.g., Mather, Henkel, & Johnson, 1997). Importantly, studies also show that illusory and veridical memories differ in rated memory characteristics (e.g., Conway, Collins, Gathercole, & Anderson, 1996; Mather et al., 1997; Norman & Schacter, 1997; see, e.g., Schacter et al., 1996, for relevant neurophysiological evidence). Such characteristics may not be used, and sufficiently thorough evaluative processes may not be engaged, under all circumstances (e.g., when source identification is not an explicit focus of the task, Jacoby et al., 1989; Lindsay & Johnson, 1989; Raye, Johnson, & Taylor, 1980;

see, Johnson, Kounios, & Nolde, 1996; Johnson, Nolde et al., 1997, for evidence that brain activity, and presumably the basis on which participants make source decisions, varies with encoding and test conditions), but people can often be more accurate in their remembering under circumstances that induce them to engage in more careful evaluation of available source-specifying information (e.g., Mather et al., 1997; Multhaup, 1995; Multhaup et al., 1999). Thus, it seems likely that continued systematic investigation of the qualitative characteristics of memory, and the phenomenal experiences they engender, will inform our understanding of both accurate and inaccurate memory.

Inducing Autobiographical Memories

Recent studies have established that some adults (approximately 25% in any given study) can be led to form (false) autobiographical memories for complex events from their childhood that never occurred—for example, that they spilled punch at a wedding (e.g., Hyman & Pentland, 1996; Loftus & Pickrell, 1995; but see Pezdek, Finger, & Hodge, 1997; see also, for example, Ceci, Croutteau Huffman, Smith, & Loftus, 1994 for similar demonstrations with children). The procedures used to induce false memories in these studies generally involve several of the factors that have been shown to produce source confusion when manipulated in isolation in the laboratory (e.g., imaging, repetition, high demand, lax criteria).

One particularly interesting direction for this research involves examining the relationship between individual difference factors (e.g., imaging ability, hypnotizability, dissociative tendencies) and the likelihood that false autobiographical memories can be created (see, for example, the Special Issue of *Applied Cognitive Psychology, 1998* (vol. 12): "Individual Differences and Memory Distortion"). Based on the SMF, individual differences related to any of the factors shown to affect source monitoring (e.g., vividness of images, emotional self-focus, feature weighting, the criteria adopted, availability of related knowledge) would be expected to predict the degree of source confusion exhibited. Consistent with this, Hyman and Billings (1998) found that among college students, scores on tests of dissociative tendencies (i.e., Dissociative Experiences Scale) and of imaging ability/

responsiveness to suggestion (i.e., Creative Imagination Scale) were positively correlated with false memory creation (see also Winograd, Peluso, & Glover, 1998). However, other factors, such as social desirability, did not appear to be related to the rate of false memory creation in this study. Although more work is needed, this line of inquiry will help to connect our understanding of the underlying mechanisms of source confusion derived from laboratory studies with individual differences that affect susceptibility to false autobiographical memory creation.

Interpersonal Reality Monitoring

Another promising line of research investigates the processes by which we judge the sources of other people's memories—*interpersonal reality monitoring* (e.g., Johnson et al., 1998; Keogh & Markham, 1998; Schooler, Gerhard, & Loftus, 1986). Results of a recent study showed that the judgment context (in this case, whether participants made judgments regarding the veracity of other people's memory accounts under high- or low-suspicion orienting conditions) influenced the weights that participants assigned to perceptual and emotional detail and the mix of heuristic and systematic processes engaged while making the judgments (Johnson et al., 1998). These data confirm that interpersonal reality monitoring can be understood in terms of basic SMF principles. Moreover, in addition to clarifying how it is we go about assessing the veridicality of others' memories, these experiments suggest questions about interpersonal reality monitoring in several applied domains, especially those in which professionals must evaluate the veracity of people's accounts of past events.

For example, *statement reality analysis* (or *statement validity analysis*) is a framework employed in German and Swedish courtrooms to expertly evaluate witness credibility. This approach exemplifies the basic tenets of the SMF: individuals engaged in statement reality analysis weigh characteristics of the information reported, such as the quantity and vividness of emotional and perceptual detail, taken together with their knowledge and beliefs about situational and motivational factors (e.g. Steller, 1989; Undeutsch, 1989). Sporer (1997) recently compared forensic assessment of the contents of witnesses' reports, known as criterion-based content analysis, and reality monitoring criteria (e.g., Johnson & Raye, 1981) and found that training with reality monitoring criteria allowed participant judges to rate the veracity of "witnesses'" accounts at greater than chance levels and slightly better than with the criterion-based content analysis criteria (although there are interpretive difficulties with the findings regarding relative accuracy with the two sets of criteria). Nevertheless, while there is empirical support for the underlying assumptions of the statement validity analysis/criterion-based content analysis approach (e.g., on average, true memories have more perceptual detail than false memories), empirical work on source monitoring also suggests caution in drawing firm conclusions about any particular memory (Johnson et al., 1993).

Cases of alleged recovered repressed memories of childhood sexual abuse especially highlight the need to understand interpersonal reality monitoring.[2] Putting aside the controversial issue of whether or not assessing the historical truth of a memory is clinically beneficial, each court case involving recovered memory experiences illustrates the importance of accurate assessment of the veracity of these accounts, not only by clients but also by their families, therapists, judges, and juries. Given what we know about source monitoring more generally, it seems likely that people involved in these cases may sometimes make this assessment with overconfidence—that is, without sufficient understanding of either intra-individual or interpersonal reality monitoring processes (e.g., the impact of imagination, lax source monitoring criteria; e.g., Lindsay & Read, 1994). Furthermore, it seems likely that the desire to believe the past was a certain way, or to find a cause for one's own (or one's client's) distress, might alter the assumed diagnosticity of some memory characteristics—for both clients and therapists. For example, people may minimize perceptual details and/or put extra trust in affective content when judging whether a memory is veridical under such circumstances (see Johnson et al., 1998, for evidence that weights assigned to different attributes may depend on people's prior assumptions). Thus, interpersonal reality monitoring among memory-exploring professionals may itself serve as a fruitful focus of scientific inquiry.

Empirical work is just beginning to investigate the processes used by memory-exploring professionals, and the effectiveness of their ability to monitor the veracity of other people's memories of past events (e.g., Sporer, 1997; Ceci et al., 1994). Nevertheless, progress is being made both in communicating theoretical ideas and empirical results from laboratory studies to memory-exploring professionals and in communicating to experimental psychologists the practical issues that these professionals face with regard to interpersonal reality monitoring (e.g., Belli & Loftus, 1994; Lindsay, in press; Lindsay & Briere, 1997; Lindsay & Read, 1995; Read & Lindsay, 1997).

Knowledge, Beliefs, and Stereotypes

Most of our discussion thus far has centered on source monitoring as it applies to episodic memory. However, recent research confirms that the SMF can also be applied to stereotypes, attitudes, beliefs, and other forms of "nonepisodic" knowledge. For example, Mather, Johnson, and De Leonardis (1999) demonstrated the impact of stereotypes on the accuracy of source memory (see also Sherman & Bessenoff, 1999). This study showed that while both younger and older adults were better at remembering the source of stereotypically consistent information (i.e., they could more accurately attribute statements to speakers if the statements were consistent with the speakers' assigned political affiliation than if they were inconsistent), older adults were at a disproportionate disadvantage when information was inconsistent with an established stereotype. In addition, this study showed that people may be somewhat more prone to the deleterious effects of stereotype-induction when something (in this case focusing on their feelings) keeps them from fully encoding source-specifying information that could be used later for accurate source discrimination (see also Hashtroudi et al., 1994; Johnson et al., 1996). Other research has investigated the role of source monitoring in producing and sustaining stereotypes (e.g., Banaji & Greenwald, 1995; Slusher & Anderson, 1987). It seems reasonable that the SMF can provide a fertile avenue for future investigations of not only stereotypes but also attitudes, beliefs, and other phenomena that typically have been investigated within the domain of social cognition (e.g., Wilson & Brekke, 1994).

Brain Mechanisms

Based on neuropsychological studies of brain-damaged patients, it appears that two regions are particularly critical for source memory. Lesions in medial-temporal or diencephalic areas disrupt the feature binding processes required for encoding and consolidating complex memories (e.g., Squire & Knowlton, 1995) and lesions in the frontal regions disrupt self-initiated processes that promote binding (e.g., through maintaining activation) and that are often critical for retrieval and evaluation (e.g., Stuss & Benson, 1986). Consistent with this pattern, relative to younger adults, older adults show source memory deficits that are related to their performance on neuropsychological tests of medial-temporal and frontal function (Craik, Morris, Morris, & Loewen, 1990; Glisky et al., 1995; Henkel et al., 1998; Schacter, Koutstaal, & Norman, 1997). Frontal damage often results in deficits on source identification tasks (e.g., Schacter, Harbluk, & McLachlan, 1984; Shimamura & Squire, 1987) and, especially combined with damage to certain other areas (e.g., basal forebrain), sometimes results in profound source confusions called confabulations (e.g., DeLuca & Cicerone, 1991; Johnson, Hayes, D'Esposito & Raye, in press). Theories of confabulation (e.g., Baddeley & Wilson, 1986; Burgess & Shallice, 1996; Johnson, 1991; Moscovitch, 1995) converge on the factors outlined in the SMF, although with varying degrees of emphasis on specific aspects (Johnson & Raye, 1998). Furthermore, in a recent discussion of memory distortion from a cognitive neuroscience perspective, Schacter, Norman, and Koutstaal (1998) adopted a general theoretical position similar to the SMF. More specific links between neural mechanisms and the theoretical ideas embodied in the SMF (e.g., Johnson, Hayes et al., in press) await more systematic studies designed to explore source monitoring using measures of cortical activity—such work is just now beginning.

Recent studies using electrophysiological (ERP; e.g., Johnson, Kounios, & Nolde, 1996; Wilding & Rugg, 1996) and neuroimaging (fMRI; e.g., Nolde, Johnson, & D'Esposito, 1998; Nyberg et al., 1996; Zorrilla, Aguirre, Zarahn, Cannon, & D'Esposito, 1996) techniques to examine the cortical activity of healthy young adults engaged in source monitoring tasks have found activation in both right and left prefrontal cortex. Furthermore, a review of studies that collected neuroimaging data during episodic memory tests suggests that relatively simple episodic remembering engages right prefrontal cortex and more reflectively demanding episodic remembering

engages left prefrontal cortex as well (Nolde, Johnson, & Raye, 1998). Taken together, these results suggest the Cortical Asymmetry of Reflective Activity (CARA) hypothesis. CARA is the working hypothesis that heuristic source monitoring processes may be supported by right prefrontal cortex and systematic processes by left (or left and right) prefrontal cortex (Johnson & Raye, 1998; Nolde et al., 1998). CARA remains to be cashed-out; specifying the component processes (e.g., Johnson, 1997) involved in heuristic and systematic mental activities, and how they interact with various attributes of memories such as visual information, cognitive operations, and emotional detail, is one of the challenges ahead.

Acknowledgment   Preparation of this chapter was supported by NIA grant AG09253. We are grateful to Carol Raye and Maria Zaragoza for lively discussions of these topics and thoughtful comments on an earlier draft. We also thank Sean Lane, Mara Mather, and John Reeder for helpful comments on an earlier draft.

Notes

1. While other types of source errors are obviously possible (e.g., witnesses might come to remember that something they did see was only suggested to them later), evidence suggests that these types of errors are more rare (Belli, Lindsay, Gales, & McCarthy, 1994; Zaragoza & Lane, 1994). For other examples of cross-modality source monitoring errors see, for example, Henkel, Franklin, and Johnson, 1999; Intraub and Hoffman, 1992.

2. Thorough reviews of the psycho-sociolegal phenomenon of alleged recovered repressed memories of childhood abuse, and the relevant empirical findings, are available elsewhere (e.g., the special issues of *Applied Cognitive Psychology, 8* (1994); *Consciousness and Cognition, 4* (1994); *Current Directions in Psychological Science, 6(3)* (1997); see also, for example, Conway, 1997; Lindsay & Read, 1994, 1995; Loftus, 1997; Read & Lindsay, 1997).

References

Ackil, J. K., & Zaragoza, M. S. (1995). Developmental differences in eyewitness suggestibility and memory for source. *Journal of Experimental Child Psychology, 60,* 57–83.

Ackil, J. K., & Zaragoza, M. S. (1998). Memorial consequences of forced confabulation: Age differences in susceptibility to false memories. *Developmental Psychology, 34,* 1358–1372.

Atkinson, R. C., & Juola, J. F. (1974). Search and decision processes in recognition memory. In D. H. Krantz, R. C. Atkinson, R. D. Luce, & P. Suppes (Eds.), *Contemporary developments in mathematical psychology* (pp. 242–293). San Francisco: Freeman.

Bacon, F. T. (1979). Credibility of repeated statements: Memory for trivia. *Journal of Experimental Psychology: Human Learning and Memory, 5,* 241–252.

Baddeley, A. D., & Wilson, B. (1986). Amnesia, autobiographical memory, and confabulation. In D. Rubin (Ed.), *Autobiographical memory* (pp. 225–252). New York: Cambridge University Press.

Banaji, M. R., & Greenwald, A. G. (1995). Implicit gender stereotyping in judgments of fame. *Journal of Personality and Social Psychology, 68,* 181–198.

Banks, W. P., Chen, Y., & Prull, M. W. (in press). Awareness and memory: Is information stratified into conscious and unconscious components? In B. H. Challis & B. M. Velichkovsky (Eds.), *Stratification of consciousness and cognition.* Amsterdam: John Benjamins Publishers.

Bartlett, F. C. (1932/1995). *Remembering: A study in experimental and social psychology.* New York: Cambridge University Press [reprint].

Batchelder, W. H., & Riefer, D. M. (1990). Multinomial processing models of source monitoring. *Psychological Review, 97,* 548–564.

Batchelder, W. H., Riefer, D. M., & Hu, X. (1994). Measuring memory factors in source monitoring: Reply to Kinchla. *Psychological Review, 101,* 172–176.

Bayen, U. J., & Murnane, K. (1996). Aging and the use of perceptual and temporal information in source memory tasks. *Psychology and Aging, 11,* 293–303.

Bayen, U. J., Murnane, K., & Erdfelder, E. (1996). Source discrimination, item detection, and multinomial models of source monitoring. *Journal of Experimental Psychology: Learning, Memory, and Cognition, 22,* 197–215.

Belli, R. F., Lindsay, D. S., Gales, M. S., & McCarthy, T. T. (1994). Memory impairment and source misattribution in postevent misinformation experiments with short retention intervals. *Memory & Cognition, 22,* 40–54.

Belli, R. F., & Loftus, E. F. (1994). Recovered memories of childhood abuse: A source monitoring perspective. In S. J. Lynn & J. W. Rhue (Eds.), *Dissociation: Clinical and theoretical perspectives* (pp. 415–433). New York: Guilford Press.

Bransford, J. D., Barclay, J. R., & Franks, J. J. (1972). Sentence memory: A constructive versus interpretive approach. *Cognitive Psychology, 3,* 193–209.

Bransford, J. D., & Johnson, M. K. (1973). Considerations of some problems of comprehension. In W. Chase (Ed.), *Visual information processing* (pp. 383–438). New York: Academic Press.

Brewer, W. F. (1988). Qualitative analysis of the recalls of randomly sampled autobiographical events. In M. M. Gruneberg, P. E. Morris, & R. N. Sykes (Eds.), *Practical aspects of memory: Current research and issues, Volume 1: Memory in everyday life* (pp. 263–268). New York: John Wiley.

Buchner, A., Erdfelder, E., & Vaterrodt-Plunnecke, B. (1995). Toward unbiased measurement of conscious and unconscious memory processes within the process dissociation framework. *Journal of Experimental Psychology: General, 123,* 137–160.

Burgess, P. W., & Shallice, T. (1996). Confabulation and the control of recollection. *Memory, 4,* 359–411.

Ceci, S. J., Crotteau Huffman, M. L., Smith, E., & Loftus, E. F. (1994). Repeatedly thinking about non-events. *Consciousness and Cognition, 3,* 388–407.

Chambers, K. L., & Zaragoza, M. S. (1993, November). *The effect of source credibility and delay on eyewitness suggestibility.* Poster presented at the annual meeting of the Psychonomic Society, Washington, DC.

Cohen, G., & Faulkner, D. (1989). Age differences in source forgetting: Effects on reality monitoring and on eyewitness testimony. *Psychology and Aging, 4,* 10–17.

Conway, M. A. (1992). A structural model of autobiographical memory. In M. A. Conway, D. C. Rubin, H. Spinnler, & W. Wagenaar (Eds.), *Theoretical perspectives on autobiographical memory* (pp. 167–193). Boston, MA: Kluwer Academic Publishers.

Conway, M. A. (Ed.). (1997). *Recovered memories and false memories.* Oxford: Oxford University Press.

Conway, M. A., Collins, A. F., Gathercole, S. E., & Anderson, S. J. (1996). Recollections of true and false autobiographical memories. *Journal of Experimental Psychology: General, 125*, 69–95.

Coxon, P., & Valentine, T. (1997). The effects of the age of eyewitnesses on the accuracy and suggestibility of their testimony. *Applied Cognitive Psychology, 11*, 415–430.

Craik, F. I. M., Morris, L. W., Morris, R. G., & Loewen, E. R. (1990). Relations between source amnesia and frontal lobe functioning in older adults. *Psychology and Aging, 5*, 148–151.

Deese, J. (1959). On the prediction of occurrence of particular verbal intrusions in immediate recall. *Journal of Experimental Psychology, 58*, 17–22.

DeLuca, J., & Cicerone, K. D. (1991). Confabulations following aneurysm of the anterior communicating artery. *Cortex, 27*, 417–423.

Dobson, M., & Markham, R. (1993). Imagery ability and source monitoring: Implications for eyewitness memory. *British Journal of Psychology, 32*, 111–118.

Dodd, D. H., & Bradshaw, J. M. (1980). Leading questions and memory: Pragmatic constraints. *Journal of Verbal Learning and Verbal Behavior, 19*, 695–704.

Dodson, C. S., Holland, P. W., & Shimamura, A. P. (1998). On the recollection of specific- and partial-source information. *Journal of Experimental Psychology: Learning, Memory, and Cognition, 24*, 1121–1136.

Dodson, C. S., & Johnson, M. K. (1993). Rate of false source attributions depends on how questions are asked. *American Journal of Psychology, 106*, 541–557.

Dodson, C. S., & Johnson, M. K. (1996). Some problems with the process-dissociation approach to memory. *Journal of Experimental Psychology: General, 125*, 181–194.

Durso, F. T., & Johnson, M. K. (1980). The effects of orienting tasks on recognition, recall, and modality confusion of pictures and words. *Journal of Verbal Learning and Verbal Behavior, 19*, 416–429.

Fiedler, K., Walther, E., Armbruster, T., Fay, D., & Naumann, U. (1996). Do you *really* know what you have seen? Intrusion errors and presuppositions effects on constructive memory. *Journal of Experimental Social Psychology, 32*, 484–511.

Finke, R. A., Johnson, M. K., & Shyi, G. C. W. (1988). Memory confusions for real and imagined completions of symmetrical visual patterns. *Memory & Cognition, 16*, 133–137.

Foley, M. A., Johnson, M. K., & Raye, C. L. (1983). Age-related changes in confusion between memories for thoughts and memories for speech. *Child Development, 54*, 51–60.

Gardiner, J. M., Ramponi, C., & Richardson-Klavehn, A. (1998). Experiences of remembering, knowing, and guessing. *Consciousness and Cognition, 7*, 1–26.

Garry, M., Manning, C. G., Loftus, E. F., & Sherman, S. J. (1996). Imagination inflation: Imagining a childhood event inflates confidence that it occurred. *Psychonomic Bulletin & Review, 3*, 208–214.

Glisky, E. L., Polster, M. R., & Routhieaux, B. C. (1995). Double dissociation between item and source memory. *Neuropsychology, 9*, 229–235.

Goff, L. M., & Roediger, H. L. (1998). Imagination inflation for action events: Repeated imaginings lead to illusory recollections. *Memory & Cognition, 26*, 20–33.

Gronlund, S. D., Edwards, M. B., & Ohrt, D. D. (1997). Comparison of the retrieval of item versus spatial position information. *Journal of Experimental Psychology: Learning, Memory, & Cognition, 23*, 1261–1274.

Gruppuso, V., Lindsay, D. S., & Kelley, C. M. (1997). The process-dissociation procedure and similarity: Defining and estimating recollection and familiarity in recognition memory. *Journal of Experimental Psychology: Learning, Memory, and Cognition, 23*, 259–278.

Hasher, L., Goldstein, D., & Toppino, T. (1977). Frequency and the conference of referential validity. *Journal of Verbal Learning and Verbal Behavior, 16*, 107–112.

Hashtroudi, S., Johnson, M. K., & Chrosniak, L. D. (1990). Aging and qualitative characteristics of memories for perceived and imagined complex events. *Psychology and Aging, 5*, 119–126.

Hashtroudi, S., Johnson, M. K., Vnek, N., & Ferguson, S. A. (1994). Aging and the effects of affective and factual focus on source monitoring and recall. *Psychology and Aging, 9*, 160–170.

Henkel, L. A., Franklin, N., & Johnson, M. K. (1999). *Cross-modal source monitoring confusions between perceived and imagined events.* Manuscript submitted for publication.

Henkel, L. A., Johnson, M. K., & De Leonardis, D. M. (1998). Aging and source monitoring: Cognitive processes and neuropsychological correlates. *Journal of Experimental Psychology: General, 127*, 251–268.

Hoffman, H. G. (1997). Role of memory strength in reality monitoring decisions:

Evidence from source attribution biases. *Journal of Experimental Psychology: Learning, Memory, and Cognition, 23*, 371–383.

Hyman, I. E., Jr., & Billings, F. J. (1998). Individual differences and the creation of false childhood memories. *Memory, 6*, 1–20.

Hyman, I. E., Jr., & Pentland, J. (1996). The role of mental imagery in the creation of false childhood memories. *Journal of Memory and Language, 35*, 101–117.

Intraub, H., & Hoffman, J. E. (1992). Reading and visual memory: Remembering scenes that were never seen. *American Journal of Psychology, 105*, 101–114.

Jacoby, L. L., Woloshyn, V., & Kelley, C. (1989). Becoming famous without being recognized: Unconscious influences of memory produced by dividing attention. *Journal of Experimental Psychology: General, 118*, 115–125.

Jenkins, J. J., & Russell, W. A. (1952). Associative clustering during recall. *Journal of Abnormal and Social Psychology, 47*, 818–821.

Johnson, M. K. (1983). A multiple entry, modular memory system. In G. H. Bower (Ed.), *The psychology of learning and motivation: Advances in research theory* (Vol. 17; pp. 81–123). New York: Academic Press.

Johnson, M. K. (1985). The origin of memories. In P. C. Kendall (Ed.), *Advances in cognitive-behavioral research and therapy* (Vol. 4; pp. 1–27). New York: Academic Press.

Johnson, M. K. (1991). Reality monitoring: Evidence from confabulation in organic disease patients. In G. P. Prigatano & D. L. Schacter (Eds.), *Awareness of deficit after brain injury: Clinical and theoretical issues* (pp. 176–197). New York: Oxford University Press.

Johnson, M. K. (1997). Identifying the origin of mental experience. In M. S. Myslobodsky (Ed.), *The mythomanias: The nature of deception and self-deception* (pp. 133–180). Mahwah, NJ: Erlbaum.

Johnson, M. K., Bransford, J. D., & Solomon, S. K. (1973). Memory for tacit implications of sentences. *Journal of Experimental Psychology, 98*, 203–204.

Johnson, M. K., Bush, J. G., & Mitchell, K. J. (1998). Interpersonal reality monitoring: Judging the sources of other people's memories. *Social Cognition, 16*, 199–224.

Johnson, M. K., De Leonardis, D. M., Hashtroudi, S., & Ferguson, S. A. (1995). Aging and single versus multiple cues in source monitoring. *Psychology and Aging, 10*, 507–517.

Johnson, M. K., Foley, M. A., & Leach, K. (1988). The consequences for memory of imagining in another person's voice. *Memory & Cognition, 16*, 337–342.

Johnson, M. K., Foley, M. A., Suengas, A. G., & Raye, C. L. (1988). Phenomenal characteristics of memories for perceived and imagined autobiographical events. *Journal of Experimental Psychology: General, 117*, 371–376.

Johnson, M. K., Hashtroudi, S., & Lindsay, D. S. (1993). Source monitoring. *Psychological Bulletin, 114*, 3–28.

Johnson, M. K., Hayes, S. M., D'Esposito, M., & Raye, C. L. (in press). Confabulation. In J. Grafman & F. Boller, *Handbook of neuropsychology* (2nd ed.). Amsterdam, Netherlands: Elsevier Science.

Johnson, M. K., Kahan, T. L., & Raye, C. L. (1984). Dreams and reality monitoring. *Journal of Experimental Psychology: General, 113*, 329–344.

Johnson, M. K., Kounios, J., & Nolde, S. F. (1996). Electrophysiological brain activity and memory source monitoring. *NeuroReport, 7*, 2929–2932.

Johnson, M. K., Kounios, J., & Reeder, J. A. (1994). Time-course studies of reality monitoring and recognition. *Journal of Experimental Psychology: Learning, Memory, and Cognition, 20*, 1409–1419.

Johnson, M. K., Nolde, S. F., & De Leonardis, D. M. (1996). Emotional focus and source monitoring. *Journal of Memory and Language, 35*, 135–156.

Johnson, M. K., Nolde, S. F., Mather, M., Kounios, J., Schacter, D. L., & Curran, T. (1997). The similarity of brain activity associated with true and false recognition memory depends on test format. *Psychological Science, 8*, 250–257.

Johnson, M. K., O'Connor, M., & Cantor, J. (1997). Confabulation, memory deficits, and frontal dysfunction. *Brain and Cognition, 34*, 189–206.

Johnson, M. K., & Raye, C. L. (1981). Reality monitoring. *Psychological Review, 88*, 67–85.

Johnson, M. K., & Raye, C. L. (1998). False memories and confabulation. *Trends in Cognitive Sciences, 2*, 137–145.

Johnson, M. K., Raye, C. L., Wang, A. Y., & Taylor, T. H. (1979). Fact and fantasy: The roles of accuracy and variability in confusing imaginations with perceptual experiences. *Journal of Experimental Psychology: Human Learning and Memory, 5*, 229–240.

Johnson-Laird, P. N. (1983). *Mental models.* Cambridge, MA: Harvard University Press.

Keogh, L., & Markham, R. (1998). Judgements of other people's memory reports: Differences in reports as a function of imagery vividness. *Applied Cognitive Psychology, 12*, 159–171.

Kinchla, R. A. (1994). Comments on Batchelder and Riefer's multinomial model for source monitoring. *Psychological Review, 101*, 166–171.

Kolers, P. A., & Roediger, H. L. (1984). Procedures of mind. *Journal of Verbal Learning and Verbal Behavior, 23*, 425–449.

Kroll, N. E. A., Knight, R. T., Metcalfe, J., Wolf, E. S., & Tulving, E. (1996). Cohesion failure as a source of memory illusions. *Journal of Memory and Language, 35*, 176–196.

Lindsay, D. S. (in press). Recovered-memory experiences. In S. Taub (Ed.), *The legal treatment of recovered memories of child sexual abuse*. Springfield, IL: Charles C. Thomas.

Lindsay, D. S. (1994). Memory source monitoring and eyewitness suggestibility. In D. F. Ross, J. D. Read, & M. P. Toglia (Eds.), *Adults eyewitness testimony: Current trends and developments* (pp. 27–55). New York: Cambridge University Press.

Lindsay, D. S., & Briere, J. (1997). The controversy regarding recovered memories of childhood sexual abuse: Pitfalls, bridges, and future directions. *Journal of Interpersonal Violence, 12*, 631–647.

Lindsay, D. S., & Johnson, M. K. (1989). The eyewitness suggestibility effect and memory for source. *Memory & Cognition, 17*, 349–358.

Lindsay, D. S., Johnson, M. K., & Kwon, P. (1991). Developmental changes in memory source monitoring. *Journal of Experimental Child Psychology, 52*, 297–318.

Lindsay, D. S., & Read, J. D. (1994). Psychotherapy and memories of childhood sexual abuse: A cognitive perspective. *Applied Cognitive Psychology, 8*, 281–338.

Lindsay, D. S., & Read, J. D. (1995). "Memory work" and recovered memories of childhood sexual abuse: Scientific evidence and public, professional, and personal issues. *Psychology, Public Policy, and Law, 1*, 846–908.

Loftus, E. F. (1993). Made in memory: Distortions in recollections after misleading information. In D. L. Medin (Ed.), *The psychology of learning and motivation: Advances in theory and research* (pp. 187–215). New York: Academic Press.

Loftus, E. F. (1997, September). Creating false memories. *Scientific American, 277*, 71–75.

Loftus, E. F., & Pickrell, J. E. (1995). The formation of false memories. *Psychiatric Annals, 25*, 720–725.

Marsh, R. L., & Hicks, J. L. (1998). Test formats change source-monitoring decision processes. *Journal of Experimental Psychology: Learning, Memory, and Cognition, 24*, 1137–1151.

Marsh, R. L., Landau, J. D., & Hicks, J. L. (1997). Contributions of inadequate source monitoring to unconscious plagiarism during idea generation. *Journal of Experimental Psychology: Learning, Memory, and Cognition, 23*, 886–897.

Mather, M., Johnson, M. K., & De Leonardis, D. M. (1999). Stereotype reliance in source monitoring: Age differences and neuropsychological test correlates. *Cognitive Neuropsychology, 16*, 437–458.

Mather, M., Henkel, L. A., & Johnson, M. K. (1997). Evaluating characteristics of false memories: Remember/know judgments and memory characteristics questionnaire compared. *Memory & Cognition, 25*, 826–837.

McGinnis, D., & Roberts, P. (1996). Qualitative characteristics of vivid memories attributed to real and imagined experiences. *American Journal of Psychology, 109*, 59–77.

Mitchell, K. J., & Zaragoza, M. S. (1999). *On the relative contribution of objective overlap and reflective processing to source confusion in an eyewitness situation.* Manuscript in preparation, Princeton University.

Moscovitch, M. (1995). Confabulation. In D. L. Schacter (Ed.), *Memory distortion: How minds, brains, and societies reconstruct the past* (pp. 226–251). Cambridge, MA: Harvard University Press.

Multhaup, K. S. (1995). Aging, source, and decision criteria: When false fame errors do and do not occur. *Psychology and Aging, 10*, 492–497.

Multhaup, K. S., De Leonardis, D. M., & Johnson, M. K. (1999). Source memory and eyewitness suggestibility in older adults. *Journal of General Psychology, 126*, 74–84.

Neisser, U. (1967). *Cognitive psychology.* New York: Appleton-Century-Crofts.

Nolde, S. F., Johnson, M. K., & Raye, C. L. (1998). The role of prefrontal cortex during tests of episodic memory. *Trends in Cognitive Sciences, 2*, 399–406.

Nolde, S. F., Johnson, M. K., & D'Esposito, M. (1998). Left prefrontal activation during episodic remembering: An event-related fMRI study. *NeuroReport, 9*, 3509–3514.

Norman, K. A., & Schacter, D. L. (1997). False recognition in younger and older adults: Exploring the characteristics of illusory memories. *Memory & Cognition, 25*, 838–848.

Nyberg, L., McIntosh, A. R., Cabeza, R., Habib, R., Houle, S., & Tulving, E. (1996). General and specific brain regions involved in encoding and retrieval of events: What, where, and when. *Proceedings of the National Academy of Science, 93*, 11280–11285.

Pezdek, K., Finger, K., & Hodge, D. (1997). Planting false childhood memories: The role of event plausibility. *Psychological Science, 8*, 437–441.

Pratkanis, A. R., Greenwald, A. G., Leippe, M. R., & Baumgardner, M. H. (1988). In search of reliable persuasion effects: III. The sleeper effect is dead. Long live the sleeper effect. *Journal of Personality and Social Psychology, 54*, 203–218.

Qin, J., Quas, J. A., Redlich, A. D., & Goodman, G. S. (1997). Children's eyewitness testimony: Memory development in the legal context. In N. Cowan (Ed.), *The development of memory in childhood* (pp. 301–341). Hove, England: Psychology Press/Erlbaum.

Rabinowitz, J. C. (1989). Judgments of origin and generation effects: Comparisons between young and elderly adults. *Psychology and Aging, 4*, 259–268.

Rajaram, S., & Roediger, H. L. (1997). Remembering and knowing as states of consciousness during retrieval. In J. D. Cohen & J. W. Schooler (Eds.), *Scientific approaches to consciousness* (pp. 213–240). Mahwah, NJ: Erlbaum.

Raye, C. L., Johnson, M. K., & Taylor, T. H. (1980). Is there something special about memory for internally generated information? *Memory & Cognition, 8*, 141–148.

Read, J. D., & Lindsay, D. S. (Eds.). (1997). *Recollection of trauma: Scientific evidence and clinical practice*. New York: Plenum.

Read, J. D., Tollestrup, P., Hammersley, R., McFadzen, E., & Christensen, A. (1990). The unconscious transference effect: Are innocent bystanders ever misidentified? *Applied Cognitive Psychology, 4*, 3–31.

Reinitz, M. T., Lammers, W. J., & Cochran, B. P. (1992). Memory-conjunction errors: Miscombination of stored stimulus features can produce illusions of memory. *Memory & Cognition, 20*, 1–11.

Reyna, V. F., & Titcomb, A. L. (1997). Constraints on the suggestibility of eyewitness testimony: A fuzzy-trace theory analysis.

In D. G. Payne & F. G. Conrad (Eds.), *Intersections in basic and applied memory research* (pp. 157–174). Mahwah, NJ: Erlbaum.

Riefer, D. M., Hu, X., & Batchelder, W. H. (1994). Response strategies in source monitoring. *Journal of Experimental Psychology: Learning, Memory, and Cognition, 20*, 680–693.

Ross, M. (1997). Validating memories. In N. L. Stein, P. A. Ornstein, B. Tversky, & C. Brainerd (Eds.), *Memory for everyday and emotional events* (pp. 49–81). Mahwah, NJ: Erlbaum.

Ross, D. F., Ceci, S. J., Dunning, D., & Toglia, M. P. (1994). Unconscious transference and lineup identification: Toward a memory blending approach. In D. F. Ross, J. D. Read, & M. P. Toglia (Eds.), *Adult eyewitness testimony: Current trends and developments* (pp. 80–100). New York: Cambridge University Press.

Sachs, J. (1967). Recognition memory for syntactic and semantic aspects of connected discourse. *Perception & Psychophysics, 2*, 437–442.

Schacter, D. L., Harbluk, J. L., & McLachlan, D. R. (1984). Retrieval without recollection: An experimental analysis of source amnesia. *Journal of Verbal Learning and Verbal Behavior, 23*, 593–611.

Schacter, D. L., Koutstaal, W., Johnson, M. K., Gross, M. S., & Angell, K. E. (1997). False recollection induced via photographs: A comparison of older and younger adults. *Psychology and Aging, 12*, 203–215.

Schacter, D. L., Koutstaal, W., & Norman, K. A. (1997). False memories and aging. *Trends in Cognitive Sciences, 1*, 229–236.

Schacter, D. L., Norman, K. A., & Koutstaal, W. (1998). The cognitive neuroscience of constructive memory. *Annual Review of Psychology, 49*, 289–318.

Schacter, D. L., Reiman, E., Curran, T., Yun, L. S., Bandy, D., McDermott, K. B., & Roediger, H. L., III. (1996). Neuroanatomical correlates of veridical and illusory recognition memory: Evidence from positron emission tomography. *Neuron, 17*, 267–274.

Schooler, J. W., Gerhard, D., & Loftus, E. F. (1986). Qualities of the unreal. *Journal of Experimental Psychology: Learning, Memory, and Cognition, 12*, 171–181.

Sherman, J. W., & Bessenoff, G. R. (1999). Stereotypes as source monitoring cues: On the interaction between episodic and semantic memory. *Psychological Science, 10*, 106–110.

Shimamura, A. P., & Squire, L. R. (1987). A neuropsychological study of fact memory and source amnesia. *Journal of Experimental Psychology: Learning, Memory, and Cognition, 13*, 464–473.

Slusher, M. P., & Anderson, C. A. (1987). When reality monitoring fails: The role of imagination in stereotype maintenance. *Journal of Personality and Social Psychology, 52*, 653–662.

Sporer, S. L. (1997). The less travelled road to truth: Verbal cues in deception detection in accounts of fabricated and self-experienced events. *Applied Cognitive Psychology, 11*, 373–397.

Squire, L. R., & Knowlton, B. J. (1995). Memory, hippocampus, and brain systems. In M. S. Gazzaniga (Eds.), *The cognitive neurosciences* (pp. 825–837). Cambridge, MA: MIT Press.

Steller, M. (1989). Recent developments in statement analysis. In J. C. Yuille (Ed.), *Credibility assessment* (pp. 135–154). Dordrecht, The Netherlands: Kluwer Academic Publishers.

Stuss, D. T., & Benson, D. F. (1986). *The frontal lobes.* New York: Raven Press.

Suengas, A. G., & Johnson, M. K. (1988). Qualitative effects of rehearsal on memories for perceived and imagined complex events. *Journal of Experimental Psychology: General, 117*, 377–389.

Sulin, R. A., & Dooling, D. J. (1974). Intrusion of a thematic idea in retention of prose. *Journal of Experimental Psychology: General, 103*, 255–262.

Tulving, E. (1962). Subjective organization in free recall of "unrelated" words. *Psychological Review, 69*, 344–354.

Tulving, E. (1985). Memory and consciousness. *Canadian Psychology, 26*, 1–12.

Underwood, B. J., & Pezdek, K. (1998). Memory suggestibility as an example of the sleeper effect. *Psychonomic Bulletin and Review, 5*, 449–453.

Undeutsch, U. (1989). The development of statement reality analysis. In J. C. Yuille (Ed.), *Credibility Assessment* (pp. 101–119). Dordrecht, The Netherlands: Kluwer Academic Publishers.

Wilding, E. L., & Rugg, M. D. (1996). An event-related potential study of recognition memory with and without retrieval of source. *Brain, 119*, 889–905.

Wilson, T. D., & Brekke, N. (1994). Mental contamination and mental correction: Unwanted influences on judgments and evaluations. *Psychological Bulletin, 116*, 117–142.

Winograd, E. (1968). List differentiation, recall, and category similarity. *Journal of Experimental Psychology, 78*, 510–515.

Winograd, E., Peluso, J. P., & Glover, T. A. (1998). Individual differences in susceptibility to memory illusions. *Applied Cognitive Psychology, 12*, S5–S27.

Yonelinas, A. P. (1994). Receiver operating characteristics in recognition memory: Evidence for a dual process model. *Journal of Experimental Psychology: Learning, Memory, and Cognition, 20*, 1341–1354.

Zaragoza, M. S., & Koshmider, J. W., III. (1989). Misled subjects may know more than their performance implies. *Journal of Experimental Psychology: Learning, Memory, and Cognition, 15*, 246–255.

Zaragoza, M. S., & Lane, S. M. (1994). Source misattributions and the suggestibility of eyewitness memory. *Journal of Experimental Psychology: Learning, Memory, and Cognition, 20*, 934–945.

Zaragoza, M. S., & Lane, S. M. (1998). Processing resources and eyewitness suggestibility. *Journal of Legal and Criminological Psychology, 3*, 305–320.

Zaragoza, M. S., Lane, S. M., Ackil, J. K., & Chambers, K. L. (1997). Confusing real and suggested memories: Source monitoring and eyewitness suggestibility. In N. L. Stein, P. A. Ornstein, B. Tversky, & C. Brainerd (Eds.), *Memory for everyday and emotional events* (pp. 401–425). Mahwah, NJ: Erlbaum.

Zaragoza, M. S., & Mitchell, K. J. (1996). Repeated exposure to suggestion and the creation of false memories. *Psychological Science, 7*, 294–300.

Zaragoza, M. S., Mitchell, K. J., & Drivdahl, S. B. (1997). Imagery and false memory creation. Abstract reprinted in J. D. Read & D. S. Lindsay (Eds.), *Recollection of trauma: Scientific evidence and clinical practice* (p. 585). New York: Plenum.

Zorrilla, L. T. E., Aguirre, G. K., Zarahn, E., Cannon, T. D., & D'Esposito, M. (1996). Activation of the prefrontal cortex during judgments of recency: A functional MRI study. *NeuroReport, 7*, 2803–2806.

13

Metamemory

Theory and Data

JANET METCALFE

Historical Events of Importance in the Area

In his search for "The First Principle," Descartes (1911) questioned all of what we might now call his basic object-level cognitive processes (Nelson & Narens, 1990, 1994; Moscovitch, 1994), allowing that he could imagine that things were different than they seemed or that they might not exist at all. It was not so much thinking that was indisputable to Descartes, but rather thinking *about* thinking. What he could not imagine was that the person engaged in such self-reflective processing did not exist.The reality of the person who knows about knowing, then, was taken by Descartes as the irreducible core—the foundation upon which all other knowledge was and must be built. It seems, though, that he based his philosophy on a misnomer, *cogito ergo sum*. What he really should have said was *metacogito ergo sum*.

People's self-reflective abilities, including their knowledge about their own knowledge, skills, capabilities, and memories, have long been considered essential for understanding what human beings are. Accordingly, Descartes was not the only philosopher to emphasize the importance of metacognition. William James (1890/1981) said something interesting about almost everything of consequence. It is no surprise, then, that he commented on

a phenomenon—the tip-of-the-tongue (TOT) state—that has become a major topic in modern studies of metacognition: "Suppose we try to recall a forgotten name. The state of our consciousness is peculiar. There is a gap therein; but no mere gap. It is a gap that is intensely active. A sort of wraith of the name is in it, beckoning us in a given direction, making us at moments tingle with the sense of our closeness. ... The rhythm of a lost word may be there without a sound to clothe it; or the evanescent sense of something which is the initial vowel or consonant may mock us fitfully, without growing more distinct" (pp. 243–244).

Although little heed was paid to metacognition (or indeed to any other phenomenon intimately bound up with consciousness) during the behaviorist era, the importance of the topic was acknowledged once again as soon as the cognitive revolution took root. Some thirty years ago, Tulving and Madigan (1970)—among the groundbreakers of the new generation of cognitive psychologists—concluded their rather pessimistic review of the field of learning and memory with a hope: "What is the solution to the problem of lack of genuine progress in understanding memory? It is not for us to say, because we do not know. But one possibility does suggest itself: why not start looking for ways of experimentally studying, and incorporating into theories and models of memory, one of the truly unique characteristics of human memory: its knowledge of its own knowledge. No extant conceptualization, be it based on stimulus-response associations or an information-processing paradigm, makes provisions for the fact that the human memory system cannot only produce a learned response to an appropriate stimulus or retrieve a stored image, but it can also rather accurately estimate the likelihood of its success in doing it. . . . We cannot help but feel that if there is ever going to be a genuine breakthrough in the psychological study of memory, one that would save the students of ecphoric processes from the [ignominious] fate we talked about at the beginning of this chapter, it will, among other things, relate the knowledge stored in an individual's memory to his knowledge of that knowledge" (p. 477).

The present chapter is a progress report.

Paradigms for Studying Metamemory

Metamemory was first advanced as a phenomenon amenable to detailed scientific study by the work of Hart (1965, 1967, and see Flavell, Friedrichs, & Hoyt, 1970), who devised a paradigm that has come to be known as the recall, judge, recognize, or RJR, paradigm. Participants are presented with a series of questions, often targeting well-learned general knowledge, though sometimes directed at newly learned information, and are asked to provide the answers. Typically the feeling-of-knowing judgments are requested only for those questions to which the participant cannot recall the answer. These judgments can be provided as numerical values indicating how likely it is that the participant deems that he or she will be able to choose the correct answer when given an n-alternative forced-choice test, or by the rank-ordering of the unrecalled questions with respect to one another. Participants are then given a multiple choice test—the criterion task. The correspondence between the judgments and the memory performance on the criterion task is computed in the form of a correlation coefficient (often a nonparametric gamma correlation; see Nelson & Narens, 1980). To the extent that this correlation coefficient is greater than zero—and it nearly always is—we may say that the person has accurate metaknowledge about what he or she will know.

Although feeling-of-knowing judgments in the RJR paradigm are the most frequently studied metacognitions, there are other paradigms and judgments that are of considerable interest. For example, there is now an extensive literature on judgments of learning, in which a participant is requested to assess how well he or she has learned a particular item or event—either immediately after having studied it or at some later time. Some researchers have also asked participants for ease of learning judgments, and for interest in learning judgments. One can also ask questions directed at another kind of metacognitive indicator: people's confidence that they will be able to learn, that they have learned, or understood, or that they have produced the correct answer. If the judgments are given as probability estimates, their mean (sometimes apportioned in various ways) can also be compared to the mean level of performance to indicate calibration of confidence. Often the mean of the judgments is higher than is memory performance, indicating overconfidence. Finally, although it would be appropriate to include several other judgments under the umbrella heading of metacognitive knowledge—for example, remember/know judgments, judgments of reality (Johnson, 1988; Johnson & Raye, 1981) or judgments about the source of a memory—because these three kinds of judgments are explicitly covered elsewhere in this handbook they will not be included here.

Theory

How do we know what we will know? A general framework for understanding metacognitive monitoring and control has been provided by Nelson and Narens (1994). As figure 13.1

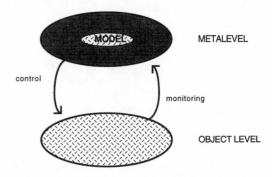

Figure 13.1 A diagram of the Nelson and Narens theoretical framework (after Nelson & Narens, 1990). Note that the metalevel contains a degraded model of the object level.

shows, they consider that both an object level and a metalevel are needed. Basic cognitive operations are conducted at the object level, whereas the metalevel makes assessments based on the information that it gleans from the object level, and returns control signals that may influence the object level operations (see Koriat's review, chapter 21). The metalevel has access to knowledge at the object level but the reverse is not true. Process-oriented models that incorporate metacognitive processes, such as those of Metcalfe (1993a) or Moscovitch (1994), also contain levels that correspond to those proposed in Nelson and Narens's framework. The proposal that there are two levels characterized in this way may allow theorists to finesse the notion of a full-blown homunculus. How these two levels actually work, and on what basis the metalevel produces its decisions, ratings, and control feedback, is the topic of more specific hypotheses, three of which have been considered in some detail in the literature, and are outlined below.

The Target Retrievability Hypothesis

The target retrievability hypothesis states that the reason people are able to make accurate judgments about their future knowledge is that even though the accessible knowledge may be insufficient to allow articulation, people nevertheless know the answer, or some part of the answer. Thus, people make accurate feeling of knowing judgments because they really do know what they will later know despite being unable to articulate it at the time the judgment is made.

Hart (1965) was one of the first to propose this idea, saying that recall was a more difficult task than recognition and hence recall required more information to reach threshold than did recognition. He thought that the threshold for feeling-of-knowing judgments might be somewhere between the two memory tasks. Since Hart's (1965) proposal, many experiments have shown that recall can sometimes be superior to recognition, in contrast to the predictions of a threshold theory of the two tasks. Therefore, the simple threshold difference cannot be correct.

Recently, a more complex target-retrievability theory not suffering from these problems has come to the fore. Burke, MacKay, Worthley, and Wade (1991; MacKay, 1982) forwarded a linguistically based model of the tip-of-the-tongue (TOT) phenomenon (i.e., the feeling that recall is imminent) and, presumably, to other feelings of knowing in which there is a semantic level of representation that is distinct from the articulatory phonemic level. Most important, from the perspective of a dissociation between knowledge and output that presumably is the basis for the TOT feeling and for accurate feelings of knowing, there are connections that may fail between the semantic and phonemic level. Persons might have excellent knowledge at the semantic level—thus really knowing what and that they know—but some confusion or breakdown might exist at the articulatory/phonemic level, or in the connections between one level and another. This notion applies especially well to older patients, in whom the connections between the semantic and phonemic levels may be particularly fragile. A recognition test allows circumvention of the articulatory requirements hard hit by the missing connections. By directly monitoring the semantic level the person can produce accurate feeling of knowing ratings.

The Cue Familiarity Hypothesis

The cue familiarity hypothesis states that feeling-of-knowing judgments may be based on the familiarity of the cue that is present at the time the judgment is made. There are two versions of the cue familiarity hypothesis. First, Reder (1987; Miner & Reder, 1994; Reder & Ritter, 1992) proposed that people make a very fast preretrieval assessment of whether to-be-remembered information exists in memory, based on cue familiarity. This fast assessment is also thought to underlie the person's feeling-of-knowing judgment. If the cue is familiar, there is a good chance that the target information exists in memory (and the participant goes on to try to retrieve it). Low cue familiarity serves as a signal that the target is not in memory and that therefore an unproductive memory search should be avoided.

Metcalfe (1993a, 1993b) has proposed an alternate cue familiarity mechanism. In Metcalfe's (e.g., 1990, 1991) CHARM model a monitor assesses the familiarity or novelty of the information being processed and sends a feedback signal that controls the weighting of the information coming into memory. She has proposed that the novelty or familiarity feeling itself is available to consciousness and that it may serve as the basis for feeling-of-knowing judgments, especially when there is no other information available on which the person may rely. In the RJR paradigm—in which the judgments are made only on those items for which participants cannot recall the targets—it is assumed that the judgments are based on the familiarity of the cue since that is all that is available. The cue-familiarity view does not preclude the possibility that participants might use other information if it were available. In Metcalfe's version, people could use accessibility information if the judgments are made on questions on which people can recall the answers. In Reder's version, there should be a time-related dominance tradeoff—cue familiarity information should be used first, and only later should the person have access to target-based information.

The Accessibility Account

Recently, Koriat (1993, 1994, 1995; Koriat & Goldsmith, 1996) has proposed a third theory called the accessibility heuristic. Participants are assumed to base their judgments upon all retrieved information, not on the mere familiarity of the cue. As well as the lexical unit itself, people may also use partial information—be it correct or incorrect. Koriat makes the important point that participants do not know whether the information that they are retrieving is correct or incorrect, much of the time. Individual elements of that information may be weighted by their strength and speed of access. The quantity of information retrieved (which is weighted by factors such as speed of access) determines the feeling of knowing judgment.

Data

Accuracy of Feeling-of-Knowing Judgments

Predictive metacognitions about later memory performance have been intensively investigated (e.g., Blake, 1973; Costermans, Lories, & Ansay, 1992; Gruneberg & Monks, 1974; Hart, 1965, 1967; Lachman, Lachman, & Thronesbury, 1979; Leonesio & Nelson, 1990; Metcalfe, 1986a, 1986b; Nelson, Leonesio, Shimamura, Landwehr, & Narens, 1982; Schacter, 1983) with different groups ranging from the very young (Butterfield, Nelson, & Peck, 1988; Cultice, Somerville, & Wellman, 1983; Schneider, 1998) to the quite old (Hertzog & Dixon,

1994) with different kinds of materials, with differing amounts of learning, and so on. Feeling-of-knowing judgments for this irretrievable information as compared to later recognition of the information are quite accurate, with correlations usually between .45 and .55. Since, by definition, participants cannot retrieve the information, part of the fascination in this general area of research is in attempting to determine how a person can know what he or she will know even though that information is demonstrably not known at the time the judgment is made.

The accuracy of the feeling-of-knowing judgments is accounted for in a straightforward manner by the target retrievability hypothesis, insofar as this hypothesis states that it is actually the target that people are basing the judgments on. The accessibility hypothesis also accounts for the correlation because of the direct retrieval of target-relevant information. The story is slightly more complicated for the accessibility hypothesis, insofar as incorrect retrieved information may also contribute to the judgments. This turns out to readily explain why the correlations are only around .5 and are not perfect.

The accuracy of feeling-of-knowing judgments seems more problematic for the cue familiarity hypothesis insofar as the judgments are not based on target information. Even so, in Reder's theory, one would expect a positive correlation between judgment and memory because the judgment determines whether a memory search will be initiated. If no search is enacted it is self-evident that memory will be poor. But even leaving a direct causal mechanism aside, there are reasons why cue familiarity might be a good predictor of target recognition. In the real world, cues and targets are often experienced in synchrony. Thus, those cues to which people are frequently exposed occur in tight conjunction with frequent exposure to their targets. The feeling-of-knowing accuracy might reflect nothing more than this cue-target correlation in the world. Indeed, in experiments lacking this real-world correlational structure—in which the cue target pairings are random and newly learned (Schwartz & Metcalfe, 1992)—the overall feeling of knowing accuracy is inconsequential.

The Tip-of-the-Tongue Phenomenon

Tip of the tongue states (TOTs—see Freedman & Landauer, 1966; Smith, 1994; Wellman,

1977) are highly correlated with high feelings of knowing. Moreover, when in such states, participants are sometimes able to provide partial information that is accurate. A. Brown (1991), R. Brown and McNeill (1966), and Koriat and Lieblich (1974) have reported that when people are in TOT states, they are able to report phonemic or orthographic information such as the first letter or the number of syllables of the to-be-remembered word. Schwartz and Smith (1997) were able to influence the probability of report of a TOT state by manipulating the amount of information that they gave participants about imaginary animals called TOTimals. This information did not change the probability of retrieval of the TOTimal name itself, however. Other researchers have also observed that partial information is available even when people cannot recall the targets. Blake (1973) has shown that partial recall of three-letter trigrams was positively correlated with feeling of knowing ratings. Schacter and Worling (1985) showed that participants could better remember the affective valence of unrecalled items given high feeling of knowing ratings than those given lower ratings. Insofar as high feeling of knowing is correlated with the TOT state, these results are consistent. Vigliocco, Antonini, and Garrett (1997) and Miozzo and Caramazza (1997) showed that Italian speakers, when in a TOT state, can retrieve the gender of the unrecalled word at better than chance accuracy, suggesting, again, that they have some partial knowledge about the actual unrecalled word. These studies provide the strongest evidence favoring the accessibility hypothesis.

Schreiber (1998; Schreiber & Nelson, 1998) has shown that feeling-of-knowing judgments can be negatively influenced by the number of different neighboring concepts that are linked to the cue. A simple interpretation of the accessibility hypothesis suggests that because more information is retrieved when there are more neighbors, people's feelings of knowing judgments should have been higher. Schreiber and Nelson suggest that a perception of response competition may contribute to people's judgments under some conditions.

Differences in Feeling of Knowing Among Different Error Types

Errors in the feeling-of-knowing task can be divided into two classes: errors of omission, where nothing is recalled; and errors of commission, where the wrong response is given. Typically, the ratings given to errors of commission are higher than are those given to omission errors (Krinsky & Nelson, 1985).

The cue-familiarity hypothesis accounts for these results by saying that it is the highly familiar cues that are likely to allow access to some information (even though that information might be wrong), whereas the unfamiliar cues may evoke no information at all. The accessibility hypothesis accounts for the finding directly—saying that people base their judgments on all information retrieved—whether right or wrong. Thus, these results are compatible with both theories.

Judgment vs. Retrieval Latency

In two studies investigating judgment versus retrieval latencies, Reder (1987, 1988) used a technique dubbed the "game show" paradigm. Participants were either asked to indicate whether they felt they knew the answers (a metacognitive judgment about future performance), or to actually provide the answers (retrieval) by hitting a bell as quickly as they could. The responses were faster in the feeling-of-knowing condition than in the retrieval condition. These latency findings provide support for the pre-retrieval locus of feeling-of-knowing judgments. She suggested that fast feeling-of-knowing judgments might provide the basis for deciding whether to initiate retrieval (or some other question answering strategy) at all.

These results seem to weigh in favor of the cue-familiarity hypothesis. It is difficult to see how the metacognitive judgments could be based on retrieved information when they are made more quickly than the person is able to initiate retrieval. However, these results also do not preclude the idea that, if given more time to deliberate about whether they will be able to recall correctly, people might use the information that they retrieve as the process proceeds.

Cue Familiarization Effects

Reder (1988) devised a cue-priming method for altering only cue familiarity. Before being given general information questions, participants rated a list of words for frequency of occurrence. Embedded in the list were some cue words that would occur later. For example, the words *golf* and *par* might have been presented on the frequency rating list. In the general-information feeling-of-knowing task, cues such as "What is the term in golf for a score of one under par?" appeared, as well as cues that were not primed. The priming of the cues spuriously increased participants' feelings of knowing without increasing their ability to answer the questions. Similarly, in an arithmetic problem experiment, Reder and Ritter (1992) found that exposure to parts of a problem, even though not in the correct configuration relevant to the requested answer, influenced participants' decisions about whether to retrieve the answer as opposed to work out the solution.

Metcalfe, Schwartz, and Joaquim (1993) contrasted the target retrievability and the cue familiarity hypotheses. An A-B A-B condition provided best target retrieval. An A-B A-D condition resulted in (slightly) negative transfer; however, as in the A-B A-B condition, the cue was repeated. The third condition was an A-B C-D condition. In this condition the cue was given only once. The target retrievability hypothesis says that feeling-of-knowing magnitudes should have been related to memory, and so the A-B/A-B condition should have had the highest ratings, and both the A-B/C-D condition and A-B/A-D condition should have produced low ratings. In contrast, the cue familiarity hypothesis predicted that the magnitude of the feeling-of-knowing judgments should have varied with the number of repetitions of the cue. Thus the A-B A-B and the A-B A-D conditions should have both been high whereas the A-B C-D condition should have had low ratings. The results closely followed the predictions of the cue-familiarity hypothesis.

Schwartz and Metcalfe (1992) also contrasted retrievability and cue familiarity. They used Reder's priming task to manipulate cue-familiarity, and Slamecka and Graf's (1978) generation task to manipulate retrievability. In other experiments they manipulated target retrievability by target priming. In three out of four of their experiments, the feeling-of-knowing judgments were unaffected by the target retrievability manipulation. In one experiment, though—where the target words were primed—an effect that might have been due to target retrievability (though the authors interpreted this finding differently) was found. In all four experiments, cue familiarity was found to have an effect on feeling of knowing judgments.

Converging evidence about the effects of cue or domain familiarity comes from a sequence of experiments by Glenberg, Sanocki, Epstein, and Morris (1987) in which participants were given short informative paragraphs to read, each on a different topic. They were then given the titles of the stories and asked to give "confidence" ratings about either their specific recall of aspects of the content of the stories or their ability to make appropriate inferences about each story. The inferences were specific to the paragraphs read during the experiment, and were intentionally designed to circumvent general domain knowledge. There was a large positive correlation between the participants' domain knowledge, or the "familiarity" of the cues, and their confidence ratings, and they exhibited no predictive accuracy.

The results of this line of research weigh in favor of the cue familiarity hypothesis. However, there is a caveat. This hypothesis seems to be revealed clearly only in certain cases such as when the data are conditionalized on nonrecall of the target, or when their domain familiarity is intentionally made irrelevant to task outcome.

Knowing the Unknown

Knowing not. Kolers and Palef (1976) made the provocative observation that people know what they do not know. If asked a question such as "What is the name of the largest department store in St. Petersburg?" many people will answer that they do not know: they give a very low feeling-of-knowing rating, and they are able to make these judgments very quickly—more quickly than would be expected if they were attempting any kind of search about knowledge of department stores or of St. Petersburg. These findings are consistent with the cue familiarity hypothesis (in a parallel processing model such as CHARM) but seem to be more problematic for the accessibility hypothesis because of the speed of the judgments. The knowledge of not knowing appears to be positively marked, and immediately accessible, rather than being attributable to an inference drawn after a failure to find the information in memory.

Knowing the nonexistent. Schwartz (in press) has reported that people sometimes report that an answer is on the tips of their tongues, when they not only never knew the information that is supposedly lurking just behind the veil of consciousness but when that information does not, in fact, exist. For example, when given questions such as: What is the last name of the great Canadian author who wrote the novel *The Last Bucket*? a remarkable number of people would claim to be in a tip-of-the-tongue state. It seems plausible that people are in this state as a result of cue familiarity. The questions in Schwartz's sample seemed similar to questions that have a real answer (such as "What is the name of the great Canadian author who wrote *The Last Spike*? Answer: Pierre Berton.).

Explicit knowledge of the unknown. In an experiment in which people were asked to decide whether the answers to certain questions were known or not known, Glucksberg and McCloskey (1981) either provided no information or gave participants statements indicating that certain answers were not known (for example, "It is not known whether Gabriel owns a violin"). They found that the explicit don't-know-information slowed people down in making their don't-know judgments. Their findings are consistent with the conjecture that fast don't-know judgments are made on the basis of the lack of familiarity with the cues (as was suggested for Kolers and Palef's data). By providing the explicit don't-know information in the context of the cue information, Glucksberg and McCloskey may have inadvertently made the cues more familiar, thus having an effect opposite from what might be expected.

Dissociation of Feeling of Knowing from Recall

Accurate feeling-of-knowing judgments are not necessarily linked to the absolute level of recall or recognition. Indeed, amnesic patients can sometimes exhibit metamemory judgments that are as accurate as those of unimpaired people. However, it appears that certain subclasses of brain-damaged patients have selective impairments in metamemory. Shimamura and Squire (1986) found that Korsakoff amnesia patients, in particular, are selectively impaired in making feeling-of-knowing judgments. Their gamma correlations relating predictions of performance and actual memory performance were not significantly different from zero. The (non-Korsakoff) amnesia patients, as well as the normals who were tested at a delay, were well above chance on their feeling-of-knowing correlations to performance. Shallice and Evans (1978) have pointed out that Korsakoff's have difficulty with many kinds of estimation (e.g., "How tall

is the average English woman?"), as well as judgments about their own memories.

It is possible that this aspect of Korsakoff patients' performance may result because they have frontal lobe impairments. Accordingly, Janowsky, Shimamura, and Squire (1989) tested a small group of patients with frontal lobe damage, but who exhibited no memory performance impairment. They obtained some suggestion that damage to the frontal lobes alone may be sufficient cause for metamemory impairments. These findings are consistent with the often-found monitoring and judgments impairments shown by frontal-lobe patients (Schacter, 1989; McGlynn & Schacter, 1989; Jouandet & Gazzaniga, 1979).

Test Effects

Study/test compatibility. Morris (1990) and Glenberg et al. (1987) have investigated how knowledge about the structure of the test may affect comprehension judgments. Similarly, Thiede (1996) suggests that metacognitions may play a complex role in study/test compatibility effects. Test effects were also shown in an experiment investigating the relation between feeling-of-knowing judgments, recognition, and perceptual identification; Nelson, Gerler, and Narens (1984) asked participants to provide feeling-of-knowing judgments about later recognition. The results showed that these judgments did, modestly, predict recognition, gamma = .29, and that they also predicted perceptual identification, gamma = −.16. However, there was no correlation between the absolute values of the gammas relating the feeling-of-knowing judgments and recognition and the gammas relating these judgments to perceptual identification, based on these scores for each participant. As Nelson et al. (1984) discussed, there does not seem to be a stable unidimensional feeling-of-knowing ability that applies to all tests. In general, then, the goodness of the metacognitive judgment appears to be a complex function of (1) people's knowledge of their knowledge, (2) their assessment of the test situation, and (3) their assessment of the congruence between their knowledge and the needs of the test.

Number of test alternatives. A simple factor that has been a pervasive confound in the literature on the accuracy of feeling-of-knowing judgments is the number of alternatives presented in the final test. Suppose the participant does not know the answer to a particular question and knows that he or she does not know, and hence gives the question a very low feeling-of-knowing rating. If he or she then gets that question wrong on the final test, this correspondence between the low rating and the incorrect performance will contribute to a positive correlation. This would be an appropriate demonstration of accurate metacognition. However, the chance that the person will get such a question wrong depends upon the number of alternatives presented at the time of test. If the test is a two-alternative recognition test, then the odds of picking a correct answer with no knowledge are quite high. Insofar as these correct guessing responses should decrease the correlation, which is the measure of metacognitive accuracy, and insofar as more of these correct guesses are expected with fewer test alternatives, we would expect to find lower gamma correlations with few than with many alternatives.

Schwartz and Metcalfe (1994) conducted a meta-analysis of experiments in the feeling of knowing literature, including all experiments, and also restricting the sample to those that had, at least, some consistency in the materials because they used the general information questions of Nelson and Narens (1980). The main variable of interest was the number of test alternatives. As can be seen from figure 13.2, which plots the gamma correlations against the number of alternatives from their paper, there was a positive correlation between gamma score and number of test alternatives. In the studies that used general knowledge questions, this factor accounted for 63% of the variability. Recall might be considered to be the logical extension of an n-alternative recognition test—an extension in which n has become extremely large. As can be seen from the figure, as might be expected, the highest correlations were, indeed, found when recall was given as the criterion test.

Thinking One Knows More Than One Does

Overconfidence. The question of whether people under or overestimate their own performance, at a macro level, is different from whether they are relatively accurate in the ordering of the to-be-remembered events. Thus, a person could have a perfectly accurate ranking of the events, but be, on average, wildly overconfident. Alternatively, a person could be entirely unable to say *which* items he or she might later answer correctly, and yet might

nevertheless be able to specify that he or she will get exactly 62% correct and be right about it. With just a few exceptions, people are overconfident (see Metcalfe, 1998). When people are asked to say how likely it is that they will get the answer to a question correct, they show an extremely well-documented tendency to overestimate this probability. Typical calibration curves have been given by Lichtenstein, Fischhoff, and Phillips (1977), and are presented in figure 13.3. As is shown in the figure, the discrepancy between what the performance should be and what the participants' estimates are is greater when the estimates are high than when they are more moderate—that is, they are more overconfident at the high extreme of the rating scale. On some calibration curves, a small underconfidence effect is shown with the extremely easy items. But the overwhelming bulk of the data point to a phenomenon of overconfidence—a phenomenon that occurs in assessment of test performance and also comprehension (e.g., Maki & Berry, 1984; Waern & Askwall, 1981; Shaughnessy, 1979). Furthermore, several groups have shown that overconfidence accrues even when people are given undiagnostic or misleading information (Oskamp, 1965; Weingardt, Leonesio, & Loftus, 1994).

Illusion of comprehension. A number of studies suggest that people are prey to what Glenberg has called an illusion of comprehension. For example, Glenberg, Wilkinson, and Epstein (1982) and Epstein, Glenberg, and Bradley (1984) had people read passages containing internal contradictions. Even when explicitly told to find the contradictions, the participants not only missed them but also voiced high confidence in their clear understanding of inherently incomprehensible passages. Similarly, when people are asked questions such as "How many animals of each kind did Moses take on the Ark?" they quickly and confidently reply two (Bredart & Modolo, 1988; Reder & Kusbit, 1991) even though, if pressed, those same people will unfailingly acknowledge that Moses had nothing to do with the Ark. Some studies have shown that calibration of comprehension is close to nonexistent—people simply have no idea of what they have understood, especially when domain familiarity is factored out (Glenberg et al., 1987; Glenberg & Epstein, 1985, 1987). Participants apparently use their self-knowledge of topic familiarity as a basis for their judgments—if they are familiar with a topic they will give high comprehension ratings

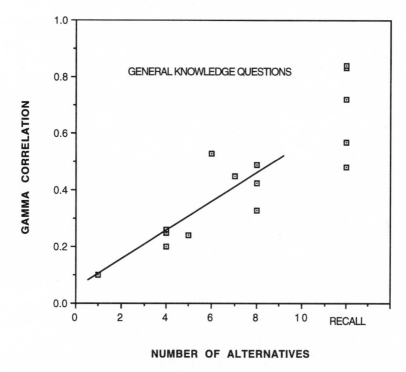

Figure 13.2 Feeling-of-knowing accuracy as a function of the number of alternatives presented in recognition, when general-information questions are the test material (after Schwartz & Metcalfe, 1994).

which, depending on the nature of the test, may or may not allow them some predictive accuracy.

Illusions of knowing. Bjork (1994) has documented a wide variety of situations in which people believe they know something, or they have adequately learned the material—and will make high judgments of learning—when, in fact they are far from mastery. For example, Jacoby and Kelley (1987) converted a task that was intrinsically very difficult (solving anagrams) into one that was ostensibly easy by providing the solutions to the anagrams. When asked for their ratings of objective difficulty, people given the unsolved anagrams thought that they were more difficult than did the people given the solutions. People who had to solve the anagrams themselves were also more accurate in assessing which anagrams were easy and which were more difficult than were people who were provided with the answers. Participants, in a variety of judgment of learning tasks, seem to use retrieval fluency (Begg, Duft, Lalonde, Melnick, & Sanvito, 1989; Bjork, 1994, Jacoby, Bjork, & Kelly, 1994) in making this judgment,

and to discount or ignore factors—like the presence of the response in short-term memory (Dunlosky & Nelson, 1992; Spellman & Bjork, 1992), or the presence of the item on the page (Jacoby & Kelley, 1987), or the fact that massed practice has poor long-term consequences (e.g., Bahrick, 1979)—that might make immediate fluency a poor barometer of future performance.

As Jacoby, Bjork, and Kelley (1994) have pointed out, it may be equally important to educate *subjective* experience as it is to educate objective experience. Bjork (1994) has documented a number of factors that lead to immediate and positive performance results and to introspective satisfaction but that fail to result in adequate long-term performance. Baddeley and Longman (1978) have demonstrated just this effect with British postal workers taught a keyboard skill under these two conditions. Immediate satisfaction was found to be a poor predictor of eventual performance. Because metacognition in learning and training situations determines how much time and effort will be invested, what kind of training procedures will be practiced, the praise the trainee

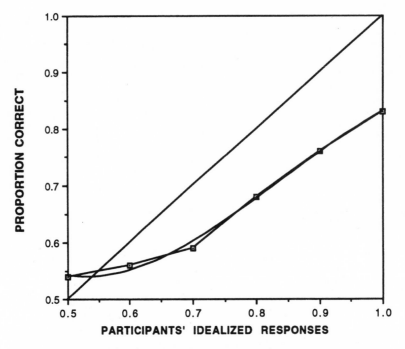

Figure 13.3 A typical graph showing people's miscalibration of confidence (after Lichtenstein, Fischhoff, & Phillips, 1977).

will bestow on the trainer (and the effects of that feedback on the behavior of the trainer), such reversals may have a particularly pernicious effect.

Thinking One Knew It All Along

Fischhoff (1975) has demonstrated that if people first make a prediction about the outcome of an event, and then, at some later time, are given feedback about the actual outcome and are asked what they said originally, they bias their memory for their original judgments in the direction of the actual outcome—that is, they exhibit a phenomenon called *hindsight bias*. Poulton (1994) has noted the difficulty that this hindsight bias phenomenon poses for researchers who have made truly exciting and unexpected discoveries. Once the scientific community has read of the nature of the discovery, it seems obvious, and the magnitude and brilliance of his or her accomplishment is nearly invariably diminished by hindsight.

Agreement?

Although one might hope that some metacognitive judgments or feelings reflect a stable

faculty that would allow predictive accuracy about performance on a variety of tasks, a number of studies suggest that the tasks and the metacognitive judgments are much more specific. Overall the conclusion seems to favor the heuristic view—that there is no one single faculty for metacognition. Rather, people's ability to make assessments of their future cognitive performance seems to depend on which performance is in question, their particular skills in that domain, their domain knowledge, and the specifics of the particular test that is given to them (as well as the compatibility between the test and the metacognitive question they are asked). In summary, then, although people's knowledge about their own knowledge varies from task to task, from person to person, and with a single person when he or she is attempting different tasks, people do show remarkable intelligence (Flavell et al., 1970) in using whatever information is available—both about themselves and about the task at hand—to solve the prediction problem.

Conclusion

So where has research on human metacognition gone in the 30 years since Tulving and

Madigan's invitation to study "the truly unique characteristics of human memory: its knowledge of its own knowledge"? There has been a blossoming of research, with widespread agreement in the field that people make their metacognitive judgments heuristically, taking whatever memory images, fragments, feelings of fluency, and real-world correlations into account, to allow relatively accurate predictions of what the future holds. Most of the spooky stuff—for example, that people have access to subliminal urges or have inexplicable premonitions—has disappeared from serious consideration. Many experiments have been conducted, and a number of fascinating phenomena have been delineated and explored. We have a fairly good understanding of the biases and errors in human metacognition, as well as a relatively detailed appreciation of the accuracy of our knowledge about our memory and the mechanisms that allow it. So some real progress has been made. Ironically, we continue to converge on the conclusion that to understand metamemory, it is necessary to understand memory.

But even so, the study of metamemory does not reduce entirely to the study of memory itself. Metamemory brings a dimension to the study of memory that lifts it out of the realm of mere responding or mere learning. Humans indisputably have a monitoring process that looks at the panoramic images as well as the fragments of basic object-level memory—assessing them and commenting upon them, making probability judgments about their diagnosticity for future performance, deciding whether this means that something really happened or is only inferred, knowing that we know it (or that we don't). This area of self-reflective knowing is, of course, fascinating in its own right. As well, though, the study of this facet of human cognition may bring researchers one step closer to understanding free will and the fact that rather than simply being passive repositories for knowledge and memories, humans can use their knowledge of what they know to exert control over what they know, will know (Mazzoni & Cornoldi, 1993; Thiede & Dunlosky, 1999), and will become. There is general agreement that a primary purpose of metacognitive knowledge is to allow control. But, although the basis of the monitoring processes, and the information on which it rests, are beginning to be understood, little is known about how that metaknowledge is systematically put to use. It is this area that

represents the most salient gap in our understanding and that begs for future study. And so this progress report, like all such reports, ends with the inevitable (but in this case true) conclusion: much has been done but more research is needed.

Acknowledgments   Preparation of this chapter was supported by NIMH grant MH48066. I thank Walter Mischel, Bennett L. Schwartz, and Lisa Son for their help.

References

Baddeley, A. D., & Longman, D. J. A. (1978). The influence of length and frequency of training session on the rate of learning to type. *Ergonomics, 21*, 627–635.

Bahrick, H. P. (1979). Maintenance of knowledge: Questions about memory we forgot to ask. *Journal of Experimental Psychology: General, 108*, 296–308.

Begg, I, Duft, S., Lalonde, P., Melnick, R., & Sanvito, J. (1989). Memory predictions are based on ease of processing. *Journal of Memory and Language, 28*, 610–632.

Bjork, R. A. (1994). Memory and metamemory considerations in the training of human beings. In J. Metcalfe & A. P. Shimamura (Eds.), *Metacognition: Knowing about knowing* (pp. 185–206). Cambridge, MA: MIT Press.

Blake, M. (1973). Prediction of recognition when recall fails: Exploring the feeling-of-knowing phenomenon. *Journal of Verbal Learning and Verbal Behavior, 12*, 311–319.

Bredart, S., & Modolo, K. (1988). Moses strikes again: Focalization effect on a semantic illusion. *Acta Psychologica, 67*, 135–144.

Brown, A. S. (1991). A review of the tip of the tongue experience. *Psychological Bulletin, 109*(2), 204–223.

Brown, R., & McNeill, D. (1966). The "tip-of-the-tongue" phenomenon. *Journal of Verbal Learning and Verbal Behavior, 5*, 325–337.

Burke, D., MacKay, D. G., Worthley, J. S., & Wade, E. (1991). On the tip of the tongue: What causes word finding failures in young and older adults? *Journal of Memory and Language, 30*, 542–579.

Butterfield, E. C., Nelson, T. O., & Peck, V. (1988). Developmental aspects of the feeling of knowing. *Developmental Psychology, 24*, 654–663.

Costermans, J., Lories, G., & Ansay, C. (1992). Confidence level and feeling of knowing in question answering: The weight of inferential processes. *Journal of Experimental Psychology: Learning, Memory and Cognition, 18,* 142–150.

Cultice, J. C., Somerville, S. C., & Wellman, H. M. (1983). Preschoolers memory monitoring: Feeling of knowing judgments. *Child Development, 54,* 1480–1486.

Descartes, R. (1911). *The philosophical works of Descartes* (E. S. Haldane & G. R. T. Ross, trans.). Cambridge: Cambridge University Press.

Dunlosky, J., & Nelson, T. O. (1992). Importance of the kind of cue for judgments of learning (JOL) and the delayed-JOL effect. *Memory & Cognition, 20,* 374–380.

Epstein, W., Glenberg, A. M., & Bradley, M. (1984). Coactivation and comprehension: Contribution of text variables to the illusion of knowing. *Memory & Cognition, 12,* 355–360.

Fischhoff, B. (1975). Hindsight is not equal to foresight: The effects of outcome knowledge on judgment under uncertainty. *Journal of Experimental Psychology: Human Perception and Performance, 1,* 288–299.

Flavell, J. H., Friedrich, A. G., & Hoyt, J. D. (1970). Developmental changes in memorization processes. *Cognitive Psychology, 1,* 324–340.

Freedman, J. L., & Landauer, T. K. (1966). Retrieval of long-term memory: "Tip of the tongue" phenomenon. *Psychonomic Science, 4,* 309–310.

Glenberg, A. M., & Epstein, W. (1985). Calibration of comprehension. *Journal of Experimental Psychology: Learning, Memory, and Cognition. 11,* 702–718.

Glenberg, A. M., & Epstein, W. (1987). Inexpert calibration of comprehension. *Memory & Cognition, 15,* 84–93.

Glenberg, A. M., Sanocki, T., Epstein, W., & Morris, C. (1987). Enhancing calibration of comprehension. *Journal of Experimental Psychology: General, 116,* 119–136.

Glenberg, A. M., Wilkinson, A. C., & Epstein, W. (1982). The illusion of knowing: Failure in the self-assessment of comprehension. *Memory & Cognition, 10,* 597–602.

Glucksberg, S., & McCloskey, M. (1981). Decisions about ignorance: Knowing that you don't know. *Journal of Experimental Psychology: Human Learning and Memory, 7,* 311–325.

Gruneberg, M. M., & Monks, J. (1974). Feeling of knowing and cued recall. *Acta Psychologica, 38,* 257–265.

Hart, J. T. (1965). Memory and the feeling of knowing experience. *Journal of Educational Psychology, 56,* 208–216.

Hart, J. T. (1967). Memory and the memory-monitoring process. *Journal of Verbal Learning and Verbal Behavior, 6,* 685–691.

Hertzog, C., & Dixon, R. A. (1994). Metacognitive development in adulthood and old age. In J. Metcalfe & A. P. Shimamura (Eds.), *Metacognition: Knowing about knowing* (pp. 227–252). Cambridge, MA: MIT Press.

Jacoby, L. L., Bjork, R. A., & Kelley, C. M. (1994). Illusions of comprehension and competence. In D. Druckman & R. A. Bjork (Eds.), *Enhancing human performance, III* (pp. 57–80). Washington, DC: National Academy Press.

Jacoby, L. L., & Kelley, C. M. (1987). Unconscious influences of memory for a prior event. *Personality and Social Psychology Bulletin, 13,* 314–336.

James, W. (1890/1981). *The principles of psychology, Vol. 1,* Cambridge, MA: Harvard University Press.

Janowsky, J. S., Shimamura, A. P., & Squire, L. R. (1989). Memory and metamemory: Comparisons between frontal lobe lesions and amnesic patients. *Psychobiology, 17,* 3–11.

Johnson, M. K. (1988). Reality monitoring: An experimental phenomenological approach. *Journal of Experimental Psychology: General, 117,* 390–394.

Johnson, M. K., & Raye, C. L. (1981). Reality monitoring. *Psychological Review, 88,* 67–85.

Jouandet, M., & Gazzaniga, M. S. (1979). The frontal lobes. In M. S. Gazzaniga (Ed.), *Handbook of behavioral neurobiology* (Vol 2, pp. 25–59). New York: Plenum Press.

Kolers, P. A., & Palef, S. R. (1976). Knowing not. *Memory & Cognition, 4,* 553–558.

Koriat, A. (1993). How do we know what we know? The accessibility model of feeling of knowing. *Psychological Review, 100,* 609–639.

Koriat, A. (1994). Memory's knowledge of its own knowledge: The accessibility account of the feeling of knowing. In J. Metcalfe & A. P. Shimamura (Eds.), *Metacognition: Knowing about knowing.* Cambridge, MA: MIT Press.

Koriat, A. (1995). Dissociating knowing from feeling of knowing: Further evidence for the accessibility model. *Journal of Experimental Psychology: General, 124,* 311–333.

Koriat, A., & Goldsmith, M. (1996). Monitoring and control processes in the strategic regulation of memory accuracy. *Psychological Review, 103,* 490–517.

Koriat, A., Lichtenstein, S., & Fischhoff, B. (1980). Reasons for confidence. *Journal of Experimental Psychology: Human Learning and Memory, 6*, 107–118.

Koriat, A., & Lieblich, I. (1974). What does a person in a "TOT" state know that a person in a "don't know" state doesn't know. *Memory & Cognition, 2*, 647–655.

Krinsky, R., & Nelson, T. O. (1985). The feeling of knowing for different types of retrieval failure. *Acta Psychologica, 58*, 141–158.

Lachman, J. L., Lachman, R., & Thronesbury, C. (1979). Metamemory through the adult life span. *Developmental Psychology, 15*, 543–551.

Leonesio, R. J., & Nelson, T. O. (1990). Do different metamemory judgments tap the same underlying aspects of memory? *Journal of Experimental Psychology: Learning, Memory, and Cognition, 16*, 464–470.

Lichtenstein, S., Fischhoff, B., & Phillips, L. D. (1977). Calibration of probabilities: The state of the art to 1980. In D. Kahneman, P. Slovic, & A. Tversky (Eds.), *Judgments under uncertainty: Heuristics and biases* (pp. 306–334). New York: Cambridge University Press.

MacKay, D. G. (1982). The problems of flexibility, fluency and speed-accuracy trade-off in skilled behavior. *Psychological Review, 89*, 483–506.

Mazzoni, G., & Cornoldi, C. (1993). Strategies in study time allocation: Why is study time sometimes not effective? *Journal of Experimental Psychology: General, 122*, 47–60.

McGlynn, S. M., & Schacter, D. L. (1989). Unawareness of deficits in neuropsychological syndromes. *Journal of Clinical and Experimental Neuropsychology, 11*, 143–205.

Maki, R. H., & Berry, S. L. (1984). Metacomprehension of text material. *Journal of Experimental Psychology: Learning, Memory, and Cognition, 10*, 663–679.

Metcalfe, J. (1986a). Feeling of knowing in memory and problem solving. *Journal of Experimental Psychology: Learning, Memory, and Cognition, 12*, 288–294.

Metcalfe, J. (1986b). Premonitions of insight predict impending error. *Journal of Experimental Psychology: Learning, Memory, and Cognition, 12*, 623–634.

Metcalfe, J. (1990). Composite holographic associative recall model (CHARM) and blended memories in eyewitness testimony. *Journal of Experimental Psychology: General, 119*, 145–160.

Metcalfe, J. (1991). Recognition failure and the composite memory trace in CHARM. *Psychological Review, 98*, 529–553.

Metcalfe, J. (1993a) Novelty monitoring, metacognition and control in a composite holographic associative recall model: Implications for Korsakoff amnesia. *Psychological Review, 100*, 3–22.

Metcalfe, J. (1993b). Monitoring and gain control in an episodic memory model: Relation to P300 event-related potentials. In A. Collins, M. Conway, S. Gathercole, & P. Morris (Eds.), *Theories of memory* (pp. 327–354). Hillsdale, NJ: Erlbaum.

Metcalfe, J. (1998). Cognitive optimism: Self deception or memory-based processing heuristics? *Personality and Social Psychological Review.* Special Issue, *Metacognition, 2*, 100–110.

Metcalfe, J., Schwartz, B. L., & Joaquim, S. G. (1993). The cue familiarity heuristic in metacognition. *Journal of Experimental Psychology: Learning, Memory, and Cognition, 19*, 851–861.

Miner, A. C., & Reder, L. M. (1994). A new look at feeling of knowing: Its metacognitive role in regulating question answering. In J. Metcalfe & A. P. Shimamura (Eds.), *Metacognition: Knowing about knowing* (pp. 47–70). Cambridge: MIT Press.

Miozzo, M., & Caramazza, A. (1997). Retrieval of lexical-syntactic features in tip-of-the-tongue states. *Journal of Experimental Psychology: Learning, Memory, and Cognition, 23*, 1410–1423.

Morris, C. C. (1990). Retrieval processes underlying confidence in comprehension judgments. *Journal of Experimental Psychology: Leaning, Memory, and Cognition, 16*, 223–232.

Moscovitch, M. (1994). Models of consciousness and memory. In M. S. Gazzaniga (Ed.), *The cognitive neurosciences* (pp. 1341–1356). Cambridge, MA: MIT Press.

Nelson, T. O., Gerler, D., & Narens, L. (1984). Accuracy of feeling of knowing judgments for predicting perceptual identification and relearning. *Journal of Experimental Psychology: General, 113*, 282–300.

Nelson, T. O., Leonesio, R. J., Shimamura, A. P., Landwehr, R. S., & Narens, L. (1982). Overlearning and the feeling of knowing. *Journal of Experimental Psychology: Learning, Memory, and Cognition, 8*, 279–288.

Nelson, T. O., & Narens, L. (1980). Norms of 300 general-information questions: Accuracy of recall, latency of recall, and feeling-of-knowing ratings. *Journal of Verbal*

Learning and Verbal Behavior, 19, 338–368.

Nelson, T. O., & Narens, L. (1990). Metamemory: A theoretical framework and new findings. In G. Bower (Ed.), *The psychology of learning and motivation* (pp. 125–173). New York: Academic Press.

Nelson, T. O., & Narens, L. (1994). Why investigate metacognition? In J. Metcalfe & A. P. Shimamura (Eds.), *Metacognition: Knowing about knowing* (pp. 1–26). Cambridge, MA: MIT Press.

Oskamp, S. (1965). Overconfidence in case-study judgments. *Journal of Consulting Psychology, 29,* 261–265.

Poulton, E. C. (1994). *Behavioral decision theory: A new approach.* Cambridge: Cambridge University Press.

Reder, L. M. (1987). Selection strategies in question answering. *Cognitive Psychology, 19,* 90–138.

Reder, L. (1988). Strategic control of retrieval strategies. *The Psychology of Learning and Motivation, 22,* 227–259.

Reder, L. M., & Kusbit, G. W. (1991) Locus of the Moses illusion: Imperfect encoding, retrieval, or match? *Journal of Memory and Language, 30,* 385–406.

Reder, L. M., & Ritter, F. E. (1992). What determines initial feeling of knowing? Familiarity with question terms, not with the answer. *Journal of Experimental Psychology: Learning, Memory, and Cognition, 18,* 435–452.

Schacter, D. L. (1983). Feeling of knowing in episodic memory. *Journal of Experimental Psychology: Learning, Memory, and Cognition, 9,* 39–54.

Schacter, D. L. (1989). Memory, amnesia, and frontal lobe dysfunction. *Psychobiology, 15,* 21–36.

Schacter, D. L., & Worling, J. R. (1985). Attribute information and the feeling of knowing. *Canadian Journal of Psychology, 39,* 467–475.

Schneider, W. (1998). The development of procedural metamemory in childhood and adolescence. In G. Mazzoni & T. O. Nelson (Eds.), *Metacognition and cognitive neuropsychology* (pp. 1–21). Mahwah, NJ: Erlbaum.

Schreiber, T. A. (1998). Effects of target set size on feelings of knowing and cued recall: Implications for the cue effectiveness and partial retrieval hypothesis. *Memory & Cognition, 26,* 553–571.

Schreiber, T. A., & Nelson, D. L. (1998). The relation between feelings of knowing and the number of neighboring concepts linked to the test cue. *Memory & Cognition, 26,* 869–883.

Schwartz, B. L. (1998). Illusory tip-of-the-tongue states. *Memory, 6,* 623–642.

Schwartz, B. L., & Metcalfe, J. (1992), Cue familiarity but not target retrievability enhances feeling-of-knowing judgments. *Journal of Experimental Psychology: Learning, Memory, and Cognition, 18,* 1074–1083.

Schwartz, B. L., & Metcalfe, J. (1994). Methodological problems and pitfalls in the study of human metacognition. In J. Metcalfe & A. P. Shimamura (Eds.), *Metacognition: Knowing about knowing* (pp. 93–114). Cambridge, MA: MIT Press.

Schwartz, B. L., & Smith, S. (1997). The retrieval of related information influences tip-of-the-tongue states. *Journal of Memory and Language, 36,* 68–86.

Shallice, T., & Evans, M. E. (1978). The involvement of the frontal lobes in cognitive estimation. *Cortex, 14,* 294–303.

Shaughnessy, J. J. (1979). Confidence-judgment accuracy as a predictor of test performance. *Journal of Research in Personality, 13,* 505–514.

Shimamura, A. P., & Squire, L. R. (1986). Memory and metamemory: A study of the feeling-of-knowing phenomenon in Amnesic patients. *Journal of Experimental Psychology: Learning, Memory, and Cognition, 12,* 452–460.

Slamecka, N. J., Graf, P. (1978). The generation effect: Delineation of a phenomenon. *Journal of Experimental Psychology: Human Learning and Memory, 4,* 592–604.

Smith, S. M. (1994). Frustrated feelings of imminent recall: On the tip of the tongue. In J. Metcalfe & A. P. Shimamura (Eds.), *Metacognition: Knowing about knowing* (pp. 27–46). Cambridge, MA: MIT Press.

Spellman, B. A., & Bjork, R. A. (1992). When predictions create reality: Judgments of learning may alter what they are intended to assess. *Psychological Science, 3,* 315–316.

Thiede, K. W. (1996). The relative importance of anticipated test format and anticipated difficulty on performance. *Quarterly Journal of Experimental Psychology, 49A,* 901–918.

Thiede, K. W., & Dunlosky, J. (1999). Toward a general model of self-regulated study: An analysis of selection of items for study and self-paced study time. *Journal of Experimental Psychology: Learning, Memory, and Cognition, 25,* 1024–1037.

Tulving, E., & Madigan, S. A. (1970). Memory and verbal learning. *Annual Review of Psychology, 21,* 437–484.

Vigliocco, G. Antonini, T., & Garrett, M. F. (1997). Grammatical gender is on the tip of Italian tongues. *Psychological Science, 8,* 314–317.

Waern, Y., & Askwall, S. (1981). On some sources of metacomprehension. *Scandinavian Journal of Psychology, 22,* 17–25.

Weingardt, K. R., Leonesio, R. J., & Loftus, E. F. (1994). Viewing eyewitness research from a metacognitive perspective. In J. Metcalfe & A. P. Shimamura (Eds.), *Metacognition: Knowing about knowing* (pp. 157–184). Cambridge, MA: MIT Press.

Wellman, H. M. (1977). Tip of the tongue and feeling of knowing experiences: A developmental study of memory monitoring. *Child Development, 48,* 13–21.

AWARENESS IN MEMORY

14

Recollection and Familiarity

Process-Dissociation

COLLEEN M. KELLEY & LARRY L. JACOBY

Alan Baddeley (1982) recounted the following story to illustrate the active processes involved in recollection. He was traveling to London by train when he noticed a familiar face. As the person did not recognize him, he assumed it was someone he had seen on the train before or around Cambridge. When he got off the train he noticed the man again, and because he had been thinking about memory and retrieval, he resolved to attempt to remember who the person was. Two associations came to mind: the name Sebastian, and something to do with children. "Sebastian" conjured up several further associations, including one friend named Sebastian from a different city, another friend whose school-age son was named Sebastian, and the teddy bear in Evelyn Waugh's *Brideshead Revisited*. All of these he rejected as irrelevant. Later, the idea of "baby-sitting" popped to mind, followed by the immediate recollection that Alan and Sebastian were members of the same baby-sitting group, with a clear image of Sebastian's sitting room with many finely printed books, a printing machine in another room, and the knowledge that Sebastian was a printer. Those details produced a strong experience of confidence in recall, as they were far more diagnostic than if he had remembered simply a room with books and a desk, which as Baddeley notes would be true of all his acquaintances.

Baddeley's anecdote beautifully illustrates the different subjective experiences of familiarity and recollection. It is a distinction that was noted by Aristotle, by William James, as well as by more contemporary psychologists (Atkinson & Juola, 1974; Mandler, 1980; Jacoby & Dallas, 1981). This chapter focuses on whether the different subjective experiences of familiarity and recollection indicate the need for two distinct processes in models of memory, or whether they simply reflect a quantitative difference in a single dimension or single process such as "trace strength." If recollection and familiarity are separate memory processes, what is the nature of those processes, and what is the relationship between the processes in the performance of a task such as a recognition memory test?

Functional Differences between Familiarity and Recollection

As indicated in Baddeley's anecdote, there are clear functional differences between familiarity and recollection. When a person looks familiar, the source of that familiarity is ambiguous: Is it a long-lost friend, someone we've seen in passing, somebody famous? Or just a person who resembles someone we know well? In contrast, recollection involves a flood of details that allows us to clearly pin down a previous encounter with the person. We took advantage of those functional differences in familiarity and recollection to demonstrate that there are two separate memory processes in a set of experiments we call the "false fame" experiments (e.g., Jacoby, Woloshyn, & Kelley, 1989). Participants in these experiments read a list of nonfamous names (e.g., Sebastian Weisdorf, no relation to Baddeley's Sebastian, as far as we know), under conditions of either full or divided attention. Our participants' attention was divided by requiring them to monitor an auditory list of random digits and to signal whenever they heard three consecutive odd digits. In the second phase of the experiment, participants were given a "fame judgment test": they were to judge whether names on a list were famous or not, and the list included famous names, some new nonfamous names, and nonfamous names that had just been read in the earlier list. Participants were informed that if they recognized any of the names as ones they had just read, they should respond "nonfamous," as all names on the earlier list were nonfamous.

Normally, recognition can be based on either familiarity or recollection. However, if the familiarity that accrues to a name because one has just read it is similar to the familiarity of the only mildly famous people's names we used on the test, our participants couldn't use familiarity as a basis for recognition, and so exclude the name from those judged "famous." To do so would lead to many misses of actual famous names that could only be judged famous because they were familiar. Instead, participants could only be sure that they recognized a name from the earlier list if they could recollect reading it. If they failed to recollect reading a nonfamous name, and yet it became familiar because of its presentation on the list, they would err and call the name "famous." That is exactly what happened when the probability of recollection was low because participants had read the names under conditions of divided attention: old nonfamous names were more likely to be judged "famous" than were new nonfamous names. In contrast, if the names had been read with full attention, participants successfully used recollection to correctly judge the name "nonfamous." Old nonfamous names were less likely to be judged "famous" than were new nonfamous names.

Dividing participants' attention with the digit monitoring task prevented participants from elaborating on or reflecting upon the nonfamous names as they read them, and so led to a very low rate of recollection. However, the rather minimal processing allowed under conditions of divided attention (which included reading the names aloud) was enough to enhance the familiarity of those nonfamous names. What does this effect tell us about the underlying process that gives rise to familiarity? Mandler (1980) suggested that recollection is supported by elaboration and interitem organizational processing whereas familiarity is a function of processing that increases the integration of representations of items. Jacoby and Dallas (1981) suggested that familiarity is generated by changes in perceptual processing of the kind that is revealed by indirect memory tests such as perceptual identification. In a visual perceptual identification test, a word or picture is presented briefly and followed by a pattern mask. Words or pictures that have been read or viewed recently show a higher probability of being identified under those degraded conditions. The subjective experience of old items on the perceptual identification test is that they "pop out" at the viewer, and in fact appear to be presented for a longer duration than the new items (Jacoby & Witherspoon, 1982). Jacoby and Dallas speculated that the subjective experience of familiarity might be based on those changes in the perceptual experience of old items, in much the same way that Tversky and Kahneman (1973) suggested that subjective probability could be based on the ease of generating examples of a class, the "availability heuristic." People could attribute their experience of perceptual fluency to having viewed a word or picture previously, and so experience a feeling of familiarity, via a "fluency heuristic." Some variables such as number of repetitions and spacing of repetitions showed parallel effects on perceptual identification test performance and recognition memory test performance, but other variables such as levels of processing affected recognition but not perceptual identification. This combination of parallel effects and dissociative effects could be accounted for by the two bases for recognition memory.

If familiarity is an interpretation of changes in processing due to prior experience, then it should be possible to bring about those changes in processing in other ways, and so create illusions of familiarity. Jacoby and Whitehouse (1989) tested that hypothesis by flashing brief previews of words prior to those words being presented in full view during a recognition test. The notion was that when the preview word matched the word presented during the recognition test, processing of the recognition test word would be more fluent, and so it would seem more familiar. However, that misattribution of the fluent processing of the test word to having studied it earlier would occur only if participants did not realize that the preview word was the source of the more fluent processing. Therefore, the illusion of familiarity was expected only when the preview word was presented so briefly that participants were unaware of it, and that is what happened. Both old test words and new test words were more likely to be judged "old" on the recognition test when preceded by a very briefly presented matching preview word, compared to control items with no preview word. In contrast, when the matching preview word was presented for a longer duration, such that participants were fully aware of it, participants were less likely to judge the test word "old." Rajaram (1993) found that the illusion of memory created by the very brief preview words acted to make words more familiar as indicated by "know" judgments, but did not affect the likelihood of recollection as indicated by "remember" judgments (see Gardiner, chapter 15).

Recognition test words read in predictive sentence contexts also can be mistakenly experienced as familiar owing to prior study as shown in a series of experiments by Whittlesea (1993). People were more likely to respond "old" to recognition test words at the end of a predictive sentence context such as, "The stormy seas tossed the *boat*," compared to test words presented in an unpredictable context, "She saved up her money and bought a *boat*." Words read in the predictable context were pronounced more quickly, which may indicate that the false familiarity is mediated by perceptual processing or speeded lexical access (Weldon, 1991), or perhaps a postpronunciation assessment of "goodness of fit" with the rest of the sentence, or even lack of novelty (Poldrack & Logan, 1998).

Past experience affects later experience in a multitude of ways, often without people's knowledge or appreciation of those effects. The false fame phenomenon is an example of such implicit memory effects in that the likelihood that a name is judged famous is increased by recent experience reading the name, in the absence of conscious recollec-

tion. The consequences of prior processing can shape a wide variety of experiences: it can make visual duration seem extended (Witherspoon & Allan, 1985), lower judgments of background noise (Jacoby, Allan, Collins, & Larwill, 1988), increase the judged validity of statements (Begg & Armour, 1991), lower judged difficulty of anagrams (Kelley & Jacoby, 1996), and increase the comprehensibility of sentences (Kelley, 1999). These effects are misattributions of the increased fluency of perceptual and conceptual processing owing to prior experience. Any of the component processes that give rise to these misattributions could be a candidate component of familiarity. Specifying the component processes of familiarity is an important task for future research. The fluency heuristic and other potential bases for familiarity are the focus of papers in a special issue of *Acta Psychologica* (Wolters, & Logan, 1998).

Separating Familiarity and Recollection: Ironic Effects

The false fame effects described earlier are an ironic effect of prior experience similar to the effects explored by Wegner (1994): Having read a list of names that one is told were all nonfamous ironically increases the probability of an error on the fame test, similar to the automatic effect of trying *not* to think about something that perversely increases the likelihood that one will think exactly that thought. Elderly adults, amnesiacs, and patients who have sustained a closed-head injury are all more susceptible to an ironic effect of past experience, in that they show a large false fame effect even after reading the nonfamous names with full attention (Bartlett, Strater, & Fulton, 1991; Cermak, Verfaellie, Butler, & Jacoby, 1993; Dywan & Jacoby, 1990; Dywan, Segalowitz, Henderson, & Jacoby, 1993; Jennings & Jacoby, 1993; Squire & McKee, 1992). This pattern of results suggests that recollection is more affected by aging and amnesia than is familiarity, although familiarity could also be affected. The method of placing recollection and familiarity in opposition does not allow one to specify precisely the degree to which either process is affected.

Repetition of events can increase ironic effects of recent exposure when increases in familiarity go unopposed by parallel increases in recollection. To place recollection and familiarity in opposition, Jacoby (1991, 1999) used a procedure logically related to the false fame studies. In the first phase, young and older adults read a list of words, with instructions to study them for a later memory test. Some of the "read" words were presented only once, and others were presented either two or three times. In the second phase, participants listened to a second list of words presented via a tape recording, and also tried to memorize those words. On the memory test, participants were given a list of words and told to respond "yes" if they *heard* the word in the second phase. However, they were warned that words read in the first phase would appear on the test, as well as new words. Therefore, if they could recollect that the word was read, they could be sure it was not heard and therefore they should say "no" on the test. However, if the word was simply familiar, they couldn't be certain that it was not heard, and so should respond "yes." Given these instructions, words that are recollected as having been read are excluded from positive responses, but words that are familiar, because they were either read or heard, will be included in the positive responses, along with words that are recollected as having been heard. Thus, recollection can be used to exclude read words, much as recollection could be used to exclude nonfamous studied names on the fame test.

If one simply focuses on recognition performance on heard items for the young versus older adults, there is a moderate deficit for the older adults (.52 for "hits" by older adults, compared to .63 for younger adults). It is not clear whether this represents problems with recollection, familiarity, or both. However, if one focuses on the failures to exclude "read" items, there is a clear problem in older adults' ability to recollect. For young adults, repetition decreased failures to exclude read items: the probabilities of saying "yes" to read items decreased for items read three times compared to items read once. Exactly the opposite pattern occurred for older adults: repetition increased failures to exclude read items (see table 14.1). Younger adults could oppose any effects of repetition on familiarity by their increased ability to recollect that an item was on the read list. Older adults were unable to keep the rising familiarity owing to repetition in check with corresponding increases in recollection.

This crossover interaction effect of repetition cannot be the result of a single process (cf. Donaldson, 1996). If one adopted a signal detection analysis by assuming, for example,

Table 14.1 Probability of responding "Yes" item was heard.

| | False Alarms | | | | Hits |
| | Read | | | | |
Group	1x	2x	3x	New	Heard
Young	.35	.31	.21	.22	.63
Elderly	.43	.53	.59	.19	.52

an ordered distribution of familiarity values corresponding to the number of presentations, such that the familiarity distribution for new items is lower than that for once-read items, which is in turn lower than the distribution for repeatedly read items—there is no placement of response criteria that could produce the pattern of results such that the probability of FA (repeatedly read) > FA (once-read) > FA (new) for elderly adults and also produce FA (repeatedly read) < FA (once-read) < FA (new) for younger adults. This pattern of results requires a form or use of memory in addition to familiarity that is different for elderly and young adults. (For similar patterns of results along with discussions of relevance to single-process models of memory, see Jacoby, Jones, & Dolan, 1998, as well as McElree, Dolan, & Jacoby, 1999.)

Estimating Recollection and Familiarity: The Process-Dissociation Procedure

Does familiarity as well as recollection diminish with aging? The method of placing familiarity and recollection in opposition does not allow one to detect such a pattern of effects, nor can it distinguish complex effects of a variable that simultaneously lowers familiarity and increases recollection from a simple increase in recollection. What is needed is some means of estimating the contributions of familiarity and recollection to performance.

An early approach to the problem of obtaining estimates of familiarity and recollection was to use performance on recall tests as a measure of recollection. Mandler (1980) took that approach in studies of recognition memory for paired associates, when he used cued-recall performance (of A given B, and of B given A) as an estimate of recollection, and solved for estimates of the familiarity of the A item, the B item, and AB pair given levels of recognition of the single items versus the pair. Given much previous work that found variables that affected recall performance and recognition performance in different ways, he assumed that recollection and familiarity make independent contributions to recognition. The equation describing such independence is recognition performance (Rg) equals Familiarity (F) plus Recollection or retrieval (R), minus the overlap of the two processes, or $Rg = F + R - FR$. He then demonstrated that when items had been presented the same number of times, estimates of F were constant across conditions with widely varying levels of recall and recognition.

Using other tasks such as recall to estimate the probability of recollection within recognition or using perceptual identification to estimate the probability of familiarity within recognition is at best a rough guide to what actually happens within the recognition task. Even if the nominal external cue were the same, the participant's goals and orientation would be different in the two tasks, and so the effective cues would differ (for a related discussion, see Kelley & Jacoby, 1998). Further, it is not necessarily the case that recall performance is a pure measure of recollection. People might produce the studied B member of an AB pair when cued with the A member, but not have an experience of recollecting the AB study episode. This production of B would be experienced as a guess, but would be a guess informed by prior experience, in much the same way that prior experience increases the production rates of items above baseline in an indirect memory test. This informed guessing process may be operating in Baddeley's anecdote, when he thought "Sebastian" when he first attempted to recall where he had previously seen that person. Ideally, estimates of recollection and familiarity should be derived from performance on the recognition memory test.

Jacoby (1991) developed a procedure to measure recollection and familiarity within a task. The method, called the Process-Dissociation Procedure, hinges on assessing recollection in terms of the control over responding it affords. Recollection is measured as the difference in responding when people are directed to *not* use responses from a particular study episode (the exclusion condition outlined earlier in the ironic effects of repetition study) compared to when they are directed *to* use responses from that study episode (the inclusion condition). So, in addition to the exclusion condition outlined earlier, participants would be directed to respond to some items on the recognition memory test by responding "yes" to all studied words, both read and heard items. In the inclusion condition, participants are told to use the test item to attempt to recollect the prior presentation of the item on either the read or heard list, but also to say "yes" if they fail to recollect the item but it is nonetheless familiar.

Assuming independence of recollection and familiarity, the probability of responding "yes" to a read item under inclusion instructions is equal to $R + F - RF$. In contrast, mistakenly responding "yes" to read items under the exclusion instructions represents failures of recollection and the operation of familiarity, or $(1 - R)F$. By subtracting the probability of "yes" to read items under exclusion instructions from the probability of "yes" to read items under inclusion instructions, one can obtain an estimate of R, which can then be used to solve for an estimate of F.

The independence assumption underlying the equations implies that there are variables that produce dissociative effects on the estimates of familiarity versus recollection. And that is indeed the case. Elderly participants show lower contributions of recollection to their recognition memory test performance compared to younger participants, but show just as much familiarity (Jennings & Jacoby, 1993, 1997; Jacoby, 1999). Returning to the ironic effects of repetition, Jacoby (1999, experiment 4) used the process-dissociation procedure to show that repeatedly reading a word served to increase both recollection and familiarity. For young adults, the probability of recollection for words read once was .38 and increased to .67 when words were read three times. The corresponding probabilities of recollection for elderly adults were much lower: .20 and .49. Estimated familiarity was lower for words read once rather than three times but did not differ for young (.45 vs. .57) and elderly (.44 vs. .58) adults.

A similar pattern of lower recollection but invariant familiarity appears for dysphoric compared to nondysphoric participants (Hertel & Milan, 1994). Forcing participants to respond quickly rather than more slowly reduces the estimates of recollection but does not affect estimates of familiarity (Yonelinas & Jacoby, 1994). Presenting longer lists of words at study reduces estimates of recollection but leaves familiarity intact. These invariances do not indicate that familiarity is unresponsive to variations in study conditions: Solving an anagram at study produces higher estimates of familiarity and recollection compared to simply reading the word (Jacoby, 1991); engaging in semantic compared to shallow processing (Toth, 1996); studying items in the form of pictures rather than words (Wagner, Gabrieli, & Verfaellie, 1997); and reinstating study context words at test (Jacoby, 1996). (For further examples see table 14.2.) These results suggest that recollection relies on the products

of elaboration and reflection, but familiarity relies on the products of more minimal perceptual and conceptual processing.

The process-dissociation procedure can be cast in the form of a multinomial model. Multinomial modeling is a statistical technique used to estimate parameters that correspond to the probabilities of hypothetical events that are discrete cognitive states. Once the cognitive events are specified that produce behavior in various categories (such as responding "old" on a recognition test), tree diagrams can be written to specify the model

Table 14.2 Estimates of recollection and automaticity as a function of aging, level of attention, study duration, habit strength, and response deadline.

Dissociating Variable	Recollection	Automaticity
Aging[a]		
Items studied once		
Young	.38	.45
Elderly	.20	.44
Items studied three times		
Young	.67	.57
Elderly	.49	.58
Attention[b]		
Full	.25	.47
Divided	.00	.46
Attention[c]		
Full	.29	.54
Divided	.14	.55
Study Duration[c]		
10 s	.44	.59
1 s	.22	.58
Habit Strength[d]		
Strong	.45	.67
Weak	.43	.48
Study Duration[d]		
1 s	.47	.62
300 ms	.27	.65
Response Deadline[d]		
3 s	.41	.62
1 s	.26	.61
Aging[e]		
Distinctive Items		
Young	.60	.70
Elderly	.30	.72
Non-distinctive Items		
Young	.44	.72
Elderly	.29	.72

Note. [a]From Jacoby (1999); [b]from Jacoby, Toth and Yonelinas (1993); [c]from Jacoby (1998); [d]from Hay and Jacoby (1996); [e]from Hay and Jacoby (1999). Estimates of "automaticity" reflect influences of familiarity, habit, bias depending on the particular paradigm.

(Rieder & Batchelder, 1988). In the case of attempting to estimate the parameters for processes underlying recognition, in addition to estimating F and R, separate parameters are included for guessing. Thus the multinomial model can handle differences in guessing (e.g., Buchner, Erdfelder, & Vaterrodt-Plünnecke, 1995; Erdfelder & Buchner, 1998). Doing so will not change the pattern of results from that obtained using the original process-dissociation procedure as long as false-alarm rates for new words, used to estimate guessing, do not differ across types of test (inclusion vs. exclusion) or groups (Jacoby, 1998; Yonelinas & Jacoby, 1996).

Yonelinas (1994) developed a dual-process model of recognition that assumes that familiarity is a continuous dimension, much as is assumed in single-process models of recognition memory, which use signal detection measures to separate memory from decision processes or response biases. However, recollection is a second process underlying recognition, and unlike familiarity, it operates as a discrete threshold process. Continuous strength processes and discrete-threshold (or high-threshold) processes produce very different relations between hits and false alarms as confidence varies. Such plots of hits versus false alarms across levels of confidence are known as receiver operating characteristics, or ROCs (see Murdock, 1974). Accordingly, familiarity alone would produce an ROC that is curvilinear and symmetrical around the negative diagonal. Recollection alone would produce a straight-line ROC that would begin at the lowest level of the hit rate and increase to 1,1. In combination, recollection and familiarity would produce ROC curves that are curvilinear but asymmetrical (see also Yonelinas, 1997).

Yonelinas, Kroll, Dobbins, Lazzara, and Knight (1998) provided evidence to support the assumption that recollection and familiarity serve as independent bases for recognition memory and found that amnesiacs suffer a deficit in familiarity as well as recollection. Re-analysis of results from published studies, as well as results from a new experiment, supported the conclusion that amnesia was associated with deficits in both recollection and familiarity but with a much greater deficit in recollection. Further, the ROCs in amnesiacs versus control participants differed in ways that supported their model with its underlying assumption of the independence of familiarity and recollection.

Extensions of the Process-Dissociation Procedure

The process-dissociation procedure has been generalized to other problems where multiple processes can contribute to performance in a single task, most importantly to the study of conscious memory (e.g., recollection and familiarity) versus unconscious or implicit memory (thought to be tapped by indirect tests such as stem completion; for reviews, see Kelley & Lindsay, 1996, and Roediger & McDermott, 1993). The procedure involves study of a single list of items, such as words. At test, cues such as word stems (e.g., *mot _ _*) are presented, with a signal to use the cue to produce a word studied on the list, but to guess if recollection fails (the inclusion condition), or with a signal to use the cue to produce a word not on the studied list (the exclusion condition). Again assuming independence of conscious and unconscious memory, the difference in producing a studied word under inclusion instructions $(C + U - CU)$ versus exclusion instructions $(1 - C)U$ is the estimate of conscious recollection. Using this procedure revealed that recollection is lowered dramatically by divided attention at study, whereas unconscious memory is unaffected, which has led to calling the unconscious memory "automatic" (Jacoby, Toth, & Yonelinas, 1993).

Hay and Jacoby (1996) applied a variant of the process-dissociation procedure in their studies that attempted to separate the contribution of experimentally established habits from the effects of recollection. Experimental habits were established in a training phase, where stimulus words were paired with a typical response on 75% of the occasions (e.g., knee-bend) and an atypical response on 25% of the occasions (e.g., knee-bone). After the habits were established, the second phase involved study of particular lists of word pairs, which included some word pairs where the right-hand member of the pair was a typical response, and some word pairs where the right-hand member of the pair was an atypical response. After studying each list, recall was cued with the left-hand member of the pair and a fragment of the right-hand member of the pair (e.g., *knee-b _ n _*). With this arrangement, correct recall of typical pairs could be based either on memory for the list (R) or on the habitual response (H). Assuming independence of the two sources for correct responding, the probability of correct recall for typical pairs can be represented as: Prob (typical) = R + H(1 − R).

When people make memory slips—that is, when they mistakenly respond with the habitual response after having studied an atypical pair—memory has failed and habit is determining their response. The probability of such errors after study of atypical pairs is represented by: Prob (typical) = H (1 − R).

By using these two equations, Hay and Jacoby were able to solve for estimates of the contributions of habit (H) and memory (R) to cued-recall performance. They found that manipulating the strength of the habit established in the first phase did not affect the estimates of R in later cued recall, but did affect the estimates of H. The estimates of H matched the probabilities established in the training phase. Manipulations of the presentation rate of the list and response time in cued recall affected the estimates of R, but did not affect the estimates of H. These dissociations support the assumption that habit and memory make independent contributions to memory performance, and converge with results from the inclusion/exclusion procedure. Hay and Jacoby (1999) showed that cued recall performance of elderly and young participants differed only because elderly participants were less able to recollect; the contribution of habit was age invariant. Again, the pattern of results is the same as found with the inclusion/exclusion procedure.

The finding that estimates of habit show probability matching suggests that habit is a form of implicit learning. Reber (e.g., 1989) has argued that probability matching reflects implicit learning of an event sequence that is acquired independently of a conscious effort to learn and without intentional strategies. Knowlton, Squire, and Gluck (1994) described probability learning as a task that relies primarily on the form of memory preserved by amnesiacs. They found that amnesiacs show evidence of probability learning but perform more poorly than people with normally functioning memory. They suggested that the poorer probability learning of amnesiacs is a result of their inability to recollect (declarative memory), a type of memory used by people with normal memory to supplement the more automatic, unintentional form of memory (procedural memory) that is fully relied on by those with amnesia for performance in probability learning tasks. The process-dissociation procedure offers the advantage of separating

the contributions of different forms or uses of memory within a task, rather than identifying processes with different tasks. Just as recall does not serve as a pure measure of recollection in recognition memory performance, performance in probability learning tasks is unlikely to serve as a pure measure of more automatic bases of responding (e.g., implicit learning or habit) in cued-recall performance.

Ratcliff and McKoon (1995, 1997) argued that many implicit memory effects are actually bias effects and proposed a counter model of such effects. We (Jacoby et. al., 1993) agree that automatic influences of memory (implicit memory) can be expressed as bias. However, we see the term "bias" as synonymous with the claim that an automatic influence of memory, such as familiarity in a test of recognition memory, can serve as an alternative to recollection as a basis for responding. Jacoby, McElree, and Trainham (1999) have shown that results reported as support for their counter model by Ratcliff and McKoon (1997) when reanalyzed, reveal striking dissociations that are the same as found by Hay and Jacoby (1996). That is, the experiments supporting the counter model reveal striking dissociations betweeen bias effects and memory, suggesting the same independence between processes as found using the process-dissociation procedure.

Controversy Surrounding the Process-Dissociation Procedure: Alternative Approaches

The assumptions underlying the process-dissociation approach have been controversial (e.g., Buchner et al., 1995; Curran & Hintzman, 1995, 1997; Graf & Komatsu, 1994; Mulligan & Hirshman, 1997; Ratcliff, Van Zandt, & McKoon, 1995). Most controversial has been the assumption that recollection and familiarity *independently* contribute to performance. Curran and Hintzman (1995) found correlations between R and A and so argued that the two bases for responding are not independent. However, through subsequent exchanges (see Curran & Hintzman, 1997, and Hintzman & Curran, 1997, along with responses by Jacoby, Begg, & Toth, 1997, and Jacoby & Shrout, 1997) agreement was reached that correlations between R and A calculated by aggregating over participants or over items cannot legitimately be used to test the independence of underlying processes. Jacoby (1998) showed that instructions can be manipulated in a way that results in violation of assumptions underlying the process-dissociation procedure, and also described other boundary conditions for those assumptions. "Paradoxical" dissociations that result from violating underlying assumptions (Curran & Hintzman, 1995) can be replicated when participants are instructed to use a particular strategy, but those dissociations were not related to correlations between R and A. Although the independence assumption underlying the process-dissociation procedure can be violated, correlations between R and A are not useful for detecting such violations.

An alternative to the independence assumption is that recollection and familiarity are in a redundant relationship—that is, recollection cannot occur unless familiarity first occurs, so recollected items are a subset of familiar items (Buchner et al., 1995; Joordens & Merikle, 1993). By this account, recollection is a late stage of processing that relies on the prior stage of computing familiarity. One way to think about the difference between independence and redundancy is with the example of generate/recognize models of recall versus models of direct retrieval. If recall is cued by a stem of the studied word, e.g., *mot- -*, people can be instructed to use that cue to generate the first word that comes to mind, and then do a recognition check of whether the generated item was on the list. With that strategy, recognition is a later stage of processing that occurs only if a studied word has been generated and, so, clearly the two cannot be independent. Generation of studied items would be above baseline because of effects of automatic or unconscious memory (Jacoby & Hollingshead, 1990). It was such generate/recognize instructions that Jacoby (1998) used to violate the independence assumption underlying the process-dissociation procedure and to establish boundary conditions for the procedure.

In contrast, the instructions in the process-dissociation procedure are to use the stem as a cue for retrieval, and so start a process of recollection. People might find also that the studied item comes automatically to mind, but in this case, recollection of the studied item does not depend on waiting for the automatic retrieval to occur—the two processes occur independently. In the case of recollection and familiarity, if recollection depended upon familiarity, the equations used to generate esti-

mates with the process-dissociation procedure would be in error, and it becomes quite amazing that so many manipulations would have produced invariance in estimates of F across wide variations in R (e.g., divided attention, elderly vs. young participants, short-deadlines to respond vs. long-deadlines to respond.) Those experiments all used instructions designed to encourage direct retrieval.

Age-related deficits in recollection are closely related to age-related deficits in source monitoring (Spencer & Raz, 1995). Source monitoring paradigms assess memory for source by examining overt source attributions (Johnson, Hashtroudi, & Lindsay, 1993; Mitchell & Johnson, chapter 12). Participants choose one of *n*-alternatives denoting whether and in what context the test item was studied. For example, participants might hear some words and read other words during study and then later judge for each test word whether it was read, heard, or not studied earlier. Those judgments are used to compute both a measure of recognition memory and a measure of source memory, often with the intention of studying possible impairments in certain types of source discrimination (e.g., Foley & Johnson, 1985; Harvey, 1985). Results from standard tests of source memory have shown that older, as compared to younger, adults are less able to remember whether information was presented visually or aurally (e.g., Light, La Voie, Valencia-Laver, Albertson-Owens, & Mead, 1992; McIntyre & Craik, 1987).

To adequately measure source memory (recollection), one must take response biases into account and make an assumption about the relation between recognition and source memory, which, in turn, requires that one adopt a model of recognition-memory performance. The treatment of source information as a late achievement is implicit in the multinomial model most often used to measure source monitoring (e.g., Buchner, Erdfelder, Steffens, & Martensen, 1997; Johnson, Kounios, & Reeder, 1994). The model that is most commonly used (Batchelder & Riefer, 1990, Model 5b) treats the probability of retrieving source information as conditional on having recognized or detected an item as "old." However, this model does not specify the processes involved in the detection parameter, D—that is, it does not specify a particular model of recognition memory. One could interpret D or recognition of old items as dependent only on familiarity, and interpret the source memory parameter as recollection. In contrast, the independence model is a dual-process model of recognition memory (see Clark & Gronlund, 1996, for a discussion of evidence for a dual-process model of recognition). McElree et al. (1999) describe how an independence assumption of the sort used to interpret ironic effects of repetition can be accommodated in the framework of global-memory models (e.g., MINERVA2, Hintzman, 1988; SAM, Gillund & Shiffrin, 1984; TODAM, Murdock, 1982). Jacoby (1999) showed that a multinomial model based on an independence assumption could account for results from his experiment using fewer parameters than required by a model based on a redundancy assumption.

The remember/know procedure (see Gardiner, chapter 15) focuses on differences in subjective experience whereas investigations of source memory and use of the process-dissociation procedure have emphasized differences in objective performance and sought to specify underlying processes. However, we agree regarding the importance of subjective experience. Estimates of recollection gained by the process-dissociation procedure are sometimes the same as the probability of a "remember" response, which is used as an index of the subjective experience of recollection. That is, subjective and objective measures of recollection often coincide. A point of controversy is how "know" responses should be interpreted. Participants are told to respond "know" on a test of recognition memory, for example, if an item seems familiar but they cannot remember encountering the item during study—a situation similar to that experienced by Baddeley in the anecdote used to begin this chapter. We have identified "know" responses with familiarity and argued that one must make an assumption about the relation between recollection and familiarity (e.g., an independence assumption) to interpret those responses in terms of the underlying processes. (For further discussion of the relation between remember/know and process dissociation, see Jacoby, Yonelinas, & Jennings, 1997; Kelley & Jacoby, 1998; Richardson-Klavehn, Gardiner, & Java, 1996).

Concluding Comments

Placing processes in opposition as in the "fame" and the "ironic effects" experiments produces results that show the necessity of a dual-process model for recognition. There is a growing consensus that contributions of different forms or uses of memory must be separated within a task rather than identified with different tasks, although there is little agreement about how that should be done.

It is important to devise means to measure deficits in recollection or source memory as part of diagnosis and treatment. As an example, older adults' greater susceptibility to false memory (e.g., Schacter, Kagan, & Leichtman, 1995) can be seen as a failure to use recollection as a basis for excluding test items that are familiar for a wrong reason. An exclusion test is not equivalent to asking people to report on memory for source. People sometimes make exclusion errors even though if directly asked they could report the source information that would allow those errors to be avoided, and this is likely to be particularly true for older adults (e.g., Dywan & Jacoby, 1990; Multhaup, 1995). Also, understanding exclusion errors requires that one consider the possibility of differences in familiarity as well as differences in recollection (Yonelinas et al., 1998). Older adults and other special populations are more prone to errors that reflect an over-reliance on habit (Hay & Jacoby, 1999).

To measure the separate contributions of the different processes to overall performance, one must adopt an assumption about the relationship between recollection and more automatic influences of memory, such as familiarity. It seems likely that an independence assumption is appropriate in some situations whereas a redundancy assumption is appropriate in other situations. That is, we expect any model to have boundary conditions. An important goal for research is to specify such boundary conditions and so reveal factors that determine the relation between underlying processes. The question about the relation between processes underlying memory performance has a parallel in the relation between the automatic versus consciously controlled processes underlying social behavior (see Chaiken & Trope, 1999). There, too, it is important to distinguish between early-selection (independence) and late-correction (redundancy) models to specify better the nature of deficits in social monitoring and to design treatments aimed at escaping the effects of such automatic processes as stereotyping (Jacoby, Kelley, & McElree, 1999).

Although recollection and automatic influences of memory are not *always* independent, there are advantages to be gained by arranging situations such that independence holds. Our proposal of independence between memory processes is consistent with the proposal by McClellend, McNaughton, and O'Reilly (1995) of independent learning systems in the hippocampus and neocortex. Aggleton and Brown (1999) describe evidence to support their claim that recollection and familiarity have different anatomical bases, and discuss the importance of techniques for separately measuring the two bases for recognition memory. Dissociations such as those presented in table 14.2 encourage us to believe that assumptions underlying the process-dissociation procedure can be met.

Acknowledgment This research was supported by grants to Larry L. Jacoby from the National Institute on Aging (NIA) #AG13845-02 and National Science Foundation (NSF) #SBR-9596209.

References

Aggleton, J. P., & Brown, M. W. (1999). Episodic memory, amnesia, and hippocampal-anterior thalamic axis. *Behavioral and Brain Sciences, 22*, 425–490.

Atkinson, R. C., & Juola, J. F. (1974). Search and decision processes in recognition memory. In D. H. Krantz, R. C. Atkinson, R. D. Luce, & P. Suppes (Eds.), *Contemporary developments in mathematical psychology, Vol.1, Learning, memory and thinking* (pp. 243–293). San Francisco, CA: Freeman.

Baddeley, A. (1982). Amnesia: A minimal model and an interpretation. In L. S. Cermak (Ed.), *Human memory and amnesia* (pp. 305–336). Hillsdale, NJ: Erlbaum.

Bartlett, J. C., Strater, L., & Fulton, A. (1991). False recency and false fame of faces in young adulthood and old age. *Memory & Cognition, 19*, 177–188.

Batchelder, W. H., & Riefer, D. M. (1990). Multinomial processing models of source monitoring. *Psychological Review, 97*, 548–564.

Begg, I., & Armour, V. (1991). Repetition and the ring of truth: Biasing comments. *Canadian Journal of Behavioral Science, 23*(2), 195–213.

Buchner, A., Erdfelder, E., Steffens, M. C., & Martensen, H. (1997). The nature of memory processes underlying recognition judgments in the Process Dissociation procedure. *Memory & Cognition, 25*, 508–517.

Buchner, A., Erdfelder, E., & Vaterrodt-Plünnecke, B. (1995). Toward unbiased measurement of conscious and unconscious memory processes within the process dissociation framework. *Journal of Experimental Psychology: General, 124*, 137–160.

Cermak, L. S., Verfaellie, M., Butler, T., & Jacoby, L. L. (1993). Attributions of familiarity in amnesia: Evidence from a fame judgment task. *Neuropsychology, 7*, 510–518.

Chaiken, S., & Trope, Y. (Eds.) (1999). *Dual process theories in social psychology.* New York: Guildford.

Clark, S. E., & Gronlund, S. D. (1996). Global matching models of recognition memory. How the models match the data. *Psychonomic Bulletin & Review, 3*(1), 37–60.

Curran, T., & Hintzman, D. L. (1995). Violations of the independence assumption in process dissociation. *Journal of Experimental Psychology: Learning, Memory, and Cognition, 21*, 531–547.

Curran, T., & Hintzman, D. L. (1997). Consequences and causes of correlations in process dissociation. *Journal of Experimental Psychology: Learning, Memory and Cognition, 23*, 496–504.

Donaldson, W. (1996). The role of decision processes in remembering and knowing. *Memory & Cognition, 24*, 523–533.

Dywan, J., & Jacoby, L. L. (1990). Effects of aging on source monitoring: Differences in susceptibility to false fame. *Psychology and Aging, 5*, 379–387.

Dywan, J., Segalowitz, S. J., Henderson, D., & Jacoby, L. L. (1993). Memory for source after traumatic brain injury. *Brain & Cognition, 21*, 20–43.

Erdfelder, E., & Buchner, A. (1998). Process-dissociation measurement models: Threshold theory or detection theory? *Journal of Experimental Psychology: General, 127*, 83–96.

Foley, M. A., & Johnson, M. K. (1985). Confusions between memories for performed and imagined actions: A developmental comparison. *Child Development, 56*, 1145–1155.

Gillund, G., & Shiffrin, R. M. (1984). A retrieval model for both recognition and recall. *Psychological Review, 91*, 1–67.

Graf, P., & Komatsu, S. (1994). Process dissociation procedure: Handle with caution! *European Journal of Cognitive Psychology, 6*, 113–129.

Harvey, P. D. (1985). Reality monitoring in mania and schizophrenia: The association of thought disorder and performance. *Journal of Nervous and Mental Disease, 173*, 67–73.

Hay, J. F., & Jacoby, L. L. (1996). Separating habit and recollection: Memory slips, process dissociations and probability matching. *Journal of Experimental Psychology: Learning, Memory and Cognition, 22,* 1323–1335.

Hay, J. F., & Jacoby, L. L. (1999). Separating habit and recollection in young and elderly adults. Effects of elaborative processing and distinctiveness. *Psychology and Aging, 14,* 122–134.

Hertel, P. T., & Milan, S. (1994). Depressive deficits in recognition: Dissociation of recollection and familiarity. *Journal of Abnormal Psychology, 103,* 736–742.

Hintzman, D. L. (1988). Judgments of frequency and recognition memory in a multiple-trace memory model. *Psychological Review, 95,* 528–551.

Hintzman, D. L., & Curran, T. (1997). More than one way to violate independence: Reply to Jacoby and Shrout (1997). *Journal of Experimental Psychology: Learning, Memory, and Cognition, 23,* 511–513.

Jacoby, L. L. (1991). A process dissociation framework: Separating automatic from intentional uses of memory. *Journal of Memory and Language, 30,* 513–541.

Jacoby, L. L. (1996). Dissociating automatic and consciously-controlled effects of study/test compatability. *Journal of Memory and Language, 35,* 32–52.

Jacoby, L. L. (1998). Invariance in automatic influences of memory: Toward a user's guide for the process-dissociation procedure. *Journal of Experimental Psychology: Learning, Memory, and Cognition, 24,* 3–26.

Jacoby, L. L. (1999). Ironic effects of repetition: Measuring age-related differences in memory. *Journal of Experimental Psychology: Learning, Memory, and Cognition, 25,* 3–22.

Jacoby, L. L., Allan, L. G., Collins, J. C., & Larwill, L. K. (1988). Memory influences subjective experience: Noise judgments. *Journal of Experimental Psychology: Learning, Memory, and Cognition, 14,* 240–247.

Jacoby, L. L., Begg, I. M., & Toth, J. P. (1997). In defense of functional independence: Violations of assumptions underlying the process-dissociation procedure? *Journal of Experimental Psychology: Learning, Memory, and Cognition, 23,* 484–495.

Jacoby, L. L., & Dallas, M. (1981). On the relationship between autobiographical memory and perceptual learning. *Journal of Experimental Psychology: General, 3,* 306–340.

Jacoby, L. L., & Hollingshead, A. (1990). Toward a generate/recognize model of performance on direct and indirect tests of memory. *Journal of Memory, and Language, 29,* 433–454.

Jacoby, L. L., Jones, T. J., & Dolan, P. O. (1998). Two effects of repetition: Support for a dual-process model of know judgments and exclusion errors. *Psychonomic Bulletin and Review, 5,* 705–709.

Jacoby, L. L., Kelley, C. M., & McElree, B. (1999). The role of cognitive control: Early selection vs. late correction. In S. Chaiken & Y. Trope (Eds.), *Dual process theories in social psychology* (pp. 383–400). New York: Guilford.

Jacoby, L. L., McElree, B., & Trainham, T. N. (1999). Automatic influences as accessibility bias in memory and Stroop-like tasks: Toward a formal model. In A. Koriat & D. Gopher (Eds.), *Attention and Performance XVII* (pp. 461–486). Cambridge, MA: MIT Press.

Jacoby, L. L., & Shrout, P. E. (1997). Toward a psychometric analysis of violations of the independence assumption in process dissociation. *Journal of Experimental Psychology: Learning, Memory, and Cognition, 23,* 505–510.

Jacoby, L. L., Toth, J. P., & Yonelinas, A. P. (1993). Separating conscious and unconscious influences of memory: Measuring recollection. *Journal of Experimental Psychology: General, 122,* 139–154.

Jacoby, L. L., & Whitehouse, K. (1989). An illusion of memory: False recognition influenced by unconscious perception. *Journal of Experimental Psychology: General, 118,* 126–135.

Jacoby, L. L., & Witherspoon, D. (1982). Remembering without awareness. *Canadian Journal of Psychology, 36,* 300–324.

Jacoby, L. L., Woloshyn, V., & Kelley, C. M. (1989). Becoming famous without being recognized: Unconscious influences of memory produced by dividing attention. *Journal of Experimental Psychology: General, 118,* 115–125.

Jacoby, L. L., Yonelinas, A. P., & Jennings, J. M. (1997). The relation between conscious and unconscious (automatic) influences: A declaration of independence. In J. D. Cohen & J. W. Schooler (Eds.), *Scientific approaches to consciousness* (pp. 13–47). Mahwah, NJ: Erlbaum.

Jennings, J. M., & Jacoby, L. L. (1993). Automatic versus intentional uses of memory: Aging, attention, and control. *Psychology & Aging, 8,* 283–293.

Jennings, J. M., & Jacoby, L. L. (1997). An opposition procedure for detecting age-related deficits in recollection: Telling effects of repetition. *Psychology and Aging, 12*, 352–361.

Johnson, M. K., Hashtroudi, S., & Lindsay, D. S. (1993). Source monitoring. *Psychological Bulletin, 114*, 3–28.

Johnson, M. K., Kounios, J., & Reeder, J. A. (1994). Time-course studies of reality monitoring and recogntion. *Journal of Experimental Psychology: Learning, Memory, and Cognition, 20*, 1409–1419.

Joordens, S., & Merikle, P. M. (1993). Independence or redundancy? Two models of conscious and unconscious influences. *Journal of Experimental Psychology: General, 122*, 462–467.

Kelley, C. M. (1999). Subjective experience as a basis for "objective judgments": Effects of past experience on judgments of difficulty. In D. Gopher & A. Koriat (Eds.), *Attention and Performance XVII* (pp. 515–536). Cambridge, MA: MIT Press.

Kelley, C. M., & Jacoby, L. L. (1996). Adult egocentrism: Subjective experience versus analytic bases for judgment. *Journal of Memory and Language, 35*, 157–175.

Kelley, C. M., & Jacoby, L. L. (1998). Subjective reports and process dissociation: Fluency, knowing, and feeling. *Acta Psychologica, 98*, 127–140.

Kelley, C. M., & Lindsay, D. S. (1996). Conscious and unconscious forms of memory. In E. L. Bjork & R. A. Bjork (Eds.), *Handbook of perception and cognition: Memory* (2nd ed.; pp. 31–63). San Diego, CA: Academic Press.

Knowlton, B. J., Squire, L. R., & Gluck, M. A. (1994). Probabilistic classification learning in amnesia. *Learning and Memory, 1*, 106–120.

Light, L. L., La Voie, D., Valencia-Laver, D., Albertson-Owens, S. A., & Mead, G. (1992). Direct and indirect measures of memory for modality in young and older adults. *Journal of Experimental Psychology: Learning, Memory, and Cognition, 18*, 1284–1297.

Mandler, G. (1980). Recognizing: The judgment of previous occurrence. *Psychological Review, 87*, 252–271.

McClelland, J. L., McNaughton, B. L., & O'Reilly, R. C. (1995). Why there are complementary learning systems in the hippocampus and neocortex: Insights from the successes and failures of connectionist models of learning and memory. *Psychological Review, 102*, 419–457.

McElree, B., Dolan, P. O., & Jacoby, L. L. (1999). Isolating the contributions of familiarity and source information to item recognition: A time-course analysis. *Journal of Experimental Psychology: Learning, Memory, and Cognition, 25*, 563–582.

McIntyre, J. S., & Craik, F. I. M. (1987). Age differences in memory for item and source information. *Canadian Journal of Psychology, 41*, 175–192.

Mulligan, N. W., & Hirshman, E. (1997). Measuring the bases of recognition memory: An investigation of the process-dissociation framework. *Journal of Experimental Psychology: Learning, Memory, and Cognition, 23*, 280–304.

Multhaup, K. S. (1995). Aging, source, and decision criteria: When false fame errors do and do not occur. *Psychology and Aging, 10*, 492–497.

Murdock, B. B., Jr. (1974). *Human memory: Theory and data.* New York: Erlbaum.

Murdock, B. B., Jr. (1982). A theory for the storage and retrieval of item and associative information. *Psychological Review, 89*, 609–626.

Poldrack, R. A., & Logan, G. D. (1998). What is the mechanism for fluency in successive recognition? *Acta Psychologica, 98*, 167–181.

Rajaram, S. (1993). Remembering and knowing: Two means of access to the personal past. *Memory and Cognition, 21*, 89–102.

Ratcliff, R., & McKoon, G. (1995). Bias in the priming of object decisions. *Journal of Experimental Psychology: Learning, Memory, and Cognition, 21*, 754–767.

Ratcliff, R., & McKoon, G. (1997). A counter model for implicit priming in perceptual word identification. *Psychological Review, 104*, 319–343.

Ratcliff, R., Van Zandt, T., & McKoon, G. (1995). Process dissociation, single-process theories, and recognition memory. *Journal of Experimental Psychology: General, 124*(4), 352–374.

Reber, A. S. (1989). Implicit learning and tacit knowledge. *Journal of Experimental Psychology: General, 118*, 219–235.

Reider, D. M., & Batchelder, W. H. (1988). Multinomial modeling and the measurement of cognitive processes. *Psychological Review, 95*(3), 318–339.

Richardson-Klavehn, A., Gardiner, J. M., & Java, R. I. (1996). Memory: Task dissociations, process dissociations and dissociations of consciousness. In G. Underwood (Ed.), *Implicit cognition* (pp. 85–158). Oxford: Oxford University Press.

Roediger, H. L., & McDermott, K. B. (1993). Implicit memory in normal human subjects. In H. Spinnler & F. Boller (Eds.), *Handbook of neuropsychology* (Vol. 8; pp. 63–131). Amsterdam: Elsevier.

Schacter, D. L., Kagan, J., & Leichtman, M. D. (1995). True and false memories in children and adults: A cognitive neuroscience perspective. *Psychology, Public Policy, and Law, 1*, 411–428.

Spencer, W. D., & Raz, N. (1995). Differencial effects of aging on memory for content and context: A meta-analysis. *Psychology and Aging, 10*, 527–539.

Squire, L. R., & McKee, R. (1992). Influence of prior events on cognitive judgments in amnesia. *Journal of Experimental Psychology: Learning, Memory, and Cognition, 18*, 106–115.

Toth, J. P. (1996). Conceptual automaticity in recognition memory: Levels-of-processing effects on familiarity. *Canadian Journal of Experimental Psychology, 50*, 123–138.

Tversky, A., & Kahneman, D. (1973). Availability: A heuristic for judging frequency and probability. *Cognitive Psychology, 5*, 207–232.

Wagner, A. D., Gabrieli, J. D. E., & Verfaellie, M. (1997). Dissociations between familiarity processes in explicit-recognition and implicit-perceptual memory. *Journal of Experimental Psychology: Learning, Memory, and Cognition, 23*, 305–323.

Wegner, D. M. (1994). Ironic processes of mental control. *Psychological Review, 101*, 34–52.

Weldon, M. S. (1991) Mechanisms underlying priming on perceptual tasks. *Journal of Experimental Psychology: Learning, Memory, and Cognition, 17*, 526–541.

Whittlesea, B. W. A. (1993). Illusions of familiarity. *Journal of Experimental Psychology: Learning, Memory, and Cognition, 19*, 1235–1253.

Witherspoon, D., & Allan, L. G. (1985). The effects of a prior presentation on temporal judgments in a perceptual identification task. *Memory & Cognition, 13*, 101–111.

Wolters, G., & Logan, G. (Eds.). (1998). Fluency and remembering. [Special Issue]. *Acta Psychologica, 98*, 121–125.

Yonelinas, A. P. (1994). Receiver operating characteristics in recognition memory: Evidence for a dual-process model. *Journal of Experimental Psychology: Learning, Memory & Cognition, 20*, 1341–1354.

Yonelinas, A. P. (1997). Recognition memory ROCS for item and associative information: The contribution of recollection and familiarity. *Memory & Cognition, 25*, 747–763.

Yonelinas, A. P., & Jacoby, L. L. (1994). Dissociations of processes in recognition memory: Effects of interference and of response speed. *Canadian Journal of Experimental Psychology, 48*(4), 516–534.

Yonelinas, A. P., & Jacoby, L. L. (1996). Response bias and the process dissociation procedure. *Journal of Experimental Psychology: General, 125*(4), 422–439.

Yonelinas, A. P., Kroll, N. E. A., Dobbins, I., Lazzara, M., & Knight, R. T. (1998). Recollection and familiarity deficits in amnesia: Convergence of remember-know, process dissociation, and receiver operating characteristics data. *Neuropsychology, 12*, 323–339.

15

Remembering and Knowing

JOHN M. GARDINER & ALAN RICHARDSON-KLAVEHN

Remembering and knowing are two subjective states of awareness associated with memory. *Remembering* refers to intensely personal experiences of the past—those in which we seem to recreate previous events and experiences with the awareness of reliving these events and experiences mentally. Remembering entails mental time travel that intimately engages one's sense of self. *Knowing* refers to other experiences of the past, those in which we are aware of knowledge that we possess but in a more impersonal way. There is no awareness of reliving any particular events or experiences. Knowing includes the general sense of familiarity we have about more abstract knowledge. Knowing also includes awareness of events that we have personally experienced when we are aware of those events as facts, without reliving them mentally. Throughout this chapter the terms remembering and knowing are used only to refer to these conscious states and to the responses subjects make when reporting them.

General Background

The idea that remembering and knowing could be studied in the memory laboratory was suggested by Endel Tulving (1985), who proposed that the two states of awareness re-flect autonoetic and noetic consciousness, two types of consciousness that respectively characterize episodic and semantic memory systems (see, too, Tulving, 1983, 1989; Wheeler, Stuss, & Tulving, 1997). He reported illustrative experiments in which subjects were instructed to report their states of awareness at the time they recalled or recognized words they had previously encountered in a study list. If they remembered what they experienced at the time they encountered the word—something they thought of at that time—they made a remember response. If they were aware they had encountered the word in the study list but did not remember anything they experienced at that time, they made a know response. The results indicated that participants could quite easily distinguish between experiences of remembering and knowing.

Though Tulving (1985) used free-recall, cued-recall, and recognition tests, it was recognition memory that became the most commonly used remember/know paradigm, not least because recognition memory is most likely to be associated with experiences of knowing, as well as remembering, especially when recognition is accompanied only by feelings of familiarity. Moreover, the two states of awareness captured by remember and know responses seemed at the time additionally relevant to dual-component theories of recognition memory, which held that recognition could be accomplished by either one of two independent processes, recollection and familiarity (e.g., Mandler, 1980).

The major premise underlying the use of remember and know responses is that the subjective states of awareness they measure cannot be reliably inferred from more conventional measures of performance (see Tulving, 1989). For example, proportion correct may be equivalent in two different experimental conditions, or in two different subject groups, yet proportions of remembering and knowing may differ. One cannot tell what subjects experience mentally from purely objective measures of their performance. If one wants to be able to take into account subjective awareness of memory, there is no alternative to the use of subjective reports. This does not, of course, mean that such reports have to be accepted at face value, since they can obviously be confabulated (see e.g., Dalla Barba, 1993). They have to be interpreted carefully, in conjunction with other evidence.

Remember and know responses are not intended as introspective measures of any underlying hypothetical constructs, such as memory systems or processes. Their use also differs from classical introspection in that all that is required is that subjects distinguish between kinds of mental experiences, rather than report the details of those experiences. Importantly too, however, when subjects are additionally asked to describe their experiences in more detail, the results confirm that remember responses reflect awareness of what was experienced when a word was encountered in a study list and know responses do not, but reflect only awareness of recent but unremembered encounters that are attributed to the study list (see Gardiner, Ramponi, & Richardson-Klavehn, 1998a).

In the remember/know paradigm, it is usual to give subjects written instructions about the two kinds of awareness measured by remember and know responses, to discuss these instructions with them, after they have read them, to ensure understanding and also to have subjects explain an arbitrary selection of their responses after the test, to check that instructions have been followed. It is quite unusual to find subjects whose explanations indicate that they have not followed the instructions. For an example of instructions used recently in our laboratory, see Appendix 1. These instructions include an important ex-

tension to the procedure, which is that subjects are required to report awareness of guessing, as well as of remembering and knowing. The implications of this extension of the original paradigm are discussed later in the chapter.

Major Findings

Studies that followed Tulving (1985) discovered various experimental manipulations that dissociate remembering from knowing. Many independent variables were found to influence remembering but not knowing, particularly variables that engage more conceptual and more elaborative processing, like level of processing, and generating versus reading at study (Gardiner, 1988; see also Gardiner, Java, & Richardson-Klavehn, 1996a). Other variables, though not nearly so many, were found to affect knowing but not remembering, particularly variables that engage perceptual processing. These variables include the presentation of a test word being preceded by an identical, masked test prime, compared with its being preceded by a masked but unrelated test prime (Rajaram, 1993), and same versus different study and test modalities following a highly perceptual orienting task (Gregg & Gardiner, 1994; see also Gardiner & Gregg, 1997). More examples of variables that influence knowing, and not remembering, have been discovered recently (e.g., Dewhurst & Hitch, 1997; Mäntylä & Raudsepp, 1996).

Some variables were found to have opposite effects on remembering and knowing. These variables include studying nonwords compared to words. Nonwords led to increased knowing and less remembering (Gardiner & Java, 1990). Massed versus spaced repetition of items within a study list was found to have a similar effect. Massed repetition led to more know responses and fewer remember responses than spaced repetition (Parkin & Russo, 1993).

Gardiner, Gawlik, and Richardson-Klavehn (1994) found a pattern of results that is analogous to showing a double dissociation between remembering and knowing within a single experiment. This experiment used an item-by-item directed forgetting paradigm to functionally manipulate the relative amounts of elaborative and maintenance rehearsal. It was assumed that elaborative rehearsal would be focused on to-be-learned, rather than on to-be-forgotten, items. Maintenance rehearsal was manipulated by varying the delay between the presentation of the item and the subsequent cue that designated it as to-be-learned or to-be-forgotten. Because it is not in the interests of subjects to rehearse items elaboratively until they are told whether the items are to be learned or to be forgotten, it was assumed also that the longer the delay, the longer the period of maintenance rehearsal. The results bore out these assumptions. Lengthening cue delay increased know but not remember responses. But item designation influenced remember but not know responses, with more remembering for the to-be-learned items. These results are summarized in table 15.1.

And there are a few studies that have found a fourth pattern of results, in which the variable has parallel effects on remembering and knowing. In one such study English subjects heard excerpts either from Polish folk songs or from classical music, either once or three times in succession (Gardiner, Kaminska, Dixon, & Java, 1996b). Both know and remember responses were greater after three presentations rather than one for the folk songs. Only remember responses, however, increased after three presentations of classical music; know responses were not affected. In another study, Gardiner, Ramponi, and Richardson-Klavehn (1998b) trained subjects to respond either 500 ms or 1500 ms after test words appeared, and found that both remember and know responses increased in parallel following the longer response deadline.

The foregoing results are summarized, along with some others, in table 15.2. The summary is illustrative rather than exhaustive.[1] Many of the earlier findings were reviewed by Gardiner and Java (1993). Richardson-Klavehn, Gardiner, and Java (1996), Rajaram and Roediger (1997), and Gardiner and Conway (in press) provide more recent, though more selective, reviews. Table 15.2 additionally serves to underscore an important

conclusion from all this evidence. The fact that the overall pattern of results demonstrates that some variables affect one or other of the two states of awareness, that some variables have opposing effects on them, and that some variables have parallel effects on them, indicates that the two states of awareness are functionally independent. This seems a remarkable discovery and its full theoretical significance has yet to be appreciated.

In addition to evidence about the ways in which various independent variables influence remembering and knowing, there is evidence about differences in remembering and knowing with respect to a number of different subject variables. Age was the first such variable to be investigated, where the general finding is of reduced remembering in elderly adults compared to young adults (Parkin & Walter, 1992; see also Mäntylä, 1993; Perfect & Dasgupta, 1997; Perfect, Williams, & Anderton-Brown, 1995; Java, 1996), but little change in knowing except under certain specific conditions in which knowing apparently increases (see Perfect et al., 1995). Young children, too, show less remembering than young adults (Toplis, 1997; see also Perner & Ruffman, 1995).

Other subject variables include Alzheimer's disease, amnesia, autism, epilepsy, and schizophrenia. With these subject variables the general finding has been that, compared to matched controls, there is less remembering, and in some cases increased or decreased knowing. Remembering is much reduced in amnesic and Alzheimer's patients, for example, and knowing is relatively unaffected (Dalla Barba, 1993, 1997; Knowlton & Squire, 1995; Schacter, Verfaellie, & Anes, 1997a), though some experiments have found differences in knowing also (e.g., Knowlton & Squire, 1995). Schizophrenic patients showed reduced remembering and little difference in knowing (Huron et al., 1995). Epileptic pa-

Table 15.1 Proportions of Responses from Gardiner et al. (1994).

| Response Categories | Cue Delay | | | | Not Studied |
| | Short | | Long | | |
	Learn	Forget	Learn	Forget	
Remember	.50	.23	.40	.26	.03
Know	.18	.20	.27	.29	.10
Overall	.68	.43	.67	.55	.13

Table 15.2 Summary of Effects of Experimental Manipulations.

Effects of Manipulation	Examples of Variables
Variable increases remember responses but does not affect know responses	• Deep versus shallow level of processing (Gardiner, 1988) • Generating versus reading at study (Gardiner, 1988) • Low versus high word frequency (Gardiner & Java, 1990) • Undivided versus divided attention at study (Gardiner & Parkin, 1990) • Shortening retention interval, if under a day (Gardiner & Java, 1991) • Vocalization at study, compared with silent reading (Gregg & Gardiner, 1991) • Intentional versus incidental learning (Maken & Hampson, 1993) • More versus less elaborative rehearsal (Gardiner et al., 1994) • Serial position in the study list (Jones & Roediger, 1995) • Listening to excerpts from famous compared with obscure pieces of classical music (Java, Kaminska, & Gardiner, 1995) • Orthographically distinctive versus orthographically common words (Rajaram, 1998) • Solving difficult compared with easy anagrams at study Dewhurst & Hitch (1999)
Variable increases know responses but does not affect remember responses	• Identical versus unrelated test primes (Rajaram, 1993) • Same versus different study and test modalities following a highly perceptual orienting task (Gregg & Gardiner, 1994) • More versus less maintenance rehearsal (Gardiner et al., 1994) • Suppression of focal attention (Mäntylä & Raudsepp, 1996) • Cohort activation from a previous lexical decision task (Dewhurst & Hitch, 1997)
Variable increases know responses and decreases remember responses	• Nonword versus word presentation (Gardiner & Java, 1990) • Massed versus spaced repetition of study list items (Parkin & Russo, 1993) • Gradually revealing test words, rather than showing them all at once (LeComte, 1995) • Encoding faces in terms of their similarities versus encoding them in terms of their differences (Mantyla, 1997)
Variable has parallel effects on remember and know responses	• Lengthening retention interval, if over a day (Gardiner & Java, 1991) • Three versus one study trials with highly unfamiliar music (Gardiner, Kaminska et al., 1996) • Long versus short response deadline (Gardiner et al., 1998b)

Table 15.3 Proportions of Responses from Bowler et al. (1998).

Response Categories	Control Group			Autistic Group		
	Studied	Not Studied	Difference	Studied	Not Studied	Difference
Remember	.46	.06	.40	.36	.05	.31
Know	.11	.03	.08	.25	.08	.17
Overall	.57	.09	.48	.61	.13	.48

tients showed huge differences between remembering and knowing (with visuo-spatial materials). Left temporal lobe epileptics largely made know rather than remember responses, and right temporal lobe epileptics largely made remember rather than know responses (Blaxton & Theodore, 1997).

Such evidence of differences in awareness in different clinical populations confirms that, in a variety of disorders, remembering is selectively impaired and knowing is relatively spared. These findings have important implications for diagnosis and remediation.

Some results from a study of autism (Bowler, Gardiner, & Grice, 1998) are summarized in table 15.3. High-functioning individuals with autism were compared with matched controls. Overall recognition performance in the two groups was very similar. But the reported states of awareness differed markedly. In the autistic group, there was less remembering and more knowing. The results shown in table 15.3 were collapsed over a manipulation of word frequency. Both subject groups showed the usual advantage to low-frequency words in remember responses and no word frequency effect in know responses (e.g., Gardiner & Java, 1990; Strack & Forster, 1995; Gardiner, Richardson-Klavehn, & Ramponi, 1997), thereby supporting the inference that autistic and control group subjects interpreted remember and know responses similarly.

A third category of evidence is from psychopharmacological treatments and from physiological measures of brain function. Both lorazepam (Curran, Gardiner, Java, & Allen, 1993) and alcohol (Curran & Hildebrandt, in press) greatly reduce remembering and leave knowing relatively unchanged. Some recent event-related potential (ERP) findings (Düzel, Yonelinas, Mangun, Heinze, & Tulving, 1997) provide somewhat more convincing evidence for qualitatively (as opposed to quantitatively) distinct patterns of neural activity in remembering and knowing than previous studies (e.g., Smith, 1993), particularly over earlier time windows. Moreover, Düzel et al. (1997) found that ERP measures of this neural activity were indistinguishable for accurate and inaccurate identification of studied words. The fact that ERPs were predicted by the subjectively reported states of awareness, and not by the studied/unstudied status of the items, provides strong physiological evidence for the psychological reality of the two kinds of awareness.

Before turning shortly to the major theoretical accounts of remembering and knowing, it should be emphasized that remember and know responses can be used without commitment to any theory, but simply to provide information about how various memory phenomena, including memory disorders, are characterized experientially.

Another particularly good example of this has been the use of these responses to characterize illusions of memory, especially false recognition effects. For example, in their revival of the procedure introduced by Deese (1959), Roediger and McDermott (1995) showed that the nonpresented words that are falsely recognized, after studying lists of words that are highly associated to them, are typically remembered, rather than known. Conversely, Schacter et al. (1997a) found that another illusion of memory, perceptually induced by presenting sets of rhyming words, increased knowing, rather than remembering (see also Dewhurst & Hitch, 1997; Mäntylä & Raudsepp, 1996). Thus it seems that both states of awareness are susceptible to illusions of memory. Moreover, the ERP study by Düzel et al. (1997) had used an extended version of the Deese/Roediger-McDermott procedure. So their physiological evidence demonstrated conjointly the psychological reality of the illusion of memory and of the neural activity that gives rise to it.

To sum up, at least three converging sources of evidence—evidence of dissociative effects of independent variables, evidence of dissociations in subject variables (particularly in various clinical populations), and evidence of differences associated with the effects of drugs and with physiological measures of brain function—all provide strong empirical support for the validity of the distinction between remembering and knowing.

Major Theories

The first major theory advanced specifically to account for remembering and knowing was Tulving's (1983, 1985) original proposal that remembering and knowing are expressions of two kinds of consciousness, autonoetic and noetic, which are properties of different memory systems, episodic and semantic memory. The distinction between episodic and semantic memory systems is, of course, supported by a number of other converging sources of evidence (Nyberg & Tulving, 1996), and the proposal that autonoetic consciousness is a property of the episodic system is particularly well supported (Wheeler et al., 1997). But the idea that noetic consciousness is a property of the semantic system even in recognition memory studies, where know responses refer to a single recent encounter with a test item, seems more controversial.

The theory assumes that encoding into different systems is serial, and that events have first to be encoded into semantic memory before they can be encoded into episodic memory (Tulving, 1994). This assumption suggests that know responses could reflect encoding that is adequate for the semantic system, but inadequate for the episodic system.

Gregg and Gardiner (1994; see also Gardiner & Gregg, 1997) devised a procedure designed to largely prevent encoding into episodic memory, but to still allow encoding into semantic memory. In this procedure, studied words were presented visually at an extremely rapid rate in conjunction with a highly perceptual orienting task. Recognition performance was quite poor following these study conditions, and very largely characterized by knowing. In addition, test modality was manipulated. Visual was compared with auditory presentation at test. Recognition performance was considerably better in the visual test, where the test mode corresponded with study mode, than it was in the auditory test, where test and study modes differed. And this modality effect occurred in know responses, not in remember responses.

The finding that following such study conditions recognition memory can be based largely on knowing, with little or no remembering, suggests that all that is necessary for encoding into the semantic system is some initial awareness of the events, however fleeting. In contrast, encoding into episodic memory must depend on greater conscious elaboration of the events. Hence the relative preservation of knowing, with normal aging, for example, and in the various clinical conditions in which remembering is greatly reduced, can be interpreted in terms of relatively unimpaired encoding into semantic memory, but impaired encoding into episodic memory because there is less conscious elaboration of events.

Conway, Gardiner, Perfect, Anderson, and Cohen (1997) investigated the acquisition of conceptual knowledge by undergraduate students, a situation that seems less controversially to involve semantic memory. Students in this study were, however, allowed to distinguish "just know" responses from "familiarity" responses, which were defined rather in the way know responses had previously been defined—that is, as feelings of some recent but unremembered encounter. One finding was that students who scored highly in initial multiple-choice questions of knowledge acquired from lecture courses remembered more correct answers than their fellow students, and that in a retest some months afterwards, there was a remember-to-know shift. These same high-scoring students now outperformed their fellow students by just knowing more correct answers, rather than by remembering more (see figure 15.1). Good memory initially meant good episodic memory, which can presumably facilitate the development of more schematized conceptual knowledge in semantic memory. Such knowledge gives rise to just knowing, rather than knowing of recent but unremembered encounters as measured by the familiarity responses.

Though Conway et al. (1997) argued that just know and familiarity responses both reflect varieties of noetic awareness (see also Gardiner & Conway, in press), there is as yet little compelling evidence that transient feelings of familiarity relating to a recent encounter reflect the same memory system that supports highly familiar long-term knowledge, and this remains a problem for the systems account.

A second major theory is the distinctiveness/fluency framework that has been developed by Rajaram (1996, 1998). This grew out of the earlier suggestion that remembering is influenced by conceptual processes, and knowing is influenced by perceptual processes, as conceived in the transfer-appropriate processing framework (see Rajaram, 1993). While this correspondence between the predominant type of processing and the state of awareness provided a reasonable summary of many of the earlier findings—including those of Gregg and Gardiner (1994), which can also be interpreted in terms of greater fluency, less distinctiveness—more recent evidence indicates that the relationship between the process distinction and the awareness distinction is more accurately regarded as orthogonal.

One perceptual factor that increases remembering is the reinstatement of identical pictorial stimuli at study and test, compared with changing the pictorial format (Rajaram, 1996). And Rajaram (1998) has shown that orthographically distinct words are more likely

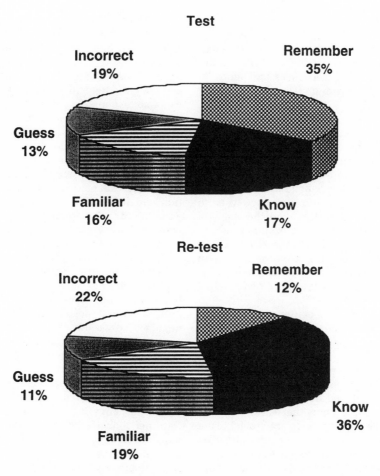

Figure 15.1 Proportions of responses from top-scoring subjects in Conway et al. (1997).

to be recognized than orthographically common words and that this effect too occurs in remembering, not knowing. Conversely, Mäntylä (1997) found that examining similarities among faces by grouping them into one of several conceptual categories, a relational task that presumably depends on the use of schemas in semantic memory, increased know responses. He also showed that studying faces by rating the distinctiveness of their features increased remembering.

Distinctiveness of processing, whether conceptual or perceptual, presumably engages a greater degree of conscious elaboration at study, and thereby enhances remembering. Knowing, in contrast, reflects fluency in processing, in either conceptual or perceptual processes. This processing framework provides a useful summary of much of the available evidence, and it is in many respects complementary to, rather than alternative to, the systems theory. For example, evidence that knowing is affected by conceptual as well as perceptual factors strengthens the semantic memory interpretation of this state of awareness just as much as it strengthens the distinctiveness/fluency framework. The two theories nonetheless differ more in their explanations of knowing than in their explanations of remembering. The notion of fluency of processing may seem more plausible when it refers to a single previous encounter with a studied item than does the notion of semantic memory. But, by the same token, the notion of semantic memory seems more plausible than does that of processing fluency when it refers to the acquisition of conceptual knowledge (Conway et al., 1977).

Both these theories have recently been challenged by a signal-detection model in which remembering reflects stronger traces and more conservative response criteria, and knowing reflects weaker traces and more lenient response criteria (Donaldson, 1996; Hirshman & Master, 1997; Inoue & Bellezza, 1998). This model can apparently mimic the various kinds of empirical relations observed between remembering and knowing by the appropriate placement of response criteria. But it does not explain why the criteria are affected by different independent and subject variables in the ways that they have to be to fit the data. Nor does it explain the states of awareness as such—how, for example, subjectively distinct states of awareness can be produced simply by shifting response criteria in one direction or another over the same memory trace. It seems capable only of modeling the responses.

There is, moreover, evidence that refutes the model's most important prediction with respect to the responses, which is that estimates of the strength of the memory trace should be the same regardless of the response criteria used in estimating it. Results from the procedure introduced by Gregg and Gardiner (1994), for example, show that estimates of the strength of the memory trace are much greater when derived from remember plus know responses than when derived only from remember responses, and meta-analyses of many different experimental conditions show highly consistent differences in the same direction (Donaldson, 1996; Gardiner & Gregg, 1997). These results show that even according to tests of the model, knowing reflects an additional source of memory, not merely a difference in response criteria. And there is other evidence that the detection model does not fit (for more discussion, see Gardiner & Gregg, 1997; Gardiner, Richardson-Klavehn, & Ramponi, 1998; Gardiner & Conway, in press).

Related Work

We next consider other related work. The most closely related work is that which has followed Mandler's (1980) more conventional dual-processing account of recognition memory. There is also related work on autobiographical memory (e.g., Brewer, 1992), and on reality and source monitoring (e.g., Johnson, Hashtroudi, & Lindsay, 1993).

Mandler proposed that recognition memory is mediated by two independent processes—elaboration, and integration—that these two processes were respectively associated with the experiences of recollection and familiarity, and that the second of these two processes was also responsible for perceptual priming in implicit memory tasks such as word stem completion (Mandler, 1980; Graf & Mandler, 1984). Almost inevitably, given this theory, among earlier suggestions for interpreting remembering and knowing was that they might reflect the independent processes of elaboration and integration. This in turn led to the expectation that there might be parallel effects between knowing in recognition memory and what happens in perceptual priming (Gardiner, 1988). The fact that level of processing typically influences neither knowing nor perceptual priming seemed promising for this hypothesis, and there are other parallels. For example, serial position effects occur in remember, not know responses (Jones & Roediger, 1995), and they occur in stem cued recall, but not in primed stem completion (Brooks, 1994).

But there are also inconsistencies. For example, the finding that word frequency influences not knowing, but remembering (e.g., Gardiner & Java, 1990), does not parallel what happens in perceptual priming because perceptual priming and recognition show similar word frequency effects (e.g., Jacoby & Dallas, 1981). There is other evidence that undermines any presumed correspondence between familiarity in recognition and perceptual priming (e.g., Snodgrass, Hirshman, & Fan, 1996; Wagner, Gabrieli, & Verfaellie, 1997).

Jacoby's (1991) process dissociation procedure retains the idea of two independent processes, and the idea that similar processes may operate in recognition and in perceptual priming. But the contrast now is between controlled and automatic processes, and it is assumed that recollection is a controlled process and familiarity is an automatic process.

Furthermore, in the process dissociation procedure as applied to recognition memory, estimates of these two independent processes are derived from what amounts to a source monitoring task (see Buchner, Erdfelder, Steffens, & Martensen, 1997). Subjects study two discriminable sets of items and are tested in an inclusion task, in which targets are defined as items from both sets; and in an exclusion task, in which targets are defined as items from one set, not the other. The difference between proportions of the critical set of targets that subjects identify rightly in the inclusion task, and wrongly in the exclusion task, is taken to reflect their conscious control and hence the recollection process. Errors in the exclusion task are taken to reflect the automatic familiarity process, but the process itself is estimated by a simple correction for independence.

Jacoby, Yonelinas, and Jennings (1997) argued for an independence remember/know model and suggested that if remembering is equated with the recollection process, and knowing with the familiarity process, but similarly corrected for independence, then the results from the remember/know procedure fall into agreement with those from the process dissociation procedure. And indeed Jacoby et al. (1997) showed examples of such convergence between the two procedures.

But there are also examples of convergence in the absence of any correction for independence (Richardson-Klavehn et al., 1996). The effects of age, for instance, and of divided versus undivided attention, leave knowing invariant and so lead to increased familiarity estimates by the independence remember/know model. But familiarity estimates for these effects are largely invariant in the process dissociation procedure. So adopting an independence remember/know model leads to divergence, not convergence, between the two procedures. Moreover, adopting an independence remember/know model sometimes leads to similar conclusions to those drawn without adopting it. For example, LeComte (1995) showed that the revelation effect, which is the increased likelihood of identifying words as previously studied if they are revealed gradually at test, rather than shown all at once, increases familiarity regardless of whether familiarity is defined simply by know responses or by know responses assuming an independence model.

The problem of the relation between the two procedures has been considered at length elsewhere (e.g., Richardson-Klavehn et al., 1996; Jacoby et al., 1997). Here we make only two other general points. First, remembering is not equivalent to the source monitoring required in exclusion tasks. Second, remembering is not equivalent to conscious control.

Remembering is broader than the source monitoring required in exclusion tasks. People remember aspects of the studied words that are not relevant to the exclusion task. Precisely this problem led Yonelinas and Jacoby

(1996) to distinguish "criterial" from "noncriterial" recollection. Noncriterial recollection is recollection that does not allow successful exclusion, and so enters into estimates of familiarity. Hence recollection consists in two components, one identified with control, the other not, and familiarity also consists in two components, if it includes automatic, irrelevant recollection. Mulligan and Hirshman (1997) made a similar point in distinguishing "diagnostic" from "nondiagnostic" recollection, where diagnostic and nondiagnostic are equivalent to criterial and noncriterial. Since noncriterial or nondiagnostic recollection will contribute to remember, not know responses, in the remember/know paradigm, the extent to which estimates of recollection in the process dissociation procedure correspond with remembering must presumably reflect the relative proportions of the two kinds of recollection.

This modification to the process dissociation procedure concedes that recollection cannot be equated with control. Other evidence distinguishing between consciousness of memory and control comes from some recent studies of perceptual priming in stem completion tasks, where it is possible to separate involuntary retrieval accompanied by awareness that the words retrieved were from a studied list, and involuntary retrieval not accompanied by such awareness (see, e.g., Richardson-Klavehn & Gardiner, 1996, 1998). Awareness of retrieval volition is dissociable from awareness of having encountered words in the study list, and that awareness of memory includes both remembering and knowing (see Java, 1994, 1996).

In autobiographical memory, involuntary remembering happens quite frequently. Much of what comes to mind in more natural settings seems more under stimulus control than under the conscious control of the person (Berntsen, 1998). Little has been done, however, to bring together related work on autobiographical memory in more natural settings and laboratory work on remembering and knowing, except for a long-term diary study of remembering and knowing in memory for actual and imagined events by Conway, Collins, Gathercole, and Anderson (1996; see also Brewer, 1992).

There is some evidence of involuntary autobiographical remembering in the laboratory. In their detailed analysis of explanations subjects provided for earlier recognition decisions, Gardiner, Ramponi et al. (1998a) found that about one-third of all decisions accompanied by remember responses reflected being reminded of some autobiographical event when words appeared in the study list, rather than the deliberate use of list learning strategies. Conway and Dewhurst (1995) showed that deliberate self-reference at study considerably increases subsequent remembering, which suggests that whatever is involuntarily remembered at study is also very likely to be remembered again at test.

Similar outcomes to that found by Gardiner, Ramponi et al. (1998a) had been found in two other studies. Huron et al. (1995) found that remembering that could be classified as autobiographical was relatively unimpaired in schizophrenic patients. Curran, Schacter, Norman, and Galluccio (1997) found that remembering that could be classified as autobiographical was relatively unimpaired in a patient with a right frontal lobe infarction. In both studies, the more general impairments in remembering appeared to reflect the less effective use of list-learning strategies. Thus it would be misleading to characterize these impairments merely as impairments in remembering, because they reflect reduced levels only of remembering that was associated with the deliberate use of list-learning strategies. The implications of this suggestion need to be followed up.

Remembering and source monitoring are obviously related. Source monitoring judgments (needed to exclude the critical set of studied items in the process dissociation procedure), such as those involving presentation modality, or speaker's voice, or orienting task, can be regarded as finer grained judgments within the state of awareness defined as remembering. Schacter, Koutstaal, Johnson, Gross, and Angell (1997) demonstrated false remembering in older, but not younger, adults induced by reviewing photographs of events related to, but not shown in, an earlier videotape. But in addition to making remember and know responses, participants made a number of further judgments in a Memory Characteristics Questionnaire (MCQ). These included judgments about what an object looked like, where it appeared, and whether there was a strong feeling of familiarity or a weak feeling of familiarity. This finer grained analysis revealed that the false remembering in older adults appeared to reflect poorer source monitoring. Mather, Henkel, and Johnson (1997) report a similar analysis of false memories, though only in young adults, in which remem-

ber and know responses were combined with MCQ ratings in order to provide a fuller characterization of memory experiences.

Some Current Problems

Both remembering and knowing define general states of awareness that may each be broken down into varieties of experiences (Gardiner & Conway, in press). Just as remembering can be broken down into more specific source monitoring judgments, other recent studies have broken down know responses into additional response categories, allowing guess responses to be reported as such, and just know responses to be reported separately from familiarity, as in Conway et al. (1997). This development partly reflects particular concern about the interpretation of know responses, which has perhaps been the most vexatious problem in the remember/know paradigm.

Where knowing is the default response, it is clearly open to abuse by subjects, who may use know responses to reflect various judgmental strategies that do not involve any awareness that the selected items were from the study list (Strack & Forster, 1995). Many earlier studies largely controlled for this by strongly discouraging guessing. Allowing subjects to report guesses instead seems a better solution to this problem (see Gardiner, Java et al., 1996a; Gardiner, Kaminska et al., 1996b; Gardiner et al., 1997; Gardiner, Ramponi et al., 1998a; Gardiner & Conway, in press) and guessing can still be strongly discouraged, even when it is allowed as a response. Evidence from these studies shows that it is guess responses, rather than know responses, that then reflect various other judgmental strategies. These strategies appear to reflect awareness of the circumstances prevailing during the memory task, such as the general characteristics of the item or the frequency of previous responses.

The evidence from these studies also shows that guess responses are more likely than know responses to be constrained by high levels of performance, as one would expect if know responses are valid measures. One dramatic demonstration of this is in Gardiner, Java et al. (1996a, exp. 1), whose results are summarized in table 15.4. The standard finding that level of processing influences remembering, and not knowing, was replicated, despite the obvious impact on guess responses of high performance following the semantic task.

Table 15.4 Proportions of Responses in Gardiner, Java et al. (1996a, exp. 1).

Response Categories	Level of Processing		Not Studied
	Semantic	Graphemic	
Remember	.72	.15	.03
Know	.18	.20	.11
Guess	.05	.24	.24
Overall	.95	.59	.38

If test conditions encourage, or compel, the use of very lenient response criteria, as in tests of a signal detection model (see, e.g., Jacoby et al., 1997; Hirshman & Henzler, 1998), and subjects are only allowed to report remember and know responses, then know responses are likely to include many guesses that subjects would report as such were they allowed to do so.[2] Consider the pattern of data in table 15.4 had subjects included guesses in know responses, rather than reported them, and adopted the same lenient recognition response criteria.

In tests of several models, Yonelinas, Dobbins, Szymanski, Dhaliwal, and King (1996) showed that a dual-process model in which recollection depends on threshold, but familiarity depends on signal detection, provides a better fit than either a pure threshold model or a pure detection model. They also showed that the independence remember/know model can predict the observed receiver operating characteristics (ROCs). But despite this success for the model, the confidence judgments as used to estimate ROCs do not correspond with knowing. A string of studies has shown dissociations between confidence judgments and know, as well as remember, responses (e.g., Gardiner & Java, 1990; Rajaram, 1993; Perfect et al., 1995; Mäntylä, 1997; Holmes, Waters, & Rajaram, 1998; Gardiner & Conway, in press). And there is discontinuity between knowing and guessing, because know responses reveal memory whereas guess responses do not (e.g., Gardiner, Java et al., 1996a, 1996b; Gardiner & Conway, in press; and see table 15.4).

The study by Conway et al. (1997) that distinguished between a just know response and a familiarity response showed that these finer grained judgments can be dissociated from each other, just as different source memory judgments can. The remember-to-know shift in that study occurred in just know responses, not in familiarity responses, which like guess responses were largely unchanged between the initial test and the retest (see figure 15.1).

Dissociations at this level are important, but they do not require any modification to the distinction between autonoetic and anoetic forms of awareness (Tulving, 1983, 1985). They only require a distinction to be made between the varieties of experience that each state of awareness may encompass (Gardiner & Conway, in press). But there is the theoretical problem of which dissociations should be taken to justify distinctions between states of awareness rather than between varieties of experience. This same kind of problem arose in relation to dissociations of implicit compared with explicit test performance and distinctions between different memory systems (see, e.g., Roediger, 1990). And there hasn't really been any satisfactory resolution of it there. Even if one accepts that its resolution will depend on many different but converging sources of evidence (Nyberg & Tulving, 1996), it still remains unclear at what point, and by what criteria, the weight of evidence will favor one resolution rather than another. The same seems true—by the same token—with respect to states of awareness and varieties of experience.

Conclusions

Following Tulving's (1985) introduction of remember and know responses as subjective reports of two states of awareness of the past, the most fundamental empirical discovery is that remembering and knowing are functionally independent. They are influenced differently, in systematic ways, by different experimental manipulations. They vary systematically in different subject populations. They are differentially susceptible to the effects of drugs, and appear to be associated with at least partially distinct patterns of neural activity.

The addition of the guess response category is an important development in the remember/know paradigm that clearly has both methodological and theoretical advantages—especially with respect to previous attempts to model remember and know responses that encouraged guessing, but did not allow guesses to be reported. Awareness of guessing, unlike awareness of remembering or of knowing, does not normally reflect memory for the specific items that elicit the response.

Remembering and knowing are not explained by a unidimensional signal detection model based on the concept of trace strength. Nor do remembering and knowing correspond to a number of other dichotomies with which they have been previously aligned. These dichotomies include (1) the distinction between explicit and implicit memory, which has sometimes been equated with conscious versus unconscious memory; (2) the distinction between conceptual and perceptual processes, from the transfer-appropriate processing framework; (3) the distinction between recollection and familiarity, conceived as independent processes in certain dual-process models of recognition; and (4) the closely related distinction between controlled and automatic processes, as represented in the process dissociation procedure.

Of theories that account for remembering and knowing, the fullest and most direct account is provided by Tulving's (1983, 1985) memory systems theory. The distinctiveness/ fluency framework developed by Rajaram (1996, 1998) provides a valuable alternative account.

More generally, the evidence reviewed in this chapter strengthens considerably the case for arguing that psychology of memory should take on board subjective reports of conscious states and not just rely on more conventional measures of performance. This evidence has established that the essential subjectivity of remembering and knowing does not make reports of these states of awareness intractable to science.

Appendix 1: Written Test Instructions

In this test you will see a series of words, one word at a time. Some of the words are those that you saw yesterday. Others are not. For each word, click the YES button if you recognize the word as one you saw yesterday and click the NO button if you do not think the word was one you saw yesterday.

Recognition memory is associated with two different kinds of awareness. Quite often recognition brings back to mind something you recollect about what it is that you recognise, as when, for example, you recognise some-

one's face, and perhaps *remember* talking to this person at a party the previous night. At other times recognition brings nothing back to mind about what it is you recognise, as when, for example, you are confident that you recognise someone, and you *know* you recognise them, because of strong feelings of familiarity, but you have no recollection of seeing this person before. You do not remember anything about them.

The same kinds of awareness are associated with recognising the words you saw yesterday. Sometimes when you recognize a word as one you saw yesterday, recognition will bring back to mind something you remember thinking about when the word appeared then. You recollect something you consciously experienced at that time. But sometimes recognizing a word as one you saw yesterday will not bring back to mind anything you remember about seeing it then. Instead, the word will seem familiar, so that you feel confident it was one you saw yesterday, even though you don't recollect anything you experienced when you saw it then.

For each word that you recognize, after you have clicked the YES button, please then click the REMEMBER button, if recognition is accompanied by some recollective experience, or the KNOW button, if recognition is accompanied by strong feelings of familiarity in the absence of any recollective experience.

There will also be times when you do not remember the word, nor does it seem familiar, but you might want to guess that it was one of the words you saw yesterday. Feel free to do this, but if your YES response is really just a guess, please then click the GUESS button.

Note to Appendix. Subjects from certain clinical populations may find the terms remembering and knowing confusing and, if so, more abstract terms such as "Memory Type A" and "Memory Type B" can be used. The descriptions of these types of memory are the same as those used to describe remembering and knowing (see, e.g., Bowler et al., 1998).

Acknowledgment The authors' research has been supported by Grant 000236225 from the Economic and Social Research Council (ESRC) of Great Britain. The study by Bowler et al. (1998) was supported by Grant 048226/Z/96 from the Wellcome Trust. We thank both the ESRC and the Wellcome Trust for their support. We also thank Cristina Ramponi for her help in the preparation of this chapter.

Notes

1. Classification is not always straightforward. Not all studies showing effects on remembering report analyses that permit conclusions about effects on knowing. Also, effects on remembering are sometimes accompanied by reverse effects on knowing that might reflect scale attenuation, and know responses tend to be more variable than remember responses for reasons we discuss later in the chapter.

2. Indeed, with a manipulation designed to encourage very lenient response criteria, Hirshman and Henzler (1998) found an increase in remember as well as in know responses. But this manipulation led to a remember false-alarm rate of 11% and a know false-alarm rate of 35%. Both false-alarm rates are exceptionally high. It seems likely that Hirshman and Henzler's subjects were induced to confabulate some of their responses. Hirshman and Henzler also reported A′ estimates of memory that were consistently lower with the more lenient response criteria, which supports this interpretation even though the reduction in those estimates was not found to be statistically significant.

References

Berntsen, D. (1998). Voluntary and involuntary access to autobiographical memory. *Memory, 6*, 113–141.

Bowler, D. M., Gardiner, J. M., & Grice, S. (1998). *Episodic memory and remembering in high-functioning individuals with autism.* Manuscript submitted for publication.

Blaxton, T. A., & Theodore, W. H. (1997). The role of the temporal lobes in recognizing visuospatial materials: Remembering versus knowing. *Brain and Cognition, 35*, 5–25.

Brewer, W. F. (1992). Phenomenal experience in laboratory and autobiographical memory. In M. A. Conway, D. C. Rubin, H. Spinnler, & W. A. Wagenaar (Eds.), *Theoretical perspectives on autobiographical memory* (pp. 31–51). Dordecht, Netherlands: Kluwer.

Brooks, B. M. (1994). A comparison of serial position effects in implicit and explicit word-stem completion. *Psychonomic Bulletin & Review, 1*, 264–268.

Buchner, A., Erdfelder, E., Steffens, M. C., & Martensen, H. (1997). The nature of memory processes underlying the process dissociation procedure. *Memory & Cognition, 25*, 508–517.

Conway, M. A., Collins, A. F., Gathercole, S. E., & Anderson, S. J. (1996). Recollections of true and false autobiographical memories. *Journal of Experimental Psychology: General, 125*, 69–95.

Conway, M. A., & Dewhurst, S. A. (1995). The self and recollective experience. *Applied Cognitive Psychology, 9*, 1–19.

Conway, M. A., Gardiner, J. M., Perfect, T. J., Anderson, S. J., & Cohen, G. (1997). Changes in memory awareness during learning: The acquisition of knowledge by psychology undergraduates. *Journal of Experimental Psychology: General, 126*, 393–413.

Curran, H. V., Gardiner, J. M., Java, R. I., & Allen, D. (1993). Effects of lorazepam upon recollective experience in recognition memory. *Psychopharmacology, 110*, 374–378.

Curran, H. V., & Hildebrandt, M. (in press). Dissociative effects of alcohol on recollective experience. *Consciousness & Cognition.*

Curran, T., Schacter, D. L., Norman, K. A., & Galluccio, L. (1997). False recognition after a right frontal lobe infarction: Memory for general and specific information. *Neuropsychologia, 35*, 1035–1049.

Dalla Barba, G. (1993). Confabulation: Knowledge and recollective experience. *Cognitive Neuropsychology, 10*, 1–20.

Dalla Barba, G. (1997). Recognition memory and recollective experience in Alzheimer's disease. *Memory, 5*, 657–672.

Deese, J. (1959). On the prediction of occurrence of particular intrusions in immediate recall. *Journal of Experimental Psychology, 58*, 17–22.

Dewhurst, S. A., & Hitch, G. J. (1997). Illusions of familiarity caused by cohort activation. *Psychonomic Bulletin & Review, 4*, 566–571.

Dewhurst, S. A., & Hitch, G. J. (1999). Cognitive operations and recollective experience in recognition memory. *Memory, 7*, 129–146.

Donaldson, W. (1996). The role of decision processes in remembering and knowing. *Memory & Cognition, 24*, 523–533.

Düzel, E., Yonelinas, A. P., Mangun, G. R., Heinze, H.-J., & Tulving, E. (1997). Event-related brain potential correlates of two states of conscious awareness in memory. *Proceedings of the National Academy of Science, 94,* 5973–5978.

Gardiner, J. M. (1988). Functional aspects of recollective experience. *Memory & Cognition, 16,* 309–313.

Gardiner, J. M., & Conway, M. A. (in press). Levels of awareness and varieties of experience. In B. H. Challis & B. M. Velichkovsky (Eds.), *Stratification of consciousness and cognition.* Amsterdam/Philadelphia: John Benjamin Publishing.

Gardiner, J. M., Gawlik, B., & Richardson-Klavehn, A. (1994). Maintenance rehearsal affects knowing, not remembering; elaborative rehearsal affects remembering, not knowing. *Psychonomic Bulletin & Review, 1,* 107–110.

Gardiner, J. M., & Gregg, V. H. (1997). Recognition memory with little or no remembering: Implications for a detection model. *Psychonomic Bulletin & Review, 4,* 474–479.

Gardiner, J. M., & Java, R. I. (1990). Recollective experience in word and nonword recognition. *Memory & Cognition, 18,* 23–30.

Gardiner, J. M., & Java, R. I. (1991). Forgetting in recognition memory with and without recollective experience. *Memory & Cognition, 19,* 617–623.

Gardiner, J. M., & Java, R. I. (1993). Recognising and remembering. In A. Collins, S. Gathercole, M. Conway, & P. Morris (Eds.), *Theories of memory* (pp. 163–188). Hillsdale, NJ: Erlbaum.

Gardiner, J. M., Java, R. I., & Richardson-Klavehn, A. (1996). How level of processing really influences awareness in recognition memory. *Canadian Journal of Experimental Psychology, 50,* 114–122.

Gardiner, J. M., Kaminska, Z., Dixon, M., & Java, R. I. (1996). Repetition of previously novel melodies sometimes increases both remember and know responses in recognition memory. *Psychonomic Bulletin & Review, 3* 366–371.

Gardiner, J. M., & Parkin, A. J. (1990). Attention and recollective experience in recognition memory. *Memory & Cognition, 18,* 579–583.

Gardiner, J. M., Ramponi, C., & Richardson-Klavehn, A. (1998a). Experiences of remembering, knowing, and guessing. *Consciousness and Cognition, 7,* 1–26.

Gardiner, J. M., Ramponi, C., & Richardson-Klavehn, A. (in press). Response deadline and subjective awareness in recognition memory. *Consciousness & Cognition.*

Gardiner, J. M., Richardson-Klavehn, A., & Ramponi, C. (1997). On reporting recollective experiences and "direct access to memory systems." *Psychological Science, 8,* 391–394.

Gardiner, J. M., Richardson-Klavehn, A., & Ramponi, C. (1998). Limitations of the signal detection model of the remember-know paradigm: A reply to Hirshman. *Consciousness and Cognition, 7,* 285–288.

Graf, P., & Mandler, G. (1984). Activation makes words more accessible, but not necessarily more retrievable. *Journal of Verbal Learning and Verbal Behavior, 23,* 553–568.

Gregg, V. H., & Gardiner, J. M. (1991). Components of conscious awareness in a long-term modality effect. *British Journal of Psychology, 82,* 153–162.

Gregg, V. H., & Gardiner, J. M. (1994). Recognition memory and awareness: A large effect of study-test modalities on "know" responses following a highly perceptual orienting task. *European Journal of Cognitive Psychology, 6,* 137–147.

Hirshman, E., & Henzler, A. (1998). The role of decision processes in conscious recollection. *Psychological Science, 9,* 61–65.

Hirshman, E., & Master, S. (1997). Modeling the conscious correlates of recognition memory: Reflections on the remember-know paradigm. *Memory & Cognition, 25,* 345–351.

Holmes, J. B., Waters, H. S., & Rajaram, S. (1998). The phenomenology of false memories: Episodic content and confidence. *Journal of Experimental Psychology: Learning, Memory, and Cognition, 24,* 1026–1040.

Huron, C., Danion, J.-M., Giacomoni, F., Grange, D., Robert, P., & Rizzo, L. (1995). Impairment of recognition memory with, but not without, conscious recollection in schizophrenia. *American Journal of Psychiatry, 152,* 1737–1742.

Inoue, C., & Bellezza, F. S. (1998). The detection model of recognition using know and remember judgements. *Memory & Cognition, 26,* 299–308.

Jacoby, L. L. (1991). A process-dissociation framework: Separating automatic from intentional uses of memory. *Journal of Memory and Language, 30,* 513–541.

Jacoby, L. L., & Dallas, M. (1981). On the relationship between autobiographical memory and perceptual learning. *Journal of Experimental Psychology: General, 110,* 306–340.

Jacoby, L. L., Yonelinas, A. P., & Jennings, J. M. (1997). The relation between conscious and unconscious (automatic) influences: A declaration of independence. In J. D. Cohen & J. W. Schooler (Eds.), *Scientific approaches to the question of consciousness* (pp. 13–47). Hillsdale, NJ: Erlbaum.

Java, R. I. (1994). States of awareness following word stem completion. *European Journal of Cognitive Psychology, 6*, 77–92.

Java, R. I. (1996). Effects of age on state of awareness following implicit and explicit word association tasks. *Psychology and Aging, 11*, 108–111.

Java, R. I., Kaminska, Z., & Gardiner, J. M. (1995). Recognition memory and awareness for famous and obscure musical themes. *European Journal of Cognitive Psychology, 7*, 41–53.

Johnson, M. K., Hashtroudi, S., & Lindsay, D. S. (1993). Source monitoring. *Psychological Bulletin, 114*, 3–28.

Jones, T. C., & Roediger, H. L. (1995). The experiential basis of serial position effects. *European Journal of Cognitive Psychology, 7*, 65–80.

Knowlton, B. J., & Squire, L. R. (1995). Remembering and knowing: Two different expressions of declarative memory. *Journal of Experimental Psychology: Learning, Memory, and Cognition, 21*, 699–710.

LeCompte, D. C. (1995). Recollective experience in the revelation effect: Separating the contributions of recollection and familiarity. *Memory & Cognition, 23*, 324–334.

Macken, W. J., & Hampson, P. (1993). Integration, elaboration, and recollective experience. *Irish Journal of Psychology, 14*, 279–285.

Mandler, G. (1980). Recognizing: The judgment of previous occurrence. *Psychological Review, 87*, 252–271.

Mäntylä, T. (1993). Knowing but not remembering: Adult age differences in recollective experience. *Memory & Cognition, 221*, 379–388.

Mantyla, T. (1997). Recollections of faces: Remembering differences and knowing similarities. *Journal of Experimental Psychology: Learning, Memory, and Cognition, 23*, 1203–1216.

Mantyla, T., & Raudsepp, J. (1996). Recollective experience following suppression of focal attention. *European Journal of Cognitive Psychology, 8*, 195–203.

Mather, M., Henkel, L. A., & Johnson, M. K. (1997). Evaluating characteristics of false memories: Remember/know judgments and memory characteristics compared. *Memory & Cognition, 25*, 826–837.

Mulligan, N. W., & Hirshman, E. (1997). Measuring the bases of recognition memory: An investigation of the process dissociation framework. *Journal of Experimental Psychology: Learning, Memory, and Cognition, 23*, 280–304.

Nyberg, L., & Tulving, E. (1996). Classifying human long-term memory: Evidence from converging dissociations. *European Journal of Cognitive Psychology, 8*, 163–183.

Parkin, A. J., & Russo, R. (1993). On the origin of functional differences in recollective experience. *Memory, 1*, 231–237.

Parkin, A. J., & Walter, B. (1992). Recollective experience, normal aging, and frontal dysfunction. *Psychology and Aging, 7*, 290–298.

Perfect, T. J., & Dasgupta, Z. R. R. (1997). What underlies the deficit in reported recollective experience in old age? *Memory & Cognition, 25*, 849–858.

Perfect, T. J., Williams, R. B., & Anderton-Brown, C. (1995). Age differences in reported recollective experience are due to encoding effects, not response bias. *Memory, 3*, 169–186.

Perner, J., & Ruffman, T. (1995). Episodic memory and autonoetic consciousness: Developmental evidence and a theory of childhood amnesia. *Journal of Experimental Child Psychology, 59*, 516–548.

Rajaram, S. (1993). Remembering and knowing: Two means of access to the personal past. *Memory & Cognition, 21*, 89–102.

Rajaram, S. (1996). Perceptual effects on remembering: Recollective processes in picture recognition memory. *Journal of Experimental Psychology: Learning, Memory, and Cognition, 22*, 365–377.

Rajaram, S. (1998). Conceptual and perceptual effects on remembering: The role of salience/distinctiveness. *Psychonomic Bulletin & Review, 5*, 71–78.

Rajaram, S., & Roediger, H. L., III (1997). Remembering and knowing as states of consciousness during recollection. In J. D. Cohen & J. W. Schooler (Eds.), *Scientific approaches to the question of consciousness* (pp. 213–240). Hillsdale, NJ: Erlbaum.

Richardson-Klavehn, A., & Gardiner, J. M. (1996). Cross-modality priming in stem completion reflects conscious memory, but not voluntary memory. *Psychonomic Bulletin & Review, 3*, 238–244.

Richardson-Klavehn, A., & Gardiner, J. M. (1998). Depth of processing effects on priming in stem completion: Tests of the voluntary contamination, conceptual processing, and lexical processing hypotheses. *Journal of Experimental Psychology: Learning, Memory, and Cognition, 24,* 593–609.

Richardson-Klavehn, A., Gardiner, J. M., & Java, R. I. (1996). Memory: Task dissociations, process dissociations, and dissociations of consciousness. In G. Underwood (Ed.), *Implicit cognition* (pp. 85–158). Oxford: Oxford University Press.

Roediger, H. L. (1990). Implicit memory: Retention without remembering. *American Psychologist, 45,* 1043–1056.

Roediger, H. L., & McDermott, K. B. (1995). Creating false memories: Remembering words not presented in lists. *Journal of Experimental Psychology: Learning, Memory, and Cognition, 21,* 803–814.

Schacter, D. L., Koutstaal, W., Johnson, M. K., Gross, M. S., & Angell, K. E. (1997). False recollection induced by photographs: A comparison of older and younger adults. *Psychology and Aging, 12,* 203–215.

Schacter, D. L., Verfaillie, M., & Anes, M. D. (1997). Illusory memories in amnesic patients: Conceptual and perceptual false recognition. *Neuropsychology, 11,* 331–342.

Smith, M. E. (1993). Neuropsychological manifestations of recollective experience during recognition memory judgements. *Journal of Cognitive Neuroscience, 5,* 1–13.

Snodgrass, J. G., Hirshman, E., & Fan, J. (1996). The sensory match in recognition memory: Perceptual fluency or episodic trace? *Memory & Cognition, 24,* 367–383.

Strack, F., & Forster, J. (1995). Reporting recollective experiences: Direct access to memory systems? *Psychological Science, 6,* 352–358.

Toplis, R. (1997). *Recollective experiences in children and adults: A comparative study.* Doctoral dissertation, University of East London, London.

Tulving, E. (1983). *Elements of episodic memory.* Oxford: Oxford University Press.

Tulving, E. (1985). Memory and consciousness. *Canadian Psychology, 26,* 1–12.

Tulving, E. (1998). Memory: Performance, knowledge, and experience. *European Journal of Experimental Psychology, 1,* 3–26.

Tulving, E. (1994). Varieties of consciousness and levels of awareness in memory. In A. Baddeley & L. Weiskrantz (Eds.), *Attention: Selection, awareness, and control. A tribute to Donald Broadbent* (pp. 283–299). Oxford: Oxford University Press.

Wagner, A. D., Gabrieli, J. D. E., & Verfaellie, M. (1997). Dissociations between familiarity processes in explicit recognition and implicit perceptual memory. *Journal of Experimental Psychology: Learning, Memory, and Cognition, 23,* 305–323.

Wheeler, M. A., Stuss, D. T., & Tulving, E. (1997). Towards a theory of episodic memory: The frontal lobes and autonoetic consciousness. *Psychological Bulletin, 121,* 331–354.

Yonelinas, A. P., Dobbins, I., Szymanski, M. D., Dhaliwal, H. S., & King, L. (1996). Signal detection, threshold, and dual process models of recognition memory: ROCs and conscious recollection. *Consciousness and Cognition, 5,* 418–441.

Yonelinas, A. P., & Jacoby, L. L. (1996). Noncriterial recollection: Familiarity as automatic, irrelevant recollection. *Consciousness and Cognition, 5,* 131–141.

16

Nonconscious Forms of Human Memory

JEFFREY P. TOTH

The relationship between memory and consciousness is one of the most fascinating aspects of cognitive research. However, it is only recently that students of psychology have truly appreciated the intimate connection between these two aspects of mental life.

Systematic research on memory began with Ebbinghaus's (1885/1964) pioneering work on memory for nonsense syllables and has since progressed through a number of phases including studies of the learning and memory capabilities of nonhuman animals (e.g., Hull, 1943; Tolman, 1932), operant-behaviorist conceptualizations of memory in terms of stimulus control (Skinner, 1969), and neo-behaviorist studies of word-list learning and the mechanisms of forgetting (Underwood, 1957). These ideas set the stage for modern cognitive conceptions of memory whereby prior experiences are viewed as mental representations, encoded, stored, and retrieved in a human information-processing system.

In contrast to research on memory, research on consciousness and awareness, although never completely absent (e.g., Adams, 1957), has been relatively sparse since the early speculations and introspective studies of psychologists such as Wundt, Titchener, and James. Although it is probably safe to say that psychologists have never doubted the existence (or at least the problem) of consciousness, much of twentieth-century psychology assumed that consciousness did not play a large role in the production of thought and behavior. And even if this view was not universally held (by psychoanalysts, for example), few methods existed for empirically approaching the problem.

This all changed in the early 1980s, however, when memory and consciousness came together in such a way as to fundamentally alter the landscape of cognitive research. In essence, it was discovered that a person's thought and behavior could be influenced by prior events of which that person was not aware; and that the nature of such nonconscious mnemonic influences—the principles by which they operated—differed significantly from the more conscious forms of memory that researchers had traditionally investigated. These findings were so important that today any serious account of memory must acknowledge the dramatic difference that obtains between "memory with awareness" and "memory without awareness." So, too, observed differences in these two kinds of *memory* have been influential in making *consciousness* and *awareness* respectable topics of inquiry in psychology and neuroscience (Barrs, 1988; Cohen & Schooler, 1997; Picton & Stuss, 1994).

The purpose of this chapter is to provide an overview of nonconscious forms of human memory. The first section ("Phenomena and Phenomenology") provides more background information and examples, essentially firming up the case that the qualitative distinction between conscious and nonconscious memory is a necessary one. This first section also introduces some of the terminology and research designs used in the field. The second section ("Paradigms") describes research methods in more detail and also provides an overview of major empirical findings. The final section ("The Future of Nonconscious Memory") briefly notes critical issues for future research and describes how ideas about nonconscious mnemonic processes are beginning to be integrated with other aspects of cognition, as well as with the study of the brain.

The reader may note the above organization does not include sections entitled "Findings" or "Theories." The reason for this is that there are simply too many relevant empirical results and theoretical positions to be included within this short chapter. More extensive reviews of the empirical literature can be found in Kelley and Lindsay (1996); Roediger and McDermott (1993); Moscovitch, Vriezen, and Goshen-Gottstein (1993); and Richardson-Klavehn and Bjork (1988). Readers interested in large-scale theoretical accounts of nonconscious processes in memory are directed to the following sources: Jacoby, Yonelinas, & Jennings, 1997; Moscovitch, 1994; Ratcliff & McKoon, 1996; Roediger, Weldon, & Challis, 1989; Schacter & Tulving, 1994a; Toth & Hunt, 1999.

Phenomena and Phenomenology

How might one establish that consciousness is a necessary concept in understanding memory? Perhaps the single most important source of evidence for answering this question comes from research with amnesic patients. Damage to the medial temporal lobes, usually involving the hippocampus and related structures, produces a profound inability to consciously recollect one's past. Patients with such damage can participate in common events, such as reading a list of words or conversing with their doctor, yet be totally unable to later recall or recognize those prior events. Indeed, for the majority of this century it was widely believed that such patients simply could not create (encode or store) a long-term record of their experience. But starting with studies by Warrington and Weiskrantz (1968; see also

Rozin, 1976) this view was shown to be incorrect. If amnesic patients are given a task that is related to their prior experiences, but which makes no reference to those experiences—such as simply rereading the list of words or completing fragmented forms of those words (me _ o _ y)—these patients show incontrovertible evidence that their prior experiences were indeed recorded and subsequently used to influence their performance.

Amnesia, then, provides a crucial piece of evidence that memory can occur without awareness: the amnesic patient fails to experience the phenomenology of remembering— she believes she is *not* remembering—but her performance shows that memory is indeed being used.

The flip side of this memory-awareness relation is also available. Patients with damage to frontal lobes, often including the basal forebrain, demonstrate a phenomenon known as confabulation in which they relate events of their past, and steadfastly assert their reality, when in fact those events *never happened* (see Kopelman, 1987; Moscovitch, 1989). The confabulating patient thus exhibits the converse of the amnesic patient's unaware form of memory: he experiences the phenomenology of remembering—believes he *is* remembering—but historical records, such as those provided by relatives, show that no memory exists.

Amnesic and confabulating patients thus indicate a complex relation between, and *dissociation* of, the retention and expression of prior experience on the one hand, and a phenomenal awareness of that experience on the other. Such patients are fascinating because they suggest that to understand memory one must also understand the phenomenal awareness of remembering. But two more issues must be addressed before the relation between memory and awareness can be viewed as fundamental. First, it must be shown that similar phenomena (i.e., memory/awareness dissociations) can occur in persons without brain damage. And second, that memory with awareness and memory without awareness operate according to different rules or principles. As described next, there is strong evidence supporting both of these points.

Imagine that a normal (non-brain-damaged) individual is presented with a list of words, half visually, half aurally. Moreover, within each presentation modality, the person makes a superficial judgment for half of the words, such as counting the number of vowels, and a more meaning-based judgment for the other half, such as deciding whether the word refers to a pleasant or unpleasant concept. If one were to assess this person's memory with an "explicit" (conscious) test of memory such as recognition or recall, it is highly likely that the individual would show superior memory for the meaningfully processed words, but that the modality of original presentation would have little impact on performance (figure 16.1).

Consider now a different test in which the subject is shown word stems (e.g., *tru__*), some of which can be completed with previously encountered words, but is simply asked to complete each stem with the first word that comes to mind. When tested in this "implicit" way (figure 16.2), performance looks dramatically different from that found with explicit tests. In particular, the meaningfulness with which words were encoded has no influence on performance, but the modality of initial presentation has a large effect. Note that performance in such implicit tests is assessed relative to a baseline condition for which no study items were presented; the increase in

performance for studied over nonstudied (baseline) items is called "priming."

Dissociations such as that shown in figures 16.1 and 16.2 have now been firmly established for a large number of experimental manipulations (see Roediger & McDermott, 1993) and thus make a strong case that conscious and nonconscious forms of memory operate according to different principles.

How do we know that the person tested implicitly is not consciously aware that his or her primed responses came from the prior encoding event (or that such awareness is not a necessary condition for the pattern of performance obtained)? This is a difficult issue that sets the stage for much of the recent research in the field (see below). But despite this difficulty, the bulk of evidence shows that neither awareness of a prior event nor an intent to remember that event is a necessary condition for prior experience to exert a significant influence on performance. Much of the research cited in the following sections shows this to be the case. Here, however, two phenomena can demonstrate the basic argument.

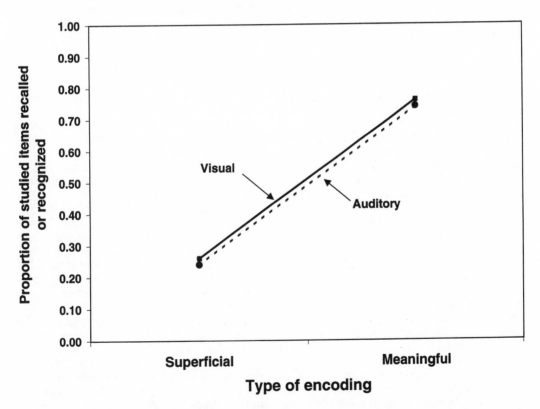

Figure 16.1 Idealized effects of semantic elaboration and study modality on an explicit test of memory.

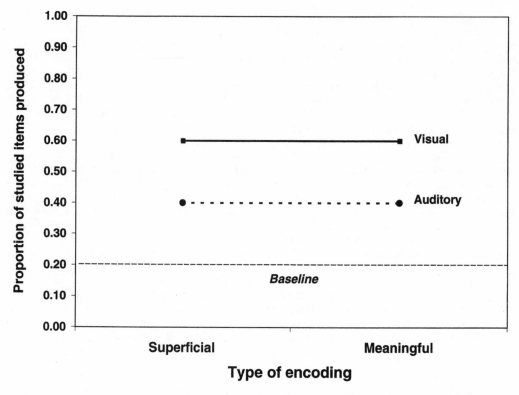

Figure 16.2 Idealized effects of semantic elaboration and study modality on a visual ("perceptual") implicit test of memory.

First, consider what is known as *stochastic independence* between memory tests. In studies examining stochastic independence, a subject is, for example, shown a list of words and then given two consecutive memory tests. One of these tests (e.g., word-fragment completion) is implicit such that, although some of the fragments can be completed with previously presented words, the subject is simply asked to complete each fragment without reference to any prior experience (with "the first word that comes to mind"). In the other test, the subject is asked to consciously recognize words from the original list, some of which are the same as those tested on the fragment test. By examining the relation between the two tests, one can ask whether performance is correlated—that is, whether recognizing a particular word predicts one's ability to complete a fragment with that word, or vice versa. In fact, results show that there is often *no* relation between performance on the two tests (i.e., the tests show stochastic independence); recognizing a word tells us nothing about whether the subject will use that word to complete a

fragment; and completing a fragment with a studied word tells us nothing about whether the subject will recognize that word as being on the study list (Jacoby & Witherspoon, 1982; Tulving, Schacter, & Stark, 1982).

Stochastic independence thus shows that conscious memory of a particular event is not a necessary condition for that event to influence performance. An even more dramatic illustration of this point comes from studies manipulating the amount of attention available for encoding an event. If subjects are asked to read a list of words while at the same time performing a difficult secondary task (such as monitoring a series of digits for a particular sequence), subsequent conscious memory (e.g., recall) will be much impaired relative to the case when the subject devotes full attention to study. In contrast, implicit tests of memory such as stem and fragment completion show little or no effect of such attentional manipulations (see figure 16.3). Such dissociations as a function of attention have been produced with a variety of tests and measurement techniques (Parkin, Reed, & Russo, 1990; Ja-

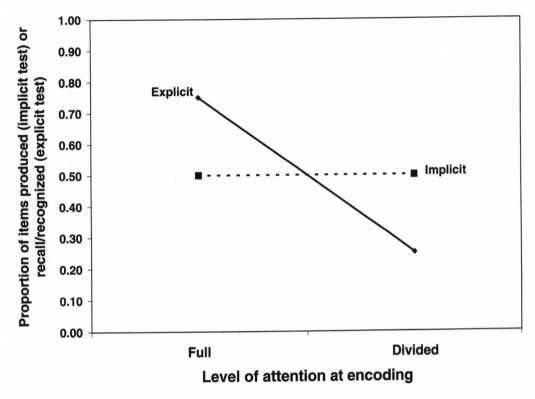

Figure 16.3 Idealized effects of full and divided attention on implicit and explicit tests of memory.

coby, Toth, & Yonelinas, 1993) and further strengthen the case that memory can occur in the absence of conscious awareness.

Stochastic independence and the effects of divided attention make a strong case that conscious and nonconscious forms of memory are distinct, qualitatively different ways in which the past can influence the present. A skeptic might further insist, however, that in both cases, the subject is aware of the earlier event and, more important, of the fact that the test bears some relation to that event. Even these worries can be addressed, however, as is shown in the following sections.

Paradigms

Mere-Exposure

How might one guarantee that subjects cannot become aware of, or attempt intentional retrieval of, a prior event? One method is to present stimuli below the threshold for aware-

ness. The notion here is that, if subjects are unaware that an item has been encoded, they cannot subsequently become aware of the relation between a later memory test and that prior encoding experience. This is exactly the strategy employed in the mere-exposure paradigm in which subjects are exposed to stimuli, such as randomly generated geometric shapes, for a "mere" 1 millisecond (one one-thousandth of a second!). As you might expect, stimuli "shown" at this duration are very difficult to see; and, in fact, subjects in such experimental conditions claim to have not seen anything (except a blank screen) and later are unable to recognize any of the briefly flashed shapes. Yet when later shown pairs of shapes and asked to choose the shape they "like best," previously flashed shapes are chosen significantly more often than shapes that were not presented earlier (Kunst-Wilson & Zajonc, 1980; Seamon et al., 1995).

Results from mere-exposure studies thus show that subjects need not even be aware that a prior event occurred for that event to influence their subsequent performance. However, mere-exposure studies are limited because, if subjects are unaware that an encoding event has occurred, they cannot act on it or process it in different ways. And getting subjects to process events in various ways is crucial to determining the different operating characteristics of conscious and nonconscious forms of memory. Thus, paradigms discussed in the following sections use the more typical procedure of showing items at easily perceivable levels, having subjects process those items in different ways, and then employing various test conditions designed to elicit nonconscious forms of memory.

Implicit Tests

The most popular way of eliciting nonconscious memory is with implicit tests such as the stem- and fragment-completion tests described above. The defining feature of an implicit memory test is simply the instructions: subjects are told to respond to test stimuli (e.g., produce a word, classify an object, solve a puzzle) without reference to past experience. Although there has been a good deal of debate as to whether such instructions are a sufficient basis on which to infer nonconscious memory (see Jacoby, 1991; Reingold & Merikle, 1990; Toth, Reingold, & Jacoby, 1994), there is no question that such tests show striking dissociations (i.e., different patterns of performance) in comparison with more traditional (conscious/explicit) tests of memory.

Table 16.1 provides a relatively comprehensive list of the many implicit tests currently in use, although new tests are invented every year. Note that the organization of this table—based on a distinction among perceptual, conceptual, and procedural processes—is not theoretically neutral. Nevertheless, it allows an extensive classification scheme that captures most, if not all, of the tests available: perceptual tests, such as word identification and fragment completion, are those that challenge the various perceptual systems in some way—for example, with a fast presentation or a degraded/fragmented stimulus. Conceptual tests, in contrast, employ retrieval cues such as category labels or general-knowledge questions designed to elicit responses that are meaningfully related to these cues. Finally, procedural implicit tests require subjects to perform extended sensory, motor, or cognitive tasks, such as learning a new perceptual-motor skill.

Most of what is known about nonconscious forms of memory is based on implicit tests. As noted earlier, this chapter will not attempt to describe all of the relevant findings. However, the major conclusions of this research can be summarized briefly: On perceptual implicit tests, nonconscious mnemonic processes appear insensitive to conceptual manipulations (i.e., they appear "presemantic") and yet show high sensitivity to changes in surface form from study to test (see figure 16.2). In contrast, conceptual tests reveal the opposite set of characteristics, being *insensitive* to changes in surface form, but showing sensitivity to conceptual-encoding manipulations such as level of processing (but see Vaidya et al., 1997).

The perceptual/conceptual theme running through the above conclusions, as well as table 16.1, has become central in theorizing about nonconscious mnemonic processes. Indeed, this distinction is the cornerstone of both "process" theories of memory (Roediger, 1990; see also Jacoby, 1983; Kolers & Roediger, 1984) as well as more "structural" multiple-memory systems approaches (see Tulving & Schacter, 1990; Schacter & Tulving, 1994a). It is important to note, however, that the perception/conception distinction, while undoubtedly important, is clearly insufficient to capture the most crucial aspect of implicit/explicit memory dissociations—namely, that in one case, the subject is aware of remembering a past event, while in the other case such awareness is absent (or at least unnecessary). This has led some researchers to deemphasize the perception/conception distinction in favor of distinctions more closely related to the phenomenological status of conscious and nonconscious memory. For example, Jacoby (1991), noting relations between nonconscious memory effects and similar phenomena in the field of attention, has advocated a distinction between mnemonic control and automaticity (see also Logan, 1990). Jacoby's view is also supplemented by a sophisticated analysis of how subjects *infer* the role of memory—thus, effectively constructing their subjective experience of remembering—on the basis of their performance and relevant task demands (see Jacoby, Kelley, & Dywan, 1989). This attributional approach is discussed more fully below.

Further questioning the usefulness of a perception/conception distinction, Masson and McLeod (1992) have conceptualized implicit/explicit dissociations in terms of the differ-

Table 16.1 Implicit tests of memory (with representative references).

Verbal tests
  Perceptual
    Word ("perceptual") identification   Jacoby & Dallas (1981)
    Word stem completion   Graf et al. (1982)
    Word fragment completion   Tulving et al. (1982)
    Lexical decision   Duchek & Neely (1989)
    Word naming   Hashtroudi et al. (1988)
    Anagram solution   Srivinas & Roediger (1990)
    Homophone spelling   Jacoby & Witherspoon (1982)
    Temporal (duration) judgments   Witherspoon & Allan (1985)
  Conceptual
    Word association   Shimamura & Squire (1984)
    Category-instance (exemplar) generation   Blaxton (1989)
    Fact (general knowledge) generation   Kelley & Lindsay (1993)
    Category verification   Vaidya et al. (1997)
    Categorization/classification judgments   Vaidya et al. (1997)
    Fame judgments   Jacoby et al. (1989b)
    Truth/credibility judgments   Begg et al. (1992)
  Procedural
    Word-based problem solving   Adams et al. (1988)
    Probability judgments   Knowlton & Squire (1994)
    Reading normal text   Levy & Kirsner (1989)
    Reading altered (e.g., mirror inverted text) Kolers (1976)
    Artificial grammar learning   Reber (1989)

Non-verbal tests
  Perceptual
    Identification of fragmented pictures   Weldon & Roediger (1987)
    Picture naming   Mitchell & Brown (1988)
    Object/non-object decision   Kroll & Potter (1984)
    Possible/impossible object decision   Schacter et al. (1990)
    Noise judgments   Jacoby et al. (1988)
    Action-decision test for dynamic events   Nilsson et al. (1992)
    Aesthetic/preference judgments   Kunst-Wilson & Zajonc (1980)
    Sensory conditioning   Benzing & Squire (1989)
    Affective conditioning   Bechara et al. (1995)
  Conceptual
    Person/trait attributions   Smith & Branscomb (1988)
    Object categorization   no published studies
    Common-uses decisions for objects   no published studies
  Procedural
    Serial reaction time   Nissen & Bullemer (1987)
    Control of complex systems   Berry & Broadbent (1984)
    Motor tracking   Corkin (1968)
    Mirror drawing   Milner (1962)
    Jigsaw puzzles   Brooks & Baddeley (1976)
    Tower of Hanoi   Cohen et al. (1985)
    Maze learning   Milner (1965)
    Motor conditioning   Weiskrantz & Warrington (1979)

ence between an initial "interpretive encoding" that involves an integration of perceptual and conceptual components, and a second, more elaborative processing phase that is predominantly conceptual. And Toth and Reingold (1996; see also Toth & Hunt, 1999) have stressed the importance of context-goal configurations in understanding both conscious and nonconscious forms of memory. It is likely that all of these ideas will figure in more mature theories of memory.

A potential problem with comparisons among implicit and explicit tests concerns the different cues they provide for access to memory. Although implicit/explicit dissociations are often taken to support a qualitative difference in memory, and thus to reveal the operating characteristics of nonconscious mnemonic processes, it is widely known that even different conscious tests of memory can show dissociations as a function of the retrieval cues they provide. As one classic example, recall and recognition dissociate as a function of frequency in the language: high-frequency words are more likely to be recalled whereas low-frequency words are more likely to be recognized. In extending such observations to implicit memory, the worry is that implicit/explicit dissociations occurring between tests that provide different retrieval cues (e.g., fragment completion and recognition) may not reflect differences in awareness or intent but rather differences in the retrieval properties of the test cues (Dunn & Kirsner, 1989).

An important development in this regard is a method known as the retrieval intentionality criterion (Schacter, Bowers, & Booker, 1989), which recommends providing *identical* cues at test (e.g., word stems) and varying only the instructions given to the subject (implicit or explicit). If one finds qualitative differences in performance as a function of instructions, one can then make a much stronger case that awareness (or intent) was the crucial factor, rather than the nature of the retrieval cues. Although the logic underlying this strategy is not unassailable (see Toth et al., 1994; Reingold & Toth, 1996) there is no question that it represents an important methodological advance in the study of implicit memory.

Before leaving implicit tests, it is worth noting another line of research—*implicit learning*—that, while proceeding somewhat independently, effectively employs the same strategy as that underlying implicit memory tests (see Reber, 1989; Seger, 1994). In studies of implicit learning, subjects are exposed to a series of stimuli that embody a complex underlying rule structure that is not readily apparent. For example, subjects may see stimuli (e.g., VTTRM) that appear to be a random collection of letters but which are actually generated by a complex rule system or grammar. In later transfer (implicit) tests, subjects are able to discriminate "legal" from "nonlegal" letter strings (i.e., those conforming vs. not conforming to the underlying grammar) despite being unable to describe the basis for their decision. Similarly, when reacting to a series of events that appear random (e.g., a sequential pattern of lights) but which actually conform to complex transition rules, reaction times become faster despite the subjects' inability to describe the underlying rule (e.g., Nissen & Bullemer, 1987). In general, implicit learning appears to be most similar to procedural implicit memory tests and it is likely that both phenomena draw on similar neurocognitive mechanisms (see Curran, 1998).

As noted above, one problem with studies employing implicit tests is the possibility that subjects are aware of, and potentially trying to retrieve, prior events. In the context of implicit/explicit test comparisons, the retrieval intentionality criterion is one way to address this problem. The next three sections describe alternative approaches to solving the vexing issue of awareness and intent in the study of nonconscious memory.

Self-Report

One strategy for isolating nonconscious processes in memory is simply to ask subjects whether they were aware of, or tried to retrieve, prior events during performance of an implicit test. Although this strategy is not widely utilized, the available research suggests two major conclusions: First, subjects *are* often aware that items presented or produced on an implicit test were previously encountered in an earlier task (e.g., Richardson-Klavehn, Lee, Joubran, & Bjork, 1994). Second, and as might be expected, subjects who are aware of the relation between an encoding event and a subsequent test are more likely to attempt intentional retrieval of items from that encoding event (Bowers & Schacter, 1990; Toth et al., 1994).

Given these potential problems, some researchers (e.g., Roediger & McDermott, 1993) have recommended disguising implicit tests through the use of long study and test lists, test lists with a high ratio of new to old items, filler tasks presented before the implicit test, and instructions that encourage fast responses to each test cue. Such techniques may indeed help disguise the nature of an implicit test, but they do so at the expense of being able to investigate variables that may turn out to be critical for understanding nonconscious mnemonic processes (e.g., long vs. short lists, high vs. low new/old ratios, fast vs. slow responses).

Self-reports themselves are not without problems. For one, subjects cannot be asked to report on their level of awareness (or intent) for each test item, at least in experiments that attempt to disguise the relation between study and a later implicit test. This means that self-reports of awareness must be assessed retrospectively (after the test is completed), a procedure that depends on the accuracy of memory for prior states of awareness and intent. Perhaps even more problematic is the questionable validity of self-reports because test demands and subsequent questions about test awareness may interact in complex ways. Implicit test instructions effectively tell subjects not to intentionally retrieve prior study items. If subjects are later asked whether they used intentional memory, answering yes is tantamount to saying that they ignored prior instructions. Subjects may be reluctant to do this, thus falsely confirming an experimenter's expectations.

Despite these problems, the available studies using self-reports suggest that test awareness does not fundamentally alter the basic expression of nonconscious (or unintentional) memory (Bowers & Schacter, 1990; Richardson-Klavehn et al., 1994). Additional research using self-report methods, as well as variations on these methods—such as the remember/know technique developed by Tulving (1985)—may provide important insights into the nature of nonconscious forms of memory, as well as how the influences of these forms of memory are "interpreted" by more conscious processes (see chapter 15; and Jacoby, 1998).

Opposition and the Process-Dissociation Procedure

One of the most important advances in the study of nonconscious influences of memory is the opposition procedure developed by Jacoby and colleagues (e.g., Jacoby, Woloshyn, & Kelley, 1989). For example, subjects might study a list of words and then later be given a test of word-stem completion. However, instead of asking subjects to complete stems with studied words, or to respond with the first words that come to mind, subjects are told to complete the stems only with words that were *not* studied. If, in contrast to instructions (and thus conscious intent), subjects complete stems with previously studied words, one has gained strong evidence for the operation of nonconscious memory because conscious memory would have resulted in the word being *excluded* as a test response.

Using the opposition procedure as a starting point, Jacoby (1991) developed a more elaborate *process-dissociation procedure* designed to quantify the strength of conscious and nonconscious forms of memory. The procedure involves combining results from the opposition (or *exclusion*) condition, with those from an *inclusion* condition in which subjects are told to *use* old words to complete test stems. By casting these two conditions into equations that embody the logical relation between conscious and nonconscious memory, one should be able to combine performance in the two conditions so as to analytically estimate the separate contributions of the two kinds of memory. And, indeed, mnemonic estimates gained from this procedure have produced a number of interesting dissociations. For example, divided attention (Jacoby, Toth et al., 1993), speed of response (Toth, 1996a; Yonelinas & Jacoby, 1995), elaborateness of study processing (Toth et al., 1994), aging (Jennings & Jacoby, 1993, 1997), and traumatic brain injury (Ste-Marie, Jennings & Finlayson, 1996; Toth, 1996b) all have been shown to affect estimates of conscious memory, but to leave estimates of nonconscious memory unchanged. Variations on the procedure have shown the opposite pattern—effects on nonconscious, but not conscious, memory (Hay & Jacoby, 1996). Importantly, many of these results agree with those from implicit/explicit test comparisons (e.g., Toth et al., 1994; Reingold & Goshen-Gottstein, 1996).

Subjects in opposition and process-dissociation experiments are aware that their memory is being tested. If this is the case, how can one speak of nonconscious processes in memory? Indeed, research based on the process-dissociation procedure breaks with tradition in this regard by assuming that nonconscious memory rarely occurs in isolation, but rather works in combination with conscious forms of memory to produce a variety of mnemonic phenomena. That is, it assumes that most acts of memory reflect a blend or co-action of conscious and nonconscious processes and thus attempts to separate the two kinds of memory within a single test. This contrasts with the implicit/explicit test approach, which attempts to create tests that selectively measure either conscious or nonconscious forms of memory. Correspondence between the two approaches, including the absolute magnitude of estimated mnemonic influences, provides some evidence that they are assessing the same underlying constructs. Yet the two approaches are obviously different, a difference that has led to numerous debates in the literature (e.g., Graf & Komatsu, 1994; Jacoby, 1998; Reingold & Toth, 1996; Toth, Reingold, & Jacoby, 1995). Irrespective of these debates, most researchers agree that nonconscious processes play a powerful role in conscious memory judgements. Thus, we next consider research that explores the complex interplay between conscious and nonconscious memory.

Fluency, Memory Attributions, and Subjective Experience

On the basis of their experiments with the implicit word-identification test, Jacoby and Dallas (1981) suggested that initial experience with a stimulus may result in more fluent (faster or more efficient) processing of that stimulus when it is encountered at a later time. They also suggested that such fluent reprocessing may be the basis for implicit memory effects (see also Masson, 1989) and that, under some conditions, subjects might use differences in fluency as the basis for conscious memory decisions. These claims have turned out to be very fruitful, and have led to a number of experiments that reveal the complex nature of nonconscious memory processes.

Research has shown that fluent processing as a function of prior experience can change how stimuli are processed in the present, and this change can have interesting, nonconscious influences on a person's subjective experience. For example, fluent reprocessing as a function of prior presentation can increase the apparent fame of nonfamous names (Jacoby, Woloshyn et al., 1989), can lengthen the apparent exposure duration of a briefly flashed word (Witherspoon & Allan, 1985), can lower the apparent loudness of background noise (Jacoby, Allan, Collins, & Larwill, 1988), and can increase the apparent truth of false statements (Begg, Anas, & Farinacci, 1992). These effects are conceptually similar to those found

with the mere exposure paradigm (Seamon et al., 1995) and are relevant, not only to understanding nonconscious memory and the nature of subjective experience but also to real-world decisions and actions because people often act on the basis of their subjective experience (see Jacoby, Kelley et al., 1989; Jacoby, Bjork, & Kelley, 1994).

In addition to influencing a person's interpretation of events in the present, fluent processing has been shown to influence interpretation of the past (i.e., conscious memory judgments). That is, by manipulating how fluently a stimulus is processed on an explicit memory test, one can increase subjects' beliefs that they are remembering, *irrespective of whether the test stimulus was actually presented earlier*. For example, Whittlesea (1993; see also Jacoby & Whitehouse, 1989) manipulated the visual clarity or semantic context in which recognition-test items were presented and found that more fluently processed items (i.e., those presented more clearly or in more congruent semantic contexts) were more likely to be judged "old." Lindsay & Kelley (1996) produced similar "illusions of memory" by manipulating the ease with which subjects completed word fragments. In addition to extending the range of nonconscious memory effects, these results may have significant implications for the interpretation of self-reports of awareness and the intention to remember. For example, fluent reprocessing may help account for the phenomenon of confabulation described earlier: even though a particular mental event may not have occurred in the past, if that event is processed fluently in the present, people may incorrectly infer that it must have occurred earlier in their life.

Taken together, the results cited in this section provide stronger evidence for a dissociation between memory and the phenomenal experience of remembering. Moreover, they reveal the operation of nonconscious processes, not only in the use of memory but also in the attribution processes that subjects use to make judgments about the past and present (Whittlesea, 1993).

The Future of Nonconscious Memory: Problems and Prospects

The reader may have noticed a change in tone that has occurred throughout this review. In particular, despite a "good start" in showing the existence of nonconscious processes in memory (based mainly on amnesic patients and implicit/explicit dissociations in neurologically intact subjects), more recent research has been characterized by increasing complexity and debate about the nature of such influences and the most appropriate way to measure them. This is to be expected, perhaps, given the relatively short time in which researchers have investigated the relationship between memory and consciousness. In this final section, a set of issues are noted that may help researchers develop more precise forms of measurement and more comprehensive conceptualizations of nonconscious mnemonic processes.

The Relation between Awareness and Intent

Schacter (1987) defined implicit memory as a facilitation of task performance "that does not require conscious or intentional recollection" (p. 507). However, recent work suggests that consciousness and intentionality can be dissociated and may even reflect different neural mechanisms (Schacter, Alpert, Savage, Rauch, & Albert, 1997). Richardson-Klavehn et al. (1994) argued that many of the mnemonic phenomena labeled as "unconscious" or "unaware" are better conceptualized as unintentional or involuntary. That is, subjects can be aware that the items they encounter or produce on a memory test were in fact encountered earlier, yet their performance can still reveal the types of dissociations normally attributed to implicit memory. However, although it seems clear that awareness and intentionality are distinct concepts, it is less clear that they are completely separate from one another, as some have suggested (e.g., Richardson-Klavehn, Gardiner, & Java., 1996). The problem is that awareness is a prerequisite for intentional control (see Jacoby, Toth, Lindsay, & Debner, 1992; Toth, Lindsay, & Jacoby, 1992) and, indeed, may sometimes even *encourage* such control. Important goals for future research are therefore to determine whether awareness per se can change the expression of memory, and the degree to which awareness and intent are dissociable.

The Role of Context and Goals

Early research and theory on nonconscious influences of memory suggested that such influences were "context free" in comparison to more explicit, episodic forms of memory that were thought to be closely tied to a specific past context (e.g., Mandler, Graf, & Kraft, 1986). Recent research, however, suggests that nonconscious memory is much more context bound than previously thought, and that such contextual specificity may even be a defining characteristic of nonconscious memory. As one striking example, Hayman and Tulving (1989) presented subjects with a list of words and then gave them two consecutive fragment completion tests. They found that when fragments on the two tests had little or no overlap (e.g., $a \_ a \_ in$ and $\_ ss \_ ss \_$) subjects showed stochastic independence between the two tests—that is, completion of one fragment did not predict a subject's ability to solve the other fragment, despite the fact that *the target word was the same*. Another example of context specificity is provided by Oliphant (1983), who showed that words presented as part of the instructions for an implicit test may produce *no* priming on that test (see also Levy & Kirsner, 1989; MacLeod, 1989).

Related to the issue of context is a subject's goals in performing some act for which nonconscious influences of memory may be operating. This is important because mental events make up a large part of the context for processing; and goals, in turn, are arguably a central aspect of mental life (Bargh, 1997; Toth & Reingold, 1996). Research on memory attributions, described above, suggest that goals may play a major role in how nonconscious memory effects are consciously interpreted. On the basis of this, and other research, Jacoby, Ste-Marie, and Toth (1993) argued that nonconscious memory processes may be relative to the goals set by conscious intentions. Research by Goschke and Kuhl (1996; see also Marsh, Hicks, & Bink, 1998) seems to confirm this: subjects who expected to perform a future action showed greater implicit memory for words describing that action, as compared to words describing similar actions that the subject did not expect to perform.

Similar to conclusions from the previous section, then, results reviewed here recommend more research into the relation between nonconscious memory and a subject's goals and intentions. As discussed next, such research would be useful, not only in helping us better understand the nature of nonconscious memory but also in bridging the gap between memory phenomena occurring in the laboratory and those occurring in the "real world."

Nonconscious Memory in Real-World Thought and Behavior

The majority of research discussed so far has been based on the processing of rather simple stimuli, such as isolated words, presented in the context of rather simple tasks, such as identifying briefly flashed stimuli. If, however, nonconscious memory processes are truly a critical aspect of everyday cognition, research must link laboratory demonstrations with phenomena observed outside of the lab. Fortunately, this enterprise has begun and the initial results, mainly reported in the social-cognition literature, are exciting (see Bargh, 1997; Greenwald & Banaji, 1995). Already, strong links have been drawn between nonconscious processes in memory and socially relevant phenomena such as impression formation, stereotyping, and prejudice (see Banaji & Greenwald, 1994; Devine, 1989). Moreover, techniques for the measurement of nonconscious forms of memory are being developed for personality assessment in the applied (e.g., job-related) sector (e.g., Dovidio & Fazio, 1992).

The role of nonconscious memory processes in clinical assessment is also maturing. Most memory-impaired populations (e.g., amnesics, the elderly) lose only conscious memory; nonconscious forms of memory appear to remain relatively intact throughout the life span. However, because people only have conscious access to the forms of memory that decline, their subjective experience may often be of a complete loss of memory. This may lead memory-impaired individuals to give up on adequately performing memory-related tasks, despite the fact that a proper arrangement of contextual cues could be used to maintain adequate levels of performance. This possibility speaks again to the complex interplay between conscious and nonconscious memory and deserves further scrutiny in the future.

Nonconscious Memory and the Brain

A final area of interest concerns the neural substrates of nonconscious memory. As was noted in the introduction, much of the modern interest in nonconscious memory was based on research with amnesic patients, and exploration of the memory capabilities of these patients continues. For example, in an extended case study of one patient (KC), Tulving, Hayman, & MacDonald (1991) uncovered a *triple dissociation* between conscious memory and two forms of nonconscious memory. That is, KC showed no conscious memory for learning episodes in which he was taught to make correct responses in a semantic knowledge task, and his semantic responses were found to be stochastically independent of his performance in an implicit fragment-completion test. Perhaps even more impressive, both forms of nonconscious memory were found to be largely intact 12 months after initial learning. Thus, detailed studies of amnesic patients continue to provide important insights into the functional (cognitive) organization of memory, a strategy that is likely to continue in the future.

Insights into the neuroanatomical organization of nonconscious forms of memory have also advanced in recent years, based largely on our ability to use modern neuroimaging techniques such as PET and fMRI to measure the neural activity of normal patients while they perform memory tasks (Buckner, chapter 39). These studies support lesion-based research in showing that the neural systems underlying nonconscious memory are anatomically distinct from the medial-temporal structures underlying conscious memory. In particular, perceptual and conceptual priming is thought to occur in the very same neocortical structures that mediate initial perception and meaning-based thought, while more procedural forms of nonconscious memory appear to rely on subcortical structures such as the basal ganglia (Gabrieli, 1998). An obviously important goal for future neurocognitive research will be to better understand the details of these brain systems, including their neuroanatomy and chemistry, as well as their points of interaction.

Summary and Conclusions

Although research on nonconscious forms of human memory can be traced back at least a hundred years (see Schacter, 1987; Schacter & Tulving, 1994b; Toth & Reingold, 1996), modern research on the subject began with the discovery that amnesic patients, previously thought unable to store their experience, could show memory for the past when tested implicitly. Subsequent research showed similar nonconscious memory phenomena in normal subjects. Since these initial demonstrations, research on nonconscious mnemonic processes has been directed toward the development of more precise methodologies for revealing and measuring these processes. These methodologies include the mere-exposure paradigm, implicit tests, and self-reports of awareness, intent, and the phenomenology of remembering. More recent methods include those that put conscious and nonconscious forms of memory in opposition, and those that attempt to quantitatively estimate their separate strengths (e.g., the process-dissociation procedure). A central theme in many of these approaches is the distinction between perception and conception (meaning-based processes), although contextual and goal-related processes are also starting to be recognized as fundamental.

Nonconscious memory plays a critical role in everyday thought and behavior both directly (e.g., by bringing a particular thought to mind) and indirectly (by influencing a person's subjective experience). These influences extend beyond the "cold cognition" studied in the lab, and into the "hot" areas of emotional and social information processing. So, too, neuroscientists are beginning to uncover the neural substrates of nonconscious memory. This will no doubt be an exciting time to remember.

References

Adams, J. K. (1957). Laboratory studies of behavior without awareness. *Psychological Bulletin, 54*, 383–405.

Adams, L. T., Kasserman, J. E., Yearwood, A. A., Perfetto, G. A., Bransford, J. D., & Franks, J. J. (1988). Memory access: The effects of fact-oriented versus problem-oriented acquisition. *Memory & Cognition, 16*, 167–175.

Banaji, M. R., & Greenwald, A. G. (1994). Implicit stereotyping and unconscious prejudice. In M. P. Zanna & J. M. Olson (Eds.), *The psychology of prejudice: The Ontario symposium* (pp. 55–76). Hillsdale, NJ: Erlbaum.

Bargh, J. A. (1997). The automaticity of everyday life. In R. S. Wyer (Ed.), *Advances in social cognition* (pp. 1–61). Mahwah, NJ: Erlbaum.

Barrs, B. (1988). *A cognitive theory of consciousness.* New York: Cambridge University Press.

Bartlett, F. (1932). *Remembering: An experimental and social study.* Cambridge: Cambridge University Press.

Bechara, A., Tranel, D., Damasio, H., Adolphs, R., Rockland, C., & Damasio, A. R. (1995). Double dissociation of conditioning and declarative knowledge relative to the amygdala and hippocampus in humans. *Science, 269*, 1115–1118.

Begg, I., Anas, A., & Frarinacci, S. (1992). Dissociation of processes in belief: Source recollection, statement familiarity, and the illusion of truth. *Journal of Experimental Psychology: General, 121*, 446–458.

Benzing, W. E., & Squire, L. R. (1989). Preserved learning and memory in amnesia: Intact adaptation level effects and learning of stereoscopic depth. *Behavioral Neuroscience, 103*, 538–547.

Berry, D. C., & Broadbent, D. E. (1984). On the relationship between task performance and associated verbalisable knowledge. *Quarterly Journal of Experimental Psychology, 36*, 209–231.

Blaxton, T. A. (1989). Investigating dissociations among memory measures: Support for a transfer appropriate processing framework. *Journal of Experimental Psychology: Learning, Memory, and Cognition, 15*, 657–668.

Bonanno, G. A., & Stillings, N. A. (1986). Preference, familiarity, and recognition after repeated brief exposures to random geometric shapes. *American Journal of Psychology, 99*(8), 403–415.

Bornstein, R. F. (1989). Exposure and affect: Overview and meta-analysis of research, 1968–1987. *Psychological Bulletin, 106*, 265–289.

Bowers, J. S., & Schacter, D. L. (1990). Implicit memory and test awareness. *Journal of Experimental Psychology: Learning, Memory, and Cognition, 16*, 404–416.

Brooks, D. N., & Baddeley, A. D. (1976). What can amnesic patients learn? *Neuropsychologia, 14*, 111–122.

Cohen, J., & Schooler, J. W. (Eds.), (1997). *Scientific approaches to consciousness.* Mahwah, NJ: Erlbaum.

Cohen, N. J., Eichenbaum, H., Deacedo, B., & Corkin, S. (1985). Different memory systems underlying acquisition of procedural and declarative knowledge. *Annals of the New York Academy of Sciences, 444*, 54–71.

Corkin, S. (1968). Acquisition of motor skill after bilateral medial temporal lobe excision. *Neuropsychologia, 6*, 225–265.

Curran, T. (1998). Implicit sequence learning from a cognitive neuroscience perspective: What, how, and where? In M. A. Stadler & P. A. Frensch (Eds.), *Handbook of implicit learning* (pp. 365–400). Thousand Oaks, CA: Sage Publications, Inc.

Devine, P. G. (1989). Stereotypes and prejudice: Their automatic and controlled components. *Journal of Personality and Social Psychology, 56,* 5–18.

Dovidio, J. F., & Fazio, R. H. (1992). New technologies for the direct and indirect assessment of attitudes. In J. Tanur (Eds.), *Questions about survey questions: Meaning, memory, attitudes, and social interaction* (pp. 204–237). New York: Russell Sage.

Duchek, J. M., & Neely, J. H. (1989). A dissociative word-frequency x levels-of-processing interaction in episodic recognition and lexical decision tasks. *Memory & Cognition, 17,* 148–162.

Dunn, J. C., & Kirsner, K. (1989). Implicit memory: Task or process? In S. Lewandowsky, J. C. Dunn, & K. Kirsner (Eds.), *Implicit memory: Theoretical issues* Hillsdale, NJ: Erlbaum.

Ebbinghaus, H. (1885/1964). *Memory: A contribution to experimental psychology* (H. A. Ruger & C. E. Bussenius, Trans.). New York: Dover Publications.

Gabrieli, J. D. E. (1998). Cognitive neuroscience of human memory. *Annual Review of Psychology, 49,* 87–115.

Goschke, T., & Kuhl, J. (1996). Remembering what to do: Explicit and implicit memory for intentions. In M. Brandimonte, G. O. Einstein, & M. A. McDaniel (Eds.), *Prospective memory: Theory and applications.* Mahwah, NJ: Erlbaum.

Graf, P., & Komatsu, S. (1994). Process dissociation procedure: Handle with caution! *European Journal of Cognitive Psychology, 6,* 113–129.

Graf, P., Mandler, G., & Hayden, P. E. (1982). Simulating amnesic symptoms in normal subjects. *Science, 218,* 1243–1244.

Greenwald, A. G., & Banaji, M. R. (1995). Implicit social cognition: Attitudes, self-esteem, and stereotypes. *Psychological Review, 102,* 4–27.

Hashtroudi, S., Ferguson, S. A., Rappold, V. A., & Chrosniak, L. D. (1988). Data-driven and conceptually driven processes in partial-word identification and recognition. *Journal of Experimental Psychology: Learning, Memory, and Cognition, 14,* 749–757.

Hay, J. F., & Jacoby, L. L. (1996). Separating habit and recollection: Memory slips, process dissociations, and probability matching. *Journal of Experimental Psychology: Learning, Memory, and Cognition, 22,* 1323–1335.

Hayman, C. A. G., & Tulving, E. (1989). Is priming in fragment completion based on

a 'traceless' memory system. *Journal of Experimental Psychology: Learning, Memory, and Cognition, 14,* 941–956.

Hull, C. L. (1943). *Principles of behavior.* New York: Appleton.

Jacoby, L. L. (1983). Remembering the data: Analyzing interactive processes in reading. *Journal of Verbal Learning and Verbal Behavior, 22,* 485–508.

Jacoby, L. L. (1998). Invariance in automatic influences of memory: Toward a user's guide for the process-dissociation procedure. *Journal of Experimental Psychology: Learning, Memory, and Cognition, 24,* 3–26.

Jacoby, L. L. (1991). A process dissociation framework: Separating automatic from intentional uses of memory. *Journal of Memory and Language, 30,* 513–541.

Jacoby, L. L., Allan, L. G., Collins, J. C., & Larwill, L. K. (1988). Memory influences subjective experience: Noise judgments. *Journal of Experimental Psychology: Learning, Memory, and Cognition, 14,* 240–247.

Jacoby, L. L., Bjork, R. A., & Kelley, C. M. (1994). Illusions of comprehension, competence, and remembering. In D. Druckman & R. A. Bjork (Eds.), *Learning, remembering, and believing: Enhancing human performance* (pp. 391–422). Washington, DC: National Academy Press.

Jacoby, L. L., & Dallas, M. (1981). On the relationship between autobiographical memory and perceptual learning. *Journal of Experimental Psychology: General, 3,* 306–340.

Jacoby, L. L., Kelley, C. M., & Dywan, J. (1989). Memory attributions. In H. L. Roediger & F. I. M. Craik (Eds.), *Varieties of memory and consciousness* (pp. 391–422). Hillsdale, NJ: Erlbaum.

Jacoby, L. L., Ste-Marie, D., & Toth, J. P. (1993). Redefining automaticity: Unconscious influences, awareness and control. In A. D. Baddeley & L. Weiskrantz (Eds.), *Attention: Selection, awareness and control. A tribute to Donald Broadbent* (pp. 261–282). Oxford, England: Oxford University Press.

Jacoby, L. L., Toth, J. P., Lindsay, D. S., & Debner, J. A. (1992). Lectures for a layperson: Methods for revealing unconscious processes. In R. F. Bornstein & T. S. Pittman (Eds.), *Perception without awareness* (pp. 81–120). New York: Guilford.

Jacoby, L. L., Toth, J. P., & Yonelinas, A. P. (1993). Separating conscious and unconscious influences of memory: Measuring recollection. *Journal of Experimental Psychology: General, 122,* 139–154.

Jacoby, L. L., & Whitehouse, K. (1989). An illusion of memory: False recognition influenced by unconscious perception. *Journal of Experimental Psychology: General, 118,* 126–135.

Jacoby, L. L., & Witherspoon, D. (1982). Remembering without awareness. *Canadian Journal of Psychology, 36,* 300–324.

Jacoby, L. L., Woloshyn, V., & Kelley, C. M. (1989). Becoming famous without being recognized: Unconscious influences of memory produced by dividing attention. *Journal of Experimental Psychology: General, 118,* 115–125.

Jacoby, L. L., Yonelinas, A. P., & Jennings, J. M. (1997). The relationship between conscious and unconscious (automatic) influences: A declaration of independence. In J. Cohen & J. W. Schooler (Eds.), *Scientific approaches to consciousness* Mahwah, NJ: Erlbaum.

Jennings, J. M., & Jacoby, L. L. (1993). Automatic versus intentional uses of memory: Aging, attention, and control. *Psychology and Aging, 8,* 283–293.

Jennings, J. M., & Jacoby, L. L. (1997). An opposition procedure for detecting age-related deficits in recollection: Telling effects of repetition. *Psychology and Aging, 12,* 352–361.

Kelley, C. M., & Lindsay, D. S. (1993). Remembering mistaken for knowing: Ease of retrieval as a basis for confidence in answers to general knowledge questions. *Journal of Memory and Language, 32,* 1–24.

Kelley, C. M., & Lindsay, D. S. (1996). Conscious and unconscious forms of memory. In E. L. Bjork & R. A. Bjork (Eds.), *Memory* (pp. 31–63). San Diego, CA: Academic Press.

Knowlton, B., & Squire, L. R. (1994). Probabilistic classification learning in amnesia. *Learning and Memory, 1,* 106–120.

Kolers, P. A. (1976). Reading a year later. *Journal of Experimental Psychology: Human Learning and Memory, 2,* 554–565.

Kolers, P. A., & Roediger, H. L. (1984). Procedures of mind. *Journal of Verbal Learning and Verbal Behavior, 23,* 425–449.

Kopelman, M. D. (1987). Two types of confabulation. *Journal of Neurology, Neurosurgery, and Psychiatry, 50,* 1482–1487.

Kroll, J. F., & Potter, M. C. (1984). Recognizing words, pictures, and concepts: A comparison of lexical, object, and reality decisions. *Journal of Verbal Learning and Verbal Behavior, 23,* 39–66.

Kunst-Wilson, W. R., & Zajonc, R. B. (1980). Affective discrimination of stimuli that cannot be recognized. *Science, 207,* 557–558.

Levy, B. A., & Kirsner, K. (1989). Reprocessing text: Indirect measures of word and message level processes. *Journal of Experimental Psychology: Learning, Memory, and Cognition, 15,* 407–417.

Lindsay, D. S., & Kelley, C. M. (1996). Creating illusions of familiarity in a cued-recall remember/know paradigm. *Journal of Memory and Language, 35,* 197–211.

Logan, G. D. (1990). Repetition priming and automaticity: Common underlying mechanisms? *Cognitive Psychology, 22,* 1–35.

MacLeod, C. M. (1989). Word Context during initial exposure influences degree of priming in word fragment completion. *Journal of Experimental Psychology: Learning, Memory, and Cognition, 15,* 398–406.

Mandler, G., Graf, P., & Kraft, D. (1986). Activation and elaboration effects in recognition and word priming. *Quarterly Journal of Experimental Psychology, 38A,* 645–662.

Marsh, R. L., Hicks, J. L., & Bink, M. L. (1998). Activation of completed, uncompleted, and partially completed intentions. *Journal of Experimental Psychology: Learning, Memory, and Cognition, 24,* 350–361.

Masson, M. E. J. (1989). Fluent reprocessing as an implicit expression of memory for experience. In S. Lewandowsky, J. C. Dunn, & K. Kirsner (Eds.), *Implicit memory: Theoretical issues.* Hillsdale, NJ: Erlbaum.

Masson, M. E. J., & MacLeod, C. M. (1992). Reenacting the route to interpretation: Enhanced perceptual identification without prior perception. *Journal of Experimental Psychology: General, 121,* 145–176.

Milner, B. (1965). Visually-guided maze learning in man: Effects of bilateral hippocampal, bilateral frontal, and unilateral cerebral lesions. *Neuropsychologia, 3,* 317–338.

Mitchell, D. B., & Brown, A. S. (1988). Persistent repetition priming in picture naming and its dissociation from recognition memory. *Journal of Experimental Psychology: Learning, Memory, and Cognition, 14,* 213–222.

Moscovitch, M. (1989). Confabulation and the frontal systems: Strategic versus associative retrieval in neuropsychological theories of memory. In H. L. Roediger & F. I. M. Craik (Eds.), *Varieties of memory and consciousness: Essays in honour of Endel Tulving* (pp. 133–156). Hillsdale, NJ: Erlbaum.

Moscovitch, M. (1994). Memory and working-with-memory: Evaluation of a component process model and comparison with other models. In D. L. Schacter & E. Tulving (Eds.), *Memory Systems 1994* (pp. 269–310). Cambridge: MIT/Bradford Press.

Moscovitch, M., Vriezen, E., & Goshen-Gottstein, G. (1993). Implicit tests of memory in patients with focal lesions or degenerative brain disorders. In F. Boller & J. Grafman (Eds.), *Handbook of neuropsychology* (pp. 133–173). Amsterdam: Elsevier.

Murphy, S. T., & Zajonc, R. B. (1993). Affect, cognition, and awareness: Affective priming with optimal and suboptimal stimulus exposures. *Journal of Personality and Social Psychology, 64,* 723–739.

Nissen, M. J., & Bullemer, P. (1987). Attentional requirements of learning: Evidence from performance measures. *Cognitive Psychology, 19,* 1–32.

Oliphant, G. W. (1983). Repetition and recency effects in word recognition. *Australian Journal of Psychology, 35,* 393–403.

Parkin, A. J., Reid, T. K., & Russo, R. (1990). On the differential nature of implicit and explicit memory. *Memory and Cognition, 18,* 507–514.

Picton, T. W., & Stuss, D. T. (1994). Neurobiology of conscious experience. *Current Opinion in Neurobiology, 4,* 256–265.

Ratcliff, R., & McKoon, G. (1996). Bias effects in implicit memory tasks. *Journal of Experimental Psychology: General, 125,* 403–421.

Reber, A. S. (1989). Implicit learning and tacit knowledge. *Journal of Experimental Psychology: General, 118,* 219–235.

Reingold, E. M., & Goshen-Gottstein, Y. (1996). Separating consciously controlled and automatic influences in memory for new associations. *Journal of Experimental Psychology: Learning, Memory, and Cognition, 22,* 397–406.

Reingold, E. M., & Merikle, P. M. (1990). On the inter-relatedness of theory and measurement in the study on unconscious processes. *Mind and Language, 5,* 9–28.

Reingold, E. M., & Toth, J. P. (1996). Process dissociations versus task dissociations: A controversy in progress. In G. Underwood (Eds.), *Implicit Cognition* (pp. 159–202). Oxford: Oxford University Press.

Richardson-Klavehn, A., & Bjork, R. A. (1988). Measures of memory. *Annual Review of Psychology, 39,* 475–543.

Richardson-Klavehn, A., Gardiner, J. M., & Java, R. I. (1996). Memory: Task dissociations, process dissociations, and dissociations of consciousness. In G. Underwood (Eds.), *Implicit Cognition* (pp. 85–158). New York: Oxford University Press.

Richardson-Klavehn, A., Lee, M. G., Joubran, R., & Bjork, R. A. (1994). Intention and awareness in perceptual identification priming. *Memory and Cognition, 22,* 293–312.

Roediger, H. L. (1990). Implicit memory: Retention without remembering. *American Psychologist, 45,* 1043–1056.

Roediger, H. L., & McDermott, K. B. (1993). Implicit memory in normal human subjects. In H. Spinnler & F. Boller (Eds.), *Handbook of neuropsychology* (pp. 63–131). Amsterdam: Elsevier.

Roediger, H. L., Weldon, M. S., & Challis, B. H. (1989). Explaining dissociations between implicit and explicit measures of retention; A processing account. In H. L. Roediger & F. I. M. Craik (Eds.), *Varieties of memory and consciousness: Essays in honour of Endel Tulving* (pp. 3–41). Hillsdale, NJ: Erlbaum.

Rozin, P. (1976). The psychobiological approach to human memory. In M. R. Rosenzweig & E. L. Bennett (Eds.), *Neural mechanisms of learning and memory* (pp. 3–46). Cambridge, MA: MIT Press.

Schacter, D. L. (1987). Implicit memory: History and current status. *Journal of Experimental Psychology: Learning, Memory, and Cognition, 13,* 501–518.

Schacter, D. L., Alpert, N. M., Savage, C. R., Rauch, S. L., & Albert, M. S. (1997). Conscious recollection and the human hippocampal formation: Evidence from positron emission tomography. *Procedures of the National Academy of Science, USA, 93,* 321–325.

Schacter, D. L., Bowers, J., & Booker, J. (1989). Intention, awareness, and implicit memory: The retrieval intentionality criteria. In S. Lewandowsky, J. C. Dunn, & K. Kirsner (Eds.), *Implicit memory* (pp. 47–65). Hillsdale, NJ: Erlbaum.

Schacter, D. L., Cooper, L. A., & Delaney, S. M. (1990). Implicit memory for visual objects and the structural description system. *Bulletin of the Psychonomic Society, 28,* 367–372.

Schacter, D. L., & Tulving, E. (Eds.). (1994a). *Memory systems 1994.* Cambridge, MA: MIT Press.

Schacter, D. L., & Tulving, E. (1994b). What are the memory systems of 1994? In D. L. Schacter & E. Tulving (Eds.), *Memory systems 1994* (pp. 1–38). Cambridge, MA: MIT Press.

Seamon, J. G., Williams, P. C., Crowley, M. J., Kim, I. J., Langer, S. A., Orne, P. J., & Wishengrad, D. L. (1995). The mere exposure effect is based on implicit memory: Effects of stimulus type, encoding conditions, and the number of exposures on recognition and affect judgments. *Journal of Experimental Psychology: Learning, Memory, and Cognition, 21,* 711–721.

Seger, C. A. (1994). Implicit learning. *Psychological Bulletin, 115,* 163–196.

Shimamura, A. P., & Squire, L. R. (1984). Paired-associate learning and priming in amnesia: A neuropsychological approach. *Journal of Experimental Psychology: General, 113,* 556–570.

Skinner, B. F. (1969). *Contingencies of reinforcement: A theoretical analysis.* New York: Appleton.

Smith, E. R., & Branscombe, N. R. (1988). Category accessibility as implicit memory. *Journal of Experimental Social Psychology, 24,* 490–504.

Srinivas, K., & Roediger, H. L. (1990). Classifying implicit memory tests: Category associations and anagram solution. *Journal of Memory and Language, 29,* 389–412.

Ste-Marie, D. M., Jennings, J. M., & Finlayson, A. J. (1996). The process dissociation procedure: Memory testing in populations with brain damage. *The Clinical Neuropsychologist.*

Tolman, E. C. (1932). *Purposive behavior in animals and man.* New York: Appleton.

Toth, J. P. (1996a). Conceptual automaticity in recognition memory: Levels of processing effects on familiarity. *Canadian Journal of Experimental Psychology, 50,* 123–138.

Toth, J. P. (1996b). Memory and attention following traumatic brain injury: Process dissociations. *Clinical Neuropsychologist, 10,* 350–351.

Toth, J. P., & Hunt, R. R. (1999). Not one versus many but zero versus any: Structure and function in the context of the multiple-memory systems debate. In J. K. Foster & M. Jelicic (Eds.), *Memory: Structure, function, or process?* (pp. 232–272). Oxford: Oxford University Press.

Toth, J. P., Lindsay, D. S., & Jacoby, L. L. (1992). Awareness, automaticity, and memory dissociations. In L. R. Squire & N. Butters (Eds.), *Neuropsychology of memory* (pp. 46–57). New York: Guilford.

Toth, J. P., & Reingold, E. M. (1996). Beyond perception: Conceptual contributions to unconscious influences of memory. In G. Underwood (Eds.), *Implicit cognition* (pp. 41–84). New York: Oxford University Press.

Toth, J. P., Reingold, E. M., & Jacoby, L. L. (1994). Toward a redefinition of implicit memory: Process dissociations following elaborative processing and self-generation. *Journal of Experimental Psychology: Learning, Memory, and Cognition, 20,* 290–303.

Toth, J. P., Reingold, E. M., & Jacoby, L. L. (1995). A response to Graf and Komatsu's critique of the process dissociation procedure: When is caution necessary? *European Journal of Cognitive Psychology, 7,* 113–130.

Tulving, E. (1985). Memory and consciousness. *Canadian Psychology, 26,* 1–12.

Tulving, E., Hayman, C. A. G., & Macdonald, C. A. (1991). Long-lasting perceptual priming and semantic learning in amnesia: A case experiment. *Journal of Experimental Psychology: Learning, Memory, and Cognition, 17,* 595–617.

Tulving, E. & Schacter, D. L. (1990). Priming and human memory systems. *Science, 247,* 301–305.

Tulving, E., Schacter, D. L., & Stark, H. A. (1982). Priming effects in word-fragment completion are independent of recognition memory. *Journal of Experimental Psychology: Learning, Memory, and Cognition, 8,* 336–342.

Underwood, B. J. (1957). Interference and forgetting. *Psychological Review, 64,* 49–60.

Vaidya, C. J., Gabrieli, J. D. E., Keane, M. M., Monti, L. A., Gutierrez-Rivas, H., & Zarella, M. M. (1997). Evidence of multiple mechanisms of conceptual priming on implicit tests. *Journal of Experimental Psychology: Learning, Memory, and Cognition, 23,* 1324–1343.

Warrington, E. K., & Weiskrantz, L. (1968). New method of testing long-term retention with special reference to amnesic patients. *Nature, 217,* 972–974.

Weiskrantz, L., & Warrington, E. K. (1979). Conditioning in amnesic patients. *Neuropsychologia, 17,* 187–194.

Weldon, M. S., & Roediger, H. L. (1987). Altering retrieval demands reverses the picture superiority effect. *Memory & Cognition, 15,* 269–280.

Whittlesea, B. W. A. (1993). Illusions of familiarity. *Journal of Experimental Psychology: Learning, Memory, and Cognition, 19,* 1235–1253.

Witherspoon, D., & Allan, L. G. (1985). The effects of a prior presentation on temporal judgments in a perceptual identification task. *Memory and Cognition, 13,* 101–111.

Yonelinas, A. P. , & Jacoby, L. L. (1995). Dissociations of processes in recognition memory: Effects of interference and response speed. *Canadian Journal of Experimental Psychology.*

Part III: Memory in Life

MEMORY IN DEVELOPMENT

17

Memory in Infancy and Early Childhood

CAROLYN ROVEE-COLLIER & HARLENE HAYNE

Since Freud (1935) first proposed that adult behavior is rooted in the infancy period, psychologists have viewed infants' experiences as the cornerstone of later development. This view presumes that infants can preserve a relatively enduring record of their experiences—a capacity that, paradoxically, infants are thought to lack. In what follows, we review the major paradigms used to study infant memory, their basic findings, and new evidence of infants' memory capacity that resolves this paradox. Finally, we consider three current issues—memory distortions, the ontogeny of multiple memory systems, and infantile amnesia.

Research Paradigms

What infants remember about their prior experiences is difficult to study. Not only can they not verbalize what they remember but also younger infants lack the motoric competence to perform most of the nonverbal tasks that have been used with older infants and children. The presence of the caregiver, the familiarity of the test setting, and the infant's momentary state of arousal also affect memory performance differently at different ages. Finally, infants are difficult subjects to come by—particularly infants of working mothers—and cannot be obtained in the numbers typical of studies with school-age children and adults. The following paradigms are used to study infant memory. For each, we describe either the seminal study or a highly representative example.

Novelty Preference

Novelty-preference paradigms used to study infant visual recognition memory are based on Sokolov's (1963) model of the habituation of the orienting reflex. In this model, each time a stimulus is encountered, an internal representation (*engram*) of it is formed. Over successive encounters with the same stimulus, the representation becomes progressively fleshed out by new information that the subject notices. As the internal representation becomes progressively more complete, subjects attend to the external stimulus progressively less; once the representation is complete, they no longer orient to it. Over time, however, the representation decays (*forgetting*). When presented again, subjects will reorient to the stimulus to the extent that their representation is no longer complete. Thus, retention of a stimulus is inferred from the extent to which infants do *not* look at it but direct their attention elsewhere (i.e., their novelty preference).

Paired-Comparison

The paired-comparison procedure was adapted from Fantz's (1956) work on infant attention and perception. Here, infants are familiarized with a particular stimulus either for a fixed number of trials or until they have accumulated a specified amount of time looking at it. During the test, they are simultaneously shown the previously exposed stimulus and a novel one (see figure 17.1). Because infants who never saw the original stimulus should fixate both test stimuli equally, retention is inferred if the percentage of total fixation time that is directed toward the novel test stimulus significantly exceeds 50%.

Most single-session studies using the paired-comparison procedure find retention within the span typical of short-term memory (0–15 s) at 4 months of age; thereafter, retention increases with age. Thus, retention is exhibited immediately but not after 75 s at 6 months, after 75–150 s at 9 months (Rose, 1981), and after 1 week at 2 years (Greco & Daehler, 1985). Multiple-session studies typically find longer retention. Fagan (1970), for example, tested infants with a set of three stimuli (e.g., A-B-C) on 3 successive days. On each day, the familiarization stimulus (A) was tested in both the right and left positions against each of the other novel stimuli (A-B, C-A). On succeeding days, another stimulus in the set was the familiarization stimulus, and the other two were the novel stimuli. Infants exhibited greater attention to novel test stimuli in session 1 only, suggesting carryover from the preceding day(s).

In a similar procedure, 5- to 6-month-olds exhibited a novelty preference for a black-and-white pattern after 2 days and for a novel facial photograph after 2 weeks (Fagan, 1973).

Habituation

In habituation studies, a stimulus is repeatedly presented until infants' attention to it has declined to some absolute or relative level. At this point, a novel stimulus is presented to some infants, while the original one is presented to others. Retention is inferred from increased responding to the novel stimulus relative to the original one. As the time between habituation and testing increases, so does responding to the original stimulus; when responding to the original stimulus has returned to its prehabituation level, forgetting is complete. In the habituation procedure, infants are tested with only a single stimulus (preexposed or novel), whereas in the paired comparison procedure, infants are tested simultaneously with the preexposed stimulus and a novel one. Because the original stimulus is absent during testing with the novel one, the habituation procedure incurs a greater memory load than the paired-comparison procedure.

Stinson (1971, in Werner & Perlmutter, 1979) obtained the first forgetting function using a variant of the habituation procedure in which 4-month-olds' high-amplitude sucks were reinforced by a visual stimulus. After infants habituated (satiated) to the original reinforcer over its successive presentations, they introduced a novel reinforcer, and the extent

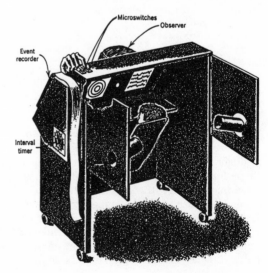

Figure 17.1 The novelty preference apparatus used in the paired-comparison procedure. The direction and duration of looking at the familiar and novel targets are recorded via a midline peephole. On the preceding trial, the familiar pattern was displayed on both panels. From R. L. Fantz, Visual perception and experience in early infancy: A look at the hidden side of behavior development. In H. W. Stevenson, E. H. Hess, & H. L. Rheingold (Eds.), *Early Behavior: Comparative and developmental approaches.* Copyright © 1967, John Wiley & Sons. Reprinted by permission of John Wiley & Sons Inc.

to which infants renewed responding indexed their novelty preference. Infants tested with the original reinforcer after delays longer than 15 s behaved as if it were novel (i.e., forgetting was complete).

Habituation studies have rarely found evidence of retention after delays longer than 15–60 s in novelty-preference tests (Cohen & Gelber, 1975), although 24-hour savings is occasionally found with measures of heart rate (Keen, Chase, & Graham, 1965) and event-related potentials (Molfese & Wetzel, 1992; Thomas & Lykins, 1995). Infants exhibit retention for facial stimuli after longer delays than other stimuli, suggesting that faces may be special (Pascalis, de Haan, Nelson, & de Schonen, 1998; see also Fagan, 1973).

Long-Term Familiarization

Long-term familiarization resembles habituation except that infants are preexposed to a stimulus for an extended period (at least 1 day) before being tested. During familiarization, the experimenter does not record responding and often is not present. In a sense, this procedure provides a degree of ecological validity to laboratory studies in which stimulus exposure and other variables are highly controlled.

Using this procedure, DeCasper and Spence (1986) asked women to recite aloud a Dr. Seuss passage from *The Cat in the Hat* twice daily during their last 6 weeks of pregnancy. During testing 56 hours after birth, infants wearing headphones could successively listen to their mother or another female reading the preexposed passage or a novel one (from *Yertle the Turtle*) by sucking on a nonnutritive nipple that controlled a tape recorder. Controls not prenatally exposed heard their mother reading both passages. Infants sucked more to hear the passage exposed *in utero* than the novel passage, irrespective of who read it, but controls displayed no preference. This and subsequent studies demonstrated that memories established *in utero* can be retained for at least 2 days after birth.

In novelty-preference studies, a novel test setting can obscure the extent of infants' memory capabilities. One day after 2 weeks of daily exposure to stimuli differing in color and form, for example, 5- and 9-week-olds looked longer at stimuli novel on a single dimension when home-tested but only at stimuli novel on both dimensions when laboratory-tested

(Bushnell, McCutcheon, Sinclair, & Tweedlie, 1984).

Visual Expectancy

In this paradigm, infants are initially exposed to a sequence of visual stimuli; their ability to anticipate the next stimulus in the sequence is tested immediately or after a delay. Smith (1984), for example, trained 5-month-olds to successively fixate four identical doors. On each trial, a signal light blinked, and then each door opened briefly, revealing a visual stimulus. During testing immediately after training, the signal light blinked, but the doors did not open. A significant number of infants fixated three locations in the correct sequence.

Using an eye-tracker, Haith, Wentworth, and Canfield (1993) reported that 3-month-olds who were exposed to a left-right sequence of light flashes anticipatorily shifted their eyes toward the next stimulus and retained this simple alternation rule for at least 4 days. Infants exposed to a left-left-right sequence also produced anticipatory eye movements.

Conditioning

Retention in conditioning paradigms is evidenced by either savings (more rapid reacquisition than in session 1) or cued recall (responding to the original stimulus in the absence of reinforcement).

Classical Conditioning

Early studies using this paradigm tracked a single infant's conditioning performance over substantial periods of time. Watson and Rayner (1917) sounded a loud gong (US: unconditional stimulus) that produced crying and withdrawal (UR: unconditional response) on two occasions when an 11-month-old infant (Albert) touched a white rat (CS: conditional stimulus). One week later, Albert still withdrew his hand when presented with the rat; afterward, he received five more CS-US pairings. Five days after that, Albert exhibited conditional emotional responses (CERs) to the rat as well as to other stimuli that resembled it (rabbit, dog, fur coat, Santa Claus mask, and cotton wool) but not to perceptually different stimuli (blocks). Ten days after the test, his CER to the rat had become muted and was "freshened" with another CS-US presentation (*reinstatement*; see "Reinstatement and Reactivation"), and the US was paired once each with the rabbit and dog. One month after the reinstatement, Albert—now 13 months old—still exhibited CERs to the rat, dog, mask, and fur coat.

Jones (1930) repeatedly paired a tapping sound (CS) and electrotactual stimulus (US) for 5 consecutive days. The anticipatory CR (galvanic skin reflex), established in session 1 at 7 months of age, was still evident 7 weeks later. Subsequently, Kantrow (1937) reported that an infant less than 10 days old still exhibited a CR (leg flexion) to a tone-CS 18 days after the final conditioning session. Little, Lipsitt, and Rovee-Collier (1984) established an eyeblink CR in a single session with 10-, 20-, and 30-day-olds, pairing a CS-tone with a US-air puff. Ten days later, all but 10-day-olds exhibited savings, and 20-day-olds outperformed 30-day-olds being trained for the first time.

Operant Conditioning

In operant conditioning studies, infants are usually trained for multiple sessions. Although designed to study learning, even early studies revealed retention from session to session. A study of conditioned vocalizations is typical (Rheingold, Gewirtz, & Ross, 1959). Three-month-olds' baseline vocalizations to an expressionless experimenter were recorded on days 1–2, and the experimenter socially reinforced their vocalizations on days 3–4. Infants vocalized more on day 4 than day 3, revealing 24-hour savings.

Mobile Task. Most studies of infant long-term memory have used the *mobile conjugate reinforcement task* (Rovee & Rovee, 1969). Here, 2- to 6-month-olds learn a motoric response—an operant footkick that moves a crib mobile via a ribbon strung from one ankle to the mobile suspension hook (see figure 17.2a). The critical information is displayed either on the mobile objects or on a cloth draped around the crib or playpen. During an initial baseline phase, the ribbon and the mobile hang from different hooks so that kicks cannot move the mobile. During acquisition, the ribbon is moved to the hook suspending the mobile, and infants' kicks move the mobile in a manner commensurate with their rate and vigor ("conjugate reinforcement"). In a final phase, baseline conditions are reinstated. Typically, this procedure is repeated the following day. During the nonreinforcement phase at the end

of day 2, infants' final level of learning and retention after 0 delay is measured. Later, infants are tested during another nonreinforcement phase with the original mobile or one that differs in some way (see figure 17.2b). If infants recognize the test mobile, then they kick robustly, as at the end of training; if they do not recognize it, then they do not kick above baseline.

The first evidence of 24-hour cued-recall in infants was found with this task (Rovee & Fagen, 1976). Three-month-olds were trained for 3 consecutive days. During the initial nonreinforcement phase of sessions 2 and 3, infants responded at the same level as they had responded at the end of the previous day's session, exhibiting perfect 24-hour cued-recall. On day 4, infants tested with the original mobile again exhibited perfect retention, but infants tested with a different mobile exhibited none, discriminating the test mobile from the training mobile they had last seen 24 hours earlier—a result replicated with 2-month-olds (Hayne, Greco, Earley, Griesler, & Rovee-Collier, 1986).

The mobile task has since been used to answer a number of fairly sophisticated questions about infants' memory processing. Timmons (1994), for example, found evidence that memories become integrated into a mnemonic network by 6 months of age. She trained 6-month-olds to move a mobile or turn on a music-box by arm-pulling or footkicking—an analog of the traditional paired-associate task. Infants learned the second cue-response pair in the same context 3 days later. Three days after that, infants produced only the appropriate response associate during cued-recall tests, irrespective of which pair they learned last. Having demonstrated that infants' memories of the paired-associates were specific, Timmons taught new groups both cue-response pairs, let them forget both pairs, and then primed them 3 weeks later with either the mobile or the music-box in a reactivation paradigm (see "Reactivation"). Twenty-four hours later, all were tested with the mobile. As expected, infants primed with the mobile produced the mobile paired-associate (i.e., if kicking was paired with the mobile, then infants kicked when tested with the mobile and did not arm-pull—the response associated with the music-box). Infants primed with the music-box and tested with the mobile, however, also produced the mobile paired-associate. Because these infants had forgotten the mobile memory and were not primed with the

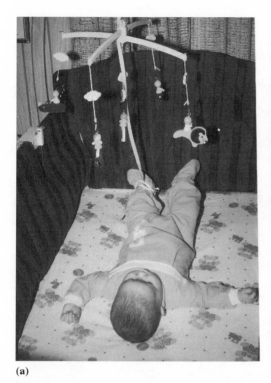 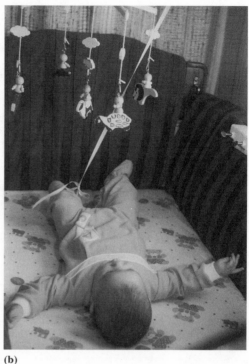

(a)   (b)

Figure 17.2 The experimental arrangement used with 2- to 6-month-olds in the mobile conjugate reinforcement task, shown here with a 3-month-old. (a) An acquisition phase: the ribbon and mobile are attached to the same overhead hook so that kicks move the mobile. (b) The delayed recognition test: the ribbon and mobile are attached to different hooks so that kicks cannot move the mobile.

mobile, the music-box prime must have indirectly activated the mobile memory via a mnemonic link (perhaps, the common training context).

Train Task. Researchers have used an upward extension of the mobile task to study retention with 6- to 18-month-olds. All aspects of training and testing are the same as in the mobile task except that instead of kicking to move a mobile, infants press a lever to move a train around a circular track (see figure 17.3). At 6 months, delayed recognition and reactivation performance, responses to cue and context changes (Hartshorn & Rovee-Collier, 1997), and priming latencies (Hildreth & Rovee-Collier, in press) are identical in both tasks. This equivalence has permitted retention data from older infants in the train task to be combined with corresponding data from younger infants in the mobile task, yielding a systematic picture of memory development

from 2–18 months of age (see "Ontogenetic Changes in Retention").

Deferred Imitation

Imitation is a "monkey see, monkey do" procedure. An individual models a behavior and the infant's ability to reproduce that behavior is assessed during a cued-recall test either immediately or after a delay (deferred imitation). Piaget (1962) assumed that infants were incapable of deferred imitation until 18–24 months of age. Meltzoff was the first to challenge this assumption, demonstrating that 14-month-olds exhibit 24-hour imitation under highly controlled conditions (Meltzoff, 1985) and still imitate at an above-chance level 4 months later (Meltzoff, 1995). Increasingly, infants have been shown to exhibit deferred imitation at younger ages. Using a new procedure in which infants watched an experimenter remove a mitten from a puppet's hand and ring

Figure 17.3 The experimental arrangement used with 6- to 18-month-olds in the train task, shown here with a 6-month-old. During baseline and the delayed retention test, the lever is deactivated so that presses cannot move the train. Note the complex array of toys in the train box.

a bell hidden inside, Barr, Dowden, and Hayne (1996) observed 6-month-olds perform this action 24 hours later (see figure 17.4). Meltzoff and Moore (1994) reported that 6-week-olds imitated an experimenter's facial movements 24 hours later. These studies demonstrate that even young infants can maintain a representation of a one-time event over relatively long periods. In general, the range of behaviors that infants imitate after a delay ex-

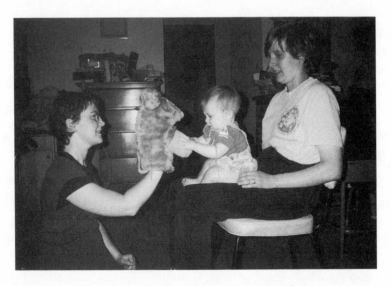

Figure 17.4 The experimental arrangement used with 6- to 24-month-old infants in the deferred imitation paradigm. Shown here is a 6-month-old removing a mitten from the puppet's hand—an action modeled by the experimenter 24 hours earlier.

pands with age from facial and body movements, to actions on objects, to intended actions and social goals (Meltzoff, 1995).

Imitation studies with older infants have followed similar procedures, but the target behaviors are more complex, and infants are usually allowed to imitate them immediately and, occasionally, during the retention interval (see Bauer, 1996). Under these conditions, 1- to 2-year-olds exhibit retention after 6 weeks (Barr & Hayne, 1996). Bauer, Hertsgaard, and Wewerka (1995) found superior retention of actions that must be performed in a specific order ("enabling" events—e.g., placing a toy bear in a bed before covering it with a blanket) instead of in an arbitrary order (e.g., putting a ring on the bear's finger and a cap on his head). The same effect has been found with older children and adults.

Object Search and Delayed Response

Object Search

The A-not-B search task, introduced by Piaget (1954), has reemerged as another method for studying memory development. In the prototypical experiment, the infant is seated between two identical wells (A, B) where an object can be hidden. The experimenter shows the infant an object, places it in well A as the infant watches, and simultaneously covers both wells. After delays from 0–10 s, the infant is permitted to reach. Infants reaching to the empty well are shown the object in the other well but are not given it. The experimenter continues to hide the object in well A until infants meet a criterion, when the procedure is repeated with the object hidden in well B. After the hiding well is reversed, infants often continue to search in well A, despite seeing the object hidden in well B (the *A-not-B error*).

Infants from 6–12 months tolerate delays that increase with age from 1–10 s. Infants tolerate slightly longer delays if tested longitudinally instead of cross-sectionally. At each age, decreasing the delay eliminates the A-not-B error, and increasing it leads to random search. Seemingly minor changes in task parameters dramatically affect retention (Diamond, 1990).

Tasks that eliminate the requirement that infants physically remove a cover or screen before recovering a hidden object have revealed evidence of retention at even younger ages. Eight-month-olds who watched a hand

retrieve an object from behind either the screen where it was hidden 15 s earlier (the *possible event*) or a second screen (the *impossible event*) looked longer at the impossible event, suggesting that they remembered where they originally saw the object hidden (Baillargeon & Graber, 1988). In traditional object search tasks, 15 s is the longest delay that infants twice as old tolerate. Hood and Willatts (1986) used darkness to hide the object. After showing 5-month-olds an object at one of two locations, they turned the lights off and removed the object. When they turned the lights back on, infants reached more to the side where the object had been than to the other side. Goubet and Clifton (1998) tested 6½-month-olds in the dark. The sound of a noisy ball rolling down a tube to infants' left or right signaled where to find the ball after a delay. Infants with previous practice reaching directionally in the light reached correctly in the dark. These studies reveal that younger infants' search errors in traditional A-not-B tasks reflect their inability to execute the coordinated motor sequence required by those tasks—not their inability to remember an object's prior location.

Delayed Response (DR)

The DR task, introduced by Hunter (1913) to measure "sensory thought" in animals and children, is almost identical to the A-not-B task. In the original study, Hunter hid a food reward behind one of three doors. A light over the door signaled the correct location and then was turned off. After a delay, subjects were allowed to respond. The maximum delay tolerated was 50 s after 507 trials at 30 months and 25 min after 15–46 trials at 6–8 years; however, all ages initially encountered difficulty at delays of 4–6 s. Subsequently, a preverbal 13- to 16-month-old watched the experimenter hide an object in one of three boxes (Hunter, 1917). During the delay, timed from when the lid was shut, the child was distracted. The delay tolerated was 12 s at 13–15 months and 24 s at 16 months.

Brody (1981) operantly trained younger infants to touch one of two locations where a light had cued an auditory-visual reward. The maximum delay tolerated was 0.25 s at 8 months and 9 s at 12 and 16 months. Overall, whether tested cross-sectionally or longitudinally, infants in the DR task tolerate linearly increasing delays from 6–12 months that are virtually the same as in the A-not-B task (Diamond, 1990).

Delayed Nonmatching to Sample (DNMS)

In the DNMS task, an object (the sample) covering a reward is placed in front of the infant. When the infant finds the reward, a screen is lowered and, after a delay, is raised to reveal the sample and a novel object. The infant responds correctly by displacing the novel object, which now covers the reward. If the child responds incorrectly, the experimenter reveals the reward but does not let the child have it. Typically, new pairs of objects are used on every trial.

Overman (1990) trained children between 12–15, 18–20, and 22–32 months to criterion on a 10-s delay and then progressively increased the delay to 30, 60, and 120 s. The youngest subjects reached criterion between 15–18 months of age. Retention was impaired at delays exceeding 10 s in the youngest group and 60 s in the oldest group.

Reenactment

"Reenactment" is the label given by some developmental psychologists to another complete training session. In this paradigm, children participate in a complex event, and their spontaneous and cued recall of its subcomponents are assessed during another training ("reenactment") session. Eighteen-month-olds, for example, performed eight different activities, returned 15 minutes, 2 weeks, or 8 weeks later for session 2, and were tested 8 weeks later (Hudson & Sheffield, 1998). Groups with more spaced sessions exhibited superior retention both during the 8-week test and 6 months later. Interestingly, reenacting only two or all eight activities after 2 weeks produced equivalent retention.

Reinstatement and Reactivation

Reinstatement and reactivation are reminder procedures that have been used in conjunction with many paradigms, including paired-comparison, auditory localization, classical and operant conditioning, deferred imitation, and reenactment. Their greatest use, however, has been in operant conditioning studies.

Reinstatement

Campbell and Jaynes (1966) hypothesized that reinstatement was the mechanism by which memories of early experiences could be perpetuated over significant periods of development. They demonstrated that trained rat pups who received periodic, partial practice throughout the retention interval still displayed retention 1 month later. Untrained pups who received the same reminders and trained pups who received no reminders (the requisite controls) exhibited no retention after that delay.

Hartshorn (1998) provided the first test of this hypothesis with human infants. Infants learned the train task at 6 months of age, received a brief reinstatement at 7, 8, 9, and 12 months, and were tested at 18 months of age. Although 6-month-olds typically forget after 2 weeks, infants receiving periodic reminders exhibited significant retention after 1 year, at 18 months of age. Immediately after the 18-month test, five infants received an additional reinstatement. When retested at 2 years, four still exhibited excellent retention despite receiving only a single reinstatement in the preceding year (at 18 months). Untrained controls who received the same reinstatement regimen exhibited no retention after any delay, confirming that the reinstatements themselves produced no new learning.

Reactivation

In the reactivation procedure, a single reminder is presented at the end of the retention interval, after forgetting is complete but before the long-term test (Spear & Parsons, 1976). The reminder, a fractional component of the original event, presumably primes the latent memory, increasing its accessibility. After reactivation, subjects exhibit retention. Trained but unreminded subjects and untrained but reminded subjects exhibit no retention after the same delay.

The first report of reactivation with human infants was by Rovee-Collier, Sullivan, Enright, Lucas, and Fagen (1980). Three-month-olds were trained in the mobile task, exposed to a reactivation reminder either 13 or 27 days later, and tested 1 day afterward. During reactivation, infants—placed in a sling-seat to reduce activity—briefly viewed the original mobile while the experimenter moved it noncontingently at the same rate each infant had moved it by kicking at the end of acquisition (see figure 17.5). Although 3-month-olds forget the mobile task after 6–8 days, the reactivation reminder completely alleviated forgetting after both delays. After reactivation, the memory was forgotten at approximately the same rate as it was forgotten originally. Untrained controls who were identically primed exhibited no retention. Researchers have since found that a reactivation reminder recovers different memory attributes at different rates. Attributes representing the general features of the mobile (which are forgotten last) are recovered before attributes representing its specific details (which are forgotten first).

In a recent mobile study, 2-month-olds received a 3-minute reminder every 3 weeks through 6½ months of age (six reminders altogether) and a final retention test at 7¼ months, when the study was terminated because infants outgrew the task (Rovee-Collier, Hartshorn, & DiRubbo, 1999). Before each reminder, infants received a preliminary retention test. Infants exhibiting no retention during the preliminary test received a reactivation reminder to recover the memory; those exhibiting retention received a reinstatement reminder to maintain it. Initially, all reminders but one were reactivations; by the end of the study, all reminders but one were reinstatements. Although 2-month-olds typically forget after 1–2 days, after repeated reminders, they exhibited significant retention 4½ months later, and most still did so 5¼ months later (see figure 17.6). Had the study not been stopped, they undoubtedly would have remembered longer. Untrained, yoked controls who received the same reminder regimen as their experimental counterparts exhibited no retention after any delay, confirming that the reminders themselves produced no new learning.

In addition to protracting retention, multiple reactivations speed memory recovery (Hayne, Hildreth, & Rovee-Collier, 1998) and reduce the accessibility of memory attributes representing contextual details (Hitchcock & Rovee-Collier, 1996).

Ontogenetic Changes in Retention

Research on infant memory development has largely followed a shotgun approach. In part, this reflects the difficulty of finding equivalent tasks for different ages. To date, the only systematic studies of retention over the entire infancy period have used operant condi-

Figure 17.5 The experimental arrangement used in reactivation procedures with the mobile task, shown here with a 3-month-old. The arrangement is identical in reinstatement procedures except that a ribbon links the ankle to the mobile hook so that kicks move the mobile.

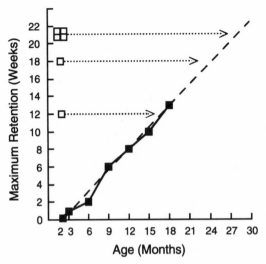

Figure 17.6 Individual data of reminded 2-month-olds (open squares) superimposed on the retention function of unreminded 2- to 18-month-olds (filled squares), shown in Figure 17.7. The dashed line extends that function through 30 months of age. Arrows indicate that after periodic nonverbal reminders, four 2-month-olds exhibited retention equivalent to 2¼-year-olds, one exhibited retention equivalent to 2-year-olds, and one exhibited retention equivalent to 17-month-olds.

olds—instead of 1–2 days (Vander Linde, Morrongiello, & Rovee-Collier, 1985).

Speed of Retrieval

The speed of memory retrieval is the time required for infants to express retention after exposure to a memory prime 1 week after forgetting has occurred. Although the duration of retention increases linearly between 3–12 months, so does the speed of memory retrieval (see figure 17.8). By 12 months, retrieval after priming is virtually instantaneous, as it is in adults (Hildreth & Rovee-Collier, in press). At any given age, however, the speed of retrieval is a function of the retention interval. If the prime is presented only 1 day after training, when the memory is more accessible, even 3-month-olds respond instantaneously (Gulya, Rovee-Collier, Galluccio, & Wilk, 1998).

Specificity of Memory

Memory specificity is determined by probing the memory with a stimulus that is the same as or different from the stimulus that was presented during encoding. If the original stimulus is an effective retrieval cue but the altered stimulus is not, then the particular information that was changed in the memory probe

tioning procedures. This work is described below.

Duration of Long-Term Memory

Infants of all ages and species exhibit equivalent retention after short delays, but with increasing age, they exhibit retention after progressively longer delays. The duration of retention in an operant conditioning paradigm with a standardized set of training parameters increases linearly from 2–18 months (Hartshorn, Rovee-Collier, Gerhardstein, Bhatt, Wondoloski, et al., 1998; see figure 17.7). Deviations from this function that have been obtained with other paradigms reflect differences in training and testing parameters—not in the underlying memory processes. Even within the same paradigm, retention is affected by session number, session duration, the memory load, and so forth. After training for three 6-minute instead of two 9-minute sessions, for example, 2-month-olds recognize the mobile for 2 weeks—the same as 6-month-

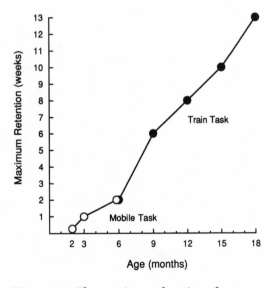

Figure 17.7 The maximum duration of retention (in weeks) of independent groups of infants over the first 18 months of life in studies in operant conditioning (mobile and train tasks) and deferred imitation paradigms.

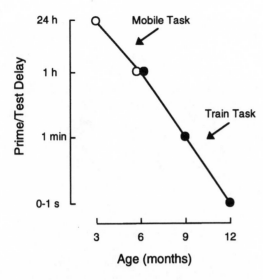

Figure 17.8 The time required for infants of different ages to express a memory after exposure to a prime. The prime was presented 1 week after each age last exhibited retention (cf. Figure 17.7). Latencies in the mobile and train tasks are identical at 6 months.

is assumed to be represented in the memory contents (for discussion of this approach, see Tulving, 1983, p. 251).

Focal Cue

Between 2–6 months, infants do not generalize to a novel mobile or train (Hartshorn, Rovee-Collier, Gerhardstein, Bhatt, Klein, et al., 1998). Effective primes are also hyperspecific: more than a single different object on a mobile prime renders it ineffective (Rovee-Collier, Patterson, & Hayne, 1985). This specificity is overridden by training with more than one mobile or merely exposing infants to a novel mobile after training is over. Under these conditions, a novel mobile is recognized 1 day later and reactivates the memory 2 weeks later (Greco, Hayne, & Rovee-Collier, 1990).

With increasing age, infants increasingly generalize to novel test cues, initially after short test delays and later after progressively longer ones (see figure 17.9, *left panel*). In conditioning studies, 9- and 12-month-olds generalize to a novel test cue after delays of 1–14 days but not longer (Hartshorn, Rovee-Collier, Gerhardstein, Bhatt, Klein, et al., 1998). In de-

ferred imitation studies, infants generalize to cues differing in color after 10 minutes at 12–14 months and 1 day at 18 months and to cues differing in both color and form after 1 day at 21 months (Hayne, MacDonald, & Barr, 1997). The fact that older infants generalize to novel test cues after short but not long delays reveals that they can discriminate the differences but *actively* disregard them.

Context

In both conditioning (Hartshorn, Rovee-Collier, Gerhardstein, Bhatt, Klein, et al., 1998) and deferred imitation (Barnat, Klein, & Meltzoff, 1996; Hanna & Meltzoff, 1993) studies, a different test context affects retention only after relatively long delays (see figure 17.9, *right panel*) at all ages except 6 months, when this pattern is reversed—perhaps as a functional adaptation that anticipates the onset of independent locomotion. This specificity is overridden by training in multiple contexts (Amabile & Rovee-Collier, 1991), exposing the cue in a novel context after training is over (Boller & Rovee-Collier, 1992), or reactivating the memory more than once (Hitchcock & Rovee-Collier, 1996).

Importantly, memories maintained over long periods may not be expressed in the same form as they were originally encoded. At 6 months, for example, the training memory is context-specific: infants trained at 6 months and reminded 3 weeks later in the original context exhibit excellent retention in that context but none in a novel one (Hartshorn & Rovee-Collier, 1997). At 8 months, however, the training memory is not context-specific. Infants trained at 6 months, reminded in the original context 4 weeks later, and tested at 8 months exhibit excellent retention whether the test context is the same or novel (Hartshorn, 1998). Apparently, the memory is converted into an age-appropriate behavior at the time of retrieval (see Tulving, 1983).

Memory Modification

Despite their specificity, infants' memories can be modified in the same way that memories are distorted in studies of eyewitness testimony with children and adults (Rovee-Collier, Borza, Adler, & Boller, 1993): new information that infants merely witness after an event is over affects their subsequent memory

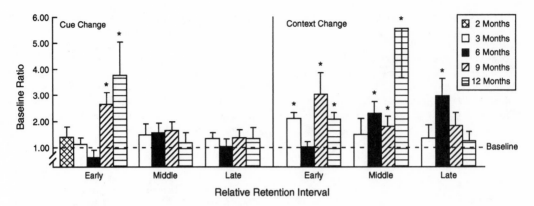

Figure 17.9 Delayed recognition performance of 2- to 12-month-olds after common relative retention intervals that correspond to the first (*Early*), middle (*Middle*), and last (*Late*) points on the forgetting function for each age. *Left panel*: Infants trained with a particular cue were tested with a different cue in the original context. *Right panel*: Infants trained in a particular context were tested in a different context with the original cue. Asterisks indicate significant retention. Vertical bars indicate ±1 *SE*.

of that event. This modification can take two forms—retention of the original event is impaired, and/or the new information is incorporated into the original memory. Memories are more easily modified when they are weaker—the longer the delay between the original event and the postevent information, the stronger the effect. If the delay is sufficiently long that details of the original cue or context have been forgotten when the postevent information is introduced, then the details of the most recent cue (Rovee-Collier, Adler, & Borza, 1994) or context (Boller, Rovee-Collier, Gulya, & Prete, 1996) are substituted for the original ones, producing a relatively permanent memory distortion.

The Ontogeny of Multiple Memory Systems

Memories of older infants and adults were long thought to be mediated by a fundamentally different system than memories of younger infants (Nelson, 1995). Presumably, a primitive memory system was functional shortly after birth, whereas a more mature system emerged late in the first year of life (Schacter & Moscovitch, 1984). The same developmental hierarchy characterized all proposed multiple memory systems, including semantic and episodic memory (Tulving, 1983), nondeclarative and declarative memory (McKee & Squire, 1993),

implicit and explicit memory (Graf & Schacter, 1985), and the habit and memory systems (Bachevalier & Mishkin, 1984). The development of these systems, however, was never studied directly with human infants but was only inferred from dissociations in the memory performance of amnesic adults on priming and recognition/recall tests (McKee & Squire, 1993).

Recently, memory dissociations have been also found in preverbal infants' memory performance on reactivation and delayed recognition tests (Rovee-Collier, 1997). These dissociations are identical to those produced by adults on priming and recognition tests, respectively, in response to the same independent variables: age, the retention interval, vulnerability (interference), the number of study trials, the amount of study time, the number of studied items, level of processing, trial and session spacing, affect, the serial position of list items, studied size, and the memory load. For both infants and adults, different levels of these variables have a major effect on performance in recognition tasks but no effect on performance in priming tasks. If memory dissociations are diagnostic of two memory systems, then both systems must be functional by 2 months of age. This evidence, combined with evidence from deferred imitation studies with 6-month-olds, suggests that the same fundamental mechanisms underlie memory processing throughout development.

Infantile Amnesia

Although some adults can remember one or two events that occurred at the age of 2 (Usher & Neisser, 1993), most cannot remember events before 3–4 years of age (White & Pillemer, 1979). This phenomenon ("infantile amnesia") has been attributed to the immaturity of the brain mechanisms responsible for maintaining information over the long term (Nelson, 1995) and to the inability of children to maintain memories over the long term before they can rehearse them by talking about them (Nelson, 1990). Four-year-olds, however, can recall some events that occurred before 2½ years of age (Fivush & Hamond, 1990), and an infant who experienced a unique event at 6 months of age verbalized about it almost 1½ years later (Myers, Clifton, & Clarkson, 1987). Additionally, multiple nonverbal reminders maintained a mobile memory encoded at 2 months through 7¼ months of age (Rovee-Collier et al., in press) and a train memory encoded at 6 months through at least 2 years of age (Hartshorn, 1998). If multiple nonverbal reminders can maintain two comparable memories over an overlapping period from 2 months through 2 years, then they should also maintain a single memory over this same period. Clearly, these studies undercut traditional accounts of infantile amnesia.

Alternative explanations of infantile amnesia are suggested by recent data. First, because the memory attributes that represent contextual information (i.e., when and where an event happened) are relatively fragile, and access to them is lost over repeated reminders, older children and adults may actually remember early-life events but be unable to pinpoint their origins. Second, because memories encoded early in life have probably been modified or updated many times, their origins are impossible to identify. Third, because memories are converted at the time of retrieval and expressed in an age-appropriate manner, they may not be recognized. And fourth, because a match between the encoding and retrieval contexts is required for memory retrieval after long delays, naturally occurring and perceived changes in context over time reduce the probability of retrieving memories acquired early in life.

Conclusions

The mechanisms that underlie memory processing are fundamentally the same in infants and adults: memories are forgotten gradually, recovered by reminders, and modified by new information that overlaps with old. The temporal parameters of memory processing, however, change with age: memories are retrieved faster and after longer delays. Also with age, infants increasingly generalize to novel retrieval cues—first after short delays and later after longer ones. The longevity and specificity of young infants' memories contradict earlier views that infants' memories are short-lived, highly generalized and diffuse, and devoid of place information. The findings reviewed in this chapter reveal that infant experiences can affect later behavior and offer insights into how this might occur.

Acknowledgment Preparation of this chapter was supported by grant nos. R37-MH32307 and K05-MH00902 from the National Institute of Mental Health (CRC) and by a Marsden grant (UOO609) from the Royal Society of New Zealand (HH).

References

Amabile, T. A., & Rovee-Collier, C. (1991). Contextual variation and memory retrieval at six months. *Child Development, 62*, 1155–1166.

Bachevalier, J., & Mishkin, M. (1984). An early and a late developing system for learning and retention in infant monkeys. *Behavioral Neuroscience, 98*, 770–778.

Baillargeon, R., & Graber, M. (1988). Evidence of location memory in 8-month-old infants in a non-search AB task. *Developmental Psychology, 24*, 502–511.

Barnat, S. A., Klein, P. J., & Meltzoff, A. N. (1996). Deferred imitation across changes in context and object: Memory and generalization in 14-month-old infants. *Infant Behavior and Development, 19*, 241–251.

Barr, R., Dowden, A., & Hayne, H. (1996). Developmental changes in deferred imitation by 6- to 24-month-old infants. *Infant Behavior and Development, 19*, 159–170.

Barr, R., & Hayne, H. (1996). The effect of event structure on imitation in infancy: Practice makes perfect? *Infant Behavior and Development, 19*, 253–257.

Bauer, P. J. (1996). What do infants recall of their lives? Memory for specific events by one- to two-year-olds. *American Psychologist, 51*, 29–41.

Bauer, P. J., Hertsgaard, L. A., & Wewerka, S. S. (1995). Effects of experience on long-term recall in infancy: Remembering not to forget. *Journal of Experimental Child Psychology, 59,* 260–298.

Boller, K., & Rovee-Collier, C. (1992). Contextual coding and recoding of infant memory. *Journal of Experimental Child Psychology, 52,* 1–23.

Boller, K., Rovee-Collier, C., Gulya, M., & Prete, K. (1996). Infants' memory for context: Timing effects of postevent information. *Journal of Experimental Child Psychology, 63,* 583–602.

Brody, L. R. (1981). Visual short-term cued recall memory in infancy. *Child Development, 52,* 242–250.

Bushnell, I. W. R., McCutcheon, E., Sinclair, J., & Tweedlie, M. E. (1984). Infants' delayed recognition memory for colour and form. *British Journal of Developmental Psychology, 2,* 11–17.

Campbell, B. A., & Jaynes, J. (1966). Reinstatement. *Psychological Review, 73,* 478–480.

Cohen, L. B., & Gelber, E. R. (1975). Infant visual memory. In L. Cohen & P. Salapatek (Eds.), *Infant perception: From sensation to cognition. Vol. 1. Basic visual processes* (pp. 347–403). New York: Academic.

DeCasper, A. J., & Spence, M. J. (1986). Prenatal maternal speech influences newborns' perception of speech sounds. *Infant Behavior and Development, 9,* 133–150.

Diamond, A. (1990). The development and neural bases of memory functions as indexed by the AB and DR tasks in human infants and infant monkeys. In A. Diamond (Ed.), *The development and neural bases of higher cognitive functions* (Vol. 608; pp. 267–309), *Annals of the New York Academy of Sciences.* New York: New York Academy of Sciences.

Fagan, J. F., III. (1970). Memory in the infant. *Journal of Experimental Child Psychology, 9,* 217–226.

Fagan, J. F., III. (1973). Infants' delayed recognition memory and forgetting. *Journal of Experimental Child Psychology, 16,* 424–450.

Fantz, R. L. (1956). A method for studying early visual development. *Perceptual and Motor Skills, 6,* 13–15.

Fivush, R., & Hamond, N. R. (1990). Autobiographical memory across the preschool years: Toward reconceptualizing childhood amnesia. In R. Fivush & J. A. Hudson (Eds.), *Knowing and remembering in young children* (pp. 223–248). Cambridge: Cambridge University Press.

Freud, S. (1935). *A general introduction to psychoanalysis.* New York: Clarion Books.

Goubet, N., & Clifton, R. K. (1998). Object and event representation in 6½-month-old infants. *Developmental Psychology, 34,* 63–76.

Graf, P., & Schacter, D. L. (1985). Implicit and explicit memory for new associations in normal and amnesic patients. *Journal of Experimental Psychology: Learning, Memory, and Cognition, 11,* 501–518.

Greco, C., & Daehler, M. W. (1985). Immediate and long-term retention of basic-level categories in 24-month-olds. *Infant Behavior and Development, 8,* 459–474.

Greco, C., Hayne, H., & Rovee-Collier, C. (1990). The roles of function, reminding, and variability in categorization by 3-month-old infants. *Journal of Experimental Psychology: Learning, Memory, and Cognition, 16,* 617–633.

Gulya, M., Rovee-Collier, C., Galluccio, L., & Wilk, A. (1998). Memory processing of a serial list by very young infants. *Psychological Science, 9,* 303–307.

Haith, M. M., Wentworth, N., & Canfield, R. L. (1993). The formation of expectations in early infancy. In C. Rovee-Collier & L. P. Lipsitt (Eds.), *Advances in infancy research* (Vol. 8; pp. 251–297). Norwood, NJ: Ablex.

Hanna, E., & Meltzoff, A. N. (1993). Peer imitation by toddlers in laboratory, home, and day-care contexts: Implications for social learning and memory. *Developmental Psychology, 29,* 701–710.

Hartshorn, K. (1998, October). *The effect of reinstatement on infant long-term retention.* Unpublished doctoral dissertation, Rutgers University, New Brunswick, NJ.

Hartshorn, K., & Rovee-Collier, C. (1997). Infant learning and long-term memory at 6 months: A confirming analysis. *Developmental Psychobiology, 30,* 71–85.

Hartshorn, K., Rovee-Collier, C., Gerhardstein, P., Bhatt, R. S., Klein, P. J., Aaron, F., Wondoloski, T. L., & Wurtzel, N. (1998). Developmental changes in the specificity of memory over the first year of life. *Developmental Psychobiology, 33,* 61–78.

Hartshorn, K., Rovee-Collier, C., Gerhardstein, P., Bhatt, R. S., Wondoloski, T. L., Klein, P., Gilch, J., Wurtzel, N., & Campos-de-Carvalho, M. (1998). The ontogeny of long-term memory over the first year-and-a-half of life. *Developmental Psychobiology, 33,* 61–78.

Hayne, H., Greco, C., Earley, L. A., Griesler, P. C., & Rovee-Collier, C. (1986). Ontogeny of early event memory: I. Encoding and retrieval by 2- and 3-month-olds. *Infant Behavior and Development, 9,* 441–460.

Hayne, H., Hildreth, K., & Rovee-Collier, C. (1998, April). *Repeated reminders facilitate memory retrieval.* Paper presented at the meeting of the International Society of Infant Studies, Atlanta, GA.

Hayne, H., MacDonald, S., & Barr, R. (1997). Developmental changes in the specificity of memory over the second year of life. *Infant Behavior and Development, 20,* 233–245.

Hildreth, K., Rovee-Collier, C. (in press). Decreases in the response latency to priming over the first year of life. *Developmental Psychobiology.*

Hitchcock, D. F. A., & Rovee-Collier, C. (1996). The effect of repeated reactivations on memory specificity in infants. *Journal of Experimental Child Psychology, 62,* 378–400.

Hood, B., & Willatts, P. (1986). Reaching in the dark to an object's remembered position: Evidence for object permanence in 5-month-old infants. *British Journal of Developmental Psychology, 4,* 57–65.

Hudson, J., & Sheffield, E. G. (1998). Deja vu all over again: Effects of reenactment on toddlers' event memory. *Child Development, 69,* 51–67.

Hunter, W. S. (1913). The delayed reaction in animals and children. *Behavioral Monographs, 2,* 52–62.

Hunter, W. S. (1917). The delayed reaction in a child. *Psychological Review, 24,* 74–87.

Jones, H. E. (1930). The retention of conditioned emotional reactions in infancy. *Journal of Genetic Psychology, 37,* 485–498.

Kantrow, R. W. (1937). An investigation of conditioned feeding responses and conditioned adaptive behavior in young infants. *University of Iowa Studies of Child Welfare, 13*(3), 64.

Keen, R., Chase, H., & Graham, F. K. (1965). Twenty-four hour retention by neonates of habituated heart rate response. *Psychonomic Science, 21,* 287–288.

Little, A. H., Lipsitt, L. P., & Rovee-Collier, C. (1984). Classical conditioning and retention of the infant's eyelid response: Effects of age and interstimulus interval. *Journal of Experimental Child Psychology, 37,* 512–524.

McKee, R. D., & Squire, L. R. (1993). On the development of declarative memory. *Journal of Experimental Psychology: Learning, Memory, and Cognition, 19,* 397–404.

Meltzoff, A. N. (1985). Immediate and deferred imitation in fourteen- and twenty-four-month-old infants. *Child Development, 56,* 62–72.

Meltzoff, A. N. (1995). What infant memory tells us about infantile amnesia: Long-term recall and deferred imitation. *Journal of Experimental Child Psychology, 59,* 497–515.

Meltzoff, A. N., & Moore, M. K. (1994). Imitation, memory, and the representation of persons. *Infant Behavior and Development, 17,* 83–89.

Molfese, D. L., & Wetzel, W. F. (1992). Short- and long-term auditory recognition in 14-month-old human infants: Electrophysiological correlates. *Developmental Neuropsychology, 8,* 135–160.

Myers, N. A., Clifton, R. K., & Clarkson, M. G. (1987). When they were very young: Almost-threes remember two years ago. *Infant Behavior and Development, 10,* 123–132.

Nelson, C. A. (1995). The ontogeny of human memory: A cognitive neuroscience perspective. *Developmental Psychology, 31,* 723–738.

Nelson, K. (1990). Remembering, forgetting, and childhood amnesia. In R. Fivush & J. A. Hudson (Eds.), *Knowing and remembering in young children* (pp. 301–316). Cambridge: Cambridge University Press.

Overman, W. H. (1990). Performance on traditional matching to sample, no-matching to sample, and object discrimination tasks by 12- to 32-month-old children: A developmental progression. In A. Diamond (Ed.), *The development and neural bases of higher cognitive functions* (Vol. 608; pp. 365–385), *Annals of the New York Academy of Sciences.* New York: New York Academy of Sciences.

Pascalis, O., de Haan, M., Nelson, C. A., & de Schonen, S. (1998). Long-term recognition memory for faces assessed by visual paired comparison in 3- and 6-month-old infants. *Journal of Experimental Psychology: Learning, Memory, and Cognition, 24,* 1–12.

Piaget, J. (1954) *The construction of reality in the child* (M. Cook, Trans.). New York: Basic Books.

Piaget, J. (1962) *Play, dreams and imitation in childhood* (C. Gattegno & F. M. Hodgson, Trans.). New York: Norton.

Rheingold, H. L., Gewirtz, J. L., & Ross, H. W. (1959). Social conditioning of vocalizations. *Journal of Comparative and Physiological Psychology, 52,* 68–73.

Rose, S. A. (1981). Developmental changes in infants' retention of visual stimuli. *Child Development, 52,* 227–233.

Rovee, C. K., & Fagen, J. W. (1976). Extended conditioning and 24-hr retention in infants. *Journal of Experimental Child Psychology, 21,* 1–11.

Rovee, C. K., & Rovee, D. T. (1969). Conjugate reinforcement of infant exploratory behavior. *Journal of Experimental Child Psychology, 8,* 33–39.

Rovee-Collier, C. (1997). Dissociations in infant memory: Rethinking the development of implicit and explicit memory. *Psychological Review, 104,* 467–498.

Rovee-Collier, C., Adler, S. A., & Borza, M. A. (1994). Substituting new details for old? Effects of delaying postevent information on infant memory. *Memory & Cognition, 22,* 644–656.

Rovee-Collier, C., Borza, M. A., Adler, S. A., & Boller, K. (1993). Infants' eyewitness testimony: Integrating postevent information with a prior memory representation. *Memory and Cognition, 21,* 267–279.

Rovee-Collier, C., Hartshorn, K., & DiRubbo, M. (1999). Long-term maintenance of infant memory. *Developmental Psychobiology, 35,* 91–102.

Rovee-Collier, C., Patterson, J., & Hayne, H. (1985). Specificity in the reactivation of infant memory. *Developmental Psychobiology, 18,* 559–574.

Rovee-Collier, C., Sullivan, M. W., Enright, M. K., Lucas, D., & Fagen, J. W. (1980). Reactivation of infant memory. *Science, 208,* 1159–1161.

Schacter, D. L., & Moscovitch, M. (1984). Infants, amnesics, and dissociable memory systems. In M. Moscovitch (Ed.), *Advances in the study of communication and affect. Vol. 9: Infant memory* (pp. 173–216). New York: Plenum.

Smith, P. H. (1984). Five-month-old infant recall of temporal order and utilization of temporal organization. *Journal of Experimental Child Psychology, 38,* 400–414.

Sokolov, E. N. (1963). Higher nervous functions: The orienting reflex. *Annual Review of Physiology, 25,* 545–580.

Spear, N. E., & Parsons, P. J. (1976). Analysis of a reactivation treatment: Ontogenetic determinants of alleviated forgetting. In D. L. Medin, W. A. Roberts, & R. T. Davis (Eds.), *Processes of animal memory* (pp. 135–165). Hillsdale, NJ: Erlbaum.

Thomas, D. G., & Lykins, M. S. (1995). Event-related potential measures of 24-hour retention in 5-month-old infants. *Developmental Psychology, 31,* 946–957.

Timmons, C. R. (1994). Associative links between discrete memories in infancy. *Infant Behavior and Development, 17,* 431–445.

Tulving, E. (1983). *Elements of episodic memory.* Oxford: Clarendon Press.

Usher, J. A., & Neisser, U. (1993). Childhood amnesia and the beginnings of memory for four early life events. *Journal of Experimental Psychology: General, 122,* 155–165.

Vander Linde, E., Morrongiello, B. A., & Rovee-Collier, C. (1985). Determinants of retention in 8-week-old infants. *Developmental Psychology, 21,* 601–613.

Watson, J. B., & Rayner, R. (1917). Emotional reactions and psychological experimentation. *American Journal of Psychology, 28,* 163–174.

Werner, J. S., & Perlmutter, M. (1979). Development of visual memory in infants. In H. W. Reese & L. P. Lipsitt (Eds.), *Advances in child development and behavior* (Vol. 14; pp. 1–56). New York: Academic.

White, S. H., & Pillemer, D. B. (1979). Childhood amnesia and the development of a socially accessible memory system. In J. F. Kihlstrom & F. J. Evans (Eds.), *Functional disorders of memory* (pp. 29–74). Hillsdale, NJ: Erlbaum.

18

Socialization of Memory

KATHERINE NELSON & ROBYN FIVUSH

Socialization of memory implies that basic memory functions, skills, strategies, and practices are affected by social learning; that in some way and for some purposes memory is improved, generally in accord with dominant cultural values, through exposure to training or practices by socialization agents, parents, teachers, or other adults. In contrast, psychological studies of memory often appear to focus on basic processes that are assumed to be unlearned and universal in nature based in neurophysiological systems. From this perspective the study of the "socialization" of memory in human childhood must seem to be a small peripheral specialization of the basic memory system. Nonetheless, the position taken by many students of the development of memory in the postinfancy years is that human memory functioning is to a great extent the result of socialization practices, beginning in early childhood and continuing into adulthood, both in and out of school.

There is a vast literature on social learning, as well as on the development of memory strategies and skills during the school years of childhood. That literature documents increases in such strategies as organization of material (e.g., clustering by semantic groups in word lists), rehearsal, and metamemory (that is, reflection on memory itself in order to improve memory functions; see Schneider &

Bjorklund, 1998, for review of these issues and literature.) For the most part this literature focuses on development with age but attends less to causal factors that may underlie these developments. In contrast, much of the research focusing on personal memory has investigated the social context and processes that facilitate children's developing memory skills. In this chapter, therefore, we focus primarily on socialization processes during early childhood that are effective in changing organization and recall of memories of personal experience. This focus provides the foundation for the argument that the developments observed during the school years are similarly the result of socialization and that human memory in general develops beyond basic memory functions to serve social, cultural, and personal purposes through socialization practices. The assertion that socialization is important to, and constitutes a unique aspect of, memory in humans is consistent with the evidence that cognitive enculturation practices define other unique aspects of human cognitive functioning (Donald, 1991; Tomasello, Kruger & Ratner, 1993; Vygotsky, 1986).

The history of memory in both oral and literate cultures implies the significance of the socialization of memory, in terms of learning effective procedures for committing material to memory. Rubin (1995) has documented the strategies and skills used to accomplish memory for oral materials such as Greek epics and traditional ballads. Throughout history and well into the twentieth century, superior memory has been considered the mark of superior intelligence. Moreover, it was universally accepted that memory needed to be trained, and the educational system in the West was designed to a large extent to impart methods for increasing memory capacity and skills. For example, the method of rehearsal through imaginatively locating sequential material to be recalled in spatially ordered locations originated with the Greeks, as is well documented (Norman, 1976). Carruthers (1990) discusses the importance of memory to scholars in medieval Europe, relating the extraordinary memory performances of scholastics such as Thomas Aquinas, who were dependent upon memory for reproducing texts available only in single copies in widely dispersed monastery libraries. In China, from ancient times until well into the modern era, following the Confucian tradition, exams for entering the civil service required years of dedicated study that consisted primarily of committing classic texts to memory (Fairbank, 1957).

The practice of memory may be seen as akin to induction into language itself, a unique human process, but one that does not develop without experience in practice with expert users. The kinds of memory to be reviewed here, particularly autobiographical memory, may also be analogous to musical performance: all humans apparently have some musical capacities, and these are variously evoked by the availability of instruments, teachers, and opportunities to engage in the practice of musical forms. In some cultures all members participate in musical activities, whereas in others the practice is confined to a few expert performers, some of whom display extraordinary abilities. Similarly, only a few expert memory practitioners become epic reciters or ballad singers in traditional oral cultures, but most members learn some poems and songs "by heart." In our contemporary society most people acquire at least minimal skills for autobiographical reminiscing and the learning of text material, as well as rote memory for spelling words or multiplication tables, but some members become expert memory practitioners within particular domains of knowledge, whether for games such as chess or bridge or for abstruse material in archeology, psychology, or history.

In contemporary Western societies memory feats are given much less emphasis in school and receive less admiration from society at large than in past centuries or in many nonliterate societies today. Yet, as Donald (1991) has argued, although we rely to a very large extent on external memory systems (writing, graphic symbols, electronic storage systems, libraries, museums, and so on), the contemporary educational process is largely devoted to the acquisition of skills for the use of these external resources, and for systems of organizing the knowledge that is externally stored in ways that can be used effectively by individual minds. Donald emphasizes that the use of this knowledge depends ultimately on the socialization practices that provide effective memory interfaces with external resources.

In this chapter we attempt to trace the emergence of forms of memory—particularly autobiographical memory—that result from socialization practices. The evidence we present here, focused primarily on the beginnings of the socialization process in the preschool years, supports the view that human memory is "tuned up" in different ways almost as soon as a child enters into a social-cultural world—that is, at birth. Memory socialization proceeds from that point, emphasizing the kinds of functions of memory that are valued in the particular culture of the child's community. To make this case, we begin with a theoretical sketch of the development of memory in early childhood.

From Procedures and Events to Episodes

Research on memory in infancy (see review by Rovee-Collier & Hayne, chapter 17) has established evidence for basic retention of information about object action sequences and action procedures, as well as imitative learning, during the first 18 months of life. Bauer and Mandler (1989) have shown that even 1-year-olds can reconstruct short action sequences that incorporate causal relations among the actions. Thus earlier suggestions that memory for specific episodes was delayed because children were incapable of accurate temporal sequencing has been ruled out. This early memory is typically referred to as procedural, or as a first implicit memory system, followed by a second explicit memory system emerging toward the end of the first year (Schacter & Moscovitch, 1984). Bauer, Hertsgaard, and Dow (1994) and

McDonough and Mandler (1994), however, argue that the retention of a specific object-action sequence observed only once, and recapitulated in action days or even months later, demonstrates "declarative" rather than "procedural" memory and recall rather than simple recognition, and they claim that this capacity is available prior to the first birthday. While accepting this point, it must be noted that recall of a relation does not necessarily demonstrate recall of the experience of the original episode (Nelson, 1994); that is, it does not demonstrate a "mental reliving" of the initial event, which is the hallmark of episodic memory as defined by Tulving (1983).

Nonetheless, research with infants (e.g. Bauer & Wewerka, 1997) and young children (e.g., Nelson, 1986) has established that, beginning at least by the end of the first year, children have acquired representations of familiar repeated events that incorporate temporal and causal relations between actions, reciprocal acts by adults and child, situationally defined boundaries of the event (e.g., bath is situated in a bathtub in the bathroom at a specific time during the day), organized around a goal or endpoint (although the goal is usually the adult's goal, not the child's). It is important to note that memory for socially organized events of this kind implies more complex memory organization than that involved in procedural memory based on individual action sequences. Memory for recurrent events composed of extended sequences of actions of self and others, in a specific spatial and situational context with specific kinds of objects, constitutes the scripts that Schank and Abelson (1977) modeled as the basis for story understanding. The event knowledge that young children acquire of recurrent events have been analogously termed "scripts" (Nelson, 1986), although not all of the implications of Schank and Abelson's theory apply to the event knowledge of the young child. Informal observation of children and systematic research demonstrating that children will readily imitate canonical scripts for bedtime and bath, but resist imitation of reversed or transformed scripts (O'Connell & Girard, 1985), has shown that children are sensitive to the temporal and causal structure of events; but they do not confuse sequences, and indeed are resistant to a change in order of actions. During the second and third year these "scripts" may be so rigidly established in the child's mind that variations in the routine (e.g., for going to bed) are met with rage. Storybook reading is an example of this memory rigidity. Young children are notoriously adept at remembering the sequence of story elements and insisting on their repetition in exactly the same way each time the story is repeated.

Generalized event memory for "how things go" contrasts with episodic memory as defined by Tulving (1983). The young child's scripts are viewed as an early form of semantic memory or general knowledge, experientially derived. No doubt other primates, and probably other mammals, also rely on this kind of general organized event memory. Nelson (1993a, 1993b) argued that the basic function of memory is for acting in the present and anticipating the future (see Glenberg, 1997, for a similar argument). This function is served by procedural and event memory for recurrent activities. Specific memories for *specific episodes* of events that have occurred in the past are not functional in the basic system, unless they predict a reoccurrence, although particular aspects of an event (an unusual object, for example) are likely to be entered into the general event knowledge system. However, a memory for a specific happening might be retained over a period of time in anticipation of its recurrence and then, in the absence of an identified recurrence, be overwritten, forgotten, or destroyed as of no value. (The relation of this function to the reinstatement process described by Rovee-Collier is obvious and will be returned to later.) The specific dating of an episode would also have no particular value to the basic event knowledge system, unless it were associated with some salient temporally significant occurrence. Event memory thus serves a basic memory function, but, for the child at least, it is dependent upon socialization practices. The child remembers events that are critical to care, such as feeding time, bathtime, bedtime, and also those that are initiated by adults as games, such as peekaboo and pattycake. These activities are socially organized and the child's participant role is well defined by parents and others.

Although we now know a great deal about memory in infancy and early childhood, some puzzles of early memory remain. In particular, it is difficult to establish whether children remember a specific episode as an episodic memory in Tulving's sense—that is, as having happened at a particular place and in a particular time. Do children have episodic memories and if so, when is this type of memory established? Is the beginning of episodic memory related to the fact that adults do not remember episodes from their early childhood, the phenomenon known as infantile or childhood amnesia? In the following section, the evidence for children's episodic memories, and their dependence on socialization practices, is reviewed. We return to a general discussion of the emergence of socialized memory in the final section.

Shaping Episodes into Narratives: The Beginnings of Autobiographical Memory

Children begin talking about the past almost as soon as they begin talking, some time between 16 and 20 months of age (Eisenberg, 1985; Sachs, 1983). However, first references to the past are most often about just completed events (Sachs, 1983) or about routine activities (Nelson, 1989). Children's ability to refer to a specific event that occurred in the more remote past develops dramatically between 2 and 3 years of age (Eisenberg, 1985; Hudson, 1990), and this development typically occurs within joint reminiscing between parents and children (see Fivush & Hudson, 1990, for reviews).

Young children's references to the past are "scaffolded" by adults, usually parents, in the sense that it is the adult who provides most of the content and structure of the narrative. In the earliest conversations about the past, parents essentially tell what happened and children confirm or repeat parental contributions. Relatively soon, however, by about 24 months of age, children become more competent participants in these conversations, providing information in response to specific questions. By 3 years of age, some children are able to provide reasonably coherent accounts of past occurrences (Fivush, Gray, & Fromhoff, 1987), and they initiate past events as topics of conversations, although their memory and narrative skills continue to improve across development (Hudson & Shapiro, 1991; Pressley & Schneider, 1986).

Research with parent-child talk about the past suggests that children learn the forms and functions of such talk through participating in parent-guided conversations. The ways in which parents structure conversations about past events appear to facilitate children's developing abilities to report past occurrences in coherent and elaborated ways. A substantial body of research has now established that

there are consistent individual differences in the ways in which mothers reminisce with their young children. Although different studies have used somewhat different methodologies, and somewhat different terminology, mothers can be conceptualized as differing along a continuum of elaborativeness (Fivush & Fromhoff, 1988; Haden, 1998; Hudson, 1990; McCabe & Peterson, 1991; Reese, Haden, & Fivush, 1993; Welch-Ross, 1997). Some mothers talk a great deal about past events with their children, providing complex and elaborated accounts, whereas other mothers talk less frequently and in less detail about past events, providing little information overall. Mothers are consistent in the level of elaborativeness, both across spans of a few weeks (McCabe & Peterson, 1991), and a few years (Reese, Haden, & Fivush, 1993). Mothers are also consistent in their level of elaborativeness across siblings, implying that reminiscing style is a function of the mother's discourse rather than a reflection of the child's abilities.

Longitudinal studies indicate that an elaborative maternal reminiscing style facilitates children's developing autobiographical skills. McCabe and Peterson (1991) found that children of mothers who were highly elaborative with their young preschoolers recalled more information 18 months later than children of less elaborative mothers. In the most comprehensive longitudinal data set collected, Reese et al. (1993) followed families across a 2½-year period during the preschool years. They found that maternal level of elaboration early in development, when children were just 40- and 46-months of age, was related to children's ability to recall episodes from their past when the children were 5, 6, and 8 years old. However, children's memory abilities at the earlier period were not significantly related either to their own subsequent memory abilities or to maternal level of elaboration later in development (see figure 18.1 showing these long-term correlations). These data clearly indicate that mothers who are highly elaborative early in development facilitate their children's developing skills to recall their past experiences in detailed episodic form.

However, reporting the past is not simply a matter of recalling many details; memory must be organized coherently for sharing with others. Children not only learn to provide details in their episodic reports through parent-guided conversations, they also learn how to structure their memories into organized narratives. The recounted event must be placed in

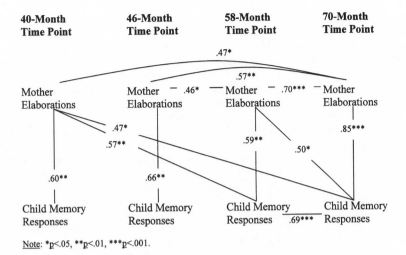

Figure 18.1 Cross-lagged correlations among maternal elaborations and children's memory responses.

an appropriate spatial-temporal context in order to orient the listener, and most important, personal narratives must include evaluative information that conveys why this event is interesting, important, and ultimately memorable (Labov, 1982; Peterson & McCabe, 1982). Evaluative information provides the subjective perspective on the event: why this event is personally significant and worth relating to others. Children also learn these narrative devices for recounting their past in parent-guided conversations.

In reminiscing with their young children, mothers display individual differences in their narrative focus; some mothers emphasize orienting information, telling who was there and where and when the event occurred. Other mothers seem more focused on evaluative information. They include a great deal of discussion of the emotional aspects of the event, what people thought and felt, and use linguistic devices to emphasize and intensify the recall. Mothers who focus on orienting information early in the preschool years have children who provide a great deal of orientation in their own independent personal narratives later in the preschool years (Peterson, 1990; Haden, Haine, & Fivush, 1997). In contrast, children of mothers who focus on evaluative information come to tell highly evaluated personal narratives later in the preschool years (Fivush, 1991; Haden et al., 1997). Again, the longitudinal patterns indicate that the direction of effects over time is from mother to child, and not from child to mother.

Thus children learn how to organize their personal experiences into coherent narratives, and which aspects of narrative organization to emphasize in their retellings, through participating in parent-guided reminiscing.

There is also growing evidence that providing emotional evaluation of past events is learned through joint reminiscing (Adams, Kuebli, Boyle, & Fivush, 1995; Kuebli, Butler, & Fivush, 1995). Those mothers who focus more on emotional reactions have children who also come to incorporate emotional reactions into their own personal narratives. Emotional aspects of the past are particularly important because they move personal narratives from stories about what happened to stories about what happened to *me*. It is emotions that link past events to self-concept, to become a part of autobiography.

Individual and Cultural Differences

The social-interactive perspective supported in the research reviewed here implies that there will be enduring individual differences in autobiographical memory resulting from differential parental scaffolding of reminiscing early in development. The longitudinal data support this prediction within white middle-class populations in the United States. In addition, there is growing evidence of gender and cultural differences in autobiography that may also result from differential socialization.

A great deal of research has established that, as adults, females' autobiographical narratives are longer, more detailed, and more emotionally laden than are males' (Cowan & Davidson, 1984; Friedman & Pines, 1991; Ross & Holmberg, 1990). Relatedly, parents tend to talk in more elaborated, embellished, and emotional ways when reminiscing with preschool daughters than with preschool sons (Reese et al., 1996; Adams et al., 1995; see Fivush, 1997, for a review). Differences between girls' and boys' autobiographical narratives are already apparent during the preschool years. Girls' autobiographical narratives are more detailed, more coherent, and more emotionally saturated than are boys' (Adams et al., 1995; Buckner & Fivush, 1998; Fivush, Haden, & Adam, 1995).

Perhaps most provocative, adult females have an earlier age of first memory than do males (Cowan & Davidson, 1984; Friedman & Pines, 1991). As adults, most of us have great difficulty recalling events that occurred before the age of about 3½, the phenomenon labeled childhood amnesia (see Pillemer & White, 1989, for a review), but age of earliest memory is as much as 6 months earlier on average for females than for males. The explanation for the paucity of early memories remains controversial, but we believe a critical component of the explanation is that of social interaction (Fivush, 1991; Nelson, 1993a). The reasoning is as follows: memories of episodes occurring before the advent of the ability to discuss specific events with others will be difficult to recall as adults, because these memories will not have the detailed, coherent character that verbal narratives allow (Fivush & Haden, 1997; Pillemer & White, 1989). Because females engage in richer, more elaborated, and coherent joint reminiscing as young children than do males, they can be expected to have an earlier age of first memory, and as noted, the evidence supports this supposition.

Related to this evidence are cross-cultural differences in autobiographical memories, specifically the findings that members of Western cultures have earlier first memories than members of Eastern cultures. Indeed, age of earliest memory for many Asian people is as late as 5 or 6 years of age (Mullen, 1994). Again, differences in early parent-child reminiscing may account for part of this difference. Several studies have indicated substantial differences in the content and structure of parent-child conversations between American and Taiwanese dyads (Miller, Wiley, Fung, &

Liang, 1997), American and Japanese dyads (Minami & McCabe, 1991), and American and Korean dyads (Han, Leichtman, & Wang, 1998). In a study focusing explicitly on this issue, Mullen (1994) confirmed that Asians have a substantially later age of first memory than do Americans, and further found that American mother-preschooler dyads engaged in talk about past experiences three times as frequently as did Asian mother-preschooler dyads (Mullen & Yi, 1995). Although this research does not establish a direct link between early parent-child reminiscing and the establishment of enduring, accessible autobiographical memories, the relations are in the direction expected from the socialization theory.

Overall, the ways in which parents reminisce with their preschool children have profound influences on children's developing autobiographical memories. But it is not just the way events are talked about in retrospect that influences children's memories; the way in which events are talked about as they are occurring also plays a role in how young children come to understand and represent those events.

Language Organizes Events

In a seminal study, Tessler and Nelson (1994) examined 4-year-old children's memories of a visit to a museum as a function of what the mother and child talked about as they toured the exhibits. Children did not recall anything about objects or activities that were only mentioned by the mother, or only by the child; only information jointly discussed was recalled. Similar findings were obtained in a second study in which mothers and children went on a photo-taking excursion together. Recent research (Haden, Didow, Ornstein, & Eckerman, 1997) replicates this effect with 2-year-old children; although their recall is quite sparse overall, they are much more likely to recall information about objects that are jointly discussed and manipulated than objects attended to by only one member of the dyad.

What is it about language during an event that facilitates memory? One possibility is that by talking about particular aspects of the event rather than others, these aspects are attended to more closely and therefore better recalled. It is also possible that there are no differences in what is actually remembered about the event, but children select to recount only those aspects that were verbally highlighted during the event. That is, language during the event may not change the memory representation but only the verbal report. Some evidence from the Tessler and Nelson study 2 suggests that this may be the case. Research by Pipe (1996), however, implies that language affects the organization of the memory representation. In Pipe's study, 5-year-old children participated in a novel "pirate" event. All children experienced exactly the same activities, but for some children the event was fully narrated as the event unfolded ("Now we are going to make the magic map. First we have to mix these colors . . . " etc.) while some children were provided only "empty" language ("Now we're going to do this."). Children were subsequently asked to recall the event verbally and to act it out after returning to the pirate room where all the objects were available. Children in the narrated condition recalled more information verbally, had fewer intrusions, and their reports were more accurately organized than children without the narrative. Most important, the same effects held for reenactment. Having a coherent verbal narrative accompanying the event as it was experienced helped children form a more organized memory representation than simply going through the actions.

The findings that language about past experiences affects recall of the memory of those episodes, and that language during the experience also affects the resulting memory for the episode, raises the question as to whether language about an anticipated future event might also affect not only the experience itself but also the subsequent memory. This question has been relatively neglected in memory development research, although educational and socialization practices seem to assume positive effects of preparation for ensuing novel experiences. Teachers and parents often take great pains to talk to children about what is to come (Benson, 1996). In a study focused on pre-bed talk, Nelson (1989) found that future-oriented talk was the most frequent by parents, organized around the topics of what would happen the next day, what the child would have for breakfast, and so on. Yet we know little about the effects of such talk on comprehension or memory for the subsequent experience. Clearly, this is an area ripe for investigation to determine at what age and under what conditions talk before an experi-

enced event affects immediate and long-term recall, and in what way.

As the research on past and present talk has documented, language appears to be a potent tool for organizing memories. Through language, memories for specific experiences take on a more organized, coherent, and therefore accessible form. Young children seem to be dependent on adults to help them construct these more organized respresentations. Children's own language skills are equally important, and the way in which an event can be talked about by the child when it occurs plays an important role in the child's subsequent ability to recall that event verbally, even early in the language development process. Bauer and Wewerka (1997) taught 20-month-old children a series of novel action sequences; all children learned the sequences easily and could recall them in action one year later. But children with more advanced language skills at 20 months were better able to recall the event verbally a year later than children less advanced in language at the time of learning.

In a different study, Peterson and Ridoux (1998) assessed young children's memories for physical injuries requiring emergency room treatment (mostly lacerations requiring sutures); children under the age of 20 months at time of injury were unable to talk about the event when it occurred and remained unable to recall it verbally over a two-year period. Children over the age of about 26 months could talk about the event when it occurred and recalled it verbally in great detail two years later. The critical group were children between 20 and 26 months of age, some of whom had the verbal skills to recall the event verbally when it occurred and some of whom did not. Of this group, only those children who could provide a verbal report of the experience could recall it verbally at 4 years of age. In a study over a longer delay period, Pillemer, Picariello, and Pruett (1994) assessed preschoolers' memories for a fire alarm event both immediately and seven years later. Only those children who could provide a coherent narrative of the experience at time of occurrence were still able to recall it after seven years.

Thus, although still preliminary, this research suggests that the ability to report verbally an event at the time of occurrence is critical for subsequent verbal recall of the event. However, the event may be retained in nonverbal form; Bauer and Wewerka (1977) report that even those children who could not verbally report the event sequences could act them out, and Peterson and Ridoux (1998) document nonverbal recall of injury and treatment by many of the children in their study. Nonetheless, on the basis of the Pipe (1996) findings discussed earlier, it may be anticipated that even the nonverbal memories will not be as well organized without language to provide structure.

It seems reasonable to conclude that children's ability to discuss an event at time of occurrence and the ways in which adults help children to discuss that event interact in producing a specific memory representation. The proposal is that the ability to verbalize an event when it occurs enables children to engage in joint reminiscing about that event, which then affects the way in which that event is represented. Events occurring before children can verbalize cannot be jointly encoded and jointly discussed, and thus will not be subject to verbal rehearsal and organization into a narrative form. Once children are able to interact verbally in somewhat more sophisticated ways, they begin the process of forming narratively organized, verbally accessible autobiographical memories, and thereafter may no longer depend on joint remembering for extended recall.

How Does Language Affect Memory?

The preceding section has stressed that talking about experiences by the child and with others has evident effects on the subsequent memory for that event. This is clearly a main vehicle through which socialization affects memory. The mediating factor implied has been organization of the memory, in particular a coherent narrative organization. There are other possible direct effects of language on memory that may operate in different ways at different points in the socialization process. The simplest effect may derive from attaching a label to some aspect of the experienced event, or the whole event, that serves as a cue for recalling a memory (Bauer & Wewerka, 1997). Another effect may derive from the use of language by the adult to draw attention to memorable aspects of the experience itself, and thus to pave the way for a more detailed elaborate representation. The fact that shared talk between parent and child was a prerequisite for remembering details of an event by 4-year-olds in Tessler's study (Tessler & Nilson, 1994) supports this supposition.

The long-term effect of talk about a shared personal experience may constitute the verbal equivalent of reinstatement through reactivation. Reinstatement of a learned association is a well-known process that extends a memory for a period of time longer than that over which it would otherwise be forgotten. Studied in animal learning, reinstatement has been demonstrated in infants in a series of studies by Rovee-Collier and her students (see chapter 17) and demonstrated in toddlers by Fivush and Hamond (1989) and Sheffield and Hudson (1994). Reinstatement, in effect, "brings back" some part of an experience (or a representation of a learned association). The implication of the reinstatement effect is that the "bringing back" reactivates the event in part or whole. It has been frequently speculated that talking about an experience might have the same effect, reactivating in essence the original experience itself on a conscious mental level rather than on an action level. Many reports in the memory development literature suggest this possibility; for example, a verbal interview about an experience leads to greater recall after a delay than other treatments such as watching a video or exposure to the original context (Ornstein, Larus, & Clubb, 1991). This finding suggests that verbalizing the event was more successful in bringing it to mind, and thus prolonging it in memory. Partial reenactment has been shown (Sheffield & Hudson, 1994) to increase delayed recall for parts of the event not reenacted as well as the parts that were. Similarly, verbalizing a partial account is expected to increase delayed recall for both the recapitulated portion and the unrehearsed portion in comparison to a no-treatment control. This outcome is expected on the grounds that the entire episode is brought to mind on the occasion of the verbal reinstatement, in effect enabling a reexperience of it as a whole event.

If talking about an experience is effective as a verbal reinstatement, it could well serve as the underlying process through which episodic memories come to be established as a semipermanent part of long-term autobiographical memory. In this way a basic memory process (reinstatement) comes to be served by the specific human capacity for verbalization, in addition to other forms of reinstatement, such as exposure to the context of an original learning experience or the reenactment of a previously learned procedure. It is important to this argument that language can be used not only between people but also for oneself; thus reminding oneself of an experience may have the same effect as talking about it with others. Self-reminding is a socially learned process (Vygotsky, 1986), established during the preschool years, a process that may account for the eventual establishment of an autobiographical memory system independent of its social origins (Nelson, 1993b).

Verbal reinstatement alone, however, could not establish autobiographical memory. Personal relevance of an episode is a necessary component of one's self-history, which is reflected in narrative coherence and the emotional valence reestablished or newly emphasized through talk or self-reflection. Autobiographical memory thus serves two related functions: it establishes an enduring semipermanent memory system that serves as a self-history, and as a consequence it constitutes a continuous self-concept deriving meaning from the personal past and future as well as the present. This concept of a self in and through time is, so far as we know, a unique characteristic of human life, not available to nonhuman animals (Nelson, 1997).

Socialization beyond Autobiographical Memory

We began this account with a brief overview of functions of memory at different periods of history and for different purposes, reflected in social practices. This sketch emphasized learning the practice of memory, increasing skills, and acquiring strategies to improve capacity and retention of culturally significant material. In contrast, the research reviewed has concentrated on children's learning to organize and verbally structure personal memories of self-experience. This review has enabled us to document the very strong effects of the process of engaging in the practice of remembering, albeit the content of the memory is of personal rather than broader cultural significance. The resulting personal memory histories, however, have their own cultural significance: as socialized individuals we are expected to remember significant events of our lives, and we are expected to remember important details of episodes that we have experienced—for example, for the purpose of supplying reliable testimony in judicial investigations.

There is a certain irony, however, in the emphasis on learning in relation to the personal function of memory, which has traditionally been viewed as relatively automatic, at least after the age of about 4 years. Most theory and evidence with regard to memory practice in psychology and education prior to the last decade has focused on learning to use strategies to organize and recall material with no particular personal relevance and without personally relevant context, presented for the specific purpose of learning and remembering. Often the favored material was (and is) a list of words, but the expectation has been that the results of the research are generalizable to other materials, such as those related to knowledge domains taught in schools. Do the kinds of practices that parents engage in with their young children learning to remember episodes from their own lives have relevance for this kind of memory practice?

Children's use of strategies include primarily organizing material for later recall, rehearsal of material, and the use of associations to provide meaningful cues. Research showing that autobiographical memory is a learned skill, socialized through interactions with adults, implies that memory strategies may be acquired in similar ways and be subject to similar variations. A recent review of strategy research from the social-cultural perspective provides evidence that social and cultural values influence the extent to which the standard findings on strategies can be generalized (Ellis, 1997).

Although the focus of most of the research reviewed here has been on facilitative effects on memory of narratives of personal experience, parents also focus on other sorts of organizing functions. For example, in Tessler's study (Tessler & Nelson, 1994), some mothers made narrative comments on scenes while others (termed "paradigmatic" by Tessler) pointed out significant details of objects and how certain categories of items go together. This style of interaction, differentiating a scene into its parts and emphasizing its relation to a knowledge domain, provides a different model of organization for the child, and mothers who adopted this style tended to expect their young children to be able to answer questions about visual details and actions of objects rather than about the motivations and activities of people. This emphasis fits naturally with the school stress on categorization and logical composition important in many school tasks. Moreover, as Tessler found, parental style of emphasis on one pattern or another was reflected in the pattern of recall by their children at later interviews.

Lange and Carroll (1997) carried out a study testing the predictions from the Tessler and Nelson (1994) study that narrative-style interactions with mothers might carry over to other task domains, in particular to the understanding of stories and other narratives in school tasks. They compared performance of the 5-year-old children on narrative and paradigmatic laboratory tasks and found differential performance, with narrative-style children performing well on story tasks and also on factual tasks but less well on object-naming and location tasks. Although preliminary, this differential pattern is significant in showing transfer of differentiated performance from personal memory to memory for text, both narrative and factual, and differential memory skills by children with different experiential socializing patterns.

Some evidence from an extensive analysis of cross-sectional and longitudinal data by Schneider and Weinert (1995) suggests that children may display differentiated memory performance patterns that could reflect influences of different socializing styles. For example, comparing performance on text recall and word lists among third graders, not a single child was consistently classified as a low, medium, or high achiever on both types of tasks. The Munich group (Schneider & Weinert, 1995) concludes that there is little evidence of a single memory function that is exhibited across tasks. Intraindividual performance differences of this kind may reflect differences in socialization practices emphasizing memory for one kind of information rather than another, as described here, that may interact with individual dispositions, habits, or capacities. These findings suggest the need for further investigations into the influence of these factors on school performance, as well as for studies of domain-dependent memory performance differences.

Conclusion

Studies of socialization of personal memory in the preschool years, resulting in long-lasting effects on autobiographical memory, have demonstrated the significance of cultural practices for memory development. Individual and cultural differences in memory reflect different emphases in socialization practices, as well as individual competence. The conclusions drawn from the study of these practices in relation to personal memory in the pre-school years cannot be generalized to later development in different domains without further study. However, they suggest the importance of learning to remember in different ways, a topic that deserves increased attention in both developmental and educational research. These directions may require revisiting research on strategies and metamemory that have primarily been seen as individual differences (c.f. Ellis, 1997). A clear implication is that there is no such thing as "natural" human memory: what we observe in development as early as the toddler years is "cultural" memory shaped to serve different purposes according to different organizational schemes.

References

Adams, S., Kuebli, J., Boyle, P., & Fivush, R. (1995). Gender differences in parent-child conversations about past emotions: A longitudinal investigation. *Sex Roles, 33*, 309–323.

Bauer, P. J., Hertsgaard, L. A., & Dow, G. A. (1994). After 8 months have passed: Long-term recall of events by 1- to 2-year-old children. *Memory, 2*, 353–382.

Bauer, P. J., & Mandler, J. M. (1989). One thing follows another: Effects of temporal structure on one- to two-year-olds' recall of events. *Developmental Psychology, 25*, 197–206.

Bauer, P., & Wewerka, S. (1997). Saying is revealing: Verbal expression of event memory in the transition from infancy to early childhood. In P. van den Broek, P. J. Bauer, & T. Bourg (Eds.), *Developmental spans in event comprehension and representation: Bridging fictional and actual events* (pp. 139–168). Hillsdale, NJ: Erlbaum.

Benson, J. B. (1996). The origins of future-orientation in the everyday lives of 9- to 36-mo-old infants. In M. M. Haith, J. B. Benson, R. J. Roberts, & B. Pennington (Eds.), *The development of future-oriented processes* (pp. 375–408). Chicago: University of Chicago Press.

Buckner, J., & Fivush, R. (1998). Gender and self in children's autobiographical narratives. *Applied Cognitive Psychology, 12*, 407–429.

Carruthers, M. J. (1990). *The book of memory: A study of memory in medieval culture.* Cambridge: Cambridge University Press.

Cowan, N., & Davidson, G. (1984). Salient childhood memories. *Journal of Genetic Psychology, 145*, 101–107.

Donald, M. (1991). *Origins of the modern mind.* Cambridge MA: Harvard University Press.

Eisenberg, A. (1985). Learning to describe past experience in conversation. *Discourse Processes, 8,* 177–204.

Ellis, S. (1997). Strategy choice in sociocultural context. *Developmental Review, 17* 490–524.

Fairbank, J. K. (1957). *Chinese thought and institutions.* Chicago: Chicago University Press.

Fivush, R. (1991). The social construction of personal narratives. *Merrill-Palmer Quarterly, 37,* 59–82.

Fivush, R. (1997). Gendered narratives: Elaboration, structure and emotion in parent-child reminscing across the preschool years. In C. P. Thompson, D. J. Herrmann, D. Bruce, J. D. Read, D. G. Payne, & M. P. Toglia (Eds.), *Autobiographical memory: Theoretical and applied perspectives* (pp. 79–104). Hillsdale, NJ: Erlbaum.

Fivush, R., & Fromhoff, F. (1988). Style and structure in mother-child conversations about the past. *Discourse Processes, 11,* 337–355.

Fivush, R., Gray, J. T., & Fromhoff, F. A. (1987). Two year olds' talk about the past. *Cognitive Development, 2,* 393–409.

Fivush, R., & Haden, C. A. (1997). Narrating and representing experience: Preschoolers' developing autobiographical recounts. In P. van den Broek, P. A. Bauer, & T. Bourg (Eds.), *Developmental spans in event comprehension and representation: Bridging fictional and actual events* (pp. 169–198). Hillsdale, NJ: Erlbaum.

Fivush, R., Haden, C. A., & Adams, S. (1995). Structure and coherence of preschoolers' personal narratives over time: Implications for childhood amnesia. *Journal of Experimental Child Psychology, 60,* 32–56.

Fivush, R., & Hamond, N. R. (1989). Time and again: Effects of repetition and retention interval on two year olds' event recall. *Journal of Experimental Child Psychology, 47,* 259–273.

Fivush, R., & Hudson, J. A. (1990). *Knowing and remembering in young children.* New York: Cambridge University Press.

Friedman, A., & Pines, A. (1991). Sex differences in gender-related childhood memories. *Sex Roles, 25,* 25–32.

Glenberg, A. M. (1997). What memory is for. *Behavioral and Brain Sciences, 20,* 1–56.

Haden, C. A. (1998). Reminiscing with different children: Relating maternal stylistic consistency and sibling similarity in talk about the past. *Developmental Psychology, 34,* 99–114.

Haden, C. A., Didow, S. M., Ornstein, P. A., & Eckerman, C. O. (1997, April). Mother-child talk about the here-and now: Linkages to subsequent remembering. In E. Reese (Chair), *Adult-child reminiscing: Theory and practice.* Symposium paper presented at the meetings of the Society for Research in Child Development, Washington, DC.

Haden, C. A., Haine, R., & Fivush, R. (1997). Developing narrative structure in parent-child reminiscing across the preschool years. *Developmental Psychology, 33,* 295–307.

Han, J. J., Leichtman, M. D., & Wang, Q. (1998). Autobiographical memory in Korean, Chinese, and American Children. *Developmental Psychology, 34,* 701–713.

Hudson, J. A. (1990). The emergence of autobiographic memory in mother-child conversation. In R. Fivush & J. A. Hudson (Eds.), *Knowing and remembering in young children* (pp. 166–196). New York: Cambridge University Press.

Hudson, J. A., & Shapiro, L. (1991). Effects of task and topic on children's narratives. In A. McCabe & C. Peterson (Eds.), *New directions in developing narrative structure* (pp. 89–136). Hillsdale, NJ: Erlbaum.

Kuebli, J., Butler, S., & Fivush, R. (1995). Mother-child talk about past events: Relations of maternal language and child gender over time. *Cognition and Emotion, 9,* 265–293.

Labov, W. (1982). Speech actions and reaction in personal narrative. In D. Tannen (Ed.), *Analyzing discourse: Text and talk* (pp. 219–247). Washington, DC: Georgetown University Press.

Lange, G., & Carroll, D. E. (1997). Relationships between mother-child interaction styles and children's laboratory memory for narrative and non-narrative materials. Paper presented at the Society for Research in Child Development biennial meeting Washington, DC, April 1997.

McCabe, A., & Peterson, C. (1991). Getting the story: A longitudinal study of parental styles in eliciting narratives and developing narrative skill. In A. McCabe & C. Peterson (Eds.), *Developing narrative structure* (pp. 217–253). Hillsdale, NJ: Erlbaum.

McDonough, L., & Mandler, J. M. (1994). Very long-term recall in infants: Infantile amnesia reconsidered. *Memory 2,* 339–352.

Miller, P. J., Wiley, A. R., Fung, H., & Liang, C-H. (1997). Personal storytelling as a medium of socialization in Chinese and American families. *Child Development, 68,* 557–568.

Minami, M., & McCabe, A. (1991). *Haiku* as a discourse regulation device: A stanza analysis of Japanese children's personal narratives. *Language in Society, 20,* 577–599.

Mullen, M. K. (1994). Earliest recollections of childhood: A demographic analysis. *Cognition, 52,* 55–79.

Mullen, M. K., & Yi, S. (1995). The cultural context of talk about the past: Implications for the development of autobiographical memory. *Cognitive Development, 10,* 407–420.

Nelson, K. (1986). *Event knowledge: Structure and function in development.* Hillsdale, NJ: Erlbaum.

Nelson, K. (Ed.). (1989). *Narratives from the crib.* Cambridge, MA: Harvard University Press.

Nelson, K. (1993a). Explaining the emergence of autobiographical memory in early childhood. In A. Collins, M. Conway, S. Gathercole, & P. Morris (Eds.), *Theories of memory.* Hillsdale, NJ: Erlbaum.

Nelson, K. (1993b). The psychological and social origins of autobiographical memory. *Psychological Science, 4,* 1–8.

Nelson, K. (1994). Long-term retention of memory for preverbal experience: Evidence and implications. *Memory, 2,* 467–475.

Nelson, K. (1997). Finding oneself in time. In J. G. Snodgrass & R. L. Thompson (Eds.), *The self across psychology: self-recognition, self-awareness and the self-concept.* Annals of the New York Academy of Sciences, 818. New York: New York Academy of Sciences.

Norman, D. A. (1976). *Memory and attention: An introduction to human information processing* (2nd ed.). New York: John Wiley.

O'Connell, B., & Girard, A. (1985). Scripts and scraps: The development of sequential understanding. *Child Development, 56,* 671–681.

Ornstein, P. A., Larus, D. M., & Clubb, P. A. (1991). Understanding children's testimony: Implications of research on the development of memory. *Annals of child development* (Vol. 8; pp. 145–176). London: Jessica Kingsley Publishers.

Peterson, C. (1990). The who, when and where of early narratives. *Journal of Child Language, 17,* 433–455.

Peterson, C., & McCabe, A. (1982). *Developmental psycholinguistics: Three ways of looking at a narrative.* New York: Plenum.

Peterson, C., & McCabe, A. (1992). Parental styles of narrative elicitation: Effect on children's narrative structure and content. *First Language, 12,* 299–321.

Peterson, C., & Rideout, R. (1998). Memory for medical emergencies experienced by 1- and 2-year-olds. *Developmental Psychology, 34,* 1059–1072.

Pillemer, D. B., Picariello, M. L., & Pruett, J. C. (1994). Very long term memories of a salient preschool event. *Journal of Applied Cognitive Psychology, 8,* 95–106.

Pillemer, D., & White, S. H. (1989). Childhood events recalled by children and adults. In H. W. Reese (Ed.), *Advances in child development and behavior* (Vol. 22; pp. 297–340). New York: Academic Press.

Pipe, M. E. (1996). Telling it like it is, was, and will be: The influence of narrative on children's event memory. Paper presented at the Second International Conference on Memory. Abano, Italy, July.

Pressley, M., & Schneider, W. (1986). *Memory development between 2 and 20.* New York: Springer-Verlag.

Reese, E., Haden, C. A., & Fivush, R. (1993). Mother-child conversations about the past: Relationships of style and memory over time. *Cognitive Development, 8,* 403–430.

Reese, E., Haden, C. A., & Fivush, R. (1996). Mothers, fathers, daughters, sons: Gender differences in autobiographical recall. *Research on Language and Social Interaction, 29,* 27–56.

Ross, M., & Holmberg, D. (1990). Recounting the past: Gender differences in the recall of events in the history of a close relationship. In M. P. Zanna & J. M. Olson (Eds.), *The Ontario Symposium: Vol 6. Self-inference processes* (pp. 135–152). Hillsdale, NJ: Erlbaum.

Rovee-Collier, C. (1995). Time windows in cognitive development. *Developmental Psychology, 31,* 147–169.

Rubin, D. C. (1995). *Memory in oral traditions.* New York: Oxford University Press.

Sachs, J. (1983). Talking about the there and then: The emergence of displaced reference in parent-child discourse. In K. E. Nelson (Ed.), *Children's language* (Vol. 4; pp. 1–28). Hillsdale, NJ: Erlbaum.

Schacter, D. L., & Moscovitch, M. (1984). Infants, amnesics, and dissociable memory systems. In M. Moscovitch (Ed.), *Infant memory: Its relation to normal and pathological memory in humans and other animals* (pp. 173–216). New York: Plenum Press.

Schank, R. C., & Abelson, R. P. (1977). *Scripts, Plans, goals, and understanding.* Hillsdale, NJ: Erlbaum.

Schneider, W., & Bjorklund, D. (1998). Memory. In W. Damon (Ed.), *Handbook of Child Psychology, 5th Edition,* (D. Kuhn & R. S. Siegler (Eds.)) *Volume 2: Cognition, perception and language* (pp. 467–522). New York: John Wiley.

Schneider, W., & Weinert, F. E. (1995). Memory development during early and middle childhood: Findings from the Munich Longitudinal Study (LOGIC). In F. E. Weinert & W. Schneider (Eds.), *Memory performance and competencies* (pp. 263–279). Mahwah, NJ: Erlbaum.

Sheffield, E. G., & Hudson, J. A. (1994). Reactivation of toddlers' event memory. *Memory, 2,* 447–466.

Tessler, M., & Nelson, K. (1994). Making memories: The influence of joint encoding on later recall by young children. *Consciousness and Cognition, 3,* 307–326.

Tomasello, M., Kruger, A. C., & Ratner, H. H. (1993). Cultural learning. *Behavioral and Brain Sciences, 16,* 495–552.

Tulving, E. (1983). *Elements of episodic memory.* New York: Oxford University Press.

Vygotsky, L. (1986). *Thought and Language.* Cambridge MA: MIT Press.

Welch-Ross, M. (1997). Mother-child participation in conversations about the past: Relations to preschoolers' theory of mind. *Developmental Psychology, 33,* 618–629.

19

Memory and Theory of Mind

JOSEF PERNER

"Theory of mind" is primarily a label for the research area that investigates the conceptual system that underlies our ability to impute mental states (what we *know, think, want, feel*, etc.) to others and ourselves. The study of these concepts is essential for our understanding of memory insofar as memory is not just storage of information, but is also dependent on knowledge of our own information-storage processes. In Tulving and Madigan's (1970) words we should "start looking for ways of experimentally studying and incorporating into theories . . . of memory one of the truly unique characteristics of human memory: its knowledge of its own knowledge" (p. 477). To have such higher order knowledge one needs a concept of knowledge and other mental states. Memory development should, therefore, be seen in the light of the acquisition of mental concepts—that is, the child's growing theory of mind.

What Is Our Theory of Mind?

Our theory of mind is constituted by our everyday mental concepts. The analysis of these concepts is influenced by traditions in analytical philosophy of mind. They are characterized as propositional attitudes (Russell, 1919) —that is, they describe a relation between an organism (person) and a proposition—for ex-

ample, the sentence, "Max *knows* that the chocolate is in the cupboard" describes knowing as a relation between Max and the proposition "the chocolate is in the cupboard."

Organism —— Attitude ——→ Proposition
   Max   knows   the chocolate
                                is in the
                                cupboard

Since cognitive science has taken on board this commonsense view of the mind, an important question is how such a relationship to a proposition can be implemented. The *representational theory of mind* (RTM; Field, 1978; Fodor, 1978) assumes that a propositional attitude consists in holding a representation of the proposition and that this representation plays a certain functional role in the economy of mental states. This can be best illustrated with the two core concepts: belief and desire. These are core concepts, since knowing what someone believes (thinks) to be the case (e.g., Max thinking the chocolate is in the cupboard and thinking that going there will get the chocolate into his possession) and what that person desires (wants) (e.g., Max wanting the chocolate to be in his possession) allows us to make a behavioral prediction that Max will approach the cupboard. This kind of inference is known since Aristotle as the practical syllogism.

Searle (1983, after Anscombe, 1957) points out that these two states are mirror images in terms of causal direction and direction of fit. The function of a belief is to be caused by reality and the believed proposition should match reality. For instance, the chocolate being in the cupboard should be responsible for Max's believing that the chocolate is in the cupboard (world to mind causation) and the proposition "the chocolate is in the cupboard" should thus match the relevant state of affairs in the world (mind should fit world). The function of desire (want) is to cause a change in the world (mind to world causation) so that the world conforms to the desired proposition (world should fit mind)—for example, if Max wants the chocolate to be in the cupboard, then this desire should cause action leading to a change of the chocolate's location such that it conforms to what Max desires.

This trivial-sounding example does highlight the important point that our mental states are not represented but are constituted by the functions that the represented propositions are to fulfill. It also serves to highlight some important distinctions.

Three Important Distinctions

First vs. Third Person

One important distinction is between first-person and third-person attribution of mental states. A third-person attribution is an attribution to another person and a first-person attribution is one to myself. For instance, if Max erroneously believes that the chocolate is still in the cupboard (because he didn't see that it was unexpectedly put into the drawer), then a third-person observer will attribute a false belief to Max. In contrast, Max himself will make a first-person attribution of knowledge to himself. The observer can capture this difference between her own and Max's subjective view by the second-order attribution that Max thinks he knows where the chocolate is. This is useful to keep in mind when it comes to false memories. Since a memory can only be a recollection of something that actually occurred, a false memory is not a memory by third-person attribution, although it is by first-person attribution.

Sense and Reference

A related second point has to do with Frege's (1892/1960) distinction between sense and reference. Since mental states involve representations, they connect us to objects and events in the real (or a possible) world. Famously, Oedipus knew and married Iocaste (referent: a particular person), but he did not know or marry her *as* his mother but *as* an unrelated queen (sense: how Iocaste was presented to Oedipus' mind). Thus, in third-person parlance we can say that Oedipus married his mother if we use the expression "his mother" to pick out (refer to) the individual whom he married without implying that he knew Iocaste under that description. In first-person description of the event Oedipus would not have used the descriptor "my mother." These distinctions are useful to keep in mind when discussing infants' ability to remember particular events: Whenever a memory trace of a unique event can be demonstrated, then one can conclude (in third-person parlance) that the infant remembers that particular event. However, one cannot conclude that the event is remembered by the infant (in first-person parlance) *as* a particular event—that is, that the infant makes cognitive distinctions that represent that event *as* a particular event.

Having vs. Representing a Mental State

The third important distinction is that between *being* in a mental state (or *having* an attitude) and *representing* that mental state. For understanding or knowing that a person is in a mental state, or to reflect on one's own mental states, one has to be able to represent that state. In order to be able to represent a state, one needs a concept of that state—that is, a rich enough theory of mind. The study of how children acquire the requisite theory of mind is therefore essential for our understanding of how children come to understand memory. Furthermore, since some memorial states are reflective or self-referential, children need a theory of mind for *being* in such states or *having* such memories.

Why We Need a Theory of Mind for Memory: Consciousness

We probably do not need a theory of mind for implicit memory, but for explicit memory we do, since "explicit memory is revealed when performance on a task requires conscious recollection of previous experiences." (Schacter, 1987). To be conscious of a fact one requires to be also aware of the state with which one beholds that fact. The higher-order-thought theories of consciousness make this their core claim (Armstrong, 1980; Rosenthal, 1986). For instance, if one *sees* a state of affairs X (e.g., that the chocolate is in the cupboard), then this seeing is a first-order mental state (attitude). To be conscious of this state of affairs means, according to theory, that one entertains a second-order thought about the seeing—that is, the second-order thought represents the first-order seeing. A weaker version does not require that one has to entertain the second-order thought, but only that one has to have the potential for having the second-order thought (Carruthers, 1996). That some such condition must be true can be seen from the following consideration: Could it ever be that I can genuinely claim that I am consciously aware of the chocolate being in the cupboard, but claim ignorance of the first-order mental state by which I behold this state of affairs— that is, by claiming that I have no clue as to whether I see, or just think of, or want the chocolate being in the cupboard?

The important point of these conceptual analyses is that to be conscious of some fact requires some minimal concept of knowledge or of some perceptual state like seeing. Unfortunately, there is no clear evidence when children understand a minimal state of this sort. There is some evidence of understanding (mother's) emotional reactions and seeing (direction of gaze) in the first year of life (see Perner, 1991, chap. 6; Baldwin & Moses, 1996; Gopnik & Meltzoff, 1997, for summaries and discussion of problems of interpretation). There is also some recent evidence that between 8 and 12 months children might be inferring people's intentions to grasp an object from where that person looks (Spelke, Phillips, & Woodward, 1995) and even between 5 to 9 months from how a person touches an object (seemingly intentional or accidentally, (Woodward 1998),[1] 1 and by 18 months (where children's understanding of mental phenomena seems to flourish in general) children imitate people's intended actions even when they observe a failed attempt (Meltzoff, 1995a) and they understand differences in preferences (e.g., that someone else can prefer cauliflower over biscuits, Repacholi & Gopnik, 1997).

Evidence that children distinguish their knowledge from ignorance is available at a relatively late age. Povinelli, Perilloux, and Bierschwale (1993) asked children to look for a sticker under one of three cups. Children were first trained to look under the cup at which the experimenter had pointed. After some training even the youngest were able to do this. When asked to look without the experimenter pointing, an interesting developmental difference emerged. Children older than 2 years and 4 months acted without hesitation when they knew which cup the sticker was under, but hesitated noticeably when—in the absence of the experimenter's pointing—they had to guess where it was. Interestingly this is also the age at which children start using the phrase "I don't know" (Shatz, Wellman, & Silber, 1983). In contrast, children younger than that showed no comparable difference in reaction time. This may indicate that young 2-year-olds do not yet reflect on what they do and do not know.

So, theory of mind research is not yet able to give a good guideline for when infants might develop explicit, conscious memories. Memory development may help out on this point. Meltzoff (1985, 1995b) demonstrated that 14-month-old infants can reenact a past event (e.g., they imitate the experimenter leaning forward to touch a panel with forehead so that panel lights up) after several months. Recently this has been demonstrated in 11-month-olds with a delay of 3 months. Since this is achieved from a brief observational period and does not require prolonged learning, and since patients with amnesia cannot do this (McDonough, Mandler, KcKee, & Squire, 1995), it is tempting to conclude that such enactment demonstrates explicit, conscious memory. One should, though, keep in mind that delayed imitation that is based on a single event (third-person view) is not to be equated with a memory (knowledge) of that event *as* a single, past event (first-person view; see chapter 18 by Nelson & Fivush for a related point on infant memory).

More impressively, Rovee-Collier (1997) reviews research on memory in infants as young as 2 or 3 months for mobiles that they had learned to activate with a foot kick. Investigation of over 10 different independent variables that produce an implicit-explicit memory dissociation in experiments with adults showed that infants' delayed recognition of the mobile behaves like explicit memory, while reactivation of foot kicking (child can activate the mobile a day after a single reexposure of the mobile) behaved like implicit memory. However tempting it is to conclude that 2- or 3-month-old infants have conscious memory, one needs to keep in mind that explicit and conscious memory may not coincide in the infant as they seem to do in the adult. Hence, the memory parameters indicating explicit, conscious memory in adults may depend on features of explicit memory that might exist without consciousness in infants (see also chapter 17 by Rovee-Collier & Hayne).

In any case, conscious knowledge of past events is not all there is to memory proper. Theory of mind research does have highly relevant findings for that further development.

Episodic Memory as a Self-Referential Mental State

For the possession of some mental states—and "memory proper" (James, 1890) is one of them—more than just a higher order mental state is required; specific features need to be represented, in particular their causal connection to the world. Searle (1983) argued that such *causal self-referentiality* is required for intentions (underlying intentional action) as well as remembering. That is, intentions to act must specify (represent as their content) that the intended action be caused by them. Similarly, proper memories of a specific event must not only specify the event but also that they have been caused by that event. This analysis fits well Tulving's (1985; see also chapter 37 by Mark Wheeler) analysis of autonoetic episodic memory as the remembering of personally experienced events that need —in Ebbinghaus's (1885) words—"be recognized as something formerly experienced." William James (1890) gave a similar definition as the distinguishing feature of memory (in the strict sense): "memory proper (or secondary memory) is the knowledge of an event, or fact . . . with the additional consciousness that we have . . . experienced it before" (p. 648). Ebbinghaus's addendum (in light of the sense-reference distinction discussed above) is critical: a personally remembered event must be remembered *as* personally experienced. Perner (1990) spoke of experiential awareness. Applied to a typical word-list memory experiment in which—for example, the word *pear* appeared, this would mean that one has to encode (or later reconstruct) a metarepresentational comment of the following kind (Perner, 1991, p. 163): "I have the information that

pear was on the list, and I have this information because I have seen *pear* on the list." It is illuminating to see an important insufficiency of this proposal and highlight a tacitly assumed but critical aspect.

Dokic (1997) astutely pointed out that this formulation leaves room for a counterexample. Let us assume I know of some event about my earliest youth, but I am not sure whether I know it because I experienced it or because I was told it. I later tell my parents, and they assure me that this indeed happened and that no one could have told me. I must have known from experience. So now I know that I know of this childhood event through experience (metarepresentational comment), but this does not turn it into an episodic memory. The criterion can be tightened (Dokic, 1997) by making it fully recursive so that the second-order knowledge (knowing that the information comes from experiencing the event) is also required to be caused by experience: "I have information (that *pear* was on the list and that I have *this information* because I have seen *pear* on the list.)[2]" This criterion rules out the above counterexample because the criterion implies that one has to have information that the second-order information—about knowledge of *pear* coming from experience— itself must come from experience. This is not the case in the example; there, the second-order information comes from parental assurance.

A critical feature that has been tacitly introduced is the use of *seen*. What is critical about it is that seeing is an instance of "experiencing something"—that is, information gained through direct (noninferential and non-truth-evaluative) contact. Sensory experiences are of this kind. The world is as I see it; the perception imposes itself as reality (for me).[3] In contrast, when I am told about an event my informational access is indirect, and I can evaluate the information before believing it. This difference is important for episodic memory. Even in Dokic's recursive formulation, if we replace *seen* with *was told*, then we do not get a genuine episodic memory.

In sum, we have identified two essential ingredients for being a genuine episodic memory: (1) it must be *causally self-referential* knowledge, and (2) the causal link must be *experiential*—that is, direct, noninferential and non-truth-evaluative informational access. There are relevant data on children's developing theory of mind that suggest that children may not be able to entertain episodic memories until the age of 4 to 6 years, because they lack the prerequisite concepts for representing causal self-referentiality.

Relevant Theory of Mind Development: Understanding Reasons for Knowing

Although by 3 years, and probably earlier, children have knowledge of whether they know something or not, Wimmer, Hogrefe, & Perner (1988a) found that 3-year-olds could not give reasons for their knowledge—for example, for knowing the contents of a box—because they had seen what was put inside or because they had been told about it. This difficulty persisted even when the task was made more obvious (Gopnik & Graf, 1988). In other words (Wimmer, Hogrefe, & Sodian, 1988b), children younger than 4 years do not understand the important link between informational access and knowledge—that some kind of information (either seeing, being told, etc.) is *necessary for knowing* what is inside the box. This lack of understanding is also reflected in the fact that 3-year-olds tend to make knowledge judgments unrelated as to whether the person did or did not have access to the relevant information (Hogrefe, Wimmer, & Perner, 1986).

There is evidence of an earlier sensitivity to a person's informational condition. Children as young as 2 years of age (O'Neill, 1996), when asking their mother to hand them a toy from a tall shelf, were more explicit in describing the box containing the toy and its location when the mother had been out of the room when the toy had been put away than when she was present. However, this knowledge may be implicit in children's information-giving behavior and not available for any other use—for example, for knowing whose advice to follow, the one who witnessed the hiding or the one who didn't (Povinelli & de-Blois, 1992). Explicit knowledge attributions on the basis of informational access can be found in 3-year-olds if differences in accessibility to information are made very salient (Pillow, 1989; Pratt & Bryant, 1990), but their performance in these tasks remains highly volatile until about 4 years of age (Marvin, Greenberg, & Mossler, 1976; Mossler, Marvin, & Greenberg, 1976; Povinelli & deBlois, 1992; Wimmer et al., 1988a). This development from implicit sensitivity to explicit understanding

can also be observed in Turkish children's natural language use of inflecting verbs (Aksu-Koc, 1988). Three-year-olds, to some degree, use inflections appropriately in their own reports, but only 4-year-olds and older children can tell whether a person had witnessed a reported event directly or not on the basis of the inflection employed.

This explicit understanding of how informational access leads to knowledge is worked out further between 4 to 6 years. O'Neill, Astington, and Flavell (1992) report that at this age children come to understand which sense organ to use in order to find out the weight (use hand to lift object) or the color (use eyes to look at it) of an object. Similarly, Taylor, Esbensen, and Bennett (1994) found that between 4 and 6 years, children become able to distinguish between words (e.g., animal or color names) that they have learned recently (e.g., maroon) and those they have known for some time (e.g., red). Similarly, they become able to realize that they don't really know whether their fictional drawing of an unknown person actually looks like that person or not (Robinson & Mitchell, 1994). Finally, it is not until 4 to 6 years that children are able to distinguish knowledge (success in finding an object after seeing where it was put) from a lucky guess (success in finding the object without having seen where it was put; e.g., Sodian & Wimmer, 1987).

Apart from the above mentioned evidence that 3-year-old children still have difficulty understanding the relationship between experiencing events and later knowledge of these events, there is suggestive evidence from their failure to understand the link between video-recorded events and viewing the video record of these events. Flavell, Flavell, Green, and Korfmacher (1990) found that between 3 and 5 years children greatly improve their understanding of how the TV image of objects relates to the objects shown. Povinelli and Simon (1998) surreptitiously put a brightly colored sticker on children's heads that the children noticed only when watching the video record. Then, only seven of sixteen 3-year-olds spontaneously tried to remove the sticker from their heads, while fourteen of sixteen 4-year-olds did so. Even more remarkably, almost as many 3-year-olds tried to retrieve the sticker when viewing a video showing the activities of 2 weeks ago while hardly any 4-year-olds tried to do so (since it is most unlikely that the sticker would still be there). This shows that 3-year-olds seem to lack an understanding of the causal link between recorded events and what they see on the video record. In stark contrast, at 4 they understand that the video record shows what just happened in the earlier experienced episode. That the observed development reflects growing understanding of self is unlikely since a similar age trend exists for children's ability to locate a teddy bear or a sticker on another person on the basis of a video record (Suddendorf, 1997; Zelazo, Sommerville, & Nichols, in press).

Impact on Memory

Memory for Source

If children up to 4 to 6 years have difficulty understanding the origin of their knowledge, then we can expect a major developmental improvement around these ages in children's ability to monitor and remember the source (Johnson, Hashtroudi, & Lindsay, 1993) of their knowledge. Indeed this seems to be the case. Gopnik and Graf (1988) found that of the few 3-year-olds who could identify the source of their current knowledge, only half could later remember the source of their knowledge about the past, whereas almost all 5-year-olds who had identified the source could also later remember it. In traditional source memory experiments, where the immediate ability to identify source is not assessed, improvements extend into later years. Lindsay, Johnson, and Kwon (1991) found that within the 2 years from 4 to 6 years, children still showed a 20% improvement in source monitoring (e.g., which of two story tellers had given a certain piece of information) when the sources were highly confusable. A similar improvement rate was reported by Ackil and Zaragoza (1995) between 7 and 9 years, with little further improvement in the years thereafter. Children younger than 4, which are particularly interesting from the point of view of their theory of mind development, have been investigated in connection with reality monitoring and suggestibility.

Reality Monitoring

Reality monitoring (Johnson & Raye, 1981)[4] refers to the ability to monitor whether the content of one's memory was a real event or fiction. Even at 3, children tend to be no worse in making and remembering this distinction than older children (Woolley & Bruell, 1996;

Woolley & Phelps, 1994), and this conforms to the original finding by Wellman and Estes (1986) that children of this age are fairly proficient in distinguishing reality from fiction.

However, the distinction between children's own acts carried out in reality and those imagined or pretended poses a problem for children as old as 6 years. Foley, Johnson, and Raye (1983) found that children had no problem remembering whether a fact was stated by someone else or by themselves, but did have problems remembering whether they themselves said it or just thought it. Recent studies show that these problems are particularly severe in 3-year-olds as opposed to 4- or 5-year-olds. For instance, the younger children have a problem remembering whether they carried out an action with a real object or a substitute (Foley, Harris, & Hermann, 1994), and they have difficulty remembering whether they had performed a real action or just a pretend action (or merely imagined the action; Welch-Ross, 1995). Under the assumption that memory for action depends strongly on motor representations or motor images (Jeannerod, 1997), then, theory of mind research indicates that between 3 and 5 years children come to understand the origins of their voluntary actions, as reported on the knee-jerk reflex by Shultz, Wells, and Sarda (1980). It is interesting that the distinction between real action and pretence poses no problem (no more than in 4- or 6-year-olds) if they have to remember the external consequences—for example, under which object they had actually hidden a chip and under which object they had pretended to hide one (Roberts & Blades, 1995). In this context it is also interesting that children with autism, who are known to have similar theory of mind problems to 3-year-olds, seem to have a problem remembering whether they themselves or someone else has placed a card (Russell & Jarrold, 1997).

Suggestibility

As a further consequence of young children's inability to encode the experiential source of their knowledge, these children might be particularly susceptible to developing "false memories." Because they do not encode the origin of their mental contents, it is more difficult to keep verbal misinformation about an event separate from the remembered experience of the event. Indeed, the susceptibility to misleading suggestions reduces strongly between 3 to 5 years (e.g., Goodman & Reed,

1986; Ceci, Ross, & Toglia, 1987). For instance, Leichtman and Ceci (1995) created expectations about a future visitor as being clumsy, then after the visit children were given misleading suggestions that the visitor had committed some acts of clumsiness (e.g., ripped a book) in repeated questioning. Under these conditions almost 45% of 3- and 4-year-olds claimed having witnessed the suggested act while only about 15% of 5- and 6-year-olds did so. Leichtman (1996) reported that suggestibility of this kind declines significantly with children's ability to pass theory of mind tests assessing the understanding of experience as the source of knowledge. Also, Welch-Ross (1997) reported that performance on such tests correlated negatively (about −.40 after age was partialed out) with suggestibility in 3- to 6-year-olds. Recognition of uncontaminated memory items also covaried with these measures, which is to be expected on theoretical grounds discussed below.

Welch-Ross, Diecidue, and Miller (1997) discovered another connection between theory of mind development and suggestibility. An important achievement around the age of 4 years is understanding that a fact can be conceived of in different ways. This makes it possible for 4- and 5-year-olds to understand false belief (Wimmer & Perner, 1983) and the distinction between appearance and reality (Flavell, Flavell, & Green, 1983)—for example, to understand that a sponge that looks like a rock is conceived of as a rock. As a result, children younger than 4 years have impaired memory for their previous false beliefs (Gopnik & Astington, 1988). Children's ability to pass false belief and appearance-reality tasks correlates negatively with children's suggestibility. Presumably, children who do not understand false belief simply let the misleading information override the original information. Children who have good memories for the original information (high control test performance) and who can understand belief have to contend with two conflicting representations. This is reflected in a significant correlation between ability to solve these theory of mind tasks and slower reaction times on incorrect answers to misleading items (Welch-Ross, 1997).

Metamemory

Metamemory is knowledge about memory (Flavell, 1971; Schneider & Pressley, 1997).

There are at least two points of contact between research on the development of metamemory and theory of mind. There is direct overlap in investigating children's growing understanding of concepts of remember and forget. After some methodological problems in earlier research (e.g., Wellman & Johnson, 1979) that led to an underestimation of children's competence, it seems now that the critical elements are understood at around 4 years—the age at which children acquire an understanding of knowledge formation. Lyon and Flavell (1994) found that after this age children have a firm understanding that only a person who once had knowledge of a fact (but not a person who has never known about it) can later *remember* or *forget* that fact. Children can also determine that a person who remembers an object's location must be the one who found the object and not the one who failed to retrieve it, and that the person who remembers must be the one who had seen the object hidden earlier and not the one who is currently looking at it. In contrast, most 3-year-olds tended to identify "remembering" with current perception and "forget" with ignorance (see Mark Wheeler, chapter 37, for related points).

Another point of contact between metamemory research and theory of mind is with children's strategic use of cognitive cues. Even though children as young as 2 years can use semantically related cues to help them find an object (deLoache, 1986), they seem to lack explicit understanding of how such cues work (Gordon & Flavell, 1977). To understand how a cognitive cue works, children have to understand that knowledge (of where an object is) can be gained from indirect sources (e.g., inference)—that is, sources other than direct perception or communication. Sodian and Wimmer (1987) found that inference as a source of knowledge is understood between 4 and 6 years. In line with this age span, Sodian and Schneider (1990) reported that children's strategic use of cognitive cues develops at the same time. That is, children become able to hide an object in a location marked with a semantically strongly related cue when the objective is to help a partner find the object but to hide it in a location with only weakly related cues for a competitor who should find the object with difficulty. The age of 4 to 6 years has also been confirmed for understanding emotional reactions to situational cues of the original event (Lagattuta, Wellman, & Flavell, 1997).

In sum, the finding from theory of mind research that children around the age of 4 years acquire an understanding of how knowledge is formed is reflected in several different areas of memory research. Children have spurts of memory development at this age or show memory development directly correlated with the relevant theory of mind development. In particular, memory for source, memory for distinctions of internally generated representations, resistance to suggestibility, and their metamemory knowledge increase around this age.

Repercussions for Self and the Individuation of Events

The metarepresentational facility for forming episodic memory may have some important repercussions for our concepts of self, of time, and of past events. Campbell (1997) argues that for having autobiographical memory it is not enough to have a picture of or narrative about self in some past episode. It is critical to see that person in the narrative as spatio-temporally connected with one's present self. It is that spatio-temporal continuity of a single self that forces a linear conception of time—that is, that the single self must have lived through and experienced the remembered narratives at particular times one after the other. To get a grip on the concept of self, we need to address the basic question of what justifies our concept that the world is inhabited by concrete objects (among them ourselves) beyond the properties that these objects carry. There are two principles (Campbell, 1995). One is that the properties and their causal effects tend to cluster because they are properties of a particular individual, and the other principle is the potentiality for propagating causal influence over time. So, what gives substance to the idea that there is one and the same thing (me) that lived through all these life episodes is that what happened to me in those episodes has a causal effect on what I am now. We can see that this conceptual basis for the notion of self gains vastly in richness once one understands that past events have not just physical effects on oneself but also mental effects (by being experienced). It is particularly interesting in this context that frontal lobe damage that is linked to the loss of episodic memory tends to be also linked to a loss of self-concern (Wheeler, Stuss, & Tulving, 1997; see also chapter 37 by Wheeler) and

that theory of mind development is closely linked to gains in self-control (Perner & Lang, in press).

Moreover, the understanding that past events affect me mentally as a perceiver should not only help the individuation of self but also help build a concept of individual events. It should help because it adds many important causal effects that cluster around a particular event—namely all the mental effects that the event has on me as a perceiver. To have a notion of individual events has important consequences. It gives additional coherence to all the aspects of the event that are otherwise only linked by association, and one can linguistically refer to the event (a defining feature of direct tests of memory, in particular, free recall (e.g., Reingold & Merikle, 1988; Richardson-Klavehn & Bjork, 1988). Moreover, free recall depends especially strongly on an understanding of the event having been experienced, since the identifying description tends to be in terms of experience—for example, "What was on the list that I've just *shown* you?" Furthermore, the individuation of events and their encoding as experienced by a spatio-temporally coherent self (see Campbell's argument above) is also important for remembering temporal order of otherwise unrelated events (i.e., events that are not structurally integrated within an encompassing event).

On the basis of these considerations, further implications for memory development can be drawn from the developmental changes in children's theory of mind around 4 years.

Development of Free Recall, Specificity of Event Knowledge, and Temporal Order

Perner and Ruffman (1995) found that between 3 and 5 years, children's improvement on free recall in particular depends significantly on their understanding of how knowledge depends on experience. Even when cued recall and verbal intelligence were partialed out, correlations stayed above .30. Figure 19.1 illustrates this point by showing that children who can distinguish a lucky guess from proper knowledge have smaller negative and even positive differences between free and cued recall than children who fail the know-guess test. Several other findings fit this pattern. For instance, as emphasized by Fivush

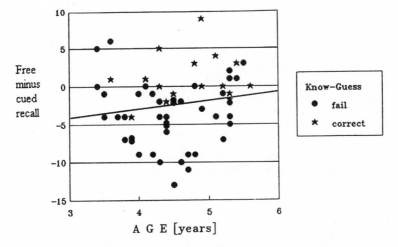

Figure 19.1 Children who correctly differentiate a lucky guess from an informed, knowledge based response show an above average difference between free and cued recall from children who fail to make this distinction (computed from data of exp. 1 in Perner & Ruffmann, 1995).

and Hamond (1990; Fivush, Hamond, Harsch, & Singer, 1991), recall in early childhood is principally structured by the semantic cues provided by the interrogator, and the information retrieved on different occasions will differ since different questions may be asked or different associations be triggered, whereas after the age of 6 years experienced events have a coherent identity that allows free recall of such events and coherence of recall over repeated interrogations.

Also, children's recall of real-life events reflects a particular improvement around the age of 4 years, as in traumatic hospital visits (Goodman & Reed, 1986; Goodman, Quas, Batterman-Faunce, & Riddlesberger, 1994; Quas et al., 1999), or an emergency school evacuation during a fire alarm. For instance, two weeks after the evacuation 4½ year olds remembered the causal and temporal sequence of the event much better than 3½ year olds (Pillemer, Picariello, & Pruett, 1994). For instance, almost all of the older but only about half of the younger children remembered that they were inside the building when the alarm rang. Seven years later only some of those who had been over 4 at the time of the alarm but none of the younger group produced a narrative memory, which is an indication that the event has gained a coherence beyond the description of its components. Over half in the older group but only 20% of the younger were able to produce memory fragments.

A recent study by McCormack and Russell (1997) used the Huppert and Piercy (1978) paradigm on 4-, 6-, and 8-year-olds. Children were presented with two different series of pictures on two consecutive days. In each series some pictures were presented once, others 3 times. After the presentation on the second day, children were asked for each picture whether it had been presented today or yesterday (recency judgment) and whether it had been presented only once or 3 times (frequency judgment). There was a marked decline in error rate on both types of judgment from 4 to 6 years, but no further improvement from 6 to 8 years.

Another relevant source of evidence comes from children with autism, most of whom are known to be deficient in those aspects of theory of mind that pose problems for 3-year-olds (Baron-Cohen, Leslie, & Frith, 1985; Baron-Cohen, Tager-Flusberg, & Cohen, 1993). These children tend to be impaired on free recall, to some degree on forced choice recognition, but not on cued recall in comparison to age-matched normally developing children or children matched on verbal ability (Boucher & Warrington, 1976; Tager-Flusberg, 1991; Boucher, 1981a). These children also tend to be impaired on memory for order and context of events (Boucher, 1981b). In contrast, high-functioning men with autism or Asperger syndrome, who tend not to have the basic problems with theory of mind of the 3-year-olds, but problems with higher order mental states (what someone thinks about someone else thinking; Happé, 1994), seem not to show a specific impairment of free recall (Rumsey & Hamburger, 1988; Minshew & Goldstein, 1993) or at least it is not very pronounced if their adult verbal IQ is fairly high (Bennetto, Pennington, & Rogers, 1996). Nevertheless, there still tends to be an impairment in temporal order and source memory. Moreover, high-functioning adults with Asperger syndrome judge correctly recognized items less often as "remembered" and more often as "known" than normal controls (Bowler, Gardiner, & Grice, 1998).

In sum, a particularly important development in children's theory of mind around 3 to 6 years is the increasing understanding that one's knowledge of the past comes through direct experience. This entails a marked improvement in free recall, memory for temporal order, and the ability to remember events for several years. Another consequence should be that events experienced before that age cannot be remembered as experienced. This is difficult to test directly with young children, but it yields a new interpretation of the phenomenon of childhood (infantile) amnesia.

Childhood Amnesia

Childhood amnesia describes the phenomenon noted by Freud as "infantile amnesia" that most adults are unable to remember their early childhood. Systematic investigations by Waldfogel (1948/1982) and many others (for reviews, see Dudycha & Dudycha, 1941; Pillemer & White, 1989; Howe & Courage, 1993; *Journal of Experimental Child Psychology, 59*(3) and *60*(1) (1995), special issues on early memory; chapters 17 by Rovee-Collier & Hayne and 18 by Nelson & Fivush, this volume) across a variety of methods suggest that very few people remember anything that happened before their third birthday. Then the number of memories sharply increases for events that happened between 3 and 5 or 6 years. For events that occurred after that age there is no distinctly greater "amnesia" than expected by normal forgetting (Wetzler & Sweeney, 1986b) as shown in figure 19.2.

Several explanations have been put forward: (1) Early experiences are less likely to be encoded in long-term memory than later events (White & Pillemer, 1979; Wetzler & Sweeney, 1986a). (2) Early experiences are encoded in an early developing system that is

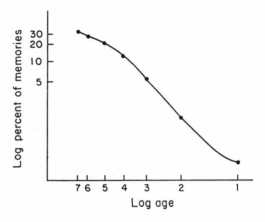

Figure 19.2 Wetzler & Sweeney's (1986b) example reanalyses of Waldfogel's (1948) data. The accelerated decline seems to begin for memories of events experienced at the age of 5 years or earlier.

spared in amnesia and supports only implicit memory inaccessible to conscious recollection (Schacter & Moscovitch, 1984; Nadel & Zola-Morgan, 1984). (3) Early experiences get encoded but become irretrievable through suppression by the superego (Freud, 1963), a change in operatory logic (Piaget, 1945/1962), assimilation to and displacement by more highly and differently schematized verbal stereotypes later in life (Neisser, 1962; Schachtel, 1947/1982). (4) Infants lack specific schemas that provide a framework for autobiographical knowledge (Hudson, 1986), which enable older children to order their life events in a coherent and retrievable form. In particular, autobiographical knowledge requires a notion of self (Howe & Courage, 1993) that extends over time and is built up by reminiscing and recounting past events over early childhood (Fivush & Hamond, 1990; Nelson, 1997).

The theory of mind explanation of childhood amnesia (Perner, 1990) sees the problem in infants' inability to encode personally experienced events *as personally experienced.* This inability creates two problems for adults trying to remember their infancy. One problem is direct: even though a representation of the experienced event may still exist, the event cannot be remembered *as* an experienced event (i.e., as a genuine memory rather than as mere knowledge about some autobiographical fact). The other problem is indirect: as argued earlier, without understanding of the mental effects of experienced events there is only weak representation of them as particular events, and these representations are prone to interference from similar events. Hence, they are unlikely to survive into adulthood as representations of individual events. The developmental data from theory of mind investigations (as outlined above) locate the critical change within the age range of 3 to 5 years. This provides a good fit to the age at which infant amnesia ends (e.g., Wetzler and Sweeney, 1986b; Sheingold and Tenney, 1982; and most other studies that looked at adults' memory for childhood events).

Conclusion

Remembering (memory in the narrow sense) is not demonstrated by just any influence of past events on our mind. Rather, it entails a reflection on past events *as* past events, as events that one knows (conscious, explicit memory) and as personally experienced (episodic, autonoetic memory). In order to represent past events in these ways, children need the prerequisite concepts—that is, an adequate "theory of mind." There is no clear evidence about when infants become able to form explicit, conscious memories. Much research effort has concentrated on the ages between 3 and 5 years, when children start to understand knowledge as something that is based on access to information. This intellectual advance has identifiable repercussions in memory. At the corresponding ages memory for source and reality monitoring improves, children become less suggestible, their understanding of memory processes (metamemory) improves, their free recall gains in relation to cued recall (a difference indicating improved episodic memory), and their recall of past events becomes more coherent. Finally, this age also marks the end of childhood amnesia, interpreted as the inability to genuinely remember early childhood events as personally experienced, rather than as an inability to reactivate any kind of knowledge about this life period.

Acknowledgments   I would like to thank Simon Baron-Cohen, Nora Newcombe, Michelle Leichtman, Jim Russell, Beate Sodian, Thomas Suddendorf, Melissa Welch-Ross for their advice and for directing me to relevant literature, and John Campbell, Jerome Dokic, Christopher Hoerl and Teresa McCormack for our ongoing email discussion of episodic memory issues.

Notes

1. It may be an overinterpretation of these data to suggest that the looking time pattern shows understanding of the observed person wanting a particular object. It might simply be that the person's intentional actions (looking, reaching, grasping) are better suited for directing infants' attention to an object than nonintentional action or artificial pointers. The recorded looking times might be the result of whether the attention is directed to the same or a different object at test. However, even this cautious interpretation attests to infants being specifically attuned to intentional actions as superior attention directors.

2. The parentheses are used to help make clear the scope of the required information.

3. This can be overridden through indirect knowledge—e.g., in the Müller-Lyer illusion after taking Psych 100. I now "know" that the two lines are the same length, yet when looking at them they still are "perceptually" different (Crane, 1992).

4. Reality monitoring is usually treated as a part of source monitoring, but I want to emphasize that whether a memory is of a real event or a fictitious event is a different distinction from that of different sources of knowledge about these events.

References

Ackil, J. K., & Zaragoza, M. S. (1995). Developmental differences in eyewitness suggestibility and memory for source. Special Issue: Early memory. *Journal of Experimental Child Psychology, 60,* 57–83.

Aksu-Koc, A. A. (1988). *The aquisition of aspects and modality.* Cambridge: Cambridge University Press.

Amsterdam, B. K. (1972). Mirror self-image reactions before age two. *Developmental Psychology, 5,* 297–305.

Anscombe, G. E. M. (1957). *Intention.* Cambridge: Cambridge University Press.

Armstrong, D. (1980). *The nature of mind and other essays.* Ithaca: Cornell University Press.

Astington, J. W. (1993). *The child's discovery of the mind.* Cambridge, MA: Harvard University Press.

Baldwin, D. A., & Moses, L. J. (1996). The ontogeny of social information gathering. *Child Development, 67,* 1915–1939.

Baron-Cohen, S., Leslie, A. M., & Frith, U. (1985). Does the autistic child have a "theory of mind"? *Cognition, 21,* 37–46.

Baron-Cohen, S., Tager-Flusberg, H., & Cohen, D. J. (1993). *Understanding other minds: Perspectives from autism.* Oxford, England: Oxford University Press.

Bennetto, L., Pennington, B. F., & Rogers, S. J. (1996). Intact and impaired memory functions in autism. *Child Development, 67,* 1816–1835.

Boucher, J. (1981a). Immediate free recall in early childhood autism: Another point of behavioral similarity with the amnesic syndrome. *British Journal of Psychology, 72,* 211–215.

Boucher, J. (1981b). Memory for recent events in autistic children. *Journal of Autism and Developmental Disorders, 11,* 293–301.

Boucher, J., & Warrington, E. K. (1976). Memory deficits in early infantile autism: Some similarities to the amnesic syndrome. *British Journal of Psychology, 67,* 73–87.

Bowler, D. M., Gardiner, J. M., & Grice, S. (1998). *Episodic memory in high functioning adults with autism.* Unpublished manuscript, City University, London, UK.

Campbell, J. (1995). The body image and self-consciousness. In J. Bermúdez, A. Marcel, & N. Eilan (Eds.), *The body and the self* (pp. 29–42). Cambridge, MA: MIT Press.

Campbell, J. (1997). The structure of time in autobiographical memory. *European Journal of Philosophy, 5,* 105–118.

Carruthers, P. (1996). *Language, thought and consciousness. An essay in philosophical psychology.* Cambridge: Cambrige University Press.

Ceci, S. J., Ross, D. F., & Toglia, M. P. (1987). Suggestibility of children's memory: Psycholegal implications. *Journal of Experimental Psychology General, 116,* 38–49.

Crane, T. (1992). The nonconceptual content of experience. In T. Crane (Ed.), *The contents of experience: Essays on perception* (pp. 136–157). Cambridge: Cambridge University Press.

DeLoache, J. S. (1986). Memory in very young children: Exploitation of cues to the location of a hidden object. *Cognitive Development, 1,* 123–137.

Dokic, J. (1997). Two metarepresentational theories of episodic memory. Paper presented at the Annual Meeting of the ESPP in Padua, Italy, August 1997.

Dudycha, G. J., & Dudycha, M. M. (1941). Childhood memories: A review of the literature. *Psychological Bulletin, 38,* 668–682.

Ebbinghaus, H. (1885). *Über das Gedächtnis.* Leipzig: Duncker und Humblot.

Field, H. (1978). Mental representation. *Erkenntnis, 13,* 9–61.

Fivush, R., & Hamond, N. R. (1990). Autobiographical memory across the preschool years: Toward reconceptualizing childhood amnesia. In R. Fivush & J. A. Hudson (Eds.), *Knowing and remembering in young children.* New York: Cambridge University Press.

Fivush, R., Hamond, N. R., Harsch, N., & Singer, N. (1991). Content and consistency in young children's autobiographical recall. *Discourse Processes, 14,* 373–388.

Flavell, J. H. (1971). First discussant's comments: What is memory development the development of? *Human Development, 14,* 272–278.

Flavell, J. H., Flavell, E. R., & Green, F. L. (1983). Development of the appearance-reality distinction. *Cognitive Psychology, 15,* 95–120.

Flavell, J. H., Flavell, E. R., Green, F. L., & Korfmacher, J. E. (1990). Do young children think of television images as pictures or real objects? *Journal of Broadcasting and Electronic Media, 34,* 399–419.

Fodor, J. A. (1978). Propositional attitudes. *The Monist, 61,* 501–523.

Foley, M. A., Harris, J. F., & Hermann, S. (1994). Developmental comparisons of the ability to discriminate between memories for symbolic play enactments. *Developmental Psychology, 30*(2), 206–217.

Foley, M. A., Johnson, M. K., & Raye, C. L. (1983). Age-related changes in confusion between memories for thoughts and memories for speech. *Child Development, 54,* 51–60.

Frege, G. (1892/1960). On sense and reference. In P. Geach & M. Black (Eds.), *Philosophical writings of Gottlob Frege* (pp. 56–78). Oxford: Basil Blackwell.

Freud, S. (1963). Introductory lectures on psycho-analysis. In J. Strachey (Ed.), *The standard edition of the complete psychological works of Sigmund Freud* (Vol. 7; pp. 135–243). London: Hogarth Press. (Original work published 1916–1917).

Goldman, A. I. (1993). The psychology of folk psychology. *Behavioral and Brain Sciences, 16,* 15–28.

Goodman, G. S., & Reed, R. S. (1986). Age differences in eyewitness testimony. *Law and Human Behavior, 10,* 317–332.

Goodman, G. S., Quas, J. A., Batterman-Faunce, J. M., & Riddlesberger, M. M. (1994). Predictors of accurate and inaccurate memories of traumatic events experienced in childhood. Special Issue: The recovered memory/false memory debate. *Consciousness and Cognition, 3,* 269–294.

Gopnik, A., & Astington, J. W. (1988). Children's understanding of representational change and its relation to the understanding of false belief and the appearance-reality distinction. *Child Development, 59,* 26–37.

Gopnik, A., & Graf, P. (1988). Knowing how you know: Young children's ability to identify and remember the sources of their beliefs. *Child Development, 59,* 1366–1371.

Gopnik, A., & Meltzoff, A. N. (1997). *Word, thoughts, and theories.* Cambridge, MA: MIT Press.

Gordon, F. R., & Flavell, J. H. (1977). The development of intuitions about cognitive cueing. *Child Development, 48,* 1027–1033.

Happé, F. (1994). *Autism: An introduction to psychological theory.* Cambridge, MA: Harvard University Press.

Hogrefe, J., Wimmer, H., & Perner, J. (1986). Ignorance versus false belief: A developmental lag in attribution of epistemic states. *Child Development, 57,* 567–582.

Howe, M. L., & Courage, M. L. (1993). On resolving the enigma of infantile amnesia. *Psychological Bulletin, 113,* 305–326.

Hudson, J. A. (1986). Memories are made of this: General event knowledge and development of autobiographic memory. In K. Nelson (Ed.), *Event knowledge: Structure and function in development* (pp. 97–118). Hillsdale, NJ: Erlbaum.

Huppert, F. A., & Piercy, M. (1978). The role of trace strength in recency and frequency judgements by amnesic and control subjects. *Quarterly Journal of Experimental Psychology, 30,* 347–354.

James, W. (1890). *The principles of psychology.* London: MacMillan.

Jeannerod, M. (1997). *The cognitive neuroscience in action.* Oxford: Blackwell.

Johnson, M. K., Hashtroudi, S., & Lindsay, D. S. (1993). Source monitoring. *Psychological Bulletin, 114,* 3–28.

Johnson, M. K., & Raye, C. L. (1981). Reality monitoring. *Psychological Review, 88,* 67–85.

Lagattuta, K. H., Wellman, H. M., & Flavell, J. H. (1997). Preschoolers' understanding of the link between thinking and feeling: Cognitive cuing and emotional change. *Child Development, 68*(6), 1081–1104.

Leichtman, M. D. (1996). What get's remembered? Patterns of memory and reminiscence in early life. Paper presented at the International Conference on Memory, Padua, Italy, July 1996.

Leichtman, M. D., & Ceci, S. J. (1995). The effects of stereotypes and suggestions on preschoolers' reports. *Developmental Psychology, 31,* 568–578, 758.

Lindsay, D. S., Johnson, M. K., & Kwon, P. (1991). Developmental changes in memory source monitoring. *Journal of Experimental Child Psychology, 52,* 297–318.

Lyon, T. D., & Flavell, J. H. (1994). Young children's understanding of "remember" and "forget." *Child Development, 65,* 1357–1371.

Marvin, R. S., Greenberg, M. T., & Mossler, D. G. (1976). The early development of conceptual perspective taking: Distinguishing among multiple perspectives. *Child Development, 47,* 511–514.

McCormack, T., & Russell, J. (1997). The development of recency and frequency memory: Is there a developmental shift from reliance on trace-strength to episodic recall? *Journal of Experimental Child Psychology, 66,* 376–392.

McDonough, L., Mandler, J. M., McKee, R. D., & Squire, L. R. (1995). The deferred imitation task as a nonverbal measure of declarative memory. *Proceedings of the National Academy of Sciences USA, 92,* 7580–7584.

Meltzoff, A. N. (1985). Immediate and deferred imitation in fourteen- and twenty-four-month-old infants. *Child Development, 56,* 62–72.

Meltzoff, A. N. (1995a). Understanding the intentions of others: Re-enactment of intended acts by 18-month-old children. *Developmental Psychology, 31,* 838–850.

Meltzoff, A. N. (1995b). What infant memory tells us about infantile amnesia: Long-term recall and deferred imitation. *Journal of Experimental Child Psychology, 59,* 497–515.

Minshew, N. J., & Goldstein, G. (1993). Is autism an amnesic disorder? *Neuropsychology, 7,* 209–216.

Mossler, D. G., Marvin, R. S., & Greenberg, M. T. (1976). Conceptual perspective taking in 2- to 6-year-old children. *Developmental Psychology, 12,* 85–86.

Nadel, L., & Zola-Morgan, S. (1984). Infantile amnesia: A neurobiological perspective. In M. Moscovitch (Ed.), *Infant memory: Its relation to normal and pathological memory in humans and other animals* (pp. 145–172). New York and London: Plenum Press.

Neisser, U. (1962). Cultural and cognitive discontinuity. In T. E. Gladwin & W. Sturtevant (Eds.), *Anthropology and human be-*

havior (pp. 54–71). Washington, DC: Anthropological Society of Washington.

Nelson, K. (1997). Finding one's self in time. In G. Snodgrass & R. Thompson (Eds.), *The self across psychology: Self recognition, self-awareness, and the self concept* (pp. 103–116). New York: Annals of the New York Academy of Sciences.

O'Neill, D. K. (1996). Two-year-old children's sensitivity to a parent's knowledge state when making requests. *Child Development, 67*, 659–677.

O'Neill, D. K., Astington, J. W., & Flavell, J. H. (1992). Young children's understanding of the role that sensory experiences play in knowledge acquisition. *Child Development, 63*, 474–490.

Perner, J. (1990). Experiential awareness and children's episodic memory. In W. Schneider & F. E. Weinert (Eds.), *Interactions among aptitudes, strategies, and knowledge in cognitive performance* (pp. 3–11). New York: Springer-Verlag.

Perner, J. (1991). *Understanding the representational mind.* Cambridge, MA: MIT Press.

Perner, J., & Lang, B. (in press). Theory of mind and executive function: Is there a developmental relationship? In S. Baron-Cohen, H. Tager-Flusberg, & D. Cohen (Eds.), *Understanding other minds: Perspectives from autism and developmental cognitive neuroscience* (2nd ed., chap. 4). Oxford: Oxford University Press.

Perner, J., & Ruffman, T. (1995). Episodic memory and autonoetic consciousness: Developmental evidence and a theory of childhood amnesia. Special Issue: Early memory. *Journal of Experimental Child Psychology, 59*, 516–548.

Piaget, J. (1945/1962). *Play, dreams, and imitation in childhood.* New York: W. W. Norton.

Pillemer, D. B., Picariello, M. L., & Pruett, J. C. (1994). Very long-term memories of a salient preschool event. *Applied Cognitive Psychology, 8*, 95–106.

Pillemer, D. B., & White, S. H. (1989). Childhood events recalled by children and adults. In H. W. Reese (Ed.), *Advances in child development and behavior* (Vol. 21; pp. 297–340). New York: Academic Press.

Pillow, B. H. (1989). Early understanding of perception as a source of knowledge. *Journal of Experimental Child Psychology, 47*, 116–129.

Povinelli, D. J., & deBlois, S. (1992). Young children's (*homo sapiens*) understanding of knowledge formation in themselves and others. *Journal of Comparative Psychology, 106*, 228–238.

Povinelli, D. J., Perilloux, H. K., & Bierschwale, D. (1993). Self-knowledge assessment in young children. Unpublished manuscript, Laboratory of Comparative Biology, New Iberia Research Centre, University of Southwestern Louisiana.

Povinelli, D. J., & Simon, B. B. (1998). Young children's understanding of briefly versus extremely delayed images of the self: Emergence of the autobiographical stance. *Developmental Psychology, 34*, 188–194.

Pratt, C., & Bryant, P. (1990). Young children understand that looking leads to knowing (so long as they are looking into a single barrel). *Child Development, 61*, 973–982.

Quas, J. A., Goodman, G. S., Bidrose, S., Pipe, M.-E., Craw, S., & Ablin, D. S. (1999). Emotion and memory: Children's long-term remembering, forgetting, and suggestibility. *Journal of Experimental Child Psychology, 72(4)*, 235–270.

Reingold, E. M., & Merikle, P. M. (1988). Using direct and indirect measures to study perception without awareness. *Perception and Psychophysics, 44*, 563–575.

Repacholi, B. M., & Gopnik, A. (1997). Early reasoning about desires: Evidence from 14- and 18-month-olds. *Developmental Psychology, 33(1)*, 12–21.

Richardson-Klavehn, A., & Bjork, R. A. (1988). Measures of memory. *Annual Review of Psychology, 39*, 475–543.

Roberts, K. P., & Blades, M. (1995). Children's discrimination of memories for actual and pretend actions in a hiding task. *British Journal of Developmental Psychology, 13*, 321–333.

Robinson, E. J., & Mitchell, P. (1994). Children's judgements of ignorance on the basis of absence of experience. *British Journal of Developmental Psychology, 12*, 113–129.

Rosenthal, D. M. (1986). Two concepts of consciousness. *Philosophical Studies, 49*, 329–359.

Rovee-Collier, C. (1997). Dissociations in infant memory: Rethinking the development of implicit and explicit memory. *Psychological Review, 104(3)*, 467–498.

Rumsey, J. M., & Hamburger, S. D. (1988). Neuropsychological findings in high-functioning men with infantile autism, residual state. *Journal of Clinical and Experimental Neuropsychology, 10*, 201–221.

Russell, B. (1919). On propositions: What they are and what they mean. *Proceedings of the Aristotelian Society, 2*, 1–43.

Russell, J., & Jarrold, C. (1997). *Memory for actions in children with autism: Self versus other.* Unpublished manuscript, Department of Experimental Psychology, University of Cambridge.

Schachtel, E. G. (1947/1982). On memory and childhood amnesia. *Psychiatry, 10,* 1–26.

Schachtel, E. G. (1982). On memory and childhood amnesia. In U. Neisser (Ed.), *Memory observed* (pp. 189–200). San Francisco: Freeman.

Schacter, D. L. (1987). Implicit memory: History and current status. *Journal of Experimental Psychology: Learning, memory and cognition, 13,* 501–518.

Schacter, D. L., & Moscovitch, M. (1984). Infants, amnesics, and dissociable memory systems. In M. Moscovitch (Ed.), *Infant memory* (pp. 173–216). New York: Plenum Press.

Schneider, W., & Pressley, M. (1997). *Memory development between two and twenty* (2nd ed.). Mahwah, NJ: Erlbaum.

Schneider, W., & Sodian, B. (1988). Metamemory-memory behavior relationships in young children: Evidence from a memory-for-location task. *Journal of Experimental Child Psychology, 45,* 209–233.

Searle, J. (1983). *Intentionality.* Cambridge: Cambridge University Press.

Shatz, M., Wellman, H. M., & Silber, S. (1983). The acquisition of mental verbs: A systematic investigation of the first reference to mental state. *Cognition, 14,* 301–321.

Sheingold, K., & Tenney, Y. J. (1982). Memory for a salient childhood event. In U. Neisser (Ed.), *Memory observed* (pp. 201–212). San Francisco: W. H. Freeman.

Shultz, T. R., Wells, D., & Sarda, M. (1980). The development of the ability to distinguish intended actions from mistakes, reflexes, and passive movements. *British Journal of Social and Clinical Psychology, 19,* 301–310.

Sodian, B., & Schneider, W. (1990). Children's understanding of cognitive cuing: How to manipulate cues to fool a competitor. *Child Development, 61,* 697–704.

Sodian, B., & Wimmer, H. (1987). Children's understanding of inference as a source of knowledge. *Child Development, 58,* 424–433.

Spelke, E. S., Phillips, A., & Woodward, A. L. (1995). Infants' knowledge of object motion and human action. In D. Sperber, D. Premack, & A. J. Premack (Eds.), *Causal cognition. A multidisciplinary debate* (pp. 44–78). Oxford: Oxford University Press.

Suddendorf, T. (1997). *Children's understanding of the relation between delayed video representation and current reality: A test for self-awareness?* Unpublished manuscript, Department of Psychology, University of Auckland.

Tager-Flusberg, H. (1991). Semantic processing in the free recall of autistic children: Further evidence for a cognitive deficit. *British Journal of Developmental Psychology, 9,* 417–430.

Taylor, M., Esbensen, B., & Bennett, R. T. (1994). Children's understanding of knowledge acquisition: The tendency for children to report they have always known what they have just learned. *Child Development, 65,* 1581–1604.

Tulving, E. (1985). Memory and consciousness. *Canadian Psychology, 26,* 1–12.

Tulving, E., & Madigan, S. (1970). Memory and verbal learning. *Annual Review of Psychology, 21,* 437–484.

Waldfogel, S. (1948/1982). The frequency and affective character of childhood memories. In U. Neisser (Ed.), *Memory observed* (pp. 73–76). San Francisco: W. H. Freeman.

Welch-Ross, M. K. (1995). Developmental changes in preschoolers' ability to distinguish memories of performed, pretended, and imagined actions. *Cognitive Development, 10,* 421–441.

Welch-Ross, M. K. (1997). Children's understanding of the mind: Implications for suggestibility. Poster presented at the Biennial Meeting of the Society for Research in Child Development, Washington, DC, April, 3–6, 1997.

Welch-Ross, M. K., Diecidue, K., & Miller, S. A. (1997). Young children's understanding of conflicting mental representation predicts suggestibility. *Developmental Psychology, 33*(1), 43–53.

Wellman, H. M., & Estes, D. (1986). Early understanding of mental entities: A reexamination of childhood realism. *Child Development, 57,* 910–923.

Wellman, H. M., & Johnson, C. (1979). Understanding of mental processes: A developmental study of "remember" and "forget." *Child Development, 50,* 79–88.

Wetzler, S. E., & Sweeney, J. A. (1986a). Childhood amnesia: A conceptualization in cognitive-psychological terms. *Journal of the American Psychoanalytic Association, 34,* 663–685.

Wetzler, S. E., & Sweeney, J. A. (1986b). Childhood amnesia: An empirical demonstration. In D. C. Rubin (Ed.), *Autobiographi-*

cal memory (pp. 191–201). Cambridge: Cambridge University Press.

Wheeler, M. A., Stuss, D. T., & Tulving, E. (1997). Toward a theory of episodic memory: The frontal lobes and autonoetic consciousness. *Psychological Bulletin, 121*, 331–354.

White, S. H., & Pillemer, D. B. (1979). Childhood amnesia and the development of a socially accessible memory system. In J. F. Kihlstrom & F. J. Evans (Eds.), *Functional disorders of memory* (pp. 29–73). Hillsdale, NJ: Erlbaum.

Wimmer, H., Hogrefe, J., & Perner, J. (1988a). Children's understanding of informational access as source of knowledge. *Child Development, 59*, 386–396.

Wimmer, H., Hogrefe, J., & Sodian, B. (1988b). A second stage in children's conception of mental life: Understanding sources of information. In J. W. Astington, P. L. Harris, & D. R. Olson (Eds.), *Developing theories of mind* (pp. 173–192). New York: Cambridge University Press.

Wimmer, H., & Perner, J. (1983). Beliefs about beliefs: Representation and constraining function of wrong beliefs in young children's understanding of deception. *Cognition, 13*, 103–128.

Woodward, A. L. (1998). *Selectivity and discrimination in infants' encoding of human behavior.* Unpublished manuscript, University of Chicago.

Woolley, J. D., & Bruell, M. J. (1996). Young children's awareness of the origins of their mental representations. *Developmental Psychology, 32*, 335–346.

Woolley, J. D., & Phelps, K. E. (1994). Young children's practical reasoning about imagination. Special Issue: Magic. *British Journal of Developmental Psychology, 12*, 53–67.

Zelazo, P. D., Sommerville, J. A., & Nichols, S. (1999). Age-related changes in children's use of external representations. *Developmental Psychology, 35*, 1059–1071.

MEMORY IN USE

20

Remembering Life Experiences

ULRIC NEISSER & LISA K. LIBBY

Two-thirds of a century have passed since Frederic Bartlett (1932) criticized standard research methods in memory as irrelevant to human life. "The psychologist, whether he uses experimental methods or not, is dealing, not simply with reactions, but with human beings. Consequently the experimenter must consider the everyday behavior of the ordinary individual, as well as render an account of the responses of his subjects within a laboratory" (p. 12). Despite Bartlett's trenchant critique, it was not until the 1980s that the ecological study of memory—especially memory for life events—began to develop as a recognizable subdiscipline in its own right. The goal of this chapter is to provide a brief overview of that discipline's achievements.

Historical and Systematic Issues

Bartlett's Contributions

Although Bartlett never studied the recall of actual life experiences, his work on stories was the first step toward an ecological study of memory. The subjects of his experiments were given a brief (and rather strange) story to read; then, at haphazard intervals varying from weeks to years, they tried to write it out from memory. Substantial distortions appeared, many resulting from the subjects' efforts to reconcile what they still remembered with their schema for what stories should be like. Similar results had been reported earlier by Henderson (1903), and there have been several replications (Johnson, 1962; Paul, 1959). Indeed, "Bartlettian" distortions appear in the recall of many kinds of material, including the scientific literature of memory (Vincente & Brewer, 1993). Interestingly, no such distortions occur if recall is immediate and subjects only report what they are sure of (Gauld & Stephenson, 1967).

Bartlett's concept of *schema* has survived in two forms. The hypothesis that people have specific "story schemas" (or sometimes "story grammars") was revived and expanded by Rumelhart (1975) and by Mandler and Johnson (1977), but it has also been strongly criticized (Black & Wilensky, 1979; Brewer & Lichtenstein, 1982). On the other hand, the notion that memories in general are supported and shaped by schematic structures is now very widely accepted—so widely that no comprehensive survey of its use is possible. (For a brief review, see Neisser, 1998.)

More Recent Developments

The modern surge of interest in memory for life experiences began with the 1978 Cardiff conference on *Practical Aspects of Memory* (Gruneberg, Morris, & Sykes, 1978). Most of the topics considered there—including eyewitness testimony, face recognition, arousal, diary studies, recall of medical information— now have substantial literatures in their own right. Like many other new ventures, the enterprise was initially defined by contrast with more traditional paradigms. This contrast, which was the thrust of Neisser's (1978) opening address at Cardiff, provoked a sharp response from Banaji and Crowder (1989). Whatever the merits of that response (cf. Neisser 1991), it did not discourage further ecological research. By now the controversy has largely abated; the present review focuses on empirical findings rather than methodological disputes.

Types of Memory

Almost all ecological research has been concerned with explicit memory, usually assessed by recall but occasionally (as in studies of eyewitness identification) by recognition. Most studies have focused on the recall of specific events (i.e., on episodic memory), and have been motivated by "correspondence" rather than "storehouse" conceptions of memory (Koriat & Goldsmith, 1996). There have also been a few notable studies of semantic memory in natural settings, especially those of Harry Bahrick and his collaborators (see Chapter 22). Note that the episodic/semantic distinction becomes blurred when the recollection itself is false—that is, when what appears to be a recalled episode is actually a construct based on semantic knowledge. Such constructions, which often represent a repeated series of similar episodes, may usefully be called *repisodic* memories (Neisser, 1981).

Targeted vs. Open Recall

Episodic memories can be elicited via either *targeted* or *open* recall (Usher & Neisser, 1993). In targeted recall the subject is asked to remember a particular past event: the birth of a younger sibling, the moment when one first heard the news of an assassination, some particular incident recorded earlier in a memory diary. Open recall, in contrast, is not directed at any specific event known to the experimenter. In the cue-word method, for example, the subject simply reports whatever memory a particular cue brings to mind (Crovitz & Shiff-

man, 1974; Galton, 1879; Robinson, 1976). In other open paradigms the participant may be asked for "memories from childhood" (Waldvogel, 1948), for especially vivid memories (Rubin & Kozin, 1984), or indeed for any memories whatever (Rubin, 1982). Studies of open recall will not be reviewed here except as they bear on the "reminiscence bump" (see below).

Involuntary memories (Salaman, 1970), which come to mind without being sought after, do not fit on either side of the targeted/open dichotomy. The best-known literary example is that described by Marcel Proust (1934), for whom the taste of a madeleine cake suddenly evoked a rich world of long-forgotten experiences. Berntsen's (1996, 1998) questionnaire and diary studies suggest that involuntary memories are quite common. Most of them, like Proust's, are apparently cued by specific environmental stimuli.

Implicit Theories

Bartlett's "schema" is not the only construct that has been used to explain memory errors. Michael Ross (1989) has proposed that memories are shaped in part by people's *implicit theories* about particular domains of experience. Many instances have been documented. Patients in pain clinics, for example, recall their pain levels of the last week as largely similar to their pain of today (Eich, Reeves, Jaeger, & Graff-Radford, 1985); the implicit theory here is that nothing much has changed. In contrast, pain patients who have received therapy tend to recall earlier levels as having been higher than they really were (Linton & Melin, 1982); here the theory is that the therapy must have done some good. Similarly, students who have just taken a study-skills course tend to underestimate the skill ratings they made before the course began (Conway & Ross, 1984). The fact that college students tend to overestimate their remembered high-school grades, documented by Bahrick, Hall, and Berger (1996), may also reflect the influence of implicit theories: the subjects knew that most of their grades had been high! (For details, see Chapter 22.)

Suggestion

There is no doubt that memories can be altered by various forms of suggestion. Hypnotic suggestion is perhaps the most obvious example (Laurence & Perry, 1983; McConkey, Barnier, & Sheehan, 1998), but it lies beyond the scope of this chapter. Other forms of suggestion can also occur in clinical contexts; in particular, false memories of sexual child abuse can result from suggestion during psychotherapy (Ofshe & Watters, 1994; Pendergrast, 1995). This does not mean that every "discovered memory" (Schooler, 1997) can be dismissed out of hand: many recollections of sexual abuse are all too valid. Generally speaking, there is no way to determine the accuracy of a given recollection without external evidence. (See Chapter 10 for a review of the false memory controversy.)

Suggestions can also be presented in less dramatic ways. In the "misinformation" paradigm (Loftus, Miller, & Burns, 1978), for example, suggestions embedded in what seem to be straightforward questions can create specific false beliefs. In a paradigm developed by Hyman, Husband, and Billings (1995), college students provide their parents' addresses so the experimenter can ask about various events that they (the students) had experienced as children. The responses are used to create individualized lists of childhood experiences, each including one spurious ("target") event that had not actually occurred. Of course, the subjects do not recall the target events, though the others are familiar enough. They are then asked to schedule a second session, and meanwhile to try to remember more about all the events. With this procedure, about 20% of the subjects report (in the second session) that they remember at least a little about the nonexistent target experiences.

While it is apparently possible to "insert" an entirely false event into someone's memory, altering the details of a firmly held recollection is a different matter. Established memories tend to resist substantive changes. This is true even if the memory in question is itself mistaken, as was the case in Neisser and Harsch's (1992) study of *Challenger* memories (see below).

Memory for Important Events

Reception Events

One's first encounter with an astonishing or dismaying piece of news is often memorable in its own right: many older Americans still recall the moment when they first learned of the assassination of President Kennedy. It was Brown and Kulik's (1977) study of such recollections that introduced the concept of "flashbulb memory" to psychology. (See Brewer, 1992, for an analysis of the Brown and Kulik paper and its impact.) This term is still widely used although the metaphor on which it is based—"permanent registration not only of the significant novelty but of all recent brain events" (p. 76)—is a poor fit to prevailing views about the role of constructive processes in memory.

The task of Brown and Kulik's informants was to recall a *reception context* (S. F. Larsen, 1992)—that is, the circumstances in which they first learned of some important event. There have been many other studies of this kind, focused not only on the 1963 Kennedy assassination (Winograd & Killinger, 1983; Yarmey & Bull, 1978), but on a variety of other events: the Japanese attack on Pearl Harbor in 1941 (Neisser, 1982, 1986; Thompson & Cowan, 1986); the murder of Olaf Palme in 1986 (Christiansson, 1989, S. F. Larsen, 1992); the attempted assassination of Ronald Reagan in 1981 (Pillemer, 1984); the 1986 explosion of the space shuttle *Challenger* (Bohannon & Symons, 1992; McCloskey, Wible, & Cohen, 1988; Neisser & Harsch, 1992; Warren & Swartwood, 1992); the 1989 Hillsborough soccer riot (Wright, 1993); the resignation of Prime Minister Thatcher in 1990 (Cohen, Conway, & Maylor, 1994; Conway et al., 1994); and the bombing of Iraq, which marked the beginning of the Gulf War in 1991 (Weaver, 1993).

The accuracy of such memories was called into question by Neisser and Harsch (1992), whose informants had recorded the details of their reception context (in which they first learned of the *Challenger* explosion) only one day after the event. Three years later, about a third of those informants produced confident but completely false accounts of what had happened; they did not readily give up those accounts even when faced with contradictory evidence.

According to Linda Levine's (1997) study of Ross Perot partisans, memory for the emotions aroused by a news event is also vulnerable to distortion. When Perot temporarily withdrew his presidential candidacy in July 1992, a large number of his supporters were asked how they had reacted to that withdrawal. When the same individuals tried to recall those reactions after the November election, their recollections were substantially biased by their current views (e.g., supporters who remained loyal to Perot underestimated how sad and angry they had felt when he withdrew). Levine (1997) also reviews other studies of memory for emotion.

Directly Experienced Events

Although hearing the news of a public event can arouse strong emotions, such events do not concern most people personally. Informants who are asked to describe vivid personal memories rarely list any reception events at all (Rubin & Kozin, 1984). What do we know about memory for experiences in which people were more directly involved— experiences that may have changed their lives (Pillemer, 1998)? Such experiences may occur in combat, but the accuracy of wartime memories is notoriously difficult to establish (Gimbel, 1992). In a study of concentration-camp survivors who were interviewed in the 1940s and again in the 1980s, Wagenaar and Groeneweg (1990) found that their recollections of salient events were generally consistent but far from perfect.

Clearer results appear in two recent studies. Thompson, Morton and Fraser (1997) compared the accounts given by 27 survivors of the *Marchioness*, a pleasure cruiser which sank in the Thames in 1989 with much loss of life. Cross-validation showed that almost all these accounts, given at delays ranging from 10 days to two years after the event, were compatible and thus presumably accurate. In Neisser et al.'s (1996) study of the 1989 Loma Prieta earthquake in California, informants were asked to record their earthquake experiences a few days after the event, and again one-and-a-half years later. There were no substantial errors; indeed, recalls were almost perfectly consistent. This remarkable accuracy cannot be ascribed to high arousal; most of Neisser et al.'s informants had been in no danger and did not report being especially alarmed. A more plausible explanation of the high accuracy levels in both these studies can be given in terms of rehearsal: people who narrowly escape drowning or are present at a major earthquake are likely to have told the story of their experiences many times.

Life Narratives

All of us can, on request, give at least some account of the course of our lives so far. That account is based on many sources of informa-

tion; it includes things we have been told (e.g., our date and place of birth) as well what we remember personally. Brewer (1986) defines *autobiographical memory* to include all forms of self-related information; in contrast, Nelson (1993) prefers to restrict the term to recollections with particular significance. Many theorists have stressed the importance of certain key memories for the life story: "momentous events" (Pillemer, 1998), "turning points" (Bruner, 1994), or "nuclear episodes," which McAdams (1985) defines as "recollections of the most significant single scenes in a person's life story" (p. 170).

These stories are central to our experience of self; they are one way of saying who we are. (There are also other ways; Neisser, 1988b, lists the "temporally extended" self as only one of five different forms of self-knowledge.) But life stories are not simply concatenations of isolated events; on the contrary, we usually organize our remembered experiences into a *narrative*. "Narrative is the cognitive process that gives meaning to temporal events by identifying them as parts of a plot" (Polkinghorne, 1991, p. 136), and that process is constantly at work as we recall our own experiences. Of course, such a definition of the life narrative says nothing about its accuracy: memories may be vivid and meaningful and yet very substantially mistaken.

The Reminiscence Bump

In most memory research, the events to be remembered are selected by the experimenter. In the method of *open recall*, however, subjects choose those events themselves. Many of the memories retrieved under these conditions are from the recent past, but older memories appear as well. In general, the probability that a recalled event stems from exactly X hours/days/years ago declines monotonically with X according to a well-defined function (Rubin, 1982; Rubin, Wetzler, & Nebes, 1986). There are two exceptions to this principle. First, "too few" memories are retrieved from the first few years of life (Rubin, Rahhal, & Poon, 1998; Rubin et al., 1986); this can be regarded as a definition of childhood amnesia. Second, middle-aged and older adults produce disproportionate numbers of memories from adolescence and early adulthood: roughly, from ages 10 to 25 (Fitzgerald & Lawrence, 1984; Rubin et al., 1986). This pattern, now called the *reminiscence bump*, also emerges in free life narratives (Fromholt & Larsen, 1991). It is not limited to episodic memory: in every cognitive domain, "things learned early in adulthood are remembered best" (Rubin et al., 1998, p. 3). This is the period that adults identify as their own "era" (Sehulster, 1996), from which their favorite books (S. F. Larsen, 1996), music (Holbrook & Schindler, 1989), and films (Sehulster, 1996) are drawn. People judge political events that occurred during this period as especially important (Schuman & Scott, 1989), and they know more about them (Rubin et al., 1998).

There are at least three possible explanations of the reminiscence bump (Rubin et al., 1998). The *maturational* hypothesis postulates that cognitive capacities are simply at their peak during this period, the *life narrative* hypothesis notes that this is the stage of life during which individuals assume their adult social identities, and the *cognitive* hypothesis assumes that encoding is best during periods of rapid change whereas memories stabilize during periods of stasis. Schrauf and Rubin's (1998) study of the reminiscence bumps of adult immigrants supports the second or third of these hypotheses.

Everyday Memory

Diary Studies

Marigold Linton (1975) was the first modern psychologist to keep a daily record of life experiences and later test her own recall. The longest (five years) study of this kind was that of Willem Wagenaar (1986), who recorded each experience in terms of *who, what, where,* and *when*, and later used the same descriptors as recall cues. Forgetting was very slow, and items that had seemed entirely forgotten could often be retrieved with additional cuing. A follow-up analysis showed that experiences that Wagenaar had rated as "self-related, very unpleasant" were remembered especially well (Wagenaar, 1994).

Other important diary studies: Thompson (1982) showed that events recorded by roommates were recalled as well as those recorded by the respondents themselves; Barclay and his associates (Barclay & DeCooke, 1988; Barclay & Wellman, 1986) found that diarists may accept false entries ("foils") as their own in recognition tests (see also Conway, Collins, Gathercole, & Anderson, 1996); S. F. Larsen (1992) reported that his memory for "news contexts" (the situations in which he had first

heard a piece of news) was especially poor. Thompson, Skowronski, Larsen, and Betz (1996) report the results of a fifteen-year program of diary research.

In most diary studies, the events to be recorded are chosen by the diarists themselves. To avoid this source of bias, Brewer's (1988) subjects carried "beepers" that sounded at random intervals. At the beep, they recorded where they were as well as what they were doing and thinking about. Actions were remembered better than thoughts, and *uniqueness* was the best predictor that an action would be remembered whereas *affect* was the best predictor for thoughts. There were few errors or distortions, though subjects recalling a given event sometimes retrieved a different "time slice" than the one they had originally recorded.

Recalling Dates and Temporal Order

Friedman (1993) and Jobe, Tourangeau, and Smith (1993) have reviewed memory for the dates of life events. Day-of-the-week judgments depend less on recall of the core aspects of an event than on memory for contextual details that help assign it to its appropriate place in a personal schedule (Larsen & Thompson, 1995). Many such schedules are cyclical (e.g., weekly, yearly), and errors in dating at different levels of temporal organization are apparently independent (Huttenlocher, Hedges, & Prohaska, 1992).

A useful strategy in linear schedules is to relate the target to a landmark event with a known date (Friedman, 1993). Prompting people to use this strategy can increase accuracy (Loftus & Marburger, 1983; Belli, 1998). "Distance" information (i.e., how long ago an event "feels") may also be helpful (Friedman, 1993); Kemp and Burt (1998) suggest that it can be used in judging whether a given action (feeding the cat, brushing one's teeth) has been performed yet on a given day.

Memory for Places

Tolman's (1948) term "cognitive map" remains popular as a way to describe what people know about specific locales. When Bahrick (1983) asked Ohio Wesleyan alumni to recall the layout of the college and the town, he found that the names of landmarks and buildings remained available for many years after graduation while street names and positions were more quickly forgotten. There has also been work on the recall of actual maps (Thorndike & Hayes-Roth, 1982; Tversky, 1981). For a recent review see Tversky (1997) and chapter 23.

Often, the task is not just to recall the layout of an environment but also to remember where a specific object was put. Winograd and Soloway (1986) conducted a study in which subjects imagined hiding various objects and later tried to recall where the objects were. The results showed that unique and unlikely locations, which seem to be good cues at the time of hiding, are difficult to remember later. For a related questionnaire study, see Brown and Rahhal (1994).

Places are often remembered in a personally significant way, comprising what Louise Chawla calls an environmental autobiography, a "detailed reminiscence of well remembered places" (Chawla, 1994, p. xx; see also Cobb, 1959; Sobel, 1990). Cooper-Marcus (1992) argues that memories of the place itself and of the emotion felt in that place are orthogonal, though both are important. G. Stanley Hall (1899), one of the founders of American psychology, devoted a long article to such memories.

Memory for Medical Information

Survey respondents tend to underreport visits to health facilities (Loftus, Smith, Klinger, & Fiedler, 1992), but to overreport procedures that they have been advised to undergo frequently (Croyle, Loftus, Klinger, & Smith, 1992, Warnecke et al. 1997). The latter tendency probably reflects the use of implicit theories as well as simple social desirability. There is also a recency bias in dating medical events (e.g., Cohen & Java, 1995; Loftus, Klinger, Smith, & Fiedler, 1990). The accuracy of medical recall can be improved with certain techniques of questioning (e.g., Cohen & Java, 1995).

Croyle and Loftus (1993) discuss medical memory as it relates to AIDS. Another important area is memory for food consumption; the amount eaten is typically underestimated (Fries, Green, & Bowen, 1995). Croyle et al. (1992) suggest that current eating patterns affect recall of past dietary intake, an effect that may reflect the influence of implicit theories. Cognitive interviewing techniques may improve memory for food consumption (Croyle et al., 1992).

Medical memory also includes memories of pain; for a review, see Erskine, Morley, and Pearce (1990). Reports of past pain intensity are positively related to current levels (Eich et al., 1985; Smith & Safer, 1993), and to previous ratings of how much pain was expected (Kent, 1985). The relationship between affect, pain, and memory is also important (Eich, Rachman, & Lopatka, 1990; see also chapter 24).

Patients often fail to remember medical information that was given to them (Ley, 1979, 1989), and parents may forget what they were told about their children (Grover, Berkowitz, & Lewis, 1994). Moreover, information that confirms patients' previous beliefs about their conditions is remembered better than information that disconfirms those beliefs (Rice & Okun, 1994). Categorizing and simplifying the critical information can improve medical recall (Bradshaw, Ley, Kincey, & Bradshaw, 1975; Ley, 1989).

Remembering What Was Said

Recall of conversation is virtually never word for word, and remains low even when scored at the level of "idea units" (Stafford, Burggraf, & Sharkey, 1987; Stafford & Daly, 1984). John Dean, the Watergate witness who testified about his conversations with President Nixon, had almost no verbatim recall and often misremembered even the basic content of those conversations (Neisser, 1981). Nevertheless, Dean's testimony was an accurate portrayal of the activities and beliefs of the president and his staff—that is, he displayed *repisodic* memory. Neisser's (1981) assessment of Dean's testimony has been criticized by Edwards and Potter (1992), who argue that no objective standard of accuracy is possible in such cases because the meanings of conversational utterances are always constructed from context and can always be disputed.

Specific colorful phrases may escape some of these limitations. The subjects of Kintsch and Bates (1977) could sometimes identify the exact wording of amusing or off-topic remarks in a lecture they had heard. Similarly, phrases with "high interactional content" can sometimes be recalled from a discussion (MacWhinney, Keenan, & Reinke, 1982), at least for short periods. People recalling statements that have "had a specific impact on their lives" often think they remember those statements word for word (Knapp, Stohl, & Reardon, 1981), but this seems unlikely.

Hyman and Neisser (1992) audiotaped the meetings of a weekly undergraduate seminar for an entire term. A few months later, participants were asked to recall what had been said on given occasions during the seminar. Recalls were generally sparse but there were few errors; the participants seemed to choose a level of specificity at which what they said was essentially correct (Neisser, 1988a; for further analysis see Koriat & Goldsmith, 1996). Although it is often assumed that people remember their own utterances better than those of others (Miller, deWinstanley, & Carey, 1996; Ross & Sicoly, 1979), this was not the case in the studies of Stafford and her collaborators (Stafford & Daly, 1984; Stafford et al., 1987) nor for the subjects of Hyman and Neisser (1992).

Eyewitness Testimony

Laboratory vs. Field Studies

For surveys of research on adult eyewitness testimony, see Ross, Read, and Toglia (1994) or Thompson et al. (1998). Most of that research has been conducted in the laboratory using videotapes or slides, so it may not generalize to the highly arousing experience of witnessing or being the victim of a violent crime (Yuille, 1993; Yuille & Cutshall, 1986). It is also noteworthy that testimony about real crime has serious consequences, in a way that laboratory "testimony" does not.

Field studies have identified certain aspects of the eyewitness situation that could affect later identification. These include the characteristics of the target (Brigham, Maass, Snyder, & Spaulding, 1982), the duration of the interaction (Naka, Itsukushima, & Itoh, 1996), and the context at questioning (Krafka & Penrod, 1985). The own-race bias in photograph identification, familiar from laboratory research (Anthony, Copper, & Mullen, 1992; Malpass, 1993), may not appear as strongly in the field (Brigham et al., 1982).

Laboratory studies have identified a phenomenon called "bystander misidentification," in which witnesses mistakenly identify an innocent bystander as the perpetrator in a photo line-up (e.g., Ross, Ceci, Dunning, & Toglia, 1994). This effect may not generalize to more natural situations. Field studies by Read, Tollestrup, Hammersley, McFadzen,

and Christensen (1990) suggest that the presence of a bystander may make identifications more rather than less accurate.

Confidence, Accuracy, and the Cognitive Interview

Among lay persons (including jurors), high confidence is generally taken as an indicator of accuracy (Penrod & Cutler, 1995). This assumption may be mistaken. Many studies, including a recent meta-analysis by Sporer, Penrod, Read, and Cutler (1995), have found little correlation between confidence and accuracy. Nevertheless, the issue is still open. Read, Lindsay, and Nichols (1998) argue that these variables are more likely to go together in situations where both exhibit a wide range of variability, as they often do for eyewitnesses in naturalistic settings.

Some ways of asking witnesses to recall what they have seen are more effective than others. The *Cognitive Interview*, developed by Edward Geiselman and Ronald Fisher, (e.g., Geiselman, Fisher, MacKinnon, & Holland, 1986), includes four specific procedures. Witnesses are asked (1) to mentally reinstate the personal and environmental context of the incident; (2) to report everything they remember, even partial information; (3) to recall the component events in a variety of orders; and (4) to recall the incident from a variety of perspectives. Fisher, McCauley, and Geiselman (1994) discuss the development and refinement of the Cognitive Interview and review relevant research; for a critique, see Bekerian and Dennett (1993).

Children's Testimony

Children's testimony raises additional concerns. Where sexual and physical abuse are alleged, for example, children may testify only after repeated questioning by potentially biased interviewers (Ceci & Bruck 1993, 1995). Children's free recall is generally accurate but also sparse: young children, especially, provide little information on their own. This means that specific questions must be asked, but such questions are often suggestive and may produce distortions. Preschoolers in particular are susceptible to repeated suggestive questioning (e.g., Ceci & Bruck, 1993, 1995; Goodman, Quas, Batterman-Faunce, Riddlesberger, & Kuhn, 1997).

In sexual abuse cases, the event to be remembered may have been physically invasive or traumatic. Unfortunately, studies of the effects of stress and trauma on children's memory have produced mixed results (Eisen, Goodman, Qin, & Davis, 1998). The frequently secretive nature of abuse must be considered. Fivush (1998) argues that children's memories of abuse may remain fragmentary because they lack the organizing support that adults often provide for other memories. Talking about traumatic experiences has been found to facilitate later recall (Goodman et al., 1994, 1997), just as it does for more ordinary events (e.g., Tessler & Nelson, 1994).

As in the case of adults, there have been attempts to improve children's verbal reports. Qin, Quas, Redlich, and Goodman (1997) discuss different formats, including the cognitive interview modified for children. The attempt to improve children's testimony by using anatomically detailed dolls remains controversial (Koocher et al., 1995). Ceci and Bruck (1993, 1995) argue that these dolls' potential for suggestion outweighs any benefits that their use might bring.

Individual Differences

Sex Differences

Seidlitz and Diener (1998) provide a recent discussion of sex differences in autobiographical memory. On average, women may have slightly better memory for life experiences than men. Females recall more events than males do (Seidlitz & Deiner, 1998), possibly because they encode more detailed representations in the first place. Ross and Holmberg (1990) found that wives had much more vivid memories (than their husbands) of past events in their lives together. Indeed, both the husbands and the wives in this sample agreed that the wives had better memories. Ross and Holmberg (1990) suggest that women may reminisce more about social events than men, thus creating more vivid memories. Women are also more accurate at dating past events (Skowronski & Thompson, 1990).

Self-Ratings of Memory

Many different memory questionnaires have been devised: the Inventory of Memory Experiences (Herrmann & Neisser, 1978); the Cognitive Failure Questionnaire (Broadbent, Cooper, Fitzgerald, & Parkes, 1982), the everyday memory questionnaire used by Sunder-

land, Harris, and Baddeley (1983), and so on. But as noted by Herrmann (1982), asking people to rate their own memories is a paradoxical enterprise. How can individuals with poor recall be expected to remember their own memory failures? Moreover, there is little evidence that self-ratings of memory correspond to actual performance (Abson & Rabbitt, 1988; Herrmann, 1982). It should be noted, however, that most research on the validity of self-ratings has used laboratory tests as their criterion; for a different approach, see Schlechter, Herrmann, and Toglia (1990).

Personality and Intelligence

Personality characteristics may affect recall of life events. One such characteristic is the "repressive coping style," operationally defined by low self-reports of anxiety together with high scores on measures of defensiveness (Weinberger, Schwartz, & Davidson, 1979). Davis and Schwartz (1987) and Davis (1987) found that repressors had poor recall of emotional experiences, especially those that involved negative feelings toward the self. Cutler, Larsen, and Bunce (1996) and Schimmack and Hartmann (1997) suggest, however, that repressors may just experience less negative emotion to start with.

Another relevant personality trait or state is depression. Depressed individuals have especially ready access to memories of negative experiences, at least in open-recall tasks (Teasdale & Barnard, 1993). Patients with diurnal mood variation tend to recall sadder life events when they are more depressed, happier events when they are less depressed (Clark & Teasdale, 1982). Lewinsohn and Rosenbaum (1987) found that depressives' recollections of their own parents' behavior varied with whether or not they were clinically depressed at the time of recall (but see Brewin, Andrews, & Gotlib, 1993). These may seem to be obvious examples of "mood congruency," but in fact memories are not always mood congruent. Parrott and Sabini (1990) found evidence of mood incongruent recall in several naturalistic studies; they suggest that people sometimes use memories to temper or offset current feelings.

Another aspect of depressives' memory is a difficulty in recalling specific (as opposed to general) positive memories (Moffitt, Singer, Nelligan, Carlson, & Vyse, 1994; Williams, 1996). Recall of life events is also affected by other traits such as neuroticism (R. J. Larsen,

1992), trait anxiety (Cutler et al., 1996), and identity status in the progression of ego development (Neimeyer & Metzler, 1994). Memory for conversation is related positively to social competence and negatively to social anxiety (Miller et al., 1996; but see Singer, 1969). Moreover. Hyman and Billings (1997) report that acceptance of false childhood memories is correlated with high scores on the Dissociative Experiences Scale and the Creative Imagination Scale.

Research on the relationship between test intelligence and everyday memory is scarce. The reported age of earliest memory is negatively related to IQ scores (Rabbitt & McInnis, 1988; Rule & Jarrell, 1983), and people with high IQs report denser recollections of early childhood (Rabbitt & McInnis, 1988). It is possible that these richer memories result directly from higher mental abilities, but we should bear in mind that high IQ individuals are likely to come from families where parents often talked about past events with their children. As we shall see, parental encouragement of children' narratives probably influences the age from which earliest memories are reported.

Social Aspects of Memory

Performances

Every culture seems to value at least some forms of memory-based performance. In many cases these are religious rituals, which must be performed in just the same way on each occasion (McCauley, 1999). In other cases, they involve the recitation of songs or poems. In the case of a song with a definitive written text, reproducing that text requires "rote" or verbatim memory. Indeed, few errors or paraphrases appear in such performances. When individuals reach the end of what they remember of "The Star-spangled Banner," for example, they just stop; they don't improvise (Rubin, 1977). This principle does not apply to professional actors, who typically focus on their character's motives and feelings (Noice, 1992). A different situation prevails when songs or poems are performed in an established oral tradition. In these traditions the performer essentially "composes" the song anew at every performance. Such songs are typically maintained over many generations with only minor changes, not because they have been memorized by rote but because they

are tightly constrained by conventions of rhythm, rhyme, imagery, or meaning (Rubin, 1995).

In these culturally significant activities, memory is a means rather than an end. An entirely different principle governs the performances of "mnemonists," individuals who seek to impress audiences with their memory abilities. Such performances lie outside the scope of this chapter; see Thompson, Cowan, Frieman, Mahadevan, and Vogl (1991) for a recent case. Noice and Noice (1996) offer an interesting comparison of the methods used by mnemonists and by professional actors.

Social Recall

Considered from the perspective of "the ecology of everyday remembering" (Edwards & Middleton, 1986, p. 424), most memory research takes place in a rather unusual social context. The subjects' only motive for remembering is the experimenter's request, and they are expected to keep on responding until they have said everything they remember. This is not how we normally use our memories. When new parents call their friends to announce the arrival of the baby, for example, they do not simply provide a linear account of the sequence of events (Tenney, 1989). When a group of friends recall a movie together—as in Edwards and Middleton's (1986) *E.T.* experiment—the result is not a linear report but a subtly negotiated social discourse. These differences appear clearly in a paradigm devised by Ira Hyman (1994). Subjects who have just read a de Maupassant short story are divided into two groups: some meet with an experimenter and recall the story in the usual way, while others discuss the story with a peer who has also just read it. In Hyman's data the peer-discussion group produced much less continuous narrative material than the experimenter-tested subjects, but offered many more personal reactions, evaluations, and analytic comments.

Social Factors in Children's Memory

Two-year-old children can answer simple questions about the past (e.g., Fivush & Hamond, 1990), so they have at least minimal episodic memory. A few isolated memories may be established even earlier: in one documented case, a 2½-year-old verbally recalled ("whale") a picture that he had been shown during an infant experiment two years earlier (Myers, Clifton, & Clarkson, 1987). At this age children's recall must be elicited by specific questions; they do not give narrative accounts of their experiences. Moreover, what they can report about a past event depends strongly on what was verbalized by adults at the time (Tessler & Nelson, 1994).

Children's interest in the order and coherence of their own experiences develops even later. The notion of a "life narrative"—that they were born at a particular point in time, have had certain memorable experiences, and can expect to have others in the future—is acquired only gradually and of course socially. Middle-class American children are introduced to that notion by their parents, typically in the course of conversation about past events (Hudson, 1990). It has been suggested that the development of such a narrative marks the end of the period of childhood amnesia (Fivush & Hamond, 1990; Nelson, 1993). Indeed, cultural differences in how much mothers talk to their children about the past are related to the reported ages of adults' earliest memories (Mullen, 1994; Mullen & Yi, 1995). For a more extensive review of the development of memory, see chapters 18 and 19.

Transactive and Group Memories

People who spend a lot of time together, such as the two members of a married couple, may come to rely on one another to remember materials of different kinds. This situation has been called "transactive memory" (Wegner, 1987; Wegner, Erber, & Raymond, 1991). Considered as a unit, such a couple has a richer memory than either partner alone. On the other hand, misunderstandings can easily occur: one partner may rely on the other for information that he or she does not actually have. Similar transactive memory systems appear in many settings, including doctor and patient, teacher and student, foreman and employee (Wegner, 1987). For a somewhat analogous analysis of an airplane crew and the technology available to them, see "How a Cockpit Remembers its Speeds" (Hutchins, 1995).

Families and other enduring groups often develop what amount to life narratives of their own (Bruner, 1990): oral histories that establish meaning and resist change just as individual narratives do. When such a family tells its story, different members adopt well-established communicative roles such as narrator,

monitor, and mentor (Hirst & Manier, 1996). In larger groups such as nations or peoples, widely accepted group narratives merge into history itself. These "collective memories" (Halbwachs, 1992) are always highly selective, and they are often substantially distorted as well. Group narratives have been intensively studied by sociologists and historians as well as psychologists; for a recent review, see Pennebaker, Paez, and Rime (1997).

Twenty years ago, one of us noted with dismay that "If X is an interesting or socially significant aspect of memory, then psychologists have hardly ever studied X" (Neisser, 1978, p. 4). That situation soon began to change; a mere 10 years later, it seemed more appropriate to say that "If X is an interesting or socially important memory phenomenon, the chances are good . . . that quite a few people are trying to study it" (Neisser, 1988a, p. 546). Today, the situation has changed again. The study of memory for life experiences, surely among the most "interesting and socially significant" of all aspects of memory, has begun to develop a substantial body of basic knowledge in its own right. We hope this brief review of that knowledge will prove to be useful as the field continues to move forward.

References

Abson, V., & Rabbitt, P. (1988). What do self rating questionnaires tell us about changes in competence in old age? In M. M. Gruneberg, P. E. Morris, & R. N. Sykes (Eds.), *Practical aspects of memory: Current research and issues* (pp. 186–191). Chichester: John Wiley.

Anthony, T., Copper, C., & Mullen, B. (1992). Cross-racial facial identification—A social cognitive integration. *Personality and Social Psychology Bulletin, 18*(3), 296–301.

Bahrick, H. P. (1983). The cognitive map of a city: Fifty years of learning and memory. In G. H. Bower (Ed.), *The psychology of learning and motivation* (pp. 125–163). New York: Academic Press.

Bahrick, H. P., Hall, L. K., & Berger, S. A. (1996). Accuracy and distortion in memory for high school grades. *Psychological Science, 7*, 265–271.

Banaji, M. R., & Crowder, R. G. (1989). The bankruptcy of everyday memory. *American Psychologist, 44*, 1185–1193.

Barclay, C. R., & DeCooke, P. A. (1988). Ordinary everyday memories: Some of the things of which selves are made. In U.

Neisser & E. Winograd (Eds.), *Remembering reconsidered: Ecological and traditional approaches to the study of memory* (pp. 91–125). New York: Cambridge University Press.

Barclay, C. R., & Wellman, H. M. (1986). Accuracies and inaccuracies in autobiographical memories. *Journal of Memory and Language, 25*, 93–103.

Bartlett, F. C. (1932). *Remembering: A study in experimental and social psychology.* New York: Cambridge University Press.

Bekerian, D. A., & Dennet, J. L. (1993). The cognitive interview technique: Reviving the issues. *Applied Cognitive Psychology, 7*(4), 275–297.

Belli, R. F. (1998). The structure of autobiographical memory and the event history calendar: Potential improvements in the quality of retrospective reports in surveys. *Memory, 6*(4), 383–406.

Berntsen, D. (1996). Involuntary autobiographical memories. *Applied Cognitive Psychology, 10*, 435–454.

Berntsen, D. (1998). Voluntary and involuntary access to autobiographical memory. *Memory, 6*, 113–141.

Black, J. B., & Wilensky, R. (1979). An evaluation of story grammars. *Cognitive Science, 3*, 213–230.

Bohannon, J. N., & Symons, V. L. (1992). Flashbulb memories: Confidence, consistency, and quantity. In E. Winograd & U. Neisser (Eds.), *Affect and accuracy in recall: Studies of "flashbulb" memories* (pp. 65–91). New York: Academic Press.

Bradshaw, P. W., Ley, P., Kincey, J. A., & Bradshaw, J. (1975). Recall of medical advice: Comprehensibility and specificity. *British Journal of Social and Clinical Psychology, 14*(1), 55–62.

Brewer, W. F. (1986). What is autobiographical memory? In D. C. Rubin (Ed.), *Autobiographical memory* (pp. 25–49). New York: Cambridge University Press.

Brewer, W. F. (1988). Memory for randomly sampled autobiographical events. In U. Neisser & E. Winograd (Eds.), *Remembering reconsidered: Ecological and traditional approaches to the study of memory* (pp. 21–90). New York: Cambridge University Press.

Brewer, W. F. (1992). The theoretical and empirical status of the flashbulb memory hypothesis. In E. Winograd & U. Neisser (Eds.), *Affect and accuracy in recall: Studies of "flashbulb" memories* (pp. 274–305). New York: Academic Press.

Brewer, W. F., & Lichtenstein, E. H. (1982). Stories are to entertain: A structural-affect theory of stories. *Journal of Pragmatics, 6*, 473–486.

Brewin, C. R., Andrews, B., & Gotlib, I. H. (1993). Psychopathology and early experience: A reappraisal of retrospective reports. *Psychological Bulletin, 113*(1), 82–98.

Brigham, J. C., Maass, A., Snyder, L. D., & Spaulding, K. (1982). Accuracy of eyewitness identifications in a field setting. *Journal of Personality and Social Psychology, 42*(4), 673–681.

Broadbent, D. E., Cooper, P. F., Fitzgerald, P., & Parkes, K. R. (1982). The Cognitive Failures Questionnaire (CFQ) and its correlates. *British Journal of Clinical Psychology, 21*, 1–16.

Brown, A. S., & Rahhal, T. A. (1994). Hiding valuables: A questionnaire study of mnemonically risky behavior. *Applied Cognitive Psychology, 8*, 141–154.

Brown, R., & Kulik, J. (1977). Flashbulb memories. *Cognition, 5*, 73–99.

Bruner, J. (1990). *Acts of Meaning.* Cambridge, MA: Harvard University Press.

Bruner, J. (1994). The "remembered self." In U. Neisser & R. Fivush (Eds.), *The remembering self: Construction and accuracy in the self-narrative.* New York: Cambridge University Press.

Ceci, S. J., & Bruck, M. (1993). Suggestibility of the child witness: A historical review and synthesis. *Psychological Bulletin, 113*(3), 403–439.

Ceci, S. J., & Bruck, M. (1995). *Jeopardy in the courtroom.* Washington, DC: American Psychological Association.

Chawla, L. (1994). *In the first country of places.* Albany, NY: State University of New York Press.

Christianson, S.-A. (1989). Flashbulb memories: Special, but not so special. *Memory and Cognition, 17*, 435–443.

Clark, D. M., & Teasdale, J. D. (1982). Diurnal variation in clinical depression and accessibility of memories of positive and negative experiences. *Journal of Abnormal Psychology, 91*(2), 87–95.

Cobb, E. (1959). The ecology of imagination in childhood. *Daedalus, 88*, 539.

Cohen, G., Conway, M. A., & Maylor, E. A. (1994). Flashbulb memories in older adults. *Psychology and Aging, 9*, 454–463.

Cohen, G., & Java, R. (1995). Memory for medical history: Accuracy of recall. *Applied Cognitive Psychology, 9*(4), 273–288.

Conway, M. A., Anderson, S. J., Larsen, S. F., Donnelly, C. M., McDaniel, M. A., McClelland, A. G. R., Rawles, R. E., & Logie, R. H. (1994). The formation of flashbulb memories. *Memory and Cognition, 22*, 326–343.

Conway, M. A., Collins, A. F., Cathercole, S. E., & Anderson, S. J. (1996). Recollections of true and false autobiographical memories. *Journal of Experimental Psychology: General, 125*, 69–95.

Conway, M., & Ross, M. (1984). Getting what you want by revising what you had. *Journal of Personality and Social Psychology, 47*, 738–748.

Cooper-Marcus, C. (1992). Environmental memories. In I. Altman & S. M. Low (Eds.), *Human behavior and environment: Advances in theory and research: Vol. 12. Place attachment* (pp. 87–112). New York: Plenum Press.

Crovitz, H. F., & Schiffman, H. (1974). Frequency of episodic memories as a function of their age. *Bulletin of the Psychonomic Society, 4*, 517–518.

Croyle, R. T., & Loftus, E. F. (1993). Recollection in the kingdom of AIDS. In D. G. Ostrow & R. C. Kessler (Eds.), *Methodological issues in AIDS behavioral research* (pp. 163–180). New York: Plenum Press.

Croyle, R. T., Loftus, E. F., Klinger, M. R., & Smith, K. D. (1992). Reducing errors in health-related memory: Progress and prospects. In J. R. Schement & B. D. Ruben (Eds.), *Information and behavior: Vol. 4. Between communication and information* (pp. 255–268). New Brunswick, NJ: Transaction Publishers.

Cutler, S. E., Larsen, R. J., & Bunce, S. C. (1996). Repressive coping style and the experience and recall of emotion: A naturalistic study of daily affect. *Journal of Personality, 64*(2), 380–405.

Davis, P. J. (1987). Repression and the inaccessibility of affective memories. *Journal of Personality and Social Psychology, 53*(3), 585–593.

Davis, P. J., & Schwartz, G. E. (1987). Repression and the inaccessibility of affective memories. *Journal of Personality and Social Psychology, 52*(1), 155–162.

Edwards, D., & Middleton, D. (1986). Joint remembering: Constructing an account of shared experience through conversational discourse. *Discourse Processes, 9*, 423–459.

Edwards, D., & Potter, J. (1992). The Chancellor's memory: Rhetoric and truth in discursive remembering. *Applied Cognitive Psychology, 6*, 187–215.

Eich, E., Rachman, S., & Lopatka, C. (1990). Affect, pain, and autobiographical memory. *Journal of Abnormal Psychology, 99*(2), 174–178.

Eich, E., Reeves, J. L., Jaeger, B., & Graff-Radford, S. B. (1985). Memory for pain: Relation between past and present pain intensity. *Pain, 23*, 375–379.

Eisen, M. L., Goodman, G. S., Qin, J., & Davis, S. L. (1998). Memory and suggestibility in maltreated children: New research relevant to evaluating allegations of abuse. In S. J. Lynn & K. M. McConkey (Eds.), *Truth in memory* (pp. 163–189). New York: Guilford Press.

Erskine, A., Morley, S., & Pearce, S. (1990). Memory for pain: A review. *Pain, 41*(3), 255–265.

Fisher, R. P., McCauley, M. R., & Geiselman, R. E. (1994). Improving eyewitness testimony with the cognitive interview. In D. F. Ross, J. D. Read, & M. P. Toglia (Eds.), *Adult eyewitness testimony: Current trends and developments* (pp. 245–269). New York: Cambridge University Press.

Fitzgerald, J. M., & Lawrence, R. (1984). Autobiographical memory across the life-span. *Journal of Gerontology, 39*, 692–699.

Fivush, R. (1998). Children's recollections of traumatic and non-traumatic events. *Development and Psychopathology, 10*, 699–710.

Fivush, R., & Hamond, N. R. (1990). Autobiographical memory across the preschool years: Toward reconceptualizing childhood amnesia. In R. Fivush & J. A. Hudson (Eds.), *Knowing and remembering in young children*. New York: Cambridge University Press.

Friedman, W. J. (1993). Memory for the time of past events. *Psychological Bulletin, 113*(1), 44–66.

Fries, E., Green, P., & Bowen, D. J. (1995). What did I eat yesterday? Determinants of accuracy in 24-hour food memories. *Applied Cognitive Psychology, 9*(2), 143–156.

Fromholt, P., & Larsen, S. F. (1991). Autobiographical memory in normal aging and primary degenerative dementia (dementia of Alzheimer type). *Journal of Gerontology, 46*(3), P85–P91.

Galton, F. (1879). Psychometric experiments. *Brain, 2*, 149–162.

Gauld, A., & Stephenson, G. M. (1967). Some experiments relating to Bartlett's theory of remembering. *British Journal of Psychology, 58*, 39–49.

Geiselman, R. E., Fisher, R. P., MacKinnon, D. P., & Holland, H. L. (1986). Enhancement of eyewitness memory with the cognitive interview. *American Journal of Psychology, 99*, 385–401.

Gimbel, C. (1992). *Memories of wartime experience: Do forty years make a difference?* Doctoral dissertation (Sociology), University of North Carolina.

Goodman, G. S., Quas, J. A., Batterman-Faunce, J. M., Riddlesberger, M. M., & Kuhn, J. (1994). Predictors of accurate and inaccurate memories of traumatic events experienced in childhood. *Consciousness and Cognition, 3*, 269–294.

Goodman, G. S., Quas, J. A., Batterman-Faunce, J. M., Riddlesberger, M. M., & Kuhn, J. (1997). Children's reactions to and memory for a stressful event: Influences of age, anatomical dolls, knowledge, and parental attachment. *Applied Developmental Science, 1*(2), 54–75.

Grover, G., Berkowitz, C. D., & Lewis, R. J. (1994). Parental recall after a visit to the emergency department. *Clinical Pediatrics*, April, 194–201.

Gruneberg, M. M., Morris, P. E., & Sykes, R. N. (Eds.). (1978). *Practical aspects of memory.* London: Academic Press.

Halbwachs, M. (1992). *On collective memory.* Chicago: University of Chicago Press. (Original work published 1950)

Hall, G. S. (1899). Note on early memories. *Pedagogical Seminary, 6*(4), 485–512.

Henderson, E. N. (1903). A study of memory for connected trains of thought. *Psychological Review Monograph Supplements, 5*, No. 6 (Whole No. 23).

Herrmann, D. J. (1982). Know thy memory: The use of questionnaires to assess and study memory. *Psychological Bulletin, 92*, 434–452.

Herrmann, D. J., & Neisser, U. (1978). An inventory of everyday memory experiences. In M. M. Gruneberg, P. E. Morris, & R. N. Sykes (Eds.), *Practical aspects of memory* (pp. 35–51). London: Academic Press.

Hirst, W., & Manier, D. (1996). Remembering as communication: A family recounts its past. In D. C. Rubin (Ed.), *Remembering our past: Studies in autobiographical memory* (pp. 271–290). New York: Cambridge University Press.

Holbrook, M. B., & Schindler, R. M. (1989). Some exploratory findings on the development of musical tastes. *Journal of Consumer Research, 16*, 119–124.

Hudson, J. A. (1990). The emergence of autobiographic memory in mother-child conversation. In R. Fivush & J. A. Hudson (Eds.), *Knowing and remembering in young children* (pp. 166–196). New York: Cambridge University Press.

Hutchins, E. (1995). How a cockpit remembers its speeds. *Cognitive Science, 19*, 265–288.

Huttenlocher, J., Hedges, L. V., & Prohaska, V. (1992). Memory for day of the week: A 5 + 2 day cycle. *Journal of Experimental Psychology: General, 121*(3), 313–325.

Hyman, I. E., Jr. (1994). Conversational remembering: Story recall with a peer versus for an experimenter. *Applied Cognitive Psychology, 8*, 49–66.

Hyman, I. E., Jr., & Billings, F. J. (1997). Individual differences and the creation of false childhood memories. *Memory, 6*, 1–20.

Hyman, I. E., Jr., Husband, T. H., & Billings, F. J. (1995). False memories of childhood experiences. *Applied Cognitive Psychology, 9*, 181–197.

Hyman, I. E., Jr., & Neisser, U. (1992). The role of the self in recollections of a seminar. *Journal of Narrative and Life History, 2*, 81–103.

Jobe, J. B., Tourangeau, R., & Smith, A. F. (1993). Contributions of survey research to the understanding of memory. *Applied Cognitive Psychology, 7*, 567–584.

Johnson, R. E. (1962). The retention of qualitative changes in learning. *Journal of Verbal Learning and Verbal Behavior, 1*, 218–223.

Kemp, S., & Burt, C. D. B. (1998). The force of events: Cross-modality matching the recency of news events. *Memory, 6*(3), 297–306.

Kent, G. (1985). Memory of dental pain. *Pain, 21*(2), 187–194.

Kintsch, W., & Bates, E. (1977). Recognition memory for statements from a classroom lecture. *Journal of Experimental Psychology: Human Learning and Memory, 3*, 150–159.

Knapp, M. L., Stohl, C., & Reardon, K. K. (1981). "Memorable" messages. *Journal of Communication, 31*(4) 27–41.

Koocher, G. P., Goodman, G. S., White, C. S., Friedrich, W. N., Sivan, A. B., & Reynolds, C. R. (1995). Psychological science and the use of anatomically detailed dolls in child sexual-abuse assessments. *Psychological Bulletin, 118*(2), 199–222.

Koriat, A., & Goldsmith, M. (1996). Memory metaphors and the real life/laboratory controversy: Correspondence versus storehouse conceptions of memory. *Behavioral and Brain Sciences, 19*, 167–228.

Krafka, C., & Penrod, S. (1985). Reinstatement of context in a field experiment on eyewitness identification. *Journal of Personality and Social Psychology, 49*(1), 58–69.

Larsen, R. J. (1992). Neuroticism and selective encoding and recall of symptoms: Evidence from a combined concurrent-retrospective study. *Journal of Personality and Social Psychology, 62*(3), 480–488.

Larsen, S. F. (1992). Potential flashbulbs: Memories of ordinary news as the baseline. In E. Winograd & U. Neisser (Eds.), *Affect and accuracy in recall: Studies of "flashbulb" memories* (pp. 32–64). New York: Cambridge University Press.

Larsen, S. F. (1996). Memorable books: Recall of reading and its personal context. In R. J. Kreuz & M. S. MacNealy (Eds.), *Empirical approaches to literature and aesthetics (advances in discourse processes* (Vol. 52; pp. 583–599). Norwood, NJ: Ablex.

Larsen, S. F., & Thompson, C. P. (1995). Reconstructive memory in the dating of personal and public news events. *Memory & Cognition, 23*(6), 780–790.

Laurence, J.-R., & Perry, C. (1983). Hypnotically created memory among highly hypnotizable subjects. *Science, 222,* 523–524.

Levine, L. J. (1997). Reconstructing memory for emotions. *Journal of Experimental Psychology: General, 126,* 165–177.

Lewinsohn, P. M., & Rosenbaum, M. (1987). Recall of parental behavior by acute depressives, remitted depressives and nondepressives. *Journal of Personality and Social Psychology, 52,* 611–619.

Ley, P. (1979). Memory for medical information. *British Journal of Social and Clinical Psychology, 18*(2), 245–255.

Ley, P. (1989). Improving patients' understanding, recall, satisfaction and compliance. In A. K. Broome (Ed.), *Health psychology: Processes and applications* (pp. 74–102). London: Chapman & Hall.

Linton, M. (1975). Memory for real-world events, In D. A. Norman & D. E. Rumelhart (Eds.), *Explorations in cognition.* San Francisco: Freeman.

Linton, S. J., & Melin, L. (1982). The accuracy of remembering chronic pain. *Pain, 13,* 281–285.

Loftus, E. F., Klinger, M. R., Smith, K. D., & Fiedler, J. (1990). A tale of two questions: Benefits of asking more than one question. *Public Opinion Quarterly, 54,* 330–345.

Loftus, E. F., & Marburger, W. (1983). Since the eruption of Mt. St. Helens, has anyone beaten you up? Improving the accuracy of retrospective reports with landmark events. *Memory & Cognition, 11*(2), 114–120.

Loftus, E. F., Miller, D. G., & Burns, H. J. (1978). Semantic integration of verbal information into a visual memory. *Journal of Experimental Psychology: Human Learning and Memory, 4,* 19–31.

Loftus, E. F., Smith, K. D., Klinger, M. R., & Fiedler, J. D. (1992). Memory and mismemory for health events. In J. M. Tanur (Ed.), *Questions about survey questions: Inquiries into the cognitive bases of surveys* (pp. 102–137). New York: Russell Sage.

MacWhinney, B., Keenan, J. M., & Reinke, P. (1982). The role of arousal in memory for conversation. *Memory and Cognition, 10,* 308–317.

Malpass, R. S. (1993). They all look alike to me. In G. G. Brannigan & M. R. Merrens (Eds.), *The undaunted psychologist: Adventures in research* (pp. 75–88). Philadelphia: Temple University Press.

Mandler, J. M., & Johnson, N. S. (1977). Remembrance of things parsed: Story structure and recall. *Cognitive Psychology, 9,* 111–151.

McAdams, D. (1985). *Power, intimacy and the life story.* Homewood, IL: Dorsey Press.

McCauley, R. N. (1999). Bringing ritual to mind. In E. Winograd, R. Fivush, & W. Hirst (Eds.), *Ecological approaches to perception and cognition: Essays in honor of Ulric Neisser.* Mahwah, NJ: Erlbaum.

McCloskey, M., Wible, C. G., & Cohen, N. (1988). Is there a special flashbulb-memory mechanism? *Journal of Experimental Psychology: General, 117,* 171–181.

McConkey, K. M., Barnier, A. J., & Sheehan, P. W. (1998). Hypnosis and pseudomemory: Understanding the findings and their implications. In S. J. Lynn & K. M. McConkey (Eds.), *Truth in memory* (pp. 227–259). New York: Guilford Press.

Miller, J. B., deWinstanley, P., & Carey, P. (1996). Memory for conversation. *Memory, 4,* 615–631.

Moffitt, K. H., Singer, J. A., Nelligan, D. W., Carlson, M. A., & Vyse, S. A. (1994). Depression and memory narrative type. *Journal of Abnormal Psychology, 103*(3), 581–583.

Mullen, M. K. (1994). Earliest recollections of childhood: A demographic analysis. *Cognition, 52,* 55–79.

Mullen, M. K., & Yi, S. (1995). The cultural context of talk about the past: Implications for the development of autobiographical memory. *Cognitive Development, 10,* 407–419.

Myers, N. A., Clifton, R. K., & Clarkson, M. G. (1987). When they were very young: Almost-threes remember two years ago. *Infant Behavior and Development, 10,* 123–132.

Naka, M., Itsukushima, Y., & Itoh, Y. (1996). Eyewitness testimony after three months: A field study on memory for an incident in everyday life. *Japanese Psychological Research, 38*(1), 14–24.

Neimeyer, G. J., & Metzler, A. E. (1994). Personal identity and autobiographical recall. In U. Neisser & R. Fivush (Eds.), *The remembering self: Construction and accuracy in the self-narrative* (pp. 105–135). New York: Cambridge University press.

Neisser, U. (1978). Memory: What are the important questions? In M. M. Gruneberg, P. E. Morris, & R. N. Sykes (Eds.), *Practical aspects of memory* (pp. 3–24). London: Academic Press.

Neisser, U. (1981). John Dean's memory: A case study. *Cognition, 9,* 1–22.

Neisser, U. (1982). Snapshots or benchmarks? In U. Neisser (Ed.), *Memory observed: Remembering in natural contexts* (pp. 43–48). New York: Freeman.

Neisser, U. (1986). Remembering Pearl Harbor: Reply to Thompson and Cowan. *Cognition, 23,* 285–286.

Neisser, U. (1988a). Time present and time past. In M. M. Gruneberg, P. E. Morris, & R. N. Sykes (Eds.), *Practical aspects of memory: Current research and issues* (Vol. 2; pp. 545–560). Chichester: John Wiley.

Neisser, U. (1988b). Five kinds of self-knowledge. *Philosophical Psychology, 1,* 35–39.

Neisser, U. (1991). A case of misplaced nostalgia. *American Psychologist, 46,* 34–36.

Neisser, U. (1998). Stories, selves, and schemata: A review of ecological findings. In M. A. Conway, S. E. Gathercole, & C. Cornoldi (Eds.), *Theories of memory* (Vol. 2; pp. 171–186). Hove, England: Psychology Press.

Neisser, U., & Harsch., N. (1992). Phantom flashbulbs: False recollections of hearing the news about *Challenger.* In E. Winograd & U. Neisser (Eds.), *Affect and accuracy in recall: Studies of "flashbulb" memories* (pp. 9–31). New York: Cambridge University Press.

Neisser, U., Winograd, E., Bergman, E. T., Schreiber, C. A., Palmer, S. E., & Weldon, M. S. (1996). Remembering the earthquake: Direct experience vs. hearing the news. *Memory, 4*(4), 337–357.

Nelson, K. (1993). The psychological and social origins of autobiographical memory. *Psychological Science, 4*(1), 7–14.

Noice, H. (1992). Elaborative memory strategies of professional actors. *Applied Cognitive Psychology, 6,* 417–427.

Noice, H., & Noice, T. (1996). Two approaches to learning a theatrical script. *Memory, 4,* 1–17.

Ofshe, R., & Watters, E. (1994). *Making monsters: False memories, psychotherapy, and sexual hysteria.* New York: Charles Scribner's.

Parrott, W. G., & Sabini, J. (1990). Mood and memory under natural conditions: Evidence for mood incongruent recall. *Journal of Personality and Social Psychology, 59*(2), 321–336.

Paul, I. H. (1959). Studies in remembering: The reproduction of connected and extended verbal material. *Psychological Issues, 1* (Monograph No. 2), 1–152.

Pendergrast, M. (1995). *Victims of memory: Incest accusations and shattered lives.* Hinesburg, VT: Upper Access Books.

Pennebaker, J. W., Paez, D., & Rime, B. (1997). *Collective memory of political events.* Mahwah, NJ: Erlbaum.

Penrod, S., & Cutler, B. (1995). Witness confidence and witness accuracy: Assessing their forensic relation. *Psychology, Public Policy, and Law, 1,* 817–845.

Pillemer, D. B. (1984). Flashbulb memories of the assassination attempt on President Reagan. *Cognition, 16,* 63–80.

Pillemer, D. B. (1998). *Momentous events, vivid memories: How unforgettable moments help us understand the meaning of our lives.* Cambridge, MA: Harvard University Press.

Polkinghorne, D. E. (1991). Narrative and self-concept. *Journal of Narrative and Life History, 1,* 135–153.

Proust, M. (1934). *Remembrance of things past.* New York: Random House.

Qin, J., Quas, J. A., Redlich, A. D., & Goodman, G. S. (1997). Children's eyewitness testimony: Memory development in the legal context. In N. Cowan (Ed.), *The development of memory in childhood* (pp. 301–342). Sussex, England: Psychology Press.

Rabbitt, P., & McInnis, L. (1988). Do clever old people have earlier and richer first memories? *Psychology and Aging, 3*(4), 338–341.

Read, J. D., Lindsay, D. S., & Nichols, T. (1998). The relationship between confidence and accuracy in eyewitness identification studies: Is the conclusion changing? In C. P. Thompson, D. J. Herrmann, J. D. Read, D. Bruce, D. G. Payne, & M. P. Toglia (Eds.), *Eyewitness memory: Theoretical and applied perspectives* (pp. 107–130). Mahwah, NJ: Erlbaum.

Read, J. D., Tollestrup, P., Hammersley, R., McFadzen, E., & Christensen, A. (1990). The unconscious transference effect: Are innocent bystanders ever misidenitified? *Applied Cognitive Psychology, 4*, 3–31.

Rice, G. E., & Okun, M. A. (1994). Older readers' processing of medical information that contradicts their beliefs. *Journal of gerontology: Psychological Sciences, 49*(3), P119–P128.

Robinson, J. A. (1976). Sampling autobiographical memory. *Cognitive Psychology, 8*, 578–595.

Ross, D. F., Ceci, S. J., Dunning, D., & Toglia, M. P. (1994). Unconscious transference and lineup identification: Toward a memory blending approach. In D. F. Ross, J. D. Read, & M. P. Toglia (Eds.), *Adult eyewitness testimony: Current trends and developments* (pp. 80–100). New York: Cambridge University Press.

Ross, D. F., Read, J. D., & Toglia, M. P. (1994). *Adult eyewitness testimony: Current trends and developments.* New York: Cambridge University Press.

Ross, M. (1989). Relation of implicit theories to the construction of personal histories. *Psychological Review, 96*, 341–357.

Ross, M., & Holmberg, D. (1990). Recounting the past: Gender differences in the recall of events in the history of a close relationship. In J. M. Olson & M. P. Zanna (Eds.), *The Ontario symposium: Vol. 6. Self-inference processes* (pp. 135–152). Hillsdale, NJ: Erlbaum.

Ross, M., & Sicoly, F. (1979). Egocentric biases in availability and attribution. *Journal of Personality and Social Psychology, 37*, 322–336.

Rubin, D. C. (1977). Very long-term memory for prose and verse. *Journal of Verbal Leaning and Verbal Behavior, 16*, 611–621.

Rubin, D. C. (1982). On the retention function for autobiographical memory. *Journal of Verbal Learning and Behavior, 19*, 21–38.

Rubin, D. C. (1995). *Memory in oral traditions: The cognitive psychology of epic, ballads, and counting-out rhymes.* New York: Oxford University Press.

Rubin, D. C., & Kozin, M. (1984). Vivid memories. *Cognition, 16*, 81–95.

Rubin, D. C., Rahhal, T. A., & Poon, L. W. (1998). Things learned early in adulthood are remembered best. *Memory and Cognition, 26*(1), 3–19.

Rubin, D. C., Wetzler, S. E., & Nebes, R. D. (1986). Autobiographical memory across the lifespan. In D. C. Rubin (Ed.), *Autobiographical memory* (pp. 202–224). New York: Cambridge University Press.

Rule, W. R., & Jarrell, G. R. (1983). Intelligence and earliest memories. *Perceptual and Motor Skills, 56*, 795.

Rumelhart, D. E. (1975). Notes on a schema for stories. In D. LaBerge & J. Samuels (Eds.), *Representation and understanding: Studies in cognitive science* (pp. 211–236). New York: Academic Press.

Salaman, E. (1970). *A collection of moments: A study of involuntary memories.* London: Longman.

Schimmack, U., & Hartmann, K. (1997). Individual differences in the memory representation of emotional episodes: Exploring the cognitive processes in repression. *Journal of Personality and Social Psychology, 73*(5), 1064–1079.

Schlechter, T. M., Herrmann, D. J., & Toglia, M. P. (1990). An investigation of people's metamemories for naturally occurring events. *Applied Cognitive Psychology, 4*(3), 213–217.

Schooler, J. W. (1997). Reflections on a memory discovery. *Child Maltreatment, 2*, 121–128.

Schrauf, R. W., & Rubin, D. C. (1998). Bilingual autobiographical memory in older adult immigrants: A test of cognitive explanations of the reminiscence bump and the linguistic encoding of memories. *Journal of Memory and Language, 39*, 1–21.

Schuman, H., & Scott, J. (1989). Generations and collective memories. *American Sociological Review, 54*, 359–381.

Sehulster, J. R. (1996). In my era: Evidence for the perception of a special period of the past. *Memory, 4*(2), 145–158.

Seidlitz, L., & Diener, E. (1998). Sex differences in the recall of affective experiences. *Journal of Personality and Social Psychology, 74*(1), 262–271.

Singer, S. (1969). Factors related to participants' memory of a conversation. *Journal of Personality, 37*, 93–110.

Skowronski, J. J., & Thompson, C. P. (1990). Reconstructing the dates of personal events: Gender differences in accuracy. *Applied Cognitive Psychology, 4*, 371–381.

Smith, W. B., & Safer, M. A. (1993). Effects of present pain level on recall of chronic pain and medication use. *Pain, 55*(3), 355–361.

Sobel, D. (1990). A place in the world: Adults' memories of childhood's special places. *Children's Environments Quarterly, 7*(4), 5–12.

Sporer, S. L., Penrod, S., Read, D., & Cutler, B. (1995). Choosing, confidence, and accuracy—A meta-analysis of the confidence-accuracy relation in eyewitness identification studies. *Psychological Bulletin, 118*(3), 315–327.

Stafford, L., Burggraf, C. S., & Sharkey, W. F. (1987). Conversational memory: The effects of time, recall mode, and memory expectancies on remembrances of natural conversations. *Human Communication Research, 14*, 203–229.

Stafford, L., & Daly, J. A. (1984). Conversational memory: The effects of recall mode and memory expectancies on remembrances of natural conversations. *Human Communication Research, 10*, 379–402.

Sunderland, A., Harris, J. E., & Baddeley, A. D. (1983). Do laboratory tests predict everyday memory? *Journal of Verbal Learning and Verbal Behavior, 22*, 341–357.

Teasdale, J. D., & Barnard, P. J. (1993). *Affect, cognition, and change: Remodelling depressive thought.* London: Erlbaum.

Tenney, Y. J. (1989). Predicting conversational reports of a personal event. *Cognitive Science, 13*, 213–233.

Tessler, M., & Nelson, K. (1994). Making memories: The influence of joint encoding on later recall by young children. *Consciousness and Cognition, 3*, 307–326.

Thompson, C. P. (1982). Memory for unique personal events: The roommate study. *Memory and Cognition, 10*, 324–332.

Thompson, C. P., & Cowan, T. (1986). Flashbulb memories: A nicer interpretation of a Neisser recollection. *Cognition, 22*, 199–200.

Thompson, C. P., Cowan, T., Frieman, J., Mahadevan, R. S., & Vogl, R. J. (1991). Rajan: A study of a mnemonist. *Journal of Memory and Language, 30*, 702–724.

Thompson, C. P., Herrmann, D. J., Read, D. J., Bruce, D., Payne, D. G., & Toglia, M. P. (Eds.). (1998). *Eyewitness memory: Theoretical and applied perspectives.* Mahwah, NJ: Erlabaum.

Thompson, C. P., Skowronski, J. J., Larsen, S. F., & Betz, A. L. (1996). *Autobiographical memories: Remembering what and remembering when.* Mahwah, NJ: Erlbaum.

Thompson, J., Morton, J., & Fraser, L. (1997). Memories for the *Marchioness. Memory, 5*, 615–638.

Thorndyke, P. W., & Hayes-Roth, B. (1982). Differences in spatial knowledge acquired from maps and navigation. *Cognitive Psychology, 14*, 560–589.

Tolman, E. C. (1948). Cognitive maps in rats and men. *Psychological Review, 55*, 189–208.

Tversky, B. (1981). Distortions in memory for maps. *Cognitive Psychology, 13*, 407–433.

Tversky, B. (1997). Spatial Constructions. In N. L. Stein, P. A. Ornstein, B. Tversky, & C. Brainerd (Eds.), *Memory for everyday and emotional events* (pp. 181–208). Mahwah, NJ: Erlbaum.

Usher, J. A., & Neisser, U. (1993). Childhood amnesia and the beginnings of memory for four early life events. *Journal of Experimental Psychology: General, 122*, 155–165.

Vincente, K. J., & Brewer, W. F. (1993). Reconstructive remembering of the scientific literature. *Cognition, 46*, 101–128.

Wagenaar, W. A. (1986). My memory: A study of autobiographical memory over six years. *Cognitive Psychology, 18*, 225–252.

Wagenaar, W. A. (1994) Is memory self-serving? In U. Neisser & R. Fivush (Eds.), *The remembering self* (pp. 191–204). New York: Cambridge University Press.

Wagenaar, W. A., & Groenweg, J. (1990). The memory of concentration camp survivors. *Applied Cognitive Psychology, 4*, 77–87.

Waldvogel, S. (1948). The frequency and affective character of childhood memories. *Psychological Monographs, 62*, Whole No. 291.

Warnecke, R. B., Sudman, S., Johnson, T. P., O'Rourke, D., Davis, A. M., & Jobe, J. (1997). Cognitive aspects of recalling and reporting health-related events: Papanicolaous smears, clinical breast examinations, and mammograms. *American Journal of Epidemiology, 146*(11), 982–992.

Warren, A. R., & Swartwood, J. N. (1992). Developmental issues in flashbulb memory research: Children recall the *Challenger* event. In E. Winograd & U. Neisser (Eds.), *Affect and accuracy in recall: Studies of "flashbulb" memories* (pp. 95–120). New York: Cambridge University Press.

Weaver, C. A. (1993). Do you need a "flash" to form a flashbulb memory? *Journal of Experimental Psychology: General, 122*, 39–46.

Wegner, D. M. (1987). Transactive memory: A contemporary analysis of the group mind. In B. Mullen & G. R. Goethals (Eds.), *Theories of group behavior* (pp.185–208). New York: Springer-Verlag.

Wegner, D. M., Erber, R., & Raymond, P. (1991). Transactive memory in close relationships. *Journal of Personality and Social Psychology, 61*, 923–929.

Weinberger, D. A., Schwartz, G. E., & Davidson, R. (1979). Low-anxious, high-anxious, and repressive coping styles: Psychometric patterns and behavioral and physiological responses to stress. *Journal of Abnormal Psychology, 88*, 369–380.

Williams, J. M. G. (1996). Depression and the specificity of autobiographical memory. In D. C. Rubin (Ed.), *Remembering our past* (pp. 244–267). New York: Cambridge University Press.

Winograd, E., & Killinger, W. A. (1983). Relating age at encoding in early childhood to adult recall: Development of flashbulb memories. *Journal of Experimental Psychology: General, 112*, 413–422.

Winograd, E., & Soloway, R. M. (1986). On forgetting the locations of things stored in special places. *Journal of Experimental Psychology: General, 115*(4), 366–372.

Wright, D. B. (1993). Recall of the Hillsborough disaster over time: Systematic biases of "flashbulb" memories. *Applied Cognitive Psychology, 7*, 129–138.

Yarmey, A. D., & Bull, M. P. (1978). Where were you when President Kennedy was assassinated? *Bulletin of the Psychonomic Society, 11*, 133–135.

Yuille, J. C. (1993). We must study forensic eyewitnesses to know about them. *American Psychologist, 48*(5), 572–573.

Yuille, J. C., & Cutshall, J. L. (1986). A case study of eyewitness memory of a crime. *Journal of Applied Cognitive Psychology, 71*(2), 291–301.

21

Control Processes in Remembering

ASHER KORIAT

This chapter examines some of the processes that take place in attempting to probe memory for a needed piece of information. In present-day conceptualization memory processes are divided into three phases: encoding, storage, and retrieval. Strangely enough, the distinction between storage and retrieval, so basic in current memory theorizing, is relatively new (see Baddeley, 1997; Roediger & Guynn, 1996). In classical, S-R learning theory, based primarily on animal research, storage, and retrieval were lumped together, and even the distinction between encoding and storage was not explicitly made. It was the extension of S-R principles to human verbal behavior that has brought to the fore the importance of distinguishing among encoding, storage, and retrieval.

Availability and Accessibility

The critical role of memory retrieval becomes apparent when we realize that the amount of information stored in our memory exceeds by far the amount of information that we can retrieve from it. In terms of the terminology introduced by Tulving and Pearlstone (1966), much more information is available in memory than is accessible at any moment. Thus, although we may momentarily fail to retrieve the name of an acquaintance, we may still be able to recall it on some later occasion or rec-ognize it among distractors. The discrepancy between the availability of information and its accessibility to consciousness testifies for the critical role of retrieval processes—the ability to conjure up stored information.

Two observations illustrate this discrepancy. Tulving (1967) had subjects study a list of words, and their recall was tested three times in succession. Only about 50% of the words were recalled on all three tests. For example, a subject might recall words on the second test that he failed to recall on the first test.

A second observation comes from a study (Williams & Hollan, 1981) in which subjects spent one hour every day trying to recall the names of people with whom they had graduated from high school 4–19 years earlier. Subjects were found to recall new names after as much as 10 hours in the experiment, spread over two weeks! Clearly these names must have been available even in the first hour of the experiment.

These observations raise several questions: What prevented all the items ultimately recalled to surface right from the beginning of testing? What allowed them to become accessible later on? And more generally, what is the process by which people search for and recollect stored information from long-term memory?

In attempting to address these questions, we should note that although most of our knowledge about memory processes derives from the use of relatively simple laboratory tasks, control processes in remembering are particularly transparent in the retrieval of information under naturalistic conditions, particularly when retrieval is laborious and prolonged. Therefore, this chapter will emphasize studies concerned with this type of retrieval despite the fact they do not always attain the methodological rigor characteristic of laboratory experimentation.

Retrieval as Problem Solving

Even a cursory examination of everyday episodes of recollection suggests that there is much more to remembering than simply fetching out a solicited piece of information from some storage place. Take, for example, the following episode recounted by Nickerson (1981):

> Consider the following effort to recall the name of a street that is located a few blocks from where I live. The name would not come to mind, but I did know it to be the name of a friend. The name Elliott suggested itself, but did not seem to be correct. I thought the name I was looking for was a first name, and although Elliott can be either a first or last name, it is in fact the last name of a friend of mine. I also was fairly sure the sought-for name was the first name of a female, and the Elliot in mind was a male . . . As the search continued, the name Cellier surfaced, the last name of a close friend of Elliott's, who was also a friend of mine. Next came Emil, the first name of Cellier; then Hilda, wife of Emil. Hilda was immediately recognized as the name of the street. (p. 79)

Similar experiences of wandering through the paths of one's memory in search for some longed-for record are not uncommon, and many have been reported in some detail in the literature. These reports suggest that in real-life situations, retrieval often involves a complex interplay between two types of processes (see Jacoby, 1991; Moscovitch, 1989), a controlled, strategic process that guides retrieval, coordinating between different operations directed toward the recovery of the elusive memory target, and the automatic, involuntary emergence into consciousness of ideas and associations throughout the search. Sometimes the controlled process will seize onto these ideas and use them as stepping stones on the

way to the sought-after target. At other times they may be recognized as misleading "interlopers" and effort will be exerted to oppose their interfering influence (Jones, 1989).

This interplay between top-down and bottom-up processes derives from the fact that there is hardly ever a cognitive algorithm that can safely lead from a retrieval description (e.g., "what is the name of that street") to its resolution—the memory target (e.g., "Hilda"). Therefore, while retrieval may begin with a controlled, goal-oriented search that takes off from the retrieval description, it must also be receptive to activations and associations that emerge during the search. In his analysis of problem solving, Duncker (1945) discussed this interplay in terms of the idea that the solution to a problem involves the matching of suggestions from above with suggestions coming from below. In fact, his definition of a problem aptly describes the situation in which retrieval is called for: "A problem arises when a living creature has a goal but does not know how that goal is to be reached" (p. 1).

The problem-solving character of remembering can be seen in many everyday memory tasks that tax memory, such as answering questions about course material or retrieving episodes from the distant past (see Burgess & Shallice, 1996; Reiser, Black, & Abelson, 1985). Williams and Hollan (1981), in fact, proposed a jigsaw puzzle metaphor of remembering, in which one begins with starter pieces (specified by the memory query), and by focusing on some section of the puzzle, searches for a piece that may fit, and then verifies that it indeed does. The problem-solving character of remembering makes extensive use of working memory (see e.g., Conway, 1992) in controlling the operation of several processes, coordinating between them, holding the outcome in a temporary store, and orchestrating the entire process.

Different components of the retrieval process are suggested by experimental studies as well as naturalistic studies in which subjects were asked to think aloud in the course of remembering. They are discussed in what follows.

The Importance of the Instigating Conditions

In everyday life we are generally unaware of using our memory. When walking in a familiar neighborhood, we must be constantly consulting our memory of the geographic layout to find our way, but we are hardly aware of doing so. We may become aware of using our memory when we lose our orientation, or when someone we meet asks us for directions. It is in those cases that we deliberately probe our memory for the needed information.

It is important to distinguish between two types of situations that motivate remembering. In the first, retrieval is prompted by a specific question posed by an external agent. Typical examples are a course examination, a job interview, or a police interrogation. Importantly, this type of situation is characteristic of practically all memory studies because in these studies the memory questions are presented and formulated by the experimenter. When remembering occurs in response to externally presented specific questions, it tends to be deliberate and relatively focused and restricted (see Bekerian & Dritschel, 1992).

The second type, which is more typical of naturalistic situations, is when memory queries are generated spontaneously by the person himself, or triggered by accidental encounters or task demands. A simple example was given by Mandler (1980):

Consider seeing a man on a bus whom you are sure that you have seen before; you "know" him in that sense. Such a recognition is usually followed by a search process asking, in effect, Where could I know him from? Who is he? The search process generates likely contexts (Do I know him from work, is he a movie star, a TV commentator, the milkman?) Eventually, the search may end with the insight, That's the butcher from the supermarket! (pp. 252–253)

This type of situation has hardly any analogue in memory experiments. When retrieval is initiated by the person himself, often in response to task demands or social interaction, the "retrieval description" (Norman & Bobrow, 1979) tends to be loose and ill defined. In other cases still, retrieval may be spontaneous, triggered automatically by some external cues (see Salaman, 1982). Unfortunately, because of the nature of experimental investigation, we know very little about self-generated queries and about automatic retrieval.

Because in everyday life we typically try to retrieve information from memory when we need it, the immediate, instigating conditions may play a critical role in guiding and facilitating retrieval. In fact, in naturalistic situations, the process of remembering has more in common with cued-recall than with free-recall testing. Such is not the case in many institutionalized memory testing situations (e.g., achievement tests, memory experiments), as when a person is required to answer a variety of general-information questions (e.g., Kelley & Lindsay, 1993; Koriat, 1995) that have nothing to do with the immediate goals and circumstances. This contrast helps bring to the fore two related principles of memory. The first is that retrieval depends critically on the presence of retrieval cues, and the second is that retrieval success varies depending on the match between the study and test situations.

The Contribution of Retrieval Cues

Tulving (1983) has promoted the notion that memory is a joint product of the stored memory traces and the cues that are present when retrieval is called for. This view implies that given the same conditions of study, retrieval success can vary greatly depending on the conditions of testing. For example, Tulving and Pearlstone (1966) observed that memory for a list of words was considerably better under cued-recall testing, where the cues were the semantic categories to which the words belonged, than under free recall testing. This result supports the importance of the distinction discussed earlier between availability and accessibility, and indicates that information that is not immediately accessible can become accessible when proper cues are present.

In the experiment just described, the cues were presented experimentally. In real-life situations the conditions that instigate retrieval normally provide many useful cues. In externally posed queries, the leading cues can be found in the query itself. Even when these cues are not sufficient to directly trigger the target item, they help delimit the memory regions in which that item is likely to be found.

Retrieval cues are particularly critical for prospective memory—that is, memory to perform intended acts in the future, such as showing up for an appointment or taking a medicine (Brandimonte & Ellis, 1996). What is most important in prospective memory is not the retrieval of the specific content of the to-be-performed act, but the retrieval of the intention to perform it at the appropriate time (Einstein & McDaniel, 1996). To do so, one must rely on cues that are available in the environment to trigger the intention, devise one's own aids ("the knot in the handkerchief," a timer), or rely on internal cues. Burgess and Shallice (1996) note that the context setting that occurs when a person "sets up" an intention to perform a future action (e.g., to mail a letter) involves a recollection of the context of retrieval (e.g., imagining the journey home, the mailbox), so that the potential cues for retrieving the intention are stored with the intention itself.

Often a failure to perform the planned act stems from the failure to identify the "cue" as a cue for retrieving the intention. Sometimes external cues operate retrospectively, reminding one of a scheduled intention that was missed (e.g., a smell of a burnt cake). Note that some of the cues, like the knot in the handkerchief, carry little information about the content of the act to be performed. Their function is to induce the person to retrieve the intention to perform some act.

Cues differ considerably in their effectiveness in prompting retrieval. In the case of prospective memory, the most effective cues are those that are more distinctive and less familiar (McDaniel & Einstein, 1993). In retrospective memory, in contrast, the effective cues, of course, are those that relate to the content of the solicited item. Research examining the effectiveness of extra-list words in prompting the recall of studied words (Nelson, McKinney, Gee, & Janczura, 1998) indicates that retrieval success varies considerably with a large number of associative properties of the cue and of the target. For example, the larger the number of words that a cue word elicits in word association norms, the lower its effectiveness in facilitating the retrieval of a studied word.

The most effective cues for retrieving an event are personal cues associated with the encoding of that event, because these cues get to be integrated into the memory trace of the event (e.g., Mäntylä, 1986). Methods of memory improvement make use of this principle, by having people utilize some system of cues during encoding, which they can latter use to aid retrieval.

How Do Cues Assist Retrieval?

Cues may aid retrieval either through a controlled process in which the person deliberately makes use of them, or through an automatic process in which the cue directly facilitates the emergence into memory of the solicited target (see Neely, 1976). The controlled exploitation of cues is particularly transparent when retrieval is difficult or prolonged. As we shall see below, much of the process of remembering appears then to involve the deliberate use of cues to probe one's memory for additional cues that may bring one closer to the desired target information. The starting point, of course, is the cues present in the situation that drives retrieval. These can be exploited to delimit a context for further search (Koriat & Lieblich, 1974; Norman & Bobrow, 1979).

In parallel, cues may aid retrieval through automatic activations (see Collins & Loftus, 1975; Nelson et al., 1998) emanating from the cognitive context of retrieval, or from the information already recovered. We may try in vain to recall the name of a person, but the name may suddenly pop up the moment we see that person. In fact, this is the way in which many "reminders" operate in everyday life: Passing by a drug store reminds us of a prescription that we have to take. Schank (1982), who considered reminding to be a crucial aspect of human memory, offered an extensive analysis of the type of reminding processes that occur in everyday life.

We know a great deal about automatic activations from experiments on verbal priming (e.g., Collins & Loftus, 1975; Neely & Keefe, 1989) and implicit memory (see Roediger & McDermott, 1994). For example, subjects retrieve faster the answer to a general-information question if that answer has been presented earlier in the context of an unrelated task (Kelley & Lindsay, 1993). In a word-association task subjects are more likely to respond with a word recently studied (e.g., Koriat & Feuerstein, 1976). While such activations generally aid retrieval, they may give rise to inadvertent plagiarism (e.g., Marsh, Landau, & Hicks, 1997) or produce false memories (e.g., Roediger & McDermott, 1995; see Koriat, Goldsmith, & Pansky, in press).

Automatic activations may bring to mind entire scenes or events, as when a certain smell or music conjure up emotionally laden old memories (see Conway, 1992; Salaman, 1982). Such activations might also underlie the recurrence of "flashbacks" memories in people suffering from posttraumatic stress, when memories of the traumatic event intrude into the person's consciousness against his or her will.

The Encoding-Specificity Principle

The importance of the instigating conditions for retrieval is also stressed by the encoding-specificity principle (Tulving & Thomson, 1973), which states that a cue presented during testing will be effective in aiding retrieval to the extent that it has been encoded together with the solicited memory target at study. Thus, a critical condition for effective retrieval is the extent to which the processing that occurs during retrieval reinstates the processing that took place during encoding.

Tulving and Thomson provided some counterintuitive results supporting the encoding specificity principle. For example, the word *hot* is more strongly associated with *cold* than the word *ground*, and indeed, in a free-recall task, *hot* is more effective than *ground* for prompting the recall of *cold*. Nevertheless *ground* will actually act as a better cue for recalling *cold* if *cold* has been originally encoded in the context of *ground*. What is more, when *cold* is encoded in the context of *ground*, subjects who are successful in recalling *cold* in response to *hot* sometimes fail to recognize it as one that has appeared in the study list! This is like the failure to recognize an acquaintance when we accidentally run into him in a very different context from that in which we are accustomed to see him.

Similar results consistent with the encoding specificity hypothesis have been reported by Morris, Bransford, and Franks (1977). Although memory for words is superior when during encoding subjects attend to the meaning of the words rather than to their sound, the reverse pattern was found when during retrieval subjects were induced to attend to the phonemic properties of the words.

Reinstating the Conditions of Learning during Testing

Retrieval is also affected by the extent to which the testing conditions reinstate the overall conditions of study with regard to the external stimulus conditions (context), the internal state of the person (state), or the person's emotional feelings (mood).

There is evidence that retrieval is context dependent—that is, that memory is best when testing occurs in the same physical environment in which learning took place. For exam-

ple, Godden and Baddeley (1975) studied the memory of divers when they learned a list of words either on land or underwater and were later tested in the same or in the opposite environment. Recall was better when learning and recall took place in the same environment than in different environments. Subjects have also been found to recall a larger number of words when they were tested in the same room in which they had studied than when they were tested in a different room (Smith, Glenberg, & Bjork, 1978). It would seem that context-dependent effects are more likely to be found when the environmental contexts differ substantially, and when subjects deliberately associate the studied material with features of the study environment. These effects are obtained only for recall, not for recognition (Eich, 1985), suggesting that contextual reinstatement specifically facilitates information retrieval.

A study by Smith (1979) suggests that mental reinstatement of the learning environment may be almost as beneficial for retrieval as actual, physical reinstatement. This idea has been incorporated in the cognitive interview (Fisher & Geiselman, 1992), designed to enhance witness recollection: prior to answering specific questions about a past event, witnesses are instructed to mentally recreate the contextual state that existed at the time of the original event.

Evidence for state dependency comes from findings indicating that memory performance is best when the same internal state is maintained across the learning and testing phases. What subjects learned when drunk they remembered better when drunk than when sober, and vice versa (Goodwin, Powell, Bremer, Hoine, & Stern, 1969). A similar pattern was observed in a study on the effects of marijuana on free recall (Eich, Weingartner, Stillman, & Gillin, 1975). Evidence for state-dependent retrieval is more clearly observed for free recall than for recognition or cued recall (see Eich, 1980). Several studies suggest that retrieval is also mood dependent: memory performance is better when people's moods during study and test match than when they do not (Eich & Metcalfe, 1989).

We now proceed to examine some of the processes that occur during retrieval. As noted, these processes are not easy to trace except when retrieval is effortful and extended over some period of time. Before focusing on effortful retrieval, however, we shall discuss briefly effortless retrieval.

Effortless Retrieval

Not every memory search is laborious; in many cases the solicited information will come to mind immediately (see Nickerson, 1981). The retrieval of well-practiced, well-rehearsed information often has the character of habits or stimulus-response associations.

What makes retrieval automatic? First, there is the case of incidental remembering. Automatic activations may increase the accessibility of a memory entry to the extent that it can emerge into consciousness spontaneously. Such activations have been studied extensively in connection with implicit memory. Second, as far as intentional retrieval is concerned, it would seem that practice retrieving an item from memory is what makes retrieval of that item more automatic (see Bjork & Bjork, 1992). Thus, although we know the numbers from 1 to 10 "by heart," their retrieval is more effortful when we have to list them from 10 to 1. Counting forward is a much more practiced habit than counting backwards.

Let us now focus on effortful retrieval. When memory retrieval is effortful and prolonged, complex regulatory processes of monitoring and control operate in guiding the search.

Preliminary Monitoring and Choice of Mode of Attack

When we are presented with a memory question we do not immediately proceed to answer it, unless the answer pops instantaneously into our head. Rather, in many cases a preliminary monitoring stage exists in which we make a rough assessment about the availability of the answer in memory and the effort needed to access it.

The initial feeling of knowing (FOK) associated with a question is apparently based on a process that monitors the overall familiarity of the question (Nhouyvanisvong & Reder, 1998; Schwartz & Metcalfe, 1992) and the extent to which it brings some fragmentary clues to mind (Koriat, 1993, 1995). If the question leaves us completely blank, chances are that we would not initiate a deliberate search for the answer. Note, however, that a controlled decision to interrupt search apparently does not prevent automatic activations that may ultimately lead to the solicited target (see Koriat & Lieblich, 1977).

Reder (1987) proposed that the familiarity of a question also affects the general strategy of answering that question. When the familiarity of a question is low, subjects would tend to resort to a plausibility strategy, inferring the answer from a variety of cues, rather than to a direct retrieval strategy. She noted, however, that even when familiarity is high subjects may still respond on the basis of the gist of the question. For example, when asked "How many animals of each kind did Moses take on the Ark?" many subjects reply "two," even though they know that it was Noah who did so (Erikson & Mattson, 1981).

Specifying the Initial Context of Search

When preliminary FOK is high, the next step is to determine the initial context in which the search has to be conducted. This decision is suggested by the verbal protocols of subjects produced in the course of remembering (e.g., Burgess & Shallice, 1996; Norman & Bobrow, 1979; Reiser et al., 1985; Williams & Hollan, 1981). This is analogous to that of choosing under what heading to look for a certain topic in a book, or under what directory a computer file is likely to be stored. For example, in attempting to answer questions about course material, students often begin by deliberating whether the question is "from the textbook" or "from the lecture." Or they may attempt to specify more precisely the relevant chapter in the textbook. When the question requires the retrieval of some autobiographical detail, the person may start by recovering a scene or an episode in which that detail is likely to be found. Duncker (1945) referred to this process as one in which "the jacket is sewn to the button" (p. 83).

Memory questions differ considerably in the extent to which they delimit, explicitly or implicitly, an effective search domain. Consider the type of questions that specify a particular memory entry to be retrieved—for example, a word or a name. This type of questions, designated "memory pointers" by Koriat and Lieblich (1977), have been extensively used in studies of the tip-of-the-tongue (TOT) and FOK states in which the person initially fails to retrieve the solicited target from memory (Brown & McNeill, 1966; Nelson & Narens, 1990). Such pointers differ widely in the extent to which they offer a plan for search. For example, a question such as "what biblical character allegedly lived 969 years?" is likely to activate a more useful search domain ("biblical characters") than the comparable question "Which person allegedly lived 969 years?" The delimitation of a search domain is useful not only for memory but also for metamemory: it contributes to the accuracy of the initial FOK associated with the memory pointer (Koriat & Lieblich, 1977). The most effective pointers are those that cast the specification of the solicited target in a format that simultaneously constitutes an effective plan for search. There are different strategies for specifying an initial context for search. For example, one of the strategies used for retrieval of the names of old classmates (Williams & Santos-Williams, 1980) was the location strategy: the subject searches a mental map where target items are likely to be recalled. Reiser, Black, and Kalamarides (1986) also identified several strategies in the retrieval of specific autobiographical events, which they classified into those involving finding a context, and those involving searching within a context. Impairments in the ability to generate a focused contextual description of the sought after information has been seen to underlie some of the memory errors encountered among brain damaged patients (Schacter, Norman, & Koutstaal, 1998).

Access to Partial Information and Zooming in on a Memory Target

Many observations suggest that retrieval is not an all-or-none matter. When we fail to retrieve a word or a name, we may still be able to access some of its fragments or attributes. These can sometimes provide the initial lead for retrieval. The utilization of such partial clues is nicely illustrated by the example presented at the beginning of this chapter, of searching for the name of a street. The partial clues available to Nickerson appeared to shape the entire remembering process. The remembering process sometimes looks as if the rememberer grasps the thread provided by the initial clues and follows their course as they gradually unfold.

Williams and Hollan (1981), discussing the processes involved in recalling the names of classmates, argued that a great deal of the process can be seen as a reconstruction from a variety of bits and pieces of information. They considered partial retrieval to be the central principle that constraints and determines the shape of the reconstructive retrieval process.

Some of the characteristics of partial retrieval are revealed in studies of the TOT state (see Brown, 1991). People in a TOT state are able to provide correct guesses about the number of syllables in the word they are grappling for, some of its letters, and the location of primary stress (Brown & McNeill, 1966). Subjects can also access semantic and associative aspects of the elusive word, such as whether it has a good or bad connotation (Koriat, 1993; Schacter & Worling, 1985).

The partial information initially retrieved provides a lead to a deliberate search, but it also affects the search through its automatic, implicit influence. This is suggested by findings such as that of Durso and Shore (1991): subjects can distinguish between correct and incorrect uses of rare English words even when they classify them as nonwords, suggesting that available partial clues can implicitly affect choice of response. Also, in Koriat's study (1993), when subjects responded with an incorrect word in cued recall, that word tended to have the same connotative meaning as the correct word that they failed to retrieve.

There are indications that during forgetting the more specific aspects of the encoded information are lost before the general attributes (Ceraso, 1987). This implies that generic information is accessible long after the more detailed, item-specific information has ceased to be accessible. Thus, studies of the long-term retention of course material suggest that memory for higher level, superordinate information declines less rapidly than memory for specific details (e.g., Cohen, Stanhope, & Conway, 1992). Similarly, categorical or gist information is lost less rapidly than item information (e.g., Dorfman & Mandler, 1994; see also Brainerd & Reyna, 1993): a person might remember that there was a bird on the list without recalling which bird it was. Such superordinate information may help define an initial domain for search.

The TOT state discloses some further features of retrieval. It has been proposed that a cursory analysis of a memory pointer activates a relatively broad region of memory that includes the target proper but also other entries that satisfy the retrieval description only grossly (Koriat & Lieblich, 1977). The activations emanating from the neighboring memory entries exert two conflicting effects: they interfere with accessing the correct target but at the same time enhance the subjective feeling that the target is about to emerge into consciousness (Koriat, 1998; Schwartz & Smith, 1997). Several researchers have proposed that the difficult retrieval that is characteristic of the TOT state results precisely from the interfering effect of neighboring targets, and that these compelling but wrong candidates must be first suppressed before the correct target can be retrieved (Jones, 1989).

Indeed, there is evidence suggesting that when a target item is retrieved from memory, neighboring targets are concurrently inhibited (see Dagenbach & Carr, 1994). Dagenbach, Carr, and Barnhardt (1990) found that the failure to retrieve the meaning of a word results in inhibitory priming of semantically related words. Anderson, Bjork, and Bjork (1994) observed that practice retrieving a target item from memory renders related items less accessible. The more likely were these items to interfere with the retrieval of the target item, the more they suffered from practice retrieving it.

In sum, when people fail to retrieve a memory target, they may access partial clues about it, and these can help in guiding the retrieval process. Because retrieval of the general attributes of items precedes the recovery of more specific features, retrieval sometimes looks like an attempt to close in on the target through a progressive narrowing of its description (Kolodner, 1983; Koriat & Lieblich, 1974). During this process competing memory candidates are suppressed to allow zooming in on the target.

Probing One's Memory during Retrieval

How is partial information utilized in the course of remembering? Several observations highlight the importance of self-cueing during retrieval—that is, of cognitive operations whose immediate aim is the recovery of further cues that can lead to more refined cues, and ultimately to the target itself.

How are additional clues recovered? Several studies concur in identifying a recursive pattern that occurs in the course of arduous remembering: a memory environment is specified in which a search is to be conducted, that environment is searched for additional clues, and the information retrieved is evaluated. This cycle is repeated, gradually refining the description of the information to be searched, until the search closes in on the target. For example, Williams and Hollan (1981) noted that in attempting to retrieve the names of high school classmates, subjects produced an enormous amount of information that was incidental to the task of recalling the names, including details about the school, about where people lived, and so forth. Examination of this information suggests that its main function was to probe one's memory for additional clues that can better specify a new context for search. They proposed that remembering consists of a series of "kernel retrieval" processes, each including three stages: a context is retrieved (e.g., the volley tennis group), a search is conducted within that context, and the information recovered is verified.

Reiser and his associates (Reiser et al., 1985, 1986), who studied recall of autobiographical episodes, also emphasized that one memory retrieval can be undertaken in order to provide cues for a subsequent retrieval. According to their context-plus-index model, specific personal episodes are recalled by first recovering the general context in which they were likely to have been encoded, and then specifying the features that uniquely distinguish these experiences from others in that context. They proposed that scripts (e.g., "eating in restaurants," see Schank, 1982) typically serve as convenient retrieval contexts. Burgess and Shallice (1996), too, noted that subjects did not always retrieve the target memory record directly, but sometimes recovered a useful cue first. Thus, it was not uncommon for subjects to answer the question "what was the weather like yesterday morning" by trying to remember first what they were wearing.

Similar processes seem to take place in retrieving information from semantic memory. One of the best-studied tasks in memory research is that of retrieving the members of natural categories such as vegetables, furniture, and the like (Raaijmakers & Shiffrin, 1981). A study by Walker and Kintsch (1985) suggests that even in this task retrieval relies on the recovery of contexts in which a search is conducted. Verbal protocols suggested a series of two-stage cycles: generating a context in which category members are likely to be found, and then using that context as a retrieval cue to produce the category members themselves. Importantly, most of the contexts generated were episodic rather than abstract-semantic (e.g., in searching for automobiles, one may picture a parking lot, the cars in front of the dorm, etc.).

The Strategic Regulation of Memory Retrieval

In the previous sections we discussed some of the recurrent processes in prolonged retrieval. Examination of the overall regulation of remembering, however, brings to the fore a variety of operations that are not specific to memory, but fall within the domain of higher order, executive-supervisory functions. These operations are involved in the overall regulation of the remembering process, and are so intertwined with lower level memory processes that it is difficult to understand remembering without considering their indispensable role. Unfortunately, little systematic work exists regarding the overall regulation of the remembering process.

An act of remembering often has the character of a goal-oriented process that is controlled and guided by an overriding program (see the example from Nickerson, cited earlier). This supervisory program is responsible for choosing a starting point, recruiting a strategy, monitoring its execution, and changing it when it proves unsuccessful. Thus, remembering may involve a complex set of problem-solving routines that are interlaced with processes concerned with memory retrieval proper (Burgess & Shallice, 1996).

Discussing the global structure of a remembering act, Norman and Bobrow (1979; see also Morton, Hammersley, & Bekerian, 1985) identified three general stages: specification of the information needed (and hence of the verification criteria), a matching process in which memory records are accessed and compared with the target description, and evaluation of suitability of the recovered records (see also Conway, 1992). Each of these stages calls for a variety of monitoring and control operations.

Burgess and Shallice (1996) reached similar conclusions regarding the broad structure of the prototypical retrieval process. However, their analysis suggested a more complex organization in which layers of control lie between general problem solving and specific memory retrieval, with monitoring running parallel with the different stages of the process. An important feature of their scheme is that the supervisory processes of monitoring and control are assumed to run parallel with the different stages of remembering rather than being confined to any one stage.

While there is agreement regarding the controlled, goal-oriented nature of retrieval, the role of "suggestions from below" has also been acknowledged. Often spurious activations lead the search astray. Williams and Santos-Williams (1980) noted that subjects sometimes abandon one strategy in response to the retrieval of information that appears to be particularly useful in the context of a different strategy. Furthermore, verbal protocols disclose moments in which the person seems to deliberately relinquish strategic control altogether, adopting a passive-receptive attitude. Nickerson (1981) noted that in retrieving words from lists, subjects often begin with a passive attitude, and then switch to an active, systematic search when the passive approach no longer yields a satisfactory return (see also Walker & Kintsch, 1985). Koriat and Melkman (1987) observed a similar pattern, but also showed that when attentional resources are diverted, the retrieval of words from a list becomes less controlled, moving along associative links between the words rather than along conceptual-logical relations.

The Strategic Regulation of Memory Reporting

We turn now to the final stages of the process, those involved either in selecting an answer and providing it, or in reporting "I don't know."

Consider first cases in which the person fails to provide any answer. A fast "don't know" response may be issued based on the assessment that the needed information is unavailable in memory. Examination of the latency of "don't know" responses suggests that such responses are not simply a result of scanning one's memory and failing to find the appropriate target, but actually depend on rather complex processes (see Glucksberg & McCloskey, 1981; Klin, Guzman, & Levine, 1997).

Even after initiating a memory search, a person may abort the process if the search fails to produce the solicited target. It should be noted that when the preliminary FOK associated with a question is high, subjects spend more time searching for the target before giving up than when initial FOK is low (Nelson & Narens, 1990). The decision to continue searching reflects the operation of two conflicting tendencies: the reward for finding the correct answer, and the cost for spending time searching (Barnes, Nelson, Dunlosky, Mazzoni, & Narens, 1999).

What are the processes underlying the outputting of an answer? All of the retrieval models reviewed earlier incorporate verification processes in which the memory records recovered are evaluated for suitability. These processes occur throughout the retrieval process, often leading to self-corrections. Burgess and Shallice (1996) stressed the frequent occurrence of "errors" in verbal protocols, which would normally not show up in the final response reported because they are corrected or edited out. They proposed that these might provide the key for explaining the occurrence of confabulations among patients with frontal lobe damage (see also Moscovitch, 1989). According to them, memory errors are a standard part of the normal memory retrieval so that mechanisms that guard against them must exist.

Williams and Hollan's study (1981) of the memory for classmates also revealed a considerable number of "fabrications" (about a third of the total number of names reported), some of which were later corrected by the subject. Walker and Kintsch (1985) examined a different kind of error: reporting a category member that has already been reported. Whereas subjects who were asked to think aloud produced a large number of such "errors," control subjects produced practically none, suggesting that they were able to edit out retrieved but already reported items.

Editing processes are particularly important when the accuracy of what one reports is at stake. A person on a witness stand, for example, must be concerned not only with "telling the whole truth" but also with telling "nothing but the truth." In order to meet both requirements, an eyewitness must monitor the correctness of the information that comes to mind and weigh the costs of providing a piece of information that may be incorrect against the costs of withholding a correct piece of information.

Koriat and Goldsmith (1994, 1996) examined the strategic regulation of memory reporting within the traditional, item-based memory assessment framework. Memory quantity was defined as the likelihood of remembering an input item, whereas memory accuracy was defined as the likelihood that a reported item is correct. Their results suggested that the option of free report—that is, the option to decide which items to volunteer and which to withhold, allows subjects to enhance their memory accuracy at the expense of memory quantity by screening out items that are likely to be

wrong. This was true for both recall and recognition memory testing. How do people regulate their memory accuracy? According to a model proposed by Koriat and Goldsmith (1996), when recounting past events, people monitor the likelihood that each item of information that comes to mind is correct. They then apply a control threshold to the monitoring output for the item with the highest subjective probability of being correct. The item will be reported if its assessed probability passes threshold, and will be withheld otherwise. The setting of the control threshold depends on the relative utility of providing complete versus accurate information: the stronger the motivation for accuracy, the more selective people are in their reporting, and hence the higher the level of memory accuracy attained. Several experiments provided support for the model, revealing the manner in which monitoring and control processes mediate between memory retrieval on the one hand and memory performance on the other. A quantity-accuracy tradeoff was observed: subjects could achieve a higher level of memory accuracy only by withholding a larger number of correct answers as well. The degree of tradeoff, however, varied strongly with monitoring effectiveness—that is, the ability to distinguish between correct and incorrect answers. Effective monitoring allowed a person to achieve a higher level of memory accuracy at a smaller cost in quantity.

Another means by which subjects can regulate the accuracy of their memory reports is by controlling the "grain" or level of generality of the reported information (see Goldsmith & Koriat, 1999). Rather than withhold an answer entirely, a person may choose a level of generality at which he is less likely to be wrong (e.g., "in the early afternoon" rather than "at 2 P.M."). The choice of grain size is guided by the attempt to compromise between the tendency to be accurate and the tendency to be informative (Goldsmith & Koriat, 1999; Yaniv & Foster, 1995).

In sum, in this chapter we focused on control processes in remembering. Some of these processes undoubtedly take place in simple, laboratory contexts, but most of them are more clearly apparent in the everyday use of memory retrieval, particularly when retrieval is more laborious. A greater effort is being made in recent years to bring some of these processes under systematic experimental investigation.

Acknowledgments This chapter was prepared while the author was a visiting professor at the Max Planck Institute for Psychological Research, Munich, Germany. The work was supported by the Max-Wertheimer Minerva Center for Cognitive Processes and Human Performance, University of Haifa, and by the Ebelin and Gerd Bucerius ZEIT Foundation.

References

Anderson, M. C., Bjork, R. A., & Bjork, E. L. (1994). Remembering can cause forgetting: Retrieval dynamics in long-term memory. *Journal of Experimental Psychology: Learning, Memory, and Cognition, 20*, 1063–1087.

Baddeley, A. (1997). Human memory—theory and practice. Hove, England: Psychology Press.

Barnes, A. E., Nelson, T. O., Dunlosky, J., Mazzoni, G., & Narens, L. (1999). An integrative system of metamemory components involved in retrieval. In D. Gopher & A. Koriat (Eds.), *Attention and performance XVII—Cognitive regulation of performance: Interaction of theory and application* (pp. 287–313). Cambridge, MA: MIT Press.

Bekerian, D. A., & Dritschel, B. H. (1992). Autobiographical remembering: An integrative approach. In M. A. Conway, D. C. Rubin, H. Spinnler, & W. A. Wagenaar (Eds.), *Theoretical perspectives on autobiographical memory* (pp. 135–150). Dordrecht, Netherlands: Kluwer.

Bjork, R. A., & Bjork, E. L. (1992). A new theory of disuse and an old theory of stimulation fluctuation. In A. F. Healy, S. M. Kosslyn, & R. M. Shiffrin (Eds.), *From learning processes to cognitive processes: Essays in honor of William K. Estes* (Vol. 2; pp. 35–67). Mahwah, NJ: Erlbaum.

Brainerd, C. J., & Reyna, V. F. (1993). Memory independence and memory interference in cognitive development. *Psychological Review, 100*, 42–67.

Brandimonte, M., & Ellis, J. (1996). *Prospective memory.* Mahwah, NJ: Erlbaum.

Brown, A. S. (1991). A review of the tip-of-the-tongue experience. *Psychological Bulletin, 109*, 204–223.

Brown, R., & McNeill, D. (1966). The "tip of the tongue" phenomenon. *Journal of Verbal Learning and Verbal Behavior, 5*, 325–337.

Burgess, P. W., & Shallice, T. (1996). Confabulation and the control of recollection. *Memory, 4*, 359–411.

Ceraso, J. (1987). On generic recall. In D. S. Gorfein & R. R. Hoffman (Eds.), *Memory and learning* (pp. 319–327). Hillsdale, NJ: Erlbaum.

Cohen, G., Stanhope, N., & Conway, M. A. (1992). Age differences in the retention of knowledge by young and elderly students. *British Journal of Developmental Psychology, 10*, 153–164.

Collins, A. M., & Loftus, E. F. (1975). A spreading-activation theory of semantic processing. *Psychological Review, 82*, 407–428.

Conway, M. A. (1992). A structural model of autobiographical memory. In M. A. Conway, D. C. Rubin, H. Spinnler, & W. A. Wagenaar (Eds.), *Theoretical perspectives on autobiographical memory* (pp. 167–193). Dordrecht, Netherlands: Kluwer.

Dagenbach, D., & Carr, T. H. (1994). Inhibitory processes in perceptual recognition: Evidence for a center-surround attentional mechanism. In D. Dagenbach & T. H. Carr (Eds.), *Inhibitory processes in attention, memory, and language* (pp. 327–358). San Diego: Academic Press.

Dagenbach, D., Carr, T. H., & Barnhardt, T. M. (1990). Inhibitory semantic priming of lexical decisions due to failure to retrieve weakly activated codes. *Journal of Experimental Psychology: Learning, Memory, and Cognition, 16*, 328–340.

Dorfman, J., & Mandler, G. (1994). Implicit and explicit forgetting: When is gist remembered? *Quarterly Journal of Experimental Psychology, 47A*, 651–672.

Duncker, K. (1945). On problem-solving. *Psychological Monographs, 58*, 1–113.

Durso, F. T., & Shore, W. J. (1991) Partial knowledge of word meanings. *Journal of Experimental Psychology: General, 120*, 190–202.

Eich, J. E. (1980). The cue-dependent nature of state-dependent retrieval. *Memory & Cognition, 8*, 157–173.

Eich, E. (1985). Context, memory, and integrated item/context imagery. *Journal of Experimental Psychology: Learning, Memory, and Cognition, 11*, 764–770.

Eich, E., & Metcalfe, J. (1989). Mood dependent memory for internal versus external events. *Journal of Experimental Psychology: Learning, Memory, and Cognition, 15*, 443–455.

Eich, J. E., Weingartner, H., Stillman, R. C., &

Gillin, J. C. (1975). State-dependent accessibility of retrieval cues in the retention of a categorized list. *Journal of Verbal Learning and Verbal Behavior, 14*, 408–417.

Einstein, G. O., & McDaniel, M. A. (1996). Retrieval processes in prospective memory: Theoretical approaches and some empirical findings. In M. Brandimonte, G. O. Einstein, & M. A. McDaniel (Eds.), *Prospective memory: Theory and applications* (pp. 115–141). Mahwah, NJ: Erlbaum.

Erikson, T. A., & Mattson, M. E. (1981). From words to meaning: A semantic illusion. *Journal of Verbal Learning and Verbal Behavior, 20*, 540–552.

Fisher, R. P., & Geiselman, R. E. (1992). *Memory-enhancing techniques for investigative interviewing: The cognitive interview.* Springfield, IL: Thomas.

Glucksberg, S., & McCloskey, M. (1981). Decisions about ignorance. *Journal of Experimental Psychology: Human Learning and Memory, 7*, 311–325.

Godden, D. R., & Baddeley, A. D. (1975). Context-dependent memory in two natural environments: On land and underwater. *British Journal of Psychology, 66*, 325–331.

Goldsmith, M., & Koriat, A. (1999). The strategic regulation of memory reporting: Mechanisms and performance consequences. In D. Gopher & A. Koriat (Eds.), *Attention and performance XVII—Cognitive regulation of performance: Interaction of theory and application.* (pp. 373–400). Cambridge, MA: MIT Press.

Goodwin, D. W., Powell, B., Bremer, D., Hoine, H., & Stern, J. (1969). Alcohol and recall: State dependent effects in man. *Science, 163*, 1358.

Jacoby, L. L. (1991). A process dissociation framework: Separating automatic from intention uses of memory. *Journal of Memory and Language, 30*, 513–541.

Jones, G. V. (1989). Back to Woodworth: Role of interlopers in the tip-of-the-tongue phenomenon. *Memory & Cognition, 17*, 69–76.

Kelley, C. M., & Lindsay, D. S. (1993). Remembering mistaken for knowing: Ease of retrieval as a basis for confidence in answers to general knowledge questions. *Journal of Memory and Language, 32*, 1–24.

Klin, C. M., Guzman, A. E., & Levine, W. H. (1997). Knowing that you don't know: Metamemory and discourse processing. *Journal of Experimental Psychology: Learning, Memory, and Cognition, 23*, 1378–1393.

Kolodner, J. L. (1983). Reconstructive memory: A computer model. *Cognitive Science, 7*, 281–328.

Koriat, A. (1993). How do we know that we know? The accessibility model of the feeling of knowing. *Psychological Review, 100*, 609–639.

Koriat, A. (1995). Dissociating knowing and the feeling of knowing: Further evidence for the accessibility model. *Journal of Experimental Psychology: General, 124*, 311–333.

Koriat, A. (1998). Illusions of knowing: The link between knowledge and metaknowledge. In V. Y. Yzerbyt, G. Lories, & B. Dardenne (Eds.), *Metacognition: Cognitive and social dimensions* (pp. 16–34). London, England: Sage.

Koriat, A., & Feuerstein, N. (1976). The recovery of incidentally acquired information. *Acta Psychologica, 40*, 463–474.

Koriat, A., & Goldsmith, M. (1994). Memory in naturalistic and laboratory contexts: Distinguishing the accuracy-oriented and quantity-oriented approaches to memory assessment. *Journal of Experimental Psychology: General, 123*, 297–315.

Koriat, A., & Goldsmith, M. (1996). Monitoring and control processes in the strategic regulation of memory accuracy. *Psychological Review, 103*, 490–517.

Koriat, A., Goldsmith, M., & Pansky, A. (in press). Toward a psychology of memory accuracy. *Annual Review of Psychology.*

Koriat, A., & Lieblich, I. (1974). What does a person in the "TOT" state know that a person in a "don't know" state does not know? *Memory & Cognition, 2*, 647–655.

Koriat, A., & Lieblich, I. (1977). A study of memory pointers. *Acta Psychologica, 41*, 151–164.

Koriat, A., & Melkman, R., (1987). Depth of processing and memory organization. *Psychological Research, 49*, 173–181.

McDaniel, M. A., & Einstein, G. O. (1993). The importance of cue familiarity and cue distinctiveness in prospective memory. *Memory, 1*, 23–41.

Mandler, G. (1980). Recognizing: The judgment of previous occurrence. *Psychological Review, 87*, 252–271.

Mäntylä, T. (1986). Optimizing cue effectiveness: Recall of 500 and 600 incidentally learned words. *Journal of Experimental Psychology: Human Learning and Memory, 12*, 66–71.

Marsh, R. L., Landau, J. D., & Hicks, J. L. (1997). Contributions of inadequate source monitoring to unconscious plagiarism during idea generation. *Journal of Experimental Psychology: Human Learning and Memory, 23*, 886–897.

Morris, C. D., Bransford, J. D., & Franks, J. J. (1977). Levels of processing versus transfer appropriate processing. *Journal of Verbal Learning and Verbal Behavior, 16*, 519–533.

Morton, J., Hammersley, R. H., & Bekerian, D. A. (1985). Headed records: A model for memory and its failures. *Cognition, 20*, 1–23.

Moscovitch, M. (1989). Confabulation and the frontal lobe system: Strategic vs. associative retrieval in neuropsychological theories of memory. In H. L. Roediger & F. I. M. Craik (Eds.), *Varieties of memory and consciousness: Essays in honor of Endel Tulving* (pp. 133–160). Hillsdale, NJ: Erlbaum.

Neely, J. H. (1976). Semantic priming and retrieval from lexical memory: Evidence for facilitatory and inhibitory processes. *Memory & Cognition, 4*, 648–654.

Neely, J. H., & Keefe, D. E. (1989). Semantic context effects on visual word processing: A hybrid prospective/retrospective processing theory. In G. H. Bower (Ed.), *The psychology of learning and motivation: Advances in research and theory* (Vol. 24; pp. 207–248). New York: Academic Press.

Nelson, D. L., McKinney, V. M., Gee, N. R., & Janczura, G. A. (1998). Interpreting the influence of implicitly activated memories on recall and recognition. *Psychological Review, 105*, 299–324.

Nelson, T. O., & Narens, L. (1990). Metamemory: A theoretical framework and new findings. In G. Bower (Ed.), *The Psychology of learning and motivation: Advances in research and theory* (Vol. 26; pp. 125–123). San Diego: Academic Press.

Nhouyvanisvong, A., & Reder, L. M. (1998). Rapid feeling-of-knowing: A strategy selection mechanism. In V. Y. Yzerbyt, G. Lories, & B. Dardenne (Eds.), *Metacognition: Cognitive and social dimensions* (pp. 35–52). London, England: Sage.

Nickerson, R. S. (1981). Motivated retrieval from archival memory. In J. H. Flowers (Ed.), *Nebraska symposium on motivation* (pp. 73–119). Lincoln: University of Nebraska Press.

Norman, D. A., & Bobrow, D. G. (1979). Descriptions: An intermediate stage in memory retrieval. *Cognitive Psychology, 11*, 107–123.

Raaijmakers, J. G. W., & Shiffrin, R. M. (1981). Search of associative memory. *Psychological Review, 88*, 93–134.

Reder, L. M. (1987). Strategy selection in question answering. *Cognitive Psychology, 19*, 90–138.

Reiser, B., Black, J. B., & Abelson, R. P. (1985). Knowledge structures in the organization and retrieval of autobiographical memories. *Cognitive Psychology, 17*, 89–137.

Reiser, B., Black, J. B., & Kalamarides, P. (1986). Strategic memory search processes. In D. C. Rubin (Ed.), *Autobiographical memory* (pp. 100–121). New York: Cambridge University Press.

Roediger, H. L., & Guynn, J. M. (1996). Retrieval Processes. In E. L. Bjork & R. A. Bjork (Eds.), *Handbook of perception and cognition:* Memory (Vol. 10; pp. 197–236). San Diego: Academic Press.

Roediger, H. L., & McDermott, K. B. (1994). Implicit memory in normal human subjects. In H. Spinnler & F. Boller (Eds.), *Handbook of neuropsychology* (Vol. 8; pp. 63–131). Amsterdam: Elsevier.

Roediger, H. L., & McDermott, K. B. (1995). Creating false memories: Remembering words not presented in lists. *Journal of Experimental Psychology: Learning, Memory, and Cognition, 21*, 803–814.

Salaman, E. (1982). A collection of moments. In U. Neisser (Ed.), *Memory observed: Remembering in natural contexts* (pp. 49–63). San Francisco: Freeman.

Schacter, D. L., & Worling, J. R. (1985). Attribute information and the feeling of knowing. *Canadian Journal of Psychology, 39*, 467–475.

Schacter, D. L., Norman, K. A., & Koutstaal, W. (1998). The cognitive neuroscience of constructive memory. *Annual Review of Psychology, 49*, 289–318.

Schank, R. C. (1982). *Dynamic memory.* Cambridge: Cambridge University Press.

Schwartz, B. L., & Metcalfe, J. (1992). Cue familiarity but not target retrievability enhances feeling-of-knowing judgments. *Journal of Experimental Psychology: Learning, Memory, and Cognition, 18*, 1074–1083.

Schwartz, B. L., & Smith, S. M. (1997). The retrieval of related information influences tip-of-the-tongue states. *Journal of Memory and Language, 36*, 68–86.

Smith, S. M. (1979). Remembering in and out of context. *Journal of Experimental Psychology: Human Learning and Memory, 5*, 460–471.

Smith, S. M., Glenberg, A. M., & Bjork, R. A. (1978). Environmental context and human memory. *Memory & Cognition, 6*, 342–353.

Tulving, E. (1967). The effects of presentation and recall in free recall learning. *Journal of Verbal Learning and Verbal Behavior, 6*, 175–184.

Tulving, E. (1983). *Elements of episodic memory.* New York: Oxford University Press.

Tulving, E., & Pearlstone, Z. (1966). Availability versus accessibility of information in memory for words. *Journal of Verbal Learning and Verbal Behavior, 5,* 381–391.

Tulving, E., & Thomson, D. (1973). Encoding specificity and retrieval processes in episodic memory. *Psychological Review, 80,* 352–373.

Walker, W. H., & Kintsch, W. (1985). Automatic and strategic aspects of knowledge retrieval. *Cognitive Science, 9,* 261–283.

Williams, M. D., & Hollan, J. D. (1981). The process of retrieval from very long-term memory. *Cognitive Science, 5,* 87–119.

Williams, M. D., & Santos-Williams, S. (1980). Methods for exploring retrieval processes using verbal protocols. In R. S. Nickerson (Ed.), *Attention and Performance VIII* (pp. 671–689). Hillsdale, NJ: Erlbaum.

Yaniv, I., & Foster, D. P. (1995). Graininess of judgment under uncertainty: An accuracy-informativeness trade-off. *Journal of Experimental Psychology: General, 124,* 424–432.

22

Long-Term Maintenance of Knowledge

HARRY P. BAHRICK

Historical Background

The retention of knowledge was a neglected domain of memory research before the 1970s because memory scholars remained committed to an experimental paradigm that could not accommodate the long periods involved in the acquisition and maintenance of knowledge. Semb and Ellis (1994) reviewed earlier scholarship dealing with the retention of knowledge acquired in schools; however, these investigations had little impact because they were widely scattered, they covered relatively short retention intervals, and they lacked essential controls. Memory research focused on the retention of episodic content over short time periods. As a result, memory scholarship could not address the needs of educators, whose memory-related concerns pertain to the maintenance of knowledge, not to memory for events (Kintsch, 1974). Neisser (1978) described this neglect as "scandalous."

The zeitgeist of the 1960s demanded that scientific scholarship become more responsive to the solution of societal problems, and memory scholars responded to this demand by adopting more eclectic methods. Maintenance of knowledge became a viable domain of research when computer technology facilitated naturalistic investigations that combine large sample sizes and multiple regression analyses to compensate for the loss of experimental controls. As recently as 1989 the use of naturalistic methods in memory research was evaluated negatively (Banaji & Crowder, 1989), but memory scholars now generally see experimental and naturalistic methods as complementary—that is, naturalistic strategies supplement experimental methods (Bahrick, 1989; Bruce, 1991; Klatzky, 1991; Neisser, 1991; Tulving, 1991). Control remains the hallmark of scientific investigations, and experiments therefore continue to be the preferred method. However, it is now generally agreed that important questions about memory should not be ignored just because they are not amenable to laboratory exploration. Instead, they should be investigated under the best available conditions of control. This pragmatic view has opened new domains of theoretical and applied inquiry, including research concerned with eyewitness testimony and various aspects of autobiographical memory content. As a consequence, memory scholarship has now become relevant to a broad range of previously neglected concerns of educators, historians, jurists, and psychotherapists.

Adopting an eclectic methodology not only made memory research more responsive to the needs of society but also challenged the development of memory theory. Theories of memory now must accommodate a wide range of phenomena and findings that emerged from investigations of semantic and autobiographical memory content, such as the distribution of autobiographical memories across the life span, systematic distortions of autobiographical memory content, and the permanence of unrehearsed knowledge. The task of developing theories that can accommodate such a wide range of phenomena is formidable, and comprehensive memory theories will re-emerge only after the current theories designed to accommodate the findings of specific subdomains can be integrated.

The review of the research related to maintenance of knowledge is organized on the basis of the following categories of variables: (1) conditions of training and acquisition; (2) rehearsal conditions—that is, interventions occurring after the acquisition period; (3) individual differences; and (4) variables associated with the type of memory content. The methodological and theoretical issues are discussed as they arise in connection with individual investigations. The review focuses on research using retention intervals of several years. Investigations of shorter duration are discussed when their results are necessary to clarify a significant issue.

Conditions of Training and Acquisition

The results of memory experiments often confirm what common sense would predict. The life span of memory content depends upon how well the content was originally learned. The beneficial effect of "overlearning" on retention was among the earliest findings reported from laboratory investigations of memory (Ebbinghaus, 1885). The early investigations examined relatively short retention intervals, reflecting the aforementioned constraints of the experimental paradigm. The life span of knowledge systems can extend over many years, and cross-sectional, naturalistic comparisons are needed to establish relevant functional relations. Bahrick, Bahrick, and Wittlinger (1975) described such relations in a study of 50 years of memory for the names and faces of high school classmates. The investigation showed that 35 years after graduating from high school, the participants were able to recognize 90% of the portraits of their classmates. Recognition of the names of classmates was nearly equally good, and performance was largely independent of the size of graduating classes. The mean class size was 294 graduates.

Figure 22.1 shows a finding from a later investigation (Bahrick, 1984a) of the maintenance of knowledge of the Spanish language acquired in U.S. high schools and colleges. The figure shows projected retention functions for the recall of Spanish-English and English-Spanish vocabulary. The functions show that for individuals trained to level five (equivalent to five college courses of Spanish), approximately 50% of their original recall vocabulary is projected to be retained 25 years after their training terminates. The projected performance is statistically adjusted to reflect no rehearsals of the language during the retention interval. In contrast, individuals trained to level one (a single semester of college Spanish) are projected to have lost all of their initial recall vocabulary within 3 to 5 years. Comparisons based upon tests of reading comprehension and other aspects of language recognition also yield large differences in the same direction, although they show somewhat better long-term retention for individuals with lower levels of original training. Analogous findings are obtained when the level of original training is defined on the basis of the letter grade received in the course. Students trained to a level of three courses and who earned a grade of A will maintain reading comprehension scores that are substantially higher than students who earned a grade of C. The difference remains stable for 50 years.

These naturalistic investigations, and several others (Bahrick, 1983; Bahrick & Hall, 1991a; Bahrick, Hall, Goggin, Bahrick, & Berger, 1994), make use of a common method. A large number of individuals (usually between 500 and 1,000) participate, and they have acquired the same type of knowledge at various intervals ranging from a few days to 50 years prior to being tested. Reliable indicants must be available to estimate (1) their original level of knowledge; (2) the length of the retention interval; (3) the amount and type of rehearsal of the knowledge during the retention interval; and (4) the amount of knowledge at the time of testing by the investigator. In the study of retention of Spanish, the estimate of the degree of original knowledge was based upon the number of courses taken and the grades received. The retention interval was the elapsed time between completion of the last course and the administration of the retention test. The amount of rehearsal was estimated from answers to a questionnaire in which partici-

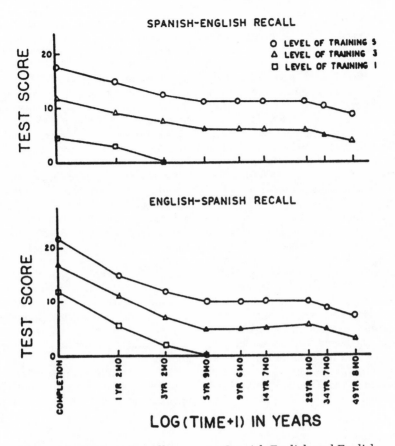

Figure 22.1 Projected recall scores on Spanish-English and English-Spanish vocabulary tests as a function of the level of original training (after Bahrick, 1984a).

pants indicated the frequency and recency of various types of uses of the Spanish language.

The data bank is entered into a computer and analyzed by hierarchical multiple regression. The criterion variable is performance on the language retention test, and the predictor variables are indicants of original knowledge, of rehearsals, and of the length of the retention interval. Higher order terms for all of these variables, and the interactions among the variables, are also used as predictors. The multiple regression equation is evaluated for successive increments of the retention interval, using various levels of the predictor variable of interest and holding other predictor variables constant at a desired level. Figure 22.1 illustrates retention functions projected in this manner. The magnitude of the multiple correlation indicates how well these functions represent actual retention performance. The investigation of the retention of Spanish lan-

guage yielded correlations from .67 to .77 for predicting retention on various subtests of Spanish. A comparable investigation of maintenance of knowledge of high school algebra (Bahrick & Hall, 1991a) over a 50-year period yielded a correlation of .80. The reliability of these correlations is very high, since they are based upon a large number of participants. Considering the many possible sources of error in naturalistic investigations, the high validity of predicting performance on a retention test was unexpected. It may be attributed to the relatively high reliability of the retention test and of the indicants of the degree of original learning used in these investigations. In contrast, single-trial indicants of recall or recognition commonly used as the dependent variable in laboratory experiments of learning and memory have much lower reliabilities that limit the validity of predicting retention (Bahrick, 1977).

An alternative treatment of the data in cross-sectional investigations involves statistical adjustments of the mean retention scores obtained by subgroups of participants tested at various retention intervals (Bahrick, Bahrick, & Wittlinger, 1975). Because these subgroups may differ in regard to the average level of original training, rehearsals, and so on, their retention performance is adjusted on the basis of the multiple regression analysis so as to reflect the overall mean level of the uncontrolled variables. Figure 22.2 shows retention data for Spanish language treated in this way (Bahrick, 1984a). The disadvantage of this method is that it fails to reveal important findings—for example, the influence of the degree of original training on the level at which retention stabilizes. This influence is apparent in figure 22.1, where it can be seen that projected performance of individuals with different degrees of training stabilizes at different levels. The influence is not apparent in figure 22.2, where the retention functions stabilize at a level that reflects the overall mean level of original training that happens to characterize the group of participants. The significance of the phenomenon of stabilized long-term retention is elaborated below.

The spaced practice effect is another finding of laboratory memory research that is greatly enhanced in investigations of maintenance of knowledge. The conclusion that a given amount of practice yields better retention if training sessions are spaced over a longer time period is one of the oldest and best-documented findings of memory research (Bruce & Bahrick, 1992; Dempster, 1990; Ebbinghaus, 1885; Glenberg, 1992). The large effects shown in figure 22.1 actually reflect the combined influence of the amount of training and the spacing of training. Individuals who take several courses in Spanish generally do not take them at the same time. Rather, they are likely to take one Spanish course per semester, so that those who have taken five courses will also have spaced their acquisition of Spanish over five semesters. Because the amount and the spacing of acquisition are confounded in all of the investigations that have been cited, their data do not permit sorting out the respective contributions of these two variables to the long-term retention of knowledge.

An independent assessment is possible, however, on the basis of longitudinal investigations designed for this purpose. In one

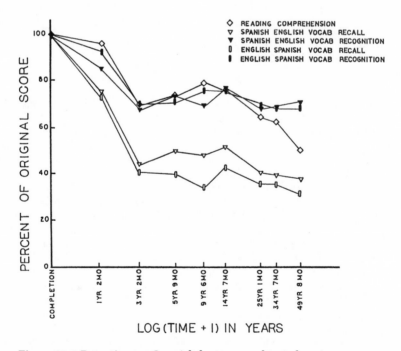

Figure 22.2 Retention on Spanish language subtests by nine groups of participants tested at various retention intervals; adjusted to equate the level of training (after Bahrick, 1984a).

such study (Bahrick, 1979), college students learned and relearned 50 English-Spanish word pairs in successive training sessions, spaced either at intervals of a few seconds, 1 day, or 30 days. Cumulative learning was somewhat faster with shorter intersession intervals, but retention between training sessions was nearly perfect after seven retraining sessions, even with a 30-day intersession interval. When a 30-day interval was introduced for the first time, it yielded substantial forgetting for subjects trained with shorter intersession intervals. That same 30-day interval yielded improved performance for individuals who were trained with that interval all along. Figure 22.3 shows the crossover effect obtained when the 30-day interval is introduced after six practice sessions. In a follow-up retention test administered eight years later (Bahrick & Phelps, 1987), students who were trained with the 30-day interval still recalled 15% of the original word pairs, those trained with a 1-day interval recalled 8%, and those trained with the shortest interval recalled 6%.

The effectiveness of practice sessions spaced at unusually long intervals was demonstrated by Bahrick, Bahrick, Bahrick, and Bahrick (1993). Four individuals learned and relearned 300 English-foreign language word pairs and were tested for retention over a 5-year period. The training program varied both the number of relearning sessions (13 or 26) and the interval between sessions (14, 28, or 56 days). This design allowed an evaluation of how retention is affected by a given number of training sessions spaced at the three intervals, or the effect of additional training sessions spaced at the same interval. The results showed that both the number of training sessions and the spacing of training sessions have large, independent effects on long-term retention. Figure 22.4 shows that the large effect of the interval between sessions is maintained over the 5-year retention period.

Current theories of the spacing effect were developed to account for findings obtained with relatively short spacing intervals. These theories are not easily applied to the very long

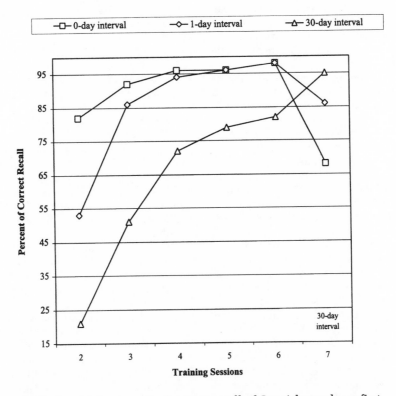

Figure 22.3 Mean percent of correct recall of Spanish words on first test trials as a function of the intersession interval (after Bahrick, 1979).

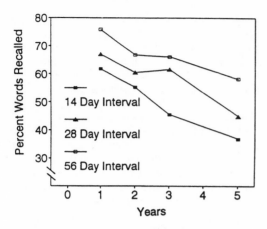

Figure 22.4 Retention of foreign language vocabulary as a function of the spacing between relearning sessions during acquisition (after Bahrick, Bahrick, Bahrick, and Bahrick, 1993).

intervals used in investigations of maintenance of knowledge. Theories of encoding variability (e.g., Glenberg, 1979; Madigan, 1969; Melton, 1970) stipulate that wider temporal spacing between successive presentations of the same target items increases the likelihood that learners will encounter a new and different encoding context at each successive presentation. The greater variability of cues present during encoding is assumed to yield a higher probability of recall in a variety of retrieval contexts. This explanation is plausible when the intervals between successive presentations range from a few seconds to several minutes. It is much less plausible as an explanation of the effect obtained in comparing a presentation interval of 28 days with one of 56 days because there is no plausible basis for assuming that the retrieval context has changed more during 56 than during 28 days.

Diminished processing theories of the spacing effect (e.g., Bregman, 1967; Cuddy & Jacoby, 1982; Greeno, 1970) hold that learners devote less processing time and attention to repeated presentations of the same content when repetitions of content follow at short intervals versus longer intervals, and that the diminished processing yields poorer encoding and ultimately poorer retention. Again, this assumption is plausible when intervals between successive presentations are relatively short (e.g., seconds or minutes), whereas differential effects for intervals of 28 versus 56

days are not easily accounted for on the basis of this rationale.

The large and long-lasting spacing effects observed in investigations of the maintenance of knowledge are better accounted for on the basis of augmented opportunities for selecting effective encoding strategies during acquisition. For instance, individuals trained to learn 50 English-Spanish word pairs with 1-day intersession intervals cannot find out whether their encoding strategies for a particular word pair are effective in maintaining access for longer than 1 day until they encounter a 30-day interval for the first time. Accordingly, as can be seen in figure 22.3, their performance declines at that time, because some of their strategies turn out to be inadequate for long-term retention. In contrast, individuals trained with a 30-day interval receive this feedback on the first trial of each retraining session, and therefore have the opportunity to modify or replace strategies that failed. After the seventh session their performance is nearly perfect—that is, almost all their strategies work for this interval (Bahrick & Phelps, 1987). Those who were trained for seven sessions with a 1-day interval also show perfect performance after seven sessions, but their performance declines sharply when a 30-day interval is introduced for the first time. By extending this principle, it is reasonable to assume that strategies selected on the basis of their effectiveness for intervals of 30 days will be more successful than strategies selected on the basis of their effectiveness for 1 day, when a retention interval of several years is used as the criterion test.

Let us consider again the phenomenon of stabilized retention functions observed in figure 22.1. The original purpose of that investigation (Bahrick, 1984a) was to determine the kind and amounts of rehearsal activities during the retention interval that would suffice to maintain the level of Spanish vocabulary, reading comprehension, and other skills acquired at the end of training. It turned out that the overwhelming majority of participants reported little or no rehearsal, and an intercorrelation matrix of rehearsal activities and performance on the retention test showed that the effects of those rehearsal levels on retention were negligible. The regression equation was then adjusted to remove these minor effects from the projected retention functions by setting the level of all rehearsal variables to zero, so that the functions in figure 22.1 show only the projected effects of varying levels of original learning. The important finding is that the decline of performance comes to a halt within 3 to 5 years after training, and performance then remains stable for approximately 25 years. Further, when the stabilized performance level is expressed as a portion of the score obtained at the end of training, this proportion largely reflects the original training level. To wit, retention of Spanish-English recall vocabulary stabilizes at a level of 0%, 29%, and 63% of the original score for those who were trained to level one, three, or five, respectively. These percentages are certain to be affected by the difficulty level of the test and other variables; however, they underline the strong influence of the level of original training on what we have called the *permastore* content, the content destined to survive for 25 years or longer in the absence of rehearsal activities.

Thus, the widely spaced, extended training yields content that withstands the normal process of forgetting. Although the influence of extended training and spaced practice was demonstrated many years ago in laboratory experiments, the cross-sectional, naturalistic investigations of the maintenance of knowledge document substantial enhancement of these effects, as well as the evidence that their interactions can yield semipermanent knowledge.

On a theoretical level, the data also permit an inference about the process by which memory content acquires permastore longevity. One may transform the projected retention functions shown in figure 22.1 into frequency distributions of the life span of individual word pairs in the participant's English-Spanish lexicon (Bahrick, 1984a). The transformation makes it apparent that a portion of the typical lexicon has a life span of 0 to 5 years, another portion has a life span of more than 30 years, and none of the lexicon has a life span between 5 and 30 years. If we assume that the prospective life span of English-Spanish word pairs increases during extended training, it follows that the increases may be gradual as life spans extend from 0 to 5 years. However, the transition must be discrete when life spans extend from 5 years to over 30 years; otherwise, some portions of the lexicon would have life spans of 10, 15, 20, or 25 years. It would appear that at a certain point during extended training, associations acquire permastore longevity.

Stabilized, long-term retention functions have now been documented in several other investigations of the retention of knowledge and skill. Conway, Cohen, and Stanhope (1991) report no decline after the third year in tests of the retention of course content in cognitive psychology. Schmidt, Peeck, Paas, and van Breukelen (in press) tested retention of streets learned incidentally by students of a Dutch elementary school. They found that recall was stable for over forty years, following an initial decline. Healy et al. (1992) report nearly perfect long-term retention in a variety of overlearned tasks and skills, as do Fleishman and Parker (1962) in a simulated flying task, Rubin (1977) for complex text (e.g., the 23rd Psalm), and Noice and Noice (1997) for the long-term retention by actors of theatrical roles.

A significant difference between the stabilized functions found by Bahrick (1984a) and Conway, Cohen, and Stanhope (1991), but not by Bahrick et al. (1975), Bahrick and Hall (1991a), Healy et al. (1992), or Fleishman and Parker (1962), pertains to losses of retention sustained during the first 3 to 5 years of the retention interval. No such losses are observed in the latter investigations; rather, they report that retention remains nearly perfect from the outset.

Whether or not early retention losses are obtained depends upon whether a portion of the memory content was added late during the acquisition period, so that it could not receive the amount or the distribution of practice required to attain permastore stability. This most recently acquired content is subject to "normal" forgetting, during the first 3 to 5 years, and only after access to that content has been lost does the retention function stabilize. In the investigations by Bahrick and Hall (1991a) and Bahrick et al. (1975), all of the memory content was subject to extended, spaced acquisition, and subsequently none of the content was lost during the early part of the retention period.

It should be a high priority for educators and trainers to explore and implement conditions of acquisition that promote permastore stability of content. So far, this has not occurred. Bjork and his associates (Christina & Bjork, 1991; Ghodsian, Bjork, & Benjamin, 1997) have emphasized that the conditions employed in training programs frequently have adverse effects on the long-term retention of knowledge and skills. This occurs because training conditions are often arranged so as to enhance performance during acquisition, and the conditions that benefit rapid acquisition may be detrimental to long-term maintenance and retention. Results of two investigations cited earlier (Bahrick & Phelps, 1987; Bahrick et al., 1993) confirm this claim. Performance during training is degraded—that is, acquisition of knowledge is slowed down when training sessions are spaced at long intervals. This happens because more forgetting occurs during long intervals between training sessions, and the loss requires some additional relearning time at the outset of each session. The results show, however, that long-term retention is greatly enhanced.

The spacing effect is only one of several conditions discussed by Bjork and his associates in this context. Other conditions that impair performance during acquisition, but support long-term maintenance, are reduced frequency of feedback to trainees (Schmidt, 1991) and variable practice—that is, experience with several versions of a task or materials during practice, as opposed to constant practice with only one version of a task. The effect of these conditions is also discussed in an important review of the literature by Healy and Sinclair (1996). Tests that require retrievals are potent learning events if the retrieval is successful (Izawa, 1970). Rather than being left in the same state it was in prior to being recalled, the retrieved information becomes more recallable in the future than it would have been without having been accessed (Bjork, 1988).

Making training too quick and easy has the additional disadvantage of giving trainees an unrealistically inflated metacognitive self-assessment of present knowledge and of the likelihood of long-term retention. Bjork (1994) and Jacoby, Bjork, and Kelley (1994) point out that a learner's metacognitive assessment of mastery may determine whether trainees will engage in additional practice or maintenance training. Overestimations of competence can have disastrous consequences in particular work environments—for example, air-traffic control, police or military operations, or nuclear power plants (Bjork, 1994). Christina and Bjork (1991) concluded that "The effectiveness of a training program should be measured not by the speed of acquisition of a task during training or by the level of performance reached at the end of training, but, rather, by the learner's performance in the post-training tasks and real-world settings that are the target of training" (p. 47).

In their review of the recent literature, Healy and Sinclair (1996) offer guidelines concerning the conditions of training and instruction designed to improve long-term retention

of knowledge and skills. In addition to the factors already discussed, they recommend the use of reinstatable procedures and of conditions that promote automaticity during learning.

The Effects of Rehearsal Conditions

It is not always possible to make a clear distinction between acquisition or training on the one hand and rehearsals or maintenance interventions on the other. Acquisition continues as long as new content is added to a knowledge domain; but acquisition sessions may also be limited to continued training with previously presented content, with the goal of improving performance (Healy, Fendrich, & Proctor, 1990). Typically, rehearsal interventions do not include new, additional content; their goal is not to improve performance, but rather to *maintain* it. Also, intervals between maintenance interventions are usually longer than intervals between acquisition sessions. In practice, however, in the case of high-level musical or athletic skills and the like, it may be difficult to distinguish categorically between acquisition and maintenance sessions.

The following strategies have been used to find rehearsal conditions that economically maintain levels of knowledge or skill: (1) statistical estimates of rehearsal that maintain knowledge; (2) experimental investigations comparing the effects of various types or schedules of maintenance interventions; and (3) investigations of the maintenance of access to marginal knowledge.

Statistical Estimates of Rehearsal that Maintain Knowledge

This strategy is illustrated with data from a naturalistic investigation (Bahrick, 1983) in which 851 students and alumni of a university took a test of their memory for the names and locations of streets and buildings in the city where the university is located. The alumni, who had graduated from 1 to 50 years prior to taking the test, also filled out a questionnaire in which they indicated the frequency, duration, and recency of visits to the city during the retention period. The data obtained from the questionnaire were the source of indicants of rehearsal activities.

Multiple regression equations predicted each aspect of performance on the retention test as a function of the time since graduation and of the various rehearsal activities. These equations were then reevaluated so as to determine the level of rehearsal activities necessary to maintain the mean score on the retention test obtained by graduating seniors. The evaluations were made for one rehearsal variable at a time, using arbitrarily fixed levels of other rehearsal variables. For example, a fixed level of 2 days was set for the duration of each visit, with the most recent visit set at 2 months earlier, and the regression equation was evaluated to determine the number of annual visits needed to maintain the test score attained at graduation. Table 22.1 gives the resulting statistical estimates of the number of visits per year needed to maintain recall of the street sequence at the graduation level, assuming various values for the duration of visits and for the most recent visit.

The validity of this technique depends upon observing a number of constraints, and upon the tenability of assumptions. The most important constraints preclude extrapolating from the available data. The values in all of the cells of table 22.1 must correspond to the data obtained from some of the participants. For example, if no participants averaged more than 8 visits per year, then the estimates of all cells with values of more than 8 visits per year lack validity. Interpolations of data are less problematic than extrapolations; for instance, if some participants visited 6 times per year and others visited 4 times per year, cells that estimate a required 5 annual visits have reasonable credibility.

An obvious constraint refers to the evaluation of hypotheses about the effects of re- hearsal variables that are not represented in the data. For example, it is not possible to evaluate whether evenly spaced visits versus visits spaced at an expanding time schedule yield superior maintenance of knowledge, unless a significant number of participants report each of the two types of rehearsal schedules.

An important assumption of this technique is the homogeneity of regression across the retention interval. This assumes that the influence of rehearsal variables on retention test performance does not systematically change with time. To test this assumption, participants were assigned to one of nine groups according to the time elapsed since their graduation, and separate multiple regression equations were obtained for each group. Overall regression weights were used only after it was determined that the regression weights obtained for the various groups did not differ systematically.

Experimental Evidence Pertaining to Rehearsal Schedules

Bjork (1988) discusses the influence of retrieval practice on the maintenance of knowledge. He points out that, in contrast to a computer, the state of information in human memory is altered by the act of retrieval, and that the key to maintaining access to knowledge in memory is to retrieve that information periodically. (It has already been pointed out that certain conditions of acquisition will yield exceptions to this rule—i.e., conditions that yield permastore content, assuring semipermanent retrievability in the absence of further rehearsals.)

Given that the maintenance of most memory content requires periodic retrieval, questions arise in regard to the optimum spacing of retrievals. Several considerations guided Landauer and Bjork (1978) in exploring these questions: (1) the spacing effect suggests that, other things being equal, retrieval rehearsals should be spaced as far apart as possible; (2) rehearsals are only effective if they involve successful retrieval, and therefore they need to occur before retrieval fails; and (3) successful retrievals facilitate future retrievals, and a cumulative effect may permit longer intervals between successive retrievals without risking retrieval failures.

On this basis Landauer and Bjork hypothesized that retrievals should be spaced as far apart as possible without retrieval failures,

Table 22.1 Number of visits per year needed to maintain recall of street sequence at the graduation level (after Bahrick, 1979).

Most Recent Visit (Months)	Duration of Each Visit (Days)				
	1	2	3	4	5
0	11.58	7.55	5.60	4.45	3.70
.50	11.72	7.64	5.67	4.51	3.74
1.00	11.82	7.71	5.72	4.55	3.77
1.50	11.90	7.76	5.76	4.58	3.80
2.00	11.96	7.80	5.79	4.60	3.82

and that cumulative retrieval effects would permit implementing this principle on the basis of an expanding retrieval schedule. The effectiveness of an expanding retrieval schedule had been demonstrated earlier by Spitzer (1939), who showed that such a schedule between successive tests was successful in maintaining academic memory content.

Landauer and Bjork (1978) systematically varied retrieval schedules in a name-learning task and compared the effects of uniform, contracting, and expanding rehearsal schedules on a delayed (30-minute) retention test. They found, in accord with their hypothesis, that the expanding retrieval schedule yielded optimum retention. Their findings were confirmed by Rea and Modigliani (1985, 1988), who tested the expanding schedule with classroom materials.

Although the available experimental data are based on time-compressed, longitudinal investigations, there is no reason to question the general applicability of an expanding retrieval principle to the long-term maintenance of knowledge. What the time-compressed experiments cannot tell us is the order of magnitude of expanding retrieval intervals that are appropriate for maintaining access to knowledge over much longer periods. In addition, the previously reported findings suggest the intriguing possibility that expanding retrieval schedules may ultimately yield permastore stability of access.

Maintenance of Access to Marginal Knowledge

A portion of semipermanent memory content is dependably available on tests of recognition, but is recalled unreliably. Success and failure of attempts at retrieval fluctuate, depending upon the momentary retrieval context. This memory content has been labeled *marginal* (Bahrick & Hall, 1991b), and it is evident that a large portion of semantic memory content is marginal. For example, the number of words we can reliably recall in any language is only a portion of the much larger lexicon available to comprehension and understood on a recognition level.

The cross-sectional investigation of memory for Spanish language (Bahrick, 1984a) showed that recall of unrehearsed vocabulary stabilizes 3 to 5 years after the acquisition period ends. It therefore seemed paradoxical that

repeated testing of participants who had terminated acquisition many years ago showed a substantial number of fluctuations of recall on successive tests for the same words. The conflict between the longitudinal and cross-sectional findings is resolved if the fluctuations are symmetrical—that is, if the number of target items not recalled in test 1, but recalled in test 2 equals the number of items recalled in test 1, but not recalled in test 2, so that the overall performance level on successive tests is stable. In actual fact, however, fluctuations are not symmetrical; rather, the number of upward fluctuations substantially exceeds the number of downward fluctuations (Bahrick & Hall, 1991b; Herrmann, Buschke, & Gall, 1987).

This observation leads to the conclusion that the asymmetry of fluctuations on successive tests of a stable memory content reflects hypermnesia induced by the retrieval practice effect of testing. Absent any retrieval interventions, the upward and downward fluctuations of accessibility must be symmetrical for an overall stable performance level, and the observed asymmetry of fluctuations must be due to retrieval practice of marginal target items. The timely retrieval has the effect of preventing, for a time, downward fluctuations that otherwise would have occurred as the retrieval context changes. Bahrick and Hall labeled this a *preventive maintenance effect*, and reasoned that one could infer the magnitude and the duration of this effect by observing how long an interval between successive tests would be required to reestablish symmetry of upward and downward fluctuations.

The Bahrick and Hall findings confirmed that the degree of asymmetry of fluctuations diminishes as the interval between repeated tests is prolonged; however, the rate of diminution is astonishingly slow. Table 22.2 shows the total number of up and down fluctuations for three types of memory content retested after 2 hours and after 1 month. Pooled for three knowledge domains (foreign language vocabulary, general knowledge questions, and naming portraits of famous individuals), down fluctuations constituted 22% of up fluctuations for the 2-hour interval and 39% of up fluctuations for the 1-month interval.

The preventive maintenance effect has dissipated when the number of down fluctuations equals the number of up fluctuations. After one month, more than half of the effect (61%) persists. Thus, a single retrieval prac-

Table 22.2 Asymmetry of up versus down fluctuations and the preventive maintenance effect (after Bahrick and Hall, 1991b).

	2-Hour Interval			1-Month Interval		
Observed Symmetry	Up	Down	Mean Prop. of Down	Up	Down	Mean Prop. of Down
PIC*	76	10	.12	56	27	.35
GEN	52	8	.12	86	23	.24
VOC	63	24	.28	72	33	.35
	191	42	.17	214	83	.31
Preventive Maintenance Index	78%			61%		

*PIC = Portraits of famous people; GEN = General knowledge; VOC = Foreign vocabulary.

tice of a marginal item learned several years earlier prevents for 1 month more than 50% of access failures that would otherwise have occurred. These findings are uniquely true for stabilized marginal memory content; they would not apply to marginal content that was acquired recently and has therefore not yet stabilized. The findings suggest intriguing possibilities for stabilizing access to marginal memory content on the basis of parsimoniously scheduled retrieval practice. If we apply the principles of expanding retrieval schedules (Landauer & Bjork, 1978) to the domain of stabilized marginal knowledge, it is reasonable to assume that a few appropriately scheduled retrievals might stabilize access to that content for many years, given that the half-life of the initial retrieval effect exceeds 1 month. Content domains of education that are not frequently accessed (e.g., foreign language vocabulary, mathematical content) could remain accessible, and therefore much more useful, by implementing brief, appropriately spaced retrieval practice sessions.

A study by McKenna and Glendon (1985) illustrates the critical need for implementation of appropriately spaced rehearsal practice. These authors investigated the retention of cardiopulmonary resuscitation (CPR) skill over a three-year period. First aid volunteers who had mastered the technique of reviving individuals who had suffered a heart attack were retested on the manikin used for training. The manikin records the subject's performance during training and provides feedback. The predicted survival rate of the resuscitable patient dropped from 100% to 15% during the first year of the retention interval.

Individual Differences

Principles of knowledge maintenance are subject to individual differences, as are all aspects of human experience. Although this topic has received relatively little attention, several investigations have explored the influence of age, gender, and traits on the maintenance of knowledge.

Age Effects

The Bahrick (1984a) data confound the age of the individual with the age of the memory trace, as is the case for all investigations of memory. During any retention interval, individuals age, and investigators do not sort out changes of the memory trace that are due to the aging process from cognitive changes that operate on the memory trace, independent of biological aging. Although this confound theoretically affects all investigations of memory, the problem is trivial when the retention interval is measured in minutes or hours, because there is little reason to assume that aging of the organism significantly affects memory over such short periods. When the retention interval is 50 years, the problem requires serious consideration.

Fortunately, one outcome of the Bahrick (1984a) investigation answers a part of the question. During the 25-plus years of stability of permastore knowledge, there is apparently no significant effect due to aging. When no losses of content are observed, the problem of apportioning losses among various causes disappears. The Bahrick (1984a) data show declines in performance beginning about 35 years after acquisition terminates and accelerating during the remaining 10 years of the 50-year retention interval. The participants who were of college age during acquisition are approximately 57 years old at the time a decline of performance resumes. It appears probable that this decline reflects an aging effect. This interpretation is also supported by results from the study of retention of names and faces of college classmates (Bahrick et al., 1975). Those retention functions show declines of performance at approximately the same age. However, the study of maintenance of the content of high school algebra (Bahrick & Hall, 1991a) shows no decline for the entire 50-year period for individuals who used the content in subsequent higher mathematics courses. It is possible that the differential retention functions reflect interactions of aging effects and content variables.

Age was an independent variable in only one study of maintenance of knowledge (Bahrick, 1984b), in which college teachers were tested for retention of names and faces of their students. Three groups of teachers, whose mean ages were 39, 54, and 68 years at the time they taught the students, were tested 1, 4, and 8 years later. They had taught the students in a single course with an average class size of 40. Performance level was not high immediately after teaching the course; only on a name recognition test did the participants average above the 80% correct level. Performance declined steadily during the 8-year retention period and showed no evidence of stabilizing. The three age groups did not differ significantly in their performance on any of the retention tests.

A similar result is reported by Cohen, Stanhope, and Conway (1992). They investigated retention of knowledge from an undergraduate course in cognitive psychology by former students aged between 25 and 77 at the time they took the course. Their retention intervals ranged from 3 months to 12 years. They found no age differences in the rate of forgetting, and concluded that intelligent, highly motivated elderly people show very little deficit in the retention of formally acquired knowledge.

The absence of significant aging effects in these investigations does not rule out age-related declines in access to knowledge that had previously been stable for many years, nor does it rule out age-related declines in the performance of skills. These questions can be answered only on the basis of an investigation in which different age groups acquired the same knowledge or skill to a level that yielded stabilized retention. If subsequent declines of retention occur when all groups reach the same age, the decline can be ascribed to biological aging, rather than aging of the memory traces.

Gender Effects

Gender effects have been examined in several of the investigations of maintenance of knowledge (Bahrick et al., 1975; Bahrick, 1983; Bahrick & Hall, 1991a) and were generally found to be small, reflecting primarily motivational, or interest variables, rather than differential cognitive processes. Stanhope, Cohen, and Conway (1993) found no gender differences in long-term retention of the content of a novel. In the study of memory for the names and faces of high school classmates (Bahrick et al., 1975), the average performance of female subjects was somewhat superior to the performance of male subjects. However, the difference reflected superior acquisition rather than superior retention, suggesting that motivational and interest variables may be responsible. Evidence for the role of motivational variables is strong in regard to the free recall of names in that investigation. Male participants recalled nearly twice as many male names as female names. Female participants recalled more female names than male names, but the difference was much smaller. Gender differences in the retention of the map of a city were small, favoring males, but the differences disappeared when adjustments were made for differential acquisition and rehearsals (Bahrick, 1983). Males were more likely to have driven a car on campus and to have made more visits during the retention interval.

Only the test of retention of high school algebra content (Bahrick & Hall, 1991a) yielded gender differences that appear to reflect cognitive processes unrelated to differential levels of acquisition or rehearsal. For individuals who took no mathematics courses at or above the level of calculus and who had received an average grade of A, no gender differences in performance appeared to exist at the end of the last algebra course. However, over time, the performance of women declined more than that of men. Rehearsal conditions were controlled (set at zero) to the extent that they were reflected by answers to a questionnaire. It is possible, of course, that differences in rehearsals that are not reflected in the answers to questionnaires may affect the data.

Trait Effects

Naveh-Benjamin, Lavi, McKeachie, and Lin (1997) examined the effects of test anxiety on long-term retention of knowledge. They tested retention of the content of a high school literature course up to 7 years after course completion, and retention of a college-level learning-to-learn course for intervals of up to 3 years after course completion. Students who reported high test anxiety performed more poorly at the end of acquisition, but not after longer retention intervals. The authors concluded that test anxiety interferes with retrieval of information, but not with storage or maintenance of knowledge. Once the anxiety has dissipated there is no evidence of diminution of the retained content.

Noice (1993) ascribes the superior, verbatim retention by professional actors to their learning strategies. These overlearned strategies include integrating the verbal text with motoric codes (Noice & Noice, 1997) and organizing each theatrical role hierarchically as a series of subgoals based upon the intentions of the assigned character. When nonactors use these strategies they recall only the gist of material, but fail to show efficient verbatim retention.

Type of Content

The effect of the type of content on maintenance of knowledge has been examined in a number of investigations. The results can be valuable for designing instructional programs that will yield longevity of content areas in accord with educational priorities. The theoretical interpretation of findings, however, is difficult because differential rates of forgetting of various content domains reflect not only differential retentivity of these content categories, but also differing degrees of original learning/overlearning. These variables are inextricably confounded not only in naturalistic investigations but also in well-controlled experiments. Underwood (1964) showed that this limitation even precludes interpreting differential rates of forgetting of nonsense syllables in memory experiments that control the level of acquisition by terminating training when a common performance criterion is reached.

The Bahrick et al. (1975) study shows that picture recognition of classmates is somewhat superior to name recognition 35 years after graduation, although performance on both tasks was approximately 90% correct at graduation. It is not possible to ascribe this difference to superior retentive properties of portraits, however, because the high performance level at graduation may conceal differential degrees of overlearning, favoring portraits over names of classmates.

Similarly, the Bahrick (1984a) study of maintenance of knowledge of Spanish language shows differential rates of loss for subtests dealing with vocabulary, grammar, idioms, reading comprehension, and so on. Since there is no way of equating the level or degree of acquisition for various aspects of knowledge of the language, one cannot attribute differential rates of forgetting to the inherent characteristics of the content. The same caveat applies to the Conway et al. (1991, 1992) investigation of long-term retention of the content of a cognitive psychology course. Names, concepts, and terms yield differential rates of forgetting, but it is impossible to rule out differential degrees of overlearning as the cause.

Naveh-Benjamin (1988) examined changes over two years in the structure of knowledge acquired in a research methods course. The course content was organized hierarchically, and Naveh-Benjamin found that most memory losses occurred for relations among concepts at the lowest level of the hierarchy. There were only slight changes in the retained structure after the first year, and Naveh-Benjamin concluded that this aspect of content may have stabilized early during the retention interval.

Although findings of differential retention of content cannot be ascribed to intrinsic characteristics of content because of the inability to equate the degree of acquisition, these findings may still be of practical value to educators who can adjust their emphasis during acquisition and rehearsals in accord with their priorities for long-term retention of content. From an applied point of view, it may not matter whether the findings regarding differential forgetting reflect inherent characteristics of content, or the degree of emphasis given during the course. The retention data can be useful in planning the emphasis during acquisition so as to yield long-term retention that reflects the educational priorities.

Concluding Comments

In contrast to research on learning, memory research has had little impact on education.

This is unfortunate, since the value of education depends largely upon the life span of what has been learned. The fault seems to be divided between memory scholars and educators. Memory scholars have focused their research on the short-term retention of episodic content, a domain that has only little relevance to the concerns of educators. Educators have emphasized the immediate achievements of students, paying little attention to the effects of their instruction on long-term retention of content.

Investigations of the maintenance of knowledge have now yielded information that is highly relevant to the goals of educators. Once it is established that instructional content may stabilize in memory for many years without the benefit of further rehearsals, it is incumbent on educators to promote conditions of instruction that yield such long-term retention, by appropriate revisions of instructional strategies, curricular modifications, and so on. Now that it is established that instructional techniques that favor rapid learning may yield poor retention, appropriate revisions of these techniques should be a priority. When it is known that spaced rehearsals can dramatically enhance the accessibility of marginal content for long periods of time, appropriate rehearsal schedules for critical aspects of instructional content should be built into the curriculum. One obvious example is to give cumulative rather than noncumulative final course examinations for maintaining information learned before the mid-term. This simple technique is frequently not observed.

The findings of knowledge-maintenance research also have significant implications for memory theory. Existing theories of the spacing effect are not suitable to explain the effect when very long intervals are involved, but the observed effects are in accord with an explanation based on opportunities to evaluate and revise encoding strategies during acquisition. Current memory theories cannot easily account for the finding that a single retrieval practice of old, marginal targets can stabilize access to such targets for several months. The method of asymmetry of fluctuations makes it possible to examine the very long-term consequences of retrieval practice of marginal, semantic memory content, and to develop appropriate theory. Memory research should now have a significant impact on education. The impact can be evaluated by assessing increases in the life span of knowledge that are achieved at an acceptable cost.

Acknowledgments Preparation of this manuscript was supported by National Science Foundation Grant SBR-9119800. The author wishes to thank Tom Nelson and Cameron Hewitt for many helpful suggestions.

References

Bahrick, H. P. (1977). Reliability of measurement in investigations of learning and memory. In I. Birnbaum & E. Parker (Eds.), *Alcohol and human memory.* Hillsdale, NJ: Erlbaum.

Bahrick, H. P. (1979). Maintenance of knowledge: Questions about memory we forgot to ask. *Journal of Experimental Psychology: General, 108,* 296–308.

Bahrick, H. P. (1983). The cognitive map of a city: 50 years of learning and memory. In G. Bower (Ed.), *The psychology of learning and motivation: Advances in research and theory* (Vol. 17; pp. 125–163). New York: Academic Press.

Bahrick, H. P. (1984a). Semantic memory content in permastore: 50 years of memory for Spanish learned in school. *Journal of Experimental Psychology: General, 113,* 1–29.

Bahrick, H. P. (1984b). Memory for people. In J. E. Harris & P. E. Morris (Eds.), *Everyday memory, actions and absent mindedness* (pp. 19–34). London: Academic Press.

Bahrick, H. P. (1989). The laboratory and the ecology: Supplementary sources of data for memory research. In L. Poon, D. Rubin, & B. Wilson (Eds.), *Everyday cognition in adulthood and late life* (pp. 73–83). Hillsdale, NJ: Erlbaum.

Bahrick, H. P., Bahrick, L. E., Bahrick, A. S., & Bahrick P. E. (1993). Maintenance of foreign language vocabulary and the spacing effect. *Psychological Science, 4,* 316–321.

Bahrick, H. P., Bahrick, P. O., & Wittlinger, R. P. (1975). Fifty years of memories for names and faces: A cross-sectional approach. *Journal of Experimental Psychology: General, 104,* 54–75.

Bahrick, H. P., & Hall, L. K. (1991a). Lifetime maintenance of high school mathematics content. *Journal of Experimental Psychology: General, 120,* 20–33.

Bahrick, H. P., & Hall, L. K. (1991b). Preventive and corrective maintenance of access to knowledge. *Applied Cognitive Psychology, 5,* 1–18.

Bahrick, H. P., Hall, L. K., Goggin, J. P., Bahrick, L. E., & Berger, S. A. (1994). Fifty years of language maintenance and language dominance in bilingual Hispanic immigrants. *Journal of Experimental Psychology: General, 123*, 264–283.

Bahrick, H. P., & Phelps, E. (1987). Retention of Spanish vocabulary over eight years. *Journal of Experimental Psychology: Learning, Memory, and Cognition, 13*, 344–349.

Banaji, M. R., & Crowder, R. G. (1989). The bankruptcy of everyday memory. *American Psychologist, 44*, 1185–1193.

Bjork, R. A. (1988). Retrieval practice and the maintenance of knowledge. In M. Gruneberg, P. Morris, & R. Sykes (Eds.), *Practical aspects of memory: Current research and issues* (Vol. 2; pp. 396–401). Chichester: John Wiley.

Bjork, R. A. (1994). Memory and metamemory considerations in the training of human beings. In J. Metcalfe & A. Shimamura (Eds.), *Metacognition: Knowing about knowing* (pp. 185–205). Cambridge, MA: MIT Press.

Bregman, A. S. (1967). Distribution of practice and between-trials interference. *Canadian Journal of Psychology, 21*, 1–14.

Bruce, D. (1991). Mechanistic and functional explanations of memory. *American Psychologist, 46(1)*, 46–48.

Bruce, D., & Bahrick, H. P. (1992). Perceptions of past research. *American Psychologist, 47*, 319–328.

Christina, R. W., & Bjork, R. A. (1991). Optimizing long-term retention and transfer. In Dr. Druckman & R. A. Bjork (Eds.), *In the mind's eye: Enhancing human performance* (pp. 23–56). Washington, DC: National Academy Press.

Cohen, G., Stanhope, N., & Conway, M. A. (1992). Age differences in very long-term retention of knowledge. *British Journal of Developmental Psychology, 10*, 153–164.

Conway, M. A., Cohen, G., & Stanhope, N. (1991). On the very long-term retention of knowledge acquired through formal education: Twelve years of cognitive psychology. *Journal of Experimental Psychology: General, 120*, 358–372.

Conway, M. A., Cohen, G., & Stanhope, N. (1992). Very long-term knowledge acquired at school and university. *Applied Cognitive Psychology, 6*, 467–482.

Cuddy, L. J., & Jacoby, L. L. (1982). When forgetting helps memory: An analysis of repetition effects. *Journal of Verbal Learning and Verbal Behavior, 21*, 451–467.

Dempster, F. N. (1990). The spacing effect: A case study in the failure to apply the results of psychological research. *American Psychologist, 43*, 627–634.

Ebbinghaus, H. (1885). *Über das Gedächtnis.* Leipzig: Duncker.

Fleishman, E. A., & Parker, J. F., Jr. (1962). Factors in the retention and relearning of perceptual motor skill. *Journal of Experimental Psychology, 64*, 215–226.

Ghodesian, D., Bjork, R. A., & Benjamin, A. S. (1997). Evaluating training *during* training: Obstacles and opportunities. In M. A. Quinones & A. Dutta (Eds.), *Training for a rapidly changing workplace: Applications of psychological research* (pp. 63–88). Washington, DC: American Psychological Association.

Glenberg, A. M. (1979). Component-levels theory of the effects of spacing of repetitions on recall and recognition. *Memory & Cognition, 7*, 95–112.

Glenberg, A. M. (1992). Distributed practice effects. In L. R. Squire (Ed.), *Encyclopedia of learning and memory* (pp. 138–142). New York: Macmillan.

Greeno, J. G. (1970). Conservation of information-processing capacity in paired-associate memorizing. *Journal of Verbal Learning and Verbal Behavior, 9*, 581–586.

Healy, A. F., Fendrich, D. W., Crutcher, R. J., Wittman, W. T., Gesi, A. T., Ericsson, K. A., & Bourne, L. E. (1992). The long-term retention of skills. In A. Healy, S. Kosslyn, & R. Shiffrin (Eds.), From *Learning process to cognitive processes: Essays in honor of William K. Estes* (Vol. 2; pp. 87–118).

Healy, A. F., Fendrich, D. W., & Proctor, J. D. (1990). Acquisition and retention of a letter-detection skill. *Journal of Experimental Psychology: Learning, Memory and Cognition, 16*, 270–281.

Healy, A., & Sinclair, G. (1996). The long-term retention of training and instruction. In E. L. Bjork & R. A. Bjork (Eds.), *Memory: Handbook of perception and cognition* (pp. 525–564). New York: Academic Press.

Herrmann, D. J., Buschke, H., & Gall, M. B. (1987). Improving retrieval. *Applied Cognitive Psychology, 1*, 27–33.

Izawa, C. (1970). Optimal potentiating effects and forgetting-prevention effects of tests in paired-associate learning. *Journal of Experimental Psychology, 83*, 340–344.

Jacoby, L. L., Bjork, R. A., & Kelley, C. M. (1994). Illusions of comprehension and competence. In D. Druckman & R. A. Bjork (Eds.), *Learning, remembering, believing: Enhancing individual and team performance* (pp. 57–80). Washington, DC: National Academy Press.

Kintsch, W. (1974). *The representation of meaning in memory.* New York: John Wiley.

Klatzky, R. L. (1991). Let's be friends. *American Psychologist, 46(1),* 43–45.

Landauer, T. K., & Bjork, R. A. (1978). Optimal rehearsal patterns and name learning. In M. M. Gruneberg, P. E. Morris, & R. N. Sykes (Eds.), *Practical aspects of memory* (pp. 625–632). London: Academic Press.

Madigan, S. A. (1969). Intraserial repetition and coding processes in free recall. *Journal of Verbal Learning and Verbal Behavior, 8,* 828–835.

McKenna, S. P., & Glendon, A. I. (1985). Occupational first aid training: Decay in cardiopulmonary resuscitation (CPR) skills. *Journal of Occupational Psychology, 58,* 109–117.

Melton, A. W. (1970). The situation with respect to the spacing of repetitions and memory. *Journal of Verbal Learning and Verbal Behavior, 9,* 596–606.

Naveh-Benjamin, M. (1988). Retention of cognitive structures learned in university courses. In M. M. Gruneberg, P. E. Morris, & R. N. Sykes (Eds.), *Practical aspects of memory: Current research and issues* (Vol. 2; pp. 283–288). New York: John Wiley.

Naveh-Benjamin, M., Lavi, H., McKeachie, W. J., & Lin, Y. (1997). Individual differences in students' retention of knowledge and conceptual structures learned in university and high school courses: The case of test anxiety. *Applied Cognitive Psychology, 11,* 507–526.

Neisser, U. (1978). Memory: What are the important questions? In M. M. Gruneberg, P. E. Morris, & H. N. Sykes (Eds.), *Practical aspects of memory* (pp. 3–24). London: Academic Press.

Neisser, U. (1991). A case of misplaced nostalgia. *American Psychologist, 46(1),* 34–36.

Noice, H. (1993). Effects of strategy on the verbatim retention of theatrical script. *Applied Cognitive Psychology, 7,* 75–84.

Noice, H., & Noice, T. (1997). Long-term retention of theatrical roles. Poster presented at the 38th annual meeting of the Psychonomic Society. Philadelphia, PA, Nov. 20–23.

Rea, C. P., & Modigliani, V. (1985). The effect of expanded versus massed practice on the retention of multiplication facts and spelling lists. *Human Learning, 4,* 11–18.

Rea, C. P., & Modigliani, V. (1988). Educational implications of the spacing effect. In M. M. Gruneberg, P. E. Morris, & R. N. Sykes (Eds.), *Practical aspects of memory: Current research and issues* (Vol. 1; pp. 403–406). New York: John Wiley.

Rubin, D. C. (1977). Very long-term memory for prose and verse. *Journal of Verbal Learning and Verbal Behavior, 16,* 611–621.

Schmidt, H. G., Peeck, V. H., Paas, F., & van Breukelen, G. J. (in press). Effects of exposure, elaborative encoding and retroactive interference on very long-term retention of street names of one's childhood neighborhood. *Memory.*

Schmidt, R. A. (1991). Frequent augmented feedback can degrade learning: Evidence and interpretations. In G. E. Stelmach & J. Requin (Eds.), *Tutorials in motor neuroscience* (pp. 59–75). Dordrecht: Kluwer Academic Publishers.

Semb, G. B., & Ellis, J. A. (1994). Knowledge taught in school: What is remembered? *Review of Educational Research, 64,* 253–286.

Spitzer, H. (1939). Studies in retention. *Journal of Educational Psychology, 30,* 641–656.

Tulving, E. (1991). Memory research is not a zero-sum game. *American Psychologist, 46(1),* 41–42.

Stanhope, N., Cohen, G., & Conway, M. A. (1993). Very long-term retention of a novel. *Applied Cognitive Psychology, 7,* 239–256.

Underwood, B. J. (1964). Degree of learning and the measurement of forgetting. *Journal of Verbal Learning and Verbal Behavior, 3,* 112–129.

23

Remembering Spaces

BARBARA TVERSKY

From the moment we enter the world, we are engaged in spatial cognition, in interacting with the world around us and in constructing mental representations of that world and our own place in it. Yet we do not conceive of the world as a geometer might, as space with three extrinsic orthogonal coordinates that specify the locations of points, objects, or regions. Rather, we adopt different frames of reference and incorporate different elements in constructing mental spaces for the real spaces important in our lives. Two milestones of the first year of life illustrate two of these functional spaces. Around the third month of life, babies begin to reach for and later manipulate objects in their environments. At the end of the first year, they begin to walk on their own. The space around the body and the space of navigation constitute natural breaks in our perception and our behavior, and in our consequent conceptions of space.

Historical Roots

Geography and Architecture

The study of spatial cognition has two separate origins that have merged, one outside psychology and applied, and the other inside psychology and theoretical. Outside psychology, spatial cognition began as the human side of architecture and geography. A seminal book was Lynch's *The Image of the City* (1960). There he observed that people's images of cities differ from reality depending on their personal experiences. He proposed that images of cities are constructed from point elements (that is, landmarks and nodes), from linear elements (that is, paths and edges), and from area elements (that is, regions). This view inspired geographers and later psychologists to investigate people's images of their environments, how they are acquired, and how they deviate from reality (see, for example, early edited books by Downs & Stea, 1973 and Moore & Golledge, 1976; review chapters by Chase (1986) and Evans (1980); more recently, a special issue of *Geoforum* in 1992 on cognitive maps, the COSIT (Conference on Spatial Information Theory) proceedings published by Springer-Verlag in 1993, 1995, 1997, and 1999, and books edited by Egenhofer & Golledge, 1998; Garling & Golledge, 1993; and Portugali, 1996.)

Psychology

Within psychology, the controversial notion of a cognitive map came to us from Tolman's paper, "Cognitive Maps in Rats and Men" (1948). Although accused by his adversaries of leaving the rat buried in thought, Tolman's point was that in solving mazes to find food, rats learned the lay of the land, not just to make left and right turns. That insight, however, did not directly stimulate research on human spatial cognition, though it left its impact on animal work (e.g., Gallistel, 1990; O'Keefe & Nadel, 1978) and thereby on current neurocognitive work. Investigations into the cognitive maps of humans was held back by two related preconceptions. One was a bias to think of memory and thought as based in language, and to regard knowledge about the visual and spatial world as reducible to language, be it labels or verbal codes or propositions. The other deterrent was a remnant of behaviorism, that mental representations of the visual and spatial were suspect; they were vague, subject to interpretation, not open to public inspection.

The view that memory for the visual/spatial world was reducible to words or propositions was first challenged by work of Paivio (1971) and others showing that words for vivid things were remembered better than other words, controlling for everything conceivable, and that pictures were remembered better than their names, and work by Shepard (1967) and others showing remarkable memory for pictures. If pictures are reduced to words in memory, how is it that pictures are remembered better than words? The view that mental representations of a visual/spatial nature are not open to scientific investigation was challenged by striking demonstrations of mental transformations, such as mental rotation and mental scanning, (e.g. Finke & Shepard, 1986; Shepard & Cooper, 1982) and mental imagery (e.g., revealed in systematic patterns of reaction times; Kosslyn, 1980).

More recently, other traditions within psychology have contributed to spatial memory. Not surprisingly, researchers in perception have been interested in people's memory for distance and direction in actual environments, with or without vision, with or without actual navigation, with imagined or actual experience (e.g., Berthoz, Israel, Georges-Francois, Grasso, & Tsuzuku, 1995; Creem & Proffitt, 1998; Loomis, Klatzky, Golledge, Cicinelli, Pellegrino, & Fry, 1993). More surprising is the interest of researchers of language use, who have studied descriptions of space because space is universal to human experience, has an objective reality for comparison to mental representation, and forms a basis for more abstract thought (e.g., in language, Lakoff & Johnson, 1980; in depiction, Tversky, 1995). These disparate traditions illustrate the broad range of inputs to spatial memory, from the lower level perceptual inputs that may be implicit to the higher level linguistic and depictive inputs that are cognitive and explicit.

From the beginning, research on memory for space and spaces has been driven more by what is special about space than by the traditional concerns of memory research, such as factors promoting encoding and retrieval of information. There is one factor that promotes memory and that makes space special—namely the way space is mentally structured, organized or schematized. Revealing the ways different spaces are schematized has been the aim of much of the research on memory for space, blurring the boundaries between spatial memory and spatial cognition.

Mental Spaces

The evidence to be surveyed supports the view that mental spaces are mental constructions, consisting of elements and the spatial relations among them. Elements may be objects, people, landmarks, regions, cities, and so forth. Elements are coded and remembered relative to each other and relative to reference frames. The spatial relations among them range from the more typical schematic or categorical to metric. To some extent, elements correspond to the "what" system and spatial relations to the "where" system distinguished in neuropsychology (e.g., Ungerleider & Mishkin, 1982).

The choices of elements, spatial relations, and reference frames depend on the space of interest, its function, and the task at hand. In the environmental psychology tradition, it has been common to distinguish between egocentric and allocentric reference frames—that is, those based on one's own perspective in contrast to those based on an external set of coordinates, such as the cardinal directions (e.g., Pick & Lockman, 1981). In the psycholinguistic tradition, a three-way distinction has been common: one based on a person, called deictic or relative or egocentric; one based on an object, usually called intrinsic, and one based on an environment, usually called extrinsic or environmental. Within this tradition, there has been debate concerning the distinction between person-based and object-based reference frames (see Levinson, 1996, for a reformulation or Taylor & Tversky, 1996, for an application and critical commentary). Spatial relation terms appropriate to person- or object-based frames include "next to," "near," "right," "in front of," and "between." Spatial relation terms appropriate to extrinsic or allocentric reference frames include "north" and "seaward."

The various perspectives provide a view or way of organizing spatial elements. More than one perspective may be used to encode even a single situation. Research on parietal patients suggests that both egocentric and allocentric reference frames are disturbed in hemineglect (Behrmann & Tipper, 1999; Bisiach, 1993), suggesting that locations are initially encoded in multiple reference frames. In language, multiple perspectives abound. Here's an example, from Taylor and Tversky (1996), "Following the loop around westwardly, you will arrive at the blizzard roller coaster, extending north as you enter the Blizzard area" (see also Carlson-Radvansky & Irwin, 1993; Schober, 1993). In addition, mental spaces may be incomplete or inconsistent, and more than one mental space may affect behavior. These properties of organization and memory of mental spaces are reflected in reaction times, errors, inferences, language, and other measures.

Places

The emphasis in this chapter is on space rather than place, on relations rather than elements. Nevertheless, a word on memory for places is appropriate. Places serve as landmarks, important in memory for space. And it appears that memory for places has special qualities not shared by memory for other, even other visual, stimuli. The first hint came from the prevalence of places among those pictures that were highly memorable (e.g., Shepard, 1967; Standing, 1973). Like other stimuli, organized scenes are remembered better than unorganized (Mandler, Seegmiller, & Day, 1977). That organization is primarily vertical, constrained by gravity. Like objects, scenes fall into natural categories. At the first level is indoors and outdoors, with house, school, and restaurant as subcategories of the former and beach, mountains, and city as subcategories of the latter (Tversky & Hemenway, 1983). Extraordinary memory for places was recognized millennia before scientific psychology became a discipline. The ancient Greeks capitalized on memory for places to facilitate memory for other information in the Method of Loci (Yates, 1966), the only European invention of interest to the late sixteenth-century Chinese court (Spence, 1985). Although remembering

locations of places may not be completely effortless or perfect, it is certainly relatively easy (cf. Hasher & Zacks, 1979; Huttenlocher, Hedges, & Duncan, 1991; Lansdale, 1998; Naveh-Benjamin, 1987). In memory for sentences, places, unlike other concepts such as people and objects, do not suffer from decreased retrieval time (fan effect) when serving as a cue for many other concepts (Radvansky, Spieler, & Zacks, 1993; Radvansky & Zacks, 1991). This is presumably because the sentences invoke mental models and mental models of places can support associations to multiple objects. The special status of places is reinforced by evidence implicating a region of the parahippocampal cortex dedicated to recognition of them (Brewer, Zhao, Desmond, Glover, & Gabrieli, 1998; Epstein & Kanwisher, 1998).

The Space of Navigation

The space of navigation is generally regarded as the space that is too large to be seen from a single vantage point. Thus, any mental representation of the space of navigation has to be put together from different views or experiences. Nevertheless, people form mental representations of these spaces, whether from navigation or from maps or from descriptions or from a combination, that allow them to arrive at their destinations and to give directions to others with some success. This is not to say that people's mental representations of the space of navigation are holistic or complete or accurate. In spite of successful navigation and direction giving, people's memories for the space of navigation differ systematically from the actual spaces. Moreover, people's memories are not simply two-dimensional simplifications, as the term "cognitive map" would imply, though they are that, too. They are in addition distorted in ways that reveal how they are constructed and organized. The evidence for these systematic distortions comes from a variety of tasks, some semantic, some episodic, some using reaction times, some using errors, some using memory, some using judgment (for reviews, see Chase, 1986; Tversky, 1992, 1993, 1997, 1998). Systematic errors and biases in reaction times have been especially informative. Errors and biases are easy to overlook as random noise unless researchers are prepared by theoretical intuitions to seek them out. Errors and biases can be interpreted as consequences of the way memory is organized, and thus as clues to memory organization. However, as with many memory tasks, it is difficult to determine whether performance in a particular situation is due to the nature of mental representation or to the nature of the retrieval or judgment task, or to both.

Relations among Elements

One way that elements—such as objects, landmarks, cities, or continents—are remembered is relative to other elements. Using other elements as references or anchors can induce distortions of direction or distance.

Alignment. In perceiving or conceiving a spatial scene, people group elements together based on proximity and similarity. They then remember grouped elements as more aligned with each other relative to a spatial reference frame than they actually are. Informants were asked to select which of two maps of the Americas was correct, the correct one or one in which South America was slid westwards to be closer to south of North America. A majority picked the incorrect map that was more aligned. Similarly, in choosing between two world maps, more informants selected the incorrect map in which east-west relations between the United States and Europe and South America and Africa were more aligned. These effects hold for directions between pairs of cities, for artificial maps, and for blobs (Tversky, 1981).

Cognitive reference points. Some elements, termed landmarks, are more salient in the geographical landscape and serve as cognitive reference points in organizing space (e.g., Couclelis, Golledge, Gale, & Tobler, 1987). For example, when people are asked where they live, they often answer relative to the nearest landmark likely to be known to the questioner (e.g., Shanon, 1983). One consequence of organizing elements relative to landmarks is a gross violation of metric assumptions in distance estimates. People judge the distance from an ordinary building to a landmark to be less than the distance from a landmark to an ordinary building (see McNamara & Diwadker, 1997; Sadalla, Burroughs, & Staplin, 1980). This asymmetry in distance judgments appears in abstract domains as well, where one category member is more representative of the category than others. For example, people judge magenta to be closer to red than red to magenta (Rosch, 1975) and North Korea as

closer to China than China to North Korea (Tversky & Gati, 1978).

Frames of Reference

In addition to being remembered relative to other elements, elements are also remembered relative to an overall frame of reference, which may distort judgements of distance and direction as well.

Hierarchical organization. Unlike actual space, but like memory for words, sentences, and discourse, memory for space is organized hierarchically. Stevens and Coupe (1978) showed this in a study whose most memorable example has become an item in the game, Trivial Pursuit. They asked students to indicate the directions between pairs of cities in the United States, most notably between San Diego and Reno. Most of their respondents correctly noted that Reno was north of San Diego, but incorrectly indicated that Reno was east of San Diego. Stevens and Coupe attributed this error to hierarchical coding of cities within states. Instead of learning the directions of every pair of cities, people learn which cities are in which states, and use the general directions of the states to infer the directions of the cities contained in them. Because Nevada is generally east of California, informants incorrectly infer that cities in Nevada are east of those in California.

Hierarchical organization is revealed not just in judgments of direction but also in judgments of relative distance. Distance judgments between elements contained within a geographic unit, even a subjectively defined one, are underestimated relative to distances between elements in separate geographic units. Hirtle and Jonides (1985) found effects of grouping for distances within or between university or town buildings in Ann Arbor, Michigan (see also Allen & Kirasic, 1985). Evidence for hierarchical organization also comes from reaction times to make direction judgments, where times to verify directions between pairs of elements in different geographic entities are faster than times for elements in the same entity (Maki, 1981; Wilton, 1979; see also Chase, 1983; McNamara, 1986, 1992). Location errors in memory of dots also implicate mental division of space into categories and adoption of the central tendency of the categories as referents (Huttenlocher et al., 1991; see also Lansdale, 1998).

Canonical axes. The location and direction of cities, buildings, and other elements are remembered relative to the canonical axes as well as relative to the larger geographic unit containing them. People remember the orientation of South America as more "upright" than it actually is, rotating its dominant axis toward the north-south axis (Tversky, 1981). This same bias is revealed in memory for orientation of cities within countries, of streets within cities, and of blobs within frames (Tversky, 1981) and has been replicated in other contexts (Glicksohn, 1994; Lloyd & Heivly, 1987).

Perspective. The external perspective taken on a mental space also biases judgments about the space. People tend to judge distances between proximal elements to be shorter relative to distances between distal elements, just as in the famous cartoons of the New Yorker's or Bostonian's view of the world. What's more, the perspective taken is flexible. Holyoak and Mah (1982) found that students in Ann Arbor who were asked to imagine themselves on the East Coast judged the distance between New York and Pittsburgh to be greater and the distance between Salt Lake City and San Francisco to be smaller than another group of students asked to imagine themselves on the West Coast.

Other Systematic Distortions

There are other ways that mental representations of space differ systematically from actual geographic spaces. Curved lines are straightened, as in residents' sketch maps of the Seine in Paris (Milgram & Jodelet, 1976) or in taxi cab drivers' representations of the city they navigate (Chase, 1983). Angles of intersections of roads are schematized to 90 degrees (Moar & Bower, 1983; Tversky, 1981). Short distances are overestimated and long ones are underestimated, a finding typical of many quantitative estimates (e.g., Lloyd, 1989; Poulton, 1989). Estimates of areas of regions shrink in memory (Kemp, 1988; Kerst & Howard, 1978). Regions are remembered as more symmetric than they actually were (Howard & Kerst, 1981; Tversky & Schiano, 1989).

Unreliability of Metric Information

The systematic distortions reviewed above, as well as others, indicate that the "metric" of mental representations of space is not Euclidean. Further support comes from estimates of distance, which are biased by a large number of factors (for a review of some, see Montello, 1997). The presence of barriers has been known to yield overestimates of distance (e.g., Kosslyn, Pick, & Fariello, 1974; Newcombe & Liben, 1982) as does the presence of clutter (Thorndyke, 1981). Similarly, overestimates of distance can result from increasing number of turns (Sadalla & Magel, 1980), number of nodes (Sadalla & Staplin, 1980b), or amount of information remembered from the environment (Sadalla & Staplin, 1980a). Even affect seems to affect distance estimates, with positive affect shortening them (Briggs, 1973; Golledge & Zannaras, 1973).

Mode of Acquisition

Knowledge of space can be acquired in a variety of ways: through direct exploration, through maps, through description, or through a combination of these. To some extent, these modes of acquisition are interchangeable—after all, spatial information from different modalities intersects in the parietal lobe—but each makes its own unique contribution. In addition, each mode has its own internal complexity and variability. For example, direct exploration typically includes visual, auditory, haptic, olfactory, proprioceptive, vestibular, and other sensory information. Maps vary extensively on what kind of detail is included and how that detail is depicted. Verbal descriptions vary in perspective, in coherence, and in detail. What is learned depends to some degree on how it is learned. Furthermore, different brain structures are activated in retrieving traversed routes than in scanning imagined maps. Recollecting routes activates parahippocampal or hippocampal structures in human brain (Aguirre & D'Esposito, 1997; Aguirre, Detre, Alsop, & D'Esposito, 1996; Ghaem et al., 1997; Maguire, Frackowiak, & Frith, 1997). These regions are closely related to regions involved in recognizing places, but separable from them. In contrast, mental scanning activates frontal-parietal regions (Ghaem et al., in press).

Exploration vs. Maps

Thorndyke and Hayes-Roth (1982) tested knowledge of direction and distance in people who had varying degrees of exposure to a two-building complex, either through maps or through direct exploration. On the whole, exploration facilitated in situ estimates of directions from one point to another and map learning facilitated estimates of distances between points. Thus, one medium was not better overall than the other, but each was better for certain kinds of information. Egocentric directions from one point to another were more accurate from exploration but distances from one point to another were more accurate from overview maps. With increased direct exploration, navigators improved first on route distance estimates and then on straight-line or survey distance estimates, suggesting that increased route exploration induced survey information. Taylor, Naylor, and Chechile (1999) replicated some of these findings, and also found effects of learners' goals. When navigators were instructed to learn the layout, they behaved more like map learners and when map learners were told to discover the fastest routes, they behaved more like navigators.

The initial benefit of exploration to direction judgments suggests that at least some of the sensory accompaniments of navigation are important to keeping track of orientation. Which aspects of sensory experience are important has been studied in acquisition of room-sized environments under varying sensory conditions. In one common paradigm, participants first studied a simple environment (Rieser, 1989). Then, while blindfolded, they either moved in the environment or else imagined moving in the environment. The movement was either by translation or by rotation. Thus, neither the actual movement group nor the imagined movement group had visual information, but the movement group had somatosensory and vestibular information from navigation, while the imagine group did not. The participants' task was to point at other objects in the room. Imagined translations were on the whole as fast and accurate as real ones, but imagined rotations were less accurate and increased with the difference between actual and imagined orientation (Easton & Sholl, 1995; Presson & Montello, 1994; Rieser, 1989). Somatosensory information, then, may be more important for keeping track of orientation than for keeping track of location. Studies in which young or old participants were asked to complete two revolutions while blindfolded implicate the importance of vestibular as well as somatosensory information in keeping track of turning motion (Takei, Grasso, & Berthoz, 1996). That cognitive information also plays a role in keeping track of motion is indicated by increased errors of distance when participants had to count backwards outloud (Takei,

Grasso, Amorim, & Berthoz, 1997). Somatosensory and vestibular information is also important in remembering the velocity and distance of passive, blindfolded motion (Berthoz et al., 1995).

The fact that participants in these studies performed quite well although blindfolded is consistent with findings that visual information is not always critical for successful acquisition and memory for environments. Studies comparing blindfolded sighted participants and blind participants have revealed comparable performance by both groups, though in complex spatial wayfinding tasks, that performance left much to be desired (Klatzky, Golledge, Loomis, Cicinelli, & Pellegrino, 1995; Loomis et al., 1993).

Mental representations of environments appear to be orientation dependent whether the environments are acquired by maps or by exploration. When acquired by maps, mental representations typically have a north-up viewpoint for canonical maps or a forward-up viewpoint for you-are-here maps, indicated by reaction times that increase with degree of misalignment (Evans & Pezdek, 1980; Levine, Jankovic, & Palij, 1982; Sholl, 1987). Although it was earlier believed that learning by exploration led to viewpoint-independent representations, more recent research suggests that representations of space acquired by exploration from many viewpoints have many viewpoints rather than being perspective free (Diwadkar & McNamara, 1997; Rieser, 1989; Roskos-Ewoldsen, McNamara, Shelton, & Carr, 1998; Shelton & McNamara, 1997).

Language

For people, language can serve as an efficient and practical way to teach and acquire spatial knowledge. Language is a portable, lightweight, easy-to-maintain, low-tech information transmission device. Well-crafted descriptions can allow people to construct accurate maps of spaces (Mani & Johnson-Laird, 1982; Taylor & Tversky, 1992a). Well-crafted descriptions can also convey travelers to their correct destinations even in such complex environments as Venice (Denis, Pazzaglia, Cornoldi, & Bertolo, 1999). Although language does not seem to be used with either reliability or validity for conveying exact metric information (e.g., Leibowitz, Guzy, Peterson, & Blake, 1993), language does seem to be adequate for conveying approximate spatial relations, like front, back, left, right, north, and south (e.g., de Vega, 1994; Franklin & Tversky, 1990; Mani & Johnson-Laird, 1982; Taylor & Tversky, 1992b; Tversky, 1991). Language has also proved adequate in communicating relative categorical distances (Morrow, Bower, & Greenspan, 1989; Glenberg, Meyer, & Lindem, 1987; Rinck, Hahnel, Bower, & Glowalla, 1997). Despite the adequacy of language for conveying approximate spatial relations, users often prefer sketch maps, though their informants frequently fail to provide them (Wright, Lickorish, Hull, & Ummelen, 1995).

Language can free viewers from their own perspectives on scenes. In describing scenes, speakers use gaze (deictic or relative), route (intrinsic), or survey (extrinsic) perspectives, or a mixture, depending in part on the nature of the scene (Taylor & Tversky, 1996). In a gaze description, akin to viewing a scene from an entrance, there is a single viewpoint and objects are described relative to other objects from that viewpoint in terms of right, left, front, and back (Ehrich & Koster, 1983). In a route description, akin to exploration, the viewpoint is the changing one of a traveler and objects are described relative to the traveler in terms of front, back, left, and right. In a survey description, akin to studying a map, the viewpoint is a stationary one from above and objects are described relative to each other in terms of north, south, east, and west (Taylor & Tversky, 1992a, 1992b). Frequently, speakers switch or mix perspectives, even without signaling. This causes few if any difficulties in comprehension (Taylor & Tversky, 1992a). Moreover, for relatively simple spaces that are completely communicated, either route or survey descriptions of a space yield functionally the same, perspective-free memory representations (Taylor & Tversky, 1992b). That is, people respond as fast and accurately to nonverbatim statements from the original perspective as from the new perspective. This finding complements the finding that maps and exploration are alternative ways to provide spatial information, even if each mode is superior for different judgments.

Levels of Acquisition

Early theories of development of spatial memory were stage theories, where the stages were Piagetian or the components of spatial knowledge or reference frames distinguished by Lynch and others (for reviews, see Hart & Moore, 1973; Montello, 1998). Piaget and his collaborators (Piaget & Inhelder, 1956; Piaget,

Inhelder, & Szeminska, 1960) proposed three stages in children's development of frames of reference, from egocentric, to fixed relative to external objects such as landmarks (akin to intrinsic), to coordinate such as the cardinal directions (extrinsic). The Piagetian group also proposed three stages in the development of spatial relations, from topological to projective to metric. In an influential paper, Siegel and White (1975) argued that children first acquire information about landmarks, then about routes, and finally about configurations—that is, survey knowledge. Pick and Lockman (1981) maintained that children progress from egocentric to allocentric representations by means of object manipulation. The latter have also been put forward as theories of acquisition as well as theories of development.

The views that either acquisition or development of spatial knowledge follows any of these progressions are controversial and have been challenged by those who observe that the proposed sequences, whether of reference frames or of spatial relations, are not necessarily acquired sequentially (e.g., Mandler, 1988; Montello, 1998). Doubt has even been cast on the intuitively compelling notion that because people typically experience space from a particular place and orientation, space must be organized egocentrically prior to allocentrically. When rats explore an environment, receptors in the hippocampus are tuned to recognize locations independent of point of view (O'Keefe & Nadel, 1978). Consistent with this, some languages use only allocentric reference frames for talking about space (Levinson, 1996), with apparent cognitive consequences. Speakers of those languages are better oriented when traveling than speakers of languages that frequently use egocentric reference frames (Levinson, 1997). Yet, there is evidence that babies, like rats (Gallistel, 1990; McNaughton, Chen, & Markus, 1991) use self as a referent for locations earlier than place as a referent (Newcombe, Huttenlocher, Drummey, & Wiley, 1998), and that children use spatial configuration earlier than landmarks (Hermer & Spelke, 1996).

Some work has demonstrated global similarities in spatial memory between children and adults, experts and novices, despite local differences. Huttenlocher, Newcombe, and Sandberg (1994), for example, found that children, like adults, use boundaries and subdivisions to remember locations. Younger children are less likely than older to subdivide spaces, and they subdivide smaller spaces earlier than larger spaces. The persistence of systematic errors and distortions calls into question the degree to which survey knowledge is coherent or accurate or metric, even in adults with extensive experience. In a large study of experienced taxi drivers, Chase (1983) found many of the same errors and distortions as those described earlier. Rather than demonstrating accurate survey knowledge, the experienced taxi drivers showed a reliance on landmarks and routes. Other evidence for long-term reliance on landmarks and routes comes from a large study of acquisition and long-term memory for a college town by students and alumni (Bahrick, 1983). Curves for both acquisition and forgetting were shallow for landmarks but steep for streets.

Models of Acquisition

In an early and influential model, Kuipers (1978; Kuipers & Levitt, 1988) attempted to account for spatial learning and navigation and to reflect what is known about human spatial knowledge, recognizing that spatial knowledge has both diverse inputs and diverse outputs. The Tour model consists of a spatial semantic hierarchy with four levels of information: sensorimotor interactions with the environment, procedural behaviors, a topological map consisting of a network of places and paths, and a metric map for actual navigation. These levels are useful for different aspects of navigation and need to be coordinated. The model captures much of the complexity of spatial memory and of navigation. Leiser and Zilbershatz (1989) describe their model, Traveller, which acquires survey knowledge through experience traversing routes. Gopal, Klatzky, and Smith (1989) developed a model that uses information-processing principles to acquire spaces from sensory information and that produces some of the well-known biases. Like the previous models, the model of Chown, Kaplan, and Kortenkamp (1995) is motivated both by robotics and by what is known about human perception and cognition. Their PLAN model uses information about prototypes and locations in an associative network to identify landmarks, select paths and directions, and abstract overviews. Epstein (in press) develops an architecture for solving way-finding problems that first tries on rapid learned reactions. If that fails, the system searches among situation-based behaviors. If that, too, fails, then the system relies on collaboration among a set of heuristics.

Cognitive Maps or Cognitive Collages?

Spatial information is inherently piecemeal, from different perspectives and different modalities and different times. There does not seem to be a central mechanism that integrates and reconciles these different sources and forms of information to a single, coherent whole. Spatial judgment, memory, and performance reflect that complexity. The many inconsistencies, biases, errors, and distortions have suggested that cognitive maps, unlike maps on paper, may be impossible figures (Tversky, 1981). Because of the partial, incomplete, inconsistent, and multimodal nature of spatial memory, cognitive collage may be a more apt metaphor than cognitive map (Tversky, 1993).

Other Spaces

Space around the Body

For the most part, the space of navigation is conceptualized in two dimensions, the plane on which navigation takes place. In contrast, the space around the body appears to be conceptualized in three dimensions. People seem to be able to keep track of the objects surrounding them as they move about in the world, even when the objects are not visible. Franklin and Tversky (1990) brought that situation into the laboratory, using descriptions to teach environments where observers appear in settings such as a museum, hotel lobby, or barn, surrounded by objects to front, back, left, right, head, and feet. After learning the description, participants were reoriented, again by description, to face another object in the scene and probed for the objects currently at the front, back, left, and so on, of the observer.

The pattern of reaction times to retrieve objects revealed how the space around the body is organized in memory. According to the Spatial Framework Theory, inspired by analyses of Clark (1973), Fillmore (1975), Miller and Johnson-Laird (1976), and others, people construct a mental spatial framework from extensions of the body axes and attach objects to the framework. Properties of the body and of the perceptual world determine the relative accessibility of objects. The head/feet axis of the body is asymmetric, and, for the upright observer, correlated with the only asymmetric axis of the world, the axis created by gravity, so it is the most accessible axis. The front/back axis is asymmetric, hence next in accessibility as the left/right axis is for the most part symmetric. In fact, retrieval times correspond to that pattern. When the observer reclines and rolls from side to front to back, no axis of the body is correlated with gravity, so properties of the body axes alone determine retrieval times. The front/back axis of the body separates the world that can be seen and manipulated from the world that cannot be seen or easily manipulated, For the reclining case, retrieval times are fastest to front/back, then to head/feet, and finally to left/right. This pattern and systematic variants of it has been replicated dozens of times (Bryant & Tversky, 1999; Bryant, Tversky, & Franklin, 1992; Franklin, Tversky, & Coon, 1992). Variants of the spatial framework pattern also emerged when the environment is acquired by model or diagram (Bryant & Tversky, 1999) or from actual viewing (Bryant, Tversky, & Lanca, in press). Franklin, Henkel, and Zangas (1995) examined description and memory for locations in the horizontal plane around the body. "Front" prescribed the largest region, followed by back, then left and right. Locations to the front were remembered most accurately, with errors toward left and right.

Diagrammatic Space

A space that is common in cultures that use writing or maps or pictures or diagrams is the space of a piece of paper. Here, the reference frame adopted depends on conceptual as well as perceptual factors. For spatial information devoid of semantic content, such as blobs and dots, the picture frame and sometimes its division into quadrants, whether present or implied, serves as a reference frame (Huttenlocher et al., 1991; Nelson & Chaiklin, 1980; Taylor, 1961; Tversky, 1981; Tversky & Schiano, 1989). For spatial information with semantic content, the reference frame selected depends on the content. For maps, the canonical axes, which typically correspond to the sides of the page, normally serve as a reference frame, but for line graphs, the implicit 45 degree line serves as a reference (Schiano & Tversky, 1992; Tversky & Schiano, 1989). For maps, lines representing roads are remembered as closer to the canonical axes (Tversky,

1981), but for graphs, lines representing functions are remembered as closer to the implicit 45 degree line (Schiano & Tversky, 1992; Tversky & Schiano, 1989).

Still More Spaces

There are many other spaces that are mentally organized, subdivided, and remembered. The space of the body is one beginning to receive attention. Because the body is experienced from the inside—kinesthetically—as well as from the outside, kinesthetic as well as visual information is important. Significant parts as indexed by relative space in sensorimotor cortex are verified faster (Morrison & Tversky, 1997) and changes in position in the upper body are more likely to be detected than changes in the lower body (Reed & Farah, 1995). Another space critical to the present and future of memory is the brain. The research community studying the brain uses several organizations simultaneously or alternatively. One is a system of absolute locations, like addresses, as in Brodmann's areas or Talairach and Tournoux coordinates (Talairach & Tournoux, 1988). Other systems use a variety of reference frames to describe locations in the brain, anterior/posterior, lateral/medial, ventral/dorsal, left/right, and more. This is probably not as chaotic as it seems. In describing environments such as recreation areas or convention centers, people often mix perspectives without signaling and others understand them (Taylor & Tversky, 1996). As for the space of navigation, the space around the body, and diagrammatic space, whatever organization that underlies memory for the body, the brain, or other spaces is likely to be revealed in biases in accuracy or retrieval time.

Finale

Spatial Mental Representations Are Not Simply Like Images

According to the classical accounts of imagery, images are like internalized perceptions (e.g., Kosslyn, 1980; Shepard & Podgorny, 1978). Images capture more or less veridically perceptual features of objects, and transformations of images reflect perception of continuous transformations of objects. The subjective impression of examining a mental image is also part of some accounts of mental imagery (Kosslyn, 1980). These properties of images do not necessarily characterize the cognitive processes accompanying spatial memory. Instead, the memory structures underlying spatial memory are biased in ways that conform to the ways space is conceived as well as the ways space is perceived. The phenomena of imagery have for the most part been demonstrated on memory for objects, whereas the phenomena of spatial memory have been demonstrated on memory for relations among objects. Conceptions of space depend on the qualities and functions of the particular space. Conceptions of space are often schematic, simplified, and categorical.

Space and Language

Spatial knowledge bears resemblances to linguistic knowledge. Neither is unitary, but rather each consists of different kinds of knowledge. For language, there is phonetics, semantics, syntax, and pragmatics, as well as the fluency and eloquence of an orator or a poet. Some of that knowledge is implicit, some explicit. Various elements of language are associated with various locations in the brain. Different principles of memory underlie the different components and processes, as surveyed in many of the chapters of this volume. The same holds true for spatial knowledge. It consists of different kinds and levels of knowledge, some explicit, some implicit, associated with different areas of the brain. Diverse spatial information is coordinated to recognize landmarks and places, to find one's way in the world, to communicate about space in words and gesture, to design buildings, to paint in words and on canvas.

But space is also special. Knowing how to find one's way to food, family, and shelter is essential to survival, not just for humans but also for our preverbal ancestors. To succeed, people must be able to recognize places, as well as landmarks and people, from different vantage points and under different conditions. They must be able to combine information from different sources and events. They must be able to use that knowledge to make estimates of distance and direction. Spatial knowledge is not reducible to language, as was earlier presumed. Evolutionarily, knowledge of space precedes knowledge of language.

By now, we have come full circle. Spatial knowledge is viewed by many as a basis for linguistic knowledge, rather than vice versa. It is apparent in the very structure or syntax of language in focus, point of view, density, boundedness, and other spatial concepts coded in grammar (e.g., Langacker, 1987; Talmy, 1983, 1988). Spatial knowledge is also apparent in semantics (e.g., Bloom, Peterson, Nadel, & Garrett, 1996; Clark & Clark, 1977; Jackendoff, 1983; Lakoff & Johnson, 1980; Talmy, 1983), pragmatics (e.g., Fauconnier, 1994), and the situation models people construct from language (e.g., Johnson-Laird, 1983; van Dijk & Kintsch, 1983). Take, for example, the simple, straight-forward spatial continuum expressed in up/down, high/low. See how these terms are extended: she's up today, he's at the top of the heap, he was at his lowest. In gesture, we give thumbs up for approval and high five for congratulations. In graphing, more and better are up, less and worse are down, even in unschooled children (Tversky, Kugelmass, & Winter, 1991). As many have observed (Clark, 1973; Cooper & Ross, 1975; Lakoff & Johnson, 1980), stronger, healthier, happier, and more things are higher, and weaker, sicker, sadder, and fewer things are lower. We don't just talk about these concepts spatially, we think about all them, and more, spatially (e.g., Banks & Flora, 1977; Boroditsky, 1997; De Soto, London, & Handel, 1965).

Acknowledgments I am indebted to Nancy Franklin, Christian Freksa, Renato Grasso, Dan Montello, Holly Taylor, and Jeff Zacks for helpful advice and comments on an earlier draft of the paper.

Correspondence concerning this article should be addressed to Barbara Tversky, Department of Psychology, Stanford University, Stanford, CA, 94305-2130.

References

Aguirre, G. K., & D'Esposito, M. (1997). Environmental knowledge is subserved by separable dorsal/ventral neural areas. *Journal of Neuroscience, 17*, 2513–2518.

Aguirre, G. K., Detre, J. A., Alsop, D. C., & D'Esposito, M. (1996). The parahippocampus subserves topographical learning in man. *Cerebral Cortex, 6*, 823–829.

Allen, G. L., & Kirasic, K. C. (1985). Effects of the cognitive organization of route knowledge on judgements of macrospatial distance. *Memory and Cognition, 13*, 218–227.

Bahrick, H. P. (1983). The cognitive map of a city: Fifty years of learning and memory. In G. H. Bower (Ed.), *The psychology of learning and motivation: Advances in research and theory* (Vol. 17; pp. 125–163). New York: Academic Press.

Banks, W. P., & Flora, J. (1977). Semantic and perceptual processes in symbolic comparisons. *Journal of Experimental Psychology: Human Perception and Performance, 3*, 278–290.

Behrmann, M., & Tipper, S. P. (1999). Attention accesses multiple reference frames: Evidence from neglect. *Journal of Experimental Psychology: Human Perception and Performance*, Feb., Vol. *25*(1), 83–101.

Berthoz, A., Israel, I., Georges-Francois, P., Grasso, R., & Tsuzuki, T. (1995). Spatial memory of body linear displacement: What is being stored? *Science, 269*, 95–98.

Bisiach, E. (1993). Mental representation in unilateral neglect and related disorders: The twentieth Barlett memorial lecture. *Quarterly Journal of Experimental Psychology, 46A*, 435–461.

Bloom, P., Peterson, M. A., Nadel, L., & Garrett, M. (Eds.). (1996). *Language and space*. Cambridge, MA: MIT Press.

Borditsky, L. (1997). Evidence for metaphoric representation: Perspective in space and time. In M. G. Shafto & P. Langley (Eds.), *Proceedings of the Nineteenth Annual Conference of the Cognitive Science Society* (pp. 869). Mahwah, NJ: Erlbaum.

Brewer, J. B., Zhao, Z., Desmond, J. E., Glover, G. H., & Gabrieli, J. D. E. (1998). Making memories: Brain activity that predicts how well visual experience will be remembered. *Science, 281*, 1185–1187.

Briggs, R. (1973). Urban cognitive distance. In R. M. Downs & D. Stea (Eds.), *Image and environment* (pp. 361–388). Chicago: Aldine.

Bryant, D. J., & Tversky, B. (1992). Assessing spatial frameworks with object and direction probes. *Bulletin of the Psychonomic Society, 30*, 29–32.

Bryant, D. J., & Tversky, B. (1999). Mental representations of spatial relations from diagrams and models. *Journal of Experimental Psychology: Learning, Memory and Cognition, 25*, 137–156.

Bryant, D. J., Tversky, B., & Franklin, N. (1992). Internal and external spatial frameworks for representing described scenes. *Journal of Memory and Language, 31*, 74–98.

Bryant, D. J., Tversky, B., & Lanca, M. (in press). Retrieving spatial relations from observation and memory. In E. van der Zee & U. Nikanne (Eds.), *Conceptual structure and its interfaces with other modules of representation*.

Carlson-Radvansky, L., & Irwin, D. E. (1993). Frames of reference in vision and language: Where is above? *Cognition, 46*, 223–244.

Chase, W. G. (1983). Spatial representations of taxi drivers. In R. Rogers & J. A. Sloboda (Eds.), *Acquisition of symbolic skills* (pp. 111–136). New York: Plenum.

Chase, W. G. (1986). Visual information processing. In K. R. Boff, L. Kaufman, & J. P. Thomas (Eds.), *Handbook of perception and human performance. Vol. III. Cognitive processes and performance* (pp. 1–73). New York: John Wiley.

Chown, E., Kaplan, S., & Kortenkamp, D. (1995). Prototypes, location, and associative networks (PLAN): Towards a unified theory of cognitive mapping. *Cognitive Science, 19*, 1–51.

Clark, H. H. (1973). Space, time, semantics, and the child. In T. E. Moore (Ed.), *Cognitive development and the acquisition of language* (pp. 27–63). New York: Academic Press.

Clark, H. H., & Clark, E. V. (1977). *Psychology and language*. New York: Harcourt Brace Jovanovich.

Cooper, W. E., & Ross, J. R. (1975). World order. In R. E. Grossman, L. J. San, & T. J. Vances (Eds.), *Papers from the parasession on functionalism* (pp. 63–111). Chicago: Chicago Linguistic Society.

Couclelis, H., Golledge, R. G., Gale, N., & Tobler, W. (1987). Exploring the anchor-point hypothesis of spatial cognition. *Journal of Environmental Psychology, 7*, 99–122.

Creem, S. H., & Proffitt, D. R. (1998). Two memories for geographical slant: Separation and interdependence of action and awareness. *Psychonomic Bulletin and Review, 5*, 22–36.

Denis, M., Pazzaglia, F., Cornoldi, C., & Bertolo, L. (1999). Spatial discourse and navigation: An analysis of route directions in the city of Venice. *Applied Cognitive Psychology, 13*, 145–174.

De Soto, C., London, M., & Handel, S. (1965). Social reasoning and spatial paralogic. *Journal of Personality and Social Psychology, 2*, 513–521.

de Vega, M. (1994). Characters and their perspectives in narratives describing spatial environments. *Psychological Research, 56*, 116–126.

Diwadkar, V. A., & McNamara, T. P. (1997). Viewpoint dependence in scene recognition. *Psychological Science, 8*, 302–307.

Downs, R. M., & Stea, D. (Eds.). (1973). *Image and environment*. Chicago: Aldine.

Downs, R. M., & Stea, D., (1977). *Maps in minds: Reflections on cognitive mapping*. New York: Harper and Row.

Easton, R. D., & Sholl, M. J. (1995). Object-array structure, frames of reference, and retrieval of spatial knowledge. *Journal of Experimental Psychology: Learning, Memory and Cognition, 21*, 483–500.

Egenhofer, M. J., & Golledge, R. G. (Eds.). (1998). *Spatial and temporal reasoning in geographic information*. New York: Oxford University Press.

Ehrich, V., & Koster, C. (1983). Discourse organization and sentence form: The structure of room descriptions in Dutch. *Discourse Processes, 6*, 169–195.

Epstein, R., & Kanwisher, N. (1998). A cortical representation of the local visual environment. *Nature, 392*, 599–601.

Epstein, S. L. (in press). Pragmatic navigation: Reactivity, heuristics, and search. *Artificial Intelligence Journal*.

Evans, G. E., & Pezdek, K. (1980). Cognitive mapping: Knowledge of real-world distance and location information. *Journal of Experimental Psychology: Human Learning and Memory, 6*, 13–24.

Evans, G. W. (1980). Environmental cognition. *Psychological Bulletin, 88*, 259–287.

Fauconnier, G. (1994). *Mental spaces: Aspects of meaning construction in natural languages*. Cambridge: Cambridge University Press.

Fillmore, C. (1975). Toward a descriptive framework for spatial deixis. In R. J. Jarvella & W. Klein (Eds.), *Speech, place, and action* (pp. 31–59). London: John Wiley.

Finke, R. A., & Shepard, R. N. (1986). Visual functions of mental imagery. In K. R. Boff, L. Kaufman, & J. P. Thomas (Eds.), *Handbook of perception and human performance* (Vol. 2; pp. 1–55). New York: Wiley-Interscience.

Franklin, N., Henkel, L. A., & Zangas, T. (1995). Parsing surrounding space into regions. *Memory and Cognition, 23*, 397–407.

Franklin, N., & Tversky, B. (1990). Searching imagined environments. *Journal of Experimental Psychology: General, 119*, 63–76.

Franklin, N., Tversky, B., & Coon, V. (1992). Switching points of view in spatial mental models acquired from text. *Memory and Cognition, 20*, 507–518.

Gallistel, C. R. (1990). *The organization of learning*. Cambridge, MA: MIT Press.

Garling, T., & Golledge, R. G. (Eds.). (1993). *Behavior and environment: Psychological and geographical approaches*. Amsterdam: North-Holland.

Ghaem, O., Mellet, E., Crivello, F., Tzourio, N., Mazoyer, B., Berthoz, A., & Denis, M. (1997). Mental navigation along memorized routes activates the hippocampus, precuneus, and insula. *NeuroReport, 8*, 739–744.

Ghaem, O., Mellet, E., Tzourio, N., Bricogne, S., Etard, O., Tirel, O. Beaudouin, V., Mazoyer, B., Berthoz, A., & Denis, M. (in press). Mental exploration of an environment learned from a map: A PET study. *Human Brain Mapping*.

Glenberg, A. M., Meyer, M., & Lindem, K. (1987). Mental models contribute to foregrounding during text comprehension. *Journal of Memory and Language, 26*, 69–83.

Glicksohn, J. (1994). Rotation, orientation, and cognitive mapping. *American Journal of Psychology, 107*, 39–51.

Golledge, R. G., & Zannaras, G. (1973). Cognitive approaches to the analysis of human spatial behavior. In W. H. Ittelson (Ed.), *Environment and cognition* (pp. 59–94). New York: Seminar.

Gopal, S., Klatzky, R. L., & Smith, T. R. (1989). NAVIGATOR: A psychologically based model of environmental learning through navigation. *Journal of Environmental Psychology, 9*, 309–331.

Hart, R. A., & Moore, G. T. (1973). The development of spatial cognition: A review. In R. Downs & D. Stea (Eds.), *Image and environment* (pp. 246–288). Chicago: Aldine.

Hasher, L., & Zacks, R. T. (1979). Automatic and effortful processes in memory. *Journal of Experimental Psychology: General, 108*, 356–388.

Hermer, L., & Spelke, E. (1996). Modularity and development: the case of spatial reorientation. *Cognition, 61*, 195–232.

Hintzman, D. L., O'Dell, C. S., & Arndt, D. R. (1981). Orientation in cognitive maps. *Cognitive Psychology, 13*, 149–206.

Hirtle, S., & Jonides, J. (1985). Evidence of hierarchies in cognitive maps. *Memory and Cognition, 13*, 208–217.

Holyoak, K. J., & Mah, W. A. (1982). Cognitive reference points in judgements of symbolic magnitude. *Cognitive Psychology, 14*, 328–352.

Howard, J. H., & Kerst, S. M. (1981). Memory and perception of cartographic information for familiar and unfamiliar environments. *Human Factors, 23*, 495–503.

Huttenlocher, J., Hedges, L. V., & Duncan, S. (1991). Categories and particulars: Prototype effects in estimating spatial location. *Psychological Review, 98*, 352–376.

Huttenlocher, J., Newcombe, N., & Sandberg, E. H. (1994). The coding of spatial location in young children. *Cognitive Psychology, 27*, 115–147.

Jackendoff, R. (1983). *Semantics and cognition*. Cambridge, MA: MIT Press.

Johnson-Laird, P. N. (1983). *Mental models*. Cambridge, MA: Harvard University Press.

Kemp, S. (1988). Memorial psychophysics for visual area: The effect of retention interval. *Memory and Cognition, 16*, 431–436.

Kerst, S. M., & Howard, J. H. (1978). Memory psychophysics for visual area and length. *Memory and Cognition, 6*, 327–335.

Klatzky, R. L., Golledge, R. G., Loomis, J. M., Cicinelli, J. G., & Pellegrino, J. W. (1995). Performance of blind and sighted persons on spatial tasks. *Journal of Visual Impairment and Blindness, 89*, 70–82.

Klatzky, R. L., Loomis, J. M., Beall, A. C., Chance, S. S., & Golledge, R. G. (1998). Updating an egocentric spatial representation during real, imagined, and virtual locomotion. *Psychological Science, 9*, 293–298.

Kosslyn, S. M. (1980). *Image and mind*. Cambridge, MA: Harvard University Press.

Kosslyn, S. M., Pick, H. L., & Fariello, G. R. (1974). Cognitive maps in children and men. *Child Development, 45*, 707–716.

Kuipers, B. J. (1978). Modelling spatial knowledge. *Cognitive Science, 2*, 129–153.

Kuipers, B. J., & Levitt, T. S. (1988). Navigation and mapping in large-scale space. *AI Magazine, 9*, 25–43.

Lakoff, G., & Johnson, M. (1980). *Metaphors we live by*. Chicago: University of Chicago Press.

Landau, B. (1988). The construction and use of spatial knowledge in blind and sighted children. In J. Stiles-Davis, M. Kritchevsky, & U. Bellugi (Eds.), *Spatial cognition: Brain bases and development* (pp. 343–371). Hillsdale, NJ: Erlbaum.

Landau, B., Spelke, E., & Gleitman, H. (1984). Spatial knowledge in a young blind child. *Cognition, 16*, 225–260.

Langacker, R. W. (1987). *Foundations of cognitive grammar, Vol. 1: Theoretical prerequisites*. Stanford, CA: Stanford University Press.

Lansdale, M. W. (1998). Modeling memory for absolute location. *Psychological Review, 105*, 351–378.

Lederman, S. J., Klatzky, R. L., Collins, A., & Wardell, J. (1987). Exploring environments by hand or foot: Time-based heuristics for encoding distance in movement space. *Journal of Experimental Psychology: Learning, Memory, and Cognition, 13*, 606–614.

Leibowitz, H. W., Guzy, L. T., Peterson, E., & Blake, P. T. (1993). Quantitative perceptual estimates: Verbal versus nonverbal retrieval techniques. *Perception, 22*, 1051–1060.

Leiser, D., & Zilbershatz, A. (1989). *The traveler: A computational model of spatial network learning*. Environment and Behavior, *21*, 435–463.

Levelt, W. J. M. (1984). Some perceptual limitations on talking about space. In A. J. van Doorn, W. A. van der Grind, & J. J. Koenderink (Eds.), *Limits on perception* (pp. 323–358). Utrecht: VNU Science Press.

Levine, M., Jankovic, I. N., & Palij, M. (1982). Principles of spatial problem solving. *Journal of Experimental Psychology: General, 111*, 157–175.

Levinson, S. C. (1996). Frames of reference and Molyneux's question: Cross-linguistic evidence. In P. Bloom, M. A. Peterson, L. Nadel, & M. Garrett (Eds.), *Space and language* (pp. 109–169). Cambridge, MA: MIT Press.

Levinson, S. C. (1997). Language and cognition: The cognitive consequences of spatial description in Guugu Yimithirr. *Journal of Linguistic Anthropology, 7*, 98–131.

Lloyd, R. (1989). Cognitive maps: Encoding and decoding information. *Annals of the Association of American Geographers, 79*, 101–124.

Lloyd, R., & Heivly, C. (1987). Systematic distortions in urban cognitive maps. *Annals of the Association of American Geographers, 77*, 191–207.

Loomis, J. M., Klatzky, R. L, Golledge, R. G., Cicinelli, J. G., Pellegrino, J. W., & Fry, P. A. (1993). Non-visual navigation by blind and sighted: Assessment of path integration ability. *Journal of Experimental Psychology: General, 122*, 73–91.

Lynch, K. (1960). *The image of the city*. Cambridge, MA: MIT Press.

Maguire, E. A., Frackowiak, R. S. J., & Frith, C. D. (1997). Recalling routes around London: Activation of the right hippocampus in taxi drivers. *Journal of Neuroscience, 17*, 7103–7110.

Maki, R. H. (1981). Categorization an ddistance effects with spatial linear orders. *Journal of Experimental Psychology: Human Learning and Memory, 7*, 15–32.

Mandler, J. M. (1988). The development of spatial cognition: On topological and Euclidean representations. In J. Stiles-Davis, M. Kritchevsky, & U. Belllugi (Eds.), *Spatial cognition: Brain bases and development* (pp. 423–432). Hillsdale, NJ: Erlbaum.

Mandler, J. M., Seegmiller, D., & Day, J. (1977). On the coding of spatial information. *Memory and Cognition, 5*, 10–16.

Mani, K., & Johnson-Laird, P. N. (1982). The mental representation of spatial descriptions. *Memory and Cognition, 10*, 181–187.

McNamara, T. P. (1986). Mental representations of spatial relations. *Cognitive Psychology, 18*, 87–121.

McNamara, T. P. (1992). Spatial representations. *Geoforum, 23*, 139–150.

McNamara, T. P., & Diwadkar, V. A. (1997). Symmetry and asymmetry of human spatial memory. *Cognitive Psychology, 34*, 160–190.

McNaughton, B. L., Chen, L. I., & Markus, E. J. (1991). "Dead reckoning," landmark learning, and the sense of direction: A neurophysiological and computational hypothesis. *Journal of Cognitive Neuroscience, 3*, 190–202.

Milgram, S., & Jodelet, D. (1976). Psychological maps of Paris. In H. Proshansky, W. Ittelson, & L. Rivlin (Eds.), *Environmental Psychology* (2nd ed.; pp. 104–124). New York: Holt, Rinehart, and Winston.

Miller, G. A., & Johnson-Laird, P. N. (1976). *Language and perception.* Cambridge, MA: Harvard University Press.

Moar, I., & Bower, G. H. (1983). Inconsistency in spatial knowledge. *Memory and Cognition, 11*, 107–113.

Montello, D. R. (1997). The perception and cognition of environmental distance: Direct sources of information. In S. C. Hirtle & A. U. Frank (Eds.), *Spatial information theory: A theoretical basis for GIS* (pp. 297–311). Berlin: Springer-Verlag.

Montello, D. R. (1998). A new framework for understanding the acquisition of spatial knowledge in large-scale environments. In M. J. Egenhofer & R. G. Golledge (Eds.), *Spatial and temporal reasoning in geographic information systems* (pp. 143–154). New York: Oxford University Press.

Moore, G., & Golledge, R. (Eds.). (1976). *Environmental knowing: Theories, research,*

and methods. Stroudsburg, PA: Dowden, Hutchinson & Ross.

Morrison, J. B., & Tversky, B. (1997). Body schemas. *Proceedings of the Meetings of the Cognitive Science Society* (pp. 525–529). Mahwah, NJ: Erlbaum.

Morrow, D. G., Bower, G. H., & Greenspan, S. (1989). Updating situation models during narrative comprehension. *Journal of Memory and Language, 28*, 292–312.

Naveh-Benjamin, M. (1987). Coding of spatial location information: An automatic process? *Journal of Experimental Psychology: Learning, Memory, and Cognition, 13*, 595–605.

Nelson, T. O., & Chaiklin, S. (1980). Immediate memory for spatial location. *Journal of Experimental Psychology: Human Learning and Memory, 6*, 529–545.

Newcombe, N., Huttenlocher, J., Drummey, A. B., & Wiley, J. G. (1998). The development of spatial location coding: Place learning and dead reckoning in the second and third years. *Cognitive Development, 13*, 185–200.

Newcombe, N., & Liben, L. (1982). Barrier effects in the cognitive maps of children and adults. *Journal of Experimental Child Psychology, 34*, 46–58.

O'Keefe, J., & Nadel, L. (1978). *The hippocampus as a cognitive map.* Oxford: Clarendon Press.

Paivio, A. (1971). *Imagery and verbal processes.* New York: Holt, Rinehart, and Winston.

Piaget, J., & Inhelder, B., (1956). *The child's conception of space.* London: Routledge & Kegan Paul.

Piaget, J., Inhelder, B., & Szeminska, A. (1960). *The child's conception of geometry.* London: Routledge and Kegan Paul.

Pick, H. L., Jr., & Lockman, J. J. (1981). From frames of reference to spatial representations. In L. S. Liben, A. H. Patterson, & N. Newcombe (Eds.), *Spatial representation and behavior across the life span: Theory and application* (pp. 39–60). New York: Academic Press.

Portugali, J. (Ed.). (1996). *The construction of cognitive maps.* The Netherlands: Kluwer.

Poulton, E. C. (1989). *Bias in quantifying judgements.* Hillsdale, NJ: Erlbaum.

Presson, C. C., & Montello, D. R. (1994). Updating after rotational and translational body movements: Coordinate structure of perspective space. *Perception, 23*, 1447–1455.

Radvansky, G. A., Spieler, D. H., & Zacks, R. T. (1993). Mental model organization.

Journal of Experimental Psychology: Learning, Memory, and Cognition, 19, 95–114.

Radvansky, G. A., & Zacks, R. T. (1991). Mental models and the fan effect. *Journal of Experimental Psychology: Learning, Memory, and Cognition, 17*, 940–953.

Reed, C. L., & Farah, M. J. (1995). The psychological reality of the body schema: A test with normal participants. *Journal of Experimental Psychology: Human Perception and Performance, 21*, 334–343.

Rieser, J. J. (1989). Access to knowledge of spatial structure at novel points of observation. *Journal of Experimental Psychology: Learning, Memory and Cognition, 15*, 1157–1165.

Rinck, M., Hahnel, A., Bower, G. H., & Glowalla, U. (1997). The metrics of spatial situation models. *Journal of Experimental Psychology: Learning, Memory, and Cognition, 23*, 622–637.

Rosch, E. (1975). Cognitive reference points. *Cognitive Psychology, 7*, 532–547.

Roskos-Ewoldsen, B., McNamara, T. P., Shelton, A. L., & Carr, W. S. (1998). Mental representations of large and small spatial layouts are orientation dependent. *Journal of Experimental Psychology: Learning, Memory, and Cognition, 24*, 215–226.

Sadalla, E. K., Burroughs, W. J., & Staplin, L. J. (1980). Reference points in spatial cognition. *Journal of Experimental Psychology: Human Learning and Memory, 5*, 516–528.

Sadalla, E. K., & Magel, S. G. (1980). The perception of traversed distance. *Environment and Behavior, 12*, 65–79.

Sadalla, E. K., & Montello, D. R. (1989). Remembering changes in direction. *Environment and Behavior, 21*, 346–363.

Sadalla, E. K., & Staplin, L. J. (1980a). An information storage model for distance cognition. *Environment and Behavior, 12*, 183–193.

Sadalla, E. K., & Staplin, L. J. (1980b). The perception of traversed distance: Intersections. *Environment and Behavior, 12*, 167–182.

Schiano, D., & Tversky, B. (1992). Structure and strategy in viewing simple graphs. *Memory and Cognition, 20*, 12–20.

Schober, M. F. (1993). Spatial perspective-taking in conversation. *Cognition, 47*, 1–24.

Shanon, B. (1983). Answers to where-questions. *Discourse Processes, 6*, 319–352.

Shelton, A. L., & McNamara, T. P. (1997). Multiple views of spatial memory. *Psychonomic Bulletin & Review, 4*, 102–106.

Shepard, R. N. (1967). Recognition memory for words, sentences and pictures. *Journal of Verbal Learning and Verbal Behavior, 6*, 156–163.

Shepard, R. N., & Cooper, L. A. (1982). *Mental images and their transformation.* Cambridge, MA: MIT Press.

Shepard, R. N., & Podgorny, P. (1978). Cognitive processes that resemble perceptual processes. In W. Estes (Ed.), *Handbook of learning and cognitive processes* (Vol. 5; pp. 189–237). Hillsdale, NJ: Erlbaum.

Sholl, M. J. (1987). Cognitive maps as orienting schema. *Journal of Experimental Psychology: Learning, Memory and Cognition, 13*, 615–628.

Sholl, M. J., & Nolin, T. L. (1997). Orientation specificity in representations of place. *Journal of Experimental Psychology: Learning, Memory, and Cognition, 23*, 1494–1507.

Siegel, A. W., & White, S. H. (1975). The development of spatial representations of large-scale environments. In H. W. Reese (Ed.), *Advances in child development and behavior* (Vol. 10; pp. 9–55). New York: Academic Press.

Spence, J. (1985). *The memory palace of Matteo Ricci.* New York: Penguin.

Standing, L. (1973). Learning 10,000 pictures. *Quarterly Journal of Experimental Psychology, 25*, 207–222.

Stevens, A., & Coupe, P. (1978). Distortions in judged spatial relations. *Cognitive Psychology, 10*, 422–437.

Takei, Y., Grasso, R., Amorim, M. A., & Berthoz, A. (1997). Circular trajectory formation during blind locomotion: A test for path integration and motor memory. *Experimental Brain Research, 115*, 361–368.

Takei, Y., Grasso, R., & Berthoz, A. (1996). Quantitative analysis of human walking trajectory on a circular path in darkness. *Brain Research Bulletin, 40*, 491–496.

Talairach, J., & Tournoux, P. (1988). *Co-planar stereotaxic atlas of the human brain: 3-dimensional proportional system: An approach to cerebral imaging.* Stuttgart: G. Thieme.

Talmy, L. (1983). How language structures space. In H. Pick & L. Acredolo (Eds.), *Spatial orientation: Theory, research and application* (pp. 225–282). New York: Plenum Press.

Talmy, L. (1988). The relation of grammar to cognition. In B. Rudzka-Ostyn (Ed.), *Topics in cognitive linguistics* (pp. 165–207). Philadelphia: John Benjamins.

Taylor, H. A., Naylor, S. J., & Chechile, N. A. (1999). Goal-specific influences on the representation of spatial perspectives. *Memory and Cognition, 27*, 309–319.

Taylor, H. A., & Tversky, B. (1992a). Descriptions and depictions of environments. *Memory and Cognition, 20*, 483–496.

Taylor, H. A., & Tversky, B. (1992b). Spatial mental models derived from survey and route descriptions. *Journal of Memory and Language, 31*, 261–282.

Taylor, H. A., & Tversky, B. (1996). Perspective in spatial descriptions. *Journal of Memory and Language, 35*, 371–391.

Taylor, M. M. (1961). Effect of anchoring and distance perception on the reproduction of forms. *Perceptual and Motor Skills, 12*, 203–230.

Thorndyke, P. W. (1981). Distance estimation from cognitive maps. *Cognitive Psychology, 13*, 526–550.

Thorndyke, P. W., & Hayes-Roth, B. (1982). Differences in spatial knowledge acquired from maps and navigation. *Cognitive Psychology, 14*, 560–589.

Tolman, E. C. (1948). Cognitive maps in rats and men. *Psychological Review, 55*, 189–208.

Tversky, A., & Gati, I. (1978). Studies of similarity. In E. Rosch & B. B. Lloyd (Eds.), *Cognition and categorization* (pp. 79–98). Hillsdale, NJ: Erlbaum.

Tversky, B. (1981). Distortions in memory for maps. *Cognitive Psychology, 13*, 407–433.

Tversky, B. (1991). Spatial mental models. In G. H. Bower (Ed.), *The psychology of learning and motivation: Advances in research and theory* (Vol. 27; pp. 109–145). New York: Academic Press.

Tversky, B. (1992). Distortions in cognitive maps. *Geoforum, 23*, 131–138.

Tversky, B. (1993). Cognitive maps, cognitive collages, and spatial mental models. In A. U. Frank & I. Campari (Eds.), *Spatial information theory: A theoretical basis for GIS* (pp. 14–24). Berlin: Springer-Verlag.

Tversky, B. (1995). Cognitive origins of graphic conventions. In F. T. Marchese (Ed.), *Understanding images* (pp. 29–53). New York: Springer-Verlag.

Tversky, B. (1996). Spatial constructions. In N. Stein, P. Ornstein, B. Tversky, & C.

Brainerd (Eds.), *Memory for emotion and everyday events* (pp. 181–208). Mahwah, NJ: Erlbaum.

Tversky, B. (1997). Memory for pictures, environments, maps, and graphs. In D. Payne & F. Conrad (Eds.), *Intersections in basic and applied memory research* (pp. 257–277). Mahwah, NJ: Erlbaum.

Tversky, B. (1998). Three dimensions of spatial cognition. In M. A. Conway, S. E. Gathercole, & C. Cornoldi (Eds.), *Theories of memory II* (pp. 259–275). Hove, Sussex: Psychological Press.

Tversky, B., & Hemenway, K. (1983). Categories of scenes. *Cognitive Psychology, 15*, 121–149.

Tversky, B., Kugelmass, S., & Winter, A. (1991). Cross-cultural and developmental trends in graphic productions. *Cognitive Psychology, 23*, 515–557.

Tversky, B., & Schiano, D. (1989). Perceptual and conceptual factors in distortions in memory for maps and graphs. *Journal of Experimental Psychology: General, 118*, 387–398.

Tversky, B., Taylor, H. A., & Mainwaring, S. (1997). Langage et perspective spatial (Language and spatial perspective). In M. Denis (Ed.), *Langage et cognition spatiale* (pp. 25–49). Paris: Masson.

Ungerleider, L. G., & Mishkin, M. (1982). Two cortical visual systems. In D. J. Ingle, R. J. W. Mansfield, & M. A. Goodale (Eds.), *The analysis of visual behavior* (pp. 549–586). Cambridge, MA: MIT Press.

van Dijk, T. A., & Kintsch, W. (1983). *Strategies of discourse comprehension.* New York: Academic Press.

Wilton, R. N. (1979). Knowledge of spatial relations: The specification of information used in making inferences. *Quarterly Journal of Experimental Psychology, 31*, 133–146.

Wright, P., Lickorish, A., Hull, A., & Ummelen, N. (1995). Graphics in written directions: Appreciated by readers but not by writers. *Applied Cognitive Psychology, 9*, 41–59.

Yates, F. A. (1966). *The art of memory.* Chicago: University of Chicago Press.

24

Memory for Emotional Events

JONATHAN W. SCHOOLER & ERIC EICH

How, if at all, do emotions influence memory for personal events? This basic question has had a longstanding and contentious history, particularly with respect to recollections of events charged with negative emotion such as sadness, shock, or terror. Discussions of the impact of strong negative emotions on memory have typically been focused within one of three research domains: eyewitness memory, flashbulb memory, and memory for traumatic experiences. Though each of these literatures has developed its own set of paradigms and idiosyncratic discussions, all three converge in their central focus on two controversial issues: (1) whether emotion enhances or diminishes the strength of memory for an event, and (2) whether special mechanisms are required to account for the effects of emotion on memory.

While both of these issues have invited strong and often sharply divided opinions in all three domains, recent analyses have become increasingly intricate. Claims regarding the effects of emotion on the strength of memory have evolved from relatively simple characterizations to more complex assessments of the distinct factors that mediate the impact of emotion. Discussions of the role of special memory mechanisms have also become more involved, shifting gradually from polarized debates to a growing appreciation of the manner in which emotion and memory interact.

Eyewitness Memory

This progression of views is well illustrated by changes in discussions of the impact of emotion on eyewitness memory. Based on the venerable Yerkes-Dodson curve, which characterizes decrements in performance on many tasks following very low or very high degrees of arousal, it was originally assumed that the strong emotion evoked by witnessing a violent act would impair memory performance (Deffenbacher, 1983). Consistent with this assumption, Clifford and Scott (1978) found that subjects who viewed a videotape depicting a violent event (a physical assault) were less accurate in answering memory items on a subsequent questionnaire than were subjects who viewed a nonviolent event (a verbal exchange between a bystander and a policeman). Relatedly, Loftus and Burns (1982) reported that exposure to a videotape that included a violent incident (a murder) impaired memory for previously seen details. Small wonder, then, that 70% of the eyewitness-memory experts surveyed by Kassin, Ellsworth, and Smith (1989) endorsed the statement that "very high levels of stress impair the accuracy of eyewitness testimony."

Accuracy of Eyewitness Memory for Emotional Events

Though the impact of negative emotion on eyewitness memory initially seemed straightforward, the picture became more complicated with the identification of a variety of mediating factors. One essential factor, foreshadowed by Easterbrook (1959), concerns memory for central in contrast to peripheral details of the to-be-remembered or target event. Easterbrook proposed that arousal may narrow the focus of attention, leading to improved memory for central details of the target event but impaired memory for peripheral details. Evidence from several sources supports this proposition (e.g., Christianson, 1992a; Heuer & Reisberg, 1990), and the idea of attention narrowing has been invoked to account for the phenomenon of weapon focus, whereby memory is impaired in the presence of a gun or knife (Loftus, Loftus, & Messo, 1987).

Retention interval has also been shown to be a potentially important mediating factor in determining the effect of emotion on eyewitness memory. It has long been known that when retention is tested immediately, high arousal at encoding impairs paired-associates learning, but that at longer retention intervals, arousal leads to superior memory performance (Kleinsmith & Kaplan, 1963, 1964). Though this same pattern has been seen in several studies involving eyewitness memory (e.g., Christianson, 1984; Burke, Heurer, & Reisberg, 1992, experiment 2), it has not been observed in others (Burke et al., 1992, experiment 1; Christianson & Loftus, 1987). Still, a recent meta-analysis (Park, 1995) suggests that the interaction of retention interval and memory for emotionally charged eyewitness events is a bona fide effect. Thus, retention interval further adds to the increasing complexity of the conditions under which emotion helps or hinders eyewitness memory.

Mechanisms of Eyewitness Memory for Emotional Events

Does eyewitness memory for emotional events draw on mechanisms that are qualitatively different from those involved in remembering nonemotional experiences? Among researchers in the area, few questions have stirred more dissent or propagated more polarized answers. On the one hand, Yuille and Cutshall (1986) investigated witnesses' memory for an actual robbery and murder and observed generally accurate recall with relatively little decline over time. Given the disparity between these results and those revealed by laboratory studies involving staged crimes, Yuille and Cutshall contended that extreme emotional events experienced in real life lead to "qualitatively different memories than innocuous laboratory events" (p. 178). Christianson, Goodman, and Loftus (1992), on the other hand, maintained that differences between lab-related and real-life emotional events may be more apparent than real (also see Christianson, 1992b).

Recent research by Cahill and his colleagues has suggested a more nuanced conclusion concerning the existence of special memory mechanisms associated with eyewitnessed emotional events. In one study (Cahill, Prins, Weber, & McGaugh, 1994), subjects were injected with either propranolol (a beta-adrenergic blocker) or a placebo before they viewed an emotionally arousing or neutral short story. Strikingly, propranolol attenuated participants' recognition advantage for the emotional elements while having no effect on their memory for the nonemotional elements (the emotional story contained both arousing and neutral parts). These findings suggest that the normal memory advantage for the central details of emotional scenes is a result of the unique involvement of adrenergic hormones, which were blocked for participants receiving propranolol.

Additional findings suggest a special role of the amygdala in facilitating emotional memory in the eyewitness paradigm. For example, Cahill, Babinksy, Markowitsch, and McGaugh, (1995) found no enhanced memory for emotional relative to nonemotional slides for a patient with bilateral degeneration of the amygdala complex. Furthermore, using a PET imaging procedure, Cahill et al. (1996) found that the degree of activation in the amygdala during the witnessing of emotional film clips predicted recall performance two weeks later (r = .92). In contrast, no reliable relation was found between amygdala activation during encoding and subsequent recall for neutral film clips.

The results of Cahill and colleagues suggest that there may be some important truths to both the claims that emotional memories involve special processes, and that laboratory-based memories are not qualitatively different from more emotional real-world ones. The unique role of adrenergic hormones and the amygdala in the processing of memories with emotional content implies the involvement of brain processes that may not be associated with nonemotional memories (see Marko-witsch, chapter 38 in this volume, for detailed discussion of the neural systems subserving memory and emotion). When considered together with the behavioral results, reviewed earlier, indicating that (1) central details of emotional memories are remembered better than peripheral details, and (2) the time course of consolidation of emotional memories may be different, these findings suggest that emotional eyewitness memories may indeed have somewhat different properties from nonemotional memories. At the same time, however, the success of Cahill and his associates in documenting the unique role of emotion in eyewitness memories in the lab suggests that memorial processes observed in the lab may not be qualitatively different from those induced in more extreme emotional situations. More generally, this analysis suggests that the question of whether or not special mechanisms exist for emotional memories may itself be an overly simplified question, as how one frames the question determines how it answered. If the question simply asks whether emotional memories draw on special processes, then the answer appears to be yes. If, however, the question challenges the pertinence of standard memory mechanisms and laboratory procedures to understanding emotional memories, then the answer seems to be no.

Rather then asking whether emotion elicits entirely unique memory processes, the more appropriate question that arises from a consideration of the eyewitness memory literature is, how and under what conditions do special emotion-related processes (such as attentional narrowing and increased amygdala activity) *interact* with standard memory encoding, consolidation, and retrieval functions? As will be seen, a similar resolution of the special-mechanism question seems appropriate for the comparable controversies associated with flashbulb memories and memory for trauma.

Flashbulb Memories

Another important area in which discussions of the peculiar properties of emotional events

have taken place has been within the context of flashbulb memories—a term coined by Brown and Kulik (1977) in their analysis of vivid memories for salient news stories, such as the assassination of President John F. Kennedy. Brown and Kulik offered two theses in their characterization of flashbulb memories: specifically, that such memories (1) are uncommonly accurate, and (2) involve unique memory processes. As the following sections will show, both of these claims have been the subjects of much controversy.

Accuracy of Flashbulb Memories

Brown and Kulik's evidence for the accuracy of flashbulb memories was rather modest. Perhaps their most compelling finding was the simple fact that almost all of their participants reported remarkably detailed recollections of their circumstances at the time of learning of Kennedy's assassination. One limitation of Brown and Kulik's evidence, however, was that they did not verify whether individuals' vivid recollections were accurate. To address this issue, a variety of subsequent studies have employed longitudinal paradigms in order to assess the consistency of flashbulb memories over time. Of course, measures of consistency do not ensure accuracy, as it is possible that individuals could be consistently inaccurate. Nevertheless, consistency is a necessary if not sufficient component of accuracy—that is, if someone is inconsistent, then at least one of his or her versions must be inaccurate. Thus, since it is generally not possible to definitively ascertain an individual's personal circumstances surrounding the learning of a major news event, consistency is often treated as a useful proxy for memory accuracy.

As an example, Pillemer (1984) tested subjects twice for their ability to recall where they were, what they were doing, and who they were with when they first learned about the attempted assassination of President Ronald Reagan. On average, about 82% of the details recollected 1 month after the assassination attempt were recalled again 7 months later—a finding that Pillemer viewed as evidence for the impressive accuracy of flashbulb memories.

However, using a similar longitudinal design, other researchers examined memory for the *Challenger* space-shuttle explosion but concluded that such memories were not especially accurate. For instance, McCloskey, Wible, and Cohen (1988) found that only 61% of the recollections were entirely consistent across two tests given 1 week and 9 months after the disaster, with 6% being more specific, 19% more general, and 8% inconsistent. Neisser and Harsch (1992) found even larger changes in recollections, with 25% of participants providing outright inconsistencies between the reports they provided 1 day after the shuttle exploded and 32–34 months later.

The above longitudinal analyses clearly illustrate that recollections of important news stories are not necessarily maintained in an immutable form. However, assessing whether there is any merit to the claim that flashbulb memories are especially accurate is problematic because it is not clear to what such memories should be compared. For example, McCloskey et al.'s findings that only 8% of participants had outright inconsistencies in their recollections could just as well be taken as evidence for the general accuracy of such recollections. A separate, but equally serious, problem is whether these events were sufficiently emotional to engender especially accurate memories in the first place. Indeed, several researchers (e.g., Bohannon, 1988; Pillemer, 1984) found reliable correlations between individuals' reported emotional response at the time of the original experience and their memory consistency across testings, suggesting that when experiences are sufficiently emotional, uniquely accurate flashbulb memories may be observed.

In an effort to finesse these problems, Conway and his colleagues (1994; see also Conway, 1995) compared the recollections of two groups of subjects—citizens of the United Kingdom versus individuals who did not live in the United Kingdom (mostly, although not entirely, U.S. citizens)—concerning the resignation of British Prime Minister Margaret Thatcher. All participants were tested at both 2-week and 11-month retention intervals. Not surprisingly, the U.K. citizens were more emotional about the experience and perceived it as more important than their North American counterparts. Nevertheless, over 90% of subjects in both groups reported recollections of sufficient detail to be classified as flashbulb memories at the 2-week interval. However, whereas 86% of the U.K. citizens retained a flashbulb memory 11 months later, only 29% of the North American residents did likewise. Moreover, the former subjects showed markedly greater consistency in their recollections between the two testing intervals than did the latter. Thus, by providing an appropriate control group, Conway et al.'s findings suggest that the quality of recollection associated with a flashbulb-type news event is indeed more detailed and accurate than that associated with a less emotionally significant news event.

Mechanisms of Flashbulb Memory

In addition to disputes over their exceptional accuracy, a second central issue in the flashbulb-memory debate has been whether such memories involve special memory mechanisms. In their original proposal, Brown and Kulik (1977) suggested that flashbulb memories entail entirely distinct memory mechanisms. Drawing on Livingston (1967), they speculated that extremely significant life experiences cause the reticular formation to discharge a *now-print* order that produces a "permanent registration not only of the significant novelty, but of all recent brain events" (Brown & Kulik, 1977, p. 76).

Critics of this special flashbulb-memory mechanism have countered that there are a variety of standard memory mechanisms—such as distinctiveness, rehearsal, and personal relevance—that could, in principle, account for the impressive though imperfect accuracy of such memories. As McCloskey et al. (1988) observed: "To the extent that we accept that ordinary memory mechanism could support reasonably good memory for experiences of learning about shocking events . . . there is no need to postulate a special flashbulb memory mechanism" (p. 180).

As in the case of eyewitness memory research, more recent findings have suggested compromise views by which flashbulb memories can be seen as the product of standard memory mechanisms that have been supplemented by the singular influences of emotion. For example, Conway et al. (1994) found that events that either did or did not eventually develop the canonical properties of flashbulb memories had distinguishing elements or features; in particular, the primary differences between the two types of recollections were the contributions of affective intensity and perceived importance. Also, recent structural-modeling analyses (Finkenauer et al., 1998) have further highlighted the importance of emotional reaction in the formation of flashbulb-type memories.

Though emotion apparently contributes to the exquisitely detailed quality of flashbulb memories, it should also be emphasized that they still share great similarity with more standard memories. For example, Anderson and Conway (1993) found that most autobiographical memories have the canonical attributes of flashbulb memories but simply not to the same degree. Moreover, the mechansims by which emotion influences flashbulb memories remain to be determined. Although emotions may alter the manner in which such memories are initially encoded, it is also possible that emotion may primarily have its impact on post encoding factors. For example the emotional salience of an experience may influence the frequency with which it is subsequently rehearsed (Neisser et al., 1998). Alternatively, or in addition, emotion elicited at the time of recall may alter the manner in which memories are retrieved (cf. Schooler, Bediksen, & Ambadar, 1997). For example, if individuals experience marked emotion during recall, such emotional intensity could in principle be conflated with sensory vividness, creating the phenomenological experience of a uniquely detailed memory.

Once again, then, a reasonable conclusion regarding the special mechanism question is both "yes" and "no". Emotional processes do seem to give flashbulb memories some unique properties—strength, vividness, and detail, in particular. However, although the precise mechanisms by which emotion imbues flashbulb memories with these properties remains to be fully determined, it seems likely that emotion related processes work in concert with—rather than apart from—standard and often reconstructive memory mechanisms. Thus, they do not ensure that flashbulb memories will be entirely veridical.

Memory for Traumatic Events

Though debates about of the impact of emotion on eyewitness and flashbulb memories have at times been heated, neither domain has ignited anything like the firestorm that has engulfed discussion of memory for trauma (see Loftus & Ketcham, 1994; Ofshe & Watters, 1994; Schacter, 1996). Nevertheless, the same two key issues that arose before apply here as well—namely, (1) assessing the impact of trauma on the accuracy of memory, and (2) determining whether trauma elicits special memory mechanisms (see Bower & Sivers,

1998, for a thorough analysis of these and related issues).

Accuracy of Traumatic Memories

Victims of trauma often lament that their traumatic experiences are associated with painfully vivid recollections, and research bears out this claim (Koss, Tromp, & Tharan, 1995). Traumatic recollections are often quite accurate, though certainly not flawless, for a variety of experiences including kidnapping (Terr, 1988), sniper attack (Pynoos & Nader, 1989), concentration camp experiences (Wagenaar & Groenweg, 1990), and emergency room visits (Howe, Courage, & Peterson, 1994). Though there has been some dispute over exactly how accurate intact memories of trauma are likely to be (Goodman, Quas, Batterman-Fauce, Riddlesberger, & Kuhn, 1994), the bigger debate in this domain has been whether traumatic memories can be completely forgotten and then later accurately recovered. This question has proved to be a divisive issue of unprecedented proportion, whose resolution has been complicated by the ethical difficulties of experimentation, the investigative constraint of corroborating clandestine activities, and the intellectual challenge of deciphering evidence that may be colored by zealotry and dogma.

As a first step in unpacking this contentious issue, it is helpful to note that the question of whether it is possible to forget and then remember traumatic memories can be usefully broken down into two separate subquestions: (1) can traumatic memories be forgotten? and (2) can traumatic memories that have been characterized as "recovered" actually be authentic?

Can Traumatic Memories Be Forgotten?

Several sorts of investigations have addressed whether traumatic memories can be forgotten, including retrospective surveys of people reporting traumatic memories, retrospective case studies of single individuals, and prospective studies of subjects identified on the basis of their exposure to trauma.

Retrospective Survey Studies. A number of studies have used retrospective questionnaires to assess individuals' traumatic memories of sexual abuse (e.g., Briere & Conte, 1993; Gold,

Hughes, & Hohnecker, 1994; Loftus, Polonsky, & Fullilove, 1994) as well as more general types of trauma (e.g. Elliott & Briere, 1995). Though reported estimates of forgetting have varied markedly, all of these studies have found significant proportions of respondents reporting that there was a time that they did not remember their trauma. Such findings are consistent with the claim that it is possible to forget traumatic experiences; nevertheless, they must be viewed with caution on two accounts. First, in none of these studies was there independent corroboration of the trauma, and as will be discussed, there are serious reasons to be uncertain about the status of recovered memories in the absence of corroboration. Second, these studies depended on respondents' ability to recall their prior memory states, and as will also be discussed, there is evidence that individuals can unknowingly exaggerate their prior degree of forgetting.

Retrospective Case Studies. A second approach to investigating the forgetting of traumatic memories is to engage in detailed review and corroboration of the claims of individuals who reportedly forgot and subsequently remembered traumas. Though such cases are useful with regard to assessing whether claims of recovered memories can involve actual abuse (see following section), they are limited with regard to documenting actual forgetting because, as with retrospective survey studies, forgetting must be estimated retrospectively. Thus, individuals may exaggerate or distort their degree of forgetting; indeed, using a case study approach, Schooler and his associates (Schooler, in press; Schooler, Ambadar, & Bendiksen, 1997; Schooler, Bendiksen, & Ambadar, 1997) provided evidence for just such distortions. Specifically, in several cases, individuals were found to have known about their traumatic experiences (i.e., they talked about it with others) at a time at which they retrospectively thought they had forgotten about it. On the basis of such errors, Schooler proposed a variant of the *knew-it-all-along effect* hindsight bias (Fischhoff, 1982) termed the *forgot-it-all-along effect*, whereby individuals underestimate rather than overestimate their prior knowledge. Accordingly, individuals may reason that "if I am this upset and agitated about this experience, then I must have previously had

no idea about it." Whereas, in fact, their agitation may stem not from discovering the memory itself, but rather from generating a new interpretation of the experience or accessing previously dormant emotions about it (see next section).

Prospective Studies. A more convincing demonstration of forgetting traumatic experiences comes from prospective studies that identify individuals on the basis of their known trauma histories (alleviating concerns of potential false memories) and that test their current recollections of abuse (alleviating concerns of retrospective assessment of forgetting). In several such studies (e.g., Widom & Morris, 1997; Williams, 1994), a substantial proportion of individuals who were known to have been abused reported no recollection of the recorded abuse incident. Though these studies provide the strongest evidence to date for the forgetting of specific incidents of trauma, they have limitations. For example, studies of this sort only address memory for individual instances of abuse and do not necessarily speak to the more general claim that individuals can forget repeated episodes of abuse. In addition, many of the individuals in these studies did not recall the particular incident of abuse for which they were treated, but nevertheless recalled other sexual assaults. Some of these individuals may have confused their recollections of abuse rather than have forgotten them completely. Despite these and other concerns (see Pope & Hudson, 1995), such studies suggest that individuals can forget single traumatic incidents. However, just because some traumatic memories can be forgotten does not mean that discovered memories of purportedly long-forgotten episodes of abuse are necessarily authentic, the issue that we turn to next.

Can Traumatic Memories That Have Been Characterized as "Recovered" Actually Be Authentic?

At the core of many discussions of recovered traumatic memories is the question of whether individuals who report having discovered long-forgotten memories of trauma are in fact recalling real events. Though such memories are typically referred to as *recovered memories*, Schooler, Ambador et al. (1997) have advocated the term *discovered memories* because it maintains agnosticity regarding whether the memory was truly forgotten or, indeed, whether the discovered event even occurred. At the same time, however, it respects the integrity of the individual's experience of having made a profound discovery (see Schooler, in press; Schooler, Ambador et al., 1997).

In recent years, an alarming number of people have reported discovering long-forgotten memories of abuse, often in the context of intense psychotherapy. The allegations sometime lead to litigation, and typically to deep family rifts. Nevertheless, there are good reasons to believe that discovered memories can be the product of therapists' over-zealous search for an explanation of their clients' symptoms. It is beyond the scope of this chapter to survey the voluminous evidence for such concern, and the reader is directed to the lucid reviews by Lindsay and Read (1994), Loftus and Ketcham (1994), Pendergrast (1996), and Schacter (1996). Suffice it to say, it is now well established that:

1. Individuals can remember, sometimes in excruciating detail, memories of events that are extraordinarily unlikely to have occurred, including alien abductions and satanic rituals (see Loftus & Ketcham, 1994; Persinger, 1992).

2. Under certain experimental conditions, subjects can be induced to recall "memories" of disturbing events that never happened, such as being lost in a shopping mall (Loftus & Pickerel, 1995) or spilling punch on the bride's parents at a wedding (Hyman, 1995).

3. A variety of psychotherapeutic techniques such as visualization (Garry, Manning, Loftus, & Sherman, 1996), repeated retrieval attempts (Hyman & Pentland, 1996), dream interpretation (Mazzoni & Loftus, 1998), and hypnosis (Putnam, 1979) can contribute to the production of false memories. These techniques correspond, with disturbing closeness, to those used by a sizable minority of clinicians in their aggressive efforts to "recover" memories of abuse (Polusny & Follette, 1996).

4. Therapists who use such techniques are the most likely to induce discovered memories (Poole, Lindsay, Memon, & Bull, 1995), and are also the most likely to have patients who ultimately retract their recollections (Nelson & Simpson, 1994).

Though the authenticity of discovered memories was originally treated as an either/ or issue (e.g., Ofshe & Watters, 1994), recent discussion has become more balanced by promoting the view that while some discovered memories may be the product of therapists suggestions, others may correspond to actual incidents (see Lindsay & Briere, 1997; Schacter, 1996; Schooler, 1994). A number of cases, documented by the news media and in the courts, have provided compelling corroborative evidence of the alleged abuse. For example, Ross Cheit's discovery of a memory of being molested by a choir counselor was corroborated by the tape-recorded confession of his perpetrator (Horn, 1993), and Frank Fitzpatrick's discovered memory of being abused by a priest was supported by similar charges levied by many other alleged victims (Commonwealth of Massachusetts v. Porter, 1993). Nevertheless, and somewhat surprisingly given the importance of the issue, there have been relatively few attempts by researchers to systematically document and corroborate allegations of recovered memories. Moreover, most of the investigations of discovered memories that have considered corroboration have primarily relied on patients' claims (e.g. Andrews, 1997; Chu, J. A., Frey, L. M., Ganzel, B. L., Mathews, J. A., 1999; Feldman-Summers & Pope, 1994; Herman & Schatzow, 1987; van der Kolk & Fisler, 1995; Roe & Schwartz, 1996)—a questionable practice, given the patients' strong biases to present their discoveries as being authentic.

A few researchers have sought to find independent corroboration for the abuse associated with discovered memories (e.g., Dalenberg, 1996; Kluft, 1998; Duggal & Stroufe, 1998; Schooler, in press; Schooler et al., 1997a, 1997b; Williams, 1995). Several of these studies are somewhat difficult to interpret however, because they do not clearly differentiate the corroboration for discovered memories of additional episodes of abuse versus the fact that one was the victim of abuse. Although the recollection of an additional abuse episode is of interest, it is clearly qualitatively less remarkable than a memory discovery that leads one to the new found conclusion that he/she was the victim of sexual abuse. Importantly, however, corroborative evidence for the abuse associated with such complete memory discovery experiences have been documented. For example, Schooler and colleagues (Schooler et al., 1997a, 1997b; Schooler, in press) investigated a number of cases involving discovered memories of alleged abuse (ranging from inappropriate fondling to rape) of individuals who believed they had been previously unaware of their abuse status. Schooler et al. sought and found independent corroboration of the abuse by seeking other individuals who had knowledge of the abuse before the victims' discovery experience, or who had evidence of the abusive tendencies of the alleged perpetrator. In addition, these corroborated cases also provided some interesting clues concerning the nature of the discovery experience. For example, in each case, the discovery of the memory was purportedly associated with conditions that shared some significant correspondence to the original trauma (e.g., seeing a movie about abuse). In addition, individuals' accounts of their initial recollection of the abuse were characterized by great surprise and sudden marked emotion, further illustrating the aptness of referring to such experiences as memory "discoveries."

Mechanisms of Traumatic Memory

As in the domains of eyewitness and flashbulb memory, the existence of special mechanisms for traumatic memory has been a topic of marked controversy, with some authors passionately promoting special mechanisms and others arguing equally strongly against them. Perhaps the most frequently mentioned special trauma-memory mechanism is the notion of repression, whereby unconscious processes deliberately keep the traumatic recollection from entering awareness (see Brewin, 1997). Though the notion of a special repression mechanism has met with marked scientific skepticism (see Holmes, 1990; Loftus & Ketcham, 1994), many authors continue to believe that repression provides the best account of certain cases of forgetting (e.g., Erdelyi, 1990; Freyd, 1996; Ramachandran, 1995; Vaillant, 1994).

A second special mechanism, dating as far back as Pierre Janet (1889), relates to the idea that during the course a trauma, individuals detach or dissociate themselves from the ongoing experience—a process that could radically alter the way in which the experience is encoded and later retrieved (Spiegel & Car-

dena, 1991). Though individuals with extreme dissociative tendencies are known to manifest marked impairments of memory (Eich, 1995; Eich, Macaulay, Loewenstein, & Dihle, 1997), the contribution of dissociation to the specific case of forgetting and subsequent remembering of traumatic memories has yet to be established empirically (see Bower & Sivers, 1998).

A third special memory mechanism that also dates back to Janet is the suggestion that some traumatic memories are recollected in a purely sensory form "without any semantic representation . . . experienced primarily as fragments of the sensory component of the event" (van der Kolk & Fisler, 1995, p. 513). In addition to their fragmentary nature, sensory memories of trauma have been hypothesized to differ from more standard narrative memories in that they (1) are relatively invulnerable to change (van der Kolk & van der Hart, 1991), and (2) are not under conscious control, but instead are invoked automatically in response to certain environmental or experiential cues (see Brewin, 1989; Brewin, Dalgleish, & Joseph, 1996).

Research with animal models has provided evidence that is broadly consistent with the existence of fragmentary sensory memories for traumatic experiences. A potentially central role of the amygdala in traumatic memories is suggested by LeDoux (1992, 1995), who has demonstrated that the amygdala is critically involved in the learning of fear responses. Moreover, LeDoux has identified two pathways from the thalamus to the amygdala: one via the cortex and the other circumventing the cortex. In principle, the latter route could "generate emotional responses and memories on the basis of features and fragments rather than full-blown perceptions of objects and events" (LeDoux, 1992, p. 277). Nadel and Jacobs (1998) review additional animal studies indicating that stress may disrupt the memory consolidation functions of the hippocampus. From such evidence, the authors posit that "when stress is high enough to impair the function of the hippocampus, resulting memories will be different than those formed under more ordinary circumstances. These empirical data suggest that memories of trauma may be available as isolated fragments rather than as coherently bound episodes" (Nadel & Jacobs, 1998, p. 156). Together, these lines of research suggest that traumatic events may simultaneously foster the amygdala-based formation of highly affective sensory representations, and hinder hippocampal binding and integration processes (for similar suggestions see Bower & Sivers, 1998; Krystal, Southwick, & Charney, 1995; Metcalfe & Jacobs, 1998; van der Kolk, 1994).

Further evidence for the sensory qualities of traumatic memories comes from recent research on posttraumatic stress disorder (see Brewin et al., 1996; Krystal et al., 1995). One study purported to compare the phenomenological quality of traumatic and nontraumatic memories (van der Kolk & Fisler, 1995). During an interview, trauma victims (who had been recruited through newspaper ads) reported that they initially remembered the traumatic event in the form of somatosensory or emotional flashback experiences, and a narrative memory began to emerge only later. In contrast, nontraumatic events were recalled as narratives without sensory components. Though consistent with the sensory account of traumatic memories, this study lacked adequate matching (e.g., age, salience, etc.) between the traumatic and nontraumatic experiences (Shobe & Kihlstrom, 1997).

Moreover, other studies comparing traumatic and nontraumatic events have produced results that seem to be at odds with the idea that the former have an especially sensory quality. For example, Tromp, Koss, Figueredo, and Tharan (1995) compared memories of a traumatic rape with pleasant and other unpleasant memories. In contrast to the predictions of the sensory hypothesis, memory of the rape was less clear, less vivid, and less detailed than were the other types of memory.

Based on the inconsistencies and unpersuasiveness of the evidence for unique traumatic-memory mechanisms, some researchers have suggested that recollections of traumatic events rely on precisely the same processes that underlie more ordinary memories. For example, noting the lack of evidence for special mechanisms and the clear applicability of standard mechanisms (e.g., lack of rehearsal) that could account for purported characteristics of traumatic recollections, Shobe and Kihlstrom (1997) concluded "nothing about the clinical evidence suggests that traumatic memories are special" (p. 74).

In their analysis of case studies of discovered memories, Schooler, Ambador et al. (1997) also noted a number of standard memory mechanisms—such as directed forgetting, encoding specificity, hypermnesia, and, as alluded to above, lack of rehearsal—that could lead to the discovery of seemingly forgotten recollections of abuse. In addition, Schooler et al. identified several other mechanisms that could create the illusion that a memory had previously been completely forgotten. For example, individuals may confuse the reinterpretation of an experience (e.g., realizing that a particular action constituted sexual abuse) with the discovery of the memory itself. Alternatively, if the memory had previously been deliberately suppressed, then individuals could misconstrue the emotional rebound that can result from thought suppression (Wegner & Gold, 1995) as having resulted from the discovery of an entirely forgotten memory of abuse.

Though many of the corroborated claims regarding traumatic memories can be accounted for on the basis of standard memory mechanisms, it seems likely that traumatic memory, like eyewitness and flashbulb memory, will be found to involve processes that are extended in particular ways owing to the unique and emotional nature of the experience. For example, in accounting for several—albeit uncorroborated—claims that memories of sexual abuse were precipitously forgotten the morning after they had occurred, Schooler (in press) speculated about the possible involvement of the forgetting processes that are unique to nocturnal experiences (e.g., those associated with the forgetting of dreams and brief awakenings). If such processes do in fact contribute to the (alleged) rapid forgetting of nocturnal abuse, they would in a sense be "special" in that they would presumably be limited to specific types of nocturnal experiences. Nevertheless, they would also be quite "ordinary" in that may be drawing on processes that occur every night (see Bonnet, 1983).

In a similar vein, even the idea that changes in the activation of normal neural systems (especially the amygdala or hippocampus) may contribute to impaired recollections of trauma can be viewed as extensions of, rather than alternatives to, standard memory processes. For example, Cahill et al.'s (1996) observation of amygdala involvement in the encoding and retrieval of emotional but less than traumatic events demonstrates that while the amygdala may be especially involved in the recollection of trauma, severe trauma is not a prerequisite for amygdala involvement.

By the same token, the suggestion that trauma may reduce the ability of the hippocampus to consolidate the components of emotional memories into a single, coherent narrative does not require the *addition* of any special memory processes. To the contrary, it actually suggests the attenuation of standard memory processes—for example, the involvement of the hippocampus in the integration or binding of diverse perceptual experiences into discrete episodes or events (McClelland, McNaughton, & O'Reilly, 1995). In the absence of such integration, traumatic memories would presumably be degraded and—contrary to claims of the unique veridicality of sensory trauma memories—especially prone to distortion and misattribution (McClelland, 1995). At the same time, lacking cohesion and integration with associated memory representations, such memories could be especially difficult to retrieve deliberately, leaving them at the mercy of situational retrieval cues (Krystal et al., 1995; van der Kolk, 1994). Such a state of affairs could resolve one of the common paradoxes of characterizations of traumatic memories—why they are sometimes retrieved excessively and other times not recalled at all. If traumatic recollections are primarily evoked by external or internal cues, then when such cues are present, recollections of trauma may be inescapable; however, when the appropriate cues are absent, so too may be the recollections.

Summary

Though researchers have, in the past, attempted to describe the impact of emotion on memory in straightforward (albeit often contradictory) ways, current findings suggest that this relation involves complex interactions among multiple variables that can lead to markedly different outcomes. Eyewitness memory for emotional events can be more or less accurate than that of nonemotional events, depending in part on both the centrality of the events' details and the amount of time that has passed since their encoding. Analogously, flashbulb memories for salient news events can be accurate or inaccurate, depending on their significance, the emotion they elicit, and ultimately to what they are being compared. And even traumatic memories can be remembered with excessive vividness or not recalled at all, depending (perhaps) on both the pattern of cognitive/neural activity at the time of encoding and the nature of the environmental and experiential cues that are encountered later.

With regard to the question of special mechanisms, although discussions have also often tended toward categorical yet contradictory positions, recent evidence suggests a more nuanced conclusion. On the one hand, emotion seems to have rather specific effects on brain activity, memory performance, and subjective experience. On the other hand, these processes are orchestrated with, and in many cases critically depend on, nonemotional processes.

Ultimately, the question of whether special memory mechanisms exist for emotional events may itself be a red herring, as its alternative presupposes a single set of neurocognitive processes that apply to all recollections. However, recent research implies that memory involves a remarkable amalgamation of distinct processes that are differentially elicited as a function of the specific circumstances surrounding event encoding, consolidation, and retrieval. Since emotional memories invoke particular subsets of these processes, they may be thought of as "special"—but perhaps no more so than the equally distinct subsets that are apt to be associated with other types of memories.

Acknowledgment Preparation of this chapter was aided by the cogent comments and advice offered by Sherry Slatten, Katie Shobe, and Tonya Schooler, and by a grant (R01-MH59636) to the second author from the National Institute of Mental Health.

References

Anderson, S. J., & Conway, M. A. (1993). Investigating the structure of autobiographical memories. *Journal of Experimental Psychology: Learning, Memory, and Cognition, 19*, 1178–1196.

Andrews, B. (1997). Forms of memory recovery among adults in therapy. In J. D. Read & D. S. Lindsay (Eds.), *Recollections of trauma: Scientific research and clinical practice* (pp. 455–467). New York: Plenum.

Bohannon, J. N. (1988). Flashbulb memories of the Space Shuttle disaster: A tale of two theories. *Cognition, 29*, 179–196.

Bonnet, M. H. (1983). Memory for events occurring during arousal from sleep. *Psychophysiology, 20*, 81–87.

Bower, G. H., & Sivers, H. (1998). Cognitive impact of traumatic events. *Development and Psychopathology, 10*, 625–653.

Brewin, C. R. (1989). Cognitive change processes in psychotherapy. *Psychological Review, 96*, 379–394.

Brewin, C. R. (1997). Clinical and experimental approaches to understanding repression. In J. D. Read & D. S. Lindsay (Eds.), *Recollections of trauma: Scientific research and clinical practice* (pp. 145–163). New York: Plenum.

Brewin, C. R., Dalgleish, T., & Joseph, S. (1996). A dual representation theory of posttraumatic stress disorder. *Psychological Review, 103*, 670–686.

Briere, J., & Conte, J. (1993). Self-reported amnesia for abuse in adults molested as children. *Journal of Traumatic Stress, 6*, 21–31.

Brown, R., & Kulik, J. (1977). Flashbulb memories. *Cognition, 5*, 73–99.

Burke, A., Heuer, F., & Reisberg, D. (1992). Remembering emotional events. *Memory & Cognition, 20*, 277–290.

Cahill, L., Babinsky, R., Markowitsch, H., & McGaugh, J. L. (1995). The amygdala and emotional memory. *Nature, 377*, 295–296.

Cahill, L., Haier, R., Fallon, J., Alkire, M., Tang, C., Keator, D., Wu, J., & McGaugh, J. L. (1996). Amygdala activity at encoding correlated with long-term, free recall of emotional information. *Proceedings of the National Academy of Sciences, 93*, 8016–8021.

Cahill, L., Prins, B., Weber, M., & McGaugh, J. L. (1994). Beta-adrenergic activation and memory for emotional events. *Nature, 371*, 702–704.

Christianson, S.-A. (1984). The relationship between induced emotional arousal and amnesia. *Scandinavian Journal of Psychology, 25*, 147–160.

Christianson, S.-A. (1992a). Remembering emotional events: Potential mechanisms. In S.-A. Christianson (Ed.), *The handbook of emotion and memory: Research and theory* (pp. 307–340). Hillsdale, NJ: Erlbaum.

Christianson, S.-A. (1992b). Emotional stress and eyewitness memory: A critical review. *Psychological Bulletin, 112*, 284–309.

Christianson, S.-A., Goodman, J., & Loftus, E. F. (1992). Eyewitness memory for stressful events: Methodological quandaries and ethical dilemmas. In S.-A. Christianson (Ed.), *The handbook of emotion and memory: Research and theory* (pp. 217–241). Hillsdale, NJ: Erlbaum.

Christianson, S.-A., & Loftus, E. F. (1987). Memory for traumatic events. *Applied Cognitive Psychology, 1*, 225–239.

Chu, J. A., Frey, L. M., Ganzel, B. L., & Matthews, J. A. (1999). Memories of Childhood Abuse; Dissociation, amnesia, and corroboration. *American Journal of Psychiatry, 156*, 749–755.

Clifford, B. R., & Scott, J. (1978). Individual and situational factors in eyewitness testimony. *Journal of Applied Psychology, 63*, 352–359.

Commonwealth of Massachusetts v. Porter. Taunton Superior Court. (1993).

Conway, M. A. (1995). *Flashbulb memories.* Hillsdale, NJ: Erlbaum.

Conway, M. A., Anderson, S. J., Larsen, S. F., Donnelly, C. M., McDaniel, M. A., McClelland, A. G. R., Rawles, R. E., & Logie, R. H. (1994). The formation of flashbulb memories. *Memory & Cognition, 22*, 326–343.

Dalenberg, C. J. (1996). Accuracy, timing and circumstances of disclosure in therapy of recovered and continuous memories of abuse. *Journal of Psychiatry and Law, 24*(2), 229–275.

Deffenbacher, K. A. (1983). The influence of arousal on reliability of testimony. In S. M. A. Lloyd-Bostock & B. R. Clifford (Eds.), *Evaluating witness evidence* (pp. 235–251). Chichester: John Wiley.

Duggal, S., & Sroufe, A. L. (1998). Recovered memory of childhood sexual trauma: A documented case from a longitudinal study. *Journal of Traumatic Stress, 2*, 301–320.

Easterbrook, J. (1959). The effect of emotion on cue utilization and the organization of behavior. *Psychological Review, 66*, 183–201.

Eich, E. (1995). Searching for mood dependent memory. *Psychological Science, 6*, 67–75.

Eich, E., Macaulay, D., Loewenstein, R. J., & Dihle, P. H. (1997). Memory, amnesia, and dissociative identity disorder. *Psychological Science, 8*, 417–422.

Elliott, D. M., & Briere, J. (1995). Posttraumatic stress associated with delayed recall of sexual abuse: A general population study. *Journal of Traumatic Stress, 8*, 629–647.

Erdelyi, M. H. (1990). Repression, reconstruction, and defense: History and integration of the psychoanalytic and experimental frameworks. In J. L. Singer (Ed.), *Repression and dissociation: Implications for personality theory, psychotherapy, and health* (pp. 1–31). Chicago: University of Chicago Press.

Feldman-Summers, S., & Pope, K. S. (1994). The experience of 'forgetting' childhood abuse: A national survey of psychologists. *Journal of Consulting and Clinical Psychology, 62*, 636–639.

Finkenauer, C., Luminet, O., Gisle, L., El-Ahmadi, A., Van der Linden, M., & Philippot, P. (1998). Flashbulb memories and the underlying mechanisms of their formation: Toward an emotional-integrative model. *Memory & Cognition, 26*, 516–531.

Fischhoff, B. (1982). For those condemned to study the past: Heuristics and biases in hindsight. In D. Kahneman, P. Slovic, & A. Tversky (Eds.), *Judgment under uncertainty: Heuristics and biases* (pp. 335–351). New York: Cambridge University Press.

Freyd, J. (1996). *Betrayal trauma: The logic of forgetting childhood abuse.* Cambridge: Harvard University Press.

Garry, M., Manning, C., Loftus, E. F., & Sherman, S. J. (1996). Imagination inflation: Imagining a childhood event inflates confidence that it occurred. *Psychonomic Bulletin and Review, 3*, 208–214.

Gold, S. N., Hughes, D., & Hohnecker, L. (1994). Degrees of repression of sexual abuse memories. *American Psychologist, 49*, 441–442.

Goodman, G. S., Quas, J. A., Batterman-Faunce, J. M., Riddlesberger, M. M., & Kuhn, J. (1994). Predictors of accurate and inaccurate memories of traumatic events experienced in childhood. *Consciousness and Cognition, 3*, 269–294.

Herman, J. L., & Schatzow, E. (1987). Recovery and verification of memories of childhood sexual trauma. *Psychoanalytic Psychology, 4*, 1–14.

Heuer, F., & Reisberg, D. (1990). Vivid memories of emotional events: The accuracy of remembered minutiae. *Memory & Cognition, 18*, 496–506.

Holmes, D. (1990). The evidence for repression: An examination of sixty years of research. In J. Singer (Ed.), *Repression and dissociation: Implications for personality theory, psychotherapy, and health* (pp. 85–102). Chicago: University of Chicago Press.

Horn, M. (1993). Memories lost and found. *US News and World Report*, November 29, 1993, 52–63.

Howe, M. L., Courage, M. L., & Peterson, C. (1994). How can I remember when "I" wasn't there: Long-term retention of traumatic experiences and emergence of the cognitive self. *Consciousness and Cognition, 3*, 327–355.

Hyman, I. E. (1995). False memories of childhood experiences. *Applied Cognitive Psychology, 9*, 181–197.

Hyman, I. E., & Pentland, J. (1996). The role of mental imagery in the creation of false childhood memories. *Journal of Memory and Language, 35*, 101–117.

Janet, P. (1889). L'automatisme continue. *Revue Generale des Sciences, 4*, 167–179

Kassin, S. M., Ellsworth, P., & Smith, V. L. (1989). The "general acceptance" of psychological research on eyewitness testimony. *American Psychologist, 44*, 1089–1098.

Kleinsmith, L. J., & Kaplan, S. (1963). Paired-associate learning as a function of arousal and interpolated interval. *Journal of Experimental Psychology, 65*, 190–193.

Kleinsmith, L. J., & Kaplan, S. (1964). Interaction of arousal and recall interval in nonsense syllable paired-associate learning. *Journal of Experimental Psychology, 67*, 124–126.

Kluft, K. P. (1998). Reflections on the traumatic memories of dissociative identity disorder patients. In S. J. Lynn & K. M. McConkey (Eds.), *Truth in Memory* (pp. 304–322). New York: Guilford Press.

Koss, M. P., Tromp, S., & Tharan, M. (1995). Traumatic memories: Empirical foundations, clinical and forensic implications. *Clinical Psychology: Research and Practice, 2*, 111–132.

Krystal, J. H., Southwick, S. M., & Charney, D. (1995). Post traumatic stress disorder: Psychobiological mechanisms of traumatic remembrance. In D. L. Schacter (Ed.), *Memory distortions* (pp. 150–172). Cambridge, MA: Harvard University Press.

LeDoux, J. E. (1992). Emotion as memory: Anatomical systems underlying indelible neural traces. In S.-A. Christianson (Ed.), *The handbook of emotion and memory: Research and theory* (pp. 269–288). Hillsdale, NJ: Erlbaum.

LeDoux, J. E. (1995). Emotion: Clues from the brain. *Annual Review of Psychology, 46*, 209–235.

Lindsay, D. S., & Briere, J. (1997). The controversy regarding recovered memories of childhood sexual abuse: Pitfalls, bridges, and future directions. *Journal of Interpersonal Violence, 12*, 631–647.

Lindsay, D. S., & Read, J. D. (1994). Psychotherapy and memories of child sexual abuse: A cognitive perspective. *Applied Cognitive Psychology, 8*, 281–338.

Livingston, R. B. (1967). Brain circuitry relating to complex behavior. In G. C. Quarton, T. Melnechuck, & F. O. Schmitt (Eds.), *The neurosciences: A study program* (pp. 499–514). New York: Rockefeller University Press.

Loftus, E. F., & Burns, T. E. (1982). Mental shock can produce retrograde amnesia. *Memory & Cognition, 10*, 318–323.

Loftus, E. F., & Ketcham, K. (1994). *The myth of repressed memory: False memories and allegations of sexual abuse.* New York: St. Martin's Press.

Loftus, E. F., Loftus, G. R., & Messo, J. (1987). Some facts about "weapon focus." *Law and Human Behavior, 11*, 55–62.

Loftus, E. F., & Pickerel, J. (1995). The formation of false memories. *Psychiatric Annals, 25*, 720–724.

Loftus, E. F., Polonsky, S., & Fullilove, M. T. (1994). Memories of childhood sexual abuse: Remembering and repressing. *Psychology of Women Quarterly, 18*, 67–84.

Mazzoni, G., & Loftus, E. F. (1998). Dream interpretation can change beliefs about the past. *Psychotherapy, 35*, 177–187.

McClelland, J. (1995). Constructive memory and memory distortions: A parallel-distributed processing approach. In D. L. Schacter (Ed.), *Memory distortions* (pp. 69–90). Cambridge, MA: Harvard University Press.

McClelland, J. L., McNaughton, B. L., & O'Reilly, R. C. (1995). Why there are complimentary learning systems in the hippocampus and neocortex: Insights from the successes and failures of connectionist models of learning and memory. *Psychological Review, 3*, 419–457.

McCloskey, M., Wible, C. G., & Cohen, N. J. (1988). Is there a special flashbulb-memory mechanism? *Journal of Experimental Psychology: General, 117*, 171–181.

Metcalfe, J., & Jacobs, W. J. (1998). Emotional memory: The effects of stress on "cool" and "hot" memory systems. In D. Medin (Ed.), *The psychology of learning and motivation, Volume 38* (pp. 187–222). San Diego: Academic Press.

Nadel, L., & Jacobs, W. J. (1998). Traumatic memory is special. *Current Directions in Psychological Science, 7*, 154–157.

Neisser, U., & Harsch, N. (1992). Phantom flashbulbs: False recollections of hearing the news about Challenger. In E. Winograd & U. Neisser (Eds.), *Affect and accuracy in recall: Studies of "flashbulb memories"* (pp. 9–31). Cambridge: Cambridge University Press.

Neisser, U., Winograd, E., Bergman, E. T., Schreiber, C. A., Palmer, S. E., & Weldon, M. S. (1996). Remembering the earthquake: Direct experience vs hearing the news. *Memory, 4*, 337–357.

Nelson, E. L., & Simpson, P. (1994). First glimpse: An initial examination of subjects who have rejected their recovered visualizations as false memories. *Issues in Child Abuse, 6*, 123–133.

Ofshe, R. J., & Watters, E. (1994). *Making monsters: False memories, psychotherapy, and sexual hysteria.* New York: Charles Schribner's Sons.

Park, J. (1995). *The effect of arousal and retention delay on memory: A meta-analysis.* Unpublished manuscript, Yale University.

Pendergrast, M. (1996). *Victims of memory: Sex abuse accusations and shattered lives* (2nd ed.). Hinesburg, VT: Upper Access.

Persinger, M. A. (1992). Neuropsychological profiles of adults who report "Sudden remembering" of early childhood memories: Implications for claims of sex abuse. *Perceptual and Motor Skills, 75*, 259–266.

Pillemer, D. B. (1984). Flashbulb memories of the assassination attempt on President Reagan. *Cognition, 16*, 63–80.

Polusny, M. A., & Follette, V. M. (1996). Remembering childhood sexual abuse: A national survey of psychologist's clinical practices, beliefs, and personal experiences. *Professional Psychology Research and Practice, 27*, 41–52.

Poole, D. A., Lindsay, D. S., Memon, A., & Bull, R. (1995). Psychotherapy and the recovery of memories of childhood sexual abuse: U.S. and British practitioners beliefs, practices, and experiences. *Journal of Consulting and Clinical Psychology, 63*, 426–437.

Pope, H. G., & Hudson, J. I. (1995). Can memories of childhood sexual abuse be repressed? *Psychological Medicine, 25*, 121–126.

Putnam, W. H. (1979). Hypnosis and distortions in eyewitness memory. *International Journal of Clinical and Experimental Hypnosis, 28*, 426–437.

Pynoos, R. S., & Nader, K. (1989). Children's memory and proximity to violence. *Journal of the American Academy of Child and Adolescent Psychiatry, 28*, 236–241.

Ramachandran, V. S. (1995). Anosognosia in parietal lobe syndrome. *Consciousness and Cognition, 4*, 22–51.

Roe, C. M., & Schwartz, M. F. (1996). Characteristics of previously forgotten memories of sexual abuse: A descriptive study. *Journal of Psychiatry and Law, 24*(2), 189–206.

Schacter, D. L. (1996). *Searching for memory.* New York: Basic Books.

Schooler, J. W. (1994). Seeking the core: The issues and evidence surrounding recovered accounts of sexual trauma. *Consciousness and Cognition, 3,* 452–469.

Schooler, J. W. (in press). Discovered memories and the "delayed discovery doctrine": A cognitive case based analysis. In S. Taub (Ed.), *Recovered memories of child sexual abuse: Psychological, legal, and social perspectives on a twentieth century controversy.* Springfield, IL: Charles C. Thomas.

Schooler, J. W., Ambadar, Z., & Bendiksen, M. A. (1997). A cognitive corroborative case study approach for investigating discovered memories of sexual abuse. In J. D. Read & D. S. Lindsay (Eds.), *Recollections of trauma: Scientific research and clinical practice* (pp. 379–388). New York: Plenum.

Schooler, J. W., Bendiksen, M. A., & Ambadar, Z. (1997). Taking the middle line: Can we accommodate both fabricated and recovered memories of sexual abuse? In M. Conway (Ed.), *False and recovered memories* (pp. 251–292). Oxford: Oxford University Press.

Shobe, K. K., & Kihlstrom, J. F. (1997). Is traumatic memory special? *Current Directions in Psychological Science, 6,* 70–74.

Spiegel, D., & Cardena, E. (1991). Disintegrated experience: The dissociative disorders revisited. *Journal of Abnormal Psychology, 100,* 366–378.

Terr, L. C. (1988). What happens to early memories of trauma? A study of twenty children under age five at the time of documented traumatic events. *Journal of the American Academy of Psychiatry, 27,* 96–194.

Tromp, A., Koss, M., Figueredo, A., & Tharan, M. (1995). Are rape memories different? A comparison of rape, other unpleasant, and pleasant memories among employed women. *Journal of Traumatic Stress, 8,* 607–627.

Vaillant, G. (1992). *Ego mechanisms of defense: A guide for clinicians and researchers.* Washington, DC: American Psychiatric Press.

van der Kolk, B. A. (1994). The body keeps score: Memory and the evolving psychobiology of post traumatic stress. *Harvard Review of Psychiatry, 1,* 253–265.

van der Kolk, B. A., & Fisler, R. (1995). Dissociation and the fragmentary nature of traumatic memories: Overview and exploratory study. *Journal of Traumatic Stress, 8,* 505–525.

van der Kolk, B. A., & van der Hart, O. (1991). The intrusive past: The flexibility of memory and the engraving of trauma. *American Imago, 48,* 425–454.

Wagenaar, W. A., & Groeneweg, J. (1990). The memory of concentration camp survivors. *Applied Cognitive Psychology, 4,* 77–87.

Wegner, D. M., & Gold, D. B. (1995). Fanning old flames: Emotional and cognitive effects of suppressing thoughts of a past relationship. *Journal of Personality and Social Psychology, 68,* 782–792.

Widom, C. S., & Morris, S. (1997). Accuracy of adult recollections of childhood victimization: Part II. Childhood sexual abuse. *Psychological Assessment, 9,* 34–46.

Williams, L. M. (1994). Recall of childhood trauma: A prospective study of women's memories of child sexual abuse. *Journal of Consulting and Clinical Psychology, 62,* 1167–1176.

Williams, L. M. (1995). Recovered memories of abuse in women with documented child sexual victimization histories. *Journal of Traumatic Stress, 8,* 649–673.

Yuille, J. C., & Cutshall, J. L. (1986). A case study of eyewitness memory of a crime. *Journal of Applied Psychology, 71,* 291–301.

MEMORY IN DECLINE

25

Memory Changes in Healthy Older Adults

DAVID A. BALOTA, PATRICK O. DOLAN, & JANET M. DUCHEK

The present chapter provides a review of the literature addressing changes in memory performance in older adults (often retired individuals with an age between 60 and 80 years), compared to younger adults (often college students around age 20). While it is well established that memory performance declines in older adults (e.g., Kausler, 1994; Ryan, 1992), it is now clear that not all aspects of memory are impaired (e.g., Balota & Duchek, 1988; Burke & Light, 1981; Craik, 1983; Schacter, Kihlstrom, Kaszniak, & Valdiserri, 1993; Shimamura, 1989). Dissociations across age groups with respect to impairments in different memory types or processes have provided (1) insights into the influence of aging on neuropsychological underpinnings of memory, and (2) leverage for memory theorists to develop a better understanding of normal memory functioning.

This chapter involves three sections: First, a summary of selected empirical findings documenting the nature of age-related changes across a wide set of memory tasks is provided. Although it is beyond the scope of the present chapter to review the rich literature concerning memory and aging, this section will acquaint the reader with examples of paradigms used to study distinct aspects of memory and the conclusions that researchers have reached regarding the influence of age on each memory type or process. Second is a discussion of

the major theoretical perspectives that have been proposed as explanatory constructs for these age-related memory deficits. Finally, an overview of recent developments that shed some light on understanding the possible neurological underpinnings of aging on memory functioning is provided.

Review of Empirical Findings

At the outset, it is useful to make a distinction between (1) memories that are revealed through intentional retrieval of a previous experience, and (2) memories that are manifested in subsequent behavior without the direct recollection of the previous event. The former is declarative (explicit) memory and is exemplified by the question "What did you have for dinner last night?" while the latter, less well-defined category, is called nondeclarative (procedural or implicit) memory (e.g., Squire, 1986), and might be reflected in one's memory for riding a bicycle. Specifically, although it may be difficult to explicitly describe how to ride a bicycle, your nondeclarative memory for the procedure is easily demonstrated by success in riding a bicycle.

Declarative Memory

Within declarative memory, one can distinguish between memories that are episodic in nature—pertaining to personally experienced events in a particular setting at a particular time (e.g., what you had for dinner last night)—and semantic memories that reflect our general knowledge of facts, words, and their meaning (e.g., who is the author of *The Adventures of Huckleberry Finn*). In general, the evidence regarding episodic and semantic memory indicates that older adults have a much larger disruption in episodic memory tasks than in semantic memory tasks.

Episodic Memory

One useful way of organizing the episodic memory literature is to use the information-processing framework (e.g., Atkinson & Shiffrin, 1968) in which stimuli are transformed into qualitatively distinct memory representations. Within this framework, one can distinguish among three major memory stores: sensory, short term, and long term.

Sensory Memory. Sensory memory systems hold information in a relatively raw (uninterpreted) format for brief periods of time. Visual/iconic (Sperling, 1960), auditory/echoic (Crowder, 1976), and tactile (Watkins & Watkins, 1974) sensory stores have been identified experimentally. The research addressing sensory memory in young and older adults indicates that there is relatively little age-related change in these systems. For example, Kline and Orme-Rogers (1978) presented participants with two fragments that were not meaningful by themselves but when fused together in the same spatial location would produce a visual word. Visual persistence of the first stimulus fragment after its offset allows the participant to combine it with the second stimulus fragment to identify the complete word. Kline and Orme-Rogers found that older adults were better at identifying the fused word with increased interstimulus intervals, suggesting that older adults' visual sensory store was slightly longer than younger adults' (also see Di Lollo, Arnett, & Kruk, 1982; Gilmore, Allan, & Royer, 1986). Parkinson and Perry (1980) found similar evidence of age invariance in the auditory analogue called echoic memory.

Primary/Short-Term Memory. Primary memory is reflected in our ability to maintain small amounts of information in immediate awareness for a short period of time—for example,

maintaining a phone number until it is dialed. In most primary memory tasks, age differences again appear to be relatively small. Consider the results from the often-used Brown-Peterson task. Participants are required to remember just three letters for a brief period of time. However, instead of allowing rehearsal during the retention interval, one ensures that attention is directed toward a secondary task (e.g., subtracting by 3s from a 3-digit number). Puckett and Stockburger (1988) found similar levels of memory for young and older adults across the delays. This suggests not only equivalent primary memory capacity but also comparable rates of forgetting (see Craik, 1977; Zacks, Hasher, & Li, 1998, for reviews).

Secondary/Long-Term Memory. It is well established that older adults, relative to younger adults, have more difficulty with episodic secondary memory tasks such as answering the question "What did you have for dinner last night?" These deficits might occur at three distinct stages of episodic secondary memory: encoding (the initial storage of the memory), retention (the maintenance of the memory across time), and retrieval (the utilization of the stored memory). Regarding *encoding*, it appears that even when instructions encourage the formation of rich, elaborate memory traces, older adults are less likely to do so (Craik & Byrd, 1982; Rabinowitz & Ackerman, 1982; see also Craik & Jennings, 1992; and Kausler, 1991, for reviews). Turning to *retention*, which is inherently more difficult to isolate because of differences in initial encoding, results suggest that when initial encoding is equated there is relatively little difference between older and younger adults in rate of forgetting across retention intervals (see Giambra & Arenberg, 1993; Park, Royal, Dudley, & Morrell, 1988; Rybarczyk, Hart, & Harkins, 1987). Finally, turning to *retrieval*, there is clear evidence of age-related changes. In particular, there is considerable evidence that age differences in memory performance diminish when retrieval is facilitated by providing additional cues at the time of the memory test. For example, largest age differences are found in tests of free-recall, diminished age differences in cued-recall, and often times little or no age differences in tests of recognition (Craik & McDowd, 1987, Rabinowitz, 1984; Smith, 1977).

Encoding Specificity. According to Tulving and Thomson's (1973) encoding specificity principle, it is important to consider the degree of match between the encoding and the retrieval operations instead of simply emphasizing either encoding or retrieval processes. This principle was explored in a study by Duchek (1984), who crossed encoding context (semantic vs. rhyme) with retrieval context (semantic vs. rhyme). The results of this study indicated that, compared to younger adults, older adults were especially poor in the conditions in which there was a match between the semantic encoding and semantic retrieval conditions. Duchek argued that the distinctiveness of the semantic encoding and retrieval operations appears to be decreased in older adults compared to younger adults (also see Craik & Byrd, 1982).

Memory for Context. Another way to consider the age deficits in secondary episodic memory is the memory of particular details or the context of prior events. Interestingly, even under conditions in which young and older adults are equated on memory for target items, older adults are poorer at recalling specific details of what they had studied. For example, Schacter, Kaszniak, Kihlstrom, and Valdiserri (1991) had older and younger adults study fictitious facts (e.g., "Bob Hope's father was a fireman") presented by either a male or female experimenter. While overall memory for the facts was similar, older adults were impaired in remembering the gender of the experimenter who presented the facts. This work falls under the important distinction between source and item memory (Johnson, Hashtroudi, & Lindsay, 1993). Specifically, one can sometimes remember an event, but cannot remember when or where it was initially experienced. There is accumulating evidence indicating that older adults have specific deficits in source information (see Hashtroudi, Johnson, & Chrosniak, 1990; Spencer & Raz, 1995, for a recent meta-analysis). We will return to the topic of source deficits in the final section of the present chapter.

Semantic Knowledge. Who wrote *The Adventures of Huckleberry Finn?* Do dogs have wings? Is *jrunsk* an English word? The fact that one can answer such questions easily and quickly suggests that we have stored a large amount of information that is well organized for rapid retrieval. One approach to understanding semantic memory is to assume our knowledge is stored as an organized network of words or concepts ("nodes") connected to other related concepts via associative/semantic pathways. When a node is "activated" (by exposure to the word or concept, or by attention directed to it), activation spreads from one activated node to other related nodes in the network, making them more accessible for subsequent processing. This mechanism of spreading activation is thought to mediate many aspects of both memory and higher order cognition (Anderson, 1983).

The principal task used to measure semantic spreading activation is the semantic priming paradigm. In this task, two stimuli are presented sequentially and the relation between them (prime and target) is manipulated. Participants are faster and more accurate to make a response (such as name the word aloud) if the second word (*nurse*) is semantically related to the first word (*doctor*), compared to an unrelated baseline (*book*). To the extent that priming occurs, researchers can infer the degree of spreading activation between nodes and the relative integrity of the underlying semantic network. The majority of these studies have found either older adults producing slightly larger semantic priming effects than younger adults or very similar semantic priming effects (see Laver & Burke, 1993, for a review). For example, Balota and Duchek (1988; see also 1989, 1991) manipulated the strength of association (strong: *animal-dog* vs. weak: *animal-swan*) and the delay (stimulus onset asynchrony, or SOA, ranging from 200 msec to 800 msec) between the prime and target words. For both younger and older adults, priming was greater for strong associates, and greater with longer SOAs. Similar findings have been reported in studies in which one measures priming among nodes that are actually instantiated within the experiment itself (e.g., Balota & Duchek, 1989; Howard, Heisey, & Shaw, 1986; Rabinowitz, 1986; Spieler & Balota, 1996). Thus, as long as one measures the automatic (nonattentional) spread of activation within the semantic memory network, this component appears to be relatively intact in older adults.

In contrast to the automatic activation of representations in memory, there are breakdowns in some semantic memory tasks that demand more attention. For example, if the participant is required to maintain the prime information for an extended period of time, older adults do produce some deficits in the semantic priming task (e.g., Balota, Black, & Cheney, 1992; see, however, Burke, White, &

Diaz, 1987). In addition, the most common memory complaint of older adults is the tip-of-the-tongue (TOT) experience in which one is trying to explicitly recall the name of a person or a low-frequency word that fits the appropriate context (Sunderland, Watts, Baddeley, & Harris, 1986). The TOT experience involves an explicit feeling of knowing the correct word, but a frustrating inability to actually produce it from memory. This problem in name and word retrieval in older adults has been demonstrated in both diary studies of memory problems and experimental studies (e.g., Burke, MacKay, Worthley, & Wade, 1991). These results may reflect a specific deficit in accessing the phonological codes necessary to retrieve a word from activated semantic/lexical codes (see Burke et al., 1991, for further discussion).

Prospective Memory.   Memory most typically involves retrieving something that has been previously stored. Recent research has focused on a different type of memory called *prospective memory*, wherein one must remember to perform some action in the future—for example, remembering to take a dose of medicine at scheduled intervals. Researchers have distinguished between prospective tasks that are time based (taking medicine every 8 hours) and those that are event based (relaying a message to a friend next time you see her; Einstein & McDaniel, 1990). Time-based tasks require more self-initiated retrieval processes and, perhaps not surprisingly (given the findings reviewed above), reveal the largest age-related deficits (see Anderson & Craik, this volume, chapter 26).

Procedural/Nondeclarative Memory

Procedural/nondeclarative memory is a broad category reflecting a number of phenomena that clearly reflect the memory of prior events or episodes, however, this type of memory typically does not require explicit recollection of the past. Some of the most intriguing evidence supporting the distinction between declarative and nondeclarative (or explicit and implicit) memories arose initially from studies of amnesics. While amnesics, by definition, perform poorly on declarative memory tasks such as free recall or recognition, they do relatively well on indirect, nondeclarative mem-

ory tasks. For example, having been exposed to the word *green*, they will be more likely to respond "green" when later asked to complete the word fragment g _ e __, even though *great* is a more common word.

Interestingly, several studies have shown nonsignificant age differences in a variety of nondeclarative repetition priming tasks such as word fragment completion (e.g., Dick, Kean, & Sands, 1989; Light, Singh, & Capps, 1986), speeded lexical decision (Balota & Ferraro, 1996), speeded naming (Spieler & Balota, 1966) and category exemplar generation (Light & Albertson, 1986). In all of these studies, the response to the stimulus is not identical across exposures to the stimulus, and so "memory" is not simply a reflection of stimulus-response practice effects. In addition to these procedural tasks, there are studies in which the subject is required to implicitly acquire a new pattern of stimulus-response mappings (e.g., acquiring a pattern of 10 randomly ordered keypresses). The results from these studies also indicate that there is relatively little age-related change in this type of implicit learning (e.g., Howard & Howard, 1992, 1997; Moscovitch, Winocur, & McLachlan, 1986). One should acknowledge that some age-related changes have been observed in certain aspects of procedural/nondeclarative memory tasks (e.g., Curran, 1997; Howard, 1988; Howard & Howard, 1997; Rose, Yesavage, Hill, & Bower, 1986). However, the general conclusion from this area of research is that studies of procedural/nondeclarative memory tasks indicate that if one observes age-related changes, these are relatively small compared to declarative tasks such as recall and recognition performance (see LaVoie & Light, 1994, for a summary).

Summary of Empirical Findings

The distinctions among types of memory systems and processes have proved valuable to our understanding of the effects of age on memory performance. It is clear that the largest memory deficits appear in the storage of long-term episodic memories, and that memories that place minimal demand on attention (such as sensory memory tasks, implicit memory tasks, and semantic priming tasks) produce relatively little age-related change in performance.

Aging and Memory: Theoretical Perspectives

We will now briefly review the major theoretical accounts of the observed age-related changes in memory performance. Each of these perspectives provides a different framework for organizing the extant literature and a theoretical explanation for the memory deficits by positing some underlying mechanism that may be impaired with aging.

Speed of Processing

According to a speed of processing perspective, aging is accompanied by a general slowing in cognitive processing that appears to include all components of processing (e.g., Birren, Woods, & Williams, 1980; Cerella, 1985). Evidence for this approach is demonstrated by predicting mean response times of older adults from the mean response times from younger adults across a set of conditions within tasks and also across tasks (Brinley, 1965). Simple linear functions often account for over 90% of the age-related variance across a wide variety of measures.

Recent versions of the processing speed perspective have further explicated the relationship between reduced processing speed and age-related memory decrements. In particular, Salthouse (1996a) has argued via large-scale psychometric studies and path analyses that processing speed serves as a mediator between age and various cognitive functions, such as memory functioning. For example, in one study, Salthouse (1996b) reported that age was related to a general speed factor (derived from a number of processing speed measures) and age was related to memory performance; however, age was only weakly related to memory performance after statistically controlling for the effect of processing speed. Likewise, the results of path analyses indicated that age is only indirectly related to memory performance and is mediated by speed of processing.

Thus, according to this framework, age differences in memory do not reflect changes in memory processing per se, but instead merely reflect age differences in the speed of processing. Although there is little doubt that older adults process information at a slower rate than younger adults, and this will be a substantial component to any theoretical account of age-related changes in cognitive performance, one potential concern with the general slowing perspective is that it does not provide a straightforward account in the patterns of age-related deficits, and lack thereof, in different components of memory performance reviewed above.

Reduced Processing Resources

The notion of reduced processing resources (also sometimes referred to as attentional capacity) represents a slightly different viewpoint from the speed of processing framework. Attentional capacity refers to the limited pool of cognitive resources available for allocation for any given cognitive task (Kahneman, 1973). A difficult cognitive task requires more attentional capacity than a simple cognitive task. It has been suggested that reduced attentional resources impair older adults' ability to engage in more cognitive demanding strategies, such as deep, elaborate encoding operations that facilitate later memory retrieval (e.g., Craik & Byrd, 1982; Salthouse, 1982). In support of this notion, Rabinowitz, Craik, and Ackerman (1982) found that older adults are less likely to encode specific contextual detail about to-be-remembered items. Instead, older adults encode information in a more general, automatic manner that typically leads to poorer retrieval cues and subsequent performance (also see Hashtroudi et al., 1990). Thus, a reduction in attentional capacity may lead to a more general encoding strategy and poorer memory performance.

The reduced attentional capacity view has been criticized as being too vague and without any clear specification and elaboration of the core construct of attentional capacity (e.g., see Salthouse, 1988). More recent attempts examining age differences in the effect of dividing attention at encoding and retrieval may provide a clearer understanding of the role of attentional control and resources in memory performance. For example, a recent study by Anderson, Craik, and Naveh-Benjamin (1998) suggests that there are no age differences in the cost of dividing attention at encoding or at retrieval on actual memory performance; instead, it is the *engagement* of encoding and retrieval operations that demands more attentional resources for older adults. Future work along these lines has considerable potential to better understand the nature of capacity reductions in older adults.

Reduced Working Memory

Similar to the attentional capacity viewpoint, the notion of reduced working memory capacity asserts that both the storage capacity and manipulation of information in working memory are limited with increasing age. According to Baddeley's (1986) model, working memory may be viewed as involving a verbal loop and visual scratchpad that maintain phonological and visual information in an active state across time. Baddeley also argues that there is an executive control system that coordinates information flow across these and other memory systems (e.g., semantic and long-term) to accomplish the goals of a given task. In support of this notion, Salthouse, Mitchell, Skovronek, and Babcock (1989) have demonstrated that older adults' performance declines as a function of the increasing complexity of mental operations involved across various tasks that tap working memory (e.g., verbal reasoning, spatial visualization). There is ample evidence of age differences across a number of working memory tasks (e.g., see Craik & Jennings, 1992). Moreover, this limitation in working memory capacity can result in poorer retention of integrated information, such as found in text comprehension where working memory demands are relatively high (e.g., Cohen, 1979; Light & Albertson, 1988; Stine, 1990). Similar to the attentional capacity view, the reduced working memory capacity notion has been criticized for its lack of specification and clarity (e.g., Hasher & Zacks, 1988). In fact, it is difficult to disentangle reduced working memory capacity from attentional capacity because most conceptualizations of working memory involve some notion of attentional resources.

Automatic vs. Controlled Processing

Based upon an empirical review of the aging and memory literature, it is clear that some aspects of memory performance decline with increasing age (e.g., episodic recall), while other aspects of performance are spared with age (e.g., semantic/implicit priming). One approach to better understanding this pattern is to rely on a distinction between automatic and attention demanding processes (see Hasher &

Zacks, 1979). According to this framework, the automatic processing of information requires little attentional capacity, is independent of conscious control, and occurs without intentional effort. Thus automatic processing does not interfere with other ongoing cognitive activities and does not benefit from practice. Hasher and Zacks further argued that certain characteristics of information were encoding automatically, such as temporal parameters, spatial location, event frequency, and word meaning. Most important for the present discussion, automatic processes are assumed to be immune to the effects of increasing age.

On the other hand, the effortful processing of information places a drain on attentional capacity, occurs under conscious control, and is executed intentionally. Thus, effortful processing interferes with ongoing cognitive activity and can benefit from practice. Although some attributes of the stimulus can be encoded in memory automatically, others require the intentional, effortful processing that is involved in more elaborate encoding and rehearsal strategies. Given that effortful processing requires attentional capacity and attentional capacity is reduced with age, it is assumed that memory tasks that involve effortful processing will be detrimentally affected by age (e.g., free recall).

While the automatic vs. effortful processing distinction has proved to be a useful way of viewing memory performance in older adults, the evidence for some of the proposed distinctions has been mixed. For example, there have been reports of age-related deficits in attributes that were assumed to be more automatic in nature, such as memory for spatial information (e.g., Light & Zelinski, 1983; Naveh-Benjamin, 1987, 1988), temporal information (e.g., Naveh-Benjamin, 1990), and event frequency (e.g., Kausler, Lichty, & Hakami, 1984; Kausler, Salthouse, & Saults, 1987). Thus, these results suggest that the encoding of such information is not impervious to the effects of aging.

Contextual/Environmental Support

The contextual/environmental support framework represents a more "functional" approach to age-related memory decline. Craik (1986) argued that the extent to which age differences will exist depends upon the specific nature of the task demands. Specifically, if the demands of the task are more "stimulus driven" and provide environmental support (i.e., context) for retrieval, then age-related memory differences will be minimized. However, if the task does not provide retrieval support and thus demands more self-initiated retrieval processes, then age-related differences will be large. This functional view of age-related memory deficits explains why age differences are larger in episodic free-recall tasks than cued-recall or recognition tasks. In free recall, there is minimal external context to guide retrieval. Both cued-recall and recognition tasks provide such context. In terms of semantic memory, age differences should not exist in priming tasks given that the context (i.e., the prime) guides the activation of the target word. Likewise, implicit memory task performance may be age independent because such tasks do not require a deliberate, self-initiated search of memory, as do explicit tasks. Of course, one may ask here what function contextual support serves within this framework. The notion is that contextual support serves to help guide memory processing. Because (as noted below) older adults have been viewed as being more susceptible to interference from irrelevant stimulation, contextual support may be especially important in keeping them "on track" during memory tasks, thereby producing the age-specific boost in memory performance.

Inhibition

Recently, there has been interest in the notion that age-related deficits in cognitive performance may arise from a decreased efficiency in the ability to inhibit partially active representations (e.g., Duchek, Balota, & Ferraro, 1995; Hamm & Hasher, 1992; Hasher, Stoltzfus, Zacks, & Rypma, 1991; Hartman & Hasher, 1991; Spieler, Balota, & Faust, 1996). The idea is that an efficient processing system must (1) activate information that is relevant to the task at hand, and (2) inhibit information that may be partially activated but irrelevant to the current task demands. This work has in large part been motivated by the theoretical framework of age differences in working memory and comprehension developed by Hasher and Zacks (1988).

According to this framework, inhibitory mechanisms serve to limit information entering working memory that is along the "goal path" of comprehension. Of course, one can assume that this attentional gating will not always be perfect and thus some "nongoal path" information may enter working memory. When this occurs, the inhibitory mechanisms serve to dampen the activation of nongoal path ideas. Thus inhibition serves two primary roles: (1) allowing only certain information to enter working memory, and (2) suppressing activation of irrelevant information in working memory.

Hasher and Zacks (1988) further contended that older adults are more distracted by irrelevant information (e.g., personal memories, environmental detail) and this reduced inhibitory control allows more "nongoal path" ideas to enter working memory and remain activated, thereby producing more difficulty in memory tasks in older adults. As a consequence, older adults tend to compensate by more heavily relying on information that is easily accessible from memory and relying on environmental cues rather than searching memory. It is important to note that this inhibitory framework moves beyond a simple reduced-capacity view of age-related memory deficits by emphasizing the contents rather than the capacity of working memory.

As noted above, there is some intriguing support for the notion that there may be age differences in the content of working memory owing to deficient inhibitory processes. Hartman and Hasher (1991) found that older adults were more likely to have unexpected endings of sentences still available in working memory after the information was disconfirmed and determined to be irrelevant. Likewise, in a comprehension task, Hamm and Hasher (1992) found that older adults were more likely to have access to competing interpretations of inferences after the correct interpretation had been confirmed. Thus, deficient inhibitory control may underlie memory decrements in old age.

It is unlikely that the cognitive architecture has only one inhibitory system, but rather involves a set of inhibitory systems. For example, Kramer, Humphrey, Larish, Logan, and Strayer (1994) have argued that inhibitory tasks that rely primarily on ventral identity-based information produce breakdowns in older adults, whereas inhibitory tasks that primarily rely on dorsal spatial processes do not produce breakdowns (also see Connelly & Hasher, 1993). Thus, an important question for future research will be to specify under what conditions one finds disproportionate age-related inhibitory breakdowns.

Summary of
Theoretical Perspectives

All of the theoretical frameworks provide unique perspectives on age-related changes in memory functioning. It also appears to be the case that each framework has both its advantages and its disadvantages. On the basis of parsimony, one might argue that the reduced speed of processing explanation for age-related deficits in memory performance is appealing. However, because of the lack of specification of component cognitive operations in a given task, and the complexity of the empirical evidence concerning age similarities and differences across memory tasks, the general slowing framework may seem a bit limited from a process-oriented cognitive perspective. As previously mentioned, the reduced processing capacity explanations have been deemed too general and vague. Also, the notion of age invariance in the automatic processing (as opposed to attention-demanding processing) of certain attributes (i.e., spatial, temporal, frequency) has not been consistently supported in the literature. In terms of contextual/environmental support, one might argue that this perspective does not really posit a theoretical construct that serves as an underlying mechanism that changes with age. Instead, this perspective merely provides a functional framework relating task and processing demands. Finally, the use of deficient inhibition as an explanatory construct for age-related cognitive deficits also has been criticized for lacking theoretical specification and an empirical definition of valid and reliable measures of inhibition (e.g. Burke, 1997; McDowd, 1997).

Although there are limitations to all the theoretical perspectives presented, each has been important in providing a framework for organizing the existing literature, stimulating research in the area, and provoking some of the more recent developments on aging and memory discussed in the next section. As we shall see, it is possible that the neurophysiological changes with age may help provide some constraints on certain theoretical accounts.

Aging and Memory:
Neuropsychological
Underpinnings

Healthy aging is an intriguing area because there is accumulating evidence regarding the aging of distinct neural substrates. For example, West (1996) has provided a review of the aging literature, and has suggested that both neurophysiological and neuropsychological evidence indicates that the frontal lobes are especially sensitive to increased aging. Interestingly, frontal areas have been tied to attention, working memory, and inhibitory control (three of the major theoretical perspectives on aging reviewed in the previous section). If indeed there are distinct patterns of aging in different cortical subsystems, then one might use aging as an assay to better understand neurological substrates of distinct components of memory.

Medial Temporal and
Frontal Contributions
to Memory

Ever since the groundbreaking study of H.M., an unfortunate epileptic who had his hippocampus removed to eliminate seizures, researchers have argued that declarative memory performance is heavily tied to the functioning of the hippocampal and surrounding parahippocampal areas—that is, the medial temporal complex. Clearly, removal of these areas has been shown to produce profound disruption in declarative memory across individuals and across species (see Cohen & Eichenbaum, 1993, for a review).

Given that the medial temporal area clearly plays a role in episodic memory, one might ask what specific function this area performs. Moscovitch and Winocur (1995) suggest that medial temporal areas are at the core of an associative system that relatively automatically binds together what is consciously apprehended (see also Cohen & Eichenbaum, 1993; Kroll, Knight, Metcalfe, Wolf, & Tulving, 1996). The notion is that at any point in time a number of distinct neural networks/pathways are activated via both internally generated and externally available stimuli. The medial temporal system has been viewed as binding these distinct patterns in a relatively automatic/modular manner to produce a record of the conscious experience.

If the medial temporal system is so important for declarative memory performance, then why is there the interest in age-related changes in frontal systems? Moscovitch and Winocur, among others (e.g., Buckner, 1996; Shimamura, 1995; Tulving, Kapur, Craik, Moscovitch, & Houle, 1994), have argued that a second frontally mediated system is also quite important in declarative memory performance. This system operates on both the input to the medial temporal system and the output from it. Presumably, the frontal areas provide control over the networks that become activated during encoding and are available during retrieval. In this sense, Moscovitch suggests that the frontal control system can be viewed as a system that works with memory—that is, providing the input and exerting control over the output. Moscovitch and Winocur (1995) have reviewed a series of experimental paradigms that indicate older adults appear to be especially disrupted by aspects of memory tasks that involve frontal structures. In addition, there is now considerable evidence from imaging studies of strong involvement of frontal areas in memory performance (e.g., Buckner, 1996; Wagner et al., 1998). Interestingly, Shimamura (1995) has argued that frontal systems provide an important gating or inhibitory function in declarative memory performance, and it is this inhibitory or gating function that appears to be disrupted in healthy older adults. This of course is quite consistent with the Hasher and Zacks (1988) inhibition model and the automatic attentional framework reviewed in the section on theoretical perspectives. It is also consistent with the general finding that increased attentional demands may play a role in the memory deficit observed in older adults.

Empirical Evidence Regarding Frontal-Type Disruption in Older Adults

If the frontal systems break down in older adults, what are the implications for the distinct types of memory performance? One area that has received considerable recent interest is not memory for information that was presented, but memory for information that is strongly related to what was presented but did not occur—that is, false memories. This work has been nurtured by a compelling experimental demonstration by Roediger and McDermott (1995), who revisited an experimental observation some 40 years earlier by Deese (1959), hereafter called the DRM paradigm. In Roediger and McDermott's first experiment, participants were presented with a list of words that converged on a critical nonpresented target word. For example, consider being presented with the following list of words: *thread, pin, eye, sewing, sharp, point, prick, thimble, haystack, pain, hurt, injection.* The

nonpresented critical target word is *needle* in this list. Roediger and McDermott reported that the likelihood of recalling the nonpresented critical word *needle* was as high as items that were actually presented in the middle of the list.

Interestingly, Norman and Schacter (1997); Tun, Wingfield, Rosen, and Blanchard (1998); and Balota et al. (1999) have recently reported evidence that healthy older adults appear to be more susceptible to false memories than healthy young adults. Norman and Schacter (1997) and Balota et al. (1999) have suggested that the increased false memories in the DRM paradigm are quite consistent with age-related decreased efficiency of frontal lobe functioning. In support of this possibility they cite Schacter, Reiman et al. (1996), who found evidence in a neural imaging study that there was increased activation in regions of prefrontal cortex when critical nonpresented lures were presented compared to the presentation of studied words. Norman and Schacter suggested that this pattern may reflect the frontal involvement in "resisting" or opposing illusory memory for the critical lures. In addition, Schacter, Curran, Galluccio, Milberg, and Bates (1996) have recently reported evidence that an individual with a lesion in the right frontal lobe produced heightened false memories. Specifically, this individual was more likely to false alarm to information that was thematically related to the earlier studied information. Thus, it appears that the increased susceptibility to false memories in older adults may be related to age-related changes in frontal functioning.

As noted earlier, there are also clear age-related differences in source memory (e.g., Brown, Jones, & Davis, 1995; Dywan & Jacoby, 1990; McIntyre & Craik, 1987; Hashtroudi, Johnson, Vnek, & Ferguson, 1994; Shimamura & Jurica, 1994). Interestingly, amnesic patients with frontal lesions also exhibit impaired source memory across a variety of tasks (e.g., Janowsky, Shimamura, & Squire, 1989; Shimamura, 1995; Shimamura, Janowsky, & Squire, 1990), although it is important to note that these individuals also typically exhibit item memory deficits. However, Schacter, Harbluk, and McLachlan (1984) found source deficits in amnesics with focal frontal lesions even when item memory was equated with control participants' performance. Furthermore, the extent of the source deficit was related to frontal dysfunction as measured by neuropsychological tests such as word fluency and Wisconsin Card Sorting Task, and not merely to the severity of the amnesia. Thus, the neuropsychological evidence seems to indicate that source monitoring is related to the integrity of frontal structures.

Glisky, Polster, and Routhieaux (1995) reported a double dissociation in older adults between frontal vs. medial temporal functioning and item and source memory performance in healthy young and older adults. Specifically, when older participants were divided into high vs. low frontal groups based on neuropsychological test performance, the high frontal group exhibited better source memory performance. On the other hand, when participants were divided into high vs. low medial temporal groups based on neuropsychological measures, the high medial temporal group exhibited better item memory performance (also see Craik, Morris, Morris, & Loewen, 1990; McDaniel, Glisky, Rubin, Guynn, & Routhieaux, 1999; Parkin, Walter, & Hunkin, 1995).

There is also evidence of an age-dissociation in some types of nondeclarative memory tasks that may involve frontal-mediated processes. As noted earlier, although older adults typically do not exhibit an age-related deficit on such tasks, there are some examples in the literature of such a deficit. Winocur, Moscovitch, and Stuss (1996) recently found a dissociation between word fragment completion (the test item is a sample of letters of an earlier presented word—e.g., *soldier*; _ o _ _ i _ r) and word-stem completion (the test item is the first few letters of an earlier presented word, e.g., *s o l _ _ _ _*). The interesting findings in this study were (1) older adults showed more of a deficit in word-stem priming than in fragment completion priming; and (2) correlations with neuropsychological tests indicated that word-stem completion was correlated with frontal measures, but not with medial temporal measures. Thus, these results suggest that one can find frontal involvement even in a nondeclarative component of memory and that it is this component that appears to show age-related change.

In sum, there appears to be converging evidence that older adults have particular deficits in frontal-type components of memory. Of course, the current descriptions have been relatively vague with respect to what the frontal areas actually do. One possibility is that the frontal areas are particularly important for maintaining representations that modulate the activated processing pathways associated with a given task. The notion is that when con-

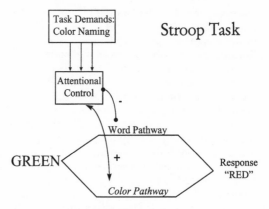

Figure 25.1 An attentional control framework for the Stroop color naming task.

fronted with a task, the participant must activate relevant processing pathways and control or inhibit partially activated but irrelevant pathways. For example, in the Stroop color naming task, the individual needs to maintain the task requirements to name the color of the stimulus instead of the word (see figure 25.1). The efficiency of a system in achieving the goals of a task depends on (1) the integrity and maintenance of the task representation across time; (2) the number of competing pathways; (3) the strength of the competing pathways. It is possible that older adults produce larger Stroop effects than younger adults (e.g., Spieler et al., 1996) because of breakdowns in the integrity of the attentional control system that maintains the task requirements across time. As shown in figure 25.2, one can also extend this framework to the false memory

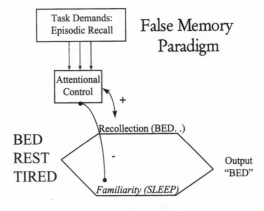

Figure 25.2 An attentional control framework for the false memory paradigm.

paradigm reviewed earlier. For example, older adults may be relatively more likely to recall/recognize highly related nonpresented words in the false memory paradigm (e.g., Norman & Schacter, 1997) because of breakdowns in the attentional control system that should inhibit/control gist related pathways, and should accentuate recollection-based pathways.

In this light, one might argue that at least some of the age-related deficits might reflect a breakdown in the integrity and maintenance of the task representations/goals across time. Frontal areas have clearly been implicated in such processes (e.g., West, 1996, for a review). An intriguing study by Multhaup (1995) provides some support for the emphasis on the integrity of maintaining task representations/goals. In this study, older adults were given additional cues during a memory test concerning sources of possible memory events. Interestingly, when older adults were given these additional cues, there was an elimination of the age-related changes in the false fame effect (i.e., an increased susceptibility to rely on familiarity of a stimulus vs direct recollection). Clearly, future work is necessary to further explore age-related changes in the integrity of task representations and goals in accounting for the observed changes in memory performance.

Conclusions

Although it is clearly the case that the stereotype of older adults showing deficits in memory performance is valid, it is also the case that healthy aging does not produce a breakdown in all memory tasks. This literature has led to a rich and diverse set of theoretical constructs proposed to accommodate the pattern of age-related changes. Given the increased knowledge of the physiological changes in both healthy aging, and in age-related diseases such as Alzheimer's disease, along with the increased sophistication in cognitive analyses in teasing apart aspects of memory performance, we believe that studies of memory and aging will provide a test bed for future theoretical advances in human memory.

References

Anderson, J. R. (1983). A spreading activation theory of memory. *Journal of Verbal Learning and Verbal Behavior, 22*, 261–295.

Anderson, N. D., Craik, F. I. M., & Naveh-Benjamin, M. (1998). The attentional demands of encoding and retrieval in younger and older adults: 1. Evidence from divided attention costs. *Psychology and Aging, 13*, 405–423.

Atkinson, R. C., & Shiffrin, R. M. (1968). Human memory: A proposed system and its control processes. In W. K. Spence & J. T. Spence (Eds.), *The psychology of learning and motivation: Advances in research and theory* (Vol. 1; pp. 89–195). New York: Academic Press.

Baddeley, A. D. (1986). *Working memory*. London: Oxford University Press.

Balota, D. A., Black, S., & Cheney, M. (1992). Automatic and attentional processes in young and old adults: A reevaluation of the two-process model of semantic priming. *Journal of Experimental Psychology: Human Perception & Performance, 18*, 485–502.

Balota, D. A., Cortese, M., Duchek, J. M., Adams, D., Roediger, H. L., McDermott, K. B., & Yerys, B. (1999). Veridical and false memories in healthy older adults and in dementia of the Alzheimer type. *Cognitive Neuropsychology, 16*, in press.

Balota, D. A., & Duchek, J. M. (1988). Age-related differences in lexical access, spreading activation, and simple pronunciation. *Psychology & Aging, 3*, 84–93.

Balota, D. A., & Duchek, J. M. (1989). Spared activation in episodic memory: Further evidence for age independence. *Quarterly Journal of Experimental Psychology, 41A*, 849–876.

Balota, D. A., & Duchek, J. M. (1991). Semantic priming effects, lexical repetition effects, and contextual disambiguation effects in healthy aged individuals and individuals with senile dementia of the Alzheimer type. *Brain & Language, 40*, 181–201.

Balota, D. A., & Ferraro, F. R. (1996). Lexical, sublexical, and implicit memory processes in healthy young and healthy older adults and in individuals with dementia of the Alzheimer type. *Neuropsychology, 10*, 82–95.

Birren, J. E., Woods, A. M., & Williams, M. V. (1980). Behavioral slowing with age: Causes, organization, and consequences. In L. W. Poon (Ed.), *Aging in the 1980's: Psychological issues* (pp. 293–308). Washington, DC: American Psychological Association.

Brinley, J. F. (1965). Cognitive sets, speed and accuracy of performance in the elderly. In

A. T. Welford & J. E. Birren (Eds.), *Behavior, aging and the nervous system* (pp. 114–149). Springfield, IL: Thomas.

Brown, A. S., Jones, E. M., & Davis, T. L. (1995). Age differences in conversational source monitoring. *Psychology & Aging, 10*, 111–122.

Buckner, R. L. (1996). Beyond HERA: Contributions of specific prefrontal brain areas to long-term memory retrieval. *Psychonomic Bulletin & Review, 3*, 149–158.

Burke, D. M. (1997). Language, aging, and inhibitory deficits: Evaluation of a theory. *Journal of Gerontology: Psychological Sciences, 52B*, 254–264.

Burke, D. M., & Light, L. L. (1981). Memory and aging: The role of retrieval processes. *Psychological Bulletin, 90*, 513–546.

Burke, D. M., MacKay, D. G., Worthley, J. S., & Wade, E. (1991). On the tip of the tongue: What causes word finding failures in young and older adults? *Journal of Memory & Language, 30*, 542–579.

Burke, D. M., White, H., & Diaz, D. L. (1987). Semantic priming in young and older adults: Evidence for age constancy in automatic and attentional processes. *Journal of Experimental Psychology: Human Perception & Performance, 13*, 79–88.

Butterfield, E. C., Nelson, T. O., & Peck, V. (1988). Developmental aspects of the feeling of knowing. *Developmental Psychology, 24*, 654–663.

Cerella, J. (1985). Information processing rates in the elderly. *Psychological Bulletin, 98*, 67–83.

Cohen, G. (1979). Language comprehension in old age. *Cognitive Psychology, 11*, 412–429.

Cohen, N. J., & Eichenbaum, H. (1993). *Memory, amnesia, and the hippocampus*. Cambridge, MA: MIT Press.

Connelly, S. L., & Hasher, L. (1993). Aging and the inhibition of spatial location. *Journal of Experimental Psychology: Human Perception and Performance, 19*, 1238–1250.

Craik, F. I. M. (1977). Age differences in human memory. In J. E. Birren & K. W. Schaie (Eds.), *Handbook of the psychology of aging* (pp. 384–420). New York: Van Nostrand Reinhold.

Craik, F. I. M. (1983). On the transfer of information from primary to secondary memory. *Philosophical Transactions of the Royal Society of London, B302*, 341–359.

Craik, F. I. M. (1986). A functional account of age differences in memory. In F. Klix & H. Hagendorf (Eds.), *Human memory and cog-*

nitive capabilities, mechanisms and performances (pp. 409–422). North Holland: Elsevier.

Craik, F. I. M., & Byrd, M. (1982). Aging and cognitive deficits. In F. I. M. Craik & S. Trehub (Eds.), *Aging and cognitive processes* (pp. 191–211). New York: Plenum.

Craik, F. I. M., & Jennings, J. M. (1992). Human memory. In F. I. M. Craik & T. A. Salthouse (Eds.), *The handbook of aging and cognition* (pp. 51–110). Hillsdale, NJ: Erlbaum.

Craik, F. I. M., & McDowd, J. M. (1987). Age differences in recall and recognition. *Journal of Experimental Psychology: Learning, Memory, and Cognition, 13*, 474–479.

Craik, F. I. M., Morris, L. W., Morris, R. G., & Loewen, E. R. (1990). Relations between source amnesia and frontal lobe functioning in older adults. *Psychology & Aging, 5*, 148–151.

Crowder, R. G. (1976). *Principles of learning and memory*. Hillsdale, NJ: Erlbaum.

Curran, T. (1997). Effects of aging on implicit sequence learning: Accounting for sequence structure and explicit knowledge. *Psychological Research, 60*, 24–41.

Deese, J. (1959). On the prediction of occurrence of particular verbal intrusions in immediate recall. *Journal of Experimental Psychology, 58*, 17–22.

Dick, M. A., Kean, M. L., & Sands, D. (1989). Memory for internally generated words in Alzheimers-type dementia. *Brain and Cognition, 9*, 88–108.

Di Lollo, V., Arnett, J. L., & Kruk, R. V. (1982). Age-related changes in the rate of visual information processing. *Journal of Experimental Psychology: Human Perception and Performance, 8*, 225–237.

Duchek, J. M. (1984). Encoding and retrieval differences between young and old: The impact of attentional capacity usage. *Developmental Psychology, 20*, 1173–1180.

Duchek, J. M., Balota, D. A., & Ferraro, F. R. (1995). Inhibitory processes in young and older adults in a picture-word task. *Aging and Cognition, 2*, 156–167.

Dywan, J., & Jacoby, L. L. (1990). Effects of aging on source monitoring: Differences in susceptibility to false fame. *Psychology & Aging, 5*, 379–387.

Einstein, G. O., & McDaniel, M. A. (1990). Normal aging and prospective memory. *Journal of Experimental Psychology: Learning, Memory, & Cognition, 16*, 717–726.

Falk, J. L., & Kline, D. W. (1978). Stimulus persistence in CFF: Overarousal or underactivation? *Experimental Aging Research,* *4,* 109–123.

Giambra, L. M., & Arenberg, D. (1993). Adult age differences in forgetting sentences. *Psychology and Aging, 8,* 451–462.

Gilmore, G. C., Allan, T. M., & Royer, F. L. (1986). Iconic memory and aging. *Journal of Gerontology, 41,* 183–190.

Glisky, E. L., Polster, M. R., & Routhieaux, B. C. (1995). Double dissociation between item and source memory. *Neuropsychology, 9,* 229–235.

Hamm, V. P., & Hasher, L. (1992). Age and the availability of inferences. *Psychology and Aging, 7,* 56–64.

Hartman, M., & Hasher, L. (1991). Aging and suppression: memory for previously irrelevant information. *Psychology and Aging, 6,* 587–594.

Hasher, L., Stoltzfus, E. R., Zacks, R. T., & Rypma, B. (1991). Age and inhibition. *Journal of Experimental Psychology: Learning, Memory, and Cognition, 17,* 163–169.

Hasher, L., & Zacks, R. T. (1979). Automatic and effortful processes in memory. *Journal of Experimental Psychology: General, 108,* 356–388.

Hasher, L., & Zacks, R. T. (1988). Working memory, comprehension, and aging: A review and a new view. In G. H. Bower (Ed.), *The psychology of learning and motivation* (Vol. 22; pp. 193–225). Orlando: Academic Press.

Hashtroudi, S., Johnson, M. K., & Chrosniak, L. D. (1990). Aging and qualitative characteristics of memories for perceived and imagined complex events. *Psychology and Aging, 5,* 119–126.

Hashtroudi, S., Johnson, M. K., Vnek, N., & Ferguson, S. A. (1994). Aging and the effects of affective and factual focus on source monitoring and recall. *Psychology & Aging, 9,* 160–170.

Howard, D. V. (1988). Implicit and explicit assessment of cognitive aging. In M. L. Howe & C. L. Brainerd (Eds.), *Cognitive development in adulthood: Progress in cognitive development research* (pp. 3–37). New York: Springer-Verlag.

Howard, D. V., Heisey, J. G., & Shaw, R. J. (1986). Aging and the priming of newly learned associations. *Developmental Psychology, 22,* 78–85.

Howard, D. V., & Howard, J. H., Jr. (1992). Adult age differences in the rate of learning serial patterns: Evidence from direct and indirect tests. *Psychology and Aging, 7,* 232–241.

Howard, J. H., & Howard, D. V. (1997). Age differences in implicit learning of higher order dependencies in serial patterns. *Psychology and Aging, 12,* 634–656.

Janowsky, J. S., Shimamura, A. P., & Squire, L. R. (1989). Source memory impairment in patients with frontal lobe lesions. *Neuropsychologia, 27,* 1043–1056.

Johnson, M. K., Hashtroudi, S., & Lindsay, D. (1993). Source monitoring. *Psychological Bulletin, 114,* 3–28.

Kahneman, D. (1973). *Attention and effort.* Englewood Cliffs, NJ: Prentice-Hall.

Kausler, D. H. (1991). *Experimental psychology, cognition, and human aging* (2nd ed.). New York: Springer-Verlag.

Kausler, D. H. (1994). Learning and memory in normal aging. San Diego, CA: Academic Press.

Kausler, D. H., Lichty, W., & Hakami, M. K. (1984). Frequency judgments for distractor items in a short-term memory task: Instructional variation and adult age differences. *Journal of Verbal Learning and Verbal Behavior, 23,* 660–668.

Kausler, D. H., Salthouse, T. A., & Saults, J. S. (1987). Frequency-of-occurrence memory over the adult lifespan. *Experimental Aging Research, 13,* 159–161.

Kline, D. W., & Orme-Rogers, C. (1978). Examination of stimulus persistence as the basis for superior visual identification performance among older adults. *Journal of Gerontology, 33,* 76–81.

Kramer, A. F., Humphrey, D. G., Larish, J. F., Logan, G. D., & Strayer, D. L. (1994). Aging and inhibition: Beyond a unitary view of inhibitory processing in attention. *Psychology and Aging, 9,* 491–512.

Kroll, N. E. A., Knight, R. T., Metcalfe, J., Wolf, E. S., & Tulving, E. (1996). Cohesion failures as a source of memory illusions. *Journal of Memory & Language, 35,* 176–196.

Laver, G. D., & Burke, D. M. (1993). Why do semantic priming effects increase in old age? A meta-analysis. *Psychology & Aging, 8,* 34–43.

LaVoie, D., & Light, L. L. (1994). Adult age differences in repetition priming: A meta-analysis. *Psychology & Aging, 9,* 539–553.

Light, L. L., & Albertson, S. (1988). Comprehension of pragmatic implications in young and older adults. In L. L. Light & D. M. Burke (Eds.), *Language, memory, and aging* (pp. 133–153). New York: Cambridge University Press.

Light, L. L., Singh, A., & Capps, J. L. (1986). Dissociation of memory and awareness in young and older adults. *Journal of Clinical and Experimental Neuropsychology, 8*, 62–74.

Light, L. L., & Zelinski, E. M. (1983). Memory for spatial information in young and old adults. *Developmental Psychology, 19*, 901–906.

McDaniel, M. A., Glisky, E. L., Rubin, S. R., Guynn, M. J., & Routhieaux, B. C. (1999). Prospective memory: A neuropsychological study. *Neuropsychology, 13*, 103–110.

McDowd, J. M. (1997). Inhibition in attention and aging. *Journal of Gerontology: Psychological Sciences, 52B*, 265–273.

McIntyre, J. S., & Craik, F. I. M. (1987). Age differences in memory for item and source information. *Canadian Journal of Psychology, 42*, 175–192.

Moscovitch, M., & Winocur, G. (1995). Frontal lobes, memory, and aging. In J. Grafman, K. J. Holyoak, & F. Boller (Eds.), Structure and functions of the human prefrontal cortex. *Annals of the New York Academy of Sciences* (Vol. 769; pp. 119–150). New York: New York Academy of Science.

Moscovitch, M., Winocur, G., & McLachlan, D. R. (1986). Memory as assessed by recognition and reading time in normal and memory impaired people with Alzheimer's disease and other neurological disorders. *Journal of Experimental Psychology: General, 115*, 331–346.

Multhaup, K. S. (1995). Aging, source, and decision criteria: When false errors do and do not occur. *Psychology & Aging, 10*, 492–497.

Naveh-Benjamin, M. (1987). Coding of spatial location information: An automatic process? *Journal of Experimental Psychology: Learning, Memory, and Cognition, 13*, 595–605.

Naveh-Benjamin, M. (1988). Recognition memory of spatial location information: Another failure of automaticity. *Memory and Cognition, 16*, 437–445.

Naveh-Benjamin, M. (1990). Coding of temporal order information: An automatic process? *Journal of Experimental Psychology: Learning, Memory, and Cognition, 16*, 117–126.

Norman, K. A., & Schacter, D. L. (1997). False recognition in younger and older adults: Exploring the characteristics of illusory memories. *Memory & Cognition, 25*, 838–848.

Park, D. C., Royal, D., Dudley, W., & Morrell, R. (1988). Forgetting of pictures over a long retention interval in young and old adults. *Psychology and Aging, 3*, 94–95.

Parkin, A. J., Walter, B. M., & Hunkin, N. M. (1995). Relationships between normal aging, frontal lobe function, and memory for temporal and spatial information. *Neuropsychology, 9*, 304–312.

Parkinson, S. R., & Perry, A. (1980). Aging, digit span, and the stimulus suffix effect. *Journal of Gerontology, 5*, 736–742.

Puckett, J. M., & Stockburger, D. W. (1988). Absence of age-related proneness to short-term retroactive interference in the absence of rehearsal. *Psychology and Aging, 3*, 342–347.

Rabinowitz, J. C. (1984). Aging and recognition failure. *Journal of Gerontology, 39*, 65–71.

Rabinowitz, J. C. (1986). Priming in episodic memory. *Journal of Gerontology, 41*, 204–213.

Rabinowitz, J. C., & Ackerman, B. P. (1982). General encoding of episodic events by elderly adults. In F. I. M. Craik & S. Trehub (Eds.), *Aging and cognitive processes* (pp. 145–154). New York: Plenum.

Rabinowitz, J. C., Craik, F. I. M., & Ackerman, B. P. (1982). A processing resource account of age differences in recall. *Canadian Journal of Psychology, 36*, 325–344.

Roediger, H. L., & McDermott, K. B. (1995). Creating false memories: Remembering words not presented in lists. *Journal of Experimental Psychology: Learning, Memory, & Cognition, 21*, 803–814.

Rose, T. L., Yesavage, J. A., Hill, R. D., & Bower, G. H. (1986). Priming effects and recognition memory in young and elderly adults. *Experimental Aging Research, 12*, 31–37.

Ryan, E. B. (1992). Beliefs about memory changes across the life span. *Journal of Gerontology, 47*, 41–46.

Rybarczyk, B. D., Hart, R. P., & Harkins, S. W. (1987). Age and forgetting rate with pictorial stimuli. *Psychology and Aging, 2*, 404–406.

Salthouse, T. A. (1982). *Adult cognition: An experimental psychology of human aging.* New York: Springer-Verlag.

Salthouse, T. A. (1988). The role of processing resources in cognitive aging. In M. L. Howe & C. J. Brainerd (Eds.), *Cognitive development in adulthood* (pp. 185–239). New York: Springer-Verlag.

Salthouse, T. A. (1996a). The processing-speed theory of adult age differences in cognition. *Psychological Review, 103*, 403–428.

Salthouse, T. A. (1996b). General and specific speed mediation of adult age differences in memory. *Journal of Gerontology: Psychological Sciences, 51B*, P30–P42.

Salthouse, T. A., Mitchell, D. R. D., Skovronek, E., & Babcock, R. L. (1989). Effects of adult age and working memory on reasoning and spatial abilities. *Journal of Experimental Psychology: Learning, Memory, and Cognition, 15,* 507–516.

Schacter, D. L., Curran, T., Galliccio, L., Milberg, W. P., & Bates, J. F. (1996). False recognition and the right frontal lobe. *Neuropsychologia, 34,* 793–808.

Schacter, D. L., Harbluk, J., & McLachlin, D. (1984). Retrieval without recollection: An experimental analysis of source amnesia. *Journal of Verbal Learning and Verbal Behavior, 23,* 593–611.

Schacter, D. L., Kaszniak, A. W., Kihlstrom, J. F., & Valdiserri, M. (1991). The relation between source memory and aging. *Psychology and Aging, 6,* 559–568.

Schacter, D. L., Kihlstrom, J. F., Kaszniak, A. W., & Valdiserri, M. (1993). Preserved and impaired memory functions in elderly adults. In J. Cerella, W. Hoyer, J. Rybash, & M. Commons (Eds.), *Adult information processing: Limits on loss* (pp. 327–350). San Diego, CA: Academic Press.

Schacter, D. L., Reiman, E., Curran, T., Yun, L. S., Bandy, D., McDermott, K. B., & Roediger, H. L., III. (1996). Neuroanatomical correlates of veridical and illusory recognition memory revealed by PET. *Neuron, 17,* 267–274.

Shimamura, A. P. (1989). Disorders of memory: The cognitive science perspective. In F. Boller & J. Grafman (Eds.), *Handbook of Neuropsychology* (pp. 35–73). Amsterdam: Elsevier.

Shimamura, A. P. (1995). Memory and frontal lobe function. In M. Gazzaniga (Ed.), *The cognitive neurosciences* (pp. 803–813) Cambridge, MA: MIT Press.

Shimamura, A. P., Janowsky, J. S., & Squire, L. R. (1990). Memory for the temporal order of events in patients with frontal lobe lesions and amnesic patients. *Neuropsychologia, 28,* 803–813.

Shimamura, A. P., & Jurica, P. J. (1994). Memory interference effects and aging: Findings from a test of frontal lobe function. *Neuropsychology, 8,* 408–412.

Smith, A. D. (1977). Adult age differences in cued recall. *Developmental Psychology, 13,* 326–331.

Spencer, W. D., & Raz, N. (1995). Differential effects of aging on memory for content and context: A meta-analysis. *Psychology and Aging, 10,* 527–539.

Sperling, G. (1960). The information available in brief visual presentations. *Psychological Monographs, 74* (Whole No. 498).

Spieler, D. H., & Balota, D. A. (1996). Characteristics of associative learning in younger and older adults: Evidence from an episodic priming paradigm. *Psychology & Aging, 11,* 607–620.

Spieler, D. H., Balota, D. A., & Faust, M. E. (1996). Stroop performance in younger adults, healthy older adults and individuals with senile dementia of the Alzheimer's type. *Journal of Experimental Psychology: Human Perception and Performance, 22,* 461–479.

Squire, L. R. (1986). Mechanisms of memory. *Science, 232,* 1612–1619.

Stine, E. L. (1990). Online processing of written text by younger and older adults. *Psychology and Aging, 5,* 68–78.

Sunderland, A., Watts, K., Baddeley, A. D., & Harris, J. E. (1986). Subjective memory assessment and test performance in elderly adults. *Journal of Gerontology, 41,* 376–384.

Tulving, E., Kapur, S., Craik, F. I. M., Moscovitch, M., & Houle, S. (1994). Hemispheric encoding/retrieval asymmetry in episodic memory: Positron emission tomography findings. *Proceedings of the National Academy of Science, 91,* 2016–2020.

Tulving, E., & Thomson, D. M. (1973). Encoding specificity and retrieval processes in episodic memory. *Psychological Review, 80,* 352–373.

Tun, P. A., Wingfield, A., Rosen, M. J., & Blanchard, L. (1998). Response latencies for false memories: Gist-based processes in normal aging. *Psychology & Aging, 13,* 23–241.

Wagner, A. D., Schacter, D. L., Rotte, M., Koutstaal, W., Maril, A., Dale, A. M., Rosen, B. R., & Buckner, R. L. (1998). Building memories: Remembering and forgetting of verbal experiences as predicted by brain activity. *Science, 281,* 1188–1191.

Watkins, M. J., & Watkins, O. (1974). A tactile suffix effect. *Memory & Cognition, 2,* 176–180.

West, R. (1996). An application of prefrontal cortex function theory to cognitive aging. *Psychological Bulletin, 120,* 272–292.

Winocur, G., Moscovitch, M., & Stuss, D. T. (1996). Explicit and implicit memory in the elderly: Evidence for double dissociation involving medial temporal- and frontal-lobe functions. *Neuropsychology, 10,* 1–9.

Zacks, R., Hasher, L., & Li, K. Z. H. (1998). Human Memory. In F. I. M. Craik & T. A. Salthouse (Eds.), *Handbook of aging and cognition II.* Mahwah, NJ: Erlbaum.

26

Memory in the Aging Brain

NICOLE D. ANDERSON & FERGUS I. M. CRAIK

In chapter 25, Balota, Dolan, and Duchek provide a comprehensive review of age-related memory decrements and the cognitive theories that have been developed in order to account for them. Our goal in this chapter is to put these findings and theories into a broader context. To facilitate this goal, we propose that the memory decrements shown by older people are mediated by a cascade of neurological and cognitive changes (see figure 26.1). First, various changes in brain structure and function occur with increasing age; these include reductions in cerebral volume, decreased brain metabolism, reduced blood flow, and altered neurochemical systems. We suggest that some of these neurological alterations mediate two general cognitive changes that have been proposed to underlie memory decrements in older adults. One is a reduction in the amount of attentional resources available for complex cognitive tasks (Craik, 1983, 1986), and the other is a reduction in the processing speed of elementary cognitive processes (e.g., Salthouse, 1996). The connection between brain aging and these cognitive consequences has already been considered. For example, Craik (1983) hypothesized that reduced attentional resources might reflect an age-related reduction in cortical tissue or in neuronal efficiency, and more recently, Anderson, Craik, and Naveh-Benjamin (1998)

suggested that reduced attentional resources may be a reflection of decreased regional cerebral blood flow to areas that are actively processing information. In a related vein, Salthouse (1985, 1988a) applied the notion of cognitive slowing to neural networks, and suggested that slowing may be a consequence of a reduced number of simultaneously active nodes (reflecting clusters of neurons), or of a reduced rate at which activation travels among nodes (reflecting neural transmission). Until recently the link between cognitive theories of aging and brain aging has remained hypothetical; however, the advent of neuroimaging techniques such as event-related potentials (ERPs), positron emission tomography (PET), and magnetic resonance imaging (MRI) has permitted a more direct investigation of the connection.

Next, we will argue that age-related reductions in attentional resources and age-related cognitive slowing both reduce cognitive control. Our use of the term cognitive control is closely linked to Jacoby's (e.g., 1991) description of intentional or conscious processes and to Hasher, Zacks, and May's (1999) description of successful working memory operations. That is, by cognitive control we mean the ability to manage one's thoughts, recollections, and actions in accordance with task-relevant goals. Finally, we will describe three

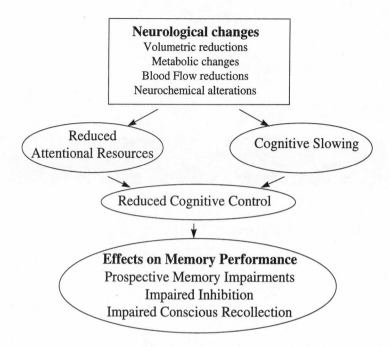

Figure 26.1 A proposed cascade of age-related neurological and cognitive changes that lead to memory impairments in older adults. Three examples of age-related memory impairments are explored in this chapter, but note that neurological and cognitive changes would lead to other types of memory impairments in addition to these.

broad consequences of reduced cognitive control for older adults' memory performance—prospective memory impairments, impaired inhibition, and reduced conscious recollection—but it should be borne in mind that there are additional adverse effects of reduced cognitive control on memory and other cognitive functions.

Neurological Alterations

Our goal in this section is to briefly review age-related alterations to the human brain that may be linked to memory deficits in older adults. A thorough review of neurological aging is beyond the scope of this chapter, and we have limited our references in this section mainly to review articles. For comprehensive reviews of the neurology of aging, see Coleman and Flood (1987), DeKosky and Palmer (1994), Haug (1997), Kemper (1994), and Raz (in press).

Before we begin our review, we would like to argue that the intricacy of cognitive aging will not be explained by global changes to brain, and perhaps not even by morphometric characteristics or resting-state metabolic activity in specific regions of the brain. As Balota et al. (chapter 25) describe, not all cognitive functions decline with age: some functions are severely disrupted in older adults, other functions are much less impaired, and still others are spared by aging. Furthermore, functional neuroimaging studies have demonstrated that different cognitive functions are mediated by different brain regions (see chapter 31). Thus, the fact that a region of the brain undergoes substantial decrements with increasing age may have little consequence for performance on a particular task if that brain region does not mediate cognitive function on that task. From a neurocognitive perspective, then, it seems clear that the link between brain aging and cognitive aging will be found at the intersection of specific brain regions and the particular cognitive functions that those regions mediate. For this reason, we will not review the effects of aging on global structure, metabolism, blood flow, or neurochemistry (for reviews, see Haug, 1997; Jagust, 1994; Kemper, 1994; Madden & Hoffman, 1997; Raz, in press), but will focus on regional changes.

A reasonable hypothesis that has received tentative support is that older adults' memory problems are linked to volumetric, metabolic, or blood-flow decrements in specific brain regions. Although the evidence is mixed and incomplete, there does seem to be an anterior-posterior gradient to the effects of aging on brain structure and function. For example, the evidence indicates that age-related volumetric reductions are greatest in the frontal lobes, smaller in the temporal lobes, and even smaller in the parietal and occipital lobes (see Raz, in press), and that age-related reductions in regional cerebral metabolism and blood flow are greatest in frontal cortex, lesser in temporal and parietal cortex, and negligible in occipital cortex (see Madden & Hoffman, 1997). Given the evidence that the hippocampus, frontal lobes, and temporal lobes play a significant role in episodic memory (see chapters 30 and 31), one would expect that these volumetric reductions are at least partly responsible for age-related decrements in episodic memory performance. Indeed, a number of investigators have reported a positive correlation between hippocampal volume and memory performance in healthy older adults (de Leon et al., 1997; Golomb et al., 1993; Soininen et al., 1994; Sullivan, Marsh, Mathalon, Lim, & Pfefferbaum, 1995). However, correlations between frontal or temporal lobe volume and episodic memory performance have been not significant (Golomb et al., 1993; Raz, Gunning-Dixon, Head, Dupuis, & Acker, 1998; Soininen et al., 1994). It is possible that the structural changes that occur in frontal and temporal regions have less impact on cognitive aging than do the functional changes that occur in these areas.

As Balota et al. describe in chapter 25, similarities exist between the memory decrements exhibited by older adults and patients with frontal lobe damage. In this sense, it is tempting to conclude that the critical link between brain aging and cognitive aging is the anterior-posterior gradient of morphometric and metabolic decrements. However, this link neglects two important facts. First, it ignores the effects of aging on neurochemistry. The cholinergic and dopaminergic systems mediate memory, and age-related reductions in both systems have been reported in the striatum, and in the cortex generally, perhaps more prominently in prefrontal cortex (see DeKosky & Palmer,

1994; Growdon & Cole, 1994; Raz, in press). These and other neurochemical changes may interact with the structural and functional changes described above, and we will explore some of these potential interactions later in the chapter. Second, measures of resting-state cerebral metabolism and blood flow are static, in that they are measured in the absence of a cognitive challenge; by contrast, cognitive aging is dynamic, in that the magnitude of age-related decrements depends on the type of cognitive challenge and its complexity (Cerella, Poon, & Williams, 1980). We stated before that the link between brain aging and cognitive aging will be found at the union of specific brain regions and the cognitive functions that these regions mediate. Now we take that statement one small but logical step further: the relationship between brain aging and cognitive aging may be evident only when regional metabolism, blood flow, or electrical activity are examined during a cognitive challenge. For that, we need to turn to *functional* neuroimaging studies of cognitive aging, particularly PET and functional magnetic resonance imaging (fMRI), because these techniques afford the spatial resolution to examine specific regions of the brain. Because these techniques are relatively new, there are few functional neuroimaging studies of memory and aging in the literature, but we will call upon the available studies in later sections of the chapter.

The Cognitive Consequences of Neurological Aging

In this section, we describe two major theories that have been developed to explain age-related memory decrements, and we attempt to link brain aging to these cognitive changes.

Reduced Attentional Resources

Craik (1983, 1986; Craik & Byrd, 1982) hypothesized that the amount of attentional resources available to fuel complex cognitive tasks is reduced by aging and, as a result, demanding cognitive processes such as encoding and retrieval deplete a greater proportion of available resources in older than younger adults. Evidence for this suggestion comes from research using a divided attention paradigm, in which subjects concurrently perform a memory task and an unrelated secondary task. The logic is that the more demanding encoding and retrieval are, the more attentional resources they will consume; consequently, fewer attentional resources will be available for the secondary task, resulting in secondary task performance decrements. Anderson et al. (1998) showed that secondary task performance was more disrupted by encoding and retrieval for older than younger adults, a result that is consistent with the claim that these processes are more attention demanding for older adults.

The reduced attentional resource theory has a more positive corollary known as the environmental support hypothesis (Craik, 1983, 1986), which refers to the notion that a supportive task environment that facilitates elaborate encoding or that guides retrieval can offset the effects of reduced attentional resources. For example, the magnitude of age-related memory decrements depends on the quality of the retrieval cue provided. When retrieval cues are absent, as in a free recall task, age-related decrements are usually substantial; by contrast, when retrieval cues are provided to guide retrieval processes, as in a recognition task, age-related decrements are much reduced (Schonfield & Robertson, 1966). Furthermore, in the divided attention paradigm, secondary task performance was much less disrupted during recognition than during recall, particularly for older adults (Anderson et al., 1998; Craik & McDowd, 1987). Together, these results demonstrate that a supportive retrieval environment reduces memory decrements and makes retrieval less attention demanding, particularly for older adults.

How can we link brain function to the very cognitive notions of attentional resources and environmental support? If attentional resources may be measured by increases in regional cerebral blood flow (rCBF) to particular brain regions in response to a cognitive challenge (Anderson et al., 1998), then rCBF in particular brain regions during encoding and retrieval should be reduced in older adults, but only when the task provides little environmental support. The particular regions of interest are those that younger adults normally activate, which are medial temporal regions during both encoding and retrieval (see chapter 30; Gabrieli, Brewer, & Poldrack, 1998), left prefrontal regions during encoding, and right prefrontal regions during retrieval (see chapter 31; Cabeza & Nyberg, 1997; Grady, 1999; Tulving, Kapur, Craik, Moscovitch, & Houle, 1994).

Thus, in order to link rCBF to reduced attentional resources, we need to examine the effects of environmental support during encoding on left prefrontal rCBF, during retrieval on right rCBF, and on medial temporal rCBF during both processes.

In two studies, the encoding task arguably required complex, attention-demanding operations (the encoding of unfamiliar faces in Grady et al., 1995, and the encoding of moderately elated word pairs in Cabeza et al., 1997), and age-related reductions in rCBF during encoding were evident in left prefrontal regions in both studies. In Grady et al.'s study, encoding-related hippocampal activation was significant in younger but not older adults; however, the interaction of age group and hippocampal activity during encoding versus a baseline task failed to reach statistical significance, possibly because one older subject (out of 10) showed encoding-related hippocampal activity equivalent to that of the younger adults. By contrast, in Madden et al.'s (in press) study, subjects made semantic judgments about individual words, a task that facilitates elaborate encoding (c.f. Craik & Tulving, 1975). When Madden et al. analyzed the two age groups' data separately, encoding was associated with rCBF increases in left prefrontal and medial temporal lobe regions in older adults *but not* in younger adults; however, when age group was included as a between-subjects variable, encoding-related brain activity in these regions did not interact with age, suggesting that the younger adults did activate left prefrontal and medial temporal regions during encoding, but not enough to surpass the statistical threshold. Thus, the limited evidence available is at least in line with the idea that an age-related reduction in encoding-related rCBF is evident during less supportive encoding tasks, but is eliminated when elaborate encoding is facilitated.

Corresponding results are available regarding the effects of environmental support during retrieval. In two studies, the retrieval tasks arguably required attention-demanding operations (cued recall and associative recognition in Cabeza et al., 1997, and word stem cued recall of perceptually encoded words in Schacter, Savage, Alpert, Rauch, & Albert, 1996), and in both studies younger adults showed greater increases in rCBF in right prefrontal regions during retrieval than did their older counterparts. By contrast, in four different cases, the retrieval task provided adequate environmental support (recognition tasks in

Grady et al., 1995, and in Madden et al., 1999, and word stem completion of semantically encoded words in Bäckman et al., 1997, and in Schacter et al., 1996), and rCBF in medial temporal/hippocampal and right prefrontal regions during retrieval was comparable in younger and older participants. Moreover, on a test of implicit memory for words, in which the level of environmental support is even greater because subjects are not trying to retrieve information from memory, Bäckman et al. (1997) found that priming was associated with the usual *reduction* in posterior rCBF, an effect which was even stronger in older than younger adults. Taken together, these data are consistent with the hypothesis that at the level of brain function, age-related reductions in attentional resources are manifested as reduced rCBF in particular brain regions that mediate attention-demanding tasks such as encoding and retrieval.

Cognitive Slowing

Forty years ago, Welford (1958) drew the very influential conclusion that aging is associated with a slowing of cognitive operations. Since then, a number of investigators have shown across a range of cognitive tasks that older adults' response latencies are approximately 1.5 times slower than younger adults' response latencies (e.g., Brinley, 1965; Myerson, Ferraro, Hale, & Lima, 1992; Salthouse, 1985). Moreover, Salthouse (e.g., 1993, 1996) has demonstrated that cognitive slowing accounts for most of the age-related variance in a number of memory tasks. Investigators assume that there is a neural basis to cognitive slowing (Birren, 1964; Cerella & Hale, 1994; Salthouse, 1985, 1988a, 1988b; Welford, 1958), but its precise nature has not been identified. Hicks and Birren (1970) hypothesized that age-related cognitive slowing may be linked to caudate dysfunction. We have already mentioned that there is an age-related reduction in dopamine receptors, particularly in the striatum and in frontal cortex (e.g., Antonini & Leenders, 1993; Wong et al., 1984), and Parkinson's patients (who undergo a much more severe dysfunction of dopaminergic function) experience motor and cognitive slowing (Lezak, 1995).

ERP studies, which have the temporal resolution needed to investigate cognitive slowing, find that aging is associated with delayed ERPs, especially in the P3 wave (Ford, Roth, Mohs, Hopkins, & Kopell, 1979; Strayer, Wickens, & Braun, 1987; for a review see Bashore, 1990) and in an associated late positivity component that is evident during successful recollection (Mark & Rugg, 1998; Swick & Knight, 1997). The P3 wave and the late positivity component have been related to conscious recollection (Smith, 1993); thus, the slowing of these ERP components may result in a diminished contribution of conscious recollection to memory performance in older adults. For example, Swick and Knight (1997) employed a continuous recognition task, in which subjects viewed a series of words. Some of the words were repeated in the series, and the lag between a word's initial presentation and its repetition was varied from 0 to 19 words. The ERP results are shown in figure 26.2, where it can be seen that the older adults' late positivity component associated with repeated words was delayed, was of shorter duration, and was eliminated at the longest lags. Furthermore, in younger adults the late positivity component was greater during word recognition than during word identification (not shown in figure 26.2), but in older adults the opposite was found. Swick and Knight concluded from these results that the contribution of conscious recollection to recognition memory declines with age, a conclusion that is well supported by the work of Jacoby and his colleagues (e.g., Jennings & Jacoby, 1993).

Reduced Cognitive Control

We believe that age-related cognitive slowing and reductions in attentional resources both reduce cognitive control, by which we mean the ability to manage one's thoughts, recollections, and actions in accordance with task-relevant goals (Hasher & Zacks, 1988; Hasher, Zacks, & May, 1999; Jacoby, 1991). Our description of cognitive control shares characteristics with the supervisory attentional system proposed by Norman and Shallice (1986), which takes control of processing in novel situations, when error detection is required, or when prepotent thoughts or responses must be avoided. In this sense, cognitive control includes interference or inhibitory control (Fuster, 1989; Knight & Grabowecky, 1995). A central tenet of Salthouse's (1996) theory is that cognitive slowing reduces the amount and quality of information simultaneously available in working memory, or the "dynamic ca-

RECOGNITION MEMORY

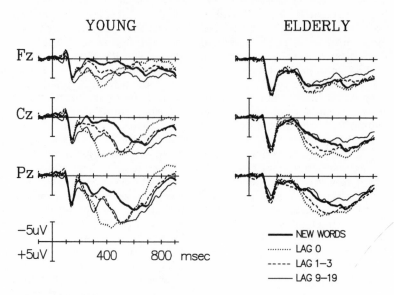

Figure 26.2 Grand average event-related potentials from three midline electrode sites are shown (Fz = frontal; Cz = central; Pz = parietal). Positive potentials are presented below and negative potentials above the x-axis. From D. Swick and R. T. Knight (1997), Event-related potentials differentiate the effects of aging on word and nonword repetition in explicit and implicit memory tasks, *Journal of Experimental Psychology: Learning, Memory, and Cognition, 23*, p. 132 (experiment 2). Copyright 1997 by the American Psychological Association. Reprinted with permission.

pacity" (p. 406) of working memory. Thus, another way to view the consequence of cognitive slowing is as a disruption of the central executive (Baddeley & Hitch, 1974) or the supervisory attentional system (Norman & Shallice, 1986). Furthermore, one distinguishing feature of controlled processes, relative to their automatic counterparts, is that they are attention demanding (Shiffrin & Schneider, 1977). Hence, a fundamental consequence of an age-related reduction in attention resources would be that fewer attentional resources would be available for cognitive control. By most accounts, cognitive control is viewed as a function of the prefrontal cortex (e.g., Baddeley & Wilson, 1988; Fuster, 1989; Knight & Grabowecky, 1995; Luria, 1966; Shallice & Burgess, 1991), and age-related impairments of cognitive control may therefore be linked to the relative vulnerability of the frontal lobes to reductions in volume, cerebral metabolic rate, and rCBF described above.

Effects of Neurocognitive Aging on Memory

In this section, we describe some of the effects of neurocognitive aging on memory performance. The cascade of neurocognitive aging that we have described would have negative implications for cognitive functions other than memory, such as attention, planning, problem solving, and abstraction. However, given that this is a handbook on memory, we restrict our discussion to three memory-related functions—prospective memory, inhibition, and conscious recollection—and attempt to elucidate the role of cognitive control in each of these functions.

Prospective Memory Impairments

Memory is usually thought of in terms of past events, but in our everyday lives we often have to remember to carry out some action at a future time, and this ability is referred to as prospective memory (PM). Craik (1983, 1986) suggested that the largest age-related decrements should be found in tasks with little environmental support. Such tasks (e.g., free recall) depend on "self-initiated activities," and it is these self-initiated mental activities that are particularly difficult for older people. In our opinion, self-initiated activities in this sense are essentially the same as those involved in conscious recollection of episodic or contextual detail in retrospective remembering; both involve controlled processing to a substantial extent, and (speculatively) both involve the frontal lobes of the brain. It would therefore be expected that older adults should show large decrements on PM tasks, and this point was made (following a suggestion by John Harris) by Craik (1983, 1986). The same point was made by Schonfield (1982), and it is also in line with the anecdotal observation that older adults are often "absent-minded" and forgetful. Surprisingly, however, Einstein and McDaniel (1990) published an influential study showing *no* age-related decrement in a PM task. In their experiment, participants carried out a short-term memory task and also responded to an occasionally occurring target word (e.g., *rake*).

Einstein and McDaniel's finding of no age differences has been modified by further studies, however. Two major factors that must be taken into consideration are, first, the distinction between time-based and event-based PM tasks, and second, the complexity of the ongoing activity in which the PM task is embedded. In their original paper, Einstein and McDaniel (1990) suggested that different patterns might emerge between situations in which the PM target is triggered by some event (e.g. "when you meet John, please give him this message"), and those that are time based (e.g., "remember to phone your friend in half an hour"). Indeed, their later work showed age-related decrements in time-based but not event-based tasks (Einstein, McDaniel, Richardson, Guynn, & Cunfer, 1995) in line with the notion that time-based tasks require more self-initiated processing and are therefore more vulnerable to the effects of aging. A similar pattern of results was reported by Park, Hertzog, Kidder, Morrell, and Mayhorn (1997); in this case, however, the investigators found age-related decrements in both types of task, although the age effect was particularly marked in the time-based task. The complex-

ity of the ongoing activity in PM tasks is a second factor that qualifies age-related decrements. There is good agreement that more demanding cover tasks are associated with poorer performance on the PM task, and that this effect is stronger in older people (Einstein, Smith, McDaniel, & Shaw, 1997; Mäntylä, 1994; Park, Hertzog, Kidder, Morrell, & Mayharn, 1997).

A further interesting finding in this area is the difference between laboratory-based and real-life PM tasks. Several investigators have used tasks such as remembering to mail postcards on specified days, or to telephone the lab at specific times, and in one such study Moscovitch (1982) reported that older adults were markedly *superior* to their younger counterparts! In a more recent study, Rendell and Thomson (in press) confirmed that older adults were superior to a younger group at real-life PM tasks, but also found (using the same participants) that the young group was superior to the old on PM tasks performed in the laboratory. It is not simply the case that older adults leave themselves more notes and reminders in real-life tasks; other factors probably include greater motivation, more rehearsal and self-reminding, and possibly a greater reliance on a more structured and stable daily routine on the part of the older adults. In line with these findings, Maylor (1990) found that older adults outperformed younger adults on a real-life PM task when participants used external cues, but that the age-related effect reversed when they relied on internal cues.

In general, then, it seems as if there can be substantial age-related decrements in PM performance, and that the size of the decrement will depend on such factors as the nature of the PM task, the availability of external cues, and the resources that must be devoted to other ongoing activities. Older people do least well when their processing resources are depleted and when the task context forces them to rely on internal self-initiated activities. That is, their generally poorer PM performance is associated with an age-related decline in cognitive control.

Impaired Inhibition

Hasher and Zacks (1988; Hasher et al., 1999; Zacks & Hasher, 1994, 1997) propose that cognitive control involves both excitatory mechanisms to enhance the activation of task-relevant information and inhibitory mechanisms to suppress the activation of task-irrelevant information. They furthermore hypothesize that aging is associated with a relative sparing of excitatory mechanisms, coupled with an impairment of inhibitory mechanisms.

Four main findings support the proposal that older adults suffer an inhibition deficit. First, older adults are more susceptible to distraction from irrelevant information. Connelly, Hasher, and Zacks (1991) and Carlson, Hasher, Connelly, and Zacks (1995) had younger and older adults read regular text passages and text passages that contained italicized text that was to be ignored. The increase in reading time due to the presence of distracting text was greater for older than younger adults. Older adults were also more likely than younger adults to select the distracting information as answers to comprehension questions, which suggests that older adults encode more of the distracting information than do younger adults.

Second, older adults are more likely to maintain no-longer-relevant information in memory. Hartman and Hasher (1991) showed younger and older adults a series of sentence frames in which the final word was highly predictable (e.g., "She ladled the soup into her _____"). Participants predicted the ending for each sentence, and then the final word was presented. On most trials, the predictable final word was confirmed (i.e., *bowl*), but on some trials it was disconfirmed (e.g., *lap*). Participants were instructed to remember the word that was presented, whether or not it matched their prediction. On an indirect test of memory for the final words, the older adults showed less priming of the confirmed words, but more priming of the disconfirmed words than their younger counterparts. These results were replicated by Hasher, Quig, and May (1997), and similar results on an explicit test were reported by Hamm and Hasher (1992). Together, these findings indicate that older adults are more likely to maintain outdated information in memory.

Third, older adults are more likely to recall information they have been instructed to forget. Zacks, Radvansky, and Hasher (1996) used a directed forgetting paradigm, in which participants were presented with a list of words, and each word was followed by the instruction to remember the word or to forget the word. At the end of the list, participants were asked to recall only the items that they were instructed to remember. The results are shown in figure 26.3. On the immediate memory test, the older adults were less likely to recall the words they were instructed to remember but were more likely to recall the words they were instructed to forget. We will discuss the results from the delayed test in a moment; for now it is important to note that the data from the immediate test suggest that older adults are less able to inhibit information that is no longer wanted in memory.

The fourth line of evidence in support of Hasher and Zacks's view is that older adults experience more memory interference. Hasher et al. (1999) argue that an age-related impairment of inhibition leads to a more "cluttered" working memory, which creates interference between relevant and irrelevant information. Therefore, older adults should be more prone to additional, experimentally imposed interference because it would combine with the interference resulting from their inability to inhibit irrelevant information. Gerard, Zacks, Hasher, and Radvansky (1991) used the fan effect paradigm (Anderson, 1974), which involves the presentation of unrelated information and the manipulation of the "fan" size, or the number of facts associated with a particular concept (e.g., a fan size of two is created by the sentences "The doctor took the car for a short test drive," and "The doctor bought a necklace for his wife"). Memory is then tested using a speeded yes/no recognition test. The fan effect refers to the fact that as fan size increases, so too does interference among information held in memory, and as a consequence, retrieval from memory operates more slowly. The fan effect is greatly exaggerated in older adults, suggesting that more irrelevant information gains access to and is not deleted from older adults' working memory, resulting in slower, less efficient retrieval (see also Cohen, 1990, and see Radvansky, Zacks, & Hasher, 1996, for important boundary conditions on this finding).

The evidence garnered by Hasher, Zacks, and their colleagues clearly demonstrates that older adults have inhibitory impairments. In an attempt to specify the nature of these deficits more precisely, Zacks and Hasher (1997) and Hasher et al. (1999) have postulated that three inhibitory functions decline with age: (1) those that control *access* of information to working memory, (2) those that control the *deletion* of unwanted information from working memory, and (3) those that exercise *restraint* over prepotent but potentially inaccurate responses. Assigning age-related deficits to these specific functions is challenging, how-

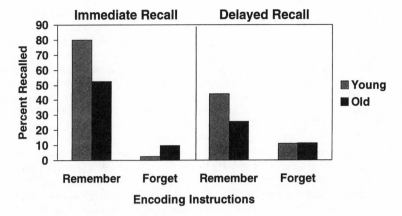

Figure 26.3 Younger and older adults' performance on immediate and delayed recall tests as a function of instructions to remember or forget the words. From R. T. Zacks, G. Radvansky, and L. Hasher (1996), Studies of directed forgetting in older adults, *Journal of Experimental Psychology: Learning, Memory, and Cognition, 22*, pp. 146–148 (Experiment 1B). Copyright 1997 by the American Psychological Association. Adapted with permission.

ever, because in order to demonstrate a failure of access control, subsequent failures of deletion and restraint must occur, and in order to demonstrate a failure of deletion, a subsequent failure of restraint must occur. For example, Hasher et al. (1999) argue that the fact that older adults are more prone to distracting text when reading passages suggests that they are more likely to allow access of irrelevant information to working memory. However, Dywan and Murphy (1996) showed that on a surprise recognition test for the distracting information, younger adults remembered more of the distracting information than did older adults. Thus, both younger and older adults allow irrelevant information to access working memory, but younger adults more successfully delete or restrain it. For a second example, let us return to the directed forgetting data of Zacks et al. (1996) shown in figure 26.3. Hasher et al. (1999) suggest that these results indicate that the older adults are less able to delete information from working memory. However, on the delayed test, the instructions were to recall *all* of the words, regardless of the previous instructions to remember or forget the words. Older adults again failed to recall as many items that they were previously instructed to remember, but they recalled as many items as younger adults that they were previously instructed to forget. These results suggest when

younger and older adults are instructed to forget information, only some of the information is successfully "forgotten," or deleted from working memory; most of the remaining information is simply prevented from being recalled (or "restrained") on the immediate test, and younger adults are more apt to restrain this information. Although these data clearly suggest an inhibitory deficit among older adults, they do not unequivocally identify the specific type(s) of inhibition that are most affected by aging.

Age-related inhibition deficits clearly reflect failures of cognitive control, in the sense that older adults' management of their thought and behavior is not well aligned with the goals of the task. Previously, we mentioned that in most theories of brain function, cognitive control is thought to be mediated by the frontal lobes (e.g., Baddeley & Wilson, 1988; Knight & Grabowecky, 1995; Luria, 1966; Shallice & Burgess, 1991). Although Hasher and Zacks's view is expressed in a cognitive framework, it shares characteristics with models that assign an inhibitory role to the prefrontal cortex (Dempster, 1992; Fuster, 1989; Shimamura, 1995). Thus, it is reasonable to suggest that age-related reductions in frontal lobe volume, cerebral metabolism, or blood flow may be partly responsible for age-related problems with inhibitory function.

Impaired Conscious Recollection

A third way in which impairments of cognitive control affect older adults' memory performance is by reducing the degree to which their memory is guided by conscious recollection, while sparing automatic, or familiarity-based memory processing (e.g., Hasher & Zacks, 1979; Jacoby & Hay, 1998). Automatic processes are fast, unintentional, and proceed unconsciously whereas conscious processes are slow, controlled, and intentional (e.g, Hasher & Zacks, 1979; Jacoby, 1991; Shiffrin & Schneider, 1977). In this section, we will discuss research that attempts to disentangle conscious recollection from automatic processes, using either the remember/know paradigm (Tulving, 1985) or the process dissociation procedure (Jacoby, 1991).

In the remember/know paradigm, for each item deemed "old" on a recognition test, participants indicate if they "remember" or consciously recollect some contextual detail of previously learning that item (e.g., what the item looked or sounded like, what images or memories the item invoked), or if they "know" that the item was presented but cannot recollect any contextual details of previously learning that item. Remember responses are reduced by aging, while know responses are unchanged (Mäntylä, 1993) or increase with age (Jacoby, Jennings, & Hay, 1996; Parkin & Walter, 1992). Thus, the remember/know data suggest that aging has a much greater impact on conscious recollection than on automatic recollection. In the remember/know paradigm, automatic processes and conscious recollection work in concert to benefit memory performance. That is, it is immaterial whether an "old" response on a recognition test is mediated by conscious "remembering" or by automatic "knowing" because both lead one to recognize a previously presented item. Other experiments have been designed so that conscious and automatic processes would work in opposition, such that conscious recollection leads to an appropriate response, whereas automatic processing leads to an inappropriate response. In this case, inappropriate responses are directly related to failures of conscious recollection.

In the false fame paradigm, participants first read a list of nonfamous names, and then a second list of famous and nonfamous names, and participants indicate whether each name on the second list refers to a famous or nonfa-

mous person. Participants are told that if they remember having seen the name on the first list, they can be sure that it was nonfamous because all of the names on the first list referred to nonfamous people. Having encountered the name on the first list should increase its familiarity, which in turn should lead to a misattribution of fame. However, if one is able to consciously recollect that the name appeared on the first list, then the tendency to make a false fame judgment would be opposed. Older adults make more false fame judgments than younger adults (Dywan & Jacoby, 1990; Jennings & Jacoby, 1993), an effect that is linked to age-related reductions in conscious recollection (Jennings & Jacoby, 1993). An age-related increase in the frequency of false fame judgments to faces was reported by Bartlett, Strater, and Fulton (1991), who additionally demonstrated that when younger and older adults completed a recency judgment task for faces seen a week ago, that day, or never, older adults were more likely provide "today" judgments for faces seen a week ago. Older adults' false recency judgments presumably arose because the faces were familiar, but the older adults' conscious recollection of when they had seen those faces was impaired. Together, these findings suggest that older adults are less able to employ conscious recollection in order to oppose the effects of familiarity on behavior.

If older adults are less able to oppose familiar information, then age-related deficits should be magnified when familiarity is enhanced. A number of studies suggest that this is the case. Bartlett et al. (1991) demonstrated that the more often a nonfamous face was presented before a fame judgment task, younger adults' false fame judgments decreased, but older adults' increased. A similar crossover interaction was reported by Jacoby (1999). Subjects first saw a list of words, in which some of the words were shown once and some three times, and then subjects heard a list of singly presented words. These lists were followed by a recognition test consisting of words subjects had seen, words subjects had heard, and new words. Participants were instructed to say yes only to words that they had heard. Younger and older adults were equally able to recognize the words they had heard, but the older adults were more likely to say yes to words they had earlier seen. Furthermore, the effect of repetition on the likelihood of incorrectly saying yes to the visually presented items was negative for the younger adults, but positive for the older adults. Similar effects of repetition have been reported by Hay and Jacoby (1999) and by Jennings and Jacoby (1997). Together, these results show that relative to older adults, younger adults are more able to oppose the effects of heightened familiarity by consciously recollecting contextual details of a prior event.

Although these results strongly suggest that the contribution of conscious recollection to memory is reduced by aging, it has not gone unnoticed that successful performance in these paradigms relies quite heavily on source memory. For example, in order to say yes on a recognition test only to items that were heard and not seen, or to be able to use the fact that all of the names on list 1 were nonfamous during a fame judgment task, one must remember the source of the information— whether it was presented visually or auditorily, or whether it was on list 1 or list 2. Given that aging impairs source memory (see Balota et al., chapter 25), the question is whether the apparent age-related deficit of conscious recollection is in fact an impairment in source memory. Indeed, Multhaup (1995) showed that when younger and older adults were encouraged to use a more stringent source decision criterion, older adults made as few false fame judgments as the younger adults. Jacoby (1999) has acknowledged the similarity between recollection and source memory, but notes that sometimes people correctly remember the source of information, but nevertheless fail to guide their remembering with conscious recollection. Such instances demonstrate that cognitive control can make an independent contribution to memory performance.

Conclusions and Future Directions

The goal of this chapter was to link the neurological and cognitive changes that occur with age, and to explain how these lead to specific types of memory impairments in older adults. This review is a first step toward that goal, but it is clear that many details of the relationship between brain aging and cognitive aging are still unknown. For example, we need to identify the specific mechanisms by which structural or functional changes to the brain affect cognition. We argued that this link will not be found at the global level, but at the intersection of specific brain regions and the cognitive functions that they mediate. This position lends a certain focus to the goal of relating brain aging to cognitive aging, but other challenges exist. For example, older adults often activate brain regions that are not activated by younger adults, an effect that may reflect compensatory mechanisms or less efficient strategy use (see Cabeza et al., 1997; Madden et al., 1999). Another question concerns the relationship between inhibitory deficits and reduced conscious recollection. Zacks and Hasher (1994) have suggested that inhibitory deficits are the primary cause of age-related memory deficits, but Jacoby (1999) has argued the very opposite—that memory deficits, or more specifically deficits in conscious recollection are the primary cause of age-related inhibitory deficits. Whether or not a causal direction between inhibition and conscious recollection impairments can be identified remains to be seen, but it seems clear that both result from impairments of cognitive control. Finally, the ultimate goal is to offset the effects of neurocognitive aging in order to alleviate older adults' problems with memory and other cognitive functions. The evidence we reviewed above indicates that the benefits of environmental support are evident at the functional, cognitive, and behavioral levels, in that it appears to reduce age-related decrements in encoding- and retrieval-related rCBF, reduces the attentional demands of these memory functions, and reduces memory decrements. That is, environmental support appears to be one factor that functionally "repairs" the cascade of neurocognitive aging, and the goal of future cognitive aging research should be to identify other factors that do the same.

Acknowledgments This work was supported by a postdoctoral fellowship from the Ontario Mental Health Foundation (N.D.A.) and by a grant from the Natural Sciences and Engineering Research Council of Canada (F.I.M.C.).

References

Anderson, J. R. (1974). Retrieval of propositional information from long-term memory. *Cognitive Psychology, 6*, 451–474.

Anderson, N. D., Craik, F. I. M., & Naveh-Benjamin, M. (1998). The attentional demands of encoding and retrieval in younger and older adults: 1. Evidence from divided attention costs. *Psychology and Aging, 13*, 405–425.

Antonini, A., & Leenders, K. L. (1993). Dopamine D2 receptors in normal human brain:

Effect of age measured by positron emission tomography (PET) and [^{11}C]-Raclopride. *Annals of the New York Academy of Sciences, 695,* 81–85.

Bäckman, L., Almkvist, O., Andersson, J., Nordberg, A., Winblad, B., Reinick, R., & Långström, B. (1997). Brain activation in young and older adults during implicit and explicit retrieval. *Journal of Cognitive Neuroscience, 9,* 378–391.

Baddeley, A., & Hitch, G. (1974). Working memory. In *The psychology of learning and motivation* (Vol. 8; pp. 47–90). New York: Academic Press.

Baddeley, A., & Wilson, B. (1988). Frontal amnesia and the dysexecutive syndrome. *Brain and Cognition, 7,* 212–230.

Bartlett, J. C., Strater, L, & Fulton, A. (1991). False recency and false fame of faces in young adulthood and old age. *Memory & Cognition, 19,* 177–188.

Bashore, T. R., Jr. (1990). Age-related changes in mental processing revealed by analysis of event-related brain potentials. In J. W. Rohrbaugh, R. Parasuraman, & R. Johnson, Jr. (Eds.), *Event-related brain potentials: Basic issues and applications* (pp. 242–275). New York: Oxford University Press.

Birren, J. E. (1964). *The psychology of aging.* Englewood Cliffs, NJ: Prentice-Hall.

Brinley, J. F. (1965). Age changes in speed of behavior: Its central nature and physiological correlates. In A. T. Welford & J. E. Birren (Eds.), *Behavior, aging, and the nervous system* (pp. 114–149). Springfield, IL: Charles C. Thomas.

Cabeza, R., Grady, C. L., Nyberg, L., McIntosh, A. R., Tulving, E., Kapur, S., Jennings, J. M., Houle, S., & Craik, F. I. M. (1997). Age-related differences in neural activity during memory encoding and retrieval: A positron emission tomography study. *Journal of Neuroscience, 17,* 391–400.

Cabeza, R., & Nyberg, L. (1997). Imaging cognition: An empirical review of PET studies with normal subjects. *Journal of Cognitive Neuroscience, 9,* 1–26.

Carlson, M. C., Hasher, L., Connelly, S. L., & Zacks, R. T. (1995). Aging, distraction, and the benefits of predictable location. *Psychology and Aging, 10,* 427–436.

Cerella, J., & Hale, S. (1994). The rise and fall in information-processing rates over the life span. *Acta Psychologica, 86,* 109–197.

Cerella, J., Poon, L. W., & Williams, D. M. (1980). Age and the complexity hypothesis. In L. W. Poon (Ed.), *Aging in the 1980s: Psychological issues* (pp. 332–340).

Washington, DC: American Psychological Association.

Cohen, G. (1990). Recognition and retrieval of proper names: Age diffferences in the fan effect. *European Journal of Cognitive Psychology, 2,* 193–204.

Coleman, P. D., & Flood, D. G. (1987). Neuron numbers and dendritic extent in normal aging and Alzheimer's disease. *Neurobiology of Aging, 8,* 521–545.

Connelly, S. L., Hasher, L., Zacks, R. T. (1991). Age and reading: The impact of distraction. *Psychology and Aging, 6,* 533–541.

Craik, F. I. M. (1983). On the transfer of information from temporary to permanent memory. *Philosophical Transactions of the Royal Society of London, B 302,* 341–359.

Craik, F. I. M. (1986). A functional account of age differences in memory. In F. Klix & H. Hagendorf (Eds.), *Human memory and cognitive capabilities, mechanisms, and performances* (pp. 409–422). North-Holland: Elsevier Science Publishers B. V.

Craik, F. I. M., & Byrd, M. (1982). Aging and cognitive deficits: The role of attentional resources. In F. I. M. Craik & S. Trehub (Eds.), *Aging and cognitive processes* (pp. 191–211). New York: Plenum.

Craik, F. I. M., & McDowd, J. M. (1987). Age differences in recall and recognition. *Journal of Experimental Psychology: Learning, Memory, and Cognition, 13,* 474–479.

Craik, F. I. M., & Tulving, E. (1975). Depth of processing and the retention of words in episodic memory. *Journal of Experimental Psychology: General, 104,* 268–294.

DeKosky, S. T., & Palmer, A. M. (1994). Neurochemistry of aging. In M. L. Albert & J. E. Knoefel (Eds.), *Clinical neurology of aging* (2nd ed.; pp. 79–101). New York: Oxford University Press.

de Leon, M. J., George, A. E., Golomb, J., Tarshish, C., Convit, A., Kluger, A., DeSanti, S., McRae, T., Ferris, S. H., Reisberg, B., Ince, C., Rusinek, H., Bobinski, M., Quinn, B., Miller, D. C., & Wisniewski, H. M. (1997). Frequency of hippocampal formation atrophy in normal aging and Alzheimer's disease. *Neurobiology of Aging, 18,* 1–11.

Dempster, F. N. (1992). The rise and fall of the inhibitory mechanism: Toward a unified theory of cognitive development and aging. *Developmental Review, 12,* 45–75.

Dywan, J., & Jacoby, L. L. (1990). Effects of aging on source monitoring: Differences in susceptibility to false fame. *Psychology and Aging, 5,* 379–387.

Dywan, J., & Murphy, W. E. (1996). Aging and inhibitory control in text comprehension. *Psychology and Aging, 11*, 199–206.

Einstein, G. O., & McDaniel, M. A. (1990). Normal aging and prospective memory. *Journal of Experimental Psychology: Learning, Memory, and Cognition, 16*, 717–726.

Einstein, G. O., McDaniel, M. A., Richardson, S. L., Guynn, M. J., & Cunfer, A. R. (1995). Aging and prospective memory: Examining the influences of self-initiated retrieval processes. *Journal of Experimental Psychology: Learning, Memory, and Cognition, 21*, 996–1007.

Einstein, G. O., Smith, R. E., McDaniel, M. A., & Shaw, P. (1997). Aging and prospective memory: The influence of increased task demands at encoding and retrieval. *Psychology and Aging, 12*, 479–488.

Ford, J. M., Roth, W. T., Mohs, R., Hopkins, W. F. III, & Kopell, B. S. (1979). Event-related potentials recorded from young and old adults during a memory retrieval task. *Electroencephalography and Clinical Neurophysiology, 47*, 450–459.

Fuster, J. M. (1989). *The prefrontal cortex* (2nd ed.). New York: Raven Press.

Gabrieli, J. D. E., Brewer, J. B., & Poldrack, R. A. (1998). Images of medial temporal lobe functions in human learning and memory. *Neurobiology of Learning and memory, 70*, 275–283.

Gerard, L., Zacks, R. T., Hasher, L., & Radvansky, G. A. (1991). Age deficits in retrieval: The fan effect. *Journal of Gerontology: Psychological Sciences, 46*, 131–136.

Golomb, J., de Leon, M. J., Kluger, A., George, A. E., Tarshish, C., & Ferris, S. H. (1993). Hippocampal atrophy in normal aging: An association with recent memory impairment. *Archives of Neurology, 50*, 967–973.

Grady, C. L. (1999). Neuroimaging and activation of the frontal lobes. In B. L. Miller & J. L. Cummings (Eds.), *The human frontal lobes: Functions and disorders* (pp. 196–230). New York: Guilford Press.

Grady, C. L., McIntosh, A. R., Horwitz, B., Maisog, J. M., Ungerleider, L. G., Mentis, M. J., Pietrini, P., Schapiro, M. B., & Haxby, J. V. (1995). Age-related reductions in human recognition memory due to impaired encoding. *Science, 269*, 218–221.

Growdon, J. H., & Cole, D. G. (1994). Pharmacology in the aging brain and neurodegenerative disorders. In M. L. Albert & J. E. Knoefel (Eds.), *Clinical neurology of aging* (2nd ed.; pp. 102–120). New York: Oxford University Press.

Hamm, V. P., & Hasher, L. (1992). Age and the availability of inferences. *Psychology and Aging, 7*, 56–64.

Hartman, M., & Hasher, L. (1991). Aging and suppression: Memory for previously relevant information. *Psychology and Aging, 6*, 587–594.

Hasher, L., Quig, M. B., & May, C. P. (1997). Inhibitory control over no-longer-relevant information: Adult age differences. *Memory & Cognition, 25*, 286–295.

Hasher, L., & Zacks, R. T. (1979). Automatic and effortful processes in memory. *Journal of Experimental Psychology: General, 108*, 356–388.

Hasher, L., & Zacks, R. T. (1988). Working memory, comprehension, and aging: A review and a new view. In G. H. Bower (Ed.), *The psychology of learning and motivation* (pp. 193–225). New York: Academic Press.

Hasher, L., Zacks, R. T., & May, C. P. (1999). Inhibitory control, circadian arousal, and age. In D. Gopher & A. Koriat (Eds.), *Attention and performance XVII* (pp. 653–675). Cambridge, MA: MIT Press.

Haug, H. (1997). The aging human cerebral cortex: Morphometry of areal differences and their functional meaning. In S. U. Dani, A. Hori, & G. F. Walter (Eds.), *Principles of neural aging* (pp. 247–261). Amsterdam: Elsevier.

Hay, J. F., & Jacoby, L. L. (1999). Separating habit and recollection in young and older adults: Effects of elaborative processing and distinctiveness. *Psychology and Aging, 14*, 122–134.

Hicks, L. H., & Birren, J. E. (1970). Aging, brain damage, and psychomotor slowing. *Psychological Bulletin, 74*, 377–396.

Jacoby, L. L. (1991). A process dissociation framework: Separating automatic from intentional uses of memory. *Journal of Memory and Language, 30*, 513–541.

Jacoby, L. L. (1999). Deceiving the elderly: Effects of accessibility bias in cued-recall performance. *Cognitive Neuropsychology, 16*, 417–436.

Jacoby, L. L. (1999). Ironic effects of repetition: Measuring age-related differences in memory. *Journal of Experimental Psychology: Learning, Memory, and Cognition, 25*, 3–22.

Jacoby, L. L., & Hay, J. F. (1998). Age-related deficits in memory: Theory and application. In M. A. Conway, S. E. Gathercole, & C. Cornoldi (Eds.), *Theories of memory II* (pp. 111–134). Hove, England: Psychology Press.

Jacoby, L. L., Jennings, J. M., & Hay, J. F. (1996). Dissociating automatic and consciously controlled processes: Implications for diagnosis and rehabilitation of memory deficits. In D. Hermann, C. McEvoy, C. Hertzog, P. Hertel, & M. K. Johnson (Eds.), *Basic and applied memory research: Theory in context* (Vol. 1; pp. 161–193). Mahwah, NJ: Erlbaum.

Jagust, W. J. (1994). Neuroimaging in normal aging and dementia. In M. L. Albert & J. E. Knoefel (Eds.), *Clinical neurology of aging* (2nd ed.; pp. 190–213). New York: Oxford University Press.

Jennings, J. M., & Jacoby, L. L. (1993). Automatic versus intentional uses of memory: Aging, attention, and control. *Psychology and Aging, 8*, 283–293.

Jennings, J. M., & Jacoby, L. L. (1997). An opposition procedure for detecting age-related deficits in recollection: Telling effects of repetition. *Psychology and Aging, 12*, 352–361.

Kemper, T. L. (1994). Neuroanatomical and neuropathological changes during aging and dementia. In M. L. Albert & J. E. Knoefel (Eds.), *Clinical neurology of aging* (2nd ed.; pp. 3–67). New York: Oxford University Press.

Knight, R. T., & Grabowecky, M. (1995). Escape from linear time: Prefrontal cortex and conscious experience. In M. S. Gazzaniga (Ed.), *The cognitive neurosciences* (pp. 1357–1371). Cambridge, MA: MIT Press.

Lezak, M. D. (1995). *Neuropsychological assessment* (3rd ed.). New York: Oxford University Press.

Luria, A. R. (1966). *Higher cortical functions in man.* New York: Basic Books.

Madden, D. J., & Hoffman, J. M. (1997). Application of positron emission tomography to age-related cognitive changes. In K. R. R. Krishnan & P. M. Doraiswamy (Eds.), *Brain imaging in clinical psychiatry* (pp. 575–613). New York: Marcel Dekker.

Madden, D. J., Turkington, T. G., Provenzale, J. M., Denny, L. L., Hawk, T. C., Gottlob, L. R., & Coleman, R. E. (1999). Adult age differences in the functional neuroanatomy of verbal recognition memory. *Human Brain Mapping, 7*, 115–135.

Mäntylä, T. (1993). Knowing but not remembering: Adult age differences in recollective experience. *Memory & Cognition, 21*, 379–388.

Mäntylä, T. (1994). Remembering to remember: Adult age differences in prospective memory. *Journal of Gerontology: Psychological Sciences, 49*, P272–P282.

Mark, R. E., & Rugg, M. D. (1998). Age effects on brain activity associated with episodic memory retrieval. *Brain, 121*, 861–873.

Maylor, E. A. (1990). Age and prospective memory. *Quarterly Journal of Experimental Psychology, 42A*, 471–493.

Moscovitch, M. (1982). A neuropsychological approach to memory and perception in normal and pathological aging. In F. I. M. Craik & S. Trehub (Eds.), *Aging and cognitive processes* (pp. 55–78). New York: Plenum Press.

Multhaup, K. S. (1995). Aging, source, and decision criteria: When false fame errors do and do not occur. *Psychology and Aging, 10*, 492–497.

Myerson, J., Ferraro, F. R., Hale, S., & Lima, S. D. (1992). General slowing in semantic priming and word recognition. *Psychology and Aging, 7*, 257–270.

Norman, D. A., & Shallice, T. (1986). Attention to action: Willed and automatic control of behavior. In R. J. Davidson, G. E. Schwartz, & D. Shapiro (Eds.), *Consciousness and self-regulation* (Vol. 4; pp. 1–18). New York: Plenum.

Park, D. C., Hertzog, C., Kidder, D. P., Morrell, R. W., & Mayhorn, C. B. (1997). Effect of age on event-based and time-based prospective memory. *Psychology and Aging, 12*, 214–327.

Parkin, A. J., & Walter, B. M. (1992). Recollective experience, normal aging, and frontal dysfunction. *Psychology and Aging, 7*, 290–298.

Radvansky, G. A., Zacks, R. T., & Hasher, L. (1996). Fact retrieval in younger and older adults: The role of mental models. *Psychology and Aging, 11*, 258–271.

Raz, N. (in press). Aging of the brain and its impact on cognitive performance: Integration of structural and functional finding. In F. I. M. Craik & T. A. Salthouse (Eds.), *Handbook of aging and cognition II.* Mahwah, NJ: Erlbaum.

Raz, N., Gunning-Dixon, F. M., Head, D. P., Dupuis, J. H., & Acker, J. D. (1998). Neuroanatomical correlates of cognitive aging: Evidence from structural MRI. *Neuropsychology, 12*, 95–114.

Rendell, P. E., & Thomson, D. M. (in press). Aging and prospective memory: Differences between naturalistic and laboratory tasks. *Journal of Gerontology: Psychological Sciences.*

Salthouse, T. A. (1985). *A theory of cognitive aging.* Amsterdam: North-Holland.

Salthouse, T. A. (1988a). Initiating the formalization of theories of cognitive aging. *Psychology and Aging, 3*, 3–16.

Salthouse, T. A. (1988b). The role of processing resources in cognitive aging. In M. L. Howe & C. J. Brainerd (Eds.), *Cognitive development in adulthood: Progress in cognitive development research* (pp. 185–239). New York: Springer-Verlag.

Salthouse, T. A. (1993). Speed mediation of adult age differences in cognition. *Developmental Psychology, 29*, 722–738.

Salthouse, T. A. (1996). The processing-speed theory of adult age differences in cognition. *Psychological Review, 103*, 403–428.

Schacter, D. L., Savage, C. R., Alpert, N. M., Rauch, S. L., & Albert, M. S. (1996). The role of the hippocampus and frontal cortex in age-related memory changes: A PET study. *NeuroReport, 7*, 1165–1169.

Schonfield, D. (1982). Attention switching in higher mental processes. In F. I. M. Craik & S. Trehub (Eds.), *Aging and cognitive processes* (pp. 309–316). New York: Plenum Press.

Schonfield, D., & Robertson, B. (1966). Memory storage and aging. *Canadian Journal of Psychology, 20*, 228–236.

Shallice, T., & Burgess, P. (1991). Higher-order cognitive impairments and frontal lobe lesions in man. In H. S. Levin, H. M. Eisenberg, & A. L. Benton (Eds.), *Frontal lobe function and dysfunction* (pp. 126–138). New York: Oxford University Press.

Shiffrin, R. M., & Schneider, W. (1977). Controlled and automatic human information processing: II. Perceptual learning, automatic attending and a general theory. *Psychological Review, 84*, 127–190.

Shimamura, A. P. (1995). Memory and frontal lobe function. In M. S. Gazzaniga (Ed.), *The cognitive neurosciences* (pp. 803–813). Cambridge, MA: MIT Press.

Smith, M. E. (1993). Neurophysiological manifestations of recollective experience during recognition memory judgments. *Journal of Cognitive Neuroscience, 5*, 1–13.

Soininen, H. S., Partanen, K., Pitkänen, A., Vainio, P., Hänninen, T., Hallikainen, M., Koivisto, K., & Riekkinen, P. J. (1994). Volumetric MRI analysis of the amygdala and the hippocampus in subjects with age-associated memory impairment: Correlation to visual and verbal memory. *Neurology, 44*, 1660–1668.

Strayer, D. L., Wickens, C. D., & Braune, R. (1987). Adult age differences in the speed and capacity of information processing II: An electrophysiological approach. *Psychology and Aging, 2*, 99–110.

Sullivan, E. V., Marsh, L., Mathalon, D. H., Lim, K. O., & Pfefferbaum, A. (1995). Age-related decline in MRI volumes of temporal lobe gray matter but not hippocampus. *Neurobiology of Aging, 16*, 591–606.

Swick, D., & Knight, R. T. (1997). Event-related potentials differentiate the effects of aging on word and nonword repetition in explicit and implicit memory tasks. *Journal of Experimental Psychology: Learning, Memory, and Cognition, 23*, 123–142.

Tulving, E. (1985). Memory and consciousness. *Canadian Psychology, 26*, 1–12.

Tulving, E., Kapur, S., Craik, F. I. M., Moscovitch, M., & Houle, S. (1994). Hemispheric encoding/retrieval asymmetry in episodic memory: Positron emission tomography findings. *Proceedings of the National Academy of Sciences USA, 91*, 2016–2020.

Welford, A. T. (1958). *Ageing and human skill*. London: Oxford University Press.

Wong, D. F., Wagner, H. N., Jr., Dannals, R. F., Links, J. M., Frost, J. J., Ravert, H. T., Wilson, A. A., Rosenbaum, A. E., Gjedde, A., Douglass, K. H., Petronis, J. D., Folstein, M. F., Toung, J. K. T., Burns, H. D., & Kuhar, M. J. (1984). Effects of age on dopamine and serotonin receptors measured by positron tomography in the living human brain. *Science, 226*, 1393–1396.

Zacks, R. T., & Hasher, L. (1994). Directed ignoring: Inhibitory regulation of working memory. In D. Dagenbach & T. H. Carr (Eds.), *Inhibitory processes in attention, memory, and language* (pp. 241–264). San Diego, CA: Academic Press.

Zacks, R. T., & Hasher, L. (1997). Cognitive gerontology and attentional inhibition: A reply to Burke and McDowd. *Journal of Gerontology: Psychological Sciences, 52B*, P274–P283.

Zacks, R. T., Radvansky, G., & Hasher, L. (1996). Studies of directed forgetting in older adults. *Journal of Experimental Psychology: Learning, Memory, and Cognition, 22*, 143–156.

27

Selective Memory Disorders

ANDREW R. MAYES

It has been known since the end of the nineteenth century that brain damage can impair memory relatively selectively (Ribot, 1881), and since World War II evidence has grown that damage to different brain regions selectively disrupts different kinds of memory (see Mayes, 1988). Memory depends on encoding (processing and representing) different kinds of information, which are then stored and later retrieved. Selective memory disorders are interesting because their existence means that memory loss occurs although information for which memory is impaired is still being processed (and hence encoded) relatively normally. Their existence challenges a widely held assumption that information is stored in the same neural network that represents it during encoding (see Ungerleider, 1995) because this implies that brain lesions that damage such networks should disturb not only storage but also the ability to process and represent the information. In other words, the assumption seems hard to reconcile with the occurrence of selective memory deficits for particular kinds of information that are still processed normally at input. It is, therefore, very important to check just how selective memory disorders are. This chapter will outline what is known about the variety of short- and long-term memory disorders caused by brain damage, and how selective they are, be-

fore briefly considering what this reveals about how the brain mediates memory.

Working or Short-Term Memory Disorders

It has been known for some time that cortical damage can impair short-term or working memory while leaving processing relatively intact. Such disorders doubly dissociate from organic amnesia (discussed later), in which fact and episode long-term memory is disrupted but short-term memory is preserved. Short-term memory disorder for phonology has been the most thoroughly explored kind of short-term memory problem. Thus, it has been shown that the ability to hold sequences of phonemes in mind for several seconds is disrupted by lesions to the left parietal lobe, particularly in the left postero-inferior parietal lobe where it conjoins with the left temporal lobe (see McCarthy & Warrington, 1990). A patient with such damage may only be able to repeat back one or two spoken digits when tested immediately after their presentation compared to the normal level of around seven digits and spoken nonword repetition ability is lost similarly fast. Despite this deficit, although some patients may be dysphasic, others show no other cognitive deficits, and not

427

only clearly understand speech but also seem to process phonemes normally when memory load is minimized (see Vallar & Papagno, 1995). Thus, one patient, PV, was unimpaired at making same-different judgments with spoken syllables (Vallar & Baddeley, 1985).

As well as showing normal phonological processing ability, patients with impaired phonological short-term memory may show normal short-term memory for other kinds of information. Short-term memory deficits that are selective in this way have been demonstrated for several kinds of information. For example, whereas PV has impaired phonological short-term memory and intact visuo-spatial short-term memory (Basso, Spinnler, Vallar, & Zanobio, 1982), Hanley, Young, and Pearson (1991) found the reverse pattern of deficit in a patient with a lesion in the region of the right Sylvian fissure (see Vallar & Papagno, 1995, for a discussion). Although Baddeley (1986) only postulated phonological and visuo-spatial short-term stores, there is evidence that visual verbal short-term memory can be selectively disrupted (see Warrington & Rabin, 1971) and Davidoff and Ostergaard (1984) reported a patient who had a selective short-term memory deficit for color information although he could process color normally when memory load was minimized. There is also evidence that relatively selective lexical semantic short-term memory deficits exist. Thus, patient AB was more impaired than patient EA (who had a phonological short-term memory deficit) on tests dependent on lexical semantic short-term memory (for example, word span tests), but performed better although not completely normally on tests primarily dependent on phonological short-term memory such as nonword span tests (see Martin, Shelton, & Yaffee, 1994). This semantic short-term memory deficit was not caused by a semantic processing impairment because AB's speech comprehension and semantic processing were usually normal when memory load was minimized. AB's lesion involved the left postero-lateral frontal lobe and adjacent parietal regions anterior to where damage probably causes phonological short-term memory deficits. Future work will explore Jonides and Smith's (1997) contention that each sensory system and the motor system has one or more short-term memory systems by exploring whether the corresponding kinds of short-term memory can be disrupted without significantly disturbing processing.

There is a widespread belief that long-term memory is preserved in patients with short-term memory deficits because patients with impaired phonological short-term memory often show normal long-term memory for spoken verbal materials. This suggests that there is not a serial relationship between short- and long-term memory, but that they operate in parallel (see McCarthy & Warrington, 1990) because information can reach long-term memory normally when short-term memory is largely absent. However, long-term memory is probably only preserved when it taps different information from that affected by the short-term memory disorder. Three pieces of evidence, which show that long-term memory is impaired when it taps the same information that is impaired by short-term memory, support this view so the belief that short- and long-term memory work in parallel must be wrong. First, Baddeley, Papagno, and Vallar (1988) found that patient PV, who has very impaired phonological short-term memory, was completely unable to learn spoken Russian words, transliterated into her native Italian. In other words, she was impaired at both short- and long-term memory for meaningless spoken words, which she had to represent as phonological sequences. This finding suggests that long-term memory for spoken verbal materials is only preserved when it draws on semantic information, which is rapidly encoded at input. Second, Hanley et al. (1991) found that their patient not only had impaired visuo-spatial short-term memory but also had severely impaired long-term memory for spatial layouts and new faces. Third, Romani and Martin (in press) found that AB was very impaired at long-term memory for lexical semantic information (for example, word lists), but showed preserved long-term memory for any information for which he had normal short-term memory. Interestingly, AB's long-term memory for stories was good, which implies that his short- and long-term memory problem was for single word semantics, and that coherent text relies on a distinct memory system.

These results suggest that short-term memory disorders are specific to particular kinds of information, can occur despite preserved processing of that information at input, and are accompanied by long-term memory deficits provided the same information is tapped by short- and long-term memory. This implies that there is a serial relationship between short- and long-term memory so that information must be initially held in short-term memory if it is to reach long-term memory.

Deficits in Previously Well-Learned Semantic Information

Neocortical lesions, particularly to the antero-lateral temporal cortex, cause impaired long-term memory for previously well-established factual information of the kind that can be found in dictionaries and encyclopaedias (Patterson & Hodges, 1995). These semantic memory deficits are found in dementing conditions such as Alzheimer's disease and the variant of frontotemporal dementia known as semantic dementia (Snowden, Goulding, & Neary, 1989) as well as following closed head injury and viral brain infections. Semantic dementia patients are impaired at naming, identifying, and describing the properties of objects, at defining spoken and written words; and at identifying semantic commonalities between pictures, but show preservation of perception, nonverbal intelligence, and syntactical and phonological abilities. It is important to know how selective to factual memory these deficits are, how selective the dissociations between different kinds of factual memory deficits are, whether the deficits reflect access or storage breakdowns, and whether the location of cortical damage determines the specific factual memories disrupted.

Patterson and Hodges (1995) noted how selective semantic dementia can be and concluded that previously well-established semantic memory (semantic dementia) and episodic memory (organic amnesia) deficits doubly dissociate, although the two memory systems clearly interact. Such interactions may explain the incompleteness of the double dissociation. Thus, semantic dementia patients typically acquire episodic memories relatively normally, but do not show completely preserved episodic memory because new episodes will often involve factual information that they have forgotten. Failure to interpret new episodes in a normal semantic fashion reduces episodic memory because people show worse episodic memory when semantic encoding is minimal (Craik & Lockhart, 1972). Conversely, amnesics may fail to learn new facts normally (for example, Gabrieli, Cohen, & Corkin, 1988) because they are impaired at episodic memory, which may underlie rapid acquisition of new fact memories, although these eventually become independent of episodic memory.

Recent work of Graham and Hodges (1997) suggests that the above view may be wrong and that semantic dementia is a misnomer. Their patients showed an inverted temporal gradient of deficit in which remote autobiographical memories (formed when semantic memory was normal) were more impaired than recent ones. and a case study found that autobiographical memories less than two years old were sometimes preserved. Similarly, Hodges and Graham (1998) found better recognition of famous faces from the current time period rather than earlier, and that a mildly impaired patient was better at retrieving detailed information about famous people from the current time period. Whether the memories are semantic or episodic may not matter. In "semantic dementia" new facts and events seem to be learned as well as remaining semantic memory permits and perhaps retained normally for a while. But the neocortical structures responsible for very long-term retention of facts and episodes are damaged so that over a period of years both kinds of information are lost pathologically. This interpretation is consistent with Squire and Alvarez's (1995) hypothesis of medial temporal lobe (MTL) amnesia, which states that fact and episode memories are initially stored in the MTL, but through gradual reorganization storage is transferred for very long-term maintenance to neocortical structures such as the anterolateral temporal cortex.

Whether different neocortical lesions can cause dissociable deficits for previously well-established semantic and episodic memories is currently unresolved. Dissociation seems likely to the extent that episodic information differs from semantic information provided one assumes that memories are stored where they are represented, and that different information is represented in different neural structures. Is nonoverlap likely? Some, but not all facts, contain perceptual and even contextual information, whereas episodes must contain this information and typically contain other factual information. Therefore, the neocortical dissociations should depend on the specific subtype of episodic or semantic memory in question.

Within semantic memory and consistent with the above suggestion, there is evidence that semantic memories for different categories break down in a dissociable manner (see Mayes, 1988; Patterson & Hodges, 1995). Thus, dissociations between impairments of word and object knowledge, and knowledge of abstract and concrete words respectively, have been reported (see Patterson & Hodges, 1995).

However, double dissociations between deficits in animate category and inanimate category knowledge have been most studied (see Patterson & Hodges, 1995; Hillis & Caramazza, 1991). Controversy continues about whether this dissociation reflects uncontrolled differences between the categories tested in variables like frequency, familiarity, and age of acquisition. Nevertheless, the dissociation might be expected if animate concepts primarily involve visual perceptual properties whereas inanimate concepts primarily involve functional properties. There is evidence that this is the case (Farah & McClelland, 1991). Lesion evidence suggests that more posterior temporal cortex lesions produce deficits in memory for man-made things whereas more anterior temporal cortex lesions disrupt memory for animate things (Hillis & Caramazza, 1991; Gainotti, Silveri, Daniele, & Giustolisi, 1995).

Shallice (1986) has proposed five criteria for deciding whether a semantic memory deficit reflects a problem with keeping fact memories in store or with accessing them. The two most plausible of these criteria involved consistency of success or failure of retrieval, and the presence or absence of item-specific implicit (unaware) memory. Shallice argued that consistently unsuccessful retrieval of particular items on different occasions implies that storage has been degraded. Conversely, if information is not recognized or recalled, but is associated with normal implicit memory, then the explicit memory deficit reflects an access problem selective to aware memory. Minimally, Shallice's argument requires that consistent failure should not be found with intact implicit memory. Although the criteria currently lack a strong theoretical base and may not easily cover the effects of partial storage damage, there is some evidence that, in semantic dementia, when previously retrievable memories become inaccessible, they remain so consistently (see Patterson & Hodges, 1995), which suggests that storage degradation is responsible.

Organic Amnesia and Frontal Lobe Damage: Episodic and Semantic Memory

Global organic amnesia is a syndrome in which there is impaired recall and recognition of facts and episodes encountered both postmorbidly (anterograde amnesia) and (more variably) premorbidly (retrograde amnesia). These deficits often occur even when intelligence and short-term memory are preserved. There is also preservation of overlearned semantic memories, various forms of skill learning and memory, and of at least some kinds of unaware memory for specific information (priming—see next section). The deficits can be produced by lesions to structures in the MTL, midline diencephalon, basal forebrain, and possibly ventromedial frontal cortex, as well as to structures, such as the fornix, that link these regions (see Mayes, 1988, for a discussion).

There is growing evidence that the syndrome is functionally heterogeneous. It has been claimed that retrograde amnesia can be produced relatively independently of anterograde amnesia, and also that lesions of different parts of the MTL and their respective projection sites cause dissociable forms of anterograde amnesia.

Several studies have found poor correlations in patients between severity of anterograde and retrograde amnesia (particularly that affecting remote premorbid memories). There have also been several reports of relatively selective retrograde amnesia (see Kapur, 1993) in which patients had a severe and enduring deficit in premorbid memory, but a relatively preserved ability to acquire new memories (so that old memories could be "relearned" to some extent). The location of lesions that cause this condition remains to be accurately resolved, but damage often includes the anterolateral temporal neocortex, particularly on the left. Kroll, Markowitsch, Knight, and von Cramon (1997) reported two patients who had damage to their temporopolar and frontal cortices, mainly on the left. These patients showed extensive retrograde amnesia, but their intelligence and new learning abilities were relatively (not completely) intact. One of the patients seemed more impaired at public information memory than at autobiographical memory, but it is hard to determine whether this was because of his relative premorbid investment in these different kinds of information or because these kinds of information were stored in different cortical regions.

The results to date suggest that old memories about autobiographical and public information may be disrupted by lesions to parts of the temporal cortex. Damage to prefrontal cortex can also disturb these memories, but it is unproved that such lesions alone can disrupt premorbid memory relatively selectively. It needs to be determined more precisely which temporal (and possibly parietal) lesions disrupt remote premorbid memories and how these relate to the damage underlying semantic dementia. Finally, there is a particular difficulty with these selective retrograde amnesia patients in proving that they are not malingering or suffering from a psychogenic deficit.

It is generally agreed that amygdala damage does not usually cause anterograde amnesia in contrast to other MTL lesions (see Zola-Morgan & Squire, 1993). However, the amygdala probably plays a role in emotional memory by modulating the effectiveness of other MTL structures in storing memories when encoding is emotionally fired up (see Sarter & Markowitsch, 1985). These issues have been very little explored in humans because of the rarity of even fairly selective amygdala lesions.

Reed and Squire (1997) have defended the view that MTL lesions, whether they are of the hippocampus or perirhinal cortex, disrupt memory in the same way, but that hippocampal lesions may have a lesser effect. This view implies that free recall and item recognition are equivalently disrupted after MTL lesions. In contrast, Aggleton and Brown (in press) have argued that hippocampal and perirhinal cortex lesions cause dissociable deficits. Their view is based on animal and human evidence. First, animals with perirhinal lesions have shown item recognition impairments (for example, Ennaceur, Neave, & Aggleton, 1996), but intact spatial memory (Gaffan, 1994), whereas the reverse effect has been found with hippocampal lesions (Aggleton, Hunt, & Rawlins, 1986). Second, a meta-analysis of human recognition data by Aggleton and Shaw (1996) suggested that there is a single dissociation in which patients with damage to the hippocampus or other parts of Papez circuit such as the fornix, mammillary bodies, or anterior thalamus are relatively unimpaired on item recognition, but as impaired as more generally lesioned global amnesics (who are also impaired at item recognition) on free-recall tests.

Although Reed and Squire (1997) have reported that several patients with apparently selective hippocampal damage were clearly impaired on item recognition when an extensive battery of tests was given, Aggleton and Brown noted that patients with selective hippocampal sclerosis related to temporal lobe epilepsy have been reported not to show impaired item recognition, and other patients with probable hippocampal damage caused by

hypoxia showed a similar preservation. Also, Vargha-Khadem, Gadian, Watkins, van Paesschen, and Mishkin (1997) have described three patients with evidence of early selective hippocampal damage, who showed completely selective free-recall deficits as their item recognition was normal on a range of tests.

Apparently selective hippocampal damage, therefore, sometimes causes severe item recognition deficits and sometimes leaves item recognition relatively or completely intact. Cerebral ischaemia often produces damage that extends beyond the hippocampus (see Bachevalier & Meunier, 1996), and as such damage may be hard to identify either by structural imaging or postmortem analysis, the most likely possibility is that those patients with more severe recognition deficits have cryptic damage extending into other brain regions important for item recognition, such as the perirhinal cortex. Such cryptic damage may be best detected by measuring whether blood flow is abnormal in nonhippocampal brain regions to a greater extent in the patients with severe item recognition deficits.

Fairly selective damage to other parts of Papez circuit (see figure 27.1) has also been found sometimes to cause little or no disruption of item recognition. Thus, Aggleton and Brown noted that relatively selective free-recall deficits have sometimes been reported after fornix lesions caused by colloid cyst surgery and also following mammillary body lesions. Lesions that affect only the anterior thalamic nucleus within the thalamus are very rare, but Hanley, Davies, Downes, and Mayes (1994) have described a patient with such very selective damage, although she also had damage to the head of her left caudate nucleus and her left fornix. This patient had completely normal recognition for items and a free-recall deficit for verbal materials.

The other memory system proposed by Aggleton and Brown (in press) comprised a circuit involving the perirhinal cortex, the dorsomedial nucleus of the thalamus and possibly the orbitofrontal cortex (see figure 27.2). As indicated above, in animals, selective perirhinal cortex lesions disrupt item recognition, but not some kinds of spatial memory. They also disrupt associations between similar kinds of items. Little relevant work has been done in humans mainly because very selective perirhinal cortex or dorsomedial thalamic lesions are extremely rare in humans or even nonexistent.

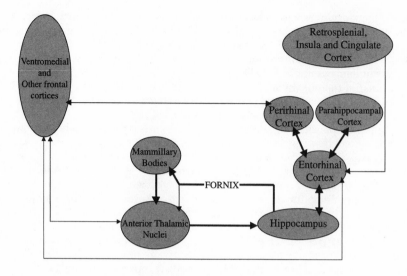

Figure 27.1 A schematic diagram of the Papez circuit structures in which thicker lines indicate the probably greater functional importance of the connections. Lesions of the hippocampus-fornix-mammillary bodies-anterior thalamus system may disrupt some kinds of associative recognition and free recall, but minimally affect item recognition. Perirhinal cortex lesions may, unlike hippocampal lesions, disrupt item recognition because this cortex also sends information to non-hippocampal regions.

Nevertheless, Buffalo, Reber, and Squire (1998) have reported that two patients with total bilateral destruction of the perirhinal cortex (as well as other regions) showed more severe impairments of recognition for complex patterns at delays of a few seconds than did other global amnesics. Interestingly, these patients performed normally at delays of zero and two seconds, as well as when making judgments when the stimulus was still present. This suggests that perirhinal cortex lesions disrupt long-term memory, but leave short-term memory and perception intact. These long-term memory deficits may be very dependent on perirhinal cortex damage being nearly total because epileptic patients with fairly selective damage that includes only part of the perirhinal cortex showed normal performance on standard tests of anterograde amnesia, but accelerated forgetting over delays of

Figure 27.2 A schematic diagram of the structures in the perirhinal cortex-dorsomedial thalamic system with the relative thickness of the lines indicating the probable degree of functional importance of the connections. Damage to this system disrupts item recognition, but the full range of mnemonic effects produced by damaging it is unknown.

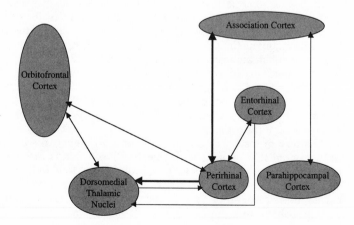

weeks. By these delays, their memory was badly impaired (see Kapur et al., 1996). Partial perirhinal cortex damage may, therefore, cause a much less severe and much delayed item-recognition deficit than does total damage to this cortex. Something similar may happen with dorsomedial thalamic lesions. Thus, Isaac et al. (1998) reported a case, shown by careful analysis of brain scan information to have fairly focal damage to a large part of this nucleus, who showed impaired item recognition as well as free recall. They indicated that other studies have found little evidence of memory deficits when only a small portion of the nucleus was damaged.

Lesions of both the Papez circuit structures and the perirhinal cortex circuit are known to cause retrograde as well as anterograde amnesia. Although severe retrograde amnesia can extend back to memories acquired decades before the causative brain damage, there often appears to be a temporal gradient in which earlier acquired memories are less disrupted (see Hodges, 1995). As Hodges notes, some evidence suggests that Papez circuit lesions cause a less severe, more steeply temporally graded retrograde amnesia than do larger lesions that involve the perirhinal cortex circuit. This would be consistent with Squire and Alvarez's (1995) hypothesis that the hippocampus (and perhaps other MTL regions) only store facts and episodes for a limited time until reorganizational processes result in neocortical storage in the sites that presumably represent the stored information. Nadel and Moscovitch (1998) have, however, challenged the claim that retrograde amnesia shows a temporal gradient at least for some kinds of information (such as spatial) so this hypothesis should be regarded as currently unproved. Future work must explore whether selective Papez circuit lesions minimally disrupt premorbid item recognition memory.

Exactly what processes are disrupted in patients with the amnesia syndrome? If the syndrome is heterogeneous, there must be several such processes. It is widely believed that many global amnesia patients process facts and episodes fairly normally because their intelligence is preserved and normal kinds of information are available to them at input when memory load is minimized (Mayes, Downes, Shoqeirat, Hall, & Sagar, 1993). Evidence from transient global amnesia (TGA) makes it unlikely that retrieval is impaired in global anterograde amnesia. TGA is a form of global amnesia that lasts for only a few hours and is usually caused by a reversible abnormality in the MTL (see Goldenberg, 1995). Upon recovery, although all premorbid memories apart from those acquired in the few minutes or hours prior to the incident typically return, as does the ability to lay down new memories, no memories for the incident itself return. As these memories do not return even when retrieval must be normal, global anterograde amnesia is probably caused by a failure to consolidate facts and episodes into long-term memory during the period immediately after input.

If Aggleton and Brown (in press) are correct, hippocampal (and Papez circuit) lesions will disrupt the consolidation of different kinds of information from those disrupted by perirhinal cortex lesions. Vargha-Khadem et al. (1997) found that their three patients with selective hippocampal lesions were normal not only at recognition memory for single items (e.g., words or faces) but also for associations between the same kind of items (e.g., word-word or face-face associations). They were, however, severely impaired at recognizing associations the components of which would be processed in different cortical regions (e.g., object-location and face-voice). As they also found that their patients remote memory for overlearned facts was relatively preserved, hippocampal and Papez circuit lesions may only disrupt consolidation of primarily episodic associations, the components of which are represented in different cortical regions.

Fairly selective right parahippocampal lesions in humans also disrupt spatial memory, although whether these deficits are different or more severe than those produced by right hippocampal lesions remains uncertain (Bohbot et al., 1997). It is unknown whether parahippocampal cortex lesions disrupt memory for similar kinds of association to those disrupted by hippocampal lesions so this requires exploration.

As Buffalo et al. (1998) showed, lesions that include the perirhinal cortex drastically impair item recognition, but little is known about the effect of selective lesions of this structure in humans. Animal studies indicate that selective damage to this cortex disrupts recognition of items and associations between similar components, but not memory for some kinds of spatial information. Ways need to be found of extending similar studies to humans to determine whether perirhinal cortex lesions merely disrupt memory for more kinds of information than hippocampal lesions or whether there are also kinds of memory (such as spatial memory) that are only disrupted by hippocampal lesions.

Prefrontal cortex damage sometimes disrupts long-term memory for post- as well as premorbidly experienced facts and episodes (see Kroll et al., 1997). Most commonly, the deficits are of free recall, temporal and source memory, and various kinds of metamemory such as making accurate feeling-of-knowing judgments when recall fails (see Mayes, 1988). However, recognition deficits typically involving high numbers of false alarms have also been reported in the presence of free recall that is relatively normal apart from the production of a pathological level of false positives (Delbecq-Derouesne, Beauvois, & Shallice, 1990).

Such memory impairments are probably secondary to the effect of frontal cortex damage on executive processes and perhaps working memory. If sophisticated encoding processes cannot be properly orchestrated, then memory will suffer and the effect is likely (as is often found) to disrupt free recall, which is more dependent than item recognition on the storage of rich inter-item associations. Similarly, if the organization of searching operations during retrieval is disrupted, then free recall will probably be affected more than item recognition. Whether this kind of explanation accounts for the disruption of temporal and source memory in frontally damaged patients (see Mayes, 1988, for a discussion) remains to be proved, but these kinds of contextual memory are likely to require considerable amounts of organization at both encoding and retrieval. The recognition deficit, reported by Delbecq-Derousne et al. (1990) is probably related to the patient's production of high numbers of false alarms in recall as well as recognition tests. This problem could be caused by impaired ability to monitor whether or not a "memory" is appropriate. Its existence suggests that differently located frontal cortex lesions may disrupt different executive processes and different aspects of fact and episode memory.

There is, however, no clearcut evidence that left and right prefrontal cortex lesions disrupt memory differently. Although there may be a weak relationship between right frontal damage and retrograde amnesia for episodes (see Kroll et al., 1997), Swick and Knight (1996) have found no evidence for episodic retrieval deficits in patients with right frontal

cortex lesions. However, a pathological tendency to make false alarms during recognition testing has been noted after both left- and right-sided frontal cortex damage (Parkin, Bindschaedler, Harsent, & Metzler, in press; Curran, Schacter, Norman, & Galluccio, 1997). Whereas in one case, performance improved when the patient performed a semantic orienting task at encoding, in the other it improved when foils were in a different semantic category from all target items.

Long-term memory for episodes and facts involves a large network of neural structures interacting with each other. The network includes several frontal cortex regions interacting with both temporal and parietal cortices, as well as subcortical structures. The precise characteristics of the memory impairments caused by lesions to specific parts of the network need further specification so as to test the functional deficit hypotheses more rigorously. For example, temporal order memory can be disrupted both by amnesia and by frontal cortex lesions. The impaired process is presumably different in the two cases, involving consolidation in the former and some kind of difficulty in executing effortful encoding and/ or retrieval processes in the latter. Mangels (1997) has shown that the frontal deficit only occurs following intentional encoding, which indicates that the source of the problem is primarily impoverished effortful encoding. If the deficit relates to deficient consolidation in amnesia, amnesics should be impaired following both intentional and incidental encoding.

Priming Deficits

Priming involves the retrieval of specific information that rememberers are typically unaware they are remembering. This kind of unaware memory is indicated by the enhanced fluency with which the remembered information is reactivated when cues that form part of the memory are encoded. Enhanced reactivation fluency of the remembered representation probably depends on storage changes at the synapses of the representing region binding the components of the memory more tightly together. One would, therefore, expect these changes to occur in different neocortical regions depending not only on whether semantic or perceptual information is being implicitly remembered but also on precisely what kinds of such information are involved. Consistent with this, functional imaging has shown that whereas visual object priming produces reduced activation of visual cortex regions where the visual object information should be represented at encoding (see Wiggs & Martin, 1998), semantic priming produced less activation in the left inferior frontal cortex (Demb et al., 1995). This implies that perceptual and semantic kinds of priming occur in different cortical regions although perceptual priming may not always be based in posterior cortex or semantic priming in frontal cortex regions. Lesions in these regions disrupt the appropriate kinds of priming.

Amnesics, who do not have damage in these neocortical regions, might be expected to show preserved priming. However, if the priming involves retrieval of the kinds of association that amnesics fail to store normally, then deficits might be expected. The evidence is still incomplete. There is good evidence that amnesics show preserved priming for information that was already in memory prior to study (such as words or famous faces), but whether they show preserved priming for some or all kinds of associative representations that were novel prior to study is uncertain as deficits have been reported (for example, see Curran & Schacter, 1997). Interpretation of such results is difficult because normal people may effortfully use explicit memory in priming tasks in hard-to-determine ways whereas amnesics cannot.

If perceptual information is processed in the posterior association cortex, then one might expect that lesions in this region will disrupt perceptual priming. This is consistent with evidence that Alzheimer patients typically show preservation of perceptual priming, but impairment in more semantic kinds of priming (see Salmon, Lineweaver, & Heindel, 1998). These patients have relative preservation of primary sensory processing regions in the posterior cortex, but marked atrophy in the temporal association cortex that with the left frontal region plays a key role in processing semantic information. Thus, Postle, Corkin, and Growdon (1996) have reported that Alzheimer patients show preservation of priming for previously novel patterns, which they argue are probably represented in the peristriate cortex, an area that should be relatively preserved in the patients. In contrast, Brandt, Spencer, McSorley, and Folstein (1988) found that Alzheimer patients were impaired at a more semantic verbal free-association priming task. There are inconsistent findings about whether these patients are impaired

at stem completion priming, which some argue may relate to this being a partially semantic priming task. However, Downes et al. (1996) have argued, on the basis of both a meta-analysis and a confirmatory experiment, that the key requirement for preserved priming was that patients should explicitly process the words phonologically during study. This interpretation is supported by evidence that they suffer from as yet inadequately characterized phonological processing problems (Biassou et al., 1995).

Alzheimer's patients are impaired not only at certain kinds of priming but also at explicit memory for facts and episodes so they do not show evidence of a dissociation between priming and recognition and/or recall. Keane, Gabrieli, Mapstone, Johnston, and Corkin (1995), however, noted this dissociation in a patient with a right posterior neocortical lesion. This patient was impaired at certain kinds of visual repetition priming. In contrast, he was relatively normal not only at semantic priming but also at recognition of visually presented words for which visual repetition priming was impaired. A double dissociation was noted between this patient and HM, who has MTL lesions that disrupt his recognition memory, but do not affect his visual priming of premorbidly familiar materials. In more recent work, this group has reported that a similar patient was unimpaired not only at the recollection component of recognition but also at the familiarity component (Gabrieli, Wagner, Stebbins, Burton, & Fleischman, 1995).

This dissociation might arise because visual word recognition usually involves retrieving primarily semantic information rather than the kinds of visual information retrieved in the perceptual priming at which both patients were impaired. However, Fleischman, Vaidya, Lange, and Gabrieli (1997) have shown that recognition of modality and font of word presentation was also preserved in the presence of impaired visual priming. If the perceptual information retrieved in the intact recognition and impaired priming tasks was truly matched, and the priming deficit was caused by a storage deficit, this finding would show that perceptual priming does not contribute to perceptual recognition. The priming deficits shown by Keane and her colleagues are, however, associated with some visual processing problems, so it still needs to be determined whether selective priming deficits can occur without corresponding processing problems.

Deficits in Other Kinds of Procedural/Implicit Memory

Amnesics perform normally on other kinds of procedural memory such as classical conditioning as well as skill learning and memory. Thus, Daum and Ackerman (1994) showed preserved delay eye blink classical conditioning in a group of amnesics. Amnesics have also been shown to acquire normally the motor skill of mirror-drawing (see Cohen, 1984), the perceptual skill of reading mirror-reversed words (Cohen & Squire, 1980), and the cognitive skill of intuitively grasping the relationship between variables to achieve a target value (Squire & Frambach, 1990). Amnesic performance has also been shown to be preserved in the acquisition of adaptation-level effects with weights and with the acquisition of the ability to perceive depth using random-dot stereograms (Benzing & Squire, 1989).

In contrast to amnesics, patients with Huntington's disease (HD), who have neostriatal damage, have been found to show impaired acquisition and retention of skills such as reading mirror-reversed words and relatively normal performance at verbal recognition tests (Martone, Butters, & Payne, 1984). In a similar way, Parkinson's patients, whose substantia nigra pathology also impacts on neostriatal function, have shown impaired acquisition of cognitive skills despite being normal at some explicit memory tasks (Saint-Cyr, Taylor, & Lang, 1988).

With respect to motor skills, Heindel, Salmon, and Butters (1991) found that, unlike amnesics, patients with HD failed to show normal adaptation-level effects with weights. This is particularly interesting because, although no correlation between motor dysfunction and motor skill acquisition dysfunction has been found in these patients (see Salmon et al., in press), uncertainty still existed over the functional deficits that underlay the motor skill acquisition deficit in HD. As the adaptation-level task is much less dependent on overt movement than motor skill acquisition, it is probable that neostriatal damage disrupts the development of motor programs vital for both normal motor skill acquisition and adaptation-level effects. The neostriatum may be particularly involved in developing motor programs for sequences of motor acts because neurodegenerative diseases affecting the neostriatum disrupt serial reaction time performance (see Salmon et al., in press). Cerebellar

atrophy disrupts performance on the serial reaction time task (Pascual et al., 1993), which suggests that the cerebellum is also involved in developing motor programs, perhaps because it indexes the temporal order of sensorimotor events.

The involvement of the striatum in perceptual and cognitive skills is supported by several reports of deficits in the development of such skills in patients with degenerative damage in the region (see Salmon et al., in press). But impairments are not always found as Huberman, Moscovitch, and Freedman (1994) found preserved acquisition of mirror-reading skill in Parkinson's disease patients. Further investigation is necessary, preferably with patients who have selective stroke damage to the basal ganglia. Whether cerebellar damage impairs these kinds of skill acquisition is uncertain because although deficits have been reported (see Salmon et al., 1998), a very careful study by Daum, Ackerman et al. (1993) found that patients with selective cerebellar degeneration showed no deficits in learning to read mirror-reversed text or solving the Tower of Hanoi problem.

Cerebellar lesions have been shown to disrupt the development of delay eye blink classical conditioning while leaving explicit memory intact (Daum, Schugens et al., 1993; Daum & Schugens, 1995). However, Daum and her colleagues found autonomic or emotional conditioning to be unimpaired in their cerebellar patients. Autonomic conditioning may well be mediated by a system that includes the amygdala so it will need to be shown what this form of conditioning shares with motoric conditioning apart from the name.

Whereas delay conditioning in which the conditioned stimulus is still present when the unconditioned stimulus appears is preserved in amnesics, more complex forms of conditioning may not be. Thus, Daum and Schugens (in press) found that amnesics were impaired at reversal discrimination conditioning and argued that this deficit arose because normal performance depends partly on the use of aware (explicit) memory, which is impaired in amnesics. Clark and Squire (1998) similarly argued that a deficit they found in amnesic trace motor conditioning (in which the conditioned stimulus ends before the unconditioned stimulus appears) occurred because such conditioning arises only in normal people who develop aware memory for the contingencies between conditioned and unconditioned stimuli. Measuring conditioned responses in the trace conditioning paradigm is difficult and Woodruff-Pak (1993) reported that trace conditioning was relatively preserved, long-lasting, and not associated with awareness in the amnesic, HM, so it remains unresolved whether trace conditioning is impaired in amnesia and whether it requires aware memory for the conditional contingencies. The problems associated with determining the relationship between trace conditioning and awareness have been well discussed by LaBar and Disterhoft (1998), who emphasize the difficulty of assessing awareness retrospectively in memory impaired patients.

Conclusion

Differently located brain damage disrupts memory for different kinds of information, often despite having little effect on the processing of the poorly remembered information. Processing may not always be unaffected (as perhaps is the case with selective priming deficits), and it is sometimes hard to determine whether it is (as with skill memory and conditioning), but, insofar as it is, the view that information is stored in the same neurons that process and represent it is challenged. At least four explanations of this apparent challenge are possible. First, the damaged region may merely modulate storage in the neural system that represents the poorly remembered information. Basal forebrain structures may play this modulatory role. Second, partial damage to the representing neural system may be sufficient to disrupt its storage abilities while having a minimal effect on its representational processing abilities. This may apply to the short-term memory disorders. Third, there are multiple representational-storage neural systems for the same information. Fourth, information is not stored exactly where it is represented. Whether amnesia necessitates the third, fourth, or other explanations is currently unknown.

The existence of multiple memory deficits suggests that there are different memory systems for different kinds of information, each with its own neural system that may mediate memory through the use of qualitatively distinct processes. Such a set of memory systems would be organized hierarchically. This is true of the influential taxonomy developed by Squire, Knowlton, and Musen (1993), which discriminates between declarative and nondeclarative memory where the former involves

all aware forms of memory and the latter all nonaware forms. If correct, all aware forms of memory should have more in common with each other than they do with any form of nonaware memory, and vice-versa. This would be untrue if amnesics have impaired priming for the same information for they which show impaired aware memory as some have claimed, and also if they are impaired at forms of conditioning that can be shown not to depend on aware memory as some believe.

The issue is very important and currently unresolved. Either memory systems are mainly organized around whether or not they produce aware memory or the kinds of information they store is more fundamental to their organization. Resolution will involve determining the relationship between unaware and aware memory and how aware memory is produced.

References

Aggleton, J. P., & Brown, M. W. (1999). Episodic memory, amnesia and the hippocampal-anterior thalamic axis. *Behavioural Brain Science, 22*, 425–489.

Aggleton, J. P., Hunt, P. R., & Rawlins, J. N. P. (1986). The effects of hippocampal lesions upon spatial and non-spatial tests of working memory. *Behavioural Brain Research, 19*, 133–146.

Aggleton, J. P., & Shaw, C. (1996). Amnesia and recognition memory: A re-analysis of psychometric data. *Neuropsychologia, 34*, 51–62.

Baddeley, A. D. (1986). *Working memory.* Oxford: Oxford University Press.

Baddeley, A. D., Papagno, C., & Vallar, G. (1988). When long-term learning depends on short-term storage. *Journal of Memory and Language, 27*, 586–595.

Bachevalier, J., & Meunier, M. (1996). Cerebral ischaemia: Are the memory deficits associated with hippocampal cell loss? *Hippocampus, 6*, 553–560.

Basso, A., Spinnler, H., Vallar, G., & Zanobio, E. (1982). Left hemisphere damage and selective impairment of auditory verbal short-term memory: A case study. *Neuropsychologia, 20*, 263–274.

Benzing, W. C., & Squire, L. R. (1989). Preserved learning and memory in amnesia: Intact adaptation-level effects and learning of stereoscopic depth. *Behavioural Neuroscience, 103*, 538–547.

Biassou, N., Grossman, M., Onishi, K., Mickanin, J., Hughes, E., Robinson, K. M., &

D'Esposito, M. (1995). Phonological processing deficits in Alzheimer's disease. *Neurology, 45,* 2165–2169.

Bohbot, V., Kalina, M., Stepankova, K., Spackova, N., Petrides, M., & Nadel, L. (1997). Spatial memory deficits in patients with lesions to the right hippocampus and to the right parahippocampal cortex. *Neuropsychologia, 36,* 1217–1238.

Brandt, J., Spencer, M., McSorley, P., & Folstein, M. F. (1988). Semantic memory activation and implicit memory in Alzheimer disease. *Alzheimer's disease and Associated Disorders, 2,* 112–119.

Buffalo, E. A., Reber, P. J., & Squire, L. R. (1998). The human perirhinal cortex and recognition memory. *Hippocampus, 8,* 330–339.

Clark, R. E., & Squire, L. R. (1998). Classical conditioning and brain systems: The role of awareness. *Science, 280,* 77–81.

Cohen, N. J. (1984). Preserved learning capacity in amnesia: Evidence for multiple memory systems. In L. R. Squire & N. Butters (Eds.), *Neuropsychology of memory* (pp. 83–103). New York: Guilford Press.

Cohen, N. J., & Squire, L. R. (1980). Preserved learning and retention of pattern analysing skill in amnesia: Dissociation of knowing how and knowing that. *Science, 210,* 207–210.

Craik, F. I. M., & Lockhart, R. S. (1972). Levels of processing: A framework for memory research. *Journal of Verbal Learning and Verbal Behavior, 11,* 671–684.

Curran, T., & Schacter, D. L. (1997). Implicit memory: What must theories of amnesia explain? *Memory, 5,* 37–48.

Curran, T., Schacter, D. L., Norman, K. A., & Galluccio, L. (1997). False recognition after a right frontal lobe infarction: Memory for general and specific information. *Neuropsychologia, 35,* 1035–1049.

Daum, I., & Ackerman, H. (1994). Dissociation of declarative and nondeclarative memory after bilateral thalamic lesions: A case report. *International Journal of Neuroscience, 75,* 153–165.

Daum, I., Ackerman, H., Schugens, M. M., Reimold, C., Dichgans, J., & Birbaumer, N. (1993). The cerebellum and cognitive functions in humans. *Behavioural Neuroscience, 107,* 411–419.

Daum, I., & Schugens, M. M. (1995). Classical conditioning after brain lesions in humans: The contribution of neuropsychology. *Journal of Psychophysiology, 9,* 109–118.

Daum, I., & Schugens, M. M. (in press). Impairment of eyeblink discrimination reversal learning in amnesia. *Society for Neuroscience Abstracts.*

Daum, I., Schugens, M. M., Ackerman, H., Lutzenberg, W., Dichgans, J., & Birbaumer, N. (1993). Classical conditioning after cerebellar lesions in humans. *Behavioural Neuroscience, 105,* 748–756.

Davidoff, J. B., & Ostergaard, A. L. (1984). Colour anomia resulting from weakened short-term colour memory. *Brain, 107,* 415–430.

Delbecq-Derouesne, J., Beauvois, M. F., & Shallice, T. (1990). Preserved recall versus impaired recognition. *Brain, 113,* 1045–1074.

Demb, J. B., Desmond, J. E., Wagner, A. D., Vaidya, C. J., Glover, G. H., & Gabrieli, J. D. E. (1995). Semantic encoding and retrieval in the left inferior prefrontal cortex: A functional MRI study. *Journal of Neuroscience, 15,* 5870–5878.

Downes, J. J., Davis, E. J., De Mornay Davies, P., Perfect, T. J., Wilson, K., Mayes, A. R., & Sagar, H. J. (1996). Stem-completion priming in Alzheimer's disease: The importance of target word articulation. *Neuropsychologia, 34,* 63–75.

Ennaceur, A., Neave, N., & Aggleton, J. P. (1996). Neurotoxic lesions of the perirhinal cortex do not mimic the behavioural effects of fornix transection in the rat. *Behavioural Brain Research, 80,* 9–25.

Farah, M., & McClelland, J. L. (1991). A computational model of semantic memory impairment: Modality specificity and emergent category specificity. *Journal of Experimental Psychology: General, 120,* 339–357.

Fleischman, D. A., Vaidya, C. J., Lange, K. L., & Gabrieli, J. D. E. (1997). A dissociation between perceptual explicit and implicit memory processes. *Brain and Cognition, 35,* 42–57.

Gabrieli, J. D. E., Cohen, N. J., & Corkin, S. (1988). The impaired learning of semantic knowledge following bilateral medial temporal-lobe resection. *Brain and Cognition, 7,* 525–539.

Gabrieli, J. D. E., Wagner, A. D., Stebbins, G. T., Burton, K. W., & Fleischman, D. A. (1995). Neuropsychological dissociation between perceptual fluency and recognition fluency in long-term memory. *Society for Neuroscience Abstracts, 21,* 753.

Gaffan, D. (1994). Dissociated effects of perirhinal cortex ablation, fornix transection and amygdalectomy: Evidence for multiple memory systems in the primate temporal lobe. *Experimental Brain Research, 99,* 411–422.

Gainotti, G., Silveri, M., Daniele, A., & Giustolisi, L. (1995). Neuroanatomical correlates of category-specific semantic disorders: A critical survey. *Memory, 3,* 247–264.

Goldenberg, G. (1995). Transient global amnesia. In A. D. Baddeley, B. A. Wilson, & F. N. Watts (Eds.), *Handbook of memory disorders* (pp. 109–133). Chichester: John Wiley.

Graham, K. S., & Hodges, J. R. (1997). Differentiating the roles of the hippocampal complex and the neocortex in long-term memory storage: Evidence from the study of semantic dementia. *Neuropsychology, 11,* 77–89.

Hanley, J. R., Davies, A. D. M., Downes, J. J., & Mayes, A. R. (1994). Impaired recall of verbal material following rupture and repair of an anterior communicating artery aneurysm. *Cognitive Neuropsychology, 11,* 543–578.

Hanley, J. R., Young, A. W., & Pearson, N. A. (1991). Impairment of the visuospatial sketch pad. *Quarterly Journal of Experimental Psychology: Human Experimental Psychology, 43A,* 101–125.

Heindel, W., Salmon, D., & Butters, N. (1991). The biasing of weight-judgements in Alzheimer's and Huntington's disease: A priming or programming phenomenon. *Journal of Clinical and Experimental Neuropsychology, 13,* 189–203.

Hillis, A. E., & Caramazza, A. (1991). Category-specific naming and comprehension impairment: A double dissociation. *Brain, 114,* 2081–2094.

Hodges, J. R. (1995). Retrograde amnesia. In A. D. Baddeley, B. A. Wilson, & F. N. Watts (Eds.), *Handbook of memory disorders* (pp. 81–107). Chichester: John Wiley.

Hodges, J. R., & Graham, K. S. (1998). A reversal of the temporal gradient for famous person knowledge in semantic dementia: Implications for the neural organization of long-term memory. *Neuropsychologia, 36,* 803–825.

Huberman, M., Moscovitch, M., & Freedman, M. (1994). Comparison of patients with Alzheimer's and Parkinson's disease on different explicit and implicit tests of memory. *Neuropsychiatry, Neuropsychology, and Behavioural Neurology, 7,* 185–193.

Isaac, C. L., Holdstock, J. S., Cezayirli, E., Roberts, J. N., Holmes, C. J., & Mayes, A. R. (1998). Amnesia in a patient with lesions limited to the dorsomedial thalamic nucleus. *Neurocase, 4,* 497–508.

Jonides, J., & Smith, E. E. (1997). The architecture of working memory. In M. D. Rugg (Ed.), *Cognitive neuroscience* (pp. 243–276). Hove, East Sussex: Psychology Press.

Kapur, N. (1993). Focal retrograde amnesia in neurological disease: A critical review. *Cortex, 29,* 217–234.

Kapur, N., Scholey, K., Moore, E., Barker, S., Brice, Thompson, S., Shiel, A., Carn, R., Abbott, P., & Fleming, J. (1996). Long-term retention deficits in two cases of disproportionate retrograde amnesia. *Journal of Cognitive Neuroscience, 8,* 416–434.

Keane, M. M., Gabrieli, J. D. E., Mapstone, H. C., Johnston, K. A., & Corkin, S. (1995). Double dissociation of memory capacities after bilateral occipital-lobe or medial temporal-lobe lesions. *Brain, 118,* 1129–1148.

Kroll, N. E. A., Markowitsch, H. J., Knight, R. T., & von Cramon, D. Y. (1997). Retrieval of old memories: The temporofrontal hypothesis. *Brain, 120,* 1377–1399.

LaBar, K. S., & Disterhoft, J. F. (1998). Conditioning, awareness, and the hippocampus. *Hippocampus, 8,* 620–626.

Mangels, J. A. (1997). Strategic processing and memory for temporal order in patients with frontal lobe lesions. *Neuropsychology, 11,* 207–222.

Martin, R. C., Shelton, J. R., & Yaffee, L. S. (1994). Language processing and working memory: Neuropsychological evidence for separate phonological and semantic capacities. *Journal of Memory and Language, 33,* 83–111.

Martone, M., Butters, N., & Payne, P. (1984). Dissociations between skill learning and verbal recognition in amnesia and dementia. *Archives of Neurology, 41,* 965–970.

Mayes, A. R. (1988). *Human organic memory disorders.* Cambridge: Cambridge University Press.

Mayes, A. R., Downes, J. J., Shoqeirat, M., Hall, C., & Sagar, H. J. (1993). Encoding ability is preserved in amnesia: Evidence from a direct test of encoding. *Neuropsychologia, 31,* 745–759.

McCarthy, R. A., & Warrington, E. K. (1990). *Cognitive neuropsychology.* San Diego: Academic Press.

Nadel, L., & Moscovitch, M. (1998). Hippocampal contributions to cortical plasticity. *Neuropharmacology, 37,* 431–439.

Parkin, A. J., Bindschaedler, C., Harsent, L., & Metzler, C. (in press). Verification impairment in the generation of memory following ruptured aneurysm of the anterior communicating artery. *Brain and Cognition.*

Pascual-Leone, A., Grafman, J., Clark, K., Stewart, M., Massaquoi, S., Lou, J., & Hallett, M. (1993). Procedural learning in Parkinson's disease and cerebellar degeneration. *Annals of Neurology, 34,* 594–602.

Patterson, K., & Hodges, J. R. (1995). Disorders of semantic memory. In A. D. Baddeley, B. A. Wilson, & F. N. Watts (Eds.), *Handbook of memory disorders* (pp. 167–186). Chichester: John Wiley.

Postle, B. R., Corkin, S., & Growdon, J. H. (1996). Intact implicit memory for novel patterns in Alzheimer's disease. *Learning and Memory, 3,* 305–312.

Reed, J. M., & Squire, L. R. (1997). Impaired recognition memory in patients with lesions limited to the hippocampal formation. *Behavioural Neuroscience, 111,* 667–675.

Ribot, T. (1881). *Les maladies de la memoire* [Diseases of memory]. Paris: Germer Baillere.

Romani, C., & Martin, R. (1999). A deficit in the short-term retention of lexical semantic information: Forgetting words, but remembering a story. *Journal of Experimental Psychology: General, 128,* 56–77.

Saint-Cyr, J. A., Taylor, A. E., & Lang, A. E. (1988). Procedural learning and neostriatal dysfunction in man. *Brain, 111,* 941–959.

Salmon, D. P., Lineweaver, T. T., & Heindel, W. C. (1998). Non-declarative memory in neurodegenerative diseases. In A. I. Troster (Ed.), *Memory in neurodegenerative disease: Biological, cognitive and clinical perspectives* (pp. 210–225). New York: Cambridge University Press.

Sarter, M., & Markowitsch, H. J. (1985). The amygdala's role in human mnemonic processing. *Cortex, 21,* 7–24.

Shallice, T. (1986). Impairments of semantic processing: Multiple dissociations. In M. Coltheart, M. Job, & Sartori, G. (Eds.), *The cognitive psychology of language.* Hillsdale, NJ: Erlbaum.

Snowden, J. S., Goulding, P. J., & Neary, D. (1989). Semantic dementia: A form of circumscribed cerebral atrophy. *Behavioural Neurology, 2,* 167–182.

Squire, L. R., & Alvarez, P. (1995). Retrograde amnesia and memory consolidation: A neurobiological perspective. *Current Opinion in Neurobiology, 5,* 169–177.

Squire, L. R., & Frambach, M. (1990). Cognitive skill learning in amnesia. *Psychobiology, 18,* 109–117.

Squire, L. R., Knowlton, B., & Musen, G. (1993). The structure and organization of memory. *Annual Review of Psychology, 44,* 453–495.

Swick, D., & Knight, R. T. (1996). Is the prefrontal cortex involved in cued recall? A neuropsychological test of PET findings. *Neuropsychologia, 34,* 1019–1028.

Ungerleider, L. G. (1995). Functional brain imaging studies of cortical mechanisms for memory. *Science, 270,* 769–775.

Vallar, G., & Baddeley, A. D. (1985). Fractionation of working memory: Neuropsychological evidence for a short-term memory store. *Journal of Verbal Learning and Verbal Behavior, 23,* 151–161.

Vallar, G., & Papagno, C. (1995). Neuropsychological impairments of short-term memory. In A. D. Baddeley, B. A. Wilson, & F. N. Watts (Eds.), *Handbook of memory disorders* (pp. 135–166). Chichester: John Wiley.

Vargha-Khadem, F., Gadian, D. G., Watkins, K. E., Van Paesschen, W., & Mishkin, M. (1997). Differential effects of early hippocampal pathology on episodic and semantic memory. *Science, 277,* 376–380.

Warrington, E. K., & Rabin, P. (1971). Visual span of apprehension in patients with unilateral cerebral lesions. *Quarterly Journal of Experimental Psychology, 23,* 432–444.

Wiggs, C. L., & Martin, A. (1998). Properties and mechanisms of perceptual priming. *Current Opinion in Neurobiology, 8,* 227–233.

Woodruff-Pak, D. S. (1993). Eyeblink classical conditioning in H.M.: Delay and trace paradigms. *Behavioral Neuroscience, 107,* 911–925.

Zola-Morgan, S., & Squire, L. R. (1993). The neuroanatomy of amnesia. *Annual Review of Neuroscience, 16,* 547–563.

28

Memory in the Dementias

JOHN R. HODGES

Work on memory in the dementias has expanded enormously over the past 10 years. The main bulk of this work has been aimed at understanding the early cognitive sequelae of Alzheimer's disease (AD) and other forms of dementia, and thus improving methods of detection and differentiation of these disorders. The second, and more innovative line of research has aimed to understand normal memory processes through the study of patients with memory failure in the context of the dementias. This chapter covers both aspects: most of the work on AD relates to the clinical issues, while that on semantic dementia concerns more theoretical questions.

Until quite recently the generally received concept of dementia was of a progressive and global intellectual deterioration, but one of the most exciting discoveries of the past decade has been the realization that each of the diseases that eventually produce "global dementia" actually produce, at least in the early stages, a distinct pattern of neuropsychological impairment that reflects the distribution of the neuropathology. To reflect this shift in emphasis a more modern definition of dementia is "a syndrome consisting of progressive impairment in both memory and at least one of the following cognitive deficits: aphasia, apraxia, agnosia or disturbance in executive abilities, sufficient to interfere with social or occupational functioning, in the absence of delirium or major non-organic psychiatric disorders (e.g., depression, schizophrenia)" (American Psychiatric Association, 1994). As will become apparent below, even this modern definition still presents problems for the diagnosis of very early cases of Alzheimer's disease who may show only memory deficits. At the other end of the spectrum, patients with frontal type dementias may not show memory deficits until very late in the course of the disease.

Most researchers now realize the limitations of standardized brief mental test schedules such as the Mini-Mental State Examination (MMSE; Folstein, Folstein, & McHugh, 1975). The MMSE is a useful instrument for grading established dementia, but is insensitive for detecting the early stages of AD (since orientation, immediate recall/registration and basic linguistic abilities are atypically preserved; see below). Furthermore, the MMSE and other similar tests are notoriously unreliable in patients with even gross frontal executive dysfunction, as in dementia of frontal type (Gregory & Hodges, 1996a, 1996b). Formal neuropsychological assessment should be performed in all cases with suspected cognitive failure, except those with clear-cut severe global impairment. The emphasis of the assessment should be to confirm deterioration in memory and/or other aspects of cognition, to quantify the degree of impairment, and to detect patterns that are atypical for AD and hence suggest other possible diagnoses particularly memory impairment in the context of depression (Greene & Hodges, 1996c).

In the following sections we will review the dementias from the perspective of separable subcomponents of memory before considering the profiles associated with the major causes of dementia.

Working (Short-Term or Immediate) Memory

Because of the nosological confusion surrounding the term "short-term memory," we prefer to use the working memory model, as defined by Baddeley (1992) with its constituent subcomponents: the central executive component, which supervises the function of two slave systems for verbal and nonverbal information, viz. the phonological loop and visuo-spatial sketchpad, respectively. Impairment of the central executive is a consistent feature of subcortical pathology such as Huntington's disease and progressive supranuclear palsy, and results in reduced digit span (especially reversed) and particularly performance on more demanding tests of dual attention (Robbins et al., 1994). Impairment in the central executive component of working memory has been found in AD (Baddeley, Bressi, Della Sala, Logie, & Spinnler, 1991), although recent work has suggested that this too may be spared in very early cases (Greene, Baddeley, & Hodges, 1995). Digit span is usually normal in the early stages but deteriorates later in the disease AD.

Episodic Memory

Episodic memory refers to memory for personally experienced and temporally specific events or episodes. Retrieval from episodic memory necessitates so-called mental time travel and successful remembering is said to be associated with a special kind of "autonoetic" conscious awareness.

A profound disruption of anterograde episodic memory is the hallmark of AD and will be discussed in more detail below. The episodic memory impairment seen in subcortical dementias not only is less striking than in cortical dementias but is due to a deficit at a different stage of memory processing. Encoding is impaired, but less so than in cortical dementias. The rate of forgetting is relatively normal in subcortical pathology (Butters et al., 1988; Moss, Albert, Butters, & Payne, 1986). The most striking difference is, however, the relative preservation of recognition memory in subcortical dementia (Butters, Wokfe, Martone, Granholm, & Cermak, 1985; Pillon, Deweer, Agid, & Dubois, 1993).

Remote Memory

Remote or retrograde memory refers to any memories that occurred prior to the onset of a pathological process. With a discrete insult such as trauma or a stroke, there is little difficulty in demarcating remote from anterograde memory. In a condition with an insidious onset such as AD, it is less easy to date the onset of the pathology.

Remote memory is impaired in AD and there is a mild temporal gradient with early-life memories being spared relative to more recent life memories (Greene & Hodges, 1996b; Kopelman, 1989). By contrast, the remote memory impairment seen in subcortical dementias shows no gradient, consistent with a retrieval deficit (Beatty, Salmon, Butters, Heindel, & Granholm, 1988; Sagar, Cohen, Sullivan, Corkin, & Growdon, 1988).

Semantic Memory

Semantic memory refers to our permanent store of representational knowledge including facts, concepts, and words and their meaning—for example, knowing the meaning of the word *panda*, that Paris is the capital of France, that the boiling point of water is 100°C, and so on. Tests of semantic memory include category fluency, naming pictures and naming from verbal description, word-picture matching, general knowledge questions, tests of vocabulary (Hodges, Patterson, Oxbury, & Funnell, 1992) and picture-picture matching tests such as the Pyramids and Palm Trees Test (Howard & Patterson, 1992).

As described below, semantic memory impairment occurs in AD (Butters, Granholm, Salmon, Grant, & Wolfe, 1987; Hodges & Patterson, 1995; Hodges, Salmon, & Butters, 1992; Martin & Fedio, 1983), but is virtually always overshadowed by the episodic memory deficit.

A profound, yet relatively pure, loss of semantic memory is the hallmark of semantic dementia (Hodges & Patterson, 1996; Hodges, Patterson et al., 1992; Snowden, Goulding, & Neary, 1989; Warrington, 1975). In this syndrome, patients present with progressive anomia and show gross deficits on a range of verbal and nonverbal tests of semantic knowledge. In contrast, episodic and working memory, perception, and nonverbal problem solving remain intact.

Patients with subcortical dementias are also impaired on fluency tasks, but tend to perform less well on letter fluency than on category fluency (Rosser & Hodges, 1994). This probably reflects impaired activation and retrieval rather than true semantic breakdown (Butters et al., 1987, 1985).

There is still considerable debate regarding the neural basis of semantic memory, which almost certainly depends upon widely distributed neural circuits, but the dominant temporal neocortex seems to play a major role, especially for verbally mediated semantic knowledge (Patterson & Hodges, 1995; Martin, Wiggs, Ungerleider, & Haxby, 1996; Mummery, Patterson, & Hodges, in press; Mummery, Patterson, Hodges, & Wise, 1996), as evidenced by studies in semantic dementia (Hodges, Patterson, Oxbury, & Funnell, 1992; Snowden et al., 1989), and Herpes simplex virus encephalitis (for review, see Gainotti, Silveri, Daniele, & Giustolisi, 1995; Garrard, Perry, & Hodges, 1997).

Alzheimer's Disease

Alzheimer's accounts for approximately two-thirds of all cases of dementia and is the commonest cause of progressive memory failure in the elderly. Despite a phenomenal increase in understanding of the molecular pathology of AD, the cause is currently unknown. AD can only be diagnosed with certainty by neuropathological confirmation of neocortical atrophy with neuronal loss, intraneuronal tangles of paired helical filaments, and extraneuronal plaques containing an amyloid core. The presence of plaques and tangles correlates significantly with the presence of dementia (Wilcock & Esiri, 1982). More recently, however, it has been claimed that synaptic loss may be the primary marker of AD, since the severity of loss correlates more closely with dementia severity (Terry et al., 1991). These neuropathological changes are found first in the transentorhinal region, and then spread to involve the hippocampal complex proper, the inferior temporal and frontal lobes, and eventually the whole of the cortex sparing only primary motor and sensory cortices (Braak & Braak, 1991; Van Hoesen, Hyman, & Damasio, 1991).

It is important to realize that AD does not result in "global" cognitive impairment from the start of the illness, but progresses in a relatively predictable pattern through various stages that will be described below. Table 28.1 is a guide to the most common order of deterioration.

The most pervasive feature of AD is undoubtedly a failure of memory. When patients present in the early stages of the disease, complaints of memory difficulty are by far the commonest symptom noticed by the patients, and more particularly by their spouses. In patients who are seen for the first time at a more advanced stage of deterioration, a retrospective history of insidiously progressive memory failure can almost invariably be elicited from the carer. As will be discussed below, there are a growing number of case reports documenting atypical presentations of AD (aphasia, apraxia, visual agnosia, etc.), but our own experience suggests that these represent only a tiny minority of cases. Contrary to popular opinion, many patients with early AD are aware of the memory impairment, although often play down the severity. There is, however, considerable variability in the degree of insight, and the factors contributing to the loss of insight (anosognosia) have been the topic of numerous recent studies; in general, insight declines with disease progression and with the onset of major psychiatric symptoms; it may also relate to the degree of working memory or executive dysfunction, although this remains controversial (Starkstein, Sabe, Chemerinski, Jason, & Leiguarda, 1996).

Episodic Memory in AD

Not all aspects of memory are affected equally in early AD. The major impairment is in the domain of anterograde episodic memory (e.g. Grady et al., 1988; Greene, Baddeley, & Hodges, 1996; Reid et al., 1996). The ability to retain new information after a period (delayed recall) is the most sensitive measure (Locascio, Growdon, & Corkin, 1995; Welsh, Butters, Hughes, Mohs, & Heyman, 1991; Welsh, Butters, Hughes, & Mohs, 1992). Figure 28.1 illus-

Table 28.1 Postulated stages of cognitive breakdown in typical Alzheimer's disease.

		Minimal	Mild	Moderate	Severe
• Memory	Working	–	+	++	+++
	Episodic	++	+++	+++	+++
	Remote	–/+	–/+	++	+++
	Semantic	–	–/+	+++	+++
• Language (syntax and phonology)		–	–	+	++
• Visuo-spatial and perceptual		–	+	++	+++
• Praxis		–	–	++	++
• Attentional and executive abilities		+/–	++	+++	+++

Key: – absent, + present, +/– variable.

trates the severity of this deficit even in patients presenting at the very earliest stage (designated in our studies "minimal AD"). Memory for both verbal and visual material is affected in the majority of cases (Greene et al., 1996; Hodges & Patterson, 1995), but a proportion of cases have material specific deficits in the early stages; Becker, Lopez, and Weiss (1992) found evidence of material specific loss in 13% of their patients based on a study in which verbal memory was assessed by imme-

diate and delayed recall of a short story and nonverbal memory by recall of the Rey Complex Figure. In our study using the Doors and People Test, which was designed to assess recall and recognition memory for both verbal and visual material matched for level of difficulty, we confirmed that up to a third of patients show a significant discrepancy across types of material (in almost all cases worse on the verbal memory tests), but this difference was hardly ever absolute; that is to say, the

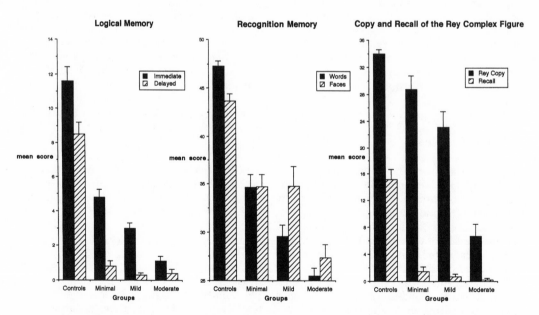

Figure 28.1 Performance of control subjects and AD patients (divided into three subgroups according to disease severity: minimal MMSE > 23, mild MMSE 18–23 and moderate MMSE <18) showing the groups' mean scores on (i) logical memory (story recall) from the WMS-R, (ii) Warrington's Recognition Memory Tests, and (iii) The Rey Complex Figure (RCF) Test: copy and delayed recall. From Hodges and Patterson (1995). Note the profound impairment of the minimal group on delayed stories and the RCF.

verbal memory scores of the patients with early AD often fell below normal (>2 z-scores), and although their visual memory scores could be considered to fall within "the normal range," they typically fell one and two z-scores below normal (Greene et al., 1996).

The profound deficit in episodic memory has been attributed principally to defective encoding of new information (Granholm & Butters, 1988; Greene et al., 1996). For instance, Granholm and Butters (1988), using an encoding-specificity paradigm, found that AD patients were impaired in their ability to either encode the semantic relationship between the word to be learned and its retrieval cue or to utilize the product of encoding at the time of retrieval.

Controversy surrounds the issue of whether there is an accelerated rate of forgetting in AD, which reflects the fact that the interpretation of forgetting functions in memory-impaired patients is, in general, fraught with problems. Certainly patients with early AD show a pathological decline between immediate and delayed recall on tests such as logical memory from the WMS-R (Butters et al., 1988), but this probably reflects the contribution of working memory (which is typically preserved) to immediate, but not to delayed, recall on such tests. When tasks that equate initial learning, and remove the effects of working memory, have been applied, AD patients show normal rates of forgetting (Becker, Boller, Saxton, & McGonigle-Gibson, 1987; Greene et al., 1996; Kopelman, 1985). In other words, patients are unable to learn new information, but the little they learn is retained reasonably well. This finding has obvious implications for the memory rehabilitation techniques that have, so far, not been widely applied to patients with early AD (see Clare, Wilson, Breen, & Hodges, 1999).

In terms of our ability to understand the very earliest cognitive deficits in AD, patients with sporadic disease provide rather limited opportunities: patients presenting to memory clinics have typically been complaining of memory failure for a number of years and rarely have an absolutely pure amnesia (Hodges & Patterson, 1995; Reid et al., 1996); it is also necessary to follow such patients for years in order to establish that they do indeed have AD pathologically. By contrast, the study of "at risk" subjects in families with genetically determined familial AD provides the unique ability to study the very beginning of the disease. In comparison to the multitude of cognitive studies of sporadic AD, such investigations are in their infancy: studies by Rossor, Warrington, and colleagues have confirmed that impairment in anterograde episodic memory is the earliest feature that may precede other cognitive deficits by a number of years. In addition, particular gene mutations may be associated with specific patterns such as early breakdown in language output or writing skills (Harvey et al., 1998; Newman, Warrington, Kennedy, & Rossor, 1994). Over the next few years we should learn a great deal more about the earliest cognitive deficits in AD and whether there are systematic differences between forms of AD (sporadic versus familial etc.).

Semantic Memory in AD

Patients with AD are also characteristically impaired on tests of semantic memory, including picture naming, naming from verbal descriptions, word-picture matching, general knowledge and vocabulary, and picture-picture matching tasks that rely on the ability to deduce the associative link between the items represented (Hodges & Patterson, 1997). The underlying cause of the semantic deficit, at a cognitive level, has been a matter of controversy. Some researchers have claimed that the deficits found on tests of semantic memory may primarily reflect impaired access to semantic memory (for review, see Bayles, Tomoeda, Kasniak, & Trosset, 1991; Nebes, 1989) and there is an extensive and controversial literature on semantic priming in AD (see chapter 27). The majority of investigators, however, support the interpretation of a breakdown in the structure of semantic memory (Chan et al., 1993; Chertkow & Bub, 1990; Hodges & Patterson, 1996; Hodges, Salmon et al., 1992).

Using a battery of tests of semantic memory, all of which test knowledge about the same consistent set of 48 items via differing modalities of sensory input and/or output, we have established that most patients presenting with even very early-stage presumed AD (which we have termed minimal AD with MMSE scores above 23) show impairment on tests of semantic memory (Hodges & Patterson, 1995). This is, however, not a universal phenomenon: some patients may be severely amnesic yet perform normally on the entire semantic battery. Certainly as the disease progresses into the moderate stages (MMSE <18), breakdown in semantic memory is a ubiquitous finding that is reflected in the increasing anomia, emptiness of language, and failure on general knowledge tests. We have also established that there is a strong item-by-item correspondence in performance for individual items in the battery. In other words, if a patient is unable to name a given item in the battery, then he or she will almost certainly be unable to generate an adequate definition when presented with the name of the same item (Hodges, Patterson, Graham, & Dawson, 1996; Lambon Ralph, Patterson, & Hodges, 1997), see figure 28.2.

Within our test battery, the tasks that show the greatest sensitivity in early AD are category fluency and generation of verbal definition (Hodges & Patterson, 1995; Hodges et al., 1996). Since category fluency is a task that calls upon a range of cognitive abilities—working memory, executive and phonological skills—as well as semantic memory, it is important to note that initial-letter based or phonological fluency (FAS) is usually preserved in AD (Rosser & Hodges, 1994). This is particularly striking since normal subjects produce consistently more items on tests of letter fluency and the latter is much more sensitive to frontostriatal pathology than category fluency. Work by Chan and colleagues (1993), using

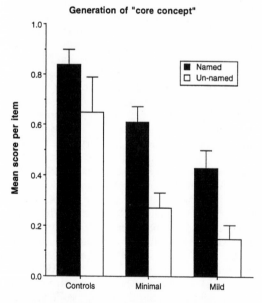

Generation of "core concept"

Figure 28.2 Ability to define the core concept in response in relationship to the ability to name pictures of the same items in our semantic battery from controls and AD patients (divided into minimal and mild). The major contrast is between named and un-named items. From Hodges et al., 1996.

multidimensional scaling techniques, has shown that the interrelationship between items produced is also disrupted in AD.

A recent PET activation study in normal subjects has confirmed that although these tasks activate an extensive network in the left peri-sylvian region, category fluency differentially activates the left inferior temporal lobe, an area known to be crucial for semantic memory, while the letter task activates the left inferior frontal lobe (Mummery et al., 1996).

There has been recent interest in the question of whether the breakdown in semantic memory affects all categories of knowledge equally in AD. Category-specific deficits are well documented in the context of focal brain damage: the most commonly observed pattern is loss of knowledge for living things (animals, fruit, and vegetables), which occurs in patients with herpes simplex virus encephalitis. The opposite pattern (i.e., disproportionate impairment for artifacts) has also been documented, thus ruling out any explanation based on test difficulty (Caramazza & Shelton, 1998; Gainotti et al., 1995; Garrard et al., 1997). Group studies of AD patients have reached contradictory conclusions with some finding an advantage for living things and others no difference across categories (for review, see Garrard et al., 1997). Recently, Gonnerman, Andersen, Devlin, Kempler, and Seidenberg (1997) have proposed a model of semantic structure that predicts that diffuse damage (of the sort that they argue occurs in AD, although—as discussed above—the pathological data clearly suggest a more orderly progression) will produce an advantage for artifacts early in the course of the disease with the opposite pattern emerging with progression. To examine this hypothesis, we have examined category effects in a group of 58 patients with various degrees of dementia and confirmed that a substantial minority do indeed show category effects (usually, but not always in the direction of worse performance on natural kinds) and that this emerges with increasing degrees of anomia, which we postulate reflects progressive left temporal lobe pathology (Garrard, Patterson, Watson, & Hodges, 1998). These findings are illustrated in figure 28.3.

Working Memory in AD

In contrast to the deficits in episodic and semantic memory, patients with AD typically

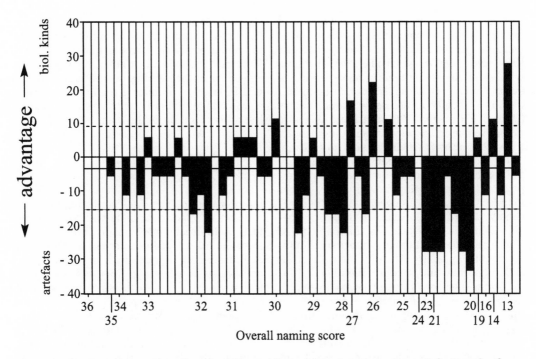

Figure 28.3 Category specific effects in AD: 58 AD patients given our semantic battery (rank-ordered according to overall naming score) to show their semantic index. The doted lines indicate the controls, mean ± 2SDs. For each AD patient, a downwards bar indicates better performance on artifacts and an upwards bar better performance on living things. Note that 13 patients show an advantage for artefacts, while 6 show the reverse pattern, usually to a minor degree. From Garrard et al. (1998).

perform normally on tests of auditory and spatial short-term memory, as exemplified by their normal digit or block-tapping span. On dual-performance tests, designed to tap the central executive component of working memory, in which subjects are required to divide their attention between two simultaneously presented streams of information, AD patients show impairment. It has also been shown that the dual-task decrement increases with disease progression even though performance on the individual tasks (e.g., digit span and tracking) does not change (Baddeley et al., 1991). In a more recent study we confirmed the impairment on two separate tests of divided attention, but only in patients with established disease (i.e., MMSE below 24). In a group of 17 patients with minimal presumed AD (MMSE >23), all of whom showed profound impairment on tests of episodic memory, dual task performance was normal (Greene et al., 1995).

Remote Memory in AD

Remote personal (or autobiographical) memory has been studied relatively little in AD, perhaps owing to the lack, until recently, of reliable and quantifiable instruments. Because patients often become preoccupied with, or indeed appear to "live in," the past, it is commonly believed that such memory is spared in AD. Recent research has shown, however, that most patients early in the course of the disease do, in fact, show impaired performance on tests of autobiographical memory, although the degree of impairment is certainly less than that seen on anterograde memory tests. This loss is temporally graded with relative sparing of more distant memories, accounting in part for the clinical observation above. Moreover, there is no clear correlation between the degree of anterograde and retrograde memory deficit (Greene & Hodges, 1996a; Kopelman, 1989).

Remote memory for famous faces and events also shows impairment with a gentle temporal gradient (Greene & Hodges, 1996a; Kopelman, 1989; Sagar et al., 1988). Patients with early AD are extremely poor at naming even very famous faces. This deficit is due, in part, to difficulty in accessing proper names (Hodges & Greene, 1998), but there is also a loss of semantic knowledge regarding people, as evidenced by (1) their inability to generate unique identifying information about the people represented, and (2) their equivalent impairment on tests using famous names rather than faces (Greene & Hodges, 1996b; Hodges & Greene, 1998). The breakdown in person-specific semantic knowledge is independent of loss of general semantic knowledge or of autobiographical memory. This finding is theoretically important and supports the idea that (1) long-term memory is organized, at least partially, according to the nature of the information stored (i.e., living vs. nonliving things; general semantic vs. person-specific knowledge), and (2) the type of retrieval and verification processes required, which are particularly crucial for the recreation of long-term autobiographical memories (for further discussion, see Evans, Breen, Antoun, & Hodges, 1996; Greene et al., 1996; Greene & Hodges, 1996a; Hodges & Patterson, 1997; Perry & Hodges, 1996).

The Role of Neuroimaging in AD

Parallel with the growth in neuropsychological studies of AD has been a burgeoning of the literature on structural and functional neuroimaging. In brief, each of the following methods have been advocated in the early diagnosis of AD: temporal orientated computed tomography (CT), volumetric magnetic resonance imaging (MRI), and single photon emission computed tomography (SPECT) (for review, see Cappa & Perani, 1996; Smith & Jobst, 1996). It remains unclear which imaging modality is the most appropriate for the early and accurate detection of particular disease states since the studies, to date, have either been very largely confined to patients with presumed AD, have not been systematically compared with neuropsychological evaluation, or have lacked long-term verification of the pathological diagnosis. Our recent experience suggests that neuropsychological evaluation is both more sensitive and specific than SPECT changes in early AD (Greene et al., 1995).

There are hints from MRI volumetric measurements that hippocampal atrophy may be detected extremely early in cases with presenile familial AD (Fox et al., 1997). There is clearly a need for further studies that compare a range of diagnostic techniques in a group of patients studied longitudinally with eventual pathological verification of the diagnosis.

Frontotemporal Dementia (Pick's Disease)

In order to understand the confusing plethora of terms applied to patients with progressive focal brain degeneration it is important to consider the history of the disorder. Arnold Pick, after describing patients with progressive fluent aphasia as a result of progressive temporal lobe atrophy, was also the first to report the syndrome of frontal dementia (Hodges, 1994). The pathological features were reported a few years later by Alzheimer, who described Pick cells and Pick bodies in association with focal brain atrophy. In the first half of the century, the term Pick's disease was applied to the clinical syndromes of progressive frontal or temporal lobe degeneration, but then mention of it faded from the literature. With the resurgence of interest in the neuropathology of the dementias, however, it became apparent that focal lobar atrophy is a relatively common cause of dementia in the presenium, but that only a minority have Pick cells and Pick bodies (Brun, 1987a; Neary et al., 1986). This finding has led to a general abandonment of the term Pick's disease in favor of labels that describe the clinical syndrome, such as frontal lobe dementia or dementia of frontal type (Miller et al., 1991; Neary et al., 1986).

In parallel with the renaissance of interest in frontal lobe dementia was the rediscovery of the syndrome of progressive aphasia in association with focal left peri-sylvian atrophy. In 1982, Mesulam reported six patients with a long history of insidiously worsening aphasia in the absence of signs of more generalized cognitive failure. Since Mesulam's seminal paper over 100 patients with progressive aphasia have been reported (for review, see Hodges & Patterson, 1996). From this literature it is clear that although the language impairment is heterogeneous, two main syndromes can be identified: (1) progressive nonfluent aphasia and (2) progressive fluent aphasia for which we prefer the term semantic dementia (see table 28.2). Patients with the latter syndrome are

Table 28.2 Major clinical subtypes of frontotemporal dementia.

- Dementia of frontal type (DFT)
- Progressive aphasic syndromes
- Semantic dementia (progressive fluent aphasia)
- Progressive nonfluent aphasia
- Progressive prosopagnosia and/or loss of person knowledge

clearly identifiable in the older Pick's disease literature as cases with amnesic aphasia and loss of conceptual knowledge (Hodges, 1994) and were also reported by Warrington as "selective loss of semantic memory" (Warrington, 1975). There are still relatively few pathological reports of patients with semantic dementia, but all 14 had either classic Pick's disease or nonspecific spongiform change of the type found in the majority of cases with the frontal form of lobar atrophy (Hodges, Garrard, & Patterson, 1998). In both forms, other nonlinguistic skills are well preserved as judged by their performance on tests of nonverbal problem solving, visuo-spatial, and perceptual abilities. Patients with the nonfluent variant present with progressive disintegration of speech production with breakdown of the phonological and syntactic aspects of language. Further discussion of this form is beyond the scope of the chapter; for review, see Hodges and Patterson (1996).

The two rather independent lines of research into dementia of frontal type and progressive aphasia associated with temporal lobe atrophy have recently reconverged with the realization that many patients eventually have features of both frontal and anterior temporal lobe atrophy. In 1994, workers from Lund and Manchester suggested the use of the term frontotemporal dementia (FTD). This has the advantage of avoiding any specific pathological connotation but blurs important differences in the clinical presentations, especially in terms of memory involvement.

Frontotemporal dementia (FTD) is clearly much less common than AD, but estimates of the ratio of the two diseases range from 1 in 5 to 1 in 20 (Snowden, Neary, & Mann, 1996). Brun (1987a) reported that 20 of the first 150 consecutive autopsied cases suffered from frontal or frontotemporal degeneration. In this and other similar studies the mean age of the total patient population was unusually young,

which may well have led to an overrepresentation of FTD patients. The peak age of onset is 45 to 65.

As with AD, the aetiology remains obscure, but a proportion of cases (estimates range from 10 to 50%) are familial. In the past few years, linkage to chromosome 17 has been established in a number of families around the world (Wilhelmsen, 1997) and to chromosome 3 in one large Danish family (Brown et al., 1995).

Dementia of Frontal Type (DFT)

In contrast to AD, the majority of patients with DFT (the frontal lobe variant of FTD) are brought to the clinic blissfully unaware of the major changes in personality and behavior observed by their relatives. Patients may appear apathetic and withdrawn, or alternatively become socially disinhibited with facetiousness and inappropriate jocularity. Their ability to plan and organize complex activities (work, social engagements, etc.) is almost invariably impaired, reflecting deficits in goal setting and attainment, mental set-shifting, and flexibility. Mental rigidity and an inability to appreciate the more subtle aspects of language (irony, punning, etc.) are common. There is often indifference to domestic and occupational responsibilities, a lack of empathy for family and friends and gradual withdrawal from all social interactions. A deterioration in self-care with a reluctance to bath, groom, and change clothes is frequently reported. Many patients show a change in eating habits with an escalating desire for sweet food coupled with reduced satiety; the increasing gluttony may lead to enormous weight gain (Snowden, Neary et al., 1996). Recently we developed clinical criteria for the diagnosis of DFT, which stress the neurobehavioural features of the disorder (Gregory & Hodges, 1996a, 1996b).

Memory is typically unaffected early in the course of the disease, and although patients may admit, when pressed, to "memory" difficulties, when this is explored further they usually have problems with attention and working memory, rather than the severe amnesia found in AD (see above). In a recent study of 9 cases, who fulfilled the criteria outlined below, we found only mild impairment on tests of episodic memory that was intermediate between that seen in controls and patients with early stage AD (Hodges et al., in press).

Similar findings have been reported by Pachana, Boone, Miller, Cummings, and Berman (1996). On tests of semantic memory, our patients performed normally. Tasks aimed at specific evaluation of the frontal lobes (such as the Wisconsin Card Sorting Test, Trail Making Test, Stroop Test, Shallice's Cognitive Estimates Test, and verbal fluency) will often show marked impairment (see Miller et al., 1991; Neary, Snowden, Northen, & Goulding, 1988), but it should be stressed that in some cases with marked neurobehavioral changes sufficient to interfere with social relations and lead to premature retirement from work, there may be very little abnormality even after rigorous neuropsychological evaluation. We have seen a number of such patients who have a "full house" of symptoms with eventually clear-cut frontal atrophy on MRI. With disease progression, episodic memory deteriorates but visuo-spatial and perceptual functions are characteristically normal even late in the disease.

Language dysfunction is an early, but subtle, finding in many patients with DFT and consists of factually empty speech that is reduced in quantity. Articulation, phonology, and syntax are typically preserved. Mild anomia may be present, but repetition is normal. In terms of classical aphasic syndromes, the picture corresponds to a dynamic aphasia (Snowden, Griffiths, & Neary, 1996a). Many patients develop spontaneous echolalia (a tendency to immediately repeat the examiner's last phrase) and other reiterative speech acts such as the repetition of phrases, words, syllables, or sounds. In advanced cases, comprehension may become impaired.

Semantic Dementia

In this variant of FTD, focal atrophy of the temporal lobe gives rise to a form of progressive fluent aphasia that we have chosen to call semantic dementia in order to convey the concept of profound and pervasive semantic deterioration that disrupts factual memory and knowledge, language, and object recognition (Hodges & Patterson, 1995, 1996; Hodges, Patterson et al., 1992; Hodges, Patterson, & Tyler, 1994; Snowden et al., 1989; Snowden, Neary et al., 1996).

Patients with semantic dementia present with loss of both receptive and expressive vocabulary, and increasing difficulty in recognizing familiar objects and people. Patients typically present complaining that they have "forgotten" the names of things and are usually unaware of the parallel decline in word comprehension. Although the most apparent early deficits may be in the domain of language, all abilities requiring access to conceptual knowledge are typically affected. Reading shows a pattern of surface dyslexia (i.e., a selective impairment in the ability to read words with irregular spelling to sound correspondence such as *pint, island*, etc., with the production of regularization errors [*pint* to rhyme with *mint*]). The selectivity of this semantic degradation is underlined by striking preservation of other aspects of cognition, including visuo-spatial skills, frontal "executive" functions, short-term memory, and nonverbally based problem-solving abilities. Spontaneous speech is characteristically empty, with word-finding difficulties and occasional semantic errors, but is fluent, reasonably well structured syntactically, and with normal articulation and phonology.

In contrast to the pattern observed in AD, memory for day-to-day events—as measured by orientation in time and place, recall of recent events, and autobiographical memory—appears to be strikingly well preserved in semantic dementia.

At first glance, these findings appear to offer strong support for the separability of semantic and episodic memory systems. Our recent study suggests, however, a more complex picture. The apparent sparing of episodic memory is itself selective: while it is true that patients remember recent life events well, their memory for more distant autobiographical information is, in fact, markedly abnormal (Graham & Hodges, 1997; Hodges & Graham, 1998; Snowden et al., 1996b). In other words, they show a reversal of the typical Ribot effect seen in amnesic patients.

In addition, there is clearly a dynamic interdependence between episodic and semantic memory: general knowledge is likely to be acquired from specific episodes, and further specific experiences are understood and encoded with reference to general knowledge. Some theorists maintain, therefore, that these two "systems" represent no more than the extremes of a single spectrum of information acquisition. According to this view, semantic memories are simply old, overlearned episodes that have lost their temporal details and become part of a fund of more context-free knowledge (Baddeley, 1990).

We favor an explanation for these findings based on recent neural network models that are grounded in both psychological and neuroanatomical data (McClelland, McNaughton, & O'Reilly, 1995; Murre, 1996). According to such models, structures in the medial part of the temporal lobe (the hippocampus, dentate gyrus, subicular complex, and entorhinal cortex)—which receive projections from all higher order areas of sensory cortex—are critical for the rapid learning of new episodic memories. The hippocampal complex thus acts as a temporary "indexer" linking together traces in other cortical areas. Over time, with repeated exposure to and retrieval of information, direct cortico-cortical connections are established that are independent of hippocampal function, a process known as consolidation. The notion that the same principles apply to learning of both general facts and specific autobiographical episodes helps to explain two different patterns. Patients with damage confined to the hippocampal complex display relative preservation of early acquired information but profoundly deficient recent learning, whether episodic or semantic (Squire, 1992); patients with damage to temporal neocortical regions, as in semantic dementia, sparing the medial temporal cortex, have the reverse pattern, with better memory for both recent personal experiences and recently encountered or reinforced general knowledge (Graham & Hodges, 1997; Hodges & Graham, 1998; Snowden et al., 1996b). There is also accruing evidence that it is possible to acquire some new semantic information in the absence of a functional hippocampal system (Vargha-Khadem et al., 1997; Kitchener, McCarthy, & Hodges, 1998); this slower, and more limited, form of direct cortical learning probably depends upon multiple stereotyped exposures.

Another interesting question that can be addressed in semantic dementia is when one no longer knows what an elephant is, can one remember seeing one? In a recent study, we used a real–nonreal object decision task. The semantic dementia patients were very impaired in the object decision test yet in a recognition test using studied plus nonstudied items they were able to identify which items had been seen earlier in the object decision test. By contrast, patients in the early amnestic stages of AD showed the opposite pattern (Graham, Becker, & Hodges, 1997). We have recently replicated this finding using the Pyramids and Palm Trees test with a later recognition memory version.

The cognitive deficits found in semantic dementia are particularly relevant to debates about the organization of semantic knowledge. A common observation is that the finer grained (subordinate) aspects of knowledge seem to be more vulnerable than higher order information. For instance, a patient may fail to demonstrate any specific knowledge about elephants but still know that an elephant is an animal. It is easy to imagine how this superordinate information might be deduced from a picture, but the same finding also applies to words (Hodges & Patterson, 1995; Hodges et al., 1994; Warrington, 1975). Furthermore, we have demonstrated an orderly progression of decreasingly specific responses in a longitudinal study of confrontation naming to 260 pictures of common objects. As a typical example of the pattern from 4 tests at roughly 6-monthly intervals, the patient's successive responses to the picture of an elephant were (1) "elephant," (2) "big African animal," (3) "horse," (4) "animal." Some commentators interpret these findings as evidence for a rather literal hierarchical structure of knowledge, in which the mental representation of a concept is analogous to a branching tree, from the superordinate at the trunk to category representations at the branches and specific instances as twigs (Warrington, 1975). The idea that a degenerative process might "prune back the semantic tree" has an obvious intuitive appeal, but the same pattern might also emerge from a more distributed feature network (McClelland et al., 1995). According to this theory, the basic units of representation are semantic properties, and semantically similar concepts are represented by largely similar patterns of activation across these units with a few distinguishing features for individual items. Even with considerable deterioration of fine-grained knowledge, the degraded network should still support judgments or responses based on category membership.

At present, one can only speculate about the distribution of neuroanatomical structures involved in representing semantic knowledge, but it already seems clear that the infero-lateral regions of the temporal lobes play a key role (Martin et al., 1996; Mummery et al., in press-a, 1996; Vandenberghe, Price, Wise, Josephs, & Frackowiak, 1996). This finding is in keeping with functional brain activation studies that have also shown activation of a left-lateralized network that includes the temporal lobe. Damage to temporal neocortex can also disrupt autobiographical information (Graham & Hodges, 1997; Snowden et al., 1996b), though multiple cortical areas probably contribute to personal memories (Evans, Breen, Antoun, & Hodges, 1996). Long-term autobiographical and more general conceptual knowledge may also differ in the nature of retrieval: remembering the details of a holiday 10 years ago is a reconstructive process involving separate fragments that need to be verified and recombined (Burgess & Shallice, 1996). It is therefore no surprise that autobiographical retrieval depends upon the integrity of executive functions requiring frontal-lobe and other closely related structures (Della Sala, Laiacona, Spinnler, & Trivelli, 1993; Hodges & McCarthy, 1993).

Structural (magnetic resonance) brain imaging in semantic dementia reveals highly focal atrophy of the anterior (polar) and inferolateral portions of the temporal lobe (Hodges & Patterson, 1996; Hodges, Patterson et al., 1992; Mummery et al., in press-a). It is as yet uncertain whether the full-blown pattern of semantic dementia requires bilateral temporal pathology, but at least some cases have shown marked abnormality only on the left.

One obvious question concerns the impact of pathology confined to parallel right temporal lobe structures. At present, limited evidence suggests that the antero-lateral right temporal lobe may have a special role in the representation of person-specific knowledge. A recently reported patient with right atrophy, VH, presented initially with a relatively selective difficulty in face recognition (prosopagnosia), which subsequently evolved to a severe and amodal loss of person knowledge but without any marked loss of more general semantic knowledge (Evans, Heggs, Antoun, & Hodges, 1995). Two previous cases with selective loss of person knowledge also had right temporal pathology in the context of HSVE and surgery for a tumor (Ellis, Young, & Critchley, 1989; Hanley, Young, & Pearson, 1989).

Subcortical Dementias

A wide range of basal ganglia and white matter diseases (see table 28.3) may result in a pattern of so-called subcortical dementia. These disorders are characterized by mental slowing, impaired attention, and frontal "executive" function (i.e., planning, problem solving, self-initiated activity). Memory is moderately impaired due to reduced attention with poor registration of new material, but se-

Table 28.3 Major causes of subcortical (frontostriatal) dementia.

- Degenerative basal ganglia diseases
    Progressive supranuclear palsy
    Huntington's disease
    Parkinson's disease
    Cortico-basal degeneration
- Vascular disorders
    Multi-infarct dementia (lacunar state)
    Binswanger's disease
    Cerebral vasculitis
- Metabolic
    Wilson's disease
- Demyelinating disease
    Multiple sclerosis
    Leucodystrophies
    AIDS dementia complex
- Miscellaneous
    Normal pressure hydrocephalus

vere amnesia of the type seen in AD does not occur in the early stages. Recognition is typically much better than spontaneous recall, suggestive of a retrieval deficit. Spontaneous speech is reduced and answers to questions are slow and laconic. Features of focal cortical dysfunction such as aphasia, apraxia, and agnosia are characteristically absent, but visuospatial deficits are consistently present (Josiassen, Curry, & Mancall, 1983). Change in mood, personality, and social conduct are very common, resulting often in an indifferent withdrawn state.

The mechanisms underlying intellectual impairment in cortical disease are relatively clear-cut, but the reason subcortical pathology results in cognitive dysfunction is perhaps less obvious: the cortex, particularly the prefrontal area, is, however, richly interconnected with subcortical structures via a number of feedback loops. Diseases affecting these structures will, therefore, functionally deactivate an otherwise normal cortex.

It should be noted that the concept of cortical and subcortical dementias is not universally accepted. AD is associated with subcortical pathology, while some basal ganglia disorders, such as Huntington's disease and progressive supranuclear palsy, show some cortical pathology (Bak & Hodges, 1998). Moreover, not all diseases can be fitted neatly into this dichotomy. The frontal form of frontotemporal dementia (dementia of frontal type) presents with features that characterize subcortical dementia and in AD, the paradigmatic cause of cortical dementia, the earliest pathological changes are found in the transentorhinal cortex, which some would not consider to be cortex proper. Hence, a better division might be into temporolimbic (AD) versus frontostriatal dementia. Table 28.4 contrasts the major features of these two types of dementia.

Parkinson's Disease

Parkinson's disease (PD) is characterized pathologically by loss of pigmented cells in the substantia nigra. Clinically, resting tremor, rigidity, bradykinesia, and postural instability occur, and may be accompanied by bradyphrenia. Although it is rare for PD to present with dementia in the absence of a movement disorder, it is commoner for PD patients to show evidence of clinically obvious cognitive dysfunction during the course of the illness, and up to 30% of PD patients fulfil the criteria for dementia. Even more PD patients show subtle subcortical deficits on neuropsychological testing (Downes et al., 1989).

The major cognitive dysfunctions occur in the fields of executive function (Dubois, Pillon, Legault, Agid, & Lhermitte, 1988; Litvan, Mohr, Williams, Gomez, & Chase, 1991; Owen, Iddon, Hodges, Summers, & Robbins,

1997; Owen et al., 1993) rather than episodic memory (Sahakian et al., 1988). On memory tasks there is typically a marked discrepancy between impaired free recall and normal, or near normal, recognition memory (Breen, 1993). The temporal ordering of newly learned information and remote memory is also defective (Sagar, Sullivan et al., 1988). In common with other subcortical disorders, language abilities are relatively spared in PD.

Huntington's Disease

This is the commonest genetic disorder to cause dementia. It is inherited in an autosomal dominant fashion, and clinical onset is usually in the fourth or fifth decade, but can be as late as the eighth. The condition is characterized neuropathologically by neostriatal degeneration (caudate nucleus and putamen) with loss of small spiny GABAergic neurones. Previous attempts to utilize neuropsychology and functional imaging to diagnose the condition preclinically have been largely superseded by confirmatory genetic testing: it has now been established that an abnormal expansion on chromosome 4 is the cause of HD.

Although characterized eventually by dementia and chorea, it is clear that cognitive and/or psychiatric changes may precede mo-

Table 28.4 Contrasting features of Cortical and Subcortical dementia.

Characteristic	Temporolimbic dementia (AD)	Frontostriatal dementia (e.g., Huntington's disease)
• Speed of cognitive processing	Normal	Slowed up (bradyphrenic)
• Attention	May be normal initially then deficits in selective, sustained and divided attention	Usually globally impaired early in course
• Frontal "executive" abilities	Preserved in early stages	Disproportionately impaired from onset
• Episodic memory	Severe amnesia Recall and recognition affected Normal forgetting	Forgetfulness Recognition better than recall
• Language	Lexico-semantic deficits prominent	Normal except dysarthria and reduced output
• Visuo-spatial and perceptual abilities	Impaired	Impaired (mild)
• Personality	Intact until late	Typically apathetic and inert
• Mood	Usually normal	Depression common

tor dysfunction by many years. There is evidence of attentional and frontal executive dysfunction very early in the disease and may even be detected at a preclinical stage (Lange, Sahakian, Quinn, Marsden, & Robbins, 1995; Lawrence et al., 1996, 1998). Memory impairment is seen in HD (Butters et al., 1985; Hodges, Salmon, & Butters, 1990; Moss et al., 1986), the deficit is primarily due to impaired retrieval of new information. On tests of remote memory, patients with HD show equivalent impairment over all decades that contrasts with the temporal gradient seen in AD and Korsakoff's patients (Beatty et al., 1988). Another difference is the impairment of working memory (e.g., digit span) early in the course of HD (Butters et al., 1985).

Vascular Dementia

Cerebrovascular disease is a common cause of dementia, accounting in some studies for up to a quarter of all cases. Unlike AD, there are no well-established criteria for the diagnosis, although the guidelines recently published by the NINDS-AIREN group are likely to become more widely used (Roman et al., 1993). The nature of the cognitive deficits have not been well defined (for review, see Bendixen, 1993) which almost certainly reflects the difficulty in case definition and the heterogeneous pathologies (major infarction, lacunes, hypertensive encephalopathy, haemorrhage, etc.) that can result in vascular dementia (Hachinski & Norris, 1994).

Cognitively, impaired attention and frontal executive features predominate (Kertesz & Clydesdale, 1994) owing to a concentration of lacunes in the basal ganglia and thalamic regions, but features of cortical dysfunction are also frequently present. Although memory is also affected, the nature of the deficit has not been well characterized (Almkvist, 1994). Multi-infarct dementia (MID) and AD patients may be separable on the basis of speech and language impairments; Powell, Cummings, Hill, and Benson (1988) found that AD patients were more impaired on linguistic features of language (especially information content), while MID patients were worse on mechanical aspects of speech (especially speech melody).

So-called thalamic dementia may arise from bilateral infarction of medial thalamic structures, which results in severe amnesia marked frontal executive deficits and vertical eye movement impairment (Hodges & McCarthy, 1993).

References

Almkvist, O. (1994). Neuropsychological deficits in vascular dementia in relation to Alzheimer's disease: Reviewing evidence for functional similarity or divergence. *Dementia, 5,* 203–209.

American Psychiatric Association. (1994). *Diagnostic and statistical manual of mental disorders* (3rd ed.). Washington, DC: American Psychiatric Association.

Baddeley, A. D. (1990). *Human memory: Theory and practice.* Hove, England: Erlbaum.

Baddeley, A. (1992). Working memory. *Science, 255,* 556–559.

Baddeley, A. D., Bressi, S., Della Sala, S., Logie, R., & Spinnler, H. (1991). The decline of working memory in Alzheimer's disease: A longitudinal study. *Brain, 114,* 2521–2542.

Bak, T., & Hodges, J. R. (1998). The neuropsychology of progressive supranuclear palsy—A review. *Neurocase, 4,* 89–94.

Bayles, K. A., Tomoeda, C. K., Kasniak, A. W., & Trosset, M. W. (1991). Alzheimer's disease effects on semantic memory: Loss of structure or impaired processing. *Journal of Cognitive Neuroscience, 3,* 166–182.

Beatty, W. W., Salmon, D. P., Butters, N., Heindel, W. C., & Granholm, E. L. (1988). Retrograde amnesia in patients with Alzheimer's disease or Huntington's disease. *Neurobiology of Ageing, 9,* 181–186.

Becker, J. T., Boller, F., Saxton, J., & McGonigle-Gibson, K. L. (1987). Normal rates of forgetting of verbal and non-verbal material in Alzheimer's disease. *Cortex, 23,* 59–72.

Becker, J. T., Lopez, O. L., & Wess, J. (1992). Material-specific memory loss in probable Alzheimer's disease. *Journal of Neurology, Neurosurgery and Psychiatry, 55,* 1177–1181.

Bendixen, B. (1993). Vascular dementia: A concept in flux. *Current Opinions in Neurology and Neurosurgery, 6,* 107–112.

Braak, H., & Braak, E. (1991). Neuropathological staging of Alzheimer-related changes. *Acta Neuropathologica, 82,* 239–259.

Breen, E. K. (1993). Recall and recognition memory in Parkinson's disease. *Cortex, 29,* 91–102.

Brown, J., Ashworth, A., Gydesen, S., Sorrensen, A., Rossor, M., Hardy, J., & Collinge, J. (1995). Familial nonspecific dementia maps to chromosome 3. *Human Molecular Genetics, 4,* 1625–1628.

Brun, A. (1987a). Frontal lobe degeneration of non-Alzheimer's type. I. Neuropathology. *Archives Gerontology and Geriatrics, 6,* 209–233.

Brun, A. (1987b). Provisional criteria for a diagnosis of frontal lobe dementia. *Archives of Gerontolgy and Geriatrics, 6,* 193–208.

Burgess, P. W., & Shallice, T. (1996). Confabulation and the control of recollection. *Memory, 4,* 359–411.

Butters, N., Granholm, E., Salmon, D. P., Grant, I., & Wolfe, J. (1987). Episodic and semantic memory: A comparison of amnesic and demented patients. *Journal of Clinical and Experimental Neuropsychology, 9,* 479–497.

Butters, N., Salmon, D. P., Cullum, M. C., Cairns, P., Troster, A. I., Jacobs, D., Moss, M. & Cermak, L. S. (1988). Differentiation of amnesic and demented patients with the Wechsler Memory Scale-Revised. *Clinical Neuropsychology, 2,* 133–148.

Butters, N., Wokfe, J., Martone, M., Granholm, E., & Cermak, L. S. (1985). Memory disorders associated with Huntington's disease; verbal recall, verbal recognition and procedural memory. *Neuropsychologia, 23,* 729–743.

Cappa, S. F., & Perani D. (1996). The functional imaging of dementia. *Neurocase, 2,* 149–153.

Caramazza, A., & Shelton, J. R. (1998). Domain-specific knowledge systems in the brain: The animate-inanimate distinction. *Journal of Cognitive Neuroscience, 10,* 1–34.

Chan, A. S., Butters, N., Paulson, J. S., Salmon, D. P., Swenson, M., & Maloney, L. (1993). An assessment of the semantic network in patients with Alzheimer's disease. *Journal of Cognitive Neuroscience, 5,* 254–261.

Chertkow, H., & Bub, D. (1990). Semantic memory loss in dementia of Alzheimer's type. *Brain, 113,* 397–417.

Clare, L., Wilson, B. A., Breen, E. K., & Hodges, J. R. (1999). Errorless learning of face-name associations in early Alzheimer's disease. *Neurocase, 5,* 37–46.

Della Sala, S., Laiacona, M., Spinnler, H., & Trivelli, C. (1993). Autobiographical recollection and frontal damage. *Neuropsychologia, 31,* 823–839.

Downes, J. J., Roberts, A. C., Sahakian, B. J., Evenden, J. L., Morris, R. G., & Robbins, T. W. (1989). Impaired extra-dimensional shift performance in medicated and unmedicated Parkinson's disease—Evidence for a specific attentional dysfunction. *Neuropsychologia, 27,* 1329–1343.

Dubois, B., Pillon, B., Legault, F., Agid, Y., & Lhermitte, F. (1988). Slowing of cognitive processing in progressive supranuclear palsy: A.comparison with Parkinson's disease. *Archives of Neurology, 45,* 1194–1199.

Ellis, A. W., Young, A. W., & Critchley, E. M. R. (1989). Loss of memory for people following temporal lobe damage. *Brain, 112,* 1469–1483.

Evans, J., Breen, E., Antoun, N., & Hodges, J. (1996). Focal retrograde amnesia for autobiographical events following cerebral vasculitis: A connectionist account. *Neurocase, 2,* 1–12.

Evans, J., Heggs, A. J., Antoun, N., & Hodges, J. R. (1995). Progressive prosopagnosia associated with selective right temporal lobe atrophy: A new syndrome? *Brain, 118,* 1–13.

Folstein, M. F., Folstein, S. E., & McHugh, P. R. (1975). "Mini-mental state." A practical method for grading the mental state of patients for the clinician. *Journal of Psychiatric Research, 12,* 189–198.

Fox, N. C., Warrington, E. K., Freeborough, P. A., Hartikainen, P., Kennedy, A. M., Stevens, J. M., & Rossor, M. N. (1997). Presymptomatic hippocampal atrophy in Alzheimer's disease: A longitudinal MRI study. *Brain, 119,* 2001–2009.

Gainotti, G., Silveri, M. C., Daniele, A., & Giustolisi, L. (1995). Neuroanatomical correlates of category specific semantic disorders: A critical survey. *Memory, 3,* 247–264.

Garrard, P., Patterson, K., Watson, P. C., & Hodges, J. R. (1998). Category specific semantic loss in dementia of Alzheimer's type: Functional-anatomical correlations from cross-sectional analyses. *Brain, 121,* 633–646.

Garrard, P., Perry, R., & Hodges, J. R. (1997). Disorders of semantic memory. *Journal of Neurology, Neurosurgery and Psychiatry, 62,* 431–435.

Gonnerman, L. M., Andersen, E. S., Devlin, J. T., Kempler, D., & Seidenberg, M. S. (1997). Double dissociation of semantic categories in Alzheimer's disease. *Brain and Language, 57,* 254–279.

Grady, C. L., Haxby, J. V., Horwitz, B., Sundaram, M., Berg, G., Schapiro, M., Friedland, R. P., & Rapoport, S. I. (1988). Longitudinal study of the early neuropsychological and cerebral metabolic changes in dementia of the Alzheimer type. *Journal of Clinical and Experimental Neuropsychology, 10,* 576–596.

Graff-Radford, N. R., Tranel, D., Van Hoesen, G. W., & Brandt, J. P. (1990). Diencephalic amnesia. *Brain, 113,* 1–26.

Graham, K. S., Becker, J. T., & Hodges, J. R. (1997). On the relationship between knowledge and memory for pictures: Evidence from the study of patients with semantic dementia and Alzheimer's disease. *Journal of the International Neuropsychological Society, 3,* 534–544.

Graham, K. S., & Hodges, J. R. (1997). Differentiating the roles of the hippocampal complex and the neocortex in long-term memory storage; evidence from the study of semantic dementia and Alzheimer's disease. *Neuropsychology, 11,* 77–89.

Granholm, E., & Butters, N. (1988). Associative encoding and retrieval in Alzheimer's and Huntington's disease. *Brain and Cognition, 7,* 335–347.

Greene, J. D. W., Baddeley, A. D., & Hodges, J. R. (1995). Autobiographical memory and executive function in early dementia of Alzheimer type. *Neuropsychologia, 33,* 1647–1670.

Greene, J. D. W., Baddeley, A. D., & Hodges, J. R. (1996). Recall and recognition of verbal and nonverbal material in early Alzheimer's disease: Applications of the Doors and People Test. *Neuropsychologia, 34,* 537–551.

Greene, J. D. W., & Hodges, J. R. (1996a). The fractionation of remote memory: Evidence from the longitudinal study of dementia of Alzheimer's type. *Brain, 119,* 129–142.

Greene, J. D. W., & Hodges, J. R. (1996b). Identification of famous faces and names in early Alzheimer's disease: Relationship to anterograde episodic and semantic memory impairment. *Brain, 119,* 111–128.

Greene, J. D. W., & Hodges, J. R. (1996c). Semantic memory in Alzheimer's disease. In R. Morris (Ed.), *The cognitive neuropsychology of Alzheimer's disease* (pp. 128–149). Oxford: Oxford University Press.

Gregory, C. A., & Hodges, J. R. (1996a). Clinical features of frontal lobe dementia in comparison with Alzheimer's disease. *Journal of Neural Transmission, 47,* 103–123.

Gregory, C. A., & Hodges, J. R. (1996b). Frontotemporal dementia: Use of consensus criteria and prevalence of psychiatric features. *Neuropsychiatry, Neuropsychology, and Behavioural Neurology, 9,* 145–153.

Hachinski, V., & Norris, J. W. (1994). Vascular dementia: An obsolete concept. *Current Opinion in Neurology, 7,* 3–4.

Hanley, J. R., Young, A. W., & Pearson, N. A. (1989). Defective recognition of familiar people. *Cognitive Neuropsychology, 6,* 179–210.

Harvey, R. J., Ellison, D., Hardy, J., Hutton, M., Roques, P. K., Collinge, J., Fox, N. C., & Rossor, M. N. (1998). Chromosome 14 familial Alzheimer's disease: The clinical and neuropathological characteristics of a family with a leucine → serine (L250S). substitution at codon 250 of the presenilin 1 gene. *Journal of Neurology, Neurosurgery and Psychiatry, 64,* 44–49.

Hodges, J. R. (1994). Pick's disease. In A. Burns & R. Levy (Eds.), *Dementia* (pp. 739–753). London: Chapman and Hall.

Hodges, J. R., Garrard, P., & Patterson, K. (1998). Semantic dementia. In A. Kertesz & D. G. Munoz (Eds.), *Pick's disease and Pick complex* (pp. 83–104). New York: Wiley-Liss, Inc.

Hodges, J. R., & Graham, K. S. (1998). A reversal of the temporal gradient for famous person knowledge in semantic dementia: Implications for the neural organisation of long-term memory. *Neuropsychologia, 36,* 803–825.

Hodges, J. R., Graham, N., & Patterson, K. (1995). Charting the progression in semantic dementia: Implications for the organisation of semantic memory. *Memory, 3,* 463–495.

Hodges, J. R., & Greene, J. D. W. (1998). Knowing people and naming them: Can Alzheimer's disease patients do one without the other. *Quarterly Journal of Experimental Psychology, 51A,* 121–134.

Hodges, J. R., & McCarthy, R. A. (1993). Autobiographical amnesia resulting from bilateral paramedian thalamic infarction: A case study in cognitive neurobiology. *Brain, 116,* 921–940.

Hodges, J. R., & Patterson, K. (1995). Is semantic memory consistently impaired early in the course of Alzheimer's disease? Neuroanatomical and diagnostic implications. *Neuropsychologia, 33,* 441–459.

Hodges, J. R., & Patterson, K. (1996). Nonfluent progressive aphasia and semantic dementia: A comparative neuropsychological study. *Journal of the International Neuropsychological Society, 2,* 511–524.

Hodges, J. R., & Patterson, K. E. (1997). Semantic memory disorders. *Trends in Cognitive Science, 1,* 67–72.

Hodges, J. R., Patterson, K., Garrard, P., Bak, T., Perry, R., & Gregory, C. (1999). The differentiation of semantic dementia and frontal lobe dementia (temporal and frontal variants of fronto-temporal dementia) from early Alzheimer's disease. *Neuropsychology, 13*, 31–40.

Hodges, J. R., Patterson, K. E., Graham, N., & Dawson, K. (1996). Naming and knowing in dementia of Alzheimer's type. *Brain and Language, 54*, 302–325.

Hodges, J. R., Patterson, K., Oxbury, S., & Funnell, E. (1992). Semantic dementia: Progressive fluent aphasia with temporal lobe atrophy. *Brain, 115*, 1783–1806.

Hodges, J. R., Patterson, K., & Tyler, L. K. (1994). Loss of semantic memory: Implications for the modularity of mind. *Cognitive Neuropsychology, 11*, 505–542.

Hodges, J. R., Salmon, D. P., & Butters, N. (1990). Differential impairment of semantic and episodic memory in Alzheimer's and Huntington's diseases: A controlled prospective study. *Journal of Neurology, Neurosurgery and Psychiatry, 53*, 1089–1095.

Hodges, J. R., Salmon, D. P., & Butters, N. (1992). Semantic memory impairment in Alzheimer's disease: Failure of access or degraded knowledge? *Neuropsychologia, 30*, 310–314.

Howard, D., & Patterson, K. (1992). *Pyramids and palm trees: A test of semantic access from pictures and words.* Bury St Edmunds, Suffolk: Thames Valley Test Company.

Josiassen, R. C., Curry, L. M., & Mancall, E. L. (1983). Development of neuropsychological deficits in Huntington's disease. *Archives of Neurology, 40*, 791–796.

Kertesz, A., & Clydesdale, S. (1994). Neuropsychological deficits in vascular dementia vs. Alzheimer's disease. *Archives of Neurology, 51*, 1226–1231.

Kitchener, E. G., McCarthy, R. A., & Hodges, J. R. (1998). Acquisition of post-morbid vocabulary and semantic facts in the absence of episodic memory. *Brain, 121*, 1313–1327.

Kopelman, M. D. (1985). Rates of forgetting in Alzheimer-type dementia and Korsakoff's syndrome. *Neuropsychologia, 23*, 623–638.

Kopelman, M. D. (1989). Remote and autobiographical memory, temporal context memory and frontal atrophy in Korsakoff and Alzheimer patients. *Neuropsychologia, 27*, 437–460.

Lambon Ralph, M. A., Patterson, K., & Hodges, J. R. (1997). The relationship between naming and semantic knowledge for different categories in dementia of Alzhei-

mer's type. *Neuropsychologia, 35*, 1251–1260.

Lange, K. W., Sahakian, B. J., Quinn, N. P., Marsden, C. D., & Robbins, T. W. (1995). Comparison of executive and visuospatial memory function in Huntington's disease and dementia of Alzheimer-type matched for degree of dementia. *Journal of Neurology, Neurosurgery and Psychiatry, 58*, 598–606.

Lawrence, A. D., Hodges, J. R., Rosser, A. E., Kershaw, A., FfrenchConstant, C., Rubinsztein, D. C., Robbins, T. W., & Sahakian, B. J. (1998). Evidence for specific cognitive deficits in preclinical Huntington's disease. *Brain, 121*, 1329–1341.

Lawrence, A. D., Sahakian, B. J., Hodges, J. R., Rosser, A. E., Lange, K. W., & Robbins, T. W. (1996). Executive and mnemonic functions in early Huntington's disease. *Brain, 119*, 1633–1645.

Litvan, I., Mohr, E., Williams, J., Gomez, C., & Chase, T. N. (1991). Differential memory and executive functions in demented patients with Parkinson's and Alzheimer's disease. *Journal of Neurology, Neurosurgery and Psychiatry, 54*, 25–29.

Locascio, J. J., Growdon, J. H., & Corkin, S. (1995). Cognitive test performance in detecting, staging, and tracking Alzheimer's disease. *Archives of Neurology, 52*, 1087–1099.

Martin, A., & Fedio, P. (1983). Word production and comprehension in Alzheimer's disease: The breakdown of semantic knowledge. *Brain and Language, 19*, 124–141.

Martin, A., Wiggs, C. L., Ungerleider, L. G., & Haxby, J. V. (1996). Neural correlates of category-specific knowledge. *Nature, 379*, 649–652.

Massman, P. J., Delis, D. C., Butters, N., Levin, B. E., & Salmon, D. P. (1990). Are all subcortical dementias alike? Verbal learning and memory in Parkinson's and Huntington's disease patients. *Journal of Clinical and Experimental Neuropsychology, 12*, 729–744.

McClelland, J., McNaughton, B., & O'Reilly, R. (1995). Why are there complementary learning systems in the hippocampus and neocortex: Insights from the successes and failures of connectionist models of learning and memory. *Psychological Review, 102*, 419–443.

Miller, B. L., Cummings, J. L., Villanueva-Meyer, J., Boone, K., Mehringer, C. M., Lesser, I. M., & Mena, I. (1991). Frontal lobe degeneration: Clinical, neuropsychological, and SPECT characteristics. *Neurology, 41*, 1374–1382.

Moss, M. B., Albert, M. S., Butters, N., & Payne, M. (1986). Differential patterns of memory loss among patients with Alzheimer's disease, Huntington's disease, and alcoholic Korsakoff's syndrome. *Archives of Neurology, 43*, 239–246.

Mummery, C. J., Patterson, K. E., & Hodges, J. R. (in press). Organisation of the semantic system: Divisible by what? *Journal of Cognitive Neuroscience.*

Mummery, C. J., Patterson, K. E., Hodges, J. R., & Wise, R. J. S. (1996). Generating "Tiger" as an animal name and a word beginning with T: Differential brain activation. *Proceeedings of the Royal Society (Series B), 263*, 989–995.

Mummery, C. J., Patterson, K., Wise, R. J. S., Price, C. J., & Hodges, J. R. (1999). Disrupted temporal lobe connections in semantic dementia. *Brain*, Jan; 122 (Pt. 1), 61–73.

Murre, J. M. J. (1996). A model of amnesia and consolidation of memory. *Hippocampus, 6*, 675–684.

Neary, D., Snowden, J. S., Bowen, D. M., Sims, N. R., Mann, D. M. A., Benton, J. S., Northen, B., Yates, P. O., & Davison, A. N. (1986). Neuropsychological syndromes in presenile dementia due to cerebral atrophy. *Journal of Neurology, Neurosurgery and Psychiatry, 49*, 163–174.

Neary, D., Snowden, J. S., Northen, B., & Goulding, P. (1988). Dementia of frontal lobe type. *Journal of Neurology, Neurosurgery and Psychiatry, 51*, 353–361.

Nebes, R. D. (1989). Semantic memory in Alzheimer's disease. *Psychological Bulletin, 106*, 377–394.

Newman, S. K., Warrington, E. K., Kennedy, A. M., & Rossor, M. N. (1994). The earliest cognitive change in a person with familial Alzheimer's disease: Presymptomatic neuropsychological features in a pedigree with familial Alzheimer's disease confirmed at necropsy. *Journal of Neurology, Neurosurgery and Psychiatry, 57*, 967–972.

Owen, A. M., Iddon, J. L., Hodges, J. R., Summers, B. A., & Robbins, T. W. (1997). Spatial and non-spatial working memory at different stages of Parkinson's disease. *Neuropsychologia, 35*, 519–532.

Owen, A. M., Roberts, A. C., Hodges, J. R., Summers, B. A., Polkey, C. E., & Robbins, T. W. (1993). Contrasting mechanisms of impaired attentional set-shifting in patients with frontal lobe damage or Parkinson's disease. *Brain, 116*, 1159–1175.

Pachana, N. A., Boone, K. B., Miller, B. L., Cummings, J. L., & Berman, N. (1996). Comparison of neuropsychological functioning in Alzheimer's disease and frontotemporal dementia. *Journal of the International Neuropsycholgical Society, 2*, 505–510.

Patterson, K., & Hodges, J. R. (1995). Disorders of semantic memory. In A. D. Baddeley, B. A. Wilson, & F. N. Watts (Eds.), *Handbook of memory disorders* (pp 167–187). Chichester: John Wiley.

Perry, R. J., & Hodges, J. R. (1996). Spectrum of memory dysfunction in degenerative disease. *Current Opinion in Neurology, 9*, 281–285.

Pillon, B., Deweer, B., Agid, Y., & Dubois, B. (1993). Explicit memory in Alzheimer's, Huntington's, and Parkinson's diseases. *Archives of Neurology, 50*, 374–379.

Powell, A. L., Cummings, J. L., Hill, M. A., & Benson, D. F. (1988). Speech and language alterations in multi-infarct dementia. *Neurology, 38*, 717–719.

Reid, W., Broe, G., Creasey, H., Grayson, D., McCusker, E., Bennett, H. (1996). Age of onset and pattern of neuropsychological impairment in mild early-stage Alzheimer disease: A study of a community-based population. *Archives of Neurology, 53*, 1056–1060.

Robbins, T. W., James, M., Owen, A. M., Lange, K. W., Lees, A. J., Leigh, P. N., Marsden, C. D., Quinn, N. P., & Summers, B. A. (1994). Cognitive deficits in progressive supranuclear palsy, Parkinson's disease, and multiple system atrophy in tests sensitive to frontal lobe dysfunction. *Journal of Neurology, Neurosurgery and Psychiatry, 57*, 79–88.

Roman, G. C., Tatemichi, T. K., Erkinjuntti, T., Cummings, J. L., Masdeu, J. C., Garcia, J. H., Amaducci, L, Orgogozo, J. M., Brun, A., Hofman, A., Moody, D. M., O'Brien, M. D., Yamaguchi, T., Gratman, J., Drayer, B. P., Bennett, D. A., Fisher, M., Ogata, J., Kokmen, E., Bermejo, F., Wolf, P. A., Gorelick, P. B., Bick, K. L., Pajeau, A. K., Bell, M. A., DeCarli, C., Culebras, A., Korczyn, A. D., Bougousslavsky, J., Hartman, A., & Scheinberg, P. (1993). Vascular dementia—Diagnostic criteria for research studies. Report of the NINDS-AIREN International workshop. *Neurology, 43*, 250–260.

Rosser, A., & Hodges, J. R. (1994). Initial letter and semantic category fluency in Alzheimer's disease, Huntington's disease and progressive supranuclear palsy. *Journal of*

Neurology, Neurosurgery and Psychiatry, *57,* 1389–1394.

Sagar, H. J., Cohen, N. J., Sullivan, E. V., Corkin, S., & Growdon, J. H. (1988). Remote memory function in Alzheimer's disease and Parkinson's disease. *Brain, 111,* 185–206.

Sagar, H. J., Sullivan, E. V., Gabrieli, J. D. E., Corkin, S., & Growdon, J. H. (1988). Temporal ordering deficits and bradyphrenia in Parkinson's disease. *Brain.*

Sahakian, B. J., Morris, R. G., Evenden, J. L., Heald, A., Levy, R., Philpot, M., & Robbins, T. W. (1988). A comparative study of visuospatial memory and learning in Alzheimer-type dementia and Parkinson's disease. *Brain, 111,* 695–718.

Smith, A. D., & Jobst, K. A. (1996). Use of structural imaging to study the progression of Alzheimer's disease. *British Medical Bulletin, 52,* 575–586.

Snowden, J. S., Goulding, P. J., & Neary, D. (1989). Semantic dementia: A form of circumscribed cerebral atrophy. *Behavioural Neurology, 2,* 167–182.

Snowden, J. S., Griffiths, H. L., & Neary, D. (1996a). Progressive language disorder associated with frontal lobe degeneration. *Neurocase, 2,* 429–440.

Snowden, J. S., Griffiths, H. L., & Neary, D. (1996b). Semantic-episodic memory interactions in semantic dementia: Implications for retrograde memory function. *Cognitive Neuropsychology, 13,* 1101–1137.

Snowden, J. S., Neary, D., & Mann, D. M. A. (1996). *Fronto-temporal lobar degeneration: Fronto-temporal dementia, progressive aphasia, semantic dementia.* New York: Churchill Livingstone.

Squire, L. R. (1992). Memory and the hippocampus: A synthesis from findings with rats, monkeys, and humans. *Psychological Review, 99,* 195–231.

Starkstein, S. E., Sabe, L., Chemerinski, E., Jason, L., & Leiguarda, R. (1996). Two domains of anosognosia in Alzheimer's disease. *Journal of Neurology, Neurosurgry and Psychiatry, 61,* 485–490.

Terry, R. D., Masliah, E., Salmon, D. P., Butters, N., DeTeresa, R., Hill, R., Hansen, L. A., & Katzman, R. (1991). Physical basis of cognitive alterations in Alzheimer's disease: Synapse loss is the major correlate of cognitive impairments. *Annals of Neurology, 30,* 572–580.

Van Hoesen, G. W., Hyman, B. T., & Damasio, A. R. (1991). Entorhinal cortex pathology in Alzheimer's disease. *Hippocampus, 1,* 1–18.

Vandenberghe, R., Price, C., Wise, R., Josephs, O., & Frackowiak, R. S. J. (1996). Functional anatomy of a common semantic system for words and pictures. *Nature, 383,* 254–256.

Vargha-Khadem, F., Gadian, D. G., Watkins, K. E., Connelly, A., Van Paesschen, W., & Mishkin, M. (1997). Differential effects of early hippocampal pathology on episodic and semantic memory. *Science, 277,* 376–380.

Warrington, E. K. (1975). Selective impairment of semantic memory. *Quarterly Journal of Experimental Psychology, 27,* 635–657.

Welsh, K. A., Butters, N., Hughes, J. P., & Mohs, R. C. (1992). Detection and staging of dementia in Alzheimer's disease: Use of the neuropsychological measures developed for the Consortium to Establish a Registry for Alzheimer's Disease. *Archives of Neurology, 49,* 448–452.

Welsh, K., Butters, N., Hughes, J., Mohs, R., & Heyman, A. (1991). Detection of abnormal memory decline in mild cases of Alzheimer's disease using CERAD neuropsychological measures. *Archives of Neurology, 48,* 278–281.

Whitehouse, P. J. (1986). The concept of subcortical and cortical dementia: Another look. *Annals of Neurology, 19,* 1–6.

Wilcock, G. K., & Esiri, M. M. (1982). Plaques, tangles and dementia: A quantitative study. *Journal of Neurological Science, 56,* 343–356.

Wilhelmsen, K. C. (1997). Frontotemporal dementia is on the MAP. *Annals of Neurology, 41,* 139–140.

Part IV: Organization of Memory

NEURAL SUBSTRATES OF MEMORY

29

Neuroanatomy of Memory

HANS J. MARKOWITSCH

Memory is a basic and at the same time a highly complex function in the animal kingdom. The range of memory functions certainly is related to the heterogeneity of the underlying nervous systems of species from planaria to humans. The broad span of behaviors subsumed under the umbrella of memory has led researchers to look for appropriate categorizations of mnestic subfunctions that range from simple forms of classical conditioning to episodic memory (Thompson & Kim, 1996; Tulving & Markowitsch, 1998). Especially in humans, memory is embedded in other complex behavioral representations such as thoughts, language, reasoning, or emotion. Localization of memory processing is difficult because cellular networks from the remotest neural periphery to the integration cortices participate in such processing. Nevertheless it is essential to unravel the circuitry of memory processing, both for the purpose of understanding brain functioning in general and for the diagnosis and treatment of individuals suffering from brain damage.

As in the case of other forms of behavior, clues for the development of enduring memories can be sought in evolution—that is, in the survival value of memory functions. Acquiring knowledge about places where food can be found is critical for the prolongation of the life of the individual, and knowledge of the scent of partners willing to engage in copulation is critical for the survival of the species. Both these examples demonstrate the embedding of memory functions in an emotional-motivational context, an insight gained already in the early days in brain research that showed that those regions involved in the processing of affective information are also involved in the processing of memory information. The "visceral brain" (MacLean, 1952) or the "rhinencephalon" (Macchi, 1989; Nieuwenhuys, Voogt, & van Huizen, 1988) were early labels for what today is termed the "limbic system" and most frequently associated with memory, though the term limbic system as such was already used in the nineteenth century (Broca, 1878).

This chapter discusses the neuroanatomical correlates for memory encoding, consolidation, storage, and retrieval on the basis of time-related and contents-related subdivisions of memory. Any discussion of brain-behavior interrelations necessarily depends on the available methodology. The last century of brain research has provided numerous examples of this contingency. Kleist's (1934) painstaking analysis of the behavioral disturbances of thousands of gun- or shrapnel-lesioned veterans from the First World War allowed him to depict a rather detailed cortical map in which at least one function is assigned to each of Brodmann's (1914) cytoarchitectonically defined areas (figure 29.1). Kleist's map probably comes closest to the old idea of establishing a *Landkartensystem* (geographical map system) of the brain, which had already been sought by Gudden (1886), the personal physician of the mad Bavarian king Ludwig II.

Work based on electrophysiological techniques has led to the formulation of views of information processing by the brain that emphasize the involvement of widely distributed (holographic) neural networks in behavior and cognition (Bartlett & John, 1973). The results of functional brain imaging techniques have shown that even for simple memory tasks numerous brain regions change their activity (Blinkenberg et al., 1996; Deiber et al., 1997). Consequently, the practice of equating the consequences of the loss of a function after damage to a certain region with the control of this function by the same region in the normal brain has been criticized (Chow, 1967; Horel, 1994; Markowitsch, 1984; Vanderwolf and Cain, 1994). The other extreme, that there is no specific brain locus for memory at all (Lashley, 1950), is also untenable at present.

The analysis of memory processes in the brain was considerably influenced by theoretical proposals on memory subdivisions that came from cognitive psychology (Tulving, 1972, 1983). Tulving's ideas helped to shape a framework for findings of memory preservation in amnesics (e.g., Warrington & Weiskrantz, 1970) and encouraged a more refined analysis of what had been earlier described as the global amnesic syndrome. Even memory research in animals profited from these content-based fractionations of memory functions (Mishkin & Petri, 1984). Tulving's (1991) subdivisions will be used here, as his specifications seem to correspond closely to observations of selective memory loss in patients with certain forms of brain damage. Consequently, long-term memory will be subdivided into episodic memory, the knowledge system (frequently named "semantic memory"), procedural memory, and priming. Episodic memory is used here as event or autobiographical memory—that is, as a memory for context-embedded events of ones own past. The knowledge system refers to context-free facts, procedural memory to various (perceptual, motor, cognitive) skills, and priming to a higher likelihood of reidentifying a previously perceived stimulus (or, for conceptual priming, a stimulus from a previously perceived set or category of stimuli).

Memory Disorders and Brain Damage

Historically, memory was regarded as one of the "intellectual faculties" and related to the frontal lobes; already in 1854, Huschke claimed that the frontal lobes were the brain of intelligence. Ribot's (1882) book, which had appeared in French in 1881 and was translated into English and German, constituted one of the major reference works for the disturbances of memory. Ribot (1882) attributed three meanings to memory: "the conservation of certain conditions, their reproduction, and their localization in the past" (p. 10). His "law" that the more recent the information is, the more likely it is lost after brain damage, while vice versa, the longer it had been stored, the more likely it is retained, is still valid, though not universally supported (Leplow et al., 1997; Snowden, Griffiths, & Neary, 1996).

At the turn of the century, memory disturbances were more and more associated with the Korsakoff's syndrome, which first had been described in 1887 (cf. Markowitsch, 1992) and which already in 1901 constituted the topic of a major book (Bonhoeffer, 1901). Subsequently both the thalamic nuclei and the mammillary bodies remained at the center of brain-memory relations for several decades (Mair, Warrington, & Weiskrantz, 1979; Victor, Adams, & Collins, 1989). The expression "amnesic syndrome" (or "amnesic symptom complex") was well known at the turn of the twentieth century (Markowitsch, 1992). The distinction between amnesia and dementia was also widely discussed at the time (Bolton, 1903; Schneider, 1901) and, following Alzheimer (1907) and Pick (1906), senile and presenile dementia was further differentiated into various forms.

Relations between temporal lobe damage and memory disturbances were much less obvious, though scattered reports again existed already at the beginning of the twentieth century (Bechterew, 1900; Knapp, 1905). Bechterew (1900) demonstrated "a brain with destruction of the anterior and medial parts of the cerebral cortex of both temporal lobes." The bilateral destruction of the uncinate and hippocampal gyri was accompanied by an "extra-ordinary anterograde amnesia, and a partial retrograde amnesia." Similarly, Knapp (1905) emphasized that "Korsakoff's syndrome has a special liking for temporal lobe tumors" (p. 254) and reported that he had

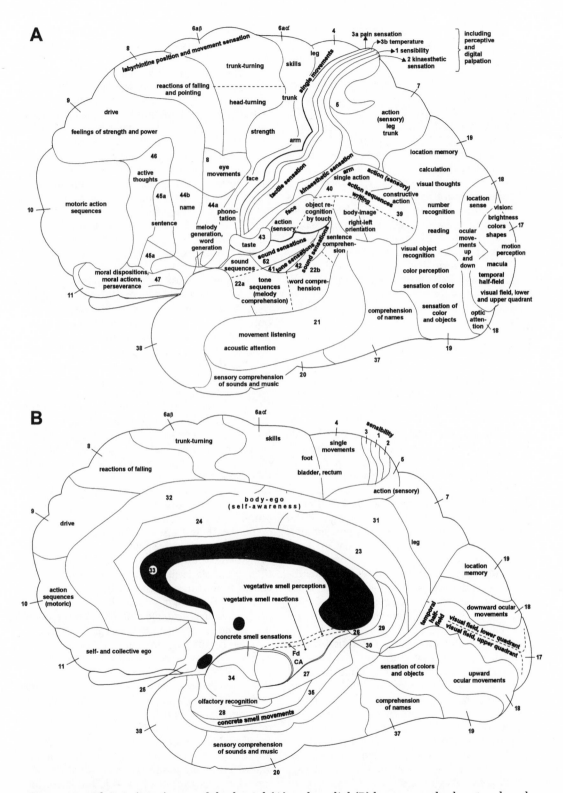

Figure 29.1 Kleist's (1934) map of the lateral (A) and medial (B) human cerebral cortex; based on his experiences with World War I veterans with traumatic brain damage. The map is based on Brodmann's (1914) cytoarchitectonic map.

found anterograde and retrograde amnesia together with a disorientation in time and space in a number of his temporal lobe damaged patients.

In the early 1950s several other papers pointed to amnesic consequences of temporal lobe damage (Glees & Griffith, 1952; Hegglin, 1953; Ule, 1951), but it was only Scoville and Milner's first detailed description of HM in 1957 that alerted scientists worldwide to the possible consequences of bilateral medial temporal damage on memory. HM received a bilateral resection of major portions of his medial temporal lobes in 1953, with the consequence of persistent anterograde and some time-restricted retrograde amnesia. Since then—and this is now nearly half a century later—his memory disturbances as well as his brain damage have been documented by numerous studies (Corkin 1984; Corkin, Amaral, Gonzalez, Johnson, & Hyman, 1997; Freed & Corkin, 1988; Freed, Corkin, & Cohen, 1987; Hebben, Corkin, Eichenbaum, & Shedlack, 1985; Keane, Gabrieli, Mapstone, Johnson, & Corkin, 1995; Milner, Corkin, & Teuber, 1968; Nissen, Cohen, & Corkin, 1981; Sagar, Gabrieli, Sullivan, & Corkin, 1990; Smith, 1988; Woodruff-Pak, 1993).

The dichotomy of medial temporal lobe and diencephalic amnesias dominated textbooks and reviews over several decades (Squire, 1987; Squire, Knowlton, & Musen, 1993), although currently some authors seem in favor of replacing the idea by the term "medial temporal-diencephalic amnesia" (Reber, Stark, & Squire, 1998), thus suggesting that the medial temporal lobes and diencephalon might be two portions of a unitary memory system (Squire, 1995).

While people with medial temporal or diencephalic damage still constitute the main group of the "amnesic patients," recently other typologies have come to be increasingly described and discussed. Thus, for example, damage to regions in the basal forebrain, usually caused by rupture of the anterior communicating artery, has also been found to result in amnesia (Damasio, Graff-Radford, Eslinger, Damasio, & Kassell, 1985; "basal forebrain amnesia"). Because all these regions belong to the limbic system, or at least to its "expanded" form (Nauta, 1979; Nieuwenhuys, 1996), the limbic system has been regarded to play a crucial role in memory processing—a finding that makes sense also from an evolutionary point of view (Markowitsch, in press).

The memory problems of most patients lie in the anterograde direction: their ability to form new memories postinjury is drastically reduced while the information stored pre-injury (retrograde memory) is largely preserved. Before the adoption of the practice of fractionating memory on the basis of its contents, the most typical group had been named "global amnesics." They were primarily characterizable by their profound inability to form new long-term episodic memories while their short-term memory and other intellectual functions appeared intact. For patients with more selective memory disturbances, the term "material-specific amnesia" was introduced; such patients, for instance, were unable to memorize faces or proper names. Furthermore, there are patient groups in whom procedural memory loss is predominant (patients with Parkinson's disease or Huntington's chorea). A large group of elderly patients have both major short-term and long-term memory deficits, and additional intellectual and personality changes; these patients are not amnesic, but demented. Patients with Alzheimer's disease constitute their largest portion, as discussed by Hodges in chapter 28. A very small group of patients have selective short-term memory deficits, though their ability to form long-term memories is largely preserved.

The widely spread and multiple sites of brain damage in demented patients suggest that the actual storage sites ("engram places") have been demolished in these patients, while focal (selective) brain damage for most other patients hampers the formation of new engrams or their transfer from short-term into long-term memory. Some researchers, however, believe that the memory impairment in these patients is attributable to the failure of access to the stored information.

In addition to patients with mainly anterograde memory problems, some do have combined anterograde and retrograde deficits (Mayes, Daum, Markowitsch, & Sauter, 1997), and others have more or less selective retrograde deficits only (Markowitsch, 1995). Although still not generally accepted, it appears logical that the brain damage leading to anterograde amnesia differs from that leading to retrograde amnesia and that patients with combined anterograde and retrograde amnesia might either have damage to both "anterograde" and "retrograde" loci, or might at least have an interruption of their interconnecting pathways. In the rest of this chapter, brain loci implicated in memory processing are discussed, divided into those necessary for information consolidation and consequently also information transfer into long-term stores, those implicated in storage itself, and those necessary for the retrieval of stored memories.

Nonlimbic structures had a less clear role in memory. Damage to neocortical regions was regarded to cause either quite restricted forms of amnesia, such as an inability to remember or retrieve names, colors, or faces (e.g., Bleuler, 1893; Damasio, 1990; Lucchelli, Muggia, & Spinnler, 1997; Reinkemeier, Markowitsch, Rauch, & Kessler, 1997), or—when it was widespread, such as in Alzheimer's disease—quite general intellectual decline. Recently, however, there have been signs of behavioral and neuropathological convergence for a limbic system–related focus in Alzheimer's disease: Braak and Braak (1997) found that the earliest neuronal damage occurs in limbic structures as well, particularly within the medial temporal lobe. And Hassing and Bäckman (1997) found that cortical dementia particularly affected the ability to transfer information from temporary to permanent storage.

Damage to nonlimbic subcortical structures usually produces other syndrome pictures in which memory complaints are less frequent and less severe. However, again stimulated by the appearance of contents-based memory subdivisions, investigations during the last decade have pointed to close relations between severe procedural memory impairments and Parkinson's disease and Huntington's chorea. Conventional neurology had regarded both diseases (and more generally damage to the basal ganglia) as resulting in major motor impairments, rigidity, tremor, and akinesia for Parkinsonism, and choreatic movements for Huntington's chorea, though it was known that (for both forms) with progression of the disease process dementia might occur ("subcortical dementia," "frontostriatal dementia"; Cummings, 1990; Darvesh & Freedman, 1996). It was found that damage to the cerebellum, like the damage to the basal ganglia, resulted in procedural memory impairments.

Finally, cortical regions surrounding the primary sensory regions, above all the unimodal nonprimary cortices, have been suggested as controlling priming (Nielsen-Bohlman, Ciranni, Shimamura, & Knight, 1997; Ochsner, Chiu, & Schacter, 1994; Seeck et al., 1997). Results from an electrophysiological study suggest the regions involved in priming are even more widespread and may include polymodal areas as well (Zhang, Begleiter, & Porjesz, 1997).

Emotion and Memory

Papez (1937) had proposed "a mechanism of emotion" and had attributed this to widely interconnected structures within the limbic system. Today these structures—hippocampal formation, fornix, mammillary bodies, mammillothalamic tract (or tract of Vicq d'Azyr), anterior thalamus, thalamo-cortical radiations, cingulate gyrus, cingulum—have kept his name ("Papez circuit"), but are more frequently discussed as memory related (figure 29.2). In line with Hebb's (1949) early assumption, the system is seen as one in which information circulates for a certain time and is associated (or brought into synchrony) with internal (emotional, motivational) states (Kornhuber, 1988), before being transmitted for long-term storage.

Other limbic structures, such as the amygdalar and septal nuclei, are regarded as much more directly involved in the processing of emotions; nevertheless, both of them modulate memory consolidation extensively via their information evaluating properties (McGaugh, Cahill, & Roozendaal, 1996; Markowitsch et al., 1994). They are part of another system, the basolateral limbic circuit, which additionally includes the mediodorsal nucleus (Sarter & Markowitsch, 1985; figure 29.3). Again, the disruption caused by damage of interconnecting fibers within this system, as may occur after capsular genu infarct, will result in a disconnection syndrome and in memory impairment (Markowitsch, von Cramon, Hofmann, Sick, & Kinzler, 1990).

Early studies that were based on more extensive temporal lesioning in monkeys attributed a number of deficits to damage within this region: visual agnosia, hypersexuality, hypermetamorphosis (the tendency to extensively attend to any kind of stimuli), hyperorality (to put everything in the mouth), tameness, bulimia, and amnesia (Klüver & Bucy, 1937; Bucy & Klüver, 1940). Later, it was found that the affect-related disturbances were mainly due to the amygdalar damage (Gallagher & Chiba, 1996; Tranel, 1997) and that amygdaloid damage may impair memory because the patients are no longer able to distinguish important from negligible informa-

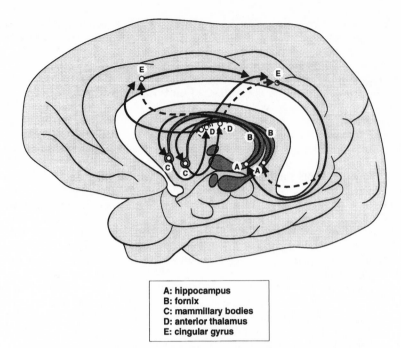

A: hippocampus
B: fornix
C: mammillary bodies
D: anterior thalamus
E: cingular gyrus

Figure 29.2 The Papez circuit interconnecting the hippocampal formation via the (postcommissural) fornix to the mammillary bodies, then via the mammillothalamic tract (or tractus Vicq d'Azyr) to the anterior thalamus, the anterior thalamus with its cortical projection targets reaches the cingulate gyrus and the subicular part of the hippocampal formation and the cingulum fibers in addition project back from the cingulate gyrus into the hippocampal formation. The precommissural fornix in addition provides a bidirectional connection between the hippocampal formation and the basal forebrain (Irle and Markowitsch, 1982).

tion (Cahill, Babinsky, Markowitsch, & McGaugh, 1995; LaBar, LeDoux, Spencer, & Phelps, 1995). A related phenomenon occurs after septal damage, though the underlying process is principally inversed: while amygdalar damage reduces emotions, septal damage enhances them (Cramon & Markowitsch, 1999). Cramon, Markowitsch, and Schuri (1993) described a patient with massive memory disorders after septal nuclear damage. The patient was unable to rationalize and evaluate information, with the consequence of grossly reduced memory abilities.

The importance of a proper emotional embedding of information also becomes apparent in patients with stress-related illnesses such as the posttraumatic stress disorder and related life-threatening experiences (Bremner et al., 1993; Bremner, Krystal, Southwick, & Charney, 1995; Krystal, Southwick, & Char-

ney, 1995; van der Kolk, 1993). Sapolsky (1996) and others have proposed that such environmental encountering may change the brain's biochemistry—release and binding of glucocorticoids or of gamma amino butyric acid (GABA) agonists—and may result in an inability to successfully store new information. The consequence is a so-called mnestic block syndrome (Markowitsch, Fink, Thöne, Kessler, & Heiss, 1997; Markowitsch, Kessler, Frölich, Schneider, & Maurer, 1998; Markowitsch, Kessler, Van der Ven, Weber-Luxenburger, & Heiss, 1998). In a few instances, even permanent brain damage in the hippocampus has been found as the likely result of such stressful events (Bremner, Randall et al., 1995; Bremmer et al., 1997).

As an example, a 23-year-old man lost his ability to store new and to retrieve old memories after he had seen a fire in his house. As it

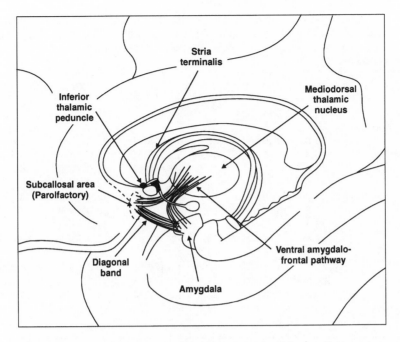

Figure 29.3 The basolateral limbic circuit. Amygdala, mediodorsal thalamic nucleus, and area subcallosa are linked with each other by distinct fiber projections, namely the ventral amygdalofugal pathway, the inferior thalamic peduncle and the bandeletta diagonalis. Note that the septal nuclei are adjacent to the subcallosal area.

turned out, he, as a child, had seen a man burning to death in his car and this event seems to have induced a shock (mnestic block) condition resulting in the observed amnesic condition. While conventional neuroradiological investigations failed to reveal any brain damage, an FDG-PET (PET = positron emission tomography) demonstrated major hypometabolism in zones of the medial and antero-lateral temporal cortex and the medial diencephalon (table 29.1), and consequently in brain regions which centrally participate in memory processing.

All this evidence strongly points to a major interaction between emotional and memory performance. The following description of regional networks specialized in information acquisition and consolidation, storage, and retrieval will demonstrate the extent of this interdependence.

Memory Acquisition

Memory acquisition refers to the sensory uptake of information, its initial encoding, and further consolidation. Of these time-related subdivisions, sensory uptake engages the appropriate sensory receptors, such as the hair cells in the cochlea and the further unimodal sensory regions of the cortex. There is some controversy as to whether memory encoding and memory consolidation should be viewed as separate processes or in fact constitute one process (Cermak, 1989, 1997). Usually, however, encoding is viewed as the more initial part of information transmission and consolidation as the more advanced part.

Based on the traditional model of separate short-term and long-term memory stores (Atkinson & Shiffrin, 1968), it is assumed that information usually reaches the cortical level initially and is stored there short term. This assumption is both in conformity with numerous descriptions of preserved short-term memory in amnesics (and therefore in patients with nonneocortical damage; Scoville & Milner, 1957; Markowitsch, von Cramon, & Schuri, 1993) and with the existence of a few case reports on patients with selective short-term memory impairment and neocortical damage (Butterworth, Cipolotti, & Warrington, 1996; Markowitsch et al., 1999; Shallice &

Table 29.1 Metabolic rates of glucose (CMRGLc; micromol/100g/min; means and standard deviations) in selected regions of the temporal lobes and the thalamus of a patient with stress-related amnesia compared to six age-matched normal control subjects.

Brain region	Patient		Control Group	
Region	R [%]	L [%]	R	L
Temporal lobe				
Li(a)	22.6 + 6.0 [67.3]	26.2 + 6.7 [75.3]	33.6 + 4.1	34.8 + 4.1
Li(m)	26.4 + 6.5 [71.9]	30.6 + 5.2 [85.5]	36.7 + 4.0	35.8 + 3.9
Li(p)	25.9 + 5.4 [76.2]	28.3 + 4.8 [81.8]	34.0 + 3.6	34.6 + 4.1
Ls(a)	26.0 + 5.0 [79.0]	26.6 + 4.1 [78.0]	32.9 + 3.6	34.1 + 3.4
Ls(m)	29.9 + 5.5 [90.9]	30.6 + 3.9 [80.1]	32.9 + 3.6	38.2 + 3.2
Ls(p)	29.5 + 5.3 [77.6]	30.5 + 4.8 [81.6]	38.0 + 4.8	37.4 + 4.4
B(a)	23.7 + 4.8 [74.3]	27.0 + 4.8 [83.6]	31.9 + 4.3	32.3 + 3.3
B(m)	22.4 + 4.3 [70.2]	23.7 + 5.2 [73.4]	31.9 + 4.2	32.3 + 4.1
B(p)	27.4 + 4.1 [80.6]	29.2 + 3.2 [86.1]	34.0 + 3.0	33.9 + 3.9
M(a)	20.9 + 3.8 [69.2]	22.6 + 3.5 [74.8]	30.2 + 4.2	30.2 + 3.8
M(m)	24.8 + 3.2 [79.7]	22.0 + 3.2 [71.7]	31.1 + 3.9	30.7 + 2.8
M(p)	29.1 + 3.6 [82.2]	27.3 + 4.3 [77.8]	35.4 + 3.9	35.1 + 4.3
Thalamus	28.6 + 4.8 [76.5]	26.7 + 5.5 [69.7]	37.4 + 5.2	38.3 + 5.8
Average (%)	77	78	(100%)	(100%)

Analysis was performed after Minoshima et al. (1994). Abbreviations: CG = Control group; R = right, L = left hemisphere; Li = inferior lateral temporal lobe region, Ls = superior lateral temporal region, B = basal temporal lobe, M = mesial temporal lobe. Indexes (a), (m), and (p) refer to the anterior, middle, and posterior portions of the respective areas [see Fig. 4].

Warrington, 1970). Confirmatory evidence also comes from results on time-limited experimental suppression of brain activity in epileptic patients (Rouleau, Labrecque, Saint-Hilaire, Candu, & Giard, 1989).

In patients with selective short-term memory impairments, the brain damage is frequently detected in the angular gyrus region of the left parietal cortex (figure 29.5), which indicates that this cortical area is centrally involved in short-term memory processing and therefore in the initial level of information acquisition. Especially, results from dynamic imaging studies speak for a role of latero-dorsal prefrontal regions in working memory (Casey et al., 1995; Manoach et al., 1997). ("Working memory" can be defined as a system for temporarily holding and manipulating information; Baddeley, 1997). It can consequently be assumed that both anterior and posterior parts of the association cortex are engaged in the temporary or transient storage of information.

This statement has, however, to be further qualified by reserving it to those forms of information that are acquired explicitly or consciously, that it as episodic memories. For the other forms of information a more gradual acquisition process with similarities to Craik and Lockhart's (1972) depth of processing idea may be assumed to exist. For these forms, which may include conditioning processes, cerebellar, amygdaloid, and various cerebral cortical regions have been named (see, e.g., Knowlton, Mangels, & Squire, 1996; Squire et al., 1993; Thompson & Kim, 1996).

Memory Transfer

The most important part of information processing is its transfer into long-term memory. As mentioned before, various regional combinations of the limbic system take part in this process. Though there is no generally accepted definition of the constituents of the limbic system (e.g., Markowitsch, 1999; Nieuwenhuys, 1996; Nauta, 1979; Nieuwenhuys et al., 1988; Shaw & Alvord, 1997), there are a number of structures that are regularly named as either belonging to it or as closely associated with it. An overview of such structures and of their most frequently associated contributions to information processing is given in table 29.2.

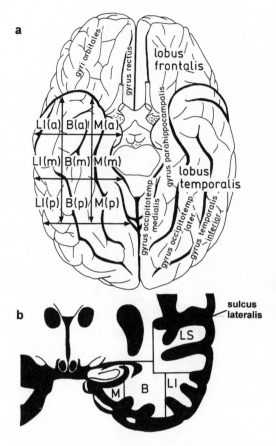

Figure 29.4 Areal partition within the temporal lobe for the measurement of metabolic glucose activity: (a) ventral view of the cortex; (b) coronal section through the temporal lobe region. Abbreviations: B = basal temporal lobe; lat = sulcus lateralis; LS = superior lateral temporal region; M = mesial temporal lobe. Indexes (a), (m), and (p) refer to the anterior, middle, and posterior portions of the respective area.

Indeed, from an anatomical point of view it seems justified to classify them, and even a number of additional structures, as components of one major memory processing system. Braak et al. (1996) have delineated an extensive scheme that represents the components of such an all-inclusive circuitry (figure 29.6). The structures within this scheme can be compared to the members of an orchestra, all of whom contribute to producing a successful concert, although their individual parts are clearly distinguishable. Similarly, structures such as the mediodorsal nucleus, which is in-

tensely connected to the prefrontal cortex, acts differently from the basal forebrain structures that have numerous cholinergic connections with widespread cortical regions, or from the hippocampal region that is widely associated with the temporal cortex. Insight, the tendency to confabulate, retrograde amnesia, conscious reflection, affective involvement, time perception, and susceptibility to interference are all examples of the features that vary quantitatively and qualitatively between structures (Cramon, Markowitsch, & Schuri, 1993; Markowitsch, Cramon et al., 1993, 1994; Tulving & Markowitsch, 1997; Vargha-Khadem et al., 1997).

Although the individual components of these limbic-system structures serve different functions, bilateral and largely complete damage to them usually results in a common syndrome—persistent amnesia. Each of these structures can therefore be regarded as a bottleneck through which information has to pass for successful consolidation. Bilateral damage to any of these bottleneck structures may consequently result in a disconnection syndrome that is termed amnesia.

There are, however, some exceptions to this general picture that throw doubt on the universal involvement of the limbic system in (episodic) memory transfer. Patient HM, for example, was capable of learning of the assassination of President Kennedy, the death of his own parents, or a favorite melody. These exceptions, together with some additional arguments, have led some researchers to postulate the existence of a nonlimbic, neocortical system that makes memory encoding possible, even though it is slow and quite limited in its capacity to bring about permanent information storage. This neocortical system also seems to be more pertinent to the encoding and storage of frequently repeated facts than of individual episodes (Kapur, 1994; McClelland, McNaughton, & O'Reilly, 1995).

Memory Storage

There is little concrete evidence available regarding the actual storage of information in the human brain. Animal research indicates that successful information acquisition first requires bioelectrical changes such as long-term potentiation and long-term depression, followed by induced changes in neuronal morphology: dendritic spine growth, synaptic enlargement, expansion of the neuropil, and the like. Furthermore, the evidence that even

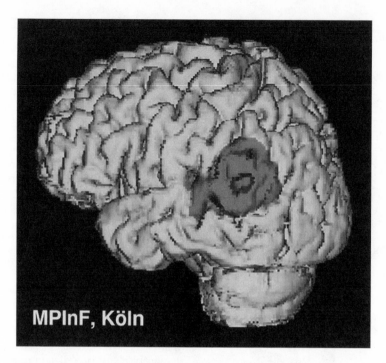

MPInF, Köln

Figure 29.5 Three-dimensional reconstruction of the left hemisphere revealing the tumor-caused brain damage (including the penumbra region) of a patient with major short-term memory impairments. The case has been described in Markowitsch et al. (1999).

complete bilateral damage of any one of the limbic bottleneck structures does not necessarily eliminate successful retrieval of old information suggests that none of these structures (e.g., medial thalamus, hippocampal region) is a long-term memory storage site. Instead, frequently proposed loci for long-term storage of information are the cerebral cortical areas and here especially the association or polymodal regions (Eichenbaum, 1997).

Evidence for the involvement of these regions in memory storage comes from dynamic imaging studies that indicate that widespread cortical sites become active during memorizing in normal subjects, and from the strong correlation between prevalent cortical damage in patients with major memory problems such as in cortical dementia (Beatty, English, & Ross, 1997; Daum, Riesch, Sartori, & Birbaumer, 1996; Giannakopoulos, Hof, Michel, Guimon, & Bouras, 1997; Laine, Vuorinen, & Rinne, 1997). Furthermore, a strong correlation has been observed between a major decrease in regional cerebral glucose metabolism across anterior and posterior cortical asso-

ciation areas and the inability to remember or newly acquire episodic and semantic memories (Markowitsch, Weber-Luxenburger, 1997b).

It is, however, still unknown whether singular neuronal modules or widespread neuronal networks represent particular bits and chunks of information. It is not even known in what form and complexity (e.g., singular bits, large-scale agglomerates) an event or item is represented and whether glial cells might also play a role in representation. Furthermore, it is an unsolved question whether cortical regions alone are able to represent an event or whether they might need assistance by emotion-coding regions such as the amygdala or the septum.

In this chapter it is assumed that information is represented in widespread networks (Abeles, 1992; Bartlett & John, 1973; Fuster, 1997) that nevertheless may be based on modular organization (Szentágothai, 1983). For the storage of procedural memories, components within the basal ganglia and the cerebellum most likely are relevant. Squire et al. (1993)

Table 29.2 Structures of the limbic system and their principal functional involvements.

Structure	Functional implication(s)
Telencephalic, cortical	
Cingulate gyrus	attention, drive, pain perception
Hippocampal formation	memory, spatial-temporal integration
Entorhinal region	memory
Telencephalic, subcortical	
Amygdala	emotional evaluation, motivations, olfaction
Basal forebrain	emotional evaluation, memory
Diencephalic	
Mammillary bodies	memory, emotion?
Anterior nucleus	memory, emotion, attention
Mediodorsal nucleus	memory, consciousness?/sleep, emotion
Non-specific thalamic nuclei	consciousness?
Associated regions ("paralimbic cortex"; expanded limbic system, Nauta, 1979)	
Medial and orbitofrontal cortex	emotional evaluation, social behavior, initiative (initiation of retrieval)
Insula	sensory-motivational integration?
Temporal pole (area 38)	memory-related sensory integration, initiation of recall

Note. The ventral striatum might be mentioned as a structure bridging between the motivational-emotional and the motor sites (Nauta, 1979). Nieuwenhuys (1996) shifted the regional agglomerate of limbic structures down to the medullar region and included among others the major noradrenergic and adrenergic nuclei in it.

have suggested that storage of skills and habits might occur "at the synapses between cortical neurons and neurons in the neostriatum" (p. 482; see also Knowlton et al., 1996).

Memory Recall

Memory recall is meant here in a wide sense, including various forms of evidence for the availability of stored information. In fact, as discussed by Tulving (1983) and also evident from the results on "false memories" (Loftus, 1998), environmental conditions influence the retrieval of information to a considerable degree. Tulving (1983) consequently reintroduced the term "ecphory" to describe the process by which retrieval cues interact with stored information to effect the creation of an image or a conscious representation of the information in question. One question is whether in the normal (nondamaged) brain, the retrieval of information occurs independent of the encoding regions (limbic system) or activates them as well. Because every form of retrieval always simultaneously entails re-encoding of the information just retrieved, dynamic imaging studies up to now have not

been able to answer this question (see, e.g., Fink, Markowitsch, Reinkemeier, Kessler, & Heiss, 1996).

A number of findings (e.g., ecphory under hypnosis, ecphory with strong retrieval cues) demonstrate that the nervous system has stored enormous amounts of information, of which only minor parts are constantly available without appropriate retrieval cues. The idea that for the recall of information regions independent of those involved in long-term transfer may also be active arose only in the last decade. It has emerged from single case reports of patients with focal brain damage outside of the classical limbic regions who have lost access to old memories, but who still possess a preserved ability to successfully form new memories (Kapur, Ellison, Smith, McLellan, & Burrowa, 1992; Markowitsch, Calabrese et al., 1993; O'Connor, Butters, Miliotis, Eslinger, & Cermak, 1992). Shortly thereafter Tulving and coworkers (1994) had formulated their HERA-model (HERA = Hemispheric Encoding/Retrieval Asymmetry) on the basis of PET-results in normal subjects. They proposed a left-hemispheric prefrontal activation for episodic memory encoding and

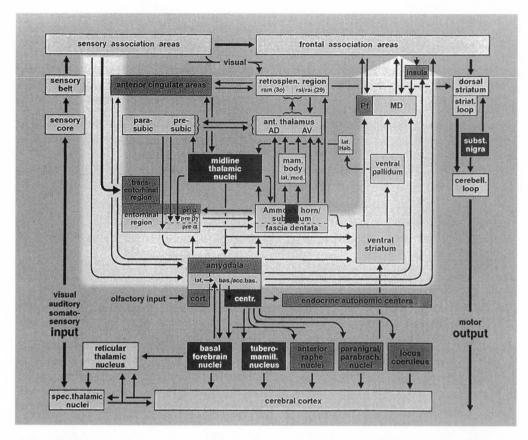

Figure 29.6 The limbic loop and additional structures are shown in detail. The amygdala integrates exteroceptive sensory data with interoceptive stimuli from autonomic centers. A large number of amygdalar efferents terminate in nuclei regulating endocrine and autonomic functions. In addition, the amygdala generates efferent connections to all nonthalamic nuclei that in a nonspecific manner project on the cerebral cortex. Abbreviations: ant. thalamus AD and AV = anterodorsal and anteroventral nuclei of the anterior thalamus; cerebell. loop = cerebellar loop; lat. Hab. = lateral habenula; lat. bas., acc. bas., cort., and centr. = lateral, basal, accessory-basal, cortical, and central amygdalar nuclei; mam. body lat. and med. = lateral and medial nuclei of the mamillary body; MD = mediodorsal thalamic nucleus; paranigral/parabrach. = paranigral and pigmented parabrachial nuclei; para subic and pre subic = parasubiculum and presubiculum; Pf = parafascicular nucleus; Pri-, Pre-, Pre-, Pre- = layers of the entorhinal region; retrosplen, region rsm (30) and rsl/rsi (29) = medial retrosplenial area (Brodmann's area 30) and lateral and intermediate retrosplenial areas (Brodmann's area 29) of the retrosplenial region; spec. thalamic nuclei = specific projection nuclei of the thalamus; striat. loop = striatal loop; subst. nigra = substantia nigra; tuberomamill. = tuberomamillary nucleus. (After Fig. 5 of Braak H, Braak E, Yilmazer D, and Bohl J: Functional anatomy of human hippocampal formation and related structures. *J Child Neurol* 1996;11:265-276; with permission from Decker Periodicals and Dr. H. Braak.)

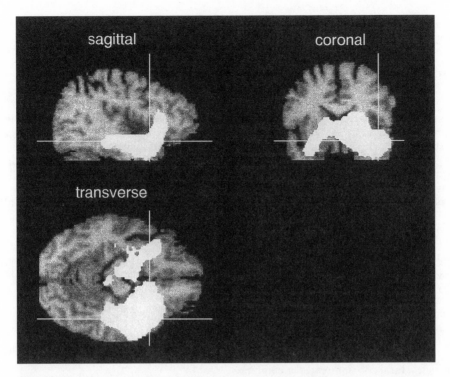

Figure 29.7 Positron-emission-tomographical (PET) representations of brain activations during ecphorizing affect-laden autobiographical memories (displayed on top of arbitrary magnetic resonance images of sagittal, coronal, and transverse brain images. The cross-hair indicates the local maximum within the area of activation. To obtain these activation patterns PET-activations during ecphorizing biographical information from an unknown individual were subtracted from those obtained during ecphorizing events from the tested subject's own biography. Note that the activations are predominantly on the right.

right-hemispheric one for episodic retrieval. Autobiographical memories, which have more emotional content and date from more distant past, have been observed to engage temporo-polar region to an even higher extent than prefrontal ones (Fink et al., 1996; Markowitsch, 1997b; Markowitsch, Fink et al., 1997; figure 29.7).

A combination of infero-lateral prefrontal and temporo-polar regions was consequently assumed to trigger the retrieval of stored old memories. For patients with normal left-hemispheric language representation it was proposed that mainly right-hemispheric (but also some left-hemispheric) damage of this regional combination will result in profound retrograde amnesia for episodic (autobiographical) material (Markowitsch, 1995, 1996). The reverse pattern, with mainly left-hemispheric damage, should result in retrograde amnesia

for information of the knowledge system. This hypothesis was largely confirmed by the results of case studies of brain-damaged patients (e.g., Calabrese et al., 1996; De Renzi, Liotti, & Nichelli, 1987; Kroll, Markowitsch, Knight, & von Cramon, 1997).

A special form of the mnestic block syndrome may also occur in memory recall: patients with psychogenic or functional amnesia (De Renzi, Lucchelli, Muggia, & Spinnler, 1997), who have no detectable brain damage (Markowitsch, 1996), may be incapable of retrieving information of autobiographical character. PET-results from a case reported by Markowitsch, Fink et al. (1997) suggest, however, that their brain function may be different from that of nonamnesic (normal) individuals, and that it may show an activation pattern indicating that such patients indeed fail to ecphorize biographical material because their brains do not engage the proper right-hemispheric fronto-temporal trigger structures.

Conclusions

Memory is a basic function for survival of the individual and the species, and memory functions are represented in a wide number of brain structures. The successful storage of memory depends on a number of associated functions, of which its emotional embedding is of special importance. The combined application of modern neuroradiological, neuropsychological, and neurological methods, which allow the in vivo study of the healthy as well as the damaged brain, has resulted in a degree of functional localization that until recently was unpredictable. Psychological insights into memory classification (short-term memory, long-term memory, episodic memory, knowledge, procedural memory, priming) and the formulation of neuropsychological mechanisms of information transfer, storage, and retrieval have resulted in the specification of selective structural conglomerates or combinations that are essential, and of others that are supportive in the acquisition, storage, and retrieval of memory. Generally, the division into short-term and long-term memory has its continuing value. Short-term memory is seen as a mechanism of cortical association regions, particularly within prefrontal and parietal areas. The limbic system is viewed as engaged in the transfer of episodes and facts for long-term storage in cortical networks. Unimodal cortical regions process, and most likely store, primed information. And subcortical, in particular basal ganglia and cerebellar structures, process, and most likely store, procedural information. Retrieval is seen as engaging a combination of fronto-temporo-polar regions: the left hemisphere dominates retrieval of factual information and the right dominates retrieval of episodic information.

Memory processing by the brain still constitutes one of the most fascinating riddles in neuroscience. The machinery of the brain with its many constituents allows a much more flexible and versatile processing and representation of information than do the most advanced computers. Nevertheless, the composition of the nervous system provides the framework for any kind of information representation in the animal kingdom. Consequently, an understanding of the circuitry within the brain provides the starting point for all models dealing with the possibilities of memory representation.

Opening of the "black box" is approached most successfully from the periphery of the brain. Indeed, available knowledge is richest with respect to the neuronal input and output channels of mnemonic information. The center of processing and storage, on the other hand, still is governed more by speculation than by firm knowledge. The extension of the present-day possibilities of neuroimaging will, however, in interaction with sophisticated neuropsychological designs, help to brighten the dark core of the brain's processing of information.

Acknowledgments Support by grants from the German Research Council (DFG; Ma 795/ 25-1 + 2, Ma 795/26-1, and He 21/1) is gratefully acknowledged.

References

Abeles, M. (1992). *Corticonics*. Cambridge: Cambridge University Press.

Alzheimer, A. (1907). Ueber eine eigenartige Erkrankung der Hirnrinde. *Allgemeine Zeitschrift für Psychiatrie, 64*, 146–148.

Atkinson, R. C., & Shiffrin, R. M. (1968). Human memory: A proposed system and its control processes. In K. W. Spence & J. T. Spence (Eds.), *The psychology of learning and motivation: Advances in research and theory* (pp. 89–195). New York: Academic Press.

Baddeley, A. (1997). *Human memory: Theory and practice* (Rev. ed.). Hove, England: Psychology Press.

Bartlett, F., & John, E. R. (1973). Equipotentiality quantified: The anatomical distribution of the engram. *Science, 181*, 764–767.

Beatty, W. W., English, S., & Ross, E. D. (1997). Retrograde amnesia for medical and other knowledge in a physician with Alzheimer's disease. *Neurocase 3*: 297–305.

Bechterew, W., von (1900). Demonstration eines Gehirnes mit Zerstörung der vorderen und inneren Theile der Hirnrinde beider Schläfenlappen. *Neurologisches Zentralblatt, 19*, 990–991.

Bleuler, E. (1893). Ein Fall von aphasischen Symptomen, Hemianopsie, amnestischer Farbenblindheit und Seelenlähmung. *Archiv für Psychiatrie und Nervenkrankheiten, 25*, 32–73.

Blinkenberg, M., Bonde, C., Holm, S., Svarer, C., Andersen, J., Paulson, O. B., & Law, I.

(1996). Rate dependence of regional cerebral activation during performance of a repetitive motor task: A PET study. *Journal of Cerebral Blood Flow and Metabolism, 16*, 794–803.

Bolton, J. S. (1903). The histological basis of amentia and dementia. *Archives of Neurology* (London), *2*, 424–620.

Bonhoeffer, K. (1901). *Die akuten Geisteskrankheiten der Gewohnheitstrinker.* Fischer: Jena.

Braak, H., & Braak, E. (1997). Frequency of stages of Alzheimer-related lesions in different age categories. *Neurobiology of Aging, 18*, 351–357.

Braak, H., Braak, E., Yilmazer, D., de Vos, R. A. I., Jansen, E. N. H., & Bohl, J. (1996). Pattern of brain destruction in Parkinson's and Alzheimer's diseases. *Journal of Neural Transmission, 103*, 455–490.

Bremner, J. D., Krystal, J. H., Southwick, S. M., & Charney, D. S. (1995). Functional neuroanatomical correlates of the effects of stress on memory. *Journal of Traumatic Stress, 8*, 527–553.

Bremner, J. D., Randall, P., Scott, T. M., Bronen, R. A., Seibyl, J. P., Southwick, S. M., Delaney, R. C., McCarthy, G., Charney, D. S., & Innis, R. B. (1995). MRI-based measurement of hippocampal volume in patients with combat-related posttraumatic stress disorder. *American Journal of Psychiatry, 152*, 973–981.

Bremner, J. D., Randall, P., Vermetten, E., Staib, L., Bronen, R. A., Mazure, C., Capelli, S., McCarthy, G., Innis, R. B., & Charney, D. S. (1997). Magnetic resonance imaging-based measurement of hippocampal volume in posttraumatic stress disorder related to childhood physical and sexual abuse—a preliminary report. *Biological Psychiatry, 41*, 23–32.

Bremner, J. D., Scott, T. M., Delaney, R. C., Southwick, S. M., Mason, J. W., Johnson, D. R., Innis, R. B., McCarthy, G., & Charney, D. S. (1993). Deficits in short-term memory in posttraumatic stress disorder. *American Journal of Psychiatry, 150*, 1015–1019.

Broca, P. (1878). Anatomie comparée des circonvolutions cérébrales. Le grand lobe limbique et la scissure limbique dans le série des mammifères. *Revue Anthropologique, 2*, 385–498.

Brodmann, K. (1914). Physiologie des Gehirns. In P. von Bruns (Hrsg.), *Neue deutsche Chirurgie* (Bd. 11, Tl. 1; pp. 85–426). Stuttgart: Enke.

Bucy, P. C., & Klüver, H. (1940). Anatomic changes secondary to temporal lobectomy. *A.M.A. Archives of Neurology and Psychiatry, 44*, 1142–1146.

Butterworth, B., Cipolotti, L., & Warrington, E. K. (1996). Short-term memory impairment and arithmetical ability. *Quarterly Journal of Experimental Psychology 49A*, 251–262.

Cahill, L., Babinsky, R., Markowitsch, H. J., & McGaugh, J. L. (1995). Involvement of the amygdaloid complex in emotional memory. *Nature, 377*, 295–296.

Calabrese, P., Markowitsch, H. J., Durwen, H. F., Widlitzek, B., Haupts, M., Holinka, B., & Gehlen, W. (1996). Right temporofrontal cortex as critical locus for the ecphory of old episodic memories. *Journal of Neurology, Neurosurgery and Psychiatry, 61*, 304–310.

Casey, B. J., Cohen, J. D., Jezzard, P., Turner, R., Noll, D. C., Trainor, R. J., Giedd, J., Kaysen, D., Hertz-Pannier, L., & Rapoport, J. L. (1995). Activation of prefrontal cortex in children during a nonspatial working memory task with functional MRI. *Neuroimage, 2*, 221–229.

Cermak, L. S. (1989). Encoding and retrieval deficits of amnesic patients. In E. Perecman (Ed.), *Integrating theory and practice in clinical neuropsychology* (pp. 139–154). Hillsdale, NJ: Erlbaum.

Cermak, L. S. (1997). A positive approach to viewing processing deficit theories of amnesia. *Memory, 5*, 89–98.

Chow, K. L. (1967). Effects of ablation. In Herausgegeben von G. C. Quarton, T. Melnechuk, & F. O. Schmitt (Eds.), *The neurosciences* (pp. 705–713). New York: Rockefeller University Press.

Corkin, S. (1984). Lasting consequences of bilateral medial temporal lobectomy: Clinical course and experimental findings in H.M. *Seminars in Neurology, 4*, 249–259.

Corkin, S., Amaral, D. G., Gonzalez, R. G., Johnson, K. A., & Hyman, B. T. (1997). H.M.'s medial temporal lobe lesion: Findings from magnetic resonance imaging. *Journal of Neuroscience, 17*, 3964–3979.

Craik, F. I. M., & Lockhart, R. S. (1972). Levels of processing. A framework for memory research. *Journal of Verbal Learning and Verbal Behavior, 11*, 671–684.

Cramon, D. Y. von, & Markowitsch, H. J. (1999). The septal region and human memory. New York: Springer.

Cramon, D. Y. von, Markowitsch, H. J., & Schuri, U. (1993). The possible contribution of the septal region to memory. *Neuropsychologia, 31*, 1159–1180.

Cummings, J. L. (Ed.). (1990). *Subcortical dementia*. New York: Oxford University Press.

Damasio, A. R. (1990). Category-related recognition defects as a clue to the neural substrates of knowledge. *Trends in Neurosciences, 13*, 95–98.

Damasio, A. R., Graff-Radford, N. R., Eslinger, P. J., Damasio, H., & Kassell, N. (1985). Amnesia following basal forebrain lesions. *Archives of Neurology, 42*, 263–271.

Darvesh, S., & Freedman, M. (1996). Subcortical dementia: A neurobehavioral approach. *Brain and Cognition, 31*, 230–249.

Daum, I., Riesch, G., Sartori, G., & Birbaumer, N. (1996). Semantic memory impairment in Alzheimer's disease. *Journal of Clinical and Experimental Neuropsychology, 18*, 648–665.

Deiber, M.-P., Wise, S. P., Honda, M., Catalan, M. J., Grafman, J., & Hallett, M. (1997). Frontal and parietal networks for conditional motor learning: A positron emission tomography study. *Journal of Neurophysiology, 78*, 977–991.

De Renzi, E., Liotti, M., & Nichelli, P. (1987). Semantic amnesia with preservation of autobiographic memory. A case report. *Cortex, 23*, 575–597.

De Renzi, E., Lucchelli, F., Muggia, S., & Spinnler, H. (1997). Is memory without anatomical damage tantamount to a psychogenic deficit? The case of pure retrograde amnesia. *Neuropsychologia, 35*, 781–794.

Eichenbaum, H. (1997). To cortex: Thanks for the memories. *Neuron, 19*, 481–484.

Fink, G. R., Markowitsch, H. J., Reinkemeier, M., Kessler, J., & Heiss, W.-D. (1996). A PET-study of autobiographical memory recognition. *Journal of Neuroscience, 16*, 4275–4282.

Freed, D. M., & Corkin, S. (1988). Rate of forgetting in H.M.: 6-months recognition. *Behavioral Neuroscience, 102*, 823–827.

Freed, D. M., Corkin, S., & Cohen, N. J. (1987). Forgetting in H.M.: A second look. *Neuropsychologia, 25*, 461–471.

Fuster, J. M. (1997). Network memory. *Trends in Neuroscience, 20*, 451–459.

Gallagher, M., & Chiba, A A. (1996). The amygdala and emotion. *Current Opinion in Neurobiology, 6*, 221–227.

Giannakopoulos, P., Hof, P. R., Michel, J.-P., Guimon, J., & Bouras, C. (1997). Cerebral cortex pathology in aging and Alzheimer's disease: A quantitative survey of large hospital-based geriatric and psychiatric co-

horts. *Brain Research Reviews, 25*, 217–245.

Glees, P., & Griffith, H. B. (1952). Bilateral destruction of the hippocampus (Cornu ammonis) in a case of dementia. *Monatsschrift für Psychiatrie und Neurologie, 123*, 193–204.

Gudden, B. von (1886). Ueber die Frage der Localisation der Functionen der Grosshirnrinde. *Allgemeine Zeitschrift für Psychiatrie und ihre Grenzgebiete, 42*, 478–499.

Hassing, L., & Bäckman, L. (1997). Episodic memory functioning in population-based samples of very old adults with Alzheimer's disease and vascular dementia. *Dementia and Geriatric Cognitive Disorders, 8*, 376–383.

Hebb, D. O. (1949). *The organization of behavior*. New York: John Wiley.

Hebben, N., Corkin, S., Eichenbaum, H., & Shedlack, K. (1985). Diminished ability to interpret and report internal states after bilateral medial temporal resection: Case H.M. *Behavioral Neuroscience, 99*, 1031–1039.

Hegglin, K. (1953). Über einen Fall von isolierter, linksseitiger Ammonshornerweichung bei präseniler Demenz. *Monatsschrift für Psychiatrie und Neurologie, 125*, 170–186.

Horel, J. A. (1994). Some comments on the special cognitive functions claimed for the hippocampus. *Cortex, 30*, 269–280.

Huschke, E. (1854). *Schaedel, Hirn und Seele des Menschen und der Thiere nach Alter, Geschlecht und Race*. Jena: F. Mauke.

Irle, E., & Markowitsch, H. J. (1982). Connections of the hippocampal formation, mamillary bodies, anterior thalamus and cingulate cortex. A retrograde study using horseradish peroxidase in the cat. *Experimental Brain Research, 47*, 79–94.

Kapur, N. (1994). Remembering Norman Schwarzkopf: Evidence for two distinct long-term fact learning mechanisms. *Cognitive Neuropsychology, 11*, 661–670.

Kapur, N., Ellison, D., Smith, M. P., McLellan, D. L., & Burrowa, E. H. (1992). Focal retrograde amnesia following bilateral temporal lobe pathology. *Brain, 115*, 73–85.

Keane, M. M., Gabrieli, J. D. E., Mapstone, H. C., Johnson, K. A., & Corkin, S. (1995). Double dissociation of memory capacities after bilateral occipital-lobe or medial temporal-lobe lesions. *Brain, 118*, 1129–1148.

Kleist, K. (1934). Kriegsverletzungen des Gehirns in ihrer Bedeutung für die Hirnlokalisation und Hirnpathologie. In K. Bonhoeffer (Ed.), *Handbuch der Aerztlichen Erfahrungen im Weltkriege 1914/18, Vol. 4:*

Geistes- und Nervenkrankheiten (pp. 343–1360). Leipzig: Barth.

Klüver, H., & Bucy, P. C. (1937). "Psychic blindness" and other symptoms following bilateral lobectomy in rhesus monkeys. *American Journal of Physiology, 119,* 352–353.

Knapp, A. (1905). *Die Geschwülste des rechten und linken Schläfelappens. Eine klinische Studie.* Wiesbaden: J. F. Bergmann.

Knowlton, B. J., Mangels, J. A., & Squire, L. R. (1996). A neostriatal habit learning systems in humans. *Science, 273,* 1399–1402.

Kornhuber, H. H. (1988). The human brain: From dream and cognition to fantasy, will, conscience, and freedom. In H. J. Markowitsch (Ed.), *Information processing by the brain* (pp. 241–258). Toronto: Huber.

Kroll, N. E. A., Markowitsch, H. J., Knight, R., & von Cramon, D. Y. (1997). Retrieval of old memories—the temporo-frontal hypothesis. *Brain, 120,* 1377–1399.

Krystal, J. H., Southwick, S. M., & Charney, D. S. (1995). Posttraumatic stress disorder: Psychobiological mechanisms of traumatic remembrance. In D. L. Schacter (Ed.), *Memory distortion* (pp. 150–172). Cambridge, MA: Harvard University Press.

LaBar, K. S., LeDoux, J. E., Spencer, D. D., & Phelps, E. A. (1995). Impaired fear conditioning following unilateral temporal lobectomy in humans. *Journal of Neuroscience, 15,* 6846–6855.

Laine, M., Vuorinen, E., & Rinne, J. O. (1997). Picture naming deficits in vascular dementia and Alzheimer's disease. *Journal of Clinical and Experimental Neuropsychology, 19,* 126–140.

Lashley, K. S. (1950). In search of the engram. *Society for Experimental Biology,* Symposium No. 4, pp. 454–482.

Leplow, B., Dierks, Ch., Lehnung, M., Kenkel, S., Behrens, Chr., Frank, G., & Mehdorn, M. (1997). Remote memory in patients with acute brain injuries. *Neuropsychologia, 35,* 881–892.

Loftus, E. F. (1998). Creating false memories. *Scientific American, 277*(3), 70–75.

Lucchelli, F., Muggia, S., & Spinnler, H. (1997). Selective proper name anomia: A case involving only contemporary celebreties. *Cognitive Neuropsychology, 14,* 881–890.

Macchi, G. (1989). Anatomical substrate of emotional reactions. In L. Squire & G. Gainotti (Eds.), *Handbook of neuropsychology* (Vol. 3; pp. 283–304). Amsterdam: Elsevier.

MacLean, P. D. (1952). Some psychiatric implications of physiological studies on frontotemporal portion of limbic system (visceral brain). *Electroencephalography and Clinical Neurophysiology, 4,* 407–418.

Mair, W. G. P., Warrington, E. K., & Weiskrantz, L. (1979). Memory disorder in Korsakoff psychosis. A neuropathological and neuropsychological investigation of two cases. *Brain, 102,* 749–783.

Manoach, D. S., Schlaug, G., Siewert, B., Darby, D. G., Bly, B. M., Benfield, A., Edelman, R. R., & Warach, S. (1997). Prefrontal cortex fMRI signal changes are correlated with working memory load. *NeuroReport, 8,* 545–549.

Markowitsch, H. J. (1984). Can amnesia be caused by damage of a single brain structure? *Cortex, 20,* 27–45.

Markowitsch, H. J. (1992). *Intellectual functions and the brain. An historical perspective.* Toronto: Hogrefe & Huber.

Markowitsch, H. J. (1995). Which brain regions are critically involved in the retrieval of old episodic memory? *Brain Research Reviews, 21,* 117–127.

Markowitsch, H. J. (1996). Organic and psychogenic retrograde amnesia: Two sides of the same coin? *Neurocase, 2,* 357–371.

Markowitsch, H. J. (1997a). Varieties of memory: Systems, structures, mechanisms of disturbance. *Neurology, Psychiatry, and Brain Research, 5,* 37–56.

Markowitsch, H. J. (1997b). The functional neuroanatomy of episodic memory retrieval. *Trends in Neurosciences, 20,* 557–558.

Markowitsch, H. J. (1999). The limbic system. In R. Wilson & F. Keil (Eds.), *The MIT encyclopedia of cognitive science* (pp. 470–472). Cambridge, MA: MIT Press.

Markowitsch, H. J. (in press). The anatomical bases of memory. In M. S. Gazzaniga (Ed.), *The cognitive neurosciences* (2nd ed.). Cambridge, MA: MIT Press.

Markowitsch, H. J., Calabrese, P., Haupts, M., Durwen, H. F., Liess, J., & Gehlen, W. (1993). Searching for the anatomical basis of retrograde amnesia. *Journal of Clinical and Experimental Neuropsychology, 15,* 947–967.

Markowitsch, H. J., Calabrese, P., Würker, M. Durwen, H. F., Kessler, J., Babinsky, R., Brechtelsbauer, D., Heuser, L., & Gehlen, W. (1994). The amygdala's contribution to memory—A PET-study on two patients with Urbach-Wiethe disease. *NeuroReport, 5,* 1349–1352.

Markowitsch, H. J., Fink, G. R., Thöne, A. I. T., Kessler, J., & Heiss, W.-D. (1997). Persistent psychogenic amnesia with a PET-proven organic basis. *Cognitive Neuropsychiatry, 2,* 135–158.

Markowitsch, H. J., Kalbe, E., Kessler, J., von Stockhausen, H.-M., Ghaemi, M., & Heiss, W.-D. (1999). Short-term memory deficit after focal parietal damage. *Journal of Clinical and Experimental Neuropsychology,* in press.

Markowitsch, H. J., Kessler, J., Frölich, L., Schneider, B., & Maurer, K. (1999). Mnestic block syndrome. *Cortex, 35,* 219–230.

Markowitsch, H. J., Kessler, J., Van der Ven, C., Weber-Luxenburger, G., & Heiss W.-D. (1998). Psychic trauma causing grossly reduced brain metabolism and cognitive deterioration. *Neuropsychologia, 36,* 77–82.

Markowitsch, H. J., von Cramon, D. Y., Hofmann, E., Sick, C.-D., & Kinzler, P. (1990). Verbal memory deterioration after unilateral infarct of the internal capsule in an adolescent. *Cortex, 26,* 597–609.

Markowitsch, H. J., von Cramon, D. Y., & Schuri, U. (1993). Mnestic performance profile of a bilateral diencephalic infarct patient with preserved intelligence and severe amnesic disturbances. *Journal of Clinical and Experimental Neuropsychology, 15,* 627–652.

Markowitsch, H. J., Weber-Luxenburger, G., Ewald, K., Kessler, J., & Heiss, W.-D. (1997). Patients with heart attacks are not valid models for medial temporal lobe amnesia. A neuropsychological and FDG-PET study with consequences for memory research. *European Journal of Neurology, 4,* 178–184.

Mayes, A. R., Daum, I., Markowitsch, H. J., & Sauter, B. (1997). The relationship between retrograde and anterograde amnesia in patients with typical global amnesia. *Cortex, 33,* 197–217.

McClelland, J. L., McNaughton, B. L., & O'Reilly, R. C. (1995). Why there are complementary learning systems in the hippocampus and neocortex: Insights from the successes and failures of connectionist models of learning and memory. *Psychological Review, 102,* 419–457.

McGaugh, J. L., Cahill, L., & Roozendaal, B. (1996). Involvement of the amygdala in memory storage: Interaction with other brain systems. *Proceedings of the National Academy of Sciences of the USA, 93,* 13508–13514.

Milner, B., Corkin, S., & Teuber, H. L. (1968). Further analysis of the hippocampal amnesic syndrome: Fourteen year follow-up study of H.M. *Neuropsychologia, 6,* 215–234

Minoshima, S., Koeppe, R. A., Frey, K. A., & Kuhl, D. E. (1994). Diagnostic approach in Alzheimer's disease using three-dimensional stereotactic surface projections of fluorine-18-FDG-PET. *Journal of Nuclear Medicine, 35,* 1528–1537.

Mishkin, M., & Petri, H. L. (1984). Memories and habits: Some implications for the analysis of learning and retention. In L. R. Squire & N. Butters (Eds.), *Neuropsychology of memory* (pp. 287–296). New York: Guilford Press.

Nauta, W. J. H. (1979). Expanding borders of the limbic system concept. In T. Rasmussen & R. Marino (Eds.), *Functional neurosurgery* (pp. 7–23). New York: Raven Press.

Nielsen-Bohlman, L., Ciranni, M., Shimamura, A. P., & Knight, R. T. (1997). Impaired word-stem priming in patients with temporal-occipital lesions. *Neuropsychologia, 35* 1087–1092.

Nieuwenhuys, R. (1996). The greater limbic system, the emotional motor system and the brain. In G. Holstege, R. Bandler, & C. B. Saper (Eds.), *The emotional motor system* (Progress in Brain Research, Vol. 107; pp. 551–580). Amsterdam: Elsevier.

Nieuwenhuys, R., Voogt, J., & van Huizen, C. (1988). The human central nervous system. A synopsis and atlas (3rd ed.). Berlin: Springer.

Nissen, M. J., Cohen, N. J., & Corkin, S. (1981). The amnesic patient H.M.: Learning and retention of perceptual skills. *Society for Neuroscience Abstracts, 7,* 235.

Ochsner, K. N., Chiu, C.-Y. P., & Schacter, D. L. (1994). Varieties of priming. *Current Opinion in Neurobiology, 4,* 189–194.

O'Connor, M., Butters, N., Miliotis, P., Eslinger, P., & Cermak, L. S. (1992). The dissociation of anterograde and retrograde amnesia in a patient with herpes encephalitis. *Journal of Clinical and Experimental Neuropsychology, 14,* 159–178.

Papez, J. W (1937). A proposed mechanism of emotion. *Archives of Neurology and Psychiatry, 38,* 725–743.

Pick, A. (1906). Ueber einen weiteren Symptomenkomplex im Rahmen der Dementia senilis, bedingt durch umschriebene stärkere Hirnatrophie (gemischte Apraxie). *Monatsschrift für Psychiatrie und Neurologie, 19,* 97–108.

Reber, P. J., Stark, C. E. L., & Squire, L. R. (1998). Cortical areas supporting category learning identified using functional MRI. *Proceedings of the National Academy of Science of the USA, 95,* 747–750.

Reinkemeier, M., Markowitsch, H. J., Rauch, B., & Kessler, J. (1997). Memory systems for people's names: A case study of a patient with deficits in recalling, but not learning people's names. *Neuropsychologia, 35,* 677–684.

Ribot, T. (1882). *Diseases of memory.* New York: D. Appleton and Co.

Rouleau, I., Labrecque, R., Saint-Hilaire, J.-M., Cardu, B., & Giard, N. (1989). Short-term and long-term memory deficit following intracarotid amytal injection: Further support for the memory consolidation hypothesis. *Brain and Cognition, 11,* 167–185.

Sagar, H. J., Gabrieli, J. D. E., Sullivan, E. V., & Corkin, S. (1990). Recency and frequency discrimination in the amnesic patient H.M. *Brain, 113,* 581–602.

Sapolsky, R. M. (1996). Stress, glucocorticoids, and damage to the nervous system: The current state of confusion. *Stress, 1,* 1–19.

Sarter, M., & Markowitsch, H. J. (1985). The amygdala's role in human mnemonic processing. *Cortex, 21,* 7–24.

Schneider, H. (1901). Ueber Auffassung und Merkfähigkeit beim Altersblödsinn. In E. Kraepelin (Ed.), *Psychologische Arbeiten* (Vol. 3; pp. 458–481). Leipzig. Engelmann.

Scoville, W. B., & Milner, B. (1957). Loss of recent memory after bilateral hippocampal lesions. *Journal of Neurology, Neurosurgery and Psychiatry, 20,* 11–21.

Seeck, M., Mainwaring, N., Cosgrove, M. D., Blume, H., Dubuisson, D., Mesulam, M. M., & Schomer, D. L. (1997). Neurophysiologic correlates of implicit face memory in intracranial visual evoked potentials. *Neurology, 49,* 1312–1316.

Shallice, T., & Warrington, E. K. (1970). Independent functioning of the verbal memory stores: A neuropsychological study. *Quarterly Journal of Experimental Psychology, 22,* 261–273.

Shaw, C.-M., & Alvord, Jr., E. C. (1997). Neuropathology of the limbic system. *Neuroimaging Clinics of North America, 7,* 101–142.

Smith, M. L. (1988). Recall of spatial location by the amnesic patient H.M. *Brain and Cognition, 7,* 178–183.

Snowden, J. S., Griffiths, H. L., & Neary, D. (1996). Semantic-episodic memory interactions in semantic dementia: Implications for retrograde memory function. *Cognitive Neuropsychology, 13,* 1101–1137.

Squire, L. R. (1987). *Memory and brain.* New York: Oxford University Press.

Squire, L. R. (1995). Biology of memory. In H. Kaplan & B. J. Sadock (Eds.), *Comprehensive textbook of psychiatry* (pp. 317–328). Baltimore, MD: Williams and Wilkins.

Squire, L. R., Knowlton, B., & Musen, G. (1993). The structure and organization of memory. *Annual Review of Psychology, 44,* 453–495.

Szentágothai, J. (1983). The modular architectonic principle of neural centers. *Reviews of Physiology, 98,* 11–61.

Thompson, R. F., & Kim, J. J. (1996). Memory systems in the brain and localization of memory. *Proceedings of the National Academy of Sciences of the USA, 93,* 13428–13444.

Tranel, D. (1997). Emotional processing and the human amygdala. *Trends in Cogntive Sciences, 1,* 46–48.

Tulving, E. (1972). Episodic and semantic memory. In E. Tulving & W. Donaldson (Eds.), *Organization of memory* (pp. 381–403). New York: Academic Press.

Tulving, E. (1983). *Elements of episodic memory.* Cambridge: Cambridge University Press.

Tulving, E. (1991). Concepts of human memory. In L. Squire, G. Lynch, N. M. Weinberger, & J. L. McGaugh (Eds.), *Memory: Organization and locus of change* (pp. 3–32). New York: Oxford University Press.

Tulving, E., Kapur, S., Craik, F. I. M., Moscovitch, M., & Houle, S. (1994). Hemispheric encoding/Retrieval asymmetry in episodic memory: Positron emission tomography findings. *Proceedings of the National Academy of Sciences of the USA, 91,* 2016–2020.

Tulving, E., & Markowitsch, H. J. (1997). Memory beyond the hippocampus. *Current Opinion in Neurobiology, 7,* 209–216.

Tulving, E., & Markowitsch, H. J. (1998). Episodic and declarative memory. Role of the hippocampus. *Hippocampus, 8,* 198–204.

Ule, G. (1951). Korsakow-Psychose nach doppelseitiger Ammonshornzerstörung mit transneuronaler Degeneration der Corpora mamillaria. *Deutsche Zeitschrift für Nervenheilkunde, 165,* 446–456.

van der Kolk, B. A. (1993). The body keeps the score: Memory and the evolving psychobiology of posttraumatic stress. *Harvard Review of Psychiatry, 1,* 253–265.

Vanderwolf, C. H., & Cain, D. P. (1994). The behavioral neurobiolgoy of learning and memory: A conceptual reorientation. *Brain Research Reviews, 19,* 264–297.

Vargha-Khadem, F., Gadian, D. G., Watkins, K. E., Connelly, A., Van Paesschen, W., & Mishkin, M. (1997). Differential effects of early hippocampal pathology on episodic and semantic memory. *Science, 277*, 376–380.

Victor, M., Adams, R. D., & Collins, G. H. (1989). *The Wernicke-Korsakoff syndrome and related neurological disorders due to alcoholism and malnutrition* (2nd ed.). Philadelphia: F. A. Davis.

Warrington, E. K., & Weiskrantz, L. (1970).

Amnesic syndrome: Consolidation or retrieval? *Nature, 228*, 628–630.

Woodruff-Pak, D. S. (1993). Eyeblink classical conditioning in H.M.: Delay and trace paradigms. *Behavioral Neuroscience, 107*, 911–925.

Zhang, X. L., Begleiter, H., & Porjesz, B. (1997). Do chronic alcoholics have intact implicit memory? An ERP study. *Electroencephalography and Clinical Neurophysiology, 103*, 457–473.

30

The Medial Temporal Lobe and the Hippocampus

STUART M. ZOLA & LARRY R. SQUIRE

"In 1954 Scoville described a grave loss of recent memory which he had observed as a sequel to bilateral medial temporal resection in one psychotic patient and one patient with intractable seizures. In both cases . . . removals extended posteriorly along the medial surface of the temporal lobes . . . and probably destroyed the anterior two-thirds of the hippocampus and hippocampal gyrus bilaterally, as well as the uncus and amygdala. The unexpected and persistent memory deficit which resulted seemed to us to merit further investigation."

This passage comes from the first paragraph of Scoville and Milner's 1957 report, "Loss of recent memory after bilateral hippocampal lesions." This publication became a landmark in the history of memory research for two reasons. First, the severe memory impairment (or amnesia) could be linked directly to the brain tissue that had been removed, suggesting that the medial aspect of the temporal lobe was important for memory function. Second, comprehensive testing of one of the patients (HM) indicated that memory impairment could occur on a background of otherwise normal cognition. This observation showed that memory is an isolatable function, separable from perception and general intellectual functions.

These discoveries led ultimately to the development of an animal model of amnesia in the monkey (Mishkin et al., 1982; Squire & Zola-Morgan, 1983) and to the identification of the anatomical structures of what is now known as the medial temporal lobe memory system (Squire & Zola-Morgan, 1991). In this chapter, the developments that led to the establishment of an animal model of amnesia are summarized, and recent work with nonhuman primates is reviewed that addresses the specific role in memory of the hippocampal region itself (the hippocampus proper, the dentate gyrus, and the subicular complex).

In work with both humans and monkeys, there has been a longstanding imprecision in the terminology used to identify the anatomical components of the medial temporal lobe. In particular, the term *hippocampus* is sometimes used interchangeably to refer to the cell fields of the hippocampus proper, sometimes to a larger region that includes the hippocampus proper as well as the dentate gyrus and the subicular complex, and sometimes to even the adjacent cortex. In the present chapter, the following terminology is used. The term *hippocampus* includes the cell fields of the hippocampus proper and the dentate gyrus; the term *hippocampal* region includes the hippocampus proper, the dentate gyrus, and the subicular complex; and the term *hippocampal formation* includes the hippocampal region and the entorhinal cortex. Finally, the *medial temporal lobe memory system* refers to the hippocampal formation together with the adjacent perirhinal and parahippocampal cortices (figure 30.1).

A Memory System in the Temporal Lobe

The findings from patient HM (Scoville & Milner, 1957) identified a region of the brain important for human memory—that is, the medial portion of the temporal lobe. The damage was originally reported to have included the amygdala, the periamygdaloid cortex (referred to as the uncus in Scoville & Milner, 1957); the hippocampal region (referred to as the hippocampus); and the perirhinal, entorhinal, and parahippocampal cortices (referred to as the hippocampal gyrus). Recently, magnetic resonance imaging of patient HM has shown that his medial temporal lobe damage does not extend as far posteriorly as originally believed and that damage to the parahippocampal cortex is minimal (the lesion extends caudally from the temporal pole approximately 5 cm, instead of 8 cm, as originally reported; Corkin, Amaral, Gonzalez, Johnson, & Hyman, 1997). In addition, the ventrocaudal aspect of the perirhinal cortex is spared.

Although these observations identified the medial temporal lobe as important for memory, the medial temporal lobe is a large region including many different structures. To determine which structures are important required that studies be undertaken in which the effects of damage to medial temporal lobe structures could be evaluated systematically. Accordingly, soon after the findings from HM were reported, efforts were made to develop an animal model of medial temporal lobe amnesia. During the next 20 years, however, findings from experimental animals with intended hippocampal lesions or larger lesions of the medial temporal lobe were inconsistent and difficult to interpret (for a review of this work, see Squire & Zola-Morgan, 1983).

In 1978, Mishkin adopted a method for testing memory in monkeys that captured an important feature of tests sensitive to human memory impairment (Mishkin, 1978). This method allowed for the testing of memory for single events at some delay after the event occurred. The task itself is known as the trial-unique delayed nonmatching to sample task, and it measures object recognition memory. In Mishkin's study, three monkeys sustained large medial temporal lobe lesions that were intended to reproduce the damage in patient HM. The operated monkeys and three unoperated monkeys were given the delayed non-matching to sample task in order to assess their ability to remember, after delays ranging from 8 seconds to 2 minutes, which one of two objects they had recently seen. The monkeys with medial temporal lobe lesions were severely impaired on the nonmatching task, consistent with the severe impairment observed in patient HM on delay tasks. Thus, lesions that included the hippocampal region, the amygdala, as well as adjacent perirhinal, entorhinal, and parahippocampal cortices caused severe memory impairment. This work, together with work carried out in the succeeding few years, established a model of human amnesia in nonhuman primates (Mishkin et al., 1982; Squire & Zola-Morgan, 1983). Although other tasks have been useful for measuring memory in monkeys (object discrimination learning, the visual paired-comparison task, see below), much of the information about the effects of damage to medial temporal lobe structures has come, until recently, from delayed nonmatching to sample task.

Once the animal model was established, systematic and cumulative work eventually identified the structures in the medial temporal lobe that are important for memory (figure 30.1). The important structures are the hippocampal region and the adjacent perirhinal, entorhinal, and parahippocampal cortices (for reviews, see Squire & Zola-Morgan, 1991; Squire & Zola, 1997; Murray, 1992; Mishkin & Murray, 1994). The amygdala proved not to be a component of this memory system, although it can exert a modulatory action on the kind of memory that depends on the medial temporal lobe system (Cahill & McGaugh, 1998).

The medial temporal lobe is necessary for establishing one kind of memory—what is termed long-term declarative or explicit memory. Declarative memory refers to the capacity for conscious recollection of facts and events (Squire, 1992). It is specialized for rapid, even one-trial learning, and for forming conjunctions between arbitrarily different stimuli (Squire & Zola, 1997). It is typically assessed in humans by tests of recall, recognition, or cued recall, and it is typically assessed in monkeys by tests of recognition (e.g., the delayed nonmatching to sample task). The medial temporal lobe memory system performs a critical function beginning at the time of

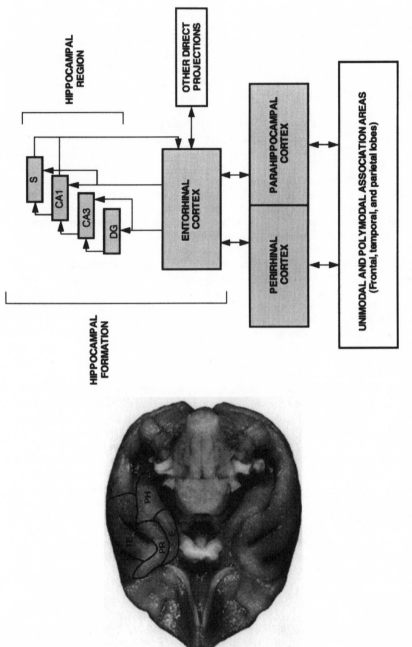

Figure 30.1 *Left.* Ventral view of a monkey brain showing the cortical components of the medial temporal lobe memory system: the perirhinal cortex (PR), the entorhinal cortex (E), and the parahippocampal cortex (PH). The hippocampal region lies deep within the medal temporal lobe. Also shown is visual association area TE. *Right.* A schematic diagram of the medial temporal lobe system. The perirhinal and parahippocampal cortices receive projections from unimodal and polymodal areas in the frontal, temporal, and parietal lobes. In turn, the perirhinal and parahippocampal cortices account for nearly two thirds of the cortical input to the entorhinal cortex. The entorhinal cortex is the primary source of cortical input to the hippocampal region (i.e., the dentate gyrus, the cell fields of the hippocampus, and the subiculum). The entorhinal cortex also receives other direct input from orbitofrontal cortex, cingulate cortex, insular cortex, and superior temporal gyrus. All these projections are reciprocal.

learning in order that representations can be established in long-term memory in an enduring and usable form.

Other kinds of abilities (including skills, habit learning, simple forms of conditioning, and the phenomenon of priming, which are collectively referred to as nondeclarative memory) lie outside the province of the medial temporal lobe memory system. Nondeclarative forms of memory are intact in amnesic patients and intact in monkeys with medial temporal lobe lesions. For example, classical delay conditioning of skeletal musculature depends on the cerebellum (Thompson & Krupa, 1994), conditioning of emotional responses depends on the amygdala (LeDoux, 1987; Davis, 1992), and habit learning (win-stay, lose-shift responding) depends on the neostriatum (Salmon and Butters, 1995; Packard, Hirsh, & White, 1989). Nondeclarative memory thus refers to a variety of ways in which experience can lead to altered dispositions, preferences, and judgments without providing any conscious memory content.

Further work with monkeys has demonstrated an association between the severity of declarative memory impairment and the locus and extent of damage within the medial temporal lobe (figure 30.2). This point was made most clearly through a retrospective analysis of behavioral data from 30 monkeys with differing extents of damage (Zola-Morgan, Squire, & Ramus, 1994). Specifically, damage limited to the hippocampal region caused significant memory impairment (this point will be discussed in detail in the next section). However, even more severe memory impairment occurred following damage that included the hippocampal region together with adjacent entorhinal and parahippocampal cortex. Finally, the severity of impairment was greater still following damage to the hippocampal region that also included the perirhinal cortex, together with entorhinal and parahippocampal cortices.

These findings in monkeys are fully consistent with the findings from human amnesia. Damage limited to the hippocampal region is associated with moderately severe amnesia (Zola-Morgan and Squire, 1986; Rempel-Clower, Zola, & Squire, 1996), and more extensive damage that includes the hippocampal region as well as adjacent cortical regions is associated with more severe memory impairment (Scoville & Milner, 1957; Corkin, 1984; Rempel-Clower et al., 1996; Reed & Squire, 1998). Taken together, these findings suggest that, whereas damage to the hippocampal region produces measurable memory impairment, a substantial part of the severe memory impairment produced by large medial temporal lobe lesions in humans and monkeys can be attributed to damage to the entorhinal, perirhinal, and parahippocampal cortices that are adjacent to the hippocampal region.

The same principle, that more extensive damage produces more severe impairment, has also been established for the hippocampus proper in the case of the rat (Jarrad, 1986; Morris, Schenk, Tweedie, & Jarrad, 1990; Moser, Moser, & Andersen, 1993; Moser et al., 1995). The dorsal hippocampus of the rat is essential for spatial learning in the water maze, and larger lesions of this region produce a larger impairment.

A final point deserves emphasis. The simple finding that larger lesions produce more severe impairment does not mean that all the components of the primate medial temporal lobe make a qualitatively similar contribution to declarative memory. The final section of this chapter considers this point more fully.

The Hippocampal Region and Memory

There is good evidence that lesions restricted to the human hippocampus impair memory. Thus, patient GD (Rempel-Clower et al., 1996), as well as patient RB (Zola-Morgan & Squire, 1986), demonstrated impaired memory in association with bilateral lesions limited to the CA1 field of the hippocampus and the CA1-subicular border zone. It is useful to note that, for patients RB and GD, as well as other amnesic patients, deficits can be demonstrated in a broad variety of verbal and nonverbal memory tasks. For example, recognition memory—that is, the ability to recognize recently presented stimuli as familiar—is impaired along with cued recall and free recall. Indeed, tests of recognition memory provide a useful and accurate index of the overall severity of declarative memory impairment, and recognition memory scores correlate closely with other measures of memory such as free recall (Haist, Shimamura, & Squire, 1992).

The findings from RB and GD notwithstanding, questions have arisen about the role of the hippocampal region and recognition memory. For example, a literature survey of results from two widely used recognition memory tests based on words and faces (War-

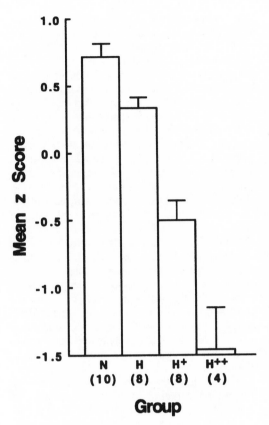

Figure 30.2 Mean z scores based on the data from four measures of memory for 10 normal monkeys (N), 8 monkeys with damage limited to the hippocampal region (H: the dentate gyrus, the cell fields of the hippocampus, and the subiculum), 8 monkeys with damage that also included the adjacent entorhinal cortex and parahippocampal cortices (H+), and 4 monkeys in which the H+ lesion was extended forward to include the anterior entorhinal and perirhinal cortices (H++). Conversion of the data from the four behavioral measures into z scores permitted tasks that used different performance measures (e.g., trials to criterion, percent correct) to be compared with each other. As more components of the medial temporal lobe were included in the lesion, the severity of memory impairment increased. This finding is also consistent with the possibility that the different structures make different contributions to memory functions. Brackets indicate standard errors of the mean. (From Zola-Morgan et al., 1994).

rington, 1984) suggested that patients with damage to the hippocampal region exhibit only a mild impairment in recognition memory and sometimes no impairment at all (Aggleton & Shaw, 1996). However, this conclusion was based on data from only three patients. One patient had damage to the CA1 region of the hippocampus (GD; Rempel-Clower et al., 1996), one had damage to the hippocampal formation (LM; Rempel-Clower et al., 1996), and one had presumed hippocampal damage, based on etiology (AB; Reed & Squire, 1997). Importantly, with one exception, all three of these patients were impaired on the test for words as well as the test for faces. Further, when performance was evaluated on a large number of tests (11–25 different recognition memory tests), and in a larger number of patients ($N = 6$), including the three patients whose data appeared in the survey, it was clear that patients with damage limited to the hippocampal region or the hippocampal formation exhibited unequivocal impairment in recognition memory (Reed & Squire, 1997). Recognition memory was impaired even when the damage was limited primarily to the CA1 region of the hippocampus proper (patients GD and RB).

The contribution of the hippocampal region to recognition memory can also be studied systematically in experimental animals. In monkeys, recognition memory has been assessed following ischemic lesions of the hippocampal region (Zola-Morgan, Squire, Rempel, Clower, & Amaral, 1992) and following stereotaxic radiofrequency lesions (e.g., Alvarez et al., 1991). More recently, it has been possible to use selective neurotoxins—for example, ibotenic acid—to make fiber-sparing lesions limited to the hippocampal region (Beason-Held et al., 1999; Murray & Mishkin, 1998; Zola et al., 2000). Ibotenic acid selectively damages the cell bodies within the target region while sparing adjacent white matter fibers (Jarrard, 1989).

At this writing four studies have described the effects on recognition memory in monkeys with lesions limited to the hippocampal region and where postmortem neurohistological analyses of the lesions have been provided (Zola-Morgan et al., 1992; Alvarez, Zola-Morgan, & Squire, 1995; Zola et al., 2000; Beason-Held et al., 1999; the latter paper refers collectively to the dentate gyrus, the hippocampus proper, and the subiculum, as the hippocampal formation). All four studies report impaired recognition memory in monkeys with hippocampal lesions. A fifth study that involved conjoint lesions of the amygdala and hippocampus found no impairment (Murray & Mishkin, 1998).

The first published study in monkeys to report that damage limited to the hippocampal region impaired recognition memory (Zola-Morgan et al., 1992) was based on an animal model of cerebral ischemia (ISC) in the monkey (figure 30.3, left panel). The second study used magnetic resonance imaging together with stereotaxic radiofrequency (RF) lesions to make substantial bilateral lesions of the hippocampal region with little or no damage to the adjacent entorhinal, perirhinal, and parahippocampal cortical regions (Alvarez et al., 1995). The monkeys with RF lesions exhibited significant and long-lasting impairment on the delayed nonmatching to sample task (figure 30.3, middle panel). The third study (Zola et al., in press) found impaired recognition in monkeys with ibotenate lesions of the hippocampal region (figure 30.3, right panel) and in a new group of monkeys with RF lesions (figure 30.6). Consistent with the findings from these three studies, Beason-Held et al. (in press) reported impaired recognition memory in monkeys that had sustained bilateral lesions of the hippocampal region made by ibotenic acid (IBO). The monkeys with ibotenic acid lesions were impaired on two different

tests of recognition memory: delayed nonmatching to sample and a delayed recognition span task. Three different versions of the latter task were administered to assess memory span for objects, color, and spatial position. Monkeys with IBO lesions were impaired on delayed nonmatching to sample and on all three version of the memory span task.

In contrast to the four studies just described, a fifth study (Murray & Mishkin, 1998) reached a different conclusion about recognition memory and the hippocampal region. This study assessed memory in monkeys with IBO lesions of the hippocampus and the amygdala on a standard version of the delayed nonmatching to sample task and on a version of the delayed nonmatching task that involved "reverse-order testing." Specifically, after a series of stimulus objects were presented, recognition memory was tested by first assessing memory for the last sample object presented and then proceeding in reverse order until memory was assessed for the first sample object. The monkeys with IBO lesions performed as well as the unoperated monkeys on both versions of the task.

Two differences between the four studies that found impaired recognition memory following lesions limited to the hippocampal region (Zola-Morgan et al., 1992; Alvarez et al., 1995; Zola et al., 2000; Beason-Held et al., 1999) and the study that did not (Murray & Mishkin, 1998) merit consideration. First, unlike the ISC, RF, and IBO monkeys in the first four studies, the IBO monkeys tested by Murray and Mishkin (1998) received preoperative

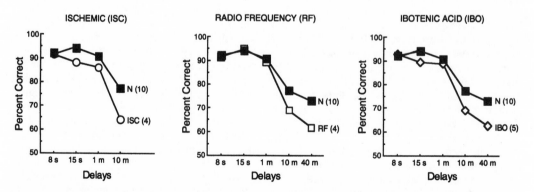

Figure 30.3 Delayed nonmatching performance in normal monkeys ($N = 10$) and monkeys with lesions limited to the hippocampal region (the dentate gyrus, the cell fields of the hippocampus, and the subiculum). Monkeys with lesions made by ischemia (ISC, $n = 4$), radio frequency (RF, $n = 4$), or ibotenic acid (IBO, $n = 5$) were similarly impaired. When the scores at all delays $\geq$ 15s were combined, each lesion group was impaired (all $ps < 0.05$).

training on the nonmatching task. During preoperative training, the nonmatching rule was first trained during several hundred trials using a delay interval of 8–10 sec. Training on the rule provides the monkey with extended practice at holding novel objects in memory across short delays, which could then make it easier to hold novel objects in memory across the longer delays from which the performance scores for this task are derived. Second, the IBO monkeys were operated on in two stages separated by at least two weeks. A unilateral lesion was made in the first stage, and the lesion on the other side was made in the other stage. Two-stage surgery sometimes results in less functional impairment than one-stage surgery (Finger, 1978; Finger & Stein, 1982). Although the mechanisms underlying this effect are poorly understood, the effect has been reported in the case of hippocampal lesions (Stein et al., 1969; Isseroff et al., 1976). Indeed, in some cases, deficits associated with one-stage hippocampal lesions were absent altogether following two-stage surgery (Stein et al., 1969). Thus, the single negative finding (Murray & Mishkin, 1998) comes from a study that differed from all the others in at least two potentially important ways.

One additional consideration about the effects of hippocampal lesions on recognition memory involves a point of experimental procedure. Alvarez et al. (1995), for practical reasons related to testing many animals at the same time, removed monkeys from the testing apparatus during the long delays but not during the short delays. Impaired performance in monkeys with RF lesions of the hippocampal region occurred only at these longer delays. Is it possible that removing animals from the testing apparatus contributed to the impaired recognition memory performance? If so, it has been suggested that the deficit could then be understood as a deficit in spatial memory rather than as a deficit in recognition memory (Nadel, 1995; Murray & Mishkin, 1998).

The effect of removing animals from the testing apparatus during the long-delay intervals has recently been addressed directly (Teng et al., 1998; also see Zola et al., 2000). A new group of four monkeys with radio-frequency lesions limited to the hippocampal region (RF2) were tested on the delayed nonmatching task at two different delay intervals: 1 minute and 10 minutes. Monkeys were tested under two conditions at each delay interval; they either remained in the testing apparatus during the delay interval (the IN

condition), or they were removed from the testing apparatus during the delay interval (the OUT condition). The monkeys with H lesions were impaired relative to the N animals at the 10-minute delay under both the IN and OUT conditions (figure 30.4). Moreover, removal from the testing box affected the normal and lesioned monkeys to a similar degree. Thus, the impairment in the RF2 monkeys cannot be accounted for by the fact that monkeys were removed from the test apparatus during the retention interval.

Figure 30.3 compares the performance of monkeys with ISC lesions, RF lesions, and IBO lesions (Zola et al., 2000). The IBO monkeys in this study sustained cell loss throughout the rostrocaudal extent of the hippocampal region, including the granule cells of the dentate gyrus, the pyramidal cells of the CA fields, and the subicular complex. On the delayed nonmatching to sample task, the IBO monkeys were impaired at the 15-sec, 10-min, and 40-min delay intervals. The performance of the ISC, RF, and IBO monkeys were quite similar. For example, at the 10-min delay, the scores for the ISC, RF, and IBO groups were 64%, 69%, and 69% correct, respectively. Normal monkeys scored 78% correct. In summary, the preponderance of evidence from monkeys with lesions of the hippocampal region is that hippocampal lesions impair recognition memory.

The Visual Paired-Comparison Task

The delayed nonmatching to sample task was important for establishing an animal model of human amnesia, and it has been useful for many years as a way of gauging the severity of memory impairment following lesions of the medial temporal lobe. However, this task provides just one specific way of measuring memory. Accordingly, it is difficult to know how well results obtained from this task generalize to other tasks of declarative memory, even to other tasks of recognition memory. If one is to understand recognition memory, it is important to study more than one task.

Tasks that depend on spontaneous novelty preference assess recognition memory by measuring an animal's tendency to look at or explore a novel object or location in comparison to a familiar object or location. These tasks appear to be particularly sensitive to hippocampal damage in rats and monkeys (Roberts, Dember, & Brodwick, 1962; Wood & Phillips,

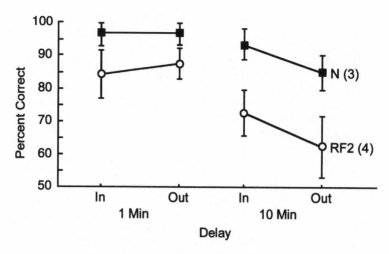

Figure 30.4 Delayed nonmatching to sample performance at two delay intervals (1 min and 10 min) in 3 normal monkeys (N) and in 4 monkeys with radio-frequency lesions limited to the hippocampal region (the dentate gyrus, the cell fields of the hippocampus, and the subiculum) (RF2). Monkeys were tested under two conditions at each delay: they remained in the testing apparatus (IN), or they were removed from the testing apparatus (OUT). Removal from the testing apparatus affected the N and RF2 groups to the same degree. Brackets indicate standard error of the mean.

1991; Bachevalier, Brickson, & Hagger, 1993; Clark, Teng, Squire, & Zola, 1996). One such task, the visual paired-comparison task, was originally designed for humans and measures how much time an individual spends looking at a new picture and a familiar picture when the new and familiar picture are presented side by side (figure 30.5). Normal subjects prefer to look at the new picture. Although the task might appear to measure habituation, or some relatively automatic behavior, it appears instead to depend, at least in part, on an individual's voluntary search of the environment in accordance with what the individual recognizes as novel or familiar. Human amnesic patients are impaired on this task (McKee & Squire, 1993). Monkeys with large medial temporal lobe lesions are also impaired (Bachevalier, Brickson, & Hagger, 1993).

Recent work shows that monkeys with more restricted lesions of the medial temporal lobe are also impaired at the visual paired-comparison task. Specifically, monkeys with radio-frequency lesions of the hippocampal region (RF2) and normal monkeys (N) performed similarly at a 1-second delay, but the RF2 group was impaired at the 10-second ($p <$ 0.05), 1-minute ($p < 0.01$), and 10-minute

($p < 0.05$) delay intervals (figure 30.6); (Zola et al., 2000). It is also worth noting that the RF2 monkeys were impaired on the delayed nonmatching to sample task at all delays greater than 8 seconds (figure 30.6). Moreover, when the data for all four lesion groups were combined (figures 30.3 and 30.6), a significant impairment was observed at all delays greater than 8 seconds (Zola et al., 2000).

Object Discrimination Learning

Tasks of recognition memory (delayed nonmatching to sample and visual paired-comparison) are not the only tasks that have been used systematically to assess memory in monkeys with medial temporal lobe lesions. Another useful task measures the ability to learn and retain simple object discriminations. An earlier analysis of 46 studies (Squire & Zola-Morgan, 1983) suggested that simple two-choice discrimination tasks—that is, ones that are learned quickly by normal animals—are dependent on the medial temporal lobe. More difficult two-choice discrimination tasks—that is, ones that are learned gradually (such as most pattern discrimination problems)—are

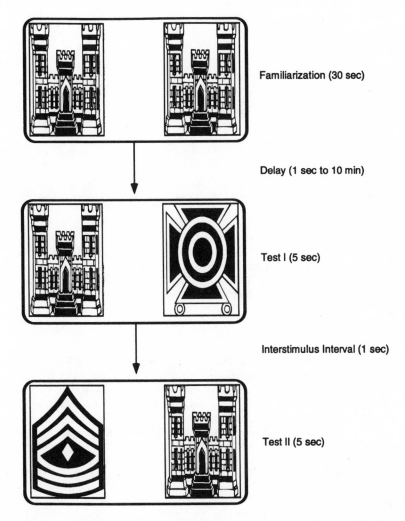

Figure 30.5 The visual paired-comparisons test. Two identical black and white line drawings were presented side by side until the monkey accumulated a total of 25 seconds of total viewing time (familiarization phase). After a delay interval (ranging from 1 sec to 10 min), the old stimulus and a new stimulus appeared on the screen side by side, until a total of 5 seconds of viewing time had accumulated (test phase). The location of the original stimulus was counterbalanced across trials to control for side preferences the monkeys might exhibit when viewing the test slides. Performance was expressed as the percentage of viewing time that the animal spent looking at the new stimulus.

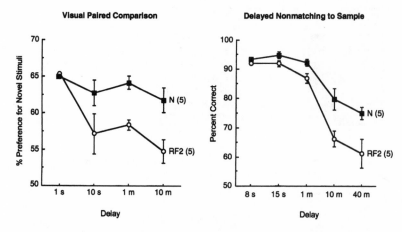

Figure 30.6 Visual paired-comparison performance and delayed non-matching to sample performance in 5 normal monkeys (N) and 5 monkeys with radio frequency lesions limited to the hippocampal region (RF2) that included the dentate gyrus, the cell fields of the hippocampus, and the subiculum.

independent of the medial temporal lobe. Difficult discrimination tasks can probably be acquired by an intact habit memory system (Mishkin & Petrie, 1984).

In one version of object discrimination learning, monkeys learn over a period of three testing days which object (of two that are presented together) is always rewarded. Twenty trials are presented each day. To obtain reliable data, this procedure is repeated with additional object pairs until a total of four object pairs have been learned. Studies of similar discrimination problems in human amnesic patients (Squire, Zola-Morgan, & Chen, 1988) suggested that the first few trials of each testing day are the most sensitive to memory impairment (figure 30.7A). The reason why the first few trials of each test day are especially sensitive to amnesia is straightforward. Amnesic patients are forgetful and have two kinds of difficulty with this task. First, during the early trials of each test day, they have difficulty remembering the feedback they receive concerning which object is the correct one. Second, they forget what they have learned from day to day. The later training trials given on each test day are therefore less sensitive to amnesia than the early trials, because the patients typically have some residual memory ability that allows them to benefit from repetition and also because they can rehearse the correct answer once they have determined what it is.

It turns out that in learning simple object discriminations, monkeys with medial temporal lobe lesions also have difficulty with the first few trials of each test day. When monkeys with lesions of the hippocampal region (the ISC group, the RF group, and the IBO group; Zola et al., 1998) were given simple object discrimination problems, and their performance evaluated on the first three trials of each testing day, learning and retention were unequivocally impaired on each test day (figure 30.7B). Further, when the data for each lesion group were examined separately, an impairment could be detected in each group. The ISC group was impaired when all 20 trials of the first test day were considered ($p < .05$; see Zola-Morgan et al., 1992). The other two groups (RF and IBO) were each impaired on the first three trials of Days 2 and 4 ($ps < .05$). Interestingly, for the latter two groups, no impairment in two-choice discrimination learning was detected when performance was based on the total number of trials correct for each test day (20 trials per day) (for the RF group, see Alvarez et al., 1995).

The data from two other groups of monkeys with medial temporal lobe lesions have also been reexamined. These two groups were ones that did not exhibit an impairment on the simple object discrimination task when the performance score was based on 20 test trials per day (monkeys with bilateral entorhinal lesions [Leonard, Amaral, Squire, & Zola-Morgan,

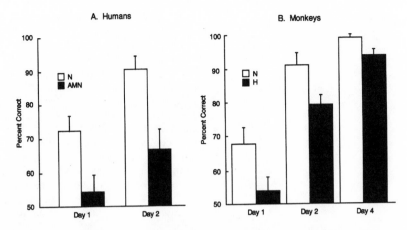

Figure 30.7 Performance on the object discrimination task. A. Mean percent correct for the first three trials of each day's testing for nine amnesic patients (AMN; $N = 14$ normal subjects; $ps < 0.01$). B. Mean percent correct scores for the first three trials of each day's testing for monkeys with lesions limited to the hippocampal region (H). The lesions were made by ischemia, $n = 4$, radio-frequency, $n = 4$, or ibotenic acid, $n = 5$. This group of 13 monkeys was impaired on each test day ($N = 10$ normal control monkeys; all $ps < 0.05$). Brackets indicate standard error of the mean.

1995] and monkeys with conjoint lesions of the perirhinal and parahippocampal cortices [Suzuki, Zola-Morgan, Squire, and Amaral, 1993]). These two groups, however, were impaired on the first three trials of each day's testing. On the basis of these observations, and previously published data for other lesion groups, it is clear that the simple object discrimination task is sensitive to medial temporal lobe damage.

Another task that is often discussed in the context of visual discrimination performance is the concurrent discrimination task. In a commonly used version of this task, 8 different pairs of objects are presented on each test day (the 8-pair concurrent discrimination task). Each pair of objects appears 5 times in a 40-trial session, and training continues until animals reach a learning criterion of 39 correct trials out of 40 in a single session. Although the concurrent discrimination task seems superficially similar to the simple object discrimination task, the two tasks are fundamentally different. Whereas the simple object discrimination task is dependent on the medial temporal lobe, the concurrent discrimination task is not. A recent review of earlier studies showed that concurrent discrimination learning is intact in monkeys with medial temporal lobe lesions unless there is also dam-

age to the adjacent visual area TE (Buffalo, Reber, & Squire, 1999). As suggested by Mishkin and Petrie (1984), the concurrent discrimination task can be acquired as a task of habit learning and is dependent on the neostriatum.

The distinction between the concurrent task and the simple object discrimination task is particularly apparent in the double dissociation that can be demonstrated between the effects of medial temporal lobe lesions and lesions of area TE (Buffalo et al., 1998). Perirhinal cortex lesions (or lesions of other medial temporal lobe structures) impair performance on the simple object discrimination task but do not impair performance on the 8-pair concurrent discrimination task. By contrast, lesions of area TE impair performance on the concurrent discrimination task but do not impair performance on the simple object discrimination task (figure 30.8).

This double dissociation can be understood as follows: First, as suggested earlier, simple object discrimination tasks are typically acquired by the kind of fast-learning strategy that is characteristic of declarative memory. By contrast, monkeys learn the concurrent task more gradually by employing a habit strategy. (Humans appear to engage a declarative strategy even for the concurrent task; (Squire et al., 1988; Hood, Postle, & Corkin, in

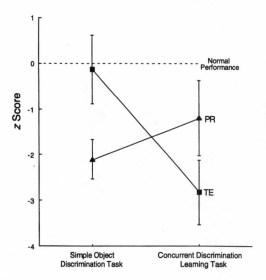

Figure 30.8 Performance on the simple object discrimination task and the concurrent discrimination learning task by monkeys with lesions of the perirhinal cortex (PR, $n = 5$), and monkeys with lesions of area TE ($n = 5$). Raw scores for each task were converted to z scores.

press) and employ a habit strategy only when special measures are taken to defeat their strong tendency to memorize [cf. Knowlton, Mangels, & Squire, 1996]). Second, the simple object discrimination task is not visually demanding. It is likely that simple discriminations can be supported by structures upstream from area TE, such as area TEO and V4. By contrast, the concurrent task involves 16 different objects with overlapping features. This more demanding task, which involves processing complex visual stimuli, depends on higher visual area TE.

A Perspective on the Hippocampal Region

How can the contribution of the hippocampal region to memory be characterized? We suggest that the hippocampus, as a result of its placement at the end of the processing hierarchy of the medial temporal lobe system (figure 30.1), combines and extends the functions of the structures that are positioned earlier in the hierarchy. Unimodal and polymodal inputs from neocortical association areas important for information processing and ultimately for

long-term memory storage converge in the medial temporal lobe. An important clue to how the components of this system function comes from the fact that different parts of the neocortex access the medial temporal lobe at different points (Suzuki & Amaral 1994). For example, the higher visual areas TE and TEO project preferentially to the perirhinal cortex. Conversely, input about spatial information that comes to the medial temporal lobe from parietal cortex arrives exclusively at the parahippocampal cortex. Based on these anatomical facts, one might expect the perirhinal cortex to be especially important for visual memory and the parahippocampal cortex to be important for spatial memory. Findings to date are consistent with this expectation (Ramus, Zola-Morgan, & Squire, 1994; Teng et al. 1997; Malkova & Mishkin 1997; Parkinson, Murray, & Miskin, 1988).

The hippocampus itself is the final stage of convergence within the medial temporal lobe, receiving input from both the perirhinal and parahippocampal cortices, as well as the entorhinal cortex. The entorhinal cortex receives about two-thirds of its cortical input from the parahippocampal and perirhinal cortices. Reasoning again from anatomy, one might expect that within the hippocampus, there is a combining of the operations of memory formation that are carried out independently by the more specialized structures that project to it. By this view, one would expect the hippocampus to be involved in both visual and spatial memory. Again, the data seem to bear out this idea. In patients with damage restricted to the CA1 region of hippocampus, the memory impairment extends across all sensory modalities and types of material, and is readily detected on tests of recognition as well as recall. The memory impairment is only modestly severe because considerable memory function can be supported by the cortical components of the medial temporal lobe system.

If there were some independent function for the hippocampal region that is not also shared by adjacent cortex, then a patient with damage limited to the hippocampal region (e.g., RB) should exhibit some deficit that is as severe as that observed in patient HM, who has damage to the hippocampal region as well as to most of the medial temporal lobe. Yet, however memory is measured, patients with damage limited to the hippocampal region appear to have a milder version of the deficit observed in patient HM. Perhaps a deficit will eventually be found in these patients that is as severe as in patient HM. However, by the view that the hippocampal region supports and extends the operations of the structures that send projections to it, studies of lesions and behavior might not reveal deficits unique to the hippocampal region that could not also be observed by damaging the perirhinal cortex, the parahippocampal cortex, or the entorhinal cortex.

It has been suggested that hippocampal lesions do not impair recognition memory and that this function can be wholly supported by adjacent cortex (Aggleton and Brown, 1999; Eichenbaum, Otto, & Cohen, 1994; Vargha-Khadem et al., 1997). This idea does not fit the available data. Further, many current proposals are compatible with the idea that recognition memory is dependent on the hippocampus. Even a recognition (or familiarity) decision requires that the stimulus presented in the retention test be identified as what was presented during learning. At the time of learning a link must therefore be made between the to-be-remembered stimulus and its context or between the stimulus and the animal's interaction with it. The recognition test does not ask whether an item has ever been seen before or whether one knows what an item is. It asks whether an item that had been presented recently now appears familiar. It is this associating, this relational work, that many have supposed is at the heart of declarative memory and hippocampal function in both humans and nonhuman animals (Eichenbaum 1997; Sutherland & Rudy 1989; Squire 1992).

Acknowledgments Address correspondence and reprint requests to Stuart M. Zola, Department of Psychiatry, U.C.S.D. School of Medicine, La Jolla, CA 92093. The research from our laboratory discussed here was supported by the Medical Research Service of the Department of Veterans Affairs and National Institutes of Health Grants NS19063 and MH24600.

References

Aggleton, J. P., & Brown, M. W. (1999). Episodic memory, amnesia, and the hippocampal-anterior thalamic axis. *Behavioral and Brain Sciences, 22*, 425–489.

Aggleton, J. P., & Shaw, C. (1996). Amnesia and recognition memory: A re-analysis of psychometric data. *Neuropsychologia, 34*, 51–62.

Alvarez-Royo, P., Clower, R. P., & Zola-Morgan, S. (1991). Stereotaxic lesions of the hippocampus in monkeys: Determination of surgical coordinates and analysis of lesions using magnetic resonance imaging. *Journal of Neuroscience Methods, 38*, 223–232.

Alvarez, P., Zola-Morgan, S., & Squire, L. R. (1995). Damage limited to the hippocampal region produces long-lasting memory impairment in monkeys. *Journal of Neuroscience, 15*, 3796–3807.

Bachevalier, J., Brickson, M., & Hagger, C. (1993). Limbic-dependent recognition memory in monkeys develops early in infancy. *NeuroReport, 4*, 77–80.

Beason-Held, L. L., Rosene, D. L., Killiany, R. J., & Moss, M. B. (1999). Ibotenic acid lesions of the hippocampal formation produce memory deficits in the rhesus monkey. *Hippocampus, 9*, 562–574.

Buffalo, E. A., Ramus, S. J., Clark, R. E., Teng, E., Squire, L. R., & Zola, S. M. (1998). Distinguishing the functions of perirhinal cortex and visual area TE. *Society for Neuroscience Abstracts, 24*, 17.

Cahill, L., & McGaugh, J. L. (1998). Mechanisms of emotional arousal and lasting declarative memory. *Trends in Neuroscience, 21*, 294–298.

Clark, R. E., Teng, E., Squire, L. R., & Zola, S. (1996). The visual paired-comparison task and the medial temporal lobe memory system. *Society for Neuroscience Abstracts, 22*, 15.

Corkin, S. (1984). Lasting consequences of bilateral medial temporal lobectomy: Clinical course and experimental findings in H. M. *Seminars in Neurobiology, 4*, 249–259.

Corkin, S., Amaral, D. G., Gonzalez, R. G., Johnson, K. A., & Hyman, B. T. (1997). H. M.'s medial temporal lobe lesion: Findings from magnetic resonance imaging. *Journal of Neuroscience, 17*, 3964–3980.

Davis, M. (1992). The role of the amygdala in fear-potentiated startle: Implications for animal models of anxiety. *Trends in Pharmacological Science, 13*, 35–42.

Eichenbaum, H. (1997). Declarative memory: Insights from cognitive psychology. *Annual Review of Psychology, 48*, 547–572.

Eichenbaum, H., Otto, T., & Cohen, N. J. (1994). Two functional components of the hippocampal memory system. *Behavioral Brain Science, 17*, 449–518.

Finger, S. (1978). *Recovery from brain damage: Research and theory.* New York: Plenum Press.

Finger, S., & Stein, D. G. (1982). *Brain damage and recovery: Research and clinical perspectives.* New York: Academic Press.

Haist, F., Shimamura, A. P., & Squire, L. R. (1992). On the relationship between recall and recognition memory. *Journal of Experimental Psychology: Learning, Memory, and Cognition, 18,* 691–702.

Hood, K. L., Postle, B. R., & Corkin, S. (in press). An evaluation of the concurrent discrimination task as a measure of habit learning: Performance of amnesic subjects. *Hippocampus.*

Isseroff, A., Leveton, L., Freeman, G., Lewis, M. E., & Stein, D. G. (1976). Differences in the behavioral effects of single-stage and serial lesions of the hippocampus. *Experimental Neurology, 53,* 339–354.

Jarrad, L. E. (1986). Selective hippocampal lesions and behavior: Implications for current research theorizing. In Isaacson, R. L., Pribaum, K. H. (Eds.) *The Hippocampus,* volume 4 (pp. 93–122). New York: Plenum Press.

Jarrard, L. E. (1989). On the use of ibotenic acid to lesion selectively different components of the hippocampal formation. *Journal of Neuroscience Methods, 29,* 251–259.

Knowlton, B. J., Mangels, J. A., & Squire, L. R. (1996). A neostriatal habit learning system in humans. *Science, 273,* 1399–1402.

LeDoux, J. E. (1987). Emotion. In J. M. Brookhart, & V. B. Mountcastle (Eds.), *Handbook of physiology: The Nervous System, V. Higher Functions of the Nervous System* (pp. 419–460). Bethesda, MD: American Physiological Society.

Leonard, B. W., Amaral, D. G., Squire, L. R., & Zola-Morgan, S. (1995). Transient memory impairment in monkeys with bilateral lesions of the entorhinal cortex. *Journal of Neuroscience, 15,* 5637–5659.

Malkova, L., & Mishkin, M. (1997). Memory for the location of objects after separate lesions of the hippocampus and parahippocampal cortex in rhesus monkeys. *Society for Neuroscience Abstracts 23,* 12.

McKee, R. D., & Squire, L. R. (1993). On the development of declarative memory. *Journal of Experimental Psychology, 19,* 397–404.

Mishkin, M. (1978). Memory in monkeys severely impaired by combined but not separate removal of the amygdala and hippocampus. *Nature, 273,* 297–298.

Mishkin, M., & Murray, E. A. (1994). Stimulus recognition. *Current Opinion in Neurobiology, 4,* 200–206.

Mishkin, M., & Petri, H. L. (1984). Memories and habits: Some implications for the analysis of learning and retention. In L. R. Squire, & N. Butters (Eds.), *Neuropsychology of memory* (pp. 287–296). New York: Guilford Press.

Mishkin, M., Spiegler, B. J., Saunders, R. C., Malamut, B. J. (1982). An animal model of global amnesia. In S. Corkin, K. L. Davis, J. H. Growdon et al., *Toward a treatment of Alzheimer's disease* (pp. 235–247). New York: Raven Press.

Morris, R. G. M., Schenk, F., Tweedie, F., Jarrad, L. E. (1990). Ibotenic lesions of hippocampus and/or subiculum: Dissociating components of allocentric spatial learning. *European Journal of Neuroscience 2,* 1016–1028.

Moser, E., Moser, M., & Andersen, P. (1993). Spatial learning impairment parallels the magnitude of dorsal hippocampal lesions, but is hardly present following ventral lesions. *Journal of Neuroscience, 13,* 3916–3925.

Moser, M., Moser, E. I., Forrest, E. et al. (1995). Spatial learning with a minislab in the dorsal hippocampus. *Proceedings of the National Academy of Sciences, USA, 92,* 9697–9701.

Murray, E. A. (1992). Medial temporal lobe structures contributing to recognition memory: The amygdaloid complex versus rhinal cortex. In J. P. Aggleton (Ed.), *The amygdala: Neurobiological aspects of emotion, memory, and mental dysfunction* (pp. 453–470). London: Wiley-Liss.

Murray, E. A., & Mishkin, M. (1998). Object recognition and location memory in monkeys with excitotoxic lesions of the amygdala and hippocampus. *Journal of Neuroscience, 18,* 6568–6582.

Nadel, L. (1995). The role of the hippocampus in declarative memory: A comment on Zola-Morgan, Squire, and Ramus (1994). *Hippocampus, 5,* 232–234.

Packard, M. G., Hirsh, R., & White, N. M. (1989). Differential effects of fornix and caudate nucleus lesions on two radial maze tasks: Evidence for multiple memory systems. *Journal of Neuroscience, 9,* 1465–1472.

Parkinson, J. K., Murray, E. A., & Miskin, M. (1988). A selective mnemonic role for the hippocampus in monkeys: Memory for the location of objects. *Journal of Neuroscience, 8,* 4159–4167.

Ramus, S. J., Zola-Morgan, S., & Squire, L. R.

(1994). Effects of lesions of perirhinal cortex or parahippo-campal cortex on memory in monkeys. *Society for Neuroscience Abstracts, 20*, 1074.

Reed, J. M., & Squire, L. R. (1997). Impaired recognition memory in patients with lesions limited to the hippocampal formation. *Behavioral Neuroscience, 111*, 667–675.

Reed, J. M., & Squire, L. R. (1998). Retrograde amnesia for facts and events: Findings from four new cases. *Journal of Neuroscience, 10*, 3943–3954.

Rempel-Clower, N., Zola, S. M., & Squire, L. R. (1996). Three cases of enduring memory impairment following bilateral damage limited to the hippocampal formation. *Journal of Neuroscience, 16*, 5233–5255.

Roberts, W. W., Dember, W. N., & Brodwick, M. (1962). Alternation and exploration in rats with hippocampal lesions. *Journal of Comparative and Physiological Psychology, 55*, 695–700.

Salmon, D. P., & Butters, N. (1995). Neurobiology of skill and habit learning. *Current Opinion in Neurobiology, 5*, 184–190.

Scoville, W. B., & Milner, B. (1957). Loss of recent memory after bilateral hippocampal lesions. *Journal of Neurology, Neurosurgery and Psychiatry, 20*, 11–21.

Squire, L. R. (1992). Declarative and non-declarative memory: Multiple brain systems supporting learning and memory. *Journal of Cognitive Neuroscience, 4*, 232–243.

Squire, L. R., & Zola-Morgan, S. (1983). The neurology of memory: The case for correspondence between the findings for human and nonhuman primate. In J. A. Deutsch (Ed.), *The physiological basis of memory* (pp. 199–268). New York: Academic Press.

Squire, L. R., & Zola-Morgan, S. (1991). Medial temporal lobe memory system. *Science, 253*, 1380–1386.

Squire, L. R., & Zola, S. M. (1997). Amnesia, memory and brain systems. *Philosophical Transactions Royal Society of London B, 352*, 1663–1674.

Squire, L. R., & Zola-Morgan, S. (1991). Medial temporal lobe memory system. *Science, 253*, 1380–1386.

Stein, D. G., Rosen, J. J., Graziadei, J. et al. (1969). Central nervous system: Recovery of function. *Science, 166*, 528–530.

Sutherland, R. W., & Rudy, J. W. (1989). Configural association theory: The role of the hippocampal formation in learning, memory and amnesia. *Psychobiology, 17*, 129–144.

Suzuki, W. A., & Amaral, D. G. (1994). Perirhinal and parahippocampal cortices of the macaque monkey: Cortical afferents. *Journal of Comparative Neurology, 350*, 497–533.

Suzuki, W. A., Zola-Morgan, S., Squire, L. R., & Amaral, D. G. (1993). Lesions of the perirhinal and parahippocampal cortices in the monkey produce long-lasting memory impairment in the visual and tactual modalities. *Journal of Neuroscience, 13*, 2430–2451.

Teng, E., Squire, L. R., Zola, S. M. (1997). Different memory roles for the parahippocampal and perirhinal cortices in spatial reversal. *Neuroscience Abstracts, 23*, 12.

Teng, E., Squire, L. R., Zola, S. M. (1998). Effects of removal from the testing apparatus on delayed nonmatching to sample performance in monkeys with lesions of the hippocampal region. *Society for Neuroscience Abstracts, 24*, 17.

Thompson, R. F., & Krupa, D. J. (1994). Organization of memory traces in the mammalian brain. *Annual Review of Neuroscience, 17*, 519–550.

Vargha-Khadem, F., Gadian, D. G., Watkins, K. E., Connelly, A., Van Paesschen, W., & Mishkin, M. (1997). Differential effects of early hippocampal pathology on episodic and semantic memory. *Science, 277*, 376–380.

Warrington, E. K. (1984). *Recognition memory test*. Windsor: FER-Nelson.

Wood, E. R., & Phillips, A. G. (1991). Deficits on a one trial object recognition task by rats with hippocampal CA1 lesions produced by cerebral ischemia. *Neuroscience Research Communications, 9*, 177–182.

Zola-Morgan, S., & Squire, L. R. (1986). Memory impairment in monkeys following lesions of the hippocampus. *Behavioral Neuroscience, 100*, 165–170.

Zola-Morgan, S., Squire, L. R., & Ramus, S. J. (1994). Severity of memory impairment in monkeys as a function of locus and extent of damage within the medial temporal lobe memory system. *Hippocampus, 4*, 483–495.

Zola-Morgan, S., Squire, L. R., Rempel, N. L., Clower, R. P., & Amaral, D. G. (1992). Enduring memory impairment in monkeys after ischemic damage to the hippocampus. *Journal of Neuroscience, 9*, 4355–4370.

Zola, S. M., Teng, E., Clark, R. E. et al. (1998). Impaired recognition memory and simple discrimination learning in monkeys following lesions limited to the hippocampal region made by radio frequency, ischemia, or ibotenic acid. *Society for Neuroscience Abstracts, 24*, 17 (abstract).

Zola, S. M., Squire, L. R., Teng, E., Stefanacci, L, & Clark, R. (2000). Impaired recognition memory in monkeys after damage limited to the hippocampal region. *Journal of Neuroscience, 20*, 451–463.

31

Brain Imaging of Memory

LARS NYBERG & ROBERTO CABEZA

Functional brain imaging makes it possible to study the human brain at work. There has been an explosive growth in this field during the last few years, and the expansion seems to continue. Several different techniques can be used for brain imaging. The focus here is on positron emission tomography (PET) and to a somewhat lesser extent on functional magnetic resonance imaging (fMRI). An important characteristic of these and related techniques is that they can simultaneously measure activity in the whole brain. This makes them well suited for adressing the notion that higher order cognitive processes result from the operations of large-scale neural networks (Mesulam, 1990). In combination with techniques that have high temporal resolution (see chapter 32), brain imaging with PET and fMRI therefore makes it possible to "observe" *in vivo* how the human brain subserves cognition.

The scope of the chapter is limited to brain imaging studies of declarative long-term memory (i.e., semantic and episodic memory) and working memory. Excellent reviews of brain imaging studies of nondeclarative memory systems such as priming (Schacter & Buckner, 1998) and procedural memory (Passingham, 1997) can be found elsewhere. The organization of the chapter is as follows: First, the principal methods for data acquisition and data analysis will briefly be discussed, fol-

lowed by a summary of results from representative studies. Thereafter, alternative data-analytic methods are introduced that more explicitly address the issue of how brain regions interact during task performance. Finally, some tentative conclusions are offered.

Data Acquisition and Analysis

PET and fMRI are hemodynamic techniques: they measure neuronal activity by assessing changes in cerebral blood flow (for a description of PET and fMRI techniques, see Raichle, 1994). The standard PET method for cognitive studies is to inject a radioactive tracer immediately before the start of a cognitive task and to average the signal generated by the tracer for 40–70 seconds. The resulting image is a time-integrated map of the distribution of blood flow during this period. In the case of fMRI, blood flow is measured by assessing changes in the blood oxygenation, without the need of a radioactive tracer. In blocked fMRI paradigms, items belonging to a particular experimental condition are presented together in a "block" and the measures of brain activity reflect averaged activity across the entire block (e.g., 10–40 sec), similar to the case of PET. In event-related fMRI paradigms, different types of items are mixed during the scan but their data are analyzed separately according to item type or performance outcome. These paradigms allow the highest temporal resolution achievable with hemodynamic techniques which is in the order of a few seconds.

Usually, the map of a PET/fMRI image from a single task cannot be interpreted by itself. Rather, a common strategy in cognitive studies has been to measure blood flow (1) while subjects are engaged in the cognitive task of interest, and (2) while subjects are engaged in a closely matched reference task. By comparing the blood flow maps associated with these tasks, it is possible to identify the regions that are differentially activated by the component process(es) that distinguishes the two tasks (so-called paired-image subtraction or cognitive subtraction). The comparison of blood flow maps is commonly done using some kind of univariate approach, such as multiple t-tests (Friston et al., 1995). An example of a brain map showing the results of a subtraction analysis is presented in figure 31.1.

There are problems associated with cognitive subtraction (cf., Price & Friston, 1997). These include difficulties with finding a reference task that effectively matches the task of interest. Another problem is that of pure insertion, or whether the addition of an extra processing component per se in the experimental task will not affect processes that are common to the experimental and reference tasks. If the "common" processes indeed are affected, it will not be possible to subtract them out and they will be reflected in the activation pattern that differentiates the tasks. Nonetheless, to date, the majority of results from PET studies of memory have been generated by "cognitive subtraction" and several robust and reliable patterns of activation have been demonstrated. Some of these findings will be discussed in the following sections. The major brain regions that will be considered in the chapter are outlined in figure 31.2.

Semantic Memory Retrieval

Semantic memory tasks tap our knowledge of the world in a very broad sense. Buckner and Tulving (1995) classified semantic retrieval tasks in terms of the extent to which the stimulus cues constrain the retrieval environment. Tasks in which the cue is readily associated with the target item—for example, reading a single word—were labeled as stimulus-driven semantic retrieval tasks. Tasks in which the cue provides a context without directly specifying the target information were labeled as elaborate semantic retrieval tasks. PET studies of elaborate semantic retrieval have used tasks such as letter fluency (generate words beginning with a specific letter) and verb generation (generate appropriate verbs to nouns; e.g., *ladder–climb*). In the latter type of task, which will be discussed here, elaboration of the cue information is needed for retrieval of the relevant information.

A previous review of the literature (Buckner & Tulving, 1995) revealed that elaborate semantic retrieval generally was associated with left prefrontal activations. The localization of these activations varied across different tasks, suggesting that they represented different components associated with specific tasks, but several tasks were associated with increased activity in or near Brodmann's areas 44 and 45.

Similarly, in a subsequent review of neuroimaging studies of cognitive processes, including semantic memory, Cabeza and Nyberg (1997) came to the conclusion that semantic retrieval tasks are generally associated with left prefrontal activations. Moreover, semantic retrieval was associated with left temporal and anterior cingulate regions. Thus, for some semantic retrieval tasks, these regions may be additionally involved.

In the context of brain activation associated with semantic retrieval, a study by Raichle et al. (1994) is intriguing. These authors studied brain regions involved during verb generation. In line with the above discussed results, they found increased activity in left prefrontal, anterior cingulate, and left posterior temporal brain regions (plus the right cerebellar hemisphere). Interestingly, after a short period of practicing the task (10–15 minutes), these regions were all significantly less active, and the neural signature of the task had become indistinguishable from that of a stimulus-driven semantic task (simple word repetition). These findings indicate that normal subjects can change the brain circuits used during task performance following short periods of practice.

Episodic Memory

Episodic memory is concerned with remembering of personally experienced events, in-

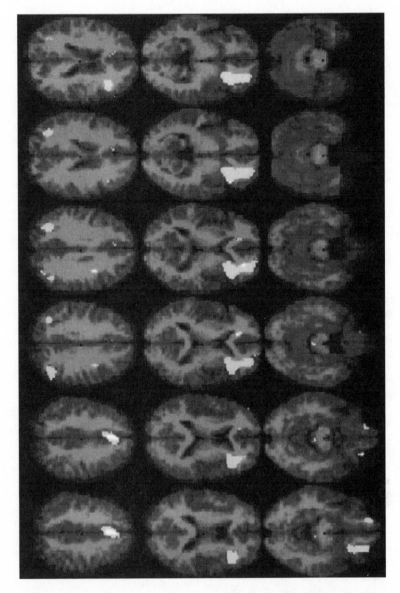

Figure 31.1 Statistical parametric map of a pairwise image comparison. From Cabeza et al. (1997). Reproduced with permission.

cluding materials presented in an experimental setting. Participants may, for example, be shown a set of words and asked to try to remember these for a subsequent test. After a retention interval, they may then be asked to think back to the study episode and recall the words that were presented. Alternatively, a mixture of studied and/or nonstudied words may be presented at test and the task of the participants is to indicate whether they recognize any words from the study episode. Theoretical proposals argue for basic similarities in the neural bases of encoding and retrieval, although empirical data suggest basic differences as well (see Craik et al., 1996). Along this vein, it has been of interest in PET studies to compare the functional anatomy of encoding and retrieval (e.g., Fletcher et al., 1995), and here episodic encoding and retrieval are discussed separately.

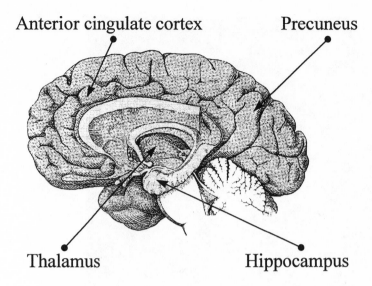

Anterior cingulate cortex   Precuneus

Thalamus   Hippocampus

Figure 31.2 Some major brain regions activated in imaging studies of working memory, episodic memory, and semantic memory. The display shows a medial view of the right hemisphere. Parts of the medial temporal cortex have been removed to visualize the hippocampus. The anatomical frame is from Kahle (1991). Reproduced with permission.

Encoding

Cabeza and Nyberg (1997) reviewed PET studies attempting to identify brain regions showing increased activity during intentional encoding. Across studies, left prefrontal, left temporal/fusiform, and anterior cingulate regions showed increased activity. In addition, increased activation in the vicinity of the hippocampal formation has been observed in studies of episodic encoding (e.g., Haxby et al., 1996; Kapur et al., 1996; Stern et al., 1996). This part of the brain has for a long time been associated with encoding of new episodes (see Squire, 1992).

Findings by Dolan and Fletcher (1997) provide evidence that one role of left hippocampus in episodic memory encoding is to register the novelty of presented verbal material (category-exemplar word pairs). In contrast, their findings indicated that the role of left prefrontal cortex is not related to novelty detection, but rather to associative semantic processing. The findings by Dolan and Fletcher, implicating left hippocampal regions in registering the novelty of verbal materials, extend findings that right hippocampal regions are involved in perceiving novel nonverbal materials (Tulving, Markowitsch, Kapur, Habib, & Houle, 1994). They also provide strong support for the novelty/encoding hypothesis put forward by Tulving and colleagues (Tulving, Markowitsch, Craik, Habib, & Houle, 1996). According to this hypothesis, encoding consists of two subprocesses: (1) novelty assess-

ment, partly mediated by hippocampal regions, and (2) meaning-based encoding operations, partly mediated by left frontal lobes. If incoming information is identified as novel, it is transmitted for further meaning-based processing. The end product of these processes is the engram or memory trace.

Further support for the importance of medial-temporal and prefrontal brain regions for episodic encoding comes from recent fMRI studies (Brewer et al., 1998; Fernandez et al., 1998; Wagner et al., 1998). These studies examined how brain activity during encoding related to subsequent retrieval, and collectively they indicate that there is a positive relation between the magnitude of activation in prefrontal and medial temporal brain regions during encoding and later memory performance.

Retrieval

Cognitive theories of episodic memory retrieval hold that several subprocesses are involved (e.g., Tulving, 1983; Moscovitch, 1992; Shallice, 1988). A major distinction is between general retrieval processes broadly related to the attempt to remember and processes related to actual retrieval of stored information. The PET evidence is largely consistent with this view, suggesting that some brain regions are generally involved in episodic retrieval whereas the involvement of others seems to be related to level of recovery.

With regard to general regions, several reviews converge on the notion that certain right prefrontal brain regions are differentially activated during episodic retrieval (Buckner, 1996; Buckner & Petersen, 1996; Buckner & Tulving, 1995; Cabeza & Nyberg, 1997; Fletcher, Frith, & Rugg, 1997; Ungerleider, 1995). In particular, a region in right anterior prefrontal cortex (area 10) has consistently been found to be involved in episodic retrieval. One interpretation of right prefrontal activation related to episodic retrieval is that it reflects processes related to maintaining a "retrieval mode" (Nyberg et al., 1995). This interpretation was based on results showing that right prefrontal activation was observed in a condition involving relatively high levels of retrieval, in a condition involving lower levels of retrieval, and in a condition involving only nonstudied items (see also Kapur et al., 1995). Subsequent analyses have confirmed the findings of a general involvement of right prefrontal cortical areas in episodic retrieval and extended them to include not only item retrieval but retrieval of spatial and temporal information as well (Köhler, Moscovitch, Winocur, Houle, & McIntosh, 1998; Nyberg, McIntosh, Cabeza, Habib et al., 1996). Moreover, sophisticated analysis of fMRI data, allowing evaluation of the response related to retrieval of individual items, has shown that right anterior prefrontal cortex is activated to a similar degree during correct rejection of nonstudied items and correct identification of studied items (Buckner et al., 1998). These findings provide evidence that right prefrontal activation is not related to actual recovery but rather to more general processes engaged by episodic retrieval.

Additional regions seem to be generally involved in episodic retrieval as well. In the Nyberg et al. (1995) study, increased activity was consistently observed in the anterior cingulate and cerebellum, in keeping with findings from several other PET studies of episodic retrieval (see Cabeza & Nyberg, 1997). Based on findings of stronger activity in the anterior cingulate and cerebellum during recall than during recognition, Cabeza et al. (1997) have proposed that the involvement of these structures in episodic retrieval is related to self-initiated processing (see also Bäckman et al., 1997). It should also be noted that several studies have found that episodic retrieval is generally associated with decreased activity in distinct brain regions (see Nyberg, 1998). For example, decreases have repeatedly been observed in bilateral temporal regions. It has

been proposed that such decreases reflect task-related inhibition from other brain regions (Andreasen et al., 1995). This issue will be discussed further in the context of network analyses.

As for regions that seem to be differentially involved in episodic retrieval depending on level of performance, activity in medial-temporal regions, including hippocampus, has been associated with higher levels of episodic retrieval in several studies (e.g., Cahill et al., 1996[1]; Eustache et al., 1995; Grasby, Frith, Friston, Frackowiak, & Dolan, 1993; Heckers et al., 1998; Nyberg, McIntosh et al., 1996; Rugg, Fletcher, Frith, Frackowiak, & Dolan, 1997; Schacter, Alpert, Savage, Rauch, & Albert, 1996). This association has been proposed to reflect recollective experience or confidence (Nyberg, McIntosh et al., 1996; Schacter et al., 1996). It is also consistent with the view that events are initially stored in the medial-temporal system (McClelland, McNaughton, & O'Reilly, 1995). According to the latter view, the hippocampus plays a time-limited role in the formation of neocortical engrams or representations. Findings of higher medial-temporal activity during retrieval in a less practiced memory state compared to a well-practiced state may be in line with this latter view (Petersson, Elfgren, & Ingvar, 1997).

The activity in other regions, as well, has been found to be sensitive to level of retrieval performance. A striking example was provided in a study by Rugg, Fletcher, Frith, Frackowiak, and Dolan (1996), showing that activity in several bilateral frontal regions was higher for successful than for unsuccessful episodic retrieval. These findings were interpreted as showing that prefrontal cortex mediates processes that act on the output of episodic retrieval operations. This may seem inconsistent with the view that right prefrontal activation reflects retrieval mode, but there are several ways to reconcile these findings. First, consistent with the retrieval mode interpretation, it is possible that right prefrontal cortex is activated when there is an intention to retrieve episodic information, although, given sufficient power to detect retrieval related differences, one will find that this region is further activated when retrieval is successful (cf. Fletcher et al., 1997). Second, in line with findings of functional heterogeneity of the prefrontal cortex (e.g., Petrides & Pandya, 1994; for a discussion of neuroimaging evidence, see

Buckner, 1996), it is possible that some areas within the right prefrontal cortex are sensitive to increased levels of recovery whereas others are activated to a similar extent regardless of level of success (cf., Nyberg, 1996).

Finally, retrieval-related activity has consistently been observed in a medial parietal cortical region; the precuneus (see, e.g., Fletcher et al., 1997). As such, this region may best be classified as a "general" episodic retrieval region, perhaps reflecting the use of imagery as a mnemonic strategy at retrieval (e.g., Dolan, Paulesu, & Fletcher, 1997, but see Buckner, Raichle, Miezin, & Petersen, 1996). However, other findings indicate that precuneus activation is related to level of retrieval success (Kapur et al., 1995), possibly by representing the reactivation of stored engrams (see also Roland & Gulyas, 1995). Thus, whereas it seems clear that precuneus is implicated in episodic retrieval, its functional role remains to be determined.

In summary, the results of activation analyses indicate that several brain regions mediate episodic memory retrieval. This extensive activation pattern is shown in figure 31.3. Additional regions to those discussed above may be involved as well. For example, in line with lesion studies (see Butters & Stuss, 1989), thalamic activations have repeatedly been observed during episodic retrieval (e.g., Cabeza et al., 1997; Fletcher et al., 1995; Petrides et al., 1995), although their functional significance is unclear. Increased activity has also been observed in the amygdala when the to-be-remembered information had a strong emotional (Cahill et al., 1996) or personal (Fink et al., 1996) flavor. Given that successful episodic retrieval requires coordinated activity in all or most of these regions, such an extensive system seems quite vulnerable. Indeed, amnesia has been conceptualized as a disconnection syndrome (see Markowitsch, 1995), and age-related episodic memory deficits have been discussed in the context of functional disconnection of relevant regions (Cabeza et al., 1997).

Working Memory

Working memory is thought to be involved in numerous activities, ranging from simple tasks, such as keeping a telephone number in mind, to complex tasks, such as planning for the future. Based on the assumption of multiple working memory components, functional neuroimaging studies have tried to determine the neural correlates of specific components. Much of this work has been inspired by the model proposed by Baddeley and Hitch (1974). According to this model, working memory consists of three dissociable components: a phonological loop for the maintenance of verbal information, a visuo-spatial sketchpad for the maintenance of visuo-spatial information, and a central executive for attentional control. In general, the results indicate that each component is mediated by multiple regions.

Phonological Loop

Activations associated with the phonological loop are usually found in posterior parietal, opercular, and premotor frontal regions (Awh et al., 1996; Cohen et al., 1997; Fiez et al., 1996; Paulesu, Frith, & Frackowiak, 1993; Schumacher et al., 1996). These activations tend to be left lateralized, thereby involving Broca's area. According to Baddeley's model, the phonological loop consists of a phonological store where information is briefly stored and a rehearsal process that refreshes the contents of this store. Functional neuroimaging studies have associated the phonological store with activations in parietal regions (Awh et al., 1996; Paulesu et al., 1993) and the rehearsal process with activations in Broca's area (Awh et al., 1996; Fiez et al., 1996; Paulesu et al., 1993).

Visuospatial Sketchpad

Data from single-cell recordings (e.g., Wilson, O'Scalaidhe, & Goldman-Rakic, 1993) and neuroimaging (e.g., Courtney, Ungerleider, Keil, & Haxby, 1996; Smith et al., 1995) indicate that the sketchpad involves two dissociable systems: one for object information and one for spatial information. Maintenance of spatial and object information tends to follow the dissociation between dorsal and ventral pathways found in perceptual networks (Ungerleider & Mishkin, 1982). Thus, activations related to the maintenance of object information are typically found in occipito-temporal and inferior prefrontal regions (Haxby, Ungerleider, Horwitz, Rapoport, & Grady, 1995; Courtney, Ungerleider, Keil, & Haxby, 1996; Smith et al., 1995), whereas activations related to the maintenance of spatial information are usually observed in occipito-parietal and superior prefrontal regions (Awh et al., 1996;

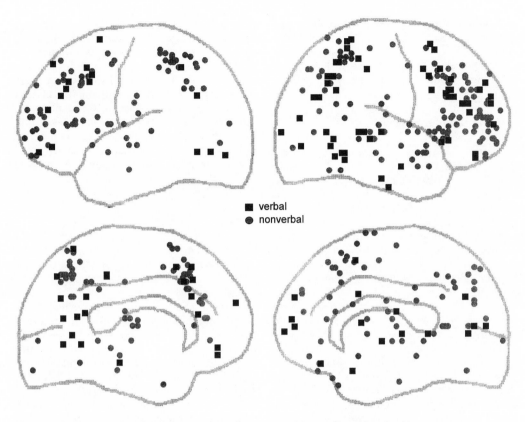

verbal
nonverbal

Figure 31.3 Summary of activations from brain imaging studies of episodic memory.

Courtney et al., 1996; Smith et al., 1995). There is also a tendency for object maintenance to be left-lateralized and for spatial maintenance to be right-lateralized (Smith et al., 1995).

Central Executive

Processes assumed to depend on the central executive are typically associated with activations in prefrontal regions. One group of executive processes includes monitoring, temporal tagging, and updating of the contents of working memory. Tasks involving these processes commonly engage the mid-dorsolateral frontal cortex (Cohen et al., 1997; Petrides, Alivisatos, Evans, & Meyer, 1993; Petrides, Alivisatos, Meyer, & Evans, 1993). Another type of executive operation is the distribution of attentional resources across simultaneous tasks. An fMRI study found that areas 9 and 46 were activated when two tasks were performed simultaneously but not when they were performed separately (D'Esposito et al., 1995), suggesting that this type of executive operation as well in-

volves the mid-dorsolateral frontal cortex. Moreover, executive operations engaged during problem solving, such as planning (Owen, Evans, & Petrides, 1996) and reasoning (Prabhakaran, Smith, Desmond, Glover, & Gabrieli, 1997), have been associated with activations in the mid-dorsolateral prefrontal cortex.

Other frontal regions, outside the mid-dorsolateral area, have also been activated during working memory tasks. Petrides (1994, 1995; see also Owen, Doyon, Petrides, & Evans, 1996a) has proposed a hierarchical model in which ventrolateral regions (areas 45 and 47) perform lower level executive operations, such as simple comparisons between items in short-term memory, and mid-dorsal regions (areas 9 and 46) perform higher level executive operations, such as monitoring and manipulation of several pieces of information in working memory. In contrast to this "process-specific" model, Goldman-Rakic (1996) has suggested a "domain-specific" model in which different prefrontal regions perform similar working memory operations but apply them to different types of information (i.e., ventrolateral regions processing object information and dorsolateral regions processing spatial information). These views are not incompatible, and there is some support for both (see Courtney, Ungerleider, & Haxby, 1997).

Intermediate Summary

The activation analyses in studies of episodic memory, semantic memory, and working memory have generated stable patterns of activation (see table 31.1). In general, these patterns involve multiple distributed regions, and it is not uncommon to see such activation patterns referred to as *networks*. Indeed, it has explicitly been argued that the statistical outcome from univariate comparisons can be conceptualized as network components. The possibility to identify systems of areas that are engaged during task performance has been emphasized as a major advantage of functional neuroimaging techniques such as PET (Zeki, 1993).

However, to more formally characterize a network, statistical techniques other than those used in "cognitive subtraction" are necessary. Alternative techniques, which take into account covariance between activity in distributed regions, are not only important in specifying a putative network as suggested by activation analyses but can also reveal the operation of several independent networks (cf., McLaughlin, Steinberg, Christensen, Law, Parving, & Friberg, 1992). As suggested in the above discussion of cognitive subtraction, depending on how well the experimental and reference tasks were designed, the activation

pattern that differentiates tasks may reflect the operation of multiple component processes. Moreover, covariance-based techniques can show that regions that do not show differential activation as revealed by univariate comparisons do indeed play a significant task-related effect by interacting differently with other network components. Next we will outline how network analyses can be conducted, followed by a presentation of network analyses of semantic memory, episodic memory, and working memory.

Network Analyses

As discussed above, cognitive subtraction identifies brain regions in which the response is sensitive to the experimental manipulation as indicated by changes in relative activation. It has been recognized that regions that do not show differential activity between conditions may still be part of the relevant network (cf., Horwitz, McIntosh, Haxby, & Grady, 1995; McIntosh, in press; for an empirical example, see Köhler, McIntosh, Moscovitch, & Winocur, 1998). Various procedures have been put forward to identify such regions. One approach, the seed-voxel technique, involves computing intercorrelations between a region (the seed) and the rest of the brain (see, e.g., Horwitz et al., 1995). This approach has been further developed in the context of partial least squares (PLS; for a discussion of PLS, see McIntosh, Bookstein, Haxby, & Grady, 1996) to be more readily applicable to analyses involving several critical regions and several conditions (McIntosh, Nyberg, Bookstein, & Tulving,

Table 31.1 Summary of results from activation analyses.

Memory operation	Typical activation pattern
Semantic memory	Left prefrontal & temporal cortex, anterior cingulate
Episodic memory	
encoding	Left prefrontal & temporal cortex, anterior cingulate, hippocampus[1]
general retrieval	Right prefrontal & *bilateral temporal*[2] cortex, anterior cingulate, cerebellum, precuneus, thalamus
successful retrieval	Prefrontal cortex, precuneus, hippocampus[1]
Working memory	
phonological loop	Left fronto-opercular (Broca's area), premotor & parietal cortex
sketchpad	Ventral (object information) & dorsal (spatial information) visual pathways
central executive	Prefrontal cortex (ventrolateral & mid-dorsal)

[1]Hippocampus refers to hippocampus proper as well as nearby cortex; [2]Italics denote decreased activation.

1997). For example, by using PLS it is possible to show that the correlations between a seed region and other brain regions vary systematically across conditions. Importantly, such a data pattern can be observed in the absence of task-related activation changes in the seed region.

A related approach to identifying network components is the use of factor-analytic techniques such as principal components analysis (PCA). The basic idea underlying this approach is that there will be systematic correlations between activity in brain regions that are functionally associated with each other in a particular condition. PCA can identify sets or components of brain regions that are related along common dimensions and have shared variance. Hence, the regions associated with each component can be thought of as representing a functional network (Horwitz et al., 1995). This approach has been applied to blood flow data measured with a single-photon emission computerized tomograph (SPECT), resulting in the identification of networks underlying auditory/linguistic, attentional, and visual imaging processes (McLaughlin et al., 1992).

The identification of networks by seed-voxel correlations or factor analysis represents a significant advance in the statistical analysis of brain imaging data in that associations between different brain regions are taken into account. Importantly, however, inferences based on correlations alone may be ambiguous. For example, neural activity in two regions may be highly correlated not only if they affect each other, directly or indirectly (i.e., through other regions) but also if they are both influenced by a third region. This issue relates to the distinction between *functional connectivity* and *effective connectivity* (e.g., Friston, 1997). To more completely characterize a network and specify direct effects (effective connectivity) and indirect effects, as well as the direction of effects, it is necessary to combine neuroanatomical information and neuroimaging data. This can be done with a technique called *structural equation modeling* or path analysis.

Structural equation modeling of PET data was developed by McIntosh and his colleagues (for a discussion of theoretical and technical issues, see McIntosh & Gonzalez-Lima, 1994). To illustrate how it is done, an analysis of cortical visual pathways will briefly be described (see McIntosh, Grady et al., 1994). Based on (1) a comparison of brain regions differentially activated during object and spatial vision tasks, (2) an analysis of interregional correlation, and (3) PCA, a set of brain regions was identified and included in the modeling. Based on existing neuroanatomical knowledge, an anatomical network model was constructed for the identified regions. This model described the connections between the included regions, and interregional correlations were used to compute weights for the different connections (functional network model). It was found that there were strong path influences from occipital to temporal regions during object vision, whereas occipito-parietal influences were stronger during spatial vision. Moreover, the analysis provided support that a frontal lobe region played a critical role by having a significant feedback effect on occipital cortex in the spatial task but not in the object task. This involvement was not evident from activation analyses. Thus, by combining the anatomical model and interregional correlations, functional networks were identified that describe how brain regions influence each other in different conditions (for an example of structural equation modeling of fMRI data, see Büchel & Friston, 1997a).

Taken together, several techniques can be used to conduct variants of network analyses (for further examples, see Friston, 1997). Below, results from various network analyses of brain imaging data from memory studies will be presented. These examples will include the use of seed-correlations, principal components analysis (PCA), and structural equation modeling.

Semantic Memory Retrieval

The activation analyses revealed that semantic retrieval involves increased activity in left frontal, temporal, and anterior cingulate regions. A PCA analysis of brain systems associated with performance on a verbal fluency task provide support that at least some of these regions are components of a common network (Friston, Frith, Liddle, & Frackowiak, 1993). The first principal component had positive loadings in the anterior cingulate, left dorsolateral prefrontal cortex, Broca's area, thalamus, and cerebellum. These findings underscore the view that left frontal and anterior cingulate regions are part of a network for elaborate semantic retrieval.

Negative loadings were observed in the posterior cingulate and in bilateral temporal regions. The negative loadings on temporal regions indicated that they were not part of the same network as the frontal and cingulate regions, perhaps reflecting the operation of more than one network within the same task (cf., McLaughlin et al., 1992). It can also be that the frequently observed co-activation of temporal regions with left frontal and cingulate regions is task specific. We will return to this issue in the discussion.

Episodic Memory

Activation analyses of episodic memory encoding have pointed to a common involvement of left frontal and hippocampal regions, as well as specific regions in temporal cortex and the anterior cingulate. Seed-correlation analysis between blood flow in right hippocampus and blood flow in all other brain areas during face encoding revealed that the right hippocampal region was strongly correlated with a region in the anterior cingulate (Grady et al., 1995). Interestingly, this pattern of correlations was observed only for young subjects. Older subjects, who did not activate right hippocampus during encoding, may thus have failed to engage the appropriate network for encoding. We noted above that the activation of hippocampal regions during encoding may be driven by novelty assessment. Recent findings, partly based on PCA, indicate that hippocampal activation may not only be related to novelty but also across-trial incremental learning (Kopelman et al., 1998).

Turning to retrieval, the activation analyses discussed above indicated that certain regions generally show decreased activity during episodic memory retrieval. This outcome has been suggested to reflect task-related inhibition from other brain regions (Andreasen et al., 1995). More direct support for this interpretation was obtained in a network analysis reported by Nyberg, McIntosh, Cabeza, Nilsson et al. (1996). This analysis revealed that regions showing increased activity during episodic retrieval, notably right prefrontal and anterior cingulate regions, had more negative influences on deactivated regions, notably bilateral temporal regions, during retrieval than during a nonepisodic reference task. The more negative effective connections in case of retrieval compared to reading is illustrated in figure 31.4. Such confirmation of the inhibition hypothesis would not have been possible based on activation analyses alone. It was

proposed that inhibition of activity could be reflecting prevention of task-irrelevant processing, and it was concluded that regional reductions in neural activity constitute an important aspect of episodic retrieval.

Regarding regions that seem to be specifically activated when retrieval is successful, a puzzling issue has been whether prefrontal brain regions are generally activated, reflecting "retrieval mode" (e.g., Nyberg et al., 1995) or whether they are activated to a higher extent when retrieval is successful (Rugg et al., 1996; see also Buckner et al., 1998). In this context it is interesting to note that a recent analysis of functional connectivity indicates that activity in certain right prefrontal regions can reflect either retrieval mode or retrieval success, depending on which other regions it is functionally linked to (McIntosh et al., 1997). This result is consistent with the idea that brain regions do not have dedicated functions in themselves, but their functional role can vary across cognitive operations as a function of the neural context.

Finally, network analysis has been used to directly compare the neural interactions underlying episodic encoding and retrieval. In a PET study by Cabeza, McIntosh et al. (1997), the functional networks of encoding and retrieval of word pairs was studied. Structural equation modeling of data from young subjects showed that there was a shift from positive interactions involving the left prefrontal cortex during encoding to positive interactions involving the right prefrontal cortex during recall. When a similar analysis was conducted on data from older subjects, it was found that frontal interactions were mixed during encoding and bilaterally positive during recall. The functional networks associated with encoding and retrieval for the young and older subjects are presented in figure 31.5. It was concluded that age-related changes in activation are partly due to age-related changes in effective connectivity.

Working Memory

The data from activation studies indicate that working memory is based on distributed networks with salient components in various parietal, temporal, and frontal regions. Only a few functional neuroimaging studies of working memory have directly approached the issue of how these different network components interact with one another. Gevins and

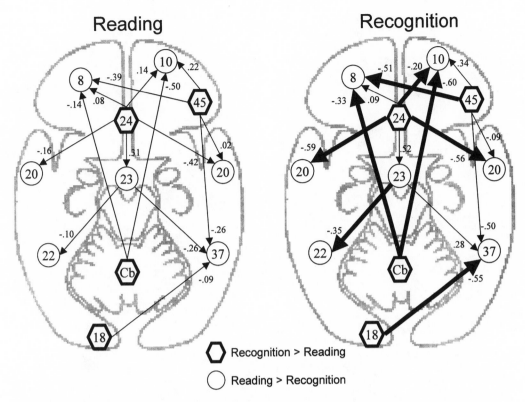

Figure 31.4 Functional network models for reading and recognition. From Nyberg, McIntosh, Cabeza, Nilsson et al. (1996). Reproduced with permission.

colleagues applied covariance analyses to electrophysiological data. In Gevins and Cutillo (1993), data recorded from a numeric working memory task were analyzed. During an awaiting stimulus interval, when responses were presumably being prepared from information maintained in working memory, electrodes over frontal scalp regions were the focus of strong covariances with occipito-parietal electrodes, particularly in the left hemisphere. These results are consistent with suggestions of interaction between frontal regions and posterior (parietal) regions during working memory, and also with the left lateralization of verbal maintenance components.

Further support for this view was provided in a study by Klingberg, O'Sullivan, and Roland (1997). The authors performed a principal component analysis on the correlations between activated regions in a PET study of nonverbal working memory (match-to-sample). The first component identified prefrontal and parietal regions. These results from human subjects were related to research suggest-

ing that activation of fronto-parietal networks forms the basis for working memory in monkeys (Friedman & Goldman-Rakic, 1994).

Finally, McIntosh, Grady et al. (1996) conducted structural equation modeling on the results of a PET study in which subjects matched faces separated by short, intermediate, and long delays. In the short-delay functional model, there were strong interactions in the right hemisphere between ventral temporal, hippocampal, anterior cingulate, and inferior frontal regions. At the long delay, right limbic interactions were attenuated in favor of bilateral frontal and fronto-cingulate interactions. This switch in effective connectivity as a function of delay is shown in figure 31.6. While cortico-limbic interactions at the short delays are consistent with short-term maintenance of iconic face representations, fronto-cingulate interactions at the longer delay suggest expanded encoding strategies necessary for further retention. This last study is an excellent example of how covariance analyses can help elucidate the complex pattern of in-

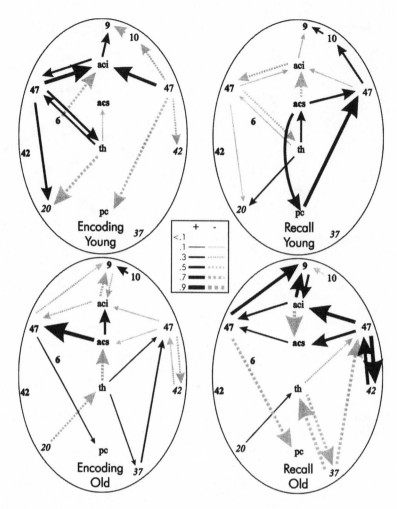

Figure 31.5 Functional network models for encoding and recall for younger and older adults. From Cabeza, McIntosh et al. (1997). Reproduced with permission.

teractions between different network components and, in line with the results by Gevins and Cutillo (1993), and Klingberg, O'Sullivan, and Roland (1997), it points to a central role of frontal brain regions in working-memory networks.

Conclusions

The results summarized above are in agreement with the view that memory is a distributed property of cortical systems (Fuster, 1997), and they start to define these systems for different memory functions. Many details remain to be worked out, but it seems fair to

say that a broad picture has emerged. One general observation is that across the examined memory domains, prefrontal brain regions are involved. For some memory operations, distinct regions within the prefrontal cortex have been found to be engaged (cf., Buckner, 1996). A striking example of this is the consistent observation that prefrontal regions in the left hemisphere tend to be differentially activated during episodic encoding and semantic retrieval, whereas right prefrontal regions tend to be differentially involved during episodic memory retrieval (for a discussion of conditions which tend to additionally activate left prefrontal regions during episodic retrieval, see Nolde, Johnson, & Raye, 1998). This regu-

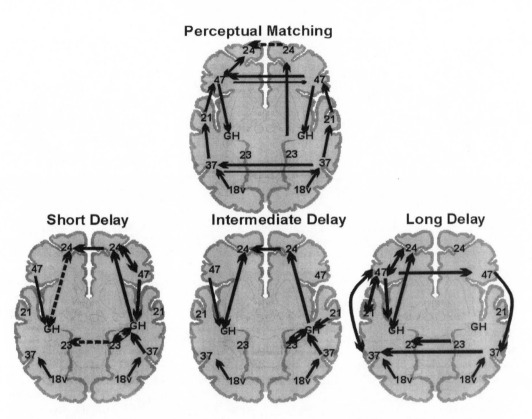

Figure 31.6 Functional network models for working memory with short and long study-test interval. From McIntosh, Grady et al. (1996). Reproduced with permission.

larity forms the basis for the hemispheric encoding/retrieval asymmetry (HERA) model proposed by Tulving and coworkers (Nyberg, Cabeza, & Tulving, 1996; Tulving, Kapur, Craik, Moscovitch, & Houle, 1994). The asymmetric involvement of left and right prefrontal brain regions in episodic encoding and retrieval is illustrated in figure 31.7.

Findings that different prefrontal regions take part in different memory networks underscore the functional heterogeneity of prefrontal cortex, but overlap in frontal activations for different memory operations has also been noted. This is true for episodic encoding and semantic retrieval and for episodic retrieval and working memory (cf., Buckner et al., 1996; Petrides et al., 1995; Rugg et al., 1996). Thus, some prefrontal regions seem to be part of more than one network subserving different memory abilities. This commonality may reflect similar functional influences, although it could also be that the same prefrontal region has a different functional role depending on the regions it interacts with (cf., McIntosh et al., 1997).

A second-general observation is that prefrontal regions seem to interact with posterior brain regions during memory encoding and retrieval. For example, the review of working memory indicated that rehearsal processes mediated by frontal regions refresh the contents of posterior "stores" during active maintenance of information. Similarly, for declarative long-term memory there is suggestive evidence that memories are represented in posterior association cortices (Fuster, 1997). As was noted in the context of semantic memory retrieval, the involvement of certain posterior regions seems to be task-specific. One interpretation of this is that the specific network nodes that are engaged will depend on the type of information that is retrieved (cf., Fuster, 1997). Empirical support for this view is provided by a study by Martin and colleagues (1995), examining brain regions associated with semantic knowledge of colors and actions associated with objects. Retrieval of both kinds of information was associated with activation of left prefrontal cortex, but material-specific activations were observed in posterior

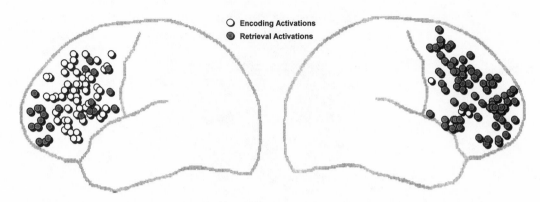

Figure 31.7 Hemispheric asymmetric involvement of left and right prefrontal cortex during episodic encoding and episodic retrieval.

brain regions. These findings were interpreted as showing that object knowledge is organized as a distributed system, and parts of this system are engaged at retrieval depending on the task demands. Thus, the topography of declarative memory networks will vary depending on the information to be retrieved, how it was acquired, and most likely also depending on the type of cues that are directing retrieval (Tulving, 1983).

Medial-temporal brain regions have had a special status in research on the neural basis for declarative memory, and divisions between memory systems have been based on whether they are hippocampal dependent or not (e.g., Squire & Zola-Morgan, 1990). Hippocampus and related structures have been suggested to play an important role in declarative memory formation and a time-limited role in declarative memory retrieval by linking distributed neocortical regions in which the memory information is represented in the long term (e.g., Squire, 1992). In light of the strong emphasis that traditionally has been put on medial-temporal structures, the relative lack of hippocampal activations in functional neuroimaging studies has been a major issue (see, e.g., Fletcher et al., 1997; Tulving & Markowitsch, 1997). Nevertheless, as noted above, hippocampal activation related to episodic encoding and retrieval has been observed in many studies (see also Gabrieli, Brewer, Desmond, & Glover, 1997; LePage, Habib, & Tulving, 1998; Schacter & Wagner, 1999), and there is some support for a time-limited role of the medial temporal lobe during retrieval (Petersson et al., 1997; but see Andreasen et al., 1995). Thus, rather than exploring whether medial temporal regions are involved in de-

clarative memory operations, an important task for future studies will be to define the interactions between hippocampal and neocortical regions during various memory operations (cf., McIntosh, Nyberg, & Tulving, 1995; McIntosh, Nyberg, Bookstein, & Tulving, 1997).

In closing, the message of this chapter is underscoring that from a recent review of network memory (Fuster, 1997), how we view the cortical organization of primate memory is changing fundamentally from localizing memories in specific areas to viewing memory as a distributed property of cortical systems. No doubt, more refined techniques for data recording and analysis will enhance our understanding of the topography of these systems. Promising attempts along these lines include analysis of the temporal dynamics of regional activations (Cohen et al., 1997; Courtney, Ungerleider, Keil, & Haxby, 1997), and the use of statistical techniques that emphasize functional integration (Büchel & Friston, 1997b; McIntosh, in press).

Acknowledgments We thank A. R. McIntosh for his insightful comments and suggestions. Thanks also to G. Neely and B. Andersson for helpful assistance. LN's work is supported by a grant from HSFR (Sweden).

Note

1. Blood flow was measured at encoding and correlated with subsequent recall performance.

References

Andreasen, N. C., O'Leary, D. S., Arndt, S., Cizaldo, T., Hurtig, R., Rezai, K., Watkins,

G. L., Boles Ponto, L. L., & Hichawa, R. D. (1995). Short-term and long-term verbal memory: A positron emission tomography study. *Proceedings of the National Academy of Sciences, USA, 92*, 5111–5115.

Awh, E., Jonides, J., Smith, E. E., Schumacher, E. H., Koeppe, R. A., & Katz, S. (1996). Dissociation of storage and rehearsal in verbal working memory: Evidence from positron emission tomography. *Psychological Science, 7*, 25–31.

Bäckman, L., Almkvist, O., Andersson, J., Nordberg, A., Winblad, B., Reineck, R., & Långström, B. (1997). Brain activation in younger and older adults during implicit and explicit retrieval. *Journal of Cognitive Neuroscience, 9*, 378–391.

Baddeley, A. D., & Hitch, G. J. (1974). Working memory. In G. A. Bower (Ed.), *The psychology of learning and motivation: Advances in research and theory*. (Vol. 8, pp. 47–89). New York: Academic Press.

Brewer, J. B., Zhao, Z., Glover, G. H., & Gabrieli, J. D. E. (1998). Making memories: Brain activity that predicts whether visual experiences will be remembered or forgotten. *Science, 281*, 1185–1187.

Buckner, R. L. (1996). Beyond HERA: Contributions of specific prefrontal brain areas to long-term memory retrieval, *Psychonomic Bulletin & Review, 3*, 149–158.

Buckner, R. L., Koutstaal, W., Schacter, D. L., Dale, A. M., Rotte, M. R., & Rosen, B. R. (1998). Functional-anatomic study of episodic retrieval: II. Selective averaging of event-related fMRI trials to test the retrieval success hypothesis. *Neuroimage, 7*, 163–175.

Buckner, R. L., & Petersen, S. E. (1996). What does neuroimaging tell us about the role of prefrontal cortex in memory retrieval? *Seminars in the Neurosciences, 8*, 47–55.

Buckner, R. L., Raichle, M. E., Miezin, F. M., & Petersen, S. E. (1996). Functional anatomic studies of memory retrieval for auditory words and visual pictures. *Journal of Neuroscience, 16*, 6219–6235.

Buckner, R. L., & Tulving, E. (1995). Neuroimaging studies of memory: Theory and recent PET results. In F. Boller & J. Grafman (Eds.), *Handbook of neuropsychology* (Vol. 10; pp. 439–466). Amsterdam: Elsevier.

Büchel, C., & Friston, K. J. (1997a). Modulation of connectivity in visual pathways by attention: Cortical interactions evaluated with structural equation modelling and fMRI. *Cerebral Cortex, 7*, 768–778.

Büchel, C., & Friston, K. J. (1997b). Characterising functional integration. In R. S. J.

Frackowiak, K. J. Friston, C. D. Frith, R. J. Dolan, & J. C. Mazziotta (Eds.), *Human brain function* (pp. 127–140). Toronto: Academic Press.

Butters, N., & Stuss, D. T. (1989). Diencephalic amnesia. In F. Boller & J. Grafman (Eds.), *Handbook of neuropsychology* (Vol. 3; pp. 107–148). Amsterdam: Elsevier.

Cabeza, R., Kapur, S., Craik, F. I. M., McIntosh, A. R., Houle, S., & Tulving, E. (1997a). Functional neuroanatomy of recall and recognition: A PET study of episodic memory. *Journal of Cognitive Neuroscience, 9*, 254–265.

Cabeza, R., McIntosh, A. R., Tulving, E., Nyberg, L., & Grady, C. L. (1997b). Age-related differences in effective neural connectivity during encoding and recall. *NeuroReport, 8*, 3479–3483.

Cabeza, R., & Nyberg, L. (1997). Imaging cognition: An empirical review of PET studies with normal subjects. *Journal of Cognitive Neuroscience, 9*, 1–26.

Cahill, L., Haier, R. J., Fallon, J., Alkire, M. T., Tang, C., Keator, D., Wu, J., & McGaugh, J. L. (1996). Amygdala activity at encoding correlated with long-term, free recall of emotional information. *Proceedings of the National Academy of Sciences, USA, 93*, 8016–8021.

Cohen, J. D., Perlstein, W. M., Braver, T. S., Nystrom, L. E., Noll, D. C., Jonides, J., & Smith, E. E. (1997). Temporal dynamics of brain activation during a working memory task. *Nature, 386* (10 April), 604–608.

Courtney, S. M., Ungerleider, L. G., & Haxby, J. V. (1997a). Response to Owen. *Trends in Cognitive Sciences, 1*, 125–126.

Courtney, S. M., Ungerleider, L. G., Keil, K., & Haxby, J. V. (1996). Object and spatial visual working memory activate separate neural systems in human cortex. *Cerebral Cortex, 6*, 39–49.

Courtney, S. M., Ungerleider, L. G., Keil, K., & Haxby, J. V. (1997b). Transient and sustained activity in a distributed neural system for human working memory. *Nature, 386* (10 April), 608–611.

Craik, F. I. M., Govoni, R., Naveh-Benjamin, M., & Anderson, N. D. (1996). The effects of divided attention on encoding and retrieval processes in human memory. *Journal of Experimental Psychology: General, 125(2)*, 159–180.

D'Esposito, M., Detre, J. A., Alsop, D. C., Shin, R. K., Atlas, S., & Grossman, M. (1995). The neural basis of the central executive system of working memory. *Nature, 378*, 279–281.

Dolan, R. J., & Fletcher, P. (1997). Dissociating prefrontal and hippocampal function in episodic memory encoding. *Nature, 388* (7 August), 582–585.

Dolan, R. J., Paulesu, E., & Fletcher, P. (1997). Human memory systems. In R. S. J. Frackowiak, K. J. Friston, C. D. Frith, R. J. Dolan, & J. C. Mazziotta (Eds.), *Human brain function* (pp. 367–404). Toronto: Academic Press.

Eustache, F., Rioux, P., Desgranges, B., Marchal, G., Petit-Taboué, M.-C., Dary, M., Lechevalier, B., & Baron, J.-C. (1995). Healthy aging, memory subsystems and regional cerebral oxygen consumption. *Neuropsychologia, 33*, 867–887.

Fernandez, G., Weyerts, H., Schrader-Bolsche, M., Tendolkar, I., Smid, H. G., Tempelmann, C., Hinrichs, H., Sheich, H., Elger, C. E., Mangun, G. R., & Heinze, H. J. (1998). Successful verbal encoding into episodic memory engages the posterior hippocampus: A parametrically analyzed functional magnetic resonance imaging study. *Journal of Neuroscience, 18*, 1841–1847.

Fiez, J. A., Raife, E. A., Balota, D. A., Schwarz, J. P., Raichle, M. E., & Petersen, S. E. (1996). A positron emission tomography study of the short-term maintenance of verbal information. *Journal of Neuroscience, 16*, 808–822.

Fink, G. R., Markowitsch, H. J., Reinkemeier, M., Bruckbauer, T., Kessler, J., & Heiss, W.-D. (1996). Cerebral representation of one's own past: Neural networks involved in autobiographical memory. *Journal of Neuroscience, 16*, 4275–4282.

Fletcher, P. C., Frith, C. D., Grasby, P. M., Shallice, T., Frackowiak, R. S. J., & Dolan, R. J. (1995). Brain systems for encoding and retrieval of auditory-verbal memory: An in vivo study in humans. *Brain, 118*, 401–416.

Fletcher, P. C., Frith, C. D., & Rugg, M. D. (1997). The functional neuroanatomy of episodic memory. *Trends in Neurosciences, 20*, 213–218.

Friedman, H. R., & Goldman-Rakic, P. S. (1994). Coactivation of prefrontal cortex and inferior parietal cortex in working memory tasks revealed by 2DG functional mapping in the rhesus monkey. *Journal of Neuroscience, 14*, 2775–2788.

Friston, K. J. (1997). Analysing brain images: Principles and overview. In R. S. J. Frackowiak, K. J. Friston, C. D. Frith, R. J. Dolan, & J. C. Mazziotta (Eds.), *Human brain function* (pp. 25–41). Toronto: Academic Press.

Friston, K. J., Frith, C. D., Liddle, P. F., & Frackowiak, R. S. J. (1993). Functional connectivity: The principal-component analysis of large (PET) data sets. *Journal of Cerebral Blood Flow and Metabolism, 13*, 5–14.

Friston, K. J., Homes, A. P., Worsley, K. J., Poline, J.-P., Frith, C. D., & Frackowiak, R. S. J. (1995). Statistical parametric maps in functional imaging: A general linear approach. *Human Brain Mapping, 2*, 189–210.

Fuster, J. M. (1997). Network memory. *Trends in Neurosciences, 20*, 451–459.

Gabrieli, J. D. E., Brewer, J. B., Desmond, J. E., & Glover, G. H. (1997). Separate neural bases of two fundamental memory processes in the human medial temporal lobe. *Science, 276* (11 April), 264–266.

Gevins, A., & Cutillo, B. (1993). Spatiotemporal dynamics of component processes in human working memory. *Electroencephalography and Clinical Neurophysiology, 87*, 128–143.

Goldman-Rakic, P. S. (1996). The prefrontal landscape: Implications of functional architecture for understanding human mentation and the central executive. *Philosophical Transactions of the Royal Society of London—Series B: Biological Sciences, 351*, 1445–1453.

Grady, C. L., McIntosh, A. R., Horwitz, B., Maisog, J. M., Ungerleider, L. G., Mentis, M. J., Pietrini, P., Schapiro, M. B., & Haxby, J. V. (1995). Age-related reductions in human recognition memory due to impaired encoding. *Science, 269* (14 July), 218–221.

Grasby, P. M., Frith, C. D., Friston, K., Frackowiak, R. S. J., & Dolan, R. J. (1993). Activation of the human hippocampal formation during auditory-verbal long-term memory function. *Neuroscience Letters, 163*, 185–188.

Haxby, J. V., Ungerleider, L. G., Horwitz, B., Maisog, J. M., Rapoport, S. L., & Grady, C. L. (1996). Face encoding and recognition in the human brain. *Proceedings of the National Academy of Science, 93*, 922–927.

Haxby, J. V., Ungerleider, L. G., Horwitz, B., Rapoport, S. I., & Grady, C. L. (1995). Hemispheric differences in neural systems for face working memory: A PET-rCBF study. *Human Brain Mapping, 3*, 68–82.

Heckers, S., Rauch, S. L., Goff, D., Savage, C. R., Schacter, D. L., Fischman, A. J., & Alpert, N. M. (1998). Impaired recruitment of the hippocampus during conscious recollection in schizophrenia. *Nature Neuroscience, 1*, 318–323.

Horwitz, B., McIntosh, A. R., Haxby, J. V., & Grady, C. L. (1995). Network analysis of brain cognitive function using metabolic and blood flow data. *Behavioural Brain Research, 66*, 187–193.

Kahle, W., Leonhardt, H., & Platzer, W. (1993). *Nervous System and Sensory Organs*. New York: Thieme Medical Publishers, Inc.

Kapur, S., Craik, F. I. M., Jones, C., Brown, G. M., Houle, S., & Tulving, E. (1995). Functional role of the prefrontal cortex in memory retrieval: A PET study. *NeuroReport, 6*, 1880–1884.

Kapur, S., Tulving, E., Cabeza, R., McIntosh, A. R., Houle, S., & Craik, F. I. M. (1996). The neural correlates of intentional learning of verbal materials: A PET study in humans. *Cognitive Brain Research, 4*, 243–249.

Klingberg, T., O'Sullivan, B. T., & Roland, P. E. (1997). Bilateral activation of frontoparietal networks by incrementing demand in a working memory task. *Cerebral Cortex, 7*, 465–471.

Köhler, S., McIntosh, A. R., Moscovitch, M., & Winocur, G. (1998). Functional interactions between the medial temporal lobes and posterior neocortex related to episodic memory retrieval. *Cerebral Cortex, 8*, 451–461.

Köhler, S., Moscovitch, M., Winocur, G., Houle, S., & McIntosh, A. R. (1998). Networks of domain-specific and general regions involved in episodic memory for spatial location and object identity. *Neuropsychologia, 36*, 129–142.

Kopelman, M. D., Stevens, T. G., Foli, S., & Grasby, P. (1998). PET activation of the medial temporal lobe in learning. *Brain, 121*, 875–887.

Lepage, M., Habib, R., & Tulving, E. (1998). Hippocampal PET activations of memory encoding and retrieval: The HIPER model. *Hippocampus, 8*, 313–322.

Markowitsch, H. J. (1995). Anatomical basis of memory disorders. In M. S. Gazzaniga (Ed.), *The cognitive neurosciences* (pp. 765–779). Cambridge, MA: MIT Press.

Martin, A., Haxby, J. V., Lalonde, F. M., Wiggs, C. L., & Ungerleider, L. G. (1995). Discrete cortical regions associated with knowledge of color and knowledge of action. *Science, 270* (6 October), 102–105.

McClelland, J. L., McNaughton, B. L., & O'Reilly, R. C. (1995). Why there are complementary learning systems in the hippo-campus and neocortex: Insights from the successes and failures of connectionist models of learning and memory. *Psychological Review, 102*, 419–457.

McIntosh, A. R. (1998). Understanding neural interactions in learning and memory using functional neuroimaging. *Annals of the New York Academy of Science, 855*, 556–571.

McIntosh, A. R., Bookstein, F. L., Haxby, J. V., & Grady, C. L. (1996). Spatial pattern analysis of functional brain images using partial least squares. *NeuroImage, 3*, 143–157.

McIntosh, A. R., & Gonzalez-Lima, F. (1994). Structural equation modeling and its application to network analysis in functional brain imaging. *Human Brain Mapping, 2*, 2–22.

McIntosh, A. R., Grady, C. L., Haxby, J. V., Ungerleider, L. G., & Horwitz, B. (1996). Changes in limbic and prefrontal functional interactions in a working memory task for faces. *Cerebral Cortex, 6*, 571–584.

McIntosh, A. R., Grady, C. L., Ungerleider, L. G., Haxby, J. V., Rapoport, S. I., & Horwitz, B. (1994). Network analysis of cortical visual pathways mapped with PET. *Journal of Neuroscience, 14*, 655–666.

McIntosh, A. R., Nyberg, L., Bookstein, F. L., & Tulving, E. (1997). Differential functional connectivity of prefrontal and medial temporal cortices during episodic memory retrieval. *Human Brain Mapping, 5*, 323–327.

McIntosh, A. R., Nyberg, L., & Tulving, E. (1995). What's new? Frontotemporal and hippocampocingulate functional connectivity during recognition of novel and familiar sentences. *Human Brain Mapping*, Supplement 1, 227.

McLaughlin, T., Steinberg, B., Christensen, B., Law, I., Parving, A., & Friberg, L. (1992). Potential language and attentional networks revealed through factor analysis of rCBF data measured with SPECT. *Journal of Cerebral Blood Flow and Metabolism, 12*, 535–545.

Mesulam, M.-M. (1990). Large-scale neurocognitive networks and distributed processing for attention, language, and memory. *Annals of Neurology, 28*, 597–613.

Moscovitch, M. (1992). Memory and working-with-memory: A component process model based on modules and central systems. *Journal of Cognitive Neuroscience, 4*, 257–266.

Nolde, S. F., Johnson, M. K., & Raye, C. L. (1998). The role of prefrontal cortex during tests of episodic memory. *Trends in Cognitive Sciences, 2,* 399–406.

Nyberg, L. (1996). *Identifying 'general' and 'specific' brain regions associated with episdic retrieval.* Invited presentation at the International Conference on Memory, Abano Terme, Italy, July 14–19.

Nyberg, L. (1998). Mapping episodic memory. *Behavioural Brain Research, 90,* 107–114.

Nyberg, L., Cabeza, R., & Tulving, E. (1996). PET studies of encoding and retrieval: The HERA model. *Psychonomic Bulletin & Review, 3,* 135–148.

Nyberg, L., McIntosh, A. R., Cabeza, R., Habib, R., Houle, S., & Tulving, E. (1996). General and specific brain regions involved in encoding and retrieval of events: What, where, and when. *Proceedings of the National Academy of Sciences, USA, 93,* 11280–11285.

Nyberg, L., McIntosh, A. R., Cabeza, R., Nilsson, L.-G., Houle, S., Habib, R., & Tulving, E. (1996). Network analysis of positron emission tomography regional cerebral blood flow data: Ensemble inhibition during episodic memory retrieval. *Journal of Neuroscience, 16,* 3753–3759.

Nyberg, L., McIntosh, A. R., Houle, S., Nilsson, L.-G., & Tulving, E. (1996). Activation of medial temporal structures during episodic memory retrieval. *Nature, 380* (25 April), 715–717.

Nyberg, L., Tulving, E., Habib, R., Nilsson, L.-G., Kapur, S., Houle, S., & McIntosh, A. R. (1995). Functional brain maps of retrieval mode and recovery of episodic information. *NeuroReport, 7,* 249–252.

Owen, A. M., Doyon, J., Petrides, M., & Evans, A. C. (1996). Planning and spatial working memory: A positron emission tomography study in humans. *European Journal of Neuroscience, 8,* 353–64.

Owen, A. M., Evans, A. C., & Petrides, M. (1996). Evidence for a two-stage model of spatial working memory processing within the lateral frontal cortex: A positron emission tomography study. *Cerebral Cortex, 6,* 31–38.

Passingham, R. (1997). Functional organization of the motor system. In R. S. J. Frackowiak, K. J. Friston, C. D. Frith, R. J. Dolan, & J. C. Mazziotta (Eds.), *Human brain function* (pp. 243–274). Toronto: Academic Press.

Paulesu, E., Frith, C. D., & Frackowiak, R. S. J. (1993). The neural correlates of the verbal component of working memory. *Nature, 362* (25 March), 342–345.

Petersson, K. M., Elfgren, C., & Ingvar, M. (1997). A dynamic role of the medial temporal lobe during retrieval of declarative memory in man. *Neuroimage, 6,* 1–11.

Petrides, M. (1994). Frontal lobes and working memory: Evidence from investigations of the effects of cortical excisions in nonhumans primates. In F. Boller & J. Grafman (Eds.), *Handbook of neuropsychology* (Vol. 9; pp. 59–82). Amsterdam: Elsevier.

Petrides, M. (1995). Functional organization of the human frontal cortex for mnemonic processing: Evidence from neuroimaging studies. In J. Grafman, K. J. Holyoak, & F. Boller (Eds.), *Structure and functions of the human prefrontal cortex.* (Vol. 769): *Annals of the New York Academy of Sciences, 769,* 85–96.

Petrides, M., Alivisatos, B., Evans, A. C., & Meyer, E. (1993). Dissociation of human mid-dorsolateral from posterior dorsolateral frontal cortex in memory processing. *Proceedings of the National Academy of Sciences USA, 90,* 873–877.

Petrides, M., Alivisatos, B., Meyer, E., & Evans, A. C. (1993). Functional activation of the human frontal cortex during the performance of verbal working memory tasks. *Proceedings of the National Academy of Sciences USA, 90,* 878–882.

Petrides, M., Alivisatos, B., & Evans, A. (1995). Functional activation of the human ventrolateral frontal cortex during mnemonic retrieval of verbal information. *Proceedings of the National Academy of Sciences USA, 92,* 5803–5807.

Petrides, M., & Pandya, D. N. (1994). Comparative architectonic analysis of the human and macaque frontal cortex. In F. Boller & J. Grafman (Eds.), *Handbook of neuropsychology* (Vol. 9; pp. 17–58). Amsterdam: Elsevier.

Prabhakaran, V., Smith, J. A., Desmond, J. E., Glover, G. H., & Gabrieli, J. D. (1997). Neural substrates of fluid reasoning: An fMRI study of neocortical activation during performance of the Raven's Progressive Matrices Test. *Cognitive Psychology, 33,* 43–63.

Price, C. J., & Friston, K. J. (1997). Cognitive conjunction: A new approach to brain activation experiments. *Neuroimage, 5,* 261–270.

Raichle, M. E. (1994). Visualizing the mind. *Scientific American, 270,* 58–64.

Raichle, M. E., Fiez, J. A., Videen, T. O., MacLeod, A.-M. K., Pardo, J. V., Fox, P. T., & Petersen, S. E. (1994). Practice-related changes in the human brain functional anatomy during nonmotor learning. *Cerebral Cortex, 4,* 8–26.

Roland, P. E., & Gulyas, B. (1995). Visual memory, visual imagery, and visual recognition of large field patterns by the human brain: Functional anatomy by positron emission tomography. *Cerebral Cortex, 5,* 79–93.

Rugg, M. D., Fletcher, P. C., Frith, C. D., Frackowiak, R. S. J., & Dolan, R. J. (1996). Differential activation of the prefrontal cortex in successful and unsuccessful memory retrieval. *Brain, 119,* 2073–2083.

Rugg, M. D., Fletcher, P. C., Frith, C. D., Frackowiak, R. S. J., & Dolan, R. J. (1997). Brain regions supporting intentional and incidental memory: A PET study. *NeuroReport, 8,* 1283–1287.

Schacter, D. L., Alpert, N. M., Savage, C. R., Rauch, S. L., & Albert, M. S. (1996). Conscious recollection and the human hippocampal formation. Evidence from positron emission tomography. *Proceedings of the National Academy of Sciences, USA, 93,* 321–325.

Schacter, D. L., & Buckner, R. L. (1998). Priming and the brain. *Neuron, 20,* 185–195.

Schacter, D. L., & Wagner, A. D. (1999). Medial temporal lobe activations in fMRI and PET studies of episodic encoding and retrieval. *Hippocampus, 9,* 7–24.

Schumacher, E. H., Lauber, E., Awh, E., Jonides, J., Smith, E. E., & Koeppe, R. A. (1996). PET evidence for an amodal verbal working memory system. Neuroimage, 3, 79–88.

Shallice, T. (1988). *From neuropsychology to mental structure.* Cambridge: Cambridge University Press.

Smith, E. E., Jonides, J., Koeppe, R. A., Awh, E., Schumacher, E. H., & Minoshima, S. (1995). Spatial versus object working memory: PET investigations. *Journal of Cognitive Neuroscience, 7,* 337–356.

Squire, L. R. (1992). Memory and the hippocampus: A synthesis from findings with rats, monkeys, and humans. *Psychological Review, 99,* 195–231.

Squire, L. R., & Zola-Morgan, S. (1990). The medial temporal lobe memory system. *Science, 253* (20 September), 1380–1386.

Stern, C. E., Corkin, S., Gonzalez, R. G., Guimares, A. R., Baker, J. R., Jennings, P. J., Carr, C. A., Sugiura, R. M., Vedantham, V., & Rosen, B. R. (1996). The hippocampal formation participates in novel picture encoding: Evidence from functional magnetic resonance imaging. *Proceedings of the National Academy of Sciences, USA, 93,* 8660–8665.

Tulving, E. (1983). Elements of episodic memory. New York: Oxford University Press.

Tulving, E., Kapur, S., Craik, F. I. M., Moscovitch, M., & Houle, S. (1994). Hemispheric encoding/retrieval asymmetry in episodic memory: Positron emission tomography findings. *Proceedings of the National Academy of Sciences, USA, 91,* 2016–2020.

Tulving, E., & Markowitsch, H. J. (1997). Memory beyond the hippocampus. *Current Opinion in Neurobiology, 7,* 209–216.

Tulving, E., Markowitsch, H., Craik, F. I. M., Habib, R., & Houle, S. (1996). Novelty and familiarity activations in PET studies of memory encoding and retrieval. *Cerebral Cortex, 6,* 71–79.

Tulving, E., Markowitsch, H., Kapur, S., Habib, R., & Houle, S. (1994). Novelty encoding networks in the human brain: Positron emission tomography data. *NeuroReport, 5,* 2525–2528.

Ungerleider, L. G. (1995). Functional brain imaging studies of cortical mechanisms for memory. *Science, 270* (3 November), 769–775.

Ungerleider, L. G., & Mishkin, M. (1982). Two cortical visual systems. In D. J. Ingle, M. A. Goodale, & R. J. W. Mansfield (Eds.), *Analysis of visual behavior* (pp. 549–586). Cambridge, MA: MIT Press.

Wagner, A. D., Schacter, D. L., Rotte, M., Koutstaal, W., Maril, A., Dale, A. M., Rosen, B. R., & Buckner, R. L. (1998). Building memories: Remembering and forgetting of verbal experiences as predicted by brain activity. *Science, 281,* 1188–1191.

Wilson, F. A. W., O'Scalaidhe, S. P., & Goldman-Rakic, P. S. (1993). Dissociation of object and spatial processing domains in primate prefrontal cortex. *Science, 260,* 1955–1958.

Zeki, S. (1993). *A vision of the brain.* Oxford: Blackwell Scientific Publications.

32

Event-Related Potential Studies of Memory

MICHAEL D. RUGG & KEVIN ALLAN

In this chapter we review studies employing event-related brain potentials (ERPs) to investigate the neural correlates of human long-term memory. Such studies have a relatively long history dating from the early 1980s (e.g., Sanquist, Rohrbaugh, Syndulko, & Lindsley, 1980). These early studies, along with those reported up to around 1994, are already the subject of comprehensive reviews (Johnson, 1995; Rugg, 1995a). Accordingly, we concentrate here on research published since that time, and focus on studies of retrieval from long-term memory, where progress has been both substantial and reasonably cumulative. We give only brief consideration to work on memory encoding, since there is little to add to the discussions of this topic in the two reviews cited above.

ERPs and the Study of Memory

General introductions to cognitive ERPs can be found in Kutas and Dale (1997); Picton, Lins, and Scherg (1995); and Rugg and Coles (1995a). ERPs are scalp-recorded changes in the brain's electrical activity (EEG) time-locked to some defineable event such as the presentation of a word. The magnitude of these changes is small in comparison to the amplitude of the "background" EEG, which constitutes the noise from which the ERP "signal" has to be extracted. ERP waveforms with satisfactory signal-to-noise ratios are obtained by averaging the EEG samples from a number of trials (typically, between 20 and 50) belonging to the same experimental condition. The averaged waveforms represent estimates of time-locked neural activity elicited by the presentation of stimuli belonging to different experimental conditions.

There are several reasons ERPs are useful for studying cognitive function in general, and memory in particular. First, neural activity associated with the processing of different classes of stimuli can be measured with a temporal resolution on the order of milliseconds. Thus, upper-bound estimates of the time required by the nervous system to discriminate between different classes of stimulus can be made directly. A second benefit of the ERP technique, central to the research reviewed below, is that ERP waveforms can be formed "off-line," after the experimental trials have been sorted into different conditions on the basis of the subject's behavior. Thus it is easy to obtain and compare records of brain activity associated with different classes of response to the same experimental items (e.g., hits vs. misses, or false alarms vs. correct rejections).

Finally, ERPs can be used to investigate

whether different experimental conditions engage functionally dissociable cognitive processes. This application of ERPs (see Rugg & Coles, 1995b) rests on the assumption that if two experimental conditions are associated with qualitatively different patterns of scalp electrical activity, then there are strong grounds for proposing that the conditions engaged at least partially nonoverlapping neural, and hence functional, processes. By contrast, differences in the ERPs associated with two conditions that are purely quantitative constitute evidence for different levels of engagement of the same neural/functional processes, so far as can be detected from scalp recordings.

There are important limitations to the use of ERPs in memory research. Some of these arise because ERP waveforms can only be used to study processes that are time-locked to a detectable event. For example, activities such as rehearsal or free recall are unlikely to be suitable for study with current ERP techniques, since there is no obvious event to which ERPs could be time-locked. Other limitations arise because of the difficulties involved in identifying the brain regions responsible for generating or modulating cognitive ERPs (Rugg & Coles, 1995b). Methods for localizing the generators of diffusely distributed, long-latency ERP effects of the kind that are typically found in studies of memory are poorly developed and have yet to be widely applied. Thus, it is difficult on the basis of ERP data alone to draw strong conclusions about the brain regions supporting memory-related cognitive operations.

ERPs and Memory Encoding

Memory encoding refers to the processes that mediate between the experience of an event and the formation of a memory of that experience. The approach taken by ERP experimenters to the investigation of encoding has largely involved variations on a single procedure. The essence of the procedure is the presentation of a series of items in a study task, during which EEG epochs time-locked to the presentation of each item are sampled and separately stored. Subsequently, memory for these items is tested. The EEG sampled at study is then used to form two classes of ERP, associated respectively with successfully and unsuccessfully retrieved items. These ERPs can be inspected for differences—"subsequent memory effects"

—that presumably reflect variation in the efficiency which the items were encoded.

Studies employing the above procedure were reviewed in detail by Rugg (1995a). The principal finding, first reported by Sanquist et al. (1980), is that the ERPs elicited by subsequently remembered items are more positive-going than those elicited by "forgotten" items. While this finding has been reported sufficiently frequently to demonstrate convincingly that ERPs recorded at study are sensitive to subsequent memory performance, the effect is by no means consistently found, and seems to be particularly inconsistent when the retrieval task is one of recognition rather than recall (e.g., Paller, McCarthy, & Wood, 1988). Furthermore, the scalp distribution of the "ERP subsequent memory effect" varies in a seemingly unsystematic fashion. In several studies the effect takes the form of a sustained, frontal-maximum wave. In other studies the effect has an even distribution over the midline, or a posterior maximum. Thus, whereas it is evident that multiple ERP components are involved in the subsequent memory effect, the circumstances under which each makes its contribution are unclear.

Since about 1994, ERP studies of memory encoding have largely fallen into abeyance, mainly, we suspect, because of uncertainty about the optimal conditions for eliciting reliable effects (for example, in our own laboratory we have consistently failed to find subsequent memory effects using either recognition or cued recall to test memory). Nonetheless, it is clear that ERPs can detect differences in neural activity at the time of learning that are "predictive" of subsequent memory, making such differences strong candidates as neural correlates of memory encoding. It is to be hoped that future work will elucidate the functional and neural significance of these findings. In this respect, fMRI findings of subsequent memory effects in specific brain regions, including parahippocampal and prefrontal cortices (Brewer, Zhao, Desmond, Glover, & Gabrieli, 1998; Wagner et al., 1998), are likely to be of relevance.

ERPs and Memory Retrieval

There have been numerous proposals about how memory for specific events might be fractionated. Perhaps the most widely accepted fractionation is between explicit (aware) and implicit (unaware) memory. This distinction is supported by the many studies (see Moscovitch, Vriezen, & Gottstein, 1993, for review) demonstrating that implicit memory, as assessed by performance on "indirect" memory tests (when memory for study items is incidental to task performance, and is expressed through changes in measures such as reaction time or identification accuracy), can be normal in amnesic patients exhibiting severe impairments on "direct" tests of memory such as recognition and recall. The distinction receives further support from the many studies with intact subjects in which dissociations between direct and indirect test performance have been reported (see Roediger & McDermott, 1993, for review). Findings from neuropsychological and normal studies suggest that implicit memory may further fractionate into "data-driven" and "conceptually driven" components (Roediger & McDermott, 1993). Data-driven implicit memory reflects processing overlap at early, presemantic processing stages, as evidenced by its relative insensitivity to the degree of semantic processing accorded study items, and its sensitivity to the perceptual similarity between study and test items. By contrast, conceptually driven implicit memory is a consequence of processing overlap at the semantic level and shows the reverse pattern: sensitivity to degree of semantic processing at study and insensitivity to perceptual factors.

A more controversial memory fractionation is between two forms of explicit memory—familiarity and recollection (episodic retrieval). According to the proponents of "dual process" models (e.g., Jacoby & Dallas, 1981; Jacoby & Kelley, 1992; Mandler, 1980; Richardson-Klavehn, Gardiner, & Java, 1996), these forms of memory reflect qualitatively different ways in which a retrieval cue can access information about a past episode. In the case of recollection, the retrieved memory contains contextual information about the learning episode and is accompanied by the phenomenological experience of having brought back to mind a specific past event. When memory is based upon familiarity, information about the context in which the test item was encoded and the phenomenal experience of "remembering" are both absent.

ERPs and Implicit Memory

Numerous studies, reviewed by Rugg and Doyle (1994) and Rugg (1995a), have demonstrated that ERPs elicited by items repeated

after an interval of up to a minute or so in indirect memory tasks demonstrate a positive-going shift relative to the ERP elicited by first presentations. The "ERP repetition effect" (figure 32.1) onsets around 200 msec poststimulus, and has been found in response to words, pronounceable nonwords, and pictures (see below). Interestingly, the effect is elicited neither by "orthographically illegal" nonwords nor by meaningless pictures, leading to the proposal that the effect reflects processes that operate on items that can be encoded into some form of unitized representation (Rugg & Doyle, 1994).

Given that the ERP repetition effect is elicited in indirect tasks in which there is no re-

.

LIGHT
STRAND
GRAPE
SNOW
JAGUAR
SPRING
TABLE
LIGHT
HARNESS

.
.
.

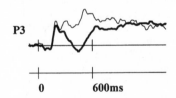

P3

0   600ms

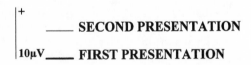

+

_____ **SECOND PRESENTATION**

10μV_____ **FIRST PRESENTATION**

Figure 32.1 Top: Part of a stimulus sequence from an indirect memory task typical of those employed to elicit the "ERP repetition effect." In this example, the task is to respond promptly to animal names (e.g., *Jaguar*) and to withhold responses to all other stimuli. Bottom: The "ERP repetition effect." Waveforms elicited by first and second presentations from a left superior parietal electrode (P3) during a task similar to that illustrated (Rugg and Nieto-Vegas, 1999).

quirement for intentional memory, it is tempting to interpret the effect as a neural correlate of implicit memory. As has been noted previously (Rugg, 1995a), however, the identification of an electrophysiological correlate of implicit memory requires more than the demonstration that ERPs vary in an indirect memory test according to the study status of the items. It is also necessary to show that the ERP effect does not reflect "incidental" or "involuntary" explicit memory for the test items (Bowers & Schacter, 1990). Because of the difficulty in satisfying this requirement it is difficult to conclude that any aspect of "ERP repetition effects" reflects implicit memory.

More recent work has attempted to overcome this problem by employing experimental manipulations known to have dissociative effects on data-driven implicit memory and explicit memory. The demonstration that an ERP memory effect is modulated by the same variables that selectively influence behavioral manifestations of implicit memory would greatly diminish the likelihood that the effect correlated with explicit memory for the test items.

One such variable is sensory modality. As assessed on a variety of indirect tasks, implicit memory is weaker when study and test items are presented in different modalities than when modality is held constant (Roediger & McDermott, 1993). In a series of studies (Rugg, Doyle, & Melan, 1993; Rugg, Doyle, & Wells, 1995; Rugg & Neito-Vegas, 1999) subjects were presented with a series of auditorally and visually presented words, some of which repeated a few items later in either the same or the alternative modality. The subjects' task was to detect and respond to occasional "target" words (animal names), and to withhold responses to the nontarget items (the items of experimental interest). Figure 32.2 illustrates the finding common to all studies. While visual-visual repetition gave rise to the "standard" ERP repetition effect, auditory-visual repetition resulted in the attenuation of the early part of this effect, most markedly over frontal and temporal scalp sites.

These findings demonstrate the existence of neural activity occurring around 200–400 msec poststimulus that is both repetition and modality sensitive, characteristics to be expected of a neural correlate of data-driven implicit memory. One possibility is that the effect reflects the modulation of perceptual processes that contribute to data-driven implicit memory for words and word-like stimuli. This hypothesis receives support from the finding (Doyle, Rugg, & Wells, 1997) that "formal" priming (e.g., *scan–scandal*), nonword repetition (e.g., *blint*; Rugg & Nagy, 1987) and word repetition all have similar effects on ERPs in the latency range occupied by the modality-sensitive effects illustrated in figure 32.2. Together with the finding that ERP repetition effects are absent for "orthographically illegal" nonwords (Rugg & Nagy, 1987), these observations suggest that the early part of the ERP repetition effect reflects the functioning of the domain-specific "perceptual representation systems" proposed by Tulving and Schacter (1990; see also Schacter, 1994) to underlie data-driven priming.

Other findings also suggest that the neural activity reflected in ERP repetition effects may, in part, reflect implicit memory. Paller and associates (Paller, Kutas, & McIssac, 1998; Paller & Gross, 1998) investigated the sensitivity of ERP repetition effects to changes in the visual format of words presented in the study and test phases of indirect tasks. These changes were intended to diminish implicit memory by reducing study-test overlap at the level of visual form. Relative to the effects elicited by words presented in the same format at study and test, format change led to a reduction in the size of the ERP repetition effects that were recorded from occipital scalp regions between approximately 400 and 500 msec post-stimulus.

The ERP correlates of implicit memory can also be investigated in direct memory tests, by contrasting ERPs elicited by studied items that subjects misclassified as new (misses) with those elicited by new items correctly judged as such. On the assumption that studied items are "missed" only when they fail to elicit explicit memory, differences between these two classes of ERP are strong candidates as neural correlates of implicit memory retrieval. This approach has two advantages over studies that investigate implicit memory with indirect tests. First, the problem of "contamination" of ERPs by explicit memory is minimal; the critical items are those not remembered explicitly at the time the ERPs were recorded. Second, the approach allows the neural correlates of implicit and explicit memory to be contrasted in the same memory test. This is important because almost all studies that have sought to dissociate brain activity associated with implicit and explicit memory have contrasted findings from direct and indirect tests. Since memory retrieval is intentional on direct tests,

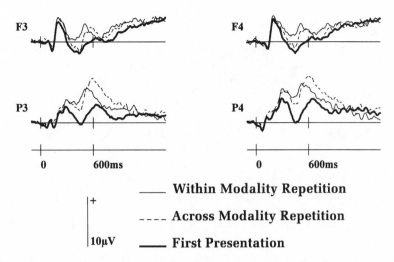

F3 F4

P3 P4

0   600ms   0   600ms

+

10µV

_____ **Within Modality Repetition**

_ _ _ _ **Across Modality Repetition**

_____ **First Presentation**

Figure 32.2 ERPs elicited by the immediate repetition of visually presented words, illustrating the differential effects of repetition within and across modality. Modality-dependent repetition effects are evident between approximately 250–400 msec poststimulus, especially at lateral frontal electrodes (F3, F4). (From Rugg and Nieto-Vegas, 1998.)

but unintentional on indirect tests, such studies confound retrieval intentionality with type of memory.

A study along these lines was described by Rugg, Mark et al. (1998b). Subjects studied a series of words under either "deep" or "shallow" encoding conditions, and were subsequently tested for their recognition memory of these words. While more than 90% of the deeply studied words were recognized, this was true for only 50% of the shallowly studied items, permitting ERPs to be formed for both shallow "hits" and shallow "misses." At posterior locations, the ERPs to both classes of old word were more positive-going than those to correct rejections (see figure 32.3). This finding represents a "pure" repetition effect—a modulation of neural activity by recently experienced words that is unaffected by whether the words were explicitly recognized. A very similar ERP modulation was found in the posterior ERPs that were elicited by deeply studied test items (see figure 32.3). Thus, despite the marked differences among the three classes of ERP after 500 msec poststimulus, "shallow misses," "shallow hits" and "deep hits" were associated with an equivalent, early (ca. 300–500 msec), posteriorly distributed effect.

These findings suggest that ERPs can detect neural activity associated with implicit memory for recently experienced words. They further suggest that this activity is topographically dissociable from that associated with explicit memory and detected at the same time at more anterior electrode sites (see figure 32.3). It is worth noting, however, that while the results show that the neural correlates of implicit memory can exist independently of the correlates of explicit memory, the reverse dissociation has not been demonstrated. If such a dissociation can be found, it will provide support for the view that the two forms of memory are independent (cf. Joordens & Merikle, 1993, and Jacoby, Toth, Yonelinas, & Debner, 1994).

In summary, the view (Rugg, 1995a) that there are no convincing examples of ERP correlates of implicit memory is no longer tenable. ERP repetition effects in indirect tasks are sensitive to the degree of perceptual match between study and test items, mimicking the sensitivity of data-driven implicit memory to this variable. Furthermore, there is evidence that ERPs are sensitive to the repetition of items for which recognition failed, and for which explicit memory was therefore either very weak or absent. It will be of considerable interest to see whether any of the brain regions responsible for generating these ERP repeti-

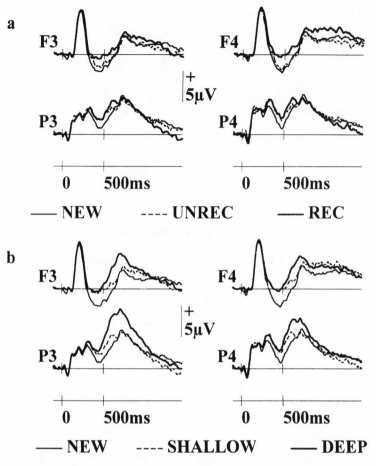

Figure 32.3 ERPs from Rugg, Mark, Walla et al. (1998), shown for lateral frontal (F3,F4) and parietal (P3,P4) sites. A—waveforms elicited by correctly rejected new items (*new*), and by recognized (*rec*) and unrecognized (*unrec*) shallowly studied items. Note the similarity at the parietal sites of the early differences between the ERPs to new items and those to each class of old item. B—waveforms elicited by correctly rejected new items, and recognized items accorded either deep or shallow study.

tion effects correspond to the repetition-sensitive brain regions identified in functional neuroimaging studies of implicit memory (for review see Schacter & Buckner, 1998).

It will also be of interest to see whether ERPs can be shown to be sensitive to conceptually driven implicit memory, as has been claimed for functional neuroimaging measures of brain activity (Demb et al., 1995). The lack of experimental variables that exert clear dissociative effects on explicit memory and conceptually driven implicit memory (e.g., depth of study processing is held to exert parallel ef-

fects on these two forms of memory) means that this may prove a difficult task.

ERPs and Explicit Memory Retrieval

Recognition Memory and Related Tasks

Numerous studies have demonstrated that event-related potentials elicited by words presented in tests of recognition memory differ according to the words' study status (see the reviews by Johnson, 1995, and Rugg, 1995a). The findings from these studies have consistently shown that, in comparison to words correctly judged to be new, the ERPs elicited by correctly detected old words demonstrate a positive-going deflection—the *left parietal ERP old/new effect*—an example of which is shown in figure 32.4. This effect onsets approximately 400 msec poststimulus, lasts around 400–600 msec, and is largest in amplitude over left temporo-parietal regions of the scalp. Because of its specificity for items correctly judged old, it has been argued (Rugg, 1995a) that the effect reflects brain activity contributing to, or contingent upon, the retrieval of information necessary to permit accurate recognition judgments.

More detailed proposals about the functional significance of the ERP old/new effect have been framed mainly in the context of dual process models of recognition memory (see "ERPs and Memory Retrieval"), and have focused on whether the effect is associated more closely with familiarity or recollection. An early proposal (Rugg & Doyle, 1992) was that the old/new effect was a correlate of familiarity-based recognition. This proposal was motivated by the finding that the effect is larger when it is elicited by low-frequency words than by high-frequency words, and depends critically on the assumption that old low-frequency words engender higher levels of familiarity at test than do old high-frequency items (as supposedly evidenced by the word frequency effect on recognition memory; Jacoby & Dallas, 1981; Mandler, 1980). The

hypothesis was seriously undermined by findings showing that the word frequency effect is at least partly attributable to the superior recollection of low-frequency words (e.g., Gardiner & Java, 1990). As will become apparent, it now appears that the old/new ERP effect is in fact closely associated with recognition based on recollection.

Early findings in favor of this idea were reported in two studies that appeared around the same time as that of Rugg and Doyle (1992). Using the remember/know procedure (Tulving, 1985), Smith (1993) found that old/new effects were almost twice as great for ERPs elicited by recognized items associated with "remember" responses as they were for effects associated with "know" responses, leading him to argue that the effects were closely tied to the recollective component of recognition. Paller and Kutas (1992) arrived at a similar conclusion on the basis of their finding that the old/new effect was sensitive to a "depth of processing" manipulation at study, a manipulation they considered to act selectively on recollection.

The research discussed above demonstrates that ERPs are sensitive to the study status of items in recognition memory tests. However, these early findings leave open the question of the functional significance of ERP old/new effects. For example, the findings of Smith (1993) are ambiguous because the remember/ know distinction was associated with a quantitative, rather than a qualitative ERP difference. And the findings of Paller and Kutas (1992) are predicated on the assumption that depth of processing has a selective influence

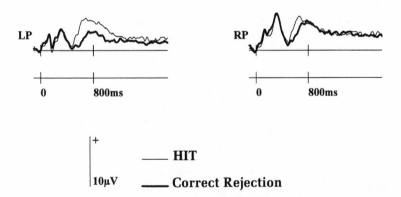

Figure 32.4 The "left parietal old/new ERP effect." ERPs from left and right parietal (LP,RP) electrodes elicited by correctly classified old and new words in a recognition memory test. Data from Allan and Rugg (1997).

on recollection (for evidence to the contrary, see Toth, 1996). More recent studies have, therefore, continued to focus on whether ERPs elicited by different classes of item in direct memory tests can dissociate different processes supporting recognition.

One way in which these putative processes can be dissociated is by employing a test of source memory. Source memory refers to memory for contextual attributes of a study episode, such as when and where it occurred and the format in which study items were presented. By definition, the accurate retrieval of such information depends upon recollection, with recognition in the absence of contextual retrieval supported either by familiarity or weak recollection.

Following this reasoning, Wilding and colleagues (Wilding, Doyle, & Rugg, 1995; Wilding & Rugg, 1996, 1997) employed tasks that allowed ERPs to correctly recognize old items to be separated according to the accuracy of a subsequent source judgment. As noted above, according to the dual-process framework, trials on which source memory was successful would be more likely to involve recollection than would trials on which memory for source was unsuccessful. Qualitative differences between the ERPs elicited by these two categories of recognized item would therefore constitute evidence that recognition memory has two functionally distinct bases.

In Wilding, Doyle, and Rugg (1995), subjects performed a lexical decision task in which half of the stimuli were presented auditorily and the remainder visually. In the subsequent test phase subjects were presented with a sequence of studied and unstudied words in one modality only. Subjects made a speeded old/new decision to each word, and, for each word judged old, a second judgment as to whether the word had been seen or heard at study. The left parietal old/new effects elicited by recognized words accorded correct and incorrect source judgments were greater in magnitude for correct judgments, but there was no evidence of any qualitative difference in their scalp topographies. Consequently, the findings offer no support for the view that recognition with and without retrieval of source depends upon different processes.

Wilding and Rugg (1996) employed the same basic procedure, but with the requirement to discriminate between visually presented test words spoken at study in one of two voices. ERP old/new effects for recognized words attracting correct source judgments were greater than the effects for words

attracting incorrect judgments, but again the two classes of effect did not differ qualitatively. Thus these findings also provide little support for the view that qualitatively distinct processes support recognition memory with and without retrieval of source.

In an important departure from previous studies, Wilding and Rugg (1996) found that the ERP old/new effects elicited in their experiments on voice memory involved two separate ERP modulations, dissociable on the basis of their time courses and their scalp distributions. The first of these ERP modulations corresponded to the left parietal old/new effect identified in previous ERP studies of recognition memory and discussed above. The second effect onset at a similar latency, but was considerably more sustained in time, and showed an amplitude maximum over the right frontal scalp. We refer to this effect as the *right frontal old/new effect*. Both effects can be seen in figure 32.5.

Findings analogous to those of Wilding and colleagues were reported by Donaldson and Rugg (1998), who investigated the ERP correlates of associative recognition. Subjects were presented at study with pairs of words. At test, they were again presented with word pairs, which were either new, representations of original study pairs, or repairings of study items. On the basis of previous research (Yonelinas, 1997), Donaldson and Rugg assumed that words that maintained their pairing between study and test (*same* pairs) would be more likely to elicit recollection than rearranged pairs, and that recognition of rearranged pairs would be more likely to be familiarity-based. As illustrated in figure 32.6, left parietal and right frontal ERP effects were larger when elicited by same than by rearranged pairs. There was, however, no evidence that the memory effects elicited by the rearranged pairs differed qualitatively from those elicited by same pairs.

In sum, the findings from the studies reviewed above (see also Wilding & Rugg, 1997) offer little support for dual-process models of recognition memory. The findings support the alternative view that recognition based on "familiarity" is better conceived of as impoverished recollection rather than as an independent basis for recognition (Johnson, Hashtroudi, & Lindsay, 1993; Mulligan & Hirshman, 1997).

The conclusion that the neural correlates of recollection and familiarity differ in degree only is qualified, however, by the findings from two studies in which a dissociation be-

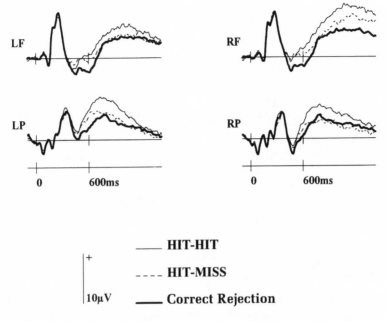

HIT-HIT

HIT-MISS

Correct Rejection

Figure 32.5 Data from Wilding and Rugg (1996, exp. 2) illustrating ERPs from lateral frontal and parietal electrodes elicited during a source memory test by words correctly classified as new (*correct rejections*), recognized and assigned to the incorrect study context (*hit-miss*), or recognized and assigned to the correct study context (*hit-hit*). Left parietal and right frontal effects, each larger for hit-hit than hit-miss items, are clearly evident.

tween the ERP correlates of recollection and familiarity may have been obtained. Düzel, Yonelinas, Mangun, Heinze, and Tulving (1997) employed the remember/know procedure to distinguish between trials on which recognition was associated with the presence or absence of a "recollective experience." In contrast to the first ERP study to employ this procedure (Smith, 1993), Düzel et al. (1997) reported that ERPs elicited by recognized words accorded either a remember or a know judgment differed qualitatively from approximately 300 to 1000 msec poststimulus. These findings suggest that, as operationalized by the remember/know procedure, recognition based upon recollection and familiarity are electrophysiologically dissociable. It will be of interest to see whether this finding generalizes to other tasks thought to be capable of dissociating the bases of recognition.

The second study to suggest that familiarity and recollection can be dissociated electrophysiologically is that of Rugg, Mark et al. (1998) described in the section "ERPs and Implicit Memory". As shown in figure 32.3, between about 300 and 500 msec poststimulus, ERPs from frontal electrodes were more posi-

tive-going for recognized old words than they were for items that were correctly rejected or missed. Unlike the prominent memory effects arising after about 500 msec, this frontal effect was insensitive to depth of study processing. These findings therefore provide evidence for two qualitatively distinct patterns of neural activity associated with successful recognition: one frontally distributed, onsetting early, and insensitive to depth of study encoding; the other parietally distributed, later in onset, and sensitive to encoding task. If one takes the view that depth of processing exclusively influences recollection (e.g., Gardiner, Java, & Richardson-Klavehn, 1996), the ERP findings provide powerful evidence that familiarity and recollection have distinct neural correlates. Unfortunately, evidence is accumulating to suggest that depth of processing does not dissociate the two putative components of recognition memory (e.g., Toth, 1996; Yonelinas, Kroll, Dobbins, & Lazzara, 1998), leaving the interpretation of these ERP findings uncertain.

In summary, the findings of Wilding and colleagues and Donaldson and Rugg (1998) offer no support for the view that the neural correlates of recognition differ qualitatively

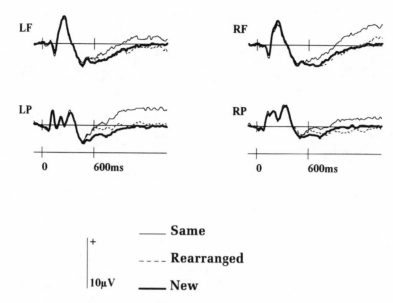

+

10μV

—— Same

---- Rearranged

—— New

Figure 32.6 ERPs from lateral frontal and parietal electrodes from the associative recognition task of Donaldson and Rugg (1998, exp. 1). *New*—correctly rejected new pairs; *Same*—word pairs that maintained their pairing between study and test, and which were correctly classified as such; *Rearranged*—word pairs that were rearranged between study and test, and correctly classified as such.

according to whether recognition is accompanied by retrieval of the encoding context. The results of other studies (Düzel et al., 1997; Rugg, Mark et al., 1998) provide grounds for modifying this conclusion but require replication and generalization. On a more positive note the findings reviewed in this section suggest that ERPs are sensitive to the *amount* of contextual information that is retrieved, in as much as ERP memory effects are larger when successful item memory is accompanied by accurate rather than inaccurate source memory. This in turn suggests that ERPs index processes that are engaged during, or as a consequence of, successful retrieval of episodic information about a prior event.

ERPs and Episodic Retrieval

Left Parietal and Right Frontal Effects

As already noted, the ERP memory effects associated with successful recollection (as operationalized in source memory and associative recognition tasks) are manifest as at least two positive-going modulations of the waveform—the left parietal and right frontal effects—dis-

sociable on both temporal and neuroanatomical criteria (Allan, Wilding, & Rugg, 1998). The different spatiotemporal characteristics of these two memory effects led Wilding and Rugg (1996) to suggest that they reflect distinct cognitive operations. Wilding and Rugg proposed that these operations involve (1) the retrieval of item and contextual information from memory, operations supported by the "medial temporal lobe memory system" (Squire, 1992); and (2) processing the products of retrieval to generate an episodic representation capable of supporting accurate source discrimination, operations dependent upon the prefrontal cortex (see Squire, Knowlton, & Musen, 1993). Wilding and Rugg (1996) linked the left parietal effect to the first of these operations, and the right frontal effect with the second, "post-retrieval" operation.

The idea that the left parietal effect indexes the contribution of the medial temporal lobe to episodic memory retrieval fits well with the findings of the research reviewed in the preceding section, and receives additional support from studies in which the ERP correlates of "false recollection" (Roediger & McDermott, 1995) were investigated. False recollection refers to the tendency of subjects in recognition memory tests to false alarm to unstudied, strong associates of study items, and to endorse such responses as remembered. Unlike ordinary false alarms, false recollections are held to depend on the engagement of the same neural system, including the hippocampus, that supports "true" recollection (Schacter et al., 1996). Thus the finding (Düzel et al., 1997; Johnson et al., 1997) that ERPs elicited by "falsely recollected" items elicit a prominent left parietal effect, comparable in magnitude to the effect elicited by items correctly endorsed as old, is consistent with the idea that this effect is a correlate of hippocampally mediated memory retrieval.

In linking the left parietal effect to retrieval operations supported by the medial temporal lobes, we are not implying that the effect originates from these regions. Indeed, current evidence suggests that neural activity in the hippocampal formation makes, at best, a very modest contribution to scalp-recorded potentials (Rugg, 1995b). A more likely possibility (Wilding & Rugg, 1996) is that the effect reflects stimulus-locked changes in cortical activity resulting from the cortico-hippocampal interactions that have been proposed to underlie episodic memory retrieval (e.g., McClelland, McNaughton, & O'Reilly, 1995).

The lack of direct methods for localizing ERP generators makes it difficult formally to test this hypothesis. Indirect evidence comes from a PET study of the effects at retrieval of study depth of processing (Rugg, Fletcher, Frith, Frackowiak, & Dolan, 1997; Rugg, Walla et al., 1998). Relative to recognition of items subjected to "shallow" study, Rugg et al. (1997) found that recognition of deeply studied items was associated with greater activation in both the left hippocampal formation and several regions of the temporal and frontal cortex of the left hemisphere. This result parallels the finding that the left parietal effect is greater when elicited by test words subjected to deep rather than shallow study (figure 32.3 and Rugg, 1998). Rugg, Walla et al. (1998) conjectured that the left parietal effect is the electrophysiological correlate of the left cortical activations identified in their PET data.

The proposal that the right frontal effect reflects "postretrieval" processing receives support from both functional and neuroanatomical evidence. The idea that the products of memory retrieval are subjected to such operations as monitoring or evaluation, and that the need for such operations varies with task demands, is central to some functional models of memory retrieval (Koriat & Goldsmith, 1996;

Shallice, 1988). On the basis of such models one might well expect to find a neural correlate of memory retrieval that is task-sensitive, onsets relatively late, and is sustained over time, all characteristics of the right frontal memory effect. Furthermore, the nature of the memory impairments that follow lesions of the prefrontal cortex suggests that this region has a key role in supporting postretrieval processes (e.g., Shallice, 1988).

The hypothesis that the right frontal effect reflects the engagement of the right prefrontal cortex during episodic retrieval receives further support from the findings of PET and fMRI studies, which have consistently demonstrated activation of this region during episodic retrieval tasks (Fletcher, Frith, & Rugg, 1997). An apparent disparity between PET and ERP findings arises from the claim (Kapur et al., 1995; Nyberg et al., 1995) that, in recognition memory tasks, right prefrontal activation is insensitive to whether test items elicit successful retrieval, and reflects instead the adoption of a tonically maintained retrieval "mode" that does not vary with the study status of the test items. This claim is incompatible with the proposal that the right frontal ERP old/new effect reflects neural activity in the right prefrontal cortex, as the effect evidently reflects neural activity that varies according to whether a test item elicits memory retrieval. The claim is contradicted however, by two other PET studies of recognition memory in which right prefrontal activity was found to vary according to the probability of successful retrieval (Rugg, Fletcher, Frith, Frackowiak, & Dolan, 1996; Rugg, Fletcher et al., 1998).

Cued Recall

The experiments described above have all investigated the ERP correlates of recollection by employing "copy" cues to elicit episodic memory retrieval. It is, of course, also possible to employ retrieval cues that provide only an incomplete specification of study item(s). A widely used task that does just this is word-stem cued recall, in the simplest version of which subjects are required to retrieve study words in response to three-letter (stem) cues (e.g., *motel* → mot _). As demonstrated in a recent series of studies (Allan, Doyle, & Rugg, 1996; Allan & Rugg, 1997, 1998), the ERP correlates of recollection engendered by such cues differ somewhat from those described in the foregoing paragraphs. All of these studies employed the same basic procedure; after studying a word list, a series of stems was pre-sented, only a proportion of which corres-ponded to study items. Subjects were in-structed to attempt to retrieve a study word in response to each stem and, following a re-sponse cue, either to provide a study word if they could, or to provide the first word to come to mind. Crucially, subjects were re-quired to accompany these responses by a judgment of whether the word they provided belonged to the study list. On the basis of these responses, it was possible to separate stems correctly completed by study words ac-cording to whether the completion was im-plicit (in which case it would be associated with the judgment that the item had not ap-peared at study) or whether it was accompa-nied by explicit memory for the study presen-tation.

The central finding from these studies is il-lustrated in figure 32.7, which contrasts wave-forms (from Allan & Rugg, 1998) elicited by stems completed with explicitly retrieved study words as opposed to unstudied items. The ERPs to the stems corresponding to the studied items show a positive-going ERP mod-ulation that onsets around 300 msec and con-tinues until the end of the recording epoch. Figure 32.8 shows the changing scalp distribu-tion of the memory effects evident in these data, which evolve from an initial anterior midline focus to include another, left tem-poro-parietal, maximum, before shifting back to a (right) anterior focus. Allan, Doyle, and Rugg (1996) reported that these memory ef-fects are absent in both ERPs elicited by stems completed with unstudied items falsely recog-nized as belonging to a study list, and in ERPs elicited by correct completions not recognized as such. These findings suggest that the ERP differences evident in figure 32.7 are a rela-tively pure reflection of episodic memory for the studied words. This proposal is further strengthened by the findings of Allan and Rugg (1998). They presented study items in one of two lists, and required subjects both to retrieve studied items and to assign these items to the correct study list. The distribution of the memory effects for correctly completed stems that were assigned to the correct list was qualitatively indistinguishable from the ef-fects elicited by stems attracting an incorrect list assignment. It would thus appear that the processes supporting memory for the encod-

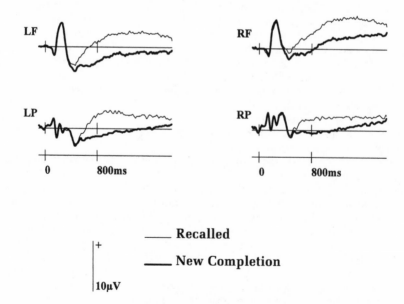

____ Recalled

____ New Completion

10μV

Figure 32.7 ERPs from lateral frontal and parietal electrodes elicited by word stems in the study of Allan and Rugg (1998). ERPs are shown for stems correctly completed with items judged to have been shown at study, collapsed across a subsequent source (study list) judgment (*recalled*), and for stems completed with unstudied items correctly endorsed as "new" (*new completion*).

400-700 msec   **800-1100 msec**   **1200-1500 msec**

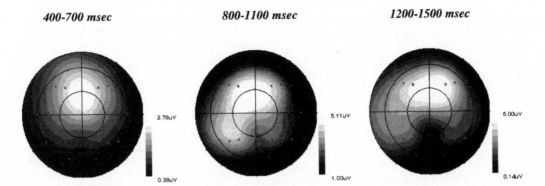

Figure 32.8 Topographic maps illustrating the scalp distribution of the cued recall memory effects in the data from Allan and Rugg (1998). Each map depicts the differences between ERPs evoked by stems correctly completed with studied items, collapsed across the subsequent source judgment, and ERPs evoked by stems completed with unstudied items correctly endorsed as "new." Maps are shown for three latency regions, 400–700msec, 800–1100msec, and 1200–1500msec.

ing context were functionally equivalent to those supporting the ability explicitly to retrieve the study items, a finding which parallels the results from ERP studies of source memory employing copy cues (see "ERPs and Explicit Memory Retrieval").

The findings from these studies of cued recall are important for two reasons. First, the findings speak to the question of the mechanism of cued recall, militating against the idea that successful retrieval on this task usually reflects the outcome of a "generate-recognize" strategy, whereby a candidate completion is first generated and then subjected to a recognition. Such a mechanism should be slower acting than recognition of the study word in its entirety, because of the time consumed by the additional process of generating candidate completions. The onset latencies of the old/new effects for recognition memory and cued recall are, however, extremely close to each other in time (Allan & Rugg, 1997), indicating that a word stem can elicit explicit retrieval virtually as quickly as a whole word. These findings are in keeping with the proposal (Toth, Reingold, & Jacoby, 1994) that explicit cued recall usually reflects the outcome of a direct retrieval process.

Second, the cued-recall findings indicate that recollection is associated with more than one pattern of ERP memory effects. While the effects for cued recall appear to include contributions from the generators of the left parietal and right frontal effects discussed previously, these effects are distributed more diffusely over the scalp than those elicited by copy cues (Allan & Rugg, 1997). Thus the findings raise the possibility that while the left parietal and right frontal effects reflect cognitive operations engaged by many tasks that elicit recollection, other more task-specific effects also exist. Dissociating these two classes of effect, and elucidating their functional and neural significance, will be an important task for future research.

Concluding Comments

We hope that readers agree with us that ERP data, especially when obtained from tasks similar to those employed by researchers using behavioral and neuropsychological methods, provide a unique perspective on the functional organization and relative timing of the component processes underlying human memory. And although seriously hampered by the lack of methods for localizing the sources of memory-related ERP effects, the existing data have none the less yielded some insights into the neural bases of different memory functions. These insights are likely to grow significantly as localization methods improve and, in particular, as ways are developed formally to incorporate functional neuroimaging data into ERP source solutions (Rugg, 1998). Indeed, we suspect that over the next few years the distinction—adhered to in the present volume—between electrophysiological and haemodynamic studies of memory will become increasingly artificial.

Acknowledgments The authors' research is supported by the Wellcome Trust and the Biotechnology and Biological Sciences Research Council (UK).

References

Allan, K., Doyle, M. C., & Rugg, M. D. (1996). An event-related potential study of word-stem cued recall. *Cognitive Brain Research, 4*, 251–262.

Allan, K., & Rugg, M. D. (1997). An event-related potential study of explicit memory on tests of word-stem cued recall and recognition memory. *Neuropsychologia, 35*, 387–397.

Allan, K., & Rugg, M. D. (1998). Neural correlates of cued recall with and without retrieval of source memory. *Neuroreport, 9*, 3463–3466.

Allan, K., Wilding, E. L., & Rugg, M. D. (1998). Electrophysiological evidence for dissociable processes contributing to recollection. *Acta Psychologica, 98*, 231–252.

Bowers, J. S., & Schacter, D. L. (1990). Implicit memory and test awareness. *Journal of Experimental Psychology: Learning, Memory and Cognition, 16*, 404–416.

Brewer, J. B., Zhao, Z., Desmond, J. E., Glover, G. H., & Gabrieli, J. D. (1998). Making memories: Brain activity that predicts how well visual experience will be remembered. *Science, 281*, 1185–1187.

Demb, J. B., Desmond, J. E., Wagner, A. D., Vaidya, C. J., Glover, G. H., & Gabrieli, J. D. E. (1995). Semantic encoding and retrieval in the left inferior prefrontal cortex: A functional MRI study of task difficulty and process specificity. *Journal of Neuroscience, 15*, 5870–5878.

Donaldson, D. I., & Rugg, M. D. (1998). Recognition memory for new associations: Electrophysiological evidence for the role of recollection. *Neuropsychologia, 37*, 377–396.

Doyle, M. C., Rugg, M. D., & Wells, T. (1997). A comparison of the electrophysiological effects of formal and repetition priming. *Psychophysiology, 33*, 132–147.

Düzel, E., Yonelinas, A. P., Mangun, G. R., Heinze, H. J., & Tulving, E. (1997). Event-related brain potential correlates of two states of conscious awareness in memory. *Proceedings of the National Academy of Sciences USA, 94*, 5973–5978.

Fletcher, P. C., Frith, C. D., & Rugg, M. D. (1997). The functional neuroanatomy of episodic memory. *Trends in Neuroscience, 20*, 213–218.

Gardiner, J. M., & Java, R. I. (1990). Recollective experience in word and non-word recognition. *Memory and Cognition, 18*, 23–30.

Gardiner, J. M., Java, R. I., & Richardson-Klavehn, A. (1996). How level of processing really influences awareness in recognition memory. *Canadian Journal of Experimental Psychology, 50*, 114–122.

Jacoby, L. L., & Dallas, M. (1981). On the relationship between autobiographical memory and perceptual learning. *Journal of Experimental Psychology: General, 3*, 306–340.

Jacoby, L. L., & Kelley, C. (1992). Unconscious influences of memory: Dissociations and automaticity. In A. D. Milner & M. D. Rugg (Eds.), *The neuropsychology of consciousness* (pp. 201–233). UK: Academic Press.

Jacoby, L. L., Toth, J. P., & Yonelinas, A. P. (1993). Separating conscious and unconscious influences of memory: Measuring recollection. *Journal of Experimental Psychology: General, 122*, 139–154.

Jacoby, L. L., Toth, J. P., Yonelinas, A. P., & Debner, J. A. (1994). The relationship between conscious and unconscious influences—independence or redundancy? *Journal of Experimental Psychology: General, 123*, 216–219.

Johnson, M. K., Hashtroudi, S., & Lindsay, D. S. (1993). Source monitoring. *Psychological Bulletin, 114*, 3–28.

Johnson, M. K., Nolde, S. F., Mather, M., Kounios, J., Schacter, D. L., & Curran, T. (1997). The similarity of brain activity associated with true and false recognition memory depends on test format. *Psychological Science, 8*, 250–257.

Johnson, R. (1995). Event-related potential insights into the neurobiology of memory systems. In J. C. Boller & J. Grafman (Eds.), *Handbook of neuropsychology* (Vol. 10; pp. 135–164). Amsterdam: Elsevier.

Joordens, S., & Merikle, P. M. (1993). Independence and redundancy? Two models of conscious and unconscious influences. *Journal of Experimental Psychology: General, 122*, 462–267.

Kapur, S., Craik, F. I. M., Jones, C., Brown, G. M., Houle, S., & Tulving, E. (1995). Functional role of the prefrontal cortex in retrieval of memories—a PET study. *Neuroreport, 14*, 1880–1884.

Koriat, A., & Goldsmith, M. (1996). Monitoring and control processes in the strategic regulation of memory accuracy. *Psychological Review, 103*, 490–517.

Kutas, M., & Dale, A. (1997). Electrical and magnetic readings of mental functions. In M. D. Rugg (Ed.), *Cognitive neuroscience* (pp. 197–242). Hove, UK: Psychology Press.

Mandler, G. (1980). Recognising: The judgment of previous occurrence. *Psychological Review, 87*, 252–271.

McClelland, J. L., McNaughton, B. L., & O'Reilly, R. C. (1995). Why are there complementary learning systems in the hippocampus and neocortex: Insights from the successes and failures of connectionist models of learning and memory. *Psychological Review, 102*, 419–457.

Moscovitch, M., Vriezen, E., & Gottstein, J. (1993). Implicit tests of memory in patients with focal lesions or degenerative brain disorders. In H. Spinnler & J. Boller (Eds.), *The handbook of neuropsychology* (Vol. 9; pp. 133–178). Amsterdam: Elsevier.

Mulligan, N. W., & Hirshman, E. (1997). Measuring the bases of recognition memory: An investigation of the process-dissociation framework. *Journal of Experimental Psychology: Learning, Memory and Cognition, 23*, 280–304.

Neville, H. J., Kutas, M., Chesney, G., & Schmidt, A. L. (1986). Event-related brain potentials during initial encoding and recognition memory of congruous and incongruous words. *Journal of Memory and Language, 25*, 75–92.

Nyberg, L., Tulving, E., Habib, R., Nilsson, L.-G., Kapur, S., Houle, S., Cabeza, R., & McIntosh, A. R. (1995). Functional brain maps of retrieval mode and recovery of episodic information. *Neuroreport, 7*, 249–252.

Paller, K. A., & Gross, M. (1998). Brain potentials associated with perceptual priming versus explicit remembering during the repetition of visual word-form. *Neuropsychologia, 6*, 559–571.

Paller, K. A., & Kutas, M. (1992). Brain potentials during retrieval provide neurophysiological support for the distinction between conscious recollection and priming. *Journal of Cognitive Neuroscience, 4*, 375–391.

Paller, K. A., Kutas, M., & McIsaac, H. K. (1998). An electrophysiological measure of priming of visual word-form. *Consciousness and Cognition, 7*, 54–66.

Paller, K. A., McCarthy, G., & Wood, C. C. (1988). ERPs predictive of subsequent recall and recognition performance. *Biological Psychology, 26*, 269–276.

Picton, T. W., Lins, O. G., & Scherg, M. (1995). The recording and analysis of event-related potentials. In J. C. Boller & J. Grafman (Eds.), *Handbook of neuropsychology* (Vol. 10; pp. 429–499). Amsterdam: Elsevier.

Richardson-Klavehn, A., Gardiner, J. M., & Java, R. I. (1996). Memory: Task dissociations, process dissociations and dissociations of consciousness. In G. Underwood (Ed.), *Implicit cognition* (pp. 85–158). Oxford, UK: Oxford University Press.

Roediger, H. L., & McDermott, K. B. (1993). Implicit memory in normal human subjects. In H. Spinnler & J. Boller (Eds.), *The handbook of neuropsychology* (Vol. 9; pp. 63–131). Amsterdam: Elsevier.

Roediger, H. L., & McDermott, K. B. (1995). Creating false memories—remembering words not presented in lists. *Journal of Experimental Psychology: Learning, Memory and Cognition, 21*, 803–814.

Rugg, M. D. (1998). Convergent approaches to electrophysiological and haemodynamic investigations of memory. *Human Brain Mapping, 6*, 394–398.

Rugg, M. D. (1995a). ERP Studies of memory. In M. D. Rugg & M. G. H. Coles (Eds.), *Electrophysiology of mind: Event-related brain potentials and cognition* (pp. 132–170). Oxford, UK: Oxford University Press.

Rugg, M. D. (1995b). Cognitive event-related potentials: Intracranial and lesion studies. In J. C. Boller & J. Grafman (Eds.), *Handbook of neuropsychology* (Vol. 10; pp. 165–186). Amsterdam: Elsevier.

Rugg, M. D., & Coles, M. G. H. (1995a). *Electrophysiology of mind: Event-related brain potentials and cognition.* Oxford, Oxford University Press.

Rugg, M. D., & Coles, M. G. H. (1995b). The ERP and cognitive psychology: Conceptual issues. In M. D. Rugg & M. G. H. Coles (Eds.), *Electrophysiology of mind: Event-related brain potentials and cognition* (pp. 27–39). Oxford, UK: Oxford University Press.

Rugg, M. D., & Doyle, M. C. (1992). Event-related potentials and recognition memory for low- and high-frequency words. *Journal of Cognitive Neuroscience, 4*, 69–79.

Rugg, M. D., & Doyle, M. C. (1994). Event-related potentials and stimulus repetition in direct and indirect tests of memory. In H. J. Heinze, T. F. Munte, & G. R. Mangun

(Eds.), *Cognitive electrophysiology* (pp. 124–148). Boston, MA: Birkhauser.

Rugg, M. D., Doyle, M. C., & Melan, C. (1993). An event-related potential study of the effects of within- and across-modality word repetition. *Language and Cognitive Processes, 8,* 337–640.

Rugg, M. D., Doyle, M. C., & Wells, T. (1995). Word and non-word repetition within- and across-modality: An event-related potential study. *Journal of Cognitive Neuroscience, 7,* 209–227.

Rugg, M. D., Fletcher, P. C., Allan, K., Frith, C. D., Frackowiak, R. S. J., & Dolan, R. J. (1998a). Neural correlates of memory retrieval during recognition memory and cued recall. *Neuroimage, 8,* 262–273.

Rugg, M. D., Fletcher, P. C., Frith, C. D., Frackowiak, R. S. J., & Dolan, R. J. (1996). Differential activation of the prefrontal cortex in successful and unsuccessful memory retrieval. *Brain, 119,* 2073–2083.

Rugg, M. D., Fletcher, P. C., Frith, C. D., Frackowiak, R. S. J., & Dolan, R. J. (1997). Brain regions supporting intentional and incidental memory: A PET study. *Neuroreport, 8,* 1283–1287.

Rugg, M. D., Mark, R. E., & Schloerscheidt, A. M. (1998). An electrophysiological comparison of two indices of recollection. *Journal of Memory and Language, 39,* 47–69.

Rugg, M. D., Mark, R. E., Walla, P., Schloerscheidt, E. M., Birch, C. S., & Allan, K. (1998). Dissociation of the neural correlates of implicit and explicit memory. *Nature, 392,* 595–598.

Rugg, M. D., & Nagy, M. E. (1987). Lexical contribution to non-word repetition effects: Evidence from event-related potentials. *Memory and Cognition, 15,* 473–481.

Rugg, M. D., & Nieto-Vegas, M. (1999). Modality-specific effects of immediate word repetition: Electrophysiological evidence. *NeuroReport, 10,* 2661–2664.

Rugg, M. D., Walla, P., Schloerscheidt, A. M., Fletcher, P. C., Frith, C. D., & Dolan, R. J. (1998). Neural correlates of depth of processing effects on recollection: Evidence from brain potentials and PET. *Experimental Brain Research, 123,* 18–23.

Sanquist, T. F., Rohrbaugh, K., Syndulko, K., & Lindsley, D. B. (1980). Electrocortical signs of levels of processing: Perceptual analysis and recognition memory. *Psychophysiology, 17,* 568–576.

Schacter, D. L. (1994). Priming and multiple memory systems: Perceptual mechanisms of implicit memory. In D. L. Schacter & E.

Tulving (Eds.), *Memory systems 1994* (pp. 233–268). Cambridge, MA: MIT Press.

Schacter, D. L., & Buckner, R. L. (1998). Priming and the brain. *Neuron, 20,* 185–195.

Schacter, D. L., Reiman, E., Curran, T., Yun, L. S., Bandy, D., McDermott, K. B., & Roediger, H. L. (1996). Neuroanatomical correlates of veridical and illusory recognition memory—evidence from positron emission tomography. *Neuron, 17,* 267–274.

Shallice, T. (1988). *From neuropsychology to mental structure.* Cambridge, UK: Cambridge University Press.

Smith, M. E. (1993). Neurophysiological manifestations of recollective experience during recognition memory judgements. *Journal of Cognitive Neuroscience, 5,* 1–13.

Squire, L. R. (1992). Memory and hippocampus: A synthesis from findings with rats, monkeys and humans. *Psychological Review, 99,* 195–231.

Squire, L. R., Knowlton, B., & Musen, G. (1993). The structure and organization of memory. *Annual Review of Psychology, 44,* 453–495.

Toth, J. P. (1996). Conceptual automaticity in recognition memory: Levels of processing effects on familiarity. *Canadian Journal of Experimental Psychology, 50,* 123–138.

Toth, J. P., Reingold, E. M., & Jacoby, L. L. (1994). Towards a redefinition of implicit memory: Process dissociations following elaborative processing and self-generation. *Journal of Experimental Psychology: Learning, Memory and Cognition, 20,* 290–303.

Tulving, E. (1985). Memory and consciousness. *Canadian Psychologist, 26,* 1–12.

Tulving, E., & Schacter, D. L. (1990). Priming and human memory systems. *Science, 247,* 301–306.

Wagner, A. D., Schacter, D. L., Rotte, M., Koutstaal, W., Maril, A., Dale, A. M., Rosen, B. R., & Buckner, R. L. (1998). Building memories: Remembering and forgetting of verbal experiences as predicted by brain activity. *Science, 281,* 1188–1191.

Wilding, E. L., Doyle, M. C., & Rugg, M. D. (1995). Recognition memory with and without retrieval of context: An event-related potential study. *Neuropsychologia, 33,* 743–767.

Wilding, E. L., & Rugg, M. D. (1996). An event-related potential study of recognition memory with and without retrieval of source. *Brain, 119,* 889–906.

Wilding, E. L., & Rugg, M. D. (1997). Event-related potentials and the recognition memory exclusion task. *Neuropsychologia, 35,* 119–128.

Yonelinas, A. P. (1997). Recognition memory ROCs for item and associative information: The contribution of recollection and familiarity. *Memory and Cognition, 25*, 747–763.

Yonelinas, A. P., Kroll, N. E. A., Dobbins, I., & Lazzara, M. (1998). Recollection and familiarity deficits in amnesia: Convergence of remember/know, process dissociation and ROC data. *Neuropsychology, 12*, 323–339.

33

Psychopharmacological Perspectives on Memory

H. VALERIE CURRAN

Drugs that act on the brain—psychoactive drugs—have been taken for their mood-altering effects ever since history was first recorded. For centuries, drugs were derived from natural plants and often used to treat ailments of the spirit as well as the body. It was not until the middle of the twentieth century that a major development occurred in the discovery of psychoactive drugs that were effective in treating many psychiatric disorders. For example, it is widely held that antischizophrenic (or neuroleptic) drugs are the most important drugs in the history of psychiatry. Their use has liberated many schizophrenics from what could have otherwise been a lifetime's confinement in mental institutions. Or again, antidepressant drugs have helped many severely depressed patients who may otherwise have contemplated suicide. Currently, there is an international research effort to develop antidementia drugs that can slow down, if not halt, cognitive deterioration in devasting dementias like Alzheimer's disease.

Many other psychoactive drugs are used recreationally rather than therapeutically. These include legal drugs like alcohol and nicotine, as well as a very wide range of illegal substances. Products of the poppy seed like opium have been used for thousands of years to control pain and induce euphoria. More recently, a wide range of chemically manufac-

tured or "synthetic" drugs have found their way onto the street with users claiming each type has distinct mood-changing and consciousness-altering properties.

Alongside the rapid development of new therapeutic drugs over the last 50 years, pharmacologists have studied how these drugs exert their effects in the brain. They have made significant advances in understanding how drugs affect neurotransmitters by influencing the processes of synaptic transmission in a variety of different ways. Psychopharmacologists study the psychological effects of drugs and, by using pharmacological knowledge of a drug's neurotransmitter action, can relate brain chemistry to psychological changes induced by a drug. There is thus a reciprocal interaction between the development and use of drugs for therapeutic purposes and the use of drugs as tools to understand the brain basis of the mind and mental disorders. This interaction is central to research on the psychopharmacology of memory.

A range of psychoactive drugs affect memory, often impairing some aspects of memory while sparing other aspects. This chapter provides an overview of research on the psychopharmacology of human memory. It looks first at why studies of the effects of drugs on memory are both clinically and theoretically important. Following a brief history, methods used in psychopharmacological studies are outlined before a summary is given of the mnemonic effects of the two most widely studied classes of drugs—cholinergic compounds and benzodiazepine receptor ligands. Areas of controversy are then discussed, including the role of drug state itself as a cue to retrieval and the degree to which the specific memory effects of drugs can be delineated from their nonmemory effects. A final section discusses treatments that aim to ameliorate organic cognitive dysfunction in Alzheimer's disease.

Relevance of Psychopharmacological Studies

Clinical Relevance

Studies of the effects of drugs on memory are important clinically for several reasons. They allow the mnemonic effects of prescribed drugs to be detailed. For example, millions of people with depression or anxiety disorders take psychoactive drugs and for them, amnesia would not be a welcome side effect. Many antidepressant and neuroleptic ("antischizophrenic") drugs have anticholinergic properties that can cause memory problems for patients (Curran, Sakulsripong, & Lader, 1991). Or again, in Western countries, 10 to 15% of people over 65 years of age regularly take a type of sleeping pill that can induce a transient memory loss. Further, it is not uncommon for older people to take several different psychoactive drugs and sometimes they can experience a drug-induced "pseudo-dementia," with confusion and memory loss sharing many similarities with organic dementia. This has implications for neuropsychological assessment where possible drug-induced impairments need to be differentiated from organic dysfunction.

From a very different clinical perspective, there are circumstances in which drug-induced amnesia is viewed *positively*. Surgeons especially value drugs that mean their patients remember nothing of their operations. Indeed, not ensuring amnesia during a surgical operation may be seen as negligence on the part of the anesthetist.

Drug studies are evidently critical in the development of new pharmacological treatments aimed at ameliorating organic cognitive dysfunctions. To date, it is true that researchers have been more successful in creating amnesia with drugs than they have in finding compounds that enhance memory in organic disorders. However, we can learn from memory impairing drugs: if by inhibiting a neurotransmitter a drug impairs memory, it may be that a drug designed to stimulate that neurotransmitter will enhance memory. A few antidementia drugs have been shown to slow down the rate of cognitive deterioration in Alzheimer's disease, and this has fired hope that new, more effective treatments may be discovered to help those with this devasting dementia.

Theoretical Relevance

Psychopharmacological studies also have theoretical importance. Because many drugs have differential effects on performance on different memory tasks, drugs can allow dissociations to be drawn between different aspects of memory. In this way, they can be complementary to research with brain-damaged people or research showing functional or developmental dissociations (cf. Nyberg & Tulving, 1996). By using drugs to explore the role of neurotransmitters, psychopharmacological studies can provide insights into the neurobiological bases of memory and its disorders. Thus drugs known to have particular effects on a neurotransmitter can be used to study the functional role of that neurotransmitter in memory. For example, in Alzheimer's disease, postmortem brains show a marked depletion in one neurotransmitter—acetylcholine—as well as less marked depletions in several other of the 80-plus neurotransmitters currently identified. To examine what role acetylcholine plays in memory, many researchers have given a drug that blocks the action of acetylcholine in normal, healthy subjects (e.g., Kopelman & Corn, 1988). They have then examined the pattern of memory and cognitive impairments induced by the drug and compared this pattern with that seen in Alzheimer's disease.

Another example stems from the robust amnestic effects of a group of drugs called benzodiazepines, which have well-known commercial names like Valium (chemical name diazepam), Xanax (alprazolam), and Halcion (triazolam). Thirty years after the discovery of these drugs, specific benzodiazepine receptors were identified in the brain. These receptors are found in greatest concentrations in the cerebral cortex, cerebellum, and limbic system (including hippocampus and amygdala)—areas which neuropsychology has long implicated in memory. Why everyone should have benzodiazepine receptors regardless of whether a benzodiazepine had ever been taken is intriguing. It suggests that there must be a natural substance (an endogenous ligand) that binds to those receptors, and the search is now on for those natural ligands. It is not clear whether these natural ligands are truly endogenous in the brain or whether they are a by-product of the gut (benzodiazepines are found in small amounts in food such as leafy vegetables, potatoes, lentils, and milk). That such ligands play a natural role in the normal regulation of memory processes is a tantalizing speculation (cf. Medina, Palandini, & Izquierdo, 1993). Thus benzodiazepines have been useful not only as tools to study pharmacological amnesia but also in providing a potential keyhole on the brain's natural chemistry.

The mood-altering properties of psychoactive drugs can also offer tools in looking at the relation between mood and memory. For example, an elegant series of studies by Cahill, Babinsky, and colleagues (1995) have shown that one drug, propanalol (which blocks beta-adrenergic receptors) impaired normal subjects' recall of emotionally arousing (but not neutral) elements of a story. Using the same task with two patients who had bilateral damage to the amygdala, they found a similar pattern of memory for the emotional and neutral story elements. Together with evidence that the neurotransmitter, noradrenaline, is released in the rat amygdala in response to learning to avoid an aversive stimulus, Cahill et al. suggest that their findings imply that adrenergic function in the amygdala mediates memory for emotional material. It might also be suggested that noradrenergic function mediates arousal or attentional function rather than memory. Nevertheless, these studies provide a good example of how neuropsychological and psychopharmacological studies can be used in parallel in research on memory.

Finally, drugs can alter levels of consciousness, and therefore offer tools for studying the relationship between memory and consciousness. To date this work has focused on anesthetic drugs and assessing memory and awareness while people are globally anesthetized and therefore unconscious (see below). However, people subjectively report that some drugs alter "states of consciousness" in a qualitative way, suggesting an intriguing possibility for a whole new area of research on memory and consciousness.

A Brief History

That drugs can affect memory was noted anecdotally many years ago. For example, in 1812, Thomas de Quincey's book *Confessions of an English Opium-Eater* attributes the author's memory loss to his favorite drug. References to the amnestic effects of excessive alcohol can be found in much earlier literature (see Polster, 1993, for an historical account). Early experimental research on the transient amnesia induced by nitrous oxide was carried out in the 1950s, most notably by Steinberg (e.g., 1954). Despite her early work showing effects of this drug on acquisition of new information that thereby reduced interference with information learned prior to drug administration, the potential to use drugs as tools to investigate memory was not developed at that time. Instead, most research on drugs and memory for the following decade was carried out by anesthesiologists who wanted to find drugs that would induce amnesia of sufficient duration and severity as to ensure that patients remembered as little as possible of events surrounding their operation. Such work was important in identifying drugs like scopolamine (hyoscine) and benzodiazepines (BDZs), which later became the most widely researched compounds in human cognitive psychopharmacology.

In the 1970s, there was a resurgence of interest in drug-induced amnesia from studies with normal, healthy volunteers that allowed more experimental control than was usually possible with surgical patients. A large series of studies by Ghoneim, Mewaldt, Berie, and Hinrichs (1981) showed how drugs like scopolamine and nitrous oxide did not affect performance on tasks that require remembering a few items for a period of seconds (e.g., digit span or the recency effect in free-recall tasks), but markedly impaired performance on tasks with greater memory loads (cf. Ghoneim & Mewaldt, 1975). These findings were interpreted as supporting the "modal model" of the day, which conceptualized memory in terms of two types of storage (short-term or primary memory and long-term or secondary memory). Much psychopharmacological research for the next decade was carried out within the framework of the modal model, reflecting a theoretical time-lag behind developments in cognitive psychology and neuropsychology. In part, this lag may have related to the close interaction between human and animal psychopharmacology. Animal researchers, for example, carry out early studies of new drugs before they are licensed for humans and can administer drugs to specific areas of an animal's brain. Their work on nonverbal memory at the behavioral level continues to focus on stages of memory. This theoretical retardation was one reason why human psychopharmacological studies have had relatively little impact to date on memory research and theory.

More recently, there has been renewed interest in studies of drugs and memory during anesthesia as one means of studying the role of consciousness in memory (cf. Andrade, 1996). When patients are fully anesthetized and therefore thought to be unconscious, researchers have sought to determine whether or not they can remember anything from their operation. In general, there is more evidence of a degree of preserved memory when implicit rather than explicit memory tests are used, although findings overall have been conflicting (Bonebakker, Jelicic, Passcher, & Bonke, 1996; Cork et al., 1996). This in part may reflect methodological difficulties in controlling drugs and doses of both premedicants and anesthetic agents in a surgical context. Often, studies have repeatedly exposed patients to stimuli during anesthesia, and there may be a threshold effect determining whether stimuli are processed at all (for reviews of this literature, see Ghoneim & Block, 1997; Kihlstrom & Schacter, 1990). Following a meta-analysis of 44 studies, Merikle and Daneman (1996) conclude that specific information can be perceived during anesthesia and retained for a period of up to 36 hours after, if appropriate measures are employed (e.g., auditory evoked potentials, sensitive memory tests). Given the limitations of working with fully anaesthetized participants, many researchers opted to carry out controlled experimental studies with healthy volunteers given doses of drugs that do not knock them completely unconscious.

Methods in Psychopharmacology

Psychopharmacologists like to point out that methodologically, studies of pharmacological amnesia have certain advantages over studies of organic amnesia. Drugs can be used to induce an amnesia that is temporary and reversible; the degree of amnesia can be manipulated by using different dose levels. By using a placebo condition (i.e., giving a chemically inert substance), each participant can act as

his or her own control. In studies of brain damage, the effects of lesions in different brain areas necessarily involve comparisons between different patients; in psychopharmacological studies, the effects of several different treatments can be examined in the same person. As normal healthy people are often the participants in such research, sample sizes can be large enough to create a powerful study. Characteristics of volunteers, such as age, psychopathology, or organic state, can also be varied.

A typical experiment in psychopharmacology might use a parallel group design, with participants randomly allocated to one of the "treatment" groups (e.g., drug A, drug B, placebo). Each treatment would be matched to appear the same—for example, tablets would be ground into powder and put into opaque gelatine capsules. This way, the participant cannot tell which treatment is given, and it is also important that the person carrying out the testing does not know this either (so-called double-blind conditions), otherwise expectations could confound drug effects. Participants would be tested a period of time after ingesting the drug, which would be calculated to allow the drug to be absorbed to reach a peak effect in the brain; this time would depend on the drug itself and how it was administered (e.g., by mouth or by intravenous injection).

The power of such experiments can be increased by testing participants before as well as after they take the drug. Alternatively, the same participant can be tested over several weeks on each of the treatments in a within-subjects or "cross-over" design. The time between each treatment (wash-out period) would be long enough to ensure the previous drug was completely eliminated (washed out) of the system and this depends a lot on the drug's plasma elimination half-life. Some drugs like diazepam have long half-lives, hanging around for days after a single dose and cannabis can still be detected four weeks after a single dose. Other drugs are more quickly metabolized and excreted. Individual factors also affect how long it takes for a drug to be eliminated. For example, because of biological changes with age, older people take longer to metabolize and excrete drugs.

In cross-over designs, it is important to balance the order in which treatments are given as a drug effect on a memory task may sometimes vary according to whether it was given first or later on in the trial. These basic designs can be elaborated to compare a range of drugs and doses, and to plot the effects of drugs over a time course. So, for example, in evaluating a potential memory enhancing drug M at doses 1, 2, 3 . . , patients allocated to each dose group of M would be compared with patients allocated to placebo before and while taking the drug each day. Often patients would be assessed again after stopping the drug to test for any residual effects. (In studies with patients who have dementia, the cognitive deterioration over time due to the disease may mean cross-over designs are not suitable.) Another kind of elaboration is seen in designs where different drugs are administered together, often seen in reversal studies where agonists and antagonists may be given to explore pharmacological interactions.

At the same time as having certain methodological advantages, psychopharmacological studies of memory have certain disadvantages, many of which relate to the lack of specificity of the pharmacological compounds that are currently available and that will improve as more specific-acting drugs are developed by the pharmaceutical industry. Rather akin to the rareness of patients with specific, localized lesions, most drugs have a diffuse effect on the brain: a drug's action on the brain is often more akin to throwing a pebble into a pond than fitting a key into a lock. There is no drug that only affects memory. Therefore one issue that is considered later in this chapter is the *specificity* of amnestic effects of drugs.

Cholinergics and Benzodiazepines

Psychopharmacological studies have researched two classes of drugs far more than any others: cholinergics and benzodiazepines (BDZs). Interest in cholinergic drugs was stimulated by the cholinergic hypothesis of Alzheimer's disease (AD) following observations of marked cholinergic depletion in the brains of patients with this devasting disease. Thus on the one hand, cholinergic drugs have been the most frequently explored pharmacological strategy in terms of enhancing memory in AD. On the other hand, drugs like scopolamine (hyoscine), which act as cholinergic blockers, were used to study the functional role of acetylcholine in memory.

Since the original work of Drachman and Leavitt (1974), the amnestic effects of this drug have been studied extensively and sco-

polamine has been put forward as a pharmacological model of AD (cf. Weingartner, 1985). Scopolamine is a selective antagonist at muscarinic acetylcholine receptors that at high doses also acts an antagonist at nicotinic receptors. Its effects can be attenuated if not fully reversed by also giving an agonist like physostigmine or arecholine. As discussed below, scopolamine's effects only partially parallelled the memory deficits observed in AD. The drug does not mimic the extensive retrograde memory loss nor the range of working memory impairments seen in AD. Despite this, the scopolamine model remains widely used today in early tests of potential cognitive enhancing drugs on the basis that if a drug can reverse or ameliorate the temporary amnesia induced in healthy volunteers by scopolamine, it may be effective in the cholinergic depletion of AD.

The amnesic effects of BDZs, initially recognized by anesthetists, were less welcome for the millions who took these drugs on a daily basis for anxiety disorders or insomnia. Some BDZs (e.g., flunitrazepam, temazepam) have now become street drugs of abuse, obtained illicitly and often taken in high doses. There are various case reports in the literature of transatlantic travelers who experienced a transient global amnesia after swallowing a single dose of triazolam (Halcion) to help them sleep during their flight. It has been suggested that the administration of BDZs to normal, healthy subjects may provide a useful model of Korsakoff's disease (Weingartner, 1985) although these drugs do not produce the retrograde impairments seen in this disease. Ghoneim and Mewaldt (1990) point out that the marketing of these drugs by pharmaceutical companies led to some inconsistencies in the information given to doctors: the physicians handbook in 1989 promoted intravenous Valium (diazepam) to anesthetists on the basis of its remarkable ability to induce total amnesia in patients for the events of their operation; a few chapters later, the very same drug given orally is promoted as a daily treatment for anxiety disorders with no mention of any effect it may have on memory.

BDZs act via specific benzodiazepine receptors and facilitate the transmission of GABA (gamma-aminobutyric acid), the major inhibitory neurotransmitter in the brain. BDZs like diazepam, lorazepam, and 30 or more similar compounds act as agonists at the GABA$_A$-BDZ receptor (the single term BDZ used here refers to these full agonists). The same

BDZ receptor can be blocked by a BDZ antagonist such as flumazenil. Compounds also exist that have opposite effects to BDZs at the same receptor—beta-carbolines act as inverse agonists to inhibit the transmission of GABA. Several other compounds act as partial agonists, binding to the receptor but producing less effect than full agonists. Thus researchers have a chemical tool kit when it comes to investigating BDZs.

Anterograde "amnesia" is a consistent finding from volunteer studies of single doses of a BDZ or scopolamine (SP): information presented after the drug is administered is poorly remembered. In contrast, no study has found objective evidence of retrograde impairments of memory: information acquired before drug administration is retained intact. These drugs therefore impede the acquisition of new information. The degree and duration of anterograde amnesia depends on several factors (dosage and route of administration; the memory assessments used; the times postdrug at which information is presented and retrieval is required; characteristics of the subject population tested; for the BDZs, the particular BDZ taken). Although there is considerable variation between studies in these factors, the relatively large number of studies carried out to date do allow some generalizations to be drawn out.

In general, tasks requiring remembering a few items for a period of seconds (e.g., digit span, block span) are unaffected by BDZs or SP. In more complex tasks where information is manipulated while it is retained, BDZ- and SP-induced deficits are found (Kopelman & Corn, 1988; Broks et al., 1988; Rusted & Warburton, 1988). On the whole, the evidence points to a reduction in the speed with which information is processed rather than qualitative effects on components of working memory. For example, error rates are generally much less affected than response times (Curran, 1991; Rusted, 1994).

There is clearly considerable debate among cognitive psychologists about how to characterize long-term remembering in terms of systems, processes, and functions, and a parallel debate about what common terminology might be used to describe memory or the dissociations found in performance on memory tasks. Although psychopharmacological dissociations are relevant to this debate, the debate itself is not within the remit of the present chapter. For discussing drug effects on memory, Tulving's (1985; Tulving & Schacter, 1990) memory systems account will be used because it most neatly embraces current findings.

A consistent and robust finding is that BDZs and SP impair performance on tasks tapping episodic memory. This impairment is clearly dose-dependent. In general, the more demands a task places on episodic memory, the clearer are the detrimental effects of BDZs. So, for example, free-recall tasks are more sensitive than cued-recall or recognition tasks; the longer the delay between acquisition and retrieval, the greater the drug effect on performance. Overall, when direct or explicit assessments of memory are used, the experimental manipulations that affect the performance of normal (nondrugged) participants produce a broadly parallel pattern of influences on the performance of participants administered single doses of BDZs. Thus if subjects are required to process information at different depths, from the relatively superficial (e.g., deciding whether a word is in capital letters or in small case) to the relatively deep (e.g., deciding whether a word belongs to a particular semantic category), BDZs will result in fewer words being subsequently recalled but the pattern of recall will be the same as normal (i.e., deeper levels of encoding lead to better recall; Curran, Schiwy, Eves, Shine, & Lader, 1988; Bishop & Curran, 1995). It also appears that rehearsal effects are normal with BDZs (Mewaldt, Hinrichs, & Ghoneim, 1983). Following acquistion, forgetting rate is not affected by BDZs or SP (Brown et al., 1983; Kopelman & Corn, 1988). Further, BDZs do not increase susceptibility to interference when initial acquisition levels on drug and placebo are matched (Gorissen, Curran, & Ehling, 1998).

Deficits in the encoding of contextual information is a possible mechanism for BDZ-induced impairment of episodic memory. Increased prior list intrusions in word-recall tasks are noted fairly frequently. Gorissen et al. (1998) used a paired associate learning task where participants first learned a series of word pairs (A-B list) and then had to learn another list where the associate to each of the first A words was changed (i.e., A-C list). Diazepam (15 mg) impaired performance on both phases of the task but only in an experiment where the word pairs were unrelated (e.g., *bird–invest*) and not in a separate experiment where they were related (e.g., *bird–crow*). Intrusion errors (B words given on the A-C phase) were not disproportionately increased by the drug, leading Gorissen et al. to conclude that diazepam disrupts the acquisition of new associations per se. Taken together with findings where contextual cues have been manipulated at study and at retrieval, it would seem that drug impairments are evident when any new associations have to be formed, whether those associations are between distinct items or between an item and its context.

Using the remember/know recognition paradigm (see chapter 15) studies have shown that remember responses are reduced by BDZs (Curran, Gardiner, Java, & Allen, 1993; Bishop & Curran, 1995). A similar pattern of effects has also been found with alcohol (Curran & Hildebrandt, in press). This is in accordance with general findings that these drugs impair episodic memory, memory requiring what Tulving (1985) terms autonoetic awareness of the study event. However, know responses are not reduced by these drugs. This pattern of drug effects parallels that on episodic and semantic memory, supporting the notion that know reponses tap semantic memory. Retrieval of well-established (semantic) knowledge is generally intact following drug administration (cf. Ghoneim & Mewaldt, 1990; Polster, 1993). For example, verbal fluency is unaffected by drugs, and in sentence-verification tasks, error rates are not increased although drugs often increase the time to complete the task. Further, a recent study has shown that conceptual priming in category generation tasks is intact following BDZs and SP even though subjects' explicit recall of studied category exemplars showed marked impairment (Bishop & Curran, 1998). Taken as a whole, these findings therefore provide evidence that episodic and semantic memory are pharmacologically dissociated.

The contents of episodic and semantic memory are thought to be directly accessible to consciousness—both personal episodes and impersonal facts can be brought to mind. In contrast, procedural memory is expressed indirectly through skilled performance. BDZs do not affect procedural learning in perceptual-learning tasks (e.g., mirror reading) or in anagram-solving tasks (e.g., Weingartner and Wolkovitz, 1988). In tasks that have a significant motor response component and/or where speed of reaction time is critical (e.g., pursuit rotor, serial reaction time) a drug effect may be found, but this is usually a general slowing of performance that relates to the drug's sedative effect (e.g., Nissen, Knopman, & Schacter,

1987; Curran, 1991). Critically, learning curves on drugs tend to parallel those on placebo.

Tasks assessing procedural memory in these ways are indirect tests of memory—remembering is inferred from changes in the performance of a skill. Another kind of indirect test of memory includes what is usually termed priming: the influence of prior exposure on subsequent performance.

Perceptual priming studies with drugs have produced an intriguing finding that one BDZ, lorazepam, produces impairments on tasks tapping perceptual priming (e.g., word-stem, word-fragment, and degraded-picture identification). Even though BDZs as a class are chemically very similar, and all produce impairments on explicit memory tasks, a range of other BDZs (alprazolam, triazolam, diazepam, oxazepam, midazolam) have been found to leave perceptual priming intact. Further, neither alcohol nor SP affects perceptual priming. That this one BDZ is qualitatively different from others in its effects lends support to the notion of a perceptual representation system that is distinct from other memory systems (Tulving & Schacter, 1990). Conceptual priming is intact following BDZs and SP. Further, that this BDZ is detrimental to perceptual priming without impairing know responses in recognition suggests that nonconscious memory revealed by priming is a different memorial entity from (self-reported) memory in the absence of conscious awareness.

Originally noted by Brown, Brown, and Bowes (1989), the effect of lorazepam on perceptual priming has been replicated and extended by several groups of researchers (e.g., Danion, Peretti, & Grange, 1992; Knopman, 1991; Curran & Gorenstein, 1993; Vidailet et al., 1994; Stewart, Rioux, Connolly, Dunphy, & Teehan, 1996). Task purity criticisms can be applied to some earlier studies on the grounds that explicit impairments contaminated performance on the implicit task. However, these could not explain findings of several studies that compared lorazepam with another drug (a different BDZ or SP) that produced the same degree of impairment on an explicit task but showed only lorazepam impaired perceptual priming (e.g., Sellal et al., 1992; Legrand et al., 1995; Bishop, Curran, & Lader, 1996). Vidailhet, Kazes, Danion, Kauffmann-Muller, and Grange (1996) used Jacoby's (1991) process dissociation procedure to examine perceptual priming effects of diazepam and lorazepam. Although findings overall were not clear-cut, when the deleterious effect of the two BDZs on conscious uses of memory were carefully matched, only lorazepam impaired the automatic use of memory. Using experimental manipulations in accordance with Schacter's retrieval intentionality criterion, Bishop and Curran (1995) found that lorazepam impaired word-stem completion and this effect was attenuated by co-administration of the benzodiazepine antagonist flumazenil. One could speculate that there is a second population of BDZ receptors, perhaps concentrated in occipital areas, to which lorazepam and flumazenil bind but not other BDZ receptor ligands. Subtypes of BDZ receptors have now been identified by microbiological studies, but their possible functional significance is not yet understood.

Drug State at Retrieval

As already discussed, no drug produces retrograde impairments of memory: information acquired before a drug is taken is retrieved intact when the person is in a drugged state. However, there is debate about two possible effects of drug state at retrieval, one concerning state-dependent retrieval and the other concerning retrieval facilitation.

The notion of state-dependency—whereby drug state itself may act as a cue to retrieving information acquired in a drug state—has a long and checkered history in drug research. State-dependency was famously portrayed by Charlie Chaplin in the 1931 movie City Lights. Chaplin starred as a tramp who made friends one day with a drunken millionaire. The following day, the then sober millionaire failed to recognize the tramp, but the next time he was drunk they returned to being old friends and so their interaction varied throughout the movie. In essence, drug state-dependency is one example of Tulving's (1985) encoding specificity principle, whereby memory is improved when cues available at retrieval are similar to cues that were available at original encoding. Drug state is simply an internal or physiological cue.

Unlike the Chaplin film, research showed that drug state-dependency was an unreliable phenomenon. The standard design of state-dependent studies is for 50% of participants to study information on a drug (D) and 50% on placebo (P); at retrieval, half of each group are given D and half P. This produces two groups

where encoding and retrieval are in congruent drug states (P-P, D-D) and two groups where drug states are incongruent (P-D; D-P). A classic review by Eich (1980) showed clearly that drug state-dependency can be demonstrated only if conditions are very controlled such that there are not other retrieval cues available except for drug-state.

However, there are several reasons why drug state-dependency does not explain drug-induced impairments of episodic memory. First, memory impairment occurs without there being any real change in drug state. For example, having taken 0.6 mg of scopolamine an hour ago, someone could now read this paragraph and find his memory for it would be very poor just a couple of minutes later, even though there has been virtually no change in his drug state over those 2 minutes. Second, where drug-state dependent effects are found, they are very small compared with acquisition deficits—for example, having studied a list of words on 2 mg of lorazepam, retrieving on the same drug may improve an individual's performance by perhaps one word compared with retrieving on placebo. But having studied on the BDZ, his recall of the words would be 30 to 70% worse than if he had studied on placebo. Third, as Eich (1980) showed clearly, tasks like cued recall or recognition do not show any drug-state dependent effects because they offer other cues at retrieval. However, robust drug-induced amnesic effects have been demonstrated on these tasks many times over. Fourth, apparent drug-state dependent effects may actually reflect mood-congruency effects (cf. Eich, 1995). Only drugs that act centrally on the brain (and not those with just peripheral actions) produce state-dependency, and this may be because the drug has induced a similar mood or state of arousal at retrieval to the mood it induced at study.

Last, state-dependent effects are asymmetrical: when information is studied on drug, recall is somewhat better if retrieval is on drug (i.e., D-D > D-P); however, when study took place on placebo, drug state at retrieval often makes no difference. Indeed, several studies have shown that subjects given a BDZ can actually remember word lists presented before the drug significantly better than subjects given placebo. This retrieval facilitation by BDZs is precisely the opposite effect to state-dependency, analogous to P-D performance being better than P-P. Often in the state-dependency literature, this asymmetry was ignored by comparing performance in both congruent drug-states (D-D plus P-P) with performance in both incongruent states (P-D plus D-P). Retrieval facilitation has also been found with alcohol. It is not clear whether SP produces the same effect, although this drug has been employed as a "truth" drug in wartime interrogations of captives. Mechanisms for retrieval facilitation are not clear but could include reduced interference from poor post-drug learning or a form of retrieval disinhibition (cf. Weingartner, Sirocco, Curran, & Wolkowitz, 1995).

Specificity of Drug Effects on Memory

Much controversy in research on the psychopharmacology of memory concerns issues of the specificity of drug effects on memory. At a psychological level, there is the question of how much a drug's effects on memory are by-products of its effects on arousal or attentional functions. At a pharmacological level, there is the question of the degree of overlap in amnesic effects of compounds like BDZs and SP which have differing pharmacological actions.

Memory and Arousal

BDZs and SP produce dose-related reductions in arousal and this may contribute to decrements in performance on tasks tapping episodic memory. How can specific mnemonic effects of drugs be differentiated from their effects on arousal? There are five main approaches and these are summarised in table 33.1. One method has been to show that different drugs may produce the same effect on sedation but different effects on memory or vice versa. For example, in a comparison of the effects of a sedative antihistamine (diphenhydramine) with SP and the BDZ lorazepam, a 50 mg dose of the antihistamine produced similar levels of sedation to SP (0.6 mg) and lorazepam (2 mg; Curran, Poovibunsuk, Dalton, & Lader, 1998). However, unlike SP and the BDZ, it did not produce any impairment on a task tapping episodic memory (continuous word recognition). Event-related potentials were also recorded and showed that earlier components of ERPs were affected similarly by all three drugs whereas later components such a P_{300} were more affected by SP and lorazepam than the antihistamine. Another method of dissociating sedation and amnesia could be to show that tolerance over repeated doses of BZs builds up differentially to the two effects. Tolerance reflects neuronal adaption to a drug whereby the same dose has less of an effect over repeated use, a phenomenon reflected in the need of drug and alcohol abusers to progressively escalate their doses over time. Overall, the evidence is that tolerance develops to drug effects on arousal much faster than it develops to a drug's amnestic effect. For example, significant impairments on word-list recall have been documented in studies of anxious patients after 8 weeks of treatment with alprazolam (Curran et al., 1994) and after at least 6 months continual use of other BDZs (Lucki, Rickels, & Geller, 1986; Tata, Rollings, Collins, Pickering, & Jacobson, 1994).

An alternative way of dissociating would be to show differential reversal of amnesic and sedative effects by an antagonist. As outlined earlier, the effects of BDZs are mediated via specific BDZ receptors on the GABA$_A$-BDZ receptor. If all of the effects of BDZs are mediated in this way, then administration of a benzodiazepine antagonist such as flumazenil should reverse the sedative, psychomotor, and amnestic effects of BZs. On the whole, however, studies with flumazenil have not produced a consistent pattern of results as different studies have used different agonist/antagonist dosages, and other procedural differences make it difficult to compare across the various studies. A fair conclusion is probably that sedative and attentional effects are more easily reversed, and at lower antagonist doses, than amnestic effects.

Psychopharmacologists would welcome drugs that had a range of memory and arousal effects (improving as well as impairing), which would enable double-dissociations to be drawn. Arousal is conceptually ill-defined and different measures (physiological, psychomotor, subjective) often show poor inter-correlations with each other. It could be that these different measures tap different aspects of arousal. Robbins and Everitt (1995) argue from psychopharmacological studies with animals that different neurotransmitter systems mediate different aspects of arousal. However, taken together, results from studies assessing co-occurrence of sedative and memory effects in the five different ways provide strong evidence that BDZs and SP have specific effects

Table 33.1 Five methods for dissociating the effects of drugs on memory (M) and arousal (A).

METHOD	TYPICAL FINDINGS	EXAMPLES
EQUATE EFFECTS ON A and determine whether two or more drugs have DIFFERENTIAL EFFECTS ON M	Different drugs produce same A effects but different M effects or *vice versa*	Weingartner et al, 1995; Curran et al, 1998.
Assess the degree of DIFFERENTIAL TOLERANCE over repeated dosing to drug effects on A and M	Tolerance to sedation develops before tolerance to memory effects	Ghoneim et al, 1981; Curran et al, 1994; Tata et al, 1994.
Assess the degree of DIFFERENTIAL REVERSAL of agonist effects on A and M by antagonist	Variable—depends on ratio of dosage of agonist to antagonist	Hommer et al, 1993; Curran & Birch, 1991.
Assess the degree of DIFFERENTIAL DOSE-RESPONSE CURVES for A and M	A and M effects show different dose-response curves	Smirne et al, 1989; Weingartner et al, 1993.
STATISTICAL—e.g., covariance	Covariance of A measures leave significant drug/placebo differences on M	See reviews Ghoneim & Mewaldt, 1990; Curran, 1991.

on memory over and above their sedative effects.

Memory, Attention, and Executive Function

It could be argued that drugs may reduce attentional resources and thereby impede initial encoding of information. Gorissen & Ehling (1998) tested this idea in two dual-task experiments. Participants performed a visual discrimination task of several levels of complexity concurrently with a paired-associate learning task. As expected, the BDZ diazepam (15 mg) impaired recall of associates. However, the degree of impairment did not interact with level of complexity of the visual discrimination task. Although dividing attention reduced memory performance, it was no more disruptive to those given diazepam than to those given placebo. This suggests that reduced attentional resources cannot account for the amnestic effects of BDZs.

The issue of whether amnestic effects are related to impaired attentional functions is a particularly heated debate in the SP literature (Broks et al., 1988; Kopelman & Corn, 1988;

Lawrence & Sahakian, 1995). Having concluded from her earlier elegant studies using dual-task paradigms that SP produced impairments of the central executive component of working memory, Rusted (1994) argues that this is not sufficient to explain the drug's effects on attention and memory. Impairment of a unitary resource allocator like the central executive would mean that attentional and memory impairments should occur together, and as Rusted shows, this clear correspondence is not often found in studies of SP. Attention is an umbrella term, and it may be that different neurobiological systems mediate different aspects of attention. Studies where a range of attentional tasks have been used show that SP has effects on some but not other aspects of attentional functions (e.g., Broks et al., 1988). Indeed, there is increasing evidence for the role of the catecholamines, especially noradrenaline, in attentional processing (Robbins & Everitt, 1995; Coull et al., 1995).

BDZs do not affect performance on verbal fluency, Tower of London, or the Wisconsin card sorting task (WCST)—traditional tests of frontal function. Other drugs do affect performance on these tests. The *N*-methyl-D-aspartate (NMDA) receptor antagonist, ketamine, is especially interesting in this respect. There is a growing interest in NMDA in light of evidence linking glutamate (an excitatory amino acid) with memory (Malhotra et al., 1996). Krystal et al. (1998) directly compared the effects of ketamine with lorazepam (2 mg), administering each drug alone and the two in combination. Ketamine produced marked impairments on "frontal tasks" (markedly increasing errors on WCST, impairing verbal fluency, and increasing distractibility on an attentional task) whereas lorazepam's effects on these tasks did not differ from those of placebo. Combining the two active drugs produced no more impairment on these tasks than ketamine alone. However, on a verbal recall task, each drug alone produced marked impairments and the combination was additive, producing a dramatically pronounced amnesia. Although the frontal effects of ketamine make it a very interesting drug for psychopharmacologists, there are problems with the specificity of its effects. NMDA receptors are very widely distributed in the brain. Further, ketamine also induces dissociative states and psychotic symptoms, in a sense putting the healthy research participant into a pseudoschizophrenic state. This is not universally appreciated by participants, although the increasing use of ketamine (a.k.a. "Special K") as an illicit recreational drug probably means that some people do enjoy this kind of experience.

Memory: Pharmacological Specificity

The cholinergic blocker, scopolamine, produces a profile of memory effects that are broadly similar to BDZs. Despite the different pharmacological actions of these compounds, their amnesic effects have proved difficult to differentiate (e.g., Frith, Richardson, Samuel, Crow, & McKenna, 1984; Curran et al., 1991; Bishop et al., 1996). Two main differences have been noted. First, SP differs from one BDZ (lorazepam) in not impairing perceptual priming. Second, patients with Alzheimer's disease show an increased sensitivity to the detrimental effects of anticholinergics like SP but no increased sensitivity to BDZs like lorazepam (Sunderland et al., 1986). However, similarities are more pervasive with both SP and BDZs producing marked anterograde impairments of episodic memory while leaving semantic, procedural, and working memory

relatively intact. This similarity in effects may reflect a common neuropharmacological action, as GABA inhibition influences cholinergic projection pathways (GABAergic mechanisms may inhibit cholinergic activity in the cortex via interaction at the level of the basal forebrain). In research with rats, one study showed that injection of a BDZ into the medial septum reduced acetyl choline release in the hippocampus by 50% while injecting the BDZ antagonist flumazenil increased hippocampal acetyl choline release by 95% (Imperato et al., 1994). These kinds of studies are beginning to reveal the interaction between different neurotransmitters and neuromodulators in memory (see McGaugh & Cahill, 1997). Other animal studies have implied that inhibition of long-term potentiation (LTP) in the hippocampus may also be a common neuropharmacological effect of BDZs and SP (Maren & Baudry, 1995), but it is not yet clear how LTP relates to any real memory process.

Pharmacological Strategies for Enhancing Memory Function

In terms of strategies for enhancement of memory, the largest effort is directed toward the development of treatments for Alzheimer's disease (AD). Although several neurotransmitters have been implicated in AD (for review, see Curran & Kopelman, 1996), cholinergic depletion is still the most well-documented neurochemical loss. Therefore much effort has focused on compounds designed to correct or moderate this cholinergic deficit. Early studies gave patients choline, which is acetylated rapidly by an enzyme to acetylcholine (ACh). This had little success and unfortunately gastrointestinal side effects made patients smell of rotting fish. The most widely discussed strategy has been to inhibit the enzyme acetylcholinesterase (AChE). AChE inhibitors prevent the hydrolysis of synaptically released ACh and therefore increase the efficiency of cholinergic transmission. Tacrine (tetrahydroaminoacridine) has a longer action and became the first antidementia drug to be given approval by the Federal Food and Drug Administration (FDA) in the United States, followed by two other AChE inhibitors, donepezil hydrochloride (Aricept) and rivastigmine.

Both tacrine and donepezil have modest effects of slowing down the rate of cognitive deterioration over time in patients with mild to moderate AD. Side effects can be problematic and only a proportion of patients will show cognitive improvement with treatment (see Knopman, 1995; American Psychiatric Association, 1997). Further, there is substantial clinical heterogeneity in patients meeting diagnostic criteria for AD, and various subtypes of AD have been suggested on the bases of neuropathological and/or cognitive variations (e.g., Richards, 1997). It is possible that different clinical subgroups will show different responses to pharmacological treatments.

It is not clear to what extent drugs produce any specific improvement in *memory* functions. Sahakian et al. (1993) showed tacrine improved choice reaction time and improved performance on a task in which patients learned to follow a simple rule and then reverse this rule. However, it had no effect compared with placebo on any memory task, leading Sahakian et al. to argue that tacrine improved attentional functions and to suggest that the cholinergic system is implicated in the control of attentional rather than memory processes.

Cholinergic agonists like nicotine increase the effect of ACh either directly or by sensitizing the receptor site. Sahakian, Jones, Levy, Gray, and Warbuton (1989) and Jones et al. (1992) showed subcutaneous nicotine improved AD patients' performance on a rapid information-processing task and psychomotor speed tasks, but had no effect on memory performance. This again suggests that tacrine and the cholinergic system are involved in attentional/information processing rather than memory (Lawrence & Sahakian, 1995). Arousal changes may also play a role in mediating these effects.

Evidence from animal studies has implicated nerve growth factor (NGF) as a possible mediator of cholinergic depletion in AD (when NGF is given to animals, cholinergic function is increased). Human studies have not yet been carried out as there are problems in using NGF therapeutically.

Other approaches have shown some promise in AD, such as estrogen therapy in postmenopausal women, and vitamin E taken over a two-year period was found to slow the progression of AD in a study by Sano et al. (1997). A range of noncholinergic techniques are currently being explored and these include vasodilators like Hydergine, which increase cerebral blood perfusion and the so-called nootropics—putative cognitive enhancers like piracetam and a range of other compounds (e.g., neuropeptides, opiate antagonists, in-

verse agonists at the BDZ receptor). There are also neurotropic agents such as oligonucleotides, which are intended to modify biosynthetic pathways involved in generation of AD pathology. Whether any of these agents have potential to improve cognitive function in AD is not yet known.

Conclusions

This chapter has focused mainly on drugs that impair memory, and mainly on the most widely studied drugs, BDZs and SP. At least 80 neurotransmitters have been identified in the brain, although most drugs act on just a few of these. Thus researchers are only beginning to explore the complexities of memory's neurochemistry. Psychopharmacologists studying memory are reliant on their tools—the chemical probes that are available—and at present, many of these have diffuse effects. Ever more specific pharmacological agents are being produced that will greatly aid researchers to tease apart neurochemical substrates of memory. The use of radio-labelled drugs in imaging studies is already allowing delineation of receptors in the living brain, and this may provide a means of assessing abnormalities in receptor populations in neurological and psychiatric disorders (e.g., Pike et al., 1995). A drug and placebo can also be administered during functional imaging and this allows drug-induced changes in activation to be monitored during performance of a memory task (cf. Fletcher, Frith, Grasby, Friston, & Dolan, 1996). Psychopharmacology will progress enormously given refinements in both the drugs available and the techniques for studying their effects. This progress will have important clinical repercussions for the treatment of memory disorders and for drug treatments in psychiatry. It will also have important theoretical implications in allowing more precise pharmacological dissociation between different aspects of human memory, which will shed further light on the role of different neurotransmitters and neuromodulators in mediating memory functions.

References

American Psychiatric Association (1997). Practice guideline for the treatment of patients with Alzheimer's disease and other dementias of later life. *American Journal of Psychiatry, 154* (Suppl. 5), 1–39.

Andrade, J. (1996). Investigations of hypesthesia: Using anesthetics to explore relationships between consciousness, learning and memory. *Consciousness and Cognition, 5*, 562–580.

Atkinson, R. C., & Shiffrin, R. M. (1971). The control of short-term memory. *Scientific American, 225*, 82–90.

Bishop, K., & Curran, H. V. (1995). Psychopharmacological analysis of implicit and explicit memory: A study with lorazepam and the benzodiazepie antagonist, flumazenil. *Psychopharmacology, 121*, 267–278.

Bishop, K., & Curran, H. V. (1998). An investigation of the effects of benzodiazepine receptor ligands and of scopolamine on conceptual priming. *Psychopharmacology, 140*, 345–353.

Bishop, K. I., Curran, H. V., & Lader, M. (1996). Do scopolamine and lorazepam have dissociable effects on human memory systems? A dose-response study with normal volunteers. *Experimental and Clinical Psychopharmacology, 4*, 292–299.

Bonebakker, A. E., Jelicic, M., Passcher, J., & Bonke, B. (1996). Memory during general anesthesia: Practical and methodological aspects. *Consciousness and Cognition, 5*, 522–561.

Broks, P., Preston, G., Traub, M., Poppleton, P., Ward, C., & Stahl, S. M. (1988). Modelling dementia: Effects of scopolamine on memory and attention. *Neuropsychologia, 26*, 685–700.

Brown, J., Brown, M. W., & Bowes, J. (1983). Effects of lorazepam on rate of forgetting, on retrieval from semantic memory and on manual dexterity. *Neuropsychologia, 21*(5), 501–512.

Brown, M. W., Brown, J., & Bowes, J. (1989). Absence of priming coupled with substantially preserved recognition in lorazepam induced amnesia. *Quarterly Journal of Experimental Psychology, 41A*, 599–617

Brown, J., Lewis, V., Brown, M. W., Horn, G., & Bowes, J. B. (1982). A comparison between transient amnesias induced by two drugs (diazepam and lorazepam) and amnesia of organic origin. *Neuropsychologia, 20*, 55–70.

Cahill, L., Babinsky, R., Markowitsch, H. J., & McGaugh, J. L. (1995). The amygdala and emotional memory. *Nature, 377*, 295–296.

Cork, R. C., Heaton, J. F., Campbell, C. E., & Kihlstrom, J. F. (1996). Is there implicit memory after propofol sedation? *British Journal of Anaesthesia, 76*, 492–498.

Cork, R. C., Kihlstrom, J. F., & Schacter, D. L. (1992). Absence of explicit or implicit

memory in patients anethetised with sufentanil/nitrous oxide. *Anesthesiology, 76*, 892–898.

Coull, J. T., Sahakian, B. J., Middleton, H. C., Young, A. H., Park, S. B., McShane, R. H., Cowen, P. J., & Robbins, T. W. (1995). Differential effects of clonidine, haloperidol, diazepam and tryptophan depletion on focussed attention and attentional search. *Psychopharmacology, 121*, 222–230.

Curran, H. V. (1991). Benzodiazepines, memory and mood: A review. *Psychopharmacology, 105*, 1–8.

Curran, H. V., & Birch, B. (1991). Differentiating the sedative and amnestic effects of benzodiazepines: A study with midazolam and the benzodiazepine antagonist, flumazenil. *Psychopharmacology, 103*, 519–523.

Curran, H. V., Bond, A., O'Sullivan, G., Bruce, M., Marks, I., Lelliot, P., Shine, P., & Lader, M. (1994). Memory functions, alprazolam and exposure therapy: A controlled longitudinal study of patients with agoraphobia and panic disorder. *Psychological Medicine, 24*, 969–976.

Curran, H. V., Gardiner, J. M., Java, R., & Allen, D. J. (1993). Effects of lorazepam on recollective experience in recognition memory. *Psychopharmacology, 110*, 374–378.

Curran, H. V., & Gorenstein, C. (1993). Differential effects of lorazepam and oxazepam on priming. *International Clinical Psychopharmacology, 8*, 37–42.

Curran, H. V., & Hildebrandt, M. (in press). Dissociative effects of alcohol on recollective experience. *Consciousness & Cognition.*

Curran, H. V., & Kopelman, M. D. (1996). The cognitive psychopharmacology of Alzheimer's Disease. In R. G. Morris (Ed.), *The neuropsychology of Alzheimer's disease.* Oxford University Press: Oxford.

Curran, H. V., Poovibunsuk, P., Dalton, J., & Lader, M. H. (1998). Differentiating the effects of centrally acting drugs on arousal and memory: An event-related potential study of scopolamine, lorazepam and diphenhydramine. *Psychopharmacology, 135*, 27–36.

Curran H. V., Sakulsripong, M., & Lader, M. H. (1991). Antidepressants and memory: An investigation of four drugs with differing anticholinergic and sedative properties. *Psychopharmacology, 95*, 520–527.

Curran, H. V., Schifano, F., & Lader, M. (1991). Models of memory dysfunction? A comparison of the effects of scopolamine and lorazepam on memory, psychomotor performance and mood. *Psychopharmacology, 103*, 83–90.

Curran, H. V., Schiwy, W., Eves, F., Shine, P., & Lader, M. H. (1988). A "levels of processing" study of the effects of benzodiazepines on human memory. *Human Psychopharmacology, 3*, 21–25.

Danion, J.-M., Peretti, S., & Grange, D. (1992). Effects of chlorpromazine and lorazepam on explicit memory, repetition priming and cognitive skill learning in healthy volunteers. *Psychopharmacology, 108*, 345–351.

Drachman, D. A., & Leavitt, J. (1974). Human memory and the cholinergic system. *Archives of Neurology, 30*, 113–121.

Eich, E. (1980). The cue-dependent nature of state-dependent retrieval. *Memory and Cognition, 8*, 157–173.

Eich, E. (1995). Searching for mood dependent memory. *Psychological Science, 6*, 67–75.

Fletcher, P. C., Frith, C. D., Grasby, P. M., Friston, K. J., & Dolan, R. J. (1996). Local and distributed effects of apomorphine on fronto-temporal function in acute unmedicated schizophrenics. *Journal of Neuroscience, 16*, 7055–7062.

Frith, C. D., Richardson, J. T. E., Samuel, M., Crow, T. J., & McKenna, P. J. (1984). The effects of intravenous diazepam and hyoscine on human memory. *Quarterly Journal of Experimental Psychology, 36A*, 133–144.

Ghoneim, M. M., & Block, R. I. (1997). Learning and memory during general anesthesia: An update. *Anaesthesiology, 87*, 387–410.

Ghoneim, M. M., & Mewaldt, S. P. (1975). Effects of diazepam and scopolamine on storage, retrieval and organisational processes in memory. *Psychopharmacologia, 44*, 257–262.

Ghoneim, M. M., & Mewaldt, S. P. (1990). Benzodiazepines and human memory: A review. *Anesthesiology, 72*, 926–938.

Ghoneim, M. M., Mewaldt, S. P., Berie, J. L., & Hinrichs, J. V. (1981). Memory and performance effects of single and 3 week administration of diazepam. *Psychopharmacology, 73*, 147–151.

Gorissen, M. E. E., Curran, H. V., & Eling, P. A. T. M. (1998). Proactive interference and temporal context encoding after diazepam intake. *Psychopharmacology, 138*, 334–343.

Gorissen, M. E. E., & Eling, P. A. T. M. (1998). Dual task performance after diazepam intake: Can resource depletion explain the benzodiazepine-induced amnesia? *Psychopharmacology, 138*, 354–361.

Hommer, D., Weingartner, H. J., & Brier, A. (1993). Dissociation of benzodiazepine induced amnesia from sedation. *Psychopharmacology, 112*, 455–460.

Imperato, A., Dazzi, L., Obinu, M. C., Gessa, G. L., & Biggio, G. (1994). The benzodiazepine receptor antagonist flumazenil increases acetylcholine release in rat hippocampus. *Brain Research, 647*, 167–171.

Jacoby, L. L. (1991). A process dissociation framework: Separating automatic from intentional use of memory. *Journal of Memory and Language, 30*, 513–541.

Jones, G. M. M., Sahakian, B. J., Levy, R., Warburton, D. M., & Gray, J. (1992). Effects of acute sub-cutaneous nicotine on attention, information processing and short-term memory in Alzheimer's disease. *Psychopharmacology, 108*, 485–94.

Kihlstrom, J. F., & Schacter, D. L. (1990). Anesthesia, amnesia and the cognitive unconscious. In B. Bonke, W. Fitch, & K. Millar (Eds.), *Memory and awareness in anaesthesia* (pp. 21–44). Lisse, The Netherlands: Swets and Zeitlinger.

Knopman, D. (1991). Unaware learning versus preserved learning in pharmacologic amnesia: Similarities and differences. *Journal of Experimental Psychology: Learning, Memory and Cognition, 17*, 1017–1029.

Knopman, D. (1995). Tacrine in Alzheimer's Disease: A promising first step. *The Neurologist, 1*, 86–94.

Kopelman, M. D., & Corn, T. H. (1988). Cholinergic 'blockade' as a model for cholinergic depletion. *Brain, 111*, 1079–1110.

Krystal, J. H., Karper, L. P., Bennett, A., D'Souza, D. C., Abi-Dargham, A. A., Morrissey, K., Suckow, R. F., Stetson, P., & Charney, D. S. (1998). Interactive effects of subanesthetic ketamine and subhypnotic lorazepam. *Psychpharmacology, 135*, 213–229.

Lawrence, A. D., & Sahakian, B. J. (1995). Alzheimer disease, attention and the cholinergic system. *Alzheimer Disease and Associated Disorders, 9*, S2, 43–49.

Legrand, F., Vidailhet, P., Danion, J.-M., Grange, D., Giersch, M., Van Der Linden, M., & Imbs, J.-L. (1995). Time course of the effects of diazepam and lorazepam on perceptual priming and explicit memory. *Psychopharmacology, 118*, 475–479.

Lucki, I., Rickels, K., & Geller, A. M. (1986). Chronic use of benzodiazepines and psychomotor and cognitive test performance. *Psychopharmacology, 88*, 426–433.

Mackell, J. A., Ferris, S. H., Mohs, R., Schneider, L., Galasko, D., Whitehouse, P., Schmitt, F., Sano, M., & Thal, L. J. (1997). Multicenter evaluation of new instruments for Alzheimer's disease clinical trials: Summary of results. *Alzheimer's Disease and Associated Disorders, 11*, S65–69.

Malhotra, A. K., Pinals, D. A., Weingartner, H., Sirocco, K., Missar, C. D., Pickar, D., & Breir, A. (1996). NMDA receptor function and human cognition: The effects of ketamine in healthy volunteers. *Neuropsychopharmacology, 14*, 301–307.

Maren, S., & Baudry, M. (1995). Properties and mechanisms of long-term synaptic plasticity in the mammalian brain: Relationship to learning and memory. *Neurobiology of Learning and Motivation, 63*, 1–18.

McGaugh, J. L., & Cahill, L. (1997). Interaction of neuromodulatory systems in modulating memory storage. *Behavioural Brain Research 83*, 31–38.

Medina, J. H., Palandini, A. C., & Izquierdo, I. (1993). Naturally occurring benzodiazepines and benzodiazepine-like molecules in the brain. *Behavioural Brain Research, 58*, 1–8.

Merikle, P. M., & Daneman, M. (1996). Memory for unconsciously perceived events: Evidence from anesthetised patients. *Consciousness and Cognition, 5*, 525–541.

Mewaldt, S. P., Hinrichs, J. V., & Ghoneim, M. M. (1983). Diazepam and memory: Support for a duplex model of memory. *Memory and Cognition, 11*, 557–564.

Nissen, M. J., Knopman, D. S., & Schacter, D. L. (1987). Neurochemical dissociations of memory systems. *Neurology, 37*, 789–794.

Nyberg, L., & Tulving, E. (1996). Classifying human long-term memory: Evidence from converging dissociations. *European Journal of Cognitive Psychology, 8*, 163–183.

Pike, V. W., McCarron, J. A., Lammertsma, A. A., Hume, S. P., Sargent, P. A., Bench, C. S., Fletcher, A., & Grasby, P. M. et al. (1995). First delineation of 5-HT$_{ia}$ receptors in human brain with PET and [^{11}c]WAY-100635. *European Journal of Pharmacology, 283*, R1–3.

Polster, M. R. (1993). Drug-induced amnesia: Implications for cognitive neuropsychological investigations of memory. *Psychological Bulletin, 114*, 477–493.

Richards, M. (1997). Neurobiological treatment of Alzheimer's disease. In R. G. M. Morris (Ed.), *The cognitive neuropsychology of Alzheimer's disease* (pp. 327–342). Oxford: Oxford University Press.

Robbins, T. W., & Everitt, B. J. (1995). Arousal systems and attention. In M. Gazzaniga et al. (Ed.), *The cognitive neurosciences* (pp. 703–725). Cambridge, MA: MIT Press.

Rogers, S. L., Friedhof, L. T., & the Donezepil Study Group (1996). The efficacy and safety of donezepil in patients with Alzheimer's disease: Results of a multicentre, randomised, double-blind, placebo-controlled trial. *Dementia, 7*, 293–303.

Rusted, J. M. (1994). Cholinergic blockade: Are we asking the right questions? *Journal of Psychopharmacology, 8*, 54–59.

Rusted, J. M., & Warburton, D. M. (1988). The effects of scopolamine on working memory in healthy volunteers. *Psychopharmacology, 96*, 145–152.

Sahakian, B. J., Jones, G. M. M., Levy, R., Gray, J., & Warburton, D. (1989). The effects of nicotine in patients with dementia of the Alzheimer type. *British Journal of Psychiatry, 154*, 797–800.

Sahakian, B. J., Owen, A. M., Morant, N. J., Eagger, S. A., Boddington, S., Crayton, L., Crockford, H. A., Crooks, M., Hill, K., & Levy, F. (1993). Further analysis of the cognitive effects of tetrahydroaminoacridine (THA) in Alzheimer's disease: Assessment of attentional and mnemonic function using CANTAB. *Psychopharmacology, 110*, 395–410.

Sano, M., Ernesto, C., Thomas, R. G., Klauber, M. R., Schafer, K., Grundman, M., Woodbury, P., Growdon, J., Cotman, C. W., Pfeiffer, E., Schneii, L. S., & Thal, L. J. (1997). A controlled trial of seleguiline, alpha-tocopherol or both as treatment for Alzheimer's disease. *New England Journal of Medicine, 336*, 1245–1247.

Sellal, F., Danion, J. M., Kauffmann-Mueller, F., Grange, D., Imbs, J. L., Van Der Linden, M., & Singer, L. (1992). Differential effects of diazepam and lorazepam on repetition priming in healthy volunteers. *Psychopharmacology, 108*, 371–379.

Smirne, S., Ferini-Strambi, L., Pirola, R., Tancredi, O., Franceschi, M., Pinto, P., & Bareggi, S. R. (1989). Effects of flunitrazepam on cognitive functions. *Psychopharmacology, 98*, 251–256.

Steinberg, H. (1954). Selective effects of anesthetic drugs on cognitive behaviour. *Quarterly Journal of Experimental Psychology, 6*, 170–180

Stewart, S. H., Rioux, G. F., Connolly, J. F., Dunphy, S. C., & Teehan, M. D. (1996). Effects of oxazepam and lorazepam on implicit and explicit memory: Evidence for possible influences of time course. *Psychopharmacology, 128*, 139–149.

Sunderland, T., Tariot, P., Weingartner, H., Murphy, D., Newhouse, P. A., Mueller, E. A., & Cohen, R. M. (1986). Anticholinergic challenge in Alzheimer patients: A controlled dose-response study. *Progress in Neuropsychopharmacology and Biological Psychiatry, 10*, 599–610.

Tata, P. R., Rollings, J., Collins, M., Pickering, A., & Jacobson, R. R. (1994). Lack of cognitive recovery following withdrawal from long-term benzodiazepine use. *Psychological Medicine, 24*, 203–213

Tulving, E. (1985). How many memory systems are there? *American Psychologist, 40*, 385–398.

Tulving, E., & Schacter, D. L. (1990). Priming and human memory systems. *Science, 247*, 301–306.

Vidailhet, P., Danion, J. M., Kauffmann-Muller, F., Grange, D., Giersch, A., Van Der Linden, M., & Imbs, J. L. (1994). Lorazepam and diazepam effects on memory acquisition in priming tests. *Psychopharmacology, 115*, 397–406.

Vidailhet, P., Kazes, M., Danion, J. M., Kauffmann-Muller, F., & Grange, D. (1996). Effects of lorazepam and diazepam on conscious and automatic memory processes. *Psychopharmacology, 127*, 63–72.

Weingartner, H. (1985). Models of memory dysfunctions. *Annals of the New York Academy of Sciences, 444*, 359–369.

Weingartner, H. J., Sirocco, K., Curran, H. V., & Wolkowitz, O. (1995). Memory facilitation following the administration of the benzodiazepine triazolam. *Experimental and Clinical Psychopharmacology, 3*, 298–330.

Weingartner, H. J., & Wolkovitz, O. (1988). Pharmacological strategies for exploring the psychobiologically distinct cognitive systems. *Psychopharmacology, S125*, 31–37.

THEORIES OF MEMORY

34

The Adaptive Nature of Memory

JOHN R. ANDERSON & LAEL J. SCHOOLER

Most research on human memory has mainly focused on the question of understanding what memory does and not on why memory does what it does. There have been requests that the field focus more on the function of memory and perhaps as a consequence applied research on memory has been a growing field. Neisser (1976, 1978, 1982) argued that the field should adopt an "ecological approach" to memory and study how memory is used in the real world. He suggests that the principles of memory in the real world might be different from the ones uncovered in the laboratory. Bruce (1985) made a serious effort to define what such an ecological approach would amount to. He noted that research under the ecological banner focused on everyday memory phenomena and he argued that more attention needed to be given to evolutionary explanations for why memory worked as it did.

The major difficulty in achieving insight from a functional approach to human memory is that its function is at once so obvious but also so apparently flawed. It is obviously valuable to have access to one's past and make one's current behavior contingent on the past. On the other hand, human memory with its many failures seems quite flawed. How much insight is there to be gained by noting that memory has an obvious function that it achieves poorly? As Bruce noted, the ecological approach is left with anecdotes about when memory seems to achieve its function well and when it does not.

However, researchers have long wondered whether human memory really was so flawed. One finds occasional arguments (e.g., Bjork & Bjork, 1992) that memory's most apparent deficit, forgetting, may be an adaptive response to the need to focus on currently relevant information. In general, arguments for the adaptiveness of human memory have taken the perspective that the memory system faces constraints and that its behavior is an optimal solution to these constraints. This theme appears in a couple of recent formal models of recognition memory (McClelland & Chappell, 1998; Shiffrin & Steyvers, 1997) that argue that recognition memory takes an optimal Bayesian solution to discriminating between the traces of foils and targets. Such optimal theories are shown capable of explaining such phenomena as the list-strength effect (Ratcliff, Clark, & Shiffrin, 1990), which had been problematical for past theories.

This chapter is organized around a proposal for understanding the adaptiveness of the memory system called *rational analysis* (J. R. Anderson & Milson, 1989; Anderson & Schooler, 1991; Schooler, 1993; Schooler & Anderson, 1997). This framework assumes that there is some cost, C, associated with retrieving a memory. This cost may reflect metabolic expenditure in maintaining and retrieving the memory and also the time to search and consider the memory. If the memory proves to be useful to the current purposes, there is some gain, G, in accessing the memory. The problem facing the memory system is to come up with some scheme that minimizes the costs in retrieval while maximizing the gains. Rational analysis also proposes that the memory system can, in effect, assign some probability P to a memory being relevant in advance of retrieving it. Given these three quantities, an adaptive memory system would search memories in order of their expected utilities, $PG - C$, and stop considering memories when a probability P is retrieved such that:

$$PG < C \qquad (1)$$

This predicts that people will be able to retrieve most rapidly memories that are most likely to be relevant to their current needs and not recall memories that are unlikely to be relevant. This framework can be elaborated into a theory that makes quantitative predictions about latency and probability of recall.

As Anderson and Milson (1989) discuss, this basic framework applies to many artificial memory systems such as information retrieval systems (Salton & McGill, 1983), libraries (Burrell, 1980, 1985), and file management systems (Stritter, 1977). For instance, libraries try to assess the probability that books will be needed, making those most likely to be needed available in special collections, others in the stacks, others in various off-site storage areas, and giving away still other books. Similarly, it is argued that the human memory system makes the most likely memories available in various sorts of working memories, makes others more or less available in long-term memory, and forgets still others.

There are three quantities in the above analysis—P, G, and C. The one that has been subjected to the most analysis is P, the probability of a memory being needed. The next section will give a formal analysis of this probability which is called *need probability* and its relationship to probability of recall and latency of recall. The subsequent two sections will discuss how this need probability is sensitive to the history of past usage of the memory as well as the current context. The last section of this chapter will discuss how G, the value of the memory, and C, the cost, might reflect effects of the content of the memory.

Part of the effort to give a rational analysis to human cognition (Anderson, 1990) was the claim that the memory system functioned optimally under this analysis. Such claims about optimality are always controversial. This chapter will not push this issue of optimality but rather simply note that this adaptive perspective does offer insight about memory. Sometimes, it yields surprising, quantitative predictions.

The Analysis of Need Probability

Need probability is the probability that a particular memory is needed in a particular context. Letting H stand for the hypothesis that the memory is needed and E the evidence of the elements in the context, the need probability can be denoted as a conditional probability $P(H \mid E)$. This conditional probability could be profitably analyzed in a Bayesian framework. Bayes theorem in odds form is:

$$\frac{P(H|E)}{P(\overline{H}|E)} = \frac{P(H)}{P(\overline{H})} * \frac{P(E|H)}{P(E|\overline{H})} \qquad (2)$$

or

Posterior-odds = prior-odds * likelihood-ratio

This offered a useful separation of factors that did involve the current context and that did not. The prior odds, $P(H)/P(\overline{H})$, reflected factors associated with the general history of use of the memory. It is called the *history factor* and will be analyzed in the next section. The likelihood ratio, $P(E \mid H)/P(E \mid \overline{H})$, reflects how the current context determines the probability of being relevant. This is called the *context factor* and will be discussed in the subsequent section. The remainder of this section will do three things. The first is to discuss the issue of possible mechanistic realizations of this mathematical formula. The other two are to articulate how need probability might map onto the dependent measures of latency and probability of correct recall.

A frequent criticism of this analysis is that the Bayesian mathematics is not intuitive and that people are poor at estimating Bayesian probabilities. It should perhaps be obvious, but there is no claim here that people are explicitly calculating these probabilities. Rather, the claim is that the human memory system is behaving as if it were calculating such probabilities. This leaves open the question of how it achieves this "as if" behavior. J. R. Anderson (1993) showed that standard connectionist activation formulas (e.g., Rumelhart & McClelland, 1986) serve to calculate a quantity related to need probability. There are two keys to this insight. The first is to note, as had J. R. Anderson and Milson (1989), that the likelihood ratio $P(E \mid H)/P(E \mid \overline{H})$ can be decomposed into the product of a number of likelihood ratios, one for each element in the context. Then the Bayesian equation above becomes:

$$\frac{P(H \mid E)}{P(\overline{H}) \mid E)} = \frac{P(H)}{P(\overline{H})} \prod_{j \in E} \frac{P(j \mid H)}{P(j \mid \overline{H})} \tag{3}$$

where the product is over the elements j in the context and the $P(j \mid H)/P(j \mid \overline{H})$ are the likelihood ratios of elements j appearing in the context if the memory is needed or not.

The quantity above reflects multiplicative operations, but neural activation is typically thought of as adding influences from various sources. One can get an additive formula by taking logs of both sides of the above equation and having a log-odds formula:

$$\log\left(\frac{P(H \mid E)}{P(\overline{H} \mid E)}\right) = \log\left(\frac{P(H)}{P(\overline{H})}\right) + \sum_{j \in E} \log\left(\frac{P(j \mid H)}{P(j \mid \overline{H})}\right) \tag{4}$$

This is basically equivalent to the following connectionist activation formula where A_i is activation of unit i, B_i is the base level activation, W_j is the input from element j, and S_{ji} is the strength of association between j and i:

$$A_i = B_i + \sum_j W_j S_{ji} \tag{5}$$

If the unit i reflects a memory, then its activation reflects log posterior odds of the memory being needed, its base-level activation reflects prior odds, and strength of association reflects the log of the likelihood ratio. The ACT-R theory, which uses these activation processes to reflect these Bayesian quantities, has been quite successful in accounting for human memory (J. R. Anderson, Bothell, Lebiere, & Matessa, 1998).

That ACT-R theory also incorporates the rational analysis of the relationship between need probability and the dependent measures of probability of recall and latency of recall. J. R. Anderson (1990) derived what the relationship should be between need odds, n, and

the observed behavioral measures. Need odds is $P(H \mid E)/P(\overline{H} \mid E)$ from the prior mathematics.

The analysis given in the introduction implied a step function for probability of recall such that all items with n over a threshold would be recalled and none below would be recalled. However, J. R. Anderson (1990) showed that, if there was some noise in the estimation of need probability, then the odds of a memory, with need odds n, being above threshold is:

$$\text{Odds of recall} = Cn^d \tag{6}$$

In words, the recall odds should be a power function of need odds. A power function means that some term (in this case n) is raised to an exponent (in this case d).[1]

The introduction described a search process that terminates when one of the following two conditions is met: (1) the needed memory is found; or (2) the need odds of the next memory falls below threshold. To predict latency of recall what is important is the first condition: the time it takes to find a needed memory that has been correctly recalled. The analysis assumes a best-first serial search of memory. Therefore, the time to retrieve a particular memory will be proportional to the rank of its need odds among the need odds of all memories. J. R. Anderson and Schooler (1991) show that, assuming need odds are distributed according to the ubiquitous Zipf's law (Ijiri & Simon, 1977), the time to recall a memory with need odds n will be:

$$\text{Time for recall} = An^{-b} \tag{7}$$

That is, the time to retrieve a particular memory should be a power function of need odds. Thus, the prediction is that two dependent measures, odds of recall and latency of recall, should both be power functions of need odds.

The History Factor

J. R. Anderson and Schooler (1991) focused on the effects of amount of practice and retention interval on recall. Somewhat obviously, it is adaptive to make more available memories that are used more often (the practice effect) and less available memories that have not been used for a while (the retention effect). If this is all that an adaptive analysis predicted it would offer only a little insight. Fortunately, more is known about the effects of practice and retention interval than these simple ordinal relationships. It has been shown that performance improves as a power function of practice (Newell & Rosenbloom, 1981). This is usually measured in terms of latency, but the relationship also holds for odds of recall. It is also known that performance deteriorates as a power function of the retention interval (Rubin & Wenzel, 1996; Wixted & Ebbesen, 1991). This is usually displayed in terms of probability of recall, but power function deterioration also describes odds of recall and latency. One of the questions addressed in Anderson and Schooler was whether this adaptive analysis could predict the behavioral power functions.

As noted, this analysis implies that the behavioral measures are related to need odds by a power function. If it turned out that need odds were related to amount of practice by a power function and to retention interval by a power function, the power laws of practice and retention interval would be predicted. That is, if the need odds, n, were related to an independent variable, X, as a power function:

$$n = Fx^g \qquad (8)$$

then odds of recall would be related to X by a power function (combining equations 6 and 8):

$$\text{Recall odds} = C(FX^g)^d = CFX^{dg} \qquad (9)$$

and latency would also be related to X by a power function (combining equations 7 and 8):

$$\text{Time for recall} = A(FX^g)^{-b} = AFn^{-bg} \quad (10)$$

Thus, the goal became to identify what relationships held between need odds and practice and retention interval. More generally the goal became to study the statistics of the information-retrieval demands that people face in their environment.

Gathering statistics about these informational demands requires detailed records of people's experience in the world. Ideally, researchers would follow people around, tallying their informational needs. Clearly, it is impractical to study the complete history of the informational demands that the environment places on an individual. Instead, J. R. Anderson and Schooler (1991) have studied three environmental databases that capture coherent "slices" of the environment. Two of these databases, word usage in speech to children and in the *New York Times* headlines, are linguistic in nature, but differ in their time scales. A third involves the daily distribution

of people who sent the first author (*JA*) electronic mail messages. This database captured aspects of his social environment.

- *Speech to children.* Each word a child hears is another demand to retrieve the meaning of that particular word. MacWhinney and Snow's (1990) CHILDES database is a collection of transcripts of children's speech interactions. Anderson and Schooler analyzed 25 hours of preschool children's verbal interactions donated by Hall and Tirre (1979) that were collected by attaching wireless microphones to the children's clothing. For the analyses based on the Hall and Tirre corpus, a word was defined to be needed each time it was mentioned in an utterance.
- *New York Times.* Reading newspaper headlines requires retrieving the meaning of words that make up the headlines. Two years' (1986 & 1987) worth of New York Times front-page headlines were studied. For the analyses based on the *New York Times* headlines, a word was defined to be needed each time it was mentioned in a headline.
- *Authors of electronic mail.* Each time someone receives mail, demands are made on the memory system to retrieve information about the person who sent it. Three years' worth of JA's mail messages were studied. For these analyses, information about a sender was defined to be needed each time JA received a message written by that sender.

Studying the effect of practice involved looking at the relationship between the probability that an item would occur in a particular interval in the past and the probability that it would occur in the next interval. It was found, as has already been documented (Ijiri & Simon, 1977), that there is a direct linear relationship between the two probabilities of the form:

Probability-in-the-future

$$= a * \text{probability-in-the-past} \qquad (11)$$

where a is a fraction typically less that 1 (in these three domains it varied from .76 to 1). Since the actual probabilities are much less than 1, this also implies the relationship between odds will be approximately of the same form:

Odds-in-the-future = $a' *$ odds-in-the-past (12)

This linear function is a special case of a power function and therefore the rational analysis does predict the power functions of practice. However, it is a somewhat degenerate and obvious power function and some of the surprise value in the result was diminished.

The situation is more interesting with respect to the retention function. When an item's environmental need odds are plotted as function of how long it has been since it was last encountered, is the resulting curve a power function? Figure 34.1 shows the results

New York Times Recency Analysis

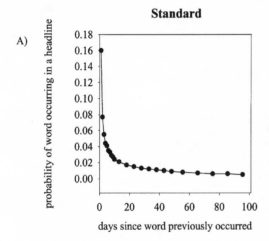

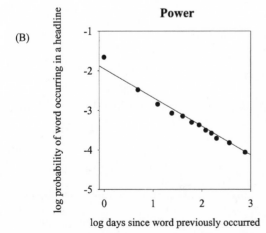

Figure 34.1 (a) Probability of a word occurring in a headline in the *New York Times* on day 101 as a function of how long it has been since the word previously occurred; (b) the same data in log-log form.

of the analysis of the *New York Times*. Figure 34.1a plots the odds of a word being included in the front page headlines as a function of the number of days since the word was last included. Figure 34.1b shows these same data in log-log coordinates. Here the curve is straight, suggesting that the environmental recency function, like its behavioral counterpart, can be described by a power function ($R^2 = .99$). Similar results held for both the analyses of speech to children and the daily distribution of the sources of electronic mail messages. Recker and Pitkow (1996) have shown that similar statistics are also found in WEB accesses.

In conclusion, need odds is both a power function of amount of practice and retention interval. In one case, this was a novel finding. Thus, in both cases, the behavioral power functions represent adaptive responses to the statistical structure in the environment. This offers some insight into the nature of memory.

Can rational analysis go beyond predicting the parametric forms of the learning and retention curves? One complication in the memory literature is the spacing effect, which involves an interaction between study lag and the retention interval. For short retention intervals memory is often best with short study intervals while the result reverses for long retention intervals. J. R. Anderson and Schooler (1991) looked at their three sources, considering situations where an item had occurred just twice in the last 100 time units. They examined how the interval between these two occurrences (analogous to study lag) interacted with the retention interval (the interval between the last occurrence and the current time—analogous to retention interval). Figure 34.2 shows the results for the three empirical domains. In each case, increasing study lag decreases the probability of encountering a stimulus for short retention intervals and increases this probability for long retention intervals. Thus, the spacing function in memory behavior seems to reflect a similar spacing function in the statistics of the environment.

Finally, J. R. Anderson and Schooler looked at the relationship between amount of practice and retention interval. There has been a history of some controversy about what the retention functions are like for different levels of practice (e.g., Bogartz, 1990; Loftus, 1985; Slamecka & McElree, 1983). When one considers odds of recall one tends to get parallel retention functions for different amounts of practice. Figure 34.3a presents some data from Hellyer (1962) looking at short retention inter-

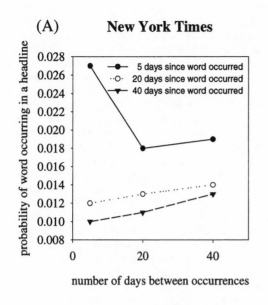

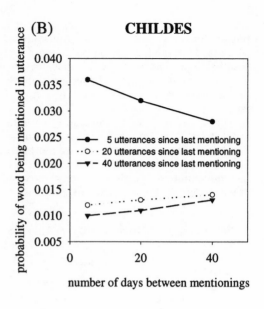

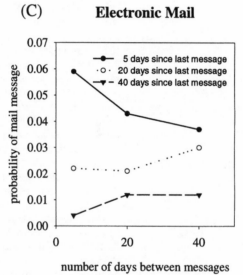

Figure 34.2 The interaction between study lag and retention lag in the (a) *New York Times*; (b) CHILDES database, and (c) electronic mail source.

vals and figure 34.3b presents data from Krueger (1929) looking at relatively longer intervals. In both of these cases, when log odds of recall is plotted as a function of log interval, there are approximately parallel curves for different levels of practice. J. R. Anderson and Schooler looked at environment retention functions in the cases where there had been many occurrences in the last 100 intervals and cases where there had been few. The results for the three data bases are shown in figure

34.4. Again there are parallel retention functions when log odds is plotted as a function of log retention interval. Figures 34.3 and 34.4 imply that when one goes back to the original scales from log scales one will find a multiplicative relationship such that the dependent measure (odds, latency) is a joint power function of practice and retention interval:

$$A \times \text{practice}^b \times \text{delay}^{-c}$$

Hellyer

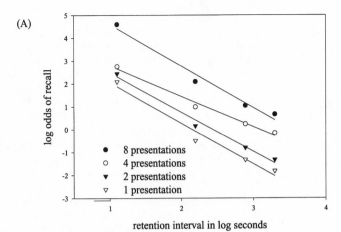

(A)

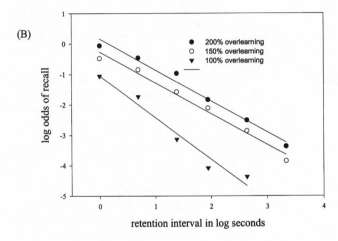

Krueger

(B)

Figure 34.3 (a) Forgetting curves at four practice levels, (from Hellyer, 1962); (b) forgetting curves at three practice levels (from Krueger, 1929).

Thus, sitting behind some of the most robust regularities in human memory there are equally robust regularities in the environment, many of which had not been suspected. This offers insight into the nature of memory and that the history factor does seem to be an adaptive response to the statistics of the environment.

One of the criticisms that has been made of that research is that the three domains investigated by J. R. Anderson and Schooler (*New York Times*, e-mail messages, and caregiver speech to children) all involve human communication. One might think that human communication is determined by human memory. Thus, it might seem circular that properties of human memory can be predicted from properties of such databases. There are

problems in making such criticisms go through in detail. For instance, one of the terms in the *New York Times* database is *Challenger* and reflects the *Challenger* explosion. It is a bit bizarre to think human memory caused the *Challenger* explosion and hence its appearance in the *New York Times*. Still, it would be nice to have databases that were free of the influence of human memory.

Human-communication databases were chosen because these tend to be represented as computer records and therefore are subject to computer-based analyses. As humans did not evolve in a world of e-mail and newspapers, one may wonder about the informational demands that were placed on early hominids during critical periods in evolution. It is, of course, impossible to study these environments di-

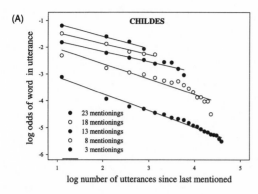

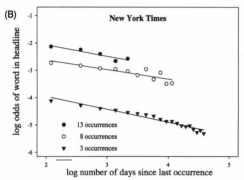

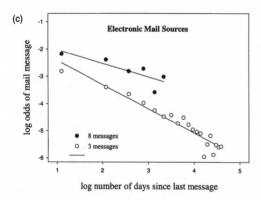

Figure 34.4 Combined frequency and recency effects in (a) the *New York Times*; (b) CHILDES database; (c) electronic mail source.

rectly. However, one can study the informational demands placed on animals whose current ecological niches share something in common with those of early hominids.

The question, then, is which animals fill the appropriate ecological niches. Milton (1981) notes that "field studies are often concerned with savanna-living primates since these are thought to offer possible analogues for hominid evolution" (p. 535). She points

out, however, that hominids evolved first in tropical forests, where "the extreme diversity of plant foods in tropical forests, and the manner in which they are distributed in space and time, have been a major selective force in the development of advanced cerebral complexity in higher primates" (p. 535). Thus, "to understand the origins of mental complexity, one must look not only at life in the savannas but also life in tropical forests." (p. 535) Therefore, studying how primates move through forests and savannas represents good starting points for understanding the informational demands that shaped early hominid evolution. The second author (L.S.), in collaboration with Juan Carlos Serio Silva[2] and Ramon Rhine,[3] is analyzing the ranging behavior of howler monkeys through forests (Serio Silva's data), and baboons through savanna (Rhine's data). While these analyses are still preliminary, it does appear that the visitation patterns of howlers and baboons match the statistics of the earlier human communication databases. For example, there appear to be similar decay functions.

Another issue is whether human memory is responsive to changes in the statistical pattern of appearance of information in the environment. In the real world at large, the probability of something appearing decreases with how long it has been since the item has been encountered. However, what if an experimenter changed this statistic and made it more likely that something would appear the longer it had not been encountered? Would human memory respond to the change in the statistics of the environment? It is just this question that has been investigated in recent research by R. B. Anderson, Tweney, Rivardo, and Duncan (1997). In fact, the retention function did change with experience and showed less decay in the case where the passage of time made the reappearance more probable. Memory did not show an increase with retention interval but the decay rate did decrease. The failure to get the retention function to rise with delay may reflect the fact that the local experience did not overwhelm the massive past experience to the contrary. Nonetheless, this is an impressive experimental demonstration that the memory system will respond to the statistics of its experience.

The Contextual Factor

It is well established that the memory system is sensitive to the match between the context in which a piece of information was studied and the context in which it was tested. This is the basic encoding specificity demonstration of Tulving (1975), where memory for a word is higher if it is tested in the context of the same word as it was studied. In analyses of the *New York Times* and the CHILDES databases, Schooler (1993) showed that a particular word was more likely to occur when other words that had occurred with it in the past were present. For instance, a headline one day mentioned both Qaddafi and Libya, and sure enough a headline the next day that mentioned Qaddafi also mentioned Libya. Stated in the context of such an example the result is rather obvious, but the example makes clear the basic adaptiveness of encoding specificity: if two items have occurred together in the past, they are more likely to occur together in the future. Therefore, an adaptive memory system should show an encoding specificity.

Schooler (1993) tried to explore the extent to which the effects of context went beyond the obvious in the *New York Times* and CHILDES databases. He collected likelihood-ratio measures of association between various words. This was measured as the associative ratio, $P(S \mid q)/P(S)$, that approximates the likelihood ratio common in Bayesian statistics. The denominator of this ratio, $P(S)$, is the base rate probability of needing a memory. The numerator is the conditional probability, $P(S \mid q)$, of needing a memory in the presence of some cue, q. The overall strength of the context is taken to be the product of the associative ratios of each of the individual cues in the context, as per equation 3.

In the same way that the environmental databases were used to investigate the history factor, they can be used to explore the context factor. Calculating the associative ratios requires estimating the base rate frequencies of the items (i.e., words) as well as the many conditional probabilities of finding one item in the presence of another. In these environmental analyses, the base rate probabilities were taken to be the proportion of all the headlines or utterances in which a word appeared. Estimating the conditional probability of finding a word in the presence of another in the same context requires a definition of context. A context was defined to be a headline or utterance; a word's context, then, was the other words that compose the headline or utterance. Table 34.1 shows some words from the headlines along with associates that had particularly high associative ratios. For example, *AIDS*

Table 34.1 Associative rates in the *New York Times* database.

| Associates | $p(AIDS)= .018$ | |
	$p(AIDS/$ associate$)$	$\dfrac{p(AIDS/\text{associate})}{p(AIDS)}$
virus	.75	41.0
spread	.54	29.4
patients	.40	21.8
health	.27	14.6
	$p(trade)= .015$	
	$p(trade/$ associate$)$	$\dfrac{p(trade/\text{associate})}{p(trade)}$
imports	.77	49.6
gap	.60	38.7
exports	.44	28.7
deficit	.35	22.7
	$p(senate)= .015$	
	$p(senate/$ associate$)$	$\dfrac{p(senate/\text{associate})}{p(senate)}$
measure	.48	19.4
veto	.46	18.6
bill	.38	15.3
votes	.35	14.3

was included in 1.8% of all headlines, and in 75% of the headlines that included *virus*. The associative ratio for the pair is 41 (i.e., .75/.018), or equivalently, *AIDS* is 41 times more likely to occur in a headline that includes *virus* than its base rate.

By definition a word is more likely to occur in a headline if a strong associate of it occurs. However, what if two strong associates occur in one headline? The earlier Bayesian statistics (see equation 3) implied that there should be a proportionate increase in the odds of the target word occurring. Indeed, this is what Schooler found. The corresponding behavioral prediction, then, is that the probability of retrieving a target word should increase if two strong associates are present rather than one. In fact, there does appear to be an effect of accumulating associates in retrieving a memory (e.g., Bowers, Regehr, Balthazard, & Parker, 1990).

Schooler (1993) and Schooler and Anderson (1997) looked at how this contextual factor combined with the historical factor. Schooler examined how these two factors combined in the *New York Times* database and the child-language database. The results are displayed in figure 34.5. Parts (a) and (b) show that both the presence of a high associate ("strong context" in figure 34.5) and the time since last appearance ("delay" in figure 34.5) affect the probability of occurrence in the critical unit of time. It might appear from parts (a) and (b) of figure 34.5 that the time factor is more important in the presence of a high associate. However, if one converts the odds scale to log odds and the time scale to log time (see J. R. Anderson & Schooler, 1991, for the justification), one gets the functions in parts (c) and (d) of figure 34.5. Those figures

show parallel linear functions, which is the additivity predicted by the Bayesian log formula given earlier (equation 4).

The interesting question is whether human memory is similarly sensitive to these factors. Schooler conducted an experiment where he asked subjects to complete word fragments and manipulated whether the fragments were in the presence of a high associate or not and the time since the target word had been seen. The data are displayed in log-log form in figure 34.6. They once again show parallel linear functions, implying that human memory is combining information about prior odds and likelihood ratio in the appropriate Bayesian fashion and making items available as a function of their posterior probability. Schooler and Anderson (1997) note that similar parallel functions have been found in other studies of human memory (e.g., Mäntylä & Nilsson, 1988; Thompson, 1972) but such data had not

Environmental Analyses of Context and Recency

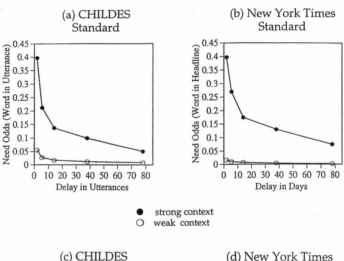

(a) CHILDES Standard

(b) New York Times Standard

● strong context
○ weak context

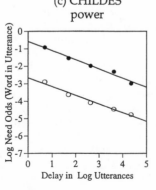

(c) CHILDES power

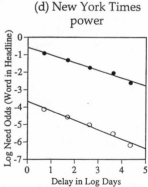

(d) New York Times power

Figure 34.5 Environmental recency curves from the analysis of the CHILDES and *New York Times* database (panels a and b). Log-log transformations are given in panels c and d.

Schooler and Anderson

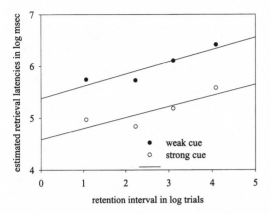

Figure 34.6 Time to retrieve memories (Schooler and Anderson, 1997). The results are plotted in log-log coordinates.

previously been analyzed in these terms. So once again there is a rather unexpected result predicted by an adaptive analysis.

The research on context discussed so far looks at situations where the context and the item are explicitly related—often because both are presented together, as in the Tulving encoding-specificity research. However, contextual effects have been shown of a more general sort where memories are associated to general cues of the environment, of drug state, or emotional mood (for a review, see J. R. Anderson, 1995). One of the interesting aspects of this literature is that the strength of these contextual effects can vary dramatically—sometimes very strong effects are obtained and sometimes null effects are obtained. This makes the point that mere statistical co-occurrence of items is not enough to ensure an association. This might seem to contradict the adaptive analysis that relates memory to the likelihood ratio measuring the statistical co-occurrence of cue and memory. However, this analysis has a significant degree of freedom, which is that it leaves open exactly what are selected as cues for a memory. Clearly, subjects cannot include everything in their current environment as potential cues. Eich and Metcalfe (1989) argue that a critical factor in getting context effects is whether the subject encodes the memory with the context at study. This shows the important role of subject encoding strategy, which is something that will be discussed further in the conclusion.

Effects of Content

Except for the issue of selection of contextual elements, the analyses so far treat memory as if it were totally a function of the statistical patterns with which people encountered events. This runs counter to all of the research that indicates that how subjects study an event and the content of an event have substantial impact on memory for the event. As J. R. Anderson and Milson (1989) show, some of the effects of study strategy can be conceived of as the subject's manipulating his experience with the target memory. For instance, different rehearsal strategies will create an environment in which the statistics will favor some items and not others. J. R. Anderson and Milson show that some of the effects associated with free recall, such as the serial position effect, reflect the statistics of such self-made environments. However, other effects do not seem to have such an explanation. These effects include the difference between shallow and deep processing (Craik & Lockhart, 1972), the effects of the concreteness and imageability of the material (e.g., Paivio, 1971), and the self-reference effect whereby memories involving the self are better (e.g., Rogers, Kuiper, & Kirker, 1977).

However, the emphasis on the statistical properties of the environment reflects only the variable P in the original P, G, and C characterization of a rational memory system. It might be less costly to process certain memories than others—that is, they have a lower value of C associated with them. Certainly, this would seem to be the implication of Paivio's analysis of the advantage of pictorial material. The claim is that the visual system is just more capable than the verbal system. Unfortunately, claims about such differences in processing costs tend to be basically circular: one winds up claiming memories are better for certain types of material because memory system is better for that material. Without some convergent evidence about processing costs, it does not seem profitable to pursue the C variable.

On the other hand, it seems possible to make objective assessments of the relative importance of various memories. One result that seems to fall out directly from an adaptive analysis is that, all other things being equal, memory should be better for more important material (i.e., higher G). For instance, people

Anderson

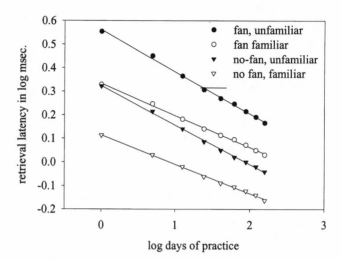

Figure 34.7 Recognition of fan and no-fan sentences about familiar and unfamiliar concepts as a function of practice. The results are plotted in log-log coordinates.

remember things about themselves and other people close to them better than about strangers (Rogers et al., 1977). One can similarly interpret the apparent superiority for flashbulb memories for details about dramatic events (e.g., Palmer, Schreiber, & Foy, 1991). Again, the framework can explain the better retention levels associated with memories that produce high arousal (Levonian, 1972). As another example of the same principle, people tend to show better memory for the meaningful aspects of an event than its unimportant superficial details (e.g., Wanner, 1968).

While it is reassuring to an adaptive analysis that memory is better for more important things, this does not offer very much insight into the nature of memory. As in the case of the history and context factor, one wants to look for detailed, nonobvious predictions. One such prediction involves the effect of practice and retention interval for memories of differential value. Rational analysis would predict that retention or practice curves for more important things would parallel those for less important on log-log scales—just as were parallel curves for different contexts in figure 34.6. This is because P and G multiply in the utility analysis and a multiplicative relationship implies an additive relationship in log-log scale. Unfortunately, in the case of at least one variable plausibly affecting importance—namely arousal—there seems to be a cross-over interaction with retention interval (Levonian, 1972). So this is evidence that the

predictions of the adaptive analysis are not always confirmed.

On the other hand, J. R. Anderson (1983) contrasted familiar (Ted Kennedy) and unfamiliar people (Bill Jones) in terms of the fan effects and practice functions for new facts learned about such people. One might assume memories about the familiar people are more important. Typical of other research, J. R. Anderson found that subjects show better memory for the more familiar material (in adaptive terms because such memories are more important) but that they show near identical practice functions (history factor) and fan effects (context factor) for the two types of material. Figure 34.7 displays the results. So this is at least one instance of the nonobvious prediction that the importance of the material elevates memory but does not change the basic memory functions.

Conclusions

Despite the generally successful tone of this review, it is not the case that all factors affecting memory can be understood in terms of an adaptive analysis. As one example, in adaptive framework it is hard to understand the effects of intention to learn on memory. Instructing a subject to learn or paying him to learn can result in differential study patterns (see J. R. Anderson, 1995, for a review) but it appears that, controlling for study pattern, there is no effect of motivation or intention to learn. An adaptive system should be able to give more resources to things that are more important. However, the only way people seem to achieve this is by changing how they study the material.

The effect of study strategy on memory also points to an Achilles' heel of the adaptive analysis. The adaptive analysis works best if one can conceive of memory as responding passively to external statistics in the environment. However, by different rehearsal patterns the subject can actively create his own unobserved environments with its own statistics. In the current terms, subjects can "trick" their memories into treating something as highly probable by giving it the statistics associated with a highly probable memory. This indicates that there are layers of adaptive consideration that go beyond just looking at environmental statistics.

Thus, the adaptive analysis here does not paint a complete picture of memory and it needs to be supplemented by other considerations. Nonetheless, some insight has been obtained about the nature of memory by taking an adaptive analysis. Nonobvious results were found that indicated human memory is adaptive in ways that had not been suspected.

Acknowledgments We would like to thank Mike Byrne for his comments on this paper. Preparation of this paper has been supported by grant SBR-94-21332 from the National Science Foundation.

Notes

1. Note that this implies that the more lawful mathematical relationships should appear if one looks at odds of recall rather than probability of recall. If P is probability of recall, $P/(1 - P)$ is the odds of recall.
2. Juan Carlos Serio Silva is at the Departamento de Ecologia Vegetal Instituto de Ecologia A.C.
3. Ramon Rhine is in the psychology department at the University of California, Irvine.

References

Anderson, J. R. (1983). *The architecture of cognition*. Cambridge, MA: Harvard University Press.

Anderson, J. R. (1990). *The adaptive character of thought*. Hillsdale, NJ: Erlbaum.

Anderson, J. R. (1993). *The rules of the mind*. Hillsdale, NJ: Erlbaum.

Anderson, J. R. (1995). *Learning and memory: An integrated approach*. New York: John Wiley.

Anderson, J. R., Bothell, D., Lebiere, C., & Matessa, M. (1998). An integrated theory of list memory. *Journal of Memory and Language, 38*, 341–380

Anderson, J. R., & Lebiere, C. (1998). *The atomic components of thought*. Mahwah, NJ: Erlbaum.

Anderson, J. R., & Milson, R. (1989). Human memory: An adaptive perspective. *Psychological Review, 96*, 703–719.

Anderson, J. R., & Schooler, L. J. (1991). Reflections of the environment in memory. *Psychological Science, 2*, 396–408.

Anderson, R. B., Tweney, R. D., Rivardo, M., & Duncan, S. (1997). Need probability affects retention: A direct demonstration. *Memory & Cognition, 25*, 867–872.

Bjork, R. A., & Bjork, E. L. (1992). A new theory of disuse and an old theory of stimulus fluctuation. In A. F. Healy, S. M. Kosslyn, & R. M. Shiffrin (Eds.), *Essays in honor of William K. Estes*, Vol. 1: *From learning theory to connectionist theory;* Vol. 2: *From learning processes to cognitive processes* (pp. 35–67). Hillsdale, NJ: Erlbaum.

Bogartz, R. S. (1990). Evaluating forgetting curves psychologically. *Journal of Experimental Psychology: Learning, Memory, and Cognition, 16*, 138–148.

Bowers, K. S., Regehr, G., Balthazard, C. G., & Parker, K. (1990). Intuition in the context of discovery. *Cognitive Psychology, 22*, 72–110.

Bruce, D. (1985). The how and why of ecological memory. *Journal of Experimental Psychology: General, 114*, 78–90.

Burrell, Q. L. (1980). A simple stochastic model for library loans. *Journal of Documentation, 36*, 115–132.

Burrell, Q. L. (1985). A note on aging on a library circulation model. *Journal of Documentation, 41*, 100–115.

Craik, F. I. M., & Lockhart, R. S. (1972). Levels of processing: A framework for memory research. *Journal of Verbal Learning and Verbal Behavior, 11*, 671–684.

Eich, E., & Metcalfe, J. (1989). Mood dependent memory for internal versus external events. *Journal of Experimental Psychology: Learning, Memory, and Cognition, 15*, 443–455.

Hall, W. S., & Tirre, W. C. (1979). *The communicative environment of young children: Social class, ethnic and situation differ-*

ences. University of Illinois, Center for the Study of Reading.

Hellyer, S. (1962). Frequency of stimulus presentation and short-term decrement in recall. *Journal of Experimental Psychology, 64*, 650.

Ijiri, Y., & Simon, H. A. (1977). *Skew distributions and the sizes of business firms*. Amsterdam: North Holland.

Krueger, W. C. F. (1929). The effects of overlearning on retention. *Journal of Experimental Psychology, 12*, 71–78.

Levonian, E. (1972). Retention over time in relation to arousal during learning: An explanation of discrepant results. *Acta Psychologica, 36*, 290–321.

Loftus, G. R. (1985). Evaluating forgetting curves. *Journal of Experimental Psychology: Learning, Memory, and Cognition, 11*, 397–406.

MacWhinney, B., & Snow, C. (1990). The child language data exchange system: An update. *Journal of Child Language, 17*, 457–472.

Mäntylä, T., & Nilsson, L. G. (1988). Cue distinctiveness and forgetting: effectiveness of self-generated retrieval cues in delayed recall. *Journal of Experimental Psychology: Learning, Memory, and Cognition, 14*, 502–509.

McClelland, J. L., & Chappell, M. (1998). Familiarity breeds differentiation: A subjective-likelihood approach to the effects of experience in recognition memory. *Psychological Review, 105*, 724–760.

Milton, K. (1981). Distribution patterns of tropical plant foods as an evolutionary stimulus to primate mental development. *American Anthropologist, 83*, 534–548.

Neisser, U. (1976). *Cognition and reality*. San Francisco: Freeman.

Neisser, U. (1978). Memory: What are the important questions? In M. M. Gruneberg, P. Morris, & R. H. Sykes (Eds.), *Practical aspects of memory* (pp. 3–24). New York: Academic Press.

Neisser, U. (1982). *Memory observed: Remembering in natural contexts*. San Francisco: Freeman.

Newell, A., & Rosenbloom, P. (1981). Mechanisms of skill acquisition and the law of practice. In J. R. Anderson (Ed.), *Cognitive skills and their acquisition* (pp. 1–55). Hillsdale, NJ: Erlbaum.

Paivio, A. (1971). *Imagery and verbal processes*. New York: Holt, Rinehart, & Winston.

Palmer, S., Schreiber, G., & Fox, C. (1991). Remembering the earthquake: "Flashbulb" memory of experienced versus reported events. Paper presented at the 32nd annual meeting of the Psychonomic Society, San Francisco.

Ratcliff, R., Clark, S., & Shiffrin, R. M. (1990). The list strength effect: I. Data and discussion. *Journal of Experimental Psychology: Learning, Memory, and Cognition, 16*, 163–178.

Recker, M., & Pitkow, J. (1996). Predicting document access in large, multimedia repositories. *ACM Transactions on Computer-Human Interaction* (ToCHI), *3*, 352–375.

Rogers, T. B., Kuiper, N. A., & Kirker, W. S. (1977). Self-reference and the encoding of personal information. *Journal of Personality and Social Psychology, 35*, 677–688.

Rubin, R. C., & Wenzel, A. E. (1996). 100 years of forgetting: A quantitative description of retention. *Psychological Review, 103*, 734–760.

Rumelhart, D. E., & McClelland, J. L. (1986). *Parallel distributed processing* (Vol. 1). Cambridge, MA: MIT Press.

Salton, G., & McGill, M. J. (1983). *Introduction to modern information retrieval*. New York: MacGraw-Hill.

Schooler, L. J. (1993). *Memory and the statistical structure of the environment*. Ph.D. Dissertation, Department of Psychology, Carnegie Mellon University.

Schooler, L. J., & Anderson, J. R. (1997). The role of process in the rational analysis of memory. *Cognitive Psychology, 32*, 219–250.

Shiffrin, R. M., & Steyvers, M. (1997). A model for recognition memory: REM—Retrieving effectively from memory. *Psychonomic Bulletin & Review, 4*, 145–166.

Slamecka, N. J., & McElree, B. (1983). Normal forgetting of verbal lists as a function of their degree of learning. *Journal of Experimental Psychology: Learning, Memory, and Cognition, 9*, 384–397.

Stritter, E. P. (1977). *File migration*. Unpublished doctoral dissertation, Stanford University, Stanford, CA.

Thomson, D. (1972). Context effects in recognition memory. *Journal of Verbal Learning and Verbal Behavior, 11*, 497–511.

Tulving, E. (1975). Ecphoric processing in recall and recognition. In J. Brown (Ed.), *Recall and recognition*. London: John Wiley.

Wanner, H. E. (1968). *On remembering, forgetting, and understanding sentences: A study of the deep structure hypothesis*. Unpublished doctoral dissertation, Harvard University.

Wixted, J. T., & Ebbesen, E. B. (1991). On the form of forgetting. *Psychological Science, 2*, 409–415.

35

Memory Models

ROGER RATCLIFF & GAIL MCKOON

The study of models of memory often seems like a backwater in the overall study of memory. Models do not have a prominent place in experimental studies of memory and they are not used or examined by most researchers in the field. This review examines the various questions that models can address, discusses why theory is not as prominent in the memory domain as in other domains of science, and presents an overview of current models. The aim is to show why models should have greater prominence and wider use.

Mainstream models for "long-term" memory take as their database the results of experiments in which subjects are asked to study and learn lists of items (words, nonsense syllables, letters, numbers, sentences, or pictures). Memory is tested in one of a number of ways: asking subjects whether or not an item occurred on the study list (recognition), asking for recall of the items on the study list, asking what item on the study list was associated with a cue, asking for the recency or frequency of appearance of an item on the study list, and so on. The dependent measures are usually accuracy, confidence ratings, or a combination of reaction time and accuracy. The eventual aim is to account for the effects on all the dependent variables for a range of experimental tasks and for a range of experimental manipulations, including the length of the study list, the strengths of the items in memory, the type of material, the similarity among study and

test items, levels of processing, rehearsal methods, and so on.

Recent development of models of long-term memory has proceeded relatively independently of other areas of memory research. For example, there has been little contact between the long-term memory models and the findings of implicit memory experiments and there has been little explicit theoretical work in the domain of implicit memory. Over the last 20 years, the domains of reaction time research and memory have not interacted in strongly productive ways, although there has been a recent resurgence of interest in random walk and diffusion reaction time models and so there may soon be more fruitful interactions. The one domain of research with which there is some sharing of representation and process assumptions is categorization. In this domain, subjects are presented with exemplars and through feedback learn how to assign the exemplars to categories. Some models of categorization are essentially long-term memory models in that they assume a representation of a category is built up with learning and the category decision process depends on retrieval from this memory representation.

Short Historical Background

The attempt to produce models of memory that can account for data both qualitatively and quantitatively has had a history of working from small models with very restricted ranges of application to more comprehensive models with wider ranges of application. Early memory models (in the 1960s to '70s) used the dichotomy between short-term memory and long-term memory as a reason either for restricting the domain of the model to short-term or long-term memory or for explaining how information progressed from short-term to long-term memory. In many of the models, component processes paralleled developments in mathematical psychology, borrowing the mechanisms of Markov chains (used in models of associations), signal detection theory (used in perception and strength based models), or serial search processes (derived from the computer metaphor and used in the influential Sternberg, 1966, serial search model). Two excellent sources for the state of the art in the early 1970s are the books, *Models of Human Memory* (Norman, 1970) and *Human Memory: Theory and Data* (Murdock, 1974). As is shown in these books, many of these were models of a particular task (e.g., paired associate learning and cued recall, or memory search and recognition) and the models were usually applied only to a restricted range of experimental data.

In the late 1960s and early 1970s, there were two more comprehensive models that were particularly influential. One was Atkinson and Shiffrin's (1968) model of short-term and long-term memory. The model provided a qualitative/theoretical basis for the separation of short- and long-term memory, although the mathematical structure of the model was not widely applied to experimental data. The model served as a focus for testing hypotheses about how the two kinds of memory might be differentiated and it was the "modal" memory model in that it represented the pinnacle of development of models of its class. It was also the stepping-off point for attacks on the simple rigid bipartite division of memory into short- and long-term components.

The second influential model was Anderson and Bower's (1973). Because the model was explicitly applied to memory both for the standard paradigms and for sentences, it was influential at the intersection of traditional memory research and the rapidly developing domain of language research. This union of memory and language theory evolved in the early 1990s into a rational model (Anderson, 1990, 1993) of memory that is intended to apply over a range of domains that includes

memory, sentence processing, and categorization. The notion of rationality has become a critical component of the newest memory models, as will be discussed below. Anderson, Bothell, Lebiere, and Matessa (1998) recently applied the Anderson (1993) model to the standard list-learning experiments targeted by more traditional models, but the model was fit only to selected aspects of data so, until more comprehensive evaluations have been carried out, it is too soon to tell how the model will fare.

Beginning in the 1980s, models were developed that were aimed at being comprehensive in both the range of tasks and the range of data to which they were applied. Murdock's (1982) TODAM model was designed to apply across the categories of information that Murdock used to classify memory, item information, associative information, and serial order information (see Murdock, 1974, p. 16), and the processes that operate on those kinds of information. Around the same time, Raaijmakers and Shiffrin's (1981) search model for free recall (SAM) accounted for many of the experimental findings from free recall experiments, and Gillund and Shiffrin (1984) extended the model to data from recognition experiments. A little later, Hintzman's (1986, 1988) MINERVA2 model was applied to recognition and categorization and then extended to judgments of recency and frequency. The next sections of this review describe these models in more detail, then describe the empirical phenomena that were inconsistent with the models, and then finally describe the next generation of models.

Global Memory Models

The SAM, MINERVA2, and TODAM models are called the global memory models for two reasons. First, for each of the models, it is assumed that a test item contacts a great deal of information in memory, possibly all stored memories. Second, the models were intended to explain data from a range of experimental tasks and a range of experimental manipulations within those tasks.

MINERVA2, SAM, and TODAM each make different assumptions about how information is represented in memory. SAM stores strengths between cues to memory (test items) and items in memory. TODAM assumes that items are vectors with random values as the elements of a vector. Memory is assumed to be a single vector into which all the item vectors are stored. MINERVA2 assumes that items are vectors with elements +1, 0, or −1, and that items are stored in separate vectors in memory. For recognition memory, the three models share the same assumption about retrieval: at test, a test item matches all of memory and a single value of familiarity is produced that serves as the basis for the decision about whether the test item was or was not on the study list. Recognition memory is the main area in which the coverage of the models overlaps, so it has become a central focus for testing and evaluation, and the two models of the next generation, to be described below, focus almost entirely on recognition memory.

A good introduction to the global memory models is presented in Neath (1998) and this would be a useful starting point for readers new to memory models.

The SAM Model

The SAM model (Gillund & Shiffrin, 1984; Raaijmakers & Shiffrin, 1981) represents information in a cued dependent structure. That is, what is stored are the strengths of the connections between cues (test items) that interrogate memory and items stored in memory ("images"). These strengths are built up by an encoding process that uses a simple short-term buffer. During the time an item to be studied is in the buffer, c units of "self strength" per unit of time are built up between the item as a cue and the image of the item in memory and a units of strength are built up between the general study context and the image of the item in memory. "Interitem strengths" (b units per unit of time) are also built up between the item as a cue and the images in memory of each of the other items that are in the buffer at the same time. There is also assumed to be some residual strength between an item as a cue and the images of each of the other items in memory; this serves the role of pre-experimental strength of connection between items.

At retrieval, a cue interrogates memory. In recognition, the cue is assumed to be the test item plus the context in which it is presented. The strength from each of these to an item in memory is calculated, and the product of these two strengths is formed. This calculation is performed for all items in memory and all the products are summed. The sum is a measure of the global familiarity of the test item. This value of familiarity is used in a signal detection analysis to produce hit and false alarm rates. A criterion is set on familiarity, and if the computed value is greater than the criterion, then the decision is that the item was on the study list and an "old" response is produced; if the computed value is lower than the criterion value, then the decision is that the item was not on the study list and a "new" response is produced. Free recall is a two-phase process, sampling and recovery. First, the context cue is used to probe memory and for each item in memory, a "sampling probability" is produced; this probability is a function of the item's strength relative to other items and it is the probability that the item will be selected for recovery. If an item is selected, then it has some probability of being recovered that is a function of its strength, so the stronger the item, the greater the probability of recovery. If recovery fails, the process resamples and attempts another recovery. An item that is successfully recovered is used as a cue along with context for an attempt to retrieve another item. This process continues until a criterion number of attempts is made without a successful retrieval. Cued recall works like free recall except that there are two cues with which to probe memory, the recall cue and the context.

SAM has been successfully applied to a wide range of experimental data. The recognition process has changed in the transition to the new generation of models, but the recall assumptions still provide the most successful explanation of recall data.

The MINERVA2 Model

In MINERVA2 (Hintzman, 1986, 1988), items are represented as vectors of features. At study, a new memory vector is created for each studied item, with the each feature of the item copied into the vector with a probability that varies as a function of study time. Features have values of plus or minus 1 or, if a feature is not copied into memory, the value for that feature is set to zero. For recognition, a test item's vector is compared with each vector in memory and a dot product (divided by the number of features) is formed to give the degree of match—the "activation" value. This value is cubed and then the activation values for all the items in memory are summed to provide an overall measure of match called "echo intensity." If this value is greater than a criterion, an "old" response is produced; if it is less, a "new" response is produced.

For recognition, the model does a good job of predicting many of the standard experimental results, including the effects of repetition and study time on performance. It also has been successfully applied to frequency judgment data and to categorization. Processes have been suggested that would allow the model to explain recall data but there have not been any specific applications.

The TODAM Model

In TODAM, an item is a vector of attributes and each attribute has a value derived from a normal distribution with mean zero. Memory is a single vector, a composite memory trace of all studied items. A study, for each studied item, the probability that an attribute is encoded is a function of study time. The vector for each studied item is simply added to the single memory vector. If two items are studied together in a pair (e.g., paired associate learning), the association between the two items is the convolution of their vectors (see Neath, 1998) and this convolution is stored in the single memory vector along with the vectors of the individual items.

For recognition, the vector for a test item is compared with the single memory vector using a dot product (i.e., multiplying corresponding attributes together and summing over attributes). The resulting sum is compared with a criterion value just as in the SAM and MINERVA2 models. The mathematics of the model would actually work in exactly the same way if it was assumed that the items are stored in separate vectors in memory instead of a composite, so the differences between this model and MINERVA2 are less than they might seem at first examination.

For cued recall, one member of a studied pair is presented and the vector for this item is correlated with the memory vector. This produces a noisy version of the other member of the pair and this is cleaned up to produce a response. Recent empirical work on the interactions of associative and item information has required a revision of TODAM; TODAM2 is the most recent version of this model (Murdock, 1997).

The Data that Challenged the Global Memory Models

It is often thought that the global memory models are unfalsifiable, that they can be manipulated to produce any pattern of data by varying parameter values or adding new parameters. Recently, Slamecka (1991) voiced this view directly: "If the models have anything, they have resilience, or to put it more precisely, their inventors have resilience, and I suspect that after some skillful patching of assumptions and/or fine-tuning of some pa-

rameters, these veterans will lumber down the runway and lift off again." If this were correct, the enterprise would truly be of little interest. Fortunately for science, and unfortunately for the global memory models (and Slamecka's argument), the models are solidly grounded in the phenomena to which they were addressed.

To understand what kinds of tests falsify the models, it is necessary to understand which are the fundamental assumptions of the models that are not subject to patching and parameter twiddling. We discuss two such assumptions. One has to do with the way the output quantities specified by the models (e.g., familiarity values) get larger as the strengths of the items stored in memory increase and the second concerns variability in the match between a test item and memory.

The easiest demonstration of the models' inabilities to handle the effects of increasing strength of items in memory is the "mirror effect." According to the models, increasing the strength of an item in memory should increase the probability that an item is called "old" for items that are indeed "old" because they were on the study list *and* for items that are not "old"—that is, items that were not on the study list. But often this is not the empirical result. For example, low-frequency words are more likely to be called old if they were studied but they are more likely to be called new if they were not (e.g., Glanzer & Adams, 1985; Glanzer, Adams, Iverson, & Kim, 1993).

One solution the models could offer for this problem is that the retrieval process begins by determining whether a test item is low versus high frequency and then alters the decision criterion for old versus new responses, but everyone agrees this is an unsatisfactory solution. Some of the problems with this solution (besides the fact that it is exactly the kind of solution that Slamecka uses to attack the modeling enterprise) are, first, that responses can be made just as quickly when frequencies are not mixed in the study and test lists as when they are; second, subjects are not very good at determining the frequencies of words; and third, in experiments with a number of different frequency values, the multiple criteria required would make the task very difficult.

The second falsifiable assumption of the models is that as the strength of an item increases, variability increases. In SAM, variability is introduced at encoding. For each unit of time that an item remains in the encoding buffer, the units of strength that are built up are not the fixed values of the strength parameters (the *c, a,* and *b* values), but instead they are these values with probability one third, .5 times these values with probability one third, or 1.5 times these values with probability one third. It follows that, as the amount of time in the buffer increases, both the encoded strength values and the variability in those values increases. Similar behavior is produced by the variability assumptions in MINERVA2 and TODAM. The assumptions about variance underlay all predictions of the models and only fundamental alteration of the basic structures of the models could change these assumptions.

For each of the models, the variance assumptions lead to the prediction of a "list strength effect." Consider a mixed study list in which some items are studied for a long time (e.g., 5s) and some for a short time (e.g., 1s) versus a pure list in which all items are studied for a short time. For SAM, when a recognition test item is matched against the items in memory, variance in familiarity is increased for the mixed list relative to the pure list because of the increased variance in the strength values of the long-study items. This increase in familiarity variance increases the chance that the familiarity value will be below criterion for an "old" response for short-study items. This results in lower accuracy for the short-study items in the mixed list relative to the pure list. This is the predicted "list strength" effect and data almost never show this effect in recognition (Murnane & Shiffrin, 1991; Ratcliff, Clark, & Shiffrin, 1990; Shiffrin, Ratcliff, & Clark, 1990), though an effect is predicted and obtained in recall (Tulving & Hastie, 1972; Shiffrin et al., 1990). MINERVA2 and TODAM make the same prediction for recognition and so they are also disconfirmed by the data.

The mirror effect and the list strength effect are two examples of predictions of the models that are testable, contradicted by experimental data, and inalterable by minor modifications to the models. These are the kinds of phenomena and tests that are at the heart of testing and evaluating the models.

New Generation Global Memory Models

Two new models have been developed to deal with the phenomena that the older global memory models could not explain, as well as all the phenomena that they could explain. The models, REM (Shiffrin & Steyvers, 1997)

and McClelland and Chappell's (1999) model, have much in common. In both, items are represented as vectors of features and, in recognition, the degree of match between a test item and memory is compared with a criterion value to make the old/new decision.

At encoding, the features of each studied item are stored in vectors in memory, a separate vector for each item. In each unit of time, some proportion of an item's features are stored, some with their accurate values and some with incorrect values. The vector for a test item is matched against all the vectors in memory. For each vector in memory, the probability is calculated that the memory vector was generated from a study item identical to the test item. A likelihood ratio is produced by dividing this probability by the probability that the memory vector was generated from some different item. For REM, the likelihood ratios for all the items in memory are summed and the result is compared with a criterion to decide whether the test item is old or new. For McClelland and Chappell's model, the maximum of the likelihood ratios is compared to the criterion. As the proportion of features stored for a study item increases, the probability of a match increases and the probability of a nonmatch decreases, essentially differentiating between old and new test items (Shiffrin et al., 1990).

The key feature of the two new models is the use of the likelihood ratio for evaluating the degree of match between a test item and memory. The models account for the mirror effect because as the likelihood ratio for a match increases (because there are more matching features), the likelihood ratio for a mismatch decreases (because there are more mismatching features). The models account for the list strength effect because strengthening an item only slightly affects the likelihood ratios for mismatches.

There are two main assumptions of these models that allow them to produce likelihood ratios. The first is that feature storage is fallible; incorrect values of features are stored with some probability. If storage were completely accurate, then there would be no mismatches when the test item is the same as the study item that produced the memory vector and the likelihood ratio could not be computed. The second is that items are represented as vectors of individual features. This makes it possible to calculate the probability of a match between a test item and an item in memory that is not the same as the test item.

The two new models are quite similar to Hintzman's MINERVA2 model in terms of their representational assumptions. They differ from MINERVA2 in their assumption about how the degree of match is computed (likelihood ratio versus echo intensity).

The new models are at the stage of development where they have been shown to account for the data that was problematic for the older memory models, but as yet no critical tests of the models have been developed. What will be needed is a clear understanding of which are the critical underlying structures of the models that cannot be altered without completely changing the predictions. These models leave the field at an exciting point, awaiting critical new challenges, applications to wider domains, and the next cycle of testing and evaluation.

Reaction Time and Memory Models

All of the global memory models, including REM and McClelland and Chappell's model, predict response accuracy; little attention is paid to the behavior of the other dependent variable they eventually will have to model, reaction time. Although there are many regularities in the relationship between reaction time and accuracy (see Atkinson & Juola, 1973; Hockley & Murdock, 1987; Ratcliff, 1978), substantive research has not been done to integrate the mechanisms that predict accuracy in these models with mechanisms to predict reaction time.

One of the important problems that will have to be faced is how to translate a dimensionless quantity, familiarity or likelihood, into a quantity with a time-related dimension (e.g., rate of processing). In the two new models, the distributions of likelihood values are highly skewed and there would be no reasonable linear translation from likelihood values to rate of accumulation of evidence. What would be needed would be a transformation (e.g., log likelihood; McClelland & Chappell, 1999) to make the distributions less highly skewed. Considerable research is needed to determine what kinds of transformations might work to correctly predict reaction time data.

What the Models Have Not Been Used For

If the memory models were having an impact on empirical research, then we would expect to see the results of experiments interpreted in terms of model parameters. But this is almost never done; the question is, why not? One reason is that many phenomena will be explained in the same way with or without a model. For example, obtaining a fit of a model to the increase in accuracy that occurs as a function of study time would not be news (even though such explicit fitting has rarely been done). Second, there are technical difficulties in fitting the models to data that have not been explored in detail. For example, in the SAM model, the effects of study time could be modeled by varying any one of several parameters. This means that the studies that show what kinds of data will constrain the models have not been presented in a way that allows nonexperts to use the models. Third, there have been few compelling demonstrations that the models are needed to interpret experimental data in domains where the experimental questions concern simple hypotheses.

The big payoff for actually fitting the models to experimental data will come with applications of the models to research in memory as a function of development in children, aging, head injury, varieties of amnesia, and so on, where the parameters of a model can be used to explain what aspects of processing and/or memory lead to the differences in performance observed across subject groups and between the individuals in a group. Variations in parameter values across individuals of different classes could be used to evaluate hypothesized explanations of their differences in performance. The models could also be used to examine performance across a range of tasks to determine if the same components or processes are affected in the same ways across tasks. This kind of evaluation of common mechanisms across tasks is not possible without theory. In ways like these, the models could be expanded from their narrow focus on standard list learning experimental procedures to questions about the larger domain of human memory.

Uses of the Memory Models: Compound Cue Models for Associative Priming

One of the phenomena that is not explained in the same way with the global memory models as it is without the models is priming in lexical decision and recognition. This kind of priming is the speedup in processing for a word that results from processing a related word just before it. For example, in making word/nonword decisions about strings of letters, if a target test word *doctor* is preceded by a related prime word, *nurse*, then the "word" response to *doctor* is speeded by 30 to 50 ms. The usual theoretical interpretation of priming is based on spreading activation: the prime word activates other words related to it in memory and this advance activation leads to a speedup on the target (see McNamara, 1992a, 1992b, 1994a, 1994b). An alternative explanation of priming is the compound cue model (Ratcliff & McKoon, 1988, 1994, 1995; McKoon & Ratcliff, 1992), which is based on the global memory models' accounts of pair recognition. In pair recognition, a pair of words is presented simultaneously and the task is to decide whether both were on the study list. If the two words were studied in a pair together, the degree of match between the test probe and memory is greater than if both words were studied but in different pairs. Ratcliff and McKoon use the same mechanism to explain priming, adding some assumptions about how reaction time is derived from degree of match. There has been considerable controversy over whether spreading activation (ACT*; Anderson, 1983) or compound cue mechanisms give the best account of priming, with no clear winner.

Models of Categorization

Categorization research has been dominated by two main classes of models, exemplar based models and decision bound models (see contrasts between the models in Ashby & Maddox, 1993; McKinley & Nosofsky, 1995). Exemplar-based models assume that a category membership decision is based on stored exemplars of the category, exemplars that were learned in the process of performing the experimental task. This means that the models are essentially memory models. Nosofsky (1991) examined the relationship between categorization and recognition memory and found that both could be explained for his experimental data with the same exemplar based memory representation but different retrieval processes for the two tasks. Apart from a few examples like this, the categorization models have largely operated independently of the memory models, and more theoretical interaction between models in the two classes is overdue.

Implicit Memory Models

The memory models examined so far deal with what has been called explicit memory, but there is another domain of research that is concerned with the effects of prior study on performance in tasks that do not require recollection of prior study; this has been called implicit memory. Much research on implicit memory has centered on the experimental finding that repetition of a stimulus produces a benefit to performance even when conscious memory of the prior episode with the stimulus is not required. A key result is the finding that on many tasks, this repetition priming effect is unimpaired in amnesics even when their explicit memory, as shown by recognition or recall tasks, is severely impaired. It has been claimed that this priming is produced by a separate memory system from the system that performs explicit memory tasks. For example, Squire (1992) proposed a hierarchy of separate systems and Schacter and Tulving (1994) produced a taxonomy of multiple memory systems. The problem with this approach is that it is driven by hypothesis testing; at no point are the hard theoretical questions asked about how information is represented within each memory system, how processing works within each system, or how processes interact among the systems. Crucially, there is no discussion of how processing works for the tasks in which repetition effects are found.

Consider, for example, what must happen in a multiple memory systems account of priming in word identification. In the tasks used to show this phenomenon, a test word is flashed briefly, then masked. A prior presentation of the word increases the probability of correctly identifying it. If the earlier encounter is stored as a new representation in a separate memory system from that used for word identification, then when the test word is presented it must contact this representation and the representation must become available to the processes that are standardly used for word identification in time to facilitate them. It seems unlikely to us that any reasonable mechanism could be constructed to work this quickly to both identify the test word in the implicit memory system and use the resulting information to aid identification.

Ratcliff and McKoon (1996, 1997) reported data that provided the basis for a different interpretation of implicit priming effects. Using experimental procedures for which costs as well as benefits could be examined, they found that the facilitative priming effect for an exact repetition of an item was accompanied by inhibition in processing when a closely similar item to the test item had been presented earlier. Ratcliff and McKoon argued that this result shows a bias in processing, not the operation of a separate memory system. They explained bias with a model for word identification (Ratcliff & McKoon, 1997), a modification of Morton's logogen model (Morton, 1969). Schooler, Shiffrin, and Raaijmakers (1998) have also proposed a model for bias that does not make use of a separate memory system; their model uses the mechanisms of REM. In both these cases, the models' primary aim is to explain standard processing, and priming is only a by-product of the standard processes (Morton, 1970). In addition, each of these models is capable of dealing with other criterial tests that have been said to identify separate memory systems: dissociations and stochastic independence (see also Ratcliff & McKoon, 1996).

At this point, the domains of implicit and explicit memory are related only by contrasts (this is implicit memory or it is explicit memory). But as models for implicit memory are developed, it is hoped that relationships between the two will become apparent (as in Schooler et al., 1998) and that theoretical progress will be made.

Connectionist Memory Models

Connectionist models might seem natural for the storage of information. Much of the early work in connectionist/neural network modeling did have a connection to memory. But there have been few recent attempts to take standard connectionist architectures and build new memory models. For a simplistic example, one might think that a multilayer connectionist network would be ideal for storing information. Vectors of features could be entered into the model and the system trained to respond positively when a learned item was presented for test. The problem is that the model will learn to respond positively for everything because it has not been presented with negative instances (people do not have to be given negative instances because they

know that any item not from the study list should be given a negative response). Another possibility might be to have every encounter with a study item add to its strength in memory (e.g., something like Anderson's, 1991, matrix model). But if this growth leads to an increase in variability, then a list strength effect is predicted, contrary to data (see Ratcliff, 1990). The key thing to keep in mind is that data constrain and rule out many simple-minded translations of many connectionist representational schemes and learning algorithms as a basis for memory models.

However, because the current memory models are distributed, they offer the possibility of translation into connectionist terms. For example, McClelland and Chappell's model (1999) is couched in connectionist terms, but is almost identical in structure to the REM model. The REM model assumes that items are stored in independent vectors in memory and these are accessed in parallel at test. The McClelland and Chappell model assumes that each item stored has a node and weights from it to vector elements. This means, for each item, there is a separate weight for each element in the vector. The correspondence with REM can be seen if the weights are equated with features in the separate memory vectors in REM. The conclusion is that there is considerable overlap in representational assumptions between the connectionist model and both the newer and the older global memory models; it follows that the insights from one of the domains should be used in theoretical development in the other.

Conclusions

In many fields of sciences, theory and experimental work go hand in glove. In cognitive psychology, experimental work and theoretical work seem to have much less interaction. Often this is because as new experimental paradigms are introduced, a lot of fruitful experimental work can be performed to examine and test verbal hypotheses. Then, often after a great deal of experimental work has been performed, the questions become more about details of methods and design than about the larger questions that started the investigation. This results in a reduction in the amount of research in the domain, especially if some other interesting empirical domain has come to prominence. The questions that generate the most interest in the empirical approach are often not critical for testing or evaluating models. This means that the models may have little to say about the empirical phenomena; they may be able to easily explain the results without adding additional insight. This is one source of an often expressed sentiment among experimentalists, that it is impossible to falsify models. But, as described above, the last 15 or 20 years of development and testing of models present a different picture and show a progression in theory development and evaluation.

Models provide a means of going beyond the more traditional empirical approach in several ways. Models are needed when we want to address issues across different experiments, across different experimental paradigms, or across different subject populations. Also, models are needed to relate different dependent variables such as reaction time, accuracy, confidence judgments, recall accuracy, forced choice accuracy, and so on.

Models should aspire to the following properties: a model should be fairly comprehensive, covering data from a range of experimental tasks and a range of manipulations of independent variables. A model should not be a restatement of the experimental data—that is, it should produce a coherent explanation of the data and classify or organize the data differently from a simple empirically based classification, perhaps by showing invariances in parameter values, performance characteristics, or structures that cannot be seen in the experimental data. Finally, a model can gain considerable power if it can deal with more than one dependent variable at a time.

The models of memory of the 1980s were designed to achieve these aims. They were comprehensive and they were able to handle most of the experimental data within their domains. They were falsifiable in that their basic assumptions could be put to empirical test. Their failures led to the new models (McClelland & Chappell, 1999; Shiffrin & Steyvers, 1997, 1998), which are now, in their turn, ripe for evaluation and testing.

Acknowledgments This research was supported by National Institute of Mental Health grant HD MH44640 and National Institute for Deafness and other Communication Disorders grant DC01240.

References

Anderson, J. A. (1991). Why, having so many neurons, do we have so few thoughts? In W. E. Hockley & S. Lewandowsky (Eds.), *Relating theory and data: Essays on human memory in honor of Bennet B. Murdock* (pp. 477–507). Hillsdale, NJ: Erlbaum.

Anderson, J. R. (1983). *The architecture of cognition*. Cambridge, MA: Harvard University Press.

Anderson, J. R. (1990). *The adaptive character of thought*. Hillsdale, NJ: Erlbaum.

Anderson, J. R. (1993). *Rules of the mind*. Hillsdale, NJ: Erlbaum.

Anderson, J. R., & Bower, G. H. (1973). *Human associative memory*. Washington, DC: Winston.

Anderson, J. R., Bothell, D., Lebiere, C., & Matessa, M. (1998). An integrated theory of list memory. *Journal of Memory and Language, 38*, 341–380.

Ashby, F. G., & Maddox, W. T. (1993). Relations between prototype, exemplar, and decision bound models of categorization. *Journal of Mathematical Psychology, 37*, 372–400.

Atkinson, R. C., & Juola, J. F. (1973). Factors influencing the speed and accuracy of word recognition. In S. Kornblum (Ed.), *Attention and performance IV* (pp. 583–612). New York: Academic Press.

Atkinson, R., & Shiffrin, R. (1968). Human memory: A proposed system and its control processes. In K. Spence & J. Spence (Eds.), *The psychology of learning and motivation* (Vol. 2; pp. 90–195). New York: Academic Press.

Gillund, G., & Shiffrin, R. M. (1984). A retrieval model for both recognition and recall. *Psychological Review, 91*, 1–67.

Glanzer, M., & Adams, J. K. (1985). The mirror effect in recognition memory. *Memory and Cognition, 13*, 8–20.

Glanzer, M., Adams, J. K., Iverson, G. J., & Kim, K. (1993). The regularities of recognition memory. *Psychological Review, 100*, 546–567.

Hintzman, D. (1986). "Schema abstraction" in a multiple-trace memory model. *Psychological Review, 93*, 411–428.

Hintzman, D. (1988). Judgments of frequency and recognition memory in a multiple-trace memory model. *Psychological Review, 95*, 528–551.

Hockley, W. E., & Murdock, B. B. (1987). A decision model for accuracy and response latency in recognition memory. *Psychological Review, 94*, 341–358.

McClelland, J. L., & Chappell, M. (1999). Familiarity breeds differentiation: A Bayesian approach to the effects of experience in recognition memory. *Psychological Review, 105,* 724–760.

McKinley, S. C., & Nosofsky, R. M. (1995). Investigations of exemplar and decision bound models in large, ill-defined category structures. *Journal of Experimental Psychology: Human Perception and Performance, 21,* 128–148.

McKoon, G., & Ratcliff, R. (1992). Spreading activation versus compound cue accounts of priming: Mediated priming revisited. *Journal of Experimental Psychology: Learning, Memory, and Cognition, 18,* 1155–1172.

McNamara, T. P. (1992a). Priming and constraints it places on theories of memory and retrieval. *Psychological Review, 99,* 650–662.

McNamara, T. P. (1992b). Theories of priming: I. Associative distance and lag. *Journal of Experimental Psychology: Learning, Memory, and Cognition, 18,* 1173–1190.

McNamara, T. P. (1994a). Priming and theories of memory: A reply to Ratcliff and McKoon. *Psychological Review, 101,* 185–187.

McNamara, T. P. (1994b). Theories of priming: II. Types of primes. *Journal of Experimental Psychology: Learning, Memory, and Cognition, 20,* 507–520.

Morton, J. (1969). The interaction of information in word recognition. *Psychological Review, 76,* 165–178.

Morton, J. (1970). A functional model for memory. In D. A. Norman (Ed.), *Models of human memory* (pp. 203–254). New York: Academic Press.

Murdock, B. B. (1974). *Human memory: Theory and data.* Potomac, MD: Erlbaum.

Murdock, B. B. (1982). A theory for the storage and retrieval of item and associative information. *Psychological Review, 89,* 609–626.

Murdock, B. B. (1997). Context and mediators in a theory of distributed associative memory (TODAM2). *Psychological Review, 104,* 839–862.

Murnane, K., & Shiffrin, R. M. (1991). Interference and the representation of events in memory. *Journal of Experimental Psychology: Learning, Memory, and Cognition, 17,* 855–874.

Neath, I. (1998). *Human memory: An introduction to research, data, and theory.* Pacific Grove, CA: Brooks/Cole.

Norman, D. A. (1970). *Models of human memory.* New York: Academic Press.

Nosofsky, R. M. (1991). Tests of an exemplar model for relating perceptual classification

and recognition memory. *Journal of Experimental Psychology: Human Perception and Performance, 17,* 3–27.

Raaijmakers, J. G. W., & Shiffrin, R. M. (1981). Search of associative memory. *Psychological Review, 88,* 93–134.

Ratcliff, R. (1978). A theory of memory retrieval. *Psychological Review, 85,* 59–108.

Ratcliff, R. (1990). Connectionist models of recognition memory: Constraints imposed by learning and forgetting functions. *Psychological Review, 97,* 285–308.

Ratcliff, R., & McKoon, G. (1988). A retrieval theory of priming in memory. *Psychological Review, 95,* 385–408.

Ratcliff, R., & McKoon, G. (1994). Retrieving information from memory: Spreading activation theories versus compound cue theories. *Psychological Review, 101,* 177–184.

Ratcliff, R., & McKoon, G. (1995). Sequential effects in lexical decision: Tests of compound cue retrieval theory. *Journal of Experimental Psychology: Learning, Memory, and Cognition, 21,* 1380–1388.

Ratcliff, R., & McKoon, G. (1996). Biases in implicit memory tasks. *Journal of Experimental Psychology: General, 125,* 403–421.

Ratcliff, R., & McKoon, G. (1997). A counter model for implicit priming in perceptual word identification. *Psychological Review, 104,* 319–343.

Ratcliff, R., Clark, S. E., & Shiffrin, R. M. (1990). The list-strength effect: I. Data and discussion. *Journal of Experimental Psychology: Learning, Memory, and Cognition, 16,* 163–178.

Schacter, D. L., & Tulving, E. (1994). What are the memory systems of 1994? In D. L. Schacter & E. Tulving (Eds.), *Memory systems 1994* (pp. 1–38). Cambridge, MA: MIT Press.

Schooler, L., Shiffrin, R. M., & Raaijmakers, J. (1998). *Theoretical note: A model for implicit effects in perceptual identification.* Manuscript submitted for publication.

Shiffrin, R. M., Ratcliff, R., & Clark, S. E. (1990). The list strength effect: II. Theoretical mechanisms. *Journal of Experimental Psychology: Learning, Memory, and Cognition, 16,* 179–195.

Shiffrin, R. M., & Steyvers, M. (1997). A model for recognition memory: REM: Retrieving effectively from memory. *Psychonomic Bulletin and Review, 4,* 145–166.

Shiffrin, R. M., & Steyvers, M. (1998). The effectiveness of retrieval from memory. In M. Oaksford & N. Chater (Eds.), *Rational*

Models of Cognition (pp. 73–95), Oxford University Press: Oxford, England.

Slamecka, N. J. (1991). The analysis of recognition. In W. E. Hockley & S. Lewandowsky (Eds.), *Relating Theory and Data: Essays on Human Memory in Honor of Bennet B. Murdock.* Hillsdale, NJ: Erlbaum.

Squire, L. R. (1992). Memory and the hippo-

campus: A synthesis from findings with rats, monkeys, and humans. *Psychological Review, 99,* 195–231.

Sternberg, S. (1966). High-speed scanning in human memory. *Science, 153,* 652–654.

Tulving, E., & Hastie, R. (1972). Inhibition effects of intralist repetition in free recall. *Journal of Experimental Psychology, 92,* 297–304.

36

Connectionist Models of Memory

JAMES L. MCCLELLAND

The study of memory has been pursued within many different paradigms, and memory has been thought of in many different ways. Often memory has been viewed as a storehouse of items. Items are created, and then filed away as if they were books in a library. Storage, loss, organization, and retrieval of memories have all been considered from this point of view. Other theories (e.g., Anderson, 1983) hold that memory is a network of nodes with associative connections among them. Typically such theories propose some primitive or elemental nodes, and additional nodes that serve to group or organize collections of other nodes via associative links. This approach provides a basis for understanding how operations at the time of storage (creation of nodes and links) affect the success of later operations (e.g., retrieval of memories following links from node to node). In all these theories, memory consists of a set of items, together with an addressing scheme that allows them to be accessed.

The view we will consider in the present chapter begins with a completely different way of thinking about memory. This view addresses phenomena that have motivated the sorts of theories mentioned above, but in doing so it lets go of the idea that items are stored in memory as such. Instead the fundamental idea is that what is stored in memory is a set of changes in the instructions neurons send to each other, affecting what patterns of activity can be constructed from given inputs. When an event is experienced, on this view, it creates a pattern of activity over a set of processing units. This pattern of activity is considered to be the representation of the event. The formation of this pattern of activity provides the trigger for the creation of the instructions. The set of instructions is then stored in the connections among the units, where it is available for use in the construction of subsequent patterns of activity. Under some circumstances—for example, when the constructive process takes place in response to a recall cue—the cue may result in the construction of a pattern of activation that can be viewed as an attempted reconstruction of the pattern that represented the previously experienced event. Such a reconstructed representation corresponds to a recollection. The patterns themselves are not stored, and hence are not really "retrieved": recall amounts not to retrieval but to reconstruction.

The goal of the present chapter is to help the reader understand and appreciate the connectionist modeling framework, which embodies this view of memory. There are other modeling frameworks that take a very similar perspective, including the matrix model of Humphreys, Bain, and Pike (1989); the convolutional model (TODAM) of Murdock (1982); and the composite holographic model of Metcalfe (1990). What sets the connectionist model apart from the others is the explicit use of the idea that the knowledge used in information processing—the instructions to which we referred just above—consists of the values, or *weights* on the connections among simple, neuronlike processing units. The approach thus taps into a vast neuroscience literature on the synaptic basis of learning and memory (see, e.g., McNaughton, 1993, for a review) as well as a complementary literature on the computational analysis of artificial neural networks (see the handbook by Arbib, 1995).

On the whole, the connectionist models have been motivated by robust and general patterns in data and by basic observations about the nature of human memory, and the focus has been on exploring general principles and understanding basic model characteristics. As the general principles become clearer, more detailed models of the quantitative aspects of experimental findings are likely soon to follow.

Local and Distributed Representation in Connectionist Networks

Some early connectionist models of memory (e.g., McClelland, 1981) made use of local representations, in which a single unit is used for each item. Typically the features of the item are represented by other units, to which the item unit is connected. Often these models can appear similar to symbolic associative models like Anderson's (1983), in that complex items are represented by units with connections to other, more elemental units. What differs is that in the connectionist model several items can contribute to the activation of elements, thus producing such phenomena as blend errors (Loftus, 1991; Nystrom & McClelland, 1992) and prototype effects (Posner & Keele, 1968).

A key question is whether the representation of knowledge in the brain is local in this way. The alternative—one that can be traced from Lashley (1950) through Willshaw (1981), Anderson (1973; Anderson, Silverstein, Ritz, & Jones, 1977) and Hinton (1981)—is an idea called *distributed representation*. This is the idea that the representation of an item is not associated with the activation of a single unit, but with the pattern of activation over a set of units; and the further idea that the knowledge

underlying the ability to activate a particular pattern is not associated with the weights coming in and out of a single unit, but is superimposed in the same set of connection weights that encode the knowledge underlying other patterns.

A simple illustration of this idea at work (McClelland, Rumelhart, & Hinton, 1986) considers knowledge that allows one pattern to be associated with another. One pattern might represent the aroma of something, perhaps a rose, and the other its appearance. Figure 36.1A shows a network that allows the input pattern—the smell of the rose—to produce the corresponding output pattern. We imagine that this association is learned by experiencing the aroma and the visual appearance of the rose at the same time, producing the indicated patterns of activation on a group of units representing the aroma and on other units representing the appearance. Learning occurs by incrementing the weight to appearance unit i from aroma unit j in proportion to the product of the activations of the two units. This rule is often called a "Hebbian" learning rule, but to avoid confusion with a later discussion of Hebb's actual proposals, we will here describe this rule as a "coincident activation" learning rule. In the example, the weights all started at 0 and were incremented by the product of the unit activations times a rate constant ε (here set to 0.25):

$$\Delta w_{ij} = \varepsilon a_i a_j \qquad (1)$$

Now that we have stored the association, we can reconstruct the appearance from the aroma by presenting the pattern representing the aroma, and then setting the activations of the appearance units based on these activations and the learned weights. For simplicity in this case the activation is set to the net or summed input to the unit,

$$net_i = \Sigma_j a_j w_{ij}. \qquad (2)$$

The reader can check that the resulting activations exactly match the appearance pattern present at the time the increments to the connection weights were computed.

One can follow the same procedure to store a second association, perhaps between the aroma and the appearance of a steak, in the same set of weights. The same learning rule is used, and the increments for the steak are added to the weights for the rose. The second

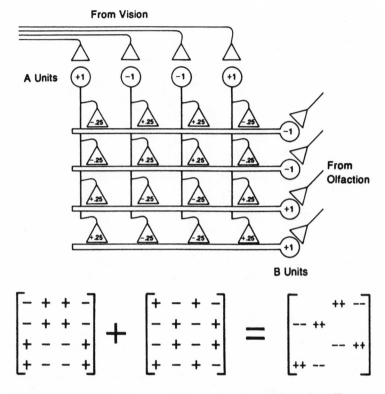

Figure 36.1 The simple associative network model used to illustrate how knowledge of two associations can be stored in the same set of weights. (A) The network with weights storing the single association between the given input and output patterns. (B) On the left, a schematic representation of the weight matrix appropriate for the same association shown in (A) and a second matrix appropriate for a second association between a different input pattern and a different output pattern. These two can be summed, creating the matrix shown on the right. Here + represents a value of +.25 and each − represents a value of −.25; ++ represents +.50, and − represents −.50. Adapted from McClelland et al. (1986), figures 12, 13, and 14, permission pending.

set of increments and the resulting summed values of the weights are shown in figures 36.1B and 36.1C. The reader can check that if one presents the rose aroma to the input, the output is the appearance of the rose, and if one presents the steak aroma, the output is the appearance of the steak.

A Distributed Auto-Associator Model of Memory

The above example demonstrates that the "memory trace" for something need not maintain a separate identity. Rather, the memory trace may be nothing more than a set of adjustments or increments to a large ensemble of widely distributed elements, the connection weights. The distributed memory model of McClelland and Rumelhart (1985) incorporates this idea. The model draws heavily on the work of James Anderson (1973; Anderson et al., 1977; Knapp & Anderson, 1984), and is a member of a class of models known as *auto-associator* or *attractor network* models (see figure 36.2). Instead of associating a pattern with another pattern, such models associate each pattern with itself. The network allows external inputs to all of the units and provides connections to each unit from every other

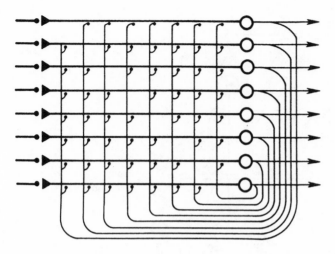

Figure 36.2 The auto-associator network from McClelland and Rumelhart (1985) Figure 1.

unit. The activation of a unit is determined by the net input, which consists of the external input plus the input coming to each unit from each of the other units via the weighted connections. The model uses an error correcting learning rule. The change in the weight to a particular unit i from another unit j is equal to:

$$\Delta w_{ij} = \varepsilon(ext_i - int_i)a_j \qquad (3)$$

This is often called the *delta* rule; learning is driven by the difference between one signal and another signal arriving at the receiving unit. The other factor in the rule, aj, is just the activation of the sending unit. As long as ε is small, this rule will tend to move connection weights toward values that bring the internal input to the unit into alignment with the external input. For example, if the internal input is smaller than the external input, and the activation of the sending unit is positive, the weight between them will be increased; this will increase the internal input, reducing *delta*.

McClelland and Rumelhart (1985) used this model to illustrate several key points about auto-associators. One is that they can act as content-addressable memories. For example, different subsets of the units might represent different aspects of a particular object. Some might represent the sight of a rose, some its aroma, some its name, some what it feels like to touch, and so on. Presentation of some aspects of the pattern will tend to lead to reconstruction of other aspects, filling them in on the other units. Another is that the network tends to clean up noisy versions of patterns on which it has been trained. Any pattern that is

similar to one of the stored patterns will tend to be modified so that it is more like the stored pattern. In networks of this type, the stored patterns are often called "attractors" because patterns that are near them tend to change over time, in the direction of becoming more similar to the stored patterns. Each attractor has a basin of attraction around it, representing the set of patterns that gets attracted to it. Both pattern completion and pattern cleanup occur in settling toward an attractor state.

Because the learning that occurs for one pattern affects the same set of weights that are used by all other patterns, there is an automatic tendency for similarity-based generalization and blending of similar patterns to occur. Thus models of this type address blend errors and prototype effects seen in memory experiments. Some authors have suggested that blend errors and prototype effects are best accounted for by models in which each study item is stored separately. In models of this type (e.g., Hintzman, 1988), presentation of a test item results in activation of all similar studied items, and the resulting activations are then summed together (this idea can be implemented in localist connectionist models such as McClelland, 1981). This makes it possible to account for the fact that, in addition to an advantage for the prototype of a category over particular studied items, there is generally also an advantage for studied items over other nonprototypical items in the category. However, McClelland and Rumelhart (1985) showed that both prototype and item effects occurred in their distributed model as well. Indeed, the connection weights in superpositional, distributed models can capture prototype and instance characteristics of several different categories at the same time, thus obviating the need to suppose that memory contains separate stored representations of every item ever experienced.

The ideas and models described above arose within the context of models that made use of either a coincident activation learning rule or an error-correcting learning rule. In the application of these ideas to models of memory and related phenomena, modelers stipulated the activations of input and output units, and used these rules to adjust the strengths of direct connections from the input units to the output units (in auto-associator models, the input and output units may be the same units). It was known from the beginning of this work that such models faced a serious computational limitation. In essence, when two input patterns activate many units in common, the patterns will tend to produce the same output, since both patterns will be using the same set of connection weights. If the outputs must be different, the few units that differ between the patterns will be left to do all of the work. If the units in question must do different work in different cases, a situation can arise in which there is no set of weights that will address all cases at once.

One way to solve this problem is to provide a mechanism for expanding the representation of an input, by pre-specifying units to represent possible conjunctions or combinations of inputs. This approach has been used successfully in some models (e.g., Gluck & Bower, 1988). However, the set of all possible conjunctions grows exponentially with the number of inputs, so that even with only 40 individual elements, the number of conjunctions exceeds the number of neurons in the brain (thought to be about 10^{11}, or 100 billion). This problem can be addressed to a degree. In one sort of solution (e.g., O'Reilly & McClelland, 1994), each of a number of conjunctive units receives inputs from a random subset of the input units, and the conjunctive units with the largest number of active inputs are chosen to represent the current input. Another approach is to create a large number of initially uncommitted units with random weights to all elements of the input. When an input is presented, the unit that it activates most strongly based on the random initial weights is selected, and its weights are tuned to match the input. This approach was taken by Grossberg (1976, 1978) and Kruschke (1992, 1996), both of whom have applied it to aspects of human

memory. A very different approach to the problem arose from the use of a sophisticated version of the error-correcting learning rule to discover useful internal representations of inputs. We will consider this approach in the context of a model of the representation and use of knowledge in semantic memory.

Connectionist vs. Symbolic Models of Semantic Memory

The classical, symbolic approach to semantic memory was proposed by Quillian (1968). It involved supposing that such information consists of a set of propositions organized into a taxonomic hierarchy. In the example shown in figure 36.3, knowledge of various kinds of plants and animals is represented hierarchically under the common superordinate "Living Thing." All propositions include a concept name, one of four relations, and another concept or property, as in the examples "canary is a bird," "canary is yellow," "bird has feathers," and "animal can move." Note that the ISA propositions encode the backbone structure of the hierarchy. According to Quillian's proposal, propositions that are true of all the concepts within a certain branch of the tree would be stored at the top of the branch; thus, since all animals can move, that proposition is stored with *animal*, but since only the birds can fly, that proposition is stored with *bird*. The result is that information is stored economically, and many inferences can easily be derived from the stored information. Thus if we simply add the proposition "sparrow is a bird," we can then infer that it can fly, that it has feathers, that it can move, etc., by following ISA propositions up the tree and reading out what is stored there.

Quillian's proposals sparked a great deal of interest in the 1970s. However, the approach is somewhat brittle in the face of exceptions and doesn't provide a very natural way of dealing with typicality effects (Rosch, 1975). Also, experiments showed that general properties did not take longer to access than specific ones, and Rips, Shoben, and Smith (1973) showed that sometimes general category membership could be verified more easily than more specific category membership. An alternative, connectionist approach that captures many of the desirable properties of Quillian's proposal and does not suffer from these difficulties was provided by Rumelhart

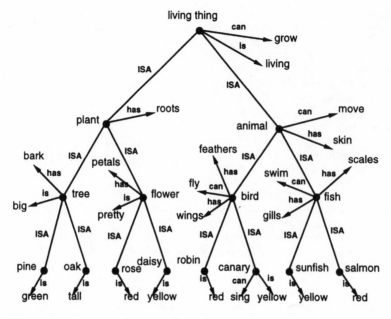

Figure 36.3 A semantic network of the type formerly used in models of the organization of knowledge in memory. All of the propositions used in training the network are based on the information actually encoded in this figure. For example, the network indicates that living things can grow; that a tree is a plant; and that a plant is a living thing. Therefore it follows that a tree can grow. All of these propositions are contained in the training set. *Note*: Redrawn with alterations from D. E. Rumelhart and P. M. Todd (1993), Learning and connectionist representations (figure 1.8, p. 14), in *Attention and performance XIV: Synergies in experimental psychology, artificial intelligence, and cognitive neuroscience*, edited by D. E. Meyer and S. Kornblum, Cambridge, MA: MIT Press. Copyright 1993 by MIT Press. Permission pending.

(1990; Rumelhart & Todd, 1993). They used the sophisticated error-correcting learning algorithm mentioned previously to train a network on the propositions stored in Quillian's hierarchical network, and showed that after training it too exhibited parsimonious representations and allowed inferences to be made from newly learned concepts. This model propagated activity in only one direction, and so it is more like the pattern associator model of the rose-steak example above. An auto-associative model with similar properties has been implemented by (O'Reilly, 1996), but we consider the Rumelhart version for simplicity.

Rumelhart's (1990) network is shown in figure 36.4. Connections run from a pool of concept units and a pool of relation units to output units for the concepts and for each of the different types of properties (*is, has,* and

can properties). Note there are two other pools of internal or "hidden" units, between the input and the output. One pool, called *concept representation* units, sits between the concept units and the other pool, called general hidden units, which receives input from the concept representation units and the relation units. This network is initialized with small random weights on all the connections. Testing of the network takes place by activating a concept input unit and a relation unit, with all other input units off, and propagating activation forward through the network. Thus we can test the network's knowledge of what a canary can do by activating *canary* and *can* on the input. Activation propagates forward: net inputs are calculated as in equation 2, with the activation of the unit a monotonic, S-shaped function of the net input.

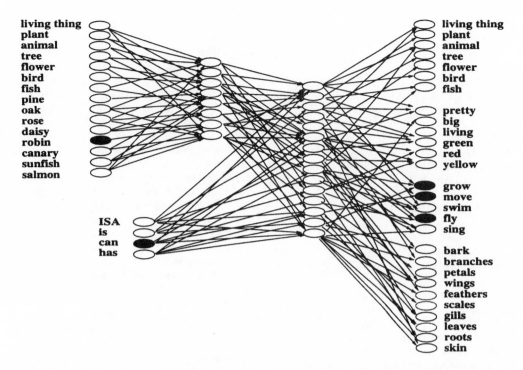

living thing
plant
animal
tree
flower
bird
fish
pine
oak
rose
daisy
robin
canary
sunfish
salmon

ISA
is
can
has

living thing
plant
animal
tree
flower
bird
fish

pretty
big
living
green
red
yellow

grow
move
swim
fly
sing

bark
branches
petals
wings
feathers
scales
gills
leaves
roots
skin

Figure 36.4 A depiction of the connectionist network used by Rumelhart to learn propositions about the concepts shown in figure 36.3. The entire set of units used in the actual
network is shown. Inputs are presented on the left, and activation propagates from left to
right. Where connections are indicated, every unit in the pool on the left (sending) side
projects to every unit in the right (receiving) side. An input consists of a concept-relation
pair; the input *robin* can is illustrated here by darkening the active input units. The network is trained to turn on all those output units that represent correct completions of the
input pattern. In this case, the correct units to activate are *grow*, *move* and *fly*; the units
for these outputs are darkened as well. Subsequent analysis focuses on the concept representation units, the group of eight units to the right of the concept input units. Reprinted
from McClelland et al. (1995), figure 5, p. 430, based on the network depicted in Rumelhart and Todd (1993), figure 1.9, page 15.

Training the Network with Back Propagation

At first, owing to the small random weights,
the activations of the hidden and output units
take on values that hover around the neutral
value of 0.5. The network must learn the content of the domain through training. The training procedure, called back propagation, was
developed independently by Rumelhart, Hinton, and Williams (1986) and other groups.
Training occurs in a series of epochs; in each
epoch, each input pattern is presented (i.e.,
each combination of a concept and a relation),
and the output is generated as described

above. The output is compared to the correct,
target output, and weights are adjusted according to the back propagation learning algorithm, which adjusts each weight a very small
amount to reduce the difference between the
desired and the obtained activation. For the
weights projecting from the general hidden
layer to the output units, a procedure very
similar to the error-correcting learning rule
presented in equation 3 is used. For each unit,
a quantity called $delta_k$, representing the extent to which changing the net input to the
unit would reduce the network's overall error,
is calculated. For output units, this quantity is
equal to the difference between the target
value t_k and the obtained activation a_k, times a

scaling factor depending on the activation of the unit

$$\delta_k = (t_k - a_k)s(a_k). \qquad (4)$$

The important innovation in the learning procedure is that it provides a way to adjust the connection weights coming into hidden units from units lower down in the processing stream. Essentially, a delta term is assigned to each such unit by considering how a change in its input would affect the error at each of the units to which it projects, and then adding up these separate effects (with a scaling factor as before):

$$\delta_i = \Sigma_k w_{ki} \delta_k s(a_i). \qquad (5)$$

Here Σ_k runs over all the units to which hidden unit i has a forward connection; w_{ki} is the weight on one such connection, and $delta_k$ is the *delta* term for the unit at the end of that connection. Thus the *delta* of each hidden unit is essentially a weighted sum of the *deltas* of all the units to which that hidden unit projects. The algorithm is called back propagation because each hidden unit's *delta* is calculated by "propagating" the delta terms associated with downstream units "backward" across the connection weights. Once *deltas* have been calculated for all of the hidden units (and this process must proceed backward by layers from the output units), all the forward-going weights to each hidden unit from all the units below it can now be adjusted according to equation 5, where i is understood to indicate the unit at the forward or receiving end of the connection and j indicates the unit at the sending end.

Back-propagation has often been criticized because, taken literally as a procedure for training connections in the brain, it appears biologically implausible. While this criticism may have some merit, it is far from clear exactly what takes place biologically. Furthermore, back propagation and other similar learning algorithms open up vast new possibilities for understanding human cognition and its development as an adaptive learning process. This is illustrated by an analysis of the outcome and time course of learning in Rumelhart's semantic network.

Cognitive and Developmental Implications

The first thing to notice about the network is that it learns by a process that might be called

progressive differentiation. This process affects both the output of the network and also its internal representations of concepts, as can be seen in figure 36.5 from a subsequent study of this network by McClelland, McNaughton, and O'Reilly (1995). The figure shows the patterns of activation assigned by the network to each of the lowest-level concepts in the hierarchy, at three stages of learning: (1) very early in learning, where the representations are determined primarily by the initial random values of the connection weights from the concept input to the concept representation units; (2) midway through learning; and (3) at the end of learning. For each concept at each point in learning, the activations of the eight concept representation units that are produced by activation of the corresponding concept unit are shown. Early in learning, the patterns or activation the network assigns to the different concepts are all very similar, with none of the units either strongly on or strongly off in any of the patterns. Midway through learning, the network has differentiated the plants from the animals, but within the plants and the animals, there are only very slight differences. At the end of training, the network has differentiated the birds from the fish and the flowers from the trees, and there are also subtle but important differences in the representations that the network assigns to the individual birds, fish, trees, and flowers. This process appears to be consistent with a corresponding process of progressive differentiation seen in child development (see McClelland et al., 1995, for discussion).

The second thing to note about the network is that it uses a parsimonious approach to representation of semantic information. By assigning very similar representations to concepts for which very similar sets of propositions are true, it can use the same set of connection weights forward of these representations to answer these questions. This use of similar representations for concepts that share propositions also allows the network to generalize what it has learned about one concept to other similar concepts. Indeed, what is common across similar concepts is more robustly represented than what is idiosyncratic. This allows the network to account naturally for the pattern of semantic loss seen in patients with a progressive deterioration of semantic memory (Warrington, 1975; Hodges, Graham, & Patterson, 1995). These patients show deterioration of knowledge of details of con-

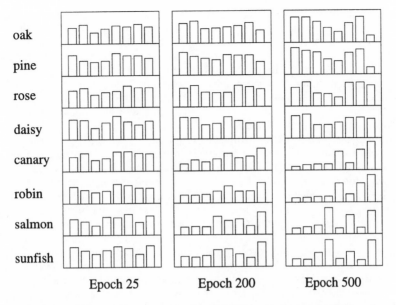

oak
pine
rose
daisy
canary
robin
salmon
sunfish

Epoch 25   Epoch 200   Epoch 500

Figure 36.5 Representations discovered in our replication of Rumelhart's learning experiment, using the network shown in figure 36.4.
The figure presents a vertical bar indicating the activation of each of
the eight concept representation units produced by activating the input unit for each of the eight specific concepts. The height of each
vertical bar indicates the activation of the corresponding unit on a
scale from 0 to 1. One can see that initially all the concepts have
fairly similar representations. After 200 epochs, there is a clear differentiation of the representations of the plants and animals, but the
trees and flowers are still quite similar as are the birds and the fish.
After 500 epochs, the further differentiation of the plants into trees
and flowers and of the animals into fish and birds is apparent. Reprinted from McClelland et al. (1995), figure 36.6, p. 431.

cepts, while still retaining their general characteristics. The same pattern is observed when
progressive damage is simulated by the addition of increasing amounts of noise into the
representations used in the network (McClelland & Rogers, 1997).

Catastrophic Interference and Complementary Systems in Memory

Connectionist learning procedures like back
propagation that train hidden units offer new
ways of thinking about semantic memory
quite different from those provided by traditional semantic network accounts that trace
their heritage back to Quillian (1968). It was,
therefore, something of a disappointment when
McCloskey and Cohen (1989) applied back

propagation to a classic memory paradigm—
paired associate learning—and discovered
that the algorithm appeared to suffer from a
problem that they labeled "catastrophic interference." They trained a connectionist network on a list of eight paired-associate patterns, then looked to see the effect on these
learned associations of subsequent training on
a second list of eight new associations involving the same input patterns but different responses. The experiment is analogous to many
classical memory experiments of retroactive
interference. Human subjects do show some
interference from learning a second list of associations on recall of a first list, but in the
network the interference was far more profound. In fact, before the network correctly
produced any of the new associations its ability to reproduce all of the old associations cor-

rectly was completely wiped out. The only way to avoid the catastrophic interference problem was to interleave learning of one set of associations with learning of the other set. In this way, the learning procedure could find a set of connection weights consistent with correct performance on both sets of associations.

This finding of catastrophic interference might seem to suggest that the back propagation model might be fatally flawed as a model of human learning and memory. However, another approach—the one taken by McClelland et al. (1995)—was to suggest that the catastrophic interference effect found by McCloskey and Cohen (1989) might be avoided in the human brain by using a back-propagation-like learning system for semantic and procedural learning, while using a different kind of learning system for the initial learning of arbitrary associations. They suggested that the areas of the neocortex of the brain in which semantic knowledge is stored may learn very slowly, so that learning of any one item can be interleaved with ongoing learning of other items. As we saw in the consideration of the learning of semantic information about plants and animals, this results in discovery of efficient representations that support generalization and robustly represent information that is shared by many things. They further suggested that other areas of the brain—particularly the medial temporal lobes, where the hippocampus and related brain structures are found—may be specialized for the rapid storage of arbitrary new information, such as paired associates. Considerable neuropsychological evidence supports the idea that the medial temporal regions of the brain plays this role; for example, individuals with extensive damage to this region are profoundly deficient in the initial acquisition of arbitrary new factual information, including episodic memory (memory for the particular contents of particular events and experiences) and paired-associate learning. What McClelland et al. (1995) proposed is that the learning system in the medial temporal lobes makes use of a conjunctive scheme like that of O'Reilly and McClelland (1994) to minimize overlap of distinct memories. Such coding schemes have been used by several investigators to model paired-associate learning without catastrophic interference (French, 1991, 1992; Sloman & Rumelhart, 1992; Kortge, 1993). Evidence from single-neuron recording studies in animals supports the idea that the hippocampus uses very sparse, conjunctive representations (e.g., Barnes, McNaughton, Mizumori, Leonard, & Lin, 1990).

Given that the catastrophic interference problem can be avoided by the use of sparse conjunctive coding, why would this approach not be used for semantic as well as episodic memory? The answer to this is key to understanding why there must be different types of learning systems in the brain. While sparse random conjunctive coding allows rapid learning of new memories, it does so in a very simple way. It assigns a distinct representation, minimizing overlap with other memories. Back propagation, on the other hand, and other learning algorithms that exploit gradual, interleaved learning, find patterns of connection weights that capture the overall structure of entire ensembles of events and experiences, and that assign representations to individual concepts that capture the position of the concept in that structure. In this regard it is interesting that the input to the medial temporal lobe systems appears to come from the neocortical regions responsible for semantic and other relatively abstract forms of representation. The arrangement suggests gradual, interleaved learning may be used to develop the representations that are then made available for storage, so that what is stored in episodic memory is not a raw copy of sensory input, but the results of sophisticated representational processes acquired throughout development in the neocortical cognitive system.

In summary, this section has reviewed different kinds of connectionist approaches to overcoming the limitations of networks containing a single layer of modifiable weights. Two kinds of solutions to these problems were considered. One of these involved some variant of a sparse random, conjunctive coding scheme, and the other involved the use of interleaved learning via back propagation to discover the structure of a domain and assign appropriate representations to concepts within it. There are strengths and weaknesses of each approach, but it appears that the brain solves the dilemma posed by this situation by making use of both solutions. Thus research on connectionist models provides a basis for understanding what might otherwise appear to be a relatively arbitrary aspect of brain organization—namely, that there appear to be separate systems in the brain subserving the initial acquisition of arbitrary information on the one hand and the systematic representation of knowledge in semantic memory on the other.

Current Directions in Connectionist Models of Memory

Attentional and Strategic Aspects of Memory

Several connectionist models now take note of the fact that encoding and retrieval of information is subject to strategic manipulation (see Cohen & O'Reilly, 1996, for a general consideration of such effects). Kruschke (1992) showed how a connectionist network could provide a mechanism implementing the distribution of attention to dimensions of input stimuli. In this earlier work and in much of his later work these ideas have been applied to learning in categorization tasks, but Dennis and Kruschke (1998) have now shown that some findings that justify the claim that attention to stimulus cues adjusts adaptively in categorization experiments are also obtained in cued-recall memory experiments. In particular, subjects appear to reduce attention to cues that they discover are ambiguous. Kruschke (1996) provides a connectionist model that captures these effects in categorization experiments and the model is extended to attention effects in memory in Dennis and Kruschke (1998). The authors suggest that such attentional effects influence the pattern of activation that arises in the neocortex when an input is experienced, affecting what is available for storage in the medial temporal lobe memory system and ultimately what is available for integration into the knowledge base stored in connections among neurons in the neocortex.

Relation of Connectionist Models to Bayesian and Other Optimal Approaches

A recent issue in memory research concerns whether it is useful to construe human memory as optimal. This question has been posed forcefully by Anderson (1990; Anderson & Milson, 1989), who has suggested that, indeed, several aspects of memory can be construed to reflect the use of optimal policies for storage, retrieval, and so on. Interestingly, there are several ways in which connectionist models may be seen as optimal or quasi-optimal (McClelland, 1998). Perhaps most fundamentally, there is a very strong connection between connectionist learning procedures and procedures for deriving optimal estimates of

parameters for complex nonlinear estimation procedures (White, 1989; MacKay, 1992). Individual connectionist units and indeed whole connectionist networks can be construed as optimal Bayesian estimators of conditional probabilities of hypotheses given evidence, and several connectionist learning rules can be viewed as procedures for deriving estimates of necessary probability relations between hypotheses and evidence in connection weights. Also, a Bayesian, probability-estimation approach has recently been applied to modeling recognition memory (Shiffrin & Steyvers, 1997; McClelland & Chappell, 1998), and McClelland and Chappell (1998) have indicated how such models might be implemented in connectionist networks.

Hebbian vs. Error-Correcting Learning Rules

The final current research direction we will consider in this article tends to undercut the idea that human learning and memory are in any general sense optimal, however. This is the idea that, perhaps, certain aspects of human learning may reflect Hebbian as opposed to error-correcting synaptic adjustment rules. Hebb's original idea was that synaptic modification works to strengthen the connection from one neuron to another, when the first appears to persistently or repeatedly take part in firing the second (the coincident activation learning rule is one example of a Hebbian-type learning rule). This rule may sometimes be counterproductive: If a stimulus activates a set of input units, and these in turn activate a pattern on some other set of units, then Hebbian learning will tend to reinforce whatever that pattern turns out to be, whether or not it is the desired response in a memory experiment. This may have the effect of reinforcing preexisting, incorrect response tendencies, and thus of actually impeding rather than enhancing progress in memory experiments.

If this is correct, the human memory system can behave far from optimally in many cases. Indeed, the idea that the mechanisms of synaptic plasticity operate according to the Hebbian principle leads to the observation that these mechanisms might be instrumental in the maintenance of maladaptive and highly nonoptimal behavior in many cases. This serves to reinforce the observation that rationality or optimality is generally conditional on the accuracy of certain (explicit or implicit) assumptions. Error-correcting learning with an exponentially decreasing learning rate can be optimal when learning in an environment when the training examples are sampled from a distribution that remains invariant over time, but is highly nonoptimal if, after considerable experience, the distribution of training examples changes. Hebbian learning may be optimal or approximately so, as long as conditions are arranged so that the activations produced by an input are predominantly desirable, but can be completely counterproductive in cases where activations produced by inputs are not the ones that are desired.

Conclusion

Connectionist models have been developed to capture what their originator's suggest may be fundamental aspects of human learning and memory systems. In most cases, these models bear strong similarities to nonconnectionist models. This observation is consistent with the idea that there may be many different frameworks within which some ideas can be captured. The connectionist framework has been fertile in allowing a range of different principles to be explored—so fertile that the framework itself is often criticized as unhelpfully general or open-ended (Massaro, 1988). While this open-endedness does have its downsides, it also has several benefits, one of which is that it has allowed the exploration of a wide range of different ideas about the nature of learning and memory. Another benefit is the naturalness with which it may be applied to addressing neuropsychological phenomena, and the ease with which it can be used to adopt specific proposals from neuroscience, including the idea that synaptic modification follows the principles of Hebbian learning, or that sparse, conjunctive representations appear to be used in the hippocampus. The approach appears to provide a useful complement to other more constrained models, many of which appear to be highly applicable to data obtained within certain classes of paradigms, but which often have little to say outside their range of applicability and which may not immediately suggest ways of incorporating findings from neuroscience. It thus appears that connectionist models play a useful role in our efforts to understand the nature of human memory, complementing other approaches.

References

Anderson, J. A. (1973). A theory for the recognition of items from short memorized lists. *Psychological Review, 80,* 417–438.

Anderson, J. A., Silverstein, J. W., Ritz, S. A., & Jones, R. S. (1977). Distinctive features, categorical perception, and probability learning: Some applications of a neural model. *Psychological Review, 84,* 413–451.

Anderson, J. R. (1983). *The architecture of cognition.* Cambridge, MA: Harvard.

Anderson, J. R. (1990). *The adaptive character of thought.* Hillsdale, NJ: Erlbaum.

Anderson, J. R., & Milson, R. (1989). Human memory: An adaptive perspective. *Psychological Review, 96,* 703–719.

Arbib, M. A. (1995). *The handbook of brain theory and neural networks.* Cambridge, MA: MIT Press.

Barnes, C. A., McNaughton, B. L., Mizumori, S. J. Y., Leonard, B. W., & Lin, L.-H. (1990). Comparison of spatial and temporal characteristics of neuronal activity in sequential stages of hippocampal processing. *Progress in Brain Research, 83,* 287–300.

Cohen, J. D., & O'Reilly, R. C. (1996). A preliminary theory of the interactions between prefrontal cortex and hippocampus that contribute to planning and prospective memory. In M. Brandimonte, G. O. Einstein, & M. A. McDaniel (Eds.), *Prospective memory: Theory and applications.* Mahwah, NJ: Erlbaum.

Dennis, S., & Kruschke, J. K. (1998). Shifting attention in cued recall. *Australian Journal of Psychology, 50,* 131–138.

French, R. M. (1991). Using semi-distributed representations to overcome catastrophic forgetting in connectionist networks. In *Proceedings of the 13th Annual Cognitive Science Conference* (pp. 173–178). Hillsdale, NJ: Erlbaum.

French, R. M. (1992). Semi-distributed representations and catastrophic forgetting in connectionist networks. *Connection Science, 4,* 365–377.

Gluck, M. A., & Bower, G. H. (1988). Evaluating an adaptive network model of human learning. *Journal of Memory and Language, 27,* 166–195.

Grossberg, S. (1976). On the development of feature detectors in the visual cortex with applications to learning and reaction-diffusion systems. *Biologcial Cybernetics, 21,* 145–159.

Grossberg, S. (1978). A theory of human memory: Self-organization and performance of sensory-motor codes, maps, and plans.

Progress in Theoretical Biology, 5, 233–374.

Hinton, G. E. (1981). Implementing semantic networks in parallel hardware. In G. E. Hinton & J. A. Anderson (Eds.), *Parallel models of associative memory* (pp. 161–187). Hillsdale, NJ: Erlbaum.

Hintzman, D. L. (1988). Judgements of frequency and recognition memory in a multiple-trace model. *Psychological Review, 95*, 528–551.

Hodges, J. R., Graham, N., & Patterson, K. (1995). Charting the progression in semantic dementia: Implications for the organisation of semantic memory. *Memory, 3*, 463–495.

Humphreys, M. S., Bain, J. D., & Pike, R. (1989). Different ways to cue a coherent memory system: A theory for episodic, semantic, and procedural tasks. *Psychological Review, 96*, 208–233.

Knapp, A., & Anderson, J. A. (1984). A signal averaging model for concept formation. *Journal of Experimental Psychology: Learning, Memory, and Cognition, 10*, 617–637.

Kortge, C. A. (1993). Episodic memory in connectionist networks. In *Proceedings of the Twelfth Annual Conference of the Cognitive Science Society* (pp. 764–771). Hillsdale, NJ: Erlbaum.

Kruschke, J. K. (1992). ALCOVE: An exemplar-based connectionist model of category learning. *Psychological Review, 99*, 22–44.

Kruschke, J. K. (1996). Base rates in category learning. *Journal of Experimental Psychology: Learning, Memory & Cognition, 22*, 3–26.

Lashley, K. S. (1950). In search of the engram. In *Society of Experimental Biology Symposium* (pp. 478–505). London, UK: Cambridge University Press.

Loftus, E. (1991). Made in memory: Distortions of recollection after misleading information. In G. Bower (Ed.), *Psychology of learning and motivation* (Vol. 27; pp. 187–215). New York: Academic Press.

MacKay, D. J. (1992). Information-based objective functions for active data selection. *Neural Computation, 4*, 590–604.

Massaro, D. W. (1988). Some criticisms of connectionist models of human performance. *Journal of Memory and Language, 27*, 213–234.

McClelland, J. L. (1981). Retrieving general and specific information from stored knowledge of specifics. In *Proceedings of the Third Annual Conference of the Cognitive Science Society* (pp. 170–172). Berkeley, CA.

McClelland, J. (1998). Connectionist models and Bayesian inference. In M. Oaksford & N. Chater (Eds.), *Rational models of cognition* (pp. 21–53). Oxford, UK: Oxford University Press.

McClelland, J. L., & Chappell, M. (1998). Familiarity breeds differentiation: A subjective-likelihood approach to the effects of experience in recognition memory. *Psychological Review, 105*, 724–760.

McClelland, J. L., McNaughton, B. L., & O'Reilly, R. C. (1995). Why there are complementary learning systems in the hippocampus and neocortex: Insights from the successes and failures of connectionist models of learning and memory. *Psychological Review, 102*, 419–457.

McClelland, J. L., & Rogers, T. T. (1997). A PDP account of basic-level category effects and semantic demantia (Abstract 133). *Abstracts of the Psychonomic Society, 2*, 14.

McClelland, J. L., & Rumelhart, D. E. (1985). Distributed memory and the representation of general and specific information. *Journal of Experimental Psychology: General, 114*, 159–188.

McClelland, J. L., Rumelhart, D. E., & Hinton, G. E. (1986). The appeal of parallel distributed processing. In D. E. Rumelhart, J. L. McClelland, & the PDP Research Group (Eds.), *Parallel distributed processing: Explorations in the microstructure of cognition* (Vol. 1; chap. 1, pp. 3–44). Cambridge, MA: MIT Press.

McCloskey, M., & Cohen, N. J. (1989). Catastrophic interference in connectionist networks: The sequential learning problem. In G. H. Bower (Ed.), *The psychology of learning and motivation* (Vol. 24; pp. 109–165). New York: Academic Press.

McNaughton, B. L. (1993). The mechanism of expression of long-term enhancement of hippocampal synapses: Current issues and theoretical implications. *Annual Review of Physiology, 55*, 375–396.

Metcalfe, J. (1990). Composite holographic associative recall model (CHARM) and blended memories in eyewitness testimony. *Journal of Experimental Psychology: General, 119*, 145–160.

Murdock, B. B. (1982). A theory for the storage and retrieval of item and associative information. *Psychological Review, 89*, 609–626.

Nystrom, L. E., & McClelland, J. L. (1992). Trace synthesis in cued recall. *Journal of Memory & Language, 31*, 591–614.

O'Reilly, R. (1996). *The leabra model of neural interactions and learning in the neocor-*

tex. PhD thesis, Department of Psychology, Carnegie Mellon University, Pittsburgh, PA.

O'Reilly, R. C., & McClelland, J. L. (1994). Hippocampal conjunctive encoding, storage, and recall: Avoiding a tradeoff. *Hippocampus, 4,* 661–682.

Posner, M. I., & Keele, S. W. (1968). On the genesis of abstract ideas. *Journal of Experimental Psychology, 77,* 353–363.

Quillian, M. R. (1968). Semantic memory. In M. Minsky (Ed.), *Semantic information processing* (pp. 216–270). Cambridge, MA: MIT Press.

Rips, L. J., Shoben, E. J., & Smith, E. E. (1973). Semantic distance and the verification of semantic relations. *Journal of Verbal Learning and Verbal Behavior, 12,* 1–20.

Rosch, E. (1975). Cognitive representations of semantic categories. *Journal of Experimental Psychology: General, 104,* 192–233.

Rumelhart, D. E. (1990). Brain style computation: Learning and generalization. In S. F. Zornetzer, J. L. Davis, & C. Lau (Eds.), *An introduction to neural and electronic networks* (pp. 405–420). San Diego, CA: Academic Press.

Rumelhart, D. E., Hinton, G. E., & Williams, R. J. (1986). Learning internal representations by error propagation. In D. E. Rumelhart, J. L. McClelland, & the PDP Research Group (Eds.), *Parallel distributed processing: Explorations in the microstructure of cognition* (Vol. 1; pp. 318–362). Cambridge, MA: MIT Press.

Rumelhart, D. E., & Todd, P. M. (1993). Learning and connectionist representations. In D. E. Meyer & S. Kornblum (Eds.), *Attention and performance XIV: Synergies in experimental psychology, artificial intelligence, and cognitive neuroscience* (pp. 3–30). Cambridge, MA: MIT Press.

Shiffrin, R. M., & Steyvers, M. (1997). A model of recognition memory: REM—Retrieving effectively from memory. *Psychonomic Bulletin & Review, 4,* 145–166.

Sloman, S. A., & Rumelhart, D. E. (1992). Reducing interference in distributed memories through episodic gating. In A. Healy, S. Kosslyn, & R. Shiffrin (Eds.), *Essays in honor of W. K. Estes* (Vol. 1; pp. 227–248). Hillsdale, NJ: Erlbaum.

Warrington, E. (1975). Selective impairment of semantic memory. *Quarterly Journal of Experimental Psychology, 27,* 635–657.

White, H. (1989). Learning in artificial neural networks: A statistical perspective. *Neural Computation, 1,* 425–464.

Willshaw, D. (1981). Holography, associative memory, and inductive generalization. In G. E. Hinton & J. A. Anderson (Eds.), *Parallel models of associative memory* (Chap. 3; pp. 83–104). Hillsdale, NJ: Erlbaum.

37

Episodic Memory and Autonoetic Awareness

MARK A. WHEELER

Perhaps the most remarkable achievement of human memory is the ability to think back and relive happenings from the past. In response to such a simple cue as, say, "high school graduation night," it is possible to mentally transport oneself back many years or decades and to reexperience parts of life that probably have not been considered in a long time. The type of memory that allows people to reflect upon personal experiences is called *episodic* memory (Tulving, 1983, 1993).

Psychological writing on the topic of episodic memory began at least as early as William James (1890). Because James's work was pioneering, he had the opportunity to select and define those psychological phenomena that he considered to be important for the developing field. It is interesting to note the way that he defined memory. James took a much more restrictive definition than do most contemporary researchers. Rather than consider memory as encompassing such acts as motor learning, habit formation, stimulus-response strengthening, and the acquisition and use of knowledge, the concept to James was equivalent to what is now called episodic memory. (These other phenomena, motor learning, etc., were all readily apparent to James, and he devoted much discussion to them, but they were not labeled as memory phenomena.) The conscious recollection that accompanied memory retrieval was taken as the defining characteristic of memory. "Memory requires more than the mere dating of a fact in the past. It must be dated in *my* past . . . I must think that I directly experienced its occurrence" (p. 612).

Episodic memory also is defined by the nature of conscious awareness that accompanies retrieval, a type of awareness now called autonoetic (self-knowing) awareness. The retrieval of episodic information, such as the recollection of a particular time that one drove one's first automobile, is not merely an objective account of what has happened or what has been seen or heard. Its contents are infused with the idiosyncratic perspectives, emotions, and thoughts of the person doing the remembering. It necessarily involves the feeling that the present recollection is a reexperience of something that has happened before.

The primary goals of this chapter are to discuss and support two theoretical propositions about episodic memory and autonoetic awareness. Because episodic remembering necessarily entails a conscious reexperience of the personal past, it is possible to conclude the following:

1. Episodic memory is critically different from all other varieties of memory (e.g., stimulus-response strengthening, general knowledge acquisition), and can be dissociated from them. An experimental dissociation occurs when one particular

variable selectively affects a certain test or class of tests, while having little or no effect on different classes of tests. There now exist at least three populations of subjects who show selective losses of episodic remembering along with spared performance on other memory measures. These subjects are described in detail later in the chapter. Such individuals show many types of memory, learning, and conditioning, yet they cannot mentally relive past experiences. The presence of these dissociations is important; without them, there would be little justification for the argument that episodic memory is a special kind of memory.

2. Episodic remembering is closely related to other higher order mental achievements that are not typically considered to be acts of memory. Individuals with autonoetic awareness are capable of reflecting upon their own experiences in the past, present, and future. Reflecting back on past happenings is episodic memory. Related behaviors are the ability to introspect upon present experiences, and also to anticipate or imagine future experiences through imagination, daydreams, and fantasies. All of these autonoetic capabilities share the fact that they require an organism to withdraw attention from the immediate sensory environment, and to reflect upon their own past, present, or future. The act of dwelling upon one's past is cognitively similar to the act of imagining one's future, although only the former is commonly labeled as "memory." For at least two, and perhaps all three, of the populations that have selective losses of episodic memory, there is a corresponding loss of the abilities to introspect upon the present, and to anticipate the future. For a description of a patient with a total loss of autonoetic awareness extending through the past, present, and future, see Tulving (1985).

Episodic and Semantic Memory

It is pretty easy to make the case that episodic remembering is distinct from procedural, or nondeclarative, or "implicit" kinds of memory; probably no one, layperson or cognitive psychologist, would confuse episodic recol-

lection with motor learning, or perceptual priming, or classical conditioning. These manifestations of memory have little surface similarity with acts of recollection.

Another form of memory, semantic memory, is more closely related to episodic remembering. Semantic memory handles knowledge about the world. When an individual reports that he was born in Chicago, or that Sacramento is the capital of California, he is almost surely retrieving the information from semantic, and not episodic, memory. It is through semantic memory that individuals are capable of "knowing things"—any information that can be expressed in terms of impersonal knowledge can be encoded, stored, retrieved, and used through semantic memory.

Although there are many proposed differences between episodic and semantic memory (Tulving, 1983), there is one attribute that best discriminates between them: the conscious awareness that occurs during retrieval. Only episodic retrieval involves autonoetic awareness and the mental reexperience of a previous moment in the past. Semantic memory, by contrast, is characterized by noetic (knowing) awareness only. There is no feeling of reliving any previous episode, and it does not correspond to William James's ideas about memory.

There are many situations, in both the laboratory and everyday life, when it can be very difficult to draw distinctions between episodic and semantic memory. As an example, consider a student's performance on an exam. When an undergraduate correctly reports information on a test, is it the case that she can autonoetically recollect a previous moment that she spent studying the material, or did she simply recall the correct response from semantic memory, or both? Either of these possibilities could be true; without interviewing the student, there is no way to know the answer to this question (see Conway, Gardiner, Perfect, Anderson, & Cohen, 1997, for an investigation of this very issue). The difference between episodic remembering and semantic knowing is of little immediate use to a testtaker. What matters is that the correct response can be recalled at all.

Dissociating Varieties of Memory and Conscious Awareness

Semantic and episodic memory have many similarities—they are both conscious, declarative varieties of memory that are commonly used to guide behavior—and it is therefore theoretically important to document cases in which they can be experimentally dissociated. In other words, it is important to find situations in which a particular variable (e.g., experimental manipulation, neurological injury) affects only one of the two kinds of memory.

Many very different lines of research have documented dissociations between episodic and semantic memory. Using functional brain imaging, it is possible to show that different brain areas are involved when healthy human adults retrieve information from these two kinds of memory (reviewed by Buckner & Tulving, 1995; Nyberg, Cabeza, & Tulving, 1996; Nyberg & Cabeza, chapter 31). Also, using the remember/know technique, researchers have identified several independent variables that selectively influence either the amount of information that research subjects claim to autonoetically remember or the amount that they say they semantically know (reviewed by Gardiner, chapter 15; Gardiner & Java, 1993). In addition, pharmacological studies have shown that certain drugs will impair episodic, but not other varieties of memory (Curran, chapter 33).

Most of the remainder of this chapter will be a summary of one particular kind of dissociation between episodic and semantic memory, and also between autonoetic and noetic awareness. There now exist at least three populations of subjects who show selective losses, or absences, of autonoetic episodic remembering, along with spared semantic memory. The presence of the dissociations is important because it lends further evidence to the proposition that these varieties of memory and conscious awareness have important differences.

Based upon the ideas about episodic memory and autonoetic awareness that have been detailed so far, it is possible to imagine the type of profile that individuals with selective losses of autonoetic, episodic memory would have. Such individuals would be able to learn new information, skills, and facts, and also be able to apply that knowledge flexibly and confidently, albeit noetically. The individuals could also report about things and situations that have been encountered, yet without mentally reliving the experiences upon which the knowledge is based. They would have knowledge about the world, including things that have happened in the past, and things that could occur in the future, yet their subjective experiences will not actually extend back into the past, or project into the future.

Groups that fit this general description are (1) patients who have sustained injuries that are restricted to the prefrontal cortical region; (2) children between the approximate ages of 2 and 5; and (3) a subset of amnesic patients who have selective damage to the hippocampus, with spared surrounding tissue. It is only fair to acknowledge at the outset that some of the relevant data are open to differing interpretations, and other people will have different ideas about how they want to think about the evidence. This review was conducted with the goal of showing dissociations between episodic autonoetic thought and noetic semantic knowledge and, with that goal in mind, there is good evidence that each of the three populations can be fairly described as selectively lacking in the former variety of memory and awareness.

Frontal Lobes and Episodic Memory

The prefrontal cortex is, in many ways, the most intriguing area of the brain. Comprising the cortical tissue in front of the motor and premotor areas, it is well accepted that this area of the brain is important for some of the most sophisticated types of cognitive functioning. The fact that the human brain differs from nonhuman animals most noticeably in the prefrontal cortex is also convergent with the general idea that this most anterior area likely plays an important role in higher order varieties of memory and conscious awareness.

Patients with frontal lobe damage seem to have an impoverished ability to consciously recollect their past, even when they know about their past. This is, of course, the distinction between autonoetic remembering and noetic knowing. A growing body of literature attests to the reality of this dissociation. Some of the best evidence comes from a phenomenon known as source amnesia (Schacter, Harbluk, & McLachlan, 1984). The phenomenon is said to occur when an individual can show the successful learning of some new fact, yet without the ability to recollect where, or how, the fact was learned. Defined this way, source amnesia is extremely common. All of us know hundreds of thousands of facts and, for the vast majority of them, we have no recollection of the origin of our knowledge. As an example, while it is commonly known that Paris is the capital of France, it is extremely difficult and usually impossible for any person to reflect back upon the instance in which the fact was originally learned. Therefore, source amnesia is a compelling phenomenon only when it occurs after recent learning episodes.

Brain lesions in the prefrontal cortex have been associated with source amnesia. In the most direct demonstration, Janowsky, Shimamura, and Squire (1989) asked both patients and control subjects to learn a series of facts (e.g., the name of the dog on the Cracker Jack box was Bingo). Following a delay of about one week, all participants returned and were asked questions that were based on either the facts they had seen the week before (e.g., What was the name of the dog on the Cracker Jack box?) or new facts that had not been studied but were potentially known. The patients had no trouble retrieving the learned information, as they recalled as many facts as the control group. Where the groups diverged was on a follow-up question that probed about the source of the recalled facts. Patients were strikingly more likely to claim that the experimentally learned facts had actually been learned at some other time, before the experiment. They were also more likely to guess that a pre-experimentally learned fact had been encountered during the study phase of the experiment when in reality it had not.

The Janowsky et al. (1989) data represent an example of a dissociation between episodic and semantic memory. Despite the presence of pathology, patients updated their semantic knowledge at levels that, at least in this experiment, were equivalent to that of healthy controls. On the fact-recall measures, they showed unimpaired noetic awareness of recently studied items. When faced with questions about source, however, there were striking difficulties. For most healthy adults, the source questions were not difficult. To answer the question, one must simply remember studying the fact one week before. Results imply that the prefrontal injuries somehow prevented the episodic recollection of the study episode, even when semantic memory was successfully updated during the episode.

Relations between frontal dysfunction and source amnesia have also been demonstrated in elderly populations, through correlational measures. Because the neurobiological changes that occur with aging occur primarily in the prefrontal cortex (Haug et al., 1983), it is possible to apply findings from research in cognitive aging to questions about frontal-lobe functioning, and vice versa (West, 1996). Of course, such applications must be made carefully.

Older adults are especially prone to source amnesia (McIntyre & Craik, 1987; Schacter, Kaszniak, Kihlstrom, & Valdiserri, 1991). Even when fact recall is equated between the two age groups, elderly subjects are much more likely to make source errors. Also, the ability to remember the source of learned facts is correlated with performance on other, nonmemory measures that are especially sensitive to frontal injury, such as the Wisconsin Card Sorting Test, and word fluency tests (Craik, Morris, Morris, & Loewen, 1990). The simple ability to recall facts was not correlated with these measures. Similar correlations have been discovered in patients with anterograde amnesia that had varying degrees of pathology extending into the prefrontal cortex (Schacter et al., 1984). Across these three populations, there is converging evidence for a dissociation between autonoetic episodic recollection and semantic learning, with only the former dependent upon the frontal lobes.

There is another way to assess the extent to which recalled or recognized items are being autonoetically recollected. The logic behind the remember/know task is relatively simple—if one wants to determine whether research participants are retrieving episodic memories, then one can simply ask them (see Gardiner, 1988; Gardiner, Richardson-Klavehn, chapter 15). Following retrieval of a previously studied item, test instructions ask subjects to respond "remember," or R, for those items on the list whose prior experience they can consciously re-experience. "Know," or K, responses represent the acknowledgment that the test item was encountered on the specified study list, but in the absence of any conscious recollection of its occurrence. The very fact that participants are readily willing to make know responses is evidence that people can make judgments about single episodes from the recent past without relying upon episodic memory.

In one comparison, Parkin and Walter (1992) required both elderly and young adults to study a list of items before taking a recognition test, followed by remember/know instructions. More recently, Wheeler and Stuss (unpublished) had both patients with focal prefrontal injuries and also healthy controls make living/nonliving decisions about study words before giving similar tests. In all of these experiments, there was some relatively minor effect of prefrontal pathology (or age) on the recognition tests. The effect reached statistical significance in the Parkin and Walter (1992) studies. There was a much larger discrepancy between the groups with respect to the episodic, or R, component. Patients with prefrontal injuries had a much more difficult time reflecting back on the learning experience, as their R scores were significantly lower than the matched control subjects (unpublished research). The elderly subjects of Parkin and Walter showed similarly depressed R scores, even when their recognition scores were matched with the younger subjects. There were substantial, significant correlations between the episodic memory measure (here, the R score) and performance on the WCST. Results from both studies resemble the prior work with source amnesia, in that frontal-related deficits do not strongly impair the ability to learn from the past, but do interfere with the autonoetic reliving of those past moments.

Autonoetic Awareness of the Present and Future

It is easy to find dissociations between episodic recollection and semantic knowing in prefrontal patients. When the definitions of these varieties of memorial awareness are made clear, it is relatively straightforward to make the case that one is impaired much more than the other. But these studies present an incomplete picture of autonoetic awareness and its relation to episodic remembering. Recent writings on autonoetic awareness suggest that it is not limited to the personal past; it encompasses the awareness of the self's experiences in the past, present, and future (Tulving, 1993; Wheeler, Stuss, & Tulving, 1997). It follows that any individuals who are unable to recollect their past should additionally have difficulty introspecting upon their current thoughts, perceptions, and feelings, and also be unable to mentally project themselves into the future.

Assessing the capacity for autonoetic awareness of the present and future is not an easy task, and it is hardly surprising that traditional cognitive and neuroscientific experiments have had little to say on the matter. Still, there exists a large clinical neuropsychological literature that bears upon the consequences of prefrontal cortical injuries. From these case reports and reviews, there is evidence from multiple converging sources that prefrontal damage leads to a disruption in patients' conscious awareness.

Several clinicians have noted that their patients are uninterested in themselves as persons, especially in their mental lives. In an early summary, Ackerley and Benton (1947) noticed that their patients with frontal damage seemed unable to self-reflect, and lacked the ability to daydream or engage in introspection. Alexander Luria (1973; Luria & Homskaya, 1964) observed a number of patients with large frontal lesions, and also reviewed many relevant case reports before concluding that a primary symptom, present in virtually every patient, was a disturbance in the critical attitude toward their own problems. The patients, according to Luria, seemed unwilling to evaluate themselves and address their cognitive or behavioral deficits appropriately. In one nineteenth-century case study, DeNobele (1835, cited in Blumer & Benson, 1975) described an open-head-injury patient with both massive prefrontal damage and blindness. The patient seemed remarkable unconcerned about the blindness. It appears that the mental changes that accompany large prefrontal injuries encompass the disturbed awareness of personal experiences across time, including a general lack of interest in those experiences.

Perhaps the largest single source of prefrontal patients came as a result of the prefrontal leucotomy procedure, a psychosurgery that was popular in the early and middle decades of this century (Moniz, 1936). With the goal of relieving various psychiatric symptoms, the technique involved severing the connections between the prefrontal cortex and the thalamus, thereby disconnecting the most anterior brain regions from more posterior areas and rendering the frontal lobes essentially useless. The benefits of the various leucotomies were never universally accepted, although several reviews reported positive benefits in a number of cases (Freeman, 1953; Sweet, 1973). Critics of the procedure considered it to be unnecessarily cruel (Valenstein, 1986) and, with the advent of psychotropic drugs, it was largely abandoned.

Freeman and Watts (1950) published a comprehensive survey, describing hundreds of individual cases of leucotomies and also drawing a number of conclusions across the cases. Although Freeman and Watts described a diverse range of postsurgical symptoms, they concluded that there was one primary characteristic lacking in their postsurgical patients, and it was a characteristic that was in abundance before the procedure. Their conclusions resemble the earlier writings of William James as he talked about the stream of consciousness and, because they do not cite James, there is no way to know whether or not the similarity was deliberate, or if they independently realized the same ideas from their own unique approach. They write:

> There is a characteristic possessed by most human beings that is conspicuous by its comparative absence in these [patients] . . . an awareness of being in some sort the person that one was yesterday and will be tomorrow, a sense (not often clearly conscious) of one's own self-continuity, of the duration of one's essential identity through changing experiences. Such self-continuity is basic to all personality development, making possible a feeling of responsibility for one's past and future behavior. . . . [Leucotomy] frees the patient from the tyranny of his own past, from the anxious self-searching that had become too terrible to endure, and at the same time renders him largely indifferent to future problems and the opinions of other people. We hypothesize, then, that psychosurgery alters the structure of the self through reducing self-continuity. (p. 316)

A recurrent theme throughout the publications (Freeman & Watts, 1950; Robinson & Freeman, 1954) is that frontal leucotomies change patients so that they are no longer interested in the sorts of past, present, and future problems that were so absorbing and incapacitating before the operations. Although the patients knew all of the personal facts (noetic awareness) that they did before, the facts were experienced with a lack of "warmth and intimacy" that William James had attributed to the way humans typically think about their lives.

Similar themes have appeared more recently. The healthy adult's conscious states have been attributed to the brain's ability to access, somehow simultaneously, information concerning the personal past, present, and future (Ingvar, 1985). After reviewing a number of case studies, Ingvar went on to consider the prefrontal cortex as important for foresight, initiative, and "memories of the future." Also, Donald Stuss has remarked that the highest level of self-awareness is the ability to reflect upon one's own essence across time, and is dependent upon the full operations of prefrontal cortex (Stuss, 1991; Stuss, Picton, & Alexander, in press). It appears that episodic recollection of the past is one component of these sophisticated, reflective abilities.

Episodic Memory in Young Children

Children between the ages of about 1 and 5 years resemble patients with frontal lobe lesions in one important respect: they are able to report about, and know about, both facts of the world and things that have happened to them, often without being able to consciously recollect the episodes upon which that knowledge is based.

One conclusion about the memory abilities of young children is inescapable: they are voracious learners, and routinely take in and retrieve vast amounts of knowledge. It is during the first several years that children learn massive amounts of new information. They learn the meanings of words and how to use those words in conversation. They also learn about the identity of people, animals, and things, and how they are expected to interact with those things. Because they are constantly updating and extending their knowledge, children above the age of 1 year must have, at a minimum, a functioning semantic memory that can be expressed through noetic awareness.

The semantic memory skills of young children are not limited to general, timeless concepts such as the meaning of the word *bench* or the way to behave around a houseguest. Infants as young as 8 months have shown impressive recall of information that was tied to a single event in their past. Evidence comes largely from a line of research called deferred imitation. In a common variant of the task, the child is an observer as an adult performs a series of actions with props. After a delay, the child is handed the props and given the chance to actively imitate what has been seen. Infants as young as 9 months are capable of imitating single actions (e.g., pressing a button on a box) that they had witnessed the previous day (Meltzoff, 1988). Performance on deferred imitation tasks becomes gradually more sophisticated throughout the next several months. Infants between the ages of 13 and 20 months at encoding later showed aspects of nonverbal and verbal recall of witnessed event sequences at retention intervals of up to 12 months (Bauer & Wewerka, 1995). Delayed recall resembles knowledge-based semantic memory much more than simple procedural, or motor, learning (McDonough, Mandler, McKee, & Squire, 1995).

Based on deferred imitation studies, it is tempting to attribute healthy infants with the operations of episodic memory. By the middle of the second year, a child can recognize and recall things that occurred several weeks before. The child has also learned to answer questions about things that he has encountered, although responses are typically limited to single words (Howe & Courage, 1993) or to short phrases that were identical or highly similar to those used by the experimenter at the time of study. It is safe to attribute the infants with event memory.

But event memory and event recall cannot be equated with episodic memory. Although a young child's verbal or nonverbal recall of a particular event seems like compelling proof of episodic memory, evidence from other sources suggests that for a period of at least several more months, young children are without the capacity to recollect their past in the rich, personal way that comprises episodic retrieval.

The most ideal tests of episodic remembering involve measures that require individuals to consciously reexperience some prior episode in order to complete the task. In practice, it is often difficult to design such a task and, with children, the enterprise becomes even more complicated. One example of a test that likely cannot be used with children is the remember/know test. If a child is truly preepisodic and has not yet developed the capacity to experience her past autonoetically, it will not make any sense to ask her to distinguish between remembering and knowing. Evidence that such terms are problematic for young children was reported by Johnson and Wellman (1980). (It is interesting that this study appeared many years before the formal cognitive distinction between remembering and knowing.) They concluded that 4-year-olds were oblivious to differences between cases of remembering, knowing, and guessing, although in some cases they could distinguish their mental state from an externally perceived state. Five-year-olds showed some ability to differentiate these mental states, while a group of first graders had a very good understanding of these terms. It is unlikely that this is a simple vocabulary problem, as kids at that age are fully capable of acquiring and using words and concepts that are much more sophisticated than words like *know* and *guess*. Difficulties with these words likely stems from the inability to monitor one's own mental life.

Much of the relevant episodic-memory data derives from experiments that are analogous to the studies of source memory previously discussed with respect to patients with prefrontal lesions. Once again, the evidence strongly implies that young children are able to report about learned information before they can reflect back upon the learning episode. One of the most striking examples of source amnesia in children comes from experiments by Gopnik and Graf (1988). They asked 3-, 4-, and 5-year-old children to learn about the contents of a drawer in one of three different ways. On some trials, children saw things that were in the drawer, in other cases they were simply told what was there, while other times they were given enough information to accurately infer what was in the drawer. Memory for both item ("What is inside this drawer?") and source information ("How do you know what is inside—did you see it, did I tell you about it, or did you figure it out?") was assessed both immediately after learning and also following a brief delay. There were no age differences in item recall; even at the longer retention interval, the recall of 3-year-olds was virtually indistinguishable from that of 5-year-olds.

On the test for source, older children had little difficulty and made very few mistakes. The majority of 3-year-olds were unable to answer the questions at levels much higher than chance, although one-third of them made no errors at all. The authors took the additional step of giving some of the children explicit training to ensure that they understood the differences among seeing, inferring, and being told about something. Even the additional instructions could not help the children travel back in their own minds to relive the learning event. Very similar results were obtained in other reports (Wimmer, Hogrefe, & Perner, 1988; O'Neill & Gopnik, 1991). Findings suggest that young children do not, or cannot, represent their knowledge as deriving from a particular time in the personal past (e.g., "I saw that there are crayons in that box"), but rather as detached, impersonal knowledge (e.g., "There are crayons in the box").

The studies just described may even overestimate children's abilities to understand how they learned information. The critical test questions used by Gopnik and Graf (1988) and the others only asked the children to discriminate between different intraexperimental sources (seeing, hearing, inferring). Many children cannot acknowledge the simple fact that a recently learned bit of information has been acquired recently (Taylor, Esbensen, & Bennett, 1994). In one experiment, 4- and 5-year-old children were taught unfamiliar color names (e.g., chartreuse, taupe). All children learned the colors easily, and were soon able to select items from an array according to color. They were then questioned about when they had learned the color names. Incredibly, a large majority of the 4-year-olds claimed to have "always" known the names, and very few could acknowledge that they had been taught the colors that day. The 5-year-olds performed markedly better, although a few of them consistently made this same source error. Across several experiments, the authors showed that young children typically are unaware of recent learning events, and claim that they have known recently learned information for a long time.

It is instructive to contrast the kinds of memory tasks that young children can and cannot perform. Recall that on deferred imitation tasks children younger than age 3 can reproduce complex, previously witnessed events in the correct temporal order after lengthy retention intervals (Bauer, 1996). Yet children the same age and even older cannot answer simple questions about recent study episodes. The difference between these tasks is surely not one of complexity or difficulty; to a healthy adult, it would seem much easier to answer source questions of the type posed by Gopnik and Graf (1988) than to reconstruct action sequences that had been witnessed weeks earlier. The difference must involve some conceptual limitation on the part of 3- and 4-year-old children; although they can learn complex actions from single events, they cannot reflect on their experience of the events by mentally traveling back in time to relive them.

Conscious Awareness in Young Children

Individuals are said to possess autonoetic awareness when they are able to reflect upon their past, introspect on their current thoughts, and actively anticipate their future. It is not difficult to show that these acts gradually develop through childhood. Unfortunately, simply proving that autonoetic behaviors gradually emerge with increasing age would not make for a very compelling argument for the distinctiveness of these behaviors. That is because all complex mental and behavioral repertoires, autonoetic and other-

wise, surely become more sophisticated throughout childhood.

The way to make the case for the relatively late emergence of autonoetic, as opposed to noetic, behaviors is to find situations in which young children show impressive amounts of knowledge that can be expressed noetically, yet seem unable to reflect upon the fact that they have the knowledge (i.e., attend to their mental states directly). Problems with autonoetic awareness of the past have already been described in the section on memory. Perner (chapter 19) relates many of the episodic memory phenomena to other changes in children's awareness between the ages of about 2 and 6 years.

There are several themes running through the developmental literature that strongly imply that young children achieve sophisticated levels of knowledge well before they are capable of attending directly to their experiences in the past, present, and future. Three- and 4-year-old children know many things, but cannot solve problems that require them to "introspectively inspect" their own minds (Gopnik & Slaughter, 1991). As an example, below the age of 5, children cannot reflect upon recently learned knowledge to overcome prepotent response tendencies in card-sorting tasks (Zelazo, Frye, & Rapus, 1996). Similarly, it has been suggested that preschoolers are not even aware of the continuous stream of consciousness that is their own mental life, and they therefore lack the ability to reflect upon their own conscious states (Flavell, 1993). These are good descriptions of the kinds of things that an autonoetic organism should be able to do.

With respect to planning and anticipating the future, it is accepted that there are marked changes between the ages of 3 and 5 in children's ability and inclination to make plans (see Zelazo, Carter, Reznick, & Frye, 1997). Unfortunately, it is difficult to know the extent to which those changes reflect the emergence of autonoetic awareness, or if they involve mainly the learning of new strategies and coping skills.

Medial Temporal Lobe Patients

Very recently, published reports describe another population that demonstrates a variant of the episodic-semantic dissociation. A group led by Faraneh Vargha-Khadem (Vargha-Khadem et al., 1997) has identified a few patients with anterograde amnesia; the patients had anoxic episodes as children (one virtually at birth, another at age 4, and the other at age 9), and have bilateral pathology that is restricted almost completely to the hippocampus. All suffered their trauma over 10 years prior to the study. They were brought to the attention of the researchers because of their severe problems whenever they attempt to remember events. None of the three was capable of taking on the types of responsibilities that are commensurate with other young adults. Formal neuropsychological testing was consistent with these observations, as all three were found to be severely impaired whenever they attempted to recall information that had been presented more than a few minutes earlier.

From the description so far, the patients' profiles match those of typical anterograde amnesics: profound losses in the ability to remember things that have occurred since the traumatic episode. But these three share one capability that sets them apart from the majority of patients with damage in the medial temporal regions: all of them have fared very well in mainstream education. Despite a seemingly complete loss of the ability to remember posttraumatic events, they are fully competent in speech and language, and have acquired seemingly normal levels of factual knowledge about the world. All three are within the normal range on the vocabulary, information, and comprehension subtests of the Intelligence Quotient scale (Vargha-Khadem et al., 1997). These retained bits of knowledge are expressed confidently and flexibly, with noetic awareness only; both anecdotal reports and formal testing strongly imply that the patients know many things and remember nothing.

These patients show a different pattern of learning and memory deficits than previously reported amnesics. The classic patient HM, for example, who had bilateral surgical excision of much of his medial temporal cortex (Scoville & Milner, 1957), exhibits clear losses in the learning of both new semantic knowledge (Cohen & Eichenbaum, 1994; Gabrieli, Cohen, & Corkin, 1988) and the recollection of postsurgical episodes (Milner, Corkin, & Teuber, 1968). Ostergaard (1987) studied a patient who, like the Vargha-Khadem et al. patients, became amnesic during childhood; after assessing the patient's progression for the next several years, the conclusion was that both episodic and semantic memory were severely disrupted.

Discrepancies between different outcomes are probably related to the specifics of the underlying pathology. A recent magnetic resonance imaging study with patient HM showed that the surgical excision had removed the rostral portion of both hippocampi, and also much of the surrounding entorhinal and perirhinal cortices (Corkin, Amaral, Gonzalez, Johnson, & Hyman, 1997). Similarly, Ostergaard's patient's lesion included the entire left hippocampus as well as the parahippocampal cortical areas. By contrast, the Vargha-Khadem patients all had bilateral lesions in the hippocampus proper with very little or no damage to the surrounding cortices. It was suggested that the integrity of these surrounding cortices is sufficient to allow for the entry of information into semantic memory, while additional processing from the hippocampus is necessary for episodic encoding (Mishkin, Suzuki, Gadian, & Vargha-Khadem, 1997).

Because these findings have been reported so recently, many questions remain unanswered. For example, although the patients clearly fail to show autonoetic awareness of the past, there is currently no way to know about their ability to reflect upon the personal present and future through such acts as introspection, planning, and anticipation. Therefore, it remains a possibility that the relation between these acts and episodic remembering is not evident in all populations. The further examination of these three patients and other similar patients is sure to provide new information about the neural substrates of the different varieties of memory and conscious awareness.

Conclusions

Episodic memory is the system of memory that allows us to experience the world autonoetically. It is this dimension—the ability to mentally travel through time—that is not shared by any other system or variety of memory. Other kinds of memory (semantic knowledge, stimulus-response strengthening, perceptual priming) are tied to the present moment—that is, one need not have any conscious awareness of the past or future to utilize these nonepisodic varieties of memory.

Episodic memory and autonoetic awareness are not obligatory for an organism to recall, recognize, report, or otherwise use information that was acquired in a recent, single episode. Indeed, the evidence reported in this chapter implies this point more strongly than any other. Although the verbal recall or recognition of a recently studied fact, or the deferred imitation of witnessed behaviors, may appear to an observer to be compelling evidence for an operational episodic memory system, a number of clever experiments have suggested otherwise. Individuals may know many things about the world, including the personal past, but be unable to mentally travel back in time to recollect the experiences upon which the knowledge is based.

Episodic remembering bears a close family resemblance to other higher order mental achievements (e.g., introspecting, daydreaming, anticipating) that are not typically considered to be acts of memory. The patients with large prefrontal lesions show these relations the most clearly, although children between the ages of about 1 and 5 years demonstrate many analogous symptoms. While neither population is amnesic, several different researchers have independently remarked that both groups do not seem to have the same kind of mental life as healthy, adult humans. They do not merely show a dissociation between semantic and episodic memory of the past; they appear to be more generally unable or unwilling to reflect upon their subjective experiences in the past, present, or future (see Wheeler et al., 1997, for a longer discussion of these populations). It is too early to know whether or not these relations will be evident in the amnesic patients reported by Vargha-Khadem and colleagues (1997).

References

Ackerley, S. S., & Benton, A. L. (1947). Report of a case of bilateral frontal lobe defect. *Research Publications: Association for Research in Nervous and Mental Disease, 27*, 479–504.

Bauer, P. J. (1996). What do infants recall of their lives? Memory for specific events by one- to two-year olds. *American Psychologist, 51*, 29–41.

Bauer, P. J., & Wewerka, S. S. (1995). One- to two-year-olds' recall of events: The more expressed, the more impressed. *Journal of Experimental Child Psychology, 59*, 475–496.

Blumer, D., & Benson, D. F. (1975). Personality changes with frontal and temporal lobe lesions. In D. F. Benson & D. Blumer (Eds.), *Psychiatric aspects of neurologic disease* (Vol. 1; pp. 151–170). New York: Grune & Stratton.

Buckner, R. L., & Tulving, E. (1995). Neuroimaging studies of memory: Theory and recent PET results. In F. Boller & J. Grafman (Eds.), *Handbook of neuropsychology* (Vol. 10; pp. 439–466). Amsterdam: Elsevier.

Cohen, N. J., & Eichenbaum, H. (1994). *Memory, amnesia, and the hippocampal system.* Cambridge, MA: MIT Press.

Conway, M. A., Gardiner, J. M., Perfect, T. J., Anderson, S. J., & Cohen, G. (1997). Changes in memory awareness during learning: The acquisition of knowledge by psychology undergraduates. *Journal of Experimental Psychology: General, 126*, 393–413.

Corkin, S., Amaral, D. G., Gonzalez, R. G., Johnson, K. A., & Hyman, D. T. (1997). H. M.'s medial temporal lobe lesion: Findings from magnetic resonance imaging. *Journal of Neuroscience, 17*, 3964–3979.

Craik, F. I. M., Morris, L. M., Morris, R. G., & Loewen, E. R. (1990). Relations between source amnesia and frontal lobe functioning in older adults. *Psychology and Aging, 5*, 148–151.

Flavell, J. H. (1993). Young children's understanding of thinking and consciousness. *Current Directions in Psychological Science, 2*, 40–43.

Freeman, W. (1953). Level of achievement after lobotomy. A study of 1000 cases. *American Journal of Psychiatry, 110*, 269–276.

Freeman, W., & Watts, J. W. (1950). *Psychosurgery* (2nd ed.). Springfield, IL: Charles S. Thomas.

Gabrieli, J. D. E., Cohen, N. J., & Corkin, S. (1988). The impaired learning of semantic knowledge following bilateral medial temporal-lobe resection. *Brain and Cognition, 7*, 157–177.

Gardiner, J. M. (1988). Functional aspects of recollective experience. *Memory and Cognition, 16*, 309–313.

Gardiner, J. M., & Java, R. I. (1993). Recognition memory and awareness: An experiential approach. *European Journal of Cognitive Psychology, 5*, 337–346.

Gopnik, A., & Graf, P. (1988). Knowing how you know: Young children's ability to identify and remember the sources of their beliefs. *Child Development, 59*, 1366–1371.

Gopnik, A., & Slaughter, V. (1991). Young children's understanding of changes in their mental states. *Child Development, 62*, 98–110.

Haug, H., Barnwater, U., Eggers, R., Fischer, D., Kuhl, S., & Sass, N. L. (1983). Anatomical changes in aging brain: Morphometric analysis of the human prosencephalon. In J. Cervois-Navarro & H. I. Sarkander (Eds.), *Brain aging: Neuropathology and neuropharamacology Vol. 21: Aging.* New York: Raven Press.

Howe, M. L., & Courage, M. L. (1993). On resolving the enigma of infantile amnesia. *Psychological Bulletin, 113,* 305–326.

Ingvar, D. H. (1985). "Memory of the future": An essay on the temporal organization of conscious awareness. *Human Neurobiology, 4,* 127–136.

James, W. (1890). *Principles of psychology.* Cambridge, MA: Harvard University Press.

Janowsky, J. S., Shimamura, A. P., & Squire, L. R. (1989). Source memory impairments in patients with frontal lobe lesions. *Neuropsychologia, 27,* 1043–1056.

Johnson, C. N., & Wellman, H. M. (1980). Children's developing understanding of mental verbs: Remember, know, and guess. *Child Development, 51,* 1095–1102.

Luria, A. R. (1973). *The working brain.* New York: Basic Books.

Luria, A. R., & Homskaya, E. D. (1964). Disturbance in the regulative role of speech with frontal lobe lesions. In J. M. Warren & K. Akert (Eds.), *The frontal granular cortex and behavior* (pp. 353–371). New York: McGraw-Hill.

McDonough, L., Mandler, J. M., McKee, R. D., & Squire, L. R. (1995). The deferred imitation task as a nonverbal measure of declarative memory. *Proceedings of the National Academy of Sciences, USA, 92,* 7580–7584.

McIntyre, J. S., & Craik, F. I. M. (1987). Age differences in memory for item and source information. *Canadian Journal of Psychology, 42,* 175–192.

Meltzoff, A. N. (1988). Infant imitation and memory: Nine-months-olds in immediate and deferred tests. *Child Development, 59,* 217–225.

Milner, B., Corkin, S., & Teuber, H. L. (1968). Further analysis of the hippocampal amnesic syndrome: 14-year followup study of H. M. *Neuropsychologia, 6,* 215–234.

Mishkin, M., Suzuki, W. A., Gadian, D. G., & Vargha-Khadem, F. (1997). Hierarchical organization of cognitive memory. *Philosophical Transactions of the Royal Society of London B., 352,* 1461–1467.

Moniz, E. (1936). *Tentatives operatoires dans le traitement de certaines psychoses.* Paris: Mason & Cie.

Nyberg, L., Cabeza, R., & Tulving, E. (1996). PET studies of encoding and retrieval: The HERA model. *Psychonomic Bulletin and Review, 2,* 134–147.

O'Neill, D. K., & Gopnik, A. (1991). Young children's ability to identify the sources of their beliefs. *Developmental Psychology, 27,* 390–397.

Ostergaard, A. L. (1987). Episodic, semantic, and procedural memory in a case of amnesia at an early age. *Neuropsychologia, 25,* 341–357.

Parkin, A. J., & Walter, B. M. (1992). Recollective experience, normal aging, and frontal dysfunction. *Psychology and Aging, 7,* 290–298.

Perner, J., & Ruffman, T. (1995). Episodic memory and autonoetic consciousness: Developmental evidence and a theory of childhood amnesia. *Journal of Experimental Child Psychology, 59,* 516–548.

Robinson, M. F., & Freeman, W. (1954). *Psychosurgery and the self.* New York: Grune & Stratton.

Schacter, D. L., Harbluk, J. L., & McLachlan, D. R. (1984). Retrieval without recollection: An experimental analysis of source amnesia. *Journal of Verbal Learning and Verbal Behavior, 23,* 593–611.

Schacter, D. L., Kaszniak, A. W., Kihlstrom, J. F., & Valdiserri, M. (1991). The relation between source memory and aging. *Psychology and Aging, 6,* 559–568.

Scoville, W. B., & Milner, B. (1957). Loss of recent memory after bilateral hippocampal lesions. *Journal of Neurological and Neurosurgical Psychiatry, 20,* 11–12.

Stuss, D. T. (1991). Self, awareness, and the frontal lobes: A neuropsychological perspective. In J. Strauss & G. R. Goethals (Eds.), *The self: Interdisciplinary approaches* (pp. 255–278). New York: Springer-Verlag.

Stuss, D. T., Picton, T. W., & Alexander, M. P. (in press). Consciousness, self-awareness, and the frontal lobes. In S. Salloway, P. Malloy, & J. Duffy (Eds.), *The frontal lobes and neuropscyhiatric illness.* Washington: American Psychiatric Press.

Sweet, W. H. (1973). Treatment of medically intractable mental disease by limited frontal leucotomy—justifiable? *New England Journal of Medicine, 289,* 1117–1125.

Taylor, M., Esbensen, B. M., & Bennett, R. T. (1994). Children's understanding of knowledge acquisition: The tendency for children to report that they have always known what they have just learned. *Child Development, 65,* 1581–1604.

Tulving, E. (1983). *Elements of episodic memory.* New York: Oxford University Press.

Tulving, E. (1985). Memory and consciousness. *Canadian Journal of Psychology, 25,* 1–12.

Tulving, E. (1993). What is episodic memory? *Current Directions in Psychological Science, 3,* 67–70.

Valenstein, G. S. (1986). *Great and desperate cures: The rise and decline of psychosurgery and other radical treatments for mental illness.* New York: Basic Books.

Vargha-Khadem, F., Gadian, D. G., Watkins, K. E., Connelly, A., Van Paesschen, W., & Mishkin, M. (1997). Differential effects of early hippocampal pathology on episodic and semantic memory. *Science, 277,* 376–380.

West, R. L. (1996). An application of prefrontal cortex function theory to aging. *Psychological Bulletin, 120,* 272–292.

Wheeler, M. A., Stuss, D. T., & Tulving, E. (1997). Towards a theory of episodic memory: The frontal lobes and autonoetic consciousness. *Psychological Bulletin, 121*(3), 331–354.

Wimmer, H., Hogrefe, G.-J., & Perner, J. (1988). Children's understanding of information access as a source of knowledge. *Child Development, 59,* 386–396.

Zelazo, P. D., Carter, A., Reznick, J. S., & Frye, D. (1997). Early development of executive function: A problem-solving framework. *Review of General Psychology, 1,* 198–226.

Zelazo, P. D., Frye, D., & Rapus, T. (1996). An age-related dissociation between knowing rules and using them. *Cognitive Development, 11,* 37–63.

38

Theories of Memory and Consciousness

MORRIS MOSCOVITCH

Having been banished from scientific investigation for nearly a century, the study of consciousness has made a triumphant return and secured a prominent place in research in cognitive neuroscience. There is no better example of this development than in research on human memory, where issues related to consciousness have been a central concern since the early 1980s. Much of the research has focused on distinguishing among types or aspects of memory that are accompanied by conscious awareness from those that are not, and on identifying the neural substrates that mediate each. In this chapter, some theories and models that guided this research or emerged from it will be presented and discussed briefly. For ease of exposition, the models and theories are classified according to whether their distinctive characteristics or primary emphasis is on structure or function. Following presentation of the models, there will be a brief review of the literature that will focus on the neuropsychological evidence of dissociations between implicit and explicit memory as revealed by behavioral studies of patients with neurological disorders and neuroimaging studies of normal people. The survey will also examine the issue of whether different types of consciousness are associated with explicit memory. The reader is referred to the relevant chapters in this book and to recent reviews for more extensive coverage (Cabeza & Nyberg, 1997; Schacter & Buckner, 1998; Buckner & Koutstaal, 1998; Gabrieli, 1998; Allen, Wilding, & Rugg, 1998).

It is noteworthy that research has advanced without a definition of consciousness that encompasses all its aspects and about which everyone can agree. There are, however, serviceable definitions that capture some important aspect of consciousness and makes the topic amenable to investigation. One of them is that consciousness is a mental state that permits one to have a phenomenological awareness of one's experience. With respect to this chapter, the concern will not be so much with the mental state as with the contents of consciousness as they relate to memory—namely, those aspects of memory that can inform conscious experience, that are the object of phenomenological awareness, and about which the person can reflect and comment. In operational terms, "one is conscious or aware of [a memory] when a verbal or nonverbal description can be provided of [it] or a voluntary response can be made that comments on it" (Köhler & Moscovitch, 1997, p. 306). As we will see, the emphasis on the mnemonic aspect of the representation as the object of reflection, as opposed to its perceptual and semantic aspects, is crucial, as is the type of phenomenological awareness that accompanies different types of explicit memory.

Functional Theories and Models of Consciousness and Memory

Process-Based Theories

Process-based theorists have associated consciousness with a particular process, such as control or attention. Control is a hallmark of conscious recollective processes in Jacoby's (1991) theories (chapter 14), so much so that the processing dissociation procedure (PDP) he uses to distinguish conscious from nonconscious memory rests on the assumption that the ability to control one's responses on memory tasks ultimately determines the assignment of a recovered memory to one or the other category. Although control processes are associated more with conscious recollection and automatic processes with implicit memory, both types of processes are implicated in important aspects of both types of memory. The PDP procedure, however, cannot distinguish between processes involved in memory recovery, only between the outcome of those processes. For example, even for explicit memory, retrieval can be either intentional and controlled or unintentional and automatic (Richardson-Klavehn, Gardiner, & Java, 1996; chapter 15). As long as both lead to a consciously apprehended memory of the item, the PDP procedure will treat them alike. Moscovitch also (1994a, 1994b) distinguished between controlled and automatic processes within explicit memory, associating one with the associative-cue-dependent, ecphoric processes centered on the medial temporal lobes, and the other with strategic retrieval processes centered on the prefrontal cortex. Dividing attention at retrieval has little effect on memory tests sensitive to medial temporal damage but strong effects on tests sensitive to frontal damage (Craik, Govoni, Naveh-Benjamin, & Anderson, 1996; but see Fernandes & Moscovitch, 1998). Conversely, recent studies by Winocur, Moscovitch, and Stuss (1996) suggest that control processes mediated by the frontal lobes play a similar role in implicit memory. Performance on implicit memory tests such as word-stem completion are correlated in the elderly with performance on tests sensitive to frontal-lobe damage and are impaired in young people if they are distracted by another task (Stone, Ladd, Vaidya, & Gabrieli, 1998).

Similar problems are encountered if explicit memory is linked to conceptually driven processes and implicit memory to perceptually driven processes, as some transfer-appropriate processing theorists have suggested (Roediger & McDermott, 1993). Though this is a good rule of thumb, it is no more than that. Explicit tests can be perceptually driven just as implicit tests can be conceptually driven (Blaxton, 1989) and spared in amnesia (Gabrieli, 1998; Schacter & Buckner, 1998).

Content-Based Theories

According to content-based explanations, conscious recollection is associated with a particular type of information in memory. Explicit and implicit memories are contrasted as context-dependent vs context-free (Mayes, Gooding, & Van Eijk 1997; Winocur & Kinsbourne, 1978), declarative vs procedural (Cohen & Eichenbaum, 1993; Squire, 1992), episodic vs. semantic (Kinsbourne & Wood, 1975), and associative vs. nonassociative (Mayes et al., 1997), to name just a few. Like the process-based theories, content-based theories work as first approximations in the sense that they can capture some, but not all, the crucial differences between explicit and implicit memory. Thus, with respect to the associative theory, implicit memory for rapidly formed, new associations has been reported in both neurologically intact people (Goshen-Gottstein & Moscovitch, 1995b) and in amnesic people (Gabrieli, Keane, Zurella, & Poldrack, 1997; Goshen-Gottstein & Moscovitch, 1995a; Moscovitch, Winocur, & McLachlan, 1986; Musen & Squire, 1993; see "Distinct Representation Models"). Similarly, context-dependent theory is contradicted by evidence that environmental context influences performance on implicit tests of memory (Graf, 1994) and even more so in amnesic patients whose explicit memory is impaired (Winocur & Kinsbourne, 1978).

Both process and content-based theories of explicit and implicit memory do not deal with consciousness in its different aspects, but rather focus on the types of memory processes and information that consciousness can support. None of the theories even attempts to account for the phenomenology of memory, the different subjective experiences that accompany one type of memory as compared to another. Essentially, both types of theories are concerned with markers of consciousness rather than with conscious experience.

Experience-Based Theories

Different types of memory are distinguished from one another not only by the information that is represented and the processes that are engaged but by the kind of conscious awareness that accompanies each type. Tulving, the leading modern proponent of this view, and his colleagues (Wheeler, Stuss, & Tulving, 1997; chapter 37) distinguish between three types: autonoetic, noetic, and anoetic. "Autonoetic (self-knowing) consciousness is the capacity that allows adult humans to mentally represent and to become aware of their protracted existence across subjective time." Autonoetic consciousness makes possible episodic memory that is defined as "conscious recollection of personal happenings and events from one's personal past and mental projection of anticipated events into one's subjective future." At the core of autonoetic awareness is a sense of a personal self and the subjective experiences associated with that self or ascribed to it. It is "autonoetic consciousness that confers the phenomenal flavor to the remembering of past events, the flavor that distinguishes remembering from other kinds of awareness such as those characterizing perceiving, thinking, imaging or dreaming" (Tulving, 1985, p. 3). Noetic awareness occurs when one thinks about something that one knows, such as a mathematical, geographical, or even personal fact, without reexperiencing or reliving the past in which that knowledge was acquired. Autonoetic and noetic consciousness are mediated by different subregions of the frontal lobes. Anoetic consciousness is associated with implicit memory because it does not involve the mental representation of different forms of knowledge but rather alterations in performance, caused by changes in speed and efficiency of perceptual, cognitive, and motor operations mediated by neocortical and subcortical regions concerned with perception, cognition, and action.

There is consensus that anoetic consciousness should be distinguished from the other two types, but not for distinguishing noetic from autonoetic consciousness. A crucial piece of evidence used to support the latter distinction comes from studies of remember/know judgments in recognition memory (chapter 15). Remember responses are given if participants revive the experience associated with that item during the study phase, whereas know responses indicate that they simply recognize the item as familiar. Autonoetic consciousness is necessary for remember (R) judgments but not for know (K) judgments for which noetic consciousness suffices. Consistent with Tulving's conception, variables associated with consciousness, such as attention, control, and depth of processing, affect remember judgments more than know judgments, whereas variations in representational format between study and test typically affect know judgments more (Rajaram & Roediger, 1997).

Memory as assessed by know judgments resembles perceptual implicit memory and has led to the suggestion, and some evidence, that they are mediated by the same system (Rajaram & Roediger, 1997). Recent studies, however, support Tulving in showing that perceptual implicit memory and familiarity on explicit recognition are distinguishable one from the other (chapter 15; Wagner & Gabrieli, 1998), the most telling evidence coming from studies of amnesic patients whose recognition memory of either type is impaired, and sometimes is at chance, even when they perform normally on perceptual implicit tests (Knowlton, 1998; Yonelinas, Kroll, Dobbins, Lazzara, & Knight, 1998).

An alternative to Tulving's theory is that awareness of a memory, once it occurs, cannot be fractionated into different subtypes. What distinguishes recollection from familiarity is the content of the memory: how elaborate it is and the extent to which the subjective sense of reexperiencing the event infuses recollection. That different variables affect one type of memory more than another is a reflection of the content of the memory and the processes involved in recovering it, not in the nature of the consciousness associated with it.

Moscovitch (1995a, 1995b) provides an experience-based theory of consciousness and memory that is compatible with both alternatives and has the advantage over other theories of explaining why explicit memory is associated with conscious awareness and implicit memory is not. Moscovitch's theory is derived from a consideration of how modules and central systems operate and interact in a components-of-processing model of memory (Moscovitch, 1992; Moscovitch & Umiltà, 1990). In his model, as in others' (Schacter, 1994; Tulving & Schacter, 1990), perceptual implicit memory or priming is mediated by modules in posterior neocortex that form presemantic structural representations of words and objects. Modules are altered by the stimuli they process so that on subsequent encounters with it processing is more efficient and accurate, which accounts for priming. By virtue of their properties—domain specificity, shallow (presemantic) output, and informational encapsulation—modules can only deliver perceptual information that leads to awareness of a percept, albeit a clearer, more rapidly formed one, but not a direct memory (as opposed to an attributed one; see below) of previous encounters with the stimulus. (See Moscovitch, 1995a, 1995b for an extended discussion.)

What distinguishes Moscovitch's theory from other ones is the conception of the processes and representations that govern explicit memory. Explicit memory begins with conscious apprehension of a stimulus event, which depends on the interaction of modules with interpretative central systems that are domain-general structures concerned with meaning and significance, whose output is deep and whose operations are cognitively penetrable. Once an event is consciously apprehended, the medial temporal lobe (the hippocampus and adjacent cortex) and related diencephalic structures mandatorily bind into a memory trace the neocortical (and other) elements that gave rise to the conscious experience of the event (see figure 38.1). The memory trace then consists of a cohesive ensemble of medial temporal/diencephalic and neocortical neurons, with the medial temporal portion acting as an index or pointer to where information about the event is represented in neocortex (and perhaps elsewhere). Based on the assumption that there is a neural correlate associated with conscious awareness of an event (say, the pattern of neural firing or the type and number of neurons firing), Moscovitch proposed that what is included in the memory trace is not just the stimulus features of the event but also those elements that made the experience conscious. Consciousness or awareness is part of the engram. At retrieval, the entire consciousness/content ensemble is reactivated. Thus, because encoding was conscious, subsequent recollection also embodies the conscious experience. According to Moscovitch's model, it is the recovery of a trace imbued with consciousness that gives rise to the felt experience of remembering or at the very least to a sense of familiarity (P. Milner, 1989).

In Moscovitch's model, as in Conway's (1999), memory traces are stored randomly like cherries in a bowl (Landauer, 1975). Encoding and retrieval are guided and organized by the frontal lobes, which act as working-with-memory structures (Moscovitch & Winocur, 1992; Moscovitch & Melo, 1997) that serve the same function in memory as they do in other domains. In Tulving's view, however, the frontal lobes are the structural correlate of autonoetic consciousness, so that their role in memory is unique.

Moscovitch's view resembles Tulving's in that consciousness is an inherent property of remembering. Moscovitch's proposal is open to the possibility that the consciousness associated with remembering and knowing are not fundamentally different from each other.[1] If a memory trace consists of a distributed set of neural elements, some may be lost during recovery of the trace. Just as it is possible to lose information about the different features of a stimulus, so it is possible to lose different aspects of the conscious experience selectively. When sufficient aspects of it are recovered, say the spatio-temporal context or multiply-associated items, remembering occurs, but when recovery is impoverished, only familiarity remains; once that is lost, all that can be sustained is an implicit memory of the event.

Conway's (1999) experience-based model has elements in common with Tulving's and Moscovitch's. In Conway's model, as in Tulving's, there is a reciprocal intimate connection between the self and autobiographical memory (AM). Autobiographical memory is the database for the working self that is conceived as a hierarchy of currently active goal structures that, in conjunction with input from autobiographical memory, sets goals, determines access to AM and encoding of information in it, and evaluates and organizes output from it. Conway's working self combines elements of Moscovitch's frontal component with Tulving's idea about the self. The sensory, phenomenological records refer to the store of near sensory experience of actual events that contribute to AM. Storage and retrieval of phenomenological records is mediated by the medial temporal lobes. As in Moscovitch's model, retrieval can be direct, via the medial temporal lobes or generative, in which case the frontal lobes are also implicated. Episodic memory is defined neither by the state of consciousness, as in Tulving, nor by the recovered trace, as in Moscovitch, but rather by the "encounter (during retrieval) of the current self with a fragment(s) of a past self," the phenomenological record, and it is this encounter which triggers recollective experience.

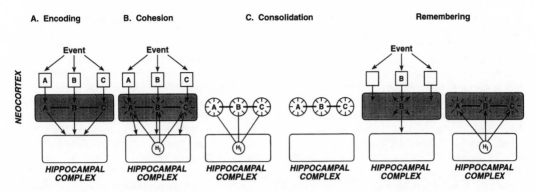

Figure 38.1 At encoding stimulus information is picked up by neocortical modules A, B, C. Consciousness is depicted as the stippled rectangular area. Although given a spatial dimension for illustrative purposes, consciousness need not be conceived as being localized to a particular region in the brain. The stippled area is meant to designate the neural correlate of information when one is consciously aware of it. The information in consciousness is automatically and obligatorily picked up by the hippocampal complex. Cohesion is the name given to the rapid process by which the hippocampal complex binds into a memory trace the neural elements that gave rise to the conscious experience, forming a consciousness/content (A-B-C) packet. (Consciousness is designated by sparkles.) Simultaneously, a neural code, Hi, is laid down which is also part of the memory trace and serves as an index file or pointer for later retrieval of the packet. The memory trace consists of an ensemble of hippocampal-cortical neurons. Consolidation begins after cohesion. Some theories hold that once consolidation is complete, the memory trace can be maintained without the hippocampal complex. Although this may be true for semantic information, the evidence suggests that the hippocampal complex always forms an integral part of the memory trace for autobiographical, episodic events (Nadel & Moscovitch, 1997). Remembering occurs when a cue, B, activates Hi, and interacts with it (ecphory). The product of that interaction (A-B-C, with sparkles), which is what is recovered from memory, contains "consciousness" along with the information that formed the content of the conscious experience. In short, what is encoded and recovered are elements of a conscious experience.

Attribution Theories of Explicit Memory

Some theorists have proposed that attribution plays an important role in determining whether an experienced event qualifies as a memory, a percept, or an image. Jacoby (1991; chapter 14) proposed that perceptual fluency is an important determinant of familiarity judgments in recognition and recollection. Because stimuli that have previously been encountered are processed more efficiently and accurately, they are perceived more easily and with greater clarity. Perceptual fluency is then used as evidence that the item had been encountered previously. The conditions under which perceptual fluency can serve as an indicator of memory, however, are limited (Watkins & Gibson, 1988) and probably restricted to circumstance that are unexpected and in which other memory cues are sparse (Whittlesea & Williams, 1998).

Attribution also plays a significant role in Johnson's source-monitoring theory. According to Johnson (1992), memory depends on the interaction of perceptual and reflective subsystems that constitute her multiple-entry modular (MEM) memory system. Whereas perceptual implicit memory depends only on the perceptual subsystems, explicit memory requires the added participation of the reflective subsystem. Conscious recollection occurs when, in the process of retrieval and monitoring, an individual attributes the source of a current representation to a past experience. Among the most important features of the representation that make it an episodic memory, or rather that influence the rememberer to judge the memory as episodic, are perceptual vividness, spatio-temporal context, affect, and consistency with other episodic and semantic memories. To the extent that the representation lacks these, the individual is likely to attribute the memory to an imagined rather than a real event, or to classify the memory as known rather than remembered.

Because Johnson does not address the issue of varieties of consciousness directly, it is difficult to tell from her writings whether or not she associates different types of explicit memory and the sources to which they are attributed with different types of consciousness. At the neuropsychological level, in Johnson's model, as in Moscovitch's and Tulving's, the medial temporal lobes are needed for binding the various features that constitute an experience into a memory trace and for reactivating it, whereas the frontal lobes are needed for the variety of reflective processes associated with encoding, retrieval, and monitoring. Insofar as consciousness is considered, it is associated with the reflective functions of the frontal lobes rather than with the medial temporal lobes (Johnson & Raye, 1998). In this way Johnson's model resembles Tulving's more than Moscovitch's where consciousness is associated with the function of both structures.

Structural Theories and Models of Consciousness and Memory

Köhler and Moscovitch (1997) and Farah and Feinberg (1997) identified four different types of structural models of consciousness and awareness. Although their surveys dealt primarily with visual perception and attention, the models apply equally to memory. None of these models currently distinguishes among different types of phenomenological awareness that accompany explicit memory, though they can be modified to incorporate these distinctions (see Moscovitch, 1995a).

Dissociation Models

The model consists of perceptual and conceptual modules in neocortex that deliver their output to a conscious awareness system (CAS), which, in turn, delivers and receives input from systems that are concerned with episodic memory, such as the medial temporal lobes, and with executive functions, such as the prefrontal cortex (for examples, see Moscovitch, 1989, 1995a; Schacter, 1994). Dissociations between implicit and explicit memory arise when either the episodic memory system or neocortical modules are disconnected from the conscious awareness system, or when

there is direct damage to the episodic memory system itself. Thus, damage to the medial temporal lobes impairs explicit memory but leaves perceptual and conceptual implicit memory intact. More interestingly, the model predicts implicit memory will be preserved, as evidence confirms, even in agnosic, dyslexic, anomic, or demented patients whose modules are intact but are disconnected from CAS (Moscovitch, 1994b; Srinivas, Breedin, Coslett, & Saffran, 1997; Schacter & Buckner, 1998).

One of the assumptions of the disconnection model is that the information or knowledge represented in neocortical modules is fundamentally similar to the information in consciousness. All that distinguishes one from the other is awareness of the information. The model also assumes that input to the CAS proceeds serially from neocortical input modules to conscious awareness. Put another way, it assumes redundancy between implicit memory and recollection, with the former being subsumed by the latter. As a result, the model predicts that it is only possible to have impaired explicit memory and intact implicit memory, but not the reverse.

Distinct Representation Models

An alternative to the disconnection model is that distinct mechanisms and representations support implicit and explicit memory (Köhler & Moscovitch, 1997). According to this view, implicit and explicit memory are different in kind and involve different cognitive and neural mechanisms so that even in normal people representations on which implicit memory is based are not available to conscious awareness, but coexist with explicit memory representations. In contrast to the previous model, modules harbor at least two distinct representations, one of which leads to conscious awareness and provides the input to the explicit memory system, and another which remains implicit but can influence behavior. (In these regards, distinct representation models resemble independence processing models (chapter 16) as well as some of the content-based theories mentioned in the previous section.) The mechanisms supporting these representations work in parallel so that it is possible to damage one without affecting the other, leading to a double dissociation between implicit and explicit memory. In this model there is no need to postulate a separate

CAS since the capacity for conscious awareness is a property of one of the neural systems but not the other.

Degraded Representations or Threshold Models

According to a third class of model, implicit and explicit memory are mediated by the same system, except that implicit memory is a degraded form of explicit memory. The quality and fullness of the representation needed to support performance on explicit tests is higher and more complete than that needed to support performance on implicit tests. Damage to the system leads to degraded, incomplete representations, which, in turn, lead to loss of explicit memory but preserved implicit memory. Computational, neural network models, particularly those dealing with perception and attention, currently provide the most compelling evidence in favor of the degraded representation model (Farah, O'Reilly, & Vecera, 1993). With regard to memory, however, the model's drawback is that it does not specify, nor do neural networks simulations indicate, exactly which structures constitute the memory system, whether damage to all or only a subset of them leads to degradation, and whether the differences between complete and degraded representations is only quantitative or is it also qualitative such that degraded representations are missing some crucial attributes or features? What the model does imply is that it is not possible to have impaired implicit memory without also having impaired explicit memory. Studies by (Jernigan & Ostergaard, 1993; Ostergaard, 1994; Ostergaard & Jernigan, 1996) provide suggestive empirical evidence in support of such a model from patients with memory disorders, including those with mesial temporal lobe lesions (but see Squire, Hamann, & Schacter for a critique).

Integrated or Interactionist Models

This class of model posits that consciousness arises when interactions across various components or processes are fully integrated with one another so that all the processes and representations are mutually consistent. For example, Cowey and Stoerig (1992; Stoerig, 1996) proposed that consciousness in vision depends on an interplay between early and late visual areas. An alternative proposal is that awareness arises from the binding of disparate neural elements into an integrated pattern by an oscillating 40 Hz signal (Singer, 1993) or by projections to and from convergence zones that serve the same binding and integrative function but with each zone assigned a particular domain (Damasio, 1989). Kinsbourne's (1988) integrated field theory is another example of this type of model. In memory, conscious awareness of a past episode may depend on the integrated action of temporal, prefrontal, and posterior neocortical neurons (see pp. 30–33).

Brief Review of the Research Literature and Evaluation of the Models and Theories

How do the various models fare against the behavioral and neuropsychological evidence on memory and consciousness? At this point in theory development and data collection, a strict evaluation of the models is premature. Typically, the models and theories act more like heuristic devices or frameworks that guide research and organize information rather than as precise formulations that can be falsified by crucial experiments. Rather than pronounce strict judgment on the models and theories, the best one can do is note their similarities and differences, and indicate their relative merits and deficiencies.

According to all the models and theories, perceptual implicit memory or priming is mediated by perceptual input modules or representation systems that are presemantic and preattentive. These modules corresponded to domain-specific posterior neocortical structures, such as those in inferior temporal cortex, that are necessary for recognizing words, faces, and objects. Conceptual priming, on the other hand, is assumed to be mediated by domain-general regions in superior left lateral temporal lobe, and inferior left prefrontal cortex that are implicated in semantic memory. Upon presentation of a stimulus, the structures that process the stimulus and derive its meaning are modified or reconfigured so that on subsequent presentations either fewer neurons, or a lower level of firing of the same neurons, are needed for processing.

With some notable exceptions (see below, pp. 20–21), the evidence on perceptual and conceptual priming is generally consistent with the models' claims at both a functional

(Roediger & McDermott, 1993) and structural level (Moscovitch, Vriezen, & Goshen-Gott-stein, 1993; Schacter & Buckner, 1998; Wiggs & Martin, 1998; see also chapter 39). Perceptual priming is preserved as long as posterior neocortical structures are sufficiently viable to support even nonconscious structural processing of stimuli even if memory, perception, naming, and comprehension is defective as it is in people with amnesia, agnosia, dyslexia, word deafness, and dementia (see Moscovitch et al., 1993; Schacter & Buckner, 1998; chapter 39). Conversely, extensive damage to posterior neocortex, especially on the right, eliminates perceptual priming for words and pictures (Gabrieli, Fleishmann, Keane, Reminger, & Morrell, 1995). Likewise, conceptual priming is typically spared in amnesics (Schacter & Buckner, 1998), but impaired in patients, such as those with Alzheimer's disease, in which areas serving semantic memory are damaged (Schacter & Buckner, 1998; chapter 39).

Recent neuroimaging and neurophysiological studies (for review, see Schacter & Buckner, 1998; Wiggs & Martin, 1998) support the hypothesis that perceptual implicit memory is associated with a reduction of activation in posterior neocortical regions, particularly in the inferior temporal lobes and temporal-occipital-parietal junctions, that are concerned with structural representations of faces, objects, and words. Reductions are not evident in early occipital visual areas and temporal auditory areas that code for elementary sensory features (Buckner et al., 1998).

Neuroimaging studies of conceptual priming show reductions in left lateral temporal lobe, but especially in left prefrontal cortex, when items are repeated in tasks that engage conceptual processes, such as verb generation to nouns, and repeated semantic classification of words and objects (Buckner et al., 1998; chapter 39).

Though the models are largely successful, recent studies indicate that they need to be modified to accommodate new evidence about the effects of level of processing and attention on perceptual priming. The differences between perceptual priming and explicit memory with regard to attention and semantic processing that were once thought to be absolute are now considered to be one of degree. Long-term perceptual priming is reduced or eliminated for words that were not attended at study (Bentin, Moscovitch, & Nirhod, 1998; and Macdonald & McLeod, 1998; Stone et al.,

in press) or were processed only at superficial sensory levels (Bentin et al., 1998). Because repetition priming was completely eliminated, not merely reduced, in some of these studies, the observed effects of attention and levels of processing cannot be attributed only to the contaminating influence of explicit memory. Even after explicit memory reaches asymptotically low levels, reduced attention and levels of processing leads to a further reduction in implicit memory, to the point of elimination. These studies indicate that conscious awareness directed at some higher order features is needed for long-term perceptual priming, and suggest that structures such as parietal and prefrontal cortices that are involved in attention and conceptual processing are also implicated in priming. As predicted, reduced activation for repeated as compared to novel items was found in those regions (Schacter & Buckner, 1998; Wiggs & Martin, 1998).

Thus, the models were correct in predicting that perceptual priming was associated with a reduction in the activity of neurons in posterior neocortex. All the models, however, failed to consider that other structures, such as parietal and prefrontal cortex are important, and will have to take them into account and specify more clearly the contribution they make.

The Relation Between Priming and Explicit Memory

Forming and Recovering New Associations

The rapid formation of new associations is thought by some to be a function of the hippocampal complex and to be dependent on conscious awareness (Squire, 1992). Early reports of single trial associative priming in a rapid reading task in amnesic patients (Moscovitch et al., 1986) were challenged by the observation that multiple repetitions were needed to observe the effect (Musen & Squire, 1993) and that on an associative stem-completion task, only moderate but not severe, amnesic people showed associative priming (Graf & Schacter, 1985). The results from these experiments were interpreted as evidence that some associative priming tests were contaminated by explicit memory so that when amnesia was severe, single-trial associative priming was eliminated. More recently, however, Goshen-Gottstein and Moscovitch (1995a) and Gabrieli, Brewer, Desmond, and Glover (1997) used associative priming tests such as two-item lexical decision and perceptual identification that are not likely contaminated by explicit memory (see also Paller & Mayes, 1994). They found intact, associative priming effects with one or two learning trials, even in severely amnesic patients. Moreover, using normal controls, Goshen-Gottstein and Moscovitch (1995b) showed that associative priming effects are perceptual in nature in that they, like single-item priming, are affected more by perceptual manipulations such as changes in format and modality than conceptual manipulations, such as levels of processing. The latter finding indicates that perceptual modules in posterior neocortex, presumably under the guidance of attentional processes of the parietal lobes and prefrontal cortex (Kinoshita, in press), can form and store structural representations between unrelated items within a single domain just as they can for novel items (Hamann & Squire, 1997).

Independence Among Perceptual Priming, Conceptual Priming, and Explicit Memory

To what extent does conceptual priming depend on repetition both of the item and of the conceptual component of the task? If perceptual and conceptual priming are related serially, conceptual priming should benefit from the expected perceptual facilitation when an item is repeated even if semantic classification of it changes from an animacy decision (living-made) on the first trial to a size decision (bigger than a breadbox) on the next. Vriezen, Moscovitch, and Bellos (1995) found that item repetition, whether of words or pictures, has little or no influence on conceptual priming unless there is overlap between the conceptual components of the task with repetition (e.g., bigger than a breadbox on trial 1 and relative width and height estimation on trial 2). In a neuroimaging variant of this experiment, Wagner, Desmond, Demb, Glover, and Gabrieli (1997) found that reductions in frontal activations on a conceptual priming task occurred only when the semantic decision was repeated along with the item, but not if the item alone was repeated. Together the results suggest that processes and mechanisms involved in perceptual and conceptual priming can operate independently of one another.

This conclusion is consistent with the observation by Gabrieli, Keane, and their coworkers (Gabrieli, Fleischman, Keane, Reminger, & Morrell, 1995; Keane, Gabrieli, Mapstone, Johnson, & Corkin, 1995) that perceptual priming can be impaired following right occipital damage without compromising conceptual priming and explicit memory. Conversely, in dementia of the Alzheimer type, conceptual priming and explicit memory are impaired but perceptual priming is preserved (Fleischman, Gabrieli, Reminger, Rinaldi, Morrell, & Wilson, 1995; Keane, Gabrieli, Fennema, Growdon, & Corkin, 1991) single unit recording studies in monkeys conducted by Miller and Desimone (1994) suggest that different neural mechansims and responses support priming and explicit memory (see Wiggs & Martin, 1998). They identified two populations of neurons that responded differently to repetition of previously presented pictures of complex objects—one whose firing rate was reduced regardless of the monkey's response to it (priming) and another one whose firing rate was increased but only when the monkey recognized the pictures as old (recognition). Together, these findings indicate that perceptual priming is independent of conceptual priming and explicit memory and can operate in parallel with them. These findings also call into question the assumption of some models, such as the dissociation, attribution, and degraded processing models, that the benefits at early stages of processing, as revealed by perceptual priming, are transferred automatically to later stages or that implicit memory always co-occurs with explicit as redundancy models assume (see chapter 16). The distinct representation or independence model fits the neuropsychological data best.

The case for independence between conceptual priming and explicit memory is more difficult to make. Conceptual priming and explicit memory typically are affected by the same variables. The neuropsychological evidence, however, suggest the two are dissociable. Neuroimaging studies show that reductions in activation, especially in the left prefrontal cortex (Schacter & Buckner, 1998; Buckner et al., 1998) are associated with conceptual priming whereas recognition typically is associated with increases in activation in right prefrontal cortex (Tulving, Kapur, Craik, Moscovitch, & Houle, 1995; Cabeza & Nyberg, 1997). Moreover, just as amnesia affects episodic memory while relatively sparing semantic memory (Vargha-Khadem et al., 1997), the reverse occurs in semantic dementia (chapter 28; Snowden, Griffiths, & Neary, 1996) a progressive degenerative disorder that affects the lateral temporal cortex and often the prefrontal cortex but spares the medial temporal lobes. Although conceptual priming has yet to be tested in these patients, it very likely is deficient in view of their greatly compromised semantic memory on which conceptual priming depends.

Because episodic memory for daily events is preserved in these patients, despite their profound semantic memory loss, it is difficult to argue in favor of theories that view semantic memory as a necessary prerequisite for episodic memory or redundant with it (Tulving, 1983). Indeed, Snowden, Neary, and Mann (1996) argue that not only does episodic memory not rely on semantic memory, but that the opposite is the case in people with semantic dementia: it is through the episodic memory system that meaning is conferred on experience. Thus, these patients can identify semantically only those objects and words with which they have a personal experience or relationship, such as objects in their house, but not similar objects with which they have no personal acquaintance.

Familiarity, Knowing, and Remembering

Experimental psychologists have long distinguished between two types of recognition: one that is based on familiarity and is considered relatively automatic and the other that is more recollective in that it requires control processes that aid in recovering the spatio-temporal and interitem context of the initial event (Mandler, 1980). There is some dispute in the literature about the mechanisms and types of processes mediating familiarity and recollective judgments of recognition, and what the relation is between them. Some attribution theorists (see Kelley & Jacoby, 1998) have proposed that judgments of familiarity are attributions based on the perceptual or conceptual fluency that underlies priming. Other investigators associate familiarity with know responses and assert that they are derived from semantic memory and reflect noetic awareness (Tulving, 1985). By a third account, familiarity-based recognition is functionally and anatomically distinct from priming and semantic memory, and is dependent, instead, on processes and mechanisms that support explicit

memory (Moscovitch, 1992; Moscovitch & Bentin, 1993; Knowlton, 1998).

The literature pertaining to all three approaches has been reviewed thoroughly recently, so it will be summarized only briefly here. Wagner and Gabrieli (1998) note that familiarity as estimated by the exclusion/inclusion method of PDP is sensitive to conceptual and perceptual variables that have little influence over perceptual priming. Moreover, damage to right occipital and adjacent temporal cortex impairs perceptual priming without affecting recognition based on familiarity or recollection whereas the reverse is obtained with amnesia (Yonelinas et al., 1998). The conclusion that Wagner and Gabrieli (1998) reach is that familiarity-based recognition is not typically derived from perceptual fluency, though the possibility that it is derived from conceptual fluency remains.

The situation is somewhat different for know responses. In their recent reviews, Rajaram and Roediger (1997), indicate that know responses are influenced more by perceptual than semantic manipulations and have suggested that they are driven by perceptual fluency. Evidence from amnesia, however, argues against this possibility because perceptual priming is intact in amnesia, but both remember and know components of recognition are impaired (Knowlton, 1998; Yonelinas et al., 1998).

The latter finding suggests that both know and remember responses are dependent on the medial temporal lobe/diencephalic system, though perhaps different regions of it, with remember responses dependent additionally on the frontal lobes (Parkin & Walter, 1992; Wheeler et al., 1997). Blaxton and Theodore (1997) found a preponderance of remember responses in people with right temporal lobectomy and know responses in people with left temporal lobectomy, suggesting that the left and right temporal lobes mediate remember and know responses, respectively. Aggleton and Brown (1999; see also chapter 27) noted that recall is impaired in patients with lesions restricted to the hippocampus proper but recognition memory is intact unless damage extends to peri-rhinal cortex and parahippocampal gyrus. One interpretation of these results is that remembering is dependent on the hippocampal formation and its diencephalic connections, whereas knowing is mediated by peri-rhinal cortex and its diencephalic projections. Recent fMRI studies lend some support to this conjecture. Schacter and Wagner (1999) and Wagner and Gabrieli (1998) note there is a suggestion that posterior regions of the medial temporal lobe, including the parahippocampus, are activated more on tests based on familiarity whereas anterior regions are activated more on tests requiring relational processing between items that can support remembering (but see Lepage, Habib, & Tulving, 1998).

The proposal that distinct regions of the medial temporal lobe mediate recollection and familiarity is most consistent with Moscovitch's component process model that the medial temporal lobes are needed even for the most elementary aspects of explicit memory. The model, however, also allows for the possibility that other component processes, such as those mediated by the frontal lobes and the posterior neocortex, can contribute to performance and to the quality and content of the memory experience.

The Self and Memory

The concept of the self is an essential aspect of autobiographical memory in humans and is a central component of experienced-based models, especially Tulving's and Conway's. In Moscovitch's it is an adjunct and has the same status as any other feature of a conscious experience that is encoded in the memory trace. Given the central role of the self, it is surprising how few studies examined the role of the self in remembering and knowing. In a meta-analysis of studies on the self-reference effect, Symons and Johnson (1997) confirmed that processing information in terms of the self is mnemonically advantageous but the effect is attenuated, or disappears entirely, if the comparison task encourages a level of organization and elaboration that is comparable to self-reference. What is crucial for the models under consideration, however, is whether the recollective experience—remembering versus knowing—is affected differently by self-reference at encoding and retrieval. Conway and Dewhurst (1995) reported that even when overall word recognition is similar across encoding conditions, successful recognition of words encoded in reference to the self is more likely to be accompanied by remembering versus knowing than of words encoded in a general semantic condition. Moroz (1998), however, found similar levels of remembering for self and social desirability conditions.

In a PET study on the self-reference effect at encoding and retrieval, the results were similarly ambiguous. Craik et al. (1999) found that during encoding, self-related words yielded left-frontal activations similar to that of other types of semantic encoding. However, they also noted distinct activations in regions BA9 and 10 of right prefrontal cortex that typically are associated with memory retrieval, not encoding (Grady, 1998). During retrieval, Moroz (1998) found that words previously encoded with respect to one's self activated anterior prefrontal cortex bilaterally whereas words encoded with respect to another person or with respect to social desirability activated more posterior regions on the left, either laterally or medially. Most interestingly, the peak activations for self in BA 8/9 bilaterally correspond closely to the areas activated in PET studies on "theory of mind," suggesting that retrieval of self-knowledge and the ability to be aware of other minds are mediated by the same structures (see Happe et al., 1996, and references therein). When activation was correlated with behavioral data, remember responses showed a positive relation with activation in the medial temporal lobes, retrosplenial cortex, and anterior cingulate cortex whereas know responses correlated positively with frontal activations. Together, these results suggest that concept of the self, and memory associated with it, is mediated, in part, by the same structures that mediate general semantic knowledge but also by some structures that are distinct. Moroz's finding that remembering preferentially activates a set of components centered on the medial temporal lobes, whereas knowing differentially activates the frontal lobes, was somewhat unexpected. A plausible interpretation is that remembered words are recovered and judged more easily than known words, which may require additional frontal monitoring, both for verification and for classification as known rather than remembered (see also Henson, Rugg, Shallice, Josephs, & Dolan, 1999).

The Frontal Lobes vs. Medial Temporal Lobes as Mediators of Explicit Memory

Except for some attribution models, all the models agree that the frontal and medial temporal lobes are needed for normal explicit memory. There is also growing consensus that the medial temporal lobes are primary in the sense that without them explicit memory, whether measured by recall or recognition, remembering or knowing, is impaired. There is a third proposition with which everyone agrees, though it is not stated explicitly except in Moscovitch's and some of the structural models—namely, that only information that is consciously apprehended can be processed by the medial temporal lobes. Recent studies on trace conditioning of the eyeblink in humans (Clark & Squire, 1998; McGlinchey-Berroth et al., 1998) underscores this point. Simple and delay classical conditioning of the eyeblink response, in which the conditioned stimulus (CS) and unconditioned stimulus (UCS) overlap, can be accomplished without the hippocampal formation (Gabrieli, McGlinchey-Berroth, Carrilo, Gluck, Cermak, & Disterhoft, 1995; Weiskrantz & Warrington, 1979; Woodruff-Pak, 1993) in both humans and animals. If there is a delay as short as 1 sec between the termination of the CS and the beginning of the UCS, conditioning does not occur in most amnesic humans and animals with hippocampal lesions, nor in some normal people. In normal humans, Clark and Squire (1998) showed that conditioning is dependent on the person having a conscious apprehension of the contingency between CS and UCS and presumably it is this information that is picked up by the medial temporal lobes.

Based on evidence that explicit memory is linked with conscious apprehension at encoding, Köhler and Moscovitch (1997) proposed that the medial temporal lobes can serve as a marker for identifying the neural substrates of consciousness: the substrates necessary for consciousness are those that project to the hippocampal formation and surrounding neocortex. At retrieval, these same substrates are reactivated via the medial temporal lobes, and support the conscious experience that is a hallmark of episodic memory. "This hypothesis does not posit that the hippocampal [complex] is the repository of consciousness or the gateway to it" (p. 363); rather, it simply is a structure that requires "conscious input" for its operation and may, therefore, serve as a guide or pointer to those regions that are involved in consciousness.

Does the pointer point to the prefrontal cortex in addition to regions in posterior neocortex? In their model of memory and consciousness, Wheeler et al. (1997) draw on a hierarchical model of frontal function developed by Stuss (1991; Stuss, Picton, & Alexander, in press) in which functions at each level, mediated by different regions of prefrontal cortex, serve a supervisory role over other functions and domains that are localized more posteriorly. Each level corresponds with the three different types of consciousness, the last being concerned with self-awareness, which is intimately related to autonoetic consciousness. It is the awareness of self, largely dependent on the frontal lobes, that serves as a foundation for this unique capacity of human consciousness. Conway's working self would correspond closely to this system.

Undoubtedly, insofar as self-awareness informs our conscious experience, it also has the potential for contributing to our explicit memory of that experience, and actually may do so on many occasions. The questions at issue is whether this (presumably) uniquely human quality that Wheeler et al. consider the essence of episodic memory is truly that or whether it is merely an aspect of it, but not a fundamental one (Moscovitch, 1996). Unfortunately, studying patients with frontal-lobe lesions does not solve this problem. On the one hand, many such patients do have a strong phenomenological awareness of recovered episodes, and distinguish clearly between semantic memory and autobiographical episodes, even when the latter are confabulated (Dalla Barba, 1995). On the other hand, remember responses are diminished in people with frontal deficits (Parkin & Walter, 1992) and in some rare cases (Levine et al., 1998), patients report that a sense of personal involvement is absent from the whatever memories can be recovered—the warmth of familiarity is lost, though the details remain. Perhaps at the moment the prudent course is not to resolve the issue but to agree with the interactionist theorists that remembering depends on the interaction of the frontal and medial temporal lobes without assigning pride of place to either (Warrington & Weiskrantz, 1982).

Conclusion

Making phenomenological awareness the object of scientific investigation is a daunting enterprise that already has achieved more success than sceptics had foreseen. We are far from understanding the relation between consciousness and memory, but investigations of the topic led to the discovery of new phenomena and to a paradigm shift in how memory is studied behaviorally and neurologically.

Acknowledgment   Preparation of this chapter was supported by Grant A8437 from the Natural Sciences and Engineering Research Council of Canada to M.M. I thank Stefan Köhler for his very helpful comments.

Note

1. It also invites speculation that explicit memory is not fundamentally different in humans than in other mammals, which in turn suggests that all species have the conscious awareness necessary for activating the medial temporal lobe system (Clark & Squire, 1997). The memory trace in humans differs from that of other species only in the nature of the experience that is represented (Moscovitch, 1996).

References

Aggleton, J. P., & Brown, M. W. (1999). Episodic memory, amnesia and the hippocampal-anterior thalamic axis. *Behavioral and Brain Sciences, 22,* 425–489.

Allan, K., Wilding, E. L., & Rugg, M. D. (1998). Electrophysiological evidence for dissociable processes contributing to recollection. *Acta Psychologica, 98,* 231–252.

Bentin, S., Moscovitch, M., & Nirhod, O. (1998). Levels of processing, selective attention, and memory encoding. *Acta Psychologica, 98,* 311–341.

Blaxton, T. A. (1989). Investigating dissociations among memory measures: Support for a transfer appropriate processing framework. *Journal of Experimental Psychology: Learning, Memory, and Cognition, 15,* 657–668.

Blaxton, T. A., & Theodore, W. H. (1997). The role of the temporal lobes in recognizing visuospatial materials: Remembering versus knowing. *Brain and Cognition, 35,* 5–25.

Buckner, R., Goodman, J., Burock, M., Rotte, M., Koutstaal, W., Schacter, D., Rosen, B., & Dale, A. (1998). Functional-anatomic correlates of object priming in humans revealed by rapid presentation event-related fMRI. *Neuron, 20,* 285–296.

Buckner, R. L., & Koutstaal, W. (1998). Functional neuroimaging studies of encoding, priming, and explicit memory retrieval. *Proceedings of the National Academy of Sciences USA, 95,* 891–898.

Cabeza, R., & Nyberg, L. (1997). Imaging cognition: An empirical review of PET studies with normal subjects. *Journal of Cognitive Neuroscience, 9,* 1–26.

Cohen, N. J., & Eichenbaum, H. (1993). *Memory, amnesia, and the hippocampal system.* Cambridge, MA: MIT Press.

Clark, E., & Squire, L. R. (1998). Classical conditioning and brain systems. The role of awareness. *Science, 280,* 77–81.

Conway, M. A. (in press). Phenomenological records and the self-memory system. In T. McCormack & C. Hoerl (Eds.), *Time and memory: Issues in philosophy and psychology.* Oxford: Oxford University Press.

Conway, M. A., & Dewhurst, S. A. (1995). The self and recollective experience. *Applied Cognitive Psychology, 9,* 1–19.

Cowey, A., & Stoerig, P. (1992). Reflections on blindsight. In A. D. Milner & M. D. Rugg (Eds.), *The neuropsychology of consciousness* (pp. 11–38). London: Academic Press.

Craik, F. I. M., Govoni, R., Naveh-Benjamin, M., & Anderson, N. D. (1996). The effects of divided attention on encoding and retrieval processes in human memory. *Journal of Experimental Psychology: General, 125,* 159–180.

Craik, F. I. M., Moroz, T. M., Moscovitch, M., Stuss, D. T., Winocur, G., Tulving, E., & Kapur, S. (1999). In search of the self: A positron emission tomography study. *Psychological Science, 10,* 27–35.

Dalla Barba, G. (1995). Consciousness and confabulation: remembering "another" past. In R. Campbell & M. A. Conway (Eds.), *Broken memories: Case studies in memory impairment* (pp. 101–114). London: Blackwell.

Damasio, A. R. (1989). Time-locked multiregional retroactivation: A system-level proposal for the neural substrates of recall and recognition. *Cognition, 33,* 25–62.

Farah, M. J., & Feinberg, T. E. (1997). Perception and awareness. In T. E. Feinberg & M. J. Farah (Eds.), *Behavioral neurology and neuropsychology* (pp. 357–368). New York: McGraw-Hill.

Farah, M. J., O'Reilly, R. C., & Vecera, S. P. (1993). Dissociated overt and covert recognition as an emergent property of a lesioned neural network. *Psychological Review, 100,* 571–588.

Fleischman, D. A., Gabrieli, J. D. E., Reminger, S., Rinaldi, J., Morrell, F., & Wilson, R. (1995). Conceptual priming in perceptual identification for patients with Alzheimer's disease and a patient with right occipital lobectomy. *Neuropsychology, 9,* 187–197.

Fernandes, M. A., & Moscovitch, M. (in press). Divided attention and memory: Evidence of substantial interference effects both at retrieval and encoding. *Journal of Experimental Psychology: General.*

Gabrieli, J. D. E. (1998). Cognitive neuroscience of human memory. *Annual Review of Psychology, 49,* 87–115.

Gabrieli, J. D. E., Brewer, J. B., Desmond, J. E., & Glover, G. H. (1997). Separate neural bases of two fundamental memory processes in the human medial temporal lobe. *Science, 276,* 264–266.

Gabrieli, J. D. E., Fleischman, D. A., Keane, M. M., Reminger, S. L., & Morrell, F. (1995). Double dissociation between memory systems underlying explicit and implicit memory in the human brain. *Psychological Science, 6,* 76–82.

Gabrieli, J. D. E., Keane, M. M., Zurella, M. M., & Poldrack, R. A. (1997). Preservation of implicit memory for new associations in global amnesia. *Psychological Science, 8,* 326–329.

Gabrieli, J. D. E., McGlinchey-Berroth, R., Carrillo, M. C., Gluck, M. A., Cermak, L. S., & Disterhoft, J. F. (1995). Intact delay-eyeblink classical conditioning in amnesia. *Behavioral Neuroscience, 109,* 819–827.

Goshen-Gottstein, Y., & Moscovitch, M. (1995a). Intact implicit memory for newly-formed verbal associations in amnesic patients. *Society for Neuroscience Meeting,* Abstract 566.15.

Goshen-Gottstein, Y., & Moscovitch, M. (1995b). Repetition priming for newly-formed associations is perceptually based: Shallow processing and format specificity. *Journal of Experimental Psychology: Learning, Memory and Cognition, 21,* 1249–1262.

Grady, C. L. (1998). Neuroimaging and activation of the frontal lobes. In B. L. Miller & J. L. Cummings (Eds.), *The human frontal lobes* (pp. 196–230). New York: Guilford Press.

Graf, P. (1994). Explicit and implicit memory: A decade of research. In C. Umiltà & M. Moscovitch (Eds.), *Attention and performance XV: Conscious and non-conscious information processing* (pp. 681–696). Cambridge, MA: MIT Press.

Graf, P., & Schacter, D. L. (1985). Implicit and explicit memory for new associations in normal subjects and amnesic patients. *Journal of Experimental Psychology: Learning, Memory, and Cognition, 11,* 501–518.

Hamann, S. B., & Squire, L. R. (1997). Intact priming for novel perceptual representations in amnesia. *Journal of Cognitive Neuroscience, 9,* 699–713.

Happ, F., Ehlers, S., Fletcher, P., Frith, U., Johnson, M., Gillberg, C., Dolan, R., Frackowiak, R., & Frith, C. (1996). "Theory of mind" in the brain: Evidence from a PET study of Asperger's syndrome. *NeuroReport, 8,* 197–201.

Henson, R. N. A., Rugg, M. D., Shallice, T., Josephs, O., & Dolan, R. J. (1999). Recollection and familiarity in recognition memory: An event-related functional magnetic resonance imaging study. *Journal of Neuroscience, 19,* 3962–3972.

Jacoby, L. L. (1991). A process dissociation framework: Separating automatic from intentional uses of memory. *Journal of Memory and Language, 30,* 513–541.

Jernigan, T. L., & Ostergaard, A. L. (1993). Word priming and recognition memory both affected by mesial temporal lobe damage. *Neuropsychology, 7,* 14–26.

Johnson, M. K. (1992). MEM: Mechanisms of recollection. *Journal of Cognitive Neuroscience, 4,* 268–280.

Johnson, M. K., & Raye, C. L. (1998). False memories and confabulation. *Trends in Cognitive Science, 2,* 137–145.

Keane, M. M., Gabrieli, J. D. E., Fennema, A. C., Growdon, J. H., & Corkin, S. (1991). Evidence for a dissociation between perceptual and conceptual priming in Alzheimer's disease. *Behavioral Neuroscience, 105,* 326–342.

Keane, M. M., Gabrieli, J. D. E., Mapstone, H. C., Johnson, K. A., & Corkin, S. (1995). Double dissociation of memory capacities after bilateral occipital-lobe or medial temporal-lobe lesions. *Brain, 118,* 1129–1148.

Kelley, C. M., & Jacoby, L. L. Subjective reports and process dissociation: Fluency, knowing, and feeling. *Acta Psychologica, 98,* 127–140.

Kinoshita, S. (in press). Context-dependent priming for new associations: Evidence for an attentional component. *Memory.*

Kinsbourne, M. (1988). Integrated field theory of consciousness. In A. J. Marcel & E. Bisiach (Eds.), *Consciousness in contemporary science* (pp. 239–256). Oxford: Oxford University Press.

Kinsbourne, M., & Wood, F. (1975). Short-term memory processes and the amnesic syndrome. In D. Deutsch & J. A. Deutsch (Eds.), *Short-term memory* (pp. 258–291). New York: Academic Press.

Knowlton, B. J. (1998). The relationship between remembering and knowing: A cognitive neuroscience perspective. *Acta Psychologica, 98,* 253–266.

Köhler, S., & Moscovitch, M. (1997). Unconscious visual processing in neuropsychological syndromes: A survey of the literature and evaluation of models of consciousness. In M. D. Rugg (Ed.), *Cognitive neuroscience* (pp. 305–373). London: UCL Press.

Kopelman, M. D., Ng, N., & Van Den Brouke, O. (1997). Confabulation extending across episodic, personal, and general semantic memory. *Cognitive Neuropsychology, 14,* 683–712.

Landauer, T. K. (1975). Memory without organization: Properties of a model with random storage and undirected retrieval. *Cognitive Psychology, 7,* 495–531.

Lepage, M., Habib, R., & Tulving, E. (1998). Hippocampal PET activations of memory encoding and retrieval: The HIPER model. *Hippocampus, 8,* 313–322.

Levine, B., Black, S. E., Cabeza, R., Sinden, M., McIntosh, A. R., Toth, J. P., Tulving, E., & Stuss, D. T. (1998). Episodic memory and the self in a case of isolated retrograde amnesia. *Brain, 121,* 1951–1973.

MacDonald, P., & MacLeod, C. M. (1998). The influence of attention at encoding on direct and indirect remembering. *Acta Psychologica, 98,* 291–310.

Mandler, G. (1980). Recognizing: The judgment of previous occurrence. *Psychological Review, 87,* 252–271.

Mayes, A. R., Gooding, P. A., & Van Eijk, R. (1997). A new theoretical framework for explicit and implicit memory. *Psyche: An Interdisciplinary Journal of Researcher Consciousness, 3.*

McGlinchey-Berroth, R., Carillo, M. C., Gabrieli, J. D. E., Brown, C. M., & Disterhoft, J. F. (1997). Impaired trace eyeblink conditioning in bilateral, medial-temporal lobe amnesia. *Behavioral Neuroscience, 111,* 873–882.

Miller, E., & Desimone, R. (1994). Parallel neuronal mechanisms for short-term memory. *Science, 263,* 520–522.

Milner, P. (1989). A cell assembly theory of hippocampal amnesia. *Neuropsychologia, 27*(1), 23–30.

Moroz, T. M. (1998). *Episodic memory for personally-relevant information: Evidence from aging, divided attention at retrieval, and positron emission tomography.* Doctoral thesis, University of Toronto, Toronto, Ontario, Canada.

Moscovitch, M. (1989). Confabulation and the frontal system: Strategic vs associative retrieval in neuropsychological theories of memory. In H. L. Roediger III & F. I. M.

Craik (Eds.), *Varieties of memory and consciousness: Essays in honour of Endel Tulving* (pp. 133–160). Hillsdale, NJ: Erlbaum.

Moscovitch, M. (1992). Memory and working with memory: A component process model based on modules and central systems. *Journal of Cognitive Neuroscience, 4,* 257–267.

Moscovitch, M. (1994a). Interference at retrieval from long-term memory: The influence of frontal and temporal lobes. *Neuropsychology, 4,* 525–534.

Moscovitch, M. (1994b). Memory and working-with-memory: Evaluation of a component process model and comparison with other models. In D. L. Schacter & E. Tulving (Eds.), *Memory systems* (pp. 269–310). Cambridge: MIT Press.

Moscovitch, M. (1995a). Models of consciousness and memory. In M. S. Gazzaniga (Ed.), *The cognitive neurosciences* (pp. 1341–1356). Cambridge, Mass.: MIT Press.

Moscovitch, M. (1995b). Recovered consciousness: A hypothesis concerning modularity and episodic memory. *Journal of Clinical and Experimental Neuropsychology, 17,* 276–291.

Moscovitch, M. (1996). Recovered consciousness: A proposal for making consciousness integral to neuropsychological theories of memory in humans and non-humans. *Brain and Behavioral Sciences, 19,* 768–770.

Moscovitch, M., & Bentin, S. (1993). The fate of repetition effects when recognition is near chance. *Journal of Experimental Psychology: Learning, Memory, and Cognition, 19,* 148–155.

Moscovitch, M., & Melo, B. (1997). Strategic retrieval and the frontal lobes: Evidence from confabulation and amnesia. *Neuropsychologia, 35,* 1017–1035.

Moscovitch, M., & Umiltà, C. (1990). Modularity and neuropsychology. In M. F. Schwartz (Ed.), *Modular deficits in Alzheimer's disease.* Cambridge, MA: MIT Press.

Moscovitch, M., Vriezen, E., & Goshen-Gottstein, Y. (1993). Implicit tests of memory in patients with focal lesions or degenerative brain disorders. In F. Boller & J. Grafman (Eds.), *Handbook of neuropsychology* (pp. 133–173). Amsterdam: Elsevier.

Moscovitch, M., & Winocur, G. (1992). The neuropsychology of memory and aging. In F. I. M. Craik & T. A. Salthouse (Eds.), *The handbook of aging and cognition* (pp. 315–372). Hillsdale, NJ: Erlbaum.

Moscovitch, M., Winocur, G., & McLachlan, D. (1986). Memory as assessed by recognition and by reading time of normal and transformed script: Evidence from normal young and old people, and patients with severe memory impairment due to Alzheimer's disease and other neurological disorders. *Journal of Experimental Psychology: General, 115,* 331–347.

Musen, G., & Squire, L. R. (1993). On the implicit learning of new associations by amnesic patients and normal subjects. *Neuropsychology, 7,* 119–135.

Nadel, L., & Moscovitch, M. (1997). Memory consolidation, retrograde amnesia and the hippocampal complex. *Current Opinion in Neurobiology, 7,* 217–227.

Ostergaard, A. L. (1994). Dissociations between word priming effects in normal subjects and patients with memory disorders: Multiple memory systems or retrieval? *Quarterly Journal of Experimental Psychology, 47A,* 331–364.

Ostergaard, A. L., & Jernigan, T. L. (1996). Priming and baseline perceptual identification performance in amnesia: A comment on Hamann, Squire, and Schacter. *Neuropsychology, 10,* 125–130.

Paller, K. A., & Mayes, A. R. (1994). New association priming of word identification in normal and amnesic subjects. *Cortex, 30,* 53–73.

Parkin, A. J., & Walter, B. (1992). Recollective experience, normal aging, and frontal dysfunction. *Psychology and Aging, 7,* 290–298.

Rajaram, S., & Roediger, H. L. III (1997). Remembering and knowing as states of consciousness during recollection. In J. D. Cohen & J. W. Schooler (Eds.), *Scientific approaches to the question of consciousness* (pp. 213–240). Hillsdale: Erlbaum.

Reingold, E. M., & Goshen-Gottstein, Y. (1996). Separating consciously controlled and automatic influences in memory for new associations. *Journal of Experimental Psychology: Learning, Memory, and Cognition, 22,* 397–406.

Richardson-Klavehn, A., Gardiner, J. M., & Java, R. I. (1996). Memory: Task dissociations, process dissociations, and dissociations of consciousness. In G. Underwood (Ed.), *Implicit cognition* (pp. 85–158). Oxford: Oxford University Press.

Roediger, H. L., III, & McDermott, K. B. (1993). Implicit memory in normal subjects. In H. Spinnler & F. Boller (Eds.), J. Grafman & F. Boller (Section Eds.), *Handbook of neuropsychology* (Vol. 8; pp. 63–131). Amsterdam: Elsevier.

Schacter, D. L. (1989). On the relation between memory and consciousness: Dissociable interactions and conscious experience. In H. L. Roediger, III & F. I. M. Craik (Eds.), *Varieties of memory and consciousness: Essays in honour of Endel Tulving* (pp. 355–389). Hillsdale, NJ: Erlbaum.

Schacter, D. L. (1994). Priming and multiple memory systems: Perceptual mechanisms of implicit memory. In D. L. Schacter & E. Tulving (Eds.), *Memory systems* (pp. 244–256). Cambridge, MA: MIT Press.

Schacter, D. L., & Buckner, R. L. (1998). Priming and the brain. *Neuron, 20,* 185–195.

Schacter, D. L., & Wagner, A. D. (1999). Medial temporal lobe activations in fMRI and PET studies of episodic encoding and retrieval. *Hippocampus, 9,* 7–24.

Singer, W. (1993). Synchronization of cortical activity and its putative role in information processing and learning. *Annual Review of Physiology, 55,* 349–374.

Snowden, J. S., Griffiths, H. L., & Neary, D. (1996). Semantic-episodic memory interactions in semantic dementia: Implications for retrograde memory function. *Cognitive Neuropsychology, 13,* 1101–1137.

Snowden, J. S., Neary, D., & Mann, D. M. A. (1996). *Fronto-temporal lobar degeneration: Fronto-temporal dementia, progressive aphasia, semantic dementia.* London: Churchill Livingstone.

Squire, L. R. (1992). Memory and the hippocampus: A synthesis from findings with rats, monkeys, and humans. *Psychological Review, 99,* 195–231.

Squire, L. R., Hamann, S. B., & Schacter, D. L. (1996). Intact baseline performance and priming in amnesia: Reply to Ostergaard and Jernigan. *Neuropsychology, 10,* 131–135.

Srinivas, K., Breedin, S. D., Coslett, H. B., & Saffran, E. M. (1997). Intact perceptual priming in a patient with damage to the anterior inferior temporal lobes. *Journal of Cognitive Neuroscience, 9,* 490–511.

Stone, M., Ladd, L. S., Vaidya, C. J., & Gabrieli, J. D. E. (1998). *Consciousness and Cognition, 7*(2), 238–258.

Stoerig, P. (1996). Varieties of vision: from blind responses to conscious recognition. *Trends in Neuroscience, 19,* 401–406.

Stuss, D. T. (1991). Self, awareness, and the frontal lobes: A neuropsychological perspective. In J. Strauss & G. R. Goethals (Eds.), *The self: Interdisciplinary approaches* (pp. 255–278). New York: Springer-Verlag.

Stuss, D. T., Picton, T. W., & Alexander, M. P. (in press). Consciousness, self-awareness and the frontal lobes. In S. Salloway, P. Malloy, & J. Duffy (Eds.), *The frontal lobes and neuropsychiatric illness.* Washington: American Psychiatric Press.

Symons, C. S., & Johnson, B. T. (1997). The self-reference effect in memory: A meta-analysis. *Psychological Bulletin, 121,* 371–394.

Tulving, E. (1983). *Elements of episodic memory.* Oxford: Clarendon Press.

Tulving, E. (1985). Memory and consciousness. *Canadian Psychology, 26,* 1–12.

Tulving, E., & Schacter, D. L. (1990). Priming and human memory systems. *Science, 247,* 301–306.

Tulving, E., Kapur, S., Craik, F. I. M., Moscovitch, M., & Houle, S. (1994). Hemispheric encoding/retrieval asymmetry in episodic memory: Positron emission tomography findings. *Proceedings of the National Academy of Sciences USA, 91,* 2016–2020.

Vargha-Khadem, F., Gadian, D. G., Watkins, K. E., Connelly, A., Van Paesschen, W., & Mishkin, M. (1997). Differential effects of early hippocampal pathology on episodic and semantic memory. *Science, 277,* 376–380.

Vriezen, E., Moscovitch, M., & Bellos, S. A. (1995). Priming effects in semantic classification tasks. *Journal of Experimental Psychology: Learning, Memory and Cognition, 21,* 933–946.

Wagner, A. D., Desmond, J. E., Demb, J. B., Glover, G. H., & Gabrieli, J. D. E. (1997). Semantic repetition priming for verbal and pictorial knowledge: A functional MRI study of left inferior prefrontal cortex. *Journal of Cognitive Neuroscience, 9,* 714–726.

Wagner, A. D., & Gabrieli, J. D. E. (1998). On the relationship between recognition familiarity and perceptual fluency: Evidence for distinct mnemonic processes. *Acta Psychologica, 98,* 211–230.

Warrington, E. K., & Weiskrantz, L. (1982). Amnesia: A disconnection syndrome. *Neuropsychologia, 20,* 233–249.

Watkins, M. J., & Gibson, J. M. (1988). On the relation between perceptual priming and recognition memory. *Journal of Experimental Psychology: Learning, Memory and Cognition, 14,* 477–483.

Weiskrantz, L., & Warrington, E. (1979). Conditioning in amnesic patients. *Neuropsychologia, 17,* 187–194.

Wheeler, M. A., Stuss, D. T., & Tulving, E. (1997). Towards a theory of episodic memory: The frontal lobes and autonoetic consciousness. *Psychological Bulletin, 121,* 331–354.

Whittlesea, B. W. A., & Williams, L. D. (1998). Why do strangers feel familiar, but friends don't? A discrepancy-attribution account of feelings of familiarity. *Acta Psychologica, 98,* 127–140.

Wiggs, C., & Martin, A. (1998). Properties and mechanisms of perceptual priming. *Current Opinion in Neurobiology, 8,* 227–233.

Winocur, G., & Kinsbourne, M. (1978). Contextual cuing as an aid to Korsakoff amnesics. *Neuropsychologia, 16,* 671–682.

Winocur, G., Moscovitch, M., & Stuss, D. T. (1996). A neuropsychological investigation of explicit and implicit memory in institutionalized and community-dwelling old people. *Neuropsychology, 10,* 57–65.

Woodruff-Pak, D. S. (1993). Eyeblink classical conditioning in H. M.: Delay and trace paradigms. *Behavioral Neuroscience, 107,* 911–925.

Yonelinas, A. P., Kroll, N. E. A., Dobbins, I., Lazzara, M., & Knight, T. (1998). Recollection and familiarity deficits in amnesia: Convergence of remember-know, process dissociation, and receiver operating characteristic data. *Neuropsychology, 12,* 323–339.

39

Memory Systems of 1999

DANIEL L. SCHACTER, ANTHONY D. WAGNER, & RANDY L. BUCKNER

In 1804, the French philosopher Maine de Biran published a monograph that contained a novel and perhaps even radical thesis. He contended that memory is not a single function or entity, instead distinguishing among three separate types or forms that can operate independently of one another: representative memory (conscious recall of facts and events), mechanical memory (learning of habits and skills), and sensitive memory (affective modifications). Maine de Biran devoted a great deal of attention to explaining, elaborating, and illustrating his key thesis (Maine de Biran, 1929; see Schacter & Tulving, 1994, for further discussion).

Although his ideas remain largely unknown today, the central message of Maine de Biran's monograph—that memory is a nonunitary entity—has assumed center stage in recent theoretical discussions regarding the nature and basis of mnemonic functions. Stimulated by neuropsychological studies showing that brain-damaged patients sometimes display normal performance on certain types of memory tasks despite exhibiting severe impairments on others, and by experimental demonstrations in healthy populations that performance on different types of memory tasks can be dissociated from one another, contemporary researchers have postulated distinctions among numerous forms of memory or memory systems. These distinctions include, but are not limited to, episodic and semantic memory (Tulving, 1972, 1983); taxon and locale memory (O'Keefe & Nadel, 1978); habit memory and cognitive memory (Mishkin & Petri, 1984); working memory and long-term memory (Baddeley, 1986); implicit and explicit memory (Graf & Schacter, 1985; Schacter, 1987); declarative and nondeclarative (Squire, 1992) or procedural memory (Cohen & Eichenbaum, 1993); and fast and slow memory systems (McClelland, McNaughton, & O'Reilley, 1995; Sherry & Schacter, 1987).

Claims concerning multiple forms of memory or multiple memory systems are associated with a variety of challenging definitional and conceptual issues: exactly what do we mean when we refer to a "form of memory" or "memory system"? What are the criteria for postulating the existence of a new memory system? And what kind of evidence is required to decide between unitary memory system theories and multiple memory system theories? Based on a consideration of these definitional and conceptual issues, and a review of evidence from cognitive and neuropsychological studies, Schacter and Tulving (1994) argued for distinctions among five major memory systems: working memory, semantic memory, episodic memory, the perceptual representation system (PRS), and procedural memory.

When Schacter and Tulving (1994) wrote their essay on memory systems, they relied mainly on cognitive studies of healthy volunteers and neuropsychological investigations of patients with focal brain injuries (as well as lesion studies of experimental animals). Since that time, however, there has been a proliferation of studies using recently developed neuroimaging techniques—positron emission tomography (PET) and functional magnetic resonance imaging (fMRI)—that are beginning to provide a host of new insights into the nature of memory and other cognitive capacities. PET and fMRI measure local changes in hemodynamic responses that are correlated with changes in neuronal activity: PET is sensitive to changes in blood flow, whereas fMRI is sensitive to oxygenation-level-dependent changes in the magnetic properties of blood (often referred to as BOLD contrast). Because both techniques allow relatively precise localization of the observed changes in hemodynamic response, it is possible to make inferences about the relative activation of particular brain regions during performance of behavioral tasks by measuring changes in blood flow or blood oxygenation level across experimental conditions (for general reviews of neuroimaging approaches, see Buckner & Koutstaal, 1998; Cabeza & Nyberg, 1997; Ungerleider, 1995).

This chapter considers whether and in what way recent neuroimaging research has enhanced or changed the understanding of each of the five major systems that had been identified on cognitive and neuropsychological grounds by Schacter and Tulving (1994). The logic and criteria introduced by Schacter and Tulving (1994) for identifying memory systems are first reviewed briefly. The neuroimaging evidence that bears on an understanding of working memory, semantic memory, episodic memory, PRS, and procedural memory is then considered and commented on.

Logic and Criteria for Memory Systems: A Brief Overview

Postulating and identifying memory systems involves a host of frequently thorny terminological and conceptual issues. Foremost among these is settling on an adequate definition of a memory system. Tulving (1985, p. 386) defined a memory system in general

terms as "a set of correlated processes." Tulving (1984) contended that memory systems could be distinguished from one another in terms of different kinds of information that they process and represent, different laws or principles that characterize their modes of operation, differences in underlying neural substrate, and differences in ontogenetic and phylogenetic development. Similarly, Sherry and Schacter (1987, p. 440) adopted a broad definition of a memory system as "an interaction among acquisition, retention, and retrieval mechanisms that is characterized by certain rules of operation." They contended that multiple memory systems could be distinguished when "two or more systems are characterized by fundamentally different rules of operation." Adopting an evolutionary orientation, they suggested that multiple systems evolved when problems of information storage and retrieval required systems with functionally incompatible properties (for a similar notion, see McClelland et al., 1995).

Drawing on these and related ideas of what constitutes a memory system, and considering possible grounds for distinguishing among systems, Schacter and Tulving (1994) proposed three main criteria for identifying memory systems: class inclusion operations, properties and relations, and convergent dissociations.

Class Inclusion Operations

A memory system allows one to perform a variety of tasks or functions within a particular class or domain, handling different kinds of information within the domain. Consider two examples. Episodic memory operates in the domain of specific personal experiences, allowing one to recollect past events that can involve many different kinds of information—objects, words, faces, places, and so forth. Semantic memory underlies the acquisition of general knowledge that is not tied to any specific personal experience and that can take a variety of forms, including words, facts, numbers, and rules. One corollary of the class inclusion criterion is that when changes in brain state (produced by neurological damage, drugs, aging, or related factors) impair performance broadly within the domain of a particular system, but have little or no effect on performance outside the domain, we have evidence for the selective operation of a specific memory system.

Properties and Relations

According to this criterion, a memory system must be described with reference to a list of properties that delineate critical features of the system and allow consideration of how these properties are related to the properties of other systems. Relevant properties of a memory system would include types of information that fall within its domain, rules by which the system operates, neural substrates, and functions of the system (what the system is "for"; cf., Glenberg, 1997; Sherry & Schacter, 1987). As Schacter and Tulving (1994) emphasized, given our presently modest understanding of memory systems, it is difficult at present to specify such critical properties as a system's rules of operations and its functions. Nonetheless, some progress has been made on these difficult but important matters. For instance, in an analysis based on evolutionary considerations, Sherry and Schacter (1987) suggested that different memory systems arise because a system that performs one class of processes sometimes proves unworkable as a solution to other problems that require incompatible processes—a condition that Sherry and Schacter (1987) referred to a "functional incompatibility." McClelland et al. (1995) took a similar approach, but grounded their analysis of functional incompatibilities in a computational model that allows a more precise formulation of the properties and relations of the two memory systems they considered. Further development of such formal models will no doubt advance the general enterprise of specifying system properties and relations.

Convergent Dissociations

Experimental demonstrations of dissociations between tasks, or classes of tasks, constitute a necessary condition for postulating memory systems. However, because it is relatively easy to produce dissociations between any two tasks, systems must not be proposed based solely on observations of a dissociation between two particular tasks (e.g., Roediger, Rajaram, & Srinivas, 1990). Rather, convergent dissociations from multiple tasks and sources of evidence are required. Such evidence may take the form of functional dissociations produced by manipulations of cognitive/behavioral task features, neuropsychological dissociations from brain-injured patients, or observations of differing physiological charac-

teristics of proposed systems. In all cases, the strongest evidence for multiple systems is provided when multiple tasks are used to tap hypothesized systems (Roediger et al., 1990), and when converging evidence from different types of measures (e.g., behavioral and physiological) is obtained (Schacter, 1992).

Systems, Processes, and Forms of Memory

The notion of multiple memory systems considered here has often been contrasted with a "processing approach" that focuses on specific operations or component processes demanded by specific tasks, rather than on the larger scale systems that have been considered (e.g., Roediger et al., 1990). However, it is now clear that the systems and processing approaches are complementary rather than incompatible (Roediger, Buckner, & McDermott, 1999; Schacter, 1990, 1992). Systems approaches focus on large-scale networks of structures and processes that operate across relatively broad domains; processing approaches focus on specific component operations that may function in one or more systems. The possibility that systems share one or more processes is consistent with the aforementioned criteria for memory systems, and can be usefully explored with functional neuroimaging techniques.

By relying on the three aforementioned criteria, it is possible to distinguish the notion of a "memory system" from the weaker notion of a "form of memory." Many different "forms of memory" have been proposed on descriptive or heuristic grounds, including such notions as recognition memory, recall memory, implicit memory, explicit memory, spatial memory, and many others. Although some forms of memory may satisfy one of the three criteria of class inclusion operations, properties and relations, and convergent dissociations, they need not and typically do not satisfy them all. Thus, the notion of "memory systems" is more restrictive than the idea of a "form of memory." The interested reader is referred to the chapter by Schacter and Tulving (1994) for consideration of these and related matters. Attention now turns to recent neuroimaging studies that have begun to explore the five major systems that Schacter and Tulving (1994) had already identified based on the criteria of class inclusion operations, properties and relations, and convergent dissociations.

Five Major Memory Systems: Evidence from Functional Neuroimaging

Working Memory

Working memory supports the temporary storage and maintenance of internal representations such that these representations can be used to guide future behavior (Baddeley, 1986; Goldman-Rakic, 1987), and mediates the controlled manipulation of these representations, often in the service of higher level cognition (Baddeley, 1986, 1994; Just & Carpenter, 1992). Although early models conceptualized working memory as a unitary faculty (Atkinson & Shiffrin, 1968), more recent models posit multiple working memory subsystems (Baddeley, 1986, 1994). According to the tripartite model, working memory consists of a central executive and two slave subsystems—the phonological loop and the visuo-spatial sketchpad (Baddeley & Hitch, 1974; Baddeley, 1986). The phonological loop supports the retrieval, temporary storage, and rehearsal of phonological representations, whereas the visuo-spatial sketchpad performs analogous functions for visual representations of stimuli and of the position of stimuli in visual space. The central executive is a limited capacity supervisory attentional system (Shallice, 1982) that coordinates the operation of the slave systems and mediates manipulation of their contents.

Considerable behavioral and neuropsychological evidence has been marshaled in support of the tripartite model (for recent reviews, see Baddeley, 1994, 1998). Nevertheless, there remain numerous functional and neuroanatomic questions about working memory. First, what are the biological underpinnings of the various subsystems and components of working memory? Second, are there separable working memory subsystems for visual and spatial information? Finally, is there a content-independent central executive that mediates the manipulation of representations in the various content-specific slave systems, or are there separate executives operating in conjunction with each slave system? PET and fMRI studies have begun to explore these issues.

Functional Neuroanatomy of Working Memory

The phonological loop is the best characterized subsystem of working memory. It consists of two components: a phonological store, and a rehearsal mechanism that maintains the contents of this store. Neuropsychological studies suggest that these components have separable neural substrates, because storage and rehearsal processes can be independently impaired (e.g., Belleville, Peretz, & Arguin, 1992; Vallar & Baddeley, 1984). Neuroimaging studies have yielded convergent evidence for this storage-rehearsal distinction.

PET and fMRI studies comparing verbal working memory to control conditions have consistently revealed activation in left inferior prefrontal (BA 44; Broca's area), dorsolateral prefrontal (BAs 46/9), supplementary motor, premotor, posterior parietal, and cerebellar cortices (e.g., Cohen et al., 1994; Fiez et al., 1996; Jonides et al., 1998). The level of activity in these regions increases with phonological memory load (Braver et al., 1997; Desmond, Gabrieli, Wagner, Ginier, & Glover, 1997; for related results see Cohen et al., 1997). Paulesu, Frith, and Frackowiak (1993) observed that performance of a task requiring both phonological storage and maintenance yielded activation in Broca's area and the supramarginal gyrus, whereas performance of a task requiring phonological coding but not storage resulted in selective activation of Broca's area. Awh et al. (1996) extended these results by demonstrating (1) activation in Broca's area and left parietal cortices when comparing a phonological storage and rehearsal task to a control task that did not require storage or rehearsal, but (2) activation only in left parietal cortices when the working memory condition was compared to a control task that did require rehearsal. Based on these dissociations, it has been proposed that Broca's area, in conjunction with supplementary motor, premotor, and cerebellar cortices, subserves phonological rehearsal mechanisms (Awh et al., 1996; Desmond et al., 1997; Paulesu et al., 1993). In contrast, posterior parietal regions, perhaps left lateralized, are thought to mediate phonological storage (Awh et al., 1996; Jonides et al., 1998; Paulesu et al., 1993; cf., Fiez et al., 1996).

Posterior parietal, inferior prefrontal (BA 47), premotor, and dorsolateral prefrontal regions also have been observed in neuroimaging studies of spatial working memory (for reviews see, Awh & Jonides, 1998; D'Esposito et al., 1998). However, whereas verbal working memory has elicited left lateralized or bilateral frontal and parietal activation, spatial working memory has yielded right lateralized or bilateral activation (Courtney, Ungerleider, Keil, & Haxby, 1996; Jonides et al., 1993; McCarthy et al., 1994; Owen, Evans, & Petrides, 1996; Smith, Jonides, & Koeppe, 1996). Extrastriate (BA 19) cortical activation also has been consistently observed during spatial working memory tasks. Although no studies have attempted to distinguish between spatial storage and rehearsal mechanisms, distinct spatial working memory components have been proposed (Awh & Jonides, 1998; Smith et al., 1996; Wilson, O'Scalaidhe, & Goldman-Rakic, 1993). Specifically, it has been suggested that extrastriate regions encode spatial information that is stored in right posterior parietal regions, whereas right inferior frontal and premotor cortices maintain these representations through tonic activation (Wilson et al., 1993; cf. Courtney et al., 1996, 1998). Such maintenance may be equivalent to spatial selective attention, where attention is allocated to the internal representations of specific locations (Awh & Jonides, 1998).

Spatial and Object Working Memory

The tripartite model of working memory (Baddeley, 1986) includes a visuo-spatial sketchpad that mediates the maintenance of visual representations and of spatial representations. However, as noted by Baddeley (1994), there is evidence indicating that spatial and object working memory may be separable. Perhaps most compellingly, single-cell recording studies in nonhuman primates have revealed a ventral-dorsal segregation in prefrontal cortex, with ventral neurons demonstrating sustained activity during object working memory delays and dorsal neurons demonstrating sustained activity during spatial working memory delays (Wilson et al., 1993).

Neuroimaging studies of object working memory have demonstrated activation in inferior prefrontal (BA 44, 45, 47), dorsolateral prefrontal, and posterior parietal cortices. Some studies have demonstrated primarily left lateralized activation (Smith et al., 1995), whereas others have demonstrated bilateral or right lateralized activation (Courtney et al., 1996; Haxby, Ungerleider, Horwitz, Rappaport, & Grady, 1995; McCarthy et al., 1996). In contrast to spatial working memory, object working memory also elicits activation in inferotemporal cortices thought to be important for object recognition processes (Ungerleider & Mishkin, 1982). Inferotemporal activation may

reflect the maintenance of object representations across working memory delays (Miller & Desimone, 1994; Wilson et al., 1993).

Within prefrontal cortex, object working memory appears to recruit bilateral inferior frontal regions. The time courses of left and right inferior frontal activation during object working memory appear to differ, with right frontal regions engaged early and left frontal regions engaged moments later (Haxby et al., 1995). One interpretation of this shift is that object representations are initially maintained in a visual code (Haxby et al., 1995; Kelley et al., 1998), perhaps by the same rehearsal mechanism subserving spatial maintenance. However, with additional time, subjects may shift strategies, translating visual codes into verbal codes that are maintained by the phonological loop. Thus, neuroimaging studies have not revealed a ventral-dorsal/object-spatial distinction within human prefrontal cortex (D'Esposito et al., 1998). Rather, it appears that similar right inferior prefrontal regions are recruited during both spatial and object delay conditions, with strategic shifts to phonological coding also supporting maintenance of object information.

Evidence for a Common Central Executive

One of the most significant questions regarding working memory concerns whether there is a single, content-independent central executive that subserves the coordination, manipulation, and updating of the contents of the slave subsystems (Baddeley, 1998). Petrides and colleagues (Owen et al., 1996) have argued for a two-stage model of working memory, with ventrolateral and dorsolateral prefrontal regions mediating distinct functions. Ventrolateral regions subserve the maintenance and evaluation of representations held in working memory, whereas dorsolateral regions subserve the monitoring and manipulation of these representations. Although these cognitive constructs are not fully characterized, this distinction between maintenance and manipulation may be related to that of working memory slave systems and the central executive.

Two recent reviews of the neuroimaging literature provide support for this ventral-dorsal distinction (Awh & Jonides, 1998; D'Esposito et al., 1998). In these reviews, working memory tasks were classified into two types: tasks that required storage, maintenance, and evaluation of representations ("maintenance" tasks), and tasks that additionally required manipulation and updating of the contents of working memory ("maintenance+" tasks). Inferior prefrontal regions were recruited during the performance of both types of tasks, with the laterality of activation depending on the nature of the representations being maintained (D'Esposito et al., 1998). In contrast, dorsolateral prefrontal cortices were less frequently engaged during maintenance tasks, but were consistently engaged during maintenance+ tasks. Engagement or laterality of dorsolateral activation did not vary across verbal, object, and spatial working memory studies (D'Esposito et al., 1998). Although not conclusive, these results are consistent with suggestions that dorsolateral prefrontal cortex performs functions that resemble the putative operations of a shared central executive (D'Esposito et al., 1995; cf., Cohen et al., 1997).

Semantic Memory

Semantic memory refers to a person's general knowledge about the world (Tulving, 1972, 1983). It encompasses a wide range of organized information, including facts, concepts, and vocabulary. Semantic memory can be distinguished from episodic memory by virtue of its lack of association with a specific learning context. A number of PET and fMRI studies have been concerned with the neuroanatomic regions associated with representations of different types of semantic knowledge, whereas others have focused on the neural mediators of semantic retrieval.

Types of Semantic Knowledge

A fascinating observation about semantic memory is that brain lesions can selectively impair knowledge about some categories while sparing knowledge about other categories (e.g., Warrington & Shallice, 1984). A recent PET study of category-specific knowledge revealed neuroanatomic dissociations that may illuminate these deficits (Martin, Wiggs, Ungerleider, & Haxby, 1996). In that study, greater activation was observed in left medial occipital cortex during naming of pictures of animals compared to naming of pictures of tools. In contrast, tool naming resulted in greater activation in left premotor and left middle temporal cortices. Discrimination among animals may require identification of

relatively subtle differences in physical features (Farah & McClelland, 1991; cf., Caramazza & Shelton, 1998). The occipital activation observed during animal naming may reflect top-down reactivation of visual processing regions necessary to make these distinctions (Martin et al., 1996). In contrast, semantic knowledge about tools is thought to include information about their function or use (Farah & McClelland, 1991). The middle temporal region observed during tool naming falls just anterior to an area active during motion perception (Tootell et al., 1995) and during action-word generation (Raichle et al., 1994). This region may store knowledge about patterns of visual motion associated with using objects (Martin et al., 1996; cf., Wagner, Gabrieli, Desmond, & Glover, 1998). The premotor region may be a site of stored knowledge about how objects are used or for the codes necessary for instantiating that movement.

Further evidence for neuroanatomic segregation of semantic domains comes from observations that retrieval of color knowledge and motion knowledge elicits distinct left temporal activations (Martin, Haxby, La Londe, Wiggs, & Ungerleider, 1995). Generation of knowledge about stimulus color results in differential activation in ventral temporal regions just anterior to an area involved in color perception (see also Chao & Martin, in press). In contrast, generation of an action word associated with a stimulus results in middle temporal activation similar to that observed during tool naming (Martin et al., 1996). Collectively, these studies suggest that semantic knowledge may be organized such that stimulus attributes are stored close to the cortical regions mediating perception of those attributes (Martin et al., 1995).

In a related PET study by Damasio, Grabowski, Tranel, Hichwa, and Damasio (1996), domain-specific activation was observed in the temporal pole during face naming, in posterior middle and inferior temporal gyri during tool naming, and in a more lateral and posterior inferotemporal region during animal naming. These findings provide further evidence for functional segregation in left temporal regions. However, there are two important differences between these results and those previously discussed. First, the region associated with tool naming appears to be ventral to the middle temporal region observed in other studies of tool and action naming (e.g., Martin et al., 1995, 1996), and the region associated with animal naming is anterior to that observed by Martin et al. (1996). Second, Damasio et al. (1996) provide neuropsychological evidence that the observed regions play a mediational role in lexical retrieval, such that these regions store lexical codes rather than abstract semantic knowledge. Additional studies are necessary to clarify these issues.

Semantic Memory Retrieval

Neuroimaging studies have consistently demonstrated activation in left prefrontal cortices during conditions thought to require extensive semantic retrieval (for reviews, see Buckner, 1996; Gabrieli, Poldrack, & Desmond, 1998; Nyberg, Cabeza, & Tulving, 1996). For example, left prefrontal regions are more active during the generation of semantic associates of words compared to baseline conditions (e.g., McCarthy, Blamire, Rothman, Gruetter, & Shulman, 1993; Petersen, Fox, Posner, Mintun, & Raichle, 1988). Similarly, activation is greater when comparing semantic classification (e.g., deciding whether a word is abstract or concrete) to nonsemantic classification (e.g., deciding whether a word is in uppercase or lowercase letters) of stimuli (e.g., Gabrieli et al., 1996; Kapur et al., 1994). Left inferior prefrontal activation during semantic retrieval (1) generalizes across input modality (i.e., auditory and visual; Petersen et al., 1988) and stimulus type (e.g., words and pictures; Buckner, Goodman et al., 1998; Vandenberghe, Price, Wise, Josephs, & Frackowiak, 1996; Wagner, Desmond, Demb, Glover, & Gabrieli, 1997); (2) is disrupted by division of attention (Fletcher, Frith, Grasby et al., 1995); and (3) does not reflect general cognitive effort, but rather appears to arise from the specific processing demands of semantic retrieval tasks (Demb et al., 1995).

The regions engaged during semantic retrieval include a posterior and dorsal extent (BAs 44/6; Broca's area) and an anterior and ventral extent (BAs 47/45) of left inferior frontal gyrus. These two regions are functionally dissociable (e.g., Poldrack, Wagner et al., 1998), indicating that they subserve distinct processes. As considered above, Broca's area has been implicated in phonological access, maintenance, and evaluation. Broca's activation during semantic retrieval tasks may reflect the greater lexical and phonological processing demands of these tasks (e.g., Buckner, 1996; Gabrieli et al., 1998). In contrast, the anterior and ventral extent of left inferior prefrontal cortex may subserve the retrieval, maintenance, and evaluation of long-term semantic knowledge (e.g., Demb et al., 1995; Kapur et al., 1994). Left prefrontal activation may be related to retrieval and evaluation operations per se or to processes that mediate the selection of relevant semantic knowledge (Thompson-Schill, D'Esposito, Aguirre, & Farah, 1997).

A number of studies have shown that the magnitude of activation in left inferior prefrontal regions is greater during initial relative to repeated semantic retrieval (for a review, see Schacter & Buckner, 1998b). These reductions in neural activation (1) are item-specific (e.g., Gabrieli et al., 1996); (2) are specific to repetition of semantic retrieval (Demb et al., 1995); (3) are correlated with behavioral changes, such as increased accuracy and decreased response latency (Raichle et al., 1994); (4) occur under implicit retrieval conditions; and (5) are not dependent upon the integrity of medial temporal or diencephalic structures (see Buckner & Koutstaal, 1998). These experience-induced reductions thus appear to be neural correlates of a conceptual form of priming (for discussion, see Schacter & Buckner, 1998b).

Episodic Memory

Episodic memory makes possible the acquisition and retrieval of information about specific personal experiences that occur at a particular time and place (Tulving, 1972, 1983). As stated recently by Tulving (1998, p. 265):

> Episodic memory does exactly what the other forms of memory do not and cannot do—it enables the individual to mentally "travel back into her personal past." . . .
>
> Episodic memory has evolved from other forms of memory, and obeys the basic time relations of its constituent mileposts: The individual does something at Time 1 and remembers it at Time 2. But, episodic memory differs from all others in that at Time 2, its time's arrow is no more an arrow, it loops back to Time 1.

Neuroimaging studies have examined brain activity both during Tulving's (1998) Time 1 (episodic encoding) and Time 2 (episodic retrieval).

Episodic Encoding

Findings from several early PET and fMRI studies focused attention on the contribution of regions within prefrontal cortex to episodic encoding. For example, several studies compared brain activity during semantic or "deep" encoding tasks that produce high levels of subsequent memory performance with brain activity during nonsemantic or "shallow" encoding tasks that produce lower levels of subsequent memory. Such studies consistently revealed greater activation in regions of left inferior prefrontal cortex (BA 44, 45, 47) during semantic encoding compared to nonsemantic encoding (e.g., Demb et al., 1995; Fletcher, Frith, Grasby et al., 1995; Kapur et al., 1994; Shallice et al., 1994). Importantly, these left inferior frontal regions are the same as the left prefrontal regions that, as noted earlier, show activation during semantic retrieval tasks. These findings highlight that retrieval from semantic memory and encoding into episodic memory share underlying component processes. In the foregoing and many other studies linking left prefrontal activity with episodic encoding, target stimuli were common words (for detailed reviews, see Buckner, 1996; Nyberg, Cabeza, & Tulving, 1996; Tulving, Kapur, Craik, Moscovitch, & Houle, 1994). More recent studies have revealed evidence of homologous right prefrontal activation during encoding of nonverbal information, including faces (Kelley et al., 1998; cf., Haxby et al., 1996) and patterns (Wagner, Poldrack et al., 1998).

In the encoding studies considered thus far, target stimuli from different encoding conditions were presented in separate "blocks," and brain activity was averaged across the encoding task performed during a particular block. While such studies allow conclusions about the neural correlates of encoding tasks that tend to produce, on average, higher or lower levels of subsequent memory performance, they do not allow examination of the trial-by-trial encoding operations that influence later remembering. It is possible, however, to examine such differences with newly developed event-related fMRI procedures, in which different trial types can be intermixed and participants' responses can be sorted according to whether or not an item is successfully remembered (for discussion of event-related fMRI methods, see Dale & Buckner, 1997).

Using event-related fMRI, Wagner, Schacter, et al. (1998) scanned participants while they made abstract/concrete judgments about a long series of words; after scanning, they tested participants' recognition memory for the studied words. Wagner, Schacter et al. (1998) reported greater activation at the time of encoding in several regions of left prefrontal cortex for words that were subsequently remembered compared to words that were subsequently forgotten. In a study using similar event-related methods to examine encoding of pictures, Brewer, Zhao, Glover, and Gabrieli (1998) reported greater activation during encoding in right prefrontal cortex for subsequently remembered pictures compared to subsequently forgotten pictures.

The foregoing studies, then, have clearly established that regions within prefrontal cortex play an important role in episodic encoding. Neuroimaging research has also been concerned with the role of the medial temporal lobe, including the hippocampus, in episodic encoding processes. Despite some early failures to obtain significant medial temporal lobe (MTL) activation, a growing number of PET and fMRI studies have reported evidence linking MTL activation with episodic encoding. In a number of such studies, MTL activation has been observed under conditions in which exposure to novel stimulus materials is compared with exposure to familiar materials (cf., Dolan & Fletcher, 1997; Gabrieli, Brewer, Desmond, & Glover, 1997; Stern et al., 1996; Tulving, Markowitsch, Craik, Habib, & Houle, 1996), thus raising the possibility that MTL contributions to episodic encoding are restricted to novelty detection processes. Contrary to this idea, several PET and fMRI studies have reported MTL encoding activations under conditions in which stimulus novelty has been held constant (for discussion of individual studies, see Schacter & Wagner, 1999). Most of these studies relied on blocked designs that allow comparisons between encoding conditions that produce higher or lower levels of memory performance. However, the two previously mentioned event-related fMRI studies both reported greater posterior MTL activity (parahippocampal gyrus) during encoding of words (Wagner, Schacter et al., 1998) or pictures (Brewer et al., 1998) that were subsequently remembered compared to those that were subsequently forgotten. As noted by Schacter and Wagner (1999), these results converge with other fMRI studies that have consistently revealed posterior MTL activations, mainly in the parahippocampal gyrus, during episodic encoding. Interestingly, PET studies have obtained evidence of both anterior and posterior MTL encoding activations (for discussion of possible sources of differences between fMRI and PET studies, see Lepage, Habib, & Tulving, 1998; Schacter & Wagner, 1999).

Episodic Retrieval

As with studies of episodic encoding, studies of episodic retrieval have focused intensively on prefrontal and medial temporal regions. PET and fMRI studies have consistently shown that when participants are asked to recall or recognize previously studied words or pictures, activation is observed in anterior prefrontal cortex (centering on BA 10), usually greater in the right than the left hemisphere (this pattern was noted initially by Tulving et al., 1994; for further review and discussion, see Buckner, 1996; Nyberg, Cabeza, & Tulving, 1996; Wagner, Gabrieli et al. 1998). Findings of right anterior prefrontal activation during episodic retrieval are particularly notable because they were largely unexpected on the basis of prior neuropsychological investigations, although recent neuropsychological evidence is consistent with such observations (e.g., Schacter, Curran, Galluccio, Milberg, & Bates, 1996).

Investigations into the nature of the right anterior prefrontal contribution to episodic retrieval have centered on the distinction between retrieval attempt or effort (trying to remember a past event, irrespective or whether one is successful) and retrieval success (recovery of stored information). Most of these studies have used blocked designs in which experimenters attempt to (1) maximize retrieval success in some scans by presenting numerous previously studied items or by testing deeply encoded items that tend to be successfully remembered; and (2) maximize retrieval effort in other scans by presenting numerous nonstudied items or by testing poorly encoded items that tend not to be successfully remembered. The results of such studies are mixed, with some data favoring the idea that right anterior prefrontal cortex is mainly involved in retrieval effort (e.g., Nyberg et al., 1995; Schacter, Alpert et al., 1996; Wagner, Gabrieli et al., 1998) and other studies indicating that it is sometimes related to successful episodic memory retrieval (e.g., Buckner, Koutstaal, Schacter, Wagner, & Rosen, 1998; Rugg, Fletcher, Frith, Frackowiak, & Dolan, 1996). Recent data from event-related fMRI procedures, which allow selective averaging based on participants' responses to individual items, indicate that on an old/new recognition task, right

anterior prefrontal cortex showed significant and similar activation for hits (successful retrieval) and correct rejections (retrieval effort only; Buckner, Koutstaal, Schacter, Dale et al., 1998; see also Schacter, Buckner, Koutstaal, Dale, & Rosen, 1997). Thus, it seems clear that retrieval success is not necessary in order to observe right anterior prefrontal activation during episodic retrieval. The relation of right anterior prefrontal activation to retrieval effort or success may depend on the specifics of the context in which retrieval is carried out (for discussion, see Buckner, Koutstaal, Schacter, Wagner et al., 1998; Schacter & Buckner, 1998a; Wagner, Gabrieli et al., 1998).

Similar issues regarding retrieval effort and success have arisen in studies that examine the role of the MTL in episodic retrieval. Several studies have provided evidence that MTL activity during episodic retrieval is associated with retrieval success (e.g., Nyberg, MacIntosh, Houle, Nilsson, & Tulving, 1996; Rugg, Fletcher, Frith, Frackowiak, & Dolan, 1997; Schacter, Alpert et al., 1996; Schacter et al., 1995). However, these observations must be tempered by the fact that studies of episodic retrieval often fail to document significant MTL activity. Among those that have, the observed activations tend to fall in parahippocampal gyrus and nearby regions of the posterior MTL (Lepage et al., 1998; see also Schacter & Wagner, 1999).

Despite the focus on prefrontal and MTL activations in many studies of episodic retrieval, it is also important to note that such studies have consistently reported evidence for the involvement of various other regions, most notably posterior medial parietal cortex, near the precuneus (e.g., Buckner et al., 1995; Buckner, Koutstaal, Schacter, Wagner et al., 1998; Fletcher, Frith, Baker et al., 1995; Fletcher, Frith, Grasby et al., 1995; Schacter, Alpert et al., 1996). The role of medial parietal cortex in episodic retrieval remains poorly understood, although some hypotheses have been suggested (e.g., Fletcher, Frith, Baker et al., 1995). Along with the evidence of right anterior prefrontal activation, the possible involvement of medial parietal cortex in episodic retrieval was largely unsuspected prior to the advent of neuroimaging studies.

Perceptual Representation System (PRS)

The PRS can be viewed as a collection of domain-specific modules that operate on perceptual information about the form and structure of words and objects (Schacter, 1990, 1994; Tulving & Schacter, 1990). For students of memory, the main interest in the PRS centers on its hypothesized role in the phenomenon of perceptual priming: a change in the ability to identify an object as a result of a specific prior encounter with the object (Tulving & Schacter, 1990; for recent reviews, see Schacter & Buckner, 1998b; Wiggs & Martin, 1998).

A number of PET and fMRI studies have examined performance on tasks that are thought to tap visual perceptual priming, and they have consistently revealed a common outcome: priming is accompanied by blood flow decreases in regions of extrastriate visual cortex. This finding has been observed across a variety of priming tasks, including visual word stem completion (e.g., Buckner et al., 1995; Schacter, Alpert et al., 1996; Squire et al., 1992), visual word fragment completion (Blaxton et al., 1996), and object naming and classification (Buckner, Goodman et al., 1998). Recent evidence indicates that priming-related decreases in extrastriate cortex are selective, in the sense that early visual regions that are activated during initial study of a visual object do not show subsequent priming-related reductions, whereas higher order extrastriate areas do (Buckner, Goodman et al., 1998).

These findings thus parallel the previously mentioned findings of inferior prefrontal blood flow reductions in association with conceptual priming. As emphasized by Schacter and Buckner (1998b), most tasks include both perceptual and conceptual components, so sharp distinctions between perceptual and conceptual priming are probably oversimplistic. Moreover, there is as yet little evidence that specifically links priming-related blood flow reductions to the modality-specific operations of the PRS. It is conceivable, for instance, that extrastriate blood flow reductions will be observed during cross-modal priming. Until appropriate analytic studies are carried out, the possible link between extrastriate blood flow reductions and perceptual aspects of priming must be viewed with interpretive caution. Nonetheless, observations of blood flow decreases in association with perceptual priming are strikingly similar to the phenomenon of "repetition suppression" observed in studies of nonhuman primates, where repeated exposure to a stimulus is associated with reduced responding of many cells in higher-order visual regions (inferior temporal

cortex; see Desimone, Miller, Chelazzi, & Lueschow, 1995). As discussed by Schacter and Buckner (1998b) and Wiggs and Martin (1998), the two phenomena might reflect the operation of a single or similar underlying mechanism. Further exploration of this possibility will likely yield important insights into the nature of the PRS.

Procedural Memory

Procedural memory refers to the learning of motor and cognitive skills, and is manifest across a wide range of situations. Learning to ride a bike and acquiring reading skills are examples of procedural memory. The procedural memory system likely includes major divisions and comprises numerous subsystems. The commonality across these subsystems is that they all enable the acquisition of new skills. Procedural memory is characterized by gradual, incremental learning and can function normally in the presence of damage to medial temporal lobe structures, thereby distinguishing it from episodic and semantic memory systems. For the purposes of this chapter, we focus on a small number of findings to illustrate how neuroimaging has illuminated brain systems underlying procedural memory (for further review and discussion, see Buckner & Tulving, 1995; Petersen, van Mier, Fiez, & Raichle, 1998; Ungerleider, 1995; Karni et al., 1998).

Procedural learning has been explored with a variety of paradigms, some of which are structurally similar to those used to examine priming. For most of these paradigms, brain activity during initial task performance is contrasted with performance after varying degrees of practice. One notable finding in such paradigms is that extensive practice on a task often produces a shift in the brain pathways used to complete the task.

For example, Raichle et al. (1994) examined a word generation task (subjects viewed nouns and generated related verbs aloud) during both its naive state and after many repetitions with the same items. The results revealed that certain areas that were characterized by significant activation in the naive state showed marked reductions in activation after numerous repetitions of target items (these regions included prefrontal cortex, anterior cingulate, and right lateral cerebellum). Such a finding is quite similar to the repetition-related decreases noted earlier in studies of priming. However, qualitative changes also appear to play a role in procedural learning. Raichle et al. also noted activity increases in bilateral Sylvian-insular and visual extrastriate cortex after extensive practice. These practice-related changes suggest that, as the pathway involving prefrontal cortex became less prominent, a separate pathway involving Sylvian-insular cortex emerged. The increased activation in visual cortex might have occurred because this pathway became increasingly stimulus driven with practice. Thus, in addition to task facilitation effects associated with reduced activation in certain pathways during early phases of repetition, alternative pathways may come to support task performance in highly practiced task states, resulting in increased activation.

This basic observation—alternative pathways are adopted during overlearned performance in contrast to naïve performance—appears to be quite general in studies of procedural memory. Similar findings have been observed both when the exact items and task are repeated (e.g., Raichle et al., 1994; Krebs et al., 1998; Petersen et al., 1998) and when task procedures are learned that generalize across specific items (e.g., Poldrack, Desmond, Glover, & Gabrieli, 1998). In this latter study, naïve performance of a mirror-reading task was associated with extensive use of ventral visual processing regions as well as parietal cortex. After practice with mirror reading, there was a significant decrease in parietal cortex and a corresponding increase in left inferior temporal cortex—a region previously associated with visual form processing. This phenomenon was observed for new words that had not been practiced previously. Poldrack et al. (1998) suggested that these results reflect a transition from a parietal-dependent strategy of visually transforming target stimuli that was used in the naïve task state to a more automatic task mode involving visual recognition of mirror-reversed letters in the practiced task state.

Tasks requiring motor and visual-motor skill learning have also shown pathway transitions with extensive practice (e.g., Grafton et al., 1992; Krebs et al., 1998). In particular, a number of motor and visual-motor tasks have been associated with increased motor area activation, especially within the supplementary motor area (SMA) and primary motor cortex, as practice progresses (e.g., Jenkins, Brooks, Nixon, Frackowiak, & Passingham, 1994; Grafton et al., 1992; Karni et al., 1995; Petersen et al., 1998). Petersen et al. (1998), for example, explored practice effects for a maze tracing task. In a series of PET studies, subjects traced mazes both in naïve states and after extensive practice. During performance in the naïve state, there was activation in a distributed network of brain areas including premotor and parietal cortex. After practice, these areas showed reduced activity together with concurrent increases in SMA and primary motor cortex, again suggesting a transition in brain pathways used during naïve and practiced task performance.

Taken together, these neuroimaging studies appear to capture an important shift in performance from naïve to practiced conditions that reflects the operation of a procedural memory system. In particular, there appears to be a tendency for tasks that require extensive prefrontal and/or premotor contributions in their naïve state to shift to more automated pathways with practice, although the specific transition noted in any individual study appears highly dependent on the exact task that is performed.

Conclusions

This review indicates that neuroimaging techniques have been used widely to investigate memory systems. This state of affairs reflects a dramatic shift within the past five years: when Schacter and Tulving (1994) reviewed evidence for memory systems, nearly all of the relevant observations were provided by cognitive studies of healthy volunteers, neuropsychological investigations of brain-damaged patients, and neurobiological studies of experimental animals. What, then, has the recent explosion in neuroimaging research revealed about the memory systems that Schacter and Tulving (1994) identified?

First, it seems clear that neuroimaging research has provided some novel insights into the nature and function of components within each of the five memory systems. For instance, within the domain of working memory, imaging data suggest a promising distinction between the contributions of ventral and dorsal prefrontal regions to the maintenance and manipulation of representations. Studies of semantic memory have led to the hypothesis that semantic attributes of a stimulus are stored near the cortical regions that underly perception of those attributes. In episodic memory, imaging studies have illuminated the contributions of distinct prefrontal regions to encoding and retrieval. Investigations of priming within the PRS have consistently revealed activation reductions in posterior cortical regions. And studies of procedural memory have uncovered evidence of a shift in pathways used during unpracticed and practiced stages of task performance. At the same time that neuroimaging has provided these and other new insights into the operation of the five memory systems, it has also highlighted that a number of the same regions are involved in multiple systems. Thus, for instance, some of the same regions within left inferior prefrontal cortex are involved in working memory, semantic memory, and episodic memory, and show changes that accompany skill learning and priming. These kinds of commonalities may provide new insights into interactions among memory systems that have been dissociated on the basis of other kinds of evidence. Future investigations that combine cognitive, neuropsychological, and neuroimaging approaches will no doubt deepen our understanding of the relations among the systems that together constitute the foundation of memory.

Acknowledgments Preparation of this chapter was supported by grants from the National Institute of Mental Health, National Institute on Aging, and Human Frontiers Science Program. We thank Carrie Racine for help with preparation of the manuscript.

References

Atkinson, R. C., & Shiffrin, R. M. (1968). Human memory: A proposed system and its control processes. In K. W. Spence & J. T. Spence (Eds.), *The psychology of learning and motivation* (Vol. 2; pp. 89–195). New York: Academic Press.

Awh, E., & Jonides, J. (1998). Spatial working memory and spatial selective attention. In R. Parasuraman (Ed.), *The attentive brain* (pp. 353–380). Cambridge, MA: MIT Press.

Awh, E., Jonides, J., Smith, E. E., Schumacher, E. H., Koeppe, R. A., & Katz, S. (1996). Dissociation of storage and rehearsal in verbal working memory: Evidence from positron emission tomography. *Psychological Science, 7*, 25–31.

Baddeley, A. (1986). *Working memory.* Oxford: Clarendon Press.

Baddeley, A. (1994). Working memory: The interface between memory and cognition. In D. L. Schacter & E. Tulving (Eds.), *Memory*

systems (pp. 351–367). Cambridge, MA: MIT Press.

Baddeley, A. D. (1998). Recent developments in working memory. *Current Opinion in Neurobiology, 8*, 234–238.

Baddeley, A. D., & Hitch, G. (1974). Working memory. In G. H. Bower (Ed.), *The psychology of learning and motivation* (Vol. 8; pp. 47–89). New York: Academic Press.

Belleville, S., Peretz, I., & Arguin, M. (1992). Contribution of articulatory rehearsal to short-term memory: Evidence from a case of selective disruption. *Brain and Language, 43*, 713–746.

Blaxton, T. A., Bookheimer, S. Y., Zeffiro, T. A., Figlozzi, C. M., Gaillard, W. D., & Theodore, W. H. (1996). Functional mapping of human memory using PET: Comparisons of conceptual and perceptual tasks. *Canadian Journal of Experimental Psychology, 50*, 42–56.

Braver, T., Cohen, J., Nystrom, L., Jonides, J., Smith, E., & Noll, D. (1997). A parametric study of prefrontal cortex involvement in human working memory. *Neuroimage, 5*, 49–62.

Brewer, J., Zhao, Z., Glover, G., & Gabrieli, J. (1998). Making memories: Brain activity that predicts whether visual experiences will be remembered or forgotten. *Science, 281*, 1185–1187.

Buckner, R. L. (1996). Beyond HERA: Contributions of specific prefrontal brain areas to long-term memory retrieval. *Psychonomic Bulletin & Review, 3*, 149–158.

Buckner, R., Goodman, J., Burock, M., Rotte, M., Koutstaal, W., Schacter, D., Rosen, B., & Dale, A. (1998). Functional-anatomic correlates of object priming in humans revealed by rapid presentation event-related fMRI. *Neuron, 20*, 285–296.

Buckner, R. L., & Koutstaal, W. (1998). Functional neuroimaging studies of encoding, priming, and explicit memory retrieval. *Proceedings of the National Academy of Sciences USA, 95*, 891–898.

Buckner, R. L., Koutstaal, W., Schacter, D. L., Dale, A. M., Rotte, M., & Rosen, B. (1998). Functional-anatomic study of episodic retrieval: Selective averaging of event-related fMRI trials to test the retrieval success hypothesis. *NeuroImage, 7*, 151–162.

Buckner, R. L., Koutstaal, W., Schacter, D. L., Wagner, A. D., & Rosen, B. R. (1998). Functional-anatomic study of episodic retrieval using fMRI: Retrieval effort versus retrieval success. *NeuroImage, 7*, 163–175.

Buckner, R. L., Petersen, S. E., Ojemann, J. G., Miezin, F. M., Squire, L. R., & Raichle,

M. E. (1995). Functional anatomical studies of explicit and implicit memory retrieval tasks. *Journal of Neuroscience, 15,* 12–29.

Buckner, R. L., & Tulving, E. (1995). Neuroimaging studies of memory: Theory and recent PET results. In F. Boller & J. Grafman (Eds.), *Handbook of neuropsychology* (Vol. 10; pp. 439–466). Amsterdam: Elsevier.

Cabeza, R., & Nyberg, L. (1997). Imaging cognition: An empirical review of PET studies with normal subjects. *Journal of Cognitive Neuroscience, 9,* 1–26.

Caramazza, A., & Shelton, J. (1998). Domain-specific knowledge systems in the brain the animate-inanimate distinction. *Journal of Cognitive Neuroscience, 10,* 1–34.

Chao, L. L., & Martin, A. (in press). Cortical regions associated with perceiving, naming, and knowing about colors. *Journal of Cognitive Neuroscience.*

Cohen, N. J., & Eichenbaum, H. (1993). *Memory, amnesia, and the hippocampal system.* Cambridge, MA: MIT Press.

Cohen, J. D., Forman, S. D., Braver, T. S., Casey, B. J., Servan-Schreiber, D., & Noll, D. C. (1994). Activation of the prefrontal cortex in a nonspatial working memory task with functional MRI. *Human Brain Mapping, 1,* 293–304.

Cohen, J., Perlstein, W., Braver, T., Nystrom, L., Noll, D., Jonides, J., & Smith, E. (1997). Temporal dynamics of brain activation during a working memory task. *Nature, 386,* 604–608.

Courtney, S. M., Petit, L., Maisog, J. M., Ungerleider, L. G., & Haxby, J. V. (1998). An area specialized for spatial working memory in human frontal cortex. *Science, 279,* 1347–1351.

Courtney, S., Ungerleider, L., Keil, K., & Haxby, J. (1996). Object and spatial visual working memory activate separate neural systems in human cortex. *Cerebral Cortex, 6,* 39–49.

Dale, A., & Buckner, R. (1997). Selective averaging of rapidly presented individual trials using fMRI. *Human Brain Mapping, 5,* 329–340.

Damasio, H., Grabowski, T., Tranel, D., Hichwa, R., & Damasio, A. (1996). A neural basis for lexical retrieval. *Nature, 380,* 499–505.

Demb, J. B., Desmond, J. E., Wagner, A. D., Vaidya, C. J., Glover, G. H., & Gabrieli, J. D. E. (1995). Semantic encoding and retrieval in the left inferior prefrontal cortex: A functional MRI study of task difficulty and process specificity. *Journal of Neuroscience, 15,* 5870–5878.

Desimone, R., Miller, E. K., Chelazzi, L., & Lueschow, A. (1995). Multiple memory systems in the visual cortex. In M. S. Gazzaniga (Ed.), *The cognitive neurosciences* (pp. 475–486). Cambridge, MA: MIT Press.

Desmond, J., Gabrieli, J., Wagner, A., Ginier, B., & Glover, G. (1997). Lobular patterns of cerebellar activation in verbal working-memory and finger-tapping tasks as revealed by functional MRI. *Journal of Neuroscience, 17,* 9675–9685.

D'Esposito, M., Aguirre, G. K., Zarahn, E., Ballard, D., Shin, R., Lease, J., & Tang, J. (1998). Functional MRI studies of spatial and nonspatial working memory. *Cognitive Brain Research, 7,* 1–13.

D'Esposito, M., Detre, J. A., Alsop, D. C., Shin, R. K., Atlas, S., & Grossman, M. (1995). The neural basis of the central executive system of working memory. *Nature, 378,* 279–281.

Dolan, R., & Fletcher, P. (1997). Dissociating prefrontal and hippocampal function in episodic memory encoding. *Nature, 388,* 582–585.

Farah, M. J., & McClelland, J. L. (1991). A computational model of semantic memory impairment: Modality specificity and emergent category specificity. *Journal of Experimental Psychology: General, 120,* 339–357.

Fiez, J., Raife, E., Balota, D., Schwarz, J., Raichle, M., & Petersen, S. (1996). A positron emission tomography study of the short-term maintenance of verbal information. *Journal of Neuroscience, 16,* 808–822.

Fletcher, P. C., Frith, C. D., Baker, S. C., Shallice, T., Frackowiak, R. S. J., & Dolan, R. J. (1995). The mind's eye: Precuneus activation in memory-related imagery. *Neuroimage, 2,* 195–200.

Fletcher, P. C., Frith, C. D., Grasby, P. M., Shallice, T., Frackowiak, R. S. J., & Dolan, R. J. (1995). Brain systems for encoding and retrieval of auditory verbal memory: An in vivo study in humans. *Brain, 118,* 401–416.

Gabrieli, J. D. E., Brewer, J. B., Desmond, J. E., & Glover, G. H. (1997). Separate neural bases of two fundamental memory processes in the human medial temporal lobe. *Science, 276,* 264–266.

Gabrieli, J. D. E., Desmond, J. E., Demb, J. B., Wagner, A. D., Stone, M. V., Vaidya, C. J., & Glover, G. H. (1996). Functional magnetic resonance imaging of semantic memory processes in the frontal lobes. *Psychological Sciences, 7*, 278–283.

Gabrieli, J., Poldrack, R., & Desmond, J. (1998). The role of left prefrontal cortex in language and memory. *Proceedings of the National Academy of Sciences USA, 95*, 906–913.

Glenberg, A. M. (1997). What memory is for. *Behavioral & Brain Sciences, 20*, 1–19.

Goldman-Rakic, P. S. (1987). Circuitry of primate prefrontal cortex and regulation of behavior by representational memory. In F. Plum (Ed.), *Handbook of physiology: Vol. V, Higher functions of the brain* (pp. 373–417). Bethesda, MD: American Physiology Society.

Graf, P., & Schacter, D. L. (1985). Implicit and explicit memory for new associations in normal subjects and amnesic patients. *Journal of Experimental Psychology: Learning, Memory, and Cognition, 11*, 501–518.

Grafton, S., Mazziota, J., Presty, S., Friston, K., Frackowiak, R., & Phelps, M. (1992). Functional anatomy of human procedural learning determined with regional cerebral blood flow and PET. *Journal of Neuroscience, 12*, 2542–2548.

Haxby, J., Ungerleider, L., Horwitz, B., Rapoport, S., & Grady, C. (1995). Hemispheric differences in neural systems for face working memory: A PET-rCBF study. *Human Brain Mapping, 3*, 68–82.

Haxby, J., Ungerleider, L., Horwitz, B., Maisog, J., Rappaport, S., & Grady, C. (1996). Face encoding and recognition in the human brain. *Proceedings of the National Academy of Sciences USA, 93*, 922–927.

Jenkins, I. H., Brooks, D. J., Nixon, P. D., Frackowiak, R. S. J., & Passingham, R. E. (1994). Motor sequence learning: A study with positron emission tomography. *Journal of Neuroscience, 14*, 3775–3790.

Jonides, J., Schumacher, E., Smith, E., Koeppe, R., Awh, E., Reuter-Lorenz, P., Marshuetz, C., & Willis, C. (1998). The role of parietal cortex in verbal working memory. *Journal of Neuroscience, 18*, 5026–5034.

Jonides, J., Smith, E. E., Koeppe, R. A., Awh, E., Minoshima, S., & Mintun, M. A. (1993). Spatial working memory in humans as revealed by PET. *Nature, 363*, 623–625.

Just, M. A., & Carpenter, P. A. (1992). A capacity theory of comprehension: Individual differences in working memory. *Psychological Review, 99*, 122–149.

Kapur, S., Craik, F. I. M., Tulving, E., Wilson, A. A., Houle, S., & Brown, G. M. (1994). Neuroanatomical correlates of encoding in episodic memory: Levels of processing effect. *Proceedings of the National Academy of Sciences USA, 91*, 2008–2011.

Karni, A., Meyer, G., Jezzard, P., Adams, M. M., Turner, R., & Ungerleider, L. G. (1995). Functional MRI evidence for adult motor cortex plasticity during motor skill learning. *Nature, 377*, 155–158.

Karni, A., Meyer, G., Rey-Hipolito, C., Jezzard, P., Adams, N., Turner, R., & Ungerleider, L. (1998). The acquisition of skilled motor performance: Fast and slow experience-driven changes in primary motor cortex. *Proceedings of the National Academy of Science USA, 95*, 861–868.

Kelley, W., Miezin, F., McDermott, K., Buckner, R., Raichle, M., Cohen, N., Ollinger, J., Akbudak, E., Conturo, T., Snyder, A., & Petersen, S. (1998). Hemispheric specialization in human dorsal frontal cortex and medial temporal lobe for verbal and nonverbal memory encoding. *Neuron, 20*, 927–936.

Krebs, H., Brasherskrug, T., Rauch, S., Savage, C., Hogan, N., Rubin, R., Fischman, A., & Alpert, N. (1998). Robot-aided functional imaging: Application to a motor learning study. *Human Brain Mapping, 6*, 59–72.

Lepage, M., Habib, R., & Tulving, E. (1998). Hippocampal PET activations of memory encoding and retrieval: The HIPER model. *Hippocampus, 8*, 313–322.

Maine de Biran. (1929). *The influence of habit on the faculty of thinking.* Baltimore, MD: Williams & Wilkins.

Martin, A., Haxby, J. V., Lalonde, F. M., Wiggs, C. L., & Ungerleider, L. G. (1995). Discrete cortical regions associated with knowledge of color and knowledge of action. *Science, 270*, 102–105.

Martin, A., Wiggs, C. L., Ungerleider, L. G., & Haxby, J. U. (1996). Neural correlates of category-specific knowledge. *Nature, 379*, 649–652.

McCarthy, G., Blamire, A. M., Puce, A., Nobre, A. C., Bloch, G., Hyder, F., Goldman-Rakic, P., & Shulman, R. G. (1994). Functional magnetic resonance imaging of human prefrontal cortex activation during a spatial working memory task. *Proceedings of the National Academy of Sciences USA, 91*, 8690–8694.

McCarthy, G., Blamire, A. M., Rothman, D. L., Gruetter, R., & Shulman, R. G. (1993). Echo-planar magnetic resonance imaging studies of frontal cortex activation during word generation in humans. *Proceedings of the National Academy of Sciences USA, 90*, 4952–4956.

McCarthy, G., Puce, A., Constable, R., Krystal, J., Gore, J., & Goldman-Rakic, P. (1996). Activation of human prefrontal cortex during spatial and nonspatial working memory tasks measured by functional MRI. *Cerebral Cortex, 6*, 600–611.

McClelland, J. L., McNaughton, B. L., & O'Reilly, R. C. (1995). Why there are complementary learning systems in the hippocampus and neocortex: Insights from the successes and failures of connectionist models of learning and memory. *Psychological Review, 102*, 419–457.

Miller, E., & Desimone, R. (1994). Parallel neuronal mechanisms for short-term memory. *Science, 263*, 520–522.

Mishkin, M., & Petri, H. L. (1984). Memories and habits: Some implications for the analysis of learning and retention. In L. Squire & N. Butters (Eds.), *Neuropsychology of memory* (pp. 287–296). New York: Guilford Press.

Nyberg, L., Cabeza, R., & Tulving, E. (1996). PET studies of encoding and retrieval: The HERA model. *Psychonomic Bulletin and Review, 3*, 135–148.

Nyberg, L., McIntosh, A. R., Houle, S., Nilsson, L.-G., & Tulving, E. (1996). Activation of medial temporal structures during episodic memory retrieval. *Nature, 380*, 715–717.

Nyberg, L., Tulving, E., Habib, R., Nilsson, L.-G., Kapur, S., Houle, S., Cabeza, R., & McIntosh, A. R. (1995). Functional brain maps of retrieval mode and recovery of episodic information. *NeuroReport, 6*, 249–252.

O'Keefe, J., & Nadel, L. (1978). *The hippocampus as a cognitive map*. Oxford: Clarendon Press.

Owen, A. M., Evans, A. C., & Petrides M. (1996). Evidence for a two-stage model of spatial working memory processing within the lateral frontal cortex: A positron emission tomography study. *Cerebral Cortex, 6*, 31–38.

Paulesu, E., Frith, C. D., & Frackowiak, R. S. J. (1993). The neural correlates of the verbal component of working memory. *Nature, 362*, 342–345.

Petersen, S. E., Fox, P. T., Posner, M. I., Mintun, M., & Raichle, M. E. (1988). Positron emission tomographic studies of the cortical anatomy of single-word processing. *Nature, 331*, 585–589.

Petersen, S., van Mier, H., Fiez, J., & Raichle, M. (1998). The effects of practice on the functional anatomy of task performance. *Proceedings of the National Academy of Science USA, 95*, 853–860.

Poldrack, R., Desmond, J., Glover, G., & Gabrieli, J. (1998). The neural basis of visual skill learning: An fMRI study of mirror reading. *Cerebral Cortex, 8*, 1–10.

Poldrack, R. A., Wagner, A. D., Prull, M. W., Desmond, J. E., Glover, G. H., & Gabrieli, J. D. E. (1998). *Distinguishing semantic and phonological processing in the left inferior prefrontal cortex*. Manuscript submitted for publication.

Raichle, M. E., Fiez, J. A., Videen, T. O., MacLeod, A. M., Pardo, J. V., Fox, P. T., & Petersen, S. E. (1994). Practice-related changes in human brain functional anatomy during nonmotor learning. *Cerebral Cortex, 4*, 8–26.

Roediger, H. L., Buckner, R. L., & McDermott, K. B. (1999). Components of processing. In J. K. Foster & M. Jelicic (Eds.), *Memory: Systems, process, or function?* (pp. 31–65), Oxford: Oxford University Press.

Roediger, H. L., Rajaram, S., & Srinivas, K. (1990). Specifying criteria for postulating memory systems. *Annals of the New York Academy of Sciences, 608*, 572–589.

Rugg, M. D., Fletcher, P. C., Frith, C. D., Frackowiak, R. S. J., & Dolan, R. J. (1996). Differential activation of the prefrontal cortex in successful and unsuccessful memory retrieval. *Brain, 119*, 2073–2083.

Rugg, M. D., Fletcher, P. C., Frith, C. D., Frackowiak, R. S. J., & Dolan, R. J. (1997). Brain regions supporting intentional and incidental memory: A PET study. *NeuroReport, 8*, 1283–1287.

Schacter, D. L. (1987). Implicit memory: History and current status. *Journal of Experimental Psychology: Learning, Memory, and Cognition, 13*, 501–518.

Schacter, D. L. (1990). Perceptual representation systems and implicit memory: Toward a resolution of the multiple memory systems debate. *Annals of the New York Academy of Sciences, 608*, 543–571.

Schacter, D. L. (1992). Understanding implicit memory: A cognitive neuroscience approach. *American Psychologist, 47*, 559–569.

Schacter, D. L. (1994). Priming and multiple memory systems: Perceptual mechanisms of implicit memory. In D. L. Schacter & E. Tulving (Eds.), *Memory systems* (pp. 244–256). Cambridge, MA: MIT Press.

Schacter, D. L., Alpert, N. M., Savage, C. R., Rauch, S. L., & Albert, M. S. (1996). Conscious recollection and the human hippocampal formation: Evidence from positron emission tomography. *Proceedings of the National Academy of Sciences USA, 93,* 321–325.

Schacter, D. L., & Buckner, R. L. (1998a). On the relations among priming, conscious recollection, and intentional retrieval: Evidence from neuroimaging research. *Neurobiology of Learning and Memory, 70,* 284–303.

Schacter, D. L., & Buckner, R. L. (1998b). Priming and the brain. *Neuron, 20,* 185–195.

Schacter, D. L., Buckner, R. L., Koutstaal, W., Dale, A. M., & Rosen, B. R. (1997). Late onset of anterior prefrontal activity during retrieval of veridical and illusory memories: A single trial fMRI study. *NeuroImage, 6,* 259–269.

Schacter, D. L., Curran, T., Galluccio, L., Milberg, W., & Bates, J. (1996). False recognition and the right frontal lobe: A case study. *Neuropsychologia, 34,* 793–808.

Schacter, D. L., Reiman, E., Uecker, A., Polster, M. R., Yun, L. S., & Cooper, L. A. (1995). Brain regions associated with retrieval of structurally coherent visual information. *Nature, 376,* 587–590.

Schacter, D. L., & Tulving, E. (1994). What are the memory systems of 1994? In D. L. Schacter & E. Tulving (Eds.), *Memory systems* (pp. 1–38). Cambridge, MA: MIT Press.

Schacter, D. L., & Wagner, A. D. (1999). Medial temporal lobe activations in fMRI and PET studies of episodic encoding and retrieval. *Hippocampus, 9/1,* 7–24.

Shallice, T. (1982). Specific impairments of planning. *Philosophical Transactions of the Royal Society London B, 298,* 199–209.

Shallice, T., Fletcher, P., Frith, C. D., Grasby, P., Frackowiak, R. S. J., & Dolan, R. J. (1994). Brain regions associated with acquisition and retrieval of verbal episodic memory. *Nature, 368,* 633–635.

Sherry, D. F., & Schacter, D. L. (1987). The evolution of multiple memory systems. *Psychological Review, 94,* 439–454.

Smith, E., Jonides, J., & Koeppe, R. (1996). Dissociating verbal and spatial working memory using PET. *Cerebral Cortex, 6,* 11–20.

Smith, E. E., Jonides, J., Koeppe, R. A., Awh, E., Schumacher, E. H., & Minoshima, S. (1995). Spatial versus object working memory: PET investigations. *Journal of Cognitive Neuroscience, 7,* 337–356.

Squire, L. R. (1992). Memory and the hippocampus: A synthesis from findings with rats, monkeys, and humans. *Psychological Review, 99,* 195–231.

Squire, L. R., Ojemann, J. G., Miezin, F. M., Petersen, S. E., Videen, T. O., & Raichle, M. E. (1992). Activation of the hippocampus in normal humans: A functional anatomical study of memory. *Proceedings of the National Academy of Sciences USA, 89,* 1837–1841.

Stern, C. E., Corkin, S., Gonzalez, R. G., Guimaraes, A. R., Baker, J. R., Jennings, P. J., Carr, C. A., Sugiura, R. M., Vedantham, V., & Rosen, B. R. (1996). The hippocampal formation participates in novel picture encoding: Evidence from functional magnetic resonance imaging. *Proceedings of the National Academy of Sciences USA, 93,* 8660–8665.

Thompson-Schill, S., D'Esposito, M., Aguirre, G., & Farah, M. (1997). Role of left inferior prefrontal cortex in retrieval of semantic knowledge: A reevaluation. *Proceedings of the National Academy of Sciences USA, 94,* 14792–14797.

Tootell, R., Reppas, J., Kwong, K., Malach, R., Born, R., Brady, T., Rosen, B., & Belliveau, J. (1995). Functional analysis of human MT and related visual cortical areas using magnetic resonance imaging. *Journal of Neuroscience, 15,* 3215–3230.

Tulving, E. (1972). Episodic and semantic memory. In E. Tulving & W. Donaldson (Eds.), *Organization of memory* (pp. 381–403). New York: Academic Press.

Tulving, E. (1983). *Elements of episodic memory.* Oxford: Clarendon Press.

Tulving, E. (1984). Multiple learning and memory systems. In K. M. J. Lagerspetz & P. Niemi (Eds.), *Psychology in the 1990s* (pp. 163–184). Amsterdam: Elsevier.

Tulving, E. (1985). How many memory systems are there? *American Psychologist, 40,* 385–398.

Tulving, E. (1998). Neurocognitive processes of human memory. In C. von Euler, I. Lundberg, & R. Llinas (Eds.), *Basic mechanisms in cognition and language* (pp. 261–281). Amsterdam: Elsevier.

Tulving, E., Kapur, S., Craik, F. I. M., Moscovitch, M., & Houle, S. (1994). Hemispheric encoding/retrieval asymmetry in episodic memory: Positron emission tomography findings. *Proceedings of the National Academy of Sciences USA, 91,* 2016–2020.

Tulving, E., Markowitsch, H., Craik, F., Habib, R., & Houle, S. (1996). Novelty and familiarity activations in PET studies of memory encoding and retrieval. *Cerebral Cortex, 6,* 71–79.

Tulving, E., & Schacter, D. L. (1990). Priming and human memory systems. *Science, 247,* 301–306.

Ungerleider, L. G. (1995). Functional brain imaging studies of cortical mechanisms for memory. *Science, 270,* 760–775.

Ungerleider, L. G., & Mishkin, M. (1982). Two cortical visual systems. In D. J. Ingle, M. A. Goodale, & R. J. W. Mansfield (Eds.), *Analysis of visual behavior* (pp. 549–586). Cambridge, MA: MIT Press.

Vallar, G., & Baddeley, A. D. (1984). Fractionation of working memory: Neuropsychological evidence for a phonological short-term store. *Journal of Verbal Learning and Verbal Behavior, 23,* 151–161.

Vandenberghe, R., Price, C., Wise, R., Josephs, O., & Frackowiak, R. (1996). Functional anatomy of a common semantic system for words and pictures. *Nature, 383,* 254–256.

Wagner, A. D., Desmond, J. E., Demb, J. B., Glover, G. H., & Gabrieli, J. D. E. (1997). Semantic repetition priming for verbal and pictorial knowledge: A functional MRI study of left inferior prefrontal cortex. *Journal of Cognitive Neuroscience, 9,* 714–726.

Wagner, A. D., Gabrieli, J. D. E., Desmond, J. E., & Glover, G. H. (1998). Prefrontal cortex and recognition memory: fMRI evidence for context-dependent retrieval processes. *Brain, 121,* 1985–2002.

Wagner, A. D., Poldrack, R. A., Eldridge, L. L., Desmond, J. E., Glover, G. H., & Gabrieli, J. D. E. (1998). Material-specific lateralization of prefrontal activation during episodic encoding and retrieval. *NeuroReport, 9,* 3711–3717.

Wagner, A. D., Schacter, D. L., Rotte, M., Koutstaal, W., Maril, A., Dale, A. M., Rosen, B. R., & Buckner, R. L. (1998). Verbal memory encoding: Brain activity predicts subsequent remembering and forgetting. *Science, 281,* 1188–1191.

Warrington, E. K., & Shallice, T. (1984). Category specific semantic impairments. *Brain, 107,* 829–854.

Wiggs, C., & Martin, A. (1998). Properties and mechanisms of perceptual priming. *Current Opinion in Neurobiology, 8,* 227–233.

Wilson, F. A. W., O'Scalaidhe, S. P., & Goldman-Rakic, P. S. (1993). Dissociation of object and spatial processsing domains in primate prefrontal cortex. *Science, 260,* 1955–1958.

EPILOGUE

The Story of Memory, and Memory of the Story

L. WEISKRANTZ

How strange this *Oxford Handbook of Memory* would seem to our forebears. That, of course, is the reconstructed fate of all forebears. I can remember when "memory" was a relatively desiccated topic assigned as compulsory reading to us as graduate students some 50 years ago—back in prehistory. It was usually linked with "learning" on the not unreasonable grounds, to quote a relatively recent (Eysenck, 1990) dictionary of cognitive psychology, that "the existence of learning is typically revealed by the use of a memory test." I turned, for old times sake, to another handbook—not of memory, of course (this being the first), but of experimental psychology (Stevens, 1951), and there it was: "Human learning and Retention" by Carl Hovland. It is a thoroughgoing account of the contemporary scene, of which the following major headings are just a subset: Conditioning, Verbal Learning, Motor Learning, the Role of Motivation, Individual Differences, Reminiscence, Unlearning, Transfer of Training, Reproductive Facilitation and Interference, Causes of Forgetting, Qualitative Changes in Retention, and Principal Phenomena of Retention. This last topic deserves a complete summary of the list of its subheadings: Conditioned Responses, Verbal Learning, Motor Learning, Limits of Retention (this last section revealing that selections of Greek material [20 lines, or 240 syllables of iambic hexameter from Sophocles' *Oedipus Tyrannus*, "tantamount to nonsense material"] heroically read aloud daily to a male infant from the age of 15 months to 3 years, subsequently yielded 30% retention at age 8 1/2, 8% at age 14, and zero at age 18).

The underlying assumptions linking that large body of work was that learning was associative (with various links, S-S, S-R, R-S), largely unitary, and amenable to strict quantitative characterization—appropriately the final section is on "Mathematical formulations of learning." Retention was treated as an imperfect residuum of such learning following a gap of time, confounded by interference or boosted by transfer of training. Admittedly, there is a brief section in Stevens's handbook, the chapter on "Qualitative Changes in Retention," with the interesting comment that "the heavy emphasis on quantitative changes in learning has almost crowded out interest in qualitative changes." It contains a short summary of Bartlett's (1932) work and research on the retention of visual forms as influenced by gestalt psychology.

What has happened to the story, meanwhile, culminating in this handbook? Well, for one thing the unity has gone. With the advent of neuropsychology, it has become clear that there is a multiplicity of memory systems or, at the very least, of dissociably different modes of processing. That is reflected here in separate treatments for words, spaces, actions, faces, short-term, and so forth. Welcome restraint is evident, however, in controlling taxonomic exuberance. In one popular dictionary of psychology (Reber, 1985), there are separate sections dealing with *33* memory qualifiers—for example, immediate, short-term, flashbulb, associative, redintegrative, primary, echoic, episodic, and semantic. This profusion, fueled by an ever-increasing number of neuropsychological dissociations, has generated a variety of taxonomic schemas over the past two or three decades, with strong allegiances and territorial imperatives. But it does seem that we may now be leaving the taxonomic era in favor of one focusing on process. Distinctions such as that between recollection and familiarity, remembering and knowing, recognition and recall, executive and automatic, enter the fray and, moreover, they have probably different developmental sequelae.

On the other hand, the varieties of memory in this handbook do share one feature—the implicit assumption that consciousness (or some viable functional equivalent) is of defining relevance. The very existence of a chapter on "unconscious processes in memory" reifies this contrast with "autonoetic awareness" that appears in a later chapter, just as the demonstration of "implicit memory processes"—made necessary by the manifold neuropsychological evidence from the amnesic syndrome—reifies the contrast with "explicit processes," not only in memory but in virtually the whole of cognitive neuropsychology. It is another matter, of course, to consider possible functions of an "off-line" conscious attribute, without any necessity to embrace dualism, but merely to note here its inclusion as a crucial distinguishing feature of remembering and recognition, in contrast with storage and retrieval without conscious acknowledgment. As a result, of course, the overwhelming substance of the present handbook is concerned with human memory (with a welcome section on development)—not that animals are not entitled to explicit processing, but the route to its study is either based on task homologies (e.g., yes/no recognition paradigms) or, more deeply, on an off-line analysis that is complex and rarely undertaken (cf., Cowey & Stoerig, 1995; Weiskrantz, 1997). It also means that memory as a subject has graduated far beyond, and is far richer—at the core of our mental life and our personal identity—than a traditional psychology dictionary definition, "the demonstration that behavior has been altered as a consequence of the previous storage of information at some point in time ranging from a few seconds ago to several decades" (which, to be fair, this dictionary goes on to elaborate, Eysenck, p. 217).

With Stevens's handbook opened in front of me, I could not resist peeking in it for any discussion of consciousness—not that it was obliged to include any. The only two references in the index are revealing, for both are dismissive of its status or its role. Thus (in relation to emotion), "an immaterial consequence or epiphenomenon," but fortunately "some . . . organic changes, especially the electrophysiological, already appear to be useful substitutes for the phenomenology of consciousness" (Stevens, 1951, p. 503).

Of more possible relevance, though, is the treatment of amnesia. Again, only two references. The first is by Hilgard to hypnosis and psychogenic amnesia, under the interesting heading of "motivational factors in forgetting,"—for example, "memory for pleasant and unpleasant items" (p. 558). Hypnotic dissociative effects appear not to have made it into the present handbook, although they can be powerful and revealing. The other reference to amnesia is a brief suggestion by Clifford Morgan that "there are primary focal areas for different memory functions but that we do not see particular memory losses localized in these areas because there is an interdependence of memory functions" (p. 784).

That prompted me to pursue the discussion of amnesia by Lashley, the influential advocate of the nonlocalizability of memory traces. Lashley was well aware of the classical evidence for an amnesic syndrome caused by brain damage—indeed, there was very little that Lashley was *not* aware of! But in keeping with his view that memories are encoded in large wavelike systems, he wrote, "I believe the evidence strongly favors the view that amnesia from brain injury rarely, if ever, is due to the destruction of specific memory traces. Rather, the amnesias represent a lowered level of vigilance, a great difficulty in activating the organized pattern of traces, or a disturbance of some broader system of organised functions" (p. 495, in Beach et al., 1960). In my notes from the pro-seminar sessions at Harvard conducted by Lashley, I also found his comment, "in man accessibility can sometimes be destroyed without traces themselves being destroyed," which was consistent, of course, with his view that memory traces were virtually indestructible anyway (unless there was destruction of large masses of cortex). His mass-action research antedated HM, of course, but I am not sure that case would have changed his mind. In any event, it postdated the strong evidence already available to him of specific and circumscribed subcortical clinical pathology linked with the Korsakoff amnesic syndrome, and there were already reports of temporal lobe pathology linked to severe memory impairment. He presumably would have interpreted the germs of residual implicit retention noted long ago by Korsakoff and Claparède as being merely "lowered levels of vigilance." As a matter of fact, the view that amnesia was just "weak memory" did not itself become weakened until relatively recently.

Lashley disliked connection*ism*—after all, the presumed short circuits caused by gold foil he placed on the brains of monkeys not only distorted the electrical d.c. fields of the gestaltists (or later, the standing potentials of Rusinov) but also short-circuited connections (Lashley, Chow, & Semmes, 1951). Neither these nor the insulating slivers of mica inserted into the brains of cats by Sperry and Miner (1955) seemed to have any but trivial disruptive effects on perception or learning. But Lashley was pursuing a conceptual journey that is intrinsically linked to contemporary connectionistic models of memory, and one doubts that he could have resisted *neural* nets forever. The conclusions associated with connectionist models reviewed in this handbook that "memory" is a function of a whole system, with graceful degradation as the system is destroyed, would have delighted him. Ironically, some connectionists today appeal to Lashley as providing historic support for graceful degradation as a universal property of memory substrates, without recognizing that Lashley was deeply wrong about the inapplicability of mass action to the devastating effects of relatively restricted lesions in generating amnesia, nor the specific effects of inferotemporal lesions in producing visual agnosia, and so forth. Had Lashley probed a bit deeper into ventral surfaces of the rat brain he would have surely been forced to modify his conclusions (cf., Kaada et al., 1961).

And so the conceptual frontier has become enriched, with lines of continuity but with important departures. Even more spectacularly are the changes in the technological frontier. Powerful advances in functional imaging are moving so quickly, allowing one to see the ac-

tivity of the brain for the different memory systems, and differentially for acquisition, rehearsal, and retrieval, that the story has to be intercepted in mid-flight. The statistical complexities in imaging are also so great, combined with the flood of new evidence, that one is certain that the section of the handbook on neural substrates, at least, will require almost continuous rewriting and updating. But that is the fate of handbooks. This is the first, but it is not going to be the last.

There is another way in which "story" intrudes into our contemporary scene: "false memories." Because of the publicity generated over the past five or six years by collective societies of accused parents of evidence that strongly held beliefs can be shown to give rise to genuinely experienced episodic memories that are patently false, the general public has had a very useful, if sometimes heated, education into the reconstructive, "story-telling" aspects of memory. No one who has seen the havoc that can be wreaked upon accused parents by adult children who have genuinely held but demonstrably false memories of abuse can fail to see the power of reconstructive processes. Distortions as evidenced in short-term recall of associative lists, reviewed by Roediger and McDermott in the handbook, also share the quality seen in the "false memory" domain of the certainty with which such memories can be held—indeed, in the long term it is part of the signature of explicit memory. Who can have a genuine memory of an event that has the very quality of being *experienced* as being "false"? In any event, one benefit of the debate provoked by the false memory epidemic is the knowledge and interest of the general public in the power of the creative, reconstructive, story-telling aspects of memories, bolstered by a string of well-informed and readable books by Pendergrast (1996), Ofshe and Watters (1994), Yapko (1994), and as a major part of the spectrum of popular treatises such as that by Schacter (1996). These aspects of the "memory story" are also penetrating, albeit slowly, into the legal and professional therapeutic professions.

Bartlett (1932) provocatively asserted that the function of memory "is *not* the re-excitation of innumerable fixed, lifeless and fragmentary traces. It is an imaginative reconstruction, or construction, built out of the relation of our attitude towards a whole active mass of organized past reactions of experience, and to a little outstanding detail" (p. 213). "I have never regarded [memory] as a faculty, as a reaction narrowed and ringed round. I have regarded it rather as one achievement in the line of ceaseless struggle to master and enjoy a world full of variety and rapid change" (p. 314). "Memory in Use" is a welcome section in this handbook because it addresses the issue of just what it *is* that memory achieves. The arcane story used by Bartlett to study serial reproduction, *The War of the Ghosts*, did not itself exactly break through into the public domain, but *his* story is still very much alive.

References

Bartlett, F. C. (1932). *Remembering*. Cambridge: Cambridge University Press.

Beach, F. A., Hebb, D., Morgan, C. T., & Nissen, H. W. (Eds.). (1960). *The Neuropsychology of Lashley*. New York: McGraw-Hill.

Cowey, A., & Stoerig, P. (1995). Blindsight in monkeys. *Nature, London, 373*, 247–249.

Eysenck, M. W. (1990). (Ed.). *The Blackwell dictionary of cognitive psychology*. Oxford: Blackwells.

Kaada, B. R., Rasmussen, E. W., & Kveim, O. (1961). Effects of hippocampal lesions on maze learning and retention in rats. *Experimental Neurology, 3*, 333–355.

Lashley, K., Chow, K. L., & Semmes, J. (1951). An examination of the electrical field theory of cerebral integration. *Psychological Review, 58*, 123–136.

Ofshe, R., & Watters, E. (1994). *Making monsters: False memories, psychotherapy, and sexual hysteria*. New York: Scribner's.

Pendergrast, M. (1996). *Victims of memory*. New York: HarperCollins.

Reber, A. S. (1985). (Ed.). *The penguin dictionary of psychology*. London: Penguin Books.

Schacter, D. L. (1996). *Searching for memory*. New York: Basic Books.

Sperry, R. W., & Miner, N. (1955). Pattern perception following insertion of mica plates into visual cortex. *Journal of Comparative and Physiological Psychology, 48*, 463–469.

Stevens, S. S. (1951). (Ed.). *Handbook of experimental psychology*. New York: John Wiley.

Weiskrantz, L. (1997). *Consciousness lost and found. A neuropsychological exploration*. Oxford: Oxford University Press.

Yapko, M. D. (1994). *Suggestions of abuse: True and false memories of childhood sexual traumas*. New York: Simon & Schuster.

Subject Index

AB (neurological patient), 428
A-B/A-C paradigm, 63
absent-mindedness, 417
abstractions, 35, 112, 119
abuse testimony, 159–60, 384, 385, 387
accessibility hypothesis, 200, 201, 202
accuracy judgments, 60
  confidence relationship, 321
  of feeling-of-knowledge judgments, 200
  of flashbulb memories, 381–82
  response time and, 576
  speed tradeoff, 49
  of traumatic memories, 383
acetylcholine, 540, 543, 549
acetylcholinesterase. See AChE inhibitiors
AChE inhibitiors, 549, 550
acoustic coding. See auditory memory
acoustic confusion, 14–15
acquisition processes, 180, 471
  knowledge retention/losses and, 353, 354
  of spatial relations, 367, 369–70
action memory, enactment paradigm and, 137–45
actors, 323, 359
ACT-R theory, 559, 577
AD. See Alzheimer's disease
adaptive expertise, 109
  characterization, 119
  transfer to novel tasks and domains, 118–19

adaptive memory system, 557–69
adaptive response, 4
adrenergic hormones, 381
age
  of children's verbal coding, 84
  contextual memory and, 96, 101
  early adulthood learning as best remembered, 319
  false fame effect and, 217–18
  as false memories susceptibility factor, 158, 159, 184
  familiarity vs. recollection patterns and, 218, 219, 220, 222, 223
  of first memory, 288
  long-term retention of formally acquired knowledge and, 357–58
  memory changes with, 55, 395–405
  memory development and, 267–79, 283
  modality judgment and, 175
  nonword repetition and, 84–85
  remember/know paradigm and, 231
  reminiscence bump and, 318–19
  socialization of memory and, 283–92
  source memory and, 96, 188, 189, 223, 224, 397, 403, 600–601
  spatial memory and, 369–70

subject-performed vs. verbal tasks memory, 144
  working memory and, 400, 401, 415–16
  See also children; infancy; older people
aging. See older people
agnosia, 441, 452, 469
AIDS, 320
akinesia, 469
alcohol effects, 545
alignments, 366
alprazolam (Xanax), 540, 545
Alzheimer's disease, 26, 231, 405, 443–48, 466, 468, 469
  cholinergic hypothesis of, 543
  diagnosis of, 443
  division of attention impairment, 87
  drug effects on, 549
  drug therapy developments, 540, 549–50
  earliest cognitive deficits of, 445
  episodic memory disruption, 442, 443–45
  explicit memory impairment, 617
  false memories tendency and, 158
  frontotemporal dementia incidence vs., 449
  limbic-system related focus, 469
  memory recency and primacy effects, 79
  memory studies, 441

Alzheimer's disease (*continued*)
neocortical damage and, 443, 469
neuroimaging and, 448
neurotransmitter depletions, 540, 549
priming and, 435, 617
as progressive cognitive breakdown, 443, 444
remember/know paradigm and, 231, 451
remote memory and, 442, 444, 447–48
scopolamine effects as partial mimic, 543
semantic memory deficits, 429, 442–43, 444, 445–46, 447, 448, 451
subcortical pathology vs., 452, 453
transentorhinal cortex and, 453
working memory impairment, 442, 444, 446–47
amnesia, drug-induced, 540, 541, 543, 548
amnesia, infantile. *See* childhood amnesia
amnesia, material-specific, 468
amnesic syndrome, 21, 36, 646–47
animal model, 485–97
aphasia, 449
autonoetic awareness vs. semantic memory, 599, 604–5
characterizations, 468, 473
dementia vs., 466, 468
episodic and semantic memory deficits, 430–34
feeling-of-knowing judgments and, 203
global, 430–34, 466, 468
impaired false memories and, 158
indirect tests indicating implicit memory, 523
ironic effects of past experience and, 217
limbic system damage and, 473
material-specific, 468
memory-judgment tasks and, 174
memory recency and primacy effects, 79
nonconscious memory retention, 246, 255, 256
object discrimination problems, 494–95
priming preservation and deficits, 435, 577
probability learning impairment, 222

procedural memory retention, 398, 436, 437, 488
psychogenic/functional, 477
recollection and familiarity deficits, 221
remember/know paradigm and, 231
source memory deficits, 403–4, 599–601, 603
stress-related, 470, 472
typologies, 466, 468
See also anterograde amnesia; dementias; retrograde amnesia
amygdala, 436, 469, 471, 485, 486
damage effects, 470, 541
emotional memory storage by, 26, 380–81, 386, 387, 431, 469, 475, 506
anesthesia, 542, 543
angular gyrus, 472
anoetic consciousness, definition of, 611
anomia, 443, 445, 446
anosognosia, 443
anterior cingulate cortex, 504, 505, 508, 509, 510, 619
anterior communicating artery, 468
anterior cortex temporal lesions, 430
anterior nucleus, 475
anterior thalamus, 469, 470
anterograde amnesia, 430, 431, 433
Alzheimer's patients, 443–45
bilateral medial temporal damage and, 468
drug-induced, 544
episodic-semantic dissociation and, 605
source amnesia and, 600
antianxiety drugs, 539, 540, 543
anticholinergic drugs, 540
antidementia drugs, 549–50
antidepressive drugs, 539, 540
antihistamines, 547
antischizophrenic drugs, 539, 540
aphasia, 441, 448–49, 450, 452.
See also semantic dementia
appearance-reality tasks, 303
apraxia, 441, 452
architecture, 363
arecholine, 543
Aricept (donepezil hydrochloride), 549–50
arousal, specificity of drug effects 547–48. *See also* emotional memories
articulatory loop. *See* phonological loop

articulatory suppression, 84, 85
artificial intelligence, 15–16
artificial memory retrieval systems, 558
Asians, age of first memory, 288
Asperger syndrome, 305–6
association cortex, 432, 478
associationism, 3–27, 179, 645
chaining hypothesis, 5, 126–27, 129
cognitivist critiques of, 16–17
connectionist models and, 583–91
declarative memory and, 497
false memories and, 152
general rejection of, 129, 130
mediates, 9–10
"mindless" vs. deeper processing, 22
nonspecific transfer, 11
positional, 128, 167–68
rote learning and, 4–7
schema labeling and, 24–25
semantic memory activation, 397
serial learning studies, 4, 5–7, 16, 126–28
terminal meta-postulate, 129
transfer of prior knowledge, 11–12
two models of, 64–65
See also paired-associates learning
associative interference, 12, 13, 63, 418
by remote associations, 126, 127, 128
associative mediators, 3, 9–10, 11, 16, 17, 18, 21, 22, 24–25
associative priming, 51, 576–77, 616–17
associative recognition
adaptive memory studies, 565–67
correlational approach, 60–61
event-related potentials correlates, 528
forming and recovering, 616–17
network model, 584–87
associative symmetry, 64–65
attention
aging and reduced capacity for, 399–400, 402, 403, 404–5, 411, 413–15
Alzheimer's vs. Huntington's patients, 453, 454
connectionist network and distribution of, 593
drug effects on, 548–49, 550
nonconscious memory effects and, 250

successful encoding and, 93, 96
working memory central executive and, 507
attention division, 249
aging and, 103, 399, 413–14
Alzheimer's disease and, 87
asymmetrical effects of, 103
dichotic listening, 53
estimates of recollection and, 220
memory source errors and, 181
See also interference
attractor network model. *See* auto-associator model
attribution, 215–16, 217
first- vs. third-person, 298
second-order, 298, 299, 300, 301
theories of explicit memory, 613–14
auditory memory
acoustic coding, 81
aging and, 396
conversation recall, 320–21, 323
modality effect, 78, 130–31, 167
phonological similarity and, 84
short-term processing, 81, 82, 150
as superior to visual memory, 130
voice recognition studies, 95
word length effects, 83–84
aural presentation. *See* auditory memory
autism
recall impairments, 305
remember/know paradigm and, 231, 233
auto-associator model, 585–87, 588
autobiographical knowledge, 306
autobiographical memories, 186, 236, 466
Alzheimer impairment, 442, 444, 447–48
brain regions and, 477
characteriztion, 23
childhood inception of, 286–91, 323
concept of self and, 27, 619
definitions of, 318, 466
directly experienced events and, 318–19
emotions and, 379–88
episodic memory as, 597
experience-based model and, 612
formation of false, 187
gender differences, 288, 322

involuntary, 237–38, 316
life narratives, 318
for locales and places, 319–20
marking events, 27
for medical information, 329
methodology, 46
psychogenic amnesic brain malfunction and, 477–78
retrieval of, 340
semantic dementia and, 429, 450, 451–52
socialization and, 284
spatio-temporal continuity and, 304
See also episodic memory; event memory
automaticity, 8, 250
automatic processing, 399, 400, 403, 420
vs. controlled processing, 400
autonoetic consciousness, 229, 233–34, 300, 442, 545, 597–606, 620, 646
capabilities, 598
in children, 604
definition of, 611
of present and future, 601–2
See also consciousness
autonomic conditioning, 436
awareness. *See* consciousness

back propagation, 589–590, 591–92
backward search, 118
bandeletta diagnalis, 471
basal forebrain, 468, 473, 475
basal ganglia, 436, 437, 478
dementias, 452–53, 454, 469
nonconscious memory forms, 256
basal temporal lobe, 473
basolateral limbic circuit, 469, 471
Bayesian models, 558–59, 565, 593
BDZs. *See* benzodiazepines
behavior. *See* brain/behavior interrelations
behavioral methods, 4, 46–56, 245, 364
brain imaging technology vs., 46, 55–56
infant conditioning memory-retention studies, 269–73, 276–77
See also classical conditioning; delay conditioning; operant conditioning; S-R theory behaviorism
behaviorism, 4–14
being, representing vs., 298
belief, 297–98
false, 303

benzodiazepines, 543–49, 550
amnestic effects of, 540–41, 543
receptor ligands, 540–41
receptors and antagonists, 543–44
scopolamine effects vs., 549
beta-carbolines, 544
bias, 222, 223
spatial judgments, 364, 365–66, 367, 370, 372
bias, self-serving, 27
binding, 402
binding problem, 94
BOLD contrast, 628
bottleneck structures, 473, 474
bradyphrenia, 453
brain aging. *See* brain regions, aging and; older people
Brain and Behavioral Sciences (journal), 23
brain/behavior interrelations, 26, 36–37, 465–78
memory-judgment tasks and, 174
working memory, 630–31
brain damage
anterograde vs. retrograde amnesia and, 468
autonoetic episodic vs. semantic remembering, 599–601
behavioral effects, 26
dementia sites, 441–54, 468, 469
from emotionally stressful events, 470–71
false memories and, 403
feeling-of-knowing judgments and, 203
ironic effects of past experience and, 217
medial temporal lobe effects, 486–88
memory/awareness dissociations, 246
memory disorders and, 427–37, 466–69
as memory variable, 55, 246, 466
selective memory losses and, 429–34, 466, 628, 632
short-term memory models and, 21–22, 472
short-term vs. long-term memory impairments, 81–83
See also specific brain areas; specific conditions
brain electrical activity. *See* event-related potentials
brain imaging, 26, 45, 55–56, 466, 501–14
advances in, 628, 629, 647
Alzheimer's disease and, 448

brain imaging (*continued*)
cognitive aging and, 413
conceptual priming and, 616
episodic memory studies,
  502–6, 507, 508, 510, 513,
  633–35, 637–38
false memories and, 403
functional dissociations and,
  55
hippocampal activation and,
  504, 514
long-term memory storage sites
  and, 474
memory recall and, 475–76
memory systems studies,
  628–38
network analysis, 508, 510–12,
  513, 514
nonconscious memory forms
  and, 256
object working memory and,
  631
procedural memory studies,
  636–37, 638
radio-labelled drug use, 550
semantic dementia and, 452
semantic memory retrieval
  studies, 509–10, 513
semantic memory studies,
  502–4, 508, 632–33
semantic vs. episodic brain
  area activation, 599
short-term and working memory studies, 77, 85, 472
working memory studies,
  506–8, 510–12, 513, 630–
  32, 637
See also brain regions
brain injury. *See* brain damage
brain-injury selective, memory
  disorders, 427–37
brain regions
aging and, 402–5, 411–21
analysis of memory processes
  and, 464–78
autobiographical memories
  and, 477
benzodiazepine receptors,
  540–41
consciousness and, 619–20
dementias and, 441–54, 468,
  469
emotional embedding and,
  469–78
emotional eyewitness memory
  and, 26, 380–81
encoding and, 475, 504, 510
episodic memory and, 26, 189,
  402, 413, 473, 475, 477, 504,
  508, 510, 592, 599–602,
  634–35, 637–38
imaging techniques. *See* brain
  imaging technology

infantile amnesia and, 279
knowing and, 618
language elements and, 372
memory for places and, 365
memory-judgment tasks and,
  173–74
memory processing and, 478
memory retrieval and, 475–78
network analysis, 508–9
new memory formation and
  storage, 95
nonconscious memory and,
  256
phonological short-term store,
  85
practice and shift in pathways,
  636
priming and, 435, 469, 488,
  611–12
procedural memory and, 474–
  75, 478, 488, 637
recall and, 26, 475–78
remember/know paradigm
  and, 233, 613
retrieval and, 475–78, 510
semantic memory and, 443,
  502, 508, 632–33
short-term memory and, 21–
  22, 26, 81, 246, 427–29,
  471–72, 474, 478
source memory and, 188–89
spatial relations, 371, 496
trauma and biochemical
  changes in, 470–71
traumatic memories and,
  386–87
visual vs. verbal short-term
  memory, 81
working memory and, 26, 472,
  506–8, 510–12, 513, 630–
  32, 637
brain volume, 411, 413
Broca's area, 85, 508, 509, 630,
  633
Brown-Peterson paradigm, 53
bundle hypothesis, 126. *See also*
  chaining hypothesis
bystander misidentification phenomenon, 321

canonical axes, 366–67
capacity, 94
CARA hypothesis, 189
Cardiff conference (1978),
  315–16
catastrophic interference, 591–93
categorization
concepts and, 34
connectionist, 593
models of, 577
priming and, 39–40
category-specific knowledge,
  446, 632

caudate dysfunction, age-related
  cognitive slowing and, 415
caudate nucleus, 453
central executive (working memory), 83, 86, 87–88, 400,
  442, 452, 506, 630
activation analysis, 508
dementia's impairment of, 441,
  442, 444, 446, 450, 452, 453
evidence for, 631–32
initial model, 87
overview, 507–8
cerebellum, 436, 469, 478, 505,
  508, 509
benzodiazepine receptors, 540
cerebral cortex, 467, 474, 540
cerebral flood flow. *See* regional
  cerebral blood flow
cerebral ischemia, 431, 490
cerebrovascular disease, 454
chaining hypothesis, 5, 126–27,
  129
Challenger explosion ((1986),
  317, 381–82, 563
CHARM model, 64, 199–200, 202
chess experts, 55, 98
CHILDES database, 560–64, 565
childhood abuse, 159–60, 188,
  317, 321–22
childhood amnesia, 279, 286,
  288, 306–7, 318
children, 299–307
abuse testimony veracity, 159,
  321–22
appearance-reality differentiation, 303
autobiographical memory beginnings, 286–91, 323
autonoetic awareness vs. semantic memory, 599, 602–4,
  606
episodic memory capacity,
  285–86, 602–4
eyewitness source monitoring
  problems, 184
false memory suggestibility,
  150, 156, 157, 158, 159, 184,
  302–3, 304, 321–22
free recall development, 304–6
future-oriented talk/memory
  relationship, 289
imagination inflation, 156
interpersonal reality monitoring, 188
learned recall strategies,
  291–92
memory recency and primacy
  effects, 79
memory scripts, 285
memory span-speed of articulation relationship, 84
metamemory, 292, 301–2,
  303–4, 307, 392

reality monitoring, 302, 307
reduced remembering, 231
socialization of memory processes, 283–92, 323–24
spatial memory development, 369–70
speech interactions study, 560–64
choline, 549
cholinergic system, 413, 473, 543–49, 550
chorea, 453
chromosome 4, 453
chromosome 17, 449
chronological illusion, 171
chunking, 129
  definition of, 11–12, 97, 115
  digit span recall, 79
  expert domain-related memory and, 115–16
  usefulness in initial encoding, 97
cingulate gyrus, 469, 470, 475
cingulum, 469, 509, 510
classical conditioning, 269–70, 436, 620
clusters, 16, 60
coding. *See* encoding
cognitive collage, 370
cognitive control, 411, 412, 415–21
Cognitive Failure Questionnaire, 322
cognitive hypothesis, 319
cognitive interview, 321, 322
cognitive map, 319, 363–64, 365, 370
"Cognitive Maps in Rats and Men" (Tolman), 363–64
cognitive memory, 627
cognitive processes, 7–8, 14–25
  age-related deficits, 399, 401, 411, 412, 413–21
  Alzheimer's progressive breakdown, 443, 444, 445
  Alzheimer's vs. Huntington's, 453
  Cartesian object-level, 197
  dementia-related deficits, 441
  effective memorization processes, 283–84
  event-related potentials studies, 521–34
  Huntington's disease impairment, 453, 454
  memory representations, 180, 245. *See also* metamemory
  nonconscious memory and, 256
  Parkinson's disease impairment, 453
  procedural memory vs., 37–38, 636

rational analysis approach, 557–69
reference points, 366
semantic dementia impairment, 450–52
source monitoring, 179–89
spatial memory and, 363–64, 368, 372
subcortical dementias, 452–54
vascular dementia impairment, 454
cognitive psychology, 14–25, 37–38, 42
  as active and constructive, 100
  antecedents, 14
  cognitive map concept, 363–64
  computer models, 15
  information processing, 14–15
  memory-consciousness relationship, 245
  memory subdivisions theories, 466
  methodological changes, 46, 47
  neuropsychology relationship, 77
  short-term memory study, 77
  verbal codes emphasis, 95
Cognitive Psychology (Neisser), 151
cognitive skills, 7–8
cognitive slowing, 411, 412, 415
collective memories, 326
communication engineering, 15–16
communication theory. *See* information processing
competing associations, 12, 13
composite holographic model of memory, 584
compound cue model, 577
comprehension, illusion of, 204–5
computed tomography (CT), 448
computer models
  artificial intelligence, 15–16
  cognition, 14
  memory encoding and retrieval, 93, 116, 558
  natural language understanding, 23
  short-term and working memory, 77, 78
concentration camp survivors, 318, 383
concept of self
  autobiographic memory and, 27, 619
  childhood development of, 299, 300, 301, 302, 306, 307
concept representation units, 588

concepts, 24–25, 33–42, 588
  connectionist network, 578, 583–94
  definition of, 24, 33–34
  knowledge acquisition of, 234
conceptual analysis, 34–35
conceptual codes, sensory codes vs., 94–95
conceptually driven implicit memory, 523
conceptual priming, 34, 40, 55, 616, 617–18, 636
conceptual process, 34
  perception vs., 250, 252, 257
concordance, doctrine of, 38
conditioned reflexes. *See* behavioral methods
confabulation, 246, 473
Confessions of an English Opium-Eater (de Quincey), 541
confidence ratings, 49
confusion errors, 9
connectionist models of memory, 578, 583–94, 647
  catastrophic interference, 591–93
  local and distributed representations, 584–85
  vs. symbolic models of semantic memory, 587–93
consciousness, 609–21
  autonoetic, 229, 233–34, 300, 442, 545, 597–606, 611
  childhood development of, 299, 300, 301–2, 306, 307
  definitions of, 609
  drug alterations of, 541, 542
  frontal vs. medial temporal lobes as mediators of, 619–20
  functional theories, 610–14
  as giving relevance to memory, 646
  intentionality relationship, 252, 255
  memory and knowing as states of, 229–30, 238–39, 245, 436, 437, 646
  memory-judgment tasks and, 174–75
  memory without, 36–37, 246–49. *See also* nonconscious memory
  mere-exposure studies, 249–50, 257
  research evaluation, 615–16
  self-report tests, 252–53
  structural theories, 614–15
  theories of, 602–21
  types of, 611
  See also episodic memory; explicit memory;

conscious recollecion. *See* recollection

conscious reflection, 473

constructive retrieval, 100, 179–80

context, 96, 99, 316
  age deficit in memory for, 397, 399, 400–401
  detail recollection and, 18, 60, 421
  encoding reinstatement and, 101
  as episodic vs. semantic memory distinction, 632
  event recency and, 18
  implicit memory and, 255
  infant memory retention, 277, 278
  memory need probability and, 558–59, 564–67
  nonconscious memory and, 255, 256
  recognition and, 401
  recollection and, 18, 60, 421, 523
  retrieval and, 101, 337, 414–15
  spatial memory and, 366–67, 369
  stimuli, 12, 17–19, 336
  study/retrieval relationship, 565
  See also cued recall; remember/know paradigm; environmental support hypothesis

context judgments, 6, 17–19

contextual support, 101, 397, 399, 400–401, 414–15, 421

contingency analyses, 59–67

continuum of sensitivity, encoding variables and, 138, 145

control, 255

controlled processing, automatic processing vs., 400

convergence-problem paradigm, 111–12, 112–14

conversation recall, 320–21, 323

convolutional model of memory. *See* TODAM model

copy cues, 47, 531

core concept, definition ability, 446

Corsi block tapping task, 80–81

cortex, 413
  Alzheimer's involvement, 443
  See also cortical damage; *specific sections*

Cortical Asymmetry of Reflective Activity (CARA) hypothesis, 189

cortical damage, 469
  episodic memory disruption, 442
  short-term memory disorders, 427–29, 471–72, 474, 478

cortical dementia, 452–53, 454, 469
  contrasted with subcortical dementia, 453
  See also Alzheimer's disease; Huntington's disease

COSIT (Conference on Spatial Information Theory), 363

Creative Imagination Scale, 158, 323

cross-cultural differences, autobiographical memories, 288

cross-indexed memories, 27

cryptomnesia, 181

CT (computed tomography), 448

cued recall, 50, 316
  children's memory and, 303, 304, 305, 307, 324
  contextual support, 401
  correlational approach, 60–61, 63–64, 65, 66, 67
  event-related potentials and, 521, 523, 531–33
  eyewitness suggestibility and, 154, 156–57, 182–84, 321
  false memory relationship, 154, 156–57, 160, 187
  free recall vs., 305, 335
  hippocampal damage impairment of, 488
  infant studies, 271–72, 277
  memory judgments, 165
  priming method, 201–2
  process-dissociation procedure and, 221–22
  recognition and, 47, 223
  retrieval intentionality criterion and, 252
  SAM model, 573
  stored information interaction, 475
  tip-of-the-tongue states and, 201
  See also cues; retrieval cues; stimulating cue

cue familiarity hypothesis, 199–200, 201–2

cues
  associative, 16–17
  children's use of cognitive, 303
  compound, 577
  conceptual tests, 250
  encoding and retrieval, 16–17, 23, 24–25, 98, 99, 100–101, 336, 337
  nonconscious, 41
  part-list inhibitions, 103
  as prospective reminders, 417
  retrieval, 98, 100–101, 250, 335–36, 414, 475
  SAM model, 573

target relation specificity, 98
  verbal, 52
  See also cued recall; free recall

curve plotting performance, 7

cytoarchitectonics, 466, 467

data-driven implicit memory, 523

date recall, for life events, 319

daydreaming, 598, 601, 606

deaf signers, 96

decay, of memories, 12, 13, 19

decision-bound models of categorization, 577

declarative memory, 598–99, 627
  associating function of, 497
  brain-imaging studies, 501
  definition of, 395–96, 486
  hippocampus and, 402, 497, 514
  medial temporal region and, 402–3, 486, 488
  procedural memory vs., 37–38, 222, 398
  See also episodic memory; explicit memory; semantic memory

decoding, 14

deep reasoning, 118, 119

defensiveness, 322

deferred imitation, infant studies, 271–73, 277, 278, 602–3, 604

delay conditioning, 436, 488, 620

delayed memories. *See* recovered memories

delayed nonmatching to sample (DNMS) task
  infant studies, 274
  monkey hippocampal damage tests, 490–91, 492

delayed recognition span task, hippocampal damage in monkeys, 490

delayed response (DR) tasks, infant studies, 273–74, 278, 299, 602

delta rule, 586, 589–90

dementia of frontal type (DFT), 448–50, 452

dementias, 441–54
  amnesia vs., 466, 468
  brain damage sites, 441–54, 468, 469
  definition of, 441
  drug-induced pseudo-, 540
  first FDA-approved drug for, 549
  frontotemporal, 448–52
  remember/know paradigm and, 231, 451
  semantic, 429, 441, 443, 448–52, 618

subcortical, 452–54, 469, 647
See also Alzheimer's disease
denotation, 35
dentate gyrus, 451, 485, 489
depression, 441
  Huntington's disease and, 453
  memory recall and, 322–23
descriptions. *See* language
designation, 35
desire, 297–98
details, memory for. *See* context
development of memory
  autonoetic awareness, 604
  infant, 267–79, 285–86
  preschool children, 602–4
  socialization process and, 283–92, 323–24
  spatial memory and, 363, 369–70
  See also age
DFT. *See* dementia of frontal type
diagrammatic space, 371
diary studies, 319
diazepam (Valium)), 540, 542, 543, 545
dichotic listening, 53
diencephalic amnesia, 468
digit-span test, 50, 79, 129, 442
diphenhydramine, 547
directed forgetting, 54, 418, 419
direction judgment, 366, 367, 368
direct tests, 16–19, 304
  vs. indirect tests, 19, 523
disasters, recollections of, 318
discovered memories. *See* recovered memories
discrimination learning, 7, 9–10, 167–68, 495–96
dissociation, 54–55
  consciousness/intentionality, 255
  consciousness/memory, 246–49, 256
  consciousness models, 598–99, 614
  direct/indirect test performance, 523
  episodic/semantic memory, 599–605
  five methods of differentiating drug effects on memory, 547, 548
  implicit/explicit, 252
  memory systems' convergent, 629
  between memory tasks, 59, 139, 145, 629
  preverbal infant memory, 278
  priming/recall, 435
  recall/recognition, 252

remembering/knowing, 230–31, 233, 239
short-term memory, 55, 59
susceptibility to false autobiographical memories and, 187
from traumatic event, 386
See also process dissociation
Dissociative Experiences Scale, 158, 323
distances, mental representations and, 366–67
distinctiveness, 98, 138
distinctiveness/fluency framework, 234, 240
distinct representation models of consciousness, 614–15
distortions of memory, 18, 149–60, 647. *See also* false memories
distractions
  automatic performance despite, 8
  older adults and irrelevant information, 401, 418, 419
distractor tasks, 53
distributed auto-associator memory model, 585–87, 612
distributed representation, 584
divided attention. *See* attention division
DNMS task. *See* delayed non-matching to sample (DNMS) task
domain-related knowledge
  expertise and, 114–18, 284
  expertise transfer to novel tasks, 119
  feeling-of-knowing task and, 202
  illusions of comprehension and, 204–5
  memory's relatedness effects and, 151
  specific memory systems and, 628, 629
donepezil hydrochloride (Aricept), 549–50
Doors and Peoples Test, 444
dopaminergic system, 413, 415
dorsomedial thalamic system, 431, 432, 433
double dissociation, 54, 55
dreams
  interpretation, 385
  memory representations of, 180
DRM paradigm, 403
DR tasks. *See* delayed response (DR) tasks
drugs. *See* psychopharmacology
drug state-dependency, 546–47
dual-code theory, 95, 138
dual-task methodology, 53, 548

dysarthric patients, 85
dysexecutive syndrome, 87
dyslexia, surface, 450
dysphasia, 427
dyspraxia, 85

echoic memory, 396
echolalia, 450
ecological validity, 26
ecphory, 475, 477–78
editing monitor, 9–10
educational system
  maintenance of knowledge and, 347–60
  memory training and, 284
EEG samples. *See* event-related potentials
effective connectivity, functional connectivity vs., 509
effortful processing, 399, 400
effortless retrieval, 338
ego development, 323
elaboration
  expert long-term working memory and, 116, 117
  recognition memory and, 236
elaborative processing, 94, 96
elderly. *See* older people
Elementary Perceiver and Memorizer (computer program), 116
e-mail (electronic mail), memory retrieval study and, 560–64
emotional memories, 379–88
  amygdala storage of, 26, 380–81, 386, 387, 431, 469, 475, 506
  embedding and, 469–78
  flashbulb, 317, 381–83, 388
  mnestic block syndrome and, 470–71, 477
  personality characteristics and, 322
  as "recovered," 159–60, 188, 384–86
  traumatic, 383–88, 470–71, 477, 478
  See also eyewitness testimony
empiricism, definition of, 3
enactment paradigm. *See* subject-performed tasks
encephalitis, 443, 446
encoding, 14, 93–103, 245
  acquisition of memory and, 471
  action vs. nonenacted events, 137–38, 142, 144, 145
  adaptive memory system and, 565
  aging and changes in, 396–97, 399, 413–15
  Alzheimer's defective, 445
  automatic, 170

encoding (*continued*)
  brain damage and, 427
  brain imaging studies and, 504, 510
  brain regions and, 475, 504, 510
  catastrophic interference problem and, 592
  childhood amnesia and, 306
  chunking and, 97
  contextual memory and, 96, 565, 567
  definition of, 93
  dementia and, 442
  divided attention and, 103
  drug-impairment of, 544–45
  dual-code hypothesis, 95
  episodic memory and, 234, 475, 504, 510, 513, 634–35, 637–38
  event-related potentials and, 522
  expertise and, 114, 116–17
  external variables, 98
  factors, 51–55
  familiarity vs. recollection, 523
  functional network model, 512
  high arousal effect on, 380
  long-term knowledge retention and, 352
  meaning involvement, 101–2
  mental spaces, 364–65
  mere-exposure studies, 249–50
  nature of memory codes and, 94–95
  nonlimbic, neocortical system and, 473
  operational factors, 96–97
  personal retrieval cues and, 336
  presentation frequency and, 169
  prior knowledge and, 96, 98, 179, 247, 248, 249
  retrieval interactions, 99, 100–102, 103, 337, 475, 513
  rule abstraction and, 119
  self-reference effect, 169
  semantic memory and, 234, 504, 634
  sensitivity continuum and, 138, 145
  specificity principle, 19, 99, 100–101, 102, 113, 234, 337, 396–97
  of subject-performed tasks, 137–39, 140
  three-store model, 93–94
  of time, 171
  of training task, 110–12, 119
  two subprocesses, 504
  types of memory code, 95–96, 100
  See also retrieval processes

engram, 468
entorhinal cortex, 432, 451, 475, 485, 487, 488, 496
environmental support hypothesis, 101, 397, 399, 400–401, 414–15, 421. *See also* context
EPAM IV (computer program), 116
epileptics, remember/know paradigm and, 231, 233
episodic memory, 466, 597–606, 627
  activation analysis, 508, 510, 514
  age deficit, 144, 189, 396–98, 401, 413
  age of emergence, 55, 284, 301
  age of learning and, 319
  Alzheimer's deficit, 443–45
  Alzheimer's vs. Huntington's patients, 453
  autobiographical as dated memory, 23
  autonoetic consciousness and, 229, 233–34, 300, 442, 597–606, 611
  brain imaging studies, 502–6, 507, 508, 510, 513, 633–35, 637–38
  brain regions and, 26, 189, 402, 413, 473, 475, 477, 504, 508, 510, 592, 599–602, 634–35, 637–38
  characteristics of, 597–98
  children's capacity for, 285–86, 602–4
  conceptual knowledge and, 234
  consolidation and, 451
  cued recall, 531–33
  decreased cerebral glucose metabolism effects, 474
  definitions of, 395–96, 442, 502–3, 597, 605, 628, 633
  dementia impairment, 442, 449–50
  in developmental hierarchy, 278, 304
  domain, 628
  drug effects on, 544–45, 547, 549, 599
  elective remembering losses, 598
  encoding, 234, 475, 504, 510, 513, 634–35, 637–38
  essential ingredients for, 300–301, 451
  event memory vs., 285
  event-related potentials study, 530–33
  experts' recall and recognition superiority, 114

experts' short-term and long-term performance, 115–18
  life events studies, 316
  for life experiences, 315–24
  memory judgments test of, 166
  retrieval of, 442, 504–6, 510, 512, 513, 514, 530–31, 597, 598, 635, 637–38
  as self-referential mental state, 300–304
  semantic dementia's selective impairment of, 450, 618
  semantic memory differentiated from, 22–23, 55, 316, 395–96, 450–51, 598–605, 618, 632
  semantic memory interaction, 151, 598–99
  source monitoring, 179–88
  successive tests, 62, 67
  targeted vs. open recall, 316
  three major memory stores within, 396
  See also false memories
ERP studies. *See* event-related potentials
error-correcting learning rule, 586–87, 588, 589, 593–94
estrogen therapy, 550
event memory
  associations and, 27
  of childhood, 285, 286–89, 301, 603
  diary studies, 319
  direct experience and, 318–19
  for emotional incidents, 379–88
  episodic memory vs., 603
  explicit vs. implicit, 522–23
  language and, 288–90, 324
  for life experiences, 315–24
  prospective remembering and, 50–51, 398, 417
  recency and, 18
  reception context for, 317–18
  See also autobiographical memories; episodic memory
event-related potentials (ERPs), 521–34
  aging and, 415, 416
  drug effects on, 547
  episodic memory cued recall and, 522, 523, 531–33
  explicit memory retrieval and, 526–30
  implicit memory and, 523–26
  limitations in memory research, 522
  old/new effect, 527, 528
  remember/know paradigm and, 233, 527, 529
everyday memory, 26–27, 319–21

evolution, 4, 84, 468, 636, 638
exclusion test, 51, 237
executive control system, 400
  dysfunction, 441, 444, 446,
    450, 452, 453, 454
  See also central executive
exemplar-based categorization
  models, 577
experience-based theories of consciousness, 611–13
  concept of self and, 301–2,
    306, 619
experiential awareness. *See* experience-based theories of consciousness
experimental methods, 45–56
  distractor tasks, 54
  eclectic, 347–48
  empirical regularities, 62–65
  encoding conditions, 51–53
  psychopharmacological effects
    on memory, 542–43
  retention interval conditions,
    53–54
  retrieval conditions, 47–55
  for serial learning pioneer stud-
    ies, 125–26
  task analysis, 59–62
  three phases, 45–46
  See also models of memory
experimenter-performed task,
  140
expertise and memory, 55, 109,
  114–19
  adaptive transfer, 118–19
  adaptive vs. routine, 109, 110,
    118, 119
  career requirements, 26–27
  deep reasoning and, 118
  domain information, 114–15,
    117, 284
  encoding and, 98
  long-term working memory as
    hallmark of, 117
  schematic representation,
    114–15
  transfer of learning and, 109,
    114, 118–19
expert memorists, 26–27
explicit memory, 47–51, 55, 102,
  627
  amnesiac impairment, 436
  attribution theories of, 613–14
  brain imaging studies, 501–14
  conscious awareness and, 611,
    612, 613–14, 620
  definition of, 486, 522
  in developmental hierarchy,
    278, 284, 285, 299
  dissociation and, 54, 250
  drug impairment of, 545
  event-related potentials and re-
    trieval of, 526–30

familiarity/recollection fractionation, 523
fluent reprocessing, 254
frontal cortex region and, 26
frontal lobes vs. medial temporal lobes as mediators of,
  619–20
  hippocampus and, 497
  implicit memory vs., 240,
    522–23, 615
  life events research, 316
  medial temporal region and,
    402–3, 486, 488, 514, 620
  priming relation, 616–18
  procedural (nondeclarative)
    vs., 37–38
  successive tests, 62
  test methods for, 16–19, 486
  theory of mind for, 298–300
  See also declarative memory;
    episodic memory; semantic
    memory
exploration, maps vs., 367–68
extra-list cues, 50
extrastriate cortex, 631
eyewitness testimony, 46, 54,
  150, 151, 159–60
  bystander misidentification,
    321
  children's testimony, 321–22
  cognitive interview and, 321
  cued recall effects on, 154,
    156–57, 182–84, 321
  effects of emotion on, 379–81,
    388
  laboratory vs. field studies, 321
  statement reality analysis,
    187–88
  suggestibility factor, 181–84
  unconscious transference, 184
face recognition studies
  Alzheimer's effects, 448, 449
  amnesia types and, 468, 469
  brain region and, 452
  encoding and, 95
  false fame paradigm, 154–55,
    181, 216, 217–18, 420
  familiarity and recognition re-
    lationship, 568
  long-term recall retention, 348,
    358, 359
  network model, 511–12
  older vs. younger adults and,
    420
  source amnesia and, 599–601
  tip-of-the-tongue state and, 398
  See also fame judgment task

factor X (unlearning), 150
fallibility of memory. *See* false
  memories
false alarm rate, recognition, 48,
  49, 50

false belief, 303
false fame effect, 154–55, 181,
  216, 217–18
  aging and, 420
false memories, 149–60, 647
  aging and susceptibility to,
    158, 224, 403, 404–5
  attentional control and, 404
  autobiographical, 187, 302
  of childhood, 302–3, 304, 323
  children's suggestibility and,
    150, 156, 158, 159, 167, 184,
    302–3, 321–22
  discovered memories as,
    385–86
  environmental conditions and,
    475
  factors creating, 151–58, 179–
    80, 181
  fluency of processing and, 254
  guessing and, 157
  hypnosis and, 157
  illusions of knowing and,
    205–6
  imagination as source, 155–56,
    159, 160
  implicit associative responses
    and, 152–53, 179–80
  individual susceptibility differ-
    ences, 158, 187
  in infancy, 277–78
  initial encoding of event and,
    100
  interference as source, 154,
    160
  interpersonal reality monitor-
    ing and, 187–88
  life experiences recall and, 315
  omission vs. commission, 148
  psychotherapeutic techniques
    eliciting, 385
  recovered memories as,
    159–60
  relatedness effect and, 152–53
  remember/know paradigm
    and, 233, 238
  retrieval processing and, 156–
    57, 342, 475
  social factors and, 157–58,
    159, 160
  source monitoring framework,
    180–89
  suggestion and, 302–3, 317
  See also eyewitness testimony
false recognition, 152–53
fame judgment task, 99, 154–55,
  216, 224
  Alzheimer's effects, 448
  false fame paradigm, 154–55,
    181, 216, 217–18
  fluent reprocessing and, 254
  older vs. younger adults and,
    420

familiarity, 10, 11, 49, 185, 215–25, 434, 497, 618
  adaptive memory and, 568
  of cues, 199–200, 201–2
  event-related potentials correlates, 529
  free recall and, 434
  functional differences between recollection and, 215–17, 523
  "just know" responses and, 224, 234, 239
  perceptual fluency and, 613
  recognition memory and, 218, 219, 221, 230, 236, 528–29, 618–19
  recollection vs., 217–18, 222–23, 224–25, 239, 523, 529, 611, 618–19
  remember/know paradigm and, 229–30, 236–37, 338, 420
  See also false fame effect
familiarization, infant memory retention and, 268, 269
famous names list
  serial learning of, 99
  See also fame judgment task
fan effect, 418
fantasies, 598
feeling-of-knowing judgments, 198, 199–206, 434
  accuracy of, 200, 205
  conceptual knowledge and, 234
  error types, 201
  factors affecting, 338
  hindsight bias, 206
  overconfidence, 204–5
  prefrontal cortex damage and, 434
  retrieval search and, 201, 338–39, 341
  test effects, 203–4
  tip-of-the-tongue states, 197, 199, 200–201, 398
  on unknown, 202–3
first-person attribution, 298
flashbacks, traumatic memories as, 336, 387
flashbulb memories, 317, 381–83, 388
fluent processing, 254
flumazenil, 544, 547, 549
flunitrazepam, 543
fMRI. *See* functional magnetic resonance imaging
Food and Drug Administration, 549
food consumption, memory for, 320
forced-choice recognition test, 47, 49

forgetting, 12–14, 149, 245
  as adaptive response, 557
  aging and, 417, 418
  Alzheimer's rate of, 445
  curve, 5, 6
  directed, 54, 418
  of early childhood events. *See* childhood amnesia
  episodic memory susceptibility to, 23
  infancy studies, 268–69, 279
  interference and, 13–14, 153–55, 160, 167
  learning spacing effect and, 354
  long-lasting priming effects on, 102
  major reasons, 12–13, 98–99
  memory distortions vs., 149
  retrieval cues and, 17
  semantic dementia complaints, 450
  short-term, 79, 81, 94
  of sources. *See* source memory
  of specific aspects over general, 339
  of traumatic memories, 383–84, 386
  See also amnesiac syndrome; dementias; recovered memories
forgot-it-all-along effect, 384
fornix, 430, 431, 469, 470
fractionating memory, 468, 523
fragmentary sensory memories, of traumatic experiences, 386
fragment completion, 51, 55, 398, 404
frames of reference. *See* context
free-association responses, 127–28
free-choice recognition test, 47–48, 49
free recall, 16–17, 21, 22, 25
  age-related deficits in, 401, 414, 417
  children and, 304–6, 307
  correlational approach, 60
  cued recall vs., 305, 335
  drug-impairment of, 544
  hippocampal damage impairment of, 488
  intra-list similarity and, 132
  memory validity vs. cued recall, 156
  modified, 54, 63, 68
  power of suggestion and, 150
  prefrontal cortex damage and, 434
  recency effect, 130
  SAM model, 224, 572, 573
  self-initiated activity and, 101

serial recall vs., 50
short-term verbal memory and, 79, 81
short-term vs. long-term memory and, 81
similarity and information type, 131
state-dependent, 337
subject-performed tasks and, 141
understanding of experienced event and, 304–6
verbal tasks and, 144
frequency-in-context judgments, 18
frequency judgments, 18, 165, 166, 168–73, 174, 175
frontal dementia, 448–450, 452
frontal leucotomy, 601–2
frontal lobes
  aging effects on, 402–4, 405, 413, 414, 415, 416, 419
  confabulation and, 246
  dementia and, 448–50, 452
  different autonoetic and noetic consciousness subregions, 611, 612, 620
  episodic memory and, 413, 510, 599–602
  executive function area specialization, 87, 453, 454
  explicit memory and, 26, 619–20
  historical memory theories and, 466
  memory-judgment tasks and, 174
  memory systems and, 633, 634, 635, 636, 637, 638
  metamemory and, 203
  progressive degeneration, 448
  short-term memory maintenance and, 81
  source memory and, 189
  working memory and, 26, 507–8, 511
  See also prefrontal cortex
frontal syndrome. *See* dysexecutive syndrome
frontostriatal dementia, 453, 469
frontotemporal dementia (Pick's disease), 448–52, 469
  introduction of term, 449
  major clinical subtypes, 449
  See also semantic dementia
FTD. *See* frontotemporal dementia
functional connectivity, effective connectivity vs., 509
functional dissociation, 54, 55
functional incompatibility, 629

functional magnetic resonance imaging, 26, 256, 505, 507, 531, 618
of aging brain, 413
data acquisition and analysis, 501–2
episodic memory studies, 634–35
as five major memory systems evidence, 630–38
semantic memory studies, 632, 634–35
technique, 628
functional networks. *See* network models of memory
functional neuroimaging, 501, 506
functional theories of consciousness, 610–14
future actions. *See* prospective remembering

GABA (gamma-aminobutyric acid), 543, 544, 549
agonists, 470–71
game show paradigm, 201
gamma-aminobuytric acid. *See* GABA
GD (neurological patient), 488
gender differences
in age of first memory, 288
in autobiographical narratives, 288, 322
in long-term retention of formally acquired knowledge, 358
general hidden units, 588
generalization-discrimination analysis, 9–10
generation effect, 52, 103
generation-recognition effect, 99, 533
genetics, dementia disorders and, 449, 453–54
geography, 363, 366
Gestalt psychology, 166
glial cells, 474
global amnesic syndrome, 430–34, 466, 468
global dementias. *See* dementias
global matching models, 173
global memory models, 224, 572–77
new generations, 575–76
test falsifications, 574–75
glucocorticoids, 470–71
glucose metabolism, 474
gluttony, 449
goal-relevant information, 114–15
nonconscious memory and, 255
goal statements, 111
grouping. *See* chunking

group narratives, 324
guessing, 47, 150, 157, 204, 219, 238
know responses vs., 239–40
Gulf War beginning (1991), memories of, 317

habit, 222, 278, 488, 496
habit memory, 627
habituation, infant memory retention and, 267, 268–69
Halcion (triazolam), 540, 543, 545
HD. *See* Huntington's disease
hearing. *See* auditory memory
Hebbian learning rule, 584–85, 593–94
hemineglect, 365
hemispheric encoding/retrieval asymmetry. *See* HERA model
HERA-model (hemispheric Encoding/Retrieval Asymmetry), 475–76, 513, 514
herpes simplex virus, 443, 446
hidden units, 588, 589
hierarchical organization
serial learning, 128–29
spatial memory, 366, 370
symbolic model of semantic memory, 587, 588
high-level skills and performance, 8
Hillsborough soccer riot (1989), memories of, 317
hindsight bias, 206, 384
hippocampal formation
conscious apprehension and, 620
definition of, 485
remembering and, 618
See also entorhinal cortex
hippocampal region, 488–97
brain imaging studies and, 514
contribution to memory, 496–97
damage effects on memory, 488
definition of, 485
episodic memory activation, 510, 514
episodic memory novelty/encoding hypothesis, 504
object discrimination learning and, 494–96
See also dentate gyrus; subicular complex
hippocampal volume, memory and, 413
hippocampus, 485–97
Alzheimer's involvement, 443
brain imaging studies, 504
and conscious memory, 246, 616

as convergence point within medial temporal lobe, 496
damage effects, 431, 433, 434, 485, 488
damage effects on short-term memory, 21, 26, 246
declarative memory and, 402, 497, 514
encoding and, 414, 415, 634
episodic memory and, 413, 451, 508, 599, 634
independent learning system in, 225
memory-judgment phenomena and, 173–74, 175
Papez circuit, 469, 470
recognition memory and, 488–89, 490, 491–92, 497
route/location recollection and, 367, 369
selective memory disorders and, 431, 475
sparse conjunctive representations and, 592
spatial relations and, 367, 369, 496
stress as functional impairment of, 386–87
temporal cortex and, 473
terminology clarifications, 485
traumatic memories and, 387–88
visual and spatial memory and, 496
volume and memory, 413
hit rate, recognition, 48, 49, 50
HM (neurological patient), 21, 81, 402, 435, 468, 473, 485, 486, 497, 605, 647
holisitic associations model, 65–65
Human Memory: Theory and Data (Murdock), 572
Huntington's disease, 436, 437, 452, 468, 469
characteristics, 453–54
Hydergine, 550
hypermnesia, 356, 387
hypnosis, pseudomemories and, 157, 187, 316, 385
hypoxia, 431

IARs. *See* implicit associative responses
iconic memory, 396
identification
definition of, 38–39
priming and, 39–40
illusions of memory. *See* false memories
illusory truth effect, 181
image association. *See* visual imagery

Image of the City, The (Lynch), 363

imagery. *See* visual imagery; visual memory

imagination
autonoetic awareness and, 598
children's reality monitoring and, 302
false memories and, 155–56, 159, 160, 184
inflation of, 156
memory representations, 180

imaging technology. *See* brain imaging technology

imitation. *See* deferred imitation

immediate memory. *See* short-term memory

implicit associative responses, 152, 179–80, 217, 316

implicit learning, 252

implicit memory, 38–40, 102, 430, 629, 646
as age independent, 400, 401
anoetic consciousness and, 611
brain injury-related deficits, 436–37
childhood, 299, 300, 306
contingency analysis, 65
definition of, 255, 522
in developmental hierarchy, 278, 284
dissociation and, 54, 250, 252, 255
event-related potentials and, 523–26, 614
explicit memory vs., 240, 522–23, 615
false fame phenomenon and, 217
familiarity and, 236
fluent reprocessing and, 254
fractionations of, 523
habit as form of, 222
memory judgments and, 174–75
models, 577–78
paradigms tapping, 102
priming effects, 51, 577–78
semantic memory deficits and, 430
study-test compatibility effects, 102
tests, 47, 51, 62, 250–53, 257, 523
See also nonconscious memory

impression formation, nonconscious memory and, 245

incidental recall, intentional vs., 117

incidental vs. intentional instructions, 52

independent associations model, 64–65

indirect tests
direct vs., 19, 524
of implicit memory, 523
perceptual identification as, 216
priming and, 545

individual differences
enactment paradigm, 140
false memory susceptibility, 158, 187
life event memories, 322–23
long-term maintenance of knowledge, 357–59
maternal reminiscing style, 287
See also age; gender differences; personality

induced cognitive state, 51–52

infancy, 55, 267–79, 284–85, 290, 299–300
conditioning studies, 269–73
context and memory retention, 277, 278
deferred imitation, 271–73, 277, 278, 602–3
explicit, conscious memories and, 299, 307
habituation studies, 267, 268–69
in utero memory retention, 269
long-term familiarization studies, 269, 299
memory familiarization, 268, 269
memory modification, 277–78
memory reactivation, 270, 274–75
novelty-preference paradigms, 267
object search and delayed response studies, 273–74, 284–85, 299
ontogeny of multiple memory systems, 278
paired-comparison procedure, 268
visual expectancy studies, 269

infantile amnesia. *See* childhood amnesia

inferences, 24
false memories and, 154, 160

inferior thalamic peduncle, 471

information processing, 14–15, 93–94, 245
aging effects, 400
codification and symbolic representation, 25
experts' goal-relevant approach, 114–15
memory images and, 26

memory storage and, 36
modal model, 81–83, 93–94
multiple memory systems and, 628
organization and, 97
psychopharmacological effects, 544
of short-term memory, 77
See also encoding; knowledge; retrieval processes; transfer of knowledge

inhibition, 10, 54, 401, 403, 417–19, 421

insight, 473

instructions, intentional vs. incidental, 52

instrumental learning. *See* trial-and-error learning

insula, 475

integration, 139
recognition memory and, 236
response, 7

intelligence
frontal lobes and, 466
life events recall and, 323

intention
awareness relationship, 255
learning effectiveness and, 98
as retrieval factor, 252

intentional recall, incidental vs., 117

intentional vs. incidental instructions, 42

interference, 4, 473
aging and, 217, 224, 418, 419
catastrophic, 591–93
factor X (unlearning), 150
as forgetting factor, 13–14, 153–55, 160, 167
by old associations, 12, 13, 63, 418
by past learning, 217–18, 224
remote associations and, 126, 127, 128
retroactive vs. proactive, 13, 51–52, 54, 79, 81, 140
See also attention division

inter-item association, 127–28, 179

inter-item similarity, 16

interpersonal reality monitoring, 187–88

interpretation, fluent processing and, 254

intoxication, 103

intra-list cues, 50, 131, 132
repetition, 132, 169–70, 171

introspection, 598, 601, 604, 606

in utero memory retention, 269

Inventory of Memory Experiences, 322

involuntary remembering
  autobiographical, 237–38
  mnemonic phenomena, 255
  specific environmental cues,
    316
item memory, source memory
  vs., 397
item-recognition tasks, 59–67
  correlational approach, 60–61,
    63–64, 65, 66, 67, 69
  perirhinal cortex lesions im-
    pairment, 433
  successive, 62–63

judgments
  of reality, 198
  about source of memory, 198
  See also memory-judgment
    tasks
"just know" responses, familiarity and, 224, 234, 239

KC (neurological patient), 256
Kennedy assassination (1963),
  memories of, 317, 381,
    473
ketamine, 549
kidnapping, 383
kinesthetic information, 371
knew-it-all-along effect. *See* hindsight bias
knowing, 229–41
  brain region and, 618
  definition of, 229
  illusions of, 205–6
  overconfidence about, 204–6
  perceptual fluency and, 618
  role of self in, 619
  as semantic memory retrieval
    characterization, 598
  of unknown and nonexistent,
    202–3
  See also feeling-of-knowing
    judgments; "just know" re-
    sponses; remember/know
    paradigm
knowledge
  autobiographical, 306
  brain injury selective effects
    on, 632
  causally self-referential,
    300–301
  children's attributions of,
    301–2, 303–4, 307
  conceptual and perceptual fac-
    tors in, 235
  content as variable in long-
    term retention, 359
  definition of, 466
  expert domain information,
    114–15
  expertise and schematic organi-
    zation of, 114

formally aquired, long-term retention of, 347–60
information encoding and
  prior, 96, 98, 113, 179
local and distributed representations, 584–85
long-term memory structures,
  23–25
maintenance of, 347–60
major theories, 233–36
marginal, 356–57
as memory base, 40
memory skills and, 284, 628
metacognitive, 198
of own knowledge. *See* metamemory
propositional, 22
of routes, 367, 368
semantic dementia decreased
  specificity of, 451
of space, 367
storage and activation of,
  397–98
theory of mind and, 297–307
See also information processing; learning; remember/
  know paradigm; semantic
  memory; transfer of knowledge
Korsakoff amnesia, 174, 203,
  466, 468, 543, 647

labeled associations, 21, 22
landmarks, 366, 369
language
  acquisition, 15–16
  Alzheimer's vs. Huntington's
    disease deficits, 453
  Alzheimer's vs. vascular de-
    mentia deficits, 454
  dementia of frontal lobe dys-
    function, 450
  impairment syndromes,
    448–49
  long-term vocabulary reten-
    tion, 348–53, 356, 359
  as memory organizer, 284,
    288–91, 324
  nonsense syllable acquisition
    and, 125
  second-language acquisition,
    85
  semantic memory and, 22–23
  serial learning and, 128–29
  spatial knowledge and, 364,
    368–69, 372
  visual memory and, 364
  See also linguistics; phonologi-
    cal loop; words
latero-dorsal prefrontal regions,
  472
learning, 7–11
  as adaptive mechanism, 4

associative cues, 16–17, 584
brain injury effects, 26
childhood, 602–3
chunking strategy, 97
of concepts, 34
conditions of acquisition/reten-
  tion relationship, 348, 353
degrees measurability, 5
discrimination tasks, 7, 9–10,
  167–68, 495–96
in early adulthood as best remembered, 319
environment/recall relationship, 101, 337, 475
error-corrector rule, 586–87,
  588, 593–94
Hebbian-type rule, 585,
  593–94
implicit studies, 252
intention as factor, 98
ironic effects of past, 217–18,
  224
long-term retention of, 347–60
memory skills and, 284, 291,
  292
multiple regression analysis,
  113
nature of materials factor, 10
nonconscious linguistic rules,
  16
procedural memory and, 636
relationship to already-known
  material, 10
retention factors, 269–77, 278,
  319, 348–49, 353, 358, 396
self-judgments of, 198
skills, 7–8, 284
spaced practice effect and,
  350–54
strategies for positive transfer,
  111–14
transfer as basic to, 10–12,
  109, 110
word memory enhancement,
  102–3
See also encoding; knowledge;
  procedural memory; re-
  trieval processes; serial
  learning
learning-to-learn, 11
left dorsolateral prefrontal cortex, 509
left parietal cortex, 472, 474
  old/new ERP effect, 527, 528,
    529, 530–31, 533
left temporal cortex, 26
legal testimony. *See* eyewitness
  testimony
levels of processing, 7–8, 94,
  102, 139
  manipulation, 52
lexical retrieval, 633
library retrieval systems, 558

life experience memory, 315–24
date recall, 319
emotional events recall,
379–88
everyday memory and, 319–21
individual differences, 322–23
memory for places, 319–20
See also autobiographical
memory; episodic memory
life narrative hypothesis, 319
limbic system
Alzheimer's disease and, 469
basolateral circuit, 469, 471
benzodiazepam receptors, 540
bottleneck structures, 473, 474
damage/persistent amnesia relationship, 473
diagram of loop, 476
early labels for, 463
as essential to memory processing, 468, 478
short-term to long-term memory transfer, 472–73, 478
structural components, 472,
473, 475
See also amygdala; hippocampus
limited capacity concept, 14
linguistics
computer models, 23
S-R theory critiques and,
15–16
See also language
list discrimination, 11, 167,
172
listening. *See* auditory memory
list learning. *See* serial learning
locale memory, 367, 369, 627
Loma Prieta earthquake (1989),
memories of, 318
long-term memory
age and, 358, 396
brain injury selective effects,
432–33, 434, 468
definition of, 78
dissociation and, 54–55, 59
errors linked with meaning,
150
event-related potential studies,
521–34
expert domain information
and, 114–15
expert episodic memory performance and, 115–18
of formally acquired knowledge, 347–60
infant, 269–71, 276, 279, 299
knowledge structures in,
23–25
modality effects, 130
models studies, 571
neuropsychological evidence,
81–83

retention and recognition studies, 348–49, 448
schematic representations, 24–
25, 114–15
semantic coding predilection,
81
separation from short-term
memory, 81
short-term memory interaction,
19–20, 21, 428
short-term memory transfer to,
82, 93–94, 472–73, 478
storage site loci, 474
See also episodic memory; explicit memory; priming; procedural memory; semantic
memory
long-term working memory, expertise and, 115, 116–18
LOP. *See* levels-of-processing effect
lorazepam, 545–46, 547, 549
LTM. *See* long-term memory
LT-WM. *See* long-term working
memory

madeleine cake (literary symbol),
316
Magical Number Seven, The
(Miller), 79
magnetic resonance imaging
of dementias, 448, 452
See also functional magnetic
resonance imaging
maintenance of knowledge,
347–60
maintenance rehearsal, 96
mammillary bodies (brain), 466,
469, 470, 475
mammillothalamic tract (tract of
Vicq d'Azyr), 469, 470
maps
exploration vs., 367–68
verbal descriptions vs., 369
See also cognitive map
Marchioness sinking (1989),
memories of, 318
marginal knowledge, 356–57
marking events, 27
Markov chains, 572
materials, learning and variability of, 10
material-specific amnesia, 468
maternal reminiscing styles,
286–88, 291, 292, 324
mathematical memory models,
64
matrix model of memory, 583
maturational hypothesis, 319
meaning
encoding and, 101–2
long-term memory errors and,
150

meaningfulness norms, 10
means-ends strategy, 111
medial temporal lobe, 485–97
aging and, 402–3, 404, 414,
415
Alzheimer's disease and, 469
amnesia model, 429, 467, 468
conscious memory and, 246,
256, 612, 614, 619, 620
damage effects on episodic-
semantic dissociation, 604–5
damage effects on short-term
memory, 21, 26
episodic encoding and, 504,
634
episodic retrieval and, 635
explicit memory and, 402–3,
486, 488, 514, 620
familiarity and recollection,
619
lesion effects, 430, 431, 433,
435
lesions' non-effect on procedural learning, 636
memory abilities outside of,
488
memory-judgment tasks and,
174
memory system, 486–88, 514
monkey cortical components,
487
object discrimination learning
and, 492–96
paired-associate learning and,
592
source memory and, 189
terminology for components,
485
medial temporal lobe memory
system
definition of, 485–86
See also hippocampal formation; parahippocampal cortex; perirhinal cortex
mediating associates. *See* associative mediators
medical information, memory
for, 320
medications. *See* psychopharmacology
mediodorsal nucleus, thalamic,
469, 471, 473, 475
memorization, 284, 323, 359
experts, 26–27
memory
acquisition processes and representations, 180, 471–72
awareness relationship, 245,
246–49
brain processing riddles, 478
concepts of, 33–42
content and, 567–68
decay of, 12, 13, 19

division into systems, 78
enhancement and impairment, 102–3
expertise and, 55, 114–19
historical concepts of, 597, 627
idioms of, 42
as isolatable function, 485
laboratory creation of, 46
levels-of-processing, 94
meanings of terms, 36–37
multiplicity of meanings, 42
multitude of qualifiers, 646
nature of codes. *See* encoding
neuroanatomy of, 465–78
neurocognitive aging effects on, 416–21
as nonunitary entity, 627
richness vs. paucity theorists, 166, 171
self-serving distortion of, 27
simple strength hypothesis, 166
socialization of, 283–92
source monitoring framework, 180–82, 302, 306
transfer of knowledge as dependent on, 110
See also memory research; models of memory; *specific memory types*
memory, nonverbal. *See* nonverbal memory
Memory Characteristics Questionnaire, 186, 238
memory disorders
brain-injury selective, 427–37
dementias, 441–54
historical theories of, 466–69
memory distortions, 18, 149–60, 647. *See also* false memories
memory for source, 302, 306. *See also* source monitoring; source monitoring framework
memory-impaired populations. *See* amnesic syndrome; older people
memory-judgment tasks, 165–75
brain mechanisms and, 173–74
conscious awareness and, 174–75
overconfidence and, 204–6
retrieval dynamics, 172–73
retrieval latency vs., 201
See also feeling-of-knowing judgments
memory models. *See* models of memory
memory recall. *See* recall
memory rehabilitation techniques, for early Alzheimer's patients, 445

memory research, 3–27
adaptiveness of memory, 557–69
animal hippocampal regions, 488–91
animal medial temporal lobe, 486–88, 492–96
associationism background, 3–4
behavioral methods, 46–56
behaviorist philosophy, 4–14, 37–38
brain imaging technology, 26, 45, 55–56, 466, 501–14
cognitive psychology, 14–25, 37–38, 95, 466
concepts and schemas, 24–25
concepts of memory, 33–42
context judgments, 17–19
contingency analyses, 59–70
dementias, 441–54
distortions and illusions, 149–51
Ebbinghaus's methodological revolution, 45–46, 245
eclectic methodology, 347–48
enactment paradigm, 137–45, 139–42
event-related potential studies, 521–34
everyday memory errors, 26–27
experimental phases, 45–46
false memories, 154–55
indirect tests, 19
infancy research paradigms, 267–78
intra-list repetition effects, 132
maintenance of formally acquired knowledge, 347–48, 360
metamemory paradigms, 198–207, 303
methods of, 45–56
models of memory, 34, 571–79, 647
multiple memory systems, 25–26, 41–42, 278, 628
nonconscious memory, 245–55, 256–57
organization of material, 129
picture superiority effect, 98
popularity of different memory tasks, 16–17
primacy and recency effect first findings, 129
psycholinguistics influence on, 16
psychopharmacological effects, 539–50
psychopharmacology experiments, 542–43

remembering and knowing, 229–33
remembering life experiences vs., 315
rote learning tradition, 4–7, 8–10, 125–33
short-term memory models, 19–21, 78–83
skills studies, 7–8
spatial memory, 363–72
subjective reports, 186–87
theories of consciousness and, 609–21
transfer of knowledge, 10–12
unitarians vs. multiple-systems, 41–42
variables in, 55
memory slips, 222
memory span, 19, 21
generate-recognize theory, 99
short-term memory study, 78–79
word length effect, 83–84
working memory, 85–87
memory storage, 36, 37, 94, 473–75, 478
connectionist models, 583–94
rehearsal distinction, 630–31
memory systems theory, 240, 627–38
brain damage selective effects on, 466, 629
five major types, 627–28
logic and criteria, 628–29
memory system definition, 628
multiple systems, 25–26, 41–42, 278, 628
neuroimaging insights into, 628, 629–38
ontogeny of multiple systems, 278, 279
processing approach complementing, 629
memory trace, 18, 36, 37, 619, 646–47
age relationship, 357
distributed memory model, 585, 612
nonavailability, 98–99
recognition as measure of, 47
Memory Type A. *See* remembering
Memory Type B. *See* knowing
MEM system (multiple-entry modular), 613–14
mental abacus calculation, 117
mentalism, 4
mental map. *See* cognitive map
mental model, 370
mental pictures, 25
mental rotation, 364, 368
mental scanning, 364
mental slips, 26–27

mental spaces. *See* spatial memory

mental state experiments. *See* theory of mind

mental transformation, 364

mere-exposure studies, 249–50, 257

metabolic processes, 12, 413, 419

metacognitive skills. *See* metamemory

metamemory, 119, 139–40, 197–207
  children and, 292, 301–2, 303–4, 307, 392
  data, 200–206
  hindsight and, 206
  paradigms for studying, 198
  prefrontal cortex damage and, 434
  retention of knowledge and, 354
  socialization of memory and, 284, 291, 292
  test effects, 203–4
  theory, 198–200
  theory of mind and, 303–4
  tip-of-the-tongue states and, 197, 199, 200–201, 202

metaphor, 370

Method of Loci, 365

midazolam, 545

mind development. *See* theory of mind

MINERVA2 model, 224, 572–74, 575, 576

Mini-Mental State Examination, 441, 444, 445, 447

mirror-drawing, 436

mirror effect, 48

mirror-reading skills, 436

misattributions, 217., *See also* source monitoring framework

misinformation paradigm, 317

misleading information, false memories and, 154

MMFR procedure, 63, 68

MMSE. *See* Mini-Mental State Examination

mnemonic devices, 11, 52
  automaticity vs., 250
  experts' short-term and long-term memory, 115, 116, 117, 118
  nonconscious, 250, 255, 256–57

mnestic block syndrome, 470–71, 477–78

mobile conjugate reinforcement task, 270–71
  reactivation studies, 274–77, 279, 299–300

modality effect, 25, 26, 78, 130–31, 167

modality judgments, 165, 166

modal model, 81–83, 93–94

Models of Human Memory (Norman), 572

models of memory, 34, 571–79, 647
  connectionist, 578, 583–84
  consciousness models, 609–21
  convolutional, 224, 572, 574, 575, 583–84
  global memory, 224, 572–77
  historical background, 571–72
  implicit memory models, 577–78
  network, 34, 508, 510–12, 513, 514, 583–94
  uses, 576–77, 579

modified free recall, 54

modified-modified free recall. *See* MMFR procedure

modules, 611–12, 615

mood
  Alzheimer's vs. Huntington's patients, 453
  encoding and, 52
  memory interrelationship, 541
  retrieval and, 337

mood-altering drugs. *See* psychopharmacology

motivation, information encoding and, 96, 358

motor component theory, subject-performed tasks and, 140–41

motor images, 302

motor skills, 436
  brain injury effects on, 16, 469
  drug effects on, 545
  nonconscious basis for, 8
  pathways transitions with extensive practice, 637
  procedural memory and, 636

movement. *See* action memory

MRI. *See* magnetic resonance imaging

MTL. *See* medial temporal lobe

multi-infarct dementia (MID), 454

multimodal dual-code theory, 138, 140, 142, 144

multinomial modeling, 220–21

multinomial processing tree (MPT), 185

multiple-entry modular (MEM) system, 613–14

multiple memory systems. *See* memory systems theory

multiple regression analysis, 113

multiple template hypothesis, 115, 117

multiple-trace hypothesis, 18, 171–72

multistore model. *See* modal model

muscarinic acetylcholine receptors, 543

musical memory, 96

names and faces. *See* face recognition studies; fame judgment task

narrative styles, 286–88, 289, 291–92, 318, 323, 324
  life narrative hypothesis, 319
  transactive memories and, 324

navigational space, 365–70

near transfer, 109

need probability, recall and, 558–59

negative emotions. *See* emotional memories; traumatic memories

negative transfer, 12, 111

neocortex
  Alzheimer's atrophy of, 443, 469
  conscious awareness and, 612, 613, 614, 615, 616, 617
  independent learning system in, 225, 473
  learning rate, 592
  lesions and selective memory disorders, 429–30, 435, 469
  points of access to medial temporal lobe, 496

neostriatal damage, 436, 453

nerve growth factor (NGF), 550

network models of memory, 34, 508–12, 513, 514
  auto-associator, 585–87
  connectionist, 578, 583–94, 647
  semantic, 588, 591

neural imaging. *See* brain imaging

neural networks, 411, 578

neuroanatomy. *See* brain-behavior interrelations; brain regions

neurochemistry, 411, 412–13, 415

neurocognitive aging, 411–21

neuroimaging studies. *See* brain imaging technology

neurological damage. *See* brain damage

neuropsychology, 55–56
  aging and memory aspects, 402–5, 411–21
  cognitive maps studies, 363–64

memory in dementias, 441–54
psychoactive drugs and,
539–50
of short-term and working
memory, 77, 85, 86
of short-term vs. long-term
memory, 81–83
See also brain regions; *specific
regions*
neuroticism, 322
neurotransmitters, 539, 540, 543
Alzheimer's involvement, 540,
549
neurotropic agents, 550
news events, flashbulb memories
for, 317, 381–83, 388
New York Times database recency analysis, 560–64, 565
nicotine, 543, 549
NINDS-AIREN group, 454
nitrous oxide, 541
NMDA (*N*-methyl-D-aspartate),
548–49
noetic consciousness, 229,
233–34
autonoetic vs., 599
definition of, 611
nonconscious memory, 36–37,
245–57, 646
awareness and intent relationship, 255
context and, 255, 256
cues and, 41
implicit tests, 250–53, 257
mnemonic processes, 250, 255,
256–57
opposition and process-dissociation tests, 253–54, 257
performance goals and, 255
in real-world situations, 256,
257
self-report, 252–53
See also implicit memory
nondeclarative memory system.
See procedural memory
nonexistent knowledge, 202–3
nonsense syllables. *See* serial
learning
non-specific thalamus nuclei,
475
nonspecific transfer, 11
nonstrategic theory, for action
events, 137–38, 144
nonverbal imagery. *See* visual
imagery
nonverbal memory
Alzheimer's loss assessment,
444
implicit test items, 251
short-term, 80–81
See also auditory memory; visual memory

nonword repetition performance,
84–85
novel tasks, expertise adaptive
transfer to, 118–19
novelty/encoding hypothesis,
504
novelty-preference studies, infant, 268–69

object discrimination learning,
492–96
object-level cognitive processes,
197
object search, 273
object working memory, 631
obscure memories, 26
occipital cortex, 26
odors memory, 81, 95
of infant memory, 276–77
older people, 395–405, 411–21
brain structure changes and,
402–5, 411–21
cognitive deficits, 399, 401,
411, 413–16, 421
conscious recollection impairment, 420–21
contextual memory, 96, 101
directed forgetting paradigm
and, 418
divided attention and, 103,
199, 413–14
encoding specificity principle
and, 396–97
episodic memory and, 144,
189, 396–98, 401, 413
extraneous information remembering by, 418
false memories susceptibility,
158, 184, 224, 403, 404–5
inhibitory impairments of,
401, 403, 417–19
ironic effects of past experience and, 217, 224, 418
long-term knowledge retention
decline, 358, 396
memory changes in, 395–405,
416–21, 468
modality judgment and, 175
nonconscious memory retention, 256
procedural memory and, 404,
468
recollection deficits, 219, 220,
222, 223, 224, 420–21
reduced remembering in, 231,
417
reduced speed of processing
and, 399–400, 402
reminiscence bump memories
of, 318–19
source forgetting, 96, 188, 189,
223, 224, 397, 403, 600–601

stereotyping by, 188
suggestibility studies, 184
tip-of-the-tongue experience
and, 398
See also Alzheimer's disease;
dementias
old-new effect, 527–28, 529, 533
old-new recognition decisions,
175
oligonucleotides, 550
On the Witness Stand (Munsterberg), 150
open recall, 316, 318–19
operant conditioning, infant
memory retention, 270–73,
276–77
operation span, working memory, 86–88
opercular region, 506
opposition procedure, 253–54,
257
oral performance tradition, 284,
323
orbitofrontal cortex, 431, 432,
475
organization, 97. *See also* chunking
overlearning, 5, 9, 348, 359
alternative brain pathways
and, 637, 638
oxazepam, 545

pain, memories of, 320
paired-associates learning, 7,
8–9, 10, 16, 25
A-B/A-C paradigm, 63
back propagation and catastrophic interference,
591–92
brain region and, 592
correlational approach problems, 65–66
drug impairment of, 544–45
emotion at encoding and impairment of, 380
and estimate of recollection
and familiarity, 218–19
as example of intra-list cues,
50
independent associations
model, 65
infant capabilities, 270
problem-solving and, 113
serial list transfer, 126–27, 128
visual imagery and, 85
paired-comparison parocedure,
infant studies, 268
pair recognition, 577
Palme murder (1986), memories
of, 317
Papez circuit, 431, 432, 433, 469,
470

parahippocampal cortex, 365, 402, 432, 433, 486, 487, 488, 495, 496, 691
parahippocampal gyrus, 634
parietal cortex, 472, 631
Parkinson's disease, 436, 468, 469
 characterization, 453
partial least squares (PLS), 508–9
part-list cueing inhibition, 103
past learning
 ironic effects of, 217–18, 224, 418
 transfer of, 10–12
 See also familiarity; recollection
path analysis, 509
pattern classification paradigm, 153
PCA analysis, 509, 510, 511
PD. *See* Parkington's disease
PDP (process dissociation procedure), 610, 618
Pearl Harbor attack (1941), memories of, 317
perception
 conception distinction, 250, 252, 257
 memory chunks, 11–12
 spatial memory, 364–72
perceptual detail, 180
 autobiographical memories and, 186
 familiarity and, 613
 identification tests, 216
 increased remembering and, 234–35, 236
 perceptual representation system and, 635–36
perceptual fluency, 613
perceptual illusions. *See* false memories
perceptual implicit memory, 616
perceptual implicit tests, 250
perceptual motor skills, 7–8, 23, 102
perceptual priming, 40, 236, 545, 616, 617–18, 636, 638
perceptual representation system, 628, 635–36, 638
performers' memory, 323, 359
periamygdaloid cortex, 486
perirhinal cortex, 431, 432, 433–34, 486, 487, 488, 495, 496, 618
peristriate cortex, 435
perisylvian region (left hemisphere), 85
personality
 Alzheimer's vs. Huntington's effects on, 453
 dementia of frontal type effects on, 449

as life events recall factor, 322–23
nonconscious memory role in assessment of, 245
subcortical dementias' effects on, 452
personal memories. *See* autobiographical memories; emotional memories; episodic memory
person-specific semantic knowledge, 448
PET. *See* positron emission tomography
Peterson Short-Term Forgetting Task, 81
pharmacology. *See* psychopharmacology
phenomenological awareness. *See* consciousness
phonological loop, 82–85, 96, 442
 components, 630
 short-term memory disorders, 427–28
 short-term store, 85
 working memory activation, 442, 506, 508, 630
 See also language; words
phonological store, 22
physostigmine, 543
PI. *See* proactive interference
Pick cells and bodies, 448
Pick's disease, 448–52, 469
pictorial memory. *See* visual memory
picture naming, 40
picture superiority effect, 98
piracetam, 550
places, memory for, 319–20, 365
PLAN model, spatial relations, 370
Plans and Structure of Behavior (Miller, Galanter, and Pribram), 15
PM tasks. *See* prospective remembering
positional association, 128, 167–68
positivism, 4
positron emission tomography, 256, 413, 446, 475, 501–14, 531, 619, 628, 630
 data analysis, 509
 ecphorizing biographical information, 477–78
 episodic memory studies, 634–35
 procedural memory and, 637
 self-referentiality and, 619
 semantic memory studies, 632–33, 634–35

shock (mnestic block) condition, 471
structural equation modeling of, 509
technique, 628
working memory studies, 630
posterior association cortex, 435
posterior neocortex, 615, 616, 617
posterior parietal regions, 26, 506, 511, 513–14, 630
posterior temporal cortex, 430
post-retrieval processing, 530, 531
posttraumatic stress disorder, 336, 387, 470
Practical Aspects of Memory (Cardiff conference, 1978), 316
practical syllogism, 298
practice of skills, 7–8, 284, 560–61
 brain pathways shift from, 636
 retention and, 350–54
precommissural formix, 470
precuneus, 504, 506, 508
predictive sentence contexts, 217
preexisting associations, 9, 13
 effects of remote, 126, 127, 128
preexisting knowledge, 96, 98, 113, 179
prefrontal cortex, 26, 473, 512
 age-related memory reductions and, 402–4, 405, 413, 414, 415, 416, 419
 consciousness types and, 620
 damage and self-reflective inability, 601, 606
 damage-related memory disruptions, 430–31, 434, 599–601
 episodic activation and, 508
 episodic encoding and, 504, 508, 512, 513, 634, 637–38
 episodic retrieval and, 505–6, 508, 513, 635, 637–38
 functional heterogeneity of, 513
 hemispheric asymmetric involvement, 513, 514
 memory networks and, 513
 posterior brain regions and, 513
 retrieval and, 510, 513
 semantic memory retrieval and, 509, 512, 513, 633, 638
 short-term memory and, 478
 source memory and, 189
 working memory and, 508, 513, 631–32, 637, 638
 See also frontal lobes
prefrontal leucotomy patients, 601–2

prejudice, nonconscious memory and, 245
premotor frontal region, 506, 508
presenile dementia, 466
preventive maintenance effect, 356–57
primacy effect, 14, 16, 21–22, 79, 129, 139
primary memory, 78, 93, 396. *See also* short-term memory
priming
  associative, 51, 576–77, 616–17
  brain injury deficits, 434–35, 437
  brain regions controlling, 435, 469, 488, 611–12
  conceptual, 34, 40, 616, 617–18, 636
  as contingency analysis drawback, 66–67
  cue-familiarity retrieval, 201–2
  definition of, 39, 247, 466
  drug effects on, 545–46
  explicit memory relation, 616–18
  implicit remembering, 51, 577–78
  memory models use and, 576–77, 615–16
  perceptual, 40, 236, 545, 616, 617–18, 636, 638
  repetition, 8–9, 19, 26, 40, 51, 132, 169–70, 171, 420–21, 523–24, 577
  types of, 38–40
  See also recency effect
principal components analysis, 509, 510, 511
prior performance. *See* transfer of knowledge
proactive interference, 13, 51–52, 79, 81
  subject-performed tasks and, 140
probability, 222, 224, 558, 593
probe techniques, 50, 80
problem solving
  adaptive expertise strategic shifts in, 118
  retrieval as, 334
procedural memory (nondeclarative), 23, 26, 398, 628
  aging and, 404, 468
  amnesic retention of, 398, 436, 437, 488
  brain injury-related deficits, 436–37, 468, 469
  brain storage sites, 474–75, 478, 488, 637
  declarative vs., 37–38, 398, 222
  definitions of, 398, 466, 636

dementias and, 468, 469
developmental hierarchy, 278
  infancy and childhood, 284, 285
  pathways shift, 637, 638
  subsystems commonality, 636
  training and transfer tasks and, 113
process dissociation, 51, 59, 219–24
  controversial aspects, 222–24
  extensions of, 221–22
  nonconscious memory tests, 253–54, 257
  recognition memory and, 236–37
  as recollection assessment, 219–21
  remember/know paradigm and, 237
  source memory and, 185
process dissociation procedure (PDP), 610, 618
processing resources, 93, 399–400, 401, 402
process theories of memory, 250, 610, 629
progressive aphasic syndromes, 448–49, 450, 452
progressive differentiation process, 590
progressive fluent aphasia. *See* semantic dementia
progressive nonfluent aphasia, 448, 449
progressive propospagnosia, 449
progressive supranuclear palsy, 452
propanalol, 541
propositional attitudes, 297
propositional knowledge, 23
prosopagnosia, 449
prospective memory, 50–51, 101, 398, 416–17
  age-related decrements, 398, 416–17
  importance of retrieval cues to, 335–36
  time-based vs. event-based, 398, 417
PRS. *See* perceptual representation system
psychoactive drugs, 539–42. *See also* psychopharmacology; *specific drugs*
psycholinguistics, 16
psychometrics, 86
psychopharmacology, 539–50, 601
  Alzheimer studies, 540, 549–50
  history, 541–42
  methods, 542–43

specificity of memory effects, 547–49, 599
  tolerance buildup, 547
psychotherapy
  false memory elicitation, 385
  memory studies and, 46
public events, memory for, 317, 381–83, 388
putamen, 453
PV (neurological patient), 428

Ranschburg effect, 132
rational analysis, of memory system adaptiveness, 557–69
rationality, 572
rationalization, 151
RB (neurological patinet), 488
rCBF. *See* regional cerebral blood flow
reaction time. *See* response time
reactivation, infant memory studies, 270, 274–75
reading, functional network model, 511
Reagan assassination attempt (1981), memories of, 317, 381
reality monitoring, 153, 180, 188, 302, 307
real-nonreal object decision test, 451
reasoning, adaptive transfer and, 118, 119
recall
  Alzheimer's patients and, 445
  brain regions and, 26, 475–78
  children's learned strategies and, 291–92, 324
  chunking and, 11–12, 79, 97, 115–16
  content and, 567–68
  of conversations, 320–21, 323
  cued. *See* cued recall
  of discovered memories, 385–86
  estimates of recollection and familiarity in, 218–21
  experts' superiority of, 114
  feeling-of-knowledge judgments and, 199, 203
  free. *See* free recall
  frontal cortex damage and, 434
  functional network model, 512
  generate-recognize theory, 99
  global organic amnesia impairment of, 430
  immediate and delayed, 419
  incidental vs. intentional, 117
  of infant memories, 279, 285–86
  learning environment and, 101, 337
  of life experiences, 315–24

recall (*continued*)
mnestic block syndrome and, 470–71, 477–78
of names and faces, 348, 358, 359
need probability and, 558–59
priming and, 66–67
recency factor and, 560–64
reminiscence bump and, 318–19
retrieval processes and, 103, 165, 475
SAM model, 573
selective memory disorders and, 430, 434
serial, 50, 125, 129, 132. *See also* serial learning
short-term verbal memory, 78–79
strength measurement, 60
study location and, 101, 337
subject-performed tasks' enhancement of, 102–3, 140–41
targeted vs. open, 316, 318–19
vs. recognition, 9, 38, 47, 61–62, 64, 67, 101, 199, 252
wet vs. dry environment, 101, 337
See also recognition memory; recollection; remembering
recall, judgment, recognize (RJR) paradigm, 198, 200
receiver-operating characteristics, 48–49, 221, 239
recency effect, 16, 18, 19, 21–22, 50, 79, 81, 129
adaptive memory studies, 560–64
aging and false recency judgments, 420
auditory memory advantage, 130
context and, 18
expert long-term working memory and, 116–17
free recall and, 130
repetition and, 167, 168, 170
study-phase retrieval and, 128
recency judgments, 165, 166, 167, 170, 174, 175
reception events, 317–18, 382
recoding, 129
recoding paradigms, 54
recognition failure paradigm, 63–64, 142
recognition memory, 17, 18–19, 429, 434
age-related decline in conscious recollection and, 415
associative, 60–61, 528, 565–67, 584–87, 616–17

conditional probability of, 63–64
contextual support and, 401
cued recall and, 47, 223
dual-process model of, 224, 230, 236, 527, 528
dual-process model rejection, 528
encoding operations and, 99–100
event-related potentials and, 526–30, 527
experts' superiority, 114
false alarm rate, 48, 49, 50
familiarity vs., 218, 219, 221, 230, 236, 528–29, 618–19
feeling-of-knowing judgments and, 199, 203
functional network model, 511
global models, 573, 574
global organic amnesia impairment of, 430
hippocampal region and, 488–89, 490, 491–92, 497
hit rate, 48, 49, 50
infant, 274–77, 279, 299–300
as judgment task, 165
knowing as basis, 234
long-term memory and, 348
measurement of, 47–50, 60–61
multiple-trace hypothesis and, 171–72
prefrontal cortex damage and, 434
priming and, 66–67
recall dependencies, 64
recall vs., 9, 38, 47, 61–62, 64, 67, 101, 199, 252
recollection and, 221, 230, 236, 237, 435, 529, 618–19
remember/know paradigm and, 229–30, 234, 240, 527, 529
retrieval dynamics, 172
selective disorders of, 429, 434
semantic dementia performances, 450, 451
subcortical dementia's retention of, 442
subject-performed tasks enhancement of, 102–3
two-process theory of, 49
young vs. elderly, 416
recollection, 185, 215–25, 430, 435
aging impairment of, 219, 220, 222, 223, 224, 412, 415, 417, 420–21
autobiographical memory as, 318–19
brain region activation and, 26
context and, 18, 60, 421, 523
criterial vs. noncriterial, 237

diagnostic vs. nondiagnostic, 237
dissociating varieties of memory and, 598–99
estimates of, 218–21
event-related potentials correlates, 529–31, 533
explicit memory and, 298–99
familiarity vs., 217–18, 222–23, 224–25, 239, 523, 529, 611, 618–19
flood of details accompanying, 216
fluent processing and, 254
frontal lobe damage disruption in, 599–601
functional differences between similarity and, 215–17
memory judgments and, 174–75
neural systems underlying false and true, 531
nonconscious vs. conscious, 245
process dissociation procedure and, 221–22
for reception events, 317–18
recognition memory and, 221, 230, 236, 237, 435, 529, 618–19
theory of mind and, 52
vividness of flashbulb memories, 381–82
See also episodic memory; knowledge; metamemory; nonconscious memory; remembering
reconstructive retrieval, 100, 179, 339–40, 647
recovered memories, 159–60, 188, 317, 384–86
interpersonal reality monitoring and, 188
memory mechanisms and, 387
recreational drug use, 539, 549
reenactment, infant studies, 274
reference, 35
sense vs., 298
reference frame, spatial memory and, 364–65, 366–67, 369, 371
regional cerebral blood flow, 411, 413, 414, 415, 416, 421
rehearsal, 21, 22, 85
encoding success and, 93, 96–97
flashbulb memories and, 383
phonological loop, 506
schedules for long-term knowledge retention, 354–57
spatial order and, 284
storage distinction, 630–31
timing of, 97
verbal, 21

rehearsal-prevention methodology, 53
rehearsal strategy, 21, 22
reinforced repetitions, 8–9
reinstatement
  event memory and, 285
  infant studies, 274, 290
  verbal, 290–91
relatedness effects, memory distortion and, 151–53
relearning, retention savings score and, 125, 149
release from PI, 52, 79
Remembering (Bartlett), 150
remembering, 42, 229–41
  brain region and, 618
  clues and targets, 339–40
  consciousness and, 611, 612, 613
  definition of, 229
  distinctiveness/fluency framework, 234
  encoding and retrieval variables, 98–99, 101
  episodic, 598, 603, 611
  implicit, 51
  involuntary, 255, 316
  involuntary autobiographical, 237–38
  knowing judgments and, 175, 619
  of life experiences, 315–24
  major theories, 233–36
  memory-judgment tasks and, 175
  perceptual factors facilitating, 234–35, 236
  prospective, 50–51, 101, 335–36, 398, 416–17
  and reflection on past events, 307
  role of self in, 27, 619
  selective episodic losses, 598
  task analysis, 69–70
  See also recollection; remember/know paradigm; retrieval processes
remember/know paradigm, 175, 186, 198, 224, 229–41, 338
  aging and, 420, 600–601
  autonoetic vs. noetic consciousness and, 611
  autonoetic vs. semantic, 599, 600
  brain region and, 233, 618
  current problems, 238–39
  dementias and, 231, 451
  event-related potentials and, 233, 527, 529
  guessing and, 239–40
  major theories, 233–36
  as nonapplicable to children, 603

psychopharmacological effects, 545
recognition memory and, 229–30, 234, 240, 527, 529
self-referentiality and, 619
signal-detection model, 236, 237
written test instructions, 240
reminding
  involuntary retrieval and, 127
  prospective remembering and, 417
reminiscence bump, 318–19
REM model, 575–76, 578
remote associations, serial learning and, 126, 127, 128
remote memory. *See* autobiographical memories
repetition effect, 523–24
repetition priming, 19, 26, 40, 51, 405
  ERP effect, 523–24
  implicit memory and, 577
  intra-list, 132, 169–70, 171
  older vs. young adults, 420–21
  recency effect and, 167, 168, 170
  reinforced, 8–9
repetition suppression, 636
representational theory of mind (RTM), 297
representing, being vs., 298
repressive coping style, 322
  traumatic memory and, 386
research. *See* memory research
response competition. *See* interference
response integration, 7
response-signal method, 172
response time, 49, 60
  aging and, 399
  infant delayed response studies, 273–74, 278, 299, 602
  measurement, 172
  memory models and, 576
retention
  aging and, 396
  of formally acquired knowledge, 347–60
  infancy studies, 269–77, 278, 602–3, 604
  overlearning benefits, 348
  preventive maintenance effect, 356–57
  rehearsal conditions and, 354–57
  serial learning savings score, 126–27
  spaced practice effect and, 350–54
retention function, 5
retention interval, 46, 53–54, 60

retrieval cues, 16–17, 23, 24–25, 98, 100–101, 250, 335–36, 414, 475
retrieval dynamics, 172–73
retrieval effort, 635
retrieval processes, 93, 98–103, 112–14, 333–42
  accessibility and, 200, 333–34, 335
  accuracy of memory reports and, 341–42
  adaptive memory system and, 558
  aging and, 396, 399, 414–15
  automatic activations and, 336, 338
  brain imaging studies, 509–10, 531
  brain regions and, 475–78, 510
  conditions, 47–55, 335, 337
  conscious awareness factor, 598
  constructive, 179–80
  constructive vs. reconstructive, 100
  as context dependent, 101, 337, 414–15
  cue familiarity and, 201–2
  cues, 16–17, 23, 24–25, 98, 100–101, 250, 335–36, 414, 475
  definition of, 93
  divided attention and, 103
  drug effects, 546–47
  effortless, 338
  elaborate semantic retrieval tasks, 502
  encoding context reinstatement and, 101
  encoding interactions, 99, 100–102, 103, 112, 475, 513
  encoding-specificity principle, 99, 337
  and episodic memory, 442, 504–6, 510, 512, 513, 514, 530–31, 597, 598, 635, 637–38
  event-related potentials and, 522–23
  expertise and, 114, 115–18
  and explicit memory, 526–30
  fabrications and, 342
  as false memory factor, 154, 156–57, 160
  feeling-of-knowing and, 201, 338–39, 341
  generality level and, 342
  Huntington's impairment, 454
  implicit vs. conceptual tests, 250
  implicit vs. explicit tests, 252
  infant speed of, 276
  intentionality criterion, 252

retrieval processes (*continued*)
knowledge long-term retention and spacing of, 355–56
memory errors and, 342
memory-judgment tasks, 172–73, 201
"memory pointers" and, 338–39
naturalistic situations, 335
nonconscious memory implicit tests, 250–52
partial information and targets, 339–40
preliminary monitoring stage, 338
preventive maintenance effect, 356–57
probability of need and, 558–69
as problem solving, 334
recency and, 116–17
recollection vs. familiarity, 217–18, 222–23, 224–25, 239, 523, 529, 611, 618–19
reconstructive, 100, 179, 339–40, 647
reminding as involuntary, 127
repeatability and, 157
self-reference effect, 619
and semantic memory, 340, 502, 509–10, 512, 513, 598, 633, 634
and similar learning environment, 101, 337, 475
state-dependent, 337
stimulus-driven semantic retrieval tasks, 502
strategic regulation of, 341
study-phase, 126, 127–28, 132
and subsequent memory performance, 103
task demands, 52–53
tip-of-the-tongue states and, 338, 339–40
and training and transfer task similarities, 112–13, 337
See also recall; recollection; remembering
retrieval success, 635
retroactive interference, 13, 54
retrograde amnesia, 430, 433, 434, 442, 468, 473, 477
drug non-effect on, 544, 546
retrospective case studies, traumatic memories, 383–84
retrosplenial cortex, 619
revisiting crime scene, 101
Ribot effect, 450
right frontal effect, 528–29, 530–31, 533
right parietal cortex, 26
right parietal old/new ERP effect, 528, 529, 530–31

rivastigmine, 549
RJR paradigm, 198, 200
ROCs. *See* receiver operating characteristics
rote learning. *See* serial learning
routes, knowledge of, 367, 368
routine expertise, 109, 110, 114, 118, 119

SAM model, 224, 572, 573, 576
schemas, 23, 24–25, 179
abstract, 112
common examples, 24
definition of, 114
distant memory recovery and, 150
as experts' domain information representation, 114–15, 117–18
personal story, 315, 647
relatedness effect and, 151
schematized verbal stereotypes, 306
schizophrenia, 441
remember/know paradigm and, 231, 238
schools. *See* educational system
scopolamine, 541, 543, 544, 547–50
benzodiazepine effects vs., 549
SDT models, 36, 48–49, 185
search model for free recall. *See* SAM model
secondary memory, 78, 93, 396, 414. *See also* episodic memory; long-term memory
second-language acquisition, 85
sedatives, differing effects on memory, 547
seed-correlation analysis, 509
self, concept of
autobiographic memory and, 27, 619
childhood development of, 299, 300, 302, 307, 306, 301
self-awareness. *See* autonoetic consciousness
self-ratings of memory, 322
self-referentiality, 300–304, 619
self-reflective knowledge. *See* metamemory
self-reminding, 291
self-reports, 252–53
self-serving bias, 27
self-transfer, 109
semantic dementia, 429, 443, 448–49, 618
characteristics, 450–52
semantic encoding, 81, 82, 96, 98, 634
network, 588, 591
semantic retrieval and, 100

semantic knowledge, organization of, 451
semantic memory, 466, 627
activation analysis and, 508
aging and, 397–98, 400, 404
Alzheimer's impairment of, 429, 442–43, 444, 445–46, 447, 448
brain imaging studies, 502–4, 509–10, 632–33
brain injury selective deficits, 429–34, 632–33
brain regions and, 443, 502, 508, 632–33
connectionist vs. symbolic models, 587–94
decreased cerebral glucose metabolism effects, 474
definitions of, 442, 502, 628, 632
dementia of frontal lobe effects, 450
developmental hierarchy, 278
domain, 628
drug non-effects on, 545
encoding, 234, 504
episodic interaction, 151, 598–99
episodic memory differentiated from, 22–23, 55, 285, 395–96, 450–51, 598–605, 618, 632
generation effect, 52
implicit memory and, 40
life experiences studies, 316
marginal knowledge and, 356
noetic consciousness and, 229, 233, 234
priming and, 435
retrieval of information, 340, 502, 509–10, 512, 513, 598, 633, 634
semantic dementia effects, 450
in young children, 602
semantic principle paradigm, 397
semipermanent memory content. *See* marginal knowledge
senile dementia, 466
sense, reference vs., 298
sensory cortices, 26
sensory memory systems, 396. *See also* auditory memory; visual memory
sensory perceptions
autobiographical memories and, 186
conceptual codes vs., 94–95
information processing and, 93
memory acquisition and, 471
traumatic memories fragmentation as, 386, 387
See also auditory memory; visual imagery; visual memory

sensory stores, 93
septal nuclei, 469, 470, 471
sequential memory, childhood
    emphasis on, 285
serial learning, 4–10, 16, 125–
    33, 126, 245
    analysis of tasks, 5–8
    as assocationism-behaviorism
        fusion, 4
    associative processes and false
        recall in, 152
    associatve cues, 16–17
    chaining hypothesis, 126–27
    children's verbal coding, 84
    critics of nonsense syllable us-
        age, 46
    digit-span test, 50, 79, 129
    discrimination task, 167–68,
        495–96
    dissociations between portions
        of position curve, 59
    of famous names, 99
    frequency-in-context judg-
        ments, 18
    frequency information and,
        169–70
    hierarchical organization,
        128–29
    intra-list similarity, 131, 132
    item information vs. order in-
        formation, 131, 132
    item position and, 128
    list-discrimination task, 167,
        172
    memorization skills and, 284
    modality effects, 78, 130–31
    part-list cueing inhibition, 103
    positional association, 128,
        131, 167–68
    position effects, 5, 6, 27, 21,
        125, 126, 129–30. See also
        subhead primacy and re-
        cency effects above
    primacy and recency effects,
        50, 79, 81, 116–17, 128, 129
    rhythmic stress, 129
    similarity effect, 131–32
    S-R theory, 8–10
    study-phase retrieval and re-
        minding, 126, 127–28, 132
    theoretical accounts, 126–29
serial position effects, 5, 6, 17,
    21, 55, 125, 126, 128,
    129–30
serial recall
    free recall vs., 50
    Ranschburg effect, 132
    strength of primacy vs. re-
        cency effect, 129
    uses for, 125
seriogram, 129
sex differences. See gender differ-
    ences

sexual abuse, 159–60, 385–87
    children's testimony and,
        321–22
    corroborations, 188, 385–86,
        387
    memory mechanisms and, 387
    restrospective case studies,
        383–84
    suggestion and false memories
        of, 317, 385
    therapeutic techniques and
        false memories of, 385
short-term memory, 19–22, 77–
    83, 396, 468
    acoustic coding predilection,
        81, 82, 150
    articulatory code, 96
    brain regions and, 21–22, 26,
        81, 246, 427–29, 471–72,
        474, 478
    chunking strategy, 97
    definition of, 78
    dementia impairment, 442
    dichotomy with long-term
        memory, 81
    dissociation and, 55, 59
    dual-task methodology, 53
    errors study, 150
    expert episodic memory perfor-
        mance and, 115
    forgetting, 79, 81, 94
    long-term memory interaction,
        19–20, 21, 428
    modal model, 81–83, 93–94
    model shortcomings, 22
    multi-component system. See
        working memory
    neuropsychological evidence,
        81–83, 85
    phonological storage, 85
    popular model, 20–22
    proactive interference impor-
        tance, 79, 81
    probe techniques, 80
    recency and primacy effects,
        79, 130
    selective disorders, 427–29
    transfer to long-term memory,
        82, 93–94, 472–73, 478
    visual and spatial separate
        components, 85
    See also working memory
signal-detection theory (SDT)
    models, 36, 48–49, 185, 236,
        237
sign language, 96
similarity effect, 127, 131–32
Simpson's paradox, 66
single dissociation, 54, 55
single-photon emission compu-
    terized tomograph, 448, 509
skill learning. See procedural
    memory

skills practice, 7–8, 284, 560–61,
    636
Skinner box, 16
sleep deprivation, 103
sleeper effect, 183
sleeping pills, 540
SMF. See source monitoring
    framework
SOA. See strength of association
socialization of memory, 283–92,
    323–24
    autobiographical memories
        and, 286–91
    gender differences, 322
    language and event recall,
        288–91
    nonconscious memory and, 256
    performances and, 323
somatosensory cortex, 26
source memory, 17–18, 179–89
    accuracy measurement,
        184–87
    age-related deficits, 96, 188,
        189, 223, 224, 397, 403, 421,
        600–601
    amnesia for, 403–4, 599–601,
        603
    as attributions, 171, 180–81
    childhood development of,
        302, 603–4
    confusion of "my external vs.
        his external" events, 18
    definition of, 528
    event-related potentials and,
        528
    eyewitness suggestibility, 154,
        156–57, 181–84
    interpersonal reality monitor-
        ing, 187–88
    item memory vs., 397
    prefrontal cortex damage and,
        434, 599–601
    recollection and, 185, 215–25
    subjective measures of qualita-
        tive characteristics of,
        186–87
    variations in source informa-
        tion and, 185
source monitoring, 165, 175,
    302, 306
source monitoring framework
    (SMF), 180–89
    accuracy measurement,
        184–87
    eyewitness suggestibility, 154,
        156–57, 181–84
    familiarity and, 217, 236–37
    interpersonal reality monitor-
        ing, 187–88
    nonconscious memory and,
        245
    reality monitoring and, 307n.4
    remembering and, 238

SP. *See* scopolamine
spaced practice effect, 350–54
spacing judgments, 165, 170
sparse random conjunctive coding, 592
spatial location judgments, 165, 171
spatial memory, 363–72
  brain region and, 367, 369, 371, 496, 631
  exploration vs. maps, 367–68
  frames of reference, 366–67
  hierarchical order and, 128–29, 366, 370, 587, 588
  object working memory and, 631
  person-based vs. object-based reference frames, 364–65
  for places, 319–20, 365
  rehearsal and, 284
  relations among elements, 366
  space around the body, 370–71
  storage and rehearsal theory, 631
  See also cognitive map; visuo-spatial sketchpad
spatial working memory, 629, 630–31
specificity
  of infant memory, 276–77
  See also encoding, specificity principle
SPECT. *See* single-photon emission computerized tomography
speech. *See* aphasia; semantic dementia; words
speed-accuracy tradeoff, 49, 173
spontaneous novelty preference tasks, 491–92
spontaneous recovery, 10
spreading activation, 397
SPT effect. *See* subject-performed tasks
S-R theory, 4–14, 37–38, 42, 245
  antecedents, 4
  cognitivist critiques of, 15–16
  forgetting and, 12–14
  infant memory retention studies, 269–73, 276–77
  intra-list repetition of items and, 132
state dependency
  drug/retrieval relationship, 546–47
  encoding specificity and, 100–101
  retrieval and, 52, 337
statement reality analysis, 187–88
stem completion, 247–50, 404

stereotyping
  nonconscious memory and, 245
  source monitoring framework and, 188
Sternberg scanning task, 86
stimulus generation, 8
stimulus-response psychology. *See* S-R theory
stimulus-specific characteristics, processing of, 97–98
STM. *See* short-term memory
stochastic independence, 248, 249, 255, 256
storage of memory. *See* memory storage
story repetition, contextual memory and, 96
story schemas, 315, 647
street drugs, 543
strength of association, 3, 397
stress
  automatic performance despite, 8
  negative effect on memory, 380, 386, 470, 472
  See also posttraumatic stress disorder
striate cortex, 26, 413, 415, 436
stroke patients, 26
Stroop color naming task, 404
structural equation modeling, 509
structural multiple-memory systems, 250
study-phase retrieval and reminding, 126, 127–28, 132
study/test compatibility, 203
subcallosal area, 471
subcortical dementias, 452–54, 647
  central executive disruption by, 441, 442
  characterizations and causes, 452, 469
  contrasted with cortical dementia, 453
subicular complex, 451, 485, 489
subjective organization, 26–27, 60, 97
subjective report, 224
subjectivity, 35, 250
  clustering, 16, 60
  fluent processing and, 254
  nonconscious memory and, 256, 257
  qualitative characteristics of memories and, 186–87
  of recollection and familiarity, 215–25, 611
  remembering and knowing, 224, 229–41
  See also autonoetic consciousness

subject-performed tasks, 102–3, 137–45
  age component, 145, 417
  data, 139–42
  enactment paradigm, 137–45
  physical movement as crucial component, 142, 145
  physical vs. imaginary movement, 143–44
  real vs. imaginary objects, 143
  theoretical approaches, 137–39
substantia nigra, 453
subthreshold recall, 9
successive tests, 62–63
  contingency analysis and, 59–67
suggestibility
  of children, 302–3, 321
  false autobiographical memories and, 187
  individual differences, 158, 187
  recollection fallibility and, 150, 158, 159–60, 181–84, 316–17
  recovered memories and, 317, 385
sulcus lateralis, 473
superior lateral temporal region, 473
Supervisory Attentional System, 87
supramarginal gyrus, 630
surface dyslexia, 450
survey knowledge, 369
synapses
  Alzheimer's loss of, 443
  decay-linked forgetting, 12
  Hebbian learning rule and, 593
systems approach, 629., *See also* network models of memory

tacrine, 549–50
tactile memory, 396
targeted recall, 316
target retrievability hypothesis, 199, 200, 202
task analysis. *See* experimental methods
taxon memory, 627
temazepam, 543
template hypothesis. *See* multiple template hypothesis
temporal details. *See* time
temporal lobes, 26, 430, 473
  Alzheimer's involvement, 443
  atrophy/progressive aphasia, 448, 449, 450, 451, 452
  damage/amnesic consequences research and, 466–68, 647
  episodic memory and, 413, 508, 510

memory systems and, 634–35, 637

remember/know responses, 618

semantic memory activation, 508

and stress-related amnesia, 472

See also medial temporal lobe

temporal order judgments, 165–66, 167–70, 171

temporal pole, 475, 477

temporolimbic dementia, 453. *See also* Alzheimer's disease

terminal meta-postulate, 129

test anxiety, 359

tests. *See* memory research

TGA (transient global amnesia), 433

thalamic dementia, 454

thalamic nuclei, 466

thalamo-cortical radiations, 469

thalamus, 431–33
  brain imaging studies, 504
  episodic retrieval and, 506
  mediodorsal nucleus, 469, 471, 473, 475
  semantic retrieval and, 509
  stress-related amnesia and, 472

Thatcher resignation (1990), memories of, 317, 382

theory of mind, 52, 297–307
  childhood amnesia explanation, 306–7
  metamemory and, 303–4
  self-referentiality, 300–304
  suggestibility and, 302–3
  three distinctions, 298
  See also knowing; socialization of memory

third-person attribution, 298

three-dimensional concept-space, 35–37

time
  autobiographical memories and, 186
  episodic memory and, 633
  memory for, 171, 473
  prospective remembering, 50, 398, 417

tip-of-the-tongue states, 197, 199, 200–201
  about nonexistent knowledge, 202–3
  in older adults, 398
  partial retrieval and, 338, 339–40

TODAM model, 224, 572, 574, 575, 583–84

TOTs. *See* tip-of-the-tongue states

Tour model, spatial semantic hierarchy, 370

trace conditioning paradigm, 437, 620

trace decay, 83–84

training task, 109, 110–14
  long-term retention relationship, 353–54
  structural similarity with transfer tasks, 99, 100–101, 102, 112–14, 119, 337
  transfer of, 10–12

trait anxiety, 323, 359

transactive memory, 324

transentorhinal cortex, 453

transfer-appropriate processing, 99, 100–101, 102, 113, 234

transfer of knowledge, 10–12, 109–18, 245
  adaptive expertise, 118–19
  awareness/memory dissociation, 245–49
  as basic learning, 109
  direction reversal, 111
  fluent reprocessing and, 254
  informed vs. uninformed, 113–14
  ironic effects of familiarity and recollection, 217–18, 224
  knowing and, 234
  as memory-dependent, 110
  negative, 12
  nonspecific vs. specific, 11–12
  optimal learning strategies, 111–12
  positive, 12, 111–12, 113
  serial learning experiments, 125, 126–27
  from short-term to long-term memory, 82, 93–94, 472–73, 478
  similarity of training and transfer task processing and, 99, 100–101, 102, 112–14, 119, 337
  as specific or general, 109–10
  See also expertise

transfer of training, 10–12

transient global amnesia, 433

traumatic memories, 383–88, 477, 478
  as flashbacks, 336, 387
  forgetting of, 383–84, 386
  mechanisms of, 386–87
  mnestic block syndrome, 470–71

trial-and-error learning, 4, 5

trial-unique delayed nonmatching to sample task, 486

triazolam (Halcion), 540, 543, 545

Tulving-Wiseman function, 63–64

Über das Gedächtnis (Ebbinghaus), 46

unconscious memory. See nonconscious memory

unconscious plagiarism. See cryptoamnesia

unconscious repression, 386

unconscious transference, 184

unitary memory system, 41–42

unknown, knowledge of, 202, 203

unlearning, 150

unlearning recovery hypothesis, 63

Valium (diazepam), 540, 542, 543, 545

vascular dementia, 454

vasodilators, 550

ventral amygdalofugal pathway, 471

ventral striatum, 475

Verbal Behavior (Skinner), 15–16

verbal behavior, 15–16, 22

verbal intelligence, 304

verbal memory
  action memory compared with, 139–40
  Alzheimer's disruption of, 444
  conversation recall, 320–21, 323
  enactment paradigm and, 137–45, 323
  encoding specificity principle, 99
  event memory relationship, 288–91
  levels-of-processing effect, 139
  memory codes types, 95
  phonological loop, 506
  serial ordering, 125–33
  short-term study techniques, 78–79, 81, 83
  visual memory as superior to, 98, 364
  for vivid concepts, 364
  word length effect, 83–84
  working memory model, 83–85, 506, 630–31

verbal rehearsal, 21

verbal symbols
  associative interference theory, 63
  memory association, 25
  posterior parietal cortex and, 26
  research materials methodology, 53
  semantic memory and, 22
  See also language; words

verbal tasks
  drug effects on, 548–49
  implicit test items, 251
  subject-performed tasks vs.,
    138–45
violent events, eyewitness memory for, 379–80
visual expectancy, infancy, 269
visual imagery, 25, 52
  diagrammatic space, 371
  infancy studies, 269
  as memory aid, 155
  paired-associates learning and,
    85
  posterior parietal cortex and,
    26
  spatial mental representations
    and, 369, 371–72
  susceptibility to false memories and, 187
visualization technique, 385
visual memory
  aging and, 396
  Alzheimer's disruption, 444,
    445
  auditory memory's superiority
    to, 130–31
  autobiographical memory and,
    186
  brain region and, 496
  face recognition studies, 95
  mental spaces, 364–65, 368
  perception-imagery relationship, 95, 102
  priming and, 435
  short-term measurement,
    80–81
  spatial representations and,
    364, 631
  as superior to verbal memory,
    98, 364
  verbal codes relationship, 95
  as working memory, 85,
    630–31
  young children's memory coding, 84
  See also visuo-spatial
    sketchpad
visual-paired comparison test,
  491–92, 493, 494, 495
visual perceptual identification
  test, 216

visual persistence, 396
visuospatial deficits, 452
  Alzheimer's vs. Huntington's
    patients, 453
visuo-spatial sketchpad (working
  memory), 83, 85, 442,
  506–7, 508, 630, 631
visuo-spatial store, 22, 25
vitamin E, 550
vocabulary. See language
voice recognition studies, 95
voluntary actions, 302
VTs. See verbal tasks

warm-up, 11
wartime memories, accuracy of,
  318
Watergate testimony, 320
Wisconsin Card Sorting Test,
  600
witness testimony. See abuse testimony; eyewitness testimony
WM. See working memory
word list learning. See serial
  learning
words
  acoustic similarity effects,
    81
  actions memory vs. memory
    for, 137–46
  encoding continuum of sensitivity and, 138, 145
  episodic memory and, 503,
    634
  fragment completion, 51, 55,
    398, 404
  imagery-arousing value, 25
  length effect, 83–84, 85
  level of processing, 97
  memory chunking and, 79
  memory enhancement, 102
  pair-testing symmetry, 65
  presentation frequency judgments, 169
  preverbal infant memory, 55
  priming and, 576–77
  processing instructions, 52
  recall/recognition dissociation
    for, 252
  recency/recall analyses,
    560–64

rhyme encoding cues, 100–101
semantic coding, 96, 98
semantic dementia comprehension failure, 450
semantic memory and, 22
stem completion, 247–50, 404
See also tip-of-the-tongue
  states
working memory, 77–78, 83–88,
  627
  activation analysis, 508,
    510–12
  aging and "cluttered," 418, 419
  aging and reduction in, 400,
    401, 415–16
  Alzheimer's deficits, 442, 444,
    446–47
  brain imaging studies, 506–8,
    510–12, 513, 630–32, 637
  brain regions and, 26, 472,
    506–8, 510–12, 513, 630–
    32, 637
  central executive, 83, 85, 86,
    87–88, 442, 506, 507–8, 630,
    631–32
  definitions of, 86, 472, 506
  dementia impairment of, 442
  functional network models,
    513
  long-term expertise and, 115,
    116–18
  model, 83
  operation span, 86–87
  phonological loop, 83, 84–85,
    96, 506, 508, 630–31
  selective disorders, 427–29
  short-term memory as component of, 77
  span differences, 84–85,
    86–88
  spatial/object separation, 631
  tripartite model, 506, 630
  visuo-spatial sketchpad, 83,
    85, 506–7, 508, 630, 631

Xanax (alprazolam), 540, 545

Yerkes-Dodson curve, 379
yes-no recognition test. See free-choice recognition test
Yule's Q, 62, 63, 64, 65, 66
  mean value, 64, 67, 68, 69

Name Index

Page locators annotated with *f* indicate figures.
Page locators annotated with *n* indicate notes.
Page locators annotated with *t* indicate tables.
Page locators in italic indicate chapter reference listings.

Aaron, F., 277, *280*
Abbott, P., 433, *439*
Abeles, M., 474, *478*
Abelson, R. P., 116, *121,* 285,
  295, 334, 338, 340, *345*
Abi-Dargham, A. A., 549, *552*
Ablin, D. S., 305, *310*
Abra, J. C., 63, 68, *70*
Abson, V., 322, *324*
Acker, J. D., 413, *424*
Ackerley, S. S., 601, *606*
Ackerman, B. P., 396, 399, *408*
Ackerman, H., 436, *438*
Ackil, J. K., 157, 158, *160,* 182,
  184, *189, 190, 195,* 302, *307*
Adams, D., 158, *160,* 403, *405*
Adams, J. A., 81, *88*
Adams, J. K., 48, *56,* 245, *257,*
  574, *579*
Adams, L. T., 251*t, 257*
Adams, M. M., 637, *640*
Adams, N., 636, *640*
Adams, R. D., 466, *484*
Adams, S., 287, 288, *292, 293*
Adelson, B., 114, *119*
Adler, S. A., 277, 278, *282*
Adolfsson, R., 144, *148*
Adolphs, R., 251*t, 257*
Aggleton, J. P., 174, *175,* 225,
  225, 431, 433, *437, 438,* 489,
  496, *497,* 618, *621*

Agid, Y., 442, 453, *455, 458*
Aguirre, G. K., 189, *195,* 367,
  372, 630, 631, 632, 633, *639,*
  642
Akbudak, E., 631, 634, *640*
Aksu-Koc, A. A., 301, *307*
Albert, M. S., 255, *260,* 414, 415,
  425, 442, 454, *458,* 505, *519,*
  635, 636, *641*
Albertson, S., 398, 400, *407*
Albertson-Owens, S. A., 223,
  227
Alexander, M. P., 602, *607,* 620,
  625
Alivisatos, B., 506, 507, 513,
  518
Alkire, M. T., 380, 387, *389,* 505,
  506, *515*
Allamano, N., 81, *89*
Allan, K., 103, 521, 525, 526*f,*
  527*f,* 529, 530, 531, 532,
  532*f,* 533, 533*f, 534, 536,*
  609, *621*
Allan, L. G., 217, *226, 228,* 251*t,*
  254, *258, 261*
Allan, T. M., 396, *407*
Allen, D., 233, *241,* 545, *551*
Allen, G. L., 366, *372*
Allen, K. C., 52, *57*
Almkvist, O., 415, *422,* 454, *454,*
  505, *515*

Alpert, N. M., 255, *260,* 414,
  415, *425,* 505, *516, 519,* 635,
  636, 637, *640, 641*
Alsop, D. C., 367, *372,* 507, *515,*
  632, *639*
Altman, L., 131, *133*
Alvarez, P., 429, 433, *440,* 489,
  490, 491, 494, *497*
Alvarez-Royo, P., 489, *497*
Alvord, E. C., Jr., 472, *483*
Alzheimer, A., 466, *478*
Amabile, T. A., 277, *279*
Amaducci, L., 454, *458*
Amaral, D. G., 468, *479,* 486,
  489, 490, 494, 495, 496, *497,*
  498, 499, 605, *606*
Ambadar, Z., 383, 384, 385, 386,
  387, *392*
American Psychiatric Asso-
  ciation, 441, *454,* 550,
  550
Amorim, M. A., 368, *377*
Amsterdam, B. K., *307*
Anas, A., 251*t,* 254, *257*
Andersen, E. S., 446, *455*
Andersen, J., 466, *478*
Andersen, P., 488, *498*
Anderson, C. A., 186, 188, *195*
Anderson, E., 87, *91*
Anderson, J. A., 80, *88,* 578, *579,*
  584, 585, *594, 595*

675

Anderson, J. R., 7, 12, 14, 15, 22, 23, 24, 25, *27, 31,* 34, *42,* 101, 101*f, 104,* 111, 112, 118, *119,* 120, 171, *175,* 397, *405,* 418, *421,* 557, 558, 559, 560, 561, 562, 563, 566, 567, 567*f,* 568, *569, 570,* 572, 577, *579,* 583, 584, 593, *594*
Anderson, M. C., *104,* 340, *343*
Anderson, N. D., 103, *105,* 398, 399, *405,* 411, 414, *421,* 503, *515,* 610, *621*
Anderson, R. B., 564, *569*
Anderson, R. C., 98, *104*
Anderson, R. E., 60, *71*
Anderson, S. J., 186, *190,* 234, 235, 235*f,* 237, 238, 239, *241,* 317, 319, *326,* 382, 383, *388, 389,* 598, *606*
Andersson, J., 415, *422,* 505, *515*
Anderton-Brown, C., 231, 239, *243*
Andrade,J., 542, *551*
Andreasen, N. C., 505, 510, 514, *514*
Andrews, B., 322, *325,* 385, *388*
Anes, M. D., 231, *244*
Angell, K. E., 184, *194,* 233, 238, *244*
Ansay, C., 200, *207*
Anscombe, G. E. M., 298, *307*
Anthony, T., 321, *324*
Antonini, A., 415, *421*
Antonini, T., 201, *211*
Antoun, N., 448, 452, *455*
Arbib, M. A., 584, *594*
Arbuckle, T. Y., 62, *72,* 139, *145*
Arenberg, D., 396, *407*
Arguin, M., 630, *638*
Armbruster, T., 184, *191*
Armour, V., 217, *225*
Armstrong, D., 299, *307*
Arndt, D. R., *374*
Arndt, S., 510, 514, *514*
Arnett, J. L., 396, *406*
Asch, S. E., 15, *27,* 64, *70,* 157, *160*
Ashby, F. G., 577, *579*
Ashworth, A., 449, *454*
Askwall, S., 204, *211*
Astington, J. W., 301, 303, *307, 309,* 310
Atkinson, R. C., 20, 21*f, 27,* 81, 82*f, 88,* 93, *104,* 130, *133,* 185, *190,* 215, *225,* 396, *405,* 471, *478, 551,* 572, 576, *579,* 630, *638*
Atlas, S., 507, *515,* 632, *639*
Atwood, M. E., 118, *121*
Austin, G., 15, *28*
Ausubel, D. P., 98, *104*
Averbach, E., 166, *177*
Avons, S., 84, *88*

Awh, E., 85, *88, 91,* 506, 507, *515, 519,* 630, 631, *638, 640, 642*
Ayers, M. S., 154, *160*
Ayres, T. J., 94, *106*

Babcock, R. L., 400, *409*
Babinsky, R., 380, *389,* 469, 470, 473, *479, 481,* 541, *551*
Bachevalier, J., 278, 279, 431, *437,* 492, *497*
Bäckman, L., 103, *106,* 138, 139, 140, 141, 142, 144, *145, 147,* 148, 415, *422,* 469, *480,* 505, *515*
Bacon, F. T., 181, *190*
Baddeley, A. D., 21, 22, *27,* 52, 53, *56,* 77, 78, 79, 80, 81, 82, 83, 83*f,* 84, 85, 87, *88, 89, 90, 91,* 95, 96, 101, 101*f,* 102, 103, *104, 105,* 150, *160,* 189, *190,* 205, *207,* 215, *225,* 251*t, 257,* 322, *331,* 333, 337, *343, 344,* 398, 400, *405, 409,* 416, 419, *422,* 428, *437,* 440, 442, 443, 444, 445, 447, 448, 450, *454, 456,* 472, *478,* 506, *515,* 627, 630, 631, *638, 643*
Bahrick, A. S., 348, 350, 351, 352*f,* 354, *360*
Bahrick, H. P., 99, *104,* 205, *207,* 316, 319, *324,* 347, 348, 349, 349*f,* 350, 350*f,* 351, 351*f,* 352*f,* 353, 354, 355*t,* 356, 357, 357*t,* 358, 359, *360, 361,* 370, *373*
Bahrick, L. E., 351, 352*f,* 354, *360*
Bahrick, P. E., 351, 352*f,* 354, *360*
Bahrick, P. O., 353, 358, 359, *360*
Baillargeon, R., 273, *279*
Bain, J. D., 64, *71,* 583, *595*
Bajo, T. M., 34, *43*
Bak, T., 449, 452, *454, 456*
Baker, J. R., 504, *519,* 634, *642*
Baker, S. C., 635, *639*
Baldwin, D. A., 299, *307*
Ballard, D., 630, 631, 632, *639*
Balota, D. A., 34, *42,* 141, *145,* 158, *160,* 395, 397, 398, 401, 403, 404, *405, 406, 409,* 412, *421,* 506, *516,* 630, *639*
Balthazard, C. G., 566, *569*
Banaji, M. R., 27, *27,* 188, *190,* 256, *257, 258,* 316, *324,* 347, *361*
Bandy, D., 158, *162,* 186, *194,* 403, *409,* 531, *536*
Banks, W. P., 48, *56,* 185, *190,* 372, *373*

Barclay, C. R., 319, *324, 325*
Barclay, J. R., 98, 99, *104,* 179, *190*
Bareggi, S. R., 548*t, 553*
Bargh, J. A., 255, 256, *257*
Barker, D., 87, *91*
Barker, S., 433, *439*
Barnard, P. J., 322, *331*
Barnat, S. A., 277, *279*
Barnes, A. E., 341, *343*
Barnes, C. A., 592, *594*
Barnes, J. M., 13, *27,* 54, *56,* 63, *70*
Barnett, S. M., 118, *119*
Barnhardt, T. M., 340, *343*
Barnier, A. J., 316, *328*
Barnwater, U., 600, *606*
Baron, J. -C., 505, *516*
Baron-Cohen, S., 305, *307, 308*
Barr, A., 15, *27*
Barr, R., 272, 273, 277, *279, 281*
Barrs, B., 245, *257*
Bartlett, F. C., 15, *28,* 46, *56,* 98, 100, *104,* 150, 151, *160,* 166, *175,* 179, *190, 257,* 315, *325,* 466, 474, *478,* 645, 647, *648*
Bartlett, J. C., 217, *225,* 420, *422*
Bartling, C. A., 69, *70,* 157, *162*
Bashore, T. R., Jr., 415, *422*
Basso, A., 428, *437*
Bassok, M., 111, 113, *119*
Batchelder, W. H., 64, *70,* 166, *175,* 185, *190, 194,* 221, 223, *225, 227*
Bates, E., 320, *327*
Bates, J., 635, *642*
Bates, J. F., 403, *409*
Batterman-Faunce, J. M., 305, *308,* 321, 322, *327,* 383, *390*
Baudry, M., 549, *553*
Bauer, P. J., 273, *279,* 284, 285, 289, 290, *292,* 602, 604, *606*
Baumgardner, M. H., 183, *194*
Bayen, U. J., 185, *190*
Bayles, K. A., 445, *454*
Beach, F. A., 646, *648*
Beall, A. C., *375*
Bean, G., 140, 143, *146*
Beasley, C. M., 111, *119*
Beason-Held, L. L., 489, 490, *497*
Beatty, W. W., 442, 454, *454,* 474, *478*
Beaudouin, V., 367, *374*
Beauvois, M. F., 434, *438*
Bechara, A., 251*t, 257*
Bechterew, W. von, 466, *478*
Becker, J. T., 444, 445, 451, *454, 456*
Begg, I., 67, 69, *70,* 205, *207,* 217, 222, *226, 225,* 251*t,* 254, *257*
Begleiter, H., 469, *484*
Behrens, Chr., 466, *481*

Behrmann, M., 95, *106,* 365, *373*
Bekerian, D. A., 27, *28,* 321, *325,* 335, 341, *343, 345*
Bell, M. A., 454, *458*
Belleville, S., 630, *638*
Bellezza, F. S., 236, *242*
Belli, R. F., 182, 184, 188, 189*n,* 190, 319, *325*
Belliveau, J., 632, *642*
Bellos, S. A., 617, *625*
Bench, C. S., 550, *553*
Bendiksen, M. A., 383, 384, 385, 386, 387, *392*
Bendixen, B., *454*
Benfield, A., 472, *481*
Benjamin, A. S., 353, *361*
Bennett, A., 549, *552*
Bennett, D. A., 454, *458*
Bennett, H., 443, 445, *458*
Bennett, R. T., 301, *311,* 603, *607*
Bennetto, L., 306, *308*
Benson, D. F., 189, *195,* 454, *458,* 601, *606*
Benson, J. B., 289, *292*
Benson, W. M., 128, *135*
Bentin, S., 616, 618, *621, 623*
Benton, A. L., 601, *606*
Benton, J. S., 448, *458*
Benzing, W. C., 436, *437*
Benzing, W. E., 251*t,* 257
Ben-zur, H., 96, *105*
Berg, G., 443, *455*
Berger, S. A., 316, *324,* 348, *360*
Bergman, E. T., 318, *329, 391*
Bergson, H., 22, *28*
Berie, J. L., 541, 548*t, 552*
Berkowitz, C. D., 320, *327*
Berman, N., 450, *458*
Bermejo, F., 454, *458*
Berntsen, D., 237, *241,* 316, *325*
Berry, D. C., 251*t,* 257
Berry, S. L., 204, *209*
Berthoz, A., 364, 367, 368, *373, 374, 377*
Bertolo, L., 368, *373*
Bessenoff, G. R., 188, *194*
Betz, A. L., 157, *160,* 319, *331*
Bever, T. G., 15, 16, *29, 30,* 129, *133*
Bhatt, R. S., 276, 277, *280*
Biassou, N., 435, *437*
Bidrose, S., 305, *310*
Biegelmann, U. E., 140, 141, *147*
Bierschwale, D., 299, *310*
Biggio, G., 549, *552*
Billings, F. J., 158, *161,* 187, *192,* 317, 323, *327*
Bindschaedler, C., 434, *439*
Binet, A., 150, 156, *160*
Bink, M. L., 255, *259*
Birbaumer, N., 436, *438,* 474, *480*
Birch, B., 548*t, 551*

Birch, C. S., 525, 526*f,* 529, 530, *536*
Birch, J. E., 399, *405,* 415, *422, 423*
Birtwistle, J., 140, *147*
Bishop, K. I., 544, 545, 546, *551*
Bishop, Y. M. M., 62, *70*
Bisiach, E., 365, *373*
Bjork, E. L., *104,* 338, 340, *343,* 557, *569*
Bjork, R. A., 19, *30,* 41, *43,* 54, *56,* 59, *72,* 102, 103, *104, 105,* 130, *133,* 157, *160,* 205, *207, 208, 210,* 246, 252, 253, 254, 255, *258, 260,* 304, *310,* 337, 338, 340, *343, 345,* 353, 354, 355, 356, 357, *361, 362,* 557, *569*
Bjorklund, D., 283, *295*
Black, J. B., 315, *325,* 334, 338, 339, 340, *345*
Black, S., 397, *405*
Black, S. E., 620, *623*
Blades, M., 302, *310*
Blake, M., 200, 201, *207*
Blake, P. T., 368, *375*
Blamire, A. M., 631, 633, *640*
Blanchard, L., 403, *409*
Blaxton, R. A., 636, *638*
Blaxton, T. A., 40, *43,* 102, *104,* 233, *241,* 251*t,* 257, 610, 618, *621*
Bleuler, E., 469, *478*
Blick, K. L., 454, *458*
Blinkenberg, M., 466, *478*
Bloch, G., 631, *640*
Block, R. A., 18, *29,* 166, 167, 169, 170, *176*
Block, R. I., 542, *552*
Bloom, P., 372, *373*
Blume, H., 469, *483*
Blumer, D., 601, *606*
Bly, B. M., 472, *481*
Bobinski, M., 413, *422*
Bobrow, D. G., 335, 336, 338, 341, *345*
Boddington, S., 550, *553*
Bogartz, R. S., 561, *569*
Bohannon, J. N., 317, *325,* 382, *388*
Bohbot, V., 433, *438*
Bohl, J., 473, 476*f, 479*
Boles Ponto, L. L., 510, 514, *515*
Boller, F., 445, *454*
Boller, K., 277, 278, *280*
Bolton, J. S., 466, *479*
Bonanno, G. A., *257*
Bond, A., 547, 548*t, 551*
Bonde, C., 466, *478*
Bonebakker, A. E., 542, *551*
Bonhoeffer, K., 466, *479*
Bonke, B., 542, *551*
Bonnet, M. H., 387, *388*

Booker, J., 252, *260*
Bookheimer, S. Y., 636, *638*
Bookstein, F. L., 508, 510, 513, 514, *517*
Boone, K. B., 448, 450, *457, 458*
Borditsky, L., 372, *373*
Born, D. G., 52, *57*
Born, R., 632, *642*
Bornstein, R. F., *257*
Boruch, R. F., 61, *72*
Borza, M. A., 277, 278, *282*
Boshuizen, H. P. A., 114, *121*
Bothell, D., 559, *569,* 572, *579*
Boucher, J., 305, *308*
Bougousslavsky, J., 454, *458*
Bouras, C., 474, *480*
Bourne, L. E., 103, *105,* 353, *361*
Bovair, S., 113, *121*
Bowen, D. J., 320, *326*
Bowen, D. M., 448, *458*
Bower, G. H., 3, 4, 11, 15, 16, 18, 19, 23, 24, 25, *27, 28, 29,* 34, 40, *42,* 52, *56,* 93, 94, 98, *104,* 128, 129, 130, *133,* 170, 171, *175, 176,* 367, 369, *376, 377,* 383, 386, 387, *388,* 398, *408,* 572, *579,* 587, *594*
Bowers, J. S., 252, 253, *257, 260,* 524, *534*
Bowers, K. S., 566, *569*
Bowes, J., 544, 545, *551*
Bowler, D. M., 232*t,* 233, 240, *241,* 306, *308*
Bowles, N., 141, *147*
Bowyer, P. A., 39, *42,* 64, 66, 69, *70, 71*
Boyle, P., 287, 288, *292*
Braak, E., 443, *454,* 469, 473, 476*f, 479*
Braak, H., 443, *454,* 469, 473, 476*f, 479*
Bradley, A., 87, *91*
Bradley, M., 204, *208*
Bradshaw, G. L., 113, *121*
Bradshaw, J. M., 183, *191,* 320, *325*
Bradshaw, P. W., 320, *325*
Brady, T., 632, *642*
Brainerd, C. J., 339, *343*
Brandimonte, M., 335, *343*
Brandt, J. P., 435, *438, 456*
Branier, A. J., 157, *160*
Branscombe, N. R., 251*t, 261*
Bransford, J. D., 52, *56,* 94, 95, 98, 99, 100*t, 104, 106,* 113, 114, *121,* 151, 152, 153, *160, 161,* 179, 180, 183, *190, 192,* 257, 257*t,* 337, *345*
Brasherskrug, T., 637, *640*
Braune, R., 415, *425*
Braver, T. S., 506, 507, 514, *515,* 630, 632, *638, 639*
Bray, N. W., 166, *175*

Brechtelsbauer, D., 469, 473, 481
Bredart, S., 204, *207*
Breedin, S. D., 614, *624*
Breen, E. K., 445, 448, 452, 453, *454, 455*
Bregman, A. S., 352, *361*
Breir, A., 549, *553*
Brekke, N., 188, *195*
Bremer, D., 337, *344*
Bremner, J. D., 470, *479*
Bressi, S., 87, *88,* 442, 447, *454*
Brewer, J. B., 365, *373,* 414, *423,* 504, 514, *515, 516,* 522, *534,* 617, *622,* 634, *638, 639*
Brewer, W. F., 152, *160,* 186, *190,* 236, 237, *241,* 315, 317, 318, 319, *325, 331*
Brewin, C. R., 322, *325,* 386, 387, *388, 389*
Brice, 433, *439*
Brickson, M., 492, *497*
Bricogne, S., 367, *374*
Brier, A., 548*t,* 552
Briere, J., 188, *193,* 383, 384, 385, *389, 390*
Briggs, G. E., 13, 14*f, 28,* 63, *70*
Briggs, R., 367, *373*
Brigham, J. C., 321, *325*
Brinley, J. F., 399, *405,* 415, *422*
Broadbent, D. E., 14, 19, *28,* 77, *89,* 251*t, 257,* 322, *325*
Broca, P., 465, *479*
Brodmann, K., 466, 467*f, 479*
Brodwick, M., 491, *499*
Brody, L. R., 273, *280*
Broe, G., 443, 445, *458*
Broks, P., 544, 548, *551*
Bronen, R. A., 470, *479*
Brooks, B. M., 144, *146,* 236, *241*
Brooks, D. J., 637, *640*
Brooks, D. N., 251*t, 257*
Brooks, L. R., 25, *28,* 85, *89, 104*
Brown, A. L., 140, *146*
Brown, A. S., 40, *43,* 201, *207,* 251*t, 259,* 320, *325,* 339, *343,* 403, *406*
Brown, C. M., 620, *623*
Brown, G. M., 505, 506, *517,* 531, *534,* 633, 634, *640*
Brown, J., 53, *56,* 81, *89,* 103, *104,* 154, *161,* 449, *454,* 544, 545, *551*
Brown, M. W., 174, *175,* 225, *225,* 431, 433, *437,* 497, *497,* 544, 545, *551,* 618, *621*
Brown, N. R., 171, *175*
Brown, R., 201, *207,* 317, *325,* 338, 339, *343,* 381, *389*
Brown, S. C., 38, 54, 93
Bruce, D., 129, *133,* 321, *331,* 347, 350, *361,* 557, *569*

Bruce, M., 547, 548*t, 551*
Bruck, M., 150, 159, *160,* 321, 322, *325*
Bruckbauer, T., 506, *516*
Bruell, M. J., 302, *312*
Brun, A., 448, 449, 454, *455, 458*
Bruner, J., 15, *28,* 318, 324, *325*
Brush, S. G., 35, *42*
Bryant, D. J., 371, *373*
Bryant, P., 301, *310*
Bryant, S., 139, 140, *146*
Bub, D., 445, *455*
Buchanan, M., 83, 84, *89*
Büchel, C., 509, 514, *515*
Buchner, A., 185, *190,* 221, 222, 223, *225,* 236, *241*
Bucht, G., 144, *148*
Buckner, J., 288, *292*
Buckner, R. L., 23, *28,* 158, *162,* 256, 402, 403, *406, 409,* 501, 502, 504, 505, 506, 510, 512, 513, *515, 519,* 522, 526, *536,* 599, *606,* 609, 610, 614, 616, 617, *621, 624,* 627, *628,* 629, 631, 633, 634, 635, 636, *638, 639, 640, 641, 642, 643*
Bucy, P. C., 469, *479, 481*
Buffalo, E. A., 432, 433, *438,* 495, *497*
Bull, M. P., 317, *332*
Bull, R., 385, *391*
Bullemer, P., 251*t,* 252, *260*
Bunce, S. C., 322, 323, *326*
Bunge, M., 35, *42*
Burgess, P. W., 87, *91,* 189, *190,* 334, 336, 338, 340, 341, 342, *343,* 416, *425,* 452, *455*
Burggraf, C. S., 320, 321, *331*
Burke, A., 380, *389*
Burke, D. M., 199, *207,* 395, 397, 398, 402, *406, 407*
Burns, B. D., 111, *122*
Burns, H. D., 415, *425*
Burns, H. J., 54, *57,* 154, 155*f,* 161, 317, *328*
Burns, T. E., 379, *391*
Burock, M., 616, 617, *621,* 633, 636, *638*
Burrell, Q. L., 558, *569*
Burroughs, W. J., 366, *377*
Burrowa, E. H., 475, *480*
Burt, C. D. B., 319, *327*
Burton, K. W., 435, *438*
Buschke, H., 81, *90,* 356, *361*
Bush, J. G., 186, 187, 188, *192*
Bushnell, I. W. R., 269, *280*
Butler, S., 287, *293*
Butler, T., 217, *225*
Butterfield, E. C., 200, *207, 406*
Butters, N., 436, *439,* 442, 443, 445, 446, 454, *454, 455, 456, 457, 458, 459,* 475, *482,* 488, *499,* 506, *515*

Butterworth, B., 471, *479*
Byrd, M., 103, *105,* 396, 397, *406,* 413, *422*

Cabeza, R., 26, *30,* 103, 189, *194,* 414, 421, *422,* 501, 502, 503*f,* 504, 505, 506, 510, 511*f,* 512*f,* 513, *515, 517, 518,* 531, *535,* 599, *607,* 609, 617, 620, *621, 623,* 628, 633, 634, 635, *639, 641*
Cahill, L., 380, 387, *389,* 469, 470, *479, 482,* 486, *497,* 505, 506, *515,* 541, 549, *551, 553*
Cain, D. P., 466, *483*
Cairns, P., 442, 445, *455*
Calabrese, P., 469, 473, 475, 477, *479, 481*
Calkins, M. W., 7, *28*
Campbell, B. A., 274, *280*
Campbell, C. E., 542, *551*
Campbell, J., 304, *308*
Campione, J. C., 140, *146*
Campos-de-Carvalho, M., 276, *280*
Canas, J., 34, *43*
Canfield, R. L., 269, *280*
Cannon, T. D., 189, *195*
Cantor, J., 186, *192*
Capelli, S., 470, *479*
Caplan, D., 85, 86, *92*
Cappa, S. F., 448, *455*
Capps, J. L., 398, *407*
Caramazza, A., 201, *209,* 430, *439,* 446, *455,* 632, *639*
Cardena, E., 386, *392*
Cardu, B., 472, *483*
Carey, P., 321, 323, *328*
Carillo, M. C., 620, *623*
Carlson, M. A., 322, *328*
Carlson, M. C., 418, *422*
Carlson-Radvansky, L., 365, *373*
Carmichael, L., 150, *160*
Carn, R., 433, *439*
Carpenter, P. A., 86, *89, 90,* 630, *640*
Carr, C. A., 504, *519,* 634, *642*
Carr, T. H., 340, *343*
Carr, W. S., 368, *377*
Carrillo, M. C., 620, *622*
Carroll, D. E., 292, *293*
Carruthers, M. J., 284, *292*
Carruthers, P., 299, *308*
Carter, A., 604, *608*
Casey, B. J., 472, *479,* 630, *639*
Catalan, M. J., 466, *480*
Caulton, D. A., 168, 172, 173*f,* 176
Ceci, S. J., 150, 159, *160,* 184, 187, 188, *190, 194,* 303, *308, 309,* 321, 322, *325, 330*
Ceraso, J., 339, *343*

Cerella, J., 399, *406*, 413, 415, 422
Cermak, L. S., 217, *225*, 442, 445, 454, *455*, 471, 475, *479*, *482*, 620, *622*
Cezayirli, E., 433, *439*
Chaiken, S., 224, *225*
Chaiklin, S., 371, *376*
Chalfonte, B. L., 94, *104, 105*
Challis, B. H., 34, *43*, 99, 102, *106*, 246, *260*
Chalom, D., 138, 140, 141, 142, *145*
Chambers, K. L., 182, 183, *190, 195*
Chan, A. S., 445, 446, *455*
Chance, S. S., *375*
Chandler, C., 49, *56*
Chao, L. L., 632, *639*
Chappell, M., 63, *70*, 557, *570*, 575, 576, 578, 579, *579*, 593, *595*
Charness, N., 109, 115, *120*
Charney, D. S., 387, 388, *390*, 470, *479, 481*, 549, *552*
Chase, H., 269, *281*
Chase, T. N., 453, *457*
Chase, W. G., 26, *28*, 98, *104*, 115, 116, 117, *120*, 363, 365, 366, 367, 370, *373*
Chawla, L., 320, *325*
Chechile, N. A., 368, *377*
Chelazzi, L., 636, *639*
Chemerinski, E., 443, *459*
Chen, K. S., 494
Chen, L. I., 369, *376*
Chen, Y., 185, *190*
Cheney, M., 397, *405*
Cheng, P. W., 112, 119, *120, 121*
Cherry, E. C., 53, *56*
Chertkow, H., 445, *455*
Chesney, G., *535*
Chi, M. T. H., 109, 110, 114, 118, *120*
Chiba, A. A., 469, *480*
Chiesi, H. L., 114, 117, 118, *120, 121*
Chiu, C. -Y. P., 469, *482*
Chomsky, N., 15, 16, *28*
Chow, K. L., 466, *479*, 647, 648
Chown, E., 370, *373*
Christal, R. E., 86, *90*
Christensen, A., 184, *194*, 321, *330*
Christensen, B., 508, 509, 510, *517*
Christianson, S. -A., 317, *325*, 380, *389*
Christie, D. F. M., 80, *91*
Christina, R. W., 353, 354, *361*
Chromiak, W., 169, *176*

Chrosniak, L. D., 181, 183, 186, *191*, 251*t, 258*, 397, 399, *407*
Chu, J. A., 385, *389*
Cicerone, K. D., 189, *191*
Cicinelli, J. G., 364, 368, *375*
Cipolotti, L., 471, *479*
Ciranni, M., 469, *482*
Cizaldo, T., 510, 514, *514*
Clare, L., 445, *455*
Clark, D. M., 322, *325*
Clark, E., 620, *621*, 621*n*
Clark, E. V., 372, *373*
Clark, H. H., 370, 372, *373*
Clark, K., 436, *440*
Clark, R. E., 436, *438*, 489, 490, 491, 492, 494, 495, *497*, *499*, 500
Clark, S., 557, *570*
Clark, S. E., 171, *175*, 224, *225*, 575, *580*
Clarkson, M. G., 279, *281*, 324, *328*
Clifford, B. R., 379, *389*
Clifton, R. K., 273, 279, *280*, *281*, 324, *328*
Clower, R. P., 489, 490, 494, *497*
Clubb, P. A., 290, *294*
Clydesdale, S., 454, *457*
Cobb, E., 320, *325*
Cochran, B. P., 181, *194*
Cocklin, T., 103, *105*
Cofer, C. N., 151, *160*
Cohen, D. J., 305, *308*
Cohen, G., 184, *190*, 234, 235, 235*f*, 238, 239, *241*, 317, 320, *325*, 339, *343*, 353, 358, 359, *361*, *362*, 400, *406*, 418, *422*, 598, *606*
Cohen, J., 245, *257*, 630, 632, *638, 639*
Cohen, J. D., 472, *479*, 506, 507, 514, *515*, 593, *594*, 630, *639*
Cohen, L. B., 269, *280*
Cohen, N. J., 174, *176*, 251*t, 257*, 317, *328*, 382, *391*, 402, *406*, 429, 436, *438*, 442, 448, *459*, 468, *480*, *482*, 497, *497*, 591, 592, *595*, *605*, *606*, 610, *621*, 627, 631, 634, *639*, *640*
Cohen, P. R., 15, *28*
Cohen, R. L., 102, *104*, 137, 138, 139, 140, 142, 143, 144, 145, *146, 148*
Cohen, R. M., 549, *554*
Cole, D. G., 413, *423*
Coleman, P. D., 412, *422*
Coleman, R. E., 415, 421, *424*
Coles, M. G. H., 521, 522, *535*
Collinge, J., 445, 449, 454, *456*
Collins, A., *375*
Collins, A. F., 186, *190*, 237, *241*, 319, *326*
Collins, A. M., 336, *343*

Collins, G. H., 466, *484*
Collins, J. C., 217, *226*, 251*t*, 254, 258
Collins, M., 547, 548*t*, *554*
Colotla, V. A., 50, *57*
Connelly, A., 451, *459*, 473, *484*, 497, *499*, 604, 605, 606, *608*, 617, *625*
Connelly, S. L., 401, *406*, 418, 422
Connolly, J. F., 545, *553*
Conrad, R., 21, *28*, 77, 81, *89*, 131, *133*, 150, *160*
Constable, R., 631, *641*
Conte, J., 383, *389*
Conturo, T., 631, 634, *640*
Convit, A., 413, *422*
Conway, A. R. A., 86, *89*
Conway, M. A., 27, *28*, 46, *56*, 186, 189*n*, *190*, 231, 234, 235, 235*f*, 236, 237, 238, 239, *241*, 242, 317, 319, *325*, *326*, 334, 336, 339, 341, *343*, 353, 358, 359, *361*, *362*, 382, 383, *388*, *389*, 598, *606*, 612, 619, *621*
Coon, V., 371, *374*
Cooper, L. A., 251*t*, *260*, 364, 377, 635, *642*
Cooper, P. F., 322, *325*
Cooper, W. E., 372, *373*
Cooper-Marcus, C., 320, *326*
Copper, C., 321, *324*
Corballis, M. C., 80, *89*, 130, *133*
Coren, S., 149, *160*
Cork, R. C., 542, *551*
Corkin, S., 251*t, 257*, 429, 435, *438*, *439*, *440*, 442, 443, 448, 453, *457*, *459*, 468, *479*, 480, *482*, 483, 486, 488, 495, *497*, 498, 504, *519*, 605, *606*, *607*, 617, *622*, 634, *642*
Corn, T. H., 540, 544, 548, *552*
Cornoldi, C., 207, *209*, 368, 373
Corsi, P., 174, *177*
Cortese, M., 403, *405*
Cortese, M. J., 158, *160*
Cosgrove, M. D., 469, *483*
Coslett, H. B., 614, *624*
Costermans, J., 200, *207*
Cotman, C. W., 550, *553*
Cotton, B., 127, *135*, 170, *177*
Couclelis, H., 366, *373*
Coull, J. T., 548, *551*
Coupe, P., 366, *377*
Courage, M. L., 306, *309*, 383, *390*, 603, *607*
Courtney, S. M., 506, 507, 508, 514, *515*, 631, *639*
Cowan, N., 84, *89*, 288, *292*
Cowan, T., 317, 323, *331*
Cowen, P. J., 548, *551*

Cowey, A., 615, *621,* 646, *648*
Coxon, P., 184, *191*
Craik, F. I. M., 22, 26, *28, 31,* 38, 50, 52, 53, 54, *56,* 82, *89,* 93, 94, 95, 96, 97, 97*f,* 98, 100, 101, 102, 103, *104, 105, 106,* 139, 140, 144, 145, *146, 147, 148,* 166, *175,* 189, *191,* 223, *227,* 395, 396, 397, 398, 399, 400, 402, 403, 404, *405, 406, 408, 409,* 411, 413, 414, 417, 421, *421, 422,* 425, 429, *438,* 472, *479, 483,* 503, 503*f,* 504, 505, 506, 513, *515, 517, 519,* 531, *534,* 567, *569,* 600, *606, 607,* 610, 617, 619, *621, 625,* 633, 634, *640, 642*
Crane, T., 307*n, 308*
Craw, S., 305, *310*
Crayton, L., 550, *553*
Creasey, H., 443, 445, *458*
Creem, S. H., 364, *373*
Cristi, C., 169, *176*
Critchley, E. M. R., 452, *455*
Crivello, F., 367, *374*
Crockford, H. A., 550, *553*
Crooks, M., 550, *553*
Crotteau Huffman, M. L., 187, 188, *190*
Crovitz, H. F., 316, *326*
Crow, T. J., 549, *552*
Crowder, R. G., 27, *27,* 77, *89,* 125, 126, 130, 131, 132, *133, 134, 135,* 154, *160,* 316, *324,* 347, *361,* 396, *406*
Crowley, M. J., 249, 254, *260*
Croyle, R. T., 320, *326*
Crutcher, R. J., 353, *361*
Cuddy, L. J., 352, *361*
Cuddy, L. L., 139, *145*
Culebras, A., 454, *458*
Cullum, M. C., 442, 445, *455*
Cultice, J., 111, *121*
Cultice, J. C., 200, *208*
Cummings, J. L., 448, 450, 454, *457, 458,* 469, *480*
Cunfer, A. R., 417, *423*
Cunitz, A. R., 59, *70*
Curran, H. V., 233, *241,* 539, 540, 544, 545, 546, 547, 548*t,* 549, *551, 552, 554,* 599
Curran, T., 158, *162,* 168, 172, *176,* 186, 187, *192, 194,* 222, 223, *225, 226,* 238, *241,* 252, *257,* 398, 403, *406, 409,* 434, 435, *438,* 531, *534, 536,* 635, *642*
Curry, L. M., 452, *457*
Cutillo, B., 512, *516*
Cutler, B., 321, 322, *329, 331*
Cutler, S. E., 323, *326*
Cutshall, J. L., 321, *332,* 380, *392*

Daehler, M. W., 268, *280*
Dagenbach, D., 340, *343*
Dale, A., 521, 522, *535,* 616, 617, *621,* 633, 634, 636, *638, 639*
Dale, A. M., 158, *162,* 403, *409,* 504, 505, 510, *515, 519,* 522, *536,* 634, 635, *638, 642, 643*
Dale, H. C. A., 80, *89*
Dalenberg, C. J., 385, *389*
Dalgleish, T., 386, 387, *389*
Dalla Barba, G., 230, 231, *241,* 620, *621*
Dallas, M., 102, *105,* 215, 216, *226,* 236, *242,* 251*t,* 254, *258,* 523, *534*
Dalton, J., 547, 548*t, 551*
Daly, J. A., 320, 321, *331*
Damasio, A. R., 251*t, 257,* 443, *459,* 468, 469, *480,* 615, *621,* 632, 633, *639*
Damasio, H., 251*t, 257,* 468, *480,* 632, 633, *639*
Daneman, M., 86, *89,* 542, *553*
Daniele, A., 430, *439,* 443, 446, *455*
Danion, J. M., 231, 238, *242,* 545, *552, 553, 554*
Dannals, R. F., 415, *425*
Dansereau, D. F., 11, *28*
Dapolito, F. J., 59, 62, 63, 70
Darby, D. G., 472, *481*
Darvesh, S., 469, *480*
Darwin, C., 4, *28*
Dary, M., 505, *516*
Dasgupta, Z. R. R., 231, *243*
Daum, I., 436, *438,* 468, 474, *480, 482*
Davidoff, J. B., 428, *438*
Davidson, G., 288, *292*
Davidson, R., 322, *332*
Davies, A. D. M., 431, *439*
Davis, A. M., 320, *331*
Davis, E. J., 435, *438*
Davis, M., 488, *497*
Davis, P. J., 322, *326*
Davis, S. L., 321, *326*
Davis, T. L., 403, *406*
Davison, A. N., 448, *458*
Dawson, K., 446, 446*f, 457*
Day, J., 365, *376*
Day, L., 84, *89*
Dazzi, L., 549, *552*
Deacedo, B., 251*t, 257*
deBlois, S., 301, *310*
Debner, J. A., 255, *258,* 525, *534*
DeCarli, C., 454, *458*
DeCasper, A. J., 269, *280*
DeCooke, P. A., 319, *324*
Deese, J., 150, 152, *160,* 179, *191,* 233, *241,* 403, *406*
Deffenbacher, K. A., 379, *389*
De Groot, A., 55, *56*
de Haan, M., 269, *281*

Deiber, M. -P., 466, *480*
DeKosky, S. T., 412, 413, *422*
Delaney, R. C., 470, *479*
Delaney, S. M., 251*t, 260*
Delbecq-Derouesne, J., 434, *438*
de Leon, M. J., 413, *422, 423*
De Leonardis, D. M., 181, 183, 184, 185, 187, 188, 189, *191, 192, 193*
Delis, D. C., *457*
Della Sala, S., 80, 81, 85, 87, *88, 89,* 442, 447, 452, *454, 455*
DeLoache, J. S., 303, *308*
Delprato, D., 68, *70*
DeLuca, J., 189, *191*
Demb, J. B., 435, *438,* 526, *534,* 617, *625,* 633, 634, *639, 643*
Dember, W. N., 491, *499*
De Mornay Davies, P., 435, *438*
Dempster, F. N., 350, *361,* 419, *422*
Denis, M., 367, 368, *373, 374*
Dennet, J. L., 321, *325*
Dennis, S., 593, *594*
Denny, L. L., 415, 421, *424*
DeNobele, 601
de Quincey, E., 541
De Renzi, E., 477, *480*
DeSanti, S., 413, *422*
Descartes, R., 197, *208*
de Schonen, S., 269, *281*
Desgranges, B., 505, *516*
Desimone, R., 617, *623,* 631, 636, *639, 641*
Desmond, J. E., 365, *373,* 435, *438,* 507, 514, *516, 518,* 522, 526, *534,* 617, *622, 625,* 630, 632, 633, 634, 635, 637, *639,* 640, *641, 643*
De Soto, C., 372, *373*
D'Esposito, M., 189, *192, 193, 195,* 367, *372,* 435, 437, 507, *515,* 630, 631, 632, 633, *639,* 642
DeTeresa, R., 443, *459*
Detre, J. A., 367, *372,* 507, *515,* 632, *639*
de Vega, M., 369, *373*
Devine, P. G., 256, *258*
Devlin, J. T., 446, *455*
de Vos, R. A. I., 473, *479*
Deweer, B., 442, *458*
Dewhurst, S. A., 230, 232*t,* 233, 238, *241,* 619, *621*
deWinstanley, P., 321, 323, *328*
Dhaliwal, H. S., 239, *244*
Diamond, A., 273, 274, *280*
Diaz, D. L., 398, *406*
Dibble, E., 118, *120*
Di Camillo, M., 113, *122*
Dichgans, J., 436, *438*
Dick, M. A., 398, *406*
Dick, M. B., 144, *146*

Didow, S. M., 288, *293*
Diecidue, K., 303, *311*
Diener, E., 322, *330*
Dierks, Ch., 466, *481*
Dihle, P. H., 386, *389*
Dijkstra, S., 81, *88*
Di Lollo, V., 396, *406*
DiRubbo, M., 275, 279, *282*
Disterhoft, J. F., *437, 439,* 620, *622, 623*
Diwadkar, V. A., 366, 368, *374, 376*
Dixon, M., 231, 232*t*, 238, *242*
Dixon, R. A., 200, *208*
Dobbins, I., 221, 224, *228,* 239, *244,* 529, *537,* 611, 618, *625*
Dobson, M., 184, *191*
Dodd, A., 84, *90*
Dodd, D. H., 183, *191*
Dodson, C. S., 181, 183, 185, *191*
Dokic, J., 300, *308*
Dolan, P. O., 218, 224, *226, 227,* 395
Dolan, R. J., 503, 504, 505, 506, 510, 513, *516, 519,* 531, *536,* 550, *552,* 619, *622,* 633, 634, 635, *639, 641, 642*
Donald, M., 283, 284, *293*
Donaldson, D. I., 528, 529, 530*f, 534*
Donaldson, W., 175, *176,* 218, *225,* 236, *241*
Donnelly, C. M., 317, *326,* 382, *389*
Donnelly, R. E., 67, *70*
Donnenwerth-Nolan, S., 137, 138, *148*
Dooling, D. J., 151, *162,* 179, *195*
Dorfman, J., 339, *343*
Dorner, D., 118, 119, *120*
Douglass, K. H., 415, *425*
Dovidio, J. F., 256, *258*
Dow, G. A., 284, *292*
Dowden, A., 272, *279*
Downes, J. J., 175, *177,* 431, 433, 435, *438, 439,* 453, *455*
Downs, R. M., 363, *374*
Doyle, M. C., 523, 524, 527, 528, 529, 531, 532, *534, 535, 536*
Doyon, J., 507, *518*
Drachman, D. A., 543, *552*
Drayer, B. P., 454, *458*
Dritschel, B. H., 335, *343*
Drivdahl, S. B., 184, *195*
Drummey, A. B., 369, *376*
D'Souza, D. C., 549, *552*
Dubois, B., 442, 453, *455, 458*
Dubuisson, D., 469, *483*
Duchek, J. M., 158, *160,* 251*t, 258,* 395, 397, 401, 403, *405, 406*
Dudley, W., 396, *408*
Dudycha, G. J., 306, *308*

Dudycha, M. M., 306, *308*
Duft, S., 205, *207*
Duggal, S., 385, *389*
Duncan, J., 87, *88*
Duncan, S., 365, 366, 371, *375,* 564, *569*
Duncker, K., 111, 113, *120,* 334, 338, *343*
Dunlosky, J., 205, 207, *208, 210,* 341, *343*
Dunn, J. C., 55, *56,* 252, *258*
Dunning, D., 184, *194,* 321, *330*
Dunphy, S. C., 545, *553*
Dupuis, J. H., 413, *424*
Durso, F. T., 184, *191,* 339, *343*
Durwen, H. F., 469, 473, 475, 477, *479, 481*
Dutta, A., 167, *177*
Düzel, E., 133, *241,* 529, 530, 531, *534*
Dywan, J., 217, 224, *225,* 250, 254, *258,* 403, *406,* 419, 420, *422, 423*

Eagger, S. A., 550, *553*
Earles, J. L., 144, *146*
Earley, L. A., 270, *280*
Easterbrook, J., 380, *389*
Easton, R. D., 368, *374*
Ebbesen, E. B., 560, *570*
Ebbinghaus, H., 4, 5, 6*f, 28,* 45, *56,* 64, *70,* 125, 126, 127, 128, 129, *133,* 149, *160,* 245, *258,* 300, *308,* 348, 350, *361*
Ebenholtz, S. M., 64, *70,* 126, 128, 130, *133, 135*
Eckerman, C. O., 288, *293*
Ecob, J. R., 80, *88*
Edelman, R. R., 472, *481*
Edwards, D., 320, 323, *326*
Edwards, M. B., 172, *176,* 191, *191*
Egenhofer, M. J., 363, *374*
Eggers, R., 600, *606*
Ehlers, S., 619, *622*
Ehling, P. A. T. M., 544, 548, *552*
Ehrich, V., 369, *374*
Eich, E., 52, *56,* 316, 320, *326,* 337, *343,* 379, 386, *389,* 546, *552,* 567, *569*
Eich, J. E., 100, *105,* 337, *343*
Eichenbaum, H., 174, *176,* 251*t,* 257, 402, *406,* 468, 474, *480,* 497, *497,* 605, *606,* 610, *621,* 627, *639*
Eimas, P. D., 81, *89*
Einstein, G. O., 50, *56,* 98, *105,* 138, *147,* 335, 336, *344,* 398, *406,* 417, *423*
Eisen, M. L., 322, *326*
Eisenberg, A., 286, *293*
Ekstrand, B. R., 64, *70*
El-Ahmadi, A., 382, *390*

Eldridge, L. L., 634, *643*
Eldridge, M., 103, *104*
Elfgren, C., 505, 514, *518*
Elger, C. E., 504, *516*
Elio, R., 112, *120*
Elliott, D. M., 384, *389*
Elliott, M. N., 131, *135*
Ellis, A. W., 452, *455*
Ellis, H. C., 110, *120*
Ellis, J., 335, *343*
Ellis, J. A., 347, *362*
Ellis, S., 291, 292, *293*
Ellison, D., 445, *456,* 475, *480*
Ellsworth, P., 379, *390*
Emmorey, K., 96, *107*
Emslie, H., 87, *88*
Engel, R. W., 86, *91*
Engelkamp, J., 53, *56,* 102, 103, *105,* 137, 138, 140, 141, 142, 143, 144, *146, 147, 148,* 156, *160*
Engen, T., 81, *89,* 95, *105*
Engle, R. W., 86, *89*
English, S., 474, *478*
Engstler-Schooler, T., 150, *162*
Ennaceur, A., 431, *438*
Enright, M. K., 274, *282*
Epstein, R., 365, *374*
Epstein, S. L., 370, *374*
Epstein, W., 202, 203, 204, *208*
Erber, R., 324, *331*
Erdelyi, M. H., 157, *161,* 386, *389*
Erdfelder, E., 185, *190,* 221, 222, 223, *225,* 236, *241*
Ericsson, K. A., 26, 27, *28,* 109, 114, 115, 116, 117, *120,* 353, *361*
Erikson, T. A., 338, *344*
Erkinjuntti, T., 454, *458*
Ernesto, C., 550, *553*
Erngrund, K., 144, *148*
Erskine, A., 320, *326*
Esbensen, B. M., 301, *311,* 603, *607*
Esiri, M. M., 443, *459*
Eslinger, P. J., 468, 475, *480, 482*
Estes, D., 302, *311*
Estes, W. K., 13, *28,* 59, 62, *70,* 109, *120,* 131, *133*
Etard, O., 367, *374*
Eustache, F., 505, *516*
Evans, A. C., 506, 507, 513, *518,* 631, *641*
Evans, G. E., 368, *374*
Evans, G. W., 363, *374*
Evans, J., 448, 452, *455*
Evans, M. E., 203, *210*
Evenden, J. L., 453, *455, 459*
Everitt, B. J., 547, 548, *553*
Eves, F., 544, *552*
Ewald, K., 474, *482*
Eysenck, M. W., 645, 646, *648*

Fagan, J. F., III, 268, 269, *280*
Fagen, J. W., 270, 274, *282*
Fairbank, J. K., 284, *293*
Falk, J. L., *406*
Fallon, J., 380, 387, *389*, 505, 506, *515*
Falloon, F., 26, *28*
Fan, J., 236, *244*
Fantz, R. L., 268, 268*f*, *280*
Farah, M. J., 25, *28*, 371, *377*, 430, *438*, 614, 615, *621*, 632, 633, *639*, *642*
Fariello, G. R., 367, *375*
Farrell, R., 118, *119*
Fauconnier, G., 372, *374*
Faulkner, D., 144, *146*, 184, *190*
Faust, M. E., 401, 404, *409*
Fay, D., 184, *191*
Fazio, R. H., 256, *258*
Fearneyhough, C., 87, *91*
Fedio, P., 442, *457*
Feigenbaum, E. A., 15, *27*, *28*, *29*, *31*
Feinberg, S. E., 62, *70*
Feinberg, T. E., 614, *621*
Feldman, J., 15, *29*
Feldman-Summers, S., 385, *389*
Feltovich, P. J., 109, 110, 114, 118, *120*
Fenandes, M. A., 610, *621*
Fendrich, D. W., 353, 354, *361*
Fennema, A. C., 617, *622*
Ferguson, S. A., 181, 184, 185, 188, *191*, *192*, 251*t*, *258*, 403, *407*
Ferini-Strambi, L., 548*t*, *553*
Fernandez, A., 131, *133*
Fernandez, G., 504, *516*
Ferraro, F. R., 398, 401, *405*, *406*, 415, *424*
Ferris, S. H., 413, *422*, *423*, *553*
Feuerstein, N., 336, *344*
FfrenchConstant, C., 454, *457*
Fiedler, J. D., 320, *328*
Fiedler, K., 184, *191*
Field, H., 297, *308*
Fiez, J. A., 502, 506, *516*, *518*, 630, 632, 633, 636, 637, *639*, *641*
Figlozzi, C. M., 636, *638*
Figueredo, A., 387, *392*
Fillmore, C., 370, *374*
Finger, K., 187, *194*
Finger, S., 491, *497*, *498*
Fink, G. R., 470, 475, 477, *480*, *482*, 506, *516*
Finke, R. A., 25, *29*, 181, 184, *191*, 364, *374*
Finkenauer, C., 382, *390*
Finlayson, A. J., 253, *261*
Fischer, D., 600, *606*
Fischhoff, B., 204, 206, 206*f*, *208*, *209*, 384, *390*

Fischman, A., 637, *640*
Fischman, A. J., 505, *516*
Fish, S. B., 131, *135*
Fisher, M., 454, *458*
Fisher, R. P., 69, *70*, 321, *326*, 337, *344*
Fisk, A. D., 170, *176*
Fisler, R., 385, 387, *392*
Fitch, F. B., 129, *134*, 166, *177*
Fitzgerald, J. M., 318, *326*
Fitzgerald, P., 322, *325*
Fivush, R., 279, *280*, 283, 286, 287, 288, 290, *292*, *293*, *294*, 299, 304, 305, 306, *308*, 322, 323, 324, *326*
Flavell, E. R., 301, 303, *308*
Flavell, J. H., 198, 206, *208*, 301, 303, *308*, *309*, 310, 604, *606*
Fleischman, D. A., 435, *438*, 616, 617, *621*, *622*
Fleishman, E. A., 353, *361*
Fleming, J., 433, *439*
Fletcher, A., 550, *553*
Fletcher, P. C., 503, 504, 505, 506, 510, 513, 514, *516*, *519*, 531, *534*, *536*, 550, *552*, 619, *622*, 633, 634, 635, *639*, *641*, 642
Flexser, A. J., 18, *29*, 63, 66, 67, *70*, 170, *176*
Flood, D. G., 412, *422*
Flora, J., 372, *373*
Flores, L., 84, *89*
Fodor, J. A., 15, 16, *29*, 129, *133*, 297, *308*
Foley, M. A., 181, 182, 183, 184, 186, *191*, *192*, 223, *225*, 302, *308*
Foli, S., 510, *517*
Follette, V. M., 385, *391*
Folstein, M. F., 415, *425*, 435, *438*, 441, *455*
Folstein, S. E., 441, *455*
Fong, G. T., 112, 119, *121*
Ford, J. M., 415, *423*
Forman, S. D., 630, *639*
Forman, T., 131, *133*
Forrest, E., 488, *498*
Forster, J., 233, 238, *244*
Foster, D. P., 342, *346*
Foster, J. K., 41, *42*
Fox, C., 568, *570*
Fox, N. C., 445, 448, *455*, *456*
Fox, P. T., 502, *518*, 632, 633, 636, 637, *641*
Fozard, J. L., 167, *176*
Frackowiak, R. S. J., 85, *91*, 367, *375*, 451, *459*, 502, 503, 505, 506, 509, 510, 513, *516*, *518*, *519*, 531, *536*, 619, *622*, 630, 633, 634, 635, 637, *639*, *640*, *641*, *642*, *643*
Frambach, M., 436, *440*

Franceschi, M., 548*t*, *553*
Frank, G., 466, *481*
Franklin, N., 189*n*, *191*, 369, 370, 371, *373*, *374*
Franks, J. J., 94, 95, 98, 99, 100*t*, *104*, *106*, 113, 114, *121*, 151, 152, 153, *160*, *161*, 179, *190*, 251*t*, *257*, 337, *345*
Frarinacci, S., 251*t*, 254, *257*
Fraser, L., 318, *331*
Freeborough, P. A., 448, *455*
Freed, D. M., 468, *480*
Freedman, J. L., 200, *208*
Freedman, M., 436, *439*, 469, *480*
Freeman, G., 491, *498*
Freeman, W., 601, 602, *606*, *607*
Frege, G., 298, *308*
French, R. M., 592, *594*
Freud, S., 267, *280*, 306, *308*
Frey, K. A., *482*
Frey, L. M., 385, *389*
Freyd, J., 386, *390*
Friberg, L., 508, 509, 510, *517*
Friedhof, L. T., *553*
Friedland, R. P., 443, *455*
Friedman, A., 288, *293*
Friedman, H. R., 511, *516*
Friedman, W. J., 171, *176*, 319, *326*
Friedrich, A. G., 198, 206, *208*
Friedrich, W. N., 322, *327*
Frieman, J., 323, *331*
Fries, E., 320, *326*
Friston, K. J., 502, *502*, 505, 509, 514, *515*, *516*, *518*, 550, *552*, 637, *640*
Frith, C. D., 85, *91*, 367, *375*, 502, 503, 505, 506, 509, 510, 513, 514, *516*, *518*, *519*, 531, *534*, *536*, 549, 550, *552*, 619, *622*, 630, 633, 634, 635, *639*, *641*, *642*
Frith, U., 305, *307*, 619, *622*
Frölich, L., 470, 471, *482*
Fromhoff, F. A., 286, *293*
Fromholt, P., 318, *326*
Frost, J. J., 415, *425*
Fry, P. A., 364, 368, *375*
Frye, D., 604, *608*
Fullilove, M. T., 384, *391*
Fulton, A., 217, *225*, 420, *422*
Fung, H., 288, *293*
Funnell, E., 442, 443, 450, 452, *457*
Fusella, V., 25, *31*
Fuster, J. M., 415, 416, 419, *423*, *480*, 512, 513, 514, *516*

Gabrieli, J. D. E., 220, *228*, 236, *244*, 250, 251*t*, 256, *258*, *261*, 365, *373*, 414, *423*, 429, 435, *438*, *439*, 453, *459*, 468,

480, 483, 504, 507, 514, *515,*
516, 518, 522, 526, *534,* 605,
606, 609, 610, 611, 616, 617,
618, 619, 620, *621, 622, 623,*
624, 625, 630, 632, 633, 634,
635, 637, 638, *639,* 640,
641, 643
Gadian, D. G., 431, 433, *440,*
451, *459,* 473, *484,* 497, *499,*
604, 605, 606, *607, 608,* 617,
625
Gaffan, D., 431, *438*
Gage, F. H., 78, *91*
Gaillard, W. D., 636, *638*
Gainotti, G., 430, *439,* 443, 446,
455
Galanter, E., 15, *30,* 78, *90*
Galasko, D., *553*
Galbraith, R. C., 168, *176*
Gale, N., 366, *373*
Gales, M. S., 184, 189*n,* 190
Gall, M. B., 356, *361*
Gallagher, M., 469, *480*
Gallistel, C. R., 364, 369, *374*
Galluccio, L., 238, *241,* 276, *280,*
403, *409,* 434, *438,* 635, *642*
Galton, F., 316, *326*
Ganzel, B. L., 385, *389*
Garcia, J. H., 454, *458*
Gardiner, J. M., 34, 36, *42,* 62,
64, 67, 69, *70, 71,* 130, *133,*
140, 144, *146, 147,* 186, *191,*
217, 224, *227,* 229, 230, 231,
231*t,* 232*t,* 233, 234, 235,
235*f,* 236, 237, 238, 239,
239*t,* 240, *241, 242, 243,*
244, 255, *260,* 306, *308,* 523,
527, 529, *534, 535,* 545, 551,
598, 599, 600, *606,* 610, *624*
Garling, T., 363, *374*
Garner, W. R., 14, *29*
Garrard, P., 443, 446, 447*f,* 449,
455, 456
Garrett, M. F., 15, 16, *29,* 129,
133, 201, *211,* 372, *373*
Garry, M., 156, *161,* 184, *191,*
385, *390*
Gathercole, S. E., 78, 84, 88, *89,*
90, 186, *190,* 237, *241,* 319,
326
Gati, I., 366, *378*
Gauld, A., 315, *326*
Gawlik, B., 230, 231*t,* 232*t,* 242
Gazzaniga, M. S., 203, *208*
Gee, N. R., 336, *345*
Gehlen, W., 469, 473, 475, 477,
479, 481
Geiselman, R. E., 321, *326,* 337,
344
Gelber, E. R., 269, *280*
Geller, A. M., 547, *552*
Gentner, D., 110, *121*
George, A. E., 413, *422, 423*

Georges-Francois, P., 364, 368,
373
Gerard, L., 418, *423*
Gerhard, D., 187, *194*
Gerhardstein, P., 276, 277, *280*
Gerler, D., 203, *209*
Gesi, A. T., 353, *361*
Gessa, G. L., 549, *552*
Gevins, A., 511, 512, *516*
Gewirtz, J. L., 270, *281*
Ghaem, O., 367, *374*
Ghaemi, M., 471, 474*f, 482*
Ghodesian, D., 353, *361*
Ghoneim, M. M., 541, 543, 544,
545, 548*t, 552, 553*
Giacomoni, F., 231, 238, *242*
Giambra, L. M., 396, *407*
Giannakopoulos, P., 474, *480*
Giard, N., 472, *483*
Gibson, E. J., 9*f,* 10, *29*
Gibson, J. M., 613, *625*
Gick, M. L., 109, 111, 112, 113,
120
Giedd, J., 472, *479*
Giersch, A., 545, *554*
Giersch, M., 545, *552*
Gilch, J., 276, *280*
Gillberg, C., 619, *622*
Gillin, J. C., 337, *344*
Gillund, G., 224, *225,* 572, 573,
579
Gilmore, G. C., 396, *407*
Gilson, A. D., 81, *90*
Gimbel, C., 318, *327*
Ginier, B., 630, *639*
Girard, A., 285, *294*
Girgus, J. S., 149, *160*
Gisle, L., 382, *390*
Giustolisi, L., 430, *439,* 443, 446,
455
Gjedde, A., 415, *425*
Glanzer, M., 48, *56,* 59, *70,* 79,
81, *90,* 128, 130, *133,* 141,
147, 574, *579*
Glaser, R., 109, 110, 114, 118,
120
Glaze, J. A., 10, *29*
Glees, P., 468, *480*
Gleitman, H., *375*
Glenberg, A. M., 130, 131, *133,*
134, 202, 203, 204, *208,* 285,
293, 337, *345,* 350, 352, *361,*
369, *374,* 629, *640*
Glendon, A. I., 357, *362*
Glicksohn, J., 367, *374*
Glisky, E. L., 184, 189, *191,* 404,
407, 408
Glover, G. H., 365, *373,* 435, *438,*
504, 507, 514, *515, 516, 518,*
522, 526, *534,* 617, *622, 625,*
630, 632, 633, 634, 635, 637,
638, 639, 641, 643
Glover, T. A., 158, *162,* 187, *195*

Glowalla, U., 369, *377*
Gluck, M. A., 222, *227,* 587, *594,*
620, *622*
Glucksberg, S., 203, *208,* 341,
344
Gobet, F., 114, 115, 116, 117,
120
Godden, D. R., 52, *56,* 101, 101*f,*
105, 337, *344*
Goetz, E. T., 98, *104*
Goff, D., 505, *516*
Goff, L. M., 156, *161,* 184, *191*
Goggin, J. P., 348, *360*
Gold, D. B., 387, *392*
Gold, S. N., 383, *390*
Goldenberg, G., 433, *439*
Golding, P. J., 443, 450, *459*
Goldman, A. I., *308*
Goldman-Rakic, P. S., 81, *90,*
506, 507, 511, *516, 519,* 630,
631, *640, 641, 643*
Goldsmith, M., 200, *208,* 316,
321, *327,* 336, 342, *344,* 531,
535
Goldstein, D., 181, *191*
Goldstein, G., 306, *309*
Goldstone, R., 110, *121*
Golledge, R. G., 363, 364, 366,
367, 368, *373, 374, 375, 376*
Golomb, J., 413, *422, 423*
Gomez, C., 453, *457*
Gonnerman, L. M., 446, *455*
Gonzalez, R. G., 468, *479,* 486,
497, 504, *519,* 605, *606,* 634,
642
Gonzalez-Lima, F., 509, *517*
Gooding, P. A., 610, *623*
Goodman, G. S., 184, *194,* 302,
305, *308, 310,* 321, 322, *326,*
327, 329, 383, *390*
Goodman, J., 380, *389,* 616, 617,
621, 633, 636, *638*
Goodnow, J., 15, *28*
Goodwin, D. W., 337, *344*
Gopal, S., 370, *374*
Gopnik, A., 299, 301, 302, 303,
309, 310, 603, 604, *606, 607*
Gordon, F. R., 303, *309*
Gore, J., 631, *641*
Gorelick, P. B., 454, *458*
Gorenstein, C., 545, *551*
Gorissen, M. E. E., 544, 548, *552*
Goschke, T., 255, *258*
Goshen-Gottstein, Y., 40, *42,*
246, 253, *260,* 610, 616, 617,
622, 623, 624
Gotlib, I. H., 322, *325*
Gott, S. P., 118, *120*
Gottlob, L. R., 415, 421, *424*
Gottstein, J., 523, *535*
Goubet, N., 273, *280*
Goulding, P., 450, *458*
Goulding, P. J., 429, *440*

Govoni, R., 103, *105,* 503, *515,* 610, *621*

Graber, M., 273, *279*

Grabowecky, M., 415, 416, 419, *424*

Grabowski, T., 632, 633, *639*

Grady, C. L., 81, *90,* 414, 415, 421, *422, 423,* 443, *455,* 504, 505, 506, 508, 509, 510, 511, 512*f,* 513*f, 515, 516, 517,* 619, *622,* 631, 634, *640*

Graf, P., 40, *42,* 52, *57,* 102, *107,* 139, *148,* 202, *210,* 222, *225,* 236, *242,* 251*t,* 254, 255, *258, 259,* 278, *280,* 301, 302, *309,* 603, 604, *606,* 610, 616, *622,* 627, *640*

Graff-Radford, N. R., *456,* 468, *480*

Graff-Radford, S. B., 316, 320, *326*

Grafman, J., 436, *440,* 466, *480*

Grafton, S., 637, *640*

Graham, F. K., 269, *281*

Graham, K. S., 429, *439,* 450, 451, *456*

Graham, N., 446, 446*f, 456, 457,* 590, *595*

Grange, D., 231, 238, *242,* 545, *552, 553, 554*

Granholm, E., 442, 443, 445, 454, *455, 456*

Grant, I., 442, 443, *455*

Grant, S., 85, *88*

Grasby, P. M., 503, 505, 506, 510, *516, 517,* 550, *552, 553,* 633, 634, 635, *639, 642*

Grasso, R., 364, 368, *373, 377*

Gratman, J., 454, *458*

Gray, C., 80, 81, 85, *89*

Gray, J., 550, *552, 553*

Gray, J. T., 286, *293*

Gray, W., 68, *72*

Grayson, D., 443, 445, *458*

Graziadei, J., 491, *499*

Greco, C., 268, 270, 277, *280*

Green, F. L., 301, 303, *308*

Green, P., 320, *326*

Green, R. L., 130, *134*

Greenberg, M. T., 301, *309*

Greene, J. D. W., 442, 443, 444, 445, 447, 448, 449, *456*

Greene, R. L., 125, 130, 131, 132, *134,* 167, *176*

Greeno, J. G., 62, 63, *70,* 352, *361*

Greenspan, S., 369, *376*

Greenwald, A. G., 27, *29,* 183, 188, *190, 194,* 256, *257, 258*

Gregg, V. H., 130, *133,* 141, *147,* 230, 232*t,* 234, 236, *242*

Gregory, C. A., 441, 449, *456*

Grice, S., 232*t,* 233, 240, *241,* 306, *308*

Griesler, P. C., 270, *280*

Griffith, H. B., 468, *480*

Griffiths, H. L., 450, 451, *459,* 466, *483,* 618, *624*

Groen, G. J., 114, 117, *120, 121*

Groeneweg, J., 383, *392*

Groenweg, J., 318, *331*

Gronlund, S. D., 171, 172, *175, 176,* 181, *191,* 224, *225*

Gross, M., 524, *535*

Gross, M. S., 184, *194,* 233, 238, *244*

Grossberg, S., 587, *594*

Grossman, M., 435, *437,* 507, *515,* 632, *639*

Grover, G., 320, *327*

Growdon, J. H., 413, *423,* 435, *440,* 442, 443, 448, 453, *457, 459,* 550, *553, 617, 622*

Gruetter, R., 633, *640*

Grundman, M., 550, *553*

Gruneberg, M. M., 200, *208,* 316, *327*

Gruppuso, V., 181, *191*

Gudden, B. von, 466, *480*

Guimaraes, A. R., 634, *642*

Guimares, A. R., 504, *519*

Guimon, J., 474, *480*

Gulya, M., 276, 278, *280*

Gulyas, B., 506, *519*

Gunning-Dixon, F. M., 413, *424*

Gutierrez-Rivas, H., 250, 251*t,* 261

Guttentag, R. E., 144, *147*

Guynn, M. J., 333, *345,* 404, *408,* 417, *423*

Guzman, A. E., 341, *344*

Guzy, L. T., 368, *375*

Gydesen, S., 449, *454*

Habib, R., 189, *194,* 504, 505, 510, 511*f,* 514, *517, 518, 519,* 531, *535,* 619, *623,* 634, 635, *640, 641, 642*

Hachinski, V., 454, *456*

Haden, C. A., 286, 287, 288, *293, 294*

Hagger, C., 492, *497*

Hahnel, A., 369, *377*

Haier, R. J., 380, 387, *389,* 505, 506, *515*

Haine, R., 287, *293*

Haist, F., 488, *498*

Haith, M. M., 269, *280*

Hakami, M. K., 400, *407*

Hakes, D. T., 128, *135*

Halbwachs, M., 324, *327*

Hale, S., 415, *422, 424*

Hall, C., 433, *439*

Hall, E. P., 118, *120*

Hall, G. S., 316, 320, *327*

Hall, J. F., 8, *29*

Hall, L. K., 316, *324,* 348, 349, 353, 356, 357*t,* 358, *360*

Hall, M., 129, *134,* 166, *177*

Hall, W. S., 560, *569*

Hallett, M., 436, *440,* 466, *480*

Halliday, M. S., 84, *90*

Hallikainen, M., 413, *425*

Hamann, S. B., 615, 617, *622, 624*

Hamburger, S. D., 306, *310*

Hamm, V. P., 401, *407,* 418, *423*

Hammersley, R., 184, *194,* 321, *330*

Hammersley, R. H., 341, *345*

Hamond, N. R., 279, *280,* 290, *293,* 305, 306, *308,* 323, 324, *326*

Hampson, P., 232*t, 243*

Han, J. J., 288, *293*

Handel, S., 372, *373*

Hanley, J. R., 428, 431, *439,* 452, *456*

Hanna, E., 277, *280*

Hänninen, T., 413, *425*

Hansen, L. A., 443, *459*

Happé, F., 306, *309,* 619, *622*

Harbluk, J. L., 96, *107,* 189, *194,* 403, *409,* 599, 600, *607*

Hardy, J., 445, 449, *454, 456*

Harkins, S. W., 396, *408*

Harman, A., 454, *458*

Harris, J. E., 322, *331,* 398, *409*

Harris, J. F., 302, *308*

Harris, M. D., 23, *29*

Harsch, N., 49, *57,* 305, *308,* 317, *329,* 382, *391*

Harsent, L., 434, *439*

Hart, J. T., 198, 200, *208*

Hart, R. A., 369, *374*

Hart, R. P., 396, *408*

Hartikainen, P., 448, *455*

Hartman, M., 401, *407,* 418, *423*

Hartmann, K., 322, *330*

Hartry, A. L., 63, 66, *71*

Hartshorn, K., 271, 274, 275, 276, 277, 279, *280, 282*

Harvey, P. D., 223, *225*

Harvey, R. J., 445, *456*

Hasher, L., 54, *57,* 169, 170, *176,* 181, *191,* 365, *374,* 396, 400, 401, 403, *406, 407, 409,* 411, 415, 417, 418, 419, 419*f,* 420, 421, *422, 423, 424, 425*

Hashtroudi, S., 18, *29,* 154, *161,* 171, 172, *177,* 180, 181, 183, 184, 185, 186, 188, *191, 192,* 223, *227,* 236, *243,* 251*t, 258,* 302, *309,* 397, 399, 403, *407,* 528, *534*

Hassing, L., 469, *480*

Hastie, R., *575, 581*

Hatano, G., 109, 117, 118, *120*

Haug, H., 412, 413, *423,* 600, *606*

Haupts, M., 475, 477, *479, 481*
Hawk, T. C., 415, 421, *424*
Haxby, J. V., 81, *90*, 414, 415, *423*, 443, 451, *455, 457*, 504, 506, 507, 508, 509, 510, 511, 513, 513*f*, 514, *515, 516, 517*, 631, 634, *639, 640*
Hay, J. F., 220*t*, 221, 222, 224, *226*, 253, *258*, 420, 421, *423, 424*
Hayden, P. E., 251*t, 258*
Hayes, S. M., 189, *192*
Hayes-Roth, B., 320, *331*, 367, *378*
Hayman, G. A. C., 62, 65, 67, *70, 72*, 255, 256, *258, 261*
Hayne, H., 38, 267, 270, 272, 273, 275, 277, *279*, 280, 281, *282*, 284, 300, 306
Head, D. P., 413, *424*
Heald, A., 453, *459*
Healy, A. F., 353, 354, *361*
Heaps, C., 156, *161*
Heaton, J. F., 542, *551*
Hebb, D. O., 81, *90*, 469, *480*, 646, *648*
Hebben, N., 468, *480*
Heckers, S., 505, *516*
Hedges, L. V., 319, *327*, 365, 366, 371, *375*
Heffernan, T. M., 84, *90*
Hegglin, K., 468, *480*
Heggs, A. J., 452, *455*
Heindel, W. C., 435, 436, *439*, *440*, 442, 454, *454*
Heinze, H. -J., 233, *241*, 504, *516*, 529, 530, 531, *534*
Heisey, J. G., 397, *407*
Heiss, W. -D., 470, 471, 474, 474*f*, 475, 477, *480, 482*, 506, *516*
Heivly, C., 367, *375*
Hellyer, S., 561, 563*f, 570*
Helstrup, T., 139, 141, 143, 144, 145, *147*
Hemenway, K., 365, *378*
Henderson, D., 217, *225*
Henderson, E. N., 315, *327*
Henkel, L. A., 184, 186, 187, 189, 189*n, 191, 193*, 238, *243*, 371, *374*
Henson, R. N. A., 87, *91*, 619, *622*
Henzler, A., 239, 241*n, 242*
Herlitz, A., 140, *145*
Herman, J. L., 385, *390*
Hermann, S., 302, *308*
Hermer, L., 369, *374*
Herrmann, D. J., 321, 322, *331, 327, 330*, 356, *361*
Hertel, P. T., 219, *226*
Hertsgaard, L. A., 273, *279*, 284, *292*

Hertzog, C., 200, *208*, 417, *424*
Hertz-Pannier, L., 472, *479*
Herz, R. S., 95, *105*
Heuer, F., 380, *389, 390*
Heuser, L., 469, 473, *481*
Heyman, A., 443, *459*
Hichwa, R. D., 510, 514, *515*, 632, 633, *639*
Hicks, J. L., 181, *193*, 255, *259*, 336, *344*
Hicks, L. H., 415, *423*
Hicks, R. Y., 128, *135*
Hildebrandt, M., 233, *241*, 545, *551*
Hildreth, K., 271, 275, 276, *281*
Hilgard, E.R., 4, *28*, 646
Hill, K., 550, *553*
Hill, L., 143, *148*
Hill, M. A., 454, *458*
Hill, R., 443, *459*
Hill, R. D., 398, *408*
Hillis, A. E., 430, *439*
Hinrichs, H., 504, *516*
Hinrichs, J. V., 132, *134*, 167, *176*, 541, 544, 548*t, 552, 553*
Hinton, G. E., 584, 585*f*, 589, *595, 596*
Hintzman, D. L., 18, *29*, 63, 64, 65, 66, *71*, 165, 166, 167, 168, 169, 169*f*, 170, 171, 172, 173*f, 176*, 222, 223, 224, *225, 226, 374*, 572, 573, *579*, 586, *595*
Hirsh, R., 488, *498*
Hirshman, E., 102, *105*, 175, *176*, 222, *227*, 236, *236*, 237, 239, 241*n, 242, 243, 244*, 528, *535*
Hirst, W., 324, *327*
Hirtle, S., 366, *374*
Hitch, G. J., 22, *27*, 53, *56*, 77, 78, 79, 83, 83*f*, 84, *88, 90*, 230, 232*t*, 233, *241*, 416, *422*, 506, *515*, 630, *638*
Hitchcock, D. F. A., 275, 277, *281*
Hockey, G. R. J., 79, *90*
Hockley, W. E., 169, *176*, 576, *579*
Hodge, D., 187, *194*
Hodges, J. R., 37, 429, 430, 433, *439, 440*, 441, 442, 443, 444, 444*f*, 445, 446, 446*f*, 447, 447*f*, 448, 449, 450, 451, 452, 453, 454, *454, 455, 456, 457, 458*, 468, 590, *595*
Hof, P. R., 474, *480*
Hoffman, H. G., 185, *191*
Hoffman, J. E., 189*n, 192*
Hoffman, J. M., 413, *424*
Hofman, A., 454, *458*
Hofmann, E., 469, *482*

Hogan, H. P., 150, *160*
Hogan, N., 637, *640*
Hogrefe, G. -J., 603, *608*
Hogrefe, J., 301, *309, 312*
Hohnecker, L., 384, *390*
Hoine, H., 337, *344*
Holbrook, M. B., 319, *327*
Holdstock, J. S., 433, *439*
Holinka, B., 477, *479*
Hollan, J. D., 333, 334, 338, 339, 340, 342, *346*
Holland, H. L., 321, *326*
Holland, P. W., 62, *70*, 181, 185, *191*
Hollingshead, A., 99, *105, 226*
Holm, S., 466, *478*
Holmberg, D., 288, *294*, 322, *330*
Holmes, C. J., 433, *439*
Holmes, D., 386, *390*
Holmes, J. B., 239, *242*
Holton, G., 35, *42*
Holyoak, K. J., 98, 109, 111, 112, 113, 119, *119, 120, 121, 122*, 367, *374*
Homa, D., 111, *121*
Homes, A. P., 502, *516*
Hommer, D., 548*t, 552*
Homskaya, E. D., 601, *607*
Honda, M., 466, *480*
Hood, B., 273, *281*
Hood, K. L., 495, *498*
Hopkins, W. F., III, 415, *423*
Horel, J. A., 466, *480*
Horn, G., *551*
Horn, M., 385, *390*
Horowitz, L. M., 131, *134*
Horwitz, B., 81, *90*, 414, 415, *423*, 443, *455*, 504, 508, 509, 510, 511, 513*f, 516, 517*, 631, 634, *640*
Houle, S., 26, *31*, 189, *194*, 402, *409*, 414, 421, *422, 425, 483*, 503*f*, 504, 505, 506, 510, 511*f*, 513, *515, 517, 518*, 519, 531, *534, 535*, 617, *625*, 633, 634, 635, *640, 641, 642*
Hovland, C. I., 6*f, 29*, 129, *134*, 166, *177*, 645
Howard, D., 442, *457*
Howard, D. V., 397, 398, *407*
Howard, J. H., 367, *375*, 398, *407*
Howe, M. L., 306, *309*, 383, *390*, 603, *607*
Hoyt, J. D., 198, 206, *208*
Hu, X., 185, *190, 194*
Huberman, M., 436, *439*
Hudson, J. A., 274, *281*, 286, 290, *293, 295*, 306, *309*, 324, *327*
Hudson, J. I., 384, *391*
Hudson, S., 87, *91*
Hughes, D., 384, *390*
Hughes, E., 435, *437*

Hughes, J. P., 443, *459*
Hull, A., 369, *378*
Hull, C. L., 4, *29*, 129, *134*, 166, *177*, 245, *258*
Hume, S. P., 550, *553*
Humphrey, D. G., 401, *407*
Humphreys, M. S., 39, *42*, 63, 64, 66, 69, *70, 71*, 583, *595*
Hunkin, N. M., 404, *408*
Hunt, P. R., 431, *437*
Hunt, R. R., 34, *43*, 98, *105*, 138, 144, *147*, 246, 252, *261*
Hunter, W. S., 273, *281*
Huppert, F. A., 174, *177*, 305, *309*
Huron, C., 231, 238, *242*
Hurtig, R., 510, 514, *514*
Husband, T. H., 317, *327*
Huschke, E., *480*
Hutchins, E., 324, *327*
Huttenlocher, J., 319, *327*, 365, 366, 369, 371, *375, 376*
Hutton, M., 445, *456*
Hyder, F., 631, *640*
Hyman, B. T., 443, *459*, 468, *479*, 486, *497*
Hyman, D. T., 605, *606*
Hyman, I. E., 156, 158, *161*, 187, *192*, 317, 321, 323, *327*, 385, *390*

Iddon, J. L., 453, *458*
Ijiri, Y., 559, 560, *570*
Imbs, J. L., 545, *552, 553, 554*
Imperato, A., 549, *552*
Inagaki, K., 109, 118, *120*
Ince, C., 413, *422*
Ingvar, D. H., 602, *607*
Ingvar, M., 505, 514, *518*
Inhelder, B., 369, *376*
Innis, R. B., 470, *479*
Inoue, C., 236, *242*
Inskeep, N. R., 166, *176*
Intraub, H., 189n, *192*
Irion, A. L., 8, 13, *29*
Irle, E., 470f, *480*
Irwin, D. E., 365, *373*
Irwin, J. M., 128, *134*, 150, *161*
Isaac, C. L., 433, *439*
Israel, I., 364, 368, *373*
Isseroff, A., 491, *498*
Itoh, Y., 321, *329*
Itsukushima, Y., 321, *329*
Iverson, G. J., 574, *579*
Izawa, C., 354, *361*
Izquierdo, I., 541, *553*

Jackendoff, R., 372, *375*
Jacobs, D., 442, 445, *455*
Jacobs, W. J., 386, 387, *391*
Jacobson, R. R., 547, 548t, *554*
Jacoby, J. D., 157, *162*

Jacoby, L. L., 49, 51, *56*, 99, 102, 103, *105*, 154, *161*, 181, 185, 186, *192*, 205, *208*, 215, 216, 217, 218, 219, 220, 220t, 221, 222, 223, 224, *225, 226*, 227, 228, 236, 237, 239, *242*, *244*, 246, 248, 249, 250, 251t, 252, 253, 254, 255, *258, 259, 261*, 334, *344*, 352, 354, *361*, 403, *406*, 411, 415, 420, 421, *422, 423, 424*, 523, 525, 527, 533, *534, 536*, 545, *552*, 610, 613, 618, *622*
Jaeger, B., 316, 320, *326*
Jagust, W. J., 413, *424*
James, C. T., 62, 63, *70*
James, M., 442, *458*
James, W., 19, *29*, 78, 81, *90*, 197, *208*, 300, *309*, 597, 598, 602, *607*
Janczura, G. A., 336, *345*
Janet, P., 386, *390*
Jankovic, I. N., 368, *375*
Janowsky, J. S., 203, *208*, 403, *407, 409*, 600, *607*
Jansen, E. N. H., 473, *479*
Jarrad, L. E., 488, 489, *498*
Jarrell, G. R., 323, *330*
Jarrold, C., 302, *311*
Jasechko, J., 154, *161*
Jason, L., 443, *459*
Java, R. I., 34, 36, *42*, 224, *227*, 230, 231, 232t, 233, 236, 237, 238, 239, 239t, *241*, *242, 243, 244*, 255, *260*, 320, *325*, 523, 527, 529, *534, 535*, 545, *551*, 599, *606*, 610, *624*
Jaynes, J., 274, *280*
Jeannerod, M., 302, *309*
Jeffries, R., 118, *121*
Jelicic, M., 41, *42*, 542, *551*
Jenkins, I. H., 637, *640*
Jenkins, J. J., 125, *134*, 179, *192*
Jennings, J. M., 145, *146*, 217, 219, 224, *226, 227*, 237, 239, *242*, 246, 253, *259, 261*, 396, 400, *406*, 414, 415, 420, 421, *422, 424*
Jennings, P. J., 504, *519*, 634, *642*
Jensen, A. R., 126, *134*
Jernigan, T. L., 615, *622, 624*
Jezzard, P., 472, *479*, 636, 637, *640*
Joaquim, S. G., 202, *209*
Jobe, J. B., 319, 320, *327, 331*
Jobst, K. A., 448, *459*
Jodelet, D., 367, *376*
John, E. R., 466, 474, *478*
Johnson, B. T., 619, *625*
Johnson, C. N., 302, 303, *311*, 603, *607*
Johnson, D. R., 470, *479*

Johnson, G. J., 5, 6f, *29*, 128, 130, *134*
Johnson, K. A., 468, *479, 480*, 486, *497*, 605, *606*, 617, *622*
Johnson, M., 364, 372, *375*, 619, *622*
Johnson, M. K., 18, *29*, 52, *56*, 94, 98, *104, 105*, 151, 152, 154, 155, *161*, 169, 171, 172, *176, 177*, 179, 180, 181, 182, 183, 184, 185, 186, 187, 188, 189, 189n, *190*, 191, *192*, *193, 194, 195*, 198, *208*, 223, *225, 227*, 233, 236, 238, *243*, *244*, 302, *308, 309*, 397, 399, 403, *407*, 512, *517*, 528, 531, *534*, 613, 614, *622*
Johnson, N. S., 315, *328*
Johnson, R., 521, 527, *534*
Johnson, R. E., 315, *327*
Johnson, T., 84, *89*
Johnson, T. P., 320, *331*
Johnson-Laird, P. N., 183, *192*, 368, 369, 370, 372, *375, 376*
Johnston, K. A., 435, *439*
Jones, C., 505, 506, *517*, 531, *534*
Jones, E. M., 403, *406*
Jones, G. M. M., 550, *552, 553*
Jones, G. V., 334, 340, *344*
Jones, H. E., 270, *281*
Jones, R. S., 584, 585, *594*
Jones, T. C., 232t, 236, *243*
Jones, T. J., 218, *226*
Jonides, J., 81, 85, 87, *88, 91*, 366, *374*, 428, *439*, 506, 507, 514, *515, 519*, 630, 631, 632, *638, 639, 640, 642*
Joordens, S., 223, *227*, 525, *534*
Joseph, S., 386, 387, *389*
Josephs, O., 451, *459*, 619, *622*, 633, *643*
Josiassen, R. C., 452, *457*
Jouandet, M., 203, *208*
Joubran, R., 252, 253, 255, *260*
Juola, J. F., 185, *190*, 215, *225*, 576, *579*
Jurica, P. J., 403, *409*
Just, M. A., 86, *90*, 630, *640*

Kaada, B. R., 647, *648*
Kagan, J., 224, *228*
Kahan, R. L., 180, *192*
Kahana, M. J., 59, 60, 62, 64, 65, 66, 67, 69, *71*
Kahle, W., 504f, *517*
Kahneman, D., 216, *228*, 399, *407*
Kalamarides, P., 339, 340, *345*
Kalbe, E., 471, 474f, *482*
Kalina, M., 433, *438*
Kaminska, Z., 231, 232t, 238, *242, 243*
Kantrow, R. W., 270, *281*

Kanwisher, N., 365, *374*
Kaplan, S., 370, *373*, 380, *390*
Kapur, N., 430, 433, *439*, 473, 475, *480*
Kapur, S., 26, *31*, 402, *409*, 414, 421, *422, 425, 483*, 503f, 504, 505, 506, 510, 513, *515, 517, 518, 519*, 531, *534, 535*, 617, 619, *621, 625*, 633, 634, 635, *640, 641, 642*
Karlin, M. B., 52, *56*
Karlsson, S., 144, *148*
Karlsson, T., 103, *106*
Karni, A., 636, 637, *640*
Karper, L. P., 549, *552*
Kasniak, A. W., 445, *454*
Kassell, N., 468, *480*
Kasserman, J. E., 251t, *257*
Kassin, S. M., 379, *390*
Kaszniak, A. W., 395, 397, *409*, 600, *607*
Katz, S., 85, *88*, 506, *515*, 630, *638*
Katzman, R., 443, *459*
Kauffmann-Muller, F., 545, *553, 554*
Kausler, D. H., 8, *29*, 395, 396, 400, *407*
Kaysen, D., 472, *479*
Kazes, M., 545, *554*
Kean, M. L., 144, *146*, 398, *406*
Keane, M. M., 250, 251t, *261*, 435, *439*, 468, *480*, 610, 616, 617, *622*
Keane, M. T., 113, *121*
Keator, D., 380, 387, *389*, 505, 506, *515*
Keefe, D. E., 336, *345*
Keele, S. W., 94, *106, 153, 161*, 584, *596*
Keen, R., 269, *281*
Keenan, J. M., 320, *328*
Keil, K., 506, 507, 514, *515*, 631, *639*
Keller, T. A., 84, 86, *89, 90*
Kelley, C. M., 49, 51, 154, *161*, 181, 185, 186, *191, 192*, 205, *208*, 215, 216, 217, 219, 221, 224, *226, 227*, 246, 250, 251t, 253, 254, *258, 259*, 335, 336, *344*, 354, *361*, 523, *534*, 618, *622*
Kelley, W., 631, 634, *640*
Kellogg, R. T., 103, *105*
Kemp, S., 319, *327*, 367, *375*
Kemper, T. L., 412, 413, *424*
Kempler, D., 446, *455*
Kenkel, S., 466, *481*
Kennedy, A. M., 445, 448, *455, 458*
Kennedy, P. T., 112, *121*
Kent, G., 320, *327*
Keogh, L., 187, *193*

Keppel, G., 79, 81, *90*
Kershaw, A., 454, *457*
Kerst, S. M., 367, *375*
Kertesz, A., 454, *457*
Kessler, J., 469, 470, 471, 473, 474, 474f, 475, 477, *480, 481, 482, 483*, 506, *516*
Ketcham, K., 27, *29*, 159, *161*, 383, 385, 386, *391*
Kidder, D. P., 417, *424*
Kieras, D. E., 113, *121*
Kiess, H. O., 10, *30*
Kihlstrom, J. F., 387, *392*, 395, 397, *409*, 542, *551, 552*, 600, *607*
Kilbane, M. C., 112, *121*
Killiany, R. J., 489, 490, *497*
Killinger, W. A., 317, *332*
Kim, I. J., 249, 254, *260*
Kim, J. J., 465, 472, *483*
Kim, K., 574, *579*
Kimball, D. R., 98, *109*
Kincey, J. A., 320, *325*
Kinchla, R. A., 185, *193*
King, L., 239, *244*
Kinoshita, S., 617, *622*
Kinsbourne, M., 610, 615, *622, 625*
Kintsch, W., 23, *29*, 81, *90*, 99, *105*, 114, 115, 116, 117, *120, 121*, 166, *177*, 320, *327*, 340, 341, 342, *346*, 347, 362, 372, *378*
Kinzler, P., 469, *482*
Kirasic, K. C., 366, *372*
Kirby, J., 80, *89*
Kirker, W. S., 567, 568, *570*
Kirkpatrick, E. A., 129, *134*
Kirsner, K., 55, *56*, 251t, 252, 255, *258, 259*
Kitchener, E. G., 451, *457*
Klatzky, R. L., 347, *362*, 364, 368, 370, *374, 375*
Klauber, M. R., 550, *553*
Klein, P. J., 276, 277, *279, 280*
Kleinsmith, L. J., 380, *390*
Kleist, K., 465, 467f, *480*
Klin, C. M., 341, *344*
Kline, D. W., 396, *406, 407*
Kline, P. J., 111, *119*
Klingberg, T., 511, 512, *517*
Klinger, M. R., 320, *326, 328*
Kluft, K. P., 385, *390*
Kluger, A., 413, *422, 423*
Klüver, H., 469, *479, 481*
Knapp, A., 466, *481*, 585, *595*
Knapp, M. L., 321, *327*
Knight, T., 181, *193*, 221, 224, 228, *242*, 402, *407*, 415, 416, 416f, 419, *424, 425*, 430, 434, *439, 440*, 469, 477, *481, 482*, 611, 618, *625*
Knopf, M., 141, 144, *147*

Knopman, D. S., 545, 550, *552, 553*
Knowlton, B. J., 189, *195*, 222, *227*, 231, *243*, 251t, *259*, 437, 440, 468, 472, 474, 475, *481, 483*, 496, *498*, 530, *536*, 611, 618, *622*
Koeppe, R. A., 85, *88, 91, 482*, 506, 507, *515, 519*, 630, 631, *638, 640, 642*
Koffka, K., 166, *177*
Koh, K., 112, *121*
Köhler, S., 505, 508, *517*, 609, 614, 620, *623*
Köhler, W., 64, *71*, 166, *177*
Koivisto, K., 413, *425*
Kokmen, E., 454, *458*
Kolb, B., 26, *29*
Kolers, P. A., 94, 99, 102, *105*, 180, *193*, 202, 203, *208*, 250, 251t, *259*
Kolodner, J. L., 340, *344*
Kolodny, J., 87, *88*
Komatsu, S., 222, *225, 258*
Konorski, J., 95, *105*
Koocher, G. P., 322, *327*
Kopell, B. S., 415, *423*
Kopelman, M. D., 246, 259, 442, 445, 447, 448, *457*, 510, *517*, 540, 544, 548, 549, *551, 552, 623*
Koppell, S., 60, *71*
Koppenaal, R. J., 68, *71*
Korczyn, A. D., 454, *458*
Korfmacher, J. E., 301, *308*
Koriat, A., 96, *105*, 199, 200, 201, *208, 209*, 316, 321, *327*, 333, 335, 336, 338, 339, 340, 341, 342, *344*, 531, *535i*
Kormi-Nouri, R., 139, 140, 141, 142, 143, 144, 145, *145, 147*, 148
Kornhuber, H. H., 469, *481*
Kortenkamp, D., 370, *373*
Kortge, C. A., 592, *595*
Koshmider, J. W., III, 183, *195*
Koslowski, B., 118, *119*
Koss, M. P., 387, 383, *390, 392*
Kosslyn, S. M., 25, 26, *29*, 364, 367, 371, 372, *375*
Koster, C., 369, *374*
Kounios, J., 181, 187, 189, *192*, 223, *227*, 531, *534*
Koutstaal, W., 158, *162*, 184, 189, *194*, 233, 238, *244*, 339, *345*, 403, *409*, 504, 505, 510, *515, 519*, 522, *536*, 609, 616, 617, *621, 628*, 633, 634, 635, 636, *638, 642, 643*
Kozin, M., 316, 318, *330*
Krafka, C., 321, *327*
Kraft, D., 255, *259*
Kramer, A. F., 401, *407*

Krampe, R. E., 26, 27, *28*
Krebs, H., 637, *640*
Krinsky, R., 201, *209*
Kroll, J. F., 251*t*, *259*
Kroll, N. E. A., 181, *193*, 221, 224, *228*, 402, *407*, 430, 434, *439*, 477, *481*, 529, *537*, 611, 618, *625*
Krueger, W. C. F., 562, 563*f*, *570*
Kruger, A. C., 283, *295*
Kruk, R. V., 396, *406*
Krumnacker, H., 137, 143, *146*
Krupa, D. J., 488, *499*
Kruschke, J. K., 587, 593, *594*, *595*
Krystal, J. H., 387, 388, *390*, 470, *479*, *481*, 549, *552*, 631, *641*
Kuebli, J., 287, 288, *292*, *293*
Kugelmass, S., 372, *378*
Kuhar, M. J., 415, *425*
Kuhl, D. E., *482*
Kuhl, J., 255, *258*
Kuhl, S., 600, *606*
Kuhn, J., 321, 322, *327*, 383, *390*
Kuiper, N. A., 567, 568, *570*
Kuipers, B. J., 370, *375*
Kuisma, J. E., 81, *89*
Kulik, J., 317, *325*, 381, 382, *389*
Kunst-Wilson, W. R., 249, 251*t*, *259*
Kusbit, G. W., 204, *210*
Kutas, M., 521, 524, 527, *535*
Kveim, O., 647, *648*
Kwon, P., 181, 183, 185, *193*, 302, *309*
Kwong, K., 632, *642*
Kyllonen, P. C., 86, *90*

LaBar, K. S., 437, *439*, 470, *481*
Labov, W., 287, *293*
Labrecque, R., 472, *483*
Lachman, J. L., 200, *209*
Lachman, R., 200, *209*
Ladd, G. L., 128, *134*
Ladd, L. S., 610, 616, *624*
Lader, M. H., 540, 544, 545, 547, 548*t*, *551*, *552*
Lagattuta, K. H., 303, *309*
Laiacona, M., 452, *455*
Laine, M., 474, *481*
Lakoff, G., 364, 372, *375*
Lalonde, F. M., 513, *517*, 632, *640*
Lalonde, P., 205, *207*
Lambert, B. L., 77, *90*
Lambon Ralph, M. A., 446, *457*
Lammers, W. J., 181, *194*
Lammertsma, A. A., 550, *553*
Lanca, M., 371, *373*
Landau, B., *375*
Landau, J. D., 181, *193*, 336, *344*

Landauer, T. K., 103, *105*, 200, 208, 355, 356, 357, *362*, 612, *623*
Landwehr, R. S., 200, *209*
Lane, D. M., 115, 117, *121*
Lane, S. M., 181, 182, 183, 184, 189*n*, *195*
Lang, A. E., 436, *440*
Lang, B., 304, *310*
Lang, K. W., 454, *457*
Langacker, R. W., 372, *375*
Lange, G., 292, *293*
Lange, K. L., 435, *438*
Lange, K. W., 442, *458*
Lange, T. E., 113, *122*
Langer, S. A., 249, 254, *260*
Långström, B., 415, *422*, 505, *515*
Lansdale, M. W., 365, 366, *375*
Larish, J. F., 401, *407*
Larsen, R. J., 322, 323, *326*, *328*
Larsen, S. F., 317, 318, 319, *326*, *328*, *331*, 382, *389*
Larus, D. M., 290, *294*
Larwill, L. K., 217, *226*, 251*t*, 254, *258*
Lashley, K. S., 15, *29*, 128, 129, *134*, 466, *481*, 584, *595*, 646, 647, *648*
Lauber, E., 506, *519*
Laurence, J. -R., 316, *328*
Laver, G. D., 397, *407*
Lavi, H., 359, *362*
LaVoie, D., 175, *177*, 223, *227*, 398, *407*
Law, I., 466, *478*, 508, 510, *517*
Law, J., 64, *71*, 99, *106*
Lawrence, A. D., 454, *457*, 548, 550, *552*
Lawrence, R., 318, *326*
Lazzara, M., 221, 224, *228*, 529, *537*, 611, 618, *625*
Leach, K., 181, 182, 186, *192*
Lease, J., 630, 631, 632, *639*
Leavitt, J., 543, *552*
Lebiere, C., 559, *569*, 572, *579*
Lechevalier, B., 505, *516*
LeCompte, D. C., 131, *135*, 232*t*, 237, *243*
Lederman, S. J., *375*
LeDoux, J. E., 386, *390*, 470, *481*, 488, *498*
Lee, M. G., 252, 253, 255, *260*
Leenders, K. L., 415, *421*
Lees, A. J., 442, *458*
Legault, F., 453, *455*
Legrand, F., 545, *552*
Lehman, D. R., 112, 119, *121*
Lehmann, A. C., 115, *120*
Lehnung, M., 466, *481*
Leibowitz, H. W., 368, *375*
Leicht, K. L., 169, *177*
Leichtman, M. D., 224, *228*, 288, *293*, 303, *309*

Leigh, P. N., 442, *458*
Leiguarda, R., 443, *459*
Leippe, M. R., 183, *194*
Leiser, D., 370, *375*
Lelliot, P., 547, 548*t*, *551*
Leonard, B. W., 494, *498*, 592, *594*
Leonard, G., 174, *177*
Leonesio, R. J., 200, 204, *209*, *211*
Leonhardt, H., *517*
Lepage, M., 514, *517*, 619, *623*, 635, *640*
Leplow, B., 466, *481*
Leslie, A. M., 305, *307*
Lesser, I. M., 448, 450, *457*
Levelt, W. J. M., *375*
Leveton, L., 491, *498*
Levin, B. E., *457*
Levine, B., 620, *623*
Levine, L. J., 317, 318, *328*
Levine, M., 368, *375*
Levine, W. H., 341, *344*
Levinson, S. C., 364, 369, *375*
Levitin, D. J., 96, *106*, 172, 173*f*, *176*
Levitt, T. S., 370, *375*
Levonian, E., 568, *570*
Levy, B. A., 251*t*, 255, *259*
Levy, F., 550, *553*
Levy, R., 453, *459*, 550, *552*, *553*
Lewandowsky, S., 127, 129, *134*
Lewinsohn, P. M., 322, *328*
Lewis, B. R., 153, *162*
Lewis, M. E., 491, *498*
Lewis, R. J., 320, *327*
Lewis, V. J., 84, *88*, 103, *104*, *551*
Ley, P., 320, *325*, *328*
Lezak, M. D., *424*
Lhermitte, F., 453, *455*
Li, K. Z. H., 396, *409*
Li, S. -C., 127, *134*
Liang, C-H., 288, *293*
Libby, L. K., 315
Liben, L., 367, *376*
Lichtenstein, E. H., 315, *325*
Lichtenstein, S., 204, 206*f*, *209*
Lichty, W., 400, *407*
Lickorish, A., 369, *378*
Liddle, P. F., 509, *516*
Lieberman, K., 85, *88*
Lieblich, I., 201, *209*, 336, 338, 339, 340, *344*
Liess, J., 475, *481*
Light, L. L., 166, 175, *177*, 223, *227*, 395, 398, 400, *406*, *407*, *408*
Lim, K. O., 413, *425*
Lima, S. D., 415, *424*
Lin, L. -H., 592, *594*
Lin, Y., 359, *362*
Lindem, K., 369, *374*

Lindsay, D. S., 18, *29,* 154, *160, 161,* 171, 172, *177,* 180, 181, 182, 183, 184, 185, 186, 188, 189*n, 190, 191, 192, 193, 194,* 221, 223, *227,* 236, *243,* 246, 251*t,* 254, 255, *258, 259, 261,* 302, *309,* 321, *329,* 335, 336, *344,* 385, *390, 391,* 397, *407,* 528, *534*
Lindsley, D. B., 521, 522, *536*
Lineweaver, T. T., 435, 436, *440*
Links, J. M., 415, *425*
Lins, O. G., 521, *535*
Linton, M., 319, *328*
Linton, S. J., 316, *328*
Liotti, M., 477, *480*
Lipsitt, L. P., 270, *281*
Little, A. H., 270, *281*
Littler, J. E., 84, *90*
Litvan, I., 453, *457*
Livingston, R. B., 382, *390*
Lloyd, R., 367, *375*
Locascio, J. J., 443, *457*
Lock, T. G., 157, *161*
Lockhart, R. S., 22, *28,* 34, 40, 45, 48, *57,* 82, *89,* 94, 95, 102, *105,* 139, *146,* 166, *175,* 429, *438,* 472, *479,* 567, *569*
Lockman, J. J., 364, 369, *376*
Loess, H., 79, *90*
Loewen, E. R., 189, *191,* 404, *406,* 600, *606*
Loewenstein, R. J., 386, *389*
Loftus, E. F., 27, *29,* 49, 54, *57,* 100, *106,* 151, 154, 155*f,* 156, 156*t,* 159, 160, *161,* 182, *184,* 187, 188, 189*n, 190, 191, 193, 194,* 204, 211, 317, 319, 320, *326, 328,* 336, *343,* 379, 380, 383, 384, 385, 386, *389, 390, 391,* 475, *481,* 584, *595*
Loftus, G. R., 60, *71,* 380, *391,* 561, *570*
Logan, G. D., 217, *227, 228,* 250, *259,* 401, *407*
Logie, R. H., 85, 87, *88, 90,* 317, *326,* 382, *389,* 442, 447, *454*
Lollis, T., 138, *147*
London, M., 372, *373*
Longman, D. J. A., 205, *207*
Loomis, J. M., 364, 368, *375*
Lopatka, C., 320, *326*
Lopez, O. L., 444, *454*
Lorch, R. F., Jr., 34, *42*
Lories, G., 200, *207*
Lou, J., 436, *440*
Lovelace, F. A., 139, *147*
Lucas, D., 274, *282*
Lucchelli, F., 469, 477, *480, 481*
Lucki, I., 547, *552*
Lueschow, A., 636, *639*
Luminet, O., 382, *390*

Luria, A. R., 416, 419, *424,* 601, *607*
Lutzenberg, W., 436, *438*
Lykins, M. S., 269, *282*
Lynch, K., 363, *375*
Lynn, S. J., 157, *161*
Lyon, T. D., 303, *309*

Maass, A., 321, *325*
Macaulay, D., 386, *389*
Macchi, G., 465, *481*
Macdonald, C. A., 65, 67, *72,* 256, *261*
MacDonald, P., 616, *623*
MacDonald, S., 277, *281*
MacKay, D. G., 199, *207, 209,* 398, *406*
MacKay, D. J., 593, *595*
Mackell, J. A., *553*
Macken, W. J., 232*t, 243*
MacKinnon, D. P., 321, *326*
MacLean, P. D., 465, *481*
MacLeod, A. M., 632, 633, 636, 637, *641*
MacLeod, C. M., 125, *134,* 250, 255, *259,* 502, *518,* 616, *623*
MacWhinney, B., 320, *328, 570*
Madden, D. J., 413, 415, 421, *424*
Maddox, W. T., 577, *579*
Madigan, S. A., 15, *31,* 97, *106,* 197, 207, *210,* 297, *311,* 352, *362*
Magel, S. G., 367, *377*
Maguire, E. A., 367, *375*
Mah, W. A., 367, *374*
Mahadevan, R. S., 323, *331*
Maine de Biran, 627, *640*
Mainwaring, N., 469, *483*
Mainwaring, S., *378*
Mair, W. G. P., 466, *481*
Maisog, J. M., 414, 415, *423,* 504, 510, *516,* 631, 634, *639, 640*
Maki, R. H., 204, *209,* 366, *376*
Malach, R., 632, *642*
Malamut, B. J., 485, 486, *498*
Malhotra, A. K., 549, *553*
Malkova, L., 496, *498*
Malmi, R. A., 61, *72*
Maloney, L., 445, 446, *455*
Malpass, R. S., 321, *328*
Mancall, E. L., 452, *457*
Mandler, G., 16, *29,* 61, *71,* 96, *106,* 111, *121,* 129, *134,* 215, 216, 218, *227,* 229, 236, *242, 243,* 251*t,* 255, *258, 259,* 335, 339, *343, 344,* 523, 527, *535,* 618, *623*
Mandler, J. M., 284, *292, 293,* 299, *309,* 315, *328,* 365, 369, *376,* 602, *607*
Mangels, J. A., 434, *439,* 472, 475, *481,* 496, *498*

Mangun, G. R., 233, *241,* 504, *516,* 529, 530, 531, *534*
Mani, K., 368, 369, *376*
Manier, D., 324, *327*
Mann, D. M. A., 448, 449, 450, *458, 459,* 618, *624*
Mann, S., 131, *133*
Manning, C. G., 156, *161,* 184, *191,* 385, *390*
Manoach, D. S., 472, *481*
Mäntylä, T., 16, 17, *29,* 230, 231, 232*t,* 233, 235, 239, *243,* 336, *344,* 417, 420, *424,* 566, *570*
Mapstone, H. C., 435, *439,* 468, *480,* 617, *622*
Marburger, W., 319, *328*
Marchal, G., 505, *516*
Maren, S., 549, *553*
Maril, A., 403, *409,* 504, *519,* 522, *536,* 634, *643*
Mark, R. E., 415, *424,* 525, 526*f,* 529, 530, *536*
Markham, R., 184, 187, *191, 193*
Markowitsch, H. J., 37, *43,* 380, 381, *389,* 430, 431, 434, *439, 440,* 465, 466, 468, 469, 470, 470*f,* 471, 472, 473, 474, 474*f,* 475, 477, *479, 480, 481,* 482, 483, 504, 506, 514, *516, 517, 519,* 541, *551,* 634, *642*
Marks, A. R., 131, *134*
Marks, I., 547, 548*t, 551*
Markus, E. J., 369, *376*
Marschark, M., 138, *147*
Marsden, C. D., 442, 454, *457, 458*
Marsh, L., 413, *425*
Marsh, R. L., 181, *193,* 255, *259,* 336, *344*
Marshuetz, C., 630, *640*
Martensen, H., 223, *225,* 236, *241*
Martin, A., 435, *440,* 442, 443, 451, *457,* 513, *517,* 616, 617, *625,* 632, 633, 636, *639, 640, 643*
Martin, E., 63, 67, 68, *71, 72,* 97, *106,* 129, *134*
Martin, R. C., 428, *439, 440*
Martone, M., 436, *439,* 442, 443, 454, *455*
Marvin, R. S., 301, *309*
Masdeu, J. C., 454, *458*
Masliah, E., 443, *459*
Mason, J. W., 470, *479*
Massaquoi, S., 436, *440*
Massaro, D. W., 594, *595*
Massman, P. J., *457*
Masson, M. E. J., 250, 254, *259*
Master, S., 175, *176,* 236, *242*
Matessa, M., 559, *569,* 572, *579*

Mathalon, D. H., *413, 425*
Mather, M., 186, 187, 188, *192, 193,* 238, *243,* 531, *534*
Matthews, J. A., 385, *389*
Mattson, M. E., 338, *344*
Maurer, K., 470, 471, *482*
Mawer, R. F., 111, 118, *121*
May, C. P., 411, 415, 417, 418, 419, *423*
Mayer, R. E., 11, *29*
Mayes, A. R., 37, 175, *177,* 427, 429, 430, 431, 433, 434, 435, *438, 439,* 468, *482,* 610, 617, *623, 624*
Mayhorn, C. B., 417, *424*
Maylor, E. A., 317, *325,* 417, *424*
Mayr, E., 35, *42*
Mazoyer, B., 367, *374*
Mazure, C., 470, *479*
Mazziota, J., 637, *640*
Mazzoni, G., 207, *209,* 341, *343,* 385, *391*
McAdams, D., 318, *328*
McCabe, A., 286, 287, 288, *293, 294*
McCarrell, N. S., 98, 99, *104*
McCarron, J. A., 550, *553*
McCarthy, G., 470, *479,* 522, *535,* 631, 633, *640, 641*
McCarthy, R. A., 427, 428, *439,* 451, 452, 454, *456, 457*
McCarthy, T. T., 184, 189*n,* 190
McCauley, M. R., 321, *326*
McCauley, R. N., 323, *328*
McClelland, A. G. R., 317, *326,* 382, 388, *389*
McClelland, J. L., 225, *227,* 388, *391,* 430, *438,* 451, *457,* 473, *482,* 505, *517,* 531, *535,* 557, 559, *570,* 575, 576, 578, 579, *579,* 583, 584, 585*f,* 586, 586*f,* 587, 589*f,* 590, 591, 592, 593, *595, 596,* 627, 628, 629, 632, *639, 641*
McCloskey, M., 203, *208,* 317, *328,* 341, *344,* 381, 382, *391,* 591, 592, *595*
McConkey, K. M., 157, *160,* 316, *328*
McConnell, J., 85, *91*
McCormack, T., 305, *309*
McCusker, E., 443, 445, *458*
McCutcheon, E., 269, *280*
McDaniel, M. A., 50, *56,* 113, *121,* 138, *147,* 317, *326,* 335, 336, *344,* 389, *389,* 398, 404, *406, 408,* 417, *423*
McDermott, K. B., 37, 100, 102, *106,* 149, 152, 153, 153*f,* 157, 158, *160, 161, 162,* 186, *194,* 221, *228,* 233, *244,* 246, 247, 252, *260,* 336, *345,* 403, *405, 408, 409,* 523, 524, 530,

531, *535, 536,* 610, 616, *624,* 629, 631, 634, *640, 641,* 647
McDonough, L., 285, *293,* 299, *309,* 602, *607*
McDowd, J. M., 102, *105,* 396, 402, *406, 408,* 414, *422*
McElree, B., 218, 222, 224, *226, 227,* 561, *570*
McFadzen, E., 184, *194,* 321, *330*
McGaugh, J. L., 380, 387, *389,* 469, 470, *479, 482,* 486, *497,* 505, 506, *515,* 541, 549, *551, 553*
McGeoch, J. A., 8, 13, *29,* 63, *71*
McGill, M. J., 558, *570*
McGinnis, D., 186, *193*
McGlinchey-Berroth, R., 620, *622, 623*
McGlynn, S. M., 203, *209*
McGonigle-Gibson, K. L., 445, *454*
McHugh, P. R., 441, *455*
McInnis, L., 323, *329*
McIntosh, A. R., 189, *194,* 414, 415, 421, *422, 423,* 503*f,* 504, 505, 506, 508, 509, 510, 511, 511*f,* 512*f,* 513, 513*f,* 514, *515, 516, 517, 518,* 531, *535,* 620, *623,* 635, *641*
McIntyre, J. S., 96, *106,* 223, *227,* 403, *408,* 600, *607*
McIsaac, H. K., 524, *535*
McKeachie, W. J., 359, *362*
McKee, R. D., 217, *228,* 278, *281,* 299, *309,* 492, *498,* 602, *607*
McKenna, P. J., 549, *552*
McKenna, S. P., 357, *362*
McKinley, S. C., 577, *580*
McKinney, V. M., 336, *345*
McKoon, G., 222, *227,* 246, *260,* 571, 577, 578, *580*
McLachlan, D. R., 96, *107,* 189, *194,* 403, *408, 409,* 599, 600, *607,* 610, 616, *623*
McLaughlin, T., 508, 509, 510, *517*
McLellan, D. L., 475, *480*
McNamara, T. P., 366, 368, *374, 376, 377,* 577, *580*
McNaughton, B. L., 225, *227,* 369, *376,* 388, *391,* 451, *457,* 473, *482,* 505, *517,* 531, *535,* 584, 589*f,* 590, 591, 592, *594, 595,* 627, 628, 629, *641*
McNeill, D., 16, *30,* 201, *207,* 338, 339, *343*
McRae, T., 413, *422*
McShane, R. H., 548, *551*
McSorley, P., 435, *438*
Mead, G., 175, *177,* 223, *227*
Medin, D. L., 24, *31,* 34, *43,* 110, *121*
Medina, J. H., 541, *553*

Mehdorn, M., 466, *481*
Mehringer, C. M., 448, 450, *457*
Melan, C., 523, *536*
Melin, L., 316, *328*
Melkman, R., 341, *344*
Mellet, E., 367, *374*
Melnick, R., 205, *207*
Melo, B., 612, *623*
Melton, A. W., 81, *90,* 128, 132, *133, 134,* 150, *161,* 352, *362*
Meltzoff, A. N., 271, 272, 273, 277, *279, 280, 281,* 299, *309,* 602, *607*
Memon, A., 385, *391*
Mena, I., 448, 450, *457*
Mensink, G. J. M., 63, *71*
Mentis, M. J., 414, 415, *423,* 510, *516*
Merikle, P. M., 86, *89,* 223, *227,* 250, *260,* 304, *310,* 525, *534,* 542, *553*
Mervis, C. B., 24, *30,* 34, *43*
Messo, J., 380, *391*
Mesulam, M. M., 469, *483, 517*
Metcalfe, J., 64, *71,* 181, *193,* 197, 199, 200, 202, 204, 205*f,* 209, 210, 337, 338, *343, 345,* 387, *391,* 402, *407,* 567, *569,* 584, *595*
Metcalfe-Eich, J., *71*
Metzler, A. E., 323, *329*
Metzler, C., 434, *439*
Metzler, J., 25, *31*
Meunier, M., 431, *437*
Mewaldt, S. P., 132, *134,* 541, 543, 544, 545, 548*t, 552, 553*
Meyer, D. E., 39, *42*
Meyer, E., 507, *518*
Meyer, G., 636, 637, *640*
Meyer, M., 369, *374*
Michel, J. -P., 474, *480*
Mickanin, J., 435, *437*
Middleton, D., 323, *326*
Middleton, H. C., 548, *551*
Miezin, F. M., 506, 513, *515,* 631, 634, 635, 636, *638, 640, 642*
Milan, S., 219, *226*
Milberg, W. P., 403, *409,* 635, *642*
Milgram, S., 367, *376*
Miliotis, P., 475, *482*
Miller, A., 80, *89*
Miller, B. L., 448, 450, *457, 458*
Miller, D. C., 413, *422*
Miller, D. G., 54, *57,* 154, 155*f, 161,* 317, *328*
Miller, E., 617, *623,* 631, *641*
Miller, E. K., 636, *639*
Miller, G. A., 12, 15, 16, *29, 30,* 78, 79, *90,* 97, *106,* 129, *134,* 150, *161,* 370, *376*
Miller, J. B., 321, 323, *328*

Miller, P.J., 288, *293*
Miller, S. A., 303, *311*
Milner, B., 81, *90*, 174, *176, 177,* 251*t, 259*, 468, 471, *482, 483,* 485, 486, 488, *499,* 605, *607*
Milner, P., 612, *623*
Milson, R., 557, 558, 567, *569,* 593, *594*
Milton, K., 564, *570*
Minami, M., 288, *294*
Miner, A. C., 199, *209*
Miner, N., 647, *648*
Minoshima, S., 85, *91, 482,* 506, 507, *519,* 631, *640, 642*
Minshew, N. J., 306, *309*
Minsky, M., 116, *121*
Mintun, M. A., 631, 633, *640, 641*
Miozzo, M., 201, *209*
Mishkin, M., 278, *279,* 364, *378,* 431, 433, *440,* 451, *459,* 466, 473, *482, 484,* 485, 486, 489, 490, 491, 494, 495, 496, 497, *498, 499, 519,* 604, 605, 606, *607, 608,* 617, *625,* 627, 631, *641, 643*
Missar, C. D., 549, *553*
Mitchell, D. B., 34, 40, *43,* 251*t, 259*
Mitchell, D. R. D., 400, *409*
Mitchell, K. J., 154, *162,* 179, 183, 184, 186, 187, 188, *192, 193, 195,* 223
Mitchell, P., 301, *310*
Miyake, A., 78, 83, 87, 88, *90, 91*
Mizumori, S. J. Y., 592, *594*
Moar, I., 367, *376*
Modigliani, V., 356, *362*
Modolo, K., 204, *207*
Moffitt, K. H., 322, *328*
Mohr, E., 453, *457*
Mohr, G., 140, 141, 142, 143, *146, 147, 148*
Mohs, R. C., 415, *423, 443, 459, 553*
Molfese, D. L., 269, *281*
Moniz, E., 601, *607*
Monks, J., 200, *208*
Montague, W. E., 10, *30*
Montello, D. R., 367, 368, 369, *376, 377*
Monti, L. A., 250, 251*t, 261*
Moody, D. M., 454, *458*
Moore, E., 433, *439*
Moore, G. T., 363, 369, *374, 376*
Moore, M. K., 272, *281*
Morant, N. J., 550, *553*
Morgan, C. T., 646, *648*
Morissey, K., 549, *552*
Morley, S., 320, *326*
Moroz, T. M., 619, *621, 623*
Morrell, F., 616, 617, *621, 622*

Morrell, R. W., 396, *408,* 417, 424
Morris, C. C., 202, 203, 204, *208, 209*
Morris, C. D., 94, 95, 98, 99, 100*t, 104, 106,* 113, *121,* 337, *345*
Morris, L. M., 600, *606*
Morris, L. W., 189, *191,* 404, *406*
Morris, P. E., 316, *327*
Morris, R. G., 189, *191,* 404, *406,* 453, *455, 459,* 600, *606*
Morris, R. G. M., 488, *498*
Morris, S., 384, *392*
Morrison, J. B., 371, *376*
Morrongiello, B. A., 276, *282*
Morrow, D. G., 369, *376*
Morton, J., 130, *133,* 318, *331,* 341, *345,* 578, *580*
Moscovitch, M., 26, *31,* 34, 40, 42, 55, *57,* 62, 65, *72,* 94, 95, 97, 100, 102, *105, 106,* 174, *177,* 189, *193,* 197, 198, *209,* 246, *259, 260,* 278, *282,* 284, *294,* 306, *311,* 334, 342, *345,* 402, 403, 404, *408, 409,* 414, 417, *424, 425,* 433, 436, *439, 483,* 504, 508, 513, *517, 519,* 522, *535,* 609, 610, 611, 612, 613*f,* 614, 616, 617, 618, 619, 620, *621,* 621*n, 622, 623, 624,* 625, 634, *642*
Moser, E., 488, *498*
Moser, M., 488, *498*
Moses, L. J., 299, *307*
Moss, M. B., 442, 445, 454, *455, 458,* 489, 490, *497*
Mossler, D. G., 301, *309*
Mueller, E. A., 549, *554*
Muggia, S., 469, 477, *480, 481*
Mullen, B., 321, *324*
Mullen, M. K., 288, *294,* 324, *328*
Müller, G. E., 153, *161*
Mulligan, N. W., 222, *227,* 237, *243,* 528, *535*
Multhaup, K. S., 181, 183, 187, *193,* 224, *227,* 405, *408,* 421, *424*
Mummery, C. J., 443, 446, 451, 452, *458*
Münsterberg, H., 150, *161*
Murdock, B. B., 17*f,* 19, *30,* 48, 49, *57,* 59, 60, 63, 64, *71,* 127, 128, 129, 130, *134,* 221, 224, *227,* 572, 574, 576, *579, 580,* 584, *595*
Murnane, K., 185, *190,* 575, *580*
Murphy, D., 549, *554*
Murphy, S. T., *260*
Murphy, W. E., 419, *423*
Murray, D. J., 84, *90*
Murray, E. A., 486, 489, 490, 491, 496, *498*

Murre, J. M. J., 451, *458*
Musen, G., 437, *440,* 468, 472, 474, *483,* 530, *536,* 610, 616, *624*
Myers, B., 157, *161*
Myers, N. A., 279, *281,* 324, *328*
Myerson, J., 415, *424*

Nadel, L., 306, *309,* 364, 369, 372, *373, 376,* 386, *391,* 433, *438, 439,* 491, *498,* 613*f, 624,* 627, *641*
Nader, K., 383, *391*
Nagy, M. E., 524, *536*
Nairne, J. S., 127, 132, *134,* 167, *177*
Naka, M., 321, *329*
Narens, L., 197, 198, 198*f,* 200, 203, 204, *209, 210,* 338, 341, *343, 345*
Nash, M., 156, *161*
Naumann, U., 184, *191*
Nauta, W. J. H., 468, 472, 475*t, 482*
Naveh-Benjamin, M., 94, 103, *105, 106,* 359, *362,* 365, *376,* 399, 400, *405, 408,* 411, 414, *421,* 503, *515, 610, 621*
Naylor, S. J., 368, *377*
Neary, D., 429, *440,* 443, 448, 449, 450, 451, *458, 459,* 466, *483,* 618, *624*
Neath, I., 130, 131, *134,* 573, 574, *580*
Neave, N., 431, *438*
Nebes, R. D., 318, *330,* 445, *458*
Neely, J. H., 141, *145,* 251*t, 258,* 336, *345*
Neimeyer, G. J., 323, *329*
Neisser, U., 15, 26, *30, 31,* 49, *57,* 98, *106,* 151, *161, 166, 177,* 179, *193,* 279, *282,* 306, *309,* 315, 316, 317, 318, 320, 321, 322, 324, *327, 329, 331,* 347, *362,* 382, 383, *391,* 557, *570*
Nelligan, D. W., 322, *328*
Nelson, C. A., 278, *279, 281*
Nelson, D. L., 34, *43,* 201, *210,* 336, *345*
Nelson, E. L., 385, *391*
Nelson, K., 269, 279, *281,* 283, 285, 286, 288, 289, 290, 291, 292, *294, 295,* 299, 306, *310,* 318, 322, 324, *329, 331*
Nelson, T. O., 69, *72, 125, 134,* 197, 198, 198*f,* 200, 201, 203, 204, 205, *207, 208, 209, 210,* 338, 341, *343, 345,* 371, *376, 406*
Neumann, C., 127, 132, *134*
Neville, H. J., *535*
Newcombe, N., 367, 369, *375, 376*
Newell, A., 15, *30, 78, 90,* 560, *570*

Newhouse, P. A., 549, *554*
Newman, S. K., 445, *458*
Ng, N., *623*
Nhouyvanisvong, A., 338, *345*
Nichelli, P., 477, *480*
Nichols, S., 302, *312*
Nichols, T., 321, *329*
Nickerson, R. S., 334, 338, 341, *345*
Nicolson, R., *90*
Niedhart, E., 144, *147*
Nielsen-Bohlman, L., 469, *482*
Nieto-Vegas, M., 523f, 524, 525f, *536*
Nieuwenhuys, R., 468, 472, 475t, *482*
Nilsson, L. -G., 17, *29*, 62, 64, 67, *71*, 99, 103, *106*, 137, 138, 139, 140, 141, 142, 143, 144, 145, *145*, *147*, 148, 251t, 505, 510, 511f, *518*, 531, *535*, 566, *570*, 635, *641*
Nirhod, O., 616, *621*
Nisbett, R. E., 112, 119, *121*
Nissen, H. W., 646, *648*
Nissen, M. J., 251t, 252, *260*, 468, *482*, 545, *553*
Nitsch, K., 98, 99, *104*
Nixon, P. D., 637, *640*
Noble, C. E., 10, *30*
Nobre, A. C., 631, *640*
Noice, H., 27, *30*, 323, *329*, 353, 359, *362*
Noice, T., 323, *329*, 353, 359, *362*
Nolde, S. F., 181, 187, 188, 189, *192*, *193*, 512, *517*, 531, *534*
Nolin, T. L., *377*
Noll, D. C., 472, *479*, 506, 507, 514, *515*, 630, 632, *638*, *639*
Nordberg, A., 415, *422*, 505, *515*
Noreen, D. L., 129, *134*
Norman, D. A., 19, 24, 25, *30*, *32*, 50, *57*, 78, 80, 81, 87, *90*, *92*, 94, *106*, 130, *135*, 284, *294*, 335, 336, 338, 341, *345*, 415, 416, *424*, *572*, *580*
Norman, K. A., 158, 159f, *161*, 186, 189, *194*, 238, *241*, 339, *345*, 403, 405, *408*, 434, *438*
Norris, J. W., 454, *456*
Northen, B., 448, 450, *458*
Nosofsky, R. M., 577, *580*
Novick, L. R., 119, *121*
Nyberg, L., 26, *30*, 59, *71*, 103, 139, 140, 141, 144, *145*, *147*, *148*, 189, *194*, 234, 239, *243*, 414, 421, *422*, 501, 502, 504, 505, 506, 508, 510, 511f, 512f, 513, 514, *515*, *517*, *518*, 531, *535*, 540, *553*, 599, *607*, 609, 617, *621*, 628, 633, 634, 635, *639*, *641*

Nystrom, L., 630, 632, *638*, *639*
Nystrom, L. E., 506, 507, 514, *515*, 584, *595*

Obinu, M. C., 549, *552*
O'Brien, M. D., 454, *458*
Ochsner, K. N., 469, *482*
O'Connell, B., 285, *294*
O'Connor, M., 186, *192*, 475, *482*
O'Dell, C. S., *374*
Ofshe, R., 317, *329*, 383, 385, *391*, 647, *648*
Ogata, J., 454, *458*
Ohrt, D. D., 172, *176*, 181, *191*
Ojemann, J. G., 635, 636, *638*, *642*
O'Keefe, J., 364, 369, *376*, 627, *641*
Okun, M. A., 320, *330*
O'Leary, D. S., 510, 514, *514*
Oliphant, G. W., 255, *260*
Ollinger, J., 631, 634, *640*
Olseth, K. L., 113, *119*
Olton, D. S., 78, *91*
O'Neil, H. F., Jr., 11, *30*
O'Neill, D. K., 301, *310*, 603, *607*
Onishi, K., 435, *437*
O'Reilly, R. C., 225, *227*, 388, *391*, 451, 457, 473, *482*, 505, *517*, 531, *535*, 587, 588, 589f, 590, 591, 592, 593, *594*, *595*, 596, 615, *621*, 627, 628, 629, *641*
Orgogozo, J. M., 454, *458*
Orme-Rogers, C., 396, *407*
Orne, P. J., 249, 254, *260*
Ornstein, P. A., 288, 290, *293*, *294*
O'Rourke, D., 320, *331*
Ortony, A., 24, *30*
Osawa, K., 117, *120*
O'Scalaidhe, S. P., 506, *519*, 631, *643*
Oskamp, S., 204, *210*
Ostergaard, A. L., 428, *438*, 605, *607*, 615, *622*, *624*
Ostrom, T. M., 157, *160*
O'Sullivan, B. T., 511, 512, *517*
O'Sullivan, G., 547, 548t, *551*
Otto, T., 174, *176*, 497, *497*
Overman, W. H., 274, *281*
Owen, A. M., 442, 453, *458*, 507, *518*, 550, *553*, 631, *641*
Owens, S. A. A., 175, *177*
Oxbury, S., 442, 443, 450, 452, *457*

Paas, F., 353, *362*
Pachana, N. A., 450, *458*
Packard, M. G., 488, *498*
Paez, D., 324, *329*
Paivio, A., 25, *30*, 95, 98, *106*, 138, *148*, 364, *376*, 567, *570*

Pajeau, A. K., 454, *458*
Palandini, A. C., 541, *553*
Palef, S. R., 202, 203, *208*
Palij, M., 368, *375*
Paller, K. A., 522, 524, 527, *535*, 617, *624*
Palmer, A. M., 412, 413, *422*
Palmer, J. C., 151, 154, 156, 156t, *161*
Palmer, S. E., 318, *329*, 391, 568, *570*
Pammer, K., 84, *88*
Pandya, D. N., 505, 507, *518*
Pansky, A., 336, *344*
Papagno, C., 84, 85, *88*, *91*, 428, *437*, *440*
Papez, J. W., 469, *482*
Pardo, J. V., 502, *518*, 632, 633, 636, 637, *641*
Park, D. C., 396, *408*, 417, *424*
Park, J., 380, *391*
Park, S. B., 548, *551*
Parker, G. V. C., 10, *30*
Parker, J. F., Jr., 353, *361*
Parker, K., 566, *569*
Parkes, K. R., 322, *325*
Parkin, A. J., 87, *91*, 230, 231, 232t, *242*, 243, 248, *260*, 404, *408*, 420, *424*, 434, *439*, 600, 601, *607*, 618, 620, *624*
Parkinson, J. K., 496, *498*
Parkinson, S. R., 396, *408*
Parrott, W. G., 322, *329*
Parsons, P. J., 274, *282*
Partanen, K., 413, *425*
Parving, A., 508, 509, 510, *517*
Pascalis, O., 269, *281*
Pascual-Leone, A., 436, *440*
Passcher, J., 542, *551*
Passingham, R. E., 501, *518*, 637, *640*
Patel, V. L., 114, 117, *120*, *121*
Patkau, J. E., 79, *91*
Patterson, J., 128, *135*, 277, *282*
Patterson, K., 429, 430, *440*, 442, 443, 444, 444f, 445, 446, 446f, 447f, 448, 449, 450, 451, 452, *455*, *456*, 457, *458*, 590, *595*
Paul, I. H., 315, *329*
Paulesu, E., 85, *91*, 506, *516*, *518*, 630, *641*
Paulson, J. S., 445, 446, *455*
Paulson, O. B., 466, *478*
Pavlov, I. P., 4, *30*
Payne, D. G., 157, *161*, 321, *331*
Payne, M., 442, 454, *458*
Payne, P., 436, *439*
Pazzaglia, F., 368, *373*
Pearce, S., 320, *326*
Pearlstone, Z., 16, *31*, 50, *57*, 79, *91*, 98, *107*, 333, 335, *346*
Pearson, N. A., 428, *439*, 452, *456*

Peck, V., 200, *207, 406*
Peeck, V. H., 353, *362*
Pellegrino, J. W., 364, 368, *375*
Peluso, J. P., 158, *162,* 187, *195*
Pendergrast, M., 317, *329,* 385, *391,* 647, *648*
Penfield, W., 166, *177*
Pennebaker, J. W., 324, *329*
Pennington, B. F., 306, *308*
Penrod, S., 321, *327, 329, 331*
Pentland, J., 156, *161,* 187, *192,* 385, *390*
Perani, D., 448, *455*
Peretti, S., 545, *552*
Peretz, I., 630, *638*
Perfect, T. J., 175, *177,* 231, 234, 235, 235*f,* 238, 239, *241, 243,* 435, *438,* 598, *606*
Perfetto, G. A., 114, *121,* 251*t, 257*
Perilloux, H. K., 299, *310*
Perkins, D. T., 129, *134,* 166, *177*
Perlmutter, M., 268, *282*
Perlstein, W. M., 506, 507, 514, *515,* 630, 632, *639*
Perner, J., 231, *243,* 297, 299, 300, 301, 303, 304, 305*f,* 306, *309, 310, 312,* 603, 604, *607, 608*
Perry, A., 396, *408*
Perry, C., 316, *328*
Perry, R. J., 443, 446, 449, *455, 456,* 448, *458*
Persinger, M. A., 385, *391*
Peters, S. C., 128, *133*
Petersen, S. E., 502, 505, 506, 513, *515, 516, 518,* 630, 632, 633, 634, 635, 636, 637, *638, 639, 640, 641, 642*
Peterson, C., 286, 287, 289, 290, *293, 294,* 383, *390*
Peterson, E., 368, *375*
Peterson, L. R., 19, 20*f, 30,* 53, *57,* 79, 81, *91,* 167, *177*
Peterson, M. A., 372, *373*
Peterson, M. J., 19, 20*f, 30,* 53, *57,* 79, 81, *91*
Petersson, K. M., 505, 514, *518*
Petit, L., 631, *639*
Petit-Taboué, M. -C., 505, *516*
Petri, H. L., 466, *482,* 494, 495, *498,* 627, *641*
Petrides, M., 433, *438,* 505, 506, 507, 513, *518,* 631, *641*
Petronis, J. D., 415, *425*
Pezdek, K., 158, *162,* 183, 187, *194, 195,* 368, *374*
Pfefferbaum, A., 413, *425*
Pfeiffer, E., 550, *553*
Phelps, E. A., 351, 352, 354, *361,* 470, *481*
Phelps, K. E., 302, *312*
Phelps, M., 637, *640*

Philippot, P., 382, *390*
Phillips, A., 299, *311*
Phillips, A. G., 491, *499*
Phillips, D., 113, *122*
Phillips, L. D., 204, 206*f, 209*
Phillips, W. A., 80, *91*
Philpot, M., 453, *459*
Piaget, J., 271, 273, *281,* 306, *310,* 369, *376*
Picariello, M. L., 289, *294,* 305, *310*
Pichert, J. W., 98, *104*
Pick, A., 466, *482*
Pick, H. L., 364, 367, 369, *375, 376*
Pickar, D., 549, *553*
Pickerel, J., 385, *391*
Pickering, A., 547, 548*t, 554*
Pickrell, J. E., 187, *193*
Picton, T. W., 245, *260,* 521, *535,* 602, *607,* 620, *625*
Piercy, M., 174, *177,* 305, *309*
Pietrini, P., 414, 415, *423,* 510, *516*
Pike, R., 64, *71, 583, 595*
Pike, V. W., 550, *553*
Pillemer, D. B., 279, *282,* 288, 289, *294,* 305, 306, *310, 312,* 317, 318, *329,* 381, 382, *391*
Pillon, B., 442, 453, *455, 458*
Pillow, B. H., 301, *310*
Pilzecker, A., 153, *161*
Pinals, D. A., 549, *553*
Pines, A., 288, *293*
Pinto, P., 548*t, 553*
Pipe, M. E., 289, 290, *294,* 305, *310*
Pirola, R., 548*t, 553*
Pitkänen, A., 413, *425*
Pitkow, J., 561, *570*
Platzer, W., *517*
Podgorny, P., 371, *377*
Poffenberger, A. T., 128, *135*
Pokorny, R. A., 118, *120*
Poldrack, R. A., 62, *71,* 217, *227,* 414, *423,* 610, *622,* 633, 634, 637, *640, 641, 643*
Poline, J. -P., 502, *516*
Polkey, C. E., 453, *458*
Polkinghorne, D. E., 318, *329*
Polonsky, S., 384, *391*
Polson, P. G., 117, 118, *120, 121*
Polster, M. R., 184, 189, *191,* 404, *407,* 541, 545, *553,* 635, *642*
Polusny, M. A., 385, *391*
Poole, D. A., 158, *161,* 385, *391*
Poon, L. W., 318, 319, *330,* 413, *422*
Poovibunsuk, P., 547, 548*t, 551*
Pope, H. G., 384, *391*
Pope, K. S., 385, *389*
Poppleton, P., 544, 548, *551*

Porjesz, B., 469, *484*
Portugali, J., 363, *376*
Posner, M. I., 53, *57,* 94, *106,* 153, *161,* 584, *596,* 633, *641*
Postle, B. R., 435, *440,* 495, *498*
Postman, L., 13, *30,* 63, 68, *71, 72,* 98, *106,* 167, *177*
Potter, J., 320, *326*
Potter, M. C., 251*t, 259*
Poulton, E. C., 206, *210,* 367, *376*
Povinelli, D. J., 299, 301, *310*
Powell, A. L., 454, *458*
Powell, B., 337, *344*
Prabhakaran, V., 507, *518*
Pradere, D., 158, *162*
Pratkanis, A. R., 183, *194*
Pratt, C., 301, *310*
Pressley, M., 286, *294,* 303, *311*
Presson, C. C., 368, *376*
Preston, G., 544, 548, *551*
Presty, S., 637, *640*
Prete, K., 278, *280*
Pribram, K. H., 15, *30,* 78, *90*
Price, C. J., 451, 452, *458, 459,* 502, *518*
Price, D., 633, *643*
Prins, B., 380, *389*
Procise, S., 131, *133*
Proctor, J. D., 354, *361*
Proffitt, D. R., 364, *373*
Prohaska, V., 319, *327*
Proust, M., 316, *329*
Provenzale, J. M., 415, 421, *424*
Pruett, J. C., 289, *294,* 305, *310*
Prull, M. W., 185, *190,* 633, *641*
Prytulak, L. S., 10, *30*
Psotka, J., 16, *31*
Puce, A., 631, *640, 641*
Puckett, J. M., 396, *408*
Putnam, W. H., 385, *391*
Pylyshyn, Z. W., 25, *30,* 98, *106*
Pynoos, R. S., 383, *391*

Qin, J., 184, *194,* 322, *326, 329*
Quas, J. A., 184, *194,* 305, *308, 310,* 321, 322, *327, 329,* 383, *390*
Quig, M. B., 418, *423*
Quillian, M. R., 587, 591, *596*
Quinn, B., 413, *422*
Quinn, G., 85, *91*
Quinn, N. P., 442, 454, *457, 458*

Raaijmakers, J. G. W., 63, *71,* 340, *345,* 572, 573, 578, *580*
Rabbitt, P., 322, 323, *324, 329*
Rabin, P., 428, *440*
Rabinowitz, J. C., 181, *194,* 396, 397, 399, *408*
Rachman, S., 320, *326*
Radvansky, G. A., 54, *57,* 365, *376, 377,* 418, 419, 419*f, 423, 424, 425*

Rahhal, T. A., 318, 319, 320, *325, 330*

Raichle, M. E., 501, 502, 506, 513, *515, 516, 518,* 630, 631, 632, 633, 634, 635, 636, 637, *638, 639, 640, 641, 642*

Raife, E. A., 506, *516,* 630, *639*

Rajaram, S., 186, *194,* 217, *227,* 230, 231, 232*t,* 234, 239, 240, *242, 243,* 611, 618, *624,* 629, *641*

Ramachandran, V. S., 386, *391*

Ramponi, C., 186, *191,* 230, 231, 233, 236, 237, 238, *242*

Ramus, S. J., 488, 489*f,* 495, 497, *498, 499*

Randall, P., 470, *479*

Rapoport, J. L., 472, *479*

Rapoport, S. I., 81, *90,* 443, *455,* 504, 509, *516, 517,* 631, *640*

Rappaport, S., 634, *640*

Rappold, V. A., 251*t, 258*

Rapus, T., 604, *608*

Rasmussen, E. W., 647, *648*

Ratcliff, R., 222, *227,* 246, *260,* 557, *570,* 571, 575, 576, 577, 578, *580*

Ratner, H. H., 143, *148,* 283, *295*

Rauch, B., 469, *483*

Rauch, S. L., 255, *260,* 414, 415, *425,* 505, *516, 519,* 635, 636, 637, *640, 641*

Raudsepp, J., 230, 232*t,* 233, *243*

Ravert, H. T., 415, *425*

Rawles, R. E., 317, *326,* 382, *389*

Rawlins, J. N. P., 431, *437*

Raye, C. L., 18, *29,* 152, 154, 155, *161,* 169, *177,* 180, 181, 182, 183, 184, 185, 186, 188, 189, *191, 192, 193, 194,* 198, *208,* 302, *308, 309,* 512, *517,* 614, *622*

Raymond, P., 324, *331*

Rayner, R., 269, *282*

Raz, N., 223, *228,* 96, *107,* 397, *409,* 412, 413, *424*

Rea, C. P., 356, *362*

Read, D. J., 95, *106,* 321, *331*

Read, J. D., 160, *161,* 184, 188, 189*n, 193, 194,* 321, *329, 330,* 385, *390*

Reardon, K. K., 320, *327*

Reber, A. S., 111, *121,* 222, *227,* 251*t,* 252, *260,* 495, 646, *648*

Reber, P. J., 432, 433, *438,* 468, *482*

Recker, M., 561, *570*

Redding, J., 132, *134*

Reder, L. M., 154, *160,* 199, 201, 202, 204, *209, 210,* 338, *345*

Redlich, A. D., 184, *194,* 322, *329*

Reed, C. L., 371, *377*

Reed, J. M., 431, *440,* 488, 489, *499*

Reed, R. S., 302, 305, *308*

Reeder, J. A., 181, *192,* 223, *227*

Reese, E, 286, 287, *294*

Reeves, J. L., 316, 320, *326*

Regehr, G., 566, *569*

Reid, T. K., 248, *260*

Reid, W., 443, 445, *458*

Reider, D. M., 221, *227*

Reiman, E., 158, *162,* 186, *194, 403, 409,* 531, *536,* 635, *642*

Reimold, C., 436, *438*

Reineck, R., 505, *515*

Reingold, E. M., 250, 252, 253, 254, 255, 256, *260, 261,* 304, *310,* 533, *536, 624*

Reinick, R., 415, *422*

Reinitz, M. T., 181, *194*

Reinke, P., 320, *328*

Reinkemeier, M., *469,* 475, 477, *480, 483,* 506, *516*

Reisberg, B., 413, *422*

Reisberg, D., 380, *380, 389, 390*

Reiser, B., 334, 338, 339, 340, *345*

Reminger, S. L., 616, 617, *621, 622*

Rempel, N. L., 489, 490, 494, *499*

Rempel-Clower, N., 488, 489, *499*

Rendell, P. E., *424*

Repacholi, B. M., 299, *310*

Reppas, J., 632, *642*

Reuter-Lorenz, P., 630, *640*

Rey-Hipolito, C., 636, *640*

Reyna, V. F., 183, *194,* 339, *343*

Reynolds, C. R., 322, *327*

Rezai, K., 510, 514, *514*

Reznick, J. S., 604, *608*

Rheingold, H. L., 268, 270, *281*

Rhine, R., 564, 569

Ribback, A., 129, *134*

Ribot, T., 427, *440,* 466, *483*

Rice, G. E., 320, *330*

Richards, M., 550, *553*

Richardson, J. T. E., 549, *552*

Richardson, S. L., 417, *423*

Richardson-Klavehn, A., 19, *30, 41, 43,* 59, *72,* 186, *191,* 224, *227,* 229, 230, 231, 231*t,* 232*t,* 233, 236, 237, 238, 239*t, 242, 243, 244,* 246, 252, 253, 255, *260,* 304, *310,* 523, 529, *534, 535,* 600, 610, *624*

Richman, C. L., 138, *147*

Richman, H. B., 15, *30,* 116, *121*

Rickels, K., 547, *552*

Riddlesberger, M. M., 305, *308,* 321, 322, *327,* 383, *390*

Rideout, R., 289, 290, *294*

Riefer, D. M., 64, *70,* 185, *190, 194,* 221, 223, *225*

Riekkinen, P. J., 413, *425*

Riesbeck, C. K., 23, *31*

Riesch, G., 474, *480*

Rieser, J. J., 368, *377*

Rime, B., 324, *329*

Rinaldi, J., 617, *621*

Rinck, M., 369, *377*

Rinne, J. O., 474, *481*

Rioux, G. F., 545, *553*

Rioux, P., 505, *516*

Rips, L. J., 587, *596*

Ritter, F. E., 199, 202, *210*

Ritz, S. A., 584, 585, *594*

Rivardo, M., 564, *569*

Rizzo, L., 231, 238, *242*

Rizzuto, D. S., 60, 62, 64, 66, 67, 69, *71*

Robbins, T. W., 87, *91,* 442, 453, 454, *455, 457, 458, 459,* 547, 548, *551, 553*

Robert, P., 231, 238, *242*

Roberts, A. C., 87, *91,* 453, *455, 458*

Roberts, J. N., 433, *439*

Roberts, K. P., 302, *310*

Roberts, P., 186, *193*

Roberts, W. W., 491, *499*

Robertson, B., 414, *425*

Robertson, L., 115, 117, *121*

Robinson, E. J., 301, *310*

Robinson, E. S., 64, *72*

Robinson, J. A., 316, *330*

Robinson, K. J., 100, *106,* 153, *162*

Robinson, K. M., 435, *437*

Robinson, M. F., 602, *607*

Rochon, E., 85, *92*

Rockland, C., 251*t, 257*

Roe, C. M., 385, *391*

Roediger, H. L., 34, 36, 37, 40, *43,* 94, 99, 100, 102, 103, *105, 106,* 149, 150, 152, 153, 153*f,* 156, 157, 158, *160, 161, 162,* 180, 184, 186, *191, 193, 194,* 221, *228,* 231, 232*t,* 233, 236, 239, *243, 244,* 246, 247, 250, 251*t,* 252, *259, 260, 261,* 333, 336, *345, 403, 405, 408, 409,* 523, 524, 530, 531, *535, 536,* 610, 611, 618, *624,* 629, *641, 647*

Rogers, M. K., 168, 169*f, 176*

Rogers, S. J., 306, *308*

Rogers, S. L., *553*

Rogers, T. B., 567, 568, *570*

Rogers, T. T., 591, *595*

Rohrbaugh, K., 521, 522, *536*

Roitblat, H. L., 15, *30*

Roland, P. E., 506, 511, 512, *517, 519*

Rollings, J., 547, 548*t, 554*

Rolls, E. T., 174, *177*

Roman, G. C., 454, *458*

Romani, C., 428, *440*
Rönnlund, M., 139, *148*
Roozendaal, B., 469, *482*
Roques, P. K., 445, *456*
Rosch, E., 24, *30,* 34, *43,* 366, *377,* 587, *596*
Rose, S. A., 268, *281*
Rose, T. L., 398, *408*
Rosen, B. R., 158, *162,* 403, *409,* 504, 505, 510, *515, 519,* 522, *536,* 616, 617, *621,* 632, 633, 634, 635, 636, *638, 642, 643*
Rosen, J. J., 491, *499*
Rosen, M. J., 403, *409*
Rosenbaum, A. E., 415, *425*
Rosenbaum, D. A., 7, *30*
Rosenbaum, M., 322, *328*
Rosenbloom, P., 560, *570*
Rosene, D. L., 489, 490, *497*
Rosenthal, D. M., 299, *310*
Roskos-Ewoldsen, B., 368, *377*
Ross, B. H., 112, 113, *121*
Ross, D. F., 184, *194,* 303, *308,* 321, *330*
Ross, E. D., 474, *478*
Ross, H. W., 270, *281*
Ross, J. R., 372, *373*
Ross, M., 27, *30,* 180, 184, *194,* 288, *294,* 316, 321, 322, *326, 330*
Ross, R. T., 129, *134,* 166, *177*
Rosser, A. E., 443, 446, 454, 457, 458
Rossman, E., 53, *57,* 454, *457*
Rossor, M., 449, *454*
Rossor, M. N., 445, 448, *455, 456, 458*
Roth, W. T., 415, *423*
Rothkopf, E. Z., 166, *177*
Rothman, D. L., 633, *640*
Rotte, M. R., 403, *409,* 504, 505, 510, *515, 519,* 522, *536,* 616, 617, *621,* 633, 634, 635, 636, *638, 643*
Rouleau, I., 472, *483*
Routhieaux, B. C., 184, 189, *191,* 404, *407, 408*
Rovee, C. K., 270, *282*
Rovee, D. T., 270, *282*
Rovee-Collier, C., 38, 267, 270, 271, 274, 275, 276, 277, 278, 279, *279, 280, 281, 282,* 284, 290, *294,* 299, 300, 306, *310*
Royal, D., 396, *408*
Royer, F. L., 396, *407*
Rozin, P., 246, *260*
Rubin, C., 166, *177*
Rubin, D. C., 27, *28, 30,* 61, *72,* 283, *294,* 316, 318, 319, 323, *330,* 353, *362*
Rubin, R., 637, *640*
Rubin, R. C., 560, *570*
Rubin, S. R., 404, *408*

Rubinsztein, D. C., 454, *457*
Rudy, J. W., 497, *499*
Ruffman, T., 231, *243,* 304, 305*f,* *310, 607*
Rugg, M. D., 103, 189, *195,* 415, *424,* 505, 506, 510, 513, 514, *516, 519,* 521, 522, 523, 523*f,* 524, 525, 525*f,* 526*f,* 527, 527*f,* 528, 529, 529*f,* 530*f,* 531, 532, 532*f,* 533, 533*f, 534, 535, 536,* 609, 619, *621, 622,* 635, *641*
Rule, W. R., 323, *330*
Rumelhart, D. E., 24, 25, *30,* 315, *330,* 559, *570,* 584, 585*f,* 586, 586*f,* 587, 588, 588*f,* 589, 589*f,* 592, *595, 596*
Rumsey, J. M., 306, *310*
Rusinek, H., 413, *422*
Russell, B., 22, *30,* 297, *310*
Russell, J., 302, 305, *309, 311*
Russell, W. A., 179, *192*
Russo, R., 230, 232*t, 243,* 248, 260
Rusted, J. M., 544, 548, *553*
Ryan, E. B., 395, *408*
Rybarczyk, B. D., 396, *408*
Rypma, B., *401, 407*

Sabe, L., 443, *459*
Sabini, J., 322, *329*
Sachs, J. S., 166, *177,* 179, *194,* 286, *294*
Sadalla, E. K., 366, 367, *377*
Safer, M. A., 320, *330*
Saffran, E. M., 614, *624*
Sagar, H. J., 433, 435, *438, 439,* 442, 448, 453, *459,* 468, *483*
Sahakian, B. J., 453, 454, *455, 457, 459,* 548, 550, *551, 552, 553*
Saint-Cyr, J. A., 436, *440*
Saint-Hilaire, J. -M., 472, *483*
Sakulsripong, M., 540, *551*
Salaman, E., 316, *330,* 335, 336, 345
Salmon, D. P., 435, 436, *439,* 440, 442, 443, 445, 446, 454, *454, 455, 457, 459,* 488, *499*
Salthouse, T. A., 399, 400, *407, 408, 409,* 411, 415, *424, 425*
Salton, G., 558, *570*
Saltz, E., 137, 138, *148*
Samuel, M., 549, *552*
Sandberg, E. H., 369, *375*
Sandler, S. P., 144, *146*
Sands, D., 144, *146,* 398, *406*
Sano, M., 550, *553*
Sanocki, T., 202, 203, 204, *208*
Sanquist, T. F., 521, 522, *536*
Santos-Williams, S., 339, 341, *346*
Sanvito, J., 205, *207*

Sapolsky, R. M., 470, *483*
Sarda, M., 302, *311*
Sargent, P. A., 550, *553*
Sarter, M., 431, *440,* 469, *483*
Sartori, G., 474, *480*
Sass, N. L., 600, *606*
Sauers, R., 118, *119*
Saults, J. S., 84, *89,* 400, *407*
Saunders, R. C., 485, 486, *498*
Sauter, B., 468, *482*
Savage, C. R., 255, *260,* 414, 415, *425,* 505, *516, 519,* 635, 636, 637, *640, 641*
Saxton, J., 445, *454*
Schaafstal, A. M., 84, *90*
Schab, F. R., 131, *135*
Schachtel, E. G., 306, *311*
Schacter, D. L., 19, *31,* 40, *42, 43,* 46, *57,* 59, 62, 65, 67, *72,* 96, 102, *107,* 139, *148,* 150, 158, 159*f, 161, 162,* 184, 186, 187, 189, *192, 194,* 200, 201, 203, *209, 210,* 224, *228,* 231, 233, 238, *241, 244, 246,* 248, 250, 251*t,* 252, 253, 255, 256, *257, 260, 261,* 278, *280, 282,* 284, *294,* 299, 306, *311,* 339, *345,* 383, 385, *391,* 395, 397, 403, 405, *408, 409,* 414, 415, *425,* 434, 435, *438,* 469, *482,* 501, 504, 505, 510, 514, *515, 516, 519,* 522, 524, 526, 531, *534, 536,* 542, 544, 545, *551, 552, 553, 554,* 577, *580,* 599, 600, *607,* 609, 610, 611, 614, 615, 616, 617, 618, *621, 622, 624, 625,* 627, 628, 629, 633, 634, 635, 636, 637, *638, 640, 641, 642, 643,* 647, 648
Schafer, K., 550, *553*
Schallert, D. L., 98, *104*
Schank, R. C., 23, *31,* 116, *121,* 285, *295,* 336, 340, *345*
Schapiro, M. B., 414, 415, *423,* 443, *455,* 510, *516*
Schatzow, E., 385, *390*
Scheinberg, P., 454, *458*
Schenk, F., 488, *498*
Scherg, M., 521, *535*
Schiano, D., 367, 371, *377, 378*
Schifano, F., 548*t, 551*
Schiffman, H., 316, *326*
Schimmack, U., 322, *330*
Schindler, R. M., 319, *327*
Schiwy, W., 544, *552*
Schlager, M. S., 113, *121*
Schlaug, G., 472, *481*
Schlechter, T. M., 322, *330*
Schloerscheidt, A. M., 529, 530, 531, *536*
Schloerscheidt, E. M., 525, 526*f,* 529, 530, *536*

Schmidt, A. L., *535*

Schmidt, H. G., 114, *121*, 353, *362*

Schmidt, R. A., 7, *31*, 354, *362*

Schmitt, F., *553*

Schneider, B., 466, 470, 471, *482*

Schneider, D. M., 157, *162*

Schneider, H., *483*

Schneider, L., *553*

Schneider, W., 170, *176*, 200, *210*, 283, 286, 292, *294, 295*, 303, *311*, 416, 420, *425*

Schneii, L. S., 550, *553*

Schober, M. F., 365, *377*

Scholey, K., 433, *439*

Scholkopf, J., 118, 119, *120*

Schomer, D. L., 469, *483*

Schonfield, D., 414, 417, *425*

Schooler, J. W., 150, *162*, 187, *194*, 245, *257*, 317, *330*, 379, 383, 384, 385, 386, 387, *391, 392*

Schooler, L. J., 557, 559, 560, 561, 562, 563, 565, 566, 567*f, 569, 570*, 578, *580*

Schrader-Bolsche, M., 504, *516*

Schrauf, R. W., 319, *330*

Schreiber, C. A., 318, *329, 391*

Schreiber, G., 568, *570*

Schreiber, T. A., 201, *210*

Schroeder, K., 144, *146*

Schugens, M. M., 436, *438*

Schultz, R. W., 128, *135*

Schumacher, E. H., 85, *88, 91*, 506, 507, *515, 519*, 630, 631, *638, 640, 642*

Schuman, H., 319, *330*

Schuri, U., 470, 471, 473, *479, 482*

Schvaneveldt, R. W., 39, *42*

Schwartz, B. L., 200, 201, 202, 204, 205*f, 209, 210*, 338, 340, *345*

Schwartz, G. E., 322, *326, 332*

Schwartz, M. F., 385, *391*

Schwarz, J. P., 506, *516*, 630, *639*

Scott, D., 79, *89*

Scott, J., 319, *330*, 379, *389*

Scott, T. M., 470, *479*

Scoville, W. B., 468, 471, *483*, 485, 486, 488, *499*, 605, *607*

Seamon, J. G., 249, 254, *260*

Searle, J., 298, 300, *311*

Seeck, M., 469, *483*

Seegmiller, D., 365, *376*

Segal, S. J., 25, *31*

Segalowitz, S. J., 217, *225*

Seger, C. A., 111, *121*, 252, *261*

Sehulster, J. R., 319, *330*

Seibyl, J. P., 470, *479*

Seidenberg, M. S., 446, *455*

Seidlitz, L., 322, *330*

Selfridge, J. A., 79, *90*

Selfridge, O. G., 15, *31*

Sellal, F., 545, *553*

Sellen, O., 140, *147*

Semb, G. B., 347, *362*

Semmes, J., 647, *648*

Serio Silva, J. C., 564, 569

Servan-Schreiber, D., 630, *639*

Service, E., 85, *91*

Shah, P., 78, 83, 87, 88, *90, 91*

Shallice, T., 22, *31*, 55, *57*, 81, 83, 84, 85, 87, 88, *90, 91*, 189, *190*, 203, *210*, 334, 336, 338, 340, 341, 342, *343*, 415, 416, 419, *424, 425*, 430, 434, *438, 440*, 452, 455, 471, *483*, 503, 504, 506, *516, 519*, 531, *536*, 619, *622*, 630, 632, 633, 634, 635, *639, 642, 643*

Shanon, B., 366, *377*

Shapiro, L., 286, *293*

Sharkey, W. F., 320, 321, *331*

Shatz, M., 299, *311*

Shaughnessy, J. J., 204, *210*

Shaw, C. -M., 174, *175*, 431, *437*, 472, *483, 497*

Shaw, J. C., 15, *30*

Shaw, P., 417, *423*

Shaw, R. J., 397, *407*

Shebilske, W., 126, 128, *135*

Shedlack, K., 468, *480*

Sheehan, P. W., 157, *162*, 317, *328*

Sheffer, D., 96, *105*

Sheffield, E. G., 274, *281*, 290, *295*

Sheich, H., 504, *516*

Sheingold, K., 307, *311*

Shelton, A. L., 368, *377*

Shelton, J., 632, *639*

Shelton, J. R., 428, *439*, 446, *455*

Shepard, R. N., 25, *31*, 364, 365, 371, *374, 377*

Sherman, J. W., 188, *194*

Sherman, S. J., 156, *161*, 184, *191*, 385, *390*

Sherry, D. F., 627, 628, 629, *642*

Shiel, A., 433, *439*

Shiffrin, R. M., 20, 21*f*, 27, 81, 82*f, 88*, 93, *104*, 130, *133*, 224, *225*, 340, *345*, 396, *405*, 416, 420, *425*, 471, *478, 551*, 557, *570*, 572, 573, 575, 578, 579, *579, 580*, 593, *596*, 630, *638*

Shimamura, A. P., 181, 185, 189, *191, 195*, 200, 203, *208, 209*, *210*, 251*t, 261*, 395, 402, 403, *407, 409*, 419, *425*, 469, *482*, 488, *498*, 600, *607*

Shin, R. K., 507, *515*, 630, 631, 632, *639*

Shine, P., 544, 547, 548*t, 551*, 552

Shobe, K. K., 387, *392*

Shoben, E. J., 587, *596*

Sholl, M. J., 368, *374, 377*

Shoqeirat, M., 433, *439*

Shore, W. J., 339, *343*

Shrout, P. E., 222, *226*

Shulman, H. G., 94, *107*

Shulman, R. G., 631, 633, *640*

Shultz, T. R., 302, *311*

Shyi, G. C. W., 181, 184, *191*

Sick, C. -D., 469, *482*

Sicoly, F., 321, *330*

Siegel, A. W., 369, *377*

Siewert, B., 472, *481*

Silber, S., 299, *311*

Silveri, M., 430, *439*

Silveri, M. C., 443, 446, *455*

Silverstein, J. W., 584, 585, *594*

Simon, B. B., 301, *310*

Simon, H. A., 12, 15, *30, 31*, 78, *90*, 98, *104*, 114, 115, 116, 117, *120, 121*, 559, 560, *570*

Simpson, P., 385, *391*

Sims, N. R., 448, *458*

Sinclair, G., 354, *361*

Sinclair, J., 269, *280*

Sinden, M., 620, *623*

Singer, J. A., 322, *328*

Singer, L., 545, *553*

Singer, N., 305, *308*

Singer, S., 323, *330*

Singer, W., 615, *624*

Singh, A., 398, *407*

Singley, M. K., 12, *31*

Sirocco, K., 547, 548*t*, 549, *553*, 554

Sivan, A. B., 322, *327*

Sivers, H., 383, 386, 387, *388*

Skinner, B. F., 4, 15, *31*, 245, *261*

Skovronek, E., 400, *409*

Skowronski, J. J., 157, *160*, 319, 322, *330, 331*

Slamecka, N. J., 52, *57*, 102, 103, *107*, 126, 127, 128, *135*, 139, *148*, 202, *210*, 561, *570*, 574, *581*

Slaughter, V., 604, *606*

Sloman, S. A., 592, *596*

Slusher, M. P., 188, *195*

Smid, H. G., 504, *516*

Smirne, S., 548*t, 553*

Smith, A. D., 396, *409*, 448, *459*

Smith, A. F., 319, *327*

Smith, E. E., 24, *31*, 34, *43*, 81, 85, 87, *88, 91*, 187, 188, *190*, 428, *439*, 506, 507, 514, *515, 519*, 587, *596*, 630, 631, *638, 639, 640, 642*

Smith, E. R., 251*t, 261*

Smith, J. A., 507, *518*

Smith, K. D., 320, *326, 328*

Smith, M. C., 157, *162*

Smith, M. E., 233, *244, 415, *425,*
  527, 529, *536*
Smith, M. L., 174, *177,* 468, *483*
Smith, M. P., 475, *480*
Smith, P. H., 269, *282*
Smith, R. E., 417, *423*
Smith, S. M., 200, 201, *210,* 337,
  340, *345*
Smith, T. R., 370, *374*
Smith, V. L., 379, *390*
Smith, W. B., 320, *330*
Snodgrass, J. G., 236, *244*
Snow, C., 560, *570*
Snowden, J. S., 429, *440,* 443,
  448, 449, 450, 451, *458, 459,*
  466, *483,* 618, *624*
Snyder, A., 631, 634, *640*
Snyder, L. D., 321, *325*
Sobel, D., 320, *330*
Sodian, B., 301, 303, *311, 312*
Soininen, H. S., 413, *425*
Sokolov, E. N., 267, *282*
Solomon, S. K., 151, *161,* 180,
  192
Soloway, R. M., 127, 170, *177,*
  135, 320, *332*
Somerville, S. C., 200, *208*
Sommers, M. S., 153, *162*
Sommerville, J. A., 302, *312*
Sorrensen, A., 449, *454*
Southwick, S. M., 387, 388, *390,*
  470, *479, 481*
Spackova, N., 433, *438*
Spaulding, K., 321, *325*
Spear, N. E., 274, *282*
Speigler, B. J., 485, 486, *498*
Speiler, D. H., 397, 404, *409*
Spelke, E. S., 299, *311,* 369, *374,*
  375
Spellman, B. A., *205, 210*
Spence, J., 365, *377*
Spence, M. J., 269, *280*
Spencer, D. D., 470, *481*
Spencer, M., 435, *438*
Spencer, W. D., 96, *107,* 223,
  228, 397, *409*
Sperling, G., 50, *57,* 80, *91,* 396,
  409
Sperry, R. W., 647, *648*
Spiegel, D., 386, *392*
Spieler, D. H., 365, *376,* 401, *409*
Spilich, G. J., 114, 117, 118, *120,*
  121
Spinnler, H., 87, *88,* 428, *437,*
  442, 447, 452, *454, 455,* 469,
  477, *480, 481*
Spiro, R. J., *162*
Spitzer, H., 356, *362*
Sporer, S. L., 187, 188, *195,* 321,
  331
Squire, L. R., 26, *31,* 38, 174,
  177, 189, *195,* 203, *208, 210,*
  217, 222, *227, 228,* 231, *243,*

251*t, 257, 259, 261,* 278,
  281, 299, *309,* 395, 403, *407,*
  409, 429, 431, 432, 433, 436,
  437, *437, 438, 440,* 451, *459,*
  468, 472, 474, 475, *481, 482,*
  483, 485, 486, 488, 489,
  489*f,* 490, 491, 492, 494,
  495, 496, 497, *497, 498, 499,*
  500, 504, 514, *519,* 530, *536,*
  577, *581,* 600, 602, *607,* 610,
  615, 616, 617, 620, *621,*
  621*n, 622, 624,* 627, 635,
  636, *638, 642*
Srinivas, K., 251*t, 261,* 614, *624,*
  629, *641*
Sroufe, A. L., 385, *389*
Stafford, L., 320, 321, *331*
Stahl, S. M., 544, 548, *551*
Staib, L., 470, *479*
Standing, L., 95, *107,* 365, *377*
Stanhope, N., 339, *343,* 353, 358,
  359, *361, 362*
Stansbury, C., 166, *177*
Staplin, L. J., 366, 367, *377*
Stark, C. E. L., 468, *482*
Stark, H. A., 62, 65, *72,* 102, *107,*
  248, 251*t, 261*
Starkstein, S. E., 443, *459*
Staszewski, J. J., 115, 116, *120,*
  121
Stea, D., 363, *374*
Stebbins, G. T., 435, *438*
Stefanacci, L., 489, 490, 491,
  492, *500*
Steffens, M. C., 223, *225,* 236,
  241
Stein, B. S., 95, 98, *104*
Stein, D. G., 491, *498, 499*
Steinberg, B., 508, 509, 510, *517*
Steinberg, H., 541, *553*
Steller, M., 187, *195*
Ste-Marie, D. M., 253, 255, *258,*
  261
Stepankova, K., *433, 438*
Stephenson, G. M., 315, *326*
Stern, C. E., 504, *519,* 634, *642*
Stern, J., 337, *344*
Stern, L. D., 169, *176*
Stern, W., 150, *162*
Sternberg, S., 59, *72,* 80, *91,* 572,
  581
Stetson, P., 549, *552*
Stevens, A., 366, *377*
Stevens, J. M., 448, *455*
Stevens, K. V., 98, *104*
Stevens, S. S., 645, 646, *648*
Stevens, T. G., 510, *517*
Stevenson, H. W., 268
Stewart, M., 140, *146, 436, 440*
Stewart, S. H., 545, *553*
Steyvers, M., 557, *570,* 575, 579,
  580, 593, *596*
Stigler, S. M., 129, *135*

Stigsdotter, A., 140, *145*
Stillings, N. A., *257*
Stillman, R. C., 337, *343*
Stine, E. L., *409*
Stinson, 268
Stockburger, D. W., 396, *408*
Stoerig, P., 615, *621, 624,* 646,
  648
Stohl, C., 321, *327*
Stoltzfus, E. R., 401, *407*
Stone, M., 610, 616, *624*
Stone, M. V., 633, *639*
Strack, F., 233, 238, *244*
Strater, L., 217, *225,* 420, *422*
Strayer, D. L., 401, *407,* 415, *425*
Stritter, E. P., 558, *570*
Stuss, D. T., 37, *43,* 174, *177,*
  189, *195,* 229, 234, *244,* 245,
  260, 304, *312,* 404, *409,* 506,
  515, 600, 601, 602, 606, *607,*
  608, 610, 611, 618, 619, 620,
  621, 623, 624, 625
Suckow, R. F., 549, *552*
Suddendorf, T., 302, *311*
Sudman, S., 320, *331*
Suengas, A. G., 182, 183, 186,
  192, 195
Sugiura, R. M., 504, *519,* 634,
  642
Sulin, R. A., 151, *162,* 179, *195*
Sullivan, E. V., 413, *425,* 442,
  448, 453, *459,* 468, *483*
Sullivan, M. W., 274, *282*
Summers, B. A., 442, 453, *458*
Summers, J. J., 167, 170, *176*
Sundaram, M., 443, *455*
Sunderland, A., 322, *331,* 398,
  409
Sunderland, T., 549, *554*
Sutherland, R. W., 497, *499*
Suzuki, W. A., 495, 496, *499,*
  605, *607*
Svarer, C., 466, *478*
Swanson, N. C., 130, 131, *134*
Swartwood, J. N., 317, *331*
Sweeney, J. A., 306, 306*f,* 307,
  311
Sweet, W. H., 601, *607*
Sweller, J., 110, 111, 118, *121*
Swenson, M., 445, 446, *455*
Swick, D., 415, 416*f, 425,* 434,
  440
Sykes, R. N., 316, *327*
Symons, C. S., 619, *625*
Symons, V. L., 317, *325*
Syndulko, K., 521, 522, *536*
Szeminska, A., 369, *376*
Szentágothai, J., 474, *483*
Szymanski, M. D., 239, *244*

Tager-Flusberg, H., 305, *308, 311*
Takei, Y., 368, *377*
Talairach, J., 371, *377*

Talmy, L., 372, *377*
Tancredi, O., 548*t*, *553*
Tang, C., 380, 387, *389*, 505, 506, 515
Tang, J., 630, 631, 632, *639*
Tardif, T., 86, *89*
Tariot, P., 549, *554*
Tarshish, C., 413, *422, 423*
Tata, P. R., 547, 548*t*, *554*
Tatemichi, T. K., 454, *458*
Taylor, A. E., 436, *440*
Taylor, H. A., 364, 365, 368, 369, 371, *377, 378*
Taylor, M., 301, *311*, 603, *607*
Taylor, M. M., 371, *378*
Taylor, T. H., 155, *161*, 169, *177*, 184, 186, *192, 194*
Teasdale, J. D., 322, *325, 331*
Teehan, M. D., 545, *553*
Tempelmann, C., 504, *516*
Tendolkar, I., 504, *516*
Teng, E., 489, 490, 491, 492, 494, 495, 496, *497, 499, 500*
Tenney, Y. J., 307, *311*, 323, *331*
Terr, L. C., 383, *392*
Terrace, H. S., 15, *30*
Terry, R. D., 443, *459*
Tesch-Romer, C., 27, *28*
Tessler, M., 288, 290, 291, 292, *295*, 322, 324, *331*
Teuber, H. L., 468, *482*, 605, *607*
Thal, L. J., 550, *553*
Tharan, M., 383, 387, *390, 392*
Theios, J., 80, *91*
Theodore, W. H., 233, *241*, 618, *621*, 636, *638*
Thiede, K. W., 203, 207, *210*
Thomas, D. G., 269, *282*
Thomas, R. G., 550, *553*
Thompson, C. P., 157, *162*, 317, 318, 319, 321, 322, 323, *328*, *330, 331*
Thompson, J., *331*
Thompson, P., 69, *70*
Thompson, R. F., 465, 472, *483*, 488, *499*
Thompson, S., 433, *439*
Thompson-Schill, S., 633, *642*
Thomson, D. M., 19, *31*, 61, 63, 65, *72*, 99, *107*, 141, 142, *148*, 337, *346*, 396, *409, 424*, 566, *570*
Thomson, N., 83, 84, 85, *88, 89*, 103, *104*
Thöne, A. I. T., 470, 477, *482*
Thorndike, E. L., 4, *31*
Thorndyke, P. W., 320, *331*, 367, *378*
Thronesbury, C., 200, *209*
Thune, L. E., 11, 11*f*, *31*
Timmons, C. R., 270, *282*
Tipper, S. P., 365, *373*
Tirel, O., 367, *374*

Tirre, W. C., 560, *569*
Titcomb, A. L., 183, *194*
Tobler, W., 366, *373*
Todd, P. M., 588, 588*f*, 589*f*, *596*
Toglia, M. P., 184, *194*, 303, *308*, 321, 322, *330, 331*
Tollestrup, P., 184, *194*, 321, *330*
Tolman, E. C., 245, *261*, 319, *331*, 363, *378*
Tomasello, M., 283, *295*
Tomoeda, C. K., 445, *454*
Tootell, R., 632, *642*
Toplis, R., 231, *244*
Toppino, T., 181, *191*
Toth, J. P., 40, 51, 102, 220, 220*t*, 221, 222, *226, 228*, 245, 246, 249, 250, 252, 253, 254, 255, 256, *258, 260, 261*, 525, 528, 529, 533, *534, 536*, 620, *623*
Toung, J. K. T., 415, *425*
Tourangeau, R., 319, *327*
Tournoux, P., 371, *377*
Trainham, T. N., 222, *226*
Trainor, R. J., 472, *479*
Tranel, D., 251*t*, *257, 456*, 469, *483*, 632, 633, *639*
Trask, F. P., 18, *32*, 167, 168*f*, *177*
Traub, M., 544, 548, *551*
Treves, A., 174, *177*
Trivelli, C., 452, *455*
Trollip, S. R., 98, *104*
Tromp, A., 387, *392*
Tromp, S., 383, *390*
Trope, Y., 224, *225*
Trosset, M. W., 445, *454*
Troster, A. I., 442, 445, *455*
Tsuzuki, T., 364, 368, *373*
Tulving, E., 15, 16, 19, 22, 23, 26, *28, 30, 31*, 33, 34, 36, 37, 38, 40, 41, *43*, 47, 50, 52, 54, 55, *56, 57*, 59, 60, 61, 62, 63, 64, 65, 67, 68, *70, 71, 72*, 79, *91*, 96, 97, 97*f*, 98, 99, 102, 103, *105, 106, 107*, 139, 141, 142, *146, 148*, 151, *162*, 174, *177*, 179, 181, 186, 189, *193, 194, 195*, 197, 206, *210*, 229, 230, 233, 234, 239, 240, *243, 244*, 246, 248, 250, 251*t*, 253, 255, 256, *258, 260, 261*, 277, 278, *282*, 285, *295*, 297, 300, 304, *311, 312*, 333, 335, 337, *345, 346*, 347, *362, 396*, 402, *407, 409*, 414, *414*, 420, 421, *422, 425*, 465, 466, 473, 475, *483*, 502, 503*f*, 504, 505, 506, 508, 510, 511*f*, 512*f*, 513, 514, *515, 517*, *518, 519*, 524, 527, 529, 530, 531, *534, 535, 536*, 540, 544, 545, 546, *553, 554*, 565, *570*, 575, 577, *580, 581*, 597, 598,

599, 601, 606, *606, 607, 608*, 610, 611, 617, 618, 619, 620, *621, 623, 625*, 627, 628, 629, 632, 633, 634, 635, 636, 637, *639, 640, 641, 642, 643*
Tun, P. A., 403, *409*
Turkington, T. G., 415, 421, *424*
Turner, A. T., 118, *121*
Turner, M. L., 86, *91*
Turner, R., 472, *479*, 636, 637, *640*
Tversky, A., 110, *122*, 216, *228*, 366, *378*
Tversky, B., 52, *57*, 320, *331*, 363, 364, 365, 366, 367, 368, 369, 370, 371, 372, *373, 374*, *376, 377, 378*
Tweedie, F., 488, *498*
Tweedlie, M. E., 269, *280*
Tweney, R. D., 564, *569*
Tyler, L. K., 450, 451, *457*
Tzeng, O. J. L., 127, *135*, 170, *177*
Tzourio, N., 367, *374*

Uecker, A., 635, *642*
Ule, G., 468, *483*
Umilta, C., 611, *623*
Ummelen, N., 369, *378*
Underwood, B. J., 10, 13, *27, 31*, 54, *56*, 61, 63, *70, 72*, 79, 81, *90*, 129, *134*, 139, *148*, 168, 170, *176, 177*, 245, *261*, 359, 362
Underwood, J., 152, 158, *162*, 183, *195*
Undeutsch, U., 187, *195*
Ungerleider, L. G., 81, *90*, 364, *378*, 414, 415, *423, 427, 440*, 443, 451, *457*, 504, 505, 506, 507, 508, 509, 510, 511, 513, 513*f*, 514, *515, 516, 517*, *519*, 628, 631, 632, 633, 634, 636, 637, *639, 640, 643*
Usher, J. A., 279, *282*, 316, *331*

Vaidya, C. J., 250, 251*t*, *261*, 435, *438*, 526, *534*, 610, 616, *624*, 633, 634, *639*
Vaillant, G., *386, 392*
Vainio, P., 413, *425*
Valdiserri, M., 395, 397, *409*, 600, *607*
Valencia-Laver, D., 175, *177*, 223, *227*
Valenstein, G. S., 601, *608*
Valentine, T., 85, *91*, 184, *191*
Vallar, G., 79, 83, 84, 85, *88, 89*, *91*, 428, *437, 440*, 630, *643*
van Breukelen, G. J., 353, *362*
Vandenberghe, R., 451, *459*, 633, *643*
Van Den Brouke, O., *623*

van der Hart, O., 386, *392*
van der Kolk, B. A., 385, 386, 387, 388, *392,* 470, *483*
Vander Linde, E., 276, *282*
Van der Linden, M., 382, *390,* 545, *552, 553, 554*
Van der Ven, C., 470, *482*
Vanderwolf, C.H., 466, *483*
van Dijk, T. A., 372, *378*
Van Eijk, R., 175, *177,* 610, *623*
Van Hoesen, G. W., 443, *456, 459*
van Huizen, C., 465, 472, *482*
van Mier, H., 633, 636, *641*
Van Paesschen, W., 431, 433, *440,* 451, *459,* 473, *484, 497, 499,* 604, 605, 606, *608,* 617, *625*
Van Zandt, T., 222, *227*
Varendonck, J., 150, *162*
Vargha-Khadem, F., 431, 433, *440,* 451, *459,* 473, *484,* 497, *499,* 604, 605, 606, *607, 608,* 617, *625*
Vaterrodt-Plünnecke, B., 185, *190,* 221, 222, 223, *225*
Vecera, S. P., 615, *621*
Vedantham, V., 504, *519,* 634, *642*
Velichkovsky, B. M., 95, *107*
Verfaellie, M., 158, *162,* 217, 220, *225, 228,* 231, 236, *244*
Vermetten, E., 470, *479*
Vesonder, G. T., 114, 117, *121*
Victor, M., 466, *484*
Vidailhet, P., 545, *552, 554*
Videen, T. O., 502, *518,* 632, 633, 636, 637, *641, 642*
Vigliocco, G., 201, *211*
Villanueva-Meyer, J., 448, 450, *457*
Vincente, K. J., 315, *331*
Vining, S. K., 69, *72*
Vnek, N., 181, 188, *191,* 403, *407*
Vogl, R. J., 323, *331*
Vollmeyer, R., 111, *122*
von Cramon, D. Y., 430, 434, *439,* 469, 470, 471, 473, 477, *479, 481, 482*
von Stockhausen, H. -M., 471, 474*f, 482*
Voogt, J., 465, 472, *482*
Voss, J. F., 114, 117, 118, *120, 121*
Vriezen, E., 246, *260,* 523, *535,* 616, 617, *623, 625*
Vuorinen, E., 474, *481*
Vygotsky, L., 283, 291, *295*
Vyse, S. A., 322, *328*

Wade, E., 199, *207,* 398, *406*
Waern, Y., 204, *211*
Wagenaar, W. A., 319, *331,* 383, *392*

Wagner, A. D., 220, *228,* 236, *244,* 403, *409,* 435, *438,* 504, 514, *519,* 522, 526, *534, 536,* 611, 617, 618, 619, *624, 625,* 627, 630, 632, 633, 634, 635, *638, 639, 641, 642, 643*
Wagner, H. N., Jr., 415, *425*
Waldfogel, S., 306, 306*f, 311*
Waldvogel, S., 316, *331*
Walker, J. A., 78, *91*
Walker, W. H., 340, 341, 342, *346*
Walla, P., 525, 526*f,* 529, 530, 531, *536*
Wallace, W. P., 69, *72*
Wallach, H., 166, *177*
Walter, B. M., 231, *243,* 404, *408,* 420, *424,* 600, 601, *607,* 618, 620, *624*
Walters, A. A., 150, *160*
Walther, E., 184, *191*
Wang, A. Y., 184, *192*
Wang, Q., 288, *293*
Wanner, H. E., 568, *570*
Warach, S., 472, *481*
Warburton, D. M., 544, 550, *552, 553*
Ward, C., 544, 548, *551*
Ward, M. R., 111, 118, *121*
Wardell, J., *375*
Warnecke, R. B., 320, *331*
Warren, A. R., 317, *331*
Warren, H. C., 3, *31*
Warrington, E. K., 22, *31,* 55, *57,* 81, 83, *89, 91,* 246, 251*t, 261,* 305, *308,* 427, 428, *439, 440,* 443, 445, 448, 449, 451, *455, 458, 459,* 466, 471, 472, *479, 481, 483, 484,* 488, *499,* 590, *596,* 620, *625,* 632, *643*
Washburn, M. F., 130, *135*
Waters, G. S., 85, 86, *92*
Waters, H. S., 239, *242*
Waters, R. M., 167, *176*
Watkins, G. L., 510, 514, *514*
Watkins, K. E., 431, 433, *440,* 451, *459,* 473, *484,* 497, *499,* 604, 605, 606, *608,* 617, *625*
Watkins, M. J., 68, *72, 82, 89,* 131, *135,* 157, *162,* 396, *409,* 613, *625*
Watkins, O. C., 131, *135,* 396, *409*
Watson, J. B., 4, *31,* 269, *282*
Watson, P. C., 446, 447*f, 455*
Watters, E., 317, *329,* 383, 385, *391,* 647, *648*
Watts, J. W., 601, 602, *606*
Watts, K., 398, *409*
Waugh, N. C., 19, *32,* 50, *57,* 78, 79, 80, 81, *90, 92,* 130, *135*
Weaver, C. A.7, 317, *331*
Weber, M., 380, *389*

Weber-Luxenburger, G., 470, 474, *482*
Wegner, D. M., 217, *228,* 324, *331,* 387, *392*
Weinberger, D. A., 322, *332*
Weinert, F. E., 292, *295*
Weinert, J. R., 167, *176*
Weingardt, K. R., 204, *211*
Weingartner, H. J., 337, *343,* 543, 545, 547, 548*t,* 549, *552, 553, 554*
Weisberg, R., 113, *122*
Weiskrantz, L., 55, *57,* 87, *91,* 246, 251*t, 261,* 466, *481, 484,* 620, *625,* 645, 646, *648*
Welch-Ross, M. K., 286, *295,* 302, 303, *311*
Weldon, M. S., 34, *43,* 99, 102, *106,* 217, *228,* 246, 251*t, 260, 261,* 318, *329, 391*
Welford, A. T., 415, *425*
Wellman, H. M., 200, *208, 211,* 299, 302, 303, *309, 311,* 319, *325,* 603, *607*
Wells, D., 302, *311*
Wells, T., 524, *534, 536*
Welsh, K., 443, *459*
Welsh, K. A., 443, *459*
Wenger, S. K., 157, *162*
Wentworth, N., 269, *280*
Wenzel, A. E., 560, *570*
Werner, J. S., 268, *282*
Wess, J., 444, *454*
West, R. L., 402, 405, *409,* 600, *608*
Wetzel, W. F., 269, *281*
Wetzler, S. E., 306, 306*f,* 307, *311,* 318, *330*
Wewerka, S. S., 273, *279,* 285, 289, 290, *292,* 602, *606*
Weyerts, H., 504, *516*
Wharton, C. M., 113, *122*
Wheeler, M. A., *37, 43,* 174, *177,* 229, 234, *244,* 300, 303, 304, *312,* 597, 600, 601, 606, *608,* 611, 618, 620, *625*
Whinney, 560
Whipple, G. M., 150, *162*
Whishaw, I. Q., 26, *29*
White, C. S., 322, *327*
White, H., 397, *406,* 593, *596*
White, L. T., 158, *161*
White, N. M., 488, *498*
White, S. H., 279, *282,* 288, *294,* 306, *310, 312,* 322, 369, *377*
Whitehouse, K., 216, *226,* 254, *259*
Whitehouse, P. J., *459, 553*
Whitten, W. B., 130, *133*
Whittlesea, B. W. A., 217, *228,* 254, *261,* 613, *625*
Wible, C. G., 317, *328,* 382, *391*
Wichawut, C., 63, 68, *72*

Wickelgren, W. A., 129, 131, *135*
Wickens, C. D., 415, *425*
Wickens, D. D., 52, *57*, 79, *92*, 140, *148*
Widing, M., 144, *148*
Widlitzek, B., 477, *479*
Widom, C. S., 384, *392*
Wiggs, C. L., 435, *440*, 443, 451, *457*, 513, *517*, 616, 617, *625*, 632, 633, 636, *640, 643*
Wight, E., 85, *88*
Wilcock, G. K., 443, *459*
Wilding, E. L., 189, *195*, 528, 529, 529*f*, 530, 531, *534, 536*, 609, *621*
Wilensky, R., 315, *325*
Wiley, A. R., 288, *293*
Wiley, J., 118, *122*
Wiley, J. G., 369, *376*
Wilhelmsen, K. C., 449, *459*
Wilk, A., 276, *280*
Wilkinson, A. C., 204, *208*
Willatts, P., 273, *281*
Williams, D. M., 413, *422*
Williams, J., 453, *457*
Williams, J. M. G., 322, *332*
Williams, L. D., 613, *625*
Williams, L. M., 384, 385, *392*
Williams, M. D., 333, 334, 338, 339, 340, 341, 342, *346*
Williams, M. V., 399, *405*
Williams, P. C., 249, 254, *260*
Williams, R. B., 231, 239, *243*
Williams, R. J., 589, *596*
Willis, C., 630, *640*
Willshaw, D., 584, *596*
Wilson, A. A., 415, *425*, 633, 634, *640*
Wilson, B. A., 79, 85, 87, *89*, 188, 189, *190*, 416, 419, *422*, 445, *455*
Wilson, F. A. W., 506, *519*, 631, *643*
Wilson, K., 435, *438*
Wilson, L., 80, 81, 85, *89*
Wilson, M., 96, *107*
Wilson, R., 617, *621*
Wilson, T. D., 188, *195*
Wilton, R. N., 366, *378*
Wimmer, H., 301, 303, *309, 311, 312*, 603, *608*
Winblad, B., 144, *148*, 415, *422*, 505, *515*
Wingfield, A., 403, *409*
Winocur, G., 95, *106*, 402, 403, 404, *408, 409*, 505, 508, *517*, 610, 612, 616, 619, *621, 623, 625*
Winograd, E., 127, *135*, 158, *162*, 167, 170, *177*, 181, 187, *195*, 317, 318, 319, *329, 332, 391*
Winograd, T., 23, *32*

Winter, A., 372, *378*
Winzenz, D., 129, *133*
Wise, R., 451, *459*, 633, *643*
Wise, R. J . S., 443, 446, 451, 452, *458*
Wise, S. P., 466, *480*
Wiseman, S., 59, 62, 63, 67, *72*
Wishengrad, D. L., 249, 254, *260*, 261
Wisniewski, H. M., 413, *422*
Witherspoon, D., 62, 65, *72*, 216, 217, *226, 228*, 248, 251*t*, 254, *259, 261*
Witmer, L. R., 10, *32*
Wittlinger, R. P., 348, 350, 353, 358, 359, *360*
Wittman, W. T., 353, *361*
Wixted, J. T., 560, *570*
Wokfe, J., 442, 443, 454, *455*
Wolf, E. S., 181, *193*, 402, *407*
Wolf, P. A., 454, *458*
Wolfe, J., 442, 443, *455*
Wolford, G., 65, *72*
Wolkowitz, O., 545, 546, 548*t*, 554
Wollen, K., 65, *72*
Woloshyn, V., 154, *161*, 181, 186, *192*, 216, *226*, 251*t*, 253, 254, *259*
Wolters, G., 217, *228*
Wondoloski, T. L., 276, 277, *280*
Wong, D. F., 415, *425*
Wood, C. C., 522, *535*
Wood, E. R., 491, *499*
Wood, F., 610, *622*
Woodbury, P., 550, *553*
Woodruff-Pak, D. S., 437, *440*, 468, *484*, 620, *625*
Woods, A. M., 399, *405*
Woodward, A. L., 299, *311, 312*
Woodworth, R. S., 128, *134, 135*
Woolley, J. D., 302, *312*
Worling, J. R., 201, *210*, 339, *345*
Worsley, K. J., 502, *516*
Worthley, J. S., 199, *207*, 398, *406*
Wright, D. B., 317, *332*
Wright, K. L., 84, *88*
Wright, P., 369, *378*
Wu, J., 380, 387, *389*, 505, 506, 515
Wu, L., 113, *119*
Würker, M., 469, 473, *481*
Wurtzel, N., 276, 277, *280*

Yaffee, L. S., 428, *439*
Yamaguchi, T., 454, *458*
Yaniv, I., 342, *346*
Yapko, M. D., 647, *648*
Yarmey, A. D., 317, *332*
Yates, F. A., 365, *378*
Yates, P. O., 448, *458*

Yearwood, A. A., 251*t, 257*
Yerys, B., 403, *405*
Yerys, B. E., 158, *160*
Yesavage, J. A., 398, *408*
Yi, S., 288, *294*, 324, *328*
Yilmazer, D., 473, 476*f, 479*
Yntema, D. B., 18, *32*, 167, 168*f*, 177
Yonelinas, A. P., 49, *57*, 185, *195*, 219, 220*t*, 221, 222, 224, *226, 228*, 233, 237, 239, *241, 242*, 244, 246, 249, 253, *258, 259, 261*, 525, 528, 529, 530, 531, *534, 537*, 611, 618, *625*
Young, A. H., 548, *551*
Young, A. W., 428, *439*, 452, *455, 456*
Young, R. K., 126, 128, *135*
Yuille, J. C., 138, *147*, 321, *332*, 380, *392*
Yun, L. S., 158, *162*, 186, *194*, 403, *409*, 531, *536*, 635, *642*

Zacks, R. T., 54, *57*, 169, 170, *176*, 365, *374, 376, 377*, 396, 400, 401, 403, *407, 409*, 411, 415, 417, 418, 419, 419*f*, 420, 421, *422, 423, 424, 425*
Zajonc, R. B., 249, 251*t, 259*, 260
Zangas, T., 371, *374*
Zannaras, G., 367, *374*
Zanobio, E., 428, *437*
Zaragoza, M. S., 154, 157, 158, *160, 162*, 181, 182, 183, 184, 189, 189*n*, 190, *193, 195*, 302, *307*
Zarahn, E., 189, *195*, 630, 631, 632, *639*
Zarella, M. M., 250, 251*t, 261*
Zeffiro,T. A., 636, *638*
Zeki, S., 508, *519*
Zelazo, P. D., 302, *312*, 604, *608*
Zelinski, E. M., 400, *408*
Zhang, X. L., 469, *484*
Zhao, Z., 365, *373*, 504, *515*, 522, *534*, 634, *638*
Zilbershatz, A., 370, *375*
Zimmer, H. D., 53, *56*, 103, *105*, 137, 138, 140, 141, 142, 143, 144, *146, 147, 148*, 156, *160*
Zola, S. M., 38, 485, 486, 488, 489, 490, 491, 492, 494, 495, 496, *497, 499, 500*
Zola-Morgan, S., 306, *309*, 431, *440*, 485, 486, 488, 489, 489*f*, 490, 491, 492, 494, 495, 496, *497, 498, 499*, 514, 519
Zorrilla, L. T. E., 189, *195*
Zurella, M. M., 610, *622*